W9-AWD-771

NTC's MASS MEDIA Dictionary

NTC's MASS MEDIA Dictionary

R. Terry Ellmore

National Textbook Company
NTC a division of *NTC Publishing Group* • Lincolnwood, Illinois USA

Library of Congress Cataloging-in-Publication Data

Ellmore, R. Terry.

NTC's mass media dictionary

1. Mass media-Dictionaries. I. Title. II. Title:
Mass media dictionary.
P87.5.E45 1990 302.23'03 89-63861
ISBN 0-8442-3185-1

1995 Printing

Published by National Textbook Company, a division of NTC Publishing Group.

Manufactured in the United States of America.

5 6 7 8 9 VP 9 8 7 6 5 4 3 2

In memory of my Father,
W. Austin Ellmore

Preface

New words are continually being coined in the various mass media; words such as *couch potato, zipping* and *zapping, uplink* and *downlink,* and acronyms such as *MERPS.* But no dictionary of the mass media would be complete without the older terms that are seldom used today; words such as *evulgate, nemo,* and *mechanical scanning,* so they too are included in the more than 20,000 entries contained in this dictionary.

This dictionary was written to aid writers, broadcasters, publishers, film and video makers, printers, advertisers, and other industry professionals, as well as teachers, students and others interested in the vocabulary of the mass media.

The vocabulary of the mass media obviously includes the major subjects of radio, television, cable television, film, newspapers, magazines, books, direct mail, and outdoor advertising. And, as they apply to the various mass media, the closely allied subjects of acting, advertising, animation, announcing, audience measurement, audio, automation, criticism, disc recording, engineering, graphic arts, history, law, lighting, magnetic recording, make-up, management, music, news, operations, printing, production, programming, public relations, regulation, research, sales, satellites, scenery, sound, statistics, video, and writing, are covered in varying degrees.

The entries themselves were culled from hundreds of sources: indexes and small glossaries in books, magazines, and articles in periodicals. No attempt was made to make the dictionary encyclopedic in nature, and the definitions are intended to be descriptive rather than proscriptive. A number of engineering terms are included, but only those engineering terms that a nonengineer might need to know are included.

No dictionary of this scope can possibly be complete, so corrections, suggestions for additional entries, and comments would not only be welcomed, but are fervently solicited.

R. Terry Ellmore, Ph.D.
Chairman
Department of Radio-TV-Film
Texas Christian University
Fort Worth, Texas 76129

Acknowledgments

I am indebted to a number of different people and organizations for permission to use standard definitions from various articles, glossaries, and other materials: Elliott Williams of the Directors Guild of America, Inc., Ron Miller of the Writers Guild of America, West, Inc., Pamm Fair of the American Federation of Radio and Television Artists, Mark Locher of the Screen Actors Guild, Jennifer Asch of the Institute of Outdoor Advertising, Mark Fine and Laura Foti Cohen of American Interactive Media, Inc., for CD-I terms, Eva J. Blinder of BME for terms found in ''Redefining Beta Splines'' in the May 1988 issue of BME, Jeffrey Friedman of the Society of Motion Picture and Television Engineers for ''Television Tape Recording Nomenclature'' from the November 1988 issue of the *SMPTE Journal*, R. H. Dowhan of GTE for lighting definitions from the Sylvania *Lighting Handbook*, Thomas F. Mocarsky of The Arbitron Company, Ray Wisbrock of Nielsen Media Research for terms from *Glossary of Cable & TV Terms*, Carolyn A. Grimes of the Eastman Kodak Company for terms from *The Complete KODAK Animation Book*, Paula S. Zimmerman of the Intel Corporation for DVI terms, Casimir J. Psujek of the National Textbook Company for terms from *Successful Direct Marketing Methods* by Bob Stone and *The Dictionary of Advertising* by Laurence Urdang, and especially to Raymond A. Collins of TAB Books for permission to use approximately 2000 definitions from the book I wrote entitled *The Illustrated Dictionary of Broadcast-CATV-Telecommunications*.

I am also indebted to a number of my friends and colleagues for assistance with a number of the definitions: John Freeman, Andy Haskett, David Barker, Larry Charlesworth, and David Green. For their many hours of work, I wish to thank five students who, at various periods during the time this dictionary was being written, accomplished numerous tasks such as searching for terms to be included, checking on the accuracy of definitions, and typing the manuscript. They are Karen Anderson, Kara Sue Allen, Beth Eley, Misty Garcia, and Kathleen McKay. A special thanks to Susan Hill of the National Association of Broadcasters for a definition of the term MERPS, an acronym that was used in a number of periodicals but never explained (an all too common practice in articles). Thanks also to Lynn Brown, my copyeditor, who was able to turn my many inconsistencies into systematic consistencies.

Finally, my thanks to my wife, Ruth, for her patience during the more than three years this dictionary was being written.

Explanatory Notes

The definitions contained in this dictionary are from a number of sources; several thousand were furnished by those individuals and companies mentioned in the acknowledgments, several hundred more were taken from various government documents such as the *Communications Act of 1934*, the *"Copyright Act of 1976,"* and the *Rules and Regulations* of the Federal Communications Commission. All other definitions are original.

All entries in this dictionary are in strict letter-by-letter alphabetical and alphanumerical order; thus, for example, "news program" is followed by "newsreel" which is followed by "news release." An ampersand (&) is treated as the word *and*, and numbers are treated as though they are spelled out. The only exceptions to this format are (1) the word *the* is ignored if it would normally begin an entry, and (2) it seemed to be a bit inane to strictly alphabetize, for example, Class IV, Class I, Class III, Class II in that order, so they are entered in the more logical order.

Many entries have multiple definitions; in one case, fourteen definitions for one entry. The definitions are not, however, listed in any particular order of significance or by subject matter.

A cross-referencing feature is the use of the words *see, see also* and *Cf.* (compare with) to aid the dictionary user in finding similar or dissimilar words.

Entries are spelled in the way they are most often found in books, periodicals, indexes, and so on. Sometimes, however, a word was spelled an almost equal number of times in different forms. For example, *close up, closeup,* and *close-up* are nearly equal in usage, without regard to whether they were verbs, nouns, or other parts of speech. In those cases, an arbitrary decision was made as to which spelling to use. In most cases the decision was made not to use the hyphenated spelling. As one writer aptly stated: "If you take hyphens seriously you will surely go mad."

NTC's MASS MEDIA Dictionary

A ☐ Accent. ☐ Advance. A wire service symbol for an advance for weekday news or for domestic news not from Washington. ☐ Agricultural programs. ☐ Ampere. ☐ Angled. ☐ Angstrom unit. ☐ Assignment. An FCC file-number prefix. ☐ Aviation. An FCC first letter file-number prefix.

AA ☐ Average audience. ☐ Advertising agency. ☐ Advertising association. ☐ Author's alterations.

AAA American Academy of Advertising.

AAAA ☐ American Association of Advertising Agencies. ☐ Associated Actors and Artistes of America.

AAAA spot contract A standardized contract between an advertising agency and a spot television supplier that specifies agreed-upon terms of a purchase; model format prepared by the American Association of Advertising Agencies. Cf. time contract.

AAAI Affiliated Advertising Agencies International.

AAAL American Academy of Arts and Letters.

AAAS American Academy of Arts and Sciences.

AACTO American Association of Cable Television Owners.

AADA American Academy of Dramatic Arts.

AAE Automatic assemble editing.

AAF American Advertising Federation.

AAIP American Association of Independent Publishers.

A and B editing The editing of film or videotape into one roll from two separate rolls of film or videotape. *See also* checkerboarding.

A and B printing A method of printing film on two rolls instead of one with black leader alternating between the shots to make splices invisible, incorporate fades, include dissolves, and so on.

A and B wind Two ways of winding single perforated film. *See also* A wind and B wind.

A and M Art and mechanical.

A and R Artists and repertoire. A recording company employee who works with performers and selects the music to be recorded.

AANR American Association of Newspaper Representatives, Inc.

AAP Association of American Publishers.

AAPOR American Association of Public Opinion Research.

AASDJ American Association of Schools and Departments of Journalism.

AAUP Association of American University Presses.

AAW Advertising Association of the West.

AB Announce booth.

ab A prefix to electrical units that indicates the corresponding units in the centimeter-gram-second (cgs) system, for example, abampere and abvolt.

ABA American Booksellers Association.

A, B, and C printing The printing of film as in A and B printing but using a third roll (the C roll) for special effects. A fourth roll would be called the D roll.

abandonment The release of a trademark by a manufacturer through nonuse or sale.

abaxial The parallel rays of light that are farthest from the optical axis of a lens. Cf. paraxial.

abaxial lens A lens in which the light rays are directed away from the axis.

ABC ☐ American Broadcasting Company. ☐ Asian Broadcasting Conference. ☐ Audit Bureau of Circulations. ☐ Australian Broadcasting Commission. A national broadcasting organization. ☐ Automatic Bass Compensation.

ABCD counties Designations by the A. C. Nielsen Company that indicate the size of counties by population. *See also* county size, A county, B county, C county, and D county.

A-B composite The electronic joining of two videotapes by using a third videotape recorder. Also called *linelock* and *intersync*. *See also* checkerboarding.

abend An acronym for *ab*normal *end*ing. The abnormal termination of a computer program due to an error. Also called an *abnormal termination*. Cf. abort.

aberration Any imperfections in a lens, mirror, prism, and so on, that cause distortion. *See also* chromatic aberration, spherical aberration, astigmatism, and coma.

ABES Association for Broadcast Engineering Standards.

abeyance A spot television advertising order for commercial time that is not available at the time of purchase.

ABI Advance book information.

abie A slang term for a talented, hardworking actor, director, writer, and so on.

ABN American Broadcasting Network. A former designation for the American Broadcasting Company radio network.

abnormal termination *See* abend.

abort □ To deliberately terminate a computer program. Cf. abend. □ To terminate an edit if the videotape player and recorder are not in synchronization.

above eye level A camera shot taken from above the subject or object.

above-the-line The costs of a production related to obtaining the rights and contracting for the services of the creative personnel, for example, producer, director, actors, and writers. Cf. below-the-line.

ABP □ American Business Press, Inc. □ Associated Business Papers.

ABPA American Book Producers Association.

ABPC American Book Publishers Council.

AB-PT American Broadcasting-Paramount Theatres, Inc. The parent company of the American Broadcasting Company.

abrasions Scratches or other unwanted marks on film.

abrasive □ Having the property of wearing down the surfaces of audio or videotape contacts as it passes through the tape path; especially having the property of wearing down the recording heads. □ A derogatory term for having the property of wearing down recording heads at an excessive rate.

abridgment The condensation of a book or other manuscript.

abrogation The repeal of legislation.

A-B roll □ A technique by which information is played back from two tape machines rolled sequentially, usually to dub the sequential information onto a third tape. □ A recording thus produced.

A-B rolling □ The preparation of a tape or film for checkerboarding. □ The use of two film projectors to produce one picture through a video switcher.

ABSAT An American Broadcasting Company television satellite used for news.

absolute address The address that is the physical location of a specific piece of data in computer storage.

absolute film A nonrepresentational, often lengthy, abstract film.

absolute playing time In CD-DA, the total time a disc has been playing. Included in the subcode and thus available for display during playback.

absolute privilege The immunity from liability for defamation granted to judges, legislators, and other government officials from remarks made during the exercise of their duties. Cf. conditional privilege.

absolute scale *See* Kelvin.

absolutism The political theory that the First and Fourteenth Amendments preclude federal or state governments from adopting any laws that may abridge freedom of expression.

absorbency A measure of a paper's ability to absorb ink or other liquids.

absorption The interception, soaking up, and dissipation of radio, light, or sound waves by sound-damping materials such as air, water, or other matter. *See also* dead. Cf. reflection.

absorption coefficient That portion of sound or energy absorbed on contact with another medium.

absorption filter A filter that transmits certain wavelengths and reflects those not transmitted. The absorbed power appears as heat, raising the temperature of the filter.

A-B split A method of selecting two groups of individuals for a survey (or a control group or test group) by selecting every other name on a list.

abstract □ A summary or abridgement of a book, manuscript, or document. □ To summarize or abridge.

abstract background A nonrealistic, decorative television set or photographic background that disassociates itself from the action but sets the mood or is purely decorative. Also called an *abstract set.*

abstract expressionism Set design characterized by amorphous shapes and decorative surfaces.

abstract film A nonrepresentational film, often one that uses line, shape, and color to create poetic images.

abstraction A composition with recognizable human, animal, or inanimate figures represented as generalized or geometric forms.

abstract set *See* abstract background.

AB switch □ A two-position switch used in a variety of electronic applications. □ A video switch designed to change a video feed from one source to another, for example, recorder input to recorder output for quality comparison.

A-B test A direct comparison made between two sound or picture sources accomplished by switching back and forth between the sources.

ABU Asian Broadcasting Union.

AC □ Adult contemporary. □ Advertising Council. □ Accumulator. □ Alternating current. □ Automatic computer. □ Analog computer.

ACA □ Advertising Council of America, Inc. □ American Communications Association. A union. □ Association of Canadian Advertisers. □ Association for Communication Administration. An association of college and university communication administrators.

AC adapter A device used to convert alternating current into direct current.

academy aperture The standard frame mask established by the AMPAS and used in theatrical motion picture projection; a ratio of 1.33 to 1. Also called *academy ratio* and *reduced aperture.* Cf. wide-screen aperture.

Academy Awards *See* Academy of Motion Picture Arts and Sciences.

academy leader The standard film leader established by the AMPAS, with special markings one second apart; used for cueing film in a projector. Cf. SMPTE universal leader.

Academy of Motion Picture Arts and Sciences (AMPAS) The organization that beginning in 1928 has awarded the Oscars, promoted the film industry, and supported film libraries and film awards.

Academy Players' Directory A voluminous work published by the AMPAS containing pictures of the various film actors and actresses.

academy ratio *See* academy aperture.

academy rolloff The standard rolloff of high frequencies used in theatre sound systems.

Academy standards The various standards established by the AMPAS, for example, academy aperture and academy ratio.

A-cart *See* NAB-A.

ACATS Advisory Committee on Advanced Television Service.

ACB Advertising Checking Bureau.

ACBB American Council for Better Broadcasts. A citizens' group.

ACC □ Air Coordinating Committee. A U.S. government committee. □ Automatic chrominance control. □ Automatic contrast control.

accelerated montage A film montage created by switching shots at an ever-increasing pace.

accelerated motion *See* fast motion.

accelerator A chemical used in film development that increases the speed of the developer.

accent □ The emphasis placed on a line, scene, musical note, and so on. □ *See* diacritical mark.

accent light A luminaire used in television and film for highlighting.

accent mark *See* diacritical mark.

accent microphone A microphone used to pick up specific sounds or voices when multiple microphone techniques are used. Also called a *spot microphone.*

accentuation *See* preemphasis.

acceptance □ A media supplier's approval of the terms of purchase offered; typically refers to negotiations for purchase of network television time. □ The agreement by a radio or television station to carry a network program at a time and date acceptable to the network. Cf. offer.

acceptance angle The maximum angle from which a lens or light meter is designed to admit light rays.

accepted interference Interference at a higher level than defined as permissible interference and higher than the level that has been agreed upon between two or more administrations without prejudice to other administrations. Used in the coordination of frequency assignments between administrations in various countries. Cf. permissible interference.

access □ The ability of a user to avail himself or herself of services, such as cable television, telephone lines, or a computer system. □ The availability of news sources to the media. □ The availability of media air time to various persons and groups, such as retail establishments or political candidates. □ The ability and liberty of the media to gain entrance to or information about places, materials, records, and so on. *See also* freedom of information, Government in the Sunshine Act, and Privacy Act. □ The process of locating and obtaining data from or placing data into storage. *See also* random access and serial access. □ To retrieve data from a computer storage device. □ The time period on television from 7:30 p.m. to 8 p.m. (ET) that immediately precedes prime time. Also called *access hour. See also* daypart. □ In CD-I, the process of locating information in a data store. □ *See* prime time access rule.

access cablecasting Channel space set aside for use by individuals and organizations within a cable community. FCC rules specify channels for public access on a first-come, nondiscriminatory basis, and for education access, local government access, and leased access.

access channel One of the cable television channels available for use by government, educational groups, or the public.

access charge A telephone company's fee to customers or long-distance carriers for use of local lines.

access controller A CD-I player component that takes drawmaps from RAM and loads them to the video decoder.

access hour *See* access.

accessibility The physical convenience to an operator of a computer or other system or peripheral device. Cf. availability.

accession The augmentation of library holdings through the addition of new materials.

accession book The place in which new library acquisitions are recorded; formerly a blank book, now often a computer database.

accession number The number assigned by a library to books, films, or other materials to indicate the order of their acquisition.

accessory A device designed to increase the effectiveness or add to the capacity of equipment.

access program A television program broadcast by a network affiliate on a weekly basis.

access protection In CD-I, the method of preventing unauthorized access to specific data of a confidential nature stored on a disc.

access rule *See* prime time access rule.

access syndication The distribution of television programs designed for public access.

access time □ The interval between the time computer data is called for and the time the data delivery is completed. □ The hour between 7 p.m. and 8 p.m. (ET) in which off-network programs may not be aired on affiliated television stations. □ The time required for a light control board memory system to accept information and make it available to the operator. □ The time between a radio or television director's command and the delivery of the sound or picture.

access to media The nonexistent right of individuals to obtain air time or print space in the media. Certain access rights do exist, however, in broadcasting for legally qualified candidates for public office, and formerly under the Fairness Doctrine.

accordion fold Paper that is folded in a zigzag fashion like the bellows of an accordion. Also called *accordion pleat.*

accordion insert An insert in a magazine with an accordion fold.

accordion pleat *See* accordion fold.

account □ An encompassing term for the business relationship between an advertising agency and a client. □ A contract between a broadcast station and an advertising agency or advertiser for the purchase of air time.

account conflict A potential conflict of interest arising when an advertising agency accepts competing clients.

account contact man *See* account executive.

account executive (AE) □ The individual in an advertising agency in charge of maintaining liaison with designated agency clients and for development and control of advertising plans for clients. Also called an *account contact person, account manager, contact executive,* and *account supervisor.* □ A representative of a marketing organization responsible for maintaining liaison with designated clients. Also called an *account representative.* □ A salesperson or serviceperson who is employed by individual companies that sell the outdoor advertising media. Also called an *account manager.*

account group The advertising agency staff that services an account; usually consists of an account executive, creative director, copy writers, and an art director.

account manager *See* account executive.

account representative *See* account executive.

account supervisor The individual in an advertising agency to whom an account executive reports.

accreditation A certification by an agency or organization as to the competence of an individual, group, company, and so on, in a profession or enterprise.

accuracy □ The freedom from error in a computer system. □ The extent to which a survey result agrees with some well-defined standard. Accuracy reflects the extent to which a result is free from errors, both sampling and nonsampling. Cf. reliability.

Accuracy in Media (AIM) A citizens' watchdog group.

ACD Associate creative director.

ac/dc Equipment capable of operating on either alternating or direct current. *See* universal receiver.

ACE American Cinema Editors.

ace □ A 1000-watt fresnel spotlight. Also called a *one K.* □ A slang term for a person with exceptional ability in directing, writing, and so on.

ACE awards Awards sponsored by the National Cable Television Association (NCTA) for excellence in original cable programs.

ACEJ American Council on Education for Journalism. *See* AEJMC.

ACET Association for Educational Communications and Technology.

acetate □ An abbreviation for *cellulose acetate,* a clear plastic material from which cels are made. Also used as a base for film. Also called an *acetate overlay.* □ *See* cel. □ A nonflammable, transparent, flexible material used as a tape, film, or disc base.

acetate base The film base that supports the emulsion layers. *See also* acetate.

acetate disc *See* disc.

acetate film A type of nonflammable safety film. Cf. nitrate base.

acetate overlay *See* acetate and acetate proof.

acetate proof A printer's proof made on transparent acetate as camera-ready copy or as an overlay.

acetic acid A colorless vinegar used in the photographic fixing process.

acetone A volatile solvent used in film cement and as a solvent and cleaner.

ACG Address Coding Guide.

A channel The left channel in a stereo system. Cf. B channel.

achromatic Without hue; colorless, for example, a gray surface or a neutral filter, or black-and-white television.

achromatic lens A lens made by combining elements made of crown glass and flint glass in order to reduce chromatic aberration.

ACI □ Adjacent channel interference. □ The Advertising Council, Inc.

acicular Needle shaped. That shape characteristic of the microstructure of gamma-ferric oxide used as the magnetizable material of videotape.

acid A chemical compound used as a stop bath to neutralize the action of a photographic developer.

acid resist A protective coating used in engraving to prevent etching in unwanted areas.

ACK An abbreviation for acknowledge.

acknowledge (ACK) A signal verifying that a block of transmitted information has been received. Also called an *acknowledgment.*

acknowledgment □ An author's recognition of help received in the preparation of a book or manuscript, often included as a separate page in the front of a book or as part of a preface. □ A form sent to a new subscriber that his or her order has been received. □ *See* acknowledge.

ACLMRS Advisory Committee for Land-Mobile Radio Services.

ACLU American Civil Liberties Union.

ACN □ A. C. Nielsen Company. □ American Cable Network, Inc.

ACNO Advisory Council of National Organizations.

A copy That part of news copy completed before the lead is written. Also called *A matter.* Cf. B copy.

A county Any county belonging to the twenty-five largest cities and consolidated urban areas in the United States. *See also* county size.

acoustic The qualities that determine the sound characteristics of an auditorium, sound stage, studio, and so on.

acoustical treatment Physical changes made to studios and other rooms to lower the noise level and absorb undesirable sound.

acoustic backing The materials used to absorb or reflect the sound in a studio or other facility, for example, draperies, polyurethane, and fiberglass.

acoustic baffle *See* baffle.

acoustic center The perceived source of sound.

acoustic coupler A device, usually used with a modem, that physically connects a telephone headset to a telephone line and allows digital data to be transmitted. Also called an *acoustic modem.*

acoustic feedback *See* feedback.

acoustic modem *See* acoustic coupler.

acoustic perspective The spatial relationship between various sound sources. *See also* binaural, stereophonic, and quadraphonic.

acoustic reflex A spontaneous tightening of the ear muscles if the ear is subjected to sounds greater than approximately 85dB.

acoustic response The sound characteristics of an auditorium, sound stage, or studio. *See also* acoustic.

acoustics □ The science that deals with the production, control, transmission, reception, and effects of sound. □ The sound qualities of a studio. Also called *acoustic.*

acoustic screen A mobile screen that has either reflective or absorptive surfaces. Used to vary the acoustic properties of a studio, that is, to make it more live or dead.

acoustic tile A form of acoustic backing made of perforated fiberboard.

acoustic wave The traveling vibration by which sound energy is transmitted.

ACP Associated Church Press.

acquisition The selection and purchase of books and other materials for addition to a library.

acquisition cost The money spent by a publisher or other organization to obtain new subscribers or customers.

acquisitions department A department charged with acquiring books, periodicals, and other materials for a library.

acquisitions editor An employee of a publishing firm who solicits, reviews, and evaluates manuscripts for possible publication. Also called a *house editor.* *See also* editor.

acquisitions librarian The person on a library staff charged with ordering books and other materials.

acquit To set free from a legal charge.

ACR Audio cassette recorder.

ACRL Association of College and Research Libraries.

acronym A group of letters that form a word from the initial letter or letters in the words of a compound term. Numerous examples are found in this dictionary.

across the board A radio or television program or advertisement that is scheduled each day at the same time; usually Monday through Friday. *See also* strip.

across the mike Speaking from the side of a microphone as opposed to directly into it. A method of reducing plosives and sibilance.

ACT □ Action for Children's Television. A citizens' group lobbying for the elimination of commercials in children's programming. □ American Citizens Television Committee, Inc. □ Association for Competitive Television. A UHF interest group.

act □ A major dramatic unit of a play, script, motion picture, teleplay, and so on, usually consisting of two or more scenes. □ To perform before an audience. □ The routine of an individual or group. □ A legislative statute.

act break The interruption of a radio or television play by commercials, fadeouts, station breaks, and so on.

acting The art of representing a character for an audience.

acting area That portion of a stage used by the actors during a performance. Often enclosed by scenery.

acting edition A script marked with the pertinent stage directions.

actinic light Light in the visible and ultraviolet spectrum that can cause chemical or electrochemical action, such as on a film or cathode ray tube. Also called *actinic rays.*

actinic rays *See* actinic light.

action □ The series of events in a program or play. □ The movement of the subject within the camera's field of view. □ A radio, television, or film director's command for talent to begin. □ The dialogue that takes place at any given instant. □ *See* AIDA.

action axis *See* imaginary line.

action central An obsolete term for a radio newsroom.

action cutting The editing of film or tape so that the transitions take place during a performer's movements, for example, during the time an individual rises from a chair.

action device A technique used in advertising to motivate responses in prospective buyers by requiring some physical action, such as pasting a stamp to show the periodicals being ordered.

action field The area covered by a camera shot.

action line A radio or television station service to listeners or viewers who have problems with local government or business firms. Called by many names: Direct Line, Consumer Help, and so on. *See also* ombudsman.

action news A television news presentation style that contains numerous visuals and a rapid pace.

action outline A written summary of a script's visual sequences; a nonvisual storyboard.

action print A quickly made silent print made from a negative. *See also* rough print.

action props Hand props that are used by talent; guns, mirrors, swords, and so on.

action replay A British term for instant replay.

action shot □ A photograph of something or someone in motion. □ *See* moving shot.

action sketch A preliminary drawing indicating the stages of action in an animated film. Cf. character sketch.

active □ A dimmer, electrical circuit, or device that has power applied to it. □ *See* active buyer, active member, and active subscriber.

active buyer A buyer who has made recent purchases in response to advertising.

active display The visual program material on a CD-I disc currently being displayed onscreen.

active file A computer file under current use or revision.

active line The horizontal scanning line carrying television picture information as opposed to the horizontal and vertical retrace lines.

active list □ Books that are in print and available for sale or distribution. Also called *active titles.* □ A list of active buyers.

active member A member of a book club who has not completed his or her original commitment or who has completed the commitment and has continued to purchase books.

actives *See* active subscriber.

active satellite A satellite carrying a station intended to transmit or retransmit radio communication signals. Cf. passive satellite.

active search A prospective buyer of goods or services who actively looks through advertising messages for a particular product or service.

active sensor A measuring instrument in the earth exploration- satellite service or in the space reach service by means of which information is obtained by transmission and reception of radio waves.

active subscriber A subscriber who continues to receive books, newspapers, magazines, and so on. Also, in the plural, called *actives.*

active switcher A television production switcher that activates the actual switching in a remotely located rack during the vertical interval. Cf. passive switcher.

active titles *See* active list.

activity A change to or reference made to an active computer file.

actor A performer hired to play a role in a motion picture, television program, stage play, and so on. The term also includes professional singers, stunt players, airplane and helicopter pilots, and puppeteers.

Actors Equity Association (AEA) The union that represents performers in legitimate theatre.

actress A female actor or performer.

ACTS ☐ Advanced Communications Technology Satellite. ☐ All-Channel Television Society. A UHF interest group. ☐ Association of Cable Television Suppliers.

ACTT Association of Cinematograph and Television Technicians.

actual A radio or television program based on a real event.

actual damages The actual loss suffered by a plaintiff in a lawsuit. Also called *compensatory damages.*

actuality ☐ A brief report, either live or recorded, from the scene of a news event. ☐ Sounds recorded at the scene of a news event. ☐ The recording of an event as opposed to a report; often used in producing documentaries. *See also* cinema verité.

actuality effects Sound effects recorded on location as opposed to library sound effects.

actual malice The publication of defamatory material with knowledge that it is false or with reckless disregard of the truth.

actual sound Sound that comes from the performer as opposed to off-stage voices.

actual time The real time from the beginning to end of a television program, motion picture, and so on.

ACTV Advanced Compatible Television.

ACUBS Association of College and University Broadcasting Stations. The first educational broadcasting organization, founded in 1925. *See also* BEA.

acuity *See* acutance.

acutance The objective measurement of the sharpness of a photographic image. Also called *acuity.*

ACVL Association of Cinema and Video Laboratories.

AD ☐ Assistant director. ☐ Associate director. ☐ Art director.

ad An abbreviation for advertisement and advertising.

A/D Audimeter/diary system.

a/d analog to digital.

ADA ☐ Automation Data Accessory. A trademark acronym for a feature of the ARCH system wherein each videocassette is automatically identified by information recorded on the cue track. ☐ Automatic data acquisition.

Ad-A-Card A trademark for a perforated tear-off coupon attached to advertisements in selected Sunday newspaper comics and supplement sections.

ad agency *See* advertising agency.

ad alley The section of a composing room used for producing display ads. Also called *ad side.*

ADAP Analog to digital audio processor.

ADAPSO Association of Data Processing Service Organizations.

adaptation A script based on a story, movie, or play originally created for another medium.

adapter ☐ A device for connecting two dissimilar parts. Also called a *gender changer.* ☐ *See* adapter ring. ☐ A connector or two connectors joined by a short length of wire; used between equipment having different types of plugs.

adapter ring A threaded device used to hold lens filters.

adaptive delta pulse code modulation (ADPCM) A technique for converting analog audio into digital audio in any CD-I level.

ADC □ Air Defense Command. □ Analog to digital converter.

a/d converter A device used to convert analog signals to digital signals.

ad copy *See* copy.

Ad Council *See* Advertising Council, Inc., The.

adcut *See* logotype.

add □ A story appended to a radio or television newscast. □ A new subscriber added to a periodical's list of subscribers. □ An abbreviation for *additional*, as in additional news copy added to the end of a previously written story. The additional material is often slugged.

Add-A-Vision A television/film camera using a prism to split the image for reception by a television and film camera at the same time.

added dialogue □ Additional dialogue recorded after the film shooting has been completed. □ Off-camera dialogue recorded for use in editing.

added entry A library catalogue entry other than the author entry, for example, subject, title, editor. Also called a *secondary entry*. Cf. main entry.

added scenes Necessary additional scenes shot after the supposed completion of a motion picture or television program.

addendum Supplementary information added to the back of a book, often for the purpose of updating or adding material inadvertently omitted. The plural is addenda. Cf. errata and supplement.

addition The production of unwarranted sounds or syllables within a word.

additional compensation The compensation paid to a film or television writer for residuals. Cf. initial compensation.

additional service Television signals carried by a CATV system in addition to those required or permitted.

additive color mix The superimposition of light sources whereby the resultant light is composed of the sums of energies at the various wavelengths. Cf. subtractive color mix.

additive color process A now-obsolete method of using three separations for each primary color to produce a single film. Also called *additive printing* and *additive process.*

additive primary colors The colors of light that are added together to form other colors. In television, red, green, and blue added together in the proper proportion produce white. *See also* primary color. Cf. subtractive primary colors.

additive printing *See* additive color process.

additive process *See* additive color process.

additive synthesis The process of reproducing colors by using the proper proportions of the primary colors.

add on □ A circuit or device that increases performance or capability of a component or system or adds memory to a computer. □ A modification or attachment that extends the power or usefulness of a machine or device. □ A record that is added to a radio station's playlist. □ *See* assemble.

add-on edit *See* assemble edit.

add-on module A discrete module in either hardware or software that extends the specified performance of a piece of equipment or a system. Cf. insert module.

add-on sales Additional purchases made at the time merchandise is ordered, usually on recommendation.

add-on service A request by a consumer to have his or her name added to a mailing list.

address □ A label, name, or number identifying where data are located in computer RAM or ROM. □ To locate information stored in a computer. □ To refer to a device or item by its address.

addressability □ The ability of a communication system to distribute programming from a central location using computers. □ The ability of a cable television system to activate, deactivate, and otherwise control from the headend the channels received by a subscriber.

addressable converter Equipment in cable television households that allows cable operators to turn on or off the converter for pay-per-view type events.

address code The SMPTE time and control code for videotape and audio tape that numbers the hours, minutes, seconds, and frames with a biphase mark containing binary coded decimal (BCD) information.

address coding guide (ACG) A publication that contains the ZIP codes for postal service by number, block, and district.

address correction requested A postal service report that advises the sender of the new address of a person who has moved.

addressing The process of imprinting names and addresses on bulk mail.

Addressograph A machine using different sizes and styles of metal plates for addressing. Largely outdated by computer mailing list programs and other electronic devices.

Addy Award An award given by the American Advertising Federation (AAF) for excellence in advertising.

adenoid A derogatory term for an announcer, singer, or speaker with a nasal voice.

adequate sample A sample large enough to minimize chance as a factor affecting the data obtained in an investigation.

adhesion □ That quality of a binder and oxide system of a videotape that enhances the system's ability to remain affixed to the base film. Also called *anchorage.* □ The tendency of adjacent layers of tape wound on a reel to stick to each other, especially during the unreeling process. Also called *blocking.*

adhesive binding *See* perfect binding.

ad hoc □ Latin, meaning "for this." A committee or group established for a specific purpose or specific set of circumstances; temporary. □ Administrative agency rulings. Cf. stare decisis.

ad hoc network A temporary radio or television network set up for the purpose of distributing specific programming, often sports.

ad hoc system Any communication link set up for a specific purpose on a temporary basis.

ADI □ American Documentation Institute. Former name for the organization named American Society for Information Science. □ Area of dominant influence.

adiactinic Materials, such as a red gel, that prevent the passage of actinic light.

ad interconnect The linking of two or more cable television systems for the purpose of distributing advertising.

adjacency □ A radio or television program or advertisement that immediately precedes or follows another program or advertisement. □ An interval between radio or television programs available as commercial time. □ The distance between two alphanumeric characters.

adjacency policy The extent to which a radio or television station or network will separate competing commercials.

adjacent ADI An ADI that is in close proximity to the home market ADI and in which there is viewing to the home market stations. Up to three adjacent ADIs may be designated for each ADI market. When more than three adjacent ADIs overlap the home market's total survey area, each adjacent ADI is ranked in descending order based on the distribution of viewing to the home station.

adjacent channel The contiguous radio or television channel above or below the channel referred to. Cf. cochannel.

adjacent channel attenuation A measure of a receiver's ability to reject unwanted signals on an adjacent radio or television channel.

adjacent channel interference Interference between adjacent radio or television channels, often caused by insufficient mileage separation. Cf. cochannel interference.

adjacent channel selectivity *See* adjacent channel attenuation.

adjective law *See* procedural law.

adjudication □ A government agency process for the formulation of an order. □ The act or process of deciding a matter judicially. Usually a process of the courts, but also FCC decisions on competing applications, petitions for denial, and so on.

adjustment A loss of outdoor advertising service requiring delivery of a similar service. Called a *make good* in other media.

ad lib □ A newspaper reporter's telephone dictation of an unwritten story to a rewrite person. □ To add improvised dialogue or music. □ To use rehearsed material so that it sounds spontaneous. *See also* impromptu.

ad lib session call Any request of a principal performer to devise dialogue.

If no dialogue is involved, the session is deemed an ad lib or creative session call when principal performer is requested to devise action not provided by the script, storyboard, or specific direction. Also called a *creative session call.*

Adlux A tradename for a backlit photo transparency; used for product displays, signs, and so on.

adman □ A person who works in the advertising industry. □ A person who writes advertising copy. □ A compositor who sets advertising copy. Also called an *advertising person.*

ad mat A pápier maché mold used to produce a duplicate for printing advertising artwork.

administration Any governmental department or service responsible for discharging the obligations undertaken in the Convention of the International Telecommunications Union and the Regulations. The Convention was the International Telecommunications Convention of the ITU, Malaga-Torremolinos, 1973.

administrative agency An authoritative, supervisory, and controlling body within the executive branch of the federal government established by an act of Congress. Included are such agencies as the Federal Communications Commission, Federal Trade Commission, Food and Drug Administration, Interstate Commerce Commission, and Atomic Energy Commission. Also called an *independent regulatory agency.*

administrative law The branch of law concerned with the manner in which administrative agencies make rules and regulations, adjudicate cases, and enforce laws and regulations. *See* Administrative Procedure Act.

Administrative Law Judge (ALJ) The FCC personnel appointed pursuant to the requirements of Section 11 of the Administrative Procedures Act to hear and adjudicate cases brought before them, other than those to be heard by the Commission en banc.

Administrative Procedure Act (APA) The 1946 law that sets forth the rights, duties, and responsibilities by which administrative agencies carry out their functions. The provisions of the Act are now incorporated in Subchapter II and Chapter 7 of Title 5 of the United States Code.

adnorm A term used by the research firm of Daniel Starch & Associates to indicate the amount of measured readership exposure of an advertisement placed in a certain periodical. It is based on experience with the periodical, the size of the advertisement, the use or nonuse of color, and the type of product advertised considered as a proportion of the norm established for advertisements of the same sort. Also called *adnorm score.* Cf. noted, read-most, and seen/associated.

adnorm score *See* adnorm.

ad-noter A term used by the research firm of Daniel Starch & Associates to designate a reader who claims to have noticed an advertisement in a certain issue of a certain periodical. Cf. noted score.

adopt To select a required or recommended textbook for use in a class, school system, or state.

adoption The selection of a textbook for school or college class use.

ADP Automatic data processing.

ad-page exposure (APX) An Alfred Politz research design used to describe the frequency at which readers are exposed to an average advertising page in a periodical.

ADPCM Adaptive delta pulse code modulation.

adperson An individual who works in the advertising industry.

ADR Automatic dialogue replacement. *See* looping.

adr An abbreviation for address.

ad retention The rate at which the consumers of advertising messages are able to correctly identify their own exposure to advertising.

ADS Alpha Delta Sigma. An advertising fraternity.

ad side *See* ad alley.

ad slick A glossy print of an advertisement.

ADSQ Audio Data Sequence.

adult □ A widely used misnomer; often used to describe motion pictures that appeal to immature audiences.

adult contemporary (AC) A radio station format designed to appeal to adults in their late twenties and thirties.

adult western A radio or television western drama, such as "Gunsmoke," with an emphasis on characterization wherein the hero sometimes fails and a lack of trite cliches is noticeable.

advance □ A news story written before an event and held for later release. Also called an *advancer. See also* advance story. □ A payment to an author against future royalties on a book. Also called an *advance on royalty.* □ Money paid by a motion picture exhibitor to a distributor before a film is shown. □ The number of frames that the sound information precedes the corresponding picture on film.

advance agent A radio or television network or station representative who makes preliminary arrangements for a remote location.

advance ball A rounded support attached to a cutter that rides on the surface of the record so as to maintain a uniform mean depth of cut and correct for small irregularities of the disc surface.

advance book information (ABI) A brief summary or description of a book sent with a copy of a book that is not yet released.

advance copy □ A copy of a new book sent to reviewers, possible bulk-copy buyers, and so on, before the publication date. □ Copy not yet assigned a publication date.

advanced compatible television (ACTV) One of the many proposals for advanced television (ATV); compatible with existing channels and receivers.

advanced television (ATV) Any television system such as EDTV, HDTV, and IDTV, that proposes standards greater than those currently used.

Advanced Television Systems Committee (ATSC) An FCC blue ribbon advisory panel that is studying HDTV.

Advanced Television Test Center (ATTC) An equipment testing facility created to evaluate terrestrial ATV television systems in conjunction with the FCC's Advisory Committee on ATV. Sponsored by the NAB, Capital Cities/ABC, CBS, INTV, NBC, PBS, and MST.

advance feed *See* line feed.

advance file *See* future file.

advance on royalty *See* advance.

advance orders Orders placed for books before the publication date.

advancer *See* advance.

advance ratings Ratings information released prior to the publication of a survey report.

advances Nielsen Station Index audience estimates available via telephone prior to client receipt of the printed report.

advance sheets Pages from a yet unpublished book distributed for purposes of review, promotion, or revision. Cf. galley proof.

advance start A periodical subscription that does not begin with the current issue but is delayed by either the subscriber or publisher. Cf. back start.

advance story A story written about an event that has not yet taken place. Also called *forecasting.* Considered unethical by some journalists.

adversary *See* antagonist.

advertise To attempt to persuade people to voluntarily produce a recommended behavior pattern by presenting them with an openly sponsored, multiply reproduced message; the message is delivered by purchased use of a medium's space or time.

advertised price □ The retail price of a single copy of a newspaper or magazine. □ The cost of a newspaper or magazine subscription as quoted by a supplier. □ The standard price for a quantity of radio or television advertising time, taking into consideration the frequency of the advertiser's commercials and the total amount of time purchased. Cf. basic price. □ The price for a product or service as stated in an advertisement.

advertisement □ A written, verbal, pictorial, graphic, and so on, announcement of goods or services for sale that uses the mass media as a vehicle. *See also* commercial matter. □ As it applies to public broadcast stations, any message or other programming material that is broadcast or otherwise transmitted in exchange for remuneration and that is intended to promote any service, facility, or product offered by any person who is engaged in such offering for profit; and to express the views of any person with respect to any matter of public importance or interest except where prohibited by law.

advertiser A national, regional, or local institution, company, retail establishment, or other organization that pays for the placement of an advertisement.

advertising □ The act or process of calling the attention of the public to goods, services, or institutions. □ The persuasive material used in advertisements. □ The business or profession of producing and placing advertisements for mass media distribution. □ The act of producing and placing advertisements. □ In general, an advertisement or advertisements.

advertising agency An independent commercial service organization that contracts with advertisers to develop and manage their advertising, for a fee or for commission derived from a standard media discount on the advertiser's spending. Also called an *ad agency.*

advertising allowance A payment or service by a source of products or services or a representative to a merchant for advertising the products or services.

advertising appropriation The amount of money budgeted by an advertiser for advertising for a specific amount of time or space.

Advertising Association of the West (AAW) A group of West Coast advertising organizations absorbed into the American Advertising Federation in 1967.

advertising availabilities *See* availabilities.

advertising campaign *See* campaign.

Advertising Checking Bureau (ACB) A service organization that supplies advertisers and agencies with tearsheets of advertisements run in publications and with other information, so that client and competitor advertising impact can be assessed.

advertising continuity □ The words written for a commercial or advertisement. □ The theme used in an advertising campaign.

advertising contract A written agreement between an advertiser and a mass medium outlet regarding the cost of advertising space or time.

Advertising Council, Inc., The (ACI) A private, nonprofit organization supported by business and advertising that conducts national advertising campaigns for nonprofit organizations. Usually referred to as the Ad Council.

advertising cutoff A rule used to separate advertisements from news, text, or other advertisements.

advertising department The department of a newspaper or magazine responsible for advertising. Often divided into classified and display units.

advertising director □ An individual within a company who is responsible for the advertising budget. □ A magazine executive who coordinates the sale of advertising space.

Advertising Federation of America (AFA) An association of organizations representing various activities relating to advertising; now part of the American Advertising Federation.

advertising insertion order *See* insertion order.

advertising lineage The number of lines of advertising carried in a publication in a given issue.

advertising manager An employee of an organization that advertises who is responsible for review and approval of advertising plans and, usually, executions of advertisements; sometimes responsible for approval of sales promotion plans. Typically reports to a marketing director. Cf. account executive.

advertising media All of the various media used to convey advertising messages.

advertising mix The proportion of time or space purchased in the different media by a single advertiser.

advertising network *See* network.

advertising penetration An index of the number of persons who have seen an advertisement for a specific product or service.

advertising person *See* adman.

advertising promotion The efforts made by the mass media to sell, increase sales, or improve advertising.

advertising rates The charges made by the mass media for advertising space or time.

advertising representative A person or agency that secures advertising for newspapers and magazines. Cf. station rep.

advertising research The investigation of a product or service to assist in discovering its marketable characteristics.

Advertising Research Foundation (ARF) An association of advertisers, advertising agencies, advertising media, and media research representatives for the purpose of advancing advertising research methodology and maintaining research standards. The ARF publishes the bimonthly *Journal of Advertising Research.*

advertising reserve An advertising budget fund established without a prior specification for its use, to be used subsequently for unanticipated contingencies.

advertising response coefficient A measure of market demand for a product or service, determined by dividing the percentage of change in sales by the percentage of change in advertising.

advertising schedule The complete listing of copy and dates for an advertising campaign.

advertising service The various forms of assistance rendered to an advertiser by the media to aid in producing advertising.

advertising specialty An inexpensive item bearing an advertiser's name used as a gift.

advertising strategy The planning and directing of advertising campaigns, including research, creativity, copy, selection of media, media use, marketing, and so on.

advertising structure In outdoor advertising, a physical structure built by a plant operator to display advertising. The advertising message is applied to the structure in several different ways, and the structures are built to standard specifications of posters or bulletins.

advertising theme The dominant subject or idea that ties an advertising campaign together.

advertising wedge The superiority of a product that may be used in designing a commercial or advertisement.

advertising weight The number of advertising messages used in or planned for a campaign. Also called *support.*

advertorial A contraction of advertisement and editorial. A point-of-view commercial; a combination of display advertising and editorial comment. Often a somewhat deceptive form of advertising. Also spelled *advetorial.*

advice program A radio or television program featuring astrologers, fortune tellers, and so on, who may tend to mislead the public.

advisory News wire advice sent to radio and television station managers, news directors, program directors, and so on.

Advisory Committee on Advanced Television Service (ACATS) The FCC's industry committee on high-definition television.

Advisory Council of National Organizations (ACNO) An organization that counsels the Corporation for Public Broadcasting on its role in relation to education.

advocacy advertising Advertising by companies or industries that are in disfavor with groups such as environmentalists.

advocacy journalist A reporter who attempts to persuade rather than report, sometimes under the guise of objective journalism.

advt An abbreviation for advertisement.

AE □ Angled end. □ Account executive.

AEA Actors Equity Association. A union.

AECT Association for Educational Communications and Technology.

AEJ Association for Education in Journalism.

AEJMC Association for Education in Journalism and Mass Communication.

AEM Association of Electronic Manufacturers, Inc.

AER □ Alpha Epsilon Rho. A college and university broadcasting fraternity. Also spelled AERho. □ Association for Education by Radio.

AERho *See* AER.

aerial A British term for an antenna.

aerial cable A cable television cable that is strung overhead on utility poles as opposed to underground.

aerial image An animation technique used to combine an optical image in space or an image on film with animation or other artwork on a cel. Also called *aerial photography.*

aerial image animation stand The animation stand used to hold the camera, cels, and associated equipment.

aerial mount A camera mount used in a helicopter or airplane.

aerial perspective The camera view as seen from an overhead shot.

aerial photography *See* aerial image.

aerial print *See* air print.

aerial shot An exterior overhead camera shot usually taken from a helicopter or airplane, but may be taken from a crane.

aerospace law The body of international law (or lack thereof) that governs the use of satellite communications in the world.

Aero-Vision A patented, antivibration mount for cameras used in helicopters. *See* helicopter mount.

AERT Association for Education by Radio-TV. *See* BEA.

AES Audio Engineering Society. A professional association.

aesthetic distance The gap between a viewer's ability to distinguish between full identification with a play or program and the full realization that it is a representational event.

aesthetics The branch of philosophy dealing with the essential nature of beauty.

AF □ Audio fidelity. □ Audio frequency.

AFA □ Actors' Fund of America. □ Advertising Federation of America.

AFC Automatic frequency control.

AFCCE Association of Federal Communications Consulting Engineers.

AFCEA Armed Forces Communications and Electronics Association.

affective behavior Advertising that attempts to affect the attitudes of consumers.

affidavit □ Any sworn statement. □ A notarized statement by a radio or television station that programs or commercials were broadcast as scheduled. Also called an *affidavit of performance.*

affidavit of performance *See* affidavit.

affiliate □ Any organization that contracts to supply goods or services, to advertise and merchandise, or in various ways to carry out the policies of a company operated in close association with it. □ A broadcasting station that receives programs from a national or regional network. *See also* affiliated station. □ A cable television system that carries the programming provided by a cable network or producer.

affiliate agreement A contract between a radio or television network and its affiliates that specifies the rights and duties of the organizations involved. Also called an *affiliation agreement.*

affiliated relationship An arrangement between publishers whereby one agrees to handle the distribution of books for a percentage of the income derived from the sales of the books.

affiliated station A television station having a regular affiliation with one of the three national television networks, under which it serves as that network's primary outlet for the presentation of its programs in a market.

affiliation agreement *See* affiliate agreement.

affirmative action A policy established to eliminate sexual and minority imbalance in the hiring and retention of employees.

afghanistanism The focusing of attention by the media on distant events in order to avoid local controversial issues of public importance.

AFI American Film Institute.

AFIPS American Federation of Information Processing Societies.

AFL-CIO American Federation of Labor-Congress of Industrial Organizations. The major American union.

AFM American Federation of Musicians. Also AF of M. A union.

AFN American Forces Network. An international broadcasting organization based in Europe and programmed primarily for American servicepeople.

afocal lens □ A lens attached to another lens to increase or decrease its focal length. □ An element in a zoom lens.

AF of M *See* AFM.

a fortiori With greater reason; a stronger argument.

AFP Agence France-Presse. One of the world's major press associations.

AFPL Alianza Federal des Pueblos Libres. A citizens' group.

AFRA American Federation of Radio Artists. Now AFTRA.

AFRS Armed Forces Radio Service.

AFRTS Armed Forces Radio and Television Service. An international broadcasting organization furnishing programming to American broadcasting stations overseas and in the United States.

AFT Automatic fine tuning.

afterglow The persistence of luminance on a television picture tube after the removal of the electron beam's excitation.

afterimage □ A picture ghost or tail. □ The image seen by the eyes after an image is no longer on a picture tube or screen. *See also* persistence of vision.

afternoon drive The time period on radio from 3 p.m. to 7 p.m. *See* daypart.

after-shows Planned entertainment for a studio audience that immediately follows a radio or television broadcast.

AFTRA American Federation of Television and Radio Artists.

AFTRCC Aerospace Flight Tests Radio Coordinating Council.

AFTS Armed Forces Television Service.

AFV Audio follow video.

AGAC American Guild of Authors and Composers. A voluntary organization for the protection of the interests of songwriters.

against the grain The direction across the fibers in a sheet of paper. *See also* grain. Cf. with the grain.

agate □ The size of type measuring 5-1/2 points in depth. □ A tool with an agate stone used to burnish gold, silver, or colored edges on books. □ *See* agate line.

agate line A unit of measurement used as a standard in selling advertising space; fourteen agate lines equals one column inch. Also called a *line.*

agate type *See* agate.

AGB Audits of Great Britain. A ratings company that operated people meters in the United States until 1988.

ag bf An abbreviation for agate boldface.

AGC □ Address coding guide. □ Automatic gain control.

age To break in a piece of equipment.

agency □ An independent news organization that sells news reports and photographs to mass media outlets on a per-story or subscription basis. □ Each authority of the government of the United States, whether or not it is within or subject to review by another agency. The term does not include, for example, the Congress or the courts of the United States. □ A talent or advertising agency.

agency action The whole or a part of an agency rule, order, license, sanction, relief, or the equivalent or denial thereof, or failure to act.

agency ad Any advertisement furnished by an organization not controlled by the media outlet.

agency commission A sum of money paid to an advertising agency by media for placing business, usually 15 percent of the value of the contract. For the outdoor advertising medium, 16-2/3 percent.

agency copy Material from an advertising agency intended for use as news copy.

Agency for Instructional Television (AIT) An organization formed in 1973 to promote education through television. Formerly, National Instructional Television (NIT).

agency group *See* network.

agency head A headline furnished by an advertising agency, often using bold or emphasized type.

agency network *See* network.

agency of record (AOR) The advertising agency designated by an advertiser from among participating agencies to handle the account for a radio or television program.

agency proceeding An administrative agency process involving rule making, adjudication, or licensing.

agency-produced program A radio or television program, often a special or spectacular, assembled as a package by an advertising agency and sold to a station or network ready for presentation.

agency recognition *See* recognition.

agency recommendation *See* recommendation.

agency record A document held by any government agency.

agency tape A British term for written material received from a news wire service.

agenda setting A supposed effect of the mass media; the ability of the mass media to set the agenda to affect the public's beliefs about what is important.

agent □ An individual who advises and represents clients in contractual negotiations. Cf. manager. □ A talent booking representative.

age/sex populations Estimates of population, broken out by various age/sex groups within a county.

agglomeration The clustering of the granules of silver in a film's emulsion.

aggregation A theory that assumes that all consumers of the mass media are similar.

aggressive cues theory The theory that exposure to violence on television leads to aggressive behavior in viewers.

agitation The process of keeping the developer or film in a state of constant motion in order to keep exhausted developer from streaking the film.

AGMA American Guild of Musical Artists. A union.

agony column The personal ads in the classified section of a newspaper.

AGREE Advisory Group on Reliability of Electronics Equipment.

agreement □ A contract or understanding reached between a broadcast station and, for example, citizens' groups, networks, advertising agency, or musical format service companies. □ A term sometimes used for a union contract.

agricultural programs (A) Programs including market reports, farming, or other information specifically addressed, or primarily of interest, to the agricultural population. An FCC program type category.

Agricultural Publishers Association (APA) A nonprofit organization of publishers of periodicals edited for farmers' interests.

AGVA American Guild of Variety Artists. A union.

A head A first-level subhead. Cf. B head and C head.

AI Artificial intelligence.

AIAA Association of International Advertising Agencies.

AICE Association of Independent Commercial Editors.

AICP Association of Independent Commercial Producers.

AID □ Arbitron's Information on Demand. □ Automatic Interaction Detector. □ Agency for International Development.

AIDA Attention, interest, desire, action. The four-step marketing procedure used in developing some advertising messages. It means gain the audience's attention, develop the audience members' interest, motivate their desire to purchase, and move them to action.

aided recall A recall interview in which the interviewer gives the respondent some help in remembering past behavior. In a broadcast survey the help may be in the form of a list of programs that were broadcast during the time periods in question. Sometimes referred to as roster recall and roster study.

AIEE American Institute of Electrical Engineers. *See also* IEEE.

AIEEE American Institute of Electrical and Electronics Engineers. *See also* IEEE.

AIGA American Institute of Graphic Arts.

AIM Accuracy in media.

AIMS Association of Independent Metropolitan Stations. An association of independent broadcasting stations in larger markets.

AIPCS Aspen Institute Program on Communications and Society. A continuing study established in 1971 to identify and develop policies concerning major issues related to the communication media.

AIPO American Institute of Public Opinion.

AIPS Automatic indexing and proofreading system.

AIR Associacion Interamericana de Radiodifusion. *See* IAAB.

air □ A slang expression for white space. □ To broadcast a radio or television program or commercial.

air agitation To introduce air into a developer in order to agitate the solution.

air bearing A low-friction bearing in which air under pressure is forced between a stationary sleeve and a surrounding, closely fitting rotating sleeve. These elements together constitute the bearing, and the air serves as the lubricant for the bearing in a quadruplex videotape recorder.

airbrush A small compressed-air spray painting device used for artwork, retouching photographs, and so on.

air check An off-the-air taping of a radio or television commercial or program. Cf. audition tape.

air date The day on which a radio or television program or announcement is scheduled.

air gap The space between a videotape and a record or playback head.

airing The broadcasting of a radio or television program or announcement.

air lease rights The rights granted to permit the broadcasting of a radio or television program.

air lock *See* sound lock.

air man Anyone who performs in front of a microphone or camera.

AIRMLC All-Industry Radio Music Licensing Committee. A broadcasting industry committee formed to work with ASCAP, BMI, and SESAC in music licensing.

air name A professional name used by disc jockeys, announcers, and so on, on radio and television stations.

air personality A well-known disc jockey or announcer.

airplane A network commercial or program that is designed for a nonspecific audience.

airplane pilot A licensed aircraft pilot who is employed to fly or taxi aircraft (including helicopters) before the camera in the filming of motion pictures.

air play □ The performance of a song, musical selection, or other musical piece on the air by a radio station. □ The amount of time devoted on the air to a specific record.

air print An aerial print, as opposed to a contact print. Also called an *aerial print.*

air squeegee A squeegee used in film processing that uses compressed air instead of rubber or foam.

air talent *See* talent.

air time □ The time a radio or television broadcast is scheduled to begin. □ The total program or commercial length.

airwaves A colloquial expression for electromagnetic waves.

AIT Agency for Instructional Television. A nonprofit American-Canadian organization established in 1973 to strengthen education through television. The successor to NIT.

AITS Association of Independent Television Stations, Inc.

AIVF Association of Independent Video and Filmmakers, Inc.

AJPA American Jewish Press Association.

AKA An acronym for *also known as.*

AL □ Assignment of license. An FCC file-number prefix. □ Assembly language.

ALA □ American Library Association. □ Authors League of America. A union.

A la carte agency An advertising agency that works on a fee basis instead of by commission. Also called a *modular agency.*

ALAI Association Litteraire et Artistique Internationale.

album □ A book consisting of blank leaves. □ A cardboard sleeve for a phonograph record. □ One or more phonograph discs enclosed in a dust cover. □ A set of compact discs.

albumen plate An offset lithography printing plate that uses the albumen from eggs as the sensitized coating.

album identifier A field of the FSVDR identifying the set of discs to which the volume belongs.

album oriented rock (AOR) A radio station format that consists primarily of all types of rock music.

ALC Automatic level control. *See* automatic gain control.

Aldine Originally, a book published by Aldus Manutius of Venice. Now used as a generic term for fine editions of books and for certain styles of type.

aleatory A filming technique that relies on unplanned camera shots and chance conditions. Often used for news or documentaries.

A lens *See* anamorphic lens.

Alexander Bill The unpassed Congressional Bill of 1918 that would have given the government a monopoly on broadcasting.

Alexanderson alternator A World War I mechanical generator capable of supplying frequencies up to 200 kHz for radio transmission. Named after its inventor, Ernst F. W. Alexanderson.

ALF Annual license fee.

algorithm □ A rule or procedure for solving a mathematical problem that frequently involves the repetition of an operation. Extensively used in 3D modeling and animation systems. □ Any of an infinite variety of computing methods.

aliasing Display artifacts caused by representing continuously variable information in the form of discrete pixels. *See also* jaggies.

alibi copy A filed duplicate of any news copy.

alien One who is not a citizen of the United States, and thus ineligible to hold a broadcasting license under Section 310 of the Communications Act.

Alien and Sedition Acts The federal and state laws passed between 1798 and 1800 that made attacks on the government, its laws, and individual officers punishable as sedition.

align To place type in a straight line, either horizontally or vertically.

alignment □ The adjusting of individual parts or components in an electronic system to work together. □ The adjustment of circuits and systems of a television tape recorder so as to provide optimal performance of the equipment. □ The condition resulting from such adjustment.

alignment chart *See* resolution chart and test pattern.

alignment tape A tape specially and carefully recorded to provide accurate signals and track patterns by which the performance of a television tape recorder can be assessed and adjusted. Also called a *standard tape.*

alive □ A current news story. □ Type that is set but not yet used. □ *See* live.

ALJ Administrative law judge.

alkali A soluble salt used in film developing solutions. Cf. acid.

all-banding A CATV term meaning the use of each band the system is capable of carrying.

all caps □ Printed matter that is set in all capital letters. □ An editor's instruction to set the type in capital letters.

all-channel A term referring to receivers, antennas, and amplifiers capable of accepting a broad range of frequencies. Television receivers shipped in interstate commerce were required to have all-channel capabilities effective April 30, 1964. Also called *all-wave.*

All Channel Receiver Act The 1962 statute that required all television receivers shipped in interstate commerce to be equipped to receive UHF as well as VHF stations.

alleged Supposed or so-called. A word used to soften an accusation against someone accused of or arrested for a crime. Also used for unproven charges and to protect newspeople against libel.

alley The aisle in a print shop or composing room.

all firsts A reference to a collection of first editions.

alligator clip A metal connector with a spring used to make temporary electrical connections.

alligator tail A swishing sound heard on some audio recordings.

all in-all out A television director's command to superimpose a picture and fade it out.

All-Inclusive Study An A. C. Nielsen report on audience data containing tabulation of four-week cumulative television audiences, used to estimate reach and frequency and to calculate gross rating points.

All-Industry Television Station Music License Committee An industry group formed to lobby for performance rights to be included in syndicated programming and against blanket licensing.

all in hand Copy that has been completed and sent to the compositor.

all market measurement period *See* sweep.

all news A radio station format.

all night The time period on radio from midnight to 6 a.m. *See* daypart.

allocation □ An entry in the Table of Frequency Allocations of a given frequency band for the purpose of its use by one or more terrestrial or space radio communication services or the radio astronomy services under specified conditions. □ The reservation of a band of frequencies for a specific radio communication service. For example, the FCC has allocated the frequencies from 88 to 108 mHz for FM broadcasting. Cf. allotment, assignment, and licensing. □ The assignment of data to specified computer storage locations. □ The sharing of story credits by more than one writer. □ The allotment of limited numbers of items to users.

all other An Audit Bureau of Circulations designation for deliveries outside the city or retail trading zone.

allotment □ The entry of a designated frequency channel in an agreed plan, adopted by a competent conference, for use by one or more administrations for terrestrial or space radio communication services in one or more identified countries or geographical areas and under specified conditions. □ The number of poster panels in an outdoor advertising showing. Generally, the larger the market, the more panels offered for sale to give a comparable advertising weight. □ Any equitable distribution of advertising space or time for which demand exceeds supply. □ The granting of a channel within an allocated band to a specific location by the FCC. Allotment applies only to FM and TV; AM channels are not allotted, but licensed on the basis of demonstrated need and noninterference with existing stations. Formerly called *assignment. See* allocation, licensing, and Table of Allotments.

allowance A payment made to others by a publisher for cooperative advertising or other expenses.

all published An incomplete set of books.

All-Purpose Linotype (APL) A small Linotype machine similar to a Ludlow.

all rights reserved A phrase used in books and other printed materials saying that the contents are copyrighted and may not be reproduced in any form without the permission of the publisher.

all-talk A radio station format consisting of two-way conversation between a communicator and the audience.

all up Copy that has been set in type.

allusion An indirect reference to a person or event; sometimes a play on words.

all-wave *See* all-channel.

ALMA Association of Literary Magazines of America.

alnico A much-used magnetic alloy for loudspeaker magnets; made from aluminum, nickel, cobalt, and steel.

alpha □ An abbreviation for *alphanumeric.* □ Computer data in alphabetic as opposed to numeric characters.

alphabet □ The letters or symbols that form the basic elements of a written language and the sounds of the spoken language. □ A computer character set that does not include numbers but may include symbols.

alphabetic-numeric *See* alphanumeric.

alphabet length The length of all the lowercase characters of the alphabet, usually stated in points.

Alpha Delta Sigma An advertising fraternity.

Alpha Epsilon Rho (AER)(AERho) A national organization of students and faculty interested in broadcast education.

alphameric *See* alphanumeric.

alphanumeric □ A character set that contains letters, numbers, and usually other symbols. Also called *alphameric* and *alphabetic-numeric.* □ *See* alphanumeric news.

alphanumeric news Printed information by a character generator in alpha and numeric characters projected on a television screen. Used for news, weather, sports results, community calendars, stock prices, and so on.

Alpha Phi Gamma A journalism fraternity.

Alphatype A keyboard photocomposing system that used a magnetic tape recorder to store keyboard information.

alpha wrap In helical scan videotape recorders, a tape path wherein the tape entering the scanner assembly passes over or under the tape as it leaves the scanner assembly, resulting in a tape-path configuration resembling the lowercase Greek letter alpha. Cf. M wrap and omega wrap.

alteration A change made in a proof after it has been set in type. *See* author's alteration and editor's alteration. Cf. printer's error.

alteration cycle The successive typesetting passes made due to changes made in proofs after the first typesetting pass.

alternate-azimuth heads *See* azimuth recording.

alternate bundles run A variety of split run in which different versions of an advertisement are printed in separate phases of a press run, the two versions of the advertisement being geographically commingled when the issues are bundled for circulation delivery.

alternate channel A radio or television channel located two channels above or below the channel in question.

alternate channel interference Interference in a radio or television channel caused by a transmitter operating in the second channel above or below the channel in question.

alternate delivery service A mail service that is not run by the United States Postal Service.

alternate relay station A broadcast station that removes its carrier from the air during an EBS activation period and stands by in operational readiness to assume broadcasting responsibilities in the event the primary relay station is unable to carry out operations.

alternate sponsor The sponsor of the next broadcast of a program series that has rotating advertisers.

alternate station A broadcast station that removes its carrier from the air during an EBS activation period and stands by in operational readiness to assume broadcasting responsibilities in the event the primary station is unable to carry out operations.

alternate title A second, often shorter title to a novel, motion picture, or other art form.

alternate transmitter A radio or television transmitter used for standby purposes.

alternate weeks (A/W) Scheduling instructions to a medium, especially to a newspaper, indicating advertisements are to appear every other week.

alternating current (ac) A continuously repeating flow of electricity that is sinusoidal in character and changes from zero to maximum potential in one direction, then decreases to zero and increases to maximum in the other direction, then returns to zero potential. In U.S. power circuits there are 60 complete cycles per second (hertz). Cf. direct current.

alternative press A term applied to antiestablishment publications; often publications dealing with protests and drugs.

alternative radio *See* underground radio.

alternative station Generally, a noncommercial radio or television station. *See also* underground radio.

alternative title The subtitle, if any, of a book or other publication.

alternator *See* Alexanderson alternator.

alum Any of various double salts (aluminum, potash, and so on) used in film hardening.

aluminum screen □ A projection screen made from a thin sheet of aluminum. □ A television picture tube with a thin layer of aluminum deposited on the back of the tube surface.

AM Amplitude modulation.

a.m. An abbreviation for a morning newspaper. Cf. p.m.

AMA American Marketing Association.

amateur A person licensed by the FCC to operate a radio transmitter as a hobby. Also called a *ham.*

amateur service A radio communication service for the purpose of self-training, intercommunication, and technical investigations carried out by amateurs, that is, by duly authorized persons interested in radio technique solely with a personal aim and without pecuniary interest.

amateur station A radio station operated by a duly authorized person interested in radio technique solely with a personal aim and without pecuniary interest.

A matter *See* A copy.

amberlith An orange-colored sheet of acetate.

ambient Encompassing the immediate area.

ambient conditions The pressure, temperature, surfaces, volume, and other states of the surrounding medium.

ambient light □ The surrounding light exclusive of that being directed on a specific location. For example, during slide presentations, the room light is ambient light. *See* available light. □ The general level of light on a set not directed specifically at the subject. *See* base-light.

ambient noise The background sounds in a studio or remote location.

ambient sound The sound that exists at any given location. Also called *environmental sound* and *nat sound.*

ambiguous Indistinct or doubtful in meaning.

ambiguous time The undefined passage of time between the scenes of a motion picture or teleplay.

ambiguous words A potentially defamatory statement capable of being understood in more than one way.

ambisonics A musical listening experience that approaches the atmosphere and realism of a live performance.

AM broadcast band The band of frequencies extending from 535 to 1605 (soon 1705) kHz.

AM broadcast channel The band of frequencies occupied by the carrier and the upper and lower sidebands of an AM broadcast signal with the carrier frequency at the center. The carrier frequencies assigned to AM broadcast stations begin at 540 kHz and are in successive steps of 10 kHz to 1600 (1700) kHz.

AM broadcast station A broadcast station licensed for the dissemination of radio communications intended to be received by the public and operated on a channel in the band 535 through 1605 kHz. The term *AM broadcast* is synonymous with the term *standard broadcast*.

ambush interview An on-the-spot interview made without prearrangement or consent; usually of persons not wishing to be interviewed.

amendment An alteration or revision of an existing legislative statute or of a constitution.

American Academy of Advertising (AAA) An organization composed of individuals who teach advertising and those who are interested in the field.

American Advertising Federation (AAF) A national association of advertising agencies, media owners, advertisers, and others whose purposes are to promote professional and public understanding of the usefulness of advertising and to raise professional standards. Founded in 1967, it is a merger of the Advertising Federation of America and the Advertising Association of the West.

American Association of Advertising Agencies (AAAA) The national organization of the advertising agency business. These agencies place nearly 80 percent of all advertising appearing in the United States. AAAA has developed the Agency Service Standards, Standards of Practice, and the copyright contracts and space- and time-buying contracts used by almost all advertising agencies. Also called the *Four A's*.

American Association of Cable Television Owners (AACTO) A cable television association designed for minority owners.

American Association of Newspaper Representatives, Inc. (AANR) The former name of the National Advertising Sales Association.

American Bar Association (ABA) The major professional association of lawyers in the United States that sets forth rules and standards for responsibilities and judicial conduct.

American Book Producers Association (ABPA) An association of individual book producers.

American Booksellers Association (ABA) A national association of owners of retail bookstores.

American Broadcasting Company (ABC) One of the major broadcasting networks in the United States. Formed in 1943 by the purchase of the Blue Network from NBC.

American Business Press, Inc. (ABP) An organization of business publishers founded in 1965 with a merger of Associated Business Publications and National Business Publications.

American Committee for Liberation *See* Radio Liberty.

American Federation of Musicians (AFM) A labor union.

American Federation of Television and Radio Artists (AFTRA) A union of actors, singers, announcers, and certain technicians in radio and television broadcasting.

American Guild of Musical Artists (AGMA) A labor union for singers and dancers.

American Guild of Variety Artists (AGVA) A labor union for circus performers, magicians, comics, and so on.

American Institute of Graphic Arts (AIGA) A national organization devoted to encouragement of the graphic arts.

American Institute of Public Opinion (AIPO) A research firm founded by George Gallup in 1935. *See also* ARI.

American Library Association (ALA) A professional association of librarians and others interested in libraries.

American Management Association A nonprofit organization devoted to education and discussion of various ideas in the field of management.

American Marconi Company A company owned by the British Marconi Company, which held a virtual monopoly on early commercial wireless operations.

American Marketing Association (AMA) A national association formed for the promotion of improved marketing practices.

American Mechanical Rights Association (AMRA) An organization that collects mechanical royalties from writers and publishers. *See also* mechanical rights.

American National Standards Institute (ANSI) An independent industry-wide association that establishes standards to promote consistency and interchangeability among manufacturers. This organization was formerly known as the United States of America Standards Institute (USASI or ASI), and previous to that as the American Standards Association (ASA).

American Newspaper Guild (ANG) A labor union of newspaper, magazine, and wire service employees.

American Newspaper Publishers Association (ANPA) An organization founded in 1887 of publishers of daily newspapers in the United States and Canada.

American point system The system by which type size is measured. *See also* point.

American Public Radio A nonprofit radio network furnishing programs to public radio stations.

American Public Transit Association (APTA) An organization of individuals and organizations involved in transit advertising.

American Radio Relay League (ARRL) An organization of amateur radio operators.

American Society of Advertising and Promotion, Inc. (ASAP) A group dedicated to providing practical information on all forms of advertising and promotion.

American Society of Cinematographers (ASC) A professional association of motion picture and television directors of photography.

American Society of Composers, Authors, and Publishers (ASCAP) An organization, formed in 1914, that licenses nondramatic performances of musical compositions on behalf of its members and collects royalties for them. Cf. BMI and SESAC.

American Society of Newspaper Editors (ASNE) The major professional organization of newspaper editors.

American Society of Television Cameramen, Inc. An organization of videographers affiliated with the international organization of videographers.

American Standard Code for Information Interchange (ASCII) A standard data transmission code designed to achieve compatibility between data devices.

American system The 525-line scan line television system used in the Western hemisphere and Japan. *See also* NTSC, PAL, and SECAM. Cf. European system.

American Television and Radio Commercials Festival The annual competition to honor excellence in broadcast advertising. The winners are awarded a golden statuette, the Clio.

American Women in Radio and Television (AWRT) A nonprofit organization of women working in the broadcasting field, whose purpose is to enhance the role of women in the industry.

AM-FM combination A situation in which both an AM and an FM station are operated in the same community by the same licensee.

AM-FM duplication *See* program duplication.

AM-FM receiver A radio receiver capable of receiving both AM and FM signals. Also called an *AM-FM tuner.*

AM-FM total A figure shown in market reports for AM-FM affiliates in time periods when they are simulcast.

AM-FM tuner *See* AM-FM receiver.

AMI Association for Multi-Image.

AMIC Asian Mass Communication Research and Information Center. Based in Singapore.

amici curiae The plural of amicus curiae.

amicus curiae Literally, friend of the court. A person who, having an interest in a case, presents evidence or legal assistance.

amidol A colorless crystalline salt used as a film developer.

AmJur *American Jurisprudence.* A legal encyclopedia.

AML Amplitude modulated link.

ammeter A meter used to measure electric current. *See also* ampere.

AMMO Audience Measurement by Market for Outdoor.

A mode The editing of videotape in the order the shots are listed on an edit decision list without leaving any blank tape. Cf. B mode.

AMOL Automated measurement of lineups.

amortization □ The depreciation of equipment and other property over a period of time. □ The allocation of costs for program acquisition over a period of time.

A mount A type of bayonet lens mount. Cf. C mount.

AMP □ Associated Music Publishers. □ Association of Media Producers.

amp An abbreviation for *ampere, amplification, amplifier,* and *amplitude.*

AMPA American Medical Publishers Association.

AMPAS Academy of Motion Picture Arts and Sciences.

ampere (A) Abbreviated amp or A. A unit of electrical current equal to the flow of one volt across a resistance of one ohm. Named after Andre M. Ampere of France.

ampersand A typographical symbol (&) for *and.*

amplification The ratio of the output of an electronic device to its input, usually expressed in decibels.

amplification factor *See* gain figure.

amplifier An electronic device or component that increases the magnitude of its input signal. May be a vacuum tube, a transistor, and so on, or it may be a combination of amplifiers.

amplify To increase the power, voltage, or amperage in a circuit.

amplitude The magnitude, range, or voltage, power, and so on, of any electrical signal or radio wave.

amplitude distortion *See* nonlinear distortion.

amplitude modulation (AM) A system of modulation in which the envelope of the transmitted wave contains a component similar to the wave form of the signal to be transmitted. Cf. frequency modulation, and phase modulation.

Amplitude Modulated Link (AML) A multichannel system for CATV that operates at 18,000 mHz.

AMPTP Association of Motion Picture and Television Producers.

AMRA American Mechanical Rights Association.

AMST Association of Maximum Service Telecasters. Now MST.

AMT Amplitude modulated transmitter.

Amtec Automatic time element compensator. A device produced by Ampex that eliminates scalloping, skewing, and quadrature error. Term now obsolete. *See also* pixlock, edit code, and Editec.

amusement tax A tax placed on entertainment for admission to motion pictures, theatres, and so on.

ANA □ American Newspaper Association. □ Association of National Advertisers.

anacom A contraction of analog and computer.

anaglyph A picture containing two views of the same object recorded from separate points.

anaglyphic projection A method of producing three-dimensional motion pictures by having an audience wear two different colored lenses (usually red and green) to view the two superimposed projected pictures.

analine printing *See* flexography.

analog The representation of numerical values using continuously changing physical quantities such as voltage or current. Cf. digital.

analog channel A communication channel that is designed for the transmission of analog data.

analog computer A computer that accepts continuously changing input as opposed to one that measures discrete units. Cf. digital computer.

analog recording A method of recording in which the information is represented by continuously variable changes that are directly proportional to the information contained in the original signal. Cf. digital recording.

analog to digital converter (ADC) A device that changes the analog output signals into digital values for use in a digital computer system. Cf. digital to analog converter.

analogue A variant spelling of *analog.*

analyst A radio or television news analyst; one who explains the meaning of news stories.

analytical density A method for determining the density of the individual dye layers in an emulsion. Cf. integral density.

analytic documentary A nonobjective resolvent documentary. Cf. persuasive documentary.

analyze To study the nature of the information received in a survey, the script of a program, and so on.

analyzer Any device that monitors a component or system for inspection or maintenance.

anamorphic A method of compressing a wide-screen motion picture to fit on standard 35 mm film.

anamorphic compression The squeezing of the width of a picture using an anamorphic lens.

anamorphic lens A special lens that enables a wide-screen picture to be economically shot on a smaller format film. The lens compresses or "squeezes" the image vertically as it is photographed; a compatible lens on the projector reverses the process, or expands the image, producing correctly proportioned images on the screen. Also called an *A lens.*

anamorphic print A motion picture print of a wide-screen film.

Anamorphoscope An anamorphic projection process developed in France in the 1920s that, upon renaming, became CinemaScope.

anastigmat A lens corrected for astigmatism.

anchor □ The main or featured talent on a television newscast who reads the news and introduces taped or filmed stories. □ To highlight a book page, newspaper page, and so on, using graphic symbols. □ To fasten a printing plate to a block with screws and solder. □ An antenna mast support, buried in the ground, to which guy wires are attached.

anchorage *See* adhesion.

anchoring *See* sweating.

anchorman A male anchor.

anchor table The desk or table at which television newscasters sit.

anchorwoman A female anchor.

ancillary doctrine The finding by a court that laws or rules are constitutional because they are necessary to the proper regulation of an industry. Sometimes referred to as *reasonably ancillary.*

ancillary exhibition The exhibition of feature films by home video and pay television. Cf. broadcast exhibition.

ancillary market □ A secondary market for programs that have completed their first run on networks, stations, pay television, motion picture circuits, and so on. □ A market made up of buyers of products and other items related to, but not consisting of, the primary product. Ancillary items may consist of toys, games, posters, and so on.

ancillary rights The legal rights granted to an individual or company to produce items that are related to specific motion picture or television programs or characters such as toys, games, posters, and so on.

ancillary services Services performed by radio, television, cable, and other stations that are not derived from the production and delivery of programs.

ancillary television Television programs that are not broadcast but are shown in hotels or motels, airplanes, and so on.

Andy Awards Awards for print and broadcasting creativity given by the Advertising Club of New York.

anecdotal lead A newspaper or magazine story that begins with a humorous characterization of a person or object.

anechoic chamber A completely dead room used for testing the frequency response of microphones and loudspeakers. Also called an *anechoic room.*

anechoic room *See* anechoic chamber.

ANG American Newspaper Guild.

angel An investor who backs a motion picture or other production but who does not participate in decision making. Also called a *backer.*

angle □ The point of view from which a news story is written. Also called a *news peg.* □ In a derogatory sense, to slant a news story. □ The degree to which type departs from the vertical; italic (to the right) or backslant (to the left). □ The point of view in looking at an animation drawing. □ A script format containing a director's cues or scene descriptions. □ *See* camera angle.

angle bars The mechanical device used to turn newspapers during the printing process.

angle brackets The symbols < and >; sometimes used as delimiters to distinguish text from codes in manuscripts.

angled (A) An outdoor advertising structure that has one end set back more than six feet from the other end of the structure.

angled end (AE) The outdoor advertising structure that is closest to the approaching vehicle when more than one structure is built in the same facing.

angled single (AS) The outdoor advertising structure that is the only panel visible to approaching traffic. Posters are considered angled single when no other panel is visible within 25 feet along the line of travel; for bulletins, when no other bulletin is visible within 50 feet.

angle of acceptance The maximum angle from which a microphone or lens will receive sound or light. *See also* polar pattern.

angle of approach The view seen by the audience as selected by the director of a television program.

angle of divergence The angle between a line drawn through the axis of a lens or electron gun to the edge of the lens or scanning area.

angle of incidence The angle between that of a radio wave or light striking a surface and a line perpendicular to the surface. Equal to the angle of reflection.

angle of reflection □ The angle between that of a radio wave or light leaving a surface and a line perpendicular to the surface. Equal to the angle of incidence. □ The maximum angle from which an acceptable projected picture may be viewed.

angle of refraction The angle of a radio wave or light beam as it passes through a different medium measured to a line perpendicular to the surface of the medium.

angle of view The maximum horizontal angle as seen through a lens or viewfinder, or by a light meter. Cf. camera angle.

angle of vision A British term for *angle of view.*

angle shot A camera shot, often an insert, that views a scene from a perspective other than straight toward a subject. *See also* another angle.

angstrom (A) One ten-billionth of a meter.

angstrom unit (AU) The unit of measurement of light wavelengths, equal to one ten-millionth of a millimeter. Visible light waves measure from 400 to 700 millimicrons (4 to 70 A).

anhysteresis Magnetization by means of a unidirectional field upon which is superimposed an alternating field of gradually decreasing amplitude.

anhysteretic duplication A tape duplication method employing anhysteresis.

Anik One of the Canadian communication satellites; from the Eskimo word for *brother.*

aniline printing An older term for flexographic printing.

animal A somewhat derogatory term for a reporter or camera operator; often used in conjunction with media personnel who accompany political candidates on trips.

Animascope A wide-screen animation process.

animate To change drawings or objects so that when they are photographed a frame at a time they produce the illusion of movement when they are projected.

animated caption Credits or title cards that are pulled or slid to reveal the information slowly.

animated film *See* animation.

animated sound The use of frame by frame drawings to produce synthetic music.

animated title □ A title used on television made to appear animated by zooming, panning, tilting, and so on. □ Titles animated on film.

animated viewer A viewer used in film editing that provides an enlarged picture. Normally mounted between two rewind arms.

animated zoom A zoom accomplished by changing the size of the artwork rather than by moving the camera.

animatic □ Pertaining to mechanical animation. □ The use of still pictures or slides on film as a substitute for limited animation. Cf. photomatic.

animatic projector A stop motion projector.

animation □ A general term that describes a wide range of frame-by-frame filmmaking techniques in which the illusion of motion is created, rather than recorded. Derived from the Latin *anima,* meaning "life" or "soul." □ The art of synthesizing apparent movement of inanimate objects or drawings. *See also* CLUT animation. Cf. limited animation. □ *See* pixillation. □ The act of performing in a vigorous, lively manner. □ Special treatment given to outdoor advertising such as moving units or flashing lights. Commonly used on rotating, permanent, or spectacular bulletins.

animation bench *See* animation board.

animation board A drawing board containing a light box covered by translucent material and fitted with registration pins. Also called an *animation bench* and *animation desk.*

animation camera A motion picture camera with single frame and reverse capabilities for animation work; mounted on a crane over the compound.

animation designer □ The art director of an animated film. □ The cartoonist who makes the extremes in an animated sequence.

animation desk *See* animation board.

animation disc A disc, of steel or heavy aluminum, mounted over a circular opening in the surface of a drawing table. A sheet of frosted plastic or glass is set into the disc. Light from a fixture below the surface shines through the glass, enabling the animator to see his drawings through several sheets of paper at once. Pegs are affixed to the disc to hold the drawing paper in register. Because the pegs hold the paper stationary, the disc rotates 360 degrees so that the animator is always working at a comfortable angle.

animation editor *See* editor.

animation effects The animation of other than character movements--rain, smoke, fire, and so on.

animation log A frame-by-frame record of an animated sequence.

animation mask A four-sided border, registered on pegs, and used to outline the limits of a drawing.

animation stand A complex mechanical device used for holding a camera and artwork. Consists of a camera mount, shadow board, zoom counter, zoom controls, compound table, floating pegs, platen, and so on. Also called a *rostrum.*

animator □ An artist who uses the techniques of frame-by-frame filmmaking to give his artwork the illusion of movement. In studio animation, the person responsible for drawing the moving characters; in independent animation, the animator is generally responsible for all phases of production. □ An electromechanical device fitted with mirrors, lights, lenses, reflectors, and so on, used for making abstract or compound illusions.

anisotropic □ Having characteristics such as magnetic permeability that are dependent upon the direction of measurement. Not isotropic. □ In reference to the base film of magnetic recording tape, having moduli of elasticity that are different for the length, width, and thickness of the base film.

ann An abbreviation for *announcer.*

anncr An abbreviation for *announcer.*

Annie Oakley *See* comp.

annotation A note to a bibliographic entry or text intended to provide further information or comment.

announce □ To introduce a performer, talent, and so on. □ To make known publicly.

announce booth (AB) A soundproof room adjacent to a television studio or control room used by announcers for delivering announcements, station breaks, narration, and so on. Also called an *announcer's booth, booth,* or *sound booth.*

announcement A radio or television commercial or noncommercial spot or brief promotion.

announcement campaign An advertising campaign using only spot announcements.

announcement program A radio or television program designed to carry the commercial messages of different noncompetitive advertisers. Cf. sponsored program and participation program.

announcer A person who delivers a message to an audience by radio or television; a communicator. May be employed by a station, network, CATV system, advertising agency, or work freelance. Abbreviated *ann* and *anncr.*

announcer voiceover *See* voiceover.

annual A serial publication issued once a year.

annual ADT *See* annual average daily traffic.

annual average daily traffic (annual ADT) In outdoor advertising, the annual average daily traffic volume for the year divided by 365 days. Counting is generally accomplished by mechanical counting instruments moved from location to location throughout a state by the state highway commission in a program of continuous traffic count sampling. The resulting counts are adjusted to an estimate of annual average daily traffic, taking into account seasonal influence, weekly variation, and other variables.

annual broadcast fee *See* annual license fee.

annual discount A discount given by a print or broadcast medium to an advertiser who purchases 52 consecutive weeks of space or time. Also called an *annual rebate.*

annual employment report The report required by the FCC of radio or television station licensees having five or more employees.

annualized disconnect rate The disconnected subscribers of cable television or pay television during any period, expressed as an annualized percentage of the subscribers existing at the beginning of the period.

annual license fee (ALF) The fee charged by the FCC of commercial broadcast stations, based on a percentage of a station's rate card. Also called *annual broadcast fee.*

annual rebate *See* annual discount.

annual report □ The report submitted by the FCC each year to Congress in compliance with section four of the Communications Act of 1934. □ The financial report and annual employment report required of licensees by the FCC. □ The financial report by a corporation required annually by the Securities and Exchange Commission.

anode The positive electrode to which a stream of electrons flows. Cf. cathode.

anodized reflector A reflector covered with an electrolytically formed coating.

anonymous A work of unknown or unavowed authorship. Cf. apocryphal.

anonymous work In copyright terms, a work on the copies or phonorecords of which no natural person is identified as author.

another angle A script notation for an angle shot.

ANP Associated Negro Press. An American news agency.

ANPA American Newspaper Publishers Association.

ANSCII American National Standards Committee for Information Interchange. Now ASCII.

ANSCR Alphanumeric system for classification of recordings.

ANSI American National Standards Institute. An independent association for establishing standards. Formerly ASA, ASI, and USASI.

answer back A response by a remotely controlled device or computer that a signal was received.

answer print The first print of a film in release form, prepared by the laboratory for the producer for acceptance, and when approved, used as a standard for all subsequent prints. Also called an *approval print, grading print, pilot print, optical print,* and *trial print. See also* married print. Cf. first trial print.

ant An abbreviation for *antenna.*

antagonist The villain or heavy or opponent of the protagonist in a play or script.

antenna The structure associated with the transition between a guided wave such as may exist in a transmission line and a free- space wave. Such a structure usually consists of radiating elements and means for distributing the energy to these elements. Antennas may be used to receive or transmit. Also called an *aerial.*

antenna array A transmitting or receiving antenna having several reflectors, directors, and so on.

antenna current The radio frequency in the antenna with no modulation.

antenna electrical beam tilt The shaping of the radiation pattern in the vertical plane of a transmitting antenna by electrical means so that maximum radiation occurs at an angle below the horizontal plane. Cf. antenna mechanical beam tilt.

antenna farm A geographical location, within established boundaries designated by the FCC, in which antenna towers with a common impact on aviation may be grouped.

antenna gain *See* gain.

antenna height above average terrain (HAAT) The average of the various heights of a radio or television antenna above the average terrain measured from 2 to 10 miles from the antenna in eight directions spaced evenly for each 45 degrees of azimuth starting with true north.

antenna lobe *See* lobe.

antenna mast *See* mast.

antenna mechanical beam tilt The intentional installation of a transmitting antenna so that its axis is not vertical, in order to change the normal angle of maximum radiation in the vertical plane. Cf. antenna electrical beam tilt.

antenna monitor A phase monitor used on directional antennas.

antenna pattern The polar pattern of a transmitting antenna from the tower to some predetermined signal strength limit.

antenna power The product of the square of the antenna current resistance at the point where the current is measured.

antenna resistance The total resistance of the transmitting antenna system at the operating frequency and at the point at which the antenna current is measured.

antenna run The lines between a receiving antenna in a CATV system and the distribution lines.

antenna structure The radiating and/or receiving system, its supporting structures, and any appurtenances mounted thereon.

antenna tower *See* tower.

anthology □ A collection of literary works with a common theme, usually written by different authors. □ *See* anthology drama.

anthology drama A dramatic television program that uses a different theme and cast each week, usually with differing content and style. Cf. series.

anthology film A motion picture that uses a different theme and cast in its various parts. Also called a *compilation film.*

antiabrasion coating A thin wax used on film to protect the emulsion.

antialiasing A technique used to disguise the effects of aliasing by averaging the color values of the background and the line that is aliased.

anticipate To take a camera shot or begin an action immediately before the shot or action is called for.

anticipation □ A pause or small countermove made by a character in preparation for a major movement; used by animators to help give the illusion of a body moving with the proper sense of weight and balance. □ The act of looking forward to give emphasis to a dramatic point in a script.

anticlimax The drop in tension following the climax, but before the denouement, of a script containing some secondary action or plot.

anticlockwise polarized wave *See* left-hand polarized wave.

anticompetitive agreement An understanding or contract that tends to lessen competition between similar businesses in prices or services. *See also* antitrust laws.

antiflare A coating sprayed on shiny surfaces in order to reduce reflections.

antihalation backing A layer applied to film to prevent light from being reflected from the base and causing halation. Also called *antihalation coating.*

antihalation coating *See* antihalation backing.

antihero A protagonist who does not have the characteristics typical of a hero.

antileapfrogging A former FCC requirement that cable systems importing distant signals select those originating in outside markets closest to the cable television community.

antimony A hardening element used to make the alloy for type metal.

Antiope An acronym for the French videotex system.

antiqua Another name for roman type.

antiquarian □ A bookseller who deals in old and rare books. □ A large sheet (31 by 53 inches) of drawing paper.

Antiquarian Booksellers' Association of America, Inc. A trade association.

antique *See* antique paper.

antique finish *See* antique paper.

antique paper A soft, unevenly textured, high-quality paper. Also called *antique* and *antique finish.*

antique tooling The blind tooling on leather book covers.

antireflection coating A thin lens coating used to decrease light loss through reflection.

antisiphoning An FCC rule limiting cable networks from competing with over-the-air broadcasters for programming fare. *See also* siphoning.

antiskating A device built into a turntable or record changer that helps prevent the tone arm from drifting toward the center of a record. *See also* skating.

antitrust laws Statutes relating to monopolies and to combinations, contracts, or agreements in restraint of trade. Sections 313 and 314 of the Communications Act convey the antitrust laws specifically applicable to broadcasting. Violations are prosecuted by the antitrust division of the Justice Department.

anvil The left or right pieces of a film cement splicer that hold the film in proper registration.

anytime *See* evergreen.

anytimer *See* evergreen.

AO Audio operator.

A/O Axis of orientation.

AOR □ Album oriented rock. □ Agency of record.

AP □ Answer print. □ Assignment of (construction) permit. An FCC file number prefix. □ Associated Press.

APA □ Administrative Procedure Act of 1946. □ Agricultural Publishers Association.

APBA Associated Press Broadcasters Association.

APBE Association for Professional Broadcast Education. Formerly, UAPRE. *See also* BEA.

APC □ Automatic Phase Control. □ Automatic Power Control.

APCL Association of Professional Color Laboratories.

APCO Associated Public-Safety Communications Officers, Inc.

aperture □ The opening in a lens, camera mask, projector mask, or printer through which the light passes. *See also* f-stop, effective aperture, equivalent aperture, and relative aperture. □ The diameter of a satellite dish.

aperture grill *See* aperture mask.

aperture lock A device on some film cameras that overrides an automatic exposure mechanism. Also called *exposure lock* and *exposure override.*

aperture mask A perforated sheet used in a color television picture tube to prevent the excitation of one color phosphor dot by another color's scanning beam. Also called *aperture grill* and *shadow mask.*

aperture plate The metal plate between the film and the lens in a camera or projector. The aspect ratio is determined by the aperture plate and vice versa.

aperture ring A movable part that controls the size of the iris opening of a lens.

aperture scale The series of f-stop numbers marked on a lens.

aperture size The generally accepted international standards for all camera and projector apertures.

apex □ A projecting point on a letter, such as the top of an *A*. Cf. arm, bar, cross stroke, ear, spur, stem, tail, and vertex. □ A diacritical mark for a long vowel.

API American Press Institute.

APL □ Assignment of (construction) permit and license. An FCC file number prefix. □ Average picture level. □ All-Purpose Linotype. □ A computer programming language.

aplanatic lens A lens with very little spherical aberration at full aperture.

APME Associated Press Managing Editors Association.

APO □ Optical answer print. □ Action print only.

apochromatic lens A lens corrected for all three primary colors. Cf. achromatic lens.

apocryphal Of doubtful authenticity. Cf. anonymous.

apogee The point in a satellite orbit at which it is most distant from the earth. Cf. perigee.

APP Associated Purchasing Publications.

apparent movement The continuous action perceived by a viewer from a succession of still pictures, as in a motion picture or television picture. *See also* persistence of vision.

appeal □ A legal challenge to a rule or decision made by an administrative agency to a court or from a court to a higher court. Cf. rehearing. □ An emotional or logical attempt to persuade an audience or prospective buyer of the quality and value of a commercial product or service. Often uses the stock appeals such as prestige, convenience, attractiveness, and so on.

appearance □ A single presentation by a performer. □ The act of coming into court or an adjudicatory proceeding before the FCC.

appellant One who appeals from a decision made by an administrative agency or who appeals from a lower to a higher court. Cf. appellee.

appellate court A court that has the power to review the decisions of a lower court. *See also* court of appeals.

appellate jurisdiction The power of a court or administrative agency to hear a case initially. Cf. original jurisdiction.

appellee One against whom an appeal is made. Cf. appellant.

appendix Matter that is added to the end of a book but that is not essential. Often consists of bibliographic material, glossaries, tables, and so on.

applause mail Fan mail from the audience; originally used as a crude form of audience survey.

apple box A low wooden box used in the studio to raise the height of an actor or object. *See also* full apple, half apple, quarter apple, and eighth apple. Cf. riser.

Appleton layer The F layer of the ionosphere.

applicable basic minimum program fee The basic, minimum commercial program fees as contained in the AFTRA Code of Fair Practices for Network Television Broadcasting.

applicant An individual or group seeking a grant to operate a business, broadcast station, cable television franchise, and so on.

application □ The problem to which data processing techniques and solutions are applied. □ The written instrument required by the FCC under Section 308 of the Communications Act of all persons desiring a construction permit, license, modification of license, and license renewal. *See also* formal application and informal application.

application for review An appeal to the U.S. Supreme Court by an appellant or by the Federal Communications Commission from a decision of a U.S. court of appeals.

application program A computer program designed to perform a specific set of tasks, for example, a word processor, spreadsheet, or database.

application software A computer program written for a specific user application.

application-specific coding flag (ASCF) An indication whether the video coding conforms to the specification of Chapter V of the Green Book or is application specific, that is, to be interpreted by the application software.

applications satellite A satellite used for specific purposes; for example, communications, weather, or navigation. Also called an *application technology satellite (ATS).*

applications technology satellite (ATS) *See* applications satellite.

applied research Research that has an immediate pragmatic use, as opposed to pure or basic research.

APPM Association of Publication Production Managers.

approach □ A camera or lens movement, often a zoom, from a long shot to a medium shot or a medium shot to a closeup. □ The distance measured along the line of travel from the point where the outdoor advertising structure first becomes fully visible to the point where copy is no longer readable.

appropriation In privacy law, the use of a person's name or likeness without his or her permission.

approval copy A textbook received from a publisher that may be kept if adopted, otherwise paid for or returned. Cf. complimentary copy and desk copy.

approval plan Books sent to libraries and others covering specific areas or subjects automatically with the understanding that unwanted books can be returned. Also called *on-approval plan*. Similar to a continuation order. Cf. blanket order.

approval print *See* answer print.

approximate equivalent simple random sample size *See* effective sample size.

APR Associated Press Radio. *See* AP Radio.

APRA American Public Relations Association.

AP Radio The audio network service of the Associated Press.

APRN Associated Press Radio Network.

apron The edge of a stage that protrudes beyond the proscenium arch.

APRS Association for Public Radio Stations.

APS Alternative Press Syndicate.

APTA American Public Transit Association.

APX Ad-page exposure.

AQH Average quarter hour.

aquadag A conductive coating of graphite used on some television picture tubes as an accelerating anode or shield. Abbreviated dag.

aquatint An etching process that produces the effect of a watercolor or india ink drawing.

aquatone A photogelatin engraving process.

AR □ Aspect ratio. □ Audience research. □ Assisted resonance.

ARA American Radio Association of the AFL-CIO.

Arabic numerals The numerals 0, 1, 2, 3, 4, 5, 6, 7, 8, 9.

ARABSAT Arab Corporation for Space Communication.

ARB American Research Bureau, Inc. *See* Arbitron.

ARBI Attitude Research Bureau, Inc.

arbitration The settling of disputes and controversies, for example, among producers and members of a union or guild.

Arbitrends Ratings information released by Arbitron that covers an extended period of time rather than only one ratings period.

Arbitron The Arbitron Company. An audience research company organized in the late 1940s as the American Research Bureau (ARB). Arbitron originally referred to a mechanical recording device used by ARB similar to the Audimeter.

Arbitron Information on Demand (AID) Sophisticated analyses of information available from an online computer system from Arbitron.

arc A curved camera movement similar to a truck.

ARCH Automatic Remote Cassette Handler. A tradename for an automatic videocassette system used in television automation.

architecture □ The interrelationship and logical structure of components in the design of a system to achieve the desired interaction. □ The protocol of a system. □ The internal design of a computer.

archive A place in which historical and other files and materials are stored.

archiving The process of maintaining computer, film, book, or other files.

arcing *See* arc.

arc lamp *See* arc light.

arc light □ A brilliant light, with a color temperature close to that of sunlight, produced by passing a current through two closely spaced carbon electrodes. Also called an *arc lamp* and *brute*. □ An arc light luminaire.

arc out A direction given to a performer to cross in front of a camera following a curved line equidistant from the lens.

area-by-area allocation (ABA) A technique for assigning an advertiser's media budget on a local basis in a manner proportionate to established or potential local sales of the advertiser's product or service. Also called *market-by-market allocation*.

area composition The placement of the elements of a page by phototypesetting for photocomposition, thus eliminating cutting and pasting.

area lighting The practice of lighting the acting space in separately controlled areas.

Area of Dominant Influence (ADI) A geographic design that defines each television market, exclusive of all others, based on measured viewing patterns. It is an area that consists of one or more Arbitron sampling units in which the commercial stations home to the ADI and satellite stations reported in combination with them received the preponderance of total viewing hours. Similar to Nielsen's designated market areas (DMAs).

area of reception Any geographic area smaller than a zone of reception in which the reception of particular radio or television programs is specifically intended and in which broadcast coverage is contemplated, such areas being indicated by countries or parts of countries.

area probability sample A probability sample for which the sampling units are well-defined geographic areas; for example, city blocks. Also called an *area sample.*

area sample *See* area probability sample.

A reel The first of two or more tapes or films to be used in a multiple chain program. Cf. B reel.

Areopagitica An essay written in 1644 by John Milton that argued for an end to the licensing of printers in order to increase freedom of expression.

ARF Advertising Research Foundation.

argon flash An electronic flash of high intensity used mainly in high-speed cinematography.

ARI Audience Research Institute. An audience research organization founded by George Gallup. *See also* AIPO.

ARIA American Radio Importers Association.

arithmetic mean *See* mean.

ARL Association of Research Libraries; a division of the American Library Association.

arm A short, horizontal or upward slanting stroke on printed characters, for example, the upward projections of a *Y* or the top of a *T.* Cf. apex, bar, cross stroke, ear, spur, stem, tail, and vertex.

armature □ The moving part of a motor, generator, or other electromechanical device. □ A jointed, metal skeletal structure onto which the figure of an animated puppet is built, providing support and shape for the figure, as well as the ability to be properly manipulated.

Armed Services Edition Paperbound books that were distributed free to members of the armed forces during World War II.

arming press A small press used for stamping heraldic arms on book bindings.

armored cable Two or more insulated conductors or coaxial cables covered by metallic and plastic sheaths. Used primarily underground.

armorial binding A book binding decorated with heraldic arms or devices of governments or other symbols of authority.

ARMS All-Radio Methodology Study. A study of audience rating methods begun in 1963 by the NAB and RAB. Cf. CRAM and RADAR.

ARMS II All Radio Marketing Study. A study in the 1970s that provided data on cross-media audiences and was designed to determine methods for improving the marketing of radio.

arm swinger *See* dolly pusher.

ARNA Association of Radio News Analysts. *See* ARTNA.

ARO Audio receive only.

A roll A videotape or film that is to be dissolved from; usually to the B roll.

arousal method A method for testing advertising effectiveness in which a galvanometer attached to a respondent measures differences in the sweating of his or her palms. Cf. galvanic skin response.

arousal theory The theory that the mass media arouses emotional responses in readers, viewers, and listeners and thus may change behavioral responses.

ARQ Automatic retransmission request for correction.

arranger An individual who scores or adapts musical compositions.

array □ An arrangement of items of data in one or more dimensions, usually ordered so that each item of data can be identified by its position. □ *See also* antenna array.

arrears Subscribers whose subscriptions to a periodical have lapsed but who are retained temporarily on active subscription lists.

ARRL American Radio Relay League. An amateur radio organization formed in 1915.

arsenic A slang term for a radio or television commercial or program that is too difficult to swallow.

art □ A general term encompassing illustrations, photographs, sketches, lettering, type, and so on, used in any medium. □ Skill in performance. □ The use of creative imagination.

art agency An organization that serves as a representative for artists.

art and mechanical (A and M) Noting or pertaining to graphic materials required for production of an advertisement.

artboard *See* board.

art buyer An employee of an advertising agency or commercial studio who is responsible for commissioning art or photography for advertising reproduction.

art card A graphics card for titles, credits, pictures, and so on; often made from illustration board.

art deco The look of the 1920s and 1930s, consisting of mixed motifs, pastel colors, glass blocks, and so on. Temporarily returned to vogue in the 1980s.

art department The motion picture studio department responsible for set design.

art director (AD) □ The person in charge of the visual aspects of a publication. Also called an *art editor.* □ The person in charge of an art department. The individual may execute and is responsible for the production of all illustrations, continuity sketches, perspectives, scenery and set designs, scale models, approving sets and properties, and so on. □ The person responsible for the design and construction supervision of sets; often designs costumes, props, graphics, and other accessories. In an advertising agency, also responsible for storyboard design.

art editor *See* art director.

art film A general term for films that ignore the commercial market and concentrate on artistic endeavors; often psychologically motivated.

art house *See* art service.

articulation The intelligible pronunciation of individual sounds and words.

artifacts Audible or visible defects in television pictures, such as cross color, chroma crawl, and ringing.

artificial intelligence (AI) □ The ability of a computer to imitate the human abilities of learning and decision making. □ The extension of human capabilities through the use of computers.

artificial language A computer language designed for a particular application. *See also* computer language.

artificial light Light produced by chemical or electrical means as opposed to natural light.

artist □ Any of a number of persons skilled in drawing, painting, set design, lighting, photography, and so on. □ An individual who specializes in arranging the elements of printed pages for newspapers or magazines. □ A synonym for talent or performer.

artist's manager *See* agent and manager.

Artists' Service Bureau (ASB) A network department in the 1930s that represented the talent that appeared on the network. Forbidden by the FCC as a conflict of interests.

ARTNA Association of Radio and Television News Analysts.

art nouveau A style of decoration of the 1890s characterized by flowing lines.

art paper A heavily coated, polished paper especially suitable for halftone printing.

art representative An individual who represents individual artists or an art service.

art service An independent company that specializes in creating advertising artwork. Also called an *art house.*

art still A professionally done portrait, usually an 8-by-10-inch size, of a performer or product; used for publicity purposes.

art type An adhesive-backed type used for artwork.

artwork A term similar to *art* and often used interchangeably; *artwork* often implies the finished product or camera-ready copy, whereas *art* is seen as being less inclusive.

ARU Audio Response Unit.

AS □ Angle shot. □ Angled single.

ASA □ American Standards Association. Now ANSI. *See* American National Standards Institute. □ Acoustical Society of America. □ American Sportscasters Association.

ASA exposure index *See* ASA rating.

ASAP American Society of Advertising and Promotion, Inc.

ASA rating A measure of a film's sensitivity to light. Also called *ASA speed* and *ASA exposure index*. Cf. DIN.

ASA speed *See* ASA rating.

ASB Artists' Service Bureau.

asbestos tapoff *See* twofer.

ASBPE American Society of Business Press Editors.

as broadcast script A radio or television script that is marked to indicate any changes made during a broadcast.

ASBU Arab States Broadcasting Union.

ASC □ American Society of Cinematographers. □ Advertising Standards Council.

ASCAP American Society of Composers, Authors, and Publishers.

ascender That portion of a lowercase character that projects upward of the mean line (for letters b, d, f, h, k, l, and t). Also called a *riser*. Cf. descender.

ascender line The highest point on an ascender. Cf. descender line.

ascending letter Any letter that rises above the mean line, as a capital letter or a lowercase letter with an ascender.

ascertainment A requirement that prospective radio and television licensees and renewal applicants determine the problems and needs of the community and design programming to help meet those problems. First required by the 1960 Programming Policy Statement. *See also* the Suburban Case.

ASCF Application Specific Coding Flag.

ASCII American Standard Code for Information Interchange. A standard data transmission code designed to achieve compatibility between data devices.

A scope *See* waveform monitor.

ascription A statistical technique that allocates radio listening proportionate to each of the conflicting stations' diaries as calculated on a county basis using TALO from the previous surveys. It excludes the most recently completed survey for those markets with back-to-back surveys. Diary credit is automatically, randomly assigned in proportion to the relative listening levels of the conflicting stations over the previous year.

ASD/PA Assistant secretary of defense/public affairs. The contact person in the Department of Defense for assistance and permission for the use of military bases, personnel, equipment, and so on, for media productions.

ASEE American Society of Electrical Engineers.

ASFA American Science Film Association.

ASFFHF Academy of Science Fiction, Fantasy, and Horror Films.

ash can A large arc light.

ASI American Standards Institute. *See* American National Standards Institute. □ Audience Studies, Inc.

Asian Broadcasting Union (ABU) An association of broadcasting organizations in the Far East founded in 1964. Associate members include ABC, CBS, NBC, and other networks from throughout the world.

Asiavision A Japanese company formed for the purpose of producing programs for transmission to other Asian countries. Cf. Eurovision and Intervision.

aside A line spoken by talent that supposedly is not heard by other characters.

ASIS American Society for Information Science.

as issued A used book or other publication purchased in its original form.

as-it-falls method A technique for assigning media weight to a test market that attempts to deliver the same level of weight that would be delivered into that market by the theoretical national plan to be tested. Cf. correct increment method, little America method, and media translation.

ASJSA American Society of Journalism School Administrators.

ASLIB Association of Special Libraries and Information Bureaus.

ASMA American Society of Music Arrangers.

ASME American Society of Magazine Editors.

ASMP American Society of Magazine Photographers.

ASNE American Society of Newspaper Editors.

as new *See* mint.

aspect ratio □ The width-to-height ratio of an image. □ The ratio of picture width to picture height. In television and standard film, the ratio is 4:3; in HDTV, 16:9; in wide-screen film, the ratio varies depending on the system. The 4:3 ratio is sometimes called the *golden dimension.*

Aspen rule The court decision that allowed groups to sponsor presidential debates without invoking the equal opportunities provision of Section 315 of the Communications Act of 1934.

aspheric lens A nonspherical lens or plate that is used in some projection and zoom lenses to correct for aberrations.

ASR □ Automatic sequence register. □ Automatic send receive.

ASRA Automatic stereophonic recording amplifier. A device developed by CBS for automatically compressing the vertical component in recording.

assemble □ To join together successive television program segments so as to form a continuous program tape. □ To direct or carry out such joining. □ A mode of television tape recorder operation for editing that permits the machine to assemble. *See also* assemble edit. □ To arrange film or tape in script sequence by mechanical or electronic editing. Also called *rough cut.* □ To translate a computer program from a programming language to machine code. □ To combine the elements of a page, chapter, book, and so on. □ To gather the components of a system. □ To make copy camera ready.

assemble edit A type of videotape edit in which a new control track is laid down, as well as new audio, video, or both. Also called an *add-on edit.* Cf. insert edit.

assemble mode The electronic addition of a picture source to a videotape following a previously recorded picture segment without using a previously laid control track. Cf. insert mode.

assembly dailies Film footage from a day's shooting that is selected and spliced in proper sequence. *See* dailies.

assembly language (AL) A computer programming language consisting of symbolic codes to translate programming languages into machine code.

assessment method A method for determining an advertising appropriation based on a specific amount per item sold in the most recent budgetary period.

assets The property, plant, equipment, program rights, good will, inventory, accounts receivable, and so on, of a broadcasting station, cable television system, or other media property.

assign To reserve a peripheral device or a portion of a computer's memory for a specific purpose.

assigned frequency The center of the frequency band allotted to a radio or television station.

assigned frequency band The frequency band within which the emission of a station is authorized; the width of the band equals the necessary bandwidth plus twice the absolute value of the frequency tolerance. Where space stations are concerned, the assigned frequency band includes twice the maximum Doppler shift that may occur in relation to any point of the earth's surface.

assigned mailing dates The dates on which a mailing list user has the obligation to mail a specific list. No other date is acceptable without specific approval of the list owner.

assigned material All material in writing or any other fixed form that a company furnishes to a writer on which a story, screenplay, or both will be based or from which it is to be, in whole or in part, adapted.

assignment □ The coverage of a news story by a reporter. □ Authorization given by an administration for a radio station to use a radio frequency or radio frequency channel under specified conditions. □ A transfer of control of a broadcast license. □ *See* allotment.

assignment board A chalkboard or bulletin board used to fulfill the function of an assignment book.

assignment book The daily record of assignments given to reporters, camera operators, crews, and so on. Also called an *assignment sheet.*

assignment desk A newsroom desk at which the assignment editor works.

assignment editor The person responsible for assigning reporters, video crews, and so on, to news events.

assignment manager A television station employee who oversees and assigns the work of reporters and remote crews.

assignment sheet *See* assignment book.

assignment slips Pieces of paper on which a reporter's assignments are written.

assistant A subordinate co-worker; as assistant cameraman, assistant director, assistant editor, assistant producer, and so on.

assistant animator In studio animation, the artist responsible for the drawings that fall between the extreme points of a movement. *See also* in-betweens and key animator.

assistant art director An assistant to the individual in charge of an advertising agency's art department; usually works on a single account at one time. *See also* art director.

assistant camera operator A cable puller or grip who assists a camera operator.

assistant director (AD) □ In television, and depending on the director, the person who often sets up the camera shots and gives the ready commands, leaving the director free to concentrate on the air commands. Also called *associate director.* □ In film, the person responsible for having the cast and crew ready to shoot.

assistant editor An individual who is assigned to assist a film editor.

assistant sportscaster Another term for an individual who does the "color" during sporting events.

assisted resonance (AR) An electronic system used to make environments that lack reverberation sound richer.

associate creative director (ACD) An advertising agency employee who devises advertisements and who reports to a creative director.

Associated Actors and Artistes of America (AAAA) An organization consisting of various trade unions: American Federation of Television and Radio Artists (AFTRA), Actors Equity Association (AEA), the Screen Extras Guild (SEG), the American Guild of Musical Artists (AGMA), and the American Guild of Variety Artists (AGVA).

associated broadcasting station The broadcasting station(s) with which a remote pickup broadcast station or system is licensed as an auxiliary and with which it is principally used.

associated equipment and facilities Facilities other than satellite terminal stations and communications satellites, constructed and operated for the primary purpose of a communications satellite system, whether for administration and management, for research and development, or for direct support of space operations.

associate director (AD) An associate director supervises the preproduction, dry rehearsal, camera rehearsal, dress rehearsal, prerecord, and sweetening broadcast, or he or she supervises others in those functions.

Associated Press (AP) One of the two major American press associations. Founded in 1848 to furnish national and international news to newspapers. Cf. United Press International (UPI).

associated television broadcast station A television broadcast station licensed to the licensee of the television auxiliary broadcast station and with which the television auxiliary station is licensed as an auxiliary facility.

associate editor □ An individual employed by a newspaper or magazine who is in charge of an editorial page or a special section. □ An individual employed by a publishing house that works with a senior editor in planning new projects and revising existing ones.

associate producer An assistant to a producer for a production company, motion picture, a television series, and so on; a creative planner.

associate writer An individual who is assigned or employed to write breakdowns.

association □ A group of individuals, usually within an industry, who share common interests and goals. Often a professional association with a code of conduct. □ Individual organizations often refer to themselves as "The Association," for example, the Outdoor Advertising Association of America (OAAA).

Association for Public Radio Stations (APRS) An association formed to represent the interests of public radio stations.

Association of American Publishers (AAP) A trade association.

Association of American University Presses (AAUP) A scholarly trade association.

Association of Data Processing Service Organizations (ADAPSO) An association of data processing industry representatives and companies.

Association of Independent Commercial Editors (AICE) An organization that deals with common interests among commercial editors.

Association of Independent Commercial Producers (AICP) A trade association that deals with advertising agencies, unions, agencies, and so on.

Association of Independent Television Stations (INTV) An association developed to represent the interests of independent television stations in regulatory and promotional concerns.

Association of Independent Video and Filmmakers (AIVF). A national association.

Association of Maximum Service Telecasters (AMST) *See* Maximum Service Telecasters.

Association of National Advertisers (ANA) The national organization of the advertising business representing advertisers of all sizes. The ANA is supported by over 400 major corporations accounting for 90 of the 100 largest users of advertising. The association represents the collective interests of advertisers; provides validated information through original research, case studies, and, on major functional aspects of advertising, marketing and communication; and helps company executives keep up with successful practices and techniques.

Association standards The Outdoor Advertising Association of America, Inc. (OAAA) sets standards to promote efficient operation and services to users of the medium.

association test A research tool used to indicate the degree to which people are able to identify brand names, logos, themes, and so on.

associative editing *See* relational editing.

AST Automatic scan tracking.

ASTA Advertiser Syndicated Television Association.

ASTD American Society for Training and Development.

asterisk A star-shaped reference mark (*), often used as a footnote symbol or as a replacement for an ellipsis.

astigmatism A defect in the eye or lens that causes blurring by the nonconvergence of light rays at a common focus point. Cf. aberration.

astonisher □ A slang term for an exclamation point. □ An attention-getting newspaper headline.

ASTVC American Society of TV Cameramen.

ASWA Antiskywave antenna.

asymmetrical A layout in which the elements may or may not balance.

asymmetrical lens A lens in which the elements are not arranged symmetrically. Cf. symmetrical lens.

asynchronous A signal that has no timed relationship with other signals; not synchronized.

asynchronous sound Sound that is not synchronized with the picture.

A system The 405-line, 25-frames-per-second, 5-mHz bandwidth, AM sound television system used in Great Britain. Cf. B, D, E, and M systems.

AT&T American Telephone and Telegraph Company. The major American telephone company furnishing local telephone service to stations, remote lines, long lines, microwave, and so on. The largest stockholder in COMSAT. Also a broadcast organization in the early days of radio.

ATFP Alliance of Television Film Producers.

ATF typesetter An American Type Foundry phototypesetting machine.

atlas *See* atlas folio.

atlas folio A large, square folio. Also called an *atlas.*

at liberty A euphemism performers use for "unemployed."

atmosphere The background sound, environment, physical setting, and so on, used to set the mood of a scene. *See also* background and background noise.

atmosphere sketch A quick sketch, generally in color, made by the director or layout artist, to indicate the mood or style of a scene.

atmospheric absorption The absorption of radio waves at high frequencies by the atmosphere. Above 30 gHz the absorption is almost immediate.

atmospheric effects Special effects that would be caused by nature in the real world: snow, rain, lightning, fog, and so on.

atmospherics □ The interference caused by electrical discharges in the atmosphere. □ The graphic identity of a corporation, as represented by the physical appearance of all of its publicly visible property, communications, and employees.

A-to-B dub □ In cartridge or cassette recorder operation, to dub a recording by replaying it on the A deck and recording the information thus produced on the B deck. □ A recording thus produced.

ATPI American Textbook Publishers' Institute.

ATR Audiotape recorder.

ATS □ American Television Society. □ Applications Technology Satellite. A series of satellites: ATS 1-6. □ Advanced Television Services. A study group of the FCC. □ Automatic transmission system.

ATSC Advanced Television Systems Committee.

attack The initial instantaneous audible sensation perceived from a sound source.

attack time The amount of time it takes for a signal to reach the maximum intended level from the previous signal level.

ATTC Advanced Television Test Center.

attended operation The operation of a radio or television station by a qualified operator on duty at the place where the transmitting apparatus is located with the transmitter in plain view of the operator. Cf. unattended operation.

attention *See* AIDA.

attention compeller *See* attention getter.

attention getter Any visual or aural sign or sound that attracts more than passing notice. Also called *attention compeller.*

attention line Any words or phrases that cause people to be attracted to a product or service. *See also* AIDA.

attention signal The signal used by broadcast stations to actuate muted receivers for interstation receipt of emergency cueing announcements and broadcasts. *See also* EBS.

attenuation The decrease in the amplitude of a signal from its transmission to reception, or from its input to output.

attenuation loss The power loss caused by the insertion of a device or component in a circuit. Also called *insertion loss.*

attenuator A device, such as a potentiometer, that provides for a reduction in amplitude of a signal.

attitude A predisposition to respond to a stimulus in one way rather than another. Cf. opinion.

attitude scale A quantitative scale used to measure a respondent's attitudinal response to a given stimulus.

attitude study A survey of attitudes toward an organization, product, service, and so on, as expressed in the answers of respondents to questions; often made before and after an advertising campaign to determine any change of attitude.

attorney general The chief attorney of the nation or state who represents the government in litigation. At the federal level, the attorney general heads the Department of Justice.

attraction A feature-length motion picture, as in "coming attraction."

attribute □ In CD-I, a word in the file descriptor indicating how a file is accessed, its owner, and the file's identification. □ An inherent characteristic or quality of a program, scene, performance, and so on.

attribution The identification of a specific person as the source of information in a news story or the identification of the person quoted.

ATV Advanced television.

ATVAS Academy of Television Arts and Sciences.

Atwater Kent An extremely popular early radio receiver. Named after A. Atwater Kent, who began manufacturing receivers in 1923.

AU Angstrom unit.

auction A method of raising money used extensively by public broadcasting stations, selling items donated by individuals and organizations to the highest bidder.

audible Capable of being heard.

audience □ Generally, a group or mass of listeners, viewers, or spectators. □ A group of households or individuals who are exposed to a television or radio program or other advertising medium. □ *See* studio audience.

audience accumulation □ The increase in the total audience viewing a television program by using reruns. Cf. reach. □ The total net audience exposed to repeated periodical outdoor, television, or radio advertising.

audience builder A radio or television program that attracts an ever-increasing audience.

audience composition The classification of a radio or television program's audience into specific categories such as age and sex.

audience duplication □ The number or percent of households or individuals reached by one program or station that are also reached by another program or station. □ The overlap of audience reached by two or more media vehicles, of the same or different media.

audience flow A measure of the change in audience during and between programs. Audience flow shows the percentages of people or households who turn on or off a program, switch to or from another channel, or remain on the same channel as the previous program.

audience fragmentation The division of the available audience into small groups because of the wide diversity of available sources of media programming and outlets.

audience-holding index An index of the degree to which an audience of a radio or television program at its beginning continues to listen or view until its completion.

audience left The same as camera left and stage right.

audience measurement Measurements expressed as percentages (ratings) or as absolute quantities (a number of households or a number of individuals).

Audience Measurement by Market for Outdoor (AMMO) AMMO reports reach and frequency by market showing sizes with demographic breaks by age, sex, and income.

audience participation program A radio or television program based on the participation of individuals in quizzes or stunts or where the moderator or master of ceremonies conducts interviews.

audience profile Demographic characteristics of individuals or households reached during a radio or television program. *See* audience composition.

audience rating *See* rating.

audience research (AR) *See* research.

audience right The same as camera right and stage left.

audience share *See* share of audience.

Audience Studies, Inc. (ASI) A qualitative research organization that studies audience reaction to commercial products.

audience survey *See* audience measurement.

audience turnover The average ratio between the cumulative audience listening to the average audience listening or viewing. If, for example, two hundred different persons listened to a particular station at a particular time and day during the 12-week survey, but only an average of 50 persons was listening at any one time, the audience turnover would be 4.0. Cf. audience accumulation.

Audilog The viewing diary used by Nielsen to gather data from the households in its national audience composition (NAC) sample.

Audimeter An A. C. Nielsen device attached to a television receiver to record whether it is turned on and to what channel it is tuned.

audio □ From the Latin "to hear." The electronic reproduction of sound. □ The equipment used for the reproduction of sound. □ The audio portion of the spectrum. □ The sound portion of a television program. Cf. video. □ The person who operates an audio control console. □ The right half of a two-column script format. Cf. video.

audio amplifier An electronic device containing transistors, integrated circuits, tubes, and so on, designed to amplify signals within the frequency range from approximately 16 to 20,000 Hz. Also called an *audio frequency amplifier.*

audio billboard *See* billboard.

audio bit In CD-I, A bit indicating that the sector contains audio information only.

audio buzz □ A low-frequency disturbance in the reproduced audio signal of a television tape recorder. □ That disturbance sometimes noted when the video tracks of a recording have been rerecorded and the original longitudinally recorded audio information has, due to machine misadjustment, been partly overwritten by the new video recording.

audiocassette *See* cassette.

audio channel □ That portion of a videotape recording machine devoted to the recording and replay of the audio. □ By extension, the signals in such a channel or the output of the channel. □ The portion of the 6-mHz bandwidth of a television carrier devoted to the sound frequencies. Cf. picture channel. □ Any channel capable of carrying audio signals.

audio conferencing A teleconference that uses audio only.

audio console *See* console.

audio control console *See* console.

audio cue channel A separate audio channel on a videotape recorder that may be used for cueing or as a second audio track.

audio cue sheet An editor's or technician's list of audio transitions and volume levels required for an audio mix.

audio dub An audio-only change made by an insert edit on a videotape containing both sound and picture. Also called an *audio-only edit.*

Audio Engineering Society Medal Award, The An award given annually to a person who has helped significantly in the advancement of the society.

audio filter *See* filter.

audio follow An automatic device on a television switcher that changes the audio portion of the program at the same time a different picture source is taken. *See* audio follow video.

audio follow video A master switching device that is preset to make the audio automatically move with the video in television tape editing.

audio frequency (AF) Any sound frequency within the range of the human ear; nominally 16 to 16,000 or 20,000 Hz.

audio frequency amplifier *See* audio amplifier.

audiographics The transmission of text, graphics, or both over ordinary voice-grade telephone lines.

audio head *See* head.

audio mix A combination of two or more audio sources.

audio mixer □ The person who operates an audio control console. Also called a *sound man* and *audio man.* □ *See* mixer.

audio No. 1 track A synonym for program audio track.

audio No. 2 track A synonym for *cue track.*

audion The three-element vacuum tube, invented by Lee DeForest in 1906, that allowed the development of radio.

audio only edit *See* audio dub.

audio operator (AO) The individual who operates an audio control console.

audiophile A person knowledgeable about, and interested in, audio recording and records or tapes.

audio quality level The reproduction quality of an audio signal. CD-I provides for five audio quality levels. They are, in decreasing order of quality, CD-DA, hi fi, mid fi, speech, and synthesized speech.

audio receive only (ARO) A small dish used by radio stations to receive audio.

audio record A record corresponding to an audio signal, especially audio record #1.

audio record #1 The record recorded in audio track #1. In present practice, the audio record number and the audio track number are identical. Thus audio record #3 is found in audio track #3.

audio recordist *See* recordist.

audio response unit (ARU) A computer device that provides voice responses to telephone inquiries.

Audio Service The national and regional press associations' audio news service to radio stations.

audio signal An electrical signal of a sound within the audio range.

audio spectrum The full range of frequencies within the audio frequency band.

audio stack A head stack comprising two or more audio heads.

audiotape An acetate, polyester, or mylar tape, usually 1/4 inch in width. The tape is coated with a backing to carry a magnetic oxide, usually iron or chromium dioxide, capable of being magnetized to record audio signals. Cf. tape and videotape.

audio track ☐ A separately addressable section of a CD-DA disc, normally carrying an individual song. It has a minimum duration of 4 seconds and a maximum duration of 72 minutes. One CD-DA disc can contain between 1 and 99 audio tracks, but the total disc playing time cannot exceed 72 minutes. ☐ A track containing an audio record.

audio track #1 ☐ An audio record track so designated in a format drawing and generally used as the primary program audio track. ☐ In quadruplex recording, a synonym for program audio track.

audio track #2 ☐ An audio record track so designated in a format drawing. ☐ In quadruplex recording, a synonym for cue track.

audio track #3 An audio record track so designated in the format drawing.

audio-visual Equipment used in radio, television, and as instructional tools, such as slide and film projectors, opaque projectors, phonographs, and so on.

audio-visual works Works that consist of a series of related images that are intrinsically intended to be shown by the use of machines or devices such as projectors, viewers, or electronic equipment, together with accompanying sounds, if any, regardless of the nature of the material objects, such as films or tapes, in which the works are embodied.

audit ☐ A formal examination of the financial or other records of an organization. ☐ A count of the number of names on a mailing list. ☐ An examination of circulation figures. *See* Audit Bureau of Circulations.

Audit Bureau of Circulations (ABC) A nonprofit, cooperative association of more than 4000 advertisers, advertising agencies, and publishers of daily and weekly newspapers, business publications, magazines, and farm publications in the United States, Canada, Puerto Rico, Bermuda, Mexico, El Salvador, and Venezuela. Established in 1914, the ABC's objectives are to issue standardized statements of circulation based on data reported by members; to verify the figures shown in these statements by an auditor's examination of any and all records considered by ABC to be necessary; and to disseminate such data, without opinion.

Audit Bureau of Marketing Services (ABMS) An organization affiliated with the Audit Bureau of Circulations, established in 1966 to offer auditing services to various advertising media and marketing services not audited by the ABC.

audited A label given by the Traffic Audit Bureau, Inc., as it verifies records and circulation for the outdoor media according to established procedures approved by its buyer and seller members. Methods are similar to the Audit Bureau of Circulations (ABC) and Business Publications Audit of Circulation (BPA). Also called *authenticated.*

audition ☐ An audio or video test of talent or program to determine suitability or acceptability for use. ☐ A position on an audio control console allowing the sound to be heard without putting it on the air. Cf. cue. ☐ According to the Screen Actors Guild, the speaking of lines the player has been required to learn outside the studio, whether or not such lines are recorded.

audition channel An off-air channel in an audio console used for checking microphones, production work, and so on. Cf. program channel and cue channel.

audition record A recording or transcription of a radio program that serves the purposes of an audition.

audition tape An audio or video tape made by talent to send to prospective employers. Also called a *casting tape.* Cf. air check.

auditory fatigue The stress caused by loud or oppressive sounds.

auditory flashback A flashback on television using only the audio, with the picture remaining in the present.

auditory perspective The use of fading sounds to create an effect of distance and sometimes direction.

audit report An annual statement issued on white paper by the Audit Bureau of Circulations disclosing the results of an audit. Also called a *white audit.*

Auntie A British nickname for the BBC.

aural Pertaining to hearing or the ear. Cf. audio.

aural broadcast intercity relay (ICR) station A fixed station for the transmission of aural program material between broadcasting stations other than international broadcasting stations, and between FM radio broadcast stations and their co-owned FM booster stations, or for other purposes as authorized.

aural broadcast microwave booster station A fixed station in the broadcast auxiliary service that receives and amplifies signals of an aural broadcast STL or intercity relay station and retransmits them on the same frequency.

aural broadcast STL station A fixed station for the transmission of aural program material between the studio and the transmitter of a broadcasting station other than an international broadcasting station.

aural carrier The portion of the carrier wave of a television signal that is modulated by the sound information. Cf. visual carrier.

aural center frequency ☐ The average frequency of the emitted wave when modulated by a sinusoidal signal. ☐ The frequency of the emitted wave without modulation.

aural perspective *See* sound perspective.

aural services The interference-free groundwave service provided by a commercial standard broadcast station with a field strength of 5 mV/m or higher, or service provided by a commercial FM broadcast station with a field strength of 3.16 mV/m (70 dBu) or higher.

aural transmitter The radio equipment for the transmission of the aural signal only.

auteur The person, usually a director, who controls all critical aspects of a production, thus stamping it with his or her personality and vision.

auteur theory The theory that the director, rather than the writer and actors, is the creator of a work of art.

authenticated *See* audited.

authenticator word lists The lists issued every six months by the FCC for use in conjunction with the procedures contained in the EBS Checklist and SOPs for tests or actual national emergency situations.

author The creator of a copyrightable work: a writer, painter, sculptor, or other artist.

author catalogue An alphabetical catalogue of books arranged by author, editor, compiler, and so on. *See also* main entry.

author earnout That point at which the revenues of a book equal the advance on royalty paid to the author.

author entry *See* main entry.

authoring In CD-I, the work involved in producing the software for an application, from the initial concept to the recording of the master tape required for the disc mastering process. Authoring embraces (a) encoding the required audio, video, text, and binary data into CD-I data formats; (b) developing and producing the application software that operates on, uses, or accesses the encoded CD-I data as required by the application; (c) structuring the encoded CD-I data and application software into the disc label, files, and records corresponding to the access and playback requirements of the application; and (d) verifying and validating the application produced.

authoring process In CD-I, the process of developing and producing the complete software for an application. It involves (a) designing the program content by creating storyboards, (b) creating and capturing data and preparing it for use, (c) developing the program that will appear on the disc, (d) simulating and testing the program in practice, and (e) preparing the final master tape.

authoring system In CD-I, the hardware and software needed for authoring CD-I discs.

Authoritarian theory One of the four theories of the press delineated by Wilbur Schramm, that official censors of the state or news editors in a democracy decide how news is to be interpreted, and thus slant it by exaggeration, selection, and so on. Cf. Libertarian theory, Social Responsibility theory, and Soviet Communist theory.

authoritative criticism A comparative approach to criticism wherein the work is evaluated by standards or precedents. Cf. impressionistic criticism.

authoritative source A term used when a government official releases information but is neither quoted nor identified. *See also* off the record.

authority interview An interview with a recognized expert.

authorization A grant or permit from the FCC to a licensee to operate a broadcast station. *See also* construction permit.

authorized bandwidth The maximum bandwidth authorized to be used by a radio or television station as specified in the station license.

authorized carrier A communications common carrier that is authorized by the Federal Communications Commission under the Communications Act of 1934, as amended, to provide services by means of communications satellites.

authorized frequency The frequency assigned to a radio station by the FCC and specified in the instrument of authorization.

authorized power The power assigned to a radio station by the FCC as specified in the instrument of authorization.

authorized user An individual or company that may, under the Communications Satellite Act, deal directly with COMSAT.

author mark *See* author number.

author number A character or characters used by a library to identify an author. Also called an *author mark*.

author-prepared copy Manuscripts or pages that are camera ready or coded for typesetting.

author-publisher An author who acts as his or her own publisher by having the work privately printed. *See also* vanity press.

author's advance *See* advance.

author's agent *See* literary agent.

author's alterations (aa) Changes made in galley or page proofs by the author. Also called *author's changes*. Cf. editor's alterations.

author's changes *See* author's alterations (aa).

author's copies The complimentary copies given by a publisher to the author.

Authors Guild A union.

author's proof The proof sent to the author for acceptance after the compositor's errors have been corrected.

author's rights *See* exclusive rights.

author-title index An alphabetical catalogue of books that includes both authors and titles.

auto An abbreviation for *automatic*.

autoassembly The automatic editing of a videotape by computer control once the information has been entered by a videotape editor into an edit decision list.

autochroma A trademark for *automatic chroma control*.

autocue A small, electrically driven device mounted on or near a camera for cueing talent. *See also* telecuer.

autodial The ability of a computer system to use telephone lines without human intervention.

autoexposure A metering system that automatically adjusts the camera lens aperture to the subject.

autofocal *See* autofocus.

autofocus A center-weighted electronic or mechanical device that automatically focuses the camera on the subject. Also called *autofocal*.

autofunctions Computer codes embedded within text for typesetting control.

auto gate A film studio automobile entrance.

autograph party The appearance of an author, usually at a bookstore, to publicize a new book and incidentally to sign autographs.

autographed A copy of a book or other printed matter signed by the author.

autolocator An audio- or videotape recorder that remembers on-the-fly functions.

auto masking A system for masking unwanted absorption in color film by using colored couplers. Also called *automatic color masking*.

automated animation The use of computers in animation to perform many of the tedious repetitious tasks formerly performed by hand.

automated channel A cable television channel that is programmed to continuously repeat text and graphics, such as for bulletin boards or community events.

automated dialogue replacement *See* automatic dialogue replacement.

automated distribution The automatic distribution of new books from publishers to bookstores based on assumed needs.

automated editing The use of videotape cue track or time code information to allow automatic computer or controller editing of preselected edit points.

automated lighting The use of preset lighting controlled by computer or automatic light board.

automated measurement of lineups (AMOL) An electronic method to decipher codes each network assigns to its programs over the airwaves or just prior to the program's signal being transmitted from the station's antenna.

automated switching The use of a computer to control the television broadcast signal—the air time, duration, source, and description.

automatic Systems, devices, and components that function without human intervention.

automatic aperture An electronic device that automatically sets the aperture to match the available light.

automatic backspace A portable videotape recorder feature that automatically reverses the tape a few frames after each shot so that clean cuts are made between shots. Also called *automatic reverse.*

automatic bass compensation (ABC) A circuit that automatically increases the volume of the bass notes at low listening levels.

automatic chroma control An apparatus for sensing and automatically correcting errors in chrominance amplitude in videotape recording.

automatic clapstick *See* automatic slate.

automatic color masking *See* auto masking.

automatic compressor An automatic sound limiter.

automatic control-track phasing □ The capability of a videotape playback apparatus to adjust automatically, by reference to the control-track signal, the motion of the tape through the tape transport, so that the paths of the video heads are centered over the recorded video track. □ The apparatus or equipment designed to carry out such an adjustment.

automatic data processing (ADP) Any type of data processing performed on automatic equipment.

automatic dialogue replacement (ADR) A computerized system for looping. Also called *automated dialogue replacement.*

automatic dissolve An animation camera mechanism that allows a preset number of frames to be set for a dissolve.

automatic distribution *See* automated distribution.

automatic dropout □ A compensation device that electronically replaces information missing on a videotape because of dropout. □ A method of reducing halftones in white spaces.

automatic exposure meter *See* autoexposure.

automatic fade An animation camera mechanism that allows a preset number of frames to be set for a fade.

automatic focus *See* autofocus.

automatic frequency control (AFC) An electronic circuit that maintains the selected frequency in a radio receiver.

automatic gain control (AGC) An electronic circuit that maintains the output volume regardless of input variations.

automatic indexing Computerized searching and listing of key words and page numbers by word processing programs.

automatic inspection The use of a high-speed film device to check for bad splices, torn perforations, and so on.

Automatic Interaction Detector (AID) A multivariate technique used for reducing large combinations of data to determine what variables and categories within these variables combine to produce the greatest discrimination in defining a dependent variable such as product or brand usage.

automatic iris An electric device that varies the aperture of a lens to conform to changing light conditions on a set.

automatic level control (ALC) In tape recording, the automatic limiting of the maximum recording level to prevent overmodulation.

automatic light control A device used in film chains to automatically compensate for variations in light intensity.

automatic logging The automatic recording of operating and program logs; approved by the FCC in 1963.

automatic mobile relay station A remote pickup broadcast base station actuated by automatic means and used to relay communications between base and mobile stations, between mobile stations, and from mobile stations licensed to broadcast stations.

automatic numbering Computerized numbering of footnotes, lines, paragraphs, pages, and so on.

automatic paster A device used to splice one roll of newsprint to another without stopping the press.

automatic projection The automatic control of the projector and house lights in motion picture theatres.

automatic purge A computer program that automatically removes unmodified copy from memory after a specified period of time.

automatic relay station A remote pickup broadcast base station that is actuated by automatic means and is used to relay transmissions between a remote pickup broadcast base and mobile stations, between remote pickup broadcast mobile stations, and from remote pickup broadcast mobile stations to broadcasting stations.

automatic retransmission request (ARQ) An automatic sequence begun to correct a satellite or other transmission that contains errors.

automatic reverse □ A tape recorder that is capable of playing in the opposite direction automatically. □ *See* automatic backspace.

automatic rewind *See* continuous projection.

automatic scan tracking (AST) A helical scan videotape head that is designed to eliminate tracking errors.

automatic sequence A record album containing more than one disc on which even numbered sides are on the same disc or discs. Cf. manual sequence.

automatic sequence register (ASR) A tradename for a device that allows a series of video cartridges to be played automatically.

automatic sheet feeder A device used to feed single sheets of paper into a computer printer. Also called a *cut sheet feeder.*

automatic shipment A book club shipment plan that sends each new selection automatically. Cf. negative option and positive option.

automatic shutoff A device that automatically stops a tape recorder or other device when the tape runs out or breaks.

automatic slate A device on some film cameras that places markers on the picture and soundtrack at the same time. *See also* beep.

automatic standards recognition An automatic switch employed on some television receivers that changes the receiver from NTSC to PAL or SECAM.

automatic threading □ The act of placing an audio- or videotape in the tape path by means of automatic machinery. □ *See* auto threading.

automatic transmission system (ATS) A self-regulating broadcast transmitter device.

automatic tuner A radio tuner that automatically scans the dial and selects stations with sufficient signal strength.

automatic tuning An electrical or mechanical button or device that allows selection of preset or predetermined radio or television stations.

automatic typewriter A typewriter that can be operated either manually or by electromechanical impulses.

automatic volume control (AVC) An electronic circuit that maintains a preset level.

automation □ The use of automatic devices to perform routine functions. Used for log keeping, technical operations, bookkeeping, and so on. □ In radio, the use of computer programmed operations through punchcards, carousels, reel-to-reel recorders, cartridges, and so on; switched by subaudible tones or silent sensing.

auto preview A preview channel in a television switcher that automatically displays the next picture to be used.

auto restart A device that provides for the automatic resumption of a system's operation after a temporary power loss.

Autoscreen film A Kodalith film used to make halftone negatives.

auto search An automatic search to any selected videotape frame using vertical interval frame code or time code.

auto tag A videotape that returns to the last frame of the previous edit to be ready for the next edit.

auto threading A camera or projector equipped with a path that automatically guides a film.

autotake An automatic device in a television switcher that "takes" the output of the preview bus and switches it to the program bus.

autotransformer A transformer with a single coil of wire around an iron core that acts as both primary and secondary transformer. Often used in light boards as a dimmer.

autotransformer dimmer A variable voltage transformer used in lighting circuits.

aux ☐ An abbreviation for *auxiliary.* ☐ *See* auxiliary channel.

auxiliary A piece of equipment used as a backup.

auxiliary broadcast services Four categories of services for broadcast stations: (a) portable or mobile stations, (b) base stations (*see* remote pickup broadcast base stations), (c) fixed stations (STL), and (d) intercity relay fixed stations.

auxiliary channel A channel used to connect external devices to an audio or video recorder. Usually marked *aux.*

auxiliary data field In CD-ROM and CD-I, the last 288 bytes of a sector, either used for extra error detection and error correction (mode 1, form 1) or available as user data area (mode 2, form 2).

auxiliary lens An afocal lens added to an existing lens.

auxiliary storage Any peripheral device on which data can be stored, as compared to internal (RAM) storage.

auxiliary transmitter A transmitter licensed for use by the FCC and maintained as a standby transmitter in case of failure of the main transmitter.

AV The abbreviation for *audio-visual.*

availabilities ☐ Unsold air time that is available for commercial use on stations, networks, or cable systems. *See also* inventory. ☐ Talent "at liberty" and available for booking. ☐ Equipment available for use. ☐ In outdoor advertising, space available for sale.

availability ☐ The first date on which a motion picture may be exhibited. ☐ The percentage of time that data processing equipment operates without error. The opposite of downtime. Cf. accessibility.

available A story or photograph that is ready to be used in a newscast.

available audience The total number of individuals or households awake and capable of receiving a broadcast signal at any given time.

available light The use of natural light in cinematography or television remotes. *See also* ambient light.

avails An abbreviation for *sales availabilities.*

avant garde ☐ New, original, sometimes extreme, or experimental ideas, films, scripts, and so on. ☐ Innovative films of the 1920s.

Avatar Award An annual award presented by the Broadcast Financial Management Association.

AVC ☐ Automatic volume control. ☐ Audio-visual communications. ☐ Association of Visual Communicators.

Avco rule The 1946 FCC rule that required licensees to solicit competitive bids for proposed license transfers. Abolished in 1949 and now forbidden by Section 310 of the Communications Act.

AV edit A videotape edit that records new audio and video.

average A statistical quantity representing the general or typical significance of a set of values. *See also* mean, median, and mode.

average audience (AA) A widely used rating by Nielsen, the AA reflects viewing to the average minute of a program and is an average of the audiences at minute 1, 2, 3, and so on. As such, it serves as an estimate of the audience (households or persons) for the average commercial; of obvious importance to the sponsor(s). It is a number used by the networks and buyers for negotiation. Also used for computing share and CPM.

average audience rating A type of rating computed for some specified interval of time such as the length of a television or radio program or for a 15- or 30-minute period. Cf. total audience rating.

average daily circulation A statistical estimate of the number of different radio or television households reached by a station on each day of a week.

average episodes per viewing household/person The average number of quarter hours viewed by each household/person reached.

average frequency The number of exposures of an average household or consumer over a specified period of time to a series of advertisements through all media carrying the advertisements. *See also* frequency.

average hours The average number of hours viewed per television household, per day, per week, or per time period.

average instantaneous-audience rating *See* average audience rating.

average minute rating *See* average audience rating.

average net paid The average circulation of a publication per issue; computed by dividing the total paid circulation of all the issues for that audit period by the total number of issues. Also called *average paid circulation.*

average paid circulation *See* average net paid.

average picture level (APL) The average luminance of a television picture during scanning.

average quarter hour (AQH) The number of persons or households estimated to be tuned to a specific radio or television program or channel for 5 continuous minutes during a 15-minute period.

average quarter-hour audience *See* quarter-hour audience.

average quarter-hour persons (AQH persons) The estimated number of persons who listened to a station for a minimum of five minutes within a given quarter hour. The estimate is based on the average of reported listening in the total number of quarter hours the station was on the air during a reported time period. This estimate is shown for the Metro, TSA, and, where applicable, the ADI.

average quarter-hour rating The average quarter-hour persons estimate expressed as a percentage of the universe. This estimate is shown in the Metro and, where applicable, the ADI.

average quarter-hour share The average quarter-hour persons estimate for a given station expressed as a percentage of the average quarter-hour persons estimate for the total listening in the Metro within a given time period. This estimate is shown only in the Metro.

average total audience rating *See* total audience rating.

AV-SYNC A nonprofit computer bulletin board service designed for the needs of users in the sound and video industries.

A/W Alternate weeks.

AWA Antique Wireless Association, Inc.

AWA Writing Awards A number of awards given by the Aviation/Space Writers Association for outstanding space writing and reporting.

away-from-home listening An estimate of listening for which the diarykeeper indicated that listening was done away from home, either in a car or some other place.

AWG American Wire Gauge. A national standard for wire diameter measurement.

A wind □ A method of winding audio- or videotape on a reel so that the magnetic surface faces the hub. □ A single perforated film winding; with the emulsion facing the core and the film unwinding clockwise, the perforations are toward the viewer. Cf. B wind.

A-wire A news service primary wire carrying worldwide news stories written in newspaper style. Cf. B-wire and radio wire.

AWR Adventist World Radio. A religious broadcasting organization.

AWRT American Women in Radio and Television.

axe grinder □ An editorial under the guise of news. □ A biased editorial. □ A press agent who furnishes information to the media to gain publicity for a client.

axis □ An imaginary line used to relate the various parts of a design. □ The straight line between the axes of the several elements of a lens. □ Any of three mutually perpendicular lines about which a body is symmetrically arranged. □ *See* imaginary line.

axis lighting The lighting of a subject from a position close to the camera lens.

axis of action *See* imaginary line.

axis of orientation (A/O) The point or points to which the eye returns automatically, as in reading lines of text.

axis of refraction The line perpendicular to the surface of the medium.

Ayer's □ A classic advertising layout formula. □ A directory of newspapers and magazines.

az/el mount A satellite dish mount that is adjustable in both azimuth and elevation.

azimuth □ The degree of rotation of a satellite dish from true north. Cf. elevation. □ The angle between the magnetic recording or reproducing head gap and the direction of tape travel.

azimuth error □ The angular deviation from the format standard of the playback and record head-pole-tip gaps. □ The error that occurs when the light path is not 90 degrees from the plane of the film passing the exciter lamp in a projector.

azimuth loss The signal loss due to misalignment of the playback head gap and the audio- or videotape recorded signal.

azimuth recording The use of a track pattern recorded on tape characterized by an alternation of the azimuths of adjacent recorded video tracks. This minimizes crosstalk resulting from mistracking and permits the reduction or elimination of guard bands. Also called *chevron pattern.*

B

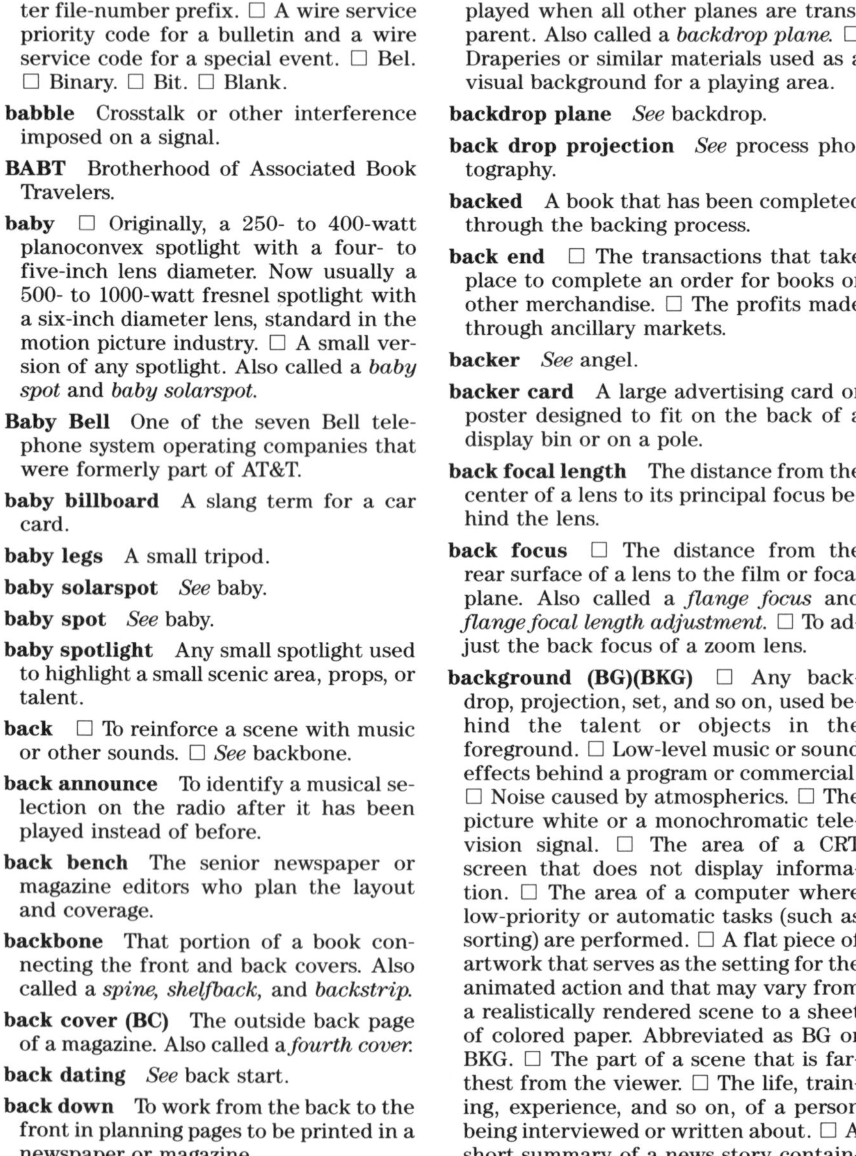

B □ Base. □ Broadcast. An FCC first letter file-number prefix. □ A wire service priority code for a bulletin and a wire service code for a special event. □ Bel. □ Binary. □ Bit. □ Blank.

babble Crosstalk or other interference imposed on a signal.

BABT Brotherhood of Associated Book Travelers.

baby □ Originally, a 250- to 400-watt planoconvex spotlight with a four- to five-inch lens diameter. Now usually a 500- to 1000-watt fresnel spotlight with a six-inch diameter lens, standard in the motion picture industry. □ A small version of any spotlight. Also called a *baby spot* and *baby solarspot.*

Baby Bell One of the seven Bell telephone system operating companies that were formerly part of AT&T.

baby billboard A slang term for a car card.

baby legs A small tripod.

baby solarspot *See* baby.

baby spot *See* baby.

baby spotlight Any small spotlight used to highlight a small scenic area, props, or talent.

back □ To reinforce a scene with music or other sounds. □ *See* backbone.

back announce To identify a musical selection on the radio after it has been played instead of before.

back bench The senior newspaper or magazine editors who plan the layout and coverage.

backbone That portion of a book connecting the front and back covers. Also called a *spine, shelfback,* and *backstrip.*

back cover (BC) The outside back page of a magazine. Also called a *fourth cover.*

back dating *See* back start.

back down To work from the back to the front in planning pages to be printed in a newspaper or magazine.

backdrop □ The image plane that is displayed when all other planes are transparent. Also called a *backdrop plane.* □ Draperies or similar materials used as a visual background for a playing area.

backdrop plane *See* backdrop.

back drop projection *See* process photography.

backed A book that has been completed through the backing process.

back end □ The transactions that take place to complete an order for books or other merchandise. □ The profits made through ancillary markets.

backer *See* angel.

backer card A large advertising card or poster designed to fit on the back of a display bin or on a pole.

back focal length The distance from the center of a lens to its principal focus behind the lens.

back focus □ The distance from the rear surface of a lens to the film or focal plane. Also called a *flange focus* and *flange focal length adjustment.* □ To adjust the back focus of a zoom lens.

background (BG)(BKG) □ Any backdrop, projection, set, and so on, used behind the talent or objects in the foreground. □ Low-level music or sound effects behind a program or commercial. □ Noise caused by atmospherics. □ The picture white or a monochromatic television signal. □ The area of a CRT screen that does not display information. □ The area of a computer where low-priority or automatic tasks (such as sorting) are performed. □ A flat piece of artwork that serves as the setting for the animated action and that may vary from a realistically rendered scene to a sheet of colored paper. Abbreviated as BG or BKG. □ The part of a scene that is farthest from the viewer. □ The life, training, experience, and so on, of a person being interviewed or written about. □ A short summary of a news story containing the details necessary to an understanding of the story. □ The stated context of previous occurrences, current environment, and desires for the future within which advertising and marketing plans are developed and executed.

background action □ The movement and sound of performers who are not the main focus of attention. □ The action that leads up to the action currently being photographed.

background artist The animation artist who paints the backgrounds.

background cyc A cyclorama used as a background.

background effects Sound effects that are used in the background.

backgrounder Information that explains the significance of a news story; often used to gain approval for the use of the story. *See also* off the record.

background light Illumination of a set or background. Also called a *set light.* Cf. back-light.

background music □ Music used to establish a mood, provide reinforcement to the action, and so on. Cf. foreground music. □ In nondramatic productions, any music used at a low level. *See also* background.

background music station A radio station, usually FM, that programs a maximum amount of neutral music and a minimum amount of talk.

background noise □ Electrical disturbances that interfere with the proper operation of electronic devices. □ The total system noise output independent of the signal.

background plate A photograph used for rear screen projection in process photography.

background processing The processing of lower priority information by a computer system, usually during the time foreground processing is not taking place.

background projection *See* rear projection.

background sound *See* background.

backing □ Any background such as a flat, drop, border, and so on, used to limit the view of an audience. □ The base material of audio- and videotape—often acetate, polyester, or PVC. □ A material applied to the backside of the base film; more properly called *backside coating.*

backing lighting The illumination provided for scenery in off- stage areas visible to the audience.

backing track A soundtrack prerecorded to accompany a vocalist.

backing up *See* backup.

backing view The construction of a set so that it conforms exactly to the scenes shot on location.

back issue A magazine or other periodical that is no longer current.

backlaying The editing of film or videotape from the end of the material rather than from the beginning.

back lead The writing of a story that then backs into a lead.

back-light Illumination of the subject from behind to produce a highlight along its edge and consequent separation between the subject and its background; light is from a direction substantially parallel to a vertical plane through the optical axis of the camera or viewer. Also called *fringe light. See also* three-point lighting. Cf. background light.

backlighting The lighting used to illuminate an animation cel.

backlining The material that is used to hold book signatures together.

backlist Books that are still in print but no longer current.

backload To schedule the use of the bulk of a budget for the latter part of a planning period; serves as a precaution against overspending a budget that may be reduced. Cf. frontload.

back lot The area of a motion picture studio that contains streets, town facades, a town square, and so on; used to simulate location shooting.

back margin The inside margin of a printed page. In a bound volume, also called a *gutter.*

back matter □ One of the three main parts of a book; contains the appendixes, notes, index, glossary, bibliography, and so on. Also called *end matter.* Cf. front matter and body matter. □ That section of a magazine that contains the continuation of stories and advertisements. Also called *back of the book matter.*

back office *See* back shop.

back of the book matter □ Printed or broadcast material that emphasizes features on science and the arts as opposed to hard news. □ The material following the editorial matter in a magazine. □ *See* back matter.

back order (BO) A book or other item temporarily out-of-stock but to be shipped when inventory is replenished.

backpack A lightweight metal frame used by a camera operator to carry a videotape recorder.

back porch The portion of a composite television picture signal between the trailing edge of a horizontal sync pulse and the trailing edge of the blanking pulse. Cf. front porch.

back projection A British term for *rear projection.*

back-rim lighting Lighting used to separate talent or objects from the background. *See also* back-light.

back room *See* back shop.

backs The edges of the book pages nearest the backbone.

back scattering The radiation of energy toward the rear of an antenna.

back shop The mechanical room of a newspaper. Also called *back office* and *back room.*

backside That side of an audio- or videotape that does not have a coating of magnetizable material. Also called *nonoxide side.*

backside coating On a videotape, a material applied to the backside of the base film, usually to minimize cinching and stiction and/or the accumulation of electrostatic charges.

backside transport A videotape transport, the majority of whose elements touch only the nonoxide side of the videotape.

backslant A letter that slants to the left; the reverse of italic.

backslash The symbol \.

backspace □ To move the carriage of a typewriter to the preceding space. □ To physically or mechanically move a videotape backward.

backspacing The backing up of a videotape prior to an edit so that the player and recorder will be up to speed and in synchronization with each other when the edit is made.

backstage The area outside the view of the audience; usually the work area. Cf. offstage.

backstage video A documentary-style video that is produced to describe in visual terms what goes on behind the scene.

back start To begin a magazine subscription with an issue that is no longer current. Also called *back dating.* Cf. advance start.

back story A personal development narrative of the life of a character in a drama.

back strip The material pasted to the edges of book pages next to the backbone.

backtime To time a script, music, or other element of a radio or television program from the end to the beginning in order to make the program end on time. Also referred to as *backtiming.*

back-to-back □ Programs, commercials, scenes, shots, and so on, that follow consecutively. □ Audio bites from two or more sources that do not contain any intervening information.

back up □ To print the reverse side of a sheet. Also called *backing up* and *perfecting.* □ To solder metal to a printing plate to increase its thickness.

backup □ A copy of a computer program, data file, tape, and so on, in case the original is accidentally destroyed or erased. Cf. dual recording. □ Equipment held in reserve to replace nonfunctioning systems or devices. □ A second reporter or photographer used as a replacement for one who cannot or does not complete an assignment.

backup copy *See* backup.

backup lead-in A silent lead-in to a sound film or video recording.

back-up page *See* back-up space.

back-up schedule Anything that is held in reserve to fill air time or print space, such as a sustaining program, evergreen copy, and so on.

back-up script A story and/or teleplay for a proposed episodic series for which a writer is employed prior to the exploitation of the television sequel rights for such proposed series, other than a pilot script.

back-up space An advertising space that must be purchased in a magazine or newspaper in order to run an insert; usually equivalent to one black and white page. Also called a *back-up page.*

backward take Reverse motion accomplished in a film by running the camera backward or by mounting the camera upside down.

backwind A mechanism that allows film to be rewound in the camera in order to accomplish special effects.

bad break An awkward-looking division of lines or paragraphs on a printed page; often occurs when stories are divided between columns or pages.

baffle □ A box, usually of wood, used to improve the bass response of a loudspeaker. □ A portable wall of sound-absorbing material. □ An acoustic screen used on a microphone to dampen unwanted noise. *See also* windscreen. □ A louvered shutter on a luminaire. Cf. barn doors.

BAFTA British Academy of Film and Television Arts.

bail □ That part of a typewriter or printer that holds the paper against the platen. □ One of the two metal clamps that holds the tympan sheets in place.

bait advertising *See* bait switch.

bait switch The advertising of low-priced goods or services designed to lure customers into purchasing higher-priced goods or services. Also called *bait advertising.*

Baker Award, W. R. G. Award given by the IEEE to the author of the outstanding paper in IEEE publications.

balance □ The blending of sound to achieve a well-proportioned mix. □ The equalization of base-light over an entire set. □ The placing of talent or visual materials to achieve the desired effect. □ Attractive picture composition. □ Well-proportioned video levels. □ Equilibrium in the elements of a page, graphic, design, set, stage picture, and so on. □ The former requirement that both sides of a controversial issue of public importance be aired. *See also* Fairness Doctrine.

balance control A potentiometer on a stereo system that increases the volume in one loudspeaker while decreasing it in the other.

balanced line A line or circuit in which the voltages of the two conductors are equal. Also called a *balanced pair.*

balanced pair *See* balanced line.

balanced print A film that has the head of each sequence of shots balanced for timing lights.

balanced programming An ambiguous term used in the 1928 Great Lakes Decision calling for a variety of program offerings by a broadcast station.

balance sheet A current business statement showing assets and liabilities.

balance stripe A stripe laid on the opposite edge of a mag stripe film so that the film can be wound evenly. Also used as a second audio channel. Also called a *balancing stripe.*

balance test A series of trial balances taken to ensure proper placement of microphones.

balancing □ A judicial test used to determine the relative merits of issues; which of two conflicting issues requires the greater protection under the law. □ The act of adjusting sound levels to account for the variation between studio equipment and receivers in the home.

balancing light A secondary light shown on a photographic subject, in a motion picture scene, television scene, and so on, intended to prevent excessive light and shade contrast from the key light.

balancing stripe *See* balance stripe.

balcony spotlight A spotlight mounted in the balcony of an auditorium, generally at the front of the balcony railing. Also called a *rail light.*

ball-and-socket A type of small camera mount.

ballast The electrical device required for all discharge lamps that limits current through the lamp. Additional functions may be incorporated for lamp starting, dimming, and so on.

ball chart *See* linearity chart.

balloon A device used in cartoons and comic strips to show the words a character is speaking.

balloon former The upper former of a printing press.

balop An abbreviation for *Balopticon* (trade name of Bausch and Lomb). A television opaque (reflection) projector. *See also* telop.

Balowstar lens An exceptionally fast (f 1.3) television lens with a seven-inch focal length.

balun An acronym for balanced/unbalanced. A device used for matching impedances; usually a transformer, for example, from a 75-ohm cable to a 300-ohm twin lead for television.

bamboo wireless A native grapevine.

BAN Black Audio Network, Inc.

ban To forbid the publication of a play, the showing of a motion picture, the televising of an event, and so on. *See also* censorship.

banana A standup comedian; usually refers to a vaudeville performer.

banana jack A jack that is built to accept a banana plug.

banana plug A small electrical connector shaped like a banana and formed from spring steel.

banana rule A form of cutoff rule.

banc *See* en banc.

band □ A group of frequencies allocated to radio communication. *See also* VLF, LF, MF, HF, VHF, UHF, SHF, and EHF. □ A range of frequencies within defined limits. □ One selection on a disc or tape. □ A group of magnetic tracks on a medium such as a magnetic drum, disk, or tape.

Band A The 10 bands of frequencies from 1990 to 2500 mHz available for assignment to television pickup, television STL, and television intercity relay stations.

Band B The 10 bands of frequencies from 6875 to 7125 mHz available for assignment to television pickup, television STL, and television intercity relay stations.

Band D The 22 bands of frequencies from 12700 to 13250 mHz available for assignment to television pickup, television STL, and television intercity relay stations.

banding □ A visual loss of television picture information appearing as evenly distributed horizontal bands. □ In video recorders designed for segmented recording, a picture fault characterized by a visible difference in parts of the picture recorded or reproduced by different heads. *See also* gauge banding, hue banding, noise banding, and saturation banding. □ A visible difference in the reproduced characteristics in that portion of a picture associated with one head channel when compared with adjacent areas associated with other head channels. In quadruplex recorders, these differences occur in horizontal bands of 16 or 17 scanning lines when reproducing a 525/60 signal.

bandoline A viscous liquid used to keep hair in place.

bandpass filter A device that allows the passage of a specified band of frequencies but attenuates frequencies on both sides of the band.

bands The horizontal cords that reinforce the spine of a book.

bandshaping The reduction of the bandwidth in color television to fit the I and Q signals into the M channel.

band sharing □ The use of an allocated radio communication band by two or more broadcast or other services. □ The use of a band of frequencies by two or more signals, for example, for the luminance and color difference signals in television.

bandwagon effect The effect caused by persons who wish to be identified with a winner and thus lend support to the front runner in a political race.

bandwidth The number of hertz expressing the difference between the limiting frequencies of a frequency band; for example, the 2.5- to 3.5-mHz band has a width of 1 mHz.

bang A slang term for an exclamation point. Also called a *soldier.*

bangtail A form of self-mailer, often with a tear-off flap used for ordering merchandise.

bank □ A group of lighting switches and/or dimmers that may be controlled together. □ A group of luminaires. □ A strip containing a number of lamps. □ A unit of computer memory, usually in multiples of 64K. □ A strip of electrical connectors. □ A British term for *video switcher bus.* □ A secondary part of a headline. Also called a *deck.* □ A storage place for type. □ A table on which type in galleys is worked on. Also called a *stone.* □ The personnel of a newspaper department.

bankable A well-known actor, director, personality, property, and so on, who through previous box office success makes it easy to raise money for a production.

banked A news story or feature that does not have a time limitation. Also called an *evergreen.*

banker A helper in a composing room.

bankroll To furnish the money necessary for a production. *See also* angel.

banner □ A headline that extends across the top of a newspaper page. Also called a *banner head, banner headline, banner line, eight-column line, line, ribbon, screamer,* and *streamer.* □ A display poster for advertising, especially one draped over a wire or cord so as to be readable from the sides.

banner head *See* banner.

banner headline *See* banner.

banner line *See* banner.

BAPSA Broadcast Advertising Producers Society of America.

BAR Broadcast Advertisers Reports.

bar In type, the enclosed horizontal line as in an *A* or *H.* Cf. apex, arm, cross stroke, ear, spur, stem, tail, and vertex.

bar-code A type of code used on products containing manufacturer and product information; may also be used on such items as library books.

bardic television A term coined by Fiske and Hartley in their book *Reading Television* to explain the functioning of television for the culture at large and the individuals who live in it. Accomplished through concentration on the messages as well as the institutions that produce the messages.

barker A large, short headline placed above the main, smaller headline. Also called a *hammer* and *reverse kicker.* Cf. kicker.

barker channel A cable television channel that is used for information about programs on the other channels.

bar line The line of type between headlines.

barn burner A speech, media event, rally, and so on that gathers an enthusiastic crowd or audience.

barn doors Shutters or flaps, usually two or four, that are attached to the front of a luminaire in order to control the shape of the light beam. Also called a *flipper.*

barn door wipe An optical wipe that imitates the opening of doors.

barney A soundproof housing or blimp used to isolate camera noise from a microphone.

barny A hollow-sounding echo.

barracuda A telescoping luminaire support.

barrel □ Either or both of the concentric tubes of a focusing lens system. □ The cylindrical sheath of a plug. □ A film-editing room wastebasket. *See also* bin. □ In Europe, an electrical pipe.

barrel adapter A short, cylindrical device used to connect two lengths of cable.

barrel distortion Television distortion wherein both sides of the raster curve outward.

barrel marks The notches on a lens that indicate the size of the diaphragm opening, the distance from camera to object, and the depth of field.

bars □ The measures of musical compositions. □ *See* color bars. □ *See* horizontal bars.

bar sheet □ A printed form, used by directors and animators in planning the movement of art and camera, on which all the elements of a film—music, voices, sound effects, visuals—are charted frame-by-frame in their relationship to time. □ *See* lead sheet.

barter □ The exchange of radio or television station time with an advertiser for goods and services. *See also* trade out. □ Free television programs furnished with commercials. Also called a *trade deal, trade out,* and *trade spot.*

barter broker An individual who arranges barters between advertisers and broadcast stations.

barter house A company that arranges barters between advertisers and broadcast stations.

barter spot A commercial in a syndicated radio or television program sold by the distributor of the program.

barter syndication The distribution of a syndicated television program wherein the station agrees to allow the syndicator to sell some of the commercial time within the program.

barter time Broadcast air time that is exchanged for goods or services.

base (B) □ That part of a lamp to which the electrical connections are made. In many cases it also forms the mechanical support of the lamp. □ A disc for supporting a luminaire. □ *See* film base. □ *See* base-light. □ The region between the collector and emitter in a transistor. □ A make-up foundation. Also called *base make-up.* □ A wooden or metal block on which a printing plate is mounted. Also called a *block* and a *mount.* □ The number upon which a set of numbers is constructed; in the decimal system, for example, the base is 10; in the binary system the base is 2. Also called a *radix.* □ A category of items or individuals from which a sample is selected. Also may be a statistical population. □ The number of households from which a sample is drawn.

baseband □ Aural transmitter input signals between 0 and 120 kHz. □ The band of frequencies to be superimposed (modulated) on a carrier wave. □ The frequencies used for local area network (LAN) transmissions.

base case The minimum characteristics of a system that may bear the CD-I name. Base case CD-I authoring systems, players, and discs conform to current CD-I specifications; those containing additional specifications are known as CDI-X.

base counts The number of in-tab households used in computation.

base distortion Film stock distortion, often caused by winding with the emulsion side out.

based on A novel, screenplay, story, or other art form that is loosely adapted from another source.

base film In audio- and videotape, the material that serves as support for the magnetizable medium.

base illumination *See* base-light.

base-light □ Uniform, diffuse illumination used to establish a sufficient ambient level of light for quality type television and film pickups at desired lens aperture. Also called *foundation light. See also* three-point lighting. □ Acceptable base level of unaccented stage illumination.

baseline □ The line on which all letters without descenders rest. Cf. mean line, ascender line, and descender line. □ A line at the bottom of a display advertisement that indicates the theme of the advertisement.

base make-up *See* base.

basement The bottom half of a page, especially of a newspaper.

base rate *See* open rate.

base side The shiny side of film stock. Cf. emulsion side.

base station A land station in the land mobile service.

base track One of the tracks laid first in multitrack recording.

basher A scoop or floodlight.

BASIC Beginner's All Purpose Symbolic Instruction Code. A simple, much-used computer programming language.

basic bus A bus in which all the transit advertising space is sold to one advertiser.

basic cable A service that transmits television signals by wire (cable) instead of through the air. This allows for improved reception and increased availability of retransmitted local and distant stations. Available at a basic monthly subscription fee.

basic cable household The number of households that subscribe to cable television service in a given area.

basic cable service □ Generally, the minimum group of channels offered to cable television subscribers at the lowest monthly fee. Usually includes local broadcast signals and some imported signals. Also called *basic service.* □ For the purpose of regulating the rates for the provision of basic cable service in circumstances in which a cable system is not subject to effective competition, any service tier that includes the retransmission of any broadcast television signals. *See* Title 47 of the *Code of Federal Regulations* (CFR), paragraph 76.5, for the extensive categories.

basic dimension A fundamental dimension to which no tolerance is applicable. Cf. derived dimension and reference dimension.

basic eligibility criteria The legal, technical, financial, and character qualifications set forth by the Federal Communications Commission for broadcast licensees. *See also* mutually exclusive criteria.

basic network □ The principal affiliates of a radio or television network, usually in the major markets, on which a sponsor must buy time. □ A cable television service that is included in basic cable service.

basic price The standard price of a periodical for which it is sold to its ordinary readership under normal conditions.

basic rate *See* one-time rate.

basic research Research that attempts to expand basic knowledge of a subject. Also called *pure research.* Cf. applied research.

basic service *See* basic cable service.

basic set A stage set without props or other stage dressing.

basic station A television station included in the basic network.

basic track An audio track containing only the rhythm portion of the music.

basic weight *See* basis weight.

basis weight The weight in pounds of a ream of paper of specified dimensions before cutting. Also called *basic weight, paper weight,* and *substance. See also* weight.

bass Sounds in the lower end of the musical scale, usually below 200 Hz.

bass boost The intentional accentuation of bass frequencies. Cf. treble boost.

bass control A potentiometer that controls the bass frequencies in an amplifier.

bass reflex A common form of loudspeaker enclosure in which the bass response is improved by the use of an opening tuned to the particular loudspeaker.

bass response The ability of a loudspeaker, microphone, or amplifier to reproduce low frequencies.

bass rolloff *See* rolloff.

bass tip-up Low-frequency exaggeration in directional microphones caused by the pressure gradient.

bassy Low-frequency overemphasis in sound reproduction.

bastard face *See* bastard type.

bastard measure A line not evenly measured in picas or half picas.

bastard size Any size that does not conform to standard sizes in typography, periodical make-up, or prescribed advertising space units.

bastard title An abbreviated title on the page preceding the title page. Also called a *half title* and *fly title.*

bastard type □ A type face inappropriate to its body size. □ Nonstandard type size. Also called *bastard face. See also* point system.

bat blacks Electronically accenting the black hues of a television picture for supers or the illusion of darkness. Also called *batting-blacks* and *hit black.*

batch □ A group of computer records processed together. □ Film manufactured at the same time and so marked to indicate uniformity between separate rolls.

batch number The number assigned by a manufacturer to a batch of film. *See also* emulsion number.

bath The chemical solutions used in film processing, such as developer, stop bath, fixer, and bleach.

batten □ A horizontal pipe on which luminaires or scenery can be hung, typically 1.25 to 2 inches in diameter. □ A metal or wooden brace used to secure flats, luminaires, mikes, and so on. □ *See* lighting batten.

battered Type that is worn or damaged and thus incapable of being printed properly.

battery An electric storage device that furnishes direct current. Used to furnish power to portable equipment.

battery belt A belt worn by a camera operator containing a series of batteries used to power a camera or sometimes a videotape recorder. Called a *battery pack* if it is inserted in equipment.

battery charger An ac converter that is used to restore power to depleted batteries. Usually nickel cadmium (ni-cad) batteries.

battery pack *See* battery belt.

battery-powered Equipment that is furnished power by batteries as opposed to alternating current sources.

batting-blacks *See* bat blacks.

batting down To decrease the brightness of a television picture.

baud A unit used to measure the number of binary units of information transmitted per second.

Baudot A coding system used for teletypewriter and telex machines. Cf. ASCII and EBCDIC.

baud rate A measure of the speed of data transmission, usually expressed in bits per second.

Bauhaus An influential German school of design characterized by functional styles.

bay □ A component of an antenna. □ A vertical rack for mounting electronic equipment. □ A storage area for flats.

Also called a *dock, scene dock,* or *scenery dock.* □ *See* jack panel.

bay mortise A portion of a halftone that is cut so that the graphic or picture covers three sides of the opening.

bayonet base (BB) *See* bayonet mount.

bayonet mount A lens mount without threads that can be locked into position with a twisting motion. Also called a *bayonet base.*

Bay Psalm Book The first book printed in English in America (1640).

bazooka An overhead luminaire supporting device.

BB □ Bayonet base. □ Books. □ Billboard.

BBB Back to the Bible Broadcast. A religious broadcasting organization.

BBC British Broadcasting Corporation. A national broadcasting organization.

BBG Board of Broadcast Governors. Former Canadian regulatory agency. Now CRTC.

BBM □ Broadcast Bureau of Measurement. A research organization. □ Bureau of Broadcast Measurement. A Canadian research organization.

BC □ Back cover. □ Broadcast. □ Binary code. □ Binary counter.

BCA □ Broadcast Credit Association. A subsidiary of IBFM. □ Broadcasting Company of America.

B-cart *See* NAB-B.

BCB □ Broadcast band. □ Button cell battery.

BCD Binary coded decimal.

BCDIC Binary Coded Decimal Interchange Code.

B channel The right channel in a stereo system.

BCI Binary coded information.

BCL Binary Coded Language.

BCN Broadband Communication Network.

B copy That part of news copy written as a follow-up to A copy; sometimes used without the A copy with a new head or with the A copy. Also called *B matter.*

B county An A. C. Nielsen designation for a county other than an A county that has more than 150,000 inhabitants in itself or that is part of a metropolitan area with more than 150,000 inhabitants. *See also* county size. Cf. A county, C county, and D county.

BCU Big close-up.

BD Board.

B/D Binary to decimal.

BDA Broadcast Design Association, Inc.

BDSA Business and Defense Services Administration of the Department of Commerce.

BEA Broadcast Education Association.

beacon system A system used for antenna obstruction marking and lighting.

beaded screen A highly directional and reflective projection screen with embedded glass beads.

beam □ A directed flow of light or electromagnetic radiation. □ The cone of light from a lighting instrument. □ The angle of greatest efficiency from which sound is received by a microphone. □ To aim a broadcast at a specific audience.

beam angle Those points of the candlepower curve where the candlepower is 50 percent of maximum candlepower that define the beam of the luminaire. The included angle is defined as the beam angle. Fifty percent of maximum candlepower is the criterion used to define the beam intensity for theatrical and photographic lighting equipment; the definition varies in other applications such as floodlighting.

beam control The television camera control that manages the electron beam setting.

beam coverage The area that is covered by the light from a luminaire.

beam current The current applied to the scanning beam in a cathode ray tube.

beamed program A technique of broadcast advertising that directs commercials to a predetermined segment of the audience.

beam light A spotlight concealed in an auditorium ceiling and used to light the downstage acting areas from above.

beam lumens The amount of light (lumens) within the beam angle of a luminaire.

beam projector A luminaire using a paraboloid reflector with the light source at the focus to produce a narrow, almost parallel, beam of light. Also called a *sun spot* and *parabolic spotlight.*

beam scanning *See* scanning.

beam shaping The use of barn doors, flags, gobos, and so on, to configure the area a light beam covers.

beam splitter □ A device in motion picture cameras that allows the beam of light to be divided into two or more images. □ A behind-the-lens prism system used to divide an image for the three primary color pickup tubes. Also called a *swan cube.*

beam spread The maximum angle to which a luminaire may be adjusted.

beamwidth The maximum angle of radiation or acceptance of a dish or antenna.

beard □ An error made by an announcer or talent. Also called a *fluff. See also* goof. □ That part of the type body that slants away from and supports the face.

bearding A picture fault characterized by long black horizontal streaks following a large black-to-white transition. The effect is usually the result of overmodulation of the FM video recording channel. Also called *overdeviation. See also* tearing.

beard line A makeup term indicating the area on a man's face where whiskers grow.

beard stick A makeup applied to cover a beard.

bearer □ The type-high strips of metal that strengthen and support a type form. □ The track on either side of a platen press. □ Type-high dead metal left around an engraved plate during the proofing and molding operations.

bearing edges The outer edges of a printing plate.

bearing surface The surface of a printing plate.

bear trap A spring device that can be clamped to pipes or battens to hold small luminaires or other small objects.

beat □ The territory or subject assigned to a reporter. Also called a *run.* □ An exclusive story; a scoop. □ To disintegrate pulp in preparation for making paper. □ A script direction for an actor to take a momentary pause before continuing dialogue or action. □ The musical tempo of a soundtrack used for timing the action in animation. □ *See* heterodyne. □ The time necessary for a computer to execute an instruction.

beat check *See* phone beat.

beat frequency (BF) Either of the two frequencies that result when two different frequencies are combined. Also called a *beat note* and *beat tone.*

beat note *See* beat frequency.

beat pattern A moiré impression in a television picture caused by interference between the image and the scanning lines.

beat tone *See* beat frequency.

beautiful music A type of music format, usually FM, consisting primarily of standards.

beauty shot A close-up of a commercial product.

bed □ The surface of a printing press against which the form is laid. □ The solution used in embossing, graining, or stamping book covers. □ A platform usually suspended from above to provide lighting positions on motion picture stages. Also called a *parallel.* □ A musical selection used as background for an audio PSA or commercial. □ The rails and supporting frame on which bellows move.

Beeb A British nickname for the BBC.

beefcake A male performer who is considered attractive to the opposite sex. Cf. cheesecake.

beep □ A short tone recorded on the audio track of a VTR for cueing or synchronization. Also called a *blip, beep tone,* or *bleep. See also* automatic slate. □ An intermittent sound signifying that a telephone conversation is being recorded. □ *See* bleep.

beeper □ A device formerly required by the FCC that places an intermittent tone on a telephone line to indicate that the conversation is being recorded. □ A telephone interview recorded on audiotape. Also called a *beeper report.*

beeper report *See* beeper.

beep tape An audiotape that contains a continuous beep.

beep tone *See* beep.

beercasting The advertising of beer on radio or television.

beginner □ A person under the age of 30 with no professional experience as an actor prior to a date 12 months before the commencement of the term of his or her employment. For such a person, chorus work or extra work, even though he or she was adjusted as an extra player for speaking lines, shall not constitute professional experience as an actor. □ A person 30 years of age or over who has had no professional experience as an actor prior to the commencement of the term of his or her employment, and for such person, chorus work or extra work shall constitute professional experience. Little theatre work shall not be considered as professional experience as an actor.

beginning of tape (BOT) The point at which the audio- or videotape leader ends and the sound and/or picture begins. Also called the *load point*.

beg your pardon A somewhat outdated term for a newspaper advertisement correction.

behavior measurement Research to determine what an audience does.

behind the lens (BTL) Viewfinders, filters, or light metering systems that are located behind the lens. Cf. through the lens (TTL).

Beirut Agreement A UNESCO-sponsored agreement that removed taxes and other restrictions on the importation of educational, cultural, or scientific audio-visual materials.

bel (b) The fundamental unit of sound measurement, equal to the logarithm of the ratio of two amounts of power. The decibel is the more commonly used unit.

belcher A slang term for a performer with a frog-like voice.

believability □ In script writing, plot segments that fit together naturally without the use of fate or coincidence to bring the script to a credible conclusion. □ The degree of acceptance as truth of advertising's contents, especially its claims, evidenced by persons exposed to it.

bell code A computer code used in a teletypewriter system for signaling precedence.

bell curve *See* normal distribution.

bellows Flexible extension tubes used for extreme close-ups.

bells A sound made on a set before recording.

Bell System The seven regional telephone companies that were formerly a part of the American Telephone and Telegraph Company.

belly board A small platform used to mount a camera for low-level shots.

below-the-line The costs of a production that are not included in above-the-line items, such as set construction, props, transportation, and film stock. Cf. above-the-line.

below-the-line listing A report of how a radio station's estimates are printed in a Radio Market Report. A station is given below-the-line listing for various reasons, such as certain special station activities.

belt To sing or speak with gusto.

belt press A printing press that has two long, continuous belts for printing each side of the paper in one pass through the press.

bench-bar-press guidelines Informal precepts voluntarily adopted by judges, lawyers, and the press covering the kinds and amount of information concerning pretrial publicity that may be published.

benchmark □ A point of reference from which comparisons between or among different pieces of equipment may be made. Cf. A-B test. □ In advertising or marketing, a type of comparison between products to determine competitors' costs, quality, and so on, versus one's own. □ Testing to compare execution speeds of various programs.

benchwork □ The work done in animation filming or film editing.

Benday A process, named after a New York printer Ben Day, that allows a variety of shading textures by using a pattern of lines or dots to produce a gray effect. Also called *shading tints*.

bend the needle A sudden excessive volume of sound as indicated by pegging the needle on a VU meter.

BER Bit error rate.

Berlin Convention The first effective international wireless agreement among nations.

Berlin wall Any barrier that prevents the free flow of information.

Berne Convention The major international copyright treaty, ratified in 1887, governing copyright use on a reciprocal basis between signatories. The treaty has been revised several times. *See also* the Berne Convention Implementation Act of 1988.

Berne Convention Implementation Act of 1988 An Act of Congress, effective in 1989, that changed the existing Copyright Act so the United States could become a signatory to the Berne Convention.

BEST Black Efforts for Soul in Television. A citizens' group.

best boy An electrician's assistant. *See also* gaffer.

best edition For the purposes of copyright, the edition of a work published in the United States at any time before the date of deposit that the Library of Congress determines to be most suitable for its purposes.

bestseller □ A book that has remained in demand; usually through several printings or over a long period of time. □ A book on one of the several compiled lists of most-purchased recent titles.

best time(s) available (BTA) The time(s) for the airing of radio or television commercial announcements as left to the discretion of the station. Same as *ROS.*

Beta An abbreviation for *Betacam* and *Betamax.*

Betacam A component analog video (CAV) format that uses metal oxide tape. Contains time code and control tracks as well as two audio channels. Cf. Betacam SP, M-II, S-VHS, and U-matic SP.

Betacam SP A videotape recording format that can use either metal-particle or metal oxide tape. Contains time code and control tracks as well as four audio channels. Cf. Betacam, S-VHS, U-matic, and M-II.

Betacart A videocassette that is designed for use in a Sony Betacam system.

Betamax A trademark name for a Sony half-inch videocassette format.

between the lens mount A shutter mounted between the front and rear lens elements.

bevel □ The slope on the edges of engravings, stereotypes, and so on, by which the plate is fastened to the base. □ To slope the edges of book boards before binding.

beyond the horizon That geographical region that is not available for line-of-sight transmission or reception.

bezel A frame or cover used to hold the edges of television picture tubes, lenses, meters, and so on.

BF □ Boldface. □ Beat frequency.

BFA Broadcasting Foundation of America.

BFC/NCC Broadcasting and Film Commission/National Council of the Churches of Christ in the U.S.A.

BFI Broadcasters' Foundation, Inc.

BFO Beat frequency oscillator.

B format A helical scan videotape recorder format.

BG Background.

BGM Background music.

B/H Binary to hexadecimal.

B-H curve A graph showing the characteristic curve of magnetic material such as magnetic tape.

B head A second-level subhead. Cf. A head and C head.

bias □ In audio recording, an ultrasonic signal applied to the record head, together with the signal to be recorded, to reduce distortion. □ An electrical force applied to an electrical device as a reference level. □ The difference between the results obtained from a survey sample and the universe sampled, other than sampling error. *See also* nonsampling error. □ A shift in color in a film due to improper processing.

biased News that is slanted by the media.

biased tape guidance The guiding of tape through a transport in such a way that at least one edge is always in contact with the reference edge of the tape as a consequence of a positive interference between the guide and the reference edge of the tape.

bias light The internal illumination that is always present in a video camera tube.

bias of nonresponse A type of nonsampling error caused by respondents differing from nonrespondents with respect to a characteristic that is being measured by a survey. *See also* nonresponse.

BIB □ Broadcast Information Bureau. □ Board for International Broadcasting.

bible □ A book delineating a radio or television network's or station's policies. □ An obsolete term for a book. □ A format containing certain characteristics and requirements. It is much more detailed than a traditional format and includes the context; framework; and central premises, themes, and progression of the multipart series or serial. It sets forth a detailed overall story development for the multipart series or serial and includes detailed story lines for all of the projected episodes of the multipart series or most of the projected episodes for the first broadcast season of the serial. The characters must be not only distinct and identifiable but must be set forth with detailed descriptions and characterizations. *See also* format.

bible paper A strong, thin, opaque paper. Also called *India paper.*

biblio A combining form from the Greek *biblion,* meaning "book."

bibliographic information interchange A service that produces bibliographic cards and records to libraries.

bibliography □ A list of works relating to a particular author, period, or subject. Also called a *reference list.* □ A list of an author's works. □ The history and description of books.

bicubic patches *See* parametric surface patches.

bicycle network A network of broadcast stations set up for bicycling.

bicycling The routing of a film, television tape, or audiotape from one broadcast station to another.

bid A response to a request from a motion picture distributor to an exhibitor or exhibition company offering a motion picture for exhibition in a particular market.

BIDEC Binary to Decimal Converter.

bidirectional □ A form of line printing wherein the printer head moves in both directions alternately. Cf. unidirectional printing. □ The use of transceivers at both ends of a communication path to receive data flow. □ Having maximum response in two directions. *See also* mike pattern.

bidirectional microphone A microphone with two lobes of maximum sound response. Its polar pattern would appear as a figure eight.

BIEM Bureau International de l'Edition Mecanique (International Bureau of Mechanical Recordings).

bifilar In videotape duplication, a method of winding two tapes onto a single reel with the oxide surfaces face to face, in preparation for further operations. *See also* contact print.

big annie A slang term for a radio or television program analyzer.

big closeup (BCU) A British term meaning extreme close-up. Similar to an ECU.

big eye □ A slang term for a fisheye lens. □ A large, 10,000-watt luminaire.

big name A slang term for a well-known entertainer.

big room A slang term for the editorial room in a newspaper.

big screen TV *See* projection television.

big seven A slang term for the seven major Hollywood motion picture studios.

big ticket Expensive merchandise with a high markup.

big time A slang term for the major studios, networks, major advertising agencies, and so on. Cf. small time.

BIH Bureau International de l'Heure. The international bureau of time. *See* Coordinated Universal Time.

bilateral Having two symmetrical sides; as in an optical, variable-area film soundtrack. Cf. duplex.

bilingual An individual who is proficient in two different languages.

bill □ A legislative proposal. □ *See* poster.

billboard □ The credits at the opening and/or closing of a radio or television program listing the talent, production personnel, and so on. □ A short sponsorship message at the opening and closing of a television program. Cf. cowcatcher and hitchhiker. □ The headlines used at the start of a television newscast. □ A newspaper headline that is surrounded by an excessive amount of white space. □ A flat, upright structure for the display of outdoor advertising. An outdoor advertising panel of 24- or 30-sheet poster size. Cf. painted bulletin and poster panel. □ A verbal identification placed at the start of a tape or track. Also called an *audio billboard* and *slate.*

bill enclosure A promotional piece or notice enclosed with a bill, an invoice, or a statement that is not directed toward the collection of all or part of the bill, invoice, or statement.

billing □ Radio or television program credits arranged in order of importance. □ Name credit to be used in publicity. □

The charge made by an agency or station to a sponsor or advertiser. ☐ A charge made to an advertiser by an advertising agency. It is based on the listed or gross charges of the media from which space or time has been purchased, along with any other charges and fees incurred by the agency that are passed on to the advertiser. ☐ Loosely, the money spent by an advertiser through an advertising agency. ☐ The actual charge made by a mass medium to an advertising agency; the gross charge less the agency discount.

billing log A broadcast station program log that contains a listing of all commercials run during a broadcast day.

Bill of Rights The first 10 Amendments to the Constitution of the United States that set forth the fundamental rights and privileges of the people: among them are freedom of speech, press, and religion; and the right to a speedy and public trial by an impartial jury.

billposter The plant operator employee who places the advertising paper on the outdoor advertising structure. Also called a *paper hanger.*

billroom The place where advertising paper is stored and prepared for the outdoor advertising billposter's use.

bimetallic plates Plates used on very long printing runs in place of the shorter-lived etched plates.

bimodality The ability of a television program to attract two disparate demographic groups.

bimodular A newspaper headline style containing two distinct parts. Sometimes abbreviated *bimo.*

bimonthly A publication issued every two months. Cf. semimonthly.

bin ☐ Large soft-sided receptacle for holding sorted but as yet unspliced film. Also called an *editing bin, editing barrel,* and *film bin.* ☐ An abbreviation for *binary.*

BINA Broadcast Institute of North America. An independent, nonprofit research organization.

binary A base numbering system using two digits: 0 and 1. Also called *binary number.*

binary code A code in which characters are represented by groups of binary digits.

binary digit *See* bit.

binary exposure system The combining of spot brightness of the subject with an overall meter reading to give an average reflected exposure index.

binary number *See* binary.

binaural Having two sources or receptors, as in binaural sound. Cf. stereophonic.

binaural disc A record with two separately recorded signals.

binaural microphone Two microphones that are separated the same distance as are human ears in order to reproduce binaural sound.

binaural recorder A two-track tape recorder employing two separate channels.

binaural sound Sound that is recorded and reproduced so that the spatial effect is that of the original sound.

binder ☐ In audio- and videotape, the material used to bond the magnetic particles to each other and to the base film. ☐ A resinous material that causes the various materials of a disc compound to adhere. ☐ A small headline on an inside page of a newspaper tying together two or more columns. Cf. banner. ☐ *See* binder line. ☐ A person who binds books. ☐ A cover or other device for holding pages together.

binder line A line or headline that ties two or more columns together. Also called a *binder.*

binder resin A resin used in the manufacture of a binder.

binder's board A stiff, high-quality composition board used in making book covers.

binder's brass A block made from brass and used for stamping cloth bindings for books.

binder's cloth The material, often cotton, used for book covers. Also called *book cloth* and *binding cloth.*

binder's dies The metal, often brass, used to stamp book covers. Also called a *book stamp.*

bindery A place where books are bound; a company that specializes in bookbinding.

bind-in card A return postcard bound into a periodical, usually for obtaining subscriptions, but often to respond to a product advertisement printed at the point of insertion. Also called an *insert card.*

binding □ The process of assembling, folding, cutting, and joining the parts of a book, magazine, or other printed material. □ The materials used to hold the pages of a book together.

binding cloth *See* binder's cloth.

binding edge The edge of the paper that is bound in a book.

bingo card A reply card inserted in a magazine and used to request information from manufacturers or suppliers. A slang term for a reader's service card.

bin stick The wood or metal strip containing pegs or clips on which to hang film during the editing process.

bio An abbreviation for *biography* or *biographical information.*

biog A biographical film, drama, or book. *See also* biopic.

Biograph An abbreviation for *American Mutoscope and Biograph,* an early American film company.

bionics The science concerned with living organisms and the application of the knowledge gained to engineering problems.

biopic A biographical film. Also called a *biog.*

Bioskop A two-projector system developed in Germany by Max Skladonowski in 1895.

biotechnology *See* ergonomics.

BIP *Books in Print.* A yearly publication (with a midyear supplement) containing an entry for each book published in the United States that is currently in print.

bipack □ The use of two films in a camera or printer in order to expose both at the same time. □ A contact printing technique wherein an already processed film is printed onto a fresh roll of film. □ The combining of an already processed film with animation artwork to produce a composite without the use of an optical printer.

bipack magazine A film magazine containing two feed and two takeup compartments.

BIPAD Bureau of Independent Publishers and Distributors.

biphase mark *See* address code.

biphonic A two-channel stereophonic recording or transmission. *See also* stereophonic sound. Cf. triphonic and quadraphonic.

bipolar A rating scale that lists two diametrically opposed choices with an odd number of steps between them, for example, hot and cold, like and dislike, and so on. *See also* semantic differential.

bipost base A lamp base with two posts capable of carrying heavy current.

bird A slang term for a communication satellite.

birdie The chirping sound produced by some electronic equipment.

birding A British term meaning "communication by satellite." Named after Early Bird.

birdseye A reflector type spotlight or floodlight.

bird's eye view A camera shot as seen from directly overhead. *See also* aerial shot.

bird's nest *See* buckle.

birefringence The refraction of light in two slightly different directions.

BIRPI International Bureau for the Protection of Intellectual Property (Berne Copyright Convention).

biscuit A small slab of plastic material used for pressing discs.

BIT *See* ILO.

bit □ An abbreviation for *binary digit.* A unit of information; yes or no, 0 or 1, and so on. □ The smallest unit of information in a computer. □ A brief appearance by a performer. Also called a *bit part.* □ A short piece of acting business. □ A small acting role.

bitch box An intercommunication system, especially applied to systems that connect the television control room to the studio.

bite □ The etching of metal printing plates by an acid. Also called *bite in.* □ *See* bite off. □ A portion of an actuality, interview, and so on, used in a radio or television news story or feature. Also called a *cut* and *sound bite.* □ An alternative spelling of *byte.*

bite cue *See* quick cue.

bite in *See* bite.

bite it off A radio or television director's command to stop immediately. Also called *cut* and *bust it.*

bite off □ To eliminate a line, cue, or musical number during the airing or taping of a radio or television program. □ To remove a portion of a story so that it fits in the available space. Also called a *bite.*

bit error *See* bit inversion.

bit error rate (BER) A measure of the capacity of a data medium to store or transmit bits without errors. Expressed as the average number of bits the medium can handle with only one bit of error. CD-ROM and CD-I, which employ three layers of error detection and error correction, have a bit error rate of 10 to the minus 18th power.

bit image printing Printing accomplished by a dot matrix printer.

bit inversion A random error causing erroneous readout of a bit; a 1 becoming a 0, or vice versa. Also called *bit inversion.*

bit-mapped display A screen display in which each pixel location corresponds to a unique memory location whose contents determine the intensity and color values of the pixel.

bit mapping A technique for creating a graphics display by describing it in terms of pixels. *See also* raster graphics.

bit part *See* bit.

bit player A film actor who specializes in bit parts. Also called a *day player.*

bit rate The number of binary digits transmitted per unit of time over a communications channel.

bits per inch A measure of magnetic tape density; often 800 or 1600 bits per inch.

bits per sample The number of bits used to express the numerical value of a digitized sample.

bits per second (BPS) The number of bits that are transmitted in one second.

biweekly A publication issued every two weeks. Cf. semiweekly.

biz □ A script abbreviation for *business.* □ A general term for show business; show biz.

bkg An abbreviation for *background.* Also called *bg.*

BKR An abbreviation for *circuit breaker.*

BL Body line.

black □ The darkest of the 10 steps of the gray scale. □ When preceded by *take, fade to,* or a similar direction, a television director's command to cut or fade the picture out. □ To silence or to jam a radio broadcast. □ A carbon-based pigment or dye. □ The absence of light.

black and white □ A designation for one-color prints or drawings. □ A reference to monochrome television or film.

Black Audio Network (BAN) A news service for black-oriented radio stations.

black balance A television camera control used to vary the black level.

blackbody A theoretical incandescent source whose spectral power distribution and color depend only on temperature.

black box □ A slang term for any of a wide variety of electrical devices; usually devices that are not understood by the user. □ An audience research program and commercial analyzer. *See* big annie, Stanton-Lazarsfeld analyzer, and program analyzer.

black clipper A circuit that eliminates black peak below a specified level of picture signal.

black comedy Comedy that derives its humor from bizarre or gruesome events or subjects.

black compression The reduction of contrast in the low-light levels of a television picture. Also called *black saturation* and *crush.*

black crush The ability of television cameras to mask seams and overlaps on black surfaces.

black disc A record that is pressed on black vinyl.

blackening The darkening of a lamp enclosure that occurs with age.

blacker than black The composite video signal amplitude region below the reference black level in the direction of the synchronizing pulses. (A voltage even more negative than the black level.)

blackface *See* boldface.

black film *See* film noir.

black leader Totally opaque film leader.

black letter A style of heavy, bold, and angular type. Also called *text, grotesque, Gothic,* and *Old English.*

black level The minimum signal level necessary to transmit the television picture blacks.

black light A misnomer for ultraviolet radiation.

blacklisting A listing of persons who are to be avoided or boycotted as the result of some real or supposed threat. *See also* Red Channels.

black on black Talent dressed in black in front of a black background.

blackout □ An interruption in radio communication caused by solar flares. □ A ban on local live (usually sports) broadcasts, often because of contractual agreements or regulations. □ A rapid dimming of all the lights on a set. □ Any interruption, as in a court-ordered news blackout. □ To switch off all illumination in a theatre except for exit lights. □ To delete a portion of a print or drawing.

black out A government order that prohibits the use of illumination on outdoor advertising structures. *See also* brown out.

blackout switch A master on/off switch used for controlling the overall production lighting for either stages or studios.

black radio Radio programming designed to solidify the black community through music and talk.

Black Rock A somewhat derogatory reference to the CBS headquarters building. *See also* Hard Rock and Thirty Rock.

black screen A television screen without a picture. Also called *black time* and *gray screen.*

black sheet A carbon copy of a story.

blacksmith A less than satisfactory worker, such as a print shop employee or writer.

black space *See* dead spot.

blacksploitation film A motion picture that improperly exploits blacks for profit-making motives. Also spelled *blaxploitation.*

black time *See* black screen.

black velour Nonreflective black velvet draperies.

black week One of the weeks wherein national audience measurements are not taken. Also called *dark week.*

blade A thin flag.

Blakeslee Award An award given by the American Heart Association for reporting on heart and circulatory diseases.

blank (B) □ Paper without printing or other marks. □ A printed card or paper with spaces left for the insertion of information. □ A typographical space. □ A dash denoting an omission. □ A piece of cardboard with a liner. □ Any medium upon which nothing is recorded. □ A binary digit representing a space. □ Clear processed film. □ A clear animation cel. □ An unused magnetic tape or other storage medium. □ A cartridge loaded with powder but no bullet. □ A sampling unit in a frame that does not represent an elementary unit that is properly part of the statistical population, such as nontelevision households and commercial listings in a telephone directory.

blank binding A binding without any letters or other marks.

blank book A book consisting of blank pages.

blank disc *See* recording disc.

blanket □ A piece of flexible material (rubber, felt, cloth, and so on) next to a platen, impression cylinder, or other part to cushion the surface. □ To cover a wide area with an electronic signal. □ To interrupt radio communication by interference. □ *See* blanket sheet.

blanket area □ The area adjacent to a radio or television transmitter in which the reception of other stations is subject to interference due to the strong signal from the station. □ A radio reception area receiving a strong signal.

blanket contour The boundaries of the blanket area.

blanket contract A contract or arrangement between a medium and an advertiser covering a number of separate advertising campaigns.

blanket coverage The ability of radio and television stations to reach all locations within a given geographical area.

blanket cylinder The impression cylinder of a press.

blanket head A headline that extends across all the columns of a story or of a department.

blanketing The interference caused by the presence of an AM broadcast signal of one volt per meter (V/m) or greater intensity in the area adjacent to the antenna of the transmitting station.

blanket license A right granted by a music licensing organization to a radio station to use any musical selections in their library for a percentage of the station's profits or for a set fee. Cf. direct license.

blanket order An agreement whereby libraries automatically receive copies of all new books in specified fields or areas by a certain publisher. Cf. approval plan.

blanket sheet □ A newspaper printed on one sheet. □ A newspaper printed on large sheets.

blank groove(s) The groove (or grooves) of a disc upon which no sound is recorded.

blanking □ Book cover impressions stamped without color, foil, or ink. Also called *blind, blind blocking, blind emboss, blind embossing, blind stamp, blind stamping,* and *blind tooling.* □ A white paper border surrounding an outdoor advertising poster copy area. It is applied, using industry standards, between the poster and the panel molding. □ The composite video signal used to make the horizontal and vertical retrace lines of a television picture invisible. *See also* field, frame, scanning, and scanning beam.

blanking interval The brief period of time necessary for blanking. Also called the *field blanking interval.*

blanking level The level of the television signal during the blanking interval, except the interval during the scanning synchronizing pulse and the chrominance subcarrier synchronizing burst.

blanking out The separation of forms for the insertion of spacing material where lines have been lifted to print in different colors. Also called *breaking for color.*

blanking paper The unprinted paper that frames a poster in outdoor advertising.

blanking pulse A positive or negative square wave used to turn off the scanning beam of a television picture during blanking.

blanking shutter A shutter used in film processing to keep the light from striking the film.

blank line A type slug line containing only spaces or blanks.

blank out Blank paper used on an outdoor advertising structure to cover over the advertising message. *See also* paint out.

blank tape *See* raw tape.

blast A momentary distortion caused by the overloading of recording or transmitting levels.

blast-in To introduce sound at an excessive level. Often caused by failure to set audio levels before the use of discs, tapes, and so on.

blasting □ Overloading a microphone by speaking too loudly. □ Overloading a loudspeaker or amplifier causing distortion.

blaxploitation film *See* blacksploitation film.

bleached whites *See* burnout.

bleaching The step in color film processing used to convert silver compounds for removal in the fixing process.

bleed □ A printed illustration or advertisement that covers one or more margins of a page. Also called a *bleed page.* □ To trim the edge of a photograph or page so much that letters or other information is lost. □ The excess area around a camera shot that compensates for the difference between the image received by the studio monitors and the home receiver. *See also* border, essential area, and scanning area.

bleed-face bulletin An outdoor advertising bulletin constructed so that the copy can cover the entire surface; similar to a bleed page in a magazine. For the poster medium, the use of blanking papers of the same color as the poster background to bring the design area up to the molding. The poster may be designed to fill the entire space inside the molding.

bleed-face poster *See* bleed-face bulletin.

bleeding The loss of distinction between different areas of a picture on film; often caused in the development process.

bleeding whites An overload condition wherein the white areas of a television picture appear to flow into the darker areas.

bleed in the gutter To run an advertisement uninterrupted across the gutter of a spread in a periodical.

bleed margin The small, extra margin in the printing medium necessary to ensure that a bleed covers the margin to the edge of the paper.

bleed page *See* bleed.

bleed poster A poster used on a billboard without a white border.

bleed through □ A production difficulty created when the previous design used on an outdoor advertising structure can be seen through the current message. This can occur because of the kind of paper used or due to chemical reactions of certain pigments. □ The transparency of a superimposed television picture.

bleep □ A sound imposed on an audio- or videotape as a cue. □ To erase a portion of a soundtrack. □ To censor a word or phrase on a soundtrack or tape. Also called a *blip, bloop,* and *beep.*

bleep tone *See* bleep.

blend The merging of one tone or color into another in an illustration.

blending lighting General illumination used to provide smooth transitions between the specific lighting areas on a stage.

blimp A soundproof housing used to eliminate motor noise in a motion picture camera. Cf. barney.

blind An impression stamped without using ink so as to create a raised or sunken design, as on heavy paper or cardboard. *See* blanking.

blind ad A classified advertisement that does not identify the advertiser.

blind bidding A prerelease bid made by an exhibitor or exhibition company without having seen the motion picture.

blind blocking *See* blanking.

blind booking The rental and scheduling of motion pictures for theatrical showing without previewing the film.

blind emboss *See* blanking.

blind embossing *See* blanking.

blind folio A book page that is counted but not numbered. *See also* folio.

blind interview An interview in which the interviewed person is not named, usually by using a phrase such as "a highly placed source."

blind keyboard A keyboard device that does not produce a display or copy of the input information.

blind lead News copy that does not immediately identify the person or object.

blind offer An offer placed inconspicuously in an advertisement; often used to measure reader attention to the advertisement. Also called a *buried offer* and *hidden offer.*

blind perforator A keyboard machine that perforates tape for typesetting.

blind query A query lacking in detail or global in scope.

blind shot A camera shot in which the sound source is not seen.

blind stamp *See* blanking.

blind stamping *See* blanking.

blind tooling *See* blanking.

blinker A signal light designed to attract the attention of television studio personnel.

blip □ A random disturbance on a cathode ray display tube. □ *See* bleep.

blister A result of paint that has separated from the surface of an outdoor advertising surface by the formation of air pockets.

blizzard head A bleached blonde performer.

block □ A splicing block. □ To set camera and talent positions and movements. *See also* blocking. □ An engraved block from which impressions are made. □ A block of wood or metal used to mount a cut to make it type high. □ A British term meaning "cut." □ A bookbinder's stamp. □ A rectangular compartment containing computer text or graphics. □ A period of time in the daily schedule of a radio or television station. *See also* strip programming. □ *See* base. □ In data processing, a group of characters, records, or words treated as a unit.

block address Thirty-two-bit integers that are converted to absolute disc addresses to access information on a compact disc.

block book A book printed from blocks.

block booking The former practice of film companies that required the rental of films in groups rather than by individual title. Now illegal. Cf. must-buy.

blockbuster □ A major motion picture. □ A motion picture, special program, and so on, that will receive wide audience attention when shown on television. Often programmed during sweeps. Cf. bomb. □ A longer than normal news story. □ A longer than normal radio or television commercial.

block converter An electronic device that changes a band of frequencies to another, higher or lower band of frequencies. Used extensively in cable television systems and satellite communication.

block device Computer mass storage equipment that reads or writes data in large sections.

block diagram A drawing that shows the essential units of a system and their interrelationships.

blocked *See* blocked station.

blocked ads Advertisements in the form of a square or rectangle.

blocked-out time Broadcast station or network time voluntarily unsold and used for sustaining programs.

blocked panel An outdoor advertising structure that has been obstructed.

blocked script A production script that includes all directions.

blocked station A radio or television station that airs syndicated and religious programs.

block flush To glue or fasten the edge of a cut.

block format A broadcast news format in which stories with similar content are placed together.

blocking □ The tendency of the adjacent layers of a roll of audio- or videotape to stick together. □ The working out and setting of the physical movements of performers by a director. Also called *breakdown.* □ The consecutive scheduling of similar program types. *See also* block programming. □ *See* stamping. □ *See* adhesion.

blocking diagram A drawing that indicates the positions of performers and cameras for a production.

blocking press. A British term meaning "stamping press."

block letter A letter or type without serifs.

blocklines *See* caption.

block out To eliminate areas from a photographic negative or print by masking or opaquing.

block preview The moving and previewing of a sequence of edits in an edit decision list.

block printing The process of printing from blocks.

block programming The consecutive scheduling of programs with similar audience appeal to create audience flow. Also called *stacking* and *blocking.*

block quotation A quotation, usually four or more lines in length, set off and indented from the rest of the text.

block time sales The sale of time by a radio or television station over which the licensee does not retain control, possibly constituting an illegal transfer of control.

block zero In CD-ROM and CD-I, the first block on a disc, with a main channel or absolute disc address of 00 minutes, 02 seconds, 00 sector number.

bloom Glare caused by the reflection of light into a camera lens. Often results in halation.

blooming The distortion of a television picture caused by a high brightness control setting.

bloop □ To erase sound from a magnetic track. □ An opaque patch used to cover the soundtrack of a film splice in order to prevent noise. □ *See* bleep. □ A noise caused by a splice in an optical soundtrack. □ *See* sync pop. □ A noise caused on a magnetic soundtrack by contact with magnetized devices.

blooper □ Any embarrassing error. *See also* goof. □ A device used to make a hole on a film soundtrack to prevent splice noise. *See also* bloop.

blooping □ The treating of a film soundtrack so that a splice is not audible. □ The recording of sync marks on a film soundtrack for synchronization purposes.

blooping ink A quick-drying, opaque black ink used for blooping.

blooping machine A device used to punch out a hole in a negative soundtrack or apply a patch to a positive soundtrack.

blooping tape Black, opaque tape used to patch a positive soundtrack.

blossom *See* bloom.

blotter □ The record of arrests kept by a police station. □ An old term for a handwritten record of newspaper sales. □ An absorbent paper used to dry photographic prints.

blow To stumble on or miss a line. *See also* goof.

blow-in cards A return postcard inserted in magazines but not attached.

Also called an *insert card.* Cf. bind-in card.

blow off *See* air squeegee.

blow up To exaggerate a news story.

blowup □ The blowing of a line by a performer. □ In photography, the optical enlargement of all or a portion of a negative. □ The enlargement of an object such as a book cover for display purposes. □ To increase the size of a film, such as from 16 mm to 35 mm; seldom used as the quality of the film decreases dramatically.

blue □ A filter used to change the color temperature of lamps. □ A filter used for viewing film. □ *See* blue coating. □ Off-color gags, material, motion pictures, and so on. □ A disc jockey who specializes in off-color material. *See also* shock jock. □ *See* blueprint.

blue background A background used to photograph objects for later use as traveling mattes. Also called *blue backing.*

blue backing *See* blue background.

Blue Book A programming statement issued in 1946 by the FCC entitled "Public Service Responsibility of Broadcast Licensees." Called the *Blue Book* because of the color of its cover.

blue coating An antireflective lens coating. Also called *blue.*

blue dupe A quickly made film print.

blue gun The electron gun whose beam strikes the phosphor dots emitting the blue primary color.

blue law A statute or ordinance that restricts business operations, usually on Sundays.

blue light Light produced by mercury vapor lamps. *See also* cold light.

blueline *See* blueprint.

blue matting *See* chromakey.

blue movie *See* blue.

Blue Network One of two networks formerly owned by NBC. The Blue Network became the American Broadcasting Company in 1943. Cf. Red Network.

blue pencil The deletion of blue material in a script by a censor or continuity acceptance department.

blueprint □ A printer's proof, blue in color, made from an offset flat or negative. Also called a *blue* and *blueline.* Cf. vandyke. □ *See* duping print.

blue screen A process in which action is photographed in front of a uniformly lit blue background. In processing, the blue background is replaced by mattes to allow different images to be inserted behind the action.

blue screen process *See* blue screen.

blue sky Proposals or promises that offer more than they can reasonably deliver, as in competing applications at license renewal time.

blur □ The indistinct picture caused by rapid camera movement or vibration. □ *See* whip pan.

blurb □ A short, promotional description of a book, story, article, or other piece. □ A derogatory term for a publicity release. □ The promotional material printed on book jackets.

blurmeter An optical device for obscuring type, trademarks, and other features of an advertisement or package associated with a brand in order to test the impact of the basic design.

blur pan *See* whip pan.

blush A dry or moist cheek rouge used in make-up.

bluster *See* ham it.

BM Beautiful music.

B matter *See* B copy.

BMB Broadcast Measurement Bureau.

BMI □ Book Manufacturers' Institute. A trade association of book manufacturers and suppliers. □ Broadcast Music, Incorporated. A music licensing organization in competition with ASCAP and SESAC.

B minus The negative terminal of a battery or the negative side of an electronic circuit supply voltage. Also called *B negative.* Cf. B plus.

B mode The checkerboard method of editing videotape, wherein all edits from one or more reels are made, leaving blank tape for later edits from other reels. Cf. A mode.

B movie *See* B picture.

BN Binary number.

BNC □ A blimped, noiseless reflex camera made by Mitchell. □ Bayonet naval connector. A commonly used electronic connector.

B negative *See* B minus.

BNF Brand Names Foundation.

BNL Broadcast News, Ltd.

BNS Broadcast News Service.

BO Back order.

board □ A shortened form for a switchboard, control board, dimmer board, audio control console, and so on. □ A general term applied to a lighting control console. □ *See* printed circuit board. □ A thick paper stock, such as cardboard, bristol board, mat board, and so on, used for illustrations, mounting copy, drawing, and other artistic uses. Also called *artboard.* □ The stiff material used for the sides of book covers.

board fade The attenuation of sound using the audio control console's potentiometers or sliders. Also called a *production fade.*

boards □ A colloquial term for outdoor advertising panels and bulletins originating during the period when theatrical and circus posters were displayed on board fences. □ A slang term for a theatre stage.

board shift A period of time during which a person is scheduled to operate a radio station audio console on the air.

bobbin An infrequently used term for a small reel, such as might be employed in an audio cartridge or audiocassette. *See also* reel.

BOC Bell Operating Company.

Bodoni □ A book published by the Italian printer Giambattista Bodoni. □ A style of type derived from Bodoni's type design.

Bodoni book The modern form of Bodoni type.

body □ That portion of a speech or program containing the central theme or idea. *See also* development. Cf. introduction and conclusion. □ The main part of a camera, less the lens and viewfinder. □ The main part of a news story. □ The solid metal block supporting a type face. □ The main text of a book. Also called *body matter.* Cf. front matter and back matter. □ Small or text type size as contrasted to larger headline or smaller footnote type. *See also* body type.

body brace *See* body pod.

body copy □ The news material that follows the lead. *See also* text. □ The text portion of a printed advertisement.

body fade A fade accomplished through the physical movement of the talent. Also called a *live fade* and *mike fade.* Cf. board fade.

body frame *See* body pod.

body height *See* body line.

body language The nonverbal cues and reactions used by a performer in acting.

body line (BL) The height of a line of type. Also called *body height. See also* x-height.

body matter *See* body.

body pod A frame, usually of metal, strapped to a camera operator to support and steady the camera. Also called a *body brace* and *body frame. See also* steadicam. Cf. monopod, shoulder pod, and tripod.

body size *See* body type.

body stabilized A satellite whose antenna is pointed toward the earth and whose solar panels are pointed toward the sun.

body type The size of type, usually 8 or 9 point, used by a majority of newspapers. *See also* type size. Cf. display type.

B of A Bureau of Advertising.

bogus □ Type that is set again because of union requirements. □ Miscellaneous matter printed in a newspaper as a filler and replaced by news in a later edition. □ Inferior quality boards.

boil To substantially reduce the length of a news story; to condense. Also called *boil down.*

boil down *See* boil.

boilerplate □ Identical sections of text or graphics that are inserted into different documents. □ Novels, television programs, stories, and so on, that are turned out in quantity by using stock formulas and writing techniques. □ Syndicated material usually furnished to small newspapers on stereotype plates. □ The plates themselves.

bold An abbreviation for *boldface.*

boldface (BF) A typeface that is heavier and darker than normal. Also called *blackface* and *overstrike.* Cf. lightface.

bold graf A paragraph set in boldface.

boldline A printed line set in boldface.

bolt A book signature with untrimmed edges.

BOM Business office must.

bomb □ A motion picture box office disaster. Also applied to television programs. Cf. blockbuster. □ To play a role badly.

bona fide Made in good faith; genuine; without fraud or deceit.

bond □ A binding agreement often guaranteed by a substantial sum of money to be forfeited in case of default or noncompliance with a government regulation. □ A superior quality opaque paper with a high rag content.

bonding Any method used to provide a solid electrical contact between parts or devices, such as soldering or welding.

bond paper *See* bond.

bone An abbreviation for *backbone.*

bonus circulation Newspaper or magazine circulation above that expected by an advertiser.

bonus spot A commercial given to an advertiser without cost, either to make up for undelivered audience or as an inducement to buy additional spots. Sometimes referred to as *make goods.*

bonus station A radio or television station that carries a network program without payment.

boob tube A derogatory term for a television receiver.

book □ To hire talent. □ A script, usually musical. □ Two-fold scenery flats. Also called *book flats* and *wings.* □ To decrease the angle between two-fold flats. □ Generally, printed material, bound or unbound, except for periodicals. □ Conversely, a magazine in the magazine industry. □ A group of stories from a wire service. *See also* take. □ To assemble a pamphlet or brochure. □ *See* blank book. □ A major division of a long literary work. □ The text of a play. □ Newspaper copy paper with a carbon paper insert. □ A magazinist's term for a magazine. □ A portfolio of an artist's, performer's, writer's, or other creative source's work.

bookaholic An individual who is inordinately fond of books and, usually, bookstores.

bookbinding The art or trade of binding books.

book clamp A clamp used to hold a book for binding, tooling, marbling, and so on.

book cloth *See* binder's cloth.

book club □ A business that sells books by mail, usually at stated intervals. □ A group that purchases books for circulation among its members. □ A booklovers' social group.

book collector A person who collects books, often rare books, books covering a specific field, or beautifully bound books.

book corner A protective, usually metal, cap for the corners of a book cover.

booked The acceptance of a contract for outdoor advertising space by a plant operator.

bookend A device used to support freestanding books.

booker □ An individual in charge of obtaining guests for a talk show. Often accomplished by a producer or assistant producer. □ An individual who monitors the distribution of motion picture release prints to the various markets.

book fair □ A book exhibition. □ A convention of book publishers and sellers at which negotiations often take place for publishing and copublishing rights. The major book fair is the annual Frankfurt, Germany, book fair.

book fast A two-fold flat or book.

book flat *See* book.

book house A book publishing or printing firm.

booking □ A performer's or writer's schedule of appearances. □ A performer's engagement to appear in a play, motion picture, television program, and so on. □ The rental of a motion picture for exhibition.

booking agent *See* agent.

booking list A calendar used to show the dates on which talk show guests are scheduled to appear.

booking memo *See* booking sheet.

booking sheet An agreement between an advertising agency and a performer that is sent to the appropriate union as a check on union membership. Also called a *booking memo.*

book insert An advertising flyer inserted in new books by a publisher.

book jacket *See* jacket.

book jobber *See* wholesaler.

booklet □ A small book, usually consisting of a few pages with a paper cover. Cf. book, brochure, and pamphlet. □ A small advertising brochure in book form.

bookmaker □ A printer or binder of books. □ A person skilled in book design.

Book Manufacturers' Institute (BMI) A trade association of book manufacturers and suppliers.

bookmark A thin strip of paper, plastic, or ribbon bound into a book to assist a reader in locating a particular page. Also called a *bookmarker* and a *register.*

bookmobile □ A bookstore or library on wheels that sells or loans books to rural dwellers. Formerly called a *book wagon.* □ A publisher's book display.

book notice A flyer used to promote a new or forthcoming title.

book packager *See* producer.

book paper Paper, other than newsprint, used for printing book and magazine pages. Often a lightly textured, bulky paper.

bookplate □ A label placed in a book to identify the owner; often containing the words *ex libris.* □ The engraved plate used for printing bookplates.

book post *See* book rate.

book printer A printer who prints complete books, as opposed to one who undertakes miscellaneous printing jobs. Cf. job printer.

book rate The special fourth-class postal rate at which books, manuscripts, educational materials, and so on may be sent. Also called *book post.*

book review A critical analysis of a book. *See also* critic.

book scout An individual who seeks out bookstores for rare and perhaps profitable books. Also called a *scout.*

book stamp *See* binder's dies.

bookstore chain *See* chain.

bookteller An individual who reads books aloud for taping; often for the blind.

book trade □ The book business in general. □ The trade book business.

book traveler *See* traveler.

book trimmer A device used to trim book edges.

book wagon *See* bookmobile.

Book Week An annual week designated by a trade or other group to promote reading, arouse interest in books, and so on.

bookworm □ The larvae of beetles or moths that feed on book bindings and adhesives. □ A person enamored of books.

bookwright A somewhat obsolete term for a writer of books.

boolean A system of thought that applies algebraic notation to logical operations; for example, AND, OR, and NOR are used to compare expressions.

boom □ A crane-like device with a projectable arm used to suspend a microphone. □ A heavy camera mount. □ A vertical pipe on which luminaires can be hung. Also called a *boomerang.* □ A metal extension used to support a matte box or lens.

boom down A television director's command to lower a microphone boom.

boomerang □ A box attached to a luminaire that holds various color frames; usually these can be changed by electrical or mechanical devices. □ *See* boom.

boomerang effect A propaganda message that produces the opposite of the intended effect.

boom light A luminaire mounted on a boom that is used to follow action.

boom man *See* boom operator.

boom microphone A microphone mounted on the end of a boom.

boom operator An individual who operates a boom microphone or boom light. Also called a *boom man.*

boom shot A high-angle shot taken from a boom-mounted camera. Cf. high angle shot.

boom up A command to raise a microphone boom.

boomy Sound that has excessive low-frequency resonance. Also called *bassy* and *tubby.*

boost □ To raise the voltage or current in a circuit or electrical device. □ To increase a portion of an audio frequency recording, such as the high frequencies. *See also* preemphasis. □ To amplify a signal and retransmit it.

booster □ A television station that picks up signals off the air and retransmits the signals without change except for amplification. Also called a *booster station* and *satellite station. See also* booster amplifier and translator. □ An autotransformer.

booster amplifier An amplifier used to increase the voltage or current in a circuit.

booster light A luminaire used to eliminate shadows on exterior sets.

booster station *See* booster.

boot □ The process of initiating action in an electronic system, usually by turning on the system. □ To load a computer program into RAM, usually from a disk. Also called *bootstrap, bootstrapping, cold boot,* and *cold start.* Cf. warm boot.

boot file An optional file on a CD-I disc containing a program to be executed when the disc is first mounted. It can be used to add or replace operating system modules in the base case system.

booth □ A small soundproof room. *See also* announce booth. □ The control room of a sound recording studio. □ An observation room in a radio or television studio. □ A film projection booth.

booth announcer An announcer who is physically located in a booth.

boothman *See* booth operator.

booth operator A film projectionist.

bootlegging The illegal (unlicensed) reproduction of tapes, records, or live performances. Cf. pirating.

boot record In CD-I, an optional record on a disc label that specifies where the boot file is on the disc. The contents of the boot file are loaded into memory when the disc is first mounted.

bootscreen The first image to appear onscreen in a computer application.

bootstrap *See* boot.

bootstrapping *See* boot.

borax A sodium borate used in film developers. □ Cheap, often shoddy merchandise. □ News or advertising copy that is poorly written or printed.

border □ A short drop of cloth or material used to represent overhead foliage or to mask microphones, luminaires, and so on. Also called a *shootoff.* □ The area outside a visual image that is reduced below the full screen size. □ An ornate or distinctive rule often used to outline advertising matter.

borderlight A striplight mounted above an acting area. Also called an *X ray.*

boresight The axis of transmission or reception of signals by an antenna or dish.

boresight point The point of maximum strength of a downlink satellite signal.

boric acid A white crystalline compound used in film developers.

BOT Beginning of tape.

both edit A videotape edit that includes both an audio and a video edit.

bottom flare The loss of detail at the bottom of a television picture.

bottom lighting When the source of illumination for photographing a scene comes from beneath the artwork, rather than above it; used for a variety of reasons, such as the creation of glowing letters or stars, or to photograph several layers of drawings at once for a pencil test. Also called *underlighting.*

bottom line An accounting term meaning the "net profit received by a business."

bounce □ An abrupt variation in the brightness of a television picture. Also called *bouncing.* □ The reflected wave of a radio signal.

bounce back Another order from a customer as a result of advertising sent with a previous shipment of goods.

bounce light Light that is not pointed toward the subject but is reflected off a surface such as a reflector, wall, or ceiling.

bounce lighting Directing light onto a large diffuse surface to use the soft indirect reflected light.

bouncing *See* bounce.

bouncing tracks The process of mixing and transferring two or more previously recorded audio tracks to an unused track in a multiple-track recorder.

bound galley A proof of a book bound for temporary use.

bourgeois Nine-point type size.

bourges A thin, colored acetate sheet used for overlays. Also called a *bourges sheet.*

bourges sheet *See* bourges.

boutique A specialized advertising agency that is usually limited to one aspect of advertising, such as the creative aspects of advertising design, writing copy, buying space or time, and so on.

bowdlerize To paraphrase or remove offensive words from books or other manuscripts. Named after Thomas Bowdler, an English physician.

bowl The circular or bowl-shaped part of a letter such as *b* or *d.*

box □ A slang term for a large, portable radio. Also called a *ghetto blaster.* □ A slug placed on a static insert in a television newscast visual. □ News or other matter enclosed by a border or rule or sometimes white space. Also called *boxed.* □ The compartments of a type case.

boxall A combination of several different items, such as a headline and news matter in a box.

box camera A simple still camera with a fixed lens.

boxed *See* box.

boxed head *See* box head.

boxed headline *See* box head.

box head A headline placed in a box. Also called a *boxed head* and *boxed headline.*

box lunch A packaged lunch provided to crews on location.

box office □ The admission booth of a theatre, auditorium, or other gathering, where tickets are purchased. □ *See* box office draw.

box office appeal *See* box office draw.

box office draw A person, usually an actor or director, who attracts attention to a film, program, stageplay, and so on, because of past successes. Also called *box office* and *box office appeal. See also* blockbuster.

box office hit *See* hit.

box office receipts The money paid by the public for admission to a particular motion picture. Also called *box office returns.*

box office returns *See* box office receipts.

box set A realistic television or stage set using working doors, windows, and so on.

box story A story placed in a box.

boy sales An obsolete term for independent agents who sell newspapers or magazines.

BP Broadcast Pioneers.

Bp Bipost.

BPA □ Broadcast Promotion Association. □ Book Publishers' Association. □ Business Publications Audit of Circulations, Inc.

BPAA Business and Professional Advertising Association.

BPEF Broadcast Pioneers Educational Fund, Inc. *See also* Broadcast Pioneers Library.

BPI Bits per inch.

B picture A low-budget, feature-length motion picture. Also called a *B movie.*

BPL Broadcast Pioneers Library.

B plus The positive terminal of a battery or the positive side of an electronic circuit supply voltage. Also called *B positive.* Cf. B minus.

BPME Broadcast Promotion and Marketing Executives.

B positive *See* B plus.

BPRA Book Publishers' Representatives Association.

BPS Bits per second.

br An abbreviation for *branch.*

brace □ A curved line, { or }, used to join two or more words or lines together. □ A type of newspaper page make-up emphasizing the right-hand side. □ A stage brace; a strut used to hold up flats or other scenery.

brace cleat A metal plate attached to a flat into which a brace is hooked.

bracket □ To make multiple exposures of film at different apertures in order to select the best exposure. Also called *bracketing.* □ To move from side to side to discover the point at which the light is most intense at a particular place on a set. □ A symbol, [or], used to enclose printed matter. Cf. parenthesis.

bracketed serif A serif that curves as it joins the main portion of a letter.

bracketing *See* bracket.

braille A system of printing or transcribing for the blind developed by Louis Braille, a French teacher of the blind.

brain A slang term for a computer that controls automated functions or devices.

brainwashing A process of thought control that attempts to produce changes in a person's value system and underlying beliefs.

branch □ The part of a cable television system between the trunk and the drop. □ A portion of an electrical or distribution system. *See also* leg. □ A departure from the normal routine in a computer program to another instruction or program. Also called a *jump.* □ A regional office of a motion picture distribution company. It licenses motion pictures, collects film rentals, and so on.

branching The ability to move into deeper levels of information in a computer system.

brand A tradename for a commercial product.

brand image A consumer's favorable, unfavorable, or neutral attitude toward a commercial product.

brand loyalty The consistent purchase and use of a specific product by a consumer over a period of time.

brand manager An individual in charge of the advertising and marketing for a specific commercial product.

brand name A word, usually trademarked, that identifies a commercial product.

brand name advertising An advertising technique that tries to persuade readers that the brand being advertised is the only legitimate or reasonable product.

Brand Names Foundation, Inc. (BNF) An organization that promotes the use of well-known products.

brand rates A broadcast station discount given to an advertiser who buys time for more than one product. Cf. contiguous rate.

brand rating A rating of the consumers' degree of product name recognition.

Brand Rating Index (BRI) A rating service that provides the marketing and media exposure patterns of adults for network television, magazines, radio, and newspapers in the fall of each year.

brand recognition A measure of the familiarity that consumers have with specific product brands.

brand share The percentage of sales that one brand has compared to all sales for the same type of product.

brand switching The consumers' lack of brand loyalty.

Brand X Any mythical product used as a comparison to an existing product.

brass check A slang term for a business office must.

brass widths The width of type characters.

Braun tube An obsolete name for a cathode ray tube. Named after its inventor, Ferdinand Braun.

brayer A small hand roller used to apply ink.

BRC □ Broadcast Rating Council. *See* EMRC. □ Business reply card.

BRE Business reply envelope.

breach of peace A violation of a law or ordinance such as disorderly conduct or inciting to riot.

breadboard A board used for mounting electrical components to construct and test a prototype.

break □ A stage of release of a motion picture, for example, first run and second run. □ Any interruption in radio or television transmission or reception. □ A recess in a rehearsal. □ A new development in a news story. □ To fold or unfold scenery. □ A pause for station identification. □ A director's command to move a camera. □ *See* commercial break. □ The place at which a story is stopped on one page to be continued on another page. Also called a *breakover, carryover,* and *runover. See also* jump. □ The time at which news is available for publication. □ *See* breaking for color. □ A disruption in printing when newsprint tears in the press.

breakaway A prop or scenery made to shatter or fall apart easily.

break back To fill in a newspaper page with matter after a jump has been completed in a right-hand column.

break camera □ A television camera positioned for a program break. □ A director's command that frees a television camera for movement.

break copy Continuity that is used during radio or television station breaks.

breakdown □ A detailed analysis of a script to determine production costs, talent, materials, time, props, and so on. □ The process of editing dailies into their component shots. □ A camera shot sheet. □ In animation, the instructions from an animator as to how the in-between drawings are to be completed. □ The rearrangement of a script so that all the shots or scenes to be made at one location are together. Also called a *script breakdown.* □ Any equipment or computer program failure. □ *See* blocking.

breakdown sheet *See* shot sheet.

breaker A circuit breaker.

breaker box A box containing a subhead as well as a headline.

breaker head A newspaper subhead.

breakeven point The number of copies of a book, magazine, or other item that must be sold so that the income equals the costs.

break for color *See* breaking for color.

breaking down *See* breakdown.

breaking for color The mechanical method of stopping printing in order to change colors. Also called a *break for color.* *See also* blanking out.

breaking story A news story that is immediate; usually broken into different sections as the news is updated. Also called a *running story.*

break it up To tape or film close-ups that are to be edited into master scenes.

breakline A line of type that does not fill the width of a column, as in the last line of a paragraph.

breakoff rule A rule used to separate columns of different matter in a newspaper.

break of the book The allocation of magazine pages to various sections.

breakout A record that suddenly moves up in the charts of records being played on the air.

breakover *See* break.

break page □ The page that contains the continuation of a story. □ Any first page of any section of a newspaper except the front page.

break rating A radio or television rating of the time periods between programs.

breakthrough A visual effect on television when part of the background is seen on or through a keyed foreground.

break-up □ A picture fault characterized by scrambling of the reproduced picture. The effect can be caused by loss of headwheel servo lock, for example. □ On a television tape recorder, to produce such a picture fault. □ To destroy a typeform so that it may not be used again.

breathing □ A slow, regular variation of the video level in a television picture. Similar to bounce. □ The in and out motion of film in a projector that causes the picture to lose focus. Usually caused by insufficient gate pressure in either the camera or the projector.

B-reel A reel of film designated to be used second (A, B, C, and so on, reels). *See also* A-reel.

breezeway In NTSC color, that portion of the back porch between the trailing edge of the sync pulse and the start of the color burst.

Bretz box A device used in instruction to demonstrate the angle of view for various focal length lenses.

brevier Eight-point type size.

BRI Brand Rating Index.

bridge □ Sound effects or music used to indicate a lapse of time, or to link dramatic scenes. □ An insert placed between two sections of the same scene. Also called a *bridge shot* and *bridging shot.* *See also* transition. □ The words between two news stories. □ Any transitional device. □ To run an advertisement across the gutter of a spread. □ Continuity written to connect two segments of tape, film, articles, and so on. □ A word, phrase, or sentence connecting the lead to the body of a news story. □ A narrow platform suspended over the acting area of a set. Luminaires and projection devices mounted on the bridge are accessible during performances. Also called a *light bridge.*

bridger *See* bridging amplifier.

bridge shot *See* bridging shot.

bridging □ The connecting of electronic devices without loss in frequency response. □ The starting of television programs earlier than the competition in order to hook the audience.

bridging amplifier An isolation transformer connected to the main trunk of a cable television system. Also called a *bridger.*

bridging shot A shot taken to show a lapse of time or change of location. *See also* bridge.

brief □ A concise, written summary of the facts, points, questions at issue, proof, and other matters pertinent to a proceeding before an administrative agency or court. □ A short news story.

bright *See* brite.

brightener *See* brite.

brightness □ The reflective index of a surface. □ The degree to which light is reflected by paper. *See also* luminance.

brightness control The television receiver control that varies the illumination of the reproduced image.

brightness range □ The variation between the lightest and darkest areas of a film frame. Also called *brightness ratio.* □ The extent of the luminance values in a television picture.

brightness ratio The ratio of the maximum to minimum luminances occurring within a scene.

bright surface A highly reflective surface.

brilliance □ The degree of "brightness" produced in high-frequency sounds. □ The degree of purity and brightness of a television picture.

brilliance control In a three-way loudspeaker system, the potentiometer used to adjust the volume of the tweeter.

brilliant □ A photograph or film with striking characteristics. □ An especially accomplished performance. □ Three-and-a-half or four-point type size.

bring it up □ A radio or television director's command to increase the sound volume. □ A direction to an engineer to peak the definition in a television picture.

bristol board A smooth-surfaced heavy paper used for printing or artwork. Also called *bristol* and *bristol paper.*

brite A short, light-hearted, often humorous news feature or story. Also spelled *bright.* Also called *brightener* and *smile. See also* kicker.

British Broadcasting Corporation (BBC) A British government chartered corporation (1927), that operates radio and television services.

British Marconi Company The company founded in 1897 to market the inventions of the inventor Guglielmo Marconi.

British Standards Institute (BSI) The British organization that sets standards and recommended practices in film and television. Similar to the ISO, AFNOR, DIN, and ASA.

broad A wide-angle floodlight.

broadband □ Transmission facilities capable of carrying frequencies greater than those necessary for voice communication. □ The multiple-channel capacity of a cable television system.

broadband communication A distribution network that carries a large number of channels spread out over a wide bandwidth. Cf. narrow band.

broadband communication network (BCN) A proposal for the implementation of cable networks that could substitute for the physical movement of persons and written matter.

broadband distribution system Any system of communication capable of carrying broadband transmissions.

BROADCAP Broadcast Capital Fund, Inc. A fund established by the National Association of Broadcasters.

broadcast □ The presentation of a radio or television program or announcement. *See also* broadcasting, telecast, and simulcast. □ The simultaneous transmission of communications to all connected computer terminals at the same time. □ Any transmission capable of being received by all subscribers.

Broadcast Advertisers Reports, Inc. (BAR) Reports of advertising on the broadcast media.

Broadcast Advertising Producers Society of America (BAPSA) An organization of radio and television commercial producers.

broadcast band A band allocated to AM, FM, or television broadcasting.

Broadcast Bureau The former division of the FCC that assisted, advised, and made recommendations to the Commission with regard to broadcast services. Now part of the Mass Media Bureau.

broadcast calendar A calendar used for accounting purposes in the broadcast industry, containing months of four or five whole weeks, each month beginning on a Monday.

broadcast chain The entire sequence through which a broadcast signal travels, from the studio to the audience.

broadcast channel *See* channel.

broadcast day The period of time between local sunrise and 12 midnight local time.

broadcast editor A videotape editor who works in a television station.

broadcast editorial *See* editorial.

Broadcast Education Association (BEA) An association of member schools and individuals interested in broadcast education.

broadcast endorsement The endorsement that was required by the FCC for a radiotelephone third-class operator's permit (slang term, "third phone" or "third-class phone") that allowed the operation of certain classes of broadcast stations.

broadcaster □ An individual or company licensed to broadcast. □ Loosely defined, anyone engaged in broadcasting.

broadcast exhibition The licensing of feature films to broadcast stations after they are licensed first to home video and pay television.

broadcast hours The aggregate number of hours broadcast during a given year.

broadcasting The process of transmitting information to the general public by electromagnetic energy. Cf. telecommunication.

Broadcasting Company of America (BCA) A subsidiary of AT&T that sold WEAF to RCA in 1926, forming the nucleus of the Red Network.

Broadcasting Foundation of America (BFA) An agency that distributes informational and cultural programs to subscribing radio stations.

broadcasting-satellite service A radio communication service in which signals transmitted or retransmitted by space stations are intended for direct reception by the general public.

broadcasting service A radio communication service in which the transmissions are intended for reception by the general public. This service may include sound transmissions, television transmissions, or other transmissions types.

broadcasting station A station in the broadcasting service.

broadcasting systems *See* national broadcasting systems.

broadcast journalism The gathering, editing, and reporting of news on radio and television. Cf. print journalism.

broadcast journalist A newscaster.

broadcast license *See* license.

Broadcast Measurement Bureau (BMB) A standard measurement service similar to publishing's Audit Bureau of Circulation. In operation from 1945 to 1950.

Broadcast Music, Inc. *See* BMI.

broadcast network-entity An organization that produces programs available for simultaneous transmission by 10 or more affiliated broadcast stations and having distribution facilities or circuits available to such affiliated stations at least 12 hours each day. Cf. cable network-entity.

Broadcast Pioneers (BP) An organization founded in 1942 by H. V. Kaltenborn called the "Twenty Year Club of Pioneers in Radio Broadcasting."

Broadcast Pioneers Library (BPL) A library consisting of oral history interviews and other historical materials. Endowed and governed by the BPAF.

Broadcast Promotion Association (BPA) A trade association composed of industry promotion executives.

Broadcast Promotion and Marketing Executives (BPME) An association designed to promote marketing and promotion techniques.

broadcast quality □ Material that is technically suitable for broadcast. □ Equipment that meets the standards of the industry.

Broadcast Rating Council (BRC) An organization founded in 1964 to represent the interests of users of syndicated audience measurement services. Name changed to Electronic Media Rating Council (EMRC).

broadcast satellite A satellite that receives and retransmits radio or television signals.

Broadcast Satellite Service (BSS) An international designation for direct broadcast satellite service to households.

broadcast service area *See* service area.

broadcast spectrum That segment of the electromagnetic spectrum allocated to radio and television broadcasting.

broadcast standards An individual or department that determines the acceptability of continuity. *See also* continuity acceptance.

broadcast station A radio or television station engaged in broadcasting. Also called a *broadcasting station, radio broadcast station, television broadcast station,* and *station.*

broadcast studio *See* studio.

Broadcast-Television Recording Engineers (BTRE) A broadcast union.

Broadcast Television Systems Committee (BTSC) An EIA committee that selected the multichannel television sound (MTS) system.

broadcast window *See* window.

broadcast wire A newswire service written in broadcast style.

broadsheet *See* broadside.

broadside □ The size of a standard newspaper page. □ A large sheet printed on only one side. Cf. tabloid. □ An advertisement printed on paper that when unfolded forms one large advertisement. Also called a *broadsheet.* □ A type of floodlight. □ An antenna array perpendicular to the direction of radiation.

brochure A well-made, printed pamphlet, sometimes stitched, often having four or a multiple of four pages.

broken box A box that has portions of the rules omitted for the purpose of inserting words or graphics.

broken head A headline that is incomplete or separated by lines. Also called a *busted head.*

broken line A line consisting of a series of dashes.

broken rule A rule that is intermittent or irregular in printing. Also called *busted rule.*

broken series A canceled television network series that is continued in syndication, usually with new episodes added.

broker An advertising time salesperson who acts as an intermediary between advertisers and broadcast stations and cable television systems.

B-roll The second of two film clips in double chain. *See also* A-roll.

bromide □ A commonplace expression or story. Also called a *stereotype.* □ A photographic processing compound.

bronze level The lowest rate charge for satellite usage. Cf. gold level and platinum level.

bronze proof *See* glassine.

bronzing The application of metallic powders to the ink on freshly printed paper to achieve an opaque quality.

broomsticking A picture fault characteristic of helical scan recorders in which the upper portion of the picture bends left or right, usually due to tape tension errors.

brown goods Radios, television receivers, and other electronic merchandise.

brownie points A slang term for the credit broadcast stations receive at renewal time for programs broadcast in the public interest.

brownline *See* brownprint.

brown out A government order that limits the amount of illumination permitted on outdoor advertising structures.

brownprint A printer's proof, identical to a blueprint, but printed in brown. Also called *vandyke* and *brownline.*

browsing A user's charting of an individual, nonsequential path through a compact disc's information.

bruning A method of producing copies of translucent originals. *See also* whiteprint.

brute A 225-ampere dc high-intensity carbon arc spotlight with a 24-inch diameter fresnel lens.

B/S Bits per second.

BSA Bibliographical Society of America.

BSI British Standards Institute. An organization similar to ANSI.

B-spline modeling A method of defining a continuous curve by recording a series of control points, each with two associated control vectors—one representing the angle of the curve as it approaches the control point and the other representing the curve's angle as it continues past the point.

BSS Broadcast satellite service.

B system The 625-line, 25-frames-per-second, 7-mHz-bandwidth, FM sound television system used in Germany, Italy, and a number of other European countries. Cf. A, D, E, and M systems.

BTA Best time(s) available.

BTL Behind the lens.

BTRE Broadcast-Television Recording Engineers. A professional organization.

BTSC Broadcast Television Systems Committee recommendation for multichannel television sound transmission and audio processing as defined in FCC Bulletin OET 60.

bubble An incandescent lamp.

bubble gum music Simple rock music designed to please people in their early teens.

buck To program against a popular show on another radio or television network or station.

bucket A headline style in which the second deck is centered under the first.

buckeye A visually crude, tasteless advertisement.

buckle A film jam in a camera. Also called a *bird's nest.*

buckle switch *See* buckle trip.

buckle trip An automatic circuit breaker in a camera that is activated by a film jam.

buckling Film breaking or tangling in a projector.

buckram □ A heavy, cotton cloth used for book covers. □ Cloth used as a base for wigs or heavy makeup.

bucktag A separate slip attached to a printed piece containing instructions to route the material to specific individuals. Also called a *routing slip.*

budget □ The amount of money allocated to run a broadcast station, produce a film, cover production costs of a program or series, and so on. □ A list of forthcoming wire service news stories. □ *See* schedule.

buff A fan or enthusiast, such as a film buff, an audiophile, discophile, or cinephile.

buffer □ In a television tape recorder, an apparatus capable of storing at least one television line of the reproduced picture and usually functioning as part of a time base corrector. □ A device on a tape transport, usually pneumatic in operating principle, that can store a variable length of moving tape as it passes over the transport. □ Any device capable of storing, but not processing, a signal. □ A substance used to maintain the acidity or alkalinity of a chemical solution. □ An audio or video insert used to isolate two scenes or sounds. *See also* bridge. □ A part of the audio and video decoders that sifts information and allows it to enter the decoder at the proper speed. □ A device or area of computer memory used to store information temporarily during data flow. Also called a *buffer store.* □ *See* buffer sample.

buffer sample An additional sample that is hand drawn by Arbitron Ratings' Data Collection department for unusual situations when there is not enough computer-drawn sample because of changes in the usability rate and/or consent rate and persons-per-household. Also called a *buffer.*

buffer store *See* buffer.

bug □ A type ornament. Also called a *dingbat.* □ A defect, often intermittent, in a device or machine that is difficult to locate. □ A slang term for a telegrapher's key. □ A slang term for an asterisk. □ An error in a computer program.

bug eye *See* fisheye.

bugging The placing of telephone taps or concealed microphones.

bug man A picky copy editor.

build The gradual increase in emotion or tension that leads to the climax of a scene.

build-up A promotional technique used to increase the popularity of a program, performer, or commercial product.

buildup □ The editing of film or videotape by using blank leader or tape to fill spaces for scenes not yet shot. □ Any unwanted deposit of oxide on magnetic recording heads, agglomeration on film, excess ink on type, and so on.

build-up announcement A promotional announcement designed to attract an audience.

built-in meter An exposure meter built into a camera; often automatic.

bulb □ A shutter setting on some cameras that allows the shutter to remain open as long as the release is held. □ The glass or quartz part of a lamp that encloses the filament or electrodes, supports, and so on. □ A universally used term for all glass-enclosed lighting elements. More properly called a *lamp.*

bulk □ The thickness of paper regardless of its weight. □ The thickness of a book without its cover. □ To make a thin book thicker by using heavier paper.

bulk circulation The distribution of a periodical in quantity as opposed to single-copy sales.

bulk degausser *See* bulk eraser.

bulk discount A quantity discount offered to advertisers for time or space purchases.

bulk eraser An electromagnetic device used to degauss a complete roll of audio- or videotape. Also called a *bulk degausser, degausser,* or *mass eraser.*

bulk mail A category of third-class mail in which large mailings are sent to different addressees at a lower rate than standard third class. Such mail is often derogatorily called "junk mail." Also called *bulk rate.*

bulk permit A post office permit granted to senders of bulk mail.

bulk rate *See* bulk mail.

bulk sale Newspapers sold at a discounted rate to hotels, restaurants, and other businesses.

bull An error or misstatement in news copy.

bulldog The earliest edition of a newspaper. Cf. bullpup.

bullet □ A large dot or other mark used as a decoration or to highlight important points in a story. □ A symbol used to indicate a record breakout.

bulletin □ A late-breaking news story. □ A news development of sufficient importance to warrant immediate airing. Cf. flash. □ New information printed as a lead in an already written story. Also called a *bulletin precede.* □ An important wire service news story or advisory. □ A short advertising announcement. □ A periodical publication, sometimes a catalogue or brochure, issued by an institution, government agency, business, and so on. □ The larger of the two standardized outdoor advertising structures. The most common size is 14 by 48 feet. Copy is reproduced by one of two methods: painting directly on the surface or posting with preprinted paper. Cf. poster.

bulletinitis The tendency of some radio or television stations to approach all news stories as if they were bulletins.

bulletin precede *See* bulletin.

bulletin spectacular A semipermanent outdoor sign, usually painted, as opposed to an outdoor board using printed poster paper.

bullfrog Talent with an extremely deep voice.

bullhorn An electronic megaphone containing a built-in microphone and loudspeaker.

bull line The heavy duty rope used to lift counterweighted scenery.

bull pen The newspaper office area, formerly enclosed by a low railing, reserved for news editors and writers.

bullpup The first mail edition of a Sunday newspaper. Cf. bulldog.

bullseye An eye-catching poster.

bump □ The sound made by a poor tape splice containing unwanted noise or sound. □ A sudden change in scene lighting intensity. A bump-up or bump-down. □ To cancel a commercial or program and replace it with other material. □ *See* bumped heads.

bump-down *See* bump.

bumped heads Headlines of similar size placed side by side. *See also* tombstone.

bumper □ The precautionary extra film or videotape footage that precedes or follows the main portion of a television commercial. Also called *safety footage.* □ A slide, photograph, or other video that serves as a transition between commercials, news stories, and so on. Also called *bumper footage.*

bump in *See* pop in.

bumping The preempting of a radio or television program.

bump mapping A technique for creating a surface texture on a three-dimensional object by wrapping a two-dimensional matrix of normals onto its surface. The matrix may or may not be random.

bump on *See* pop in.

bump out *See* pop out.

bump up To duplicate a tape using a larger format, such as from half-inch to three-quarter-inch tape.

bump-up *See* bump.

bun An abbreviation for *bulletin.*

bundled service Cable television bundling.

bundling The practice of offering two or more cable services to subscribers for a single monthly fee. Cf. unbundling.

bunk lead A temporary lead to a news story waiting for a rewrite. Also called a *trial lead.*

BUP British United Press. A subsidiary of UPI.

burden of proof □ That burden that rests on the prosecution or plaintiff to prove the fact or facts in dispute. □ The responsibility an individual has to furnish full and positive support for a position. For example, under Section 315 of the Communications Act, the burden of proof lies with the candidate requesting equal opportunities.

bureau A subordinate office of a newsgathering organization, such as ''London Bureau'' or ''Washington Bureau.''

Bureau International de Presse A French news agency.

Bureau of Advertising (B of A) A promotional agency of the American Newspaper Publishers Association.

buried ad A newspaper or periodical advertisement that is inconspicuous among other ads.

buried offer *See* blind offer.

burin A cutting tool used in line engraving.

Burke test A test service of Burke Marketing Research, Inc., which measures recall of an advertisement among those people exposed to it the preceding day.

burn □ An image retained on the face of a television camera tube. Also called a *burn-in, retained image,* and *sticking.* □ To expose type to a sensitized printing plate.

burned-in code *See* burned-in numbers.

burned-in numbers Time code numbers that are shown as video characters on a monitor. Also called *burned-in code.*

burned out *See* burn out.

burn in □ To subject a printing plate to heat in order to make it acid resistant. □ To subject portions of an image on film to additional light during the enlarging process in order to achieve more definition or a darker image. Cf. dodge. □ A double exposure of a title over previously exposed film. *See also* superimposure.

burn-in □ The operation of any device to stabilize it before use in a system. □ *See* burn.

burnish □ To rub a halftone plate in order to deepen the printed tone. □ To polish the colored edges of a book.

burnished edges The polished gilt edges of a book.

burnishing facet The portion of the cutting stylus in disc recording directly behind the cutting edge that smooths the groove.

burn out A loss of tonal quality in a television picture characterized by burned out or bleached whites. Also called *burned out.*

burnout □ A television program, usually in syndication, that has been seen too often. □ A record that is no longer popular.

burp A strange noise in an audio circuit.

burr A rough edge on type or on a metal printing plate.

burst □ A sudden increase in the strength of a signal. □ A pulse used for testing a television transmitter. *See also* color burst. □ *See* flight.

burst error The corruption of a sequence of bits.

burst transmission The transmission of data at discrete intervals as opposed to continuous transmission.

bury To obscure a story, advertisement, and so on, by placing it in a less prominent place, such as the inside page of a newspaper.

bus □ An uninsulated bar or wire in an electric circuit, such as a ground wire or mix bus. □ A row of buttons on a video switcher. Also spelled *buss.* □ Computer signal paths or lines that carry data from one place to another. □ The component of a CD-I player along which data is routed from one processing unit to another.

business Any on-stage action or pantomime by talent except a cross. Cf. bit.

business agent A union official responsible for enforcing contracts and settling grievances.

business department The department of a newspaper, magazine, broadcast station, or other medium that handles the billing, accounting, and so on.

business list The persons or companies with which an organization maintains or hopes to begin business relationships.

business magazine *See* business paper.

business manager The person who handles the business affairs of an actor or performer; sometimes an agent.

business office must (BOM) A newspaper story ordered by the business department that may not be omitted; often a front page insertion.

business paper A periodical publication devoted to a particular industry, trade, profession, and so on. Also called a *business magazine* and *business publication.*

business publication *See* business paper.

Business Publications Audit of Circulation, Inc. (BPA) A national, independent, nonprofit corporation of advertisers, advertising agencies, and business publications that are often referred to as trade books. Its function is to issue standardized statements of the circulations of its publication members; to verify the accuracy of the figures shown on these statements by means of an auditor's examination of any and all necessary published records; to issue, at least once a year, a report made by the corporation on each publication member; and to disseminate pertinent circulation data concerning its publication members for the benefit of advertisers, advertising agencies, and publishers.

business reply card (BRC) A preaddressed, return postcard, bearing specified Postal Service indicia; the postage is paid upon delivery to the addressee.

business reply envelope (BRE) A preaddressed, return envelope bearing specified Postal Service indicia; the postage is paid upon delivery to the addressee.

busorama Transit advertising on buses.

buss *See* bus.

bust To stop a rehearsal, show, program, or other event, temporarily.

busted head *See* broken head.

busted rule *See* broken rule.

bust it A television director's command to stop. *See also* cut and bite it off.

bust shot A camera shot framed from the chest to slightly above the head. Also called a *chest shot*. *See also* camera shots.

busy □ A cluttered set or background. □ A picture containing unnecessary detail. □ A scene with too much nonessential action. □ A distracting soundtrack. □ A layout, photograph, advertising message, and so on, that is cluttered or contains too much information.

butcher A film, tape, news, or copy editor who bungles, mutilates, or otherwise degrades the material.

butt □ The end of a roll of paper, tape, wire, and so on. □ To join lines of type end to end. *See also* butted slugs. □ To join film or tape without overlapping the material.

butt changeover A smooth crossover from one disc or tape to another during a program. Cf. segue.

butted Two sounds or pictures that are joined.

butted slugs Linecaster slugs that are placed end to end to make a line longer than the machine can set.

butt end The end of a piece of film prepared for a butt splice.

butterfly □ A scrim used to soften or diffuse lighting. □ A reflector used to soften sunlight in exterior shots.

butt join *See* butt splice.

button □ *See* mike button. □ A musical phrase ending.

buttonhook A question mark-shaped rod that supports the feedhorn and the low noise amplifier in a satellite dish.

butt splice A film or tape splice that does not overlap. Also called a *butt join*. Cf. overlap splice.

butt splicer A type of splicer used to make butt splices.

buy □ A take or scene that is considered good enough for use in a production. □ A purchase of media time or space.

buyer □ A purchasing agent. □ An advertising agency time buyer. □ *See* media buyer. □ A person who orders merchandise, books, records, information, or services. Unless another modifier is used, it is assumed that a buyer has paid for all merchandise to date.

BuyerGraphics An Arbitron term that is used to define viewers by the products they purchase instead of by demographics.

Buyers Guide The *Buyers Guide to Outdoor Advertising*. The official rate and allotment release from the Outdoor Advertising Association of America, Inc. (OAAA). Released twice a year, in January and September.

buying □ A misnomer for leasing the rights to show copyrighted materials such as television programs, motion pictures, and so on. □ To purchase air time, print space, or another advertising medium.

buying around The buying of less expensive book editions directly from foreign sources even though an exclusive arrangement has been made to purchase them from another publisher.

buying service An advertising agency or firm that specializes in purchasing media time and space.

buy off An individual who is paid a flat fee for performing in a commercial instead of receiving pay based on the number of times the commercial is broadcast.

buyout A one-time fee paid to talent, writers, directors, and so on, with no subsequent royalties or residuals.

buy rate The percentage of pay-per-view households that purchase a program.

buy up To place an individual artist, talent, informant, or other person under exclusive contract.

buzz An audio distortion often caused by line frequency harmonics.

buzzer A warning device, similar to a light or bell, that is used to signal the start of filming or taping.

buzz track □ A soundtrack with a low level of sound to match the background sound in a dialogue track. Used when there is no dialogue on the soundtrack. □ A test tape or film used to align recording or playback heads.

B/W Black and white.

B wind □ A single perforated film winding; with the emulsion facing the core and the film unwinding clockwise, the perforations are away from the viewer. Cf. A wind. □ A tape wound with the oxide or emulsion facing out.

B-wire A news service secondary wire carrying in-depth features and texts of speeches. Cf. A-wire and radio wire.

bye-bye A phrase used to introduce a new radio or television program segment, such as ''We take you now to Soldier's Field for. . . .''

byline A line containing the name of the author, writer, reporter, or other originator. In a newspaper, the byline is often printed above the story. Also called *title line.* Also frequently spelled *by line* or *by-line.*

B-Y signal The blue primary color difference signal in color television.

byte □ A contraction of ''by eight''; a set of eight adjacent bits that are treated as a unit. One byte can represent one complete character. □ An 8-bit unit representing one symbol before 8-to-14 modulation.

C

C □ Candle. □ Capacitance. □ Capacitor. □ Carbon. □ Celsius. □ Centigrade. □ Centimeter. □ Character. □ Clear. □ Collector. □ Commercial. An FCC file-number prefix. □ Common Carrier. An FCC first letter file-number prefix. □ Copyright. □ Coulomb. □ Cut. □ Cycle. □ Cycles per second. □ Velocity of light. □ An abbreviation for capital letters. □ A wire service designation for regular features. □ Outside front cover; first cover. Used in ordering magazine advertising.

CA □ Commercial announcement. □ Court of appeals. □ Courtesy announcement.

ca An abbreviation for *circa*.

c/a Change of address.

CAAA □ Composers, Authors, and Artists of America. □ Canadian Association of Advertising Agencies.

CAB □ Cable [Television] Advertising Bureau. □ Canadian Association of Broadcasters. □ Civil Aeronautics Board. □ Cooperative Analysis of Broadcasting.

cabinet A housing for electronic equipment. Cf. rack.

cable □ A conductor—often a wire, optical fiber, fiber bundle, or group of conductors—separately insulated and usually provided with a protective sheath. Cf. coaxial cable. □ An abbreviation for *cable television*.

Cable Advertising Bureau (CAB) A trade association of cable television systems, MSOs, and individuals who promote the concept of advertising on cable television.

cable audio *See* cable radio.

cablecast A program shown on cable television.

cablecaster A person who operates a cable television system. Cf. broadcaster.

cablecasting Programming, exclusive of broadcast signals, carried on a cable television system. *See also* local origination.

cable catalog A display of products on a television screen in catalog format, using videotape. Viewers of the catalog may order the products using an 800 number. *See also* direct response advertising.

cable channel A portion of the electromagnetic frequency spectrum used in a cable system and capable of delivering a television channel. Also called a *channel*.

Cable Communications Policy Act of 1984 The statute regulating cable television that resulted from a compromise among the National Cable Television Association, the National League of Cities, and the U.S. Conference of Mayors.

cable compatible *See* cable ready.

cable converter Equipment in the homes of cable television subscribers used to convert cable signals to normal television channels.

cable correction The electronic circuits that compensate for the loss of frequencies as the length of camera cables is increased.

cable FM *See* cable radio.

cable franchise *See* franchise.

cable guard A device used to keep the wheels of a dolly from bumping into or running over a camera cable.

cableless sync Camera and recorder synchronization accomplished by a battery-operated crystal. Also called *cordless sync*.

cable lift The number of households that subscribe to cable television in order to receive certain premium channels.

cableman A sound assistant who operates the sound recorder in double system sound.

cable network A programming service usually delivered by satellite to cable television systems.

cable network-entity An organization that produces programs available for simultaneous transmission by cable systems serving a combined total of at least five million subscribers and having distribution facilities or circuits available to such affiliated stations or cable systems. Cf. broadcast network-entity.

cable only Programming that is available only through cable television systems.

cable operator Any person or group of persons that provides cable service over a cable system and directly or through one or more affiliates owns a significant interest in such cable system, or who otherwise controls or is responsible for, through any arrangement, the management and operation of such a cable system.

cable-oriented programming service An organization that provides original programming to local cable television systems.

cable originated programming service A program service that provides to local cable systems programming that is not transmitted over the air.

cable penetration The percentage of cable television households in a given area expressed as a percentage of all television households.

cable puller A grip assigned to keep the camera and camera operator from running into the camera cable.

cable radio The FM radio signals delivered to subscribers on a cable television system. Also called *cable audio* and *cable FM.*

cable ready A general term for television receivers, videotape recorders, and so on, that are capable of tuning cable television channels directly without a cable converter.

cable release A remote control flexible cable used to trip a shutter without moving the camera.

cable rep An individual who works on commission as an independent sales operator.

cablese □ The combining of words in the sending of news by cable in order to lower transmission costs. □ The codes and abbreviations used in copy sent by cable.

cable service The one-way transmission to subscribers of video programming or another programming service; subscriber interaction, if any, that is required for the selection of such video programming or other programming service.

cable spacer A metal device used to separate a coaxial cable from a messenger.

cable subscriber A household that receives cable television service for a monthly fee.

cable synchronization In double system sound, the synchronization between a film camera and a sound recorder.

cable system □ For the purposes of copyright, a facility located in any state, territory, trust territory, or possession that in whole or in part receives signals transmitted or programs broadcast by one or more television broadcast stations licensed by the Federal Communications Commission. It makes secondary transmissions of such signals to subscribing members of the public who pay for such service. For the purposes of determining the royalty fee, two or more cable systems in contiguous communities under common ownership or control or operating from one headend shall be considered as one system. □ *See* cable television system.

cable system operator Any person or group of persons who provides cable service over a cable system and directly or through one or more affiliates owns a significant interest in such cable system; or who otherwise controls or is responsible for, through any arrangement, the management or operation of such a cable system.

cable television A communications system that delivers broadcast and other signals to a subscriber for a fee. The term is usually synonymous with *community antenna television, CATV,* and *cable TV.*

Cable Television Administration and Marketing Society (CTAM) A cable television association concerned with cable programming and marketing.

Cable [Television] Advertising Bureau (CAB) An organization established to provide promotional and advisory services to the cable television industry.

Cable Television Bureau Formerly, the Bureau of the FCC that developed, recommended, and administered policies and programs with respect to the regulation of cable television systems and related private microwave radio facilities. Now part of the Mass Media Bureau.

cable television channel A channel with a bandwidth of 6 mHz used to deliver a television signal to a subscriber from a cable television system. *See* class I, class II, class III, and class IV.

cable television coordinator A city employee who monitors cable operator performance, and often, the person in charge of the government access channel.

cable television relay (CAR) station A fixed or mobile station used to transmit television and related audio signals, signals of standard and FM broadcast stations, signals of instructional television fixed stations, and cablecasting from the point of reception to a terminal point from which the signals are distributed to the public by cable.

cable television relay pickup station A land mobile CAR station used for the transmission of television signals and related communications from the scenes of events occurring at points removed from cable television studios to cable television studios or headends.

cable television relay service A fixed service, the stations of which are used for the transmission of television and related audio signals.

cable television relay service (CARS) station A fixed or mobile station used for the transmission of television and related audio signals, signals of standard and FM broadcast stations, signals of instructional television fixed stations, and cablecasting from the point of reception to a terminal point from which the signals are distributed to the public.

cable television relay studio to headend link station (SHL) A fixed CAR station used for the transmission of television program material and related communications from a cable television studio to the headend of a cable television system.

cable television system A facility consisting of a set of closed transmission paths and associated signal generation, reception, and control equipment that is designed to provide cable service including video programming and that is provided to multiple subscribers within a community. The term does not include (a) a facility that serves only to retransmit the television signals of one or more television broadcast stations; (b) a facility that serves only subscribers in one or more multiple-unit dwellings under common ownership, control, or management, unless such facility or facilities use any public right-of-way; (c) a facility of a common carrier that is subject, in whole or in part, to the provisions of Title II of the Communications Act of 1934, as amended, except that such facility shall be considered a cable system to the extent such facility is used in the transmission of video programming directly to subscribers; or (d) any facilities of any electric utility used solely for operating its electric utility system.

cable television system operator *See* cable system operator.

cabletext The electronic delivery of alphanumeric information to homes by cable television for news, program information, advertising, and so on.

cable TV A term usually synonymous with community antenna television, CATV, or cable television.

cablevision A synonym for cable television.

caboose News that is buried at or near the end of the first section of a newspaper.

cache A buffer type of computer memory that can process information more quickly than the main memory.

cacoethes scribendi From the Latin for "the itch for writing."

CAD Computer aided design.

CADC Court of Appeals, District of Columbia. Also abbreviated *U.S. App. D.C.*

CADD Computer aided design and drafting.

cadiotropic lens A long focal length lens using mirror optics.

CAF Cable Arts Foundation, Inc. A cable program producer.

CAFM Cable FM. *See* cable radio.

cage The control area of a newspaper composing room.

Cahiers du Cinema An influential and critical film journal edited for a number of years by Andre Bazin.

CAI Computer assisted instruction.

CAIV Computer assisted interactive video.

calculator A device that can perform arithmetic and logical operations, sometimes with limited programming capabilities.

calendered Paper with a glossy finish that has been polished between smooth cylinders of steel and compressed cotton. Cf. antique paper, coated paper, and supercalendered.

calf An abbreviation for *calfskin*; a relatively expensive book cover material.

calibration □ A process of comparison between a standard and a device or piece of equipment. □ The marks on a lens barrel that indicate the f stop.

California case *See* California job case.

California job case A shallow compartmented tray for holding uppercase and lowercase type side by side. *See also* case.

call □ A public notice of a tryout or audition. □ The offer of a job to talent. □ A scheduled rehearsal or performance time. Also called a *shooting call.* □ A contact made by a reporter on a beat. □ To give a play-by-play description of a sporting event.

call-back □ A further attempt by an interviewer to obtain information from a respondent who did not, for some reason, provide information for a survey at a previously attempted interview. □ A request for talent to return for an additional test or audition.

call board *See* call sheet.

call book A book maintained by a salesperson with the locations, purchases, buying habits, and other facts about regular customers.

Callier coefficient The ratio between the diffuse and specular densities of a film's emulsion. Also called the *Q factor.*

calligraphy Elegant writing by hand.

call in □ A radio station format in which a talk show host accepts telephone calls from the audience. □ An individual who telephones a radio talk show. □ To withdraw a publication from circulation.

call-in audience research A method of research in which members of an audience call a telephone number to hear the material being evaluated.

call in radio *See* talk radio.

call letters The letters, or letters and numbers, assigned by the FCC that identify a broadcast station. Normally, the prefix *W* is used west of the Mississippi; *K,* east. Also called a *call sign.*

call out audience research A method of research in which interviewers call telephone respondents to play the material being evaluated.

call report A record of a meeting between an advertiser and an agency prepared by an agency representative. Also called a *conference report* and *contact report.*

call screener An individual who takes incoming telephone calls for a call-in radio program and screens them for acceptability; often the producer of the show. Also called a *screener.*

call sheet A posted schedule indicating rehearsal times and locations.

call sign A synonym for *call letters.*

calnicon A type of television camera pick-up tube.

calotype An early photographic process (1839) invented by William Henry Fox Talbot. Also called a *Talbotype.*

CAM Computer aided make-up. Used for newspaper and magazine composition. Also called *composition and make-up.*

cam □ An abbreviation for *camera.* □ An eccentric mechanical device for imparting motion to a roller or pin, as in an animation stand focus mechanism, viewfinder parallax mechanism, or camera or projector intermittent shutter mechanism.

camcorder A small, portable video camera and recorder combined into one unit.

cameo □ A lighting situation in film or television production when only the foreground is illuminated. The background is black and unlighted. Also called *cameo lighting.* Cf. limbo. □ A small role played by a performer.

cameo lighting *See* cameo.

camera □ An electromagnetic device that transforms an optical image into electrical impulses. The term usually refers to a complete unit: the camera itself, the viewfinder, and the optical system. □ A device that transforms an optical image to a photographic image on film. □ *See* copy camera.

camera angle The relationship between the set or performers and the position of the camera.

camera aperture *See* aperture.

camera balance The degree of uniformity between or among the electronic pictures taken by television cameras. Also called *camera match* and *picture matching.*

camera body A complete camera except for the lens(es) of a still or motion picture camera; the camera box, motor housing, and magazine housing. Also called a *camera case* and *camera head.*

camera boom A large, mobile camera mount. *See also* crane.

camera box The main housing of a camera body.

camera cable The multistranded, covered cable connecting a television camera to its CCU.

camera cam head *See* cam head.

camera can *See* can.

camera caption *See* caption.

camera cards Titles, credits, and other graphics shown by a camera. *See* graphics. Cf. cue card.

camera case *See* camera body.

camera chain A television camera, camera control unit, sync generator, power supply, monitor, interconnecting cables, and so on. The complete unit necessary to transform an optical image into a signal ready for transmission.

camera composition *See* composition.

camera control unit (CCU) An electronic component used to adjust and control the output of a television camera.

camera copy *See* camera ready.

camera crane *See* crane.

camera cue A cue to a performer taken from the tally light on a television camera.

camera cue light *See* tally light.

camera department The motion picture studio department responsible for maintaining cameras and associated equipment, as well as film loading and handling.

camera effects *See* camera opticals.

camera field angle The angle of view of a set seen by a given camera lens. The shorter the focal length, the wider the angle.

camera field angle scale A plastic scale with the angle of view for various lenses imprinted on it. Used for planning camera shots on a set floor plan.

camera head □ The device inserted between a camera and a camera mount that allows the camera to move without moving the camera mount. *See also* cam head, cradle head, fluid head, friction head, gear head, gyro head, pan and tilt head, and pan head. □ *See* camera body.

camera headlamp A British term for a camera light.

camera hog A person who tries to upstage other performers.

camera housing A waterproof camera enclosure used for underwater filming.

camera left Directions given from the camera's point of view. Cf. stage left.

camera lens *See* lens.

camera lens turret *See* turret.

cameraless animation Animation accomplished by drawing or painting directly on film.

cameraless film A film, usually animated, made by drawing directly on the film stock.

camera level □ A spirit level used to establish the proper horizontal plane for a camera and camera mount. □ The height above the ground as seen from the lens of a camera.

camera light A lighting instrument mounted on a camera for lighting on the optical axis, usually to provide eye light. Also called an *inky-dinky, eye-light,* and *kicker.* Cf. tally light.

camera log A list of shots and takes made for each roll of film. Also called a *report sheet.* Cf. log sheet.

camera lucida A device with a reflecting prism used to enlarge or decrease the size of artwork. Also called a *lucy* and *lucey.*

cameraman □ In television, the camera operator. □ In motion pictures, the person responsible for overall lighting and camera composition. *See also* cinematographer.

camera match *See* camera balance.

camera microphone A microphone attached to or built into a video camera; often a shotgun.

camera mixing The selection of television pictures for transmission or recording.

camera motor A synchronous or nonsynchronous electric or spring wound motor used to drive a camera mechanism.

camera mounts The varied devices used to steady or hold a camera for operation. *See also* baby legs, crab dolly, crane, creeper, dolly, field mount, free head, high hat, Huston crane, monster, panorama dolly, pedestal, sanner dolly, spyder, tongue, top hat, tripod, trolley, and Tyler mount.

camera movement *See* arc, chinese, chinese turn, crab, crane, dolly, gibbing, pan, pedestal, tilt, tongue, and truck.

camera negative The original negative film taken by a camera. *See also* camera original.

camera obscura Literally, "a dark chamber." A primitive type of shutterless camera with a pinhole or lens for focusing light rays inside a box.

camera operator □ The individual who moves, focuses, composes, and manages camera shots under the supervision of the director. □ In animation, the person responsible for translating the instructions on the exposure sheet into camera moves and photographing the artwork.

camera opticals Opticals made in the camera instead of by an optical printer. Also called *camera effects.*

camera optics The lens composition of various cameras.

camera original The original film used to photograph a scene. If a negative film is being used, a camera negative; if a positive film, a camera positive. Also called *original film.*

camera pen *See* camera-stylo.

camera placement The selection of positions in and around a set for taping or filming.

camera positive The original positive film taken by a camera. *See also* camera original.

camera projection The use of a camera to project pictures on an animation compound table to make layouts and traveling mattes. *See also* rotoscope.

camera pulse track *See* pulse track.

camera ready □ A notification from the camera operator to the director that the film camera has been checked for flare, film scratches, parallax, and so on, and is ready for use. □ Any copy that is finished and ready for photographic reproduction. Often said of advertising copy from a client.

camera rehearsal A rehearsal with cameras, mikes, sound, and other studio equipment.

camera report *See* dope sheet.

camera reporting The transmission of a program not designed specifically for television.

camera right Directions given from the camera's point of view. Cf. stage right.

camera rock The in-and-out or side-to-side movement of a camera between frames to simulate violent action in a static picture. Sometimes called a *rocker.*

camera room The area in which camera ready copy is reproduced. Cf. darkroom.

camera script A script with all stage directions and shots indicated. *See also* shot sheet.

camera setup □ The position from which a shot is taken. □ The alignment and warmup of cameras by an engineer or technician.

camera shadow A shadow cast by a camera and picked up by the camera shot.

camera shots The many and varied pictures taken by a camera for which there are few universally accepted definitions. *See also* aerial shot, BCU, boom shot, bust shot, chest shot, close-shot, cover shot, CU, down shot, dutch angle, ECU, extremely long shot, eye level shot, face shot, false reverse, following shot, follow shot, full shot, head shot, high-angle shot, insurance, in tight, knee shot, long shot, loose shot, low-angle shot, master shot, medium close-up, medium long shot, medium shot, mirror shot, mist shot, model shot, moving shot, mug shot, nostril shot, over-the-shoulder shot, passing shot, pocket shot, point of view, pop zoom, reaction pan, reaction shot, reveal, reverse angle, reverse shot, running shot, run through shot, shoulder shot, straight shot, swish pan, TCU, three shot, tight shot, track, tracking shot, travel shot, trick angle, trick shot, two shot, up shot, waist shot, walking shot, whip, wide-angle shot, wide shot, and zoom shot.

camera signal The video output of a television camera.

camera speed *See* frame rate.

camera spin The effect produced by rotating the animation compound table.

camera-stylo A development in filmmaking style that called for a personal statement in film similar to that in literature: a camera pen.

camera switching The selection between or among different camera shots. *See also* mix, switcher, and switching.

camera synchronism The distance, measured in frames, between the picture and the sound in a film camera. Cf. editorial synchronism.

camera test A short length of film shot to check camera operation.

camera track *See* track.

camera trap A hidden break within a set through which a camera may take pictures without being seen by an audience.

camera tube The electron beam tube in television used to convert light rays into electrical signals. *See also* pickup tube.

camera turret *See* turret.

camera viewpoint A scene as viewed from the vantage point of a camera.

cam head A type of camera head using dual cams for counterbalancing the camera.

Cammy awards Television awards made to students by the Collegiate Amateur Movie Makers of the Year.

camouflage The use of anything in a survey questionnaire to conceal the identity of the survey sponsor or to reduce bias.

camp Artwork, books, motion pictures, and so on, that are currently in vogue; often less than enduring.

campaign □ A series of related announcements distributed, printed, aired, and so on, that is designed to promote a commercial product, service, station, program, public service organization, or event. *See also* public relations. □ *See* crusade.

Campbell's Soup position The first right-hand page following the main editorial section of a magazine; so called because the Campbell Soup Company has often specified this position for its advertisements.

campus radio systems A communication system having the output of one or more low-power transmitters coupled into a power distribution network or other network of conductors. The RF signals are picked up by conductive connection to the network or by space radiation in the vicinity of the network and operated in the AM broadcasting band on the campus of an educational institution. Often called a *carrier current station.*

can □ A 1000-watt floodlight. □ A metal shield used to cover a vacuum tube. □ A round metal container used for storage of film reels and magnetic tape.

canalization The ability of the mass media to promote a product or service through the change of attitudes and behaviors.

canary A slang term for a singer.

cancel □ To omit matter already printed. □ A new leaf or leaves reprinted to replace obsolete or incorrect material. Also called *cancels.* □ To abort a computer program.

cancellation □ The signal opposition caused by a difference in phase between two signals. □ A program, commercial, advertisement, and so on, that is withdrawn after being ordered or scheduled.

cancellation date The last date that an advertisement or commercial may be canceled for a publication, broadcast, outdoor advertising, and so on. Cf. closing date.

cancels *See* cancel.

candela (cd) A unit of light intensity designed to replace the candle. It is equal to one lumen per square foot, or 98.1 percent of a candle.

candidate *See* legally qualified candidate.

candid photograph A picture taken of a subject who is unaware that he or she is being photographed; unposed. Also called *candids.*

candids *See* candid photograph.

c and lc Capital and lowercase letters. Also spelled *c/lc* and *clc.*

candle (C) A unit of light intensity. *See also* candela.

candle meter A unit of light intensity equal to one candlepower falling on a surface from one meter. Also called a *lux.*

candlepower □ A term sometimes used in place of intensity. □ The intensity of light expressed in candles. Bright sunlight has an intensity of 50 to 60,000 candlepower, and an ordinary lamp from 10 to 120 candlepower.

C and W Country and western.

can go over (CGO) Newspaper copy of lesser importance that could be held until the next edition.

canned □ Anything transcribed or recorded for later use; "in the can." □ A standardized or scripted sales pitch.

canned copy □ Publicity written by press agents. *See also* handout. □ Material received from a news syndicate. Also called *canned news. See also* boilerplate. □ *See* canned.

canned laughter *See* laugh track.

canned music A musical selection from one of a number of record cuts from a music library.

canned news *See* canned copy.

canned routine An overused, often-copied performer's act.

cannibalize To use the parts from one component to repair similar pieces of equipment.

canoe □ That portion of tape in a quadruplex transport that lies between the tape-input guide and tape-output guide and is cupped by the vacuum guide. □ Pertaining to that portion of the tape or to the elements that shape it.

canon □ The largest type size (48 point) having a name. □ A critical standard set by a professional organization, such as a code of judicial ethics.

Canon 3A(7) The Canon that replaced Canon 35 as part of the American Bar Association's Canon of Judicial Conduct in 1972 but retains the prohibition against broadcasting, recording, or taking pictures in or near a courtroom, unless authorized by the judge.

Canon 20 An American Bar Association Canon of Professional Ethics adopted in the early 1900s that provided "newspaper publications by a lawyer as to pending or anticipated litigation may interfere with a fair trial in the courts and otherwise prejudice the due administration of justice. Generally, they are to be condemned."

Canon 35 An American Bar Association Canon of Professional Ethics adopted in 1937 that forbade the taking of photographs in the courtroom. Later Canon 35 was updated to include restrictions on radio and television. *See also* Canon 3A(7).

Canon plug *See* XLR connector.

Canons of Journalism The code of ethics developed by the American Society of Newspaper Editors in 1923.

canopy *See* canopy head.

canopy head A headline that covers several columns and often has second decks. Also called a *canopy.*

cans A slang term for headphones. Cf. headset.

canted shot A shot wherein the subject or object appears tilted away from the vertical.

cap □ A lens cover made from rubber, metal, or plastic. □ To cover a lens. Also called *capping.* □ An electronic device used to shield a television camera lens from stray light automatically. □ An abbreviation for *capital letter.*

capacitance (C) The property that permits the storage of an electrical charge. The unit of capacitance is the farad (f).

capacitance disc *See* video disc.

capacitor (C) A device consisting of two conductors separated by an insulator.

capacitor loudspeaker *See* electrostatic loudspeaker.

capacitor microphone *See* electrostatic microphone.

capacity The amount of information a storage device is able to hold or accommodate.

caper film An adventure film, usually containing the planning of a robbery, its execution, and the obligatory chase scenes.

capital □ An uppercase letter. Cf. lowercase. □ The initial letter of a sentence, proper noun, title, and so on.

cap line *See* ascender line.

capping *See* cap.

caps An abbreviation for *capital letters.*

caps lock The key on a typewriter or computer keyboard that causes only capital letters to be printed or displayed.

capstan □ The driven spindle in a tape machine—sometimes the motor shaft itself—that rotates in contact with the tape and meters the tape through the tape transport. □ Pertaining to the circuits and apparatus associated with the capstan to carry out the metering function. Cf. pressure roller.

capstan idler *See* pressure roller.

capstan modulator *See* modulator.

capstan oscillator An electronic device used to control the speed of the capstan motor in a videotape recorder.

capstan servo The servo mechanism that controls the startup and running of the capstan.

capsule □ A brief news report. □ A tape cartridge.

CAPTAIN Character and Pattern Telephone Access Information Network. The videotext system used in Japan.

captain The individual in charge of a production company's transportation requirements.

caption □ A title or explanation for a picture; usually above the picture. Also called *blocklines* and *figure legends*. Cf. cutline and legend. □ A headline in a newspaper. □ The descriptive text that accompanies artwork. □ A chapter or table heading. □ The words translating foreign languages superimposed at the bottom of motion picture frames. □ A British term for a title card.

caption roller A British term for a roller title.

caption scanner A British term for a graphics camera.

caption stand A British term for a graphics stand.

captive audience A group of individuals who are forced to listen to a radio station, commercial message, and so on, because they have little choice other than to leave. Occurs in a store or restaurant that plays music, often obviously selected by the employees.

captured keystrokes Manuscripts that are electronically recorded on disks or tape for direct computer typesetting instead of the conventional process requiring rekeyboarding.

capture effect The ability of an FM tuner to reject the weaker of two signals.

CAR Cable Television Relay. Formerly CARS.

CARA Classification and Rating Administration of the Motion Picture Association of America.

carbon (C) A nonmetallic, conductive element.

carbon arc An ac or dc arc source in which the arc is formed in air between a pair of electrodes. These electrodes—frequently carbon with additives—burn away and must be advanced during operation. *See also* arc light.

carbon copy A duplicate made with carbon paper.

carbon microphone A low-quality microphone that uses carbon granules.

carbon paper. A thin paper coated with lampblack that, when struck by typewriter keys, forms an impression on the paper behind it.

carbons The rods of carbon used in arc lights.

carbon tetrachloride A dangerous, toxic chemical formerly used as a film and equipment cleaning agent.

carbro process A carbon-bromide print process, usually made from three different colored negatives. Also called an *oxotype*.

car card A transit advertising sheet for display inside or outside a vehicle of public transportation. Car cards are generally 11 inches high by 28 inches long.

card □ A postcard. □ A piece of pasteboard. *See also* bristol board. □ A large advertising display. □ A note, published in a newspaper, containing an advertisement, statement, explanation, and so on. □ A card indicating union membership. □ *See* punched card. □ *See* printed circuit board. □ *See* title card.

card ad A card published in a newspaper.

cardboard A general term given to paper products that are thicker than normal paper.

cardboard engineer An individual who designs displays and packages.

card deck *See* deck.

cardholder An individual who has been given permission to borrow books from a library.

card image The representation of a punched card on computer disks or tape.

carding To increase the space between lines of type.

carding out To space slugs by the insertion of thin paper or other material. Also called *carding*. Cf. leaded.

cardioid microphone A microphone with a unidirectional, heart-shaped sound polar pattern. *See also* mike pattern.

card out *See* carding out.

card plate An advertising or table of contents page placed opposite a title page.

card punch A machine that punches holes in punched cards in designated locations to store data.

card rate The undiscounted cost of broadcast time or print media space as listed on the rate card.

card reader (CR) A machine that senses data on punched cards for transfer into computer memory.

card stand *See* easel.

caret The ‸ mark, used by proofreaders to indicate the place an insertion is to be made.

CARF Canadian Advertising Research Foundation.

caricature A picture or description that exaggerates or distorts a person or object, usually for humorous purposes.

Carnegie Commission A commission created in 1964 to study noncommercial television. Its report was instrumental in the passage of the Public Broadcasting Act of 1967.

carousel □ A device invented by Bill Moulic to automatically prepare cartridges for insertion and playback. □ A mechanism of a videocassette recorder designed to hold a number of cassettes and deliver them, on command, to a transport for recording or playback. Also spelled *carrousel.* □ A cartridge tape player used by automated radio stations. □ A circular tray designed to hold slides.

carpenter shop The motion picture studio department responsible for the construction of sets.

carriage □ The dissemination or retransmission of a broadcast signal by a cable television system. □ The transportation or conveyance of merchandise, as from a publisher to a library, bookstore, and so on.

carriage return (CR) A nonprinting character that causes the cursor of a CRT or the carriage of a printer to return to a preset left-hand margin.

carriage rule The FCC rule that required cable television systems to carry local television station signals. Cf. nonduplication.

carrier □ An organization that provides telecommunication service. □ A person who delivers newspapers. □ *See* common carrier. □ In a frequency-stabilized system, the sinusoidal component of a modulated wave whose frequency is independent of the modulating wave; the output of a transmitter when the modulating wave is made zero; a wave generated at a point in the transmitting system and subsequently modulated by the signal; or a wave generated locally at the receiving terminal that, when combined with the side bands in a suitable detector, produces the modulating wave. □ The unmodulated signal from the FM modulator of a videotape recorder. □ The J0 term of a Bessel function representing the spectral distribution of an FM signal during a relatively long period of constant luminance. □ A medium on which digital data or other information is stored or transmitted. □ The metal casting that holds a videotape head. □ The enlarger frame that holds the negative. □ *See* carrier wave.

carrier current □ The carrier wave current. □ A radio station, often found on college campuses, using wires for the dissemination of programming instead of a broadcast channel. *See also* campus radio systems.

carrier frequency The frequency of the carrier wave of a transmitter.

carrier power The average power supplied to the antenna transmission line by a transmitter during one radio frequency cycle under conditions of no modulation.

carrier presort Bulk mailings that are sorted by zip code and receive a discount from the postal service.

carrier-to-noise ratio (c/n) The ratio of the carrier magnitude to the noise magnitude of a signal.

carrier wave (CW) The transmitted radio wave that is modulated by the sound and/or picture information.

Carroll case The decision by the Court of Appeals for the District of Columbia that required the FCC to consider the subject of economic injury when the effect of another station would be detrimental to the public interest. Cf. Sanders Brothers case.

carrousel *See* carousel.

carryover *See* breakover.

carry-over audience *See* inherited audience.

carry-over effect The ability that advertising has on consumers to affect buying habits even after the advertising campaign has been completed through a delayed response effect or customer holdover effect.

CARS Community Antenna Relay Service. Now CAR.

CAR station *See* cable television relay station.

cart An abbreviation for an *audio-* or *videotape cartridge.*

CARTA Catholic Apostolate of Radio, Television, and Advertising.

carted Commercials, promos, and so on, that have been recorded on audio- or videotape cartridges.

Carter Mountain case The 1962 case wherein the FCC established jurisdiction over CATV by denying a microwave relay application of a cable television system.

Carterphone Decision The 1968 decision that allows telephone subscribers to purchase their own equipment and connect it to telephone company terminals.

carting The process of dubbing or recording material onto audio- or videotape cartridges.

cart machine A device that is able to play back audio or video cartridges, and, in many cases, record cartridges. Extensively used in radio stations for promos, commercials, and so on.

cartoon □ A motion picture produced by photographing a series of drawings by animation. □ A preparatory drawing or painting. □ A comic strip. □ A satirical or humorous drawing; a pictorial caricature, often political.

cartooning The production of a cartoon.

cartoonist An individual who draws cartoons.

cartouche □ An ornamental, scroll-like design. □ A decorative panel that may be used to outline a graphic. □ An obsolete term for a roll of paper.

cartridge □ The transducer located in a tone arm that changes the mechanical motion of the attached stylus into electrical impulses. □ A plastic or metal enclosure containing an endless loop of lubricated magnetic tape, wound on a rotatable hub in such a fashion as to allow continuous tape motion. *See also* cart machine, NAB-A, NAB-B, and NAB-C. Cf. cassette. □ A container with feed and take-up reels capable of being loaded with film or purchased already loaded with film.

cartridge machine *See* cart machine.

cartridge notches The coded notches on a film cartridge that provide the camera with light metering information.

cartridge paper A rough drawing paper.

cartridge tape A continuously looped audio- or videotape used in a cart machine. *See also* cartridge.

cartridge tape recorder *See* cart machine.

cascade A sequence of two or more devices, such as line amplifiers in a cable television system, in which the output of one feeds the input of the next.

case □ A shallow compartmented box used for holding type; the upper case for capital letters, the lower case for lowercase letters. *See also* California job case. □ An action in law or equity. □ A slipcase. □ To affix a cover to a book. □ To place pied type in its proper box in a case. □ An inflectional form of nouns, pronouns, and adjectives denoting the syntactic relationship between these words and other words in a sentence. □ Uppercase or lowercase letters.

casebound A hardcover book.

case in *See* casing in.

case law *See* common law.

case reporter *See* reporter.

case study A system of research or teaching that uses selected or precedent-setting cases. Used extensively in legal research and marketing.

cash buyer In direct marketing, a buyer who encloses the payment with the order.

cash discount The deduction from the cost of advertising allowed for prompt payment of agency bills, equipment, and so on.

cash flow The amount of money received by a business as compared to the amount of money spent; the difference is the cash flow.

cash option *See* cash rider.

cash plus An arrangement in which a station pays for a syndicated program but gives the syndicator several minutes of commercial time on the program as part of the deal.

cash rider An order form that offers installment terms but also contains a postscript that offers the option of sending full cash payment with order. Usually it provides a savings over the credit price as an incentive. Also called *cash up* and *cash option.*

cash up *See* cash rider.

casing The plastic housing for an audio- or videotape cartridge or cassette.

casing in The process of inserting and fastening a hardcover book to its cover. Also called *case in. See also* hardbound.

Cassandra A computerized program analysis system acquired by the A. C. Nielsen Company in 1980. With a database of pure program and time period trend data going back for more than three years, all report periods, Cassandra is designed to provide telecast information for selected programs on a market-by-market basis. Available programs include syndicated, network, local news, local movies, and local sports. Output data can include household data and all NSI-reported or derivable demographics for the selected program, for comparison with lead-in, lead-out, competition, or prior history in a variety of formats.

cassegrain antenna An antenna design that incorporates a waveguide and a secondary reflector to direct the signal to the main reflector. Used extensively in satellite communication.

cassette From the French for "K-7." □ An assembly composed of a case and one or more spools for storing or reeling tape and designed to be put into a transport for automatic playback or recording. Also called a *cassette player, cassette recorder,* and *cassette tape recorder.* Cf. cartridge. □ A plastic or metal film cartridge. A small film magazine containing two spools.

cassette player *See* cassette.

cassette recorder *See* cassette.

cassette tape recorder *See* cassette.

cast □ The performers engaged in a production, motion picture, and so on. Also called a *cast list.* □ To assign the parts in a script to actors, performers, talent, and so on. □ A list of the parts in a play. □ An abbreviation for *newscast.* □ To stereotype or electrotype. □ A slug or other molded metal used for printing purposes. □ To calculate the amount of manuscript copy required to fill a certain area when set in a specified type size. Also called *fit.* □ The hue of a photograph.

cast breakdown A list of the roles in a motion picture, television program, radio show, or other medium used by agents, casting directors, and so on.

cast coated A coated paper stock with a high gloss.

cast commercial A radio or television commercial acted out by members of the program to which it belongs. Cf. star commercial.

caster Any machine that sets type.

casting □ A plate made by pouring molten metal over a mat or matrix. *See also* stereotype and electrotype. □ The process of selecting talent. *See also* audition, booking, call, and call-back.

casting box A box used for making casts for stereotypes.

casting copy *See* casting off.

casting couch An imaginary piece of furniture (usually a bed) on which aspiring young actresses are encouraged to have affairs with men who can help them get acting breaks.

casting director The individual or member of a studio in charge of selecting actors and actresses for the roles in motion pictures, television programs, and commercials.

casting files The cross-indexed files kept by directors, advertising agencies, and so on, containing the names, ages, characteristics, and other details about talent.

casting off The process of calculating how much column space or what number of pages a given amount of copy will take when set in a specific size of type. *Cast off* is used as frequently. Also called *casting copy, copyfit,* and *copyfitting.* Cf. scaling.

casting tape *See* audition tape.

cast list *See* cast.

cast off *See* casting off.

CAT Computer aided typesetting.

CATA Community Antenna Television Association.

catadioptric lens A long focal length camera lens that uses mirrors and reflective and refractive elements to shorten the lightpath in the lens.

catalist cinema *See* cinema verité.

catalog □ A book or booklet showing merchandise with descriptions and prices. □ A publisher's list containing the books currently in print. □ To index a set of items by author, title, subject, computer file, and so on. Also called a *directory.* □ A library card file, by author, title, or subject. □ To make a list or catalog. Also spelled *catalogue.*

catalog buyer A person who has bought products or services from a catalog.

Cataloging in Publication (CIP) A program established by the Library of Congress in 1971 wherein publishers provide galleys or first typeset proofs to the Library so that they may be cataloged.

catalog request A request for a catalog by a prospective buyer.

catalogue A now less-used spelling of *catalog.*

catchlight □ A small spotlight used for highlighting. Also called an *eyelight.* □ Reflections caused by bright objects.

catchline □ An identifying line at the top of a news story. Also called a *guideline. See also* slug. □ A line within a news story designed to attract the attention of the reader. □ A line in a play designed to make the audience laugh. □ A line at the bottom of a page containing a catchword.

catchword □ A word at the bottom of a page that repeats the first word of the following page. This practice is seldom used today. □ The first word of an entry in a dictionary; as in this entry, the word *catchword.* □ A word printed at the top of a dictionary page to allow entries to be found more easily; usually the first or last defined term on the page. □ A word that cues an actor.

catchword entry The most important or easily remembered word entry in a catalog, list, or index of book titles.

catharsis A classical theory that pity and fear can be purged by vicarious participation in viewing aggression.

cathode (K) □ A negative electrode. □ The element in a vacuum tube that emits electrons. Cf. anode.

cathode ray The stream of electrons emitted from the cathode of a vacuum tube under the influence of a magnetic field.

cathode ray oscilloscope (CRO) A test instrument that transforms electrical energy into a light display for viewing the signals passing through a circuit.

cathode ray tube (CRT) A vacuum tube in which electrons from a cathode are directed to a luminescent screen that glows in direct proportion to the intensity of the light. *See also* pickup tube. Cf. picture tube. □ A video display device.

cathode sputtering *See* sputtering.

CATI Computer assisted telephone interviewing.

catoptric Light produced by reflection.

CATS Center for Advanced Television Studies. A British organization.

cattle call A casting call for a large group of actors or extras.

CATV □ Community antenna television. □ Cable television.

CATV system *See* cable television system.

CATV Task Force The former name of the FCC Cable Television Bureau.

catwalk An overhead walkway allowing access to flies, lights, and so on, on a stage or in a large studio. Also called a *walkway.*

CAV □ Component analog video. □ Constant angular velocity.

caveat emptor Literally, from the Latin for ''let the buyer beware.'' A consumer warning for ''as is'' merchandise, restricted by consumer protection and deceptive advertising laws.

cavity The inside of a square, rectangular, or circular waveguide.

CB □ Citizens band. A land-mobile service. □ Circuit breaker.

CBA □ Catholic Broadcasters Association. □ Commonwealth Broadcasting Association. A British Commonwealth association of national public service broadcast organizations. □ Christian Booksellers Association.

C band The frequencies from 4 to 6 gHz. Used for satellite communication. Cf. Ku band.

CBBB Council of Better Business Bureaus.

CBC □ Canadian Broadcasting Corporation. A national broadcasting organization. □ Commonwealth Broadcasting Conference of the British Commonwealth.

CBEMA Computer and Business Equipment Manufacturers Association.

CBI Cumulative Book Index.

CBN □ Christian Broadcasting Network. □ Commonwealth Broadcasting Network.

CBO Control board operator.

CBS Columbia Broadcasting System. The second major broadcasting network launched in the United States, founded in 1927 by the United Independent Broadcasters with financial support from the Columbia Phonograph Record Company.

CBU Caribbean Broadcasting Union.

CC □ Closed captioning. □ Commercial continuity. □ Controlled circulation.

CCA □ Citizens for Cable Awareness. □ Controlled circulation audit.

C-cart *See* NAB-C.

CCB Common Carrier Bureau (of the FCC).

CCBS Clear Channel Broadcasting Service.

CCC □ Citizens Communication Center. □ Copyright Clearance Center.

CCD Charge coupled device.

CCD camera A video camera using a CCD instead of a pickup tube.

CCF Catholic Communications Foundation.

CC filter Color compensating filter used in color photography and for making color prints.

CCI □ Co-channel interference. □ Chambre de Commerce International (International Chamber of Commerce).

CCIF Comité Consultatif International Téléphonique (International Telephone Consultative Committee). An intergovernmental organization.

CCIR Comité Consultatif International Technique des Communications Radioélectriques (International Radio Consultative Committee). An intergovernmental organization.

CCIR standards The recording and reproducing specifications outlined by the CCIR.

CCIS Coaxial Cable Information System. A Japanese multipurpose cable system.

CCIT Comité Consultatif International Télégraphique (International Telegraph Consultative Committee). An intergovernmental organization.

CCITT International Telegraph and Telephone Consultative Committee. An intergovernmental organization.

C-clamp An adjustable metal clamp made in the shape of a *C* so it fits over a pipe. Often used to hang luminaires.

CCMM Council on Children, Media, and Merchandising. A citizens' group.

C copy *See* C roll.

C county An A. C. Nielsen designation for any county other than an A or B county that has either more than 35,000 inhabitants or that is in a metropolitan area with more than 35,000 inhabitants. *See also* county size. Cf. A county, B county, and D county.

CCRT Closed circuit radio transmitter.

CCS Continuous Commercial Service. The rating of components used by broadcast stations.

C/CS County/Coverage Service.

CCT Committee for Competitive Television. An association of UHF broadcasters.

CCTA Canadian Cable Television Association.

CCTI Committee on Children's Television, Inc. A citizens' group.

CCTS Coordinative Committee for Transmissions by Satellite.

CCTV Closed circuit cable television or closed circuit television.

CCU Camera control unit.

CCW Counterclockwise.

CD □ Complete drawing. □ Compact disc. □ Creative director.

cd Candela.

CD-DA Compact disc-digital audio.

CD-DA track An audio track.

CD device driver The lowest software level to handle CD drives. The only software to communicate directly with the CD control unit; it resides in ROM on a CD-I player.

CD disc master A CD master disc, produced by exposing a photosensitive coating on a glass substrate to a laser beam. The laser is modulated by the digital program information from the CD master tape, together with subcode, which is generated during the disc mastering process from the subcode cue code, also on the CD master tape. The exposed coating is developed, covered with a silver coating, and then nickel-plated to form a metal father recording mold.

CD-FM A CD file manager.

CD-4 A recording and playback system for discrete discs encompassing four channels. Also called a *quadradisc.*

CD graphics In CD-DA, a technique for generating text, still pictures, or animated graphics related to the music. The graphic information is recorded in subcode channels R-W. Not related to the graphics facilities of CD-I.

CD-I Compact disc-interactive.

CDI-X An extended form of the CD-I format able to accommodate more functions than can base case players and discs.

CDL A computerized videotape editing system.

CD-ROM Compact disc-read only memory. A format standard for placing any kind of digital data on a compact disc; the underlying structure for both DVI and CD-I. CD-ROM discs use a beam of laser light to follow data tracks on the CD and can store as much as 648 megabytes of data. Basically the same as a CD audio player mechanism.

CD-RTOS Compact Disc-Real Time Operating System.

CdS Cadmium sulfide. A photochemical compound used in light meters.

CdS meter A through-the-lens light meter used in some 8, super 8, and 16 mm cameras using CdS technology.

CD-V Compact disc-video.

CE Chief engineer.

cease and desist An order from a court or administrative agency to stop and not begin again any prohibited action. FCC cease and desist orders are issued under Section 312 of the Communications Act. *See also* show cause order.

CEC Centre Européen de la Culture (European Cultural Center). An international organization.

Cecil Award, Russell L. An award given to the media by the Arthritis Foundation for outstanding writing on the subject of arthritis.

CEE The International Commission on Rules for the Approval of Electrical Equipment.

Ceefax The British teletext system.

CEEM Council for Education on Electronic Media; formerly COBE.

CEG Consumer Electronics Group of the EIA.

CEI Commission Electrotechnique Internationale. An international organization. Also IEC.

cel □ A sheet of cellulose acetate used for titles and graphics. Also spelled *cell.* □ A thin, flexible, transparent sheet of acetate that has been punched, onto which the animators' finished drawings are transferred—either by inking or xerography—and painted. The clear cel does not show when photographed, so when it is placed over the background, the characters appear to be within the setting.

cel animation An animation technique in which the figures to be animated are drawn and painted on cels, placed over a background, and photographed frame by frame. Cel animation has been the standard technique for studio animation since its invention in 1915.

cel flash *See* flash.

cell □ *See* cel. □ One compartment of a battery. □ An abbreviation for *photocell.* □ The smallest unit of computer memory, capable of storing a single bit. □ A small homogeneous group within a larger sample. □ A geographic area used in cellular radio.

cel level The position of a cel when more than one cel is positioned on the animation table pegs.

cellular radio A mobile telephone system that uses low-powered transmitters in small geographic areas called cells. The calls are automatically switched from cell to cell as the user moves. Also called a *cellular telephone* and *cellular mobile.*

celluloid □ Cellulose nitrate. Formerly used as a film base. *See also* acetate. □ An obsolete slang term for a motion picture. □ *See* cel.

cellulose A complex polymeric carbohydrate used in film bases.

cellulose acetate *See* acetate.

cellulose nitrate A substance used in making lacquer discs.

cellulose triacetate The most common form of film base.

cel sandwich A combination of three or more cels.

Celsius A temperature scale wherein the freezing point of water is 0 degrees and the boiling point is 100 degrees. Also called *centigrade*.

cement An adhesive used for film splicing.

cement splicer A film splicer that uses a solvent (cement) to join overlapped film joints.

CEN Central Educational Network.

censor A person charged with deleting objectionable or illegal materials from scripts. *See also* continuity acceptance.

censorship An act of prior restraint prohibiting the publication of information. *See also* gag order. Censorship of radio and television stations by the FCC is forbidden by Section 326 of the Communications Act. *See also* prior restraint.

census □ A survey in which one canvasses all sampling units in the frame. □ An enumeration of every member of a statistical population. Cf. survey and poll.

census tract A geographical area that has clearly identifiable boundaries and that contains a relatively homogeneous population segment of about 1200 households.

center □ The middle of a set, picture, lens, page, and so on. □ *See* centered.

center channel A monophonic combination of the left and right stereo channels.

centered A line of type with equal white space on each side. Also called *center* and *center justified*.

centered dot □ A bullet used as an ornament to highlight words, paragraphs, and so on. □ A raised period used to separate letters or syllables.

centerfold □ A center spread that unfolds to reveal two more pages. □ A type of center spread made famous by *Playboy* magazine.

center frequency □ The average frequency of the emitted wave when modulated by a sinusoidal signal. □ The frequency of the emitted wave without modulation.

center headline A centered headline.

centering control The horizontal or vertical control that moves the entire television picture. Also called a *framing control*.

center justified *See* centered.

center of attention The talent or object that is emphasized by camera shots or movement.

center of interest That portion of a picture to which the viewer's attention is drawn.

center pin The cylindrical projection on a turntable that fits into the hole in a disc.

center-span tension A calculated value of the tape tension at a point midway between the tape entrance and exit guides of the scanner in a videotape recording system.

center spread □ An advertisement that fills the two facing pages in the center of a newspaper or magazine. Also called a *double spread, double truck,* and *spread*. Cf. double truck. □ Two outdoor billboards containing advertisements from the same company.

center stage □ The place on a set where the main action takes place. □ The middle of a stage or set. □ For a performer to be the center of attention. □ The center of attention in artwork.

center up A director's command to a camera operator to adjust the picture so the talent or object is in the middle of the screen.

center weighted Through-the-lens metering that places greater weight to the center of the object being photographed.

centigrade (C) *See* Celsius.

centile One of the 99 points that divide a frequency distribution into 100 equal parts. Cf. decile and percentile.

centimeter candle *See* phot.

central character The protagonist in a story, program, screenplay, and so on.

central masking The masking of a sound in one ear caused by noise in the other ear.

central microprism A series of small prisms used in a viewfinder focusing mechanism to accomplish precise focusing.

central office exchange The switching and processing office of a telephone company or other communications network.

central processing unit (CPU) The unit of a computing system that controls and coordinates the circuits containing the arithmetic, logic, and control units.

central tendency A numerical measure of the mean, median, or mode of a frequency distribution.

Centrex The telephone equipment in a central office exchange that services subscribers' PABX systems.

Centronics cable A 25-wire cable used for connecting computers to printers.

CEPT Comité Européen de Poste et Télégraphe (European Conference of Postal and Telecommunications Administrations). An intergovernmental organization.

ceramic microphone A microphone element made of barium titanate. Similar to a crystal microphone.

ceramic pickup A phonograph cartridge element made of barium titanate. Similar to a crystal pickup.

Certificate of Compliance (COC) Formerly, the authority from the FCC for the operation of a cable television system or for the carriage of additional television broadcast signals. No longer required. *See also* franchise.

Certificate of Rating *See* Classification and Rating Administration (CARA).

certification The acceptance by a government agency or standards bureau of an individual's qualifications or equipment compliance to specified standards.

Certified Radio Marketing Consultants (CRMC) A media sales representative accredited by the Radio Advertising Bureau.

certiorari A writ of a superior court calling up the records of an inferior court or an administrative agency.

CETS Conference Européene des Telecommunications par Satellites.

cf. An abbreviation for *compare with.*

CFA Call for Action. A citizens' group.

CFDA Christian Film Distributors Association.

C format A type of one-inch helical scan videotape format.

CFR Code of Federal Regulations. The official codification of the rules of administrative agencies.

CG Completion guarantor.

CGO An abbreviation for *can go over.*

CGS Centimeter-gram-second. The three basic units of the metric system of measurement.

CH ☐ Channel. ☐ Character. ☐ Critical hours.

chain ☐ An audio signal path in a control console, including the input, potentiometer, key, and preamp. ☐ A company that owns two or more newspapers, bookstores, theatres, and so on. ☐ *See* camera chain. ☐ *See* film chain. ☐ *See* chain broadcasting.

chainbreak ☐ The time during which a network-affiliated station identifies itself. ☐ A commercial delivered during this time.

chain broadcasting The original name for network broadcasting. The simultaneous transmission of an identical program by two or more connected stations. *See also* network.

chaining The linking of segments of computer programs so that the next required segment is called for automatically.

chain line *See* chain mark.

chain mark One of the wide lines in watermarked paper. *See also* laid paper.

chair A seat of authority; sometimes refers to a newspaper editor.

chairman One of the members of the FCC, FTC, or other administrative agency designated by the president to serve as the chief executive officer of the agency.

chalk To mark a performer's position.

chalk engraving A printing process accomplished by stereotyping a drawing etched on a chalk-covered metal plate.

challenge ☐ A copyreader's notification to an editor of doubt concerning the authenticity of a news story. ☐ The contesting of a broadcast station's license renewal application by a citizens' group; often accomplished by filing a competing application. *See also* mutually exclusive.

chamfered splice A film splice made with the ends of the film beveled instead of overlapped.

chance One of the three elements that constitute a lottery, wherein each participant has an equal likelihood of being selected. Cf. consideration and prize.

change To vary the emphasis, mood, tempo, and so on, of a speech or program.

change of venue A motion requesting that a legal case be transferred to another judge, court, or location.

changeover The change from one projector or VTR to another at the end of a reel.

changeover cue A small dot or other mark placed in the upper right-hand corner of a film frame to indicate the time to start the motor on the other projector. At the second mark, the actual changeover is accomplished. Also called *changeovers* and *projection cue.*

changeovers *See* changeover cue.

changer *See* record changer.

changing bag A flexible, lightproof, cloth bag used for loading and unloading film when a darkroom is not available.

channel □ A signal path for conveying information. □ Any communication link between two points. □ A link between two data terminals. □ An electronic path along which signals are sent. □ A complete set of recording or playback equipment. □ An individual signal path, especially a signal path dedicated to the conveying of signals to or from a record or playback head. *See also* head channel and audio channel. □ A portion of the spectrum designed to carry the information from one broadcasting station. *See also* clear channel, local channel, and regional channel. □ *See* class I, class II, class III, and class IV cable channel. □ A complete sound signal path; for example, stereo systems have two channels. □ In compact discs, data blocks within a real-time record can be labeled according to logical "channels" that can be selected in real time. It is by selecting these channels that the user can change audio, video, and text sources during the playing of a real-time record. □ *See* cable channel.

channel balance The varied programming received within a community from the different broadcasting stations or cable television systems.

channel capacity □ The maximum rate at which information can be transmitted on a given channel of communication. □ The number of channels or signals available to subscribers of a cable television system for current or future use. The number of channels and the services available are normally established by agreement between the franchising authority and the cable television system.

channel compatible Any advanced television system that would be contained within the standard 6 MHz bandwidth of a television channel.

channel letters Sheet metal letters with recessed surfaces designed to accommodate incandescent lamps or luminous tubing.

channel noise Any interference or disturbance in the transmission or reception of a message, from static to blurred printing.

channel piggybacking *See* piggyback.

channel research Research into one or more aspects of the mass media.

channel selector □ The control used to select the desired channel on a receiver. Cf. tuning control. □ The person who selects the radio or television program to be listened to or viewed.

channel separation The difference between the left and right stereo channels or the four channels in quadraphonic sound.

chapbook An obsolete term for a small book containing popular literature.

chapel A local union organization of workers in a printshop.

chapter A main division of a book, thesis, and so on.

chapter heading The heading printed at the beginning of a chapter.

chapter opening The number and title of a chapter.

character □ An individual role in a production. □ A type of performer, such as a gangster or old man. □ Any one of a set of symbols: alphabetic, numeric, punctuation marks, or other special symbols. *See also* byte. □ An animated cartoon animal or individual.

character actor A performer who plays other than straight roles.

character animation The art of making an animated figure move like a unique individual; sometimes described as acting through drawings. The animator must understand how the character's personality and body structure will be reflected in its movements.

character code A specific combination of bits used to represent a standardized byte for each printed character. Systems of character codes include ASCII and EBCDIC.

character compensation *See* tracking.

character considerations One of the four basic qualifications for a broadcast license. *See also* financial considerations, technical considerations, and legal considerations.

character count The number of characters and spaces in a manuscript. Cf. unit count.

character generation The appearance of an alphanumeric typographical image on a display screen.

character generator □ An electronic device that prints text to a display screen for photocomposition. □ An electronic device that keys in letters or symbols directly on a television screen.

characteristic curve A diagram relating the response between film density and exposure. Also called the *D log E curve* and *H and D curve.*

characteristic frequency A frequency that can be easily identified and measured in a given emission. For example, a carrier frequency may be designated as a characteristic frequency.

characterization The act of exhibiting the individual qualities of a character in a play or script.

character pitch □ The distance between successive characters. □ The number of characters per inch in a line of text.

character printer A typewriter or printer that prints one character at a time. Cf. line printer.

character recognition The electronic sensing of handwritten, printed, or otherwise reproduced characters for use by a computer.

character reel A tape or soundtrack of one actor's speaking role.

character set The characters and other symbols found on a standard typewriter. *See also* extended character set.

character sketch A drawing of a proposed animated cartoon character. Cf. action sketch.

characters per pica The number of characters of a specified point size and type face that will fit in one pica. A pica is one-sixth of an inch, or 72 points.

character string A group of characters. *See also* string.

character style The features of a type face that distinguish it from others.

charge □ The electrical energy stored in a battery or capacitor. □ To restore power to a battery.

charge coupled device (CCD) A semiconductor image detector designed to replace a television camera tube.

charger An electrical device used to convert alternating current into direct current for the restoration of power to a battery.

charge sheet A list of newspaper advertising charges. *See also* rate card.

chart A music industry trade paper list of the bestselling records of the week.

charted A musical recording that has appeared on record charts.

charting the showing The process of selecting the individual panel distribution on city streets for outdoor advertising. This process involves specific requests from the buyer and is planned to achieve maximum reach and frequency.

chase □ An overused action wherein one character pursues another, usually in cars. Also called a *chase scene.* □ The rectangular metal frame in which printing plates are locked up to make a page.

chase film A motion picture characterized by a number of chases or one long, often interminable chase.

chaser □ A new newspaper page with updated information or corrections for replating. □ Music used to mark a performer's exit.

chaser lights A linear string of lamps wired in several circuits; equally spaced lamps (generally four or five apart) are connected to the same circuit; because the circuits are sequentially energized, spots of light appear to be chasing along the string.

chase scene *See* chase.

chassis A metal frame or box used for mounting electronic components.

chatter The distortion caused by the vibration of a stylus in a groove.

C head A third-level subhead.

cheat □ The movement of a performer away from another performer to allow for a better camera angle. Also called *cheat the look* and *counter.* □ To deprive an audience of the facts necessary to solve the crime in a whodunit.

cheat shot □ A camera shot using a cheat. □ A tight camera shot used to eliminate the necessity of building a larger set.

cheat the look *See* cheat.

check □ To verify information, equipment, and so on. □ The step in production in which all elements of a scene are examined and checked against the exposure sheet to ensure they are correct before being filmed. In studio animation, the person responsible for this step is the checker.

checkbook journalism The payment of large sums of money to well-known individuals in return for exclusive interviews or for news information. Considered less than ethical.

checker □ In animation, the person assigned to review the completed cels before they are photographed. □ *See* check.

checkerboard □ A television programming practice that places programs of the same or similar types in the same time period during the week. Cf. stripping. □ A unit of magazine advertising that consists of quarter pages or spread half pages placed in diagonal opposition.

checkerboard assembly *See* checkerboarding.

checkerboard cutting *See* checkerboard editing.

checkerboard editing The preparation of a reel of film for checkerboarding by inserting leader in the proper positions on the A and B rolls.

checkerboarding □ A method of preparing film or tape for use. Odd-numbered scenes or sounds are placed on one roll, usually designated the A-roll, and the even-numbered scenes on the other roll, the B-roll. The two rolls are then processed or electronically edited together. Also called *checkerboard assembly.* □ The practice of scheduling two or more different television programs in the same time slot during the week.

checking □ The process of verifying the printing, broadcasting, showing, and so on, of advertising. □ Physical inspections in each market to choose the outdoor advertising structure to be included in a contract or to verify that the delivery meets contract specifications.

checking copy A copy of a publication sent to an advertiser as proof an advertisement was run. Cf. tear sheet.

check light An indicator light signifying an error or problem in equipment. Cf. tally light.

checklist □ An interviewer's list of items to be accomplished. □ *See* flash cards. □ A list of items that are necessary for a remote, location shoot, and so on.

checkout A procedure for maintaining inventory control over equipment.

check print An examination print of a film made by a laboratory for testing and evaluation.

cheesecake A publicity photo of an attractive model or actress. Sometimes called *leg art.* Cf. beefcake.

cheese roll *See* quarter roll.

chemical booster *See* booster.

chemical fade A type of fade made by immersing film in a chemical solution frame by frame; each frame is held in the solution for an increasing length of time.

chemical fog Film fog caused by overdevelopment.

chemical paper Paper made entirely from a chemical pulp without groundwood. Cf. groundwood paper.

chemical printing *See* lithography.

chemical pulp A paper made from wood by using a sulfite, sulfate, or soda process. Cf. groundwood pulp.

chemistry The indefinable interaction that takes place between two performers who work well together, such as Bogart and Bacall, and Laurel and Hardy.

cherry picker □ A large, wheeled ladder with a cage built into the top for working on scenery, lights, and so on. □ A large, motorized camera crane.

cherry picking The selection of television or satellite signals for distribution on a cable television system from a number of sources on a program-by-program basis as opposed to full carriage.

cherry pie Money, in addition to regular wages, earned as overtime or for additional jobs.

cheshire labels Specially prepared paper used to reproduce names and addresses to be mechanically affixed, one at a time, to a mailing piece.

chest shot The same as a bust shot in picture dimensions.

chevron pattern *See* azimuth recording.

chiaroscuro The effect of light and shadow without regard to color.

chief engineer (CE) The person in charge of the engineering department of a broadcast station.

chief operator A person with an FCC radiotelephone operator's permit who, together with the licensee, is responsible for the technical operation of a broadcast station.

children For the purposes of copyright, a person's immediate offspring, legitimate or not, and any children legally adopted by that person.

Children's Program Review Committee A former NBC committee organized to review children's television programs.

Children's Television Workshop (CTW) An independent production company that produces such programs as "Sesame Street."

chiller A motion picture or television program that is designed to send "chills up your spine."

chilling effect The result of a court interpretation that restricts the First Amendment to the U.S. Constitution by imposing limits on the freedom of expression.

chimney A vent on a large carbon arc luminaire.

china girl A slide or film of a girl's face used for checking television color and/or alignment.

chinagraph *See* china marker.

china marker A grease pencil used to mark film and tape edit points.

china paper A thin, soft paper made from bamboo.

chinese A camera movement combining a dolly or a zoom out and a pan left or right. *See also* camera movement.

Chinese style A book that has thick, uncut leaves. Also called *Japanese style.*

chinese turn A camera movement that moves through a complete 360-degree arc. *See also* camera movement.

chip □ A monochrome test pattern for television alignment. □ The material removed from the recording medium by the recording stylus while it cuts the groove. Also called *swarf.* □ *See* integrated circuit.

chipboard An inexpensive substitute for binder's board.

chip camera A television camera that uses light-sensitive chips instead of pickup tubes.

chip chart A gray scale test pattern used to adjust television cameras.

chippy A slang term for a studio carpenter.

chi square A measure of statistical validity, often used in communication research.

chiz biz An abbreviation for *chiseling business. See also* payola, plugola, and double billing.

choke □ An inductive device used to impede the flow of electric current. □ To forget or blow a line due to nervousness. *See also* goof. □ An accumulation of paper in a newspaper press, often caused by a break.

choke point The point at which subscribers to magazines, cable television services, book clubs, and so on, become saturated.

chop *See* chopmark.

chopmark A symbol used by printers as a trademark attesting to the quality of the product. Also called a *chop.*

choreographer A person who creates and directs the execution of dances.

CHR Contemporary hit radio.

christmas tree □ A pattern on a television picture tube caused by the failure of the horizontal oscillator. □ A pattern on a disc caused by a beam of light.

chroma The saturation of a color without white. Cf. hue, intensity, and luminance.

chroma control A device for controlling the amount of color saturation.

chroma crawl The moving of the edges of a saturated color in a television picture.

chroma flutter A picture fault characterized by a rapid nonsynchronous fluctuation of chrominance level.

chromakey A television special effect that electronically uses a monochromatic color background to key the insertion of another background picture. Deep ultramarine blue commonly is used for the background when the foreground involves people. This process is analogous to the traveling-matte systems used in motion picture photography. *See also* color key.

chroma noise □ Noise appearing predominantly in the portion of the video spectrum conveying chrominance information. Also called *color noise.* □ The picture fault resulting from such noise. □ A picture fault characterized by unwanted hue and chrominance shifts, usually at a scan-line rate. Often called *streaky noise.*

chroma streaking *See* streaky noise.

chromatic Pertaining to color.

chromatic aberration A lens aberration caused by the refraction of white light into colors. *See also* achromatic lens.

chromaticity The hue and saturation aspects of colored light considered together; it is independent of the brightness aspect.

chromatic scale The musical scale consisting of half tones.

chrominance The colorimetric difference between any color and a reference color of equal luminance; the vividness of an image. Expressed as U and V signals. Cf. luminance.

chrominance channel The red, green, or blue channel used in color television.

chrominance signal The portion of the color television signal containing the color information. Cf. luminance signal.

chrominance subcarrier The carrier that is modulated by the chrominance information.

chromium dioxide (CrO_2) A magnetizable substance often employed as the magnetizable medium in high-coercivity tapes.

chronograph camera A camera capable of being triggered at intervals for time studies.

chronophotography A method of analyzing an action by taking pictures of moving subjects at predetermined intervals.

church law The ecclesiastical law developed in England as opposed to common law.

churn The turnover of cable television subscribers as a result of disconnects and new customers.

churn rate A numerical statement of the number of changes in cable television households during a churn period.

CHUT Cable households using television. A cable television rating similar to HUT.

Chyron A trademark for a brand of character generator that has become almost generic for all character generators.

CI □ Column inch. □ Color index.

CICR Comité International de la Croix Rouge. Also ICRC.

CICT International Technical Control Center. The EBU center for technical coordination.

CIE Commission International d'Éclairage (International Commission of Illumination).

CIESJ Centre International d'Enseignement Supérieur de Journalisme. A UNESCO documentation center.

CIE system Commission Internationale d'Éclairage (illumination). A set of standards for color specifications and descriptions.

CIM Conseil International de la Musique. Also IMC.

CIN Cooperative Information Network. An electronic link between libraries.

cinching Tangential slippage between tape layers occurring when a loosely wound reel of tape is subjected to high rotational acceleration or deceleration. This interlayer slippage usually results in physical damage to the tape, manifested in a series of scratches, buckles, creases, or folds in the areas that have slipped.

cinch marks Random vertical scratches on film often caused by tight winding or pulling too hard on the end of a roll of film.

CINE Council on International Non-Theatrical Events.

cine An abbreviation for *cinema.*

cineaste An eager and insatiable film buff.

cine camera A camera capable of exposing a number of frames of film at a constant rate in rapid sequence.

cinedome A circular motion picture theatre with a domed roof.

cine film Film in a number of widths or gauges containing perforated film stock wound on a core or reel.

cinema From the Greek *kinema,* meaning "motion." □ A motion picture. □ A motion picture theatre. □ The motion picture industry. □ The art of making motion pictures. □ An abbreviation for *cinematograph.*

cinemacrography The cinematography of small objects.

cinema noir *See* film noir.

cinema novo A Brazilian film movement that combines melodrama and fantastic subjects.

CinemaScope The first extensively used wide-screen filming system. A wide aspect ratio of 2.35:1 is squeezed horizontally by an anamorphic lens to fit a standard 1.33:1 film frame.

cinematic time Compressed or expanded time for the purposes of dramatic necessity. Cf. real time.

cinematograph A motion picture camera or projector.

Cinematographe A motion picture camera, printer, and projector invented by the Lumiere brothers in France.

cinematographer The film supervisor responsible for lighting and photography. Also called a *lighting cameraman* and *director of photography.*

cinematography The art or technique of motion picture photography.

cinematology The study of film.

cinema verité A style of documentary filmmaking characterized by location shooting using mobile equipment and often off-camera direction and narration. Also called *catalist cinema.* Cf. direct cinema.

cinemicrography Microscopic cinematography.

Cinemiracle A wide-screen process developed in the 1950s by National Theatres, an organization of exhibitors. *See also* wide-screen.

cinemobile A self-contained, mobile vehicle used for filming on location.

Cineorama An early form of a 360-degree projection system using 10 cameras. Cf. Circarama.

cinephile A film buff.

Cinerama A wide-screen process that used three synchronized cameras and three synchronized projectors. Later became an anamorphic system.

cine structuralism *See* structuralism.

cinetabs *See* trim tab.

cinex A short series of film frames printed with various exposures to allow the camera operator to judge the camera exposure. Also called a *cinex strip* and *control strip.*

cinex strip *See* cinex.

CIP Cataloging in Publication.

CIP data *See* Cataloging in Publication.

CIP information *See* Cataloging in Publication.

cir An abbreviation for *circuit, circulate,* and *circulation.*

CIRC Cross-Interleaved Reed-Solomon Code.

circa (ca) From the Latin meaning "about" or "around." Often used to list approximate dates.

Circarama A 360-degree wide-screen system used in Disneyland, similar to Cineorama, but smaller in scope.

circle in *See* circle wipe.

circle of confusion The blurred image around a light source caused by the inherent aberration of a lens. Also called the *circle of least confusion.*

circle of least confusion *See* circle of confusion.

circle out *See* circle wipe.

circle wipe A special effect used to replace one picture with another by wiping in or out from the center. Also called *circle in* or *circle out.*

circuit □ An electronic path between two or more points. □ An electronic path interconnecting two or more pieces of equipment; as a talkback circuit. □ A path for conducting electrical energy to a device such as a lighting instrument. □ A chain of motion picture theatres. □ A number of theatres at which a traveling troupe performs.

circuit binding A book binding with rounded corners. *See also* divinity circuit binding.

circuit board *See* printed circuit board.

circuit breaker (CB) An automatic device for opening a circuit to prevent damage to a component. Cf. fuse.

circuit court A court that has jurisdiction over more than one judicial district. *See also* court of appeals.

circuit diagram *See* schematic.

circuit edges *See* circuit binding.

circular A general term for a flyer, leaflet, insert, and so on, usually advertising or promotional pieces intended for wide distribution.

circular file A slang term for a wastebasket; a repository for unsolicited manuscripts, screenplays, and so on. Also called *file thirteen.*

circular polarization A pattern of polarization in an antenna; used extensively for FM antennas and proposed for television antennas.

circulating library A library, usually privately owned, that rents books to subscribers or the public. Also called a *lending library* and *rental library.*

circulating system The system of pumps and pipes used in film-processing equipment to circulate the chemicals to and from storage and replenishing tanks.

circulation □ The number of subscribers to a newspaper, magazine, journal, and so on. Cf. readership. □ *See* circulation department. □ The activity of lending books and other materials from a library to borrowers. □ The number of households or individuals, regardless of where they are located, that are estimated to be in the audience of a given television or radio network or station at least once during some specified period of time. Cf. coverage, frequency, and reach. □ The number of television households or individuals that tune to a broadcast signal or cable signal during a day or week. □ *See* cumulative audience. □ The count of potential viewers to determine the value of the outdoor advertising medium. Traffic volume is obtained by counting the number of pedestrians and automobiles passing any advertising structure during a specified time period, and the number of persons riding in mass transit vehicles.

circulation area The geographic area that is covered by a broadcast station, newspaper, flyer, and so on. Cf. coverage area.

circulation department The department in charge of newspaper or periodical distribution. Also called *circulation.*

circulation director A newspaper employee who is in charge of increasing the paper's circulation.

circulation guarantee The minimum number of copies of a periodical that are to be sent or delivered to subscribers.

circulation promotion The efforts made to maintain or increase circulation.

circulation research A study designed to elicit information concerning print media circulation.

circumlocution A wordy, redundant statement or expression.

circus *See* circus make-up.

circus make-up A newspaper page format with various styles and sizes of type, multiple headlines, and so on, resulting in an inconsistent appearance. Also called a *circus.*

CIRM International Radio Maritime Committee.

CIS Congressional Information Service.

CISAC Confederation Internationale des Sociétés d'Auteurs et de Compositeurs (International Confederation of Authors' and Composers' Societies).

CISPR Comité International Spécial des Perturbations Radioélectriques (International Special Committee on Radio Interference).

citation A footnote or other indicator of the source of material. A citation normally includes the author, title, publisher, place of publication, date of publication, volume number, and so on. A legal citation may appear in the form 319 U.S. 190, indicating Volume 319 of the United States Reports (Supreme Court), page 190.

citizens band (CB) A range of frequencies authorized for short-range communications by the general public.

Citizens Communications Center (CCC) case The 1971 decision by the Court of Appeals for the District of Columbia that overturned the 1970 FCC renewal policy statement.

city circulation The number of newspapers delivered or sold within a metropolitan area.

city desk The desk or office of a city editor in a newspaper.

city edition The final edition of a morning newspaper intended for delivery in a metropolitan area. Cf. mail edition.

city editor The newspaper employee in charge of local news and local reporters.

city room The local newsroom of a newspaper, presided over by a city editor.

city symphony A motion picture that contained camera shots of ordinary street life.

city western A slang term for a gangster film.

city wire A major press association's wire serving a large city and carrying news of special interest to that city.

civil law The laws that govern the private rights of individuals. Cf. criminal law.

Civil Rights Act The statute of 1964 that created the Equal Employment Opportunity Commission (EEOC) to attempt to eliminate discrimination in employment.

CJS Corpus Juris Secundum. A legal encyclopedia.

ck An abbreviation for *check*.

cladding A covering for the core of an optical fiber.

claim A statement made in an advertisement or commercial for a product or service.

clambake A badly produced, directed, or acted program or rehearsal.

clamper A device that functions during the horizontal blanking or sync interval to fix the level of the picture signal at some predetermined reference level at the beginning of each scanning line.

clamping A process that establishes a fixed level for the picture signal at the beginning of each scanning line.

clap board *See* clapstick.

clapper The grip who operates a clapstick. Also called a *clapper boy*.

clapperboard *See* clapstick.

clapper boy *See* clapper.

clapstick Two hinged boards that, when struck together, make a sound used for synchronization. Also called a *clap board* and *clapper board*. *See also* slate.

claque A group of devoted fans; formerly, members of an audience paid to applaud a performer or performance.

Clarion Awards Awards given by Women in Communications Inc. (WICI) for creative work in women's rights, the environment, and community service.

Clarke orbit *See* geostationary orbit.

Class I cable television channel A signaling path provided by a cable television system to relay to subscriber terminals television broadcast programs that are received off-the-air, are obtained by microwave, or are obtained by direct connection to a television broadcast station.

Class II cable television channel A signaling path provided by a cable television system to deliver to subscriber terminals television signals that are intended for reception by a television broadcast receiver without the use of an auxiliary decoding device and that are not involved in a broadcast transmission path.

Class III cable television channel A signaling path provided by a cable television system to deliver to subscriber terminals television signals that are intended for reception by equipment other than a television broadcast receiver or by a television broadcast receiver only when equipped with auxiliary decoding equipment.

Class IV cable television channel A signaling path provided by a cable television system to transmit signals of any type from a subscriber terminal to another point in the cable television system.

class I outside station A commercial television station or superstation that delivers at least 50 percent or greater net weekly circulation in an ADI other than its home ADI, Sunday through Saturday, 6 a.m. to 2 a.m. Cf. class II outside station.

class II outside station A commercial television station, superstation, or cable-originated television programming that delivers a 20 percent to 49 percent net weekly circulation in an ADI other than its home ADI, Sunday through Saturday, 6 a.m. to 2 a.m. Cf. class I outside station.

class I station An AM dominant station operating on a clear channel and designed to render primary and secondary service over an extended area and at relatively long distances with an operating power of not less than 10 kW nor more than 50 kW.

class II station An AM secondary station operating on a clear channel and designed to render service over a primary service area that is limited by and subject to such interference as may be received from a class I station. Class II stations are designated II-A, II-B, or II-D.

class II-A station An unlimited time class II AM station operating on a clear channel with a power of not less than 10 kW nor more than 50 kW.

class II-B station An unlimited time class II AM station other than those included in class II-A operating within a power of not less than 250 watts nor more than 50 kW.

class II-D station A class II AM station operating daytime or limited time with a power of not less than 250 watts nor more than 50 kW.

class III station An AM station that operates on a regional channel and that is designed to render service primarily to a principal center of population and the rural area contiguous thereto. Class III stations are designated as class III-A or class III-B.

class III-A station A class III AM station operating with a power of not less than 1 kW nor more than 5 kW.

class III-B station A class III AM station operating with a power of not less than 500 watts nor more than 1 kW night and 5 kW daytime.

class IV station An AM station operating on a local channel and designed to render service primarily to a city or town and the suburban and rural areas contiguous thereto with a power of not less than 250 watts nor more than 250 watts nighttime and 1 kW daytime.

class A group, set, or category of persons or items sharing common attributes.

class A Commercials used in 21 or more cities or 2 or more of the major cities.

class AA line A telephone company line ordered for continuous use having a frequency range from 50 to 8000 Hz.

class AAA line A telephone company line ordered for continuous use having a frequency range from 50 to 15,000 Hz.

class A channel The 20 FM channels designated in Title 47 of the *Code of Federal Regulations* (CFR), paragraph 73.206 (a)(1) for use by class A stations.

class action suit A suit brought by a person or group affected by a law in which the outcome of the suit affects all others similarly involved. Also called a *class suit.*

Class A library binding A book that meets the standards for library books as set by the Library Binding Institute and the American Library Association.

class A line A telephone company line ordered for continuous use having a frequency range from 100 to 5000 Hz.

class A station An FM station designed to render service to a relatively small community, city, or town and the surrounding rural area with an effective radiated power of not more than 3 kW.

class B Commercials used in 6 to 20 cities exclusive of New York, Chicago, and Los Angeles or used in one of these cities and 9 other cities.

class BB line A telephone company line ordered for occasional use having a frequency range from 50 to 8000 Hz.

class BBB line A telephone company line ordered for occasional use having a frequency range from 50 to 15,000 Hz.

class B-C channels All of the FM channels from 222 to 300 except for those listed in Title 47 of the *Code of Federal Regulations* (CFR), paragraph 73.206.

class B line A telephone company line ordered for occasional use having a frequency range from 100 to 5000 Hz.

class B station An FM station that operates on a class B-C channel and is designed to render service to a sizable community, city, or town or to the principal city or cities of an urbanized area and to the surrounding area with an effective radiated power of not more than 50 kW.

class C Commercials used in 1 to 5 cities, exclusive of New York, Chicago, and Los Angeles.

class catalog *See* classed catalog.

class C line A telephone company line ordered for continuous use having a frequency range from 200 to 3500 Hz.

class C station An FM station that operates on a class B-C channel and is designed to render service to a community, city, or town and large surrounding area with an effective radiated power of not more than 100 kW.

class D line A telephone company line ordered for occasional use having a frequency range from 200 to 3500 Hz.

class D station A noncommercial educational station operating on channels 201 through 220 with no more than 10 watts transmitter power output.

classed catalog A library catalog arranged by subject or classes. Also called a *class catalog.*

class E line A telephone company line ordered for occasional use having a frequency range from 300 to 2500 Hz.

classic A work of excellence that has withstood the test of time.

classical cutting A picture taking or editing style characterized by dramatic and emotional emphasis.

classic western *See* western.

classification □ A system of arranging books in a library by classes. □ The categorization of government secret documents into various classes: top secret, secret, confidential, and so on. *See also* classified materials.

Classification and Rating Administration (CARA) of the Motion Picture Association of America A full-time rating board composed of seven people headed by a chairperson that rates feature films as G, PG, PG-13, R, or X. The X may be self-applied by pornographic filmmakers; the other ratings are registered and cannot be used unless the film has been submitted for rating.

classified Newspaper or magazine advertisements grouped by subjects. Also called *want ad, line ad,* and *classified ad.*

classified ad *See* classified.

classified advertising Advertising appearing in a newspaper or magazine classified section and subdivided into want ads, for rent, help wanted, and so on.

classified materials Government documents and other materials not available to the public or the media.

classified section The part of a newspaper or magazine set aside for classified advertising.

classifier A person in charge of classification, for example, in a library or advertising department.

classify To identify and systematically arrange like items according to predetermined criteria.

class magazine *See* class publication.

class of emission The set of characteristics of an emission, designated by standard symbols, for example, type of modulation, modulating signal, or type of information to be transmitted.

class publication A periodical designed to appeal to a specific group of individuals with common interests. Also called a *class magazine.*

class rate The cost of broadcast time for the different time periods. Sometimes designated as class AAAA, AAA, AA, A, B, C, or D, depending on the individual network or station. Class AAAA time has the highest rate; class D, the lowest. *See also* rate class.

class suit *See* class action suit.

class time *See* class rate, rate book, rate card, and rate class.

claw The camera or projector mechanism that moves the film by engaging the perforations. Also called a *pulldown.*

clay animation An animation technique involving the use of pliable clay figures that are manipulated before each exposure. Also called *Claymation.*

Claymation A trademark for clay animation.

Clayton Act The 1914 statute that directed the Federal Trade Commission (FTC) to prevent unfair methods of competition in commerce. *See also* Wheeler-Lea Act.

c/lc Capital and lowercase letters. Also spelled *c and lc.*

clean □ A signal that is free from static, noise, distortion, and so on. □ *See* clean copy. □ *See* cleaning.

clean copy Copy that needs little or no revision. Also called *clean* and *good copy.*

clean cue A fade in or take of music or sound effects without a wow or other distortion.

clean effects *See* clean sound.

clean entrance □ An unobtrusive entrance onto a stage or set made by a performer. □ To roll tape or film before the action begins to allow for smooth edits.

clean exit To continue to roll tape or film after the action ends to allow for smooth edits.

clean feed A network or remote feed that is technically acceptable; without interference.

cleaning The process of correcting or removing a name and address from a mailing list because it is no longer correct or because the listing is to be shifted from one category to another.

clean it up To revise directions, camera shots, talent movement, and so on, during a rehearsal in order to alleviate problems.

clean proof A manuscript proof that is without errors.

clean rough A layout in which major elements of a printed page, poster, advertisement, and so on, are sketched in considerable detail.

clean sound Background sound without anything added.

clean tape A typesetting tape without errors or extraneous codes.

clean type Type set without errors.

cleanup The process of retracing the animators' rough, sketchy drawings and converting them into finished drawings with smooth outlines that can be transferred to cels. In studio animation, this is done by the cleanup artist. *See also* roughs.

cleanup artist *See* cleanup.

clear □ To obtain the rights to use copyrighted music, scripts, and so on. Also called *clear a number* and *close the rights.* □ To make a radio or television station time available to a network or advertiser. □ A recording that is crisp, bright, and lacking in distortion. □ A film or television set ready for action. □ A newspaper or magazine department that has finished its work for an edition or issue. □ To reset or erase computer memory. Cf. hold.

clearance □ The rights obtained to use a literary, dramatic, or musical work on radio or television. □ The acceptance of a network program by an affiliate. □ The release of a motion picture to an exhibitor or exhibition company. □ The purchase of a syndicated program by a television station.

clear and present danger A test devised by Justice Oliver Wendell Holmes in 1919 that states that freedom of expression can be suspended if the words used are of such a nature that they may bring about substantive evils that Congress has a right to prevent.

clear a number *See* clear.

clear channel An AM channel on which a dominant station or stations render service over wide areas without objectionable interference. Clear channel stations are designated as class I, class II, class II-A, or class II-B. Originally, a clear channel had only one station assigned to it.

Clear Channel Broadcasting service (CCBS) An association of radio broadcasters operating clear channel stations.

clearing bath A bath used in film processing to eliminate any residue from a previous solution.

clear leader Transparent film leader.

clear the frame A command similar to "ready on the set."

clear time To arrange for free air time with a radio or television station or network.

CLeaR-TV Christian Leaders for Responsible Television. A citizens' group.

clear yourself A direction to a performer to move so that the camera view is not obstructed by another performer or object.

CLGA Composers and Lyricists Guild of America. A labor union representing employees in motion pictures and television.

cliché An overworn, trite phrase or situation. Also called a *bromide.*

clicker A British term for a compositor.

click stops The detents built into a lens housing so that the f stop settings may be felt.

click track A timing device used when elements of the soundtrack are added after the animation has been completed. The beat to which the animation is matched is recorded onto tape and played through earphones for the conductor, sound effects creator, and/or voice artists, enabling them to match their sounds to the film.

client □ An individual or organization that employs a business manager, advertising agency, public relations firm, and so on. □ A potential or actual sponsor or advertiser.

clientitis An allergy developed by television directors (and others) when advertisers or sponsors decide to "help."

cliff hanger A suspense-filled dramatic program.

climax The point in a story at which the conflict or situation is resolved.

Clio An award given by the American TV and Radio Festival to recognize excellence in radio and TV advertising.

clip □ A short piece of film or tape. Also called a *cut* and *trim.* □ To cut off abruptly. □ An abbreviation for *clipping.* □ An item cut out of a newspaper or magazine. Also called a *cutting.* □ A story filed in a news library. □ *See* film clip.

clip art □ Commercially prepared artwork sold on sheets or in books ready to photograph or cut out and use. □ A computer program designed to produce clip art.

clip book A book of clip art.

clipper A potentiometer on a video switcher used to adjust a television key.

clipping □ The removal of a portion of a signal above and/or below a selected level by a limiter. □ The removal of the portion of a CRT display that is too large for the screen. □ The loss of the beginning and/or ending of sounds; usually on voice-activated devices. □ An item cut out of a newspaper or magazine. Also called a *clip.* □ *See* stock shot. □ *See* network clipping.

clipping bureau A commercial service that clips items in various categories from numerous newspapers, magazines, and journals and sells them to clients.

clipsheet □ A prepared sheet resembling a newspaper page containing publicity material, news stories, fillers, photographs, and so on, that may be used by a newspaper. □ *See* clip art.

clock □ A device that synchronizes the operation of components in an electronic system. □ A device that counts hours, minutes, seconds, and frames in video editing. □ A digital electronic device that generates pulses at fixed intervals to control the timing of events in a computer system. *See also* synchronization.

clock format *See* wheel.

clocking A technique used to permit the synchronous transmission of data at high speed.

clock speed The rate of timing pulses in a computer.

clock time □ The time on the frame in a videotape editing system that uses time code. □ *See* real time.

clogged head A tape head with a built-up residue of oxide causing tape damage, loss of picture, or noise.

clogging □ The accumulation of debris on a pole tip, usually through removal of oxide and binder from the tape. It creates increased separation between pole tip and tape, resulting in a partial or complete loss of signal. □ The picture fault thus caused.

clone □ A television program that is in many ways identical to another; a copy of a successful program. □ A computer that is made to conform to the operating system developed by another company, usually an IBM clone.

cloning The unauthorized manufacture of a chip to decode encoded satellite or other signals.

close □ To finish work on a newspaper edition or magazine issue. *See also* put to bed. □ The standard conclusion of a radio or television program. Also called *closing.* Cf. outro.

close bolt A style of book binding in which the edge folds are left uncut.

closed A newspaper page that is locked up and ready for printing.

closed architecture A design for a device that is complete; one that will not accept additional components or circuits. Cf. open architecture.

closed captioning (CC) A system of visual messages, actually encoded captioning, that contains messages for the hearing impaired. Sent during the vertical blanking interval. CC requires a special decoder to be seen.

closed circuit A television distribution system wherein monitors are connected to the studio by coaxial cable or microwave. Cf. broadcasting.

closed end A series of books containing a set number of volumes. Cf. open end.

closed-end diary A type of diary listing specific time segments for each broadcast day to be covered by a survey. Cf. open-end diary.

closed-end item A set of alternative responses for an interview question.

closed-end question *See* fixed-alternative question.

closed-end series *See* miniseries.

closed-loop system A system containing automatic feedback so that the system is always in synchronization, output remains the same, and so on.

closed-loop tape system A tape transport that contains a capstan and pinch roller on each side of the tape heads.

closed negotiation A restricted negotiation between a broadcast station or station representative and a buyer when either the station air time is sold out or the buyer desires more time than is available for sale. No price negotiation is available to the buyer. Cf. open negotiation.

closed set A rehearsal, taping, or live broadcast not open to an audience.

closed shelf A library that does not have open stacks for access to users. Cf. open shelf.

closed shop A workplace in which union membership is required for continuing employment. Cf. open shop.

close on A performer working near a microphone.

closer □ The ending words of a television standupper, track, or package. □ The closing announcement or segment of a radio or television program.

close shot *See* close-up.

closet drama A script more suitable for reading than production.

close the rights *See* clear.

close up To tighten loose type or to make one word out of two.

close-up (CU) A tightly framed camera shot showing details of a person or object. Also called a *close shot. See also* camera shots.

close-up camera A television camera reserved for taking close-ups.

close-up lens *See* meniscus lens.

closing *See* close.

closing credits The credits that may appear at the end of a television program or motion picture, often those for technical staff or secondary characters. Cf. opening credits.

closing date The last day on which a publication will accept an advertisement to appear in a specific edition or issue. Sometimes called a *deadline*. Cf. cancellation date.

closing hour The last time during a day on which a radio or television station will accept a commercial. Similar to a closing date except that the deadline time is often shorter.

closing shot The final shot of a motion picture, television program, commercial, and so on, which may vary from a long shot in a motion picture to a close-up in a commercial. Cf. opening shot.

cloth *See* book cloth.

clothbound A book bound in cloth with stiff boards. A hardbound book.

clouding A television picture condition caused by a scene with too much contrast.

cloze procedure A method of testing readability by leaving out words or letters to be filled in by the reader.

clr An abbreviation for *clear*.

clubbing Two magazine subscriptions purchased at less than the cost of the individual subscriptions.

clump A British term for a slug.

clumping The depositing of silver salts in clumps during the development process.

cluster □ A sampling unit that represents two or more elementary units in a survey. □ A group of advertisements or commercials.

clustering □ The sequential presentation of news stories that have a common or similar theme. □ The joining of the operation of two or more cable television systems. □ The location of two satellites in approximately the same geostationary orbit.

ClusterPlus A market segmentation system developed by Donnelley Market Information Services that profiles a market or audience by 47 different lifestyles.

cluster sample A survey sample wherein the sample elements are groups of units and not individual units. Each element is identified with only one cluster in the selection process. *See also* probability sample.

CLUT Color look-up table.

CLUT animation In CD-I, a technique used to impart motion to graphic objects by repeatedly changing the data in the color look-up table. For CLUT-coded images, the 256 values in the CLUT control the colors of the entire image; therefore, some simple animation effects are possible simply by redefining some or all of the CLUT contents as a function of time.

clutter The total of all the messages, announcements, station identification, and other nonprogram elements aired by a television station or cable channel. *See also* overcommercialization.

CLV Constant linear velocity.

CM □ Centimeter. □ Commercial matter.

CMA Country Music Association, Inc., The. A professional organization of the country music industry.

CMOS Complementary metal oxide semiconductor. A technology for making large scale integration (LSI) chips that feature extremely low power consumption.

C-mount A standard screw-in lens mount.

cmp An abbreviation for *computer.*

cmptr An abbreviation for *computer.*

CMSA Consolidated Metropolitan Statistical Area.

CMTT Commission Mixte CCIR/CCITT pour les Transmissions Télévisuelles et Sonores. An intergovernmental organization.

C/N Carrier-to-noise ratio. Also CNR.

CNN Cable News Network.

CNR Carrier-to-noise ratio. Also C/N.

C-O Company owned. *See* O&O.

coach A vocal, dramatic, dialect, or other type of tutor hired to work with performers, actors, and so on.

coarse screen A halftone screen with 100 or fewer dots per linear inch; used for printing newspaper pictures.

coated *See* coated paper.

coated cover A paper stock suitable for magazine and brochure covers.

coated lens A lens that has a transparent film of magnesium fluoride or calcium fluoride to reduce light loss.

coated offset A coated paper suitable for offset printing.

coated paper Paper that has been coated with a mineral-based substance to give it a smooth finish. Also called *art paper* and *coated stock.*

coated stock *See* coated paper.

coater A coating used on compact discs.

coating □ The thin, transparent layer of magnesium fluoride or other material applied to the outer surface of a lens to reduce reflection. Also called an *antireflection coating.* □ The emulsion applied to a film base. □ The layer of bonded, polished oxide on a magnetic audiotape. □ Of videotape, any substance applied to the base film, such as the magnetic coating or backside coating.

coating resistivity The electrical resistivity, stated in ohms per square unit, of the magnetic coating of a videotape.

coat out The process of covering a painted outdoor advertising message with white or gray paint before new copy is painted. *See also* paint out.

coax An abbreviation for *coaxial cable.*

coaxial cable A cable consisting of a conductor completely surrounding another conductor and separated from it by a solid dielectric or by air with spacing insulators. Also called *coaxial line* and *coax.*

coaxial line *See* coaxial cable.

coaxial speaker A loudspeaker that combines both a high- and a low-frequency unit or cone.

cobalt-doped oxide An oxide, usually gamma-ferric oxide, that has a higher magnetic coercivity as a consequence of having small quantities of cobalt added during manufacture.

cobalt doping □ The act of adding cobalt or a cobalt compound to the material destined for use as the magnetizable medium of a videotape. □ The cobalt or cobalt compound itself.

COBE Council on Broadcast Education. Now CEEM.

cobweb spinner A fan-driven machine used for special effects to spin spiderlike cobwebs from a rubber cement compound.

COC Certificate of Compliance. A former FCC file-number prefix for cable television.

co-channel The same channel as specified; for example, two broadcast stations authorized the same frequency would be called co-channel. Cf. adjacent channel.

co-channel interference Any interference caused by the operation of two radio or television stations on the same frequency.

cockled □ A bumpy or puckered paper surface. □ A puckered or wrinkled book or paper; usually resulting from dampness or uneven drying. Also called *cockling.*

cockling *See* cockled.

cocktail bar *See* sound truck.

cocktail party A sound effect in which a listener can hear a single conversation in a group.

code ☐ Any self-regulatory body of rules. ☐ A union talent agreement. ☐ The representation of data in symbolic characters. ☐ The instructions in a computer program. ☐ A set of symbols used to represent computer routines, functions, or instructions. Also called a *code set.* ☐ A system of signals used for communication. ☐ A system of characters or symbols used to represent words. ☐ A systematically arranged body of laws or regulations, such as the United States Code.

Code Authority Director The director of the Radio or Television Code of the National Association of Broadcasting who was responsible for the administration, interpretation, and enforcement of the code. The codes have been eliminated.

codec A combination of coder and decoder. A device that takes an analog television image and converts it into digital form for transmission by computer.

cod effects Sound effects that are exaggerated for a comic purpose.

code generator *See* time code generator.

code message A broadcast message not understandable by all listeners; a private communication. Forbidden by the FCC.

code number A number printed in ink on motion picture film for use in editing. Cf. edge numbers.

code of ethics A set of principles governing conduct and practices, such as the Outdoor Advertising Association of America, Inc., voluntary set of rules pledging member plants to operate for and in the public interest.

coder/decoder *See* codec.

codes Numbers or symbols used on a survey questionnaire for ease in tabulation.

code set *See* ASCII, code, DEC ASCII, and EBCDIC.

codex A manuscript; often refers to an ancient manuscript such as the Bible.

coding ☐ The classification of responses on a questionnaire, schedule, or diary according to specified rules, to facilitate their tabulation and summarization or to enable data processing. ☐ The marking of motion picture film with code numbers or edge numbers. ☐ Identifying devices used on reply devices to identify the mailing list or other source from which the address was obtained. ☐ A structure of letters and numbers used to classify characteristics of an address on a list. ☐ The process of inserting codes into manuscripts for computer-controlled typesetting.

coding form A sheet containing computer program instructions for use by optical character readers.

coding information byte In CD-I, the fourth and eighth bytes of subheader, indicating the exact data type of the sector.

coding machine A machine that prints edge numbers on film stock.

coedition An edition of a book published by two or more companies at the same time.

coefficient of variation A statistical measure equal to the standard deviation divided by the arithmetic mean.

coercive force The reverse magnetizing force needed to cancel the remanent magnetism of a magnetic material.

coercive practices The practices prohibited under Section 506 of the Communications Act, including threats of violence, intimidation, or duress; featherbedding; and so on.

coercivity That property of a magnetic material characterized by the maximum coercive force needed to cancel the largest remanent magnetism possible for that material, that is, the remanent magnetism resulting from saturation induction of the material. In magnetic tape, coercivity becomes an indicator of maximum energy available from a recorded tape.

coffee table book A slang term for a large, richly illustrated book that is designed to be displayed.

coherent light Single frequency, continuously advancing light waves. *See also* holography.

coherer The first detector of wireless waves, developed in 1890 by Edouard Branly of France.

coil A number of turns of wire.

coincidental interview A type of interview in which the respondent is asked to state behavior with regard to radio or television activity at the precise time the interview is being conducted, or perhaps the instant immediately prior to the time the interview began. Also called *coincidental measurement, coincidental rat-*

ing, and *coincidental survey.* Cf. recall interview.

coincidental measurement *See* coincidental interview.

coincidental rating *See* coincidental interview.

coincidental survey *See* coincidental interview.

coincidental telephone survey A coincidental interview carried out on the telephone.

coined word A word that is invented or fabricated, especially one that is a tradename for a product. Examples are Advil, Spring Air, Kleenex, and Frigidaire.

COL Computer oriented language.

col An abbreviation for *column.*

cold □ A performance or audition taken without specific preparation. Also called a *cold reading.* □ To begin a radio or television program without an introduction. □ A nonenergized circuit. Cf. hot. □ A mailing list that doesn't produce customers; a performer who does not draw an audience; a previous buyer who no longer responds to advertising; and so on.

cold boot *See* boot.

cold call A sales call made without a prior warning being given to the prospective advertiser.

cold color A color that goes toward the blue end of the spectrum so as to become unnatural; for example, green flesh tones.

cold composition Typesetting accomplished without the use of molten metal. Cf. hot composition.

cold copy News copy that is out-of-date.

cold drama A dramatic radio or television program without background or transition music.

cold light Light tending toward the blue end of the spectrum, such as fluorescent light.

cold mirror A dichroic coated surface that reflects light but transmits infrared so that the reflected beam contains less heat.

cold reading *See* cold.

cold start *See* boot.

cold type Type matter that is set by photographic or strike on methods instead of by molten metal. *See also* photographic type. Cf. hot type.

collage □ A montage obtained by combining multiple picture or light sources. □ Artwork made from piecing different elements together, often photographs, colored paper, and so on. Cf. montage.

collage film An animated film usually consisting of numerous cutouts, overlays, inserts, and so on.

collate □ To assemble individual elements of a mailing in sequence for inserting into a mailing envelope. □ A computer program that combines two or more ordered files to produce a single ordered file. Also the act of combining such files. Synonymous with merge as in merge-purge. □ To check the completeness and order of a book or manuscript. □ To examine the signatures or forms of a book for arrangement. □ To make a complete set of pages from many copies of pages. □ *See* gathering.

collateral Any visual materials used in sales presentations that are not prepared as part of the commercial or advertisement.

collateral service Any additional service, such as the preparation of brochures, market research, promotion, and so on, performed by an advertising agency for an additional fee.

collating *See* collate.

collating mark A mark placed on the outside fold of a signature to make it easier to collate a book.

collating posters The organization of individual outdoor advertising sheets in the sequence needed so that the bill poster can post the advertising message properly.

collator A machine used for matching or merging two or more punched card files, or for card selection from one file.

collected edition The publication of the works of a single author in uniform bindings.

collection An aggregation of books, motion pictures, videotapes, magazines, and so on, gathered in one place.

collective mark A symbol used by a group, organization, association, union, and so on, that serves as an identifying sign.

collective work A work, such as a periodical issue, anthology, or encyclopedia, in which a number of contributions constituting separate and independent works in themselves are assembled into a collective whole.

collector (C) The element of a transistor to which the charge carriers flow. Similar in function to the plate of a vacuum tube. Cf. base and emitter.

collect run A run in which a complete newspaper is printed each cycle instead of each half cycle. Effectively doubles the page capacity of a press. Cf. straight run.

college library collection The books and other manuscripts of a college or university library that support teaching and research.

college representative A book publisher's representative who calls on textbook users to promote current and new publications. Also called a *college traveler. See also* traveler.

college traveler *See* college representative.

collimator A device used to align, calibrate, and correct the light beams in lenses, viewfinders, and other optical equipment.

collodion A viscous solution of pyroxylin used in film emulsions.

collotype *See* photogelatin.

colophon □ Originally, the information at the end of a book detailing the designer, typeface used, paper stock, and so on. □ A book publisher's trademark or imprint. Also called a *press mark.* Cf. printer's mark.

color □ An encompassing term referring to the characteristics of light other than spatial and temporal inhomogeneities; principally, the aspect of hue, saturation, and brightness. Object color involves the capacity of a surface to modify the color of light. □ The different wavelengths of the spectrum that appear to the eye as varying hues. *See also* additive primary colors, chroma, intensity, luminance, and saturation. □ The subtractive primary colors. □ The setting used to describe or indicate a mood or atmosphere. □ The historical, statistical, and incidental information used during periods of temporary inactivity in a play-by-play sports broadcast. □ Colored artwork or printing. □ To bias or exaggerate news, reports, publicity, and so on. □ Color photography as opposed to black and white.

coloration The change in a pure sound by the individual characteristics or resonances of a microphone or loudspeaker.

color balance □ The balance between the colors produced by two or more television cameras. □ The adjustment made within a television camera or receiver to compensate for the different efficiencies of the three color scanning beams. □ A design factor in indoor or outdoor film made to correct for the difference in color temperature between sunlight and incandescent or fluorescent light. *See also* color correction filter. □ A measure of the difference in colors in a print or slide to one another.

color balancing filter A filter used to change the color of a luminaire, enlarger, and so on. Also called a *color temperature filter.* Cf. color correction filter.

color banding A change in hue running horizontally across a television picture. Also called *hue banding* and *hue shift banding. See also* banding.

color bars An electronically generated set of color standards, set by the SMPTE, used as a reference to test the chrominance of a videotape recorder. Also called *steps.*

colorblind film Film stock sensitive to one color instead of three.

color breakup A brief separation of a color picture into its component colors caused by a rapid movement of the camera or talent.

color burst A special color-synchronizing signal transmitted to enable the receiver to separate the color information from the other signals.

color cards A set of different colored strips used to check the color balance of film. Similar in function to color bars.

colorcast An outdated term for a television program broadcast in color.

color chart □ A card containing both color cards and a gray scale. □ A chart containing samples of the standard colors, as approved by the Bulletin Color Conference sponsored by the OAAA. It is available from paint manufacturers for use as a guide for designing painted advertising structures or wall surfaces.

color chips Color samples painted on wood, plastic, or paper that are sent to outdoor advertising plant operators to enable them to match colors for artwork in which nonstandard colors have been used. Also called *color swatches*.

color code A set of colors that represent numbers; for example, for resistors, black, brown, red, orange, yellow, green, blue, violet, gray, and white represent the numbers 0 through 9, respectively.

color commentator A sportscaster who supports the play-by-play announcer with statistics, highlights, background information, and so on. Also called a *color man*.

color compensation filter *See* color correction filter.

color conversion filter *See* color correction filter.

color corrected lens A lens corrected for chromatic aberration.

color correction The changing of tonal qualities of objects by the use of gels, filters, lights, and so on.

color correction filter (CC) A filter used to enable daylight film to be used with tungsten lamps or to enable film balanced for tungsten light to be used with daylight. Also called *color compensation filter*, *conversion filter*, and *color conversion filter*. Cf. color balancing filter.

color crosstalk A low-frequency pattern in a color television picture.

color cylinder A printing couple used to print color on one side of a web.

color decoder The television receiver circuit that derives the color signal from the color picture signal and the color burst.

color difference signal The television signal produced by the difference between a color signal and the luminance signal. Usually designated as R-Y, B-Y, and G-Y.

color edging Unwanted colors outlining other colors in a television picture.

colored news News that is written to make it more interesting to the reader.

color encoder The circuit in a television transmitter that combines the camera signals and the chrominance subcarrier into the color picture signal. Cf. color decoder.

colorer *See* opaquer.

color fidelity The degree to which a color film or television picture reproduces the colors of the actual scene.

color film Film with one or more emulsions sensitive to color.

color filter A filter that allows only one color of light to pass. *See also* color correction filter.

color flicker The disturbance in a television picture that results from the fluctuation of both chrominance and luminance.

color form The printing plate used to print one color.

color frame A metal housing used to support color media at the front of a luminaire.

color fringing The spurious chromaticity that causes colors to become separated.

color guide A sketch prepared by an artist as a guide in preparing color plates from black and white copy.

color image The image formed on color film.

colorimeter A device used for matching colors visually.

colorist A British term for an animation opaquer.

colorize To use computer techniques to color existing black and white motion pictures.

colorizer □ An electronic device used to convert a monochrome signal into any desired color. □ An electronic device capable of converting monochrome pictures into colored pictures.

color key □ A system based on pixel-by-pixel color matching to control overlay transparency. A technique in which parts of an image are determined to be transparent based on the color values. Also called *chromakey*. □ *See* color model. □ The process of using separate acetate overlays to produce a colored picture.

color killer The circuit in a television receiver that removes the chrominance signal when a monochrome signal is received.

colorless filter *See* ultraviolet filter.

color lock A potentiometer on a videotape recorder that adjusts the phase of the color signal.

color look-up table (CLUT) A means of compressing the amount of information needed to store pictorial information by allowing only 256 colors (tints and brightness) and holding these absolute

RGB values in a table. The color of a given picture element or pixel is then defined as a value from this table, which contains all the colors that may be used in an individual picture. The picture is then encoded using the table addresses rather than absolute values. *See also* CLUT animation.

color man *See* color commentator.

color match The extent to which separate color sources are perceived to be identical, whether from a luminaire, through a lens, or by the eye.

color media Any colored transparent material that can be placed in front of a lighting instrument to color the light. These are often referred to as "gels" (for gelatin); cut glass and plastic materials are also used.

color meter *See* color temperature meter.

color model In animation, a representative drawing or cel of a character, with all of the colors labeled, that serves as a reference for the painters. Also called a *color key* and *model drawing.*

color noise *See* chroma noise.

coloroto A colored rotogravure.

color overlay A transparent overlay superimposed on black and white camera copy as a key for the addition of colors in printing.

color person *See* assistant sportscaster.

color picture signal The complete color television signal less the blanking and synchronizing signals.

color plate □ An illustration printed in color. □ A plate used to print one of a desired number of colors for such an illustration.

colorplexer The television signal encoding device. *See also* encoder.

color print A positive, full-color reproduction on photographic paper or in printed form.

color printing In the print media, the printing of any color, including black.

color proof A print made from plates to check their alignment and accuracy.

color radio A promotional term used to describe a "colorful" radio station.

color receiver A compatible television receiver capable of displaying color as well as monochrome pictures.

color registration chart A television aid used to align and test the accuracy of registration of triple-pickup color television cameras. The chart contains fine black horizontal and vertical lines on a white background.

color rendering index (CRI) A single-number, approximate evaluation of the effect of a light source on the visual appearance of colored surfaces.

color response The relation of the output of a television camera to the color of light or object seen.

color reversal film *See* reversal film.

color reversal intermediate (CRI) A procedure for making a duplicate negative without an intermediate positive.

color saturation *See* saturation.

color sensitivity The response of color film emulsions to the different wavelengths of visible light.

color separation □ The process of making single color negatives to produce color prints. □ One of the negatives made by the process. □ The use of dichroic prisms in color television cameras to form three separate color images on pickup tubes. □ The separation of colors from a color negative or internegative into three separate films.

color separation overlay (CSO) A British term for a chromakey.

color shading The use of color in a manuscript to emphasize material.

color signal A general term for a color television signal used for controlling the chrominance of the signal.

color subcarrier The color television signal that is added to the monochrome signal to carry color information.

color swatches *See* color chips.

Colortec An Ampex device for reducing the time errors in videotape playback.

color television Television pictures produced by the three primary colors of light as opposed to monochrome television. *See also* NTSC color, PAL color system, and SECAM.

color temperature The temperature of a blackbody that generates light with the closest visual color match to the source being specified.

color temperature filter *See* color balancing filter.

color temperature meter A meter designed to read the color temperature of light in degrees Kelvin. Also called a *color meter.*

color test Footage of a film that has been timed and that is used as a check to make sure that colors, characters, and backgrounds do not clash in the finished film. *See also* timing.

color timing The processing of color film so that the color tones are as close as possible to the original scene.

color toning The coloration of a black and white photograph.

color transmission The transmission of color television signals that can be reproduced with different values of hue, saturation, and luminance.

color transparency A color slide or other film viewed or projected by passing light through it.

color under A reduced-bandwidth method of recording color video signals that uses a filtered heterodyne down-conversion of the color subcarrier to generate a separated, lower-frequency chrominance signal. This lower-frequency signal is then directly recorded on the videotape without undergoing FM modulation.

color wheel □ A device holding several different color media that can be rotated by hand or motor to change the color in front of the luminaire. □ A wheel containing transparent material in the three primary colors that rotated in front of a television receiver designed by CBS in the 1940s. The RCA compatible system was adopted. □ An early 1900s process for color film using a two-color wheel.

colporteur A distributor of religious tracts and books. Also spelled *colporter.*

COLRAM Committee on Local Radio Audience Measurement. A National Association of Broadcasters committee for radio audience measurement problems and procedures.

COLTAM Committee on Local Television Audience Measurement. A technical advisory group to the NAB research committee.

COLTRAM Committee on Local Television and Radio Audience Measurement. A former NAB committee that combined the work of COLRAM and COLTAM.

Columbia Journalism Award A plaque given annually for distinguished service in the field of journalism by Columbia University.

columbian □ A 16-point type size. □ An early American printing press.

column □ A newspaper or magazine feature, usually with a byline. □ One of a number of vertical lines of type on a page. Cf. row. □ An area of print running down a page of a periodical, composed of lines of equal width. □ The typical or standard width of such an area of print, used as a measure of size for such a periodical.

column conductor One who conducts a column; an outmoded term for a columnist.

column guide A special aid used in desktop publishing to indicate the available space in a column.

column inch A measure of space on a printed page; the width of the column and one inch deep. Used especially to determine the cost of an advertisement.

column inch rate The cost for a column inch in a newspaper or magazine advertisement or other matter.

columnist A writer of a special newspaper or magazine column. Also called a *column conductor.*

column rule A vertical line printed between columns.

COM □ Committee for Open Media. A citizens' group. □ Computer output microfilm.

coma A nonaxial lens defect in which the image of a point appears as a comet tail.

comb filter A filter network that passes frequencies within a very narrow band.

combination Two or more pictures, films, cuts, and so on, used together. Also called a *combo.*

combination buy A media buy made at a combination rate.

combination commercial A television commercial that combines various techniques such as live action, a film, or the display of still photographs or drawings. Cf. integrated commercial.

combination cut *See* combination plate.

combination halftone *See* combination plate.

combination head A newspaper or magazine headline that extends over several smaller headlines.

combination microphone A housing containing two or more microphones.

combination plate A printing plate made from halftone and line negatives. Also called a *combination cut* and *combination halftone.*

combination rate A reduced rate charged to advertisers who buy space or time in two or more newspaper editions, magazine issues, broadcast stations, and so on. Also called a *combo rate.*

combination run A combination rate offered by printers who combine a number of smaller jobs on a large press and run them at the same time.

combination term contract A contract in which a contract player is employed under a contract for both television motion pictures and theatrical motion pictures.

combined audio harmonics The arithmetical sum of the amplitudes of all the separate harmonic components.

combined dupe *See* composite dupe.

combined move *See* compound move.

combined print *See* married print.

combiner A passive device that mixes two or more signals into one for distribution on a coaxial cable.

combining amplifier An amplifier that mixes two or more signals together.

combining filter An electronic device used to feed the output of two circuits into one input.

combo An abbreviation for *combination.* □ A radio station employee who functions both as an announcer and board operator. Also called a *combo operator* and *dual.* □ A small group of musicians.

combo operator *See* combo.

combo rate *See* combination rate.

comeback □ A sharp or witty response. □ To return to a former state, as in a situation in which an unemployed performer is again accepted for roles.

comedy A theatrical production, motion picture, television program, book, and so on, with a light and amusing plot, lines, and characterization, usually with a happy ending.

comedy-variety program A radio or television program of a unit series or a single unit program that consists of various entertainment elements, such as comic acts, sketches, and musical numbers. Also called a *variety program.*

come in To respond to a casting call.

come-on spot *See* teaser.

comet tail *See* lag.

comic book A magazine that contains one or more comic strips.

comic relief □ The emotional release given to an audience by a light moment in a serious drama. □ The performer who provides comic relief.

comic strip A panel of consecutive drawings presenting humorous situations and adventures; usually found in newspapers.

comic supplement A separate newspaper section, usually in color, containing a number of comic strips.

coming up □ The next program on a radio or television network or station. □ A warning command that a radio or television program is about to begin. *See also* standby.

comm An abbreviation for *communication.*

comma chaser A slang term for a copy editor.

commag Composite magnetic. A film with an optical soundtrack. Cf. comopt.

command □ The portion of a computer instruction to start, stop, continue, or change a program. □ A radio or television director's order to a production crew or individual to perform a required task immediately.

commentary □ The descriptive narration or opinion used to explain or expand upon news or action in a program. □ The material written or delivered by a commentator. □ The off-screen descriptive narration used to explain or expand upon the action in a program or motion picture. Also called *commentative sound.*

commentative sound *See* commentary.

commentator □ A radio or television news analyst who gives his or her own views about the meaning of political or other news events. *See also* editorial. □ A narrator.

commercial (C) □ A radio or television announcement that is paid for, as opposed to a public service announcement. *See also* commercial announcement. □ A short advertising or commercial message made as a motion picture and intended for showing over television. Advertising or commercial messages include any narration, dialogue, songs, jingles, or other matter that depicts or mentions the advertiser's name, product, or service.

commercial ad An advertisement contracted for by a business as opposed to an individual.

commercial announcement (CA) Any advertising message—including bonus spots, trade-out spots, and promotional announcements—for which a charge is made or other consideration is received, but not including commercial continuity (CC).

commercial art Artwork prepared for advertising purposes.

commercial audience The television or radio audience for a specific commercial.

commercial billboard A standard program opening or closing and standard lead-in or lead-out made for a designated radio or television program. Also called *program opening* and *program closing.*

commercial break An interruption in a radio or television program for a commercial.

commercial code number A series of four letters followed by four numbers used to identify a television commercial film print's sponsor and content; assigned by the originating advertising agency in accordance with a standard industry system.

commercial competition *See* competition.

commercial continuity (CC) The advertising message of a radio or television program sponsor.

commercial copy A sales message of an advertiser. Cf. commercial continuity.

commercial credit The specific naming of a sponsor or a product on radio or television.

commercial deadline The date and time after which no further advertising will be accepted by an advertising medium.

commercial delivery The exposure of a radio or television commercial measured by the size of the commercial audience.

commercial exposure potential The ratio of the number of receivers actually tuned to a radio or television station at the time when a commercial is delivered to the number of receivers able to receive the commercial.

commercial expression doctrine *See* commercial speech doctrine.

commercial FM translator An FM broadcast translator station that rebroadcasts the signals of a commercial FM radio broadcast station.

commercial impression A unit for measuring gross message weight, representing the exposure to a radio or television commercial. Cf. exposure and gross rating points.

commercial integration charge A charge made by a radio or television station or network for the inclusion of a commercial into its broadcast schedule. Cf. networking.

commercial killer A device that is programmed to delete commercials during the home videotaping of a television program.

commercial lead in The program segment that precedes the first commercial on a television program.

commercial load The number of minutes devoted to commercial matter in a given hour.

commercial matter (CM) Network and nonnetwork commercial continuity and commercial announcements.

commercial minute One minute of actual radio or television commercial time.

commercial occasion *See* occasion.

commercial pool The selection of a radio or television commercial that an advertiser has available for airing at any one time. Also called a *pool.*

commercial program A radio or television program that is paid for by a sponsor or by the sale of time for commercial matter.

commercial protection The amount of time or space between announcements or commercial messages for competing products or services.

commercial sign A privately owned advertising structure used on roofs, walls, or other outdoor areas of business establishments or factories for purposes of identification or direction.

commercial speech Speech that is used to promote goods and services for a for-profit organization.

commercial speech doctrine The doctrine developed in several court cases since the 1960s that places most advertising under First Amendment protection. Also called *commercial expression doctrine.*

commercial straight A nonintegrated radio or television commercial, delivered during a break in a program or during a station break.

commercial time *See* nonprogram material.

commissary The restaurant in a motion picture studio lot.

Commission A shortened version of the name for a federal administrative agency, such as the Federal Communications Commission, the Federal Trade Commission, or the Interstate Commerce Commission.

commission □ A state or local agency that assists film and television producers to obtain the use of facilities in their areas. □ An agent's or advertising agency's percentage of the sum paid to talent or paid for station time.

commissioned representative A print media sales representative who works on a commission instead of salary. Cf. house representative.

commissioned writer A writer who has a contract to write a particular script or series. Cf. freelance and staff writer.

commissioner One of the members of an administrative agency such as the Federal Communications Commission. Appointed by the president, with the advice and consent of the Senate, to serve for a period of seven years.

Commission personnel All members, officers, and employees of an administrative agency.

commitment A verbal or written agreement by talent to perform on a radio or television program.

Committee on Local Television and Radio Audience Measurements (COLTRAM) An organization founded in 1964 to review methodologies used in local rating services. Composed of research directors of major group stations, station representatives, and representatives of industry associations.

Committee on Nationwide Television Audience Measurement (CONTAM) An industry group established in 1963 to evaluate the network audience estimates then being provided by Arbitron and Nielsen. Originally composed of one representative from each of the three television networks, membership has been expanded to include broader network representation plus participation by the NAB.

commodity advertising Generic advertising for a class of products as opposed to advertising for a specific brand. Examples include Idaho potatoes, Wisconsin cheese, and Florida orange juice.

common carriage The prime time programs carried by most PBS stations at the same time. Also called a *core schedule.*

common carrier (CC) A communications service, such as a telephone company, that offers wire and/or microwave facilities for rates set by local, state, or federal government.

common custom The traditional practice of reporters to enter private places in which a newsworthy event is taking place without being liable for charges of trespassing.

common language A computer language, such as BASIC, that can be used on a number of different computers; portable language.

common law That body of law based on custom and usage or judicial decisions as opposed to law decreed by statute. Also called *case law, judge-made law,* and *discovered law. See also* stare decisis.

common law copyright The form of copyright eliminated by the general revision of the copyright law in 1976 (effective 1978). All copyright is now statutory.

Common Program Control Station (CPCS) An EBS primary station in an operational (local) area that is responsible for coordinating the carriage of a common emergency program for its area.

communication The use of language and nonverbal signs to establish social interaction.

communication band The band of frequencies occupied by the signal in radio communication.

communication by radio *See* radio communication.

communication by wire *See* wire communication.

communication channel □ A channel for the transmission of data between two physically separate points. □ Any means of communication, from a studio talkback system to a satellite downlink.

communication device Any electrical or mechanical device that allows the exchange of data between computer systems.

communication mix The use of two or more of the mass media for advertising, services, information, and so on.

communication overload The plight that exists when an audience, message recipient, or any recipient of messages can no longer process the meaning of conversation, television, bad news, and so on.

communication policy The existing and proposed laws, regulations, and plans for the technological, economic, and social development of the means of communication.

communications Two or more letters, messages, telephone calls, and so on. The process of communicating is the singular word *communication.*

Communications Act of 1934 The federal statute (47 USC 151 et seq.) that replaced the Radio Act of 1927 and established the Federal Communications Commission (FCC). The purpose of the act is to "make available, so far as possible, to all the people of the United States, a rapid, efficient, Nation-wide, and world-wide wire and radio communication service. . . ."

communication satellite *See* satellite.

communication-satellite earth station complex The transmitters, receivers, and communications antennas at the earth station site together with the interconnecting terrestrial facilities and modulating and demodulating equipment. This equipment processes traffic received from the terrestrial distribution system(s) prior to transmission via satellite and traffic received from the satellite prior to transfer of channels of communication to terrestrial distribution system(s).

communication satellite system A system of communications satellites and earth stations that transmit television, telephone, data, and so on, between terrestrial points.

communications common carrier *See* common carrier.

communications revolution The period from the invention of the printing press to the present explosion of new communication technologies.

communications satellite An earth satellite that is intentionally used to relay telecommunication information.

Communications Satellite Corporation (COMSAT) The government-private corporation authorized by the Communications Satellite Act of 1962 to operate an international satellite relay system and represent the United States in Intelsat.

communications satellite system A system of communications satellites in space whose purpose is to relay telecommunication information between satellite terminal stations, together with such associated equipment and facilities for tracking, guidance, control, and command functions as are not part of the generalized launching, tracking, control, and command facilities for all space purposes.

communication theory The statistical analysis of the basic features of communication including the measurement of information content and channel capacity. Based primarily on the ideas of C. D. Shannon.

communicator □ One who communicates. □ A radio talk show host.

community A geographical area, regardless of size, that is served by one or more broadcast stations. *See also* hyphenated market, market, and MSA.

community access channel A cable television channel programmed by members of the community. Also called a *community channel.*

community antenna television The early name for the dissemination of television signals by cable. Now more commonly referred to as *cable television* or *CATV.*

Community Antenna Television Association (CATA) An organization of smaller cable television system operators. Cf. NCTA.

community ascertainment *See* ascertainment.

community channel *See* community access channel.

community problems The needs and problems of a local community for which a broadcaster must design programs. *See also* ascertainment.

community reception The reception of emissions from a space station in the broadcasting-satellite service by receiving equipment, which in some cases may be complex and have antennae larger than those for individual reception, and intended for use by a group of the general public at one location, or through a distribution system covering a limited area. Cf. individual reception.

community relations director A radio or television station employee who is in charge of determining local public needs and problems and who designs programs to meet those needs and problems. *See also* ascertainment.

community service grant (CSG) A grant from the Corporation for Public Broadcasting (CPB) to public radio and television stations for the purchase of programming and for other costs.

community station A low-powered radio or television station that serves a small local community or area.

community unit A cable television system serving a particular community. *See also* system community unit.

comopt Composite optical. A film with an optical soundtrack. Cf. commag.

comp □ An abbreviation for *complimentary.* A free ticket to a production. Also called an *Annie Oakley* and *freebie.* Cf. hard ticket. □ An abbreviation for *compositor, composition, comprehensive, computer,* and so on.

compact A newspaper similar in size to a tabloid but more conservative in style.

compact cassette An obsolete term for *audiocassette. See also* minicassette.

compact disc (CD) A system for the reproduction of high-density digital data from an optical disc. Originally conceived as a medium for high-fidelity music reproduction, for which CD-DA is now an accepted world standard. Because of the large disc data storage capacity, the term *compact disc* is now being applied as a text/data medium for electronic publishing (CD-ROM), an audio-video medium (CD-V), and a multiple-function (audio/video/text/data) medium for interactive programs (CD-I).

compact disc-digital audio (CD-DA) Developed jointly by Philips and Sony, and launched in 1982, this system records and plays back music in the form of digital data, onto and from a 12-cm diameter disc. Also, the audio quality level of the encoded material.

compact disc-interactive (CD-I) Compact disc-based multimedia system that is mainly real-time audio-and video-driven but also has text, binary data, and computer program capabilities. Cf. digital video interactive (DVI).

compact disc player A device specifically designed to read CD-DA discs. If provided with digital output and control interface, it can also be used, in conjunction with a suitable signal processor, to read CD-ROM or CD-I discs.

compact disc-read-only memory (CD-ROM) Defined by Philips and Sony in 1985, CD-ROM makes use of the identical physical characteristics—disc size, rotational speed, and read-out mechanism as well as disc mastering and replication processes—as used for CD-DA. The CD-ROM specification limits itself to defining the method by which data is stored on the disc, and no more. The nature of the data and the purpose for which it is to be interpreted are left to the information providers making use of the medium.

compact disc-real-time operating system (CD-RTOS) The operating system used in CD-I, specified so that the real-time capabilities of CD-I are usable, as far as possible, in a device-independent way.

compander A combination of the words *compressor* and *expander.* A device that compresses a signal at a transmitter and expands the signal at the receiver. May be used for multichannel television sound, telephone lines, and so on, to increase the quality of the received signal. Also spelled *compandor.*

companion page Either of the two pages that make up one block of complementary material.

company switch A disconnect switch and power source for portable lighting equipment.

comparable use rule The rule that broadcast stations may not charge legally qualified candidates more than what is charged other advertisers. Cf. lowest unit charge.

comparative advertising Advertising in which two or more competing products are compared; the product that pays for the commercial always wins the competition.

comparative broadcasting systems The four types of internal broadcasting systems often mentioned are private ownership and operation, government ownership and operation, government ownership and public operation, and public ownership and public operation.

comparative criteria The factors used in the selection between or among applicants for a broadcast license. Those most often used by the FCC are diversification of control of the media of mass communication, integration of ownership and management, local residence, civic participation, previous broadcasting experience, past broadcast record, and proposed programming.

comparative hearing A hearing conducted before the FCC between or among mutually exclusive applicants for a broadcast license.

compatibility □ The ability of computer software and hardware to work on or with different systems without special modifications. □ In compact discs, the extent to which different types of discs can be interpreted by different types of players or drives. For example, all CD-DA discs are fully compatible with all CD-DA players, so that any player can reproduce music from any disc regardless of manufacturer.

compatible □ A monochromatic television receiver capable of displaying color broadcasts. □ Components, devices, and machines capable of working well together. □ The degree to which a wide-screen motion picture can be viewed on television. Also called *compatible composition.*

compatible color system The television color system developed by RCA that allows the reception of a monochrome picture.

compatible composition *See* compatible.

comp copy *See* complimentary copy.

compensation □ The amount that radio or television networks pay affiliates for carrying programs. □ *See* initial compensation and additional compensation. Cf. reverse compensation. □ The control of balance between sound sources. □ The altering of the frequency response of an amplifier for record equalization, bass boost, loudness contour, and so on.

compensator *See* equalizer.

compensatory damages *See* actual damages.

competition The radio or television programs being broadcast at the same time over the other stations or networks.

competitive plants One or more outdoor advertising operators offering services in the same market area.

compilation □ A work formed by the collection and assembling of preexisting materials or of data selected, coordinated, or arranged in such a way that the resulting work as a whole constitutes an original work of authorship. The term includes collective works. □ *See* compilation television program.

compilation film □ A film made up of clips and other footage shot for other feature films, documentaries, newsreels, and so on. Also called a *compilation sequence. See also* compilation. □ An anthology film.

compilation sequence *See* compilation film.

compilation television program A program using excerpts from television films, or from theatrical films and television films. Examples include twenty-five years of Lucy on television and shows whose titles begin "The Best of. . . ."

compiled list The names and addresses derived from directories, newspapers, public records, registrations, and other sources that identify groups of people, companies, or institutions with something in common.

compiler An organization that produces compiled lists.

complainant A cable television system operator, a cable television system association, a utility, or an association of utilities that file a complaint.

complaint A filing by a cable television system operator, a cable television system association, a utility, or an association of utilities alleging that a rate, term, or condition for a pole attachment is not just and reasonable.

complementary angles Camera shots that match each other; often used in over-the-shoulder shots wherein two performers are seen from opposite angles.

complementary color □ Any two colors that when combined in the proper proportions produce white light. *See also* additive primary colors. □ Any two pigment colors that when combined in the proper proportions produce black. *See also* subtractive primary colors.

complete cancel An individual who cancels a membership in a book club or other service after having completed a specific commitment.

complete census A redundant term for *census*; a survey in which all sampling units in a frame are canvassed.

complete drawing (CD) An animation term meaning "complete the drawing."

completion bond An insurance bond taken to ensure that the motion picture or other project being insured will be finished.

completion guarantor (CG) An individual who arranges the guarantee for financial backing for the completion of a motion picture or other project.

complex wave A periodic wave made up of more than one frequency.

compliance The inverse of stiffness, such as the vertical and lateral ease of movement of a tone arm or loudspeaker cone.

complication An unexpected dramatic development in a play that hinders the protagonist's search for a solution.

complimentary copy A copy of a book, magazine, or other item given without charge. Also called a *comp copy.*

complimentary ticket *See* comp.

comp list A periodical's list of individuals and organizations that receive complimentary copies. *See also* controlled circulation.

COMPO Council of Motion Picture Organizations.

component A self-contained part of a system, such as an amplifier, a loudspeaker, or a sync generator.

component analog video (CAV) A half-inch videotape recording format that approaches the quality of one-inch tape. The Betacam and M-format systems are examples.

component recording A video recording process in which the luminance and chrominance information is recorded on separate tracks. Also called *component video.*

component television A television system in which the chrominance and luminance signals are handled separately. Cf. composite television.

component video *See* component recording.

compool A contraction of *communication pool. See also* pool.

compose □ To set type for printing. □ To arrange the performers in a scene; a stage picture.

composer The person who creates the score for a film, program, play, and so on.

Composers and Lyricists Guild of America (CLGA) A union.

composing manager An individual who supervises artists and typesetters to ensure quality in the finished product.

composing room The department or area of a print shop or newspaper in which type is set.

composing stick A small metal tray used to hold hand-set type.

composite □ The complete video signal, including sync. Cf. noncomposite. □ A film containing both picture and soundtrack. Also called a *marriage.* □ An actor or model's brochure, depicting the person's appearance and other vital data.

composite baseband signal A signal that is composed of all program and other communications signals that frequency modulates the FM carrier.

composite color signal The color picture signal, including blanking and sync pulses.

composite copy A copy made from the first composite negative.

composite daily print *See* answer print.

composite dupe A duplicate negative film containing both picture and soundtrack.

composite dupe master A composite dupe used for printing release prints.

composite image The positive dye image in a tripack color film.

composite master A completed videotape or film containing both sound and picture.

composite negative A negative film used for printing positive prints.

composite objects Graphic designs that are combined by computer.

composite photograph *See* composograph.

composite picture The complete composite video signal.

composite print A print of a film that contains both picture and soundtrack. Films regularly shown in theatres are composite prints. Also called a *release print.*

composite shot A shot presenting two or more separate scenes simultaneously. *See also* split screen.

composite signal A television signal containing both picture and synchronizing information.

composite story A news story or feature made up from several different angles.

composite television A television system in which the chrominance and luminance signals are combined. Cf. component television.

composite video signal The complete video signal. For monochrome, it consists of the picture signal and the blanking and synchronizing signals. For color, additional color-synchronizing signals and color-picture information are added.

composite week Seven days selected by the FCC for which licensees were required to submit a program log, such as Monday, February 1, Tuesday, April 12, Wednesday, June 7, and so on.

composition □ The setting of type according to a predetermined layout in a form suitable for printing. □ The layout of a page, advertisement, artwork, and so on. □ The art of arranging persons or objects in a shot for a pleasing effect. □ The balance between light and shade in a picture. □ An intellectual creation, such as a musical composition or a piece of writing. □ The work of a compositor.

composition house A company that specializes in typesetting and in preparing repro proofs.

composition-set type Type that is set by a composition house. Cf. publication-set type.

compositor □ A person who sets type; a typesetter. □ A company that performs typesetting services.

composograph A composite photograph; a picture made from two or more negatives.

compound The flat, tablelike part of an animation stand on which the artwork rests while it is being photographed. Also called a *compound table.*

compound lens A lens containing more than one element.

compound move An animation stand movement combining, for example, a pan and a zoom.

compound shutter A camera shutter containing leaves that open from the center.

compound table *See* compound.

compre *See* comprehensive.

comprehensive A layout used in advertising and promotion to illustrate how the finished artwork will appear. Also called a *comp, comprehensive layout,* and *compre. See also* layout. Cf. rough.

comprehensive layout *See* comprehensive.

compressed *See* condensed.

compressed time The decrease in the length of time of a motion picture or other dramatic presentation is perceived to be by a viewer. Cf. expanded time, experienced time, objective time, screen time, and subjective time.

compressed video A video signal that has been condensed by digitizing in order to eliminate the transmission of redundant information. Also called *video compression.*

compressing The act of increasing the rate of speech in order to shorten the time necessary to deliver a line, speech, and so on.

compression □ The movement of air molecules that are closely spaced. Cf. rarefaction. □ The automatic reduction made in an audio or video signal to minimize distortion.

compression/decompression algorithms Algorithms that allow storage of more than one hour of DVI full-motion video on a standard CD-ROM disc for decompression in real time.

compression molding The process of forming a disc by means of compressing a charge of suitable plastic in a cavity.

compression ratio The ratio of the input to the output signals of a compressor.

compression threshold The point at which a compressor begins to operate.

compressor A signal processor that is designed to reduce the dynamic range of an audio or video signal.

compulsory license An automatic license granted to certain users under the Copyright Act (a) for mechanical rights to musical compositions, (b) for cable television systems, and (c) for noncommercial broadcasting, and until 1988, (d) for jukeboxes. The rates for such uses are set by the Copyright Act. Sometimes called a *mandatory license.*

compunications A general term that refers to the use of computers in communication.

computer A device capable of receiving and storing a set of instructions, processing data, and supplying the results of the processing in a specified format. A general-purpose computer normally contains a CPU, memory, and input/output facilities. Computers may be analog, digital, or hybrid. *See also* analog computer, desktop computer, digital computer, mainframe, microcomputer, minicomputer, and personal computer.

computer aided design (CAD) Computer programs written to assist in producing automated architectural, industrial, and other types of drawings.

computer aided instruction (CAI) Computer programs written to provide students with tutorials in various subjects.

computer aided typesetting The preparation of typeset materials for composition, page make-up, justification, phototypesetting, and other uses to relieve writers, compositors, and so on, of mechanical and repetitive tasks. Also called *computer typesetting.*

computer animation A field of animation that takes advantage of the computer's ability to direct and generate a video image based on preprogrammed input. Also called *computer assisted animation* and *electronic animation.*

computer assisted animation *See* computer animation.

computer assisted interactive video (CAIV) A system for controlling videotape and videodisc recorders and players.

computer editing The use of a computer in conjunction with a controller and videotape recorders to perform video edits.

computer enhancement The improvement made in photographs, tapes, graphics, and so on, by digital manipulation of the image.

computer flooring Flooring consisting of raised, removable panels so that wiring may be hidden and protected.

computer freak *See* hacker.

computer-generated graphics *See* computer graphics.

computer-generated letter *See* computer letter.

computer graphics The generation of charts, graphs, drawings, and so on, by a computer.

computerist An individual who uses a computer.

computerized animation An animation technique that allows the programming of the animation camera movements.

computerized animation stand A specialized animation stand that allows all camera moves to be preprogrammed and activated when the shutter is pressed, permitting greater accuracy and speed in filming.

computerized composition The use of computers to drive typesetting machines.

computer language A language that is designed to express language for a particular type of computer.

computer letter A personalized form letter with personal insertions. Also called a *computer printed letter* and *computer-generated letter. See also* computer personalization.

computer literacy The state of having a general knowledge of and familiarity with computers and their use.

computer output microfilm (COM) A microfilm, microform, or microfiche that is produced by a computer.

computer personalization The printing of letters or other promotional pieces by a computer using names, addresses, special phrases, or other information based on data appearing in one or more computer records. The objective is to make use of the information in the computer record to tailor the message to a specific individual.

computer printed letter *See* computer letter.

computer printout *See* printout.

computer program A set of instructions that directs a computer to perform specified operations, solve a problem, or complete an assignment.

computer service bureau An internal or external facility providing general or specific data processing services.

computer system A combination of parts consisting of a central processing unit (CPU), memory, input/output (I/O) devices, and peripheral equipment such as disk drives, printers, modems, and so on.

COMSAT Communications Satellite Corporation.

COMSTAR A communications satellite.

concave lens A lens with its faces curved inward so that the light waves disperse or spread. Cf. convex lens.

concealment In digital signal processing, the hiding of errors, such as by an interpolation scheme.

concentration of control *See* diversification of control.

concentric groove On a disc, a locked circular groove, the center of which is coincident with the center of the recording spiral. Also called *stopping groove* and *locked groove.*

concentricity Of a rotary quadruplex video head assembly, that condition in which the center of rotation of the heads coincides with the center of curvature of the vacuum guide.

concept A program development idea produced in brief or outline form.

concert border A borderlight mounted immediately behind the proscenium arch.

Concert Music Broadcasters Association An organization of broadcasters who air classical music.

conclusion The third major division of a speech. Cf. introduction and body.

concordance An alphabetical index of all the words or subjects in a book that shows where they may be found.

concurring opinion An opinion written by a judge that agrees with the majority opinion but that differs in reasoning or interpretation.

condensed A type that is narrower (by approximately 40 percent) than the normal size of the same typeface. Also called *compressed, condensed face,* and *condensed type.*

condensed face *See* condensed.

condensed radio market Generally a small to midsized radio market; most are surveyed once a year for the Arbitron Company's Spring Report. The Metro and TSA sample objectives are considerably smaller than those for standard radio markets, and an abbreviated version of the Standard Radio Market Report is produced.

condensed radio report A radio ratings summary made for smaller markets.

condensed type *See* condensed.

condenser □ A plano-convex lens. □ An obsolete term for *capacitor.*

condenser lens The lens in a projection system that directs light from the lamp into the gate or film aperture and into the projection lens.

condenser loudspeaker An obsolete term for an electrostatic loudspeaker. Also called a *condenser speaker.*

condenser microphone An obsolete term for an electrostatic microphone.

condenser speaker *See* condenser loudspeaker.

conditional access Access to a courtroom granted to a reporter based upon conditions specified by the presiding judge.

conditional grant □ An authorization made by the FCC subject to its later withdrawal. □ A grant made by the FCC subject to its being withdrawn after a comparative hearing.

conditional privilege *See* qualified privilege.

conditional question A survey question to be asked only when a specified response is given to the preceding question. Cf. filter question.

conditional renewal A broadcast license that is renewed by the FCC subject to specified changes or actions. *See also* short-term renewal.

conditioning bias A survey error that results when respondents change their activities, preferences, and so on, simply because they have been included in the study. *See* nonsampling error.

conduct clause A phrase inserted in a contract that gives the employer the right to cancel the contract for misconduct by the performer.

conductive coating A low-resistivity nonmagnetic backside coating for audio-

or videotape, used to lessen the buildup of static electrical charges.

conductor Any material—such as a wire or coaxial cable—capable of carrying an electric current.

conduit A thin metal pipe used for protecting wires or cables.

cone □ The radiating diaphragm of a loudspeaker; often made of corrugated paper. □ A large floodlight. Also called a *cone light.* □ One of the color sensory organs of the retina. Cf. rod.

cone light *See* cone.

Conelrad Control of Electromagnetic Radiation. The emergency warning system now replaced by the Emergency Broadcasting System (EBS).

cone wrap A computer-controlled method of wrapping an image to a cone-shaped object.

conference □ The daily planning meeting of a newspaper editorial staff. □ Used also in obvious ways, such as *script conference* or *legislative conference.*

conference call □ A conference of less than one hour in duration to acquaint a union employee with the staff, script, production plan, and the like. Conference calls are not considered working time and are not compensated. □ A nonbroadcast program sent to affiliates by a network.

conference report *See* call report.

confetti The small flecks of color seen in a television picture similar to snow in a monochrome picture.

confidence head In helical recorders, an auxiliary head positioned in the scanner to read just recorded signals.

confidence level The likelihood that the sampling error in a survey result will fall within a specified range, usually expressed in terms of standard errors. The chances are about 68.26 out of 100 that an estimate from a perfect probability sample will differ from a census of the same sampling frame by less than one standard error. The chances are about 95 out of 100 that the difference would be plus or minus two standard errors. The term expresses the probability that the specified range will include the complete census result.

configuration The structure and arrangement of the parts of a computer, schedule, machine, device, and so on.

configure To design or install a piece of equipment so that it will work with other devices.

confirmation □ A statement by a radio or television station or network that a specific time period is available for purchase. □ The acceptance of an order by a station or network for broadcast time.

conflict □ The struggle between the protagonist and antagonist in a story, between the protagonist and the environment, or internal discord. □ Two jobs scheduled at the same time. □ Two or more qualifying stations using the same or similar slogan, program, personality, sports, or frequency identification in the same county.

conflicting views on issues of public importance A phrase in the Communications Act of 1934 that was used by the FCC in reference to the Fairness Doctrine, which required broadcasters to present such views.

conformer An individual who is in charge of conforming.

conforming The process of cutting the original film footage to match the finished workprint. Also called *matching.*

confrontation The point in a script where goals are in conflict between opposing forces.

conglomerate An organization that owns companies in more than one industry.

conjugate foci The focal points on each side of a lens, one the subject, the other the film or pickup tube surface.

conjugate leaves The leaves of the same signature of a book joined at the fold.

conk out A slang term meaning to become inoperative.

connector □ A mechanical or electrical device used to join two or more wires, cables, circuits, or components. □ A symbol used to indicate the connection between two points on a flowchart.

connect time The period of time in which a user is using a computer.

connotative headline A headline that entices a reader to read the story that follows. *See also* teaser.

consecutive action Action that immediately follows in real time but not necessarily in dramatic time.

consecutive announcements Back-to-back commercials.

consecutive weeks discount (CWD) A discount given to advertisers who buy radio or television advertising time for a continuous period, usually between 26 and 52 weeks.

consent A legal defense that a person who agrees to the publication of defamatory statements or invasion of privacy may not recover damages in a lawsuit.

consent decree An agreement between a court or the U.S. Justice Department and a company requiring some action to resolve or remove an obstacle to competition in commerce. An example is the decision in the 1940s that required motion picture studios to divest themselves of motion picture theatres. *See also* consent order.

consent order The most common method of settling disputes between the Federal Trade Commission and advertisers. In a consent order, an advertiser agrees to discontinue a questionable practice but does not admit engaging in false or deceptive advertising. Also called a *consent decree.*

conservation The support of existing public opinion to maintain the status quo.

consideration One of the three elements that constitute a lottery. Consideration is the furnishing of any money or thing of value or requiring the purchase of a product to be eligible to compete for the prize. *See also* chance and prize.

consignment The commissioned sale of goods. *See also* on consignment.

consistency theory A theory that individuals desire to reduce inconsistencies in their attitudes and behaviors. Also called *dissonance theory.*

console □ A series of electronic devices housed together in a control room; the devices provide for mixing, amplifying, fading, and routing audio inputs. Also called a *board, audio console,* and *audio control console.* □ A lighting control board resembling an organ console in terms of size and arrangement of parts, generally placed so that the operator can see the studio. *See also* lighting control console. □ The part of a computer used by the operator to communicate with the computer. □ A film editing machine such as a moviola.

consolette A small console usually containing four or five pots.

consolidated A combined order for different goods, usually shipped together.

Consolidated Metropolitan Statistical Area (CMSA) As defined by the U.S. Office of Management and Budget, a grouping of closely related Primary Metropolitan Statistical Areas.

consolidation The grouping by the FCC of cases that involve the same applicant or involve substantially the same issues, or any applications that present conflicting claims.

consonant A speech sound characterized by the constriction or blocking of the breath channel. Cf. vowel.

constant □ A fixed, invariable value. □ Data that remains the same during the running of a computer program. □ *See* standing.

constant-amplitude recording A mechanical recording characteristic wherein, for a fixed amplitude of a sinusoidal signal, the resulting recorded amplitude is independent of frequency.

constant angular velocity (CAV) A disc rotation mode in which the disc always rotates at the same speed, so that the time of one revolution is always the same. Used in interactive LaserVision. Cf. constant linear velocity.

constant linear velocity (CLV) A disc rotation mode in which the disc rotation speed changes as the read radius changes so that the linear reading speed —the speed at which the read-out device scans the track—is always the same. Maximizes disc information storage capacity. Used in CD and in noninteractive LaserVision. Cf. constant angular velocity.

constant speed motor A motor that is designed to run at the same speed without adjustment.

constant-tension transport A tape transport in which the tension of the tape is regulated to be constant, especially at some critical point in the tape path such as the video-head assembly. Constant tension is maintained despite such variables as supply reel or take-up reel diameter or the quantity of the tape on either reel.

constant-velocity recording A mechanical recording characteristic wherein, for a fixed amplitude of a sinusoidal signal, the resulting amplitude is inversely proportional to frequency.

constitution The basic law of a country or state outlining the structure and powers of the various branches of the government, and often the rights and responsibilities of its citizens.

constitutional law Law based on the Constitution of the United States or a state constitution.

constitutional privilege *See* constitutional right.

constitutional right A privilege guaranteed by a constitution, such as freedom of speech and of the press. Also called *constitutional privilege.*

construct An idea or image synthesizing a theoretical proposition.

construction □ As applied to educational broadcasting facilities, the acquisition and installation of transmission apparatus necessary for broadcasting, but not the construction or repair of structures to house such apparatus. □ A scene shop or carpenter shop.

construction permit (CP) The instrument of authorization required by the Communications Act or the Rules and Regulations of the Federal Communications Commission made pursuant to the Act for the construction of a station or the installation of apparatus for the transmission of energy, communications, or signals by radio by whatever name the instrument may be designated by the FCC. Also called a *permit for construction.*

construction units Stock flats and other pieces used to build a set. Also called *scenic elements.*

consultant An individual, usually an expert, hired by a company to evaluate and suggest changes in order to improve the product or service.

consumer □ The ultimate user of a product or service. □ The viewer, listener, reader, or other recipient of a radio or television program, motion picture, book, periodical, and so on.

consumer advertising Advertising directed at the public as a whole rather than to a profession, industry, and so on.

consumer goods Products that directly satisfy human wants, desires, and needs.

consumerism The development of laws and regulations that protect consumers' right to have a choice, right to be informed about products, right to have redress for inferior products, and so on.

consumer list A list of names, usually with home addresses, compiled or resulting from a common inquiry or buying activity indicating a general or specific buying interest.

consumer magazine A magazine intended for the general public rather than for a trade or profession. Cf. professional magazine and trade magazine.

consumer panel A long-term sample of individuals or households to obtain information concerning media habits and product purchases.

consumer profile The delineated traits—age, sex, income, buying habits, and so on—of a consumer.

consumer research *See* marketing research.

contact □ A source of information, often a news source. □ A mechanical device for carrying current from a relay or switch.

contact executive *See* account executive.

contact microphone A microphone designed to pick up vibrations through physical contact with an object or person.

contact print A copy of a magnetic recording made by placing the tape to be copied in close contact with the blank tape that is to become the copy, and exposing the tapes to some process, such as the anhysteretic duplication process, designed to accomplish the transfer of the magnetic patterns to the blank tape. *See also* bifilar.

contact printer A device for reproducing film. *See also* contact printing. Cf. optical printer.

contact printing The reproduction of a negative by placing the negative in physical contact with the photographic paper or film stock. Cf. optical printing.

contact producer □ A producer representing a network, station, or advertising agency who assists or advises the program or commercial producer. □ A producer who acts as liaison between an advertising agency and a station or network.

contact report *See* call report.

contact screen A halftone screen on film.

contact sheet A single piece of photographic paper on which all the pictures on a roll of film are printed, usually as proofs.

CONTAM Committee on Nationwide Television Audience Measurement. A ratings evaluation committee established by the networks.

conte A brief narrative story.

contemporary A newspaper, magazine, or other periodical that is printed at approximately the same time as another.

contemporary binding A binding made in the style of the period in which a book was originally published.

contemporary hit radio (CHR) Another term for a top 40 radio station. Also called *hit radio.*

contemporary music A radio music format characterized by a mixture of top-40 and other, basically rock, records. Cf. country, middle-of-the-road, rock, and so on.

contempt A direct or indirect act of disobedience, disrespect, or obstruction toward a court, judge, or legislative body. Contempt may be either civil or criminal.

contempt of court *See* contempt.

content analysis □ The separation of qualitative or subjective responses to interview questions into manageable categories. □ The systematic study of the content of mass media messages and the process of inferring effects from the analysis of programs, messages, or even camera shots, angles, and so on.

content curve The time necessary for a viewer to absorb the information contained in a camera shot.

content provider In CD-I, the writer, publisher, or other party(ies) supplying information, usually copyrighted, for an application.

content regulation The regulation of what is expressed as opposed to time, place, and manner regulation.

contents page A front matter page listing the contents of a book.

contest Any broadcast by a radio station in connection with which any money or any other thing of value is offered as a prize or prizes to be paid or presented by the program sponsor or by any other person or persons, as announced in the course of the broadcast.

contiguity □ Proximity without intervening elements as that of radio programs following one directly after the other. □ A condition regarded as equivalent for billing purposes, created by an advertiser's purchase of a minimum amount of time either in one day or in one week. *See also* horizontal contiguity and vertical contiguity.

contiguity rate A reduced rate offered an advertiser who sponsors separate programs in adjacent time periods or whose sponsorship creates situations of vertical or horizontal contiguity. Also called *contiguous rate.* Cf. brand rates.

contiguous areas Geographical areas, such as cities or counties, that share a common border.

contiguous rate *See* contiguity rate.

contingency The amount of money set aside for unexpected expenses of a production.

contingent deferment *See* fixed deferments.

continuance The postponement of a pending court action.

continuation □ A book or other publication issued as part of a series. □ One of the parts of a series.

continuation line A newspaper or magazine line that continues a story from a previous page.

continuation order *See* standing order.

continuing discount A previously earned radio or television advertising discount continued under a new contract.

continuing zoom A zoom wherein the movement is continued past what would be considered normal composition, for example, a zoom past a head shot to a portion of the head or some other point of interest past the person.

continuity □ Any written script material. □ The detailed plan of a radio or television program. □ Smooth transitions between camera shots or sounds. □ The path taken by electrical currents. □ The flow of pictures, lines, camera angles, and so on, used to advance a story. □ The individual responsible for ensuring that there are no differences in costume, props, and so on, between takes in a motion picture or other production. Also called a *continuity girl* and *script girl.*

continuity acceptance A department or censor delegated the task of screening commercial matter and programs for possible violation of law, regulations, or self-regulatory standards. *See also* standards and practices.

continuity book A folder that contains, in proper order, all of the commercials to be read over a radio or television station on a given day. Also called a *copy book.*

continuity cutting The systematic editing of film or tape in a smooth, logical manner acceptable to an audience. Also called *continuity editing.*

continuity department A broadcast station individual or department charged with writing continuity and often with continuity acceptance.

continuity editing *See* continuity cutting.

continuity girl *See* continuity.

continuity in media The repeated use of an advertising message.

continuity link A device used to establish continuity between shots, scenes, and so on.

continuity program Products or services bought as a series of small purchases rather than all at one time. Generally based on a common theme and shipped at regular or specific time intervals.

continuity shot A shot taken after the completion of a film or program to cover some previously undetected continuity error.

continuity sketch A continuity storyboard.

continuity strip An advertisement in comic strip format.

continuity title A subtitle or key used in motion pictures and television to bridge a change of time or place, such as the name of a city or the year.

continuity writer □ A broadcast station, advertising agency, or network employee who writes copy. □ A motion picture writer who adapts a story for a screenplay.

continuous action A series of scenes that are uninterrupted by flashbacks, cutbacks, or cutaways.

continuous exposure The movement of film past a camera aperture without interruption.

continuous feed paper Paper with continuous pin feed holes on each side and perforations between pages. Also called *fanfold paper.*

continuous motion A television projector capable of moving film evenly at the rate of 30 frames per second. Cf. intermittent movement.

continuous power The amount of power that an amplifier is able to deliver on a prolonged basis.

continuous printer An optical or contact printer for film in which the raw stock and the processed film move past the aperture of the printer in a continuous motion. Cf. step printer.

continuous processing The use of automatic film processing equipment wherein the film passes through the various processing stages without interruption.

continuous projector □ A telecine projector. □ A projector with a continuous loop mechanism or cassette that allows a film to be shown repeatedly.

continuous receiver A device that automatically receives and records messages, such as a teleprinter.

continuous roll insert *See* hi-fi insert.

continuous season The scheduling of the start of new television programs throughout the year rather than just at the start of the fall season.

continuous tape *See* idiot tape.

continuous tone □ A photographic image that contains shades or hues that gradually merge into one another rather than in halftones. □ The range of values from white through gray to black.

continuous wave (CW) □ Identical electromagnetic wave oscillations that can be modulated to carry information. □ Electromagnetic radiation formed by identical oscillations.

contour The area subsumed by a line encompassing the outer limits of a radio or television station's coverage. *See also* grade A and grade B.

contour effect The alteration of the voltage output from a magnetic reproducing head at long wavelengths due to the shape of the pole pieces and the presence of magnetic shielding close to the tape.

contouring □ The action by which the shape of a video head's tape-contacting surface slowly adapts itself to the tensions and pressures of the tape it is contacting. The result of such action is normally an improvement in the intimacy of head-to-tape contact; the action therefore usually results in better performance. Also called *head contouring.* □ Horizontal and vertical aperture correction in a television camera. Also called *edge enhancement.*

contour light *See* back-light.

contract A binding agreement, enforceable under law, between two or more parties to do or not do a particular thing. Examples include a licensing agreement between a record company and a musician, an agreement between a publisher and an author, a broadcast station and a network, and so on.

contract classifieds Classified advertisements run in a newspaper or magazine on a continuing basis rather than on a one-time basis.

contract film A motion picture made under a contract wherein the director, players, and so on, receive a percentage of the profits instead of salaries.

contractor □ An individual or company that selects the musical talent for a recording session. □ A program supplier for the Independent Broadcasting Authority in Great Britain.

contract player A player employed under a contract for television motion pictures or theatrical motion pictures or both. The contract is for a term of at least 10 out of 13 weeks and may not specify any role, picture, or series, unless otherwise requested by the player and approved by the Screen Actors Guild. *See also* combination term contract. Cf. day player, deal player, free-lance player, multiple picture player, stunt player, and term player.

contract rate A discounted rate given to an advertiser upon the purchase of a specific number of ads or spots in a given time period.

contract year The period from the first insertion of an advertisement in a periodical to the end of the 12-month period following.

contrapuntal sound Sound used in counterpoint to the action of a film or videotape production.

contrast □ The range of light and dark values in a picture or the ratio between the maximum and minimum brightness values. For example, in a high-contrast picture there are intense blacks and whites, whereas a low-contrast picture contains only various shades of gray. □ The effect achieved through the placement of different ideas, objects, people, and so on, together for comparison or composition. □ In a script, the range of emotions or conditions exhibited.

contrast control The potentiometer in a television receiver or monitor used to vary the contrast.

contrast filter A filter used with monochrome film to heighten the contrast between tonal values.

contrast glass A film director's neutral density filter eyepiece for viewing a scene.

contrasting characters Characters that act in counterpoint to each other.

contrast range *See* contrast ratio.

contrast ratio The ratio between the brightest and darkest portions of a television picture. The ratio should not exceed 20 to 1 for an acceptable picture. Also called *contrast range.*

contrasty A high-contrast picture lacking mid-range tones.

contre jour Shooting into the light to produce a backlit subject.

contribution factor A percentage of red, green, and blue as related to individual pixels to create visual effects.

contributor list The names and addresses of persons who have donated to a specific fund-raising effort.

contrived A created motion picture, television production, work of art, and so on. A term sometimes used in criticism to mean artificial or labored.

control □ As used by the FCC, a term of ownership not limited to majority stock ownership but that includes actual working control in whatever manner exercised. □ To adjust sound and/or picture levels. □ A potentiometer or other variable device.

control and telemetry transmissions Signals transmitted on a multiplex subcarrier intended for any form of control and switching functions or for equipment status data and aural or visual alarms.

control board An electrical panel containing controls for production lighting, including dimmer controllers, faders, nondim switches, and so on. Cf. dimmer board and lighting control console.

control character A character in a computer program or file that has no graphic representation but is used to initiate an action such as inserting a line feed or form feed, or turning a peripheral device on or off.

control circuit A telephone ring-down circuit used for communication between a radio or television studio and a remote location.

control code □ Any code placed in a video recording, either in auxiliary tracks or encoded within the video signal, for the purpose of editing, cueing, or otherwise controlling the video recorder or its playback signal. □ The SMPTE time and control code.

control desk *See* control panel.

control group A group selected for a research experiment to which the experimental factor is not applied.

control key A key on a computer keyboard that, when pressed in conjunction with another key, performs special functions, such as changing a file name, deleting a block of text, or calculating page numbers.

controlled circulation (CC) A newspaper or magazine that is sent free to individuals or companies on the basis of their occupations or professions. Also called *qualified circulation.*

Controlled Circulation Audit (CCA) An organization that audits the circulation statements of controlled circulation publications. *See also* Audit Bureau of Circulations.

controlled circulation newspaper *See* controlled circulation and shopper.

controlled duplication A method by which names and addresses from two or more computer lists are matched to eliminate extra mailings to the same name or address.

controller A microprocessor that converts signals from a computer to operate a disk drive, printer, or other peripheral device. Also called a *control unit.*

controller/decoder The hardware needed to play a CD-I disc and to decode the information coming from the disc to the digital output port.

control panel □ A sound monitoring device. □ A desk used for the operational control of sound, picture, or animation. Also called a *control desk* and *mixing panel.* □ A patch panel.

control room An area, usually adjacent to a radio or television studio, into which sound and/or picture signals are fed and from which a production is directed.

control signal An electronic pulse used to synchronize a film camera and recorder.

control station An international television receiving and distributing terminal.

control strip *See* cinex.

control track The area on the tape containing a record used by the tracking servo to control longitudinal motion of the tape during playback in a television tape recorder system. The control track may contain other signals that, for example, identify a color field or frame sequence used for editing.

control track editor An edit control unit that uses the frame pulses on the videotape control track to synchronize edits. Also called a *pulse code editor.*

control track head A head positioned on the transport so as to record or replay the control track record. The control track head is normally positioned near the rotating head assembly to minimize errors caused by variable tensions in the tape.

control track phase The temporal relationship between the flux of the control track record and a specified point in a reference video signal.

control track pulse *See* frame pulse.

control track record The record recorded in the control track.

control track simulplay head A head used to monitor the control track signal. The position of this head is less critical than the position of the control track head.

control track signal The signal recorded on the control track.

control unit *See* controller.

control variable A condition—such as place, time, environment, and so on—that is controlled by a researcher in an experimental study.

controversial public issues Another term for conflicting views on issues of public importance.

CONUS An acronym for continental United States.

convenience sample A nonscientific sample selected, not on a probability basis, but on the basis of interviewee availability, or convenience, the results of which may be very misleading. Commonly referred to as a "poll." Cf. probability sample.

convention ☐ A familiar bit, line, action, dialogue, and so on, used in dramatic works. ☐ The intellectual acceptance by a viewer of nonlogical or artificial situations and shot sequences.

conventional processing The rekeyboarding of manuscripts by a typesetter. Cf. electronic processing.

convergence The process of aligning the scanning beam to strike the correct color dots.

converging lens *See* positive lens.

conversation station A radio station using an all-talk format.

conversion ☐ The process of changing data from one format to another. ☐ The process of changing a computer program from one language or type of hardware to another. ☐ The procedure involved in replacing or updating equipment. ☐ The creation of wants in a consumer by persuasive advertising.

conversion filter *See* color correction filter.

conversion table A table that lists items in two or more different systems, such as paper weight to size, metric measurements to English equivalents, and motion picture film gauge to running time.

converter ☐ A device used to change direct current to alternating current. Cf. rectifier. ☐ A device used to change the frequency of a television signal, as in shifting signals from television stations to other channels on a cable television system. *See also* cable converter. ☐ A device for changing a television signal from one standard to another, such as from 525 lines to 625. Also called an *electronic converter.* ☐ A device for changing impulses from one form to another, for example, from analog to digital.

convex lens A lens with its faces curved outward so that the light waves converge. Cf. concave lens.

cook ☐ To determine the reliability of electronic components by leaving them on for an extended period of time before being placed in service. ☐ *See* cucoloris.

cookie *See* cucoloris.

cook system An early stereophonic disc system using two pickups mounted side-by-side and traversing two separate bands. Cf. 45/45.

cool ☐ A relaxed performance. ☐ Between hot and cold. ☐ The colors toward the blue end of the spectrum. Cf. warm.

cool color Generally in the range of green-blue-violet. Cool light sources are of high color temperature. Cf. warm color.

cool filter A filter that reduces the amount of red in a picture. Also called a *cooling filter.*

cooling filter *See* cool filter.

co-op *See* cooperative advertising.

cooperation rate *See* response rate.

cooperative advertising ☐ Advertising time paid for by apportioning the cost between the manufacturer and the local distributor or merchant. Also called *co-op.* ☐ In film, an agreement between an exhibitor and a distributor to share the expense of advertising and promotion.

Cooperative Analysis of Broadcasting (CAB) A radio survey company that produced the Crossley ratings. In operation from 1930 to 1946.

cooperative commercial A radio or television commercial aired on the basis of cooperative advertising.

cooperative mailing Advertising or promotional material mailed to prospective buyers containing the advertising matter of two or more advertisers.

cooperative program A network program designed for the insertion of local advertising.

cooperative publishing A publishing arrangement wherein the writer pays all or most of the cost of publication. *See also* vanity press.

cooperative sales An advertising agreement wherein the media representative agrees to advertise the product in return for a fixed amount for each unit sold. *See also* per inquiry.

co-op mailing A mailing in which two or more offers are included in the same envelope or other carrier, with each participating mailer sharing mailing costs according to a predetermined formula.

coordinated advertising Advertising and promotion through various media centered on a single theme or visual motif so that each type of advertisement supports the impact of the others.

Coordinated universal time (UTC) (CUT) A time scale, based on the second (SI), as defined and recommended by the CCIR, and maintained by the Bureau International de l'Heure (BIH). For most practical purposes associated with communication, UTC is equivalent to mean solar time at the prime meridian (0 degrees longitude), formerly expressed in Greenwich mean time (GMT).

coordinates Any of a set of numbers used to specify the position of a point in space or on a CRT.

coordination area The area associated with an earth station outside of which a terrestrial station sharing the same frequency band neither causes nor is subject to interfering emissions greater than permissible level.

coordination distance The distance from an earth station, within which there is a possibility of the use of a given transmitting frequency at this earth station causing harmful interference to stations in the fixed or mobile service, sharing the same band, or of the use of a given frequency for reception at this earth station receiving harmful interference from such stations in the fixed or mobile service.

copies Material objects, other than phonorecords, in which a work is fixed by any method now known or later developed, and from which the work can be perceived, reproduced, or otherwise communicated, either directly or with the aid of a machine or device. The term includes the material object, other than a phonorecord, in which the work is first fixed.

coplanar Pertaining to objects that lie or rotate in a single plane, especially the video heads in a headwheel or drum.

coplanarity □ The condition of being coplanar. □ The degree to which that condition is met.

copper engraving □ An engraving or etching made on a copper plate. Also called *copperplate engraving* and *copperplate etching.* □ A print made from a copper engraving. *See also* intaglio.

coppering The process of making old news sound or read like fresh copy.

copperplate engraving *See* copper engraving.

copperplate etching *See* copper engraving.

coprocessor A microprocessor that replaces the main processor in a computer to enable it to emulate a different operating system.

coproduction A motion picture jointly produced by two or more individuals or companies. Often, a motion picture shot in another country.

copter mount *See* helicopter mount.

copublishing An agreement made between two publishers to cooperate in printing and distributing a book edition.

COPUOS Council on the Peaceful Use of Outer Space (of the United Nations).

copy □ In general, any written material: a script, radio, or television commercial matter, the body of a news story, a manuscript ready to be set in type, a magazine or newspaper, and so on. Also called a *typescript.* □ A reproduction of an original work. □ A duplicate of a book, tape, film, and so on. □ To duplicate. □ A name for a 16- by 20-inch piece of paper. □ To dub. □ To duplicate a tape by any means, including direct recording as well as contact duplication methods. □ A tape produced by a duplication process. □ The complete advertising message to be displayed on an outdoor advertising structure. □ To reproduce a portion of a computer file in a new location in the same or a different file. □ A positive copy of an original film.

copy approach The theme or major point of emphasis in a commercial or advertisement.

copy area *See* type page.

copy block □ A body of type, often part of a printed ad with artwork. □ The right-hand half of a television script or newscast containing the words to be spoken by an announcer, narrator, or other performer.

copy book □ A folder or book containing sheets of paper for accounts or writing copy. □ *See* continuity book.

copy boy A newspaper employee who runs errands and carries copy to and from the various departments. Also called *copy girl.*

copy camera A camera used to reproduce still photographs.

copy casting The counting of the number of characters in a manuscript or copy to determine the amount of space it will use.

copy chief An individual who supervises the work of advertising copy writers.

copy code chip A CBS development made to prevent the duplication of digital audiotapes.

copy cutter An employee in a newspaper composing room who cuts stories into sections for the Linotype operators.

copy desk The center of editorial activity in a newspaper or magazine where copy is edited and headlined.

copy edit *See* copy editing.

copy editing □ The duplication of edited portions of a tape. □ To check a manuscript for errors in structure, style, syntax, coherence, and so on. Also called *copy edit. See also* proofreading marks. Cf. copy preparation.

copy editing marks The symbols used to indicated changes to be made in copy. Cf. proofreading marks.

copy editor *See* copyreader.

copy factor The increase in film contrast caused as a result of copying. The contrast increases with each generation.

copy fighter A slang term for a copyreader who makes unnecessary changes in copy.

copyfit *See* casting off.

copyfitting *See* casting off.

copy flow The movement of news copy from reporting to printing.

copy girl *See* copy boy.

copy guard A signal placed on a tape that is designed to prevent unauthorized duplication. Also called *copy protect.*

copy heavy Display ads that are too wordy.

copy holder □ A proofreader's assistant; one who reads copy to a proofreader. □ A device designed to hold copy.

copy hook The spike on which copy is placed on a Linotype machine.

copyist An individual who copies hastily written notes, news, musical scores, and so on, in order to make them legible.

copy lens A film printer lens.

copy line The phrase in an advertisement designed to be remembered. Examples are "Ask the man who owns one," and "Nothing touches you but the spray itself."

copy log A record made of all copy that passes through the hands of a copy editor.

copy negative A photographic negative made by photographing other photographic material.

copy paper Leftover newsprint used for writing copy.

copy pencil A soft-lead, number one pencil used for marking copy.

copy platform □ A creative plan prepared by an advertising agency for a commercial product. Also called *copy policy.* □ *See* fact sheet.

copy policy *See* copy platform.

copy preparation The act of preparing a manuscript or copy for the compositor after the copy editor has finished. Cf. copy editing.

copy print A photographic print.

copy protect *See* copy guard.

copyreader □ A newsroom employee who corrects, cuts, and adds headlines to newspaper copy. Also called a *reader.* □ A book publishing editor who reviews manuscripts for style, syntax, coherence, and so on.

copy record A new recording by a different artist of a record that has already been released.

copyright The exclusive legal right granted under copyright law to publish, reproduce, or sell a literary, musical, or artistic work. Copyrights are granted for the life of the author plus 50 years. Cf. patent.

Copyright Act The 1976 law (effective January 1, 1978) that completely revised the 1909 Act.

Copyright Clearance Center (CCC) A private organization created by authors and publishers to collect and distribute royalties for the duplication of printed, copyrighted works.

copyright fee The money paid to the Copyright Office to register a work. Cf. copyright royalty.

copyright infringement *See* infringement.

copyright notice The words and symbols used to indicate that material is copyrighted. The form of the notice requires that the copyrighted work contain (a) the letter *C* in a circle, the word "copyright," or the abbreviation "Copr."; (b) the year of first publication of the work; and (c) the name of the owner of the copyright.

copyright owner With respect to any one of the exclusive rights composing a copyright, refers to the owner of that particular right.

copyright page The page in a book, magazine, newspaper, or other publication that contains the notification of copyright.

copyright royalty The money paid for the rights to use a copyrighted work. Cf. copyright fee.

Copyright Royalty Tribunal An administrative agency headed by five commissioners to determine royalty rates for the use of certain copyrighted materials under compulsory licensing and to distribute the royalties deposited with the Register of Copyrights.

Copyright Service Bureau, Ltd., The An administrative agency representing publishers in the licensing, collecting, and payment of royalties.

copyright symbol *See* copyright notice.

copy schedule The list of news stories to be used in a newspaper edition.

copy slant *See* copy approach.

copy stand A table containing lights and a vertical pipe designed to hold an overhead camera.

copytaker A newspaper writer who takes information over the telephone from reporters and writes copy from the information received.

copy taster A newspaper employee designated to evaluate incoming copy to see whether it is usable.

copy testing Research into the appeal of advertising copy.

copy writer An individual who writes advertising copy.

cord A flexible, insulated conductor, usually with jacks, plugs, or clips at each end.

cording A sixteenth century term for the outside quire of a ream of paper. Also called *cording quires.*

cording quires *See* cording.

cordless sync *See* cableless sync.

core □ The light-carrying part of an optical fiber. □ The plastic or metal center of a reel on which film or tape is wound. Cf. flange. □ The center rod of a roll of newsprint. □ A hollow space in body type, electrotype, or stereotype. □ An obsolete term for computer storage that consisted of small ferrite cores capable of holding a magnetic charge. This system of storage has been replaced by semiconductors; however, the term is still occasionally used when referring to the primary storage area in a mainframe. Also called *core memory* and *main memory.*

core market The primary market for a product.

core schedule *See* common carriage.

Cork Award The former name of the award given by the Irish Advertising Awards Festival for radio and television tapes and commercial films.

corn Obvious or unsophisticated copy or material.

corner bullet A small dot placed at each corner of an advertisement to define the column width and lineage depth of an advertisement. Also called a *corner dot.*

corner card The printed material in the upper left corner of an envelope or letterhead containing the name, address, and business.

corner dot *See* corner bullet.

corner insert An insert in one of the corners of a picture.

corner key A television key in one of the corners of the picture.

corner post *See* return.

corner quadrat An L-shaped quadrat.

corner resolution The resolution at the corners of a television camera tube. Resolution is less at the corners than it is at the center.

corona A luminous discharge of electricity caused by the ionization of the surrounding air. A corona often precedes the breakdown of electric or electronic equipment.

corporate advertising The advertising of the merits of a company to improve its image, as opposed to the advertising of a specific product.

corporate defamation Defamation that would tend to damage the corporation's ability to make a profit, or defamation of a nonprofit corporation if the defamation would tend to damage its ability to obtain financial support.

corporate underwriter A national, regional, or local corporation that pays for the cost of producing or purchasing a noncommercial radio or television program.

corporation Any corporation, joint stock company, or association.

Corporation for Public Broadcasting (CPB) A federally chartered organization created by the Public Broadcasting Act of 1967 to promote and help finance the development of public radio and television. *See also* PBS.

correct increment method A technique used to assign media weight to a test market that attempts to apply the same rate of test versus nontest weight levels as used for the national theoretical versus local plans. Cf. as-it-falls method, little America method, and media translation.

correct *See* sic.

correction A published revision or apology for a mistake in a printed item.

correction line A line of type changed to replace an incorrect line.

corrective advertising Advertising that is placed pursuant to a Federal Trade Commission rule that requires an advertiser to correct previously broadcast or printed misleading advertisements for a period of time in future advertisements. Advertising that is designed to correct impressions created by earlier false advertising; may be required under a consent order issued by the Federal Trade Commission. Cf. counter advertising.

corrective commercial A commercial that is required by the corrective advertising rule of the Federal Trade Commission.

corrective maintenance The work required to repair equipment malfunctions. Cf. preventive maintenance and routine maintenance.

correlation A mathematical measure of the degree of similarities and differences between two attributes of or measurements on the same group.

correlation coefficient A measure, from -1 to +1, of correlation. Plus 1 is perfect correlation; -1, perfect negative correlation; and 0, no correlation.

correspondent An individual permanently or temporarily employed to report news from out-of-town.

corrigendum An error in a printed manuscript. *See also* errata.

corx An instruction to a printer to correct the copy. Also called *cx.*

cosine equalizer □ An electrical filter exhibiting a cosinusoidal amplitude-versus-frequency response and a linear phase-versus-frequency response. □ In videotape recorders, such a filter, equipped for knob adjustment of its amplitude-versus-frequency response, can be used for equalization of high-frequency attenuation caused by magnetic head-gap-length losses.

cosmetic make-up Make-up designed to hide imperfections, especially on the face and hands.

COSPAR Committee for Space Research (of the International Council of Scientific Unions).

cosponsored A radio or television program that has two or more sponsors who share the cost on a proportional basis.

cost efficiency The effectiveness of an advertising medium measured with reference to its actual or potential audience and its cost for advertising placement; usually expressed in cost per thousand persons, households, or other units reached or able to be reached.

cost per episode The cost of a single syndicated television program. Cf. cost per series.

cost per gross rating point (CPGRP) *See* cost per point.

cost per inquiry (CPI) The cost of reaching one person who responds to a mailing or advertisement.

cost per order (CPO) Similar to cost per inquiry except based on actual orders rather than inquiries.

cost per point (CPP) The cost of a rating point for a specific schedule. May be determined by the cost per spot divided by the average rating or the cost of the schedule divided by the gross rating points. Also called *cost per rating point* and *cost per gross rating point.*

cost per rating point (CPP) The cost of each rating point delivered for a specific schedule.

cost per series The cost of the total number of programs in a syndicated series. Cf. cost per episode.

cost per thousand (CPM) The ratio of the cost of a television or radio advertisement (in dollars) to a number of households (in thousands) or to a number of individuals (in thousands) estimated to be in the audience at the time the advertisement is broadcast. It can also be determined by dividing the cost of the publication by the circulation or number of readers in thousands. Cf. households per dollar.

cost plus An advertising campaign, advertisement, commercial, and so on, that is produced for the cost plus expenses.

cost ratio A term used by Daniel Starch and Associates for an estimate of relative advertising readership efficiency. Readership is divided by the number of dollars spent on an advertisement and the resulting figure is stated as a percentage of the average number of readers per dollar spent for all advertisements in the same issue.

costs *See* above the line and below the line.

costume The clothing worn by a performer during a program or production.

costume and wardrobe supervisor A motion picture company employee who is in charge of packing, sorting, cataloging, pressing, repairing, altering, and maintaining wardrobes.

costume call A line-up of talent in costume for a director's approval.

costume department *See* wardrobe.

costume designer The individual responsible for costume breakdown, the production of costume designs, color sketches, and so on, for a motion picture studio or network television program.

costume film A period motion picture that uses costumes from that period.

costume house A firm that rents costumes.

costume light A luminaire used to make dark costumes appear lighter.

costumer A person who works under the supervision of a costume and wardrobe supervisor.

couch potato An individual who spends hours a day in front of a television receiver.

cough button A momentary contact switch used in radio so that an announcer may turn his or her microphone off for a brief period. Also called a *cough key* and *cut key.*

cough key *See* cough button.

coulomb (C) A unit of electrical charge equal to the quantity of electricity passing a point in one second when one ampere is maintained.

counselor An individual or company that furnishes advice concerning public relations.

count down To count, usually in reverse order from 10 to 1, to the beginning of a scene, sequence, film or tape roll, and so on.

countdown □ A signal recorded just ahead of the desired television program, providing an aural and visual indication of the number of seconds remaining before the start of the program. □ That portion of a tape containing such a signal. □ The marks on a film leader that allow exact cueing. Also called *countdown leader.*

countdown leader *See* countdown.

counter □ The white space within a letter, such as in the center of an *O.* □ A device that registers the number of revolutions of a printing press, the travel of a tape deck, the number of frames on a video editor, and so on. For a tape deck, also called a tape timer. □ A device used to keep track of time or numbered events. □ A frame, revolution, or footage indicator. Also called an *index counter.* □ *See* cheat.

counter advertising Announcements made under the Fairness Doctrine by groups or organizations opposed to a commercial product or products. Applied only to cigarette advertising. Also called *counter commercials.* Cf. corrective advertising.

counter card A point-of-sale sign containing the name of the product and its price.

counter commercials *See* counter advertising.

counterfeit An illegally made duplicate of a record, tape, book, and so on. *See also* pirating.

counterfeiting *See* pirating.

counter-key Illumination on a subject from a direction opposite to that of the key-light. *See also* modeling light.

counterpoint The use of contrast in music, drama, writing, and so on.

counter programming □ The television network or station practice of scheduling a program with a different audience appeal or that appeals to a different segment of the audience from that of the competition. *See also* hammocking, lead in, and tent polling. ☐ The radio station practice of using a format different from that of the competition.

countershading In make-up, a color opposite to a shading color; a highlight.

counting keyboard A tape-perforating typesetting machine that signals the operator when justification and hyphenation information is to be entered.

counting mode A computer keyboard routine that automatically justifies a line of type when enough characters have been entered.

counting station A defined point on a street where vehicles and/or pedestrians are recorded to determine circulation for outdoor advertising.

count mode *See* counting mode.

country An abbreviation for *country music*; a radio station format.

country and western (C&W) ☐ A music category characterized by simple, straightforward melody and harmony. ☐ A radio music format.

country copy News copy from rural areas, often written by a stringer.

country edition An edition of a newspaper distributed nationally and dated the day of its distribution; predate.

country laning An undesirable wandering of tape motion as the tape passes through a transport, often due to physical defects in the tape, including slitting errors.

country newspaper A small town newspaper, often a weekly.

country press Small town and rural newspapers.

county/coverage service (C/CS) County-by-county audience data compiled from NSI's November, February, and May all-market measurement cycles. Data includes average daily and weekly circulation as well as average quarter hour audience estimates by major dayparts and fringe half hours. A cable supplement supplies separate estimates of station audiences in cable versus noncable households, plus audience estimates for cable origination and pay cable.

county size An A. C. Nielsen classification of the size of counties. *See also* A county, B county, C county, and D county.

coupler ☐ A chemical used in film processing to produce a colored dye image. ☐ A device used to connect two or more television receivers to an antenna.

coupon The portion of a promotion piece of advertisement intended to be filled in by an inquirer or customer and returned to the advertiser to complete the action intended.

coupon clipper A person who has given evidence of responding to free or nominal-cost offers out of curiosity with little or no serious interest or buying intent.

courseware Computer programs that are designed to enhance classroom teaching.

court A federal, state, county, or municipal adjudicatory body. For broadcasting, the two most important courts are the Court of Appeals for the District of Columbia (CADC) and the Supreme Court.

courtesy An announcement made at the beginning and ending of a preempted program that mentions the name of the sponsor of the program usually seen at that time. Also called a *courtesy announcement.*

courtesy announcement. *See* courtesy.

court of appeals The federal district courts that may be called upon to enforce compliance with orders issued by the FCC, the FTC, the FDA, and so on, or to which parties aggrieved by a decision of an administrative agency may appeal. The Court of Appeals for the District of Columbia (CADC) receives the majority of FCC cases. The citation used for the court of appeals is F. or F.2d.

cover ☐ To gather news at the scene of an event. ☐ To be responsible for a news beat. ☐ To report a news story. ☐ The four outside sheets of a magazine, periodical, catalogue, and so on. *See also* front cover, second cover, third cover, and fourth cover. ☐ A book binding or case. ☐ Insurance shots taken to ensure that at least one shot will be usable when retakes, as of an exploding building, would not be feasible. ☐ The partial obscuring of a camera's view by a performer. Also called *covering.*

cover ad An advertisement placed on the cover of a magazine.

coverage ☐ The extent of a publication's circulation. ☐ The extent of a newspaper's or other mass medium's reporting of an event. ☐ The number of households or individuals, regardless of location, that are able to receive a given television or radio station, or group of stations. Cf. circulation. □ In film, the close-ups taken in addition to the master shot. □ The defined parameters of a market; most usually refers to a county or counties, and the percent of this universe exposed to outdoor advertising structures purchased.

coverage area □ A geographic area within which a television or radio station can be received. *See also* contour and field strength. Cf. circulation area. □ The geographical area reached by a radio or television station's signal. Also called *listening* or *viewing area. See also* contour and coverage map.

coverage map A geographical map showing the Grade A and Grade B contours of a broadcasting station.

covering *See* cover.

covering power The capacity of a lens to produce a sharp image over the entire picture at wide apertures.

cover line A line of type on the front cover of a magazine that lists some of the inside contents.

cover paper *See* cover stock.

cover rate The price charged for advertising on magazine and other periodical covers.

cover record Any recording of a song by someone other than the original artist.

cover set A set, usually indoors, held in readiness if the selected outdoor set is not available because of inclement weather.

cover shot □ A long shot of a set. Also called a *master long shot.* □ A shot held in reserve for safety; one a television director can take immediately if something unexpected happens. Also called *insurance* and *protection shot.*

cover stock A heavy paper used as covers for magazines, paperback books, and so on.

cowcatcher A commercial shown before the beginning of a radio or television program. Cf. hitchhiker.

CP □ Canadian Press, The. A Canadian news agency. □ Construction Permit. □ Candlepower. □ Control Panel.

CPA □ Caribbean Press Association. □ Catholic Press Association.

CPB Corporation for Public Broadcasting.

CPB qualified A public radio station that is recognized by the Corporation for Public Broadcasting on the basis of sufficient staff, budget, facilities, and other factors.

CPCS Common program control station.

CPGRP Cost per gross rating point.

CPI □ Center for Public Interest. A consumer group. □ Cost per inquiry.

CPL Characters per line.

CPM □ Cost per thousand. □ Cycles per minute.

CPO Cost per order.

CPP Cost per point or cost per rating point.

C print A glossy, four-color print usually taken from a transparency.

CPS Cycles per second.

CPU □ Central processing unit. □ Commonwealth press union.

CQ An abbreviation for *correct.* The printed material is correct even if it appears to be incorrect. Also written *sic. See also* cx.

CR □ Carriage return. □ Card reader.

crab □ *See* crowfoot. □ *See* truck.

crabbing *See* truck.

crab dolly A four-wheeled, steerable camera dolly.

crack To turn on a microphone.

crack a lens To rack a lens partially so that only a portion of the picture is seen.

cradle □ A device used as a support for heavy lenses. □ *See* rocker.

cradle book *See* incunabula.

cradle head A cradle-shaped camera head that allows smooth tilting.

Craftint A trademark for a variety of acetate sheets used in making shading tints. *See also* Benday.

craft union A labor union of skilled workers performing similar tasks. Cf. industrial union.

CRAM Cumulative Radio Audience Method.

crane □ A large camera dolly that holds both a camera and the camera operator. Also called a *cherry picker* and *crane truck.* To move the camera boom up or down. □ A microphone dolly that has a long arm. □ In animation, the mounting that supports the camera over the compound.

crane operator An individual who operates a crane.

crane shot A horizontal or vertical panoramic shot taken from a moving crane.

crane truck *See* crane.

craning The movement of a camera vertically on a crane. Cf. pedestal.

crank up To increase the volume of sound.

crash □ a computer system that has become unusable due to a temporary malfunction. □ A physical collision between the head and the recording surface of a disk. □ A paper with a coarse finish. Also called *crash finish.* □ *See* super.

crash finish *See* crash.

crawl □ The vertical or horizontal movement of graphics mounted on a large drum or between two rollers. □ The device itself. Also called *crawling title, creeper, creeping title, title crawl,* and *title roll. See also* roller title.

crawling title *See* crawl.

crawl space The space on a television screen used for alphanumeric characters; usually at the bottom of the screen.

crawl title *See* crawl.

CRBC Canadian Radio Broadcasting Commission. Canada's original radio regulatory agency. Now CBC.

CRC Cyclic redundancy check.

crease □ A tape deformity remaining after a fold in the tape has been corrected. □ The picture degradation resulting from such a deformity.

creasing □ The compression of a signature at the place where the pages are to be folded. Cf. scoring. □ A defect in an audio- or videotape caused by bending or folding.

created A copyrighted work fixed in a copy or phonorecord for the first time. Where a work is prepared over a period of time, the portion of it that has been fixed at any particular time constitutes the work as of that time. Where the work has been prepared in different versions, each version constitutes a separate work.

created news News of an event deliberately planned for its potential news value.

creative boutique *See* boutique.

creative department The advertising agency department charged with the responsibility to develop commercials and/or campaigns.

creative direction The strategy devised by the creative department of an advertising agency for a campaign.

creative director An advertising agency employee who designs, coordinates, and supervises artwork and copy for advertisements or commercials. Cf. account executive, associate creative director, and executive creative director.

creative editor A videotape editor who is responsible for the aesthetics of a program or commercial but who does not perform the actual editing.

creative session call *See* ad lib session call.

credit □ An allowance made for loss of outdoor advertising service given by a plant operator. Credits that are common include extended service, extra service, or cash refunds. Similar to a make good in other media. □ A plug for a commercial product or advertiser.

credit hold A withholding of further shipments until a previous shipment of books, magazines, and so on, is paid for.

credit line A line giving the name of the producer, artist, writer, photographer, and others responsible for the artwork, story, motion picture, and so on.

credits Audible or visual graphics placed at the beginning or ending of a television program or motion picture that list the names of the production staff and cast. Also called a *credit title* and *creeping title.*

credit title *See* credits.

creed □ A set of principles adhered to by members of an industry. *See also* canon. □ A telegraphic printer.

creep The movement of videotape past the head at a rate other than normal.

creeper □ A performer who constantly edges closer to a microphone or camera. □ A small camera dolly. □ *See* crawl.

creepie peepie A small, portable, handheld television camera, usually monochrome.

creeping The running together of the lines of a photoengraving.

creeping title *See* crawl and credits.

crew □ Generally, a group of persons assembled for a common purpose; as a film crew, press crew, stage crew, and so on.

☐ The production personnel; everyone except talent.

crew call A call for the technical personnel to report for work at a given time.

CRI ☐ Color rendering index. ☐ Color reversal intermediate.

crib card *See* shot sheet.

Criminal Code Title 18 of the United States Code. Three sections of the Criminal Code are of particular interest to broadcasters: Section 1304 concerning lotteries, Section 1343 concerning fraud, and Section 1464 concerning obscene language. Violation of each carries a possible prison sentence and/or fine.

criminal law The law that covers the relationship between government and its citizens; the law of crime and its punishment.

criminal libel Libel that is malicious in nature or that may tend to cause a breach of the peace, or formerly, defamation against the government. Cases involving criminal libel are now rare.

crimp To attach a wire to a connector by squeezing the connector with a crimping tool or pliers.

crisis A turning point in dramatic action. *See also* climax.

crisp ☐ A picture that contains well-defined elements. ☐ A sound that contains high frequencies as well as intermediate and low frequencies.

crispening The process of electronically adjusting the sharpness of a television picture. *See also* sharpening.

crit An abbreviation for *criticism.*

criteria ☐ The standards or principles of judgment used in evaluating the quality of work. ☐ *See* comparative criteria.

critic A professional analyzer and evaluator of books, motion pictures, television programs, the media, works of art, and so on. Cf. reviewer.

critical angle ☐ The maximum angle a radio wave may strike the ionosphere and still be refracted back to earth. ☐ The minimum angle a light ray may be refracted after passing through one medium into another.

critical area *See* essential area.

critical directional antenna An AM broadcast directional antenna that is required, by the terms of a station authorization, to be operated with the relative currents and phases within the antenna elements at closer tolerances of deviation than those permitted under FCC Rules (paragraph 73.62).

critical focus The point or points in front of a camera that are in sharp focus. *See also* depth of field.

critical hours (CH) ☐ The two-hour period immediately following local sunrise and the two-hour period immediately preceding local sunset. ☐ The hours of broadcast transmission when interference is greatest.

criticism The application of a suitable standard to an event, program, industry, characterization, medium, and so on.

critique An evaluation of the strengths and weaknesses of a book, manuscript, performance, advertisement, and so on.

CRMC Certified radio marketing consultant.

CRN Children's Radio Network.

CRO Cathode ray oscilloscope.

CrO_2 Chromium dioxide.

C roll The third roll used in checkerboarding. Also called *C copy.* Cf. A roll and B roll.

crony journalism A lack of ethics displayed by a journalist who ignores negative news about friends or influential acquaintances.

crop ☐ To trim the edges of a picture by moving a camera closer to the talent or object. ☐ To trim a photograph to the desired aspect ratio. Also called *cropping.*

crop mark A line or other mark used to indicate the places where pictures should be cropped.

cropping *See* crop.

cross A movement by talent from one side of the set or stage to the other. Abbreviated *X* on a script.

crossbar ☐ A metal bar used to strengthen a large chase. ☐ A printing press guide used to turn or guide paper. ☐ *See* cross stroke.

cross channel affiliation The ownership of two different electronic media by the same individual or organization. Also called *cross ownership.* Cf. cross media ownership and group ownership.

cross connect circuit A connecting system that permits studio outlets to be temporarily connected to various dimmers and nondim circuit outputs. Cf. patch panel and selector switch system.

cross cut ☐ To cut back and forth between two different scenes in order to give the impression that the two events are occurring simultaneously. Also called *cross cutting, parallel cutting,* and *intercut.* ☐ To cut, often rapidly, from one picture to another within a scene.

cross-cut A British term for cut.

cross cutting *See* cross cut.

cross-dissolve *See* dissolve.

cross examination The legal act of questioning a witness by the opposing side on an issue in question.

cross-fade ☐ In television, a dissolve. ☐ In radio, a segue. ☐ In lighting, the transition from one light source to another.

cross hairs The markings engraved in a camera viewfinder and used for centering the subject.

crosshatch ☐ A series of crossed lines used for line shading. ☐ A test pattern containing crossed lines used for television picture adjustments.

crosshead A centered headline in the body of a story.

cross-interleaved Reed-Solomon code (CIRC) An error correction code especially developed for compact discs. CIRC makes it possible for a CD player/decoder to detect and correct or conceal large burst errors. Errors up to 4000 bits (2.5 mm of track) can be corrected. Errors up to 12,304 data bits can be concealed.

cross keying The use of two key lights to provide equal illumination to two subjects or objects.

cross-lap *See* dissolve.

Crossley ratings *See* Cooperative Analysis of Broadcasting (CAB).

cross-licensing An agreement among manufacturers to pool patent rights.

crosslighting Illumination from two sources on opposite sides of the subject. Often different color media are used in the luminaires for a given area to give the illusion of shadow while providing sufficient illumination for good visibility.

crossline A one-line headline that runs across a column.

cross media ban *See* diversification of control.

cross media ownership The ownership of two or more different media outlets, such as a newspaper and a television station. Cf. cross channel affiliation.

cross modulation ☐ Interference between two broadcasting stations or channels that causes video or audio distortion. ☐ Distortion introduced in variable area optical soundtracks due to light scatter.

crossover ☐ The frequency at which a crossover network begins the rolloff. ☐ The times when television audiences normally change channels; on the hour and half-hour. ☐ The frequencies between the different signals on a cable television system. ☐ To change from one style of music to another.

crossover network An electronic device that separates the audio frequencies of an amplifier's output so as to feed separate loudspeakers.

crossover spiral *See* lead-over groove.

cross ownership *See* cross channel affiliation.

cross plug ☐ A commercial announcement, usually at the end of a radio or television program, by an alternate sponsor. ☐ A plug on different media, such as a radio spot promoting a television program, a television program promoting a book, and so on.

crosspoint A solid-state active element used in television switchers to change signal sources.

cross polarization A means of increasing the number of signals a transmission is able to carry.

cross reference A reference from one part of a book, catalogue, and so on, to another.

cross stroke A part of a letter that cuts across the stem. Also called a *crossbar.*

cross-talk An undesired signal occurring in one channel caused by an electrical signal in another channel. Cf. print-through.

cross the line To cross the imaginary line.

cross-validation *See* validation.

crowd noise Background sound, usually conversational.

crowd scene A scene in which a number of extras are shown; from a party scene to a mob scene. Also called a *mob scene.*

crowd work Extras who respond to directions as groups and are not required to perform individual business.

crowfoot A folding device used to hold the legs of a tripod stationary on slippery surfaces. Also called a *crab* and *spider.*

crown A standard size of printing paper, 15 by 19 inches (15 by 20 inches in England).

crown folio Printing paper one half the size of crown.

crown glass An optical glass that has a relatively low index of refraction.

crown octavo Printing paper one eighth the size of crown.

crown quarto Printing paper one quarter the size of crown.

CRT □ Cathode ray tube. □ Copyright Royalty Tribunal.

CRTC Canadian Radio and Television Commission. Replaced the Board of Broadcast Governors (BBG) in 1968.

CRT composition The use of a computer program to generate an image on the face of a cathode ray tube for later production as hard-copy type.

CRT feedback The editing of text or graphics using a touch screen.

CRTPB Canadian Radio Technical Planning Board.

cruise To drive a mobile radio unit with no specific destination looking for news.

cruise control A knob or joystick that controls the speed of a magnetic tape past the heads of a videotape recorder.

cruiser A mobile radio unit.

crusade A newspaper or magazine campaign that advocates reform or change in a matter of public concern. Also called a *campaign.*

crush *See* white crush and black crush.

crushout A British term for bloom.

crystal A piece of quartz ground to vibrate at a specific frequency when electrically excited.

crystal black *See* video black.

crystal controlled *See* crystal sync.

crystal cutter A cutter in which the mechanical displacements of the recording stylus are derived from the deformations of a piezoelectric material.

crystallization The creating of an awareness of vague attitudes or opinions held by individuals or the public. *See* selective perception.

crystal microphone An inexpensive, low-quality microphone.

crystal oven An enclosed heating device used to maintain a crystal at a constant temperature and thus decrease frequency drift.

crystal pickup An inexpensive, low-quality phonograph cartridge. Also called a *piezoelectric pickup.* Cf. magnetic pickup.

Crystal Radio Awards Awards given by the NAB to radio stations for community service and involvement.

crystal set The early form of radio receiver, using a tuning coil, a crystal detector, and a pair of earphones.

crystal sync Camera and recorder speed synchronization accomplished by crystal controlled timer. Also called *crystal controlled.*

CS □ CinemaScope. □ Communication system. □ Close-shot. *See also* close-up.

C/S Characters per second.

CSC Cable/show cause. An FCC file-number prefix for cable television filed after March 31, 1972.

CSO Color separation overlay.

CSPA Columbia Scholastic Press Association.

C-SPAN A cable television satellite public affairs network.

CSR Cable/special relief. An FCC file-number prefix for cable television filed after March 31, 1972.

CSTA Cable/special temporary authority. An FCC file-number prefix for cable television.

CT □ Color temperature. □ Cartridge tape. □ Commercial television. An FCC file-number prefix.

CTAB Cable Television Advertising Bureau. A trade association.

CTAC Cable Television Technical Advisory Committee of the FCC.

CTAM Cable Television Administration and Marketing Society.

CTCM Chroma time compressed multiplex. A multiplex system in which the signals are separated into R-Y and B-Y chrominance signals and time compressed before being recorded in the C-track.

CTG Copy to go.

CTIC Cable Television Information Center.

ctr An abbreviation for *center.*

CTS Communication technology satellite.

CTV □ Cable television. □ Canadian Television. A national broadcasting organization.

CTW Children's Television Workshop.

CU □ Close-up. □ Control unit.

CUB Council for UHF Broadcasting. An organization of UHF licensees and organizations dedicated to obtain UHF parity with VHF.

cub An apprentice reporter.

cucoloris An opaque material that has a cutout that allows light to pass through the cutout area in order to project a form, such as a cloud formation, on the scenery or cyclorama. Also called a *cookie, cuke, kookie,* and a *pattern projector.*

cuddling Broadcasting on adjacent channels.

cue □ A prearranged signal to start a radio or television program, a sound, a picture, a movement or speech by talent, and so on. Cues may be given by hand signal, cue cards, light, music, the action of a performer, and so on. □ To prepare recorded material for playback. □ A hand signal or verbal command by a director or floor manager to begin. □ In an automated lighting setup, to prepare a lighting sequence for use. □ An event in a production that is the signal for a specific action; a signal given in order to cause such an action; the response to such a signal, which may include intensity setting for all luminaires in use in the production. □ To prepare a tape and machine for playback by positioning the tape in the transport at a point just prior to the beginning of a program. Also called *cue up.*

cue bite A line begun by a performer before the line by another performer is finished.

cue board *See* cue card.

cue box *See* cue speaker.

cue card A large card held near a camera used to prompt a performer. Also called an *idiot card, idiot sheet, cue board, cue sheet,* and *prompter card.* Cf. teleprompter.

cue channel □ A second audio channel on a recorder used for cueing purposes. □ A channel in an audio console that allows the operator to hear records, tapes, and so on, being cued. Cf. audition channel and program channel. □ That portion of a videotape recorder devoted to the recording and replay of the cueing information or time code signals relating to the video. □ By extension, the signals in such a channel or the output of the channel.

cue circuit □ A unidirectional voice circuit used to convey program information. Cf. talkback. □ A circuit used for camera, microphone, and other types of warning lights.

cue clock An elapsed time clock used to indicate the time remaining in a radio broadcast or television program until a station break or other event.

cue code In compact discs, a code used in tape mastering. Recorded on audio track 1 of the CD master tape, it contains the information necessary to generate subcode during disc mastering.

cue control The control mechanism on an audio recorder that lifts the tape from the heads.

Cue Dot The first automation system designed for radio in the late 1950s by Paul Schafer.

cue dots *See* changeover cue.

cue-in *See* cue.

cueing □ The act of preparing recorded material for playback. □ The act of delivering a cue.

cue light A British term for a tally light.

cue line □ A telephone company line from a remote to a studio. Also called a *control circuit* and *ring-down line.* □ A line delivered by talent that cues another performer.

cue marks Circles in the upper right-hand corner of film frames used to indicate the end of the reel. Also called a *cue punch* and *film cue. See also* changeover cue.

cue material Information given to a scriptwriter.

cue print A specially marked film for musicians to perform postproduction work. *See also* click track.

cue program A network or remote feed of material before the actual radio or television program. Used for setting levels and cueing.

cue punch *See* cue marks.

cue rehearsal A rehearsal of the portions of a radio or television program with difficult or complicated cues.

cue sheet □ An orderly list of all the cues in a program. □ A camera shot sheet. □ *See* cue card. □ A list of the sound cues with instructions for the film sound mixer. Also called a *mixing sheet.* □ A list of film camera filters, lenses, and so on, used by a cinematographer.

cue sheet timing A listing of the times at which specific radio or television program segments should begin or end. Cf. rundown sheet.

cue speaker A loudspeaker used by an audio operator to hear records or tapes being cued.

cue system An audio console circuit used for cueing records and tapes. Cf. audition.

cue tone One of the three possible tones placed on cart machine tapes: 1000 Hz, the primary cue tone, 150 Hz, the secondary cue tone, and 8 kHz, the tertiary cue tone. The primary cue tone is used to cue the cart machine; the secondary and tertiary cue tones are used for auxiliary switching functions.

cue track The area reserved on the tape for an audio record that may relate to production requirements, contain electronic editing information, or serve as an ancillary program signal.

cue up To prepare a recording for playback. *See also* cue.

CUFC Consortium of University Film Centers.

cuffo A slang term for work done on speculation or without pay.

cuke *See* cucoloris.

culling The process of removing unwanted material, footage, dialogue, and so on.

cult film A motion picture that has become popular with a group of individuals.

cultivation theory A theory based on the idea that heavy media consumption influences attitudes and beliefs.

cultural imperialism The result of media imperialism: a cultural (and political or economic) control over underdeveloped geographic areas and nations.

cume An abbreviation for *cumulative audience.* An estimate of the number of different television households or different resident persons within those households that view at least once during the average week for five minutes or more during the reported time. This is an unduplicated or cumulative estimate for *circulation* or *reach.*

cume daypart combinations The unduplicated audience for combinations of dayparts.

cume persons The estimated number of different persons who listened to a station for a minimum of five minutes within a given daypart. Cume estimates may also be referred to as *cumulative, unduplicated,* or *reach estimates.*

cume rating The estimated number of cume persons expressed as a percentage of the universe. This estimate is shown for the Metro only.

cum privilegio From the Latin meaning "with privilege." A book published with proper licensing or authorization. *See also* imprimatur and nihil obstat.

cumulative audience The total nonduplicated audience for one or a series of telecasts, programs, messages, or time periods, expressed as a percentage of a given universe. A household or person counts once no matter how many times he or she may have viewed the telecasts. This is sometimes referred to as *reach, net unduplicated audience,* or *net reach.* If the context is the actual number of households or persons reached at least once during a specific period of time by a network or station, this number is referred to as the *circulation.* Usually abbreviated *cume.* Cf. gross audience.

cumulative book index *See* cumulative index.

cumulative catalogue *See* cumulative index.

cumulative index An index of previously published material. Also called a *cumulative catalogue.*

cumulative influence The effects of exposure to the mass media on individuals that take place over an extended period of time.

Cumulative Radio Audience Method (CRAM) An in-depth NBC telephone audience study carried on in the 1960s. *See also* ARMS and RADAR.

cumulative rating *See* cumulative audience.

cumulative reach *See* cumulative audience.

cumulative time The total elapsed time since the beginning of a radio or television program. Also called *running time.* Cf. playing time.

cuneiform The wedge-shaped writing initiated by the Sumerians some 6000 years ago.

cupping The undesired curvature of a magnetic tape in the lateral direction. Also called *transverse curl.*

CUPUOS Committee on the Peaceful Uses of Outer Space (of the United Nations).

Curie point That temperature above which a ferromagnetic substance, such as a magnet, loses virtually all of its ferromagnetic properties.

curiosa Strange or unusual books.

curl A movement similar to a page turn in television.

current (I) The rate of movement of electrons through a conductor measured in amperes.

current carrying capacity The maximum current a conductor or device can carry without overheating or throwing a circuit breaker.

current issue The issue of a periodical that is being mailed and displayed on newsstands.

cursive A graceful type style that is similar to handwriting. Cf. script and italic.

cursor A symbol or character on a screen that indicates a position or a path to be followed. Moved by a computer application program to guide the user and by the user to define a requirement.

cursor plane In multiplane video representations, the one-pixel-deep plane in which the graphical image cursor is presented. This plane can be moved around the display or made invisible as required and can be positioned at any other point over other planes.

curtain □ Any material that separates an audience from a stage. Also called a *house curtain, main curtain, front curtain,* and *show curtain.* □ The end of a program or play. □ A headline with rules on three sides.

curtain call The applause by a live audience that requests the performers to take a bow, play an encore, and so on.

curtain line *See* tagline.

curved plate A printing plate used on a rotary press.

curved screen A wide-screen process screen used for a system such as Cinerama. Used to avoid lateral distortion at the ends of the screen.

cushion Extra material, sound, picture, or lines, which can be inserted into or deleted from the end of a radio or television program so that it ends on time.

custom binding □ A book cover designed and bound to the specifications of the buyer. □ A specially designed book binding.

custom book A book printed to the specifications of the buyer.

customer service A department of a company that handles orders, complaints, questions, and, sometimes, billing.

custom label A company that produces records under its own name but has a major record company distribute them.

CUT Coordinated universal time. Formerly GMT.

cut □ Any of the separate bands on a disc. □ A radio or television director's command to stop action. Cf. freeze. □ To edit a tape or film. □ To delete lines or scenes from a script. □ To make a disc recording. □ To switch from one picture to another. *See also* take. □ To delete the end of a radio or television program that is running too long. □ To shorten copy. □ A woodcut. □ An engraved block or plate for printing. □ An illustration embedded in text. □ To trim the edges of book pages. □ To cut apart full printed sheets in preparation for binding. □ To eliminate a performer from a role. □ *See* clip. □ *See* bite. □ A direct or immediate transition from one scene to the next. □ The removal of unwanted footage from a film during editing.

cut and hold A director's command for cameras to stop recording and performers to freeze.

cut and paste An electronic technique for the manipulation of textural or pictorial information on a screen in a manner similar to the cut and paste technique used in editing such information on paper.

cutaway A shot that focuses on something other than the main action; a reaction shot. Also called a *cutaway shot.*

cutaway questions Questions asked by a reporter after an interview for use as cutaways in editing.

cutaway shot *See* cutaway.

cutback A shot that returns to a scene or character previously shown. Cf. continuous action.

cut bank A row of buttons on a video switcher used for cutting between pictures.

cut edges Book edges that have been trimmed. Also called *cut*.

cut film *See* sheet film.

cut flush To trim a book cover so that it does not overlap the edges of the paper.

cut in □ A local commercial substituted for one being fed by a network. Also called a *local cut in*. □ A camera shot inserted in a master shot. □ To eliminate text so that other—more important or newer—material may be inserted without increasing the length. □ *See* cut in head. □ An announcement inserted in a network program but which is released to a lesser portion of the network (but consisting of more than one station). □ An audio promo added near the end of a television program; usually while the credits are running. Also called a *cut in tag*.

cut in head A side headline or explanatory matter surrounded on three sides by text.

cut in letter A large initial letter, sometimes illustrated, that begins a chapter or heading.

cut in tag *See* cut in.

cut key *See* cough button.

cut length *See* cutoff.

cutline A caption printed below a picture or illustration; a legend. Also called an *underline*.

cutoff □ A thin dividing line between different elements on a printed page. Also called a *cutoff rule*. □ The cut length of a completed newspaper. Also called *cut length*. □ The portion of a television picture not seen on a receiver. Cf. essential area.

cut-off frequency The frequency above and below which no appreciable energy is radiated by an antenna.

cutoff rule *See* cutoff.

cutout □ An unused portion of recorded tape or film. Also called *overs*. □ A visual device affixed to the surface of an outdoor bulletin to give it a three-dimensional effect. □ *See* cutouts.

cut out To cut from a close-up to a long shot.

cutout animation The use of jointed cutout figures that are moved slightly between each frame of an animated sequence.

cut-outs Letters, packages, figures, or mechanical devices that are attached to the face of an outdoor advertising bulletin to provide a three-dimensional effect. Also called an *embellishment*.

cutouts An animation technique in which small, flat, jointed figures, usually made of heavy paper, are placed over a background and manipulated under the camera, then photographed.

cutouts on cels An animation technique combining the cel and cutout methods. The cutout figures are pasted onto cels, placed over a background, and photographed.

cut picture *See* workprint.

cutrate subscription A periodical subscription offered at a special low rate to stimulate circulation.

cuts The eliminated portions of a script. Cf. provisional cut.

cut sheet A list that instructs an editor how a television or motion picture sequence is to be edited.

cut sheet feeder *See* automatic sheet feeder.

cuts only A simple videotape editor that is capable of making straight cuts only.

cutter □ An electromechanical transducer that transforms an electric input into mechanical motions of a cutting stylus. □ *See* gobo. □ The person, usually under the direction of an editor, who does the physical splicing of film.

cutting □ The editing of film. □ The making of a disc or tape. □ *See* clip. □ *See* die cut.

cutting copy □ A duplicate of a film or videotape used for editing purposes. □ A British term for a workprint.

cutting cylinder The printing cylinder containing the knives that cut a newspaper to the proper length.

cutting on A method of editing in which there is motivation for the cut. Examples include cutting on action, cutting on motivation, cutting on mood, and cutting on the beat.

cutting print A British term for a workprint.

cutting rate The number of grooves per inch on a disc. For micro-groove discs, 200 to 300 grooves per inch.

cutting room A film editing room.

cutting room floor Often, the receptacle for the scenes from a motion picture that are not to be used.

cutting rubber The long rubber block against which the cutting knives move to cut newspapers to length.

cutting stylus A stylus having its cutting edge at a plane substantially different from the cutting facet for the purpose of cutting and polishing the groove in an acetate disc.

cutting sync *See* editorial sync.

CW □ Carrier wave. □ Clockwise. □ Continuous wave.

CWA Communications Workers of America. A union.

CWD Consecutive weeks discount.

CWPR Committee on Women in Public Relations.

cx An abbreviation for *correction*. Also spelled *corx*. *See also* CQ.

cyan One of the three primary subtractive colors. *See also* primary color.

cybernetics A comparative study of the interaction between men and machines; the basis of communication theory. The word was coined by Norbert Wiener in 1948.

cyc An abbreviation for *cyclorama*.

cycle □ One complete alternation of sound or radio waves. The rate of repetition of cycles is the frequency. □ A series of drawings that are photographed again and again. The last drawing moves logically into the first to create the appearance of continuous, repetitive motion. Cycles are normally used for movements that are repeated without variation, such as walks or runs. □ A period, often a quarter of 13 weeks, used as a unit of time in negotiations for purchase of commercial occasions or for the payment of commercial performers. □ *See* cycle time. □ The time required to complete one complete computer operation. □ A sequence performed repeatedly in the same order.

cycle animation *See* cycle.

cycle discount A discount for the purchase of radio or television time to run during an entire cycle, at a rate increasing according to the number of cycles purchased.

cycles per second (CPS) An obsolete term for *hertz*.

cycle time □ The total time required to extract a cartridge or cassette just played and replace it with another cartridge or cassette, properly cued for play. □ The minimum duration of a series of cartridges or cassettes that may be played without suffering an interruption in the continuous flow of video. □ *See* cycle.

cyclic animation A film that creates a story or a repeated sequence. *See also* cycle.

cyclic programming The proposition that television program types reach a peak, fall in numbers, then return.

cyclic redundancy check (CRC) In compact discs, a separate error detection scheme for the compact disc subcode.

cyc light A luminaire that produces a soft light capable of lighting a cyclorama evenly from a relatively close distance.

cyclodrum A rotating drum with regularly spaced openings and a light source, used to create the effect of a passing train or automobile lights. *See also* gloccamorra.

cyclorama A vertical surface that forms the background for a theatrical type setting. Although it can be fabricated of a solid material, which is referred to as a "hard cyc," usually it is made of heavy cloth that is drawn taut in both the horizontal and vertical planes to achieve a smooth, flat surface. Usually referred to as a *cyc*. Also called a *panorama cloth*.

cyclorama strip lights A striplight mounted horizontally at the top or bottom of a cyclorama to light it in a smooth or uniform manner. Also called a *cyc strip*.

cyc strip *See* cyclorama strip lights.

cylinder press *See* flatbed press.

cylinder scanning *See* drum scanning.

cylindrical A normal projection lens, as opposed to an anamorphic lens.

cylindrical screen A 360-degree projection screen.

D

D □ Daytime. □ Deci. □ Deleted. □ Deferred. A wire service code for stories of secondary importance. □ Density. □ Digit. □ Digital. □ Display. □ Dissolve. □ Distance. □ Domain.

DA □ Directional antenna. □ Distribution amplifier.

d/a Digital to analog.

DAC Digital to analog converter.

DAD Digital audio disc.

DAF Demographic adjustment factor.

dag An abbreviation for *aquadag*.

dagger A reference mark, †.

daguerreotype The first practical photographic process, invented by Louis Jacques Mande Daguerre in 1839. It consisted of a positive image on a silver-coated copper plate.

dailies A print of the previous day's shooting, used to check the results for correctness. Used mainly in feature production. Also called *rushes*.

daily A newspaper, bulletin, or other publication that is published at least five times a week.

daily effective circulation (DEC) The audience that has an opportunity to see an outdoor advertising structure(s) in a 24-hour period.

daily electronic feed (DEF) An ABC news service fed to its affiliates. Cf. A News.

daily fee *See* session fee.

daily location work Location work on an assignment that does not require a performer to stay away from home overnight. Cf. location work and overnight location work.

daily newspaper *See* daily.

daily rate The advertising space rate charged by a daily newspaper for all editions published Monday through Friday or Saturday.

daily service A telephone company line that is supplied on a one-time basis to a television station or network for 24 hours, usually for special events.

daisy chaining □ The connection of computer peripheral devices in series. □ The term also refers to disk drives that are connected in parallel from a controller.

daisy wheel A type of print element with raised characters on spokes emanating from a central hub. Cf. dot matrix printer.

dakota Any script material or lines that lead directly into a song.

damages The compensation awarded by a court to a person who has suffered loss or injury in, for example, a suit for defamation.

damped ballistics A method of damping a VU meter so that it reads averages instead of peaks.

damped oscillation Oscillation that—because the driving force has been removed—gradually dies out, each swing being smaller than the preceding in smooth, regular decay.

dampen To deaden vibration by absorption, usually by using draperies, nonreflective walls, and so on. *See also* reverberation.

damping A mechanical or electrical reduction of oscillations.

damping control A potentiometer used to eliminate horizontal distortion in a television receiver.

dance-in A stand-in for a dancer.

dancer □ An individual who dances in a motion picture or television program. According to the Screen Actors Guild, the term includes both swimmers and skaters when the performance is choreographed. □ *See* dandy roll.

dandy roll A wired cylinder that impresses watermarks or lines on paper. Also called a *dancer*.

DAR Day-after recall.

dark □ A set or studio that is not being used at the time. □ *See* regular.

dark current *See* electrode dark current.

dark end The loading end of a film-developing machine. Cf. light end.

darkroom A light-proof area used to process film.

dark week *See* black week.

DASH Digital audio stationary head.

dash □ A punctuation mark (—). □ A short horizontal rule used to separate parts of a headline, story, and so on. *See also* em dash, en dash, jim dash, thirty dash. □ The longer of the two sounds made by a telegrapher's key. Cf. dot.

DAT Digital audiotape.

data Factual material such as information, numbers, symbols, or letters used to describe persons, objects, situations, or other items for analysis, discussion, or decision.

data bank □ A comprehensive data file that is updated regularly for various reasons, such as the production of mailing lists. □ A summary compilation of audience estimates for the various media made by BBDO.

database A systematic organization of data files containing information concerning a particular subject.

database manager A computer or computer program that handles the flow of news from its reception to its composition.

database publishing *See* electronic publishing.

data bit-indicator A CD-I sector containing software, text, or data used by the application.

data capture The process of converting information into computer readable form; keyboarding and scanning are such processes.

data channel □ An analog or digital communication channel used to carry data between two points. □ A cable television channel that carries weather information, messages, promotions, and so on. □ In CD, a channel carrying data, as opposed to audio information. □ In CD-ROM, a channel carrying mode 1 data.

data collection The gathering of data for processing.

data communication *See* data transmission.

data compression The act of automatically removing or compressing redundant or unnecessary information from computer storage to save space.

data driven action tagging In CD-I, the technique for identifying or tagging events on the different data streams (audio, video, and text/data) so that they can be synchronized according to the requirements of the application program.

data entry The process of entering individual data items, usually after they have been coded, onto a computerized record or data file. Normally, this is accomplished through manually keying or keypunching each item; however, data entry may be totally automated using optical scanners and similar electronic devices.

Data Interchange Format (DIF) A file format used to allow data to be exchanged among incompatible formats. *See also* ASCII.

data link A communications circuit used for the transmission of data between two points.

Datanews The high-speed digital news service of United Press International.

data processing □ The classifying, sorting, storing, reporting, and so on, of information to produce records and reports. □ The coding, editing, and tabulating of factual material obtained in an audience survey or other study.

data radio *See* teletext.

data reduction The selection of specific information from a large volume of raw data in a computer database.

Datastream The high-speed digital news service of the Associated Press.

data tablet A device with a pen-shaped stylus that is used to input graphics into a computer on a television screen.

data terminal *See* terminal.

Data terminal equipment (DTE) Equipment such as terminals and computers that are connected to a modem using the RS-232 standard for serial connections.

data transmission The high-speed transfer of data from one computer to another or from a terminal to a mainframe.

DATE Digital audio for television. A system designed to deliver improved television sound.

datebook *See* future book.

dated Material, especially news, that is outdated and no longer usable.

dateline □ The point of origin of a news story. □ The opening phrase of a news story that names the source.

dateline technique A transitional device used in some newscasts calling for the use of a dateline before each story.

dating An extension of credit received by postdating an invoice.

datum A singular form of *data*.

Davis Amendment An amendment to the Radio Act of 1927 that required the FCC to make an equal allocation of broadcast stations among five zones. Later, part of Section 307 of the Communications Act until repealed.

dawn patrol The radio or television station personnel who have an early morning shift.

day □ An abbreviation for *daylight* and *benday*. □ Any twenty-four-hour period beginning 0100 GMT and ending 0100 GMT.

day-after recall (DAR) Audience recall measured the day after an advertisement is exposed.

day-after survey An advertising research survey made 15 to 24 hours after a test treatment, such as the broadcast of a test commercial.

daybook A book in which news stories are listed for use in making assignments.

day for night Photographing during the day with filters to achieve a nighttime effect. Cf. night for night.

Day-Glo A trademark for certain inks and lacquers that become fluorescent when activated by ultraviolet rays of light or the near ultraviolet rays of blacklight.

daylight □ The color temperature of sunlight, usually considered to be 5600 degrees K, although it is actually often much higher. Cf. sunlight. □ Film balanced for daylight.

daylight cassette *See* daylight loading.

daylight film Film that is designed for use in daylight or with electronic flash.

daylight filter A filter used to balance light from a source such that the spectral distribution will approximate daylight; used when a camera or film balanced to daylight response is employed with sources such as incandescent lamps.

daylight loading A spool or cassette designed to be loaded in subdued light without subsequent film fogging.

daylight loading tank A film processing device that allows the use of light in the darkroom after the film is loaded.

daylight spool *See* daylight loading.

daypart Any of the time segments of a broadcast day for which listening or viewing estimates are calculated and recognized in the industry. Dayparts for television are usually daytime, early fringe, access, prime time, late fringe, and late night; for radio, morning drive, daytime, afternoon drive, night, and all night.

dayparting The changing of programming to fit the needs and desires of the various dayparts on radio and television.

day player A player employed by the day, other than an extra, stunt player, professional singer, or airplane pilot. Cf. contract player, deal player, free-lance player, multiple picture player, stunt player, and term player.

day shift *See* day side.

day side The daytime staff of a newspaper. Cf. night side.

daytime (D) □ The period of time between local sunrise and local sunset. □ *See* daytime operation. □ The time period on television from sign on to approximately 5 p.m. *See also* daypart. □ The radio time from approximately 10 a.m. to 3 p.m. *See also* daypart.

Daytime Broadcasters' Association (DBA) An organization of broadcasters licensed for daytime operation dedicated to achieving parity with full-time stations.

daytime drama *See* soap opera.

daytime only operation *See* daytime operation.

daytime operation An AM broadcast license that permits broadcasting from approximately sunrise to approximately sunset only.

daytimer An AM station licensed for daytime operation.

daytime station *See* daytime operation.

DB Delayed broadcast.

dB Decibel.

d/b Digital to binary.

DBA □ Daytime Broadcasters Association. □ Doing business as. A fictitious name under which an individual or company operates.

dBk Decibels above one kw.

dB meter A meter calibrated to read directly in decibels. Cf. VU meter.

DBMS Database management system. Computer software designed to organize data.

DBS Direct broadcast satellite.

DBSA Direct Broadcast Satellite Association. *See* STIA.

dBu Decibels above one mv/m.

DC □ Data check. □ Digital computer. □ Direct coupled. □ Direct current. □ Disconnect. □ Display code. □ Double contact. A lamp base type. □ Double column.

D county An A. C. Nielsen designation for any county that is not an A, B, or C county. Cf. A county, B county, and C county.

DCP Display control program.

DDC Defense Documentation Center.

DDR Digital disc recorder.

dead □ A studio dampened by draperies, carpeting, and other sound-absorbing materials so that little or no sound is reflected. Also called *dead acoustic*. Cf. live. □ A microphone, potentiometer, or other equipment that is not activated. □ Copy or type that is no longer needed. Also called *dead matter*. □ A periodical subscription that has expired and has not been renewed.

dead acoustic A studio in which little or no sound is reflected. *See also* dead.

dead air □ The transmission of a carrier wave without modulation. □ A brief lapse in a radio or television program usually due to a missed cue or other mistakes by talent.

dead area A geographical location where broadcast reception is difficult or impossible. *See also* silent zone.

dead bank A holder that contains unusable type.

deadbeat A person who has ordered a product or service and, without just cause, has failed to pay for it.

dead book Radio and television programs that have been aired.

deaden *See* dampen.

dead end The end of a studio with the least amount of reverberation.

dead front An electrical panel or switchboard that has no exposed wires or current-carrying parts. Cf. hot front.

dead groove *See* unmodulated groove.

deadhorse Printing that is paid for before it is run.

deadline The latest time or date material to be used on a broadcast may be received or approved.

dead matte A photographic print with a dull finish that can be easily marked with a pencil or pen.

dead matter *See* dead.

dead metal □ The areas on a printing plate that are to be trimmed away. □ Metal that is to be remelted.

dead microphone A disconnected or inoperative microphone.

deadpan The reading of a line by talent without facial expression or interpretation.

dead pot A potentiometer set at maximum attenuation.

dead roll The process of beginning a tape, film, record, and so on, at a designated time so as to have it end on time. Used when a live radio or television program is running over its allotted time.

dead room A studio that has little or no reverberation. A completely dead room is called an *anechoic chamber*.

dead season The time of year when no new productions are being filmed or taped.

dead side The side(s) of a microphone that has a low response compared to the live side.

dead space *See* dead spot.

dead spot □ A geographical area in which radio signals are received with a low signal strength or are not received. Also called *dead space*. □ The time period in which a commercial or program is scheduled but not shown. Also called *black space*. □ A small area on a set where the light level drops. □ A gap in a pickup pattern caused by improper microphone placement.

dead time *See* downtime.

dead zone An area in which radio and television reception is difficult or impossible.

deaf aid A slang term for an inconspicuous earphone worn by talent for cueing purposes.

deal To apportion work, as in assigning news stories to reporters.

dealer A company that sells merchandise at retail or wholesale.

dealer imprint The name and address of a dealer printed on a leaflet, pamphlet, poster, and so on, usually printed or stamped in a space provided for the purpose.

dealer space The space on a brochure, flyer, and so on, used for a dealer's imprint.

dealer spot A radio or television commercial furnished by a manufacturer for use in local markets.

dealer super *See* local tag.

dealer tie-in A listing of local dealers in an advertisement paid for entirely by a manufacturer.

dealer use Commercials produced by manufacturers or distributors and used by retail merchants on local radio or television stations where the station time is contracted for by the retail merchant. Cf. program use and wild spot.

deal player A player who is employed for one or more motion pictures at a guaranteed salary of $25,000 or more per picture. Cf. contract player, day player, free-lance player, multiple picture player, stunt player, and term player.

deblooping A film that has had words or phrases blooped but upon rerelease has the words or phrases reinserted in the soundtrack.

debrief To interview an individual after a news event.

debriefing log A radio or television station record of news events or guests; contains notes and comments about events and individuals.

debug □ The process of locating and removing mistakes in a computer program or a computer system or other electronic device. □ To correct a malfunction.

deburn A process of defocusing a television camera pointed toward a light source to eliminate an image burned on the face of the pickup tube.

debut An actor's, singer's, dancer's, or other performer's first performance.

DEC Daily effective circulation.

deca A metric prefix for 10.

decalcomania A design or logo printed on paper, glass, metal, and so on. Also called *transfer printing.*

DEC ASCII A form of ASCII computer codes.

decay □ The deterioration that takes place over a period of time. May be said of a sound, equipment, survey respondents, and so on. □ The rate at which a sound decreases in intensity. □ The length of time until a stored tape becomes unusable. Also called *decay time.*

decay rate The time period necessary for an electronic device to go from on to off.

decay time *See* decay rate.

Decency in Broadcasting (DIB) An organization formed in 1985 to protest the blue humor of two Indianapolis, Indiana, disc jockeys.

deceptive advertising *See* false advertising.

deceptive program A program or portion thereof designed with the intent to deceive the listening or viewing public. Prohibited by Section 509 of the Communications Act.

deci A prefix meaning one-tenth.

decibel (dB) One tenth of a bel. The standard measure of relative intensity, power, or voltage. A change of one decibel is barely discernible by the human ear; 20 decibels is equivalent to the rustling of leaves; 130 decibels is the threshold of pain. *See also* loudness. Cf. phon.

decile The 9 percentile points that divide a distribution into 10 equal parts.

decimal An integer represented by a character from 0 to 9.

decimal classification *See* Dewey decimal system.

decision □ An operation performed by a computer in choosing between two or more possible courses of action. □ A determination made by an administrative agency or a court of a matter before it. *See also* initial decision and final decision.

decision list *See* edit decision list.

decision-making Commission personnel Federal Communications Commission personnel in restricted adjudicative or rule-making proceedings: the Commissioners and their personal office staffs; the chief of the Office of Opinions and Review and staff; the Review Board and staff; the chief administrative law judge, the administrative law judges; the general counsel and staff; the chief engineer and staff; and the chief of the Cable Television Bureau and staff when participating in proceedings involving service by common carriers to community antenna television systems.

decisive moment That one instant in which a subject or object is positioned perfectly for a photograph or shot.

deck □ The plate of a tape transport that serves as the main support for the elements of the transport. □ The complete audio- or videotape transport itself. □ A collection of business reply postcards, often in the form of a booklet, to be returned to businesses by consumers requesting products or information. Also called a *card deck* and *direct response cards.* □ A portion of a headline. Also called a *bank* and *deck head.* □ The holder from which sheets are fed into a press. □ A pack of punched cards belonging to a specific file.

deck head *See* deck.

deckle A frame that forms the paper pulp and fixes the size of a sheet of paper.

deckle edge Book paper with rough, untrimmed edges.

deck panel Two outdoor advertising structures with the same facing built one above the other. *See also* double decker.

declaratory ruling An action by the FCC terminating a controversy or removing uncertainty in a proceeding.

declination angle The angle between the polar axis and the plane of a satellite.

decode The opposite of encode. To alter data from one format to the original format.

decoder □ An electronic device in a television receiver that separates the encoded red, green, and blue components of the signal. Cf. encoder. □ A device used to detect and activate circuitry to demute a broadcast receiver for the EBS two-tone attention signal. □ A device used to unscramble an encoded television signal. Also called a *decrypter* and *descrambler.* □ A device that translates a set of coded data.

decor The overall appearance of a set; a combination of the furniture, wall covering, lighting, and so on.

decoupage The breakdown of the action and the setup of the camera shots to be used in a scene.

decoy A unique or fictitious name inserted in a mailing list (or dictionary) to check for possible usage by unauthorized individuals. Also called a *dummy name.*

decree A judicial decision or order.

decrypter *See* decoder.

dedicated A machine, device, port, service, circuit, system, and so on, that is used for only one purpose, service, or operator.

dedicated channel □ A cable television channel devoted to a single source for its programming. □ A cable television channel used for local government access, education access, leased access, or public access. □ *See* dedicated line.

dedicated device *See* dedicated.

dedicated key A computer keyboard multitask key that accomplishes a function that would normally take two or more keystrokes.

dedicated line A communications link between two devices that is reserved for that use only. Also called a *dedicated channel.*

dedicated machine A videotape recorder or player whose versatility is limited—either by its construction or by its operator—to optimize its performance for a particular function. Examples include features such as record only, commercial-playing, and network time-delay machine.

dedicated system *See* dedicated.

dedicated word processor A computer used primarily for producing short, uncomplicated letters and simple documents.

dedication A name, and often a brief thought, inscribing a book to a person.

dedication page The front matter page used for a dedication.

deduction The process of reasoning from the general to the specific. Cf. induction.

deejay A slang term for a radio disc jockey. Also spelled *DJ.*

deemphasis An operation, complementary to preemphasis, by which signal frequencies emphasized before transmission or recording are restored to their normal relative amplitudes. *See also* postemphasis.

deep A source of information that may not be identified; as in *deep throat.*

deep etch An offset lithographic process in which the plates are deeply etched. Used for critical work and long runs.

deep field Great depth of field. *See also* deep focus.

deep focus A style of cinematography in which everything is kept in focus, from close-up to infinity. Also called *deep field.* Cf. differential focus and shallow focus.

deep space Space at a distance from the earth approximately equal to, or greater than, the distance between the earth and the moon.

deesser A compressor that is used to reduce sibilance and other high-frequency audio sounds.

DEF Daily electronic feed.

de facto pilot A television series pilot that is accepted and produced for a network or syndicator. A consideration in compensation for a pilot made on speculation.

defamacast Broadcast defamation.

defamation A statement made orally or in writing that exposes a person to ridicule, hatred, contempt, and scorn; injures him or her in business; or lowers his or her reputation in the community. *See also* libel and slander.

default A predetermined setting or outcome automatically made unless another option is selected or substituted.

defective pleading Any pleading filed in a formal complaint not in conformity with the requirements of applicable FCC rules and regulations.

defendant The person against whom charges are brought in a civil lawsuit or criminal action.

deferred A wire service code for news stories of less than immediate importance; stories that may be run at later dates. Cf. advance, bulletin, flash, regular, and urgent.

deficit financing An arrangement whereby motion picture studios lease productions to television networks for less than the cost of the picture. The deficit is, hopefully, recouped in syndication and/or foreign distribution.

defining power *See* definition.

definition □ The degree of sharpness, detail, or fidelity with which the elements of a television picture are reproduced. *See also* resolution. □ The sharpness of a lens. Also called *defining power.* □ The clarity with which an emulsion renders an image on film. □ The fidelity with which a sound is reproduced.

definitive edition An authoritative book edition, presumably correct and often annotated.

definitive head A descriptive headline.

deflection The horizontal and vertical movement of the scanning beam in a television camera or receiver controlled by an electromagnetic or electrostatic field. *See also* yoke.

deflection coil An electromagnetic field produced by an inductance to deflect the scanning beam in a television camera or receiver.

deflection yoke *See* yoke.

defocus To cause a picture to be out of focus.

defocusing *See* defocus transition.

defocusing dissolve *See* defocus transition.

defocus mix *See* defocus transition.

defocus transition A transitional device wherein one scene goes out of focus as another comes into focus. Also called *defocusing, defocusing dissolve, defocus mix,* and *out of focus dissolve.*

degauss □ To remove remanent magnetism from a material by subjecting it to an alternating magnetic field of gradually diminishing strength. *See also* erase. □ To remove a magnetic field from a color television receiver. □ To erase a tape in a magnetic field. *See also* bulk eraser.

degausser A device used to remove the magnetic field that builds up around a color television receiver. *See also* demagnetizer.

degradation □ A gradual decrease in the ability of a component to work satisfactorily. □ The decrease in picture or sound quality caused by interference. □ The loss of image quality on film or tape through duplication or dubbing.

degrees Kelvin *See* Kelvin.

deintermixture The FCC allotment plan giving either UHF or VHF television stations but not both to a market.

de jure From the Latin, according to law. An entity that has complied with all legal conditions.

del An abbreviation for *delay*.

delay □ The time necessary for a signal to travel between two components or devices. □ *See* delay line.

delay cable A coaxial cable capable of delaying a signal for a few microseconds per foot.

delayed action An electronic or mechanical shutter release that opens the shutter a few seconds later, allowing the photographer to get in the picture.

delayed broadcast (DB) The transmission of a network program at some time after the nationally scheduled period.

delayed carriage The taping of a radio or television program for later playback.

delayed lead A newspaper or magazine story that does not contain one of the five W's in the lead.

delay line □ A tape recording that is a few seconds long and is designed to retard playback. Often used in radio talk programs, allowing time for the station to cut objectionable remarks made by a call-in guest. □ A cable or other length of conductor used to delay a signal for synchronizing purposes.

delay time The amount of time one signal lags behind another.

dele An abbreviation for *delete*.

delegated authority A person, panel, or board authorized to act for the Federal Communications Commission pursuant to Section 5(d) of the Communications Act.

delegation The assigning of input and output switches or potentiometers on a console to various peripheral devices.

delete □ A proofreader's or copy editor's word or symbol designating a letter, word, or other unit of characters to be deleted from copy. □ To eliminate a character, record, program, and so on, from a computer CRT, memory, or storage.

deletion The removal by the FCC or federal court of a license to broadcast. *See also* revocation.

delimiter A character used to define the end of a string or message. *See also* EOM.

delinquent A person who has fallen behind in payments or has stopped scheduled payment for products or services.

delivery □ The physical or electronic distribution of signals, books, periodicals, and other communication to a viewer, reader, and so on. □ The physical and vocal style of communicating a word, line, or speech.

delivery date The date on which a specific list order is to be received from the list owner by the list user or designated representative of the list user.

delta A triangular shape used in some television picture tubes for the placement of the three electron guns.

delta modulation In data communications, a form of differential PCM in which only one bit for each sample is used.

delta pulse code modulation (DPCM) *See* delta modulation.

delta-YUV (DYUV) A high-efficiency image-coding scheme for natural pictures used in CD-I. DYUV coding takes advantage of the fact that there is a high correlation between adjacent pixel values, making it possible to encode only the differences between the absolute YU or YV pixel values. This coding scheme is applied per line, that is, in one dimension. *See also* YUV encoding and compression.

deluxe edition A special, often elegant edition of a book.

deluxe urban bulletin A painted outdoor advertising bulletin 13 feet, 4 inches high by 46 feet, 10 inches wide.

demagnetizer A device used to remove the magnetic field that builds up on a tape recording and playback heads. Cf. bulk eraser.

demassification The move by the mass media from attempting to reach the greatest possible audience to appealing to smaller, often upscale, audiences. *See also* fragmentation.

de minimis A trifling or insignificant legal matter.

demo □ An abbreviation for *demonstration*. □ A disc, audiotape, film, videotape, or other medium containing commercials, programs, air checks, and so on; used by production studios, directors, performers, advertising agencies, and other people for auditions.

demodulation The electronic elimination of the carrier wave of a broadcast signal by a receiver. Also called *detection.* Cf. modulation.

demodulator □ The apparatus for recovering from a signal the information input to it by a modulator. □ In a videotape recorder, the apparatus that recovers the original video from the reproduced FM signal. □ *See* processor.

demographic adjustment factor (DAF) A factor used in computation of NSI persons data to compensate for the difference in persons per television household between the in-tab sample and the universe.

demographic breakout A section of a demographic publication.

demographic characteristics A broad term that refers to the various social and economic characteristics of a group of households or group of individuals, such as age, sex, education, and occupation.

demographic edition *See* demographic publication.

demographic publication A magazine or other periodical aimed at a specific market—geographical, age, sex, occupation, ethnic group, and so on. Also called a *demographic edition.* If only a part of the publication is aimed at a specific demographic audience, it may be called a demographic breakout.

demographics The classification of audience characteristics based on social and economic conditions. Among the classifying characteristics in general use are age and sex of individuals; and education, income, race, and working status of a household member.

demographic weight *See* weight.

demographic weighting A statistical procedure designed to reduce the effects of differences between the demographic characteristics of a sample and the characteristics, either known or estimated, of the universe the sample is intended to represent.

demos An abbreviation for *demographics.*

demo tape *See* demo.

demurrer A contention in a lawsuit that even if the facts are true, they do not constitute a cause for action.

demy A standard size of printing paper, 16 by 21 inches.

denouement The action in a drama following the climax.

de novo New, again; used in the sense of beginning a trial again.

dense An overexposed film negative. Cf. thin.

densitometer A device used to measure the density of a film.

density □ The degree of compactness of magnetic particles on recording tape. □ The bits per unit of recording material. □ *See* packing density. □ The degree of opacity of a film. □ The number of characters in a given space. □ Population density, the average number of persons in a square mile.

dentelle A style of lacelike book cover decoration.

department A newspaper or magazine section.

departmental library representative A college or university professor selected to represent the academic department to the campus library in the selection of manuscripts and periodicals.

Department of Justice The part of the executive branch of the federal government charged with the administration of the law.

deposit copies The copies of books and other copyrighted materials that are required by the Copyright Act of 1976 to be filed with the Library of Congress.

deposition □ A sworn statement made by a witness who is unable to appear in court or whose appearance in person is not required. □ Any written statement made under oath.

depreciation schedule The recommended length of time in years that broadcast station assets may be depreciated for tax purposes. Typically, the period for studio equipment is 6 years; towers and antennas, 20 years; and buildings, 45 years.

depth □ The number of inches or agate lines in a newspaper or magazine column. □ The accumulated line spacing, expressed in inches or lines, displayed by a computer word processor. □ The distance on a printing plate between the printing surface and the level to which the nonprinting portions of the plate have been etched. □ The third dimension (in addition to height and width).

depth interview An interview characterized by intensive questioning.

depth of exposure The extent to which the size and duration of an advertisement or the frequency of its repetition heightens the consciousness of it on the part of a newspaper reader, television viewer, and so on.

depth of field (df) That distance—from the closest to the farthest point from the camera—in which objects appear to be in focus. Depth of field is dependent upon three factors: the focal length of the lens, the f stop used, and the distance between the object and the camera. *See also* critical focus. Cf. depth of focus.

depth of focus The distance between the lens and the film or television pickup tube target in which the object is in sharp focus. Depth of focus is dependent upon the focal length of the lens and the f stop. Cf. depth of field.

depth perception The ability to judge the distance of objects and their spatial relationships.

depth staging An arbitrary plan that divides a stage or set into foreground, middleground, and background.

depthy A slang term for a three-dimensional motion picture.

deregulate To remove controls from previously regulated industries or from previously regulated practices or procedures.

deregulation In general, the repeal of laws and rules; specifically, the removal by the FCC of unnecessary and archaic rules, which decreased paperwork and streamlined application procedures. Also called *reregulation* and *unregulation.*

derivative work A copyrighted work based upon one or more preexisting works, such as a translation, musical arrangement, dramatization, fictionalization, motion picture version, sound recording, art reproduction, abridgment, condensation, or any other form in which a work is recast, transformed, or adapted. A work consisting of editorial revisions, annotations, elaborations, or other modifications that, as a whole, represents an original work of authorship, is a derivative work.

derived dimension A dimension obtained by computation from other fundamental dimensions and given for informational purposes only. Cf. basic dimension and reference dimension.

desaturation □ A reduction in television color saturation. □ The separation of the colors in an original film negative during processing.

descender □ A character that extends below the base line, such as *g, j, p, q,* and *y.* □ The portion of a character that is between the base line and the descender line. Also called a *descending letter.*

descender line The imaginary line limiting the lowest part of a type character. Cf. ascender line.

descending letter *See* descender.

descrambler A device used to decode a signal that has been encoded. Used for cable television premium channels, satellite transmissions, and so on. Also called a *decoder* and *decrypter.*

descriptive statistics A generalized classification and report of a statistical study.

descriptive survey A survey that describes attitudes, opinions, demographic characteristics, and so on, of a statistical population.

descriptor In a computer-based information search and retrieval system, a word or title used to identify a specific document.

desensitization The theory that exposure to repeated antisocial acts on television leads to indifference to the same kinds of acts in real life.

desiderata A list of books or other items searched for.

design □ The arrangement of the visual elements of a book, magazine, pamphlet, and so on. □ To prepare visual or research plans. □ The pattern of procedures used in a research project.

designated community The community listed in Title 47 of the *Code of Federal Regulations* (CFR), paragraph 76.51, as the primary community of a major television market.

designated market area (DMS) Generally a group of counties in which commercial stations in a metro/central area achieve the largest audience share. Counties are assigned annually on the basis of Nielsen Station Index audience estimates. DMA's are nonoverlapping areas used for planning, buying, and evaluating television audiences.

designer □ The person who invents and combines form and color to produce an artistic work; a book designer, scene designer, costume designer, and so on. □ In studio animation, the person responsible for the overall look and style of the film.

desiccator A dry chemical, such as silica gel, used to absorb moisture from the air to protect equipment, film, and so on.

desire *See* AIDA.

desk A shortened form of city desk or copy desk.

desk and sofa show A slang term for a stock interview show with comedy and variety, such as the "Johnny Carson Show."

desk assistant *See* news assistant.

desk chief *See* desk editor.

desk copy A textbook furnished free to an instructor who has adopted the book for classroom use. Cf. approval copy and complimentary copy.

desk editor The person in charge of making assignments to reporters. Also called a *desk chief.*

deskman A copy editor. Also appears as *deskwoman.*

desk mike A microphone mounted on a low stand for placement on a table or desk.

desk mount A small stand used to hold a desk mike.

desktop computer A small, single-user microcomputer used for a variety of applications.

desktop publishing The use of a desktop computer to design and produce manuscripts. Also called *self-publishing.* Cf. electronic publishing.

deskwoman A copy editor. Also appears as *deskman.*

destination volume The computer disk that is being written to. Cf. source volume.

detail The degree of sharpness of a television picture or other reproduced image. *See also* resolution. Cf. definition.

detail set *See* insert set.

detail shot An extreme close-up camera shot.

detection *See* demodulation.

detector The portion of a radio receiver that captures a broadcast signal. *See also* demodulator.

detent One of a number of preset positions in a switch or stop lock such as the cue position on a potentiometer or a station position on a television receiver rotary dial.

deuce A 2000-watt fresnel spotlight. Also called a *junior* and *two-K. See also* lights.

Deus Ex Machina From the Latin for a "god from a machine." A contrived script device that allows the intervention of outside forces to resolve a plot or extricate the protagonist from a hopeless situation.

Deutsche Industrie Norm (DIN) The German industry standards organization.

developer The chemical solution used to make film or prints visible.

developing agent *See* reducing agent.

developing shot A camera shot from one angle or position that changes because of the movement of the camera or object.

developing story A news story for which new angles and information are disclosed over a period of time.

development □ A process by which a latent image on a film is made visible. □ The unfolding of plot and character in a script. □ *See* body. □ The step of obtaining the rights to a literary work, screenplay, story outline, or published work. Development is the first step in feature film production.

developmental broadcast station A station licensed experimentally to carry on development and research primarily in radiotelephony for the advancement of the broadcast services.

developmental journalism The use of the media in developing countries to help achieve the aims of the government. Also called *developmental news.*

developmental news *See* developmental journalism.

development fog *See* fog.

deviation □ In FM systems used for videotape recording, the difference between the frequency corresponding to sync-tip amplitude and that corresponding to peak-white amplitude. □ The numerical distance of a score, rating, number, and so on, from a central point such as a mean or median.

device A general term for electrical, electronic, or mechanical apparatus.

devil A printer's apprentice or helper.

devitrification A change of state in quartz from a glassy to a minutely crystalline state that reduces strength and integrity; often due to the combination of surface contaminants and high temperature, evidenced by a diffused etched appearance.

Dewey decimal system A system devised by Melvil Dewey in 1876 for classifying books and other publications into 10 main classes of knowledge. Cf. Library of Congress system.

dew light A light on a videotape recorder that illuminates if the dew sensor is activated.

dew sensor A protection circuit that deactivates a videotape recorder if excessive moisture is present.

df Depth of field.

DGA Directors Guild of America.

D/H Digital to hexadecimal (conversion).

DI Dolly in.

dia An abbreviation for *dialogue, diameter,* and *diaphragm.*

diacritical mark An accent mark or symbol attached to a letter to distinguish it from another or to indicate a different pronunciation from other sounds.

diagnosis The process of locating errors or problems in equipment, computer software, systems, and so on.

diagnostic program A computer program designed to aid in the location of problems within the computer system.

dial A graduated face, usually with a pointer or other indicator, used to set or calibrate equipment, such as a tuning dial, potentiometer, and so on.

dial access A CATV retrieval system wherein the subscriber uses a telephone type dial to select a desired program.

dialect A national or regional language variation characterized by atypical pronunciation, vocabulary, or grammar.

Dial-It 900 An AT&T telephone service often used for public opinion polls.

dialog A variant spelling of *dialogue.*

dialogue □ The lines spoken by a character in a performance. □ The conversation by two or more performers. □ Lip synchronous sound. □ The written conversation lines in a script. □ In animation, the portion of the soundtrack recorded by the voice artists and spoken by the characters on the screen.

dialogue coach An expert in diction, pronunciation, dialects, and so on, who instructs or assists a performer.

dialogue cue A script direction concerning how a line should be read.

dialogue director An expert in the delivery of dialogue.

dialogue looping *See* looping.

dialogue picture *See* direct recording.

dialogue recording *See* dialogue replacement.

dialogue replacement A postproduction technique wherein the voices of performers are rerecorded to replace poor quality sound. Also called dialogue recording. *See also* post synchronization.

dialogue track A magnetic tape soundtrack containing dialogue as opposed to music or effects.

dialogue triangle A situation in which a third actor hears or sees action or dialogue between two other actors.

dial position The location on a dial of a radio or television frequency or channel.

dial-up A terminal that uses a modem and telephone lines to access a remote computer.

diamond The smallest of the usable type sizes; four and a half points.

diamond dash A dash divided by a diamond-shaped mark used to mark page and column divisions. Also called a *swell dash.*

Diamond Memorial Award, Harry An award given by the IEEE to a person in government service in any country as evidenced by publication in professional society journals.

diamond stylus A record stylus made from an industrial grade diamond.

diaphote An early mechanical television device.

diaphragm □ The flexible portion of some microphones and loudspeakers that serves as a transducer. □ The movable metal blades used to adjust the size of a lens opening. Also called *iris* and *stop. See also* f stop. □ Any device that controls the amount of light passing through a lens.

diaphragm marks The calibrations on a lens that indicate the size of the aperture.

diapositive A transparent photographic positive; a transparency, glass slide, and so on.

diary □ A folder or bound book used to keep a record of news events to be covered by appointment. □ A special type of questionnaire wherein a respondent is asked to furnish a written record of behavior for a specified period of time.

diary reinterview An interview conducted with a household that has already cooperated in one of the diary measurements. Diary reinterviews are valuable because they allow the researcher to prescreen respondents by information previously collected in the original diary measurement. Diary reinterviews generally have extremely high cooperation rates.

diary story A news event covered by appointment.

diascope A simple optical projector.

diazo A light-sensitive reproduction process used to make photocomposition proofs on translucent materials. Also called a *whiteprint.* Cf. blueprint.

DIB Decency in Broadcasting.

diced A tooling found on some book covers resembling dice or small squares.

dichroic filter A filter that transmits certain wavelengths and reflects those not transmitted; the absorption is small.

dichroic mirror The filter in a color television camera that directs the primary colors to the appropriate pickup tube.

dichroic rangefinder A rangefinder using a dichroic filter to produce two different colors for focusing.

dichroism The property of a surface to selectively reflect light of different colors.

Dickinson rule A rule developed from a court decision that an order must be obeyed even though it is obviously unconstitutional.

dicta *See* obiter dicta.

diction The pronunciation and enunciation of words by performers.

dictionary A lexicon containing alphabetized and defined words and phrases of a language or body of knowledge.

dictionary catalog A catalog of books that has the subject, title, and author categories arranged alphabetically instead of being organized alphabetically by category.

DI/DO Data input/data output.

die □ A metal block, often brass, containing letters or designs used to stamp impressions on book covers or paper. □ A knife-edged metal used to cut paper into predetermined shapes.

die cut □ Paper or thin cardboard that has been cut to shape by a die. □ A cut made by a die.

dielectric An insulating material; usually ceramic, plastic, mica, air, or impregnated paper.

diesis *See* double dagger.

die stamping Intaglio printing accomplished by the use of a die.

DIF Data Interchange Format.

diff An abbreviation for *diffused.*

differential The price difference between the amount charged local and national advertisers. Also called *rate differential.*

differential focus A style of cinematography in which the entire acting area is in focus and the background and foreground are not as sharply defined. Also called *split focus. See also* zone focusing. Cf. deep focus.

differential gain The ratio of the output to the input signal of an amplifier.

differential PCM In data communications, a version of pulse code modulation in which the difference in value between a sample and the previous sample is encoded. Because fewer bits are required for transmission than under PCM, this technique is used in satellite communications. In CD-I, this technique is applied in video encoding as well as audio encoding. *See also* adaptive delta pulse code modulation and delta YUV.

differential phase The change in phase between the black level and white level in a television system.

differential survey treatment (DST) A standard diary sampling method used as an alternative to daily calling to encourage black and Hispanic households to complete and return their diaries. Target respondents in predesignated areas are mailed diaries and receive increased premiums. Three follow-up calls are made to all DST homes.

differentiation □ The concept created in the minds of listeners and viewers that the various broadcast stations, when contrasted with one another, are somehow not alike but varied and creative in their differences. □ The diversity of programming between various pay cable and STV services.

diffracted wave A wave that has been bent or deflected by diffraction. Cf. reflected wave and refracted wave.

diffraction The spreading or bending of light, radio, or sound waves caused by contact with objects.

diffraction grating A glass surface etched with parallel lines and used to break down a beam of light into the different colors of the spectrum.

diffraction lens A lens with a diffraction grating used for special effects.

diffraction region The point at which radio waves begin to diffract, usually at the horizon unless a building, high terrain, or other object obstructs the path of the wave.

diffuse □ A reflecting or transmitting media for which the reflected/transmitted light is distributed uniformly in all directions. □ When used in reference to light, the term indicates a soft light.

diffused illumination Lighting accomplished using floodlights.

diffused light Lighting softened by the use of a diffuser.

diffuser □ A translucent material, such as frosted glass or gel, used to soften lighting. □ A reflective or absorptive panel used to make a studio more live or dead.

diffusing screen *See* matte screen.

diffusion □ The scattering or spreading of light or sound waves. Cf. diffraction. □ The softening of hard lines in an image.

diffusion filter A lens filter that softens hard lines. Also called an *effects filter.*

diffusion lens A supplementary lens that acts as a diffusion filter.

diffusion screen *See* diffuser and matte screen.

dig To investigate a news story thoroughly.

digest □ A systematically arranged compilation of laws, rules and regulations, or court decisions. □ A magazine containing condensed material from other sources.

digest sized page A unit of magazine advertising space measuring five by seven inches, included in a magazine of larger page size.

digetic time Screen time; the time that is taking place within the context of the story of each shot or scene.

digit (D) Any of the symbols of a base numbering system.

digital (D) Referring to the use of discrete integral numbers or characters to represent data, as opposed to analog representation. Cf. analog.

digital/analog converter A device that converts a digital signal into the continuously changing electrical signal suitable for use by an analog computer.

digital audio Audio that has been changed from the normal analog form to digital form.

Digital audio stationary head (DASH) An audio recording method using a stationary head as opposed to using helical scan methods for recording digital signals. The same concept applies here as in video.

digital camera A camera that is capable of recording images directly in digital form.

digital clock *See* clock.

digital computer A computer that processes information represented by discrete elements, as opposed to analog representation. Cf. analog computer, desktop computer, mainframe, microcomputer, minicomputer, and personal computer.

digital counter *See* counter.

digital delay An electronic delay unit used on radio call-in talk shows. *See also* delay line.

digital disc recorder (DDR) A video disc recorder.

digital effects A general term for special effects generated by digital means. *See also* digital video effects.

digital frame store An electronic device capable of storing a complete frame of digital video information.

digital leader A film or videotape leader containing digits at one-second intervals for countdown.

digital optical recording (DOR) A system that can write and read data. Its principal application is large-scale archiving.

digital production master In CD-DA, digitally recorded audiotape used in editing to produce a master tape. It may be a studio mix, an equalized copy from a mastering suite, or a transfer from a previous master.

digital programmer A digital system used for radio automation.

digital recorder A device that records digital data as discrete points on a magnetic recording medium.

digital recording A recording in which the recorded signal is made by rapidly sampling the audio or video material. Cf. analog recording.

digital sampling *See* sampling.

digital sync *See* crystal sync.

digital television A proposed television system that would largely eliminate distortion and picture quality degradation by using digital encoding for long-distance transmission.

digital transmission The sending of a signal in discrete bits as opposed to analog modulated waves.

digital video effects (DVE) Special effects created by the use of digitized video signals. Examples of their use are to reduce or enlarge images, compress or expand images, and rotate and wrap images.

digital video interactive (DVI) A technology for an interactive all-digital system that can work with and display any kind of audio-visual material, including motion images, still images, audio, graphics, computer data, or text. Materials can be placed on any digital storage medium including the low-cost and popular CD-ROM compact disc. Seventy-two minutes of full-screen, full-motion video is possible on a standard compact disc. Cf. CD-I.

digital video recording (DVR) The recording of digitized video rather than conventional analog video.

digitization The process of changing an analog signal into a digital signal; performed by sampling.

digitize To convert to digital form.

digitized video *See* video chip.

digitizer A device that converts analog data such as a drawing or sketch into digital form. *See also* graphics tablet.

dihedral The angular relationship, on the scanner, of the rotating heads of a television tape recorder.

DiLitho The use of offset planographic plates with the direct transfer of the image from plate to web. Used in newspaper printing.

Dill-White Bill The Radio Act of 1927, named after its cosponsors.

dilute To decrease the strength of a solution such as a developer.

dim □ To change the amount of light either by increasing it or decreasing it, namely, to dim up or to dim down. □ To raise or lower the intensity of a lamp.

dime novel An obsolete term for an inexpensive, usually sensational or melodramatic, novel; often written for a young adult audience.

Dimension 150 A wide-screen projection system covering 150 degrees on a deeply curved screen.

dimensional animation Animation accomplished through three-dimensional drawings and paintings.

dimensional stability The ability of a tape, film, or other medium to retain its original length, width, and so on.

dimmer A device used for controlling the amount of light radiated from a luminaire. Common types are resistance, autotransformer, magnetic amplifier, silicon controlled rectifier or semiconductor, thyratron, and iris.

dimmer board A panel board containing switches, dimmers, and outlets for the luminaires to be controlled. Also called a *control board* and *switch board.* A lighting control console.

dimmer curve The performance characteristics of a dimmer indicated in terms of the light output of a lamp controlled by the dimmer versus the arbitrary linear scale of 0 to 10 associated with the dimmer control.

dimmer room A room or space in which remotely controlled dimmers are housed.

DIN Deutsch Industrie Norm. The West German standards organization system of rating film emulsion speed. Also referred to as *Das Ist Normal.*

DIN connector A common form of European connector used for various electronic applications.

dingbat □ Type ornaments of various designs. □ A boxed story.

dinky dash A special, short dash used to separate items in a list or story. Cf. jim dash.

dinky-inky A low-wattage lamp used for highlights. Also called an *inky-dinky.*

dinky roll *See* quarter roll.

DIN speed The German system emulsion speed rating.

diode □ A vacuum tube that has only a cathode and an anode. □ A two-element semiconductor used as a rectifier.

diopter A unit of measurement of the refractive power of a lens.

diopter lens A supplemental lens used in close-up photography; available in several different diopters.

diorama □ A model or miniature set. □ An advertising display, usually three-dimensional, specially lighted, and often animated.

DIP Dual in-line package. The standard integrated circuit container having two rows of pins, each separated by one-tenth of an inch.

dipless cross-fade A lighting cross-fade in which all lighting instruments change slowly and smoothly.

diplexer A coupling unit used to combine television video and audio signals for radiation by the same antenna.

dipole A high-frequency single bay transmitting or receiving antenna.

DIP switch One of a number of small on/off switches mounted on a dual in-line package (DIP) and used for changing the configuration of a circuit board.

direct advertising Printed advertising materials that are distributed by hand or mail to prospective buyers. Includes direct mail advertising.

direct broadcast satellite (DBS) A geostationary satellite that broadcasts television signals directly to households on conventional television receivers.

direct broadcast satellite service A radio communication service in which signals transmitted or retransmitted by space stations are intended for direct reception by the general public.

direct cinema A style of documentary filmmaking characterized by location shooting using mobile equipment and minimal intervention by the director. Cf. cinema verité.

direct current (DC) A current of one value that flows in one direction. Cf. alternating current.

direct cut A redundant term for television cut or take.

direct cut disc A cellulose nitrate disc made by cutting the grooves instead of stamping.

direct distance dialing (DDD) A telephone service that permits users to make long distance calls without operator assistance.

direct distribution expense The costs incurred in distributing a product or service such as a motion picture or book. Usually includes publication costs, advertising, and so on.

direct halftone A halftone made as an object is photographed rather than from a photographic negative or print. *See also* direct halftone process.

direct halftone process In color engraving, the production by photography of halftone separation negatives for each color, using appropriate color filters and halftone screens simultaneously. Also called *direct process.*

direct impression □ The method used by a typewriter to print characters on paper. □ A limited capability typesetter. Also called a *direct impression typesetter. See also* cold type and strike-on.

direct impression typesetter *See* direct impression.

direction □ A scene as viewed by the audience or performer. *See also* audience left, audience right, camera left, camera right, stage left, stage right, and so on. □ The direction a performer glances or looks.

directional antenna An antenna that is designed or altered for the purpose of obtaining a noncircular radiation pattern.

directional continuity The continuation of a performer's movements in the same screen direction from shot to shot in a filmed or taped sequence.

directional illumination Lighting produced by luminaires with a narrow beam.

directional microphone A microphone with a narrow angle of acceptance pattern. *See also* mike pattern and unidirectional microphone.

directional pattern *See* radiation pattern.

directional radiation Electromagnetic radiation that is focused and concentrated by an antenna or other device.

directional screen A projection screen that concentrates the reflected light in a narrow angle.

directional station A radio station that uses a directional antenna for signal radiation.

directions A scriptwriter's instructions for talent and cameras.

directive gain The differential gain in a geographical direction derived by using a directional antenna instead of a nondirectional antenna.

directive interview *See* structured interview.

direct license A license to use a copyrighted work received directly from the copyright holder. Cf. blanket license.

direct mail *See* direct mail advertising.

direct mail advertising Advertising or promotional material sent to prospective buyers through the mail or other direct delivery service.

Direct Mail Advertising Association (DMAA) An organization of national and local users of direct mail advertising; formed to further member interests and promote this advertising medium.

direct mail agency A company that sells magazine subscriptions through the mail; usually accomplished through massive promotions and prizes.

direct mail campaign A promotional or sales campaign designed to maximize the number of responses in the shortest possible period of time.

direct marketing (DM) The selling of goods or services directly to a consumer.

Direct Marketing Association (DMA) An international trade association of suppliers, advertisers, and other professionals of direct marketing.

direct master An offset plate made of paper or plastic.

direct media The communication outlets that are used for direct marketing, such as telephone and mail. Cf. indirect media.

direct memory access (DMA) The movement of data without going through a computer's CPU.

direct meter A light-meter reading taken from the position of the camera.

direct method An FCC-approved method for measuring antenna power; defined as the product of the antenna resistance at the operating frequency and the square of the unmodulated antenna current at that frequency, measured at the point where the antenna resistance has been determined. Cf. indirect method.

director □ The individual in charge of all artistic aspects of a radio or television program or commercial, including lighting, sets, acting, camera composition, audio, and so on. Others may be in charge of various aspects—for example, a lighting director—but the director is responsible for their actions and decisions. Cf. producer. □ A parasitic antenna element. □ The part of an operating system that has control over the execution of a computer's functions. □ The individual who directs the production of motion pictures and whatever is seen and heard in the finished product. He or she also directs all related functions and activities required for translating and transferring the script, premise, or idea and/or concept to the audio-visual images. Cf. employee director. □ In studio animation, the creative head of the film, responsible for the concept of how the script will be portrayed, and conveying the concept to the people involved; the unifying artistic force of the production.

director of photography (DP) *See* cinematographer.

director of research *See* research director.

Directors Guild of America (DGA) A professional organization of motion picture and television directors.

director's script *See* shooting script.

Directory *See* Academy Player's Directory.

directory □ A list of files stored in a computer memory. □ The most general division of a CD-I disc's program area. Each directory is subdivided into files. □ *See* catalog.

directory advertising Advertising that appears in a specialized directory such as the commercial telephone pages.

direct pickup The transmission of live, as opposed to recorded, radio and television programs.

direct positive □ A positive print made from a negative. □ The positive image resulting from reversal processing.

direct pressure machine A hydraulic press used to mold stereotype mats.

direct process *See* direct halftone process.

direct questionnaire A questionnaire with straightforward, pointed questions. Cf. indirect questionnaire.

direct quote A word-for-word report of a person's remarks. Cf. indirect quote, paraphrase, and partial quote.

direct reception In the broadcasting satellite service, the term encompasses both individual reception and community reception.

direct recording The recording of audio or video without subsequent dubbing.

direct response advertising Advertising that requires a simple reply from the prospective customer to the advertiser, such as mail order, direct mail, and cable television home shopping channels.

direct response card *See* deck.

direct sales Sales of products or services made without the services of a broker or third party. An example is a magazine subscription ordered directly from the publisher instead of a subscription agent.

direct sequence system A spread spectrum system in which the incoming information is usually digitized, if it is not already in binary format, and modulo 2 added to a higher-speed code sequence. The combined information and code are then used to modulate an RF carrier. Because the high-speed code sequence dominates the modulating function, it is the direct cause of the wide spreading of the transmitted signal.

direct signal A signal from a sound source such as a musical instrument fed directly into an audio console instead of through a microphone.

direct sound □ The recording of sound simultaneously with the motion picture image. □ The sound that travels from the source to a microphone without reflection.

direct sound camera A camera equipped to record sound on film. *See also* single system.

direct subscriber A subscriber who orders magazines and other periodicals directly from the publisher. Cf. indirect subscriber.

direct take *See* cut.

direct view A television picture that is seen directly as opposed to a projected picture.

direct viewfinder A form of viewfinder, often camera mounted, in which the scene is viewed directly instead of through the lens or by means of a mirror.

direct voice (DV) *See* lip-sync.

direct wave An electromagnetic wave that is propagated from a transmitting to a receiving antenna. Cf. ground wave, reflected wave, and sky wave.

dirty □ Audio- or videotape that has been used but not completely erased. □ Film containing scratches, abrasions, and so on. □ *See* dirty copy.

dirty copy Copy that contains numerous errors, strikeovers, corrections, and so on.

disable To override an interrupt facility.

disaster film A motion picture that features earthquakes, fires, hurricanes, airline crashes, and so on, as its primary plot.

disc □ A phonograph record consisting of a solid substrate coated with a plasticized cellulose nitrate lacquer made either by direct-cut or pressing. □ *See* disk. □ *See* video disc. □ A flat photomatrix used in phototypesetting equipment that contains a selection of typefaces.

discard To withdraw a book, periodical, or other item permanently from a library.

disc bootstrap routine An optional routine on a CD-I disc to add or replace operating system capabilities in a base case system.

discharge lamp A lamp in which an electric charge causes a gas to produce light.

disc jockey (DJ) A radio station personality who plays records interspersed with comments, information, humor, and so on. Also called a *deejay, DJ,* and *jock.*

disc label In CD-I, the disc identity in terms of its volume and album description. Recorded in the first track of the disc. *See also* super table of contents.

disclaimer An announcement that attempts to limit the possible liability of a station, advertiser, and other responsible parties for the claims made by a product or service.

disclosure □ The requirement that broadcast station employees reveal the receipt of money, service, or other valuable consideration for the broadcast of matter over the station before the broadcast, as required by Section 508 of the Communications Act. □ The full and accurate publication of the rules of a contest.

disc map The organization of data on magnetic tape as it will be on the CD. *See also* memory management.

disc memory *See* disc storage.

discography A compilation of phonograph records by title, mood, performer, and so on; a bibliography.

disconnect rate The percentage of cable television subscribers in a given area who have discontinued service during a certain time period.

disconnects Subscribers who have terminated cable service or have been terminated because of failure to pay subscription fees.

discontinuous spectrum A characteristic of some light sources that emit energy over only a portion of the spectrum rather than throughout the visible spectrum.

discophile An individual who is knowledgeable about and collects phonograph records.

discount □ Any reduction from a stated price or rate of payment, made for various reasons, such as frequency, time of day, amount of space or time, or volume book buying. *See also* class rate, rate, rate card, and rate cutting. □ A reduction in quoted base space rates earned by contract continuity.

discovered An actor or object brought to the attention of the audience during a scene by a line, action, or camera movement. Also called a *discovery.*

discovered law *See* common law.

discovery □ The pretrial procedure in which opposing participants are allowed to examine documents or objects germane to the case. □ *See* discovered.

DiscoVision A trademark for a video disc system.

disc recorder A mechanical device consisting of a record head with a cutting stylus and a properly driven turntable to inscribe a signal on a recording disc.

discrepancy □ An incongruity between two related things, as media space or time ordered and that billed to the advertiser. □ An inadequacy of competitive separation or commercial protection provided by a medium. □ A change made in the operation of a broadcast station at the last minute and noted in the operating, maintenance, or program log.

disc replication The production of a copy disc from a master disc, usually for commercial distribution.

discrete □ Consisting of separate, distinct parts. □ A system of broadcasting a four-channel signal on FM radio. *See also* matrix.

discrete data Noncontinuous data that is characterized by gaps in the scale. For example, children and other audience members come in discrete quantities; few families have 2.7 children.

discrete demographics Uncombined or nonoverlapping sex/age groupings for listening estimates. Typical groupings include men and/or women 18 to 24, 25 to 34, 35 to 44, as opposed to target group demographics such as men and/or women 18 or older, 18 to 34, 18 to 49, 25 to 49. Also called *uncombined listening estimates.*

discrete function A keyboard movement in which each keystroke performs a single action.

discretionary hyphen A computer code for a hyphen that may be used depending on whether the hyphenated word falls at the end of a line after justification. *See also* hyphenation.

discretionary time The time left to an individual after sleeping, eating, working; time left for mass media consumption.

discriminator An electronic device, such as an FM receiver, in which amplitude variations are derived from frequency or phase variations.

disc storage Data storage on an optical or magnetic disc, characterized by lower cost and faster data access than tape storage.

disengagement *See* disinvolved move.

dish □ An antenna reflector usually in the shape of a truncated paraboloid used for microwave transmission and reception. □ A long-distance microphone reflector, often circular instead of parabolic. Also called a *dishpan*. *See also* parabola.

dishpan *See* dish and parabola.

disinformation A term typically associated with governments or government agencies wherein incorrect information is disseminated on purpose.

disinvolved move A stage movement by a character used to show rejection, disapproval, or disbelief. Also called a *disengagement*.

disk □ A circular storage medium coated on both surfaces with a ferromagnetic material. *See also* floppy disk and hard disk. □ A variant spelling of *disc*.

disk based Word processing programs that save sections of a file on disk and retrieve them as needed.

disk cartridge *See* disk pack.

disk crash *See* crash.

disk drive A random access storage device using a read/write head to store and retrieve information on a disk.

diskette *See* floppy disk.

disk file Any information that is stored on a disk.

disk operating system (DOS) A set of computer instructions that controls the way information is stored on and retrieved from disks.

disk pack A group of magnetic disks used for computer storage. Also called a *disk cartridge*.

disk storage (DS) The storage of computer-generated information on magnetic disks as opposed to on magnetic tape, in RAM, and so on.

dismissal without prejudice An action that terminates a case before a court or application before an administrative agency wherein the case or application may again be brought before the court or administrative agency. Cf. dismissal with prejudice.

dismissal with prejudice An action that terminates a case before a court or application before an administrative agency wherein the case or application may not be pursued further. Cf. dismissal without prejudice.

disorientation An editing or shooting scheme used to confuse an audience as to time, place, or identity.

dispatcher An individual who works with a radio or television assignment editor to maintain radio communication with remote units.

dispersion □ The distribution of magnetic oxide particles throughout a disk, tape, and so on. □ The separation, often by a prism, of a beam of light into its component colors. □ The degree to which individual measurements scatter around a measure of central tendency.

dispersion pattern □ The audience flow at the end of a radio or television program. □ The placing of advertising messages, in terms of coverage and frequency, to attain an objective.

displacement magazine A film magazine in which the feed reel becomes smaller to make room for the film as it increases in size on the takeup reel.

displacement recorder A recorder used to rerecord a single system soundtrack so that it is in edit sync with the picture.

display (D) □ A large, conspicuous, advertising layout. □ *See* display type. □ A printed poster. □ To show a copy of a copyrighted work, either directly or by means of a film, slide, television image, or any other device or process or, in the case of a motion picture or other audiovisual work, to show individual images nonsequentially. □ *See* display ad. □ A term that refers to the information presented on a television receiver or monitor; the term also refers to LED and LCD displays. Also called a *display tube*.

display ad Any newspaper or magazine advertisement except for classified ads; usually set in type larger than body type and separated from text by rules. Also called a *display advertisement*.

display advertisement *See* display ad.

display advertising □ Advertising designed to attract attention by the use of large type, borders, white space, illustrations, and so on. □ Advertising mounted in a display.

display classified advertising Classified advertising that uses display type, illustrations, and other special features, and that occupies more space for its text content than the regular advertising of a classified section.

display controller A two-path device that takes pixel data from the two banks of RAM in a CD-I player and combines them to produce a single RGB video output.

display control program (DCP) A set of command codes that is interrupted by the hardware during either the horizontal or vertical retrace periods. The codes can then be used to perform a variety of functions such as background colors and CLUT entries.

display face *See* display type.

display line The line displaying the cursor on a video display monitor.

display mode A television picture movement, such as a roll, crawl, or wipe.

display period The exposure time during which the individual outdoor advertising message is on display. Posters are normally contracted for monthly exposure; bulletins, rotating or permanent, usually display the same copy for a four-month period.

display resolution The measure of the number of pixels, and thus the amount of detail, that a screen can display.

display size A size of type; for newspapers, 14 points or larger. *See also* type size. Cf. body size (text size).

display tube *See* display and video display terminal.

display type Large and heavy type used for headlines, chapter headings, advertising, banners, and so on. Also called *display.* Cf. body type.

display unit *See* video display.

diss An abbreviation for *dissolve.*

dissector A television camera pickup tube developed in the 1920s by Philo T. Farnsworth.

dissemination The act of spreading news, information, materials, and so on.

dissent A statement by a judge or justice who disagrees with the majority opinion of the court. Also called a *dissenting opinion.*

dissenting opinion *See* dissent.

dissolve (D) □ A variable-speed transition between two pictures, one fading in as the other is fading out. When both pictures are at half-strength, the image is called a superimposition. Also called a *cross-dissolve, cross-lap, lap, lap-dissolve,* and *mix. See also* optical. Cf. cut. □ A camera effect in which one scene gradually fades out as another simultaneously fades in to replace it. Dissolves are commonly used as scene transitions in animation. □ A television director's command to dissolve from one picture to another. Abbreviated *X* on a script.

dissolve in A television director's command to begin a dissolve and hold when the superimposition is at its maximum. Cf. dissolve out.

dissolve out A television director's command to end a superimposition by fading out to the second picture. Cf. dissolve in.

dissonance The disturbance felt by individuals when a message does not agree with their preconceived attitudes or opinions.

dissonance theory *See* consistency theory.

distance (D) The amount of separation between two points; often the distance between the camera and the subject.

distance meter A rangefinder.

distance scale The calibrations on a camera lens barrel that indicate the distance between camera and object.

distance shot *See* long shot.

distant locations Locations on which an actor or actress is required to remain away and be lodged overnight.

distant signal □ A television signal received from beyond the Grade B contour of the station. *See also* imported signal. □ A signal received by satellite or microwave.

distant signal equivalent A value assigned to the secondary transmission of any nonnetwork television programming carried by a cable system in whole or in part beyond the local service area of the primary transmitter of such programming. It is computed by assigning a value of one to each independent station and a value of one-quarter to each network station and noncommercial educational station for the nonnetwork programming so carried.

distant signal importation Television stations that are brought in to a market by a cable television system. Often a superstation.

distant station A television station that is located in another market.

Distinguished Service Award An award given by the NAB for "significant and lasting contribution to the American system of broadcasting by virtue of a singular achievement or continuing service for or in behalf of the industry."

distortion □ Any undesired change in waveform. The difference between the recorded and reproduced quality. *See also* harmonic distortion and intermodulation distortion. □ The presence of frequencies at the output of an electronic device that are not present at the input. □ Imperfections in a lens that cause asymmetry or deformation of the image. □ Sometimes used to refer to the difference in perspective between the use of a dolly shot and a zoom. □ A false light tort wherein facts are omitted or pictures are used out of context. □ The false recognition of an experience, such as one in an advertising message, that makes the message fit readily into a personal frame of reference. □ Intentional distortion of the width of a newspaper advertisement in order to accommodate individual newspaper column width requirements; an alternative to cropping or completely resizing an advertisement.

distress sale A transfer of control of a broadcast station whose license may be revoked or not renewed by the FCC.

distribute To separate and return type to its case after use.

distribution □ The act of separating and returning type to its case. □ The method by which subscriptions to newspapers and magazines are delivered. □ The marketing and merchandising of media products. □ The location of the individual outdoor advertising structures within a market. □ Any method by which programming is conveyed to the listener or viewer: broadcasting, CATV, audio- or videotapes or discs, and so on. □ *See* frequency distribution.

distribution amplifier (DA) An amplifier used to boost a signal for distribution.

distribution channel □ The means by which motion pictures, television programs, books, magazines, and other media are distributed to end users. Also called *distribution flow.* □ *See* distribution system.

distribution expenses All costs and expenses—incurred, paid, payable, or accrued—in connection with the distribution, advertising, exploitation, and turning to account of the photoplay of whatever kind or nature. Also included are costs and expenses that are customarily treated as distribution expenses in connection with customary accounting procedures in the motion picture industry.

distribution fee A fee of gross film rentals received by a distributor from exhibitors (usually about 30 percent—foreign may be 40 percent).

distribution flow *See* distribution channel.

distribution rights The licensing of motion pictures, television programs, and other media to someone who distributes the finished products to various exhibitors.

distribution system The part of a cable television system used to carry the signals from the head end to the subscriber's receiver; includes the trunk, feeder lines, and house drops. Also called a *distribution channel.*

distribution tap A cable television connection that splits signals to feeder lines and subscriber drops.

distribution window *See* window.

distributor □ A company organized to distribute motion pictures and other media products to various exhibitors. □ A producer when he or she distributes a motion picture through his or her own distribution facilities for telecasting of free television or, if applicable, for supplemental markets' use, and all other distributors engaged by a producer to distribute such motion picture for telecasting on free television or, if applicable, for supplemental markets use. □ An individual who markets programs to television stations and cable television systems. □ A person who sells or delivers newspapers, magazines, and so on.

distributor's foreign gross With respect to any television film, the absolute gross income realized by the distributor from the foreign telecasting and including, in the case of a foreign territorial sale by any such distributor, the income realized from such sale by the purchaser or licensee. There are extensive exceptions to what is included in a distributor's foreign gross.

distributor's gross receipts The absolute gross income received by all distributors of a motion picture from the telecasting thereof on free television anywhere in the world and, if applicable, from the supplemental markets' use thereof anywhere in the world.

district An area covered by a reporter; a beat.

district man A news reporter assigned to cover a district or specific geographic area. Also called a *legman* and *legger.*

dither □ To cause to vary in position or path, randomly or periodically, from a central location or path. □ In a dynamic tracking system, to cause the video head to vary its tracking so that the head scans alternately to one side of the video track, then the other. Usually there are several such alternations per headpass, for determining the average location of the video track and adjusting the system tracking accordingly. □ The motion or path of an object undergoing such a position or path variation. □ Pertaining to the signal applied to cause such a position or path variation.

ditto □ To repeat. □ *See* hectograph.

ditty bag A small, usually flexible, container used to hold an assortment of articles used in remotes and on location: screwdrivers, cores, gaffer tape, filters, and so on. Also called a *ditty box.*

ditty box *See* ditty bag.

diva A prima donna.

divergence The spreading of light rays. *See also* diffusion.

diversification of business interests A minor factor considered in comparative hearings before the FCC's 1965 Policy Statement was instituted; this factor gave credit for different business interests to applicants for broadcast licenses.

diversification of control of the media of mass communication A hoped-for deconcentration of control of the media of mass communication to prevent domination by the few over the attitudes and opinions of the public. The major criterion used in mutually exclusive applications for broadcasting licenses; not limited to broadcast ownership but inclusive of CATV and newspaper ownership.

diversity reception A method used to maximize a received signal using two receivers or two antennas.

dividend A book given or sold at a greatly reduced price by a book club to a subscriber who has fulfilled a commitment or has recruited a new subscriber.

dividing network *See* crossover network.

divinity circuit binding A book binding characterized by rounded corners and flexible covers; often used for Bibles.

division A subdivision of a newspaper section, book, and so on.

division label The heading given to a newspaper division.

division title The heading given to a book division.

DIZ An abbreviation for *dissolve.*

DJ □ Disc jockey. □ Dust jacket.

DJA Disc Jockey Association.

D layer The lowest of the ionospheric layers. *See also* D region.

D log E curve *See* characteristic curve.

DM □ Direct marketing. □ Data management.

DMA □ Designated market areas. □ Direct Marketing Association. □ Direct memory access.

DMAA Direct Mail Advertising Association.

DMM Direct metal mastering. A mastering process that does not use an intermediate process.

DMMA Direct Mail Marketing Association.

DMMA mail order action line (MOAL) A service provided by DMMA to assist consumers who have encountered problems while they shopped by mail that they cannot resolve themselves.

DMS Data management system.

DNA Deutscher Normenausschus (German Standards Committee). A standards organization similar to the EIA.

DNP Did not play.

DO Dolly out.

do An abbreviation for *ditto.*

DOA Department of the Army.

DOC □ Department of Commerce. □ Dropout compensator.

doc An abbreviation for *docket* and *document.*

dock A scene storage bay.

docket The FCC designation of cases designated as mutually exclusive or designated for hearing.

docket numbers The FCC consecutive numbers assigned to dockets. Cf. file number.

doctor To rewrite, revise, or otherwise attempt to improve a script, screenplay, manuscript, and so on.

doctor blade A metal scraper used to wipe excess ink from a printing plate.

doctrine A principle formed from law, regulation, or court decision.

docudrama A contraction of *documentary drama.* A fictionalized, dramatic motion picture or television program that is based primarily on fact and shot in documentary style.

document A term used to distinguish a word processing file from computer programs, spreadsheets, database files, and so on.

documentary A factual film or radio or television program often using a sociological theme, and based on actual events in the life of a person or group, or the analysis of a phenomenon.

documentation □ The materials or evidence offered to substantiate a claim, research, news item, and so on. □ The printed materials furnished by a seller, such as operator manuals and schematics, needed to explain and maintain equipment. □ The requirement by the Federal Trade Commission that advertisers substantiate the claims made in commercials and advertisements. □ The written materials that explain the use of computer hardware and software. Often referred to as *manuals.*

documercial A television commercial that is shot in documentary style.

DOD Department of Defense.

dodge A technique used in enlarging to lighten a portion of a print. See also burn in.

dodger □ A small circular. □ A small piece of metal or paper used to keep portions of enlargements from becoming overexposed.

dog □ A box on page one of a newspaper, usually in one of the upper corners, used to indicate the edition or a special feature. Also called a *dog ear.* □ A gripping device used to lock a film magazine lid. □ A poor program, script, actor, and so on.

dog and pony show A presentation made by an ad agency, publisher, prospective employee, and so on, to demonstrate his, her, or its qualifications to excel at a given task. Often, a well-rehearsed lecture or presentation.

dog ear *See* dog.

doghouse □ A small building at the base of an antenna tower. □ An early morning radio board shift. Cf. dog watch.

dog station A broadcasting station that does not show a profit, is poorly managed, or has poor programming.

dog watch □ A late night radio board shift. Cf. doghouse. □ *See* lobster trick.

Dolby A One of the methods of increasing the signal-to-noise ratio of an audio signal. Signals are divided into four bands: up to 80 Hz, 80 to 3000 Hz, 3000 to 9000 Hz, and over 9000 Hz, and then recombined. Cf. Dolby B, Dolby C, Dolby HX Pro, and Dolby SR.

Dolby B One of the methods of increasing the signal-to-noise ratio of an audio signal. Frequencies above 5000 Hz are encoded and boosted 10 dB, then decoded. Cf. Dolby A, Dolby C, Dolby HX Pro, and Dolby SR.

Dolby C One of the methods of increasing the signal-to-noise ratio of an audio signal. Frequencies in two bands, midrange and high frequency, are preemphasized and then decoding is required for acceptable signals. Cf. Dolby A, Dolby B, Dolby HX Pro, and Dolby SR.

Dolby HX Pro One of the methods of increasing the signal-to-noise ratio of an audio signal. An active biasing system accomplished by adding six dB of headroom to the high frequency range by reducing the bias fed to the tape. Cf. Dolby A, Dolby B, Dolby C, and Dolby SR.

Dolby SR A spectral recording system used to expand headroom. Cf. Dolby A, Dolby B, Dolby C, and Dolby HX Pro.

Dolby system An audiotape recording and playback circuit used to improve the signal-to-noise ratio. Named after its inventor. *See also* Dolby A, Dolby B, Dolby C, Dolby HX Pro, and Dolby SR.

dolly □ A movable camera support that allows flexibility of movement. Also called a *trolley.* □ A movable microphone support. □ A camera movement toward or away from the subject. □ A director's command to move the dolly: dolly in or dolly out. ☐ A type of stage wagon.

dolly back *See* dolly out.

dolly camera A camera mounted on a dolly.

dolly forward *See* dolly in.

dolly in (DI) ☐ To move a camera toward the subject. ☐ A director's command to dolly in. Also called *dolly forward* and *push in*. Cf. zoom in.

dollying The act of moving a camera forward or backward.

dolly out (DO) ☐ To move a camera away from the subject. ☐ A director's command to dolly out. Also called *dolly back, pull back,* and *push out*. Cf. zoom out.

dolly pusher A grip who moves a large camera mount during productions.

dolly shot (DS) A shot taken while the camera is moving toward or away from the subject.

dolly track A flange attached to a dolly that pushes the camera cables out of the way.

domestic comedy A television program form that focuses on humorous family interrelationships. Similar to a situation comedy.

domestic release *See* domestic version.

domestic satellite (domsat) A satellite whose transponders are for lease to commercial customers, in addition to military and government use.

domestic version A motion picture made for release in English-speaking countries. Also called a *domestic release*. Cf. foreign version.

dominant ☐ A focal point in a scene, script, print, and so on. ☐ A satellite used for cable and broadcast programming.

dominant area *See* Area of Dominant Influence (ADI).

dominant character The major character in a script.

dominant contrast The area in a picture that commands the viewer's attention.

dominant head The headline on a newspaper or magazine page that draws first attention from a reader.

dominant station A class I station operating on a clear channel in the AM band.

domsat A domestic satellite.

Donald Duck ☐ The effect obtained by playing a recording too fast; a 33-rpm recording at 45 rpm, or a 7-1/2-ips tape at 15 ips. ☐ A type of sound made by ACSB.

D-1 A high-quality videotape recording format that records the video signal digitally in its component form using standard oxide tape. Cf. D-2 and D-3.

donkey An electric stage winch.

Don Lee Broadcasting System An early regional radio network and experimental television broadcasting company.

donor acknowledgment An announcement made on a noncommercial broadcasting station specifically mentioning the person or company that donated money or goods.

donor list *See* contributor list.

donut A radio commercial that contains a music bed between the intro and outro, over which an announcer fills in the hole. Also called a *sandwich* and *wraparound*.

door stepper A British term for a shotgun interview.

dope ☐ A slang term for information, facts, or rumor based on advance information. ☐ A cellulose derivative used in photography for film bases and retouching.

dope sheet ☐ A news cameraperson's list of filming requirements: location, footage, developing instructions, and so on. Also called a *poop sheet* and *spot sheet*. ☐ A chart detailing instructions for filming animation. Also called a *camera report, exposure sheet, short card,* and *shot sheet*. ☐ A slang term for a description of a stock shot.

dope story A news story based on opinions or predictions.

doppler effect The increase or decrease of sound or light frequency caused by a change in distance between the sound source and the microphone or observer. Also called *doppler shift*.

doppler shift *See* doppler effect.

DOR Digital optical recording.

DOS Disk operating system.

dos a dos A book binding containing two complete books back-to-back, one upside down from the other.

dot ☐ One element of a color television line. ☐ A small metal disc used as a light diffuser. *See also* gobo. ☐ One of the individual elements of a halftone. □ A small type mark such as a period or the point over a lowercase *i*. □ The shorter of the two sounds made by a telegrapher's key. Cf. dash. □ A round, adhesive circle used to seal envelopes and doubled postcards.

dot formation The arrangement and relative size of the dots of a halftone film or plate.

dot leader A line of type formed by dots.

dot matrix printer An impact printer that fashions characters from dots formed by a matrix of wires. Also called a *dot printer* and *matrix printer.*

dot pitch The distance between the color dots in a television picture tube.

dot printer *See* dot matrix printer.

dot sequential The color television system of scanning successive primary color dots along the scanning line.

dots per inch (DPI) A measure of the quality of the print by a dot matrix printer; the greater the number of dots per inch, the greater the quality.

double □ To play more than one role in a production. Also called a *dual role.* □ A stunt person who performs dangerous or difficult tasks. Also called a *photo double.* Cf. stand-in. □ A musician who plays two or more instruments in a production. □ *See* doublet.

double action Action that is repeated; often shot from a different angle.

double apple *See* apple box.

double-arming The mounting of two tone arms on one turntable. May be used to segue from one arm to the other on the same record for continuous sound effects.

double atlas A size of paper; 35-1/2 by 55 inches.

double back A double photographic plate holder.

double band *See* sepmag.

double bank A set erected downstage of another set.

double bill A motion picture double feature.

double billing The illegal practice of submitting identical invoices for radio or television station time to a local advertiser and a national manufacturer.

double blind An experimental method in which neither the researcher nor the subjects know in which category the subjects fall.

double broad A two-lamp floodlight, usually of rectangular shape, used as a source of fill light.

double cap A size of paper; 17 by 28 inches.

double chain The simultaneous use of two film chains.

double coated film Film with emulsion layers on each side; used to increase the latitude of the film.

double coating An unusually heavy paper coating; the term is used regardless of the number of coating operations.

double column (DC) A story or advertisement two columns wide.

double copy A size of paper; 20 by 33 inches.

double dagger A reference mark: ‡. Also called a *diesis* and *double obelisk.*

double dash *See* Oxford rule.

double decker An outdoor advertising display in two separate tiers. Also called *deck panels.*

double demy A size of paper; 21 by 32 inches.

double density A technique used to double the bit density on a disk so that more information can be stored in the same space.

double double A size of paper; 28 by 34 inches.

double eight An 8-mm camera that uses 16-mm film with double perforations. The film is run through the camera twice, once upside down, and then split in processing. The same procedure is followed for double super eight.

double elephant A size of paper; 27 by 40 inches.

double exposure □ A motion picture that is shown on a television station more than once in a week; sometimes refers to the same motion picture shown on two different stations. □ The superimposure of two images. Also called *double run.* Cf. multiple exposure.

double feature Two motion pictures shown in a theatre back-to-back; one usually a B picture. No longer a common practice.

double folio A size of paper; 33 by 34 inches.

double foolscap A size of paper; 17 by 27 inches.

double four pound A size of paper; 22 by 31 inches.

double frame The exposure of two frames of film instead of one to halve the speed of the motion.

double-frequency scanning A method of scanning a television picture at twice the normal frequency so that double the number of lines can be shown within one frame, without the loss of quality or the line flicker of normal interlace scanning. Improves the vertical resolution of a display.

double headed projection Projection accomplished by a projector equipped with two film mechanisms. *See also* interlock.

double image *See* ghost.

double imperial A size of paper; 30 by 44 inches.

double jump Two jumps.

double key Key lighting accomplished from two different angles, usually to cover two subjects or objects.

double leading The spacing of printed lines farther apart than normal.

double letter □ *See* ligature. □ A size of paper; 16 by 20 inches.

double medium A size of paper; 23 by 36 inches.

double numbered A book or other manuscript whose page numbers indicate both chapter and section, paragraph, or page number within the chapter, such as 1:34 indicates Chapter 1, section or paragraph 34 or Chapter 1, page 34.

double obelisk *See* double dagger.

double outcue An outcue on an audio- or videotape that is repeated; the cue is always the second of the two cues.

double packet A size of paper; 19 by 24 inches.

double-page spread *See* double spread.

double perforation Film that has perforations along each edge. Cf. single perforation.

double play An audiotape containing twice as much tape as normal; however, the tape is thin and prone to stretch.

double post A size of paper; 19-1/2 by 31-1/2 inches.

double pott A size of paper; 15 by 25 inches.

double prime The accent mark ″.

double print □ A combination on a printing plate of line and halftone, created by the photographic exposure of two different negatives in register in the same area, type overprinting the photographic area. □ A sheet printed from such a plate. □ To expose a negative twice from two separate sources. □ To print each frame of a film twice. □ To produce two images from one negative.

doubleprint *See* surprint.

double pyramid A form of newspaper layout in which a center section of editorial matter is flanked by columns of advertising.

double reel A film reel containing the film from two smaller reels; often a release print.

double resolution In CD-I, a display resolution mode between the normal- and high-resolution modes, with 768 pixels (twice as many as normal resolution) and 280 vertical pixels (the same as normal resolution). Cf. high resolution and low resolution.

double royal A size of paper; 24 by 38 inches.

double rule *See* Oxford rule.

double run *See* double exposure.

double sideband Transmission comprising the upper and lower sidebands in addition to the carrier frequency.

double small A size of paper; 3-1/2 by 5 inches.

double small post A size of paper; 19 by 30-1/2 inches.

double spacer □ A news wire term used to indicate a significant story. □ A story or news, double-spaced to indicate its importance.

double spotting The broadcasting of two commercials consecutively. Stations and networks also use triple spotting.

double spread Two opposing pages in a newspaper or magazine made up as a unit. Also called a *double-page spread.* Cf. center spread and double truck.

doublestrike A print mode in which each character is printed twice; the second strike is slightly off-center. Similar to emphasized.

double struck □ An impression made by a die that is struck twice, one slightly different from the other. □ An erroneous use of term to mean "double truck."

double super eight *See* double eight.

double superroyal A size of paper; 27-1/2 by 41 inches.

double system The use of two cameras or one camera and a synchronized tape recorder to record a scene. Usually used in motion picture work but can be accomplished with videotape. Cf. single system.

double-system sound □ A sound recording system characterized by the use of audio recording apparatus separate from the videotape recorder. □ Film sound that is recorded separately from the picture.

doublet □ An item or story printed twice in the same edition or issue. Also called a *dupe*. □ Type set twice by mistake. Also called a *double* and *doubleton*. □ A pair of lenses.

double take A delayed reaction by an actor to achieve comic effect.

doubleton *See* doublet.

double truck An advertising message using two facing pages in a newspaper or magazine; often the center pages. The message usually covers the gutter as well as the pages.

double truck head A headline or advertising material that extends across two pages of a newspaper or magazine.

double width *See* expanded.

double word A numeric entry comprising twice the number of bits contained in a normal computer word. For a 16-bit processor the double word is 32 bits wide; for a 32-bit processor, it is 64 bits wide. Occupies two successive memory locations.

double written In CD-I, data written twice with a four-byte separation. This achieves a data integrity level equivalent to mode 1.

doubling □ To play a dramatic role as a double. □ To play two or more roles in one performance. Also called *dual role*. □ To double frame.

doubling up The use of two light sources to cover one area of a set.

doublure A special lining made for a book cover; leather, brocade, and so on.

douse An order to turn the lights off on a set.

douser A mechanical element in a follow spot or similar device to cut off the light without extinguishing the lamp or arc. In a carbon arc, such a device protects the lens while the arc is struck.

down □ Lowercase type. □ Toward the front of a stage. □ The location of the pressroom. □ The lower half of a newspaper page. Also called *downstairs*. □ A script direction for talent to lower his or her voice or for music or sound effects to decrease in volume.

down and under A radio or television director's command to decrease the volume of music or sound effects and hold it under for background.

downbeat A musical or timing beat, usually the first.

down conversion The change of television standards to a lesser number of lines, such as from 625 to 525. Cf. up conversion.

downconverter A satellite receiver that automatically lowers the frequency of the signal to a lower frequency for subsequent relay.

down fade A decrease in light levels on a stage set.

downgrade □ To lower a performer's professional standing. Cf. outgrade and upgrade. □ A change by a cable television subscriber to a lower tier or to discontinue a premium service.

down in the mud Any sound so low in volume that the VU meter barely moves.

down in the noise A weak signal showing little difference in the signal-to-noise ratio.

down lead □ The wire or wires that couple an antenna to a receiver or transmitter. □ *See* lead-in.

downlight An overhead light with its beam directed downward and confined to a nearly vertical direction.

downlink The path of a signal from a communication satellite to a ground station. Cf. uplink.

downlink antenna A satellite antenna that radiates the downlink signal.

download To transfer a file or program from one computer to another, often by means of a modem.

downscale A market or audience that has a lower-than-average socioeconomic base. Cf. upscale.

down shot A camera shot taken from a high angle.

downside The lower portion of a rotating digital video effect (DVE). Cf. upside.

downstage The direction toward the cameras or audience. Cf. upstage.

downstairs *See* down.

downstream Pertaining to the locations on the tape longitudinally displaced from a given reference point in the direction of tape motion. Cf. upstream. □ The movement of signals in a CATV system from the head end to the subscriber's receiver.

downstream key A key that is introduced downstream from the output of a television video switcher.

downstyle Type that contains a minimum of uppercase lettering. Cf. upstyle.

downtime The period in which equipment cannot be used because of malfunction or other equipment failure. Also called *dead time* and *fault time.*

downtrend A gradual decrease in ratings, sales, subscribers, and so on, over a period of time. Cf. uptrend.

dowser A shutter on a film projector that cuts off the light source.

DP □ Data processing. □ Director of photography.

DPC Data processing center.

DPCM *See* delta modulation.

DPI Dots per inch.

DPR Day press rate. A reduced telegraphic rate. Cf. NPR.

DPS Data processing system.

draft □ A low-quality, high-speed print mode on dot matrix printers. □ A preliminary script or outline of a screenplay, manuscript, story, and so on.

drag The mechanical slowing of a tape transport mechanism causing wow and flutter. *See also* stylus drag.

dragon's blood A red powder used to prevent acid undercutting in photoengraving.

drain To reduce the power of a battery through use.

drama A vehicle, usually in prose, used to portray plot, characters, action, and so on, to an audience or reader. A drama may be classified as tragedy, comedy, melodrama, farce, or another category, and also as realism, expressionism, impressionism, and so on.

dramatic anthology *See* anthology.

dramatic irony The irony produced by incongruity between situations and words or actions.

dramatic license Any liberty taken with convention by a writer or director.

dramatic lighting Lighting used to establish mood.

dramatic rights The right of presentation in dramatic form on the speaking stage with living actors appearing and performing in the immediate presence of an audience, without any recordation, transmission, or broadcast thereof intended for aural or visual reception at places away from the place of performance.

dramatic time The period covered by the plot of a script. Cf. real time.

dramatis personae The characters in a dramatic work.

dramatist A playwright.

dramatization A fictionalized representation of a real or imagined event.

drape □ A scenic drop or background cyc. More properly called *draperies.* □ To drape a set.

draw □ The number of copies of a newspaper edition or magazine issue. □ A box office attraction. □ The amount of money advanced to someone in sales against future earnings.

draw card A title card or other graphic that is removed or placed horizontally. Cf. crawl and flip card.

drawing card A performer or feature that attracts people.

drawmap A RAM location containing CD-I visual information. Cf. soundmap.

drawn edge A marbled paper.

drawn on A cover for a paperbound book or magazine.

drawn-on-film An animation technique in which the image is drawn, painted, or scratched directly on the film stock.

drawn-on-paper An animation technique in which the animator's drawings are photographed, rather than transferred to cels. Some artists prefer this technique because they feel it gives them a chance to make a more immediate and personal statement or because the look of the drawing style may be suited to the film's content. The drawings may be done in a variety of media—

pencil, pen and ink, pastels, charcoal, and so on.

draw sheet A sheet used to hold overlays in place.

dream factory A slang term for a motion picture studio.

dream machine A slang term for the television industry.

D region The region above the earth extending to approximately 50 miles. *See also* ionosphere.

dress □ A dress rehearsal. Cf. dry run and run-through. □ To put the finishing touches on a stage set. □ The neat placement of leads in an electronic component. □ The style and appearance of a newspaper or other publication.

dresser □ The person responsible for costumes during the rehearsal and performance of a motion picture or television program. □ *See* set dresser.

dress extra An extra who wears something other than ordinary clothing.

dressing The props, decorations, and other items or materials added to a basic set to make it look lived-in.

dressing room The room or rooms in which cast members change into their costumes. Sometimes also used for applying make-up.

dress off A direction to a performer to line up or move by the placement of another performer or set piece.

dress parade A lineup of cast members so that the director may check their costumes.

dress rehearsal The final rehearsal of a play or television program before it is performed; done without stopping and as if the play or program were being presented to an audience or broadcast. Cf. dry run, run-through, and walk-through.

drier A cabinet or enclosure used for drying film during processing.

drift □ The movement of a tuner or other device away from the selected frequency. □ A random rate of deviation in frequency or pitch close to zero cycles per second. Cf. flutter and wow. □ A slow, deliberate movement by a performer.

drip loop A U-shaped loop formed in a cable television subscriber drop to keep moisture from entering the building.

drive □ A general term for any mechanism that moves a recording or playback system, such as a tape transport, disk drive, or turntable. □ An abbreviation for *disk drive.* A device that accesses disks to retrieve or store information. □ A device or player specifically designed to read digital data from CD-ROM or CD-I discs. CD-I drives can also play CD-DA discs.

drive in An outdoor motion picture theatre that caters to persons in automobiles.

drive in theatre *See* drive in.

drive mechanism *See* drive.

drive motor A motor that operates both a film camera and a tape recorder in synchronization. *See also* double system.

drive out To space words so as to fill a line of type. *See also* wordspacing.

drive pin A pin similar to a center pin but located to one side thereof; used to prevent a disc from slipping on the recording turntable.

drive player *See* compact disc.

driver □ An electronic circuit that supplies input power to another circuit. □ The transducing element of a midrange- or high-frequency horn. □ A computer program that controls the operation of peripheral devices or interfaces. □ Hardware-specific features of CD-I players and implement functions of file managers and isolate software for hardware functions.

drive side The side of a printing press containing the drive mechanism. Cf. operating side.

drivetime The commuting hours on weekdays when the radio audience is greatest; radio's prime time. Comprises approximately 6 to 10 a.m. and 3 to 7 p.m. *See also* evening drive and morning drive.

drooling A slang term for a DJ talking about nothing of importance.

drop □ An abbreviation for *backdrop.* A suspended drapery or canvas on which a scene is painted. □ A transmitter that receives a videotape feed, and in turn, feeds the stations connected to it. □ The connection from a CATV system to a subscriber's receiver; a subscriber drop. □ A subscriber's telephone line connection. □ A headline from a streamer.

drop arm A vertical pole on which a luminaire may be clamped or hung.

drop cable A cable that connects a subscriber's television receiver to the feeder cable in a cable television system.

drop folio A book page number printed at the bottom. Cf. folio.

drop-frame Pertaining to a mode of operation of the SMPTE time and control code characterized by periodic and deliberate omission of one frame count. Such omissions occur at a rate that causes elapsed time indicated by the code to correspond exactly with elapsed time indicated by a clock. This technique is used in NTSC television systems because of the nonsynchronous relationship between the NTSC signal and the usual 60-Hz powerline frequency. Necessary because the color frame rate is 29.97 instead of an exact 30 frames per second.

drop head A subordinate headline. Also called a *step head* or *step lines* when it consists of two or more indented lines. Also called a *drop headline, drop line,* and *hanger.*

drop headline *See* drop head.

drop in □ The accidental generation of random bits during reading from or writing to a computer disk. Cf. dropout. □ A method of changing graphics on camera wherein the cards fall into place. Cf. drop out. □ A television allotment made without consideration of the Table of Allotments. □ A local television commercial inserted in a nationally sponsored network program.

drop in ad An advertisement for one product contained within the space allocated to another advertisement; often used by advertisers to promote public service events.

drop in allotment A VHF television allotment made by the FCC without regard to the required minimum mileage separation.

drop initial A cut-in letter that uses part of the space of several text lines. Also called a *drop letter. See also* initial. Cf. rising initial.

drop letter *See* drop initial.

drop line *See* drop head.

drop out □ An accidental loss of information on a computer disk during read/write operations. Cf. drop in. □ A method of changing graphics on camera wherein the cards fall out of place to reveal another card. Cf. drop in.

dropout □ A halftone in which no dots appear in the white spaces. Also called a *dropout halftone* and *highlight halftone.* □ A temporary loss of sound or picture caused by faulty magnetic tape coating or backing. □ A fault in tape playback characterized by a brief loss of the FM signal, such loss usually but not necessarily being of less than one scan line duration. □ The picture fault resulting from such a loss. □ The periodic and predictable signal loss in a helical scan recorder, resulting when the scanning head finishes the scanning of one video track and momentarily leaves the tape to begin the scanning of the next track.

dropout compensation The action of a dropout compensator.

dropout compensator (DOC) □ An apparatus that detects the presence of a dropout and acts to minimize its visibility in the reproduced television picture. □ An apparatus that accomplishes the foregoing by replacing the missing information from another part of the signal, such as from the preceding scan line.

dropout counter A device that measures the number of dropouts per unit of magnetic tape.

drop out halftone A halftone in which dots are dropped out in the highlight areas of the plate to give the whitest effect possible for good contrast.

dropout rate The rate at which dropouts occur, usually measured in dropouts per minute.

dropped cue A missed cue.

dropped head A book chapter heading that is lower than the point where the first line of type would normally be located.

drop shipment Orders sent from a manufacturer to a consumer that are billed to a retail seller.

drop shutter A camera shutter with an aperture opening in a metal plate.

drop start A quick start method for discs. *See also* slip start.

dross The waste material, commonly referred to as scum, that results from the melting of type metal.

drum □ A rotating cylinder used for graphics. □ A cylindrical device used for drying film. □ A rotating slide holder. □ The flywheel next to a projector's sound head. □ A cylinder, one section of which holds video heads, around which magnetic tape is at least partially wrapped to form the head-to-tape interface of a television tape recording system. The preferred synonym for the quadruplex recording system is *head wheel.* Also called a *head drum. See also* scanner. □ *See* magnetic drum.

drumbeater A slang term for a press agent.

drum modulator *See* modulator.

drum scanning □ The use of a rotational head and cylindrical guiding assembly in a helical scan videotape recorder. □ The form of scanning used in facsimile. Also called *cylinder scanning.*

drum servo An electromechanical device on a videotape recorder that controls the rotational speed of the headwheel. Also called a *headwheel servo. See also* headwheel and servo.

dry A day in which there is little newsworthy material. *See also* silly season.

dry brush A painting technique in which the brush is dipped in paint, brushed against some unneeded surface to remove most of the paint, then used to produce brush strokes with a rough, grainy, irregular look. Used on cels to create such effects as speed lines and on paintings for such textures as wood grain.

dry groove *See* unmodulated groove.

dry ice Frozen carbon dioxide. Produces the special effects of fog and mist when mixed with water.

drying The process of eliminating moisture in film processing.

drying cabinet *See* drier.

drying marks The spots left on processed film after the water has evaporated.

drymount A photographic mount that uses a heated solvent or rubber cement as opposed to paste.

dry offset A printing method in which an image is offset to a rubber blanket for transfer to paper without the use of water. Also called *letterset.*

dry point □ A method of engraving without acid, wherein a plate is etched with a fine needle. □ A print made by the dry point process. □ The needle used for making the print.

dry processing A type of film requiring heat instead of chemicals for processing.

dry rehearsal *See* dry run.

dry run A complete rehearsal but without costumes, props, or cameras. Also called a *dry rehearsal.* Cf. dress rehearsal, run through, and walk-through.

dry sound Any sound that is lacking in reverberation or equalization of any kind. Also called *non-EQ'd sound.* Cf. wet sound.

DS □ Disk storage. □ Downstream. □ Dolly shot.

DSA Distinguished Service Award of the NAB.

DST Differential survey treatment.

D system The 625-line, 25-frames per second, 8-mHz bandwidth, FM sound television system used in the Soviet Union and other communist countries. Cf. A, B, E, and M systems.

dt An abbreviation for *date.*

DTE Data terminal equipment.

D-3 A half-inch composite digital videotape format that uses metal particle tape for duplication without generational loss. Cf. D-1 and D-2.

DTM Director of telecommunication management of the IEP.

DTS Data transmission system.

DTTR Digital television tape recorder.

D-2 A high-quality videotape recording format that uses azimuth recording with metal tape to produce completely digital video, audio, and control data. Each dub is therefore equal to the master tape with the audio quality on four channels superior to that of CDs. Cf. D-1 and D-3.

dual □ *See* combo. □ *See* double.

dual capstan A tape transport that has a capstan on both sides of the tape heads.

dual channel market A geographic area that receives at least two television channels.

dual coded lamp ANSI-coded lamps carrying two code designations. The first three-letter code identifies the lamp. The lamp is the suggested substitution for applications indicated by the second three-letter code.

dual feedhorn A satellite dish feedhorn that can receive both horizontally and vertically polarized signals.

dual gauge Equipment capable of handling more than one size of film, such as super 8 and standard 8 mm.

dual imprint An imprint by two or more publishers. Also called *joint imprint. See also* copublishing.

dual kicker Two short headlines over one story. *See also* kicker.

dual licensees Licensees operating more than one radio or television station. *See also* duopoly rule and multiple ownership.

dual microphones Two small, side-by-side microphones that are used by the same person in case one should become inoperative. Often used in television news.

dual network The operation by the same organization of two or more networks that are operated simultaneously or with substantial overlap in coverage.

dual pickup *See* turnover cartridge.

dual purpose □ A luminaire capable of producing flood or spot lighting. □ A lens designed for either television or film cameras. □ A projector capable of displaying two different sizes of film, such as 35 mm and 70 mm. □ A studio or stage constructed for easy conversion between television and motion picture production.

dual rate A radio or television station that has two rate cards; usually national and local.

dual receiver □ A television receiver capable of receiving both VHF and UHF bands. □ A television receiver capable of receiving more than one line standard or more than one system, such as PAL and NTSC.

dual recording The making of two master tapes or disks at the same time to provide a replacement should one be accidentally destroyed. Cf. backup.

dual role *See* double and doubling.

dual track recorder *See* half track recorder.

dub □ To make a copy of a recording by rerecording. □ A copy that is thus made. Cf. dupe. □ To record lip-sync on film for later mixing. Also called *looping.* □ *See* RF dub. □ *See* dubbing and video dub.

dubbed version *See* dubbing.

dubber □ A sound playback unit, either tape or mag film. □ A tape recorder used in its playback mode.

dubbing □ Any copying or joining together of picture and/or sound on film, videotape, or audiotape. □ To change the medium on which the sound or picture is recorded, as from film to tape or vice versa. □ The replacing of a film soundtrack in one language with another. Also called *looping. See also* foreign version. □ To add sound to a visual presentation by adding additional tracks of music, dialogue, sound effects, and so on. □ To record a voice in lip-sync with a film image.

dubbing cue sheet A multitrack audio cue sheet used in dubbing sound for film or tape.

dubbing mixer A multichannel audio console used for dubbing.

dubbing session The time spent in planning and accomplishing dubbing.

dubbing stage The studio or soundstage where music or sound effects are added to dialogue tracks or where foreign language versions are lip-synced.

dub down To dub to a videotape smaller in width or to an audiotape at a slower speed. Cf. dub up and mix down.

dub in To add anything to a soundtrack after the original recording has been made.

dub off To dub a portion of a tape or film.

dub up To dub to a videotape greater in width or to an audiotape at a faster speed. Cf. dub down.

ducting The temporary trapping of a broadcast signal between two layers of the earth's atmosphere. When released, the broadcast signal may receive widespread coverage.

due A newspaper insertion owed to an advertiser.

due bill □ An agreement for the barter of services from an advertiser, such as a hotel or airline, in exchange for space or time in a mass medium. □ A statement of radio or television barter time acquired.

due care A court-enunciated doctrine holding a licensee guilty for all defamatory and other statements made over the air unless the licensee could demonstrate that he or she took "due care" to prevent the airing of such material.

due process The administration of law carried out in accordance with proper procedures through the courts.

dull Not glossy; uncalendered paper.

dull coated A paper that has a nonglossy coating.

dulling spray A spray used in motion pictures and television to reduce the reflection from bright surfaces.

dumb terminal A computer terminal that is unable to process information without being connected to a mainframe. Cf. smart terminal.

dummy □ A layout or diagram of a newspaper or magazine page showing the location of each item. Also called a *map.* □ A sample copy of a book, often made with blank pages, showing the general appearance of the finished product. □ A stuffed, human form used as a double for action that is too dangerous for a human stunt person. □ A microphone that is used as a prop.

dummy load *See* phantom load.

dummy name *See* decoy.

Dumont Television Network A short-lived (1950 through 1955) television network.

dump □ A computer routine that moves stored information to another location or output; as in a screen dump. □ To place type in galleys.

dunning process An early, special effects self-matting process.

duodecimo A size of book pages; from the folding of a sheet into 12 leaves. Colloquially referred to as a twelvemo.

duograph *See* duotone.

duo play A replay of a dual track recording, either from the same tape or from tape and mag stripe.

duopoly rule The FCC rule that forbids the ownership of two or more stations of the same kind in the same service area. *See also* multiple ownership.

duoscopic A television receiver designed to receive two programs at one time.

duotone A two-color reproduction of a halftone from two separate plates; usually black and one other color. Also called a *duograph.*

dupe □ A duplicate or carbon copy of a news story. □ *See* doublet. □ An abbreviation for *duplicate.* A copy of a film. Cf. master. A duplicate tape is more properly called a *dub.* □ *See* picture dupe negative.

dupe elimination *See* duplication elimination.

dupe negative A negative film prepared from an original negative, often by duping. Also called a *picture duplicate negative.*

duping □ An abbreviation for *duplicating.* □ In film, the process of making a negative from a positive. □ The making of duplicates by rerecording.

duping print A special fine grain print made from an original negative in order to make a high-quality dupe negative. Also called a *blue print.*

duplex □ A symmetrical, variable-area soundtrack that is opaque on the negative film. Cf. bilateral. □ A microfilm system containing a mirror so that both sides of a document may be recorded simultaneously.

duplex operation Electronic communication in which transmission is possible simultaneously in both directions. *See also* full duplex and half duplex.

duplex paper Paper with a different tint on each side.

duplex technique A telephone audience interviewing technique in which the activities of a potential audience at the time of the interview and over the previous 15 minutes are examined.

duplicate A tape recording produced by dubbing; a replica. Also called a *duplicate tape. See also* dub.

duplicate audience The audience common to two or more programs or commercials.

duplicated newspaper A short-run newspaper, often a high school paper, run off using stencils.

duplicate master Another negative or positive master made as insurance against damage to the original master.

duplicate negative *See* dupe negative.

duplicate plates Backup printing plates made to provide plates in case of damage to the original plates or for exact duplication of advertisements in several different publications.

duplicate tape *See* duplicate.

duplicating process The process of making positive or negative prints of original camera film.

duplicating stock A fine grain film used for making duplicates.

duplication □ The act of producing a replica of a previously recorded tape, by dubbing, anhysteretic duplication, thermal duplication, or any other suitable process. □ The process of making a copy of a disc, disk, book, and so on. □ A CATV system's carriage of a distant signal that is the same as that broadcast by a local station. □ The receipt by a household or individual of the advertising messages of two or more different media. □ The exposure of a household or individual to the same commercial or program more than once. *See also* program duplication. □ The amount of exposure of the known audience of a medium of the same type carrying the same advertising, or to more than one appearance of the same advertising in the same medium, such as successive issues of the same magazine. □ The purchase of more than one copy of a newspaper or magazine by a reader. □ *See* audience duplication.

duplication elimination A controlled mailing system that provides that no matter how many times a name and address is on a list and no matter how many lists contain that name and address, it will be accepted for mailing only one time by that mailer. Also called *dupe elimination.*

duplicator A copying machine used for short runs; a hectograph, stencil duplicator, and so on.

duPont Award, Alfred I. Awards given by Columbia University for "outstanding performance in news and public affairs."

durability The extent to which an audio- or videotape can repeatedly pass across the heads of a recorder before it becomes too worn for use.

duration The length of time a program, segment, cut, scene, edit, advertisement insertion, production, and so on, lasts.

duration averaging Averaging radio or television programs together by weighting according to the length of each program.

dust cover A protective paper folder for discs. Also called a *dust jacket.*

dust jacket □ A paper cover that is used to wrap a book. The cover often contains information about the author, a brief synopsis, and reviews. Also called a *dust wrapper* and *jacket.* □ *See* dust cover.

dust wrapper *See* dust jacket.

dutch angle A camera shot taken from an unusual position. *See also* trick angle.

dutch break Copy that extends beyond a headline. Also called a *dutch turn, dutch wrap,* and *raw wrap.*

dutch door A unit of space in a magazine, produced under special circumstances; consists of two-part, full-page gatefolds folding to a common center, or stacked or single half-page gatefolds.

dutchman □ The extra lens added to the front of a P.C. spotlight to serve as a condenser before adding a projection head. □ A piece of wood used in a form to tighten and hold type in forms. □ Any of various devices for concealing poor workmanship or discontinuities in the shape of something. □ A cloth strip that is pasted over the crack or hinges between two flats.

dutch paper A fine, handmade paper.

dutch turn *See* dutch break.

dutch wrap *See* dutch break.

duty cycle The amount of time a device designed for intermittent use may be operated without damage, such as a relay, solenoid, or tape eraser.

duvetyn A smooth, velvety fabric used to dull reflective surfaces.

DV Direct voice.

DVE Digital video effects.

DVI Digital video interactive. A technological development that compresses different kinds of digital data—audio, video, computer-created images—onto CDs or other storage media. Up to 72 minutes of video can be stored on a single compact disc. Cf. CD-I.

Dvorak keyboard A keyboard designed by August Dvorak in the 1930s that is easier and faster to use than a standard keyboard. Cf. QWERTY.

DVR Digital video recording.

DW Dust wrapper.

DX Long distance.

dye A film or art coloring material or chemical.

dye coupler A chemical ingredient added to film or developing solutions that produces a color image.

dye transfer An opaque color print made from artwork or transparency; permits a wide range of color correction during the laboratory process or a match to the color of the original. *See also* imbibition.

Dynalens The tradename of a gyroscopically compensated lens that decreases the effect of camera vibration.

dynamic cutting Television or film editing marked by continuous, often vigorous transitions. Also called *dynamic editing.* Cf. static cutting.

dynamic editing *See* dynamic cutting.

dynamic frame An experimental motion picture process that used variable moving mattes to control different aspect ratios between and within camera shots.

dynamic loading In CD-I, updating the contents of the color look-up table during the horizontal retrace period (up to 4 colors), or during the vertical retrace period (up to 256 colors).

dynamic loudspeaker A loudspeaker that contains a moving coil in a magnetic field. Also called a *moving coil loudspeaker.*

dynamic microphone A pressure microphone that employs a diaphragm connected to a moving coil transducer. Also called a *moving coil microphone* and *pressure microphone. See also* cardioid microphone, condenser microphone, and velocity microphone.

dynamic pickup A disc cartridge transducer, the electric output of which results from the motion of a coil in a magnetic field. Also called a *dynamic reproducer* and *moving coil pickup. See also* pickup.

dynamic range The difference, in decibels, between the lowest and highest sound pressure levels. For example, FM radio has far greater dynamic range than AM radio.

dynamic reproducer *See* dynamic pickup.

dynamics □ The way in which sound quality varies. □ The moving, vibrant, nonstatic qualities of a script or program. □ The use of lines, brushwork, sounds, balance, tension, and so on, in layouts, dramas, scripts, and other forms.

dynamic tracking A technique for maintaining tracking in a television tape recorder in an operating mode in which the linear tape speed is abnormal.

dynode An element in a cathode ray or other tube that produces a secondary emission of electrons.

dynode flare A flare in a cathode ray tube similar in effect to a lens flare.

DYUV *See* delta YUV.

E

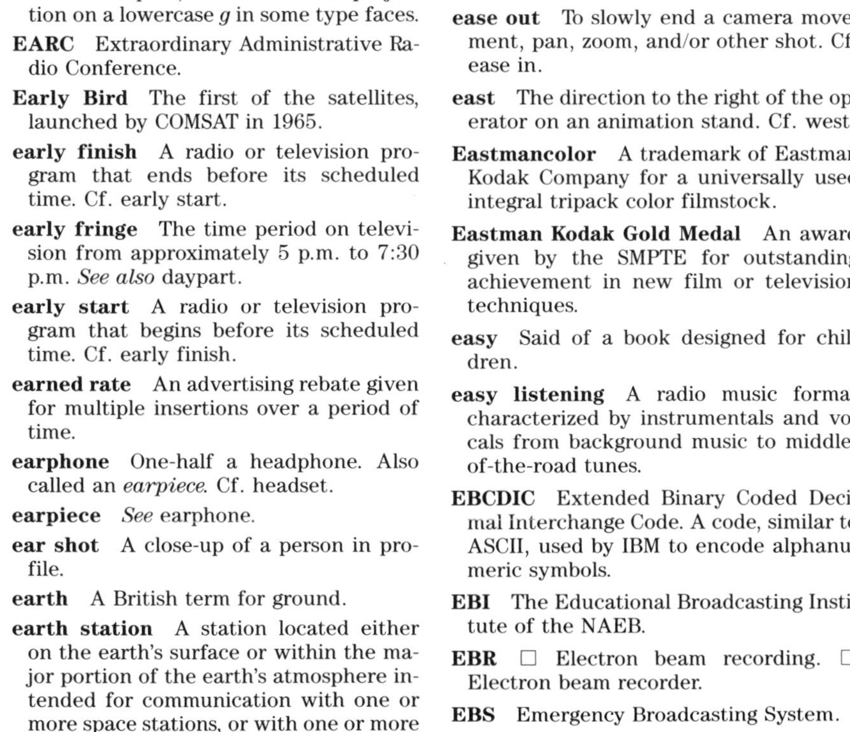

E □ Edition. □ Electricity. □ Electron. □ Engineering. □ Entertainment programs. □ A wire service code for entertainment or cultural material.

ea □ Editorial assistant. □ Editor's alteration.

EAM The Evangelical Alliance Mission. A religious broadcasting organization.

EAN Emergency Action Notification.

EANA European Alliance of News Agencies.

ear □ A small box in an upper corner of a newspaper page containing a slogan, weather report, and so on. □ A projection on a lowercase *g* in some type faces.

EARC Extraordinary Administrative Radio Conference.

Early Bird The first of the satellites, launched by COMSAT in 1965.

early finish A radio or television program that ends before its scheduled time. Cf. early start.

early fringe The time period on television from approximately 5 p.m. to 7:30 p.m. *See also* daypart.

early start A radio or television program that begins before its scheduled time. Cf. early finish.

earned rate An advertising rebate given for multiple insertions over a period of time.

earphone One-half a headphone. Also called an *earpiece.* Cf. headset.

earpiece *See* earphone.

ear shot A close-up of a person in profile.

earth A British term for ground.

earth station A station located either on the earth's surface or within the major portion of the earth's atmosphere intended for communication with one or more space stations, or with one or more stations of the same kind by means of one or more reflecting satellites or other objects in space. *See also* downlink and uplink.

ease in To slowly begin a camera movement, pan, zoom, or other shot. Cf. ease out.

easel □ A holder with adjustable borders used to support photographic paper on an enlarger base. □ A device used to hold graphics. Also called a *card stand.*

easel shot A television studio camera shot of pictures or illustrations displayed on an easel.

easement A right granted to use the land of another. Specifically, in CATV, the right to use the land of another for laying cables.

ease out To slowly end a camera movement, pan, zoom, and/or other shot. Cf. ease in.

east The direction to the right of the operator on an animation stand. Cf. west.

Eastmancolor A trademark of Eastman Kodak Company for a universally used integral tripack color filmstock.

Eastman Kodak Gold Medal An award given by the SMPTE for outstanding achievement in new film or television techniques.

easy Said of a book designed for children.

easy listening A radio music format characterized by instrumentals and vocals from background music to middle-of-the-road tunes.

EBCDIC Extended Binary Coded Decimal Interchange Code. A code, similar to ASCII, used by IBM to encode alphanumeric symbols.

EBI The Educational Broadcasting Institute of the NAEB.

EBR □ Electron beam recording. □ Electron beam recorder.

EBS Emergency Broadcasting System.

EBS Authenticator List A list issued every six months by the FCC to be used in conjunction with procedures contained in the EBS Checklist and SOPs for tests or actual national emergency situations.

EBS Checklist The document that states the actions to be taken by a station's personnel upon receipt of an Emergency Action Notification, Emergency Action Termination, or test messages.

EBU European Broadcasting Union.

EBU time code The EBU's designation for the SMPTE time code.

EC □ Electronic cinematography. □ Electronic computer.

ECATV Educational cable television. A system designed for two-way educational CATV.

ECC □ Error correction code. □ East Coast Council, a New York-based film union.

eccentric A device that turns circular motion into reciprocating motion; used for intermittent film advance in some cameras.

eccentric circle *See* eccentric groove.

eccentric groove The groove at the end of a disc used to trip an automatic record player's reject mechanism. Also called an *eccentric circle.*

eccentricity □ Of a quadruplex rotary video-head assembly, the degree to which the center of rotation of the video heads fails to coincide with the center of curvature of the vacuum guide. A prescribed degree of eccentricity is employed in normal operating practice to compensate partially for differences between the radius of the vacuum guide used in recording and the vacuum guide used in playback. □ The displacement of the center of the recording groove spiral with respect to the disc center hole.

Eccles-Jordan circuit *See* flip-flop.

echo A wave that has been reflected at one or more points in the transmission medium with sufficient magnitude and time difference to be perceived in some manner as a wave distinct from that of the main or primary transmission. Echoes may be either leading or lagging the primary wave and appear in the television picture as reflections or ghosts.

echo chamber An electronic device or room used to produce reverberation or delay in an audio signal. A tape recorder by itself may act as an echo chamber. Cf. reverberation.

echo effect A sound effects reverberation accomplished by an echo chamber or a delay line.

echo equalizer A device used to reduce ghosting in television reception.

echo return A control that adjusts the amount of signal received from a reverberation or echo device by an audio control console. Cf. echo send.

echo send A control that adjusts the amount of signal sent to a reverberation or echo device from an audio control console. Cf. echo return.

eclectic A radio, television, magazine, or other format that contains varied types of materials.

ECM Electronic countermeasures.

ECOM Electronic Computer Originated Mail. An electronic mail system run by the U.S. Postal Service.

economic injury The alleged injury that might occur to an existing radio or television station by the introduction of a new station into a market. The FCC need not consider economic injury unless it might result in a loss of service to the public. *See also* Carroll case.

ECS □ Experimental communications satellite. □ Educational Communications System. A former project of the NAEB.

ECU Extreme close-up.

ECUI Extreme close-up indeed. A British term for an ECU.

ED □ Educational. An FCC file-number prefix. □ Educational institution programs. □ Every day.

ed An abbreviation for *edit, edited, edition, editor,* and *editorial.*

ED-Beta A Sony half-inch videotape format similar in quality to S-VHS.

EDC □ Error detection code. □ Electronic digital computer.

Eddie Award An award given by the American Cinema Editors for outstanding achievement in feature film and TV editing.

EDFM Educational FM station. *See also* noncommercial broadcasting.

edge beat *See* twinkling.

edge curl The curl on the outside edges of magnetic tape often caused by incorrect winding resulting in tape deformity and the subsequent loss of recorded information.

edge effect □ The density differences at boundaries between different parts of the image in developed photographic film. □ An increased emphasis of outlines common to the image orthicon. □ The bordering of objects on a television screen by the inherent properties of the system. *See also* following blacks, following whites, leading blacks, and leading whites.

edge enhancement *See* contouring.

edge flare A loss of contrast at the edges of a television picture.

edge fog The film fogging that occurs along one or both film edges due to improper handling, exposure to strong light, and so on. Also called *edge fogging.*

edge fogging *See* edge fog.

edge index An alphabetical index formed by placing rules to the edge of book pages that can be seen as black blocks. Cf. thumb index.

edge key A graphic key that has letters with drop shadows, outlines, and so on.

edge light A luminaire used to form a halo around an object. *See also* backlight.

edge marking A general term for edge numbers and code numbers.

edge numbers (EN) The identification numbers printed by the manufacturer on film stock to indicate footage. Also called *footage numbers* and *negative numbers.* Cf. code numbers and key number.

edge roll A tool used to make decorative book covers.

edge stripe The magnetic tape track added to a film for audio recording. Cf. optical sound.

edging The outlining of a colored object by another color in a television picture.

edging in A transitional technique of fading in a new portion of a radio or television program being aired so that it does not blast-in.

edgy A subjective description of a lack of smoothness in mid- and high-frequency loudspeaker reproduction.

Edison base The standard screw thread base used on ordinary household light bulbs (lamps).

Edison effect The transfer of current in a vacuum tube from one element to another generated by heating one element. Named after its discoverer, Thomas Alva Edison. Also called the *Richardson effect.*

Edison Medal An award given by the IEEE for a "career of meritorious achievement in electrical science or electrical engineering."

edit □ To alter the contents of a recorded tape either by selectively erasing a portion of the tape and recording new material, or by appending new material to a previously unrecorded section at the end of the tape. *See also* assemble edit and insert edit. □ To direct or carry out such an operation. □ A point or location in a tape at which such an alteration has been made. □ The program material in the immediate vicinity of such an alteration. □ An abbreviation for *editorial,* an FCC programming category. □ To arrange the various shots, scenes, and sequences, or the elements of the sound track, in the order desired to create the finished film. □ To physically or electronically change the sequence of shots or to change the length of film or video- or audiotape. □ To change the arrangement of words, sentences, stories, and so on. □ An abbreviation for *edited* and *edition.* □ To supervise the publication of a newspaper, magazine, and so on. □ To physically or electronically change the sequence of shots or scenes of a video or audiotape or film. □ To change the arrangement of words, sentences, stories, and so on, by deleting extraneous matter or adding matter for clarity. □ To prepare material for publication in book form. □ To arrange, delete from or add to a computer file.

Editall A tradename for an audiotape splicing block.

edit code □ Generally, any coded pulse train designed to facilitate the tape editing process by locating program segments on a tape. □ Specifically, the SMPTE time and control code. □ The magnetic pattern recorded on tape to represent such a code.

edit control A device on an audiotape recorder that makes the tape slack for editing purposes.

edit decision list (EDL) A handwritten or computer list of videotape edits to be performed. Used to edit the final tape in the proper sequence. Also called a *decision list* and *edit list.*

Editec An automatic computer-controlled editing device for videotape.

edit error Dropout, distortion, flashing, or color shifting caused by poor splicing of videotape. On audiotape it causes dropout, deletions of sound, or more sound than desired.

editing □ The step of reviewing responses on questionnaires, schedules, or diaries for apparent completeness, consistency, and accuracy. □ The process of arranging and/or eliminating scenes or sounds on a magnetic tape. □ The process of arranging and/or eliminating scenes or sound on film. □ The process of reviewing and revising news copy, manuscripts, motion pictures, television programs, and so on. □ The process of arranging and perfecting news copy. *See also* edit.

editing barrel *See* bin.

editing bench A bench containing rewinds, viewers, splicers, and so on, used for editing film. Also called an *editing table.*

editing bin *See* bin.

editing block *See* splicing block.

editing controller An electronic device that controls the operation of videotape recorders and players during editing. Also called an *editing control unit.*

editing control unit *See* editing controller.

editing house A company that specializes in postproduction work in videotape and film.

editing machine □ A vertical or horizontal viewing and synchronizing device for editing film. *See also* flatbed and Moviola. □ A videotape editing machine.

editing room assistant A person engaged in and about the editing room, film library and vault, whose duties may include splicing, patching, rewinding, coding film, and carrying materials to and from the editing room, library, and splicing machines.

editing script The script used to select the scenes and edit points for a television program or commercial, and to make the edit decision list.

editing session A period of time spent editing film, audio- or videotape, and so on. Also called an *edit session.*

editing sync *See* editorial sync.

editing table *See* editing bench.

editing tempo The pacing of the sound and picture on a videotape or film, whether to music, dialogue, action, mood, or other variable.

editing terminal A computer terminal designed for the preparation of text and graphics.

editing videotape recorder A videotape recorder containing the circuitry necessary for it to be able to interface with an editing controller.

edition □ One of a number of printings of the same work from the same type. □ A periodical issue. □ The form in which a literary work is published. □ The number of copies of a work printed at one time; as first or second edition. Cf. impression. □ One of several printings of a newspaper during a day, such as city edition, mail edition, and final edition.

edition binding A commercial binding of a large number of books or complete editions.

editio princeps □ From the Latin for "first edition." □ The first edition of a work that was printed from a manuscript after the invention of printing. □ Any work that is newly printed. Normally called a *first edition.*

edit-level video (ELV) A DVI technique that captures and compresses motion video images in real time.

edit list *See* edit decision list.

edit mode The computer text mode that allows editing.

editor □ A person who edits material for publication. □ A person who edits tape or film into its final form. □ An editorial writer. □ A department head or other employee, as in titles such as managing editor, acquisitions editor, city editor, sports editor, and editor in chief. □ An apparatus designed to accomplish or facilitate the editing of a tape. □ A person who edits tape recordings or directs such editing. □ A computer program that facilitates the entry and editing of text. □ The IATSE designation for a person actually engaged in cutting or selecting in dramatic continuity, revising or correcting all motion picture material. The editor's function is to contribute to all of the creative elements of a motion picture and to participate in molding and integrating them into one cohesive and aesthetic whole.

editorial □ An announcement or program presented for the purpose of stating the opinions of the licensee of a broadcast station or the management of a publication. □ The interjection of opinion into news stories by editors and reporters. □ A statement of a point of view regarding public issues expressed by the management of a periodical. *See also* editorial matter. □ Noting or pertaining to editorial matter.

editorial alteration *See* editor's alteration (ea).

editorial authority □ A credibility advantage established by a media vehicle's public reputation for accuracy and objectivity in its editorial content. □ A goal of advertising, sought either by placement of advertisements in media vehicles judged to be of high authority to purchase prospects, or by designing advertisements to imitate the appearance of editorial matter in the media in which they appear.

editorial calendar A plan that contains the editorial content of a magazine or other publication.

editorial cartoon A cartoon, often political or issue oriented, found on editorial pages of newspapers.

editorial classification The system of major sections or departments used to organize a periodical, especially a newspaper.

editorial content *See* editorial matter.

editorial department The newspaper department responsible for all matter except advertising.

editorial environment The standard editorial content, tone, and philosophy of a medium; seen as potentially supportive or destructive of the effectiveness of advertising using this medium.

editorialization □ The expression of opinions by broadcast licensees. Forbidden by the FCC in the Mayflower Decision but later approved in 1949. □ To inject opinions into newscasts or news reports.

editorial material All material in a newspaper except advertising.

editorial matter □ The reading matter prepared by the staff of a publication or accepted from contributors, as opposed to advertising. Also called *editorial* and *editorial content.* □ The programs on radio and television exclusive of commercial matter.

editorial page The newspaper page devoted to editorials, often page two. *See also* op-ed page.

editorial policy The principle followed by a newspaper, broadcast station, magazine, and so on, in presenting news and other matter.

editorial process The process of preparing the raw materials of the media (tape, film, scripts, news, and so on) for dissemination.

editorial program *See* editorial.

editorial sync The code numbers placed on separate picture and sound frames so that the sound is exactly even with the corresponding picture frame so that the film may be edited. Also called *cutting sync, editing sync, editorial synchronism, editorial synchronization, level sync,* and *recording sync.* Cf. projection sync.

editorial synchronism *See* editorial sync.

editorial synchronization *See* editorial sync.

editor in chief □ The head of a newspaper news department. Also called an *editor.* □ A policymaking executive of a publishing house.

editor's alteration (ea) A change made to newspaper or magazine copy or to a manuscript by an editor. Cf. author's alteration (aa) and printer's error (pe).

edit out A somewhat redundant term for eliminating a portion of a shot, sound, and so on.

edit point The entry and exit (in and out) points of a single video scene within a television program, commercial, and so on.

edit program A computer program that automatically controls the operation of an audio or video editing system.

edit pulse □ Originally, a pulse derived from and occurring during the vertical interval of the even field of the television signal and recorded on the control track to facilitate mechanical editing procedures. □ The magnetic pattern recorded on tape representing such a pulse. Occasionally called an *editing pulse.* The preferred term is *frame pulse.*

edit session *See* editing session.

edit sync guide (ESG) Audible beeps placed at one-second intervals on videotape for editing purposes. Now largely obsolete. Also called *talking clock.*

Edivue A tradename for one of the rapidly evaporating fluids (Freon TF) used to make the frame pulses on videotape visible for mechanical splicing.

EDP Electronic data processing.

EDPA Exhibit Designers and Producers Association.

EDRS ERIC Document Reproduction Service.

edsat A satellite used for educational purposes.

EDTV □ Extended definition television. □ Enhanced definition television.

education access channel A specifically designated cable television channel for use by local educational authorities.

Educational Communications Association An organization of persons interested in educational communication.

educational institution programs (ED) Programs prepared by, on behalf of, or in cooperation with educational institutions, educational organizations, libraries, museums, PTAs, or similar organizations. Sports programs are not included. An FCC program type category.

Educational Media Council (EMC) A federation of professional and trade organizations concerned with developments and problems in the educational media field.

educational program *See* educational institution programs.

educational radio *See* noncommercial broadcasting.

educational reservations The allotment of radio and television channels to various communities throughout the United States for noncommercial radio and television stations.

educational television *See* noncommercial broadcasting.

Educational Television and Radio Center (ETRC) The forerunner of National Educational Television (NET).

Educational Television Facilities Act The Act of 1962 that provided the first direct federal aid to noncommercial broadcasting.

educational television or radio programs Programs designed for educational or cultural purposes. *See also* educational institution programs.

edutainment A portmanteau word signifying educational entertainment; learning in an easy, enjoyable way.

EE Electrical engineer.

EEN Eastern Educational Television Network.

EEO Equal employment opportunities.

EEOC Equal Employment Opportunity Commission. A federal government agency.

EF English finish.

effect A technique or device for producing a visual or auditory illusion, as in sound effects, special effects, or optical effects.

effective aperture The difference between the f stop setting of a lens and the actual amount of light transmitted by the lens. Also called the *working aperture.* Cf. relative aperture.

effective circulation An estimate of the number of passersby who might reasonably be considered to see an outdoor advertisement. Calculated as half of pedestrian, truck, and automotive traffic, and a quarter of public transit riders, by the Traffic Audit Bureau.

effective drum diameter The value of drum diameter that, when used in calculations, will produce tape record dimensions equal to those of an actual video recording produced by a given helical-scan television tape recording system. The effective value is equal to or greater than the actual drum diameter.

effective field The root-mean-square (RMS) value of the inverse distance fields at a distance of one mile from the antenna in all directions in the horizontal plane. Also called the *effective field intensity.*

effective field intensity *See* effective field.

effective field strength *See* effective field.

effective focal length (EFL) The working value of a camera lens focal length.

effective gap length The apparent gap length of a tape playback system as deduced from measured gap losses. In practice, the effective gap length is found to be greater than the physical gap.

effective isotropic radiated power (EIRP) A measure of a satellite's signal strength as received on the earth.

effective radiated power (ERP) The product of the antenna power (transmitter output power less transmission line loss) times the antenna power gain, or the antenna field gain squared.

effective radiated power above isotropic *See* equivalent isotropically radiated power.

effective sample base (ESB) An estimate of the size of a simple random sample that would provide the same standard error as the actual sampling plan and methodology on which a survey result is based. Also called *effective sample base* and *equivalent simple random sample size.*

effective sample size The size of a simple random sample that provides the same standard error as the actual sampling plan on which a survey result is based. Also called *approximate equivalent simple random sample size, effective sample base,* and *equivalent simple random sample size.*

effects □ The patterns generated by a special effects generator. □ *See* optical effects. □ *See* sound effects. □ *See* special effects.

effects animation The animation of noncharacter movements, such as rain, smoke, lightning, or water.

effects bank The buttons, knobs, and levers on a television switcher used to accomplish special effects. Cf. cut bank.

effects box *See* matte box.

effects bus The bus on a video switcher that controls the type, duration, size, and so on, of wipes, dissolves, fades, and other shots.

effects filter *See* diffusion filter.

effects generator An electronic device used to create video effects such as wipes, quad splits, rotations, and so on.

effect shot A camera shot that produces the desired result.

effects machine A device used to create special effects such as snow, fog, and thunder. *See also* effects projector.

effects projector A scenic projector, often involving multiple slides and/or motion. Also called an *effects machine* and *scenic projector.*

effects track The soundtrack that carries the special effects to be mixed later with the music and dialogue tracks.

efficacy The effectiveness of a light source in converting electric power (watts) to luminous flux (lumens) expressed in lumens per watt (LPW). In the past this concept was called *luminous efficiency. See also* lumens per watt.

efficiency The ratio of a specifically designated output flux (lumens) to the flux (lumens) generated by the lamps in a luminaire, such as beam efficiency, field efficiency, luminaire efficiency, and so on. Various utilization efficiencies involve the ratio of flux delivered to a specific location divided by the total flux generated by the lamps used. □ The degree to which the media are effective in reaching audiences for the presentation of commercial messages at a reasonable cost. □ The ratio of the usable output of a device or circuit compared to its input. Usually expressed as a percentage.

Effie An award presented by the advertising industry for excellence in advertising.

EFL Effective focal length.

EFLA Educational Film Library Association, Inc. A clearinghouse for nontheatrical film information.

EFM Eight-to-fourteen modulation.

EFP Electronic field production.

EFX A script abbreviation for *special effects.*

eggshell A relatively smooth antique paper that resembles the shell of an egg.

Egyptian *See* square serif.

EHF Extremely high frequency.

EI Exposure index.

EIA □ Education Industries Association. An association of manufacturers of products for education. □ Electronic Industries Association.

EIAJ Electronic Industry Association of Japan. An organization similar to the EIA in the United States.

Eidophor A theatre television projection system.

eigentone The room resonance produced by reflections between parallel walls.

eight ball A round, nondirectional dynamic microphone.

eight column line *See* banner.

eighth apple An apple box 18 by 12 by 1-1/2 inches.

eight hundred number *See* WATS.

eight millimeter A now largely obsolete film size, superseded by super 8.

eight-to-fourteen modulation (EFM) In compact disc technology, the pulse code modulated signal produced by analog-to-digital conversion is a simple nonreturn-to-zero bit stream of ones and zeros. EFM is applied to produce a signal format suitable for recording and introduces a unique synchronization pattern to each frame of audio information.

eighty column A standard display screen and transmission system that uses 80 columns of characters.

eighty column card A standard Hollerith punched card that contains 80 columns and 12 rows.

EIRP Equivalent isotropically radiated power.

EJ Electronic journalism. *See* ENG.

Ektachrome An Eastman Kodak Company tradename for a tripack color reversal film widely used in 16-mm cameras.

E layer The ionospheric layer lying just above the D layer.

elbow A hook used to hold a luminaire suspended from a lighting grid.

ELDO European Launcher Development Organization. A satellite organization.

electret microphone A capacitor microphone that uses a metallized diaphragm of a dielectric material. A reliable, low noise, small, and inexpensive microphone.

electric *See* electrical.

electrical Of, relating to, or operated by electricity.

electrical etching The use of electrolysis to etch relief printing plates.

electrical potential The difference in the electrical charge between two points.

electrical transcription (ET) Originally, a 16-inch disc used to record a 15-minute radio program or several bands of music for broadcast use. An ET may now refer to any phonograph record or disc.

electric eye An advertising term for a camera with an automatic aperture control.

electrician The stagehand responsible for execution of production lighting. *See also* gaffer.

electrician's knot A special knot used to tie wires together mechanically to reduce the strain on the electrical connections.

electricity A fundamental property of nature that certain particles have to possess a force field. *See also* alternating current and direct current.

electric spectacular An outdoor advertisement in which the words and designs are formed by lights.

electro *See* electrotype.

electroacoustic transducer *See* transducer.

electrode A conducting element capable of having an electrical charge.

electrode dark current That component of electrode current that flows without ionizing radiation or optical photons. Also called *dark current.*

electrodynamic braking A method of stopping a tape transport motor by impressing a voltage upon it.

electrodynamics The branch of physics concerned with the effects of the interactions between magnets and electric currents. Cf. electrostatics.

electroluminescence Fluorescence or phosphorescence caused by cathode rays, X rays, or radioactivity.

electrolytic processing A system of processing film by passing an electric current through the chemical baths.

electromagnetic Relating to or produced by electricity and magnetism.

electromagnetic deflection A method of deflecting an electron beam by using an electromagnetic deflection yoke.

electromagnetic energy Energy that may consist of radio waves, infrared, light waves, ultraviolet X rays, gamma rays, or cosmic rays and that travels at approximately 186,000 miles or 300,000,000 meters per second.

electromagnetic focusing The focusing produced by a coil mounted around the neck of a television picture tube. Cf. electrostatic focusing.

electromagnetic interference (EMI) Any electromagnetic energy that causes an adverse effect on an electronic circuit or radio wave.

electromagnetic radiation The form of energy characterized by electric and magnetic fields that travels at the speed of light in a vacuum.

electromagnetic spectrum The portion of the spectrum that runs from approximately 19 kHz to 10 (to the 20th power) mHz.

electromagnetic wave The energy produced by the oscillation of electric and magnetic charges.

electromechanical A device, such as a loudspeaker, that changes electrical energy into mechanical energy.

electromotive force (EMF) The pressure of a system or circuit that forces the current to flow. The unit is the volt.

electron An elementary particle of matter with a negative electrical charge.

electron beam The electromagnetically or electrostatically focused beam of electrons that strikes the target in a cathode ray tube.

electron beam recording (EBR) A method for converting television signals directly to film.

electron gun The electronic device used to form the electron beam that scans the image in a television cathode ray tube.

electronically variable delay line (EVDL) A delay line whose electrical length can be altered by means of an electronic control signal.

electronic animation *See* computer animation.

electronic blackboard A tablet with a conductive surface used to write on with an electronic pen.

electronic camera Another term for a filmless video camera.

electronic church A somewhat derogatory term for a highly commercial approach to religion as seen on a number of religious television programs.

electronic cinematography (EC) Cinematography accomplished with the use of video cameras instead of film cameras.

electronic clapper *See* electronic clapstick.

electronic clapstick An electronic device used in double system filming to mark the picture frame and place a tone on the magnetic tape for use as editorial sync. Also called an *electronic clapper* and *electronic slate.*

electronic composite A composite accomplished electronically in television as opposed to an optical composite in film.

electronic composition Any use of a computer or computerized system for the composition of typed or typeset pages.

electronic converter *See* converter.

electronic countermeasures (ECM) A term borrowed from the military in describing, for example, VLSI techniques to decrease the likelihood that decoding chips could be illegally cloned.

electronic darkroom A room in which photographs are processed by computer instead of by chemicals.

electronic data processing (EDP) Data processing performed by an electronic machine such as a computer.

electronic edit An edit carried out by electronic means, without recourse to physical cutting and rejoining of tapes.

electronic editing A postproduction procedure involving selecting and electronically reassembling a tape without mechanical editing.

electronic field production (EFP) □ Production accomplished through the use of portable video cameras, recorders, and associated equipment. Also called *field production.* □ The portable equipment itself.

electronic files The computer files created to organize storage and recall of information.

electronic film transfer *See* kinescope.

electronic flash A reusable, high-voltage, gas-filled tube fired by a capacitor furnished current. Used extensively in still photography. Also called a *strobe.* Cf. photoflash.

Electronic Industries Association (EIA) A standards-setting association of electronic equipment manufacturers. Formerly known as the RMA and RETMA.

electronic journalism (EJ) The coverage of news events by radio and television. *See also* electronic news gathering.

electronic mail The sending of letters, data, and so on, using computer modems and telephone lines to deliver copies instantly.

electronic manuscript A book or other manuscript that contains not only the text of the material, but typesetting, formatting, and other codes.

electronic matteing *See* matte.

electronic media The mass media: radio, television, cable television, direct broadcast satellites, and so on. Cf. print media.

Electronic Media Rating Council (EMRC) An organization of advertising agencies, broadcasters, and others that accredits rating companies.

electronic monitoring *See* Mediawatch.

electronic music Music constructed from electronic devices such as a Moog synthesizer.

electronic news gathering (ENG) The use by networks or stations of small, portable television cameras and videotape recorders to replace film cameras in news work.

electronic newspaper The use of a home CRT to receive newspaper-type textual material such as news, stock listings, and sports. Rudimentary systems exist in teletext and videotex.

electronic newsroom A newspaper newsroom that uses computer-assisted word processing for news writing and text storage and retrieval.

electronic paste-up The integration of graphics and text by a computer program.

electronic pointer A device used to highlight a part of a television picture; an arrow, spot, line, and so on.

electronic printer A computer printer.

electronic processing The conversion of disks or tapes for use on a computer typesetting system without the necessity of rekeyboarding. Cf. conventional processing.

electronic projection The use of lenses and cathode ray tubes to project a large television picture on a screen.

electronic publishing □ *See* desktop publishing. □ The use of computers for design, text composition, editing, proofs, indexing, and so on.

electronics The branch of physics that deals with the emission, behavior, and effects of electrons and their action in tubes, transistors, devices, and so on.

electronic scanner □ A device used to scan printed text or graphics for input to a computer. □ A device used to produce color separations for lithography or letterpress printing. □ A device used in airports to scan luggage. Tapes may be ruined and film may be fogged by such devices.

electronic shutter A shutter used to show motion picture film on television by operating in sync with the vertical blanking interval.

electronic slate *See* electronic clapstick.

electronic smog The radiation produced by radio, television, and other forms of electromagnetic transmissions.

electronic splicing The editing of audio- or videotape through electronic means as opposed to mechanical editing.

electronic stylus *See* light pen.

electronic tablet An electrically conductive surface that may be used with a light pen or electrical stylus.

electronic television Television accomplished through electronic means as opposed to the mechanical television systems proposed from the 1800s through the early 1930s.

electronic text The letters, words, spaces, and punctuation in a manuscript, excluding the computer codes.

electronic video recording (EVR) Any of the noncompatible cartridge or cassette video recording devices designed for home use, such as CBS's EVR, RCA's SelectaVision, Kodak's Supermatic 60, or Teldec's Video Disc.

electronic viewfinder A television viewfinder.

electron image The pattern of electrons emitted from the scanning gun corresponding to the light and shade or color patterns of the object seen by the television camera.

electron multiplier The plates that multiply the number of electrons received from the return beam in a television pickup tube.

electron tube *See* vacuum tube.

electrophotography The generic term for a xerographic process.

electroprint *See* electroprinting.

electroprinting A process for transferring a magnetic tape soundtrack to an optical track on film; an electroprint.

electros *See* electrotypes.

electrostatic deflection A method of deflecting an electron beam by using charged plates.

electrostatic focusing (EF) A method of focusing the electron beam in a television picture tube wherein charged plates are used. Cf. electromagnetic focusing.

electrostatic loudspeaker A loudspeaker made by suspending a charged diaphragm between two perforated plates. The diaphragm vibrates when power is applied to the plates. Also called a *capacitor* and *condenser loudspeaker.*

electrostatic microphone A pressure microphone in which the signal is generated by the variations in capacitance between two charged plates. Also called a *capacitor* and *condenser microphone.*

electrostatic printer A printer that forms characters by using an electrostatic charge with burned-in dry ink.

electrostatic printing A technique wherein a powder is electrostatically adhered to paper to produce a duplicate. Also called electrostatic reproduction.

electrostatic reproduction *See* electrostatic printing.

electrostatics The branch of physics concerned with the phenomena due to attraction or repulsion of charges at rest. Cf. electrodynamics.

electrotype A durable reproduction of an engraving or type form, produced by the electrolysis of copper onto an original and then cast into a mold. Also called *electros.*

Electrozoom A tradename for a zoom lens.

eleemosynary organization A charitable organization.

element □ The smallest detail distinguishable in a television scanning line. In color television, a dot. □ An individual part of an antenna. □ One optical part of a lens. □ A single shot in a television commercial. □ A member of a collection of items; for example, bits are elements of words. □ A letter, word, rule, picture, and so on, printed on a page. □ A typewriter or printer head such as a daisy wheel or type ball. □ A constituent part of a circuit, device, picture, soundtrack, and so on.

elemental area *See* essential area.

elementary sampling unit *See* elementary unit.

elementary unit The basic unit about which a statistical survey is intended to gather information. In broadcast surveys, the elementary unit is often either a household or an individual. Also called an *elementary sampling unit.*

elephant folio A size of paper; 23 by 28 inches.

elevation □ A drawing that shows the vertical configuration of a stage or set. Cf. floor plan. □ The angular position of a satellite perpendicular to the earth's surface. Cf. azimuth.

elevator shot A vertical crane shot.

ELF Extremely low frequency.

elhi An abbreviation for textbooks intended for the elementary and high school markets.

eligibility criteria The basic legal, technical, financial, and character qualifications set forth by the FCC for broadcast licensees. *See also* mutually exclusive criteria.

elite One of the two most common sizes of type pitch: 12 characters per inch. Cf. pica.

elite press The publishers of newspapers designed for an upscale and high-level socioeconomic readership.

ellipsis Three spaced periods denoting an intentional omission in a line of type; often used in quotations.

ellipsoidal spotlight A luminaire embodying a lamp, a reflector, a framing device, and a single or compound lens system, together with provisions for accommodating a pattern hold and patterns. Also called a *Leko. See also* hard light.

elliptical orbit A random or nonsynchronous satellite orbit. Used to provide coverage above the 75th parallel. Cf. geostationary orbit.

elliptical stylus A stylus with an elliptical rather than a round shape; usually more expensive than the round one.

ELS Extreme long shot.

ELV □ Edit-level video. □ Expendable launch vehicle. A nonrecoverable rocket used to launch satellites.

EM Electronic mail.

em A unit of measurement of line width, based on the width of a capital *M* in any size of type. Also called a *mutton. See also* em dash and em quad. Cf. en.

E mail An abbreviation for *electronic mail.*

embargo A hold placed on a news story until it is cleared for release.

embellished painted bulletin *See* semispectacular.

embellishment A shaped piece that extends a visual image beyond its customary frame, as in a storyboard cel or outdoor bulletin; in outdoor, a standard embellishment size is 5 feet 6 inches at top, 2 feet at its sides, and 1 foot to 2 feet at its base. Also called an *extension.*

embellishments Letters, packages, figures, or mechanical devices that are attached to the face of an outdoor advertising structure to provide a three-dimensional effect.

emboss To raise the surface of paper, book covers, or other material in a relief pattern by use of a die.

embossing press *See* blocking press.

embossing stylus A recording stylus with a rounded tip that displaces the material in the recording medium to form a groove.

EMC Educational Media Council.

emcee A variant spelling of MC.

em dash A dash the length of an em.

EMEP Extended mogul end prong. A lamp base type.

emerald A British type size that measures between six and seven points.

Emergency Action Notification (EAN) The notice to all licensees and regulated services of the FCC, participating nongovernmental industry entities, and the general public, of the existence of an emergency situation.

Emergency Action Termination The notice to all licensees and regulated services of the FCC, participating nongovernmental industry entities, and the general public of the termination of an emergency situation.

Emergency Broadcast System (EBS) A system of providing the president and the federal government, as well as heads of state and local governments or their designated representatives, with a means of communicating with the general public in times of emergency. EBS replaced the former Conelrad system in 1964.

emergency power A battery or generator that furnishes backup power in case of a power line failure.

emergency powers The authorization given to the president of the United States in time of war or national emergency by Section 606 of the Communications Act to suspend or amend all FCC rules and regulations.

Emergency Relocation Board The FCC board designed to function in place of the FCC in the event of war or disaster.

emergent ray A light ray that has been deflected by a lens or other material. Cf. incident ray.

EMF Electromotive force.

EMI Electromagnetic interference.

em indention A paragraph indention specified to be one em, two ems, and so on.

emission □ Radiation produced, or the production of radiation, by a radio transmitting station. □ The emitting of a stream of electrons, as in a cathode ray tube.

emission types The international classification of modes of operation for various radio communication services, including Type AO, Unmodulated continuous-wave transmission; Type A1, Telegraphy, or pure continuous waves; Type A4, Facsimile; and Type A5, Television.

emit To give off or radiate.

Emitron A British adaptation of Zworykin's iconoscope.

emitted signal Any program-carrying signal that goes to or passes through a satellite.

emitted wave The emission transmitted by a radio or television station.

emitter The transistor terminal that gives off charge carriers. *See also* base and collector.

Emmy The awards given by the National Academy of Television Arts and Sciences in recognition of outstanding work in many categories of television production.

emote A slang term for issuing emotion, meaning to act with feeling.

empathy An emotion aroused in a viewer or listener involving a personal identification with the emotion of a character in a dramatic presentation.

emperor A size of paper; 40 by 60 inches.

emphasis The use of dialogue, camera angles, special effects, lines, words, and so on, used to give special importance to a shot, script, or article. □ *See* preemphasis.

emphasized A computer printing mode in which each dot is printed twice; the second strike is slightly below the first. Similar to doublestrike. Also called *enhanced.*

emphasized text Type matter that is printed in italics, emphasized, doublestrike, boldface, small caps, and so on.

empirical Research based on observation or experience.

employee director A director who works continuously and exclusively for a producer and is sometimes engaged in crafts or functions other than directing, and who is also assigned to direct productions.

empty dialogue Dialogue that does not further the plot or contribute to character development.

em quad A blank spacer the length of an em. Also called an *em space* and *mutton quad.*

EMRC Electronic Media Rating Council.

em space *See* em quad.

emulate To imitate one computer system with another so that it will accept the original system's software.

emulation A part of the CD-I production process. A CD-I image is emulated when it has been coded and stored in CD-I format and the coding is used to reproduce the image using the same techniques a CD-I player would use.

emulator A device that assists in allowing computers to interface with one another.

emulsion The photosensitive coating applied to a film base or photographic paper.

emulsion batch *See* batch.

emulsion coating *See* coating.

emulsion number A manufacturer's identification number for a film type. Cf. batch number.

emulsion position The position of film emulsion in a camera or projector; normally toward the subject or screen.

emulsion side The film side that contains the emulsion.

emulsion speed A measure of the sensitivity of a film emulsion to light; usually expressed by an ASA number. The higher the number, the faster the speed. Also called *film speed.*

EN Edge number.

en One half of an em. Also called a *nut.*

enamel The calendered finish of clay and sizing on a coated paper.

enameled paper *See* coated paper.

enamel proof *See* repro proof.

en banc A session in which all members of a court or administrative agency sit to hear a case. Cf. panel.

encipher *See* encode.

enclosed captioning *See* closed captioning.

enclosure □ A loudspeaker cabinet designed to improve bass response. □ Anything mailed in an envelope or the like, especially in addition to the principal content. Also called an insert.

encode □ To change characters or symbols into digital form. □ To prepare program information for a computer. □ In communication theory, to substitute a symbol for an idea or emotion. Cf. decode and encrypt.

encoded signal A television signal containing the chrominance, luminance, and synchronizing information.

encoder □ An electronic device used to combine the red, green, and blue television signals so that they can be transmitted. Cf. decoder. □ A device for the generation of the EBS two-tone attention signal. □ In information theory, the sender of a message.

encore □ A presentation made by a performer immediately following the scheduled performance. □ The demand made by an audience, by applause or voice, for an encore or reprise.

encore presentation A euphemism for a television rerun.

encrypt □ To scramble a message, signal, program, and so on. □ In satellite cable programming, to transmit such programming in a form whereby the aural or visual characteristics or both are modified or altered to prevent the unauthorized receipt of such programming by persons without authorized equipment designed to eliminate the effects of such modification or alteration. Cf. encode.

encryption The process of electronically changing a signal so that a decoder is required to receive the signal. Used extensively in satellite transmissions.

end □ A word denoting the end of a computer program. □ *See* end mark.

en dash A dash the length of an en.

end code A computer code used to mark the end of italics, boldface, indention, and so on. Cf. exit code.

end cue Any cue intended to indicate the end of a program or program segment. Cf. outcue.

end dash *See* thirty dash.

ending A short appendage to the body of a commercial. *See also* tag. Cf. introduction.

end leaf *See* end paper.

end mark A code, such as "30" or "#," used to signify the end of a story, message, or other written material. Also called an *end. See* thirty dash. □ An end-of-message signal used by a character generator to stop keying in a roll or crawl; sometimes indicated by EOM.

end matter *See* back matter.

endnotes Footnotes that are compiled as part of the back matter or at the end of a chapter of a book or manuscript instead of at the bottom of each page.

end of message (EOM) A character or symbol indicating the point at which a message ends. *See also* end mark.

end of tape (EOT) In a video cartridge or cassette, a mark placed near the end of the unrecorded tape to allow appropriate sensors to detect the approach of the end of the tape.

end of tape sensor A device that automatically stops an audio- or videotape when the end of the tape is reached.

endorsement A statement by a well-known individual in a commercial or advertisement that encourages people to buy the product or service.

end paper The single-fold sheet at the beginning and end of a book next to the covers; one side pasted to the inside of the cover, the other half bound to the book. Also called an *end leaf, end sheet, pastedown,* and *lining paper.*

end point The last frame of a videotape edit containing a wipe or dissolve. Does not apply to cuts.

end rate The actual rate the advertiser pays for commercial time or space after all discounts have been applied.

end sheet *See* end paper.

end sign *See* thirty dash.

end slate A clapstick held upside down at the end of a filmed or taped segment.

end sync Sync marks placed at the tail of a reel of film. Also called *tail sync.*

end titles Titles at the end of a motion picture that are normally placed at the beginning, such as producer or director credits.

energize To activate a circuit or device.

energy The capacity for doing work.

ENG Electronic news gathering.

engagement The employment of a performer or player who has given written notice of acceptance, has signed a contract, or has been given a verbal call by a producer, authorized representative, and so on. Usually extends for a relatively short period of time.

engineer A person charged with the technical operation of a radio, television, or CATV studio or transmitter, or someone with an individual responsibility for camera alignment, quality of sound, lighting, and so on. *See also* chief engineer and technical director.

Engineering Award An award given by the National Association of Broadcasters for contributions that "measurably advance the technical state of the broadcasting industry."

engineering service An interconnection among network stations for the use of operations and maintenance personnel.

engineering standards Technical standards set by the FCC for the selection of equipment, power, frequency, operation, and so on.

English A type size of 14 points.

English finish (ef) A paper with a hard, unpolished surface.

English line fall A page that is set with an unjustified right-hand margin. Also called *ragged right.*

engraver's proof A proof made of an engraving, usually on fine paper.

engraving □ A metal plate used to reproduce a design or drawing. Also called a *cut. See also* halftone and line cut. □

A print made from an engraving. □ *See* intaglio.

engrossing Decorative hand lettering.

enhanced *See* emphasized.

Enhanced Definition Television (EDTV) An attempt to produce a high-quality, NTSC-compatible television picture at a lower resolution than HDTV.

enhanced services Cable television services that require two-way interaction, such as direct home shopping, polling, and so on.

enhancement A signal processing technique that increases the definition, color, brightness, and so on, of a television picture or recorded sound.

enjoin To order a person to perform or abstain from some act, as by court order.

enlarged type Type that is expanded to approximately twice its normal width without raising its corresponding height. Also called *wide type.*

enlargement A photographic print that is larger than the negative from which it was made.

enlargement print An optical film print from smaller to larger stock, such as from 16 mm to 35 mm.

enlargement printing *See* projection printing.

enlarger A projection printing device used in a darkroom to produce enlargements.

enlarger lens A lens designed to decrease internal reflections, increase image contrast, and produce a sharp image.

en quad A blank spacer the length of an en. Also called an *en space* and *nut quad.* Cf. em quad.

enrichment A presentation of instructional television materials that are not part of a basic course of study.

ensemble A group of players, singers, dancers, or other entertainers who work together in various vehicles.

en space *See* en quad.

entering station A public broadcasting station that submits a Station Program Cooperative (SPC) bid for a program.

enter key The carriage return key on many computers and dedicated word processors.

enterprise copy □ News or feature copy that is treated more in depth than the assignment required. Often includes investigative reporting. □ Copy written without an assignment. Also called an *enterprise story.*

enterprise shot □ A news or feature photograph that is given more time, skill, or care than required by the assignment. □ A photograph taken without an assignment.

enterprise story *See* enterprise copy.

entertainer A professional performer, such as an actor, comedian, musician, singer, or dancer.

entertainment A book, periodical, or other means of providing a public performance of a play, motion picture, television program, and so on, designed to divert, engage, gratify, and relax an audience.

entertainment programs (E) Programs intended primarily as entertainment, such as music, drama, variety, comedy, quiz, and so on. An FCC program type category.

entrance Any initial or subsequent appearance by a character in a play, program, sketch, and so on.

entrance radius The radius in a quadruplex recorder vacuum guide that defines the curvature of the uppermost section of the active guide surface, where the guide surface curves away from the tape to facilitate an impact-free entrance of the video pole tip onto the tape.

entry □ A unit of information used by a computer. □ A word or words defined or described in a dictionary.

envelope □ The glass or metal casing of a vacuum tube. □ The enclosure of a modulated waveform. □ A paper sleeve that protects a floppy disk and its jacket.

envelope stuffer Any advertising or promotional material enclosed in an envelope with business letters, statements, or invoices.

Environmental Protection Agency The federal administrative agency that enforces environmental protection laws concerning, among other items, land use, radiation, and toxic substances.

environmental sound *See* ambient sound.

EOD □ Every other day. □ End of data.

EOE Equal opportunity employer.

EOF End of file. A character or symbol indicating the end of a computer file or sequence.

EOM End of message.

EOP □ End of program. □ Executive office of the president.

EOR □ End of record. □ End of reel.

EOS Extraordinary occasion service. An old AP newspaper wire slug indicating an important message or story.

EOT □ End of transmission. A signal indicating that the end of the transmission has been reached. □ End of tape.

EOW Every other week.

EOWTF Every other week till forbid.

EP Extended play.

EPA Evangelical Press Association.

EPAA Educational Press Association of America.

EPC Educational Publishers Council.

ephemera Printed matter, television programs, and so on, that are of only transitory interest and without lasting value.

ephemeral recording A copy of a recording used and retained solely by the transmitting organization that made it for the purpose of transmission or archival preservation.

epic □ An unusually long book, motion picture, or television special that often presents a heroic historical figure or a legendary tale. □ Sometimes refers to a long documentary.

epigraph A quotation, usually on a separate page, included in the front matter of a book.

epilogue □ The last section of a literary work. □ An explanatory speech by an actor at the end of a play.

Episcope A European term for an opaque projector.

episode □ A single broadcast in a series. □ A single scene in a television program.

episodic A script or novel structured as a series of brief units of action.

episodic promo A promotional announcement that highlights upcoming episodes of a television series.

episodic series A series of films, each of which contains a separate complete story with a character or characters common to each of the films in the series. The designation provides, however, that such series shall remain an episodic series even though a two-, three-, four-, or five-multipart story is used in the series. Cf. unit series.

episodic series format *See* format.

EPP Electronic postproduction.

EPRN Eastern Public Radio Network.

eq An abbreviation for *equalize, equalizer,* and *equalization.*

EQ'd sound *See* wet sound.

equal access The quest by broadcasters for equality with the print media for entrance into legislative and judicial chambers and courtrooms.

equalization □ The process of modifying the amplitude-frequency response characteristics in a recording and reproducing system to produce a flat overall frequency response. The term also applies to matching the signal-handling capabilities of the recording system to the frequency distribution of the signal to be recorded and/or to minimize the audible noise of the reproducer in order to produce the maximum audible signal-to-noise ratio. □ The increase of the high-frequency record level with respect to the decreasing groove speed (velocity) in recording to compensate for reproducing losses. *See also* translation loss. □ Amplitude modulation of certain frequencies in a video signal to compensate for deficiencies in the record/reproduce system.

equalize To compensate for or balance the amplitude or frequency of an electronic circuit or device.

equalizer A device designed to modify the amplitude-frequency response of a system or component. Also called a *compensator.*

equal-loudness contours *See* Fletcher-Munson curve.

equal opportunities The requirements set forth in Section 315 of the Communications Act for the use of air time by legally qualified candidates. Candidates may not be discriminated against in any particular: rates, total time, use of facilities, and so on. Popularly, but incorrectly, called "equal time."

equal space law A Florida statute that required newspapers to devote equal space for opposing candidates. The law was overturned in 1975.

equal time A widely popular misnomer for equal opportunities.

equipment A general term for components, devices, machines, systems, and so on.

equipment performance measurements The measurements performed to determine the overall performance characteristics of a broadcast transmission system from point of program origination at a main studio to sampling of signal as radiated.

equipment test Tests made for the purpose of adjustments and measurements necessary to ensure compliance with the terms of a radio or television station construction permit.

Equity A British actors trade union. □ An abbreviation for *Actors Equity*. *See also* Actors Equity Association.

equity □ The amount of capital invested. □ A system of jurisprudence, similar to but distinct from common law, in which cases are decided not on precedence but on the basis of fairness.

equivalent aperture The optical efficiency of a lens. Cf. effective aperture.

equivalent focus *See* focal length.

equivalent isotropically radiated power (EIRP) The product of the antenna input power and the antenna gain in a given direction relative to an isotropic antenna.

equivalent live time program A radio or television program recorded so as to be broadcast at the same clock time in more than one time zone.

equivalent monopole radiated power (EMRP) The product of the power supplied to the antenna and its gain relative to a short vertical antenna in a given direction.

equivalent satellite link noise temperature The noise temperature referred to the output of the receiving antenna of the earth station corresponding to the radio frequency noise power that produces the total observed noise at the output of the satellite link. It excludes the noise due to interference coming from satellite links using other satellites and from terrestrial systems.

equivalent simple random sample size *See* effective sample size.

erasability The degree to which a medium can be erased without damaging the paper, tape, disk, or other surface.

erasable □ A medium that can be reused after the signal has been erased. □ *See* magneto-optical.

erasable storage Media, such as tape or magnetic disk, that are capable of being reused by degaussing.

erase □ To remove, destroy, nullify, or eliminate a magnetic recording by degaussing. □ Pertaining to equipment or an apparatus used to erase magnetic tape, for example, an erase head, erase current, and so on. □ To remove, by degaussing, all previously recorded signals on a magnetic tape. □ To delete data from a computer memory or storage device.

erase head A device on a tape transport used to produce the magnetic field necessary to remove a recorded signal.

erasure □ A process by which a signal recorded on tape is removed and the tape is prepared for a new recording. □ An area or segment on tape that has been erased. □ The act of erasing.

erect image An image that is produced by a concave lens as opposed to an inverted image that is produced by a convex lens.

erecting system A series of wooden or metal pieces that are connected together from which to suspend microphones, luminaires, and so on.

E region The region above the earth's atmosphere from about 50 to 100 miles. *See also* ionosphere.

ERES Electronic reflected energy system. A system that enables electronically generated walls and surfaces in order to improve acoustics.

ergonomics The aspect of technology relating to the interactive problems between the user and the machine. Also called *biotechnology*.

ERIC Educational Resources Information Center. The Stanford University clearinghouse on educational media and technology.

erotica Literary or artistic works containing amorous themes. *See also* pornography.

ERP □ Effective radiated power. □ The arrangement of heads on a tape recorder: erase, record, and playback.

errata A list of errors made in printing. If in a book, the errata is usually listed on a separate page and included with the book. If in a periodical, the errata list is usually included in the next issue. Also called *corrigenda* and *corrections*.

error A general term denoting a malfunction of equipment, defective software, or operator carelessness. *See also* operator error.

error concealment A variety of techniques used to conceal errors in visual images displayed from a CD-I disc.

error correction code (ECC) Identification and correction of errors arising in the transfer of bits of information. Used extensively in computer storage media such as compact discs. In CD-ROM and CD-I, error correction code identifies the incorrect bit and replaces it with the correct one. *See also* cross-interleaved Reed Solomon code, cyclic redundancy check, and error detection code.

error detection code (EDC) A code designed to detect but not correct an error.

error line A typeset line containing an error in spelling, punctuation, or other feature.

error rate The percentage of errors in a manuscript; the ratio between, for example, the number of lines with an error compared with the total number of lines.

ESB ☐ Effective sample base. ☐ Electrical Standards Board.

ESbus An SMPTE and EBU standard for remote control automation; a two-way high-speed pathway for television intersystem communication.

ESC Engineering service circuit. A telephone company order wire.

escalator clause An automatic salary increase built into a performer's contract.

escape (ESC) A computer keyboard key normally used in conjunction with another key to perform specific cursor movements, select print options, and so on.

escapement The typewriter mechanism that controls the carriage movement.

escapism The diversion of the mind from reality or routine using the entertainment media.

ESDAC European Space Data Center. A satellite organization.

ESF ☐ Expanded sample frame. ☐ Electrostatic focusing.

ESG Edit sync guide.

esquisse A rough layout sketch; a thumbnail.

ESRIN European Space Research Institute. A satellite organization.

ESRO European Space Research Organization. A satellite organization.

ESSA Environmental Science Services Administration. The forerunner of the EPA.

essential area ☐ The television picture area that is seen on a properly aligned home receiver. ☐ In graphics, the "safe" area for lettering, drawings, pictures, and so on, that is smaller than the scanning area. Also called the *critical area, elemental area, safe action area, safe area, safety, safety area,* and *usable area.* ☐ The geographical area around a television station in which the picture is received without undue degradation. *See also* grades 1–6.

establish ☐ To make the total atmosphere of a scene or sequence clear. *See also* establishing shot. ☐ To play music or another sound long enough for it to set a mood before decreasing the sound pressure level. *See also* up and under. Cf. down and under.

established serial or episodic series A serial or episodic series based upon material that has been published or exploited in any manner or by any medium whatsoever, or based upon a story in the public domain or owned by the company producing the serial or series.

establishing approach A scriptwriter's method of beginning a story visually. Usually a move from a long shot to a close-up.

establishing shot The opening shot of a program or scene that provides the viewer with the interrelationships of the subsequent close-ups. *See also* camera shots.

ESTEC European Space Technology Center. A satellite organization.

estimate ☐ A notice of anticipated costs, often sent from an advertising agency to a client as a request for approval of anticipated cost details. ☐ To produce such a notice.

estimated rating A predicted rating for a radio or television program that is to be broadcast.

estimator An advertising agency employee who prepares media cost estimates, usually for media buys.

estrangement effect The effect caused by the intellectual distance between the audience and the performers.

E system The 819-line, 25-frames-per-second, 14-mHz-bandwidth, AM-sound television system used in France. Cf. A, B, D, and M systems.

ET □ Educational television. An FCC file-number prefix. □ Electrical transcription.

ETA Estimated time of arrival.

et al. An abbreviation for *et alii,* which is Latin meaning "and others."

etaoinshrdlu The line of type resulting from a compositor running a finger down the first two rows of keys on a line-casting machine.

etch To selectively remove metal from an intaglio or letterpress printing plate by means of corrosive chemicals or electrolysis. In the strictest sense, etching differs from engraving in that an engraved plate is incised with a tool. Cf. intaglio.

etched circuit A printed circuit made by chemical and/or electrolytic methods to remove the unwanted material.

etched depth The depth to which a printing plate has been etched.

etching □ The process of making prints or designs from glass or metal plates corroded by the application of an acid. □ An impression made by this process. □ Removing imperfections in film emulsions. □ Removing portions of film emulsion for animation effects.

etching ground The varnish, wax, or other material used on a plate to keep the acid from the printing areas.

etching proof □ A paper proof used to make an etching. □ *See* reproduction proof.

ether A rarefied element in the atmosphere formerly believed to be the carrier of radio waves. *See also* electromagnetic wave.

ethics The study of the ideal human character; the nature of the highest good; a system of moral principles; and so on.

ethnic controls Arbitron ratings placement and weighting techniques used in the qualifying Metros of Arbitron Radio Markets to establish better representation of the black and/or Hispanic populations.

ethnic film A motion picture that deals with a specific anthropological subgroup, such as Arabs, Jews, or Indians. Cf. ethnographic film.

ethnic media Any communication medium that is designed to reach specific ethnic groups.

ethnic press Newspapers that are designed to reach specific ethnic groups.

ethnic radio A broadcast station format designed for one or more minority groups.

ethnographic film A descriptive anthropological motion picture that deals with preliterate cultures, such as Eskimos or Indians. Cf. ethnic film.

ethos The distinguishing character of a performer or speaker. Cf. empathy.

ethritus The inflammation and hardening of the eardrums caused by listening to sounds exceeding a reasonable level, such as jack hammers and amplified rock music. Ethritus can produce a permanent loss of hearing.

E to E □ Electronic to electronic. *See* E to E mode. □ End to end.

E to E mode A test or standby mode of a videotape recorder in which the FM output of the record electronics is fed directly to the playback electronics, bypassing the record/play process.

ETRAC Educational Radio and Television Center.

ETS Educational Television Stations. A division of the NAEB.

et seq. An abbreviation for *et sequens,* which is Latin meaning "and the following."

ETV Educational television. *See* PTV.

ETVS Educational television by satellite.

European Broadcasting Union (EBU) A broadcasting association composed of broadcasting organizations from Western Europe with associate members from most other parts of the world. Also UER. Cf. International Radio and Television Organization (OIRT).

European system The 625-scan line television system used in Europe. Cf. American system.

Eurovision An abbreviation for *European Television.* A West European television network operated under the auspices of the European Broadcasting Union (EBU). Cf. Intervision.

EUTELSAT The European Telecommunications Satellite Organization.

E value The radial distance from the outermost layer of tape wound on a reel to the circumferential edge of the reel flange. Sometimes called *freeboard.*

EVDL Electronically variable delay line.

evening drive The time period on radio from approximately 3 p.m. to 7 p.m. Also called *drivetime. See also* daypart.

evening programming Programs starting and concluding on a network between the hours of 7:30 p.m. and 11 p.m. local time (one hour earlier in the Central time zone), plus all programs other than regular newscasts starting on the network between 7 and 7:30 p.m. local time (one hour earlier in the Central time zone). It does not include portions broadcast after 7 p.m. of programs starting earlier, or portions broadcast after 11 p.m. of programs starting earlier. Nonnetwork evening programming has no specified time period.

even parity *See* parity.

event □ A special happening. □ Any significant part of a scene. □ Any action that affects an item in a data file.

event number A number on an edit decision list assigned to each piece of videotape footage to be edited.

evergreen □ A timeless feature or news story. Also called a *banked story.* □ *See* standard.

every day (ED) A term used in scheduling or ordering newspaper advertising, as in "Insert a scheduled newspaper advertisement each day."

every other day (EOD) A term used in scheduling or ordering newspaper advertising, as in "Insert a scheduled newspaper advertisement every other day."

every other week (EOW) A term used in scheduling or ordering newspaper advertising, as in "Insert a scheduled newspaper advertisement every other week."

every other week till forbid (EOWTF) A term used in scheduling or ordering newspaper advertising, as in "Insert a scheduled newspaper advertisement every other week until the order is canceled."

evidence Matter submitted to the FCC or a court as proof.

evo *See* octavo.

EVR □ Electronic video recording. □ Electronic video recorder.

evulgate To publish.

EX Developmental. An FCC file-number prefix. *See also* developmental broadcast station.

exaggeration The overstatement or broadening of a gesture so that it is perceived clearly by an audience. An essential element of character animation, as the subtleties possible in live-action become lost or appear weak when animated.

examination copy A textbook requested by a teacher from a publisher. The invoice is usually canceled if the textbook is adopted for classroom use or returned to the publisher. Cf. desk copy.

examiner *See* administrative law judge.

excelsior □ Written material used as a filler. □ A three point type size.

exception dictionary A set of words or codes stored in computer memory used by a program that automatically hyphenates words that do not fit standard patterns of hyphenation.

exceptions Brief objections filed with an administrative agency or a court to a decision made by that body, such as "Exceptions to initial decisions must be filed within 30 days."

exchange □ An arrangement between publishers to exchange newspaper or periodical subscriptions. □ An arrangement whereby two mailers exchange equal quantities of mailing list names. □ A situation wherein performers exchange appearances on each other's radio or television programs.

exchange ad An arrangement between publishers of newspapers or periodicals to give free space on an equal basis to the other. *See also* barter.

exchange area A geographical area designated by a telephone company; usually a single metropolitan area or city.

exchange commercial The final commercial presented on a program by a program's alternate sponsor.

exchange editor A newspaper or periodical editor who selects material from other publications to reprint.

exchange program A program produced by two or more television stations or organizations and broadcast by each.

exciter An oscillator that generates the carrier frequency of a transmitter.

exciter lamp A high-intensity incandescent lamp used to record and reproduce optical soundtracks on film.

exclusive □ A news story, feature, article, and so on, acquired by one newspaper, broadcast station, or other news outlet. If news, also called a *scoop* and *beat*. □ A cable television franchise awarded to a single entity for an entire area or city. □ An individual who listens, watches, or reads one broadcasting station, newspaper, and so on, most of the time.

exclusive affiliation A radio or television station that bound itself to carrying the programs from only one national network.

exclusive contract A contract that binds a performer to an individual or company granting sole rights to the performer's services.

exclusive cume listening The estimated number of cume persons in the Metro who listened to one and only one station within a given daypart.

exclusive franchise *See* exclusive.

exclusive market area A group of counties or other areas whose radio or television audiences are predominantly drawn to stations in a designated market area; used for spot broadcast audience measurement data. Each measurement service employs a proprietary, synonymous term to describe such areas, such as designated market area or area of dominant influence.

exclusive rights The rights granted to copyright holders under copyright law to reproduce, prepare derivative works, distribute copies, perform, or display the copyrighted works.

exclusive run A motion picture clearance that allows only one theatre within a specified geographical area to run a film.

exclusive to A written lead often used for an exclusive.

exclusivity □ The right of media to broadcast or publish material on a nonduplicated basis within the immediate service or circulation area. *See also* network exclusivity and syndicated exclusivity. □ Freedom from competing advertising within a given communication medium enjoyed by one advertiser; requires major space or time purchases. □ A contract between a record company and a recording artist for the exclusive right to record the performer.

executable code A set of instructions, or a computer program in the machine language for a specific computer or microprocessor that can be executed or run directly.

executable object code The output from a compiler's or assembler's linkage editor or linker that is in the machine code for a particular processor, with each loadable program being one named file (module). In CD-I, such an object file does not contain audio or video data. *See also* executable code.

execute To perform the operations indicated by a computer program.

execution An advertisement prepared to a stated creative strategy.

Executive Advisory Council An FCC council that provides a forum for the interchange of information and ideas among the Commission's principal staff members.

executive creative director An advertising agency employee responsible for managing the operations and personnel of a creative department.

executive editor The senior editor of a newspaper.

executive privilege An asserted right of the president or other government executives to withhold documents from examination by the public, the press, and other government bodies, especially Congress.

executive session A euphemism for a meeting closed to the press.

exhausted A developer or other chemical solution that has lost its strength.

ex-height *See* x-height.

exhibit A document or supporting materials presented to an administrative agency or court.

exhibition The presentation of feature motion pictures in a theatre; a public showing of books, magazines, and so on; a broadcast presentation or other transmission.

exhibition chain A group, usually national or regional, of motion picture theatres.

exhibitor A theatre chain or independent theatre owner who shows feature films. Cf. ancillary exhibition and broadcast exhibition.

exhibs An abbreviation for *exhibitors.*

existing light *See* natural lighting.

existing stations Broadcast stations authorized before a new rule is adopted by the FCC. Such stations are often exempt from the new rule.

exit □ To terminate a computer program, usually when the last instruction has been completed. □ Talent movement from on stage to off stage, or from on camera to off camera. Cf. entrance.

exit code A computer code used to return the typesetter to the default type style. Cf. end code.

exit line A line spoken by a performer immediately before an exit.

exit poll A series of interviews made with voters as they leave an election polling place so that the media may report the expected results of the election.

ex libris A heading on a bookplate, from the Latin meaning "from the library of."

exp An abbreviation for *exposed* and *exposure.*

expanded A typeface that is twice as wide as normal. Also called *double-width, extended,* and *fat type.* Cf. condensed.

expanded basic A cable television tier that adds several other channels to the basic cable service for an additional fee.

expanded cinema Motion pictures that used bright lights, flashing lights, changing colors, and so on, to produce a different way of looking at life.

expanded sample frame (ESF) A universe that consists of unlisted telephone households; households that do not appear in the current or available telephone directories either because they have requested their telephone number not to be listed or because their telephone service began after publication of the most recent directory.

expanded time The increase in the length of time of a motion picture or other dramatic presentation as perceived by a viewer. Cf. compressed time, experienced time, objective time, screen time, and subjective time.

expander An electronic device used to increase the dynamic range of a signal.

expanding square A special effect wherein a second image wipes out the television picture from the center of the scene in a square shape. Other such effects include expanding circle, expanding diamond, and so on.

ex parte An oral or written communication not on the public record with respect to which reasonable prior notice to all parties is not given. It shall not include requests for status reports on any matter or proceeding covered by Subchapter II of Title 5, United States Code.

ex-parte presentation Any written presentation made to decision-making FCC personnel by any other person, that is not served on the parties to the proceeding, or any oral presentation made to decision-making Commission personnel by any other person without advance notice to the parties to the proceeding and without opportunity for them to be present. Often, ex-parte presentations are made for the purpose of influencing adjudicatory or rule-making proceedings.

expedite charge An additional charge for overtime made by a telephone company for installing remote lines or other services.

experienced time The length of time of a segment of a motion picture or other dramatic presentation as felt by a viewer. Cf. compressed time, expanded time, objective time, screen time, and subjective time.

experimental A research design based on or derived from empirical observation; often contains statistical procedures.

experimental broadcast station A station licensed for experimental or developmental transmission of radio telephony, television, facsimile, or other types of telecommunication services intended for reception and use by the general public.

experimental film A motion picture that reflects the personal conceptions of the filmmaker.

experimental period The time between 12 midnight local time and local sunrise, used by AM stations for tests, maintenance, and experimentation.

experimental radio service A service in which radio waves are employed for experimentation in the radio art or for providing essential communications for research projects that could not be conducted without the benefit of such communications.

experimental station A station using radio waves in experiments with a view to the development of science or technique.

expiration date The date on which a subscription expires.

expire □ A former subscriber to a publication. □ A mail order customer who is no longer an active buyer.

expired A subscription that is not renewed.

explanatory title A seldom-used technique in which words are inserted in a picture to explain something not made clear by the dialogue, action, or location.

exploitation The use of advertising or promotional matter to advertise a motion picture or television program.

exploitation film A low-budget motion picture that appeals to a limited audience.

explosion wipe An extremely fast wipe, usually from the center of the picture out or in.

expose □ A news story that discloses information of a discreditable nature. □ To subject film or photographic paper to a light source.

exposé A motion picture, television program, magazine article, and so on, that tends to discredit situations or people.

exposition The information given an audience by a narrator, announcer, or character about a motion picture or broadcast program to set the scene by revealing events prior to the action.

ex post facto A law or rule changed after an act or event so as to make further similar acts or events illegal. Cf. grandfathering.

exposure (X) □ The amount of light allowed to enter a lens and fall on the emulsion. □ An advertisement or program presented to an audience. □ The number of persons who see a given advertisement, motion picture, newspaper edition, and so on. □ In surveys of print media, the act of opening a publication to a space containing advertising.

exposure counter A mechanical device on some film cameras that indicates the number of frames that have been exposed.

exposure factor □ Any consideration, such as filters, depth-of-field, and so on, that would tend to change the normal shutter speed or aperture setting. □ A BBDO estimate of the proportion of viewers who will have the opportunity to see a television commercial.

exposure index (EI) A measure of film speed or sensitivity to light; usually expressed as an ASA or DIN number. *See also* film speed.

exposure latitude A measure of the ability of a film to produce an acceptable image under varying exposure conditions. Also called *latitude*.

exposure lock *See* aperture lock.

exposure meter *See* light meter.

exposure override *See* aperture lock.

exposure range *See* exposure latitude.

exposure sheet □ A photographic cue sheet that indicates exposure times. *See also* dope sheet. □ In animation, the frame-by-frame instructions for the camera operator that accompany the artwork when it is sent to be photographed.

expressionism A dramatic style that depicts subjective emotions of the writer or director rather than objective reality.

express mail A special mail classification with guaranteed next-day delivery.

expurgated A book or publication from which objectionable material has been removed.

ex rel An abbreviation for *ex relatione*, from the Latin meaning "in relation to."

ext An abbreviation for *exterior*.

EXTEL Exchange Telegraph. A British news agency.

extended *See* expanded.

extended character set A set of type characters that contain extra symbols in addition to those found on a standard keyboard.

extended control A single-throw, push-button switch on the end of a long lead that can close or open the grand master from a remote point. Also called a *foreign control*.

extended cover A pamphlet or brochure cover that extends beyond the trim of the pages. Also called *overhang* and *overlap*.

Extended Definition Television (EDTV) One of the many forms of advanced television (ATV). Generally, a system with less resolution than HDTV. Also called *enhanced definition television.*

extended frame A camera shot or drawing that allows the viewer to complete the image with his or her imagination. Also called an *extended image.*

extended image *See* extended frame.

extended play (EP) □ The six-hour mode on a VHS recorder. Cf. SP and SLP. □ A forty-five rpm, seven-inch disc with long-playing characteristics. Cf. long playing record.

extended scene A filmed scene that is expanded in length by an extension.

extended service A method of adjusting a loss of outdoor advertising service by exposing the advertiser's message to the public beyond the period specified in the contract.

extension □ The area of design made as a cutout that extends beyond the basic space of an outdoor advertising structure. Added costs are normal practice for the use of extensions. □ A trim added to a filmed scene to extend the length. □ A seller's agreement to prolong the time available to a prospect for consideration of an option to purchase radio or television time. □ An additional period of time granted by a periodical after a closing date for receipt of printing materials. □ *See* link. □ *See* embellishment. □ In CD-I, an upwardly compatible module to replace an existing system module in ROM. During initialization, all modules in CD-RTOS (except the protection modules) may be replaced by extended modules such as a keyboard. □ In CD-I, a hardware module supporting a functional extension. During initialization, CD-RTOS identifies the extension and includes the software modules from it.

extension meter A radio or television station monitoring device mounted away from the equipment it is monitoring.

extension tubes Hollow cylinders of varying lengths used between a camera body and a lens for close-up photography.

exterior (ext) □ An outdoor scene. □ An indoor shot photographed to appear as outdoor.

external broadcasting A term generally synonymous with international broadcasting.

external house organ *See* house organ.

external memory *See* mass storage.

external microphone Any microphone that is not mounted on or contained within a camera.

external motivation Motivation that is necessitated by script requirements rather than the emotions of the actor. Cf. internal motivation.

external publication Any publication intended for sale or distribution to anyone not associated with the publisher. Cf. internal publication.

external sync A synchronizing signal that is not generated within a device or component but is received from another source such as a sync generator. Cf. internal sync.

external validity A somewhat redundant term for *validity.*

extinction frequency The frequency at which a signal can no longer be used.

extinction meter An exposure meter that uses a graduated density wedge with figures that are illuminated by the scene.

extra □ A newspaper edition run in addition to the regular editions. A rare occurrence now. □ An additional composing room employee hired for a day or week. □ A performer who does not speak any lines whatsoever as an individual, but who also may be heard—singly or in concert—as part of a group or crowd. Also called an *extra player. See also* crowd work, general extra, insert, omnies, silent bit, and special ability extra. Cf. special extra.

extra binding A high-quality book binding.

extra bold Type that is darker than bold.

extra close-up *See* extreme close-up.

extra condensed A typeface narrower than condensed.

extract □ A quotation. □ *See* flashback.

extra illustrated A book or other manuscript that is illustrated with engravings or other decorative matter.

extraneous wrap A stock closing for a newscast.

Extraordinary Administrative Radio Conference (EARC) Several international special administrative conferences convened to discuss the use of worldwide frequency bands. *See also* IFRB.

extra play An audiotape that is only one mil thick, so that a reel can hold 50 percent more tape.

extra service A method of adjusting the loss of outdoor advertising service by posting additional panels beyond the number specified in the contract. In the case of a bulletin, a mutually acceptable substitute location may be offered.

extra size folio A size of paper; 19 by 24 inches.

extreme close-up (ECU) (also XCU) The closest possible shot of an object or person. Also called an *extra close-up.* Similar to BCU and LCU.

extreme long-shot The longest possible shot of an object, person, or scene. Outdoors, usually a panoramic view; indoors, the complete set. Cf. extreme close-up.

extremely high frequency (EHF) The band of frequencies from 30 to 300 gHz.

extremely low frequency (ELF) The frequencies below 300 Hz.

extremes Drawings of the key or extreme points of a movement, for example, where weight shifts, balance changes, or the greatest squash and stretch occurs. In pose-to-pose animation, the extremes are drawn by the key animator; an assistant animator draws the in-betweens, the action that falls between the extremes.

extrusion A method of creating a three-dimensional model from a two-dimensional shape by adding thickness.

eyebrow *See* kicker.

eye camera A camera used to record the eye movements of research subjects to measure the relative amounts of visual stimulation. Used extensively in advertising copy testing.

eye level shot Any camera shot taken at eye level, such as a scene showing what a person walking down the street would see.

eye-light Illumination to produce a specular reflection from the eyes (and teeth) without adding a significant increase of light on the subject. Also called a *catchlight* and *kicker.*

eyeline □ The direction a subject appears to be looking from the point of view of the camera. □ The part of the face where eyecolor make-up is used.

eyepatch A distinctive visual or symbolic device used to identify a specific series of advertisements; derived from the prop used in ''classic'' Hathaway shirt advertisements.

eye picture The idea communicated by an actor's stage business.

eyepiece □ The lens at the viewing end of an optical device. □ A rubber or plastic cup used with some cameras to cradle the eye and eliminate extraneous light.

eyewitness □ An individual who reports or testifies to an act done by another. □ An informal news format wherein newscasters feel free to comment on what they are reporting.

eyewitness story A news story, often told in the first person, usually about tragic or unusual events.

EZ Easy listening; a radio music format.

F

F ☐ Fahrenheit. ☐ Federal Reporter. ☐ Ferrule contact. A lamp base type. ☐ Filament. ☐ Focal length. ☐ Frequency. ☐ Fuse. ☐ Financial. A wire service code for financial news. ☐ Flash. A wire service code for stories of utmost importance.

f ☐ Following, as in *(and the following page). See also* ff. ☐ Folio. *See also* ff.

FA Full aperture.

FAA ☐ Federal Aviation Administration. ☐ Film Artists' Association of Great Britain.

face ☐ The front surface of a lens, cathode ray tube, light meter, or other equipment. ☐ To select the position for an illustration in a book. ☐ To be on the page opposite. ☐ The printed side of paper. ☐ The printing surface of a piece of type or plate. ☐ A particular design or style of type. *See also* type face. Cf. font. ☐ The front or edge of a book. ☐ To position film or tape in relation to the light source or magnetic head. ☐ The surface of an outdoor advertising structure on which the advertising message is posted or painted.

faceplate *See* face.

face shot *See* head shot.

facetiae Witty, sometimes coarse, humorous books or writings.

face-to-face An interview situation in which an interviewer and respondent are physically together.

facilities (fax) A general term applied to the technical equipment of a broadcast station. Cf. production facilities.

facilities man *See* grip.

facility form *See* station information form.

facing The direction the outdoor advertising poster face may be seen to traffic flow; for example, a south-facing panel can be read by northbound traffic.

facing text The preferred position for printed advertising matter in a newspaper or magazine. Cf. Campbell's Soup position.

FACS Foundation for American Communications.

facsimile (Fax) (FX) ☐ A form of telegraphy for the transmission of fixed images, with or without halftones, with a view to their reproduction in a permanent form. ☐ The reproduction of an original document. ☐ A copy of a book or manuscript. ☐ A copy of a label or entry form used in contests.

facsimile broadcast station A station licensed to transmit images of still objects for record reception by the general public.

facsimile edition *See* facsimile.

facsimile test chart A chart with a variety of patterns intended to facilitate the checking of modulation characteristics, square wave testing, power supply regulation and clamping, definition, halftone characteristics, index of cooperation, readability, jitter, and other parameters of transmitted facsimile copy.

fact Information having objective reality as opposed to opinion.

factor ☐ The various ratings of the sensitivity or speed of a film's emulsion. ☐ *See* filter factor.

fact sheet ☐ A list of items to be covered in a radio or television program. Also called a *run-down sheet.* ☐ A list of commercial highlights to be delivered ad-lib. Also called a *copy platform.* ☐ A page of information about a person or event used as a handout to assist media personnel.

fade ☐ A camera effect in which the image either gradually appears from black (fade-in) or disappears to black (fade-out). ☐ A gradual increase or decrease in audio or video signal strength. ☐ A radio or television director's command to fade in or fade out picture or sound. Cf. black, cut, dissolve, and take. ☐ A gradual increase or decrease in set illumination, often used as a transitional device.

faded A loss of color brilliance in an outdoor advertising poster or bulletin due to length of exposure, weather conditions, or technical weakness of production.

fade down To lower or attenuate the sound level.

fade in □ A gradual transition from black to a picture. □ A television director's command to bring up the picture from black. □ A radio or television director's command to bring up music or other sound. Also called a *fade up.*

fade off The physical movement of talent away from a microphone while he or she is speaking. Also called *moving off.*

fade on The physical movement of talent toward a microphone while he or she is speaking. Also called *moving on.*

fade out □ The reverse of fade in. □ The gradual dimming of lights at the end of a scene or program. □ The closing moments of the final scene of a radio or television program or motion picture. □ The loss of radio wave propagation at great distances.

fader □ A potentiometer, attenuator, or other device used to control sound, video, and lighting. *See also* slider. □ A device used to progressively increase or decrease the amount of light reaching a film emulsion. May be accomplished by a shutter, variable density glass, or other means. Also called a *fading glass* and *fading shutter. See also* fading solution. □ A term sometimes applied to master dimmers controlling many dimming circuits.

fader bar A device on a video switcher that controls the rate of a fade, dissolve, wipe, and so on. Also called a *fader.*

fader wheel A device used to control the intensity of a light source. Also called a *fader.*

fade to black A television director's command to fade the picture to black. Also called *go to black.*

fade up □ To raise the sound level. □ A radio or television director's command to fade in.

fading □ The loss of sound or picture quality due to deterioration of the broadcast signal. □ A decrease in sound volume.

fading area A geographical area within normal broadcasting range in which fading of signals from a radio or television station is common.

fading glass *See* fader.

fading shutter *See* fader.

fading solution A dye used to make fades on processed film.

failing newspaper For the purpose of the Newspaper Preservation Act, a newspaper publication that—regardless of ownership or affiliations—is in probable danger of financial failure.

Failing Newspaper Bill *See* Newspaper Preservation Act.

failure Any malfunction of equipment that causes a complete loss of use. Cf. fault.

fair comment and criticism A limited or qualified privilege defense against a charge of defamation concerning such comments as those made by a reporter about commercial products, movies, books, or restaurants.

Fairness Doctrine A former requirement that licensees editorializing or allowing the presentation of controversial issues afford reasonable opportunities for the discussion of conflicting views on such issues. Originally an administrative interpretation by the FCC, the Fairness Doctrine was, it was assumed, added to Section 315 of the Communications Act in 1959. *See also* editorializing, Mayflower Decision, and Red Lion case. As of 1990 the Fairness Doctrine had become, in general, inapplicable; however, codification was being considered by the Congress.

Fairness Primer An FCC document issued in 1964 that attempted to clarify the intent of the Fairness Doctrine.

Fairness Report An FCC document issued in 1974 further detailing the requirements of the Fairness Doctrine. The most important sentence in the report reads in part: "We regard strict adherence to the Fairness Doctrine—including the affirmative obligation to provide coverage of issues of public importance —as the single most important requirement of operation in the public interest . . . ."

fair trade law A state law that allowed a manufacturer to set a minimum price for goods sold at retail. An anticompetitive practice outlawed in 1975.

fair use The limited privilege of persons other than a copyright holder to use the copyrighted material in a reasonable manner without consent for purposes such as review and criticism.

fairy godmother A derogatory term for an uncreative musical director.

fake □ To improvise. □ A falsified news story.

fake process A full-color reproduction of a black and white illustration or photograph made from handmade separations.

faking □ The use of tricks, props, or other artifice to make the unreal seem real. □ To play music as if it were familiar when it is not.

fall off The decrease in the intensity of light (square of the distance) as the distance from the source increases.

false advertising An advertisement that is misleading in a material respect. False advertising is forbidden by Title 15 of the USC, section 55. *See also* fraud.

false ceiling A partial or fabricated ceiling on a set designed to give the illusion of reality.

false cue A second stop cue placed by accident on an audio cart.

false impression *See* false light.

false light A violation of privacy law wherein a person is portrayed in an unflattering or even an overenthusiastic manner. False light often arises in dramatizations of real events or using pictures unrelated to the specific event. Also called a *false impression.*

false move A mistimed or misdirected movement by a performer.

false plant A defect in a script that misleads an audience. *See also* plant.

false reverse A camera shot taken at some angle other than that of a reverse shot but that appears the same.

false signals False or fraudulent broadcast communications; forbidden by Section 325 of the Communications Act.

FAM A rating index of the degree of public familiarity with a performer or program.

family □ All the type of any single design. *See also* race and series. □ The elements used in different advertisements that constitute the common theme, symbol, act, and so on, of a campaign. □ A group of two or more persons related by blood, marriage, or adoption, living in the same housing unit.

Family Communications, Inc. (FCI) A public television broadcasting organization.

family diary *See* household diary.

family hour *See* family viewing time.

family viewing time An FCC requirement that television networks present programs suitable for the entire family during the early evening hours (7 p.m. to 9 p.m. Eastern time).

fan □ An electrical device used to cool cameras, projectors, computers, and so on. □ An ardent admirer of a film, television series, performer, and so on.

F and G Folded and gathered signatures.

fanfare Several bars of music announcing an entrance or the start of something special.

fanfold paper *See* continuous feed paper.

fan mail Letters, usually unsolicited, that are sent to actors, personalities, performers, and so on. Often contain requests for autographed pictures, unwarranted adulation, proposals of marriage, and so on.

fan wipe A wipe in the form of a line moving radially so as to pass through an arc.

FAO Food and Agriculture Organization of the United Nations. An intergovernmental organization.

farce A dramatic comedy marked by broad, often ridiculous humor.

Farmer's reducer A chemical used to reduce the amount of silver in a film print.

farm out To subcontract work such as printing, artwork, writing, and photography.

farm publication A periodical edited to interest farmers and their families.

Farnsworth system An early television system developed by Philo T. Farnsworth.

far shot A term sometimes used for a long shot.

FAST An acronym for *focus, aperture, shutter, tachometer.* Items to check before filming.

fast □ A lens with a large maximum aperture. □ A film with a high emulsion speed. Cf. slow.

fast breaking A developing, current news story.

fast charger A battery charger capable of recharging a battery in a shorter than normal period of time.

fast cut A series of brief shots, usually accomplished in the editing process.

fast evening persons report (FEP) A weekly report from Nielsen Television Index (NTI) that provides estimates of audience composition data for prime time network television programs.

fast film *See* fast.

fast forward An operational mode of an audio- or videotape recorder characterized by the winding of the tape from the supply reel to the take-up reel at a rate greater than the normal rate used for playback.

fast groove *See* fast spiral.

fast lens *See* fast.

fast motion The action that appears when film is projected at a speed greater than that at which it was shot. Also called *accelerated motion* and *quick motion*. Cf. slow motion.

fast spiral An unmodulated groove on a disc having a spacing that is much greater than that of the modulated grooves. Also called a *fast groove*.

fast stock *See* fast.

fast weekly household (FWH) audience report A weekly report from Nielsen Television Index (NSI) that provides estimates of household audiences for all sponsored network television programs.

fat head A headline too large or long to fit in the allotted space.

father A metal negative for a compact disc (CD).

fat line A line of type too long to fit in the allotted space.

fat matter An easily set up page; one containing standing type, illustrations, or other already set up material. Also spelled *phat*. Also called *fat page* and *fat take*. Cf. lean matter.

fat page *See* fat matter.

fat part A role in a production that offers greater than normal opportunities for a performer to excel.

fat take *See* fat matter.

fat type *See* expanded.

fault Any malfunction of equipment that decreases its efficiency. Cf. failure.

fault time *See* downtime.

favor *See* favoring shot.

favoring shot A camera shot that gives a pictorial advantage to one performer over another.

Fax □ An abbreviation for *facilities*. □ An abbreviation for *facsimile*. Also abbreviated *Fx*.

fay light A luminaire that uses incandescent parabolic reflector lamps with a dichroic coating to provide daylight illumination.

FB Feedback.

FBC Fox Broadcasting Company.

FC □ Footcandle. □ Foolscap.

FCA Federal Code Annotated. The former name of USCS.

FCBA Federal Communications Bar Association.

FCC □ Federal Communications Commission. □ Foreign Correspondents Club (of Japan).

FCCA Forestry, Conservation Communications Association.

FCI Family Communications, Inc.

F connector A common form of connector used on coaxial cables.

FD Floppy disk.

FDA Food and Drug Administration.

FDM Frequency division multiplex.

FD ratio The ratio of the focal length of a satellite dish to its diameter.

FE □ First edition. □ Foreign editor.

fearless dolly A small boom type dolly.

feather edge A book paper with a deckle edge.

featherweight A light, bulky paper.

feature □ To give special importance to a story, sketch, or talent. □ A news story in which immediacy is not important and human interest is stressed. Cf. hard news. □ A break in a radio station segment of news, music, or other continuing programming. □ A special article, page, or section of a newspaper or magazine. □ A story written from a human interest angle. Also called a *feature story* and *soft news*. □ To give special prominence to a story or part of a story. □ A full-length motion picture. Also called a *feature film*. Cf. short. □ *See* featured player. □ A distinctive article or story in a newspaper or magazine. □ A full-length animated film, usually 60 to 120 minutes in length.

featured □ A motion picture, television program, and so on, advertised as a special attraction. □ *See* featured player.

featured player □ A performer who receives billing below that of the stars and costars of a motion picture. Also referred to as *featured.* □ A performer better known than a bit player but less well known than a star. *See also* billing.

feature film A film made originally for distribution to movie theatres, usually five or more reels in length.

feature lead *See* soft lead.

feature length A motion picture that normally runs more than 70, 75, or 90 minutes, depending on the source of the information. Cf. short.

feature story *See* feature.

feature syndicator □ A packager of television programs for distribution to stations. □ *See* syndicate.

featurette A short feature.

featurize To develop a feature from straight news.

FEB Field Engineering Bureau (of the FCC). Now Field Operations Bureau.

FEC First Edition Club.

FeCr Ferrichrome recording tape.

federal agency Any agency of the United States. *See also* administrative agency.

Federal Aviation Administration (FAA) One of the federal government's independent regulatory agencies that, in addition to its primary functions, approves applications for broadcasting towers that might involve hazards to air navigation.

Federal Communications Act The 1934 statute that created the Federal Communications Commission to accomplish the licensing and regulation of broadcasting.

Federal Communications Bar Association (FCBA) An organization of attorneys authorized to practice before the Federal Communications Commission.

Federal Communications Commission (FCC) One of the federal government's administrative agencies. Established by the Federal Communications Act of 1934, the Commission is charged with regulating interstate and foreign communication originating in the United States (radio, television, telephone, telegraph, and so on) in the public interest, convenience and necessity. Successor to the Federal Radio Commission (FRC).

Federal Election Campaign Act The Congressional Act of 1971 that amended the Communications Act to require broadcasting stations to allow "reasonable access" to candidates for federal office (Section 312) and charge candidates only the lowest unit charge for time (Section 315).

Federal Open Meetings Law *See* Government in the Sunshine Act.

Federal Radio Commission (FRC) Established by the Radio Act of 1927, the FRC was charged with regulating radiocommunication but not telephone and telegraph. Replaced by the FCC in 1934.

Federal Register (FR) The official government daily report of actions taken by federal agencies.

Federal Reporter (F) (F.2d) The official records of the courts of appeals.

Federal Trade Commission (FTC) One of the federal government's independent regulatory agencies. In the media, the FTC is primarily concerned with false advertising and consumer protection.

Federal Trade Commission Improvements Act of 1975 The congressional law that gave the Federal Trade Commission the authority not only to regulate advertising in commerce but also to regulate advertising affecting commerce. Also called the *Moss-Magnuson Act.*

Federal Trademark Act The 1946 statute that grants to manufacturers the exclusive right to use names and symbols associated with their products or services. Also known as the Lanham Act. *See also* trademark.

fee □ An amount charged by an advertising agency to an advertiser for services rendered in addition to the agency commission, or as an agreed-upon alternative to commission compensation. □ A payment made for services, such as session fees.

feed □ To transmit a program from a network or remote. □ To send a signal from one component to another. *See also* pipe. □ To insert paper into a typewriter or printer. □ To furnish a forgotten line or action to a performer.

feedback □ A loud howl caused by a microphone picking up the sound from a loudspeaker and reamplifying it, or when the output of a tape playback head is fed into the record circuit. Also called *acoustic feedback.* □ Random streaks on a television monitor caused by overamplification of a reentered video signal. □ The response of a listener or viewer to the stimulation received from a communication. □ The use of information output as input to the same or another machine or process.

feedback cable A coaxial cable used in a CATV system to connect the head end through the trunk amplifier to the subscriber taps.

feedback cutter An electromechanical transducer that performs the same function as a cutter.

feeder □ A worker who places paper in a press. □ A subordinate acting role.

feeder cable *See* feeder line.

feeder line The coaxial cable used in a CATV system to connect bridge and line amplifiers to subscriber taps. Also called a *feeder cable.*

feeder link A radio link from an earth station at a specified point to a space station, or vice versa, conveying information for a space radio communication service other than for the fixed-satellite service.

feedhorn A device that channels microwave or satellite signals from the dish to the LNA.

feed line A dialogue line that serves to cue a performer but is unnecessary to the understanding of the action.

feed reel The supply reel on a tape recorder or film camera or projector. Also called a *free reel* and *stock reel.* Cf. take-up reel.

feed spool *See* feed reel.

feed through *See* print-through.

feet per minute (fpm) A measure of the speed of tape or film through a camera, recorder, projector, and so on.

feet per second (fps) A measure of the speed of tape or film through a camera, recorder, projector, and so on.

feevee A slang term for subscription television.

felony A crime more serious in nature than a misdemeanor, punishable by death or imprisonment.

felt A web of fabric used to hold newly formed paper.

felt side The side of the paper next to the felt in a paper-manufacturing machine. Cf. wire side.

female A recessed device, such as a jack, into which a male device, such as a plug, fits.

female guide The preferred term is *vacuum guide.*

femcee A female emcee.

feminine stanza A slang term for a woman's radio or television program.

FEP Fast evening persons report.

ferric oxide The minute particles of iron oxide used as a magnetic substance on audio- and videotape.

ferrite core A ring-shaped ferromagnetic material used to hold an electromagnetic charge.

ferrite head A tape recorder head in which a long-wearing ferrite material is used to manufacture the pole piece.

ferromagnetic Relating to substances with a high magnetic permeability.

ferrotype *See* tintype.

fest A film festival.

festschrift A collection of books, papers, and so on, issued by colleagues, former students, admirers, and so on, on a special occasion or anniversary.

festspiel A festival play.

FF □ Form feed. □ Flip-flop. □ Fast forward.

ff □ Following, as in *(and the following pages). See also* f. □ Folios. *See also* f.

fg An abbreviation for *foreground.*

FI Fade in.

FIAPF Fédération Internationale des Associations de Producteurs de Films (International Federation of Associations of Film Producers).

fiber bundle A collection of optical fibers. *See also* fiber optics.

fiber optics A technology that uses tiny, precision optical glass fibers to transmit information, such as a television signal, on a modulated light emitting source such as a laser or LED.

fibre The material used to manufacture paper; it may consist of various types depending upon the intended use and price. Some types are abaca, coir, cotton linter, flax, kapok, linen, and sisal.

fiction An imaginative or invented story; a novel.

fictionalization A false light tort wherein words, mannerisms, and so on, are attributed to actual persons.

fictitious name An assumed name under which business is carried out. Also called *DBA*.

FIDAERS International Federation of Amateurs of Sound Recording and Reproduction. An international organization.

fidelity The accuracy of a reproduced sound or picture as compared to the original sound or picture.

fiduciary A stewardship obligation wherein one person acts for another in trust. Considered a broadcaster's responsibility to the public.

FIEJ International Federation of Newspaper Publishers.

field □ An area under the influence of an electromagnetic or electrostatic charge. □ One-half of a television picture; the odd or even scanning lines. Two fields are interlaced to form one frame or complete picture. □ An area within a computer record designed to hold a specific amount or type of information. □ The framed area of a camera shot. Also called *action field* and *field area*. □ *See* field area. □ In animation, the area that will be photographed by the camera for a given shot and, therefore, the area in which the animator draws. The largest field in standard use is the 12-field (12″ × 9″); the smallest is the 4-field (4″ × 3″).

field angle Those points of the candlepower curve where the candlepower is 10 percent of the maximum candlepower define the field of the luminaire. The included angle is defined as the field angle. Also called *field coverage*.

field area The frame area of a camera shot, usually marked on a cel for use in animation or graphics.

field blanking interval *See* blanking interval.

field camera □ A portable film or video camera used for location shooting or remotes. Cf. studio camera. □ A plate or sheet film camera.

field chart *See* field guide.

field coverage *See* field angle.

field frequency The number of fields scanned per second. In the United States, 60 fields per second is the rate; in Europe, 50 fields per second. Also called *field repetition rate*.

field guide In animation, a punched sheet of heavy acetate printed to indicate the sizes of all standard fields which, when placed over the artwork, indicates the area in which the action will take place. Used by the director, animators, and camera operator to check the size of the area the camera will photograph. Also known as *field chart*.

field inspection A review of a radio or television station by representatives of the Federal Communications Commission.

field intensity *See* field strength.

field intensity contours The Grade A and Grade B contours that describe the field strength of a television signal.

field interviewers Interviewers who work from their homes and function as independent contractors under Arbitron's supervision and direction. The role of Arbitron's field interviewers is to contact, recruit, and follow up with sample households.

field lens A telephoto lens usually used on remotes.

field mask An opaque rectangular guide in the shape of a picture frame used for print or animation composition.

field mount A stationary camera tripod used primarily for remotes.

field of action *See* field of view.

field of view The area subtended by the angle of acceptance of a lens, expressed in degrees. Also called *field of action*.

field of vision The area subtended by the angle of acceptance of the human eye, expressed in degrees; normally, 150 degrees horizontally and 120 degrees vertically.

Field Operations Bureau One of the major divisions of the FCC, responsible for Commission engineering activities performed in the field. Formerly called the Field Engineering Bureau.

field pattern *See* polar pattern.

field period The time necessary to scan one field. In the United States, one-sixtieth of a second; in Europe, one-fiftieth of a second.

field pickup *See* remote.

field position The height of a camera above an animation compound.

field producer An individual who supervises a remote broadcast.

field production ☐ *See* electronic field production. ☐ *See* remote.

field pulse A pulse derived from each vertical interval of a composite video signal. In NTSC systems, the rate of such a pulse is 59.94 Hz.

field rate The number of fields per second in a television system.

field repetition rate *See* field frequency.

field sequential color television A system in which the primary colors are presented in successive fields.

field size The size of the area being filmed on an animation stand; from 1 size to 12 size.

field strength The intensity of a radio or television station's electric field, usually measured in the horizontal plane in millivolts per meter at any given distance from the antenna. Also called *field intensity.*

field strength meter (FSM) A calibrated, frequency-selective instrument used to measure field strength.

field test ☐ To test equipment. ☐ *See* pretest.

field work The collecting or gathering of audience research data through interviews or observation.

field zoom An extremely long focal length zoom lens used for remotes; formerly three or more feet long.

FIFO First-in, first-out. A computer routine that first uses the data entered first. Cf. LIFO.

fifteen and two The terms allowed an advertising agency by a broadcasting station, for example, 15 percent agency commission plus 2 percent discount for prompt payment.

fifteener *See* incunabulum.

fifteen-Hertz edit pulse An edit pulse that occurs at a 15-Hz rate; used for identifying NTSC color television frames.

fifteen ips *See* supplementary tape speeds.

fifth estate The electronic media: radio, television, and so on, as distinguished from the print media. Cf. fourth estate.

fifth generation A new class of computers expected in the early 1990s that should use such advancements as ultralarge scale integrated circuits and parallel processing architectures.

fifty-fifty ☐ A plan by which the cost of cooperative advertising is shared equally by a manufacturer and a wholesaler or retailer. ☐ A half-silvered mirror used to split or super an image.

fighting words A doctrine that words that may incite to riot or violence may be subject to prior restraint as a "clear and present danger" to individuals or property.

fight the music To be off the beat in singing or reading lines to music.

figure ☐ A character that represents a number. ☐ A representation of an object or person. ☐ A British term for a type cut.

figure eight The polar pattern of a bidirectional microphone.

figure legend A caption accompanying a figure.

figure of speech A comparative expression using simile, metaphor, or personification.

filament (F) ☐ The heating element in a vacuum tube. ☐ The wire in an electric lamp that, when heated, glows.

file ☐ Originally, to send copy by wire; now applies to any electronic means. ☐ To submit copy (usually by a reporter). ☐ An organized collection of records with a distinctive name that is treated by a computer as one unit. ☐ In CD-I, a subdivision of a directory, in turn subdivided into any number of records.

file descriptor record A sector found in all CD-I files, containing a list of the data segments, their starting logical sector number, size, and file attributes. Needed to access files on a disc.

file label A code or symbol used to identify the contents of a computer file, the type of file, and sometimes the file name.

file maintenance *See* file management.

file management The periodic task of adding to, correcting, copying, and deleting records and files to maintain their accuracy.

file manager In CD-I, a system software module that handles I/O requests for the CD drive. Provides random access to files at the byte level through system calls.

file name The set of alphanumeric characters used to identify a file.

file number The sequential number assigned by the FCC to applications. Cf. docket number.

file-number prefix The letters that precede an FCC file number. Each letter has a specific meaning; for example, *B* stands for "broadcast" and *R* stands for "renewal."

filer A program that controls and manipulates computer files on peripheral storage devices.

file structure volume descriptor record (FSVDR) A record of the disc label describing all necessary items related to the files or parts of the files recorded on the volume.

file thirteen A wastebasket, often the receptacle for poorly written stories or copy. Also called a *circular file.*

filing fee Payment made to the FCC for filing an application as authorized by Title 31 of the USC, section 483(a).

fill □ Material used to pad a radio or television program if it runs short. Also called *padding.* □ A radio or television program substituted for a scheduled program. □ *See* fill leader.

fill copy *See* filler.

filler □ A short news item used to fill an empty space on a news page. Also called *CGO, fill copy, plug, punk, red dog, reserve,* and *stuff. See also* when room. □ Material used to pad a radio or television program if it runs short. Also called *fill copy.* □ The base material of a disc. Cf. binder. □ A clay-like substance added to paper in its manufacture. □ A short act or skit used to fill in time.

fillet □ An ornamental line, usually gold, used on a book cover. □ The stamp or wheeled tool used for making fillets. □ The material or design that completes the outline on a book cover.

fill in □ A news release or other story written so that local names or other information can be inserted. □ A name, address, or other words added to a preprinted letter. □ *See* filler. □ To substitute for someone who does not show; to serve as an understudy.

fill in light *See* fill light.

fill leader □ A short piece of film used in editing to stretch a soundtrack to synchronize it with the picture. Also called *fill.* □ A piece of film used to substitute for a section of film not yet processed, damaged, or to be reshot.

fill light One of the three major lights in three-point lighting. Supplementary illumination used to reduce shadow or contrast range. Cf. back light, base-light, and key light.

film □ A flexible, usually sprocketed, cellulose-based material with a photosensitive emulsion used for taking pictures. □ To photograph, especially motion pictures. □ The film industry. □ A motion picture.

film archive □ A reference library of films. □ A collection of stock shots. □ A collection of posters, books, periodicals, and other materials relating to film. Also called a *film library.*

film artist A director who places his or her personal stamp on a film in conjunction with other key personnel. Cf. auteur.

film auteur *See* auteur.

film base The acetate to which the light sensitive emulsion is bonded.

film bin *See* bin.

film break An interruption in a filmed television program due to missing sprocket holes, broken splices, or other mechanical malfunctions.

film camera A camera that exposes film, as opposed to a videotape camera.

film cameraman *See* cinematographer.

film cement The liquid adhesive used to produce a chemical weld between pieces of film.

film chain The complete set of components, including one or more projectors, television camera, controls, cables, power supply, and so on, used to convert motion picture film into electronic images. Also called a *telecine. See also* multiplexer.

film chamber A camera housing that holds the exposed and unexposed film. *See also* magazine.

film cleaner A chemical or ultrasonic machine used to clean motion picture film.

film clip □ A short film segment used in a television program. □ A short film segment taken from a longer sequence. □ A stainless steel or plastic clip used to hold film for drying.

film commercial A commercial for television on film as opposed to live or on tape.

film continuity *See* continuity.

film conversion table A table that converts the running time for different sizes of motion picture film, such as 16mm to 35mm. Also called a *film footage table.*

film counter A device that measures the amount of film that has passed through a camera, projector, and so on.

film criticism *See* criticism.

film cue A perforation on a film, usually in the upper right-hand corner, indicating the end of the film. *See also* cue marks.

filmdom A slang term for the motion picture industry and its personnel.

film editor The individual who physically cuts the film for motion pictures. *See also* editor.

film festival An event that shows a group of motion pictures of a particular director, actor, genre, or year. Often the festival contains critical discussions and awards. Also called a *fest.*

film footage table *See* film conversion table.

film format *See* format.

film frame *See* frame.

film gate The projector opening through which the projection lamp shines and the film frame is shown.

film gauge The width of the various filmstocks, expressed in millimeters.

film geometry The relationship of the film emulsion to the core. *See also* A wind and B wind.

film gloves *See* gloves.

film holder The receptacle that contains sheet film for a field or view camera.

film horse *See* horse.

filmic Relating to the creative elements found in motion pictures.

filmic space *See* filmic time and space.

filmic time and space The power of the film medium to expand, contract, or suspend time and space through the use of various devices: flashbacks, flashforwards, shot combinations, special effects, and so on.

film island The space occupied by the slide and film chains. *See also* telecine.

film laboratory *See* laboratory.

film leader *See* leader.

film library *See* film archive.

film lineup The list indicating the order of projection of a number of films to be used during a television program or for an entire day.

film loader The individual on a motion picture crew assigned to load and unload film in the cameras. Often an assistant camera operator.

film logging *See* logging.

film loop □ A short length of motion picture film spliced head to tail and used as a continuing background or for special effects. Cf. tape loop. □ *See* loop.

film magazine *See* magazine.

filmmaker A person who is in charge of all aspects of producing a film.

film movement A joining of filmmakers, their films, and others in a group to promote a common goal; often a political or social aim as well as artistic.

film noir A motion picture characterized by dark, often violent characters, depressing plots, and usually urban settings. Also called *black cinema* and *cinema noir.*

filmograph A motion picture in which the movement of the camera instead of the subject simulates motion.

filmography □ A film bibliography. □ The study of filmographs.

film perforation *See* perforation.

film pickup *See* film scanning.

film plane *See* focal plane.

film print A motion picture film reproduction, complete with all visual and audio components, for projection or transmission.

film ratio The ratio between the total film footage shot to the total footage used in the final cut.

film registration The holding of a film in proper alignment. *See also* registration and pilot pin.

film review A critique of a motion picture. *See also* criticism.

film rundown A list of cues for a filmed news story.

film running speed *See* film speed.

film scanner A method used to change the 24-frames-per-second film speed to a rate of 60-fields-per-second television picture.

film scanning The process of converting motion picture film into a television picture. Also called *film pickup.*

film scratch test The running of film through a camera to check for possible scratching by the mechanism or foreign matter.

film sequence Those parts of a telecast using film clips.

film speed □ A measure of the film sensitivity to light, generally in numerical terms of ASA exposure index. More sensitive films have higher numbers, and the total required exposure is less. Also called *emulsion speed.* □ The rate at which film passes through a camera or projector; usually measured in feet per second. Also called *film running speed.*

film splice *See* splice.

film stock Unexposed film. Also called *virgin film.*

film storage A film vault.

filmstrip (FS) An audio-visual 35-mm film with a different picture in each frame. It is not intended to run as a motion picture.

film structure The interrelated elements such as plot and characterization that are arranged to form a cohesive whole.

film studio □ A studio in which motion picture films are recorded. □ A firm that specializes in arranging the production of movies or commercials.

film talent agency *See* talent agency.

film-to-tape transfer Any process by which images originally recorded on photographic film are recorded on tape. Cf. tape-to-film transfer.

film transfer A film copy of a television production. *See also* kinescope.

film transport The mechanism in a camera or projector that moves the film from the supply reel through the mechanism to the take-up reel. *See also* intermittent movement.

film treatment *See* breakdown.

film type The different selections of film available, such as black and white, color, negative, positive, reversal, and infrared.

film vault *See* vault.

film viewer A hand operated or motor driven device used to view processed film; often used during editing.

filter □ A combination of resistors, capacitors, and or inductances that allows some frequencies to pass and attenuates others. □ A sound-effects device used to change the characteristics of a voice or other sound. □ A glass or gelatin disc used to balance or change the light received by a lens.

filter effects *See* effects filter.

filter factor A number by which the exposure length must be multiplied to compensate for the light loss caused by a filter.

filter holder Any device used to hold a filter in front of a luminaire or a camera or enlarger lens.

filter microphone A microphone used for special effects, such as reproducing the limited frequency sound of a telephone.

filter question A question used in a survey to determine whether to continue an interview. If the survey is concerned with television, for example, and the respondent does not own a television set, the interview is terminated. Cf. conditional question.

filter wheel A round filter holder used between a television camera lens and a pickup tube. Also used for capping a television camera.

FIM □ Facing identification mark. □ Fédération Internationale des Musiciens (International Federation of Musicians).

final consumer *See* ultimate consumer.

final cut The finished version of a motion picture or film, ready for duplication. *See also* first answer print. Cf. fine cut.

final decision A decision made by the FCC in an adjudicatory matter. Appeals from final decisions may be made to the Court of Appeals. Cf. initial decision.

final draft The finished sketch, story, version, and so on, of a story, screenplay, advertisement, or other communication that is ready for approval. Cf. first draft.

finale The closing act, scene, musical selection, and so on, of a performance.

final mile The ground link from a satellite dish to the audience, regardless of the length of the link.

final shooting script A motion picture script that has been approved for production.

final trial composite A corrected, ready for release, composite print of a film. Also called a *sample print.* Cf. first trial composite.

financial considerations One of the four basic qualifications for a broadcast license. *See also* character considerations, legal considerations, and technical considerations.

financial interest rule An FCC rule that prohibits television networks from having a financial interest in syndication rights for network programs.

financial qualifications One of the basic qualifications necessary for a broadcast license. The others are technical, legal, and character qualifications.

financial report The annual financial statement of commercial broadcast stations and CATV systems required by the FCC.

finder *See* viewfinder.

fine art Art created without regard to its commercial value.

fine cut The last, refined version of a workprint, subject to little revision, if any. Cf. final cut and rough cut.

fine grain A film with a low emulsion speed that produces a high-quality negative or print.

fine grain dupe A duplicate negative made from a master positive or original negative.

fine grain master positive A black and white positive made from an original negative.

fine groove *See* microgroove.

fines and forfeitures Penalties imposed by the FCC as authorized by Section 503 of the Communications Act. Fines and forfeitures are imposed for various technical violations, deceptive programming, failure to identify sponsors, or failure to observe any rule or regulation of the FCC. *See also* forfeiture.

fine screen A halftone with a large number of lines per inch.

finger A translucent device used in front of a luminaire to reduce the intensity or to cast shadows.

fingernails A slang term for parentheses.

finish The quality and texture of the surface of paper.

finished art Camera ready artwork.

finishing □ The completion of the binding, mounting, ornamentation, and so on, of a book or other printed material. □ The smoothing of the edges of a type casting.

finishing line A rule that sets off or limits artwork.

finish size The completed size of a book after trimming.

FIRC Forest Industries Radio Communications.

fire brigade A slang term for a news unit that covers remotes on short notice.

fire shutter A metal plate in a projector that drops into place if the film catches fire.

fire up An instruction to an operator to make a piece of equipment—a camera, projector, amplifier, and so on—ready for use.

firm order An advertiser's positive order for media space or time.

firm order date A date after which an order for advertising space or time cannot be canceled.

firmware Computer programs that are stored permanently in ROM, as opposed to programs stored temporarily in RAM.

First Amendment The First Amendment of the Constitution of the United States, which reads in part: "Congress shall make no law . . . abridging the freedom of speech or of the press. . . ."

first answer print The first composite print. *See also* answer print.

first assistant director In motion picture production, an individual who specifically organizes the preproduction preparation—including organizing the crew, securing equipment, breaking down the script (or storyboard), preparing strip-board and shooting schedule. During production he or she assists the director with the on-set production details, coordinates and supervises crew and cast activities, and facilitates and organizes flow of production activity.

first call *See* right of first refusal.

first camera operator The first assistant to the cinematographer in a motion picture production.

first class The postal service category of sealed written matter. Cf. fourth class, second class, and third class.

first class permit *See* radiotelephone operator's permit.

first cover The front cover of a magazine or periodical.

first day story A news story printed or released for the first time. Cf. follow.

first draft □ A preliminary sketch, outline, version, and so on, of a story, screenplay, advertisement, or other copy. Cf. final draft. □ According to the WGA, the first complete draft of any script in continuity form, including full dialogue. Cf. polish and rewrite.

first draft screenplay *See* first draft.

first draft teleplay A first complete draft of any script in continuity form, including the full dialogue. Also called a *first draft telescript. See also* teleplay.

first draft telescript *See* first draft teleplay.

first edition □ The entire number of copies of a book printed for the first time. □ A single copy of a rare or antique book. *See also* editio princeps.

First Edition Club (FEC) An organization in existence from 1922 to 1932 that promoted the study of book collecting and bibliography, issued books, and arranged exhibitions.

first generation □ A duplicate tape, film, copy, and so on, of a master or original. □ An original recording. Also called a *master. See also* generation.

first generation computer Computers that used vacuum tubes; developed before the invention of solid state devices.

first grip *See* key grip.

first impression The side of paper that is printed first.

first night *See* premiere.

first nighter A person who attends the first performance of a play, motion picture, and so on.

first page The front page of a newspaper.

first person A news story, feature, script, and so on, written in the first person voice.

first person narration A stream-of-consciousness narration in which a character expresses his or her inner emotions as well as what is happening.

first person shot *See* point of view.

first proof The first copy of an advertisement or news story pulled for checking purposes.

first refusal *See* right of first refusal.

first revise A first proof after corrections have been made.

first run □ The first release of a motion picture for theatre exhibition; often a limited release. Cf. general release, premiere, preview, and rerun. □ *See* first-run nonseries programs. □ *See* first-run series.

first-run nonseries programs Programs, other than series, that have no national network television exhibition in the United States and no regional network exhibition in the relevant market.

first-run series A series whose episodes have had no national network television exhibition in the United States and no regional network exhibition in the relevant market.

first-run syndication A television program series produced to be syndicated instead of broadcast by the networks.

firsts First editions of books.

first sale doctrine The right, under copyright law, given to the owner of a lawfully made copy of a copyrighted work to rent, lease, or sell the copy.

first serial rights The rights granted to a magazine or periodical to publish portions of a book prior to the publication of the book. Cf. second serial rights.

first string The major performers in a production as opposed to doubles or stand-ins. Also called *first team.*

first stripe *See* main stripe.

first team *See* first string.

first time buyer A person who buys a product or service from a specific company for the first time.

first trial composite The first trial print in projection synchronism. Used to check the sound and picture quality. Cf. final trial composite.

first trial print *See* answer print.

fishbowl A radio or television studio observation booth often used by sponsors and visitors.

fisheye An extreme wide-angle lens, often 180 degrees, that produces a distorted image.

fish him out A slang term for lower the microphone boom.

fishing rod *See* fishpole.

fishpole A lightweight, handheld microphone boom. Also called a *fishing rod.*

fishpole boom *See* fishpole.

FIT Foundation to Improve Television. A citizens' group.

fit *See* cast.

fitting The adjusting and alteration of a performer's costumes.

fitting fee The money paid to a performer for the time spent in costuming.

five *See* five K.

500 Net Test Transmissions A weekly test of the national-level interconnection facilities of the EBS system.

525 lines The number of scanning lines on a television receiver in the United States and a number of other countries. *See also* line.

five K A 5000-watt fresnel spotlight. Also called a *five*, *fiver*, and *senior*.

fiver *See* five K.

five W's The five basic questions answered in a news story lead: who, what, when, where, and why.

five W's and H The five W's and how.

fix □ To establish a sound or picture level. □ To establish the blocking and business in a scene. □ To harden a photographic film or print. Also called *fixing*. □ To make a correction in copy.

fixation The process of fixing photographic film or prints. Also called *fixing*.

fixative A clear spray used to cover artwork to keep it from smearing.

fixed A copyrighted work is "fixed" in a tangible medium of expression when its embodiment in a copy or phonorecord, by or under the authority of the author, is sufficiently permanent or stable to permit it to be perceived, reproduced, or otherwise communicated for a period of more than transitory duration. A work—consisting of sounds, images, or both that are being transmitted—is "fixed" for purposes of the Copyright Act if a fixation of the work is being made simultaneously with its transmission.

fixed-alternative question A question for which the possible answers have been prelisted on a questionnaire or schedule. Also called a *closed-end question* and *structured question*. Cf. open-end question.

fixed aperture A camera or projector that does not allow the aperture to be changed.

fixed deferments Payments made to parties who have deferred their cash compensation for work done on a film. Also called a *contingent deferment*.

fixed earth station An earth station intended to be used at a specified fixed point.

fixed field A computer database field that always has a definite number of positions available for use.

fixed focus □ A lens in which the focus cannot be changed. □ A lens setting used to keep objects in focus at varying distances from the camera.

fixed installation A permanent studio, set, instrument, and so on.

fixed lens A nonvariable focal length lens.

fixed location □ A space in a periodical occupied by one advertiser for two or more consecutive issues. □ A space in a periodical specified by an advertiser.

fixed mileage zone An area for which a standard rate is paid for travel, as determined by unions or guilds.

fixed position announcement A broadcast commercial that is run at specified times and that usually carries a fixed rate. Cf. run-of-schedule.

fixed rate A premium rate paid for a broadcast commercial for which the specific time on the schedule is guaranteed. Cf. preemptible rate.

fixed record A computer database record of prescribed length.

fixed-satellite service A radio communication service between earth stations at specified fixed points when one or more satellites are used; in some cases this service includes satellite-to-satellite links, which may also be effected in the intersatellite service; the fixed-satellite service may also include feeder links for other space radio communication services.

fixed service A radio communication service between specified fixed points.

fixed space A variable length, user-defined computer type space. Cf. variable space.

fixed station A station in the fixed service.

fixed storage A computer storage device, such as ROM, that stores data that cannot be altered by computer instructions.

fixed word length A prescribed number of characters or bits used in a computer program. Cf. variable word length.

fixer □ A British term for a remote location coordinator. □ A chemical solution, usually sodium thiosulfate, used to harden a photograph by removing the silver salts.

fixing *See* fix.

fixture A name applied to luminaires.

FL Focal length.

fL Footlambert.

flack □ A slang term for a press agent. □ Releases sent out by a press agent.

flag □ A tear in paper used on an outdoor advertising structure that causes the paper to hang loose and flap. *See also* flagging. □ A computer code that indicates the next signal received will require special treatment; for example, a typesetting code. □ The front page title of a newspaper. Also called a *flag line*, *nameplate*, and *title line*. Cf. logo and masthead. □ A piece of paper or cardboard inserted between lines of type to denote a need for correction. □ A sheet of metal or cloth used to shield light from a camera. Also called a *french flag*, *gobo*, and *mask*. □ Opaque material placed in front of a light source to produce a shadow in the area illuminated.

flagging □ The peeling of outdoor posters at corners and edges. □ *See* flag waving.

flag line *See* flag.

flagship station The main station of a network.

flag waver A story, newspaper, or periodical that emphasizes patriotic themes.

flag waving A picture fault characterized by a random left-and-right motion of picture elements near the top of the picture. Also called *broomsticking*, *flagging*, and *hooking*.

flaking The shedding of pieces of oxide from magnetic tape.

flange □ A projection extending around the hub of a tape reel and arranged to give support and guidance to the tape stored on that reel. □ One of the two sides of a film reel. Cf. core.

flange focal length adjustment *See* back focus.

flange focus *See* back focus.

flanger An audio special-effects generator that combines two versions of the same audio source. *See also* delay line and feedback.

flanging The effect that occurs when two signals that are slightly out of phase with each other are combined. Also called *phasing*.

flap A protective sheet of paper attached to the back top of a piece of artwork and folded over the front.

flare An undesirable streak in a television picture or film emulsion caused by light reflections from a lens or object, or by a mechanical defect. May also cause a reduction of image contrast on film emulsions.

flare check A visual, through-the-lens check for flares from sunlight or lighting instruments.

flash □ An extremely brief scene or camera shot. □ The excess compound generated at the edge of a disc during the compression molding operation. □ Momentary interference in a television picture. Also called a *hit*. □ A bright reflection from a cel. Also called a *cel flash*. □ *See* flash frame.

flash (F) A wire service code for news stories of utmost importance. Cf. advance, bulletin, deferred, regular, and urgent.

flash approach An outdoor advertising space position value factor. Specifically, the term is applied to a panel that is visible for less than 40 feet to pedestrian traffic, less than 100 feet to traffic traveling faster than 35 miles per hour, or less than 75 feet to traffic moving slower than 35 miles per hour.

flashback □ A scene in which past action is inserted to show character or previous plot development. □ A return to a previously shown scene. Also called a *cutback* and *retrospect*.

flash box A special-effects device used to produce a bright flash of light using flash powder. Also called a *flash pot*.

flashbulb A small glass enclosure containing oxygen and aluminum foil or wire; used in amateur photography as a light source. Now replaced by electronic flash attachments.

flash cards Cards shown to interviewees in a survey that list various possible responses, such as income brackets and age breakdowns.

flashcube A cube shaped device that holds four flashbulbs. Used for amateur photography. Cf. electronic flash.

flash cutting The editing of film or videotape into short, rapidly paced segments. Also called *flash editing* and *flutter cutting.*

flash editing *See* flash cutting.

flashes Commercial announcements of 30 seconds or less. *See also* spot.

flash forward A scene in which future action is inserted. Cf. flashback.

flash frame The first or last frame or frames of a shot that are overexposed because the camera is not running at the proper speed.

flashing □ A technique in which film or enlarging paper is exposed to subdued light in order to decrease the contrast range. □ The exposing of the negative in the making of halftones.

flash pan *See* whip.

flash pot *See* flash box.

flashtube □ An extremely bright lamp used in antenna lighting. □ The light source in an electronic flash.

flat □ A piece of scenery usually made of wood covered with canvas. □ A picture that is lacking in contrast. □ An indentation on a turntable drive wheel caused by leaving the turntable in "gear" for an extended period. □ The surface of a worn stylus. □ *See* flat lighting. □ *See* flat response. □ A series of cutouts in a paper used to hold film positives or negatives in the process of making printing plates. □ The thick glass used to support the paper cutouts. □ A group of negatives processed together. □ A magazine with large pages. □ Paper with a fine texture and finish. □ An unfolded sheet of paper. Also called a *flat piece.* □ A large sheet of zinc containing several engravings that are etched at one time.

flat advertising rate *See* flat rate.

flat angle A camera shot taken on a horizontal plane with the object or subject; often an eye-level shot.

flat animation Animation done in two dimensions without any attempt to add depth.

flat back A book binding that is not rounded.

flatbed □ A film-editing machine with a horizontal work surface as opposed to a vertical editing machine. Also called a *flatbed editor* and *horizontal editor.* Cf. Moviola. □ *See* flatbed press.

flatbed cylinder press *See* flatbed press.

flatbed editor *See* flatbed.

flatbed press A printing press that has a bed with a flat form for holding type. Also called a *cylinder press, flatbed,* and *flatbed cylinder press,* although technically, a cylinder press is a rotary press if it carries a curved type form. Cf. rotary press.

flat color Color printing that does not overlap to form other colors. *See also* spot color.

flat display □ A two-dimensional display. □ A liquid crystal or other video display device that has a flat face.

flat fee *See* flat rate.

flat film *See* sheet film.

flat foolscap A size of paper; 13 by 16 inches.

flat letter A size of paper; 10 by 16 inches.

flat lighting Lighting that lacks definition, highlights, or contrast.

flat packet A size of paper; 12 by 19 inches.

flat piece *See* flat.

flat plate antenna A phased array antenna used for satellite reception.

flatplate printing Any printing made from a flatbed press.

flat print A film print suitable for projection with a normal lens. Cf. anamorphic.

flat proof A proof of type that has not yet been printed on a press; often used for proofreading and the positioning of the elements in an advertisement.

flat rate A uniform charge for advertising space or time regardless of the frequency, number of insertions, or amount of time purchased. Also called *flat advertising rate* and *flat fee.*

flat rental The payment of a set amount instead of a percentage or sliding scale for motion picture exhibition.

flat response The frequency response of a component or system that does not vary significantly throughout its range.

flat screen A newer form of television display that uses light-emitting elements instead of a cathode ray tube, thus allowing the thin screen to hang, for example, on a wall.

flat tension mask (FTM) A television display technology now used for computer displays but being developed for general video display applications.

flat type Any type that is not made from metal, such as output from phototypesetting and laser printing.

F layer The ionosphere layer lying just above the E layer. Most radio waves are reflected from this layer. *See also* F region.

Flesch formula An index of readability; based on the length of words and sentences.

flesh peddler A derogatory term for a performer's agent.

Fletcher-Munson curve A group of curves showing the sensitivity of the human ear to varying sound pressure levels. Also called *equal-loudness contours. See also* loudness control.

flex clock A flexible clock; a radio network format that allows affiliates to insert their own news, IDs, and commercials.

FlexForm A printed advertisement not contained by the usual boundary rules; not square or rectangular.

flexible binding A bendable, often limp book cover. Also called a *flexible cover* and *limp binding.*

flexible cover *See* flexible binding.

flexible disk *See* floppy disk.

flexichrome A black and white photograph that has been hand-colored to approximate natural colors when reproduced.

flexitron A special effects device used to make a picture waver.

flexographic printing *See* flexography.

flexography A method of printing using rubber plates; used for printing paper bags and other commercial products. Formerly called *analine printing.*

flick □ A brief cue light. □ A method of changing graphic cards quickly. □ A slang term for a motion picture. Also called a *flicker.*

flicker □ A rapid fluctuation in a television picture. □ A rapid fluctuation in a film caused by a slow film-projection rate or malfunction. *See also* persistence of vision. □ *See* flick.

flier *See* flyer.

flies The overhead area of a studio or stage used to fly scenery, usually operated from a fly floor or fly gallery.

flight □ The length of an advertising schedule. □ To alternate active and inactive or hiatus periods of advertising schedules.

flighting A technique used by advertisers in which a broadcast commercial is scheduled to run for a specific time period, usually a minimum of three weeks, instead of continuously. *See also* hiatus.

flight saturation A maximum concentration of spot radio or television advertising within a short period, to a point at which any further advertising would presumably have diminishing or negative effects.

flimsy A thin carbon paper copy.

flint glass A heavy glass with a high index of refraction used in lens systems.

flip □ A television director's command to change a graphic on a flip stand. □ To rack a lens turret. □ An optical effect in which a graphic, such as a card, rotates horizontally or vertically to reveal a different picture on the opposite side. Also called a *flip over.* □ A story that is continued on the next page of a newspaper or magazine. □ A computerized edit procedure that assigns aberrated call letters to legal call letters; or the AM designation of a set of call letters may be changed to an FM designation. For example, WODC-AM flips to WOBC-AM, and WOBC-FM flips to WOBC-AM. □ A method used by animators to check the effect of their work at the pencil stage. The drawings are held at the top with one hand and released sequentially with the thumb and forefinger of the other.

flip book A small booklet of sequential drawings that appear to move when thumbed through. *See also* flip.

flip cards A set of title cards or other graphics mounted in sequence so that they may be changed by a quick hand motion. Also called a *flop. See also* graphic.

flip-flop An electronic bistable circuit capable of storing one bit of information in either of two stable states: 0 or 1. Also called an *Eccles-Jordan circuit.*

flip over *See* flip.

flipover cartridge An old-style tone arm cartridge that has two styli; one for microgroove, one for 78 rpm discs.

flipover wipe A flip wipe.

flipper ☐ A small flat hinged to a larger flat. ☐ *See* barn door.

flipping To thumb through a sequence of drawings to check for proper animation.

flip shot *See* flop.

flip side A slang term for the other side of a phonograph disc.

flip stand An easel for holding graphics that are to be flipped on the air. Also called a *nod*.

float ☐ The footlights on a theatrical stage. ☐ To center a design or copy in the available space. ☐ Money received from client billing but not yet paid to the supplier of the merchandise or services billed. ☐ To run an advertisement within a space that is larger than that for which its printing plate was intended. ☐ To unground a circuit.

floater ☐ A piece of scenery used in a shot and then removed. ☐ A radio announcer or other station personnel who move from job to job.

floating announcement An announcement that can be broadcast at the discretion of a station. *See also* ROS.

floating flag A newspaper nameplate displayed below the top of the page. Also called a *floating nameplate*.

floating multiple Interconnected jacks on a patch panel that are not connected to another circuit. Also called a *floating mult*.

floating nameplate *See* floating flag.

floating pegbars *See* floating pegs.

floating pegs The pegbars used for registration on an animation table. Also called *floating pegbars*.

floating pulley The weighted pulley used to keep film taut in automatic processing machines.

floating time *See* run-of-schedule.

flock ☐ A coated paper used as a nonreflective surface. ☐ A turntable padding material made of felt.

flong A sheet of papier maché used to make a mold or matrix for stereotyping.

flood ☐ To adjust a luminaire usually by moving the lamp closer to the lens; enlarging the diameter of the beam of light emitted. ☐ The widest field of illumination from a luminaire. ☐ An abbreviation for *floodlight*.

floodlight A luminaire consisting of only a lamp and reflector with fixed spacing; generally, the reflector has a diffused finish and is often physically large in size. Also called a *scoop*.

flood lighting Wide-area lighting. *See* flat lighting.

floor ☐ A studio floor. Cf. stage. ☐ The studio itself.

floor director *See* floor manager.

floor lamp *See* floor light.

floor light ☐ A luminaire mounted on a floor stand. Also called a *floor lamp*. ☐ A luminaire mounted at floor level.

floor man A television production grip.

floorman A compositor or printer.

floor manager The member of the television production crew assigned to direct the activities of the talent and the crew physically present in the studio by relaying commands from the director in the control room. Also called *floor director*.

floor plan A scale drawing of the physical details of a studio or stage, used to show the location of sets, props, lights, and so on. Also called a *plot plan*. Cf. elevation.

floor stand ☐ A device used to hold luminaires above the floor of a studio. ☐ An easel used to hold camera graphics.

flop ☐ A motion picture, radio or television program, advertising campaign, and so on, that is not well-received. ☐ An optical effect used to reverse a frame horizontally. Also called a *flip shot* and *flop over*. ☐ An illustration that was printed or photographed on the wrong side. Cf. reverse. ☐ *See* flip card.

flop over *See* flop.

floppy disk A flexible, circular, magnetically coated mylar disk used by computer disk drives to record data. Also called a *diskette* and *floppy*. Cf. hard disk.

floret *See* flower.

floss Any overwritten script or story.

flow ☐ A sequence of events. ☐ *See* audience flow. ☐ The smoothness with which scenes, stories, animated pictures, and so on, move.

flow chart □ A scheduling calendar used for advertising campaigns. □ To create a flowchart.

flowchart □ A graphical representation of a sequence of events such as found in problem solving, computer program instructions, and so on. □ A chart indicating the interactive and pseudolinear structure of a CD disc.

flower □ A flower-shaped ornament used to decorate book bindings. Also called a *floret*. □ The tool used to make a flower.

flslk Feels like. A wire service weather report category that follows the current temperature to indicate the chill factor, if any.

flub □ Generally, an error by a member of a film or tape crew. □ *See* fluff.

fluff □ Any mistake or distortion that results in a noticeable error. Also called a *flub*. *See also* goof. □ Dust gathered by a stylus from a disc. □ A story lacking in depth.

fluid duplicator *See* spirit duplicator.

fluid head A lightweight camera head with a smooth action. Also called a *free head*.

fluorescence □ The property of some substances to absorb ultraviolet energy and emit visible light of various colors. *See also* ultraviolet. □ The emission of light by the ionization of a gas during excitation. *See also* electroluminescence.

fluorescent bank A series of fluorescent lamps mounted together.

fluorescent light Light produced by the ionization of a gas that activates the lining of the tube-shaped envelope. Cf. incandescent lamp.

fluorescent printing *See* luminescent printing.

flush Margins that are even on the left or right edge, or both edges.

flush and hang A style of printing in which the first line is flush with the left margin and subsequent lines are indented. Also called *flush and indent*. Similar to hanging indention.

flush and indent *See* flush and hang.

flush binding A book binding in which the boards and leaves are even. Cf. overlap.

flush blocking The mounting of a printing plate so that its edges are flush with those of its block.

flush cover A cover of a booklet or the like trimmed even with its pages.

flush head A headline that is aligned with the left margin.

flush left Type set so that it is aligned with the left margin, leaving the right margin ragged. *See also* quad left. Cf. flush left and right, and flush right.

flush left and right Type set so that it is aligned with the left and right margins. *See also* justification.

flush right Type set so that it is aligned with the right margin, leaving the left margin ragged. Also called *ragged left* and *right justified*. *See also* quad right. Cf. flush left, and flush left and right.

flutter □ In recording or reproducing, the deviation in frequency or pitch that results from minor periodic or random changes in the motion of the medium. Usually cyclic deviations occurring at a relatively high rate, as, for example, 10 cycles per second. Cf. drift and wow. □ A rapid, irregular movement in a film camera, printer, or projector that causes uneven exposure.

flutter cutting *See* flash cutting.

flutter echo A rapid succession of reflected pulses resulting from a single initial pulse. If the flutter echo is periodic and if the frequency is in the audible range, it is called a musical echo.

flutter rate The number of cyclical variations per second of the flutter.

flux □ A measure of the amount of light. The unit is the lumen. □ The rate of transfer of magnetic particles. □ A substance used to promote the fusion of metals. In electrical soldering, resin. □ The magnetic lines of force.

fly □ The point at which folded newspapers enter the conveyor or are removed from the press. □ A machine used to remove papers from a printing press. □ An abbreviation for *flyleaf*. □ The space above a stage. □ To raise scenery from the studio floor to above the grid.

flyback The horizontal or vertical return of the television scanning beam during blanking. *See also* retrace.

flyboy The person who removed folded newspapers from a printing press; now accomplished by a fly.

flyer A single-sheet handbill or mailing piece designed to promote or advertise a product or service. Also spelled *flier*.

fly floor A narrow catwalk above the stage or studio floor next to a wall from where the flies are operated. Also called a *fly gallery.*

fly gallery *See* fly floor.

flying erase head A moving head next to a record head on a videotape recorder that erases specific frames so as to make insert editing possible.

flying head The read/write heads on a disk drive that move on a cushion of air above the recording medium.

flying spot scanner A facsimile or television pickup device that illuminates the film, slide, or other material with a tiny spot of light by scanning back and forth across the picture. Also called *indirect scanning.*

flying squad A group of reporters without specific assignments that are used to cover news when and where needed.

fly it A direction to raise a suspended flat, drop, mike, and so on.

flyleaf The blank half of the leaf at the beginning or end of a book closest to the book itself. Cf. endpaper.

fly loft The space above a stage.

fly page One side of a flyleaf.

fly press A handscrew press.

fly sheet A single-page advertising circular.

fly title *See* bastard title.

FM Frequency modulation.

FMA FM Association. An association of FM broadcasters.

FM blanketing A form of interference to the reception of other broadcast stations that is caused by the presence of an FM broadcast signal of 115 dBu or greater signal strength in the area adjacent to the antenna of the transmitting station. The 115-dBu contour is referred to as the blanketing contour and the area within this contour is referred to as the blanketing area.

FM broadcast band The band of frequencies extending from 88 to 108 mHz and continuing in successive steps of 200 kHz to and including 107.9 mHz.

FM broadcast booster station A station in the broadcasting service operated for the sole purpose of retransmitting the signals of an FM radio broadcast station by amplifying and reradiating such signals without significantly altering any characteristic of the incoming signal other than its amplitude.

FM broadcast channel A band of frequencies 200 kHz wide and designated by its center frequency.

FM broadcast station A station employing frequency modulation in the FM broadcast band and licensed primarily for the transmission of radiotelephone emissions intended to be received by the general public.

FM broadcast translator station *See* FM translator.

FM microphone A wireless microphone that transmits a frequency-modulated signal.

FM multiplex The transmission of facsimile or other signals in addition to the regular broadcast signal. *See also* multiplex transmission.

FM stereophonic broadcast The transmission of a stereophonic program by a single FM broadcast station using the main channel and a stereophonic subchannel.

FM system Those circuits of a television tape recorder that generate and process the FM signal prior to recording, and after playback, process and demodulate it.

FM translator A station in the broadcasting service operated for the purpose of retransmitting the signals of an FM radio broadcast station or another FM broadcast translator station without significantly altering any characteristics of the incoming signal other than its frequency and amplitude, in order to provide FM broadcast service to the general public.

FMX A new system that enhances the range of an FM signal without a corresponding increase in power.

f-number ☐ The number used to indicate the aperture of the lens opening. ☐ The ratio of the focal length of a lens to its diameter.

FO ☐ Fiber optics. ☐ Fade out.

FOB Field Operations Bureau (of the FCC).

focal character The main character in a play, often the hero or heroine.

focal distance The distance between the lens and the object or subject.

focal length (F or FL) The distance between a particular point of a lens or reflector and the focal point. For simple lenses in lighting instruments it is usually adequate to measure this distance from the center of the lens.

focal plane The area in space at which an image is in sharp focus. Also called *film plane.*

focal plane camera A still camera with a shutter mounted near to the focal plane.

focal plane matte A matte mounted closely in front of the film.

focal plane shutter A camera shutter that allows light to pass the film through a moving slit in front of the film.

focal point The small region where a lens or reflector concentrates all light rays received from a distant source of light.

focimeter An instrument used to measure the focal length of a lens.

focus □ The sharp definition of television picture elements. □ The point where light rays converge to form an image. *See also* depth of field and depth of focus. □ The most brilliantly lit portion of a set. □ That portion of a drawing or illustration that draws first attention. □ The aiming and adjusting of a luminaire or camera.

focus coil An electromagnetic coil used in a cathode ray tube or video camera tube used to focus the beam.

focus group A selection of individuals who, in group discussion, reveal attitudes, opinions, and other information for a qualitative study of radio or television programs, commercials, products, performer, and so on.

focus in A television director's command to focus a picture purposely out-of-focus.

focusing The act of changing the focus of a television or film camera so that the image is sharply detailed.

focusing control The control on a television camera or receiver used to sharpen definition.

focusing mount The lens mount that holds the lens to the camera body and allows the distance from the lens to the focal plane to be adjusted.

focusing scale The lens markings that indicate the distance to the subject or object.

focusing screen Any of a number of devices, such as a ground glass viewfinder, that allows an image to be seen.

focusing tube A film camera focusing screen contained in an attachment on the side of the camera.

focus out A television director's command to defocus.

focus pull A focusing or refocusing of a camera lens. Also called a *pull focus.*

focus puller A film camera crew member whose primary job is to focus the lens.

focus ring The device that is used to focus a lens on objects at varying distances from a camera.

focus up A film or television director's command to sharpen focus.

fog To ruin undeveloped film by exposing it to light, radiation, incorrect storage, and so on.

fog density The characteristic density of film caused by age, moisture, temperature, and so on.

fog filter A special effects filter used to diffuse and soften an image.

fogged track A film soundtrack that has been blacked out so that no sound is heard upon projection.

fogging The exposure of film to stray light either in shooting or processing; may be accidental or deliberate.

fog index A broadcast journalism formula for testing the readability of copy.

fog maker A special device used to create the effects of fog, smoke, haze, and so on.

FOH spot Front of house spot. Luminaires mounted in auditorium or front-of-house positions. *See also* balcony spotlight, beam light, and rail light.

FOI Freedom of information.

FOIA Freedom of Information Act.

foil A thin sheet of metal, often gold, used for stamping books.

fold □ A tape deformity in which the tape is doubled or bent over on itself, either transversely or longitudinally. □ The line at which a newspaper is folded in half. □ The pages or leaves of a book. □ A variation of a special-effects curl, wherein the edge is creased.

foldback □ A highly directional loudspeaker. □ A British term for a talkback system.

folded and gathered sheets The assembled signatures of a book.

folded sideband In the FM modulation process usually applied to analog videotape recording, a lower sideband whose calculated position in the spectrum is in the negative portion of the frequency axis, and whose actual position is in the positive portion, displaced upward from zero frequency an amount equal to the calculated negative displacement from zero. The direction of motion of such a sideband, in response to a change in either carrier frequency or modulating frequency, is contrary to the normal direction of motion of a lower sideband.

folder □ An advertising or promotional flyer, usually folded several times. □ A machine used to fold a newspaper. □ A person who operates a folder.

folding stick A knife-like wooden or metal instrument used to fold paper.

foldover A horizontal or vertical television picture distortion in which the picture appears to bend backward and overlap itself.

foley A method of adding sound to a scene already photographed by looping or otherwise recording sound in sync with a picture. Also called *foleying.*

foleying *See* foley.

foley stage A sound studio or stage that contains various baffles, reflective surfaces, and so on, for sound recording.

foliation The numbering of the leaves of a book instead of the pages.

folio □ A page number, usually placed at the top right-hand margin. Cf. drop folio. □ The largest regular book size. □ A book made from standard-sized sheets folded once. □ To paginate; to number the pages of a book or manuscript. □ A leaf of a book or manuscript. □ A sheet of paper folded once. □ A size of paper; 17 by 22. □ A case made to hold loose papers. □ A book or manuscript made up of folio sheets. □ A line or box on a newspaper page containing name, date, edition, volume number, and so on. Also called *folio line.* □ A book with large pages.

folio letterheads A size of paper; 8-1/2 by 11 inches.

folio line *See* folio.

folio noteheads A size of paper; 5-1/2 by 8-1/2 inches.

folio publishing The publishing of large books.

folio recto (FR) A right-hand page.

follow A news story that furnishes new information about a previously published article or story. Also called a *follow-up story, folo, folo story, second cycle story, second day story, shirttail,* and *supplementary story. See also* add.

follow action *See* follow shot.

follow copy An instruction to a compositor to print the copy exactly as written even if it appears to be incorrect. Also spelled *folo copy.*

follow focus A process of keeping talent in focus as either the camera or the talent moves closer or farther from the camera.

follow focus cam A device used on an animation stand to keep the camera in focus when the camera is moved up or down.

follow f stop To change the f stop during shooting when following the action from areas of different light intensity.

following and next to reading matter Immediately after and alongside part of the main editorial section of a periodical; used in ordering advertising. Also called *Campbell Soup position.*

following blacks A television picture condition in which the edge of a white object is followed by a black border. Also called *edge effect* and *trailing blanks.* Cf. leading blacks.

following focus. *See* follow focus.

following ghost A ghost displaced to the right of the primary image in a television picture. Also called a *lagging ghost.*

following shot A shot in which the camera moves in the same direction and at the same speed as the subject. Also called a *moving shot, running shot,* or *tracking shot.* Cf. follow shot.

following whites television picture condition in which the edge of a black object is followed by a white border. Also called *edge effect* and *trailing whites.* Cf. leading whites.

follow shot (FS) A camera shot in which the action of a performer is seen from a fixed camera position. Also called *follow action.* Cf. following shot.

follow spot A high-power, narrow beam spotlight suited for long throws (typically 100 to 300 feet), generally with iris, shutters, color boom, and other controls. It is designed for hand operation to follow the movement of performers.

follow style An instruction to a typesetter to set in accordance with a previously established style.

follow-up □ A mailing to a potential customer who has expressed interest in a product or service. □ The actions subsequent to the introduction of a new product or advertising campaign. □ *See* follow.

followup A news story that includes events subsequent to the original report.

follow-up contact A contact made to sample persons or households after the initial contact and recruitment stage. The purpose may be to remind respondents to complete and return their diaries, obtain missing data items, convert prior refusals, or thank respondents for cooperating with the survey.

folo □ *See* follow. □ A subordinate headline. □ The subsequent developments to a news story.

folo copy *See* follow copy.

folo head *See* folo.

folo story *See* follow.

font The complete selection of one size and style of type characters.

fonted Anything printed from a font.

font editor A computer program that allows the user to design fonts.

font mark A symbol used on metal type to identify its font.

Food and Drug Administration (FDA) A U.S. government administrative agency created in 1938 to regulate the content, labeling, recommended use, and advertising claims for a variety of food and drug products, as specified in the Food, Drug, and Cosmetic Act.

Food, Drug, and Cosmetic Act A 1938 federal statute prohibiting the misbranding, falsification, or adulteration of any of certain articles of interstate commerce; enforced by the Food and Drug Administration.

foolscap A standard size of paper; 13 by 16 inches.

foolscap folio Paper one-half the size of foolscap.

foolscap octavo Paper one-eighth the size of foolscap.

foolscap quarto Paper one-quarter the size of foolscap.

foot □ A unit of measure of film length; one foot is approximately equal to 16 frames of 35-mm film or 40 frames of 16-mm film. Cf. film speed. □ *See* tail. □ The lowest part of a type body. □ The bottom of a page. Cf. head. □ An abbreviation for *footnote*.

footage □ The length of a piece of film or tape, usually expressed as the amount of film or tape recorded or projected. □ A method of measuring film length and, therefore, screen time. As 90 feet of 35 mm film equal one minute of screen time, 35 mm footage is used in many studios as a measure of an animator's weekly output. Animators also refer to the length of scenes in feet, rather than in seconds or minutes—a 30-foot scene, rather than a 20-second one.

footage counter □ An indicator built into a film camera that shows the amount of film used. □ An indicator on an audio- or videotape recorder that shows the amount of tape used.

footage number *See* edge number.

footage time calculator A device used to correlate film footage with running time.

footcandle (fc) A unit of illumination equal to one lumen distributed evenly over a square foot. Cf. footlambert.

footcandle meter A light meter designed to measure footcandles.

footer A title or document identification printed at the bottom of a page. Cf. header.

foot iron A steel brace used to attach scenery to a floor.

footlambert (fL) A unit of luminance. A diffuse surface emitting one lumen per square foot has a luminance of one fL. Cf. footcandle.

footlights A row of downstage lights placed at floor or stage level. Cf. borderlight.

footnote A reference note or citation placed at the bottom of a page. Cf. endnote.

footprint The area on the earth's surface covered by a satellite's transmissions.

footroom The distance between a performer's feet and the bottom of a picture. Cf. headroom.

foot slug A slug used at the bottom of a column.

force □ The physical cause of motion. □ *See* push. □ The overdevelopment of film beyond its emulsion rating. Also called *push.*

forced combination An association of media, particularly newspapers, whose advertising space must be purchased in equal quantities by an advertiser in one of them.

forced development A method of improving the density of underexposed film by increasing the temperature of the developer or the development time. Also called *forced processing.*

forced distribution The advertising of commercial products that are not yet locally available, which causes a demand for merchants to stock the products.

forced perspective Scenic design and construction that is not in normal perspective so that performers appear larger or smaller than normal. Cf. free perspective.

force majeure A superior or irresistible force. A suspension of an individual or contract for extenuating circumstances.

forcing The effective increasing of film speed by underexposing the film and using forced development. Also called *pushing.*

forecasting *See* advance story.

fore edge The edge of a book opposite the back.

foreground (fg) □ The area nearest the cameras; the downstage area of a set, stage, or animation cels. Cf. background. □ The area in a computer that can be used by an operator to perform interactive tasks. □ The area in a mainframe where priority tasks are performed. Cf. background.

foreground music Music that is synchronized with the performers, for example, music played by a band, sung by a vocalist, and so on. Cf. background music.

foreground processing Computer handling and processing of high-priority tasks. Cf. background processing.

foreign Advertising placed in a newspaper by an advertiser from outside its circulation area.

foreign communication A program prepared in the United States and delivered to a station in a foreign country for the purpose of transmitting it to the United States. Section 325 of the Communications Act requires a permit from the FCC for such transmissions.

foreign control *See* extended control.

foreign picture release negative A dupe negative used for printing foreign release prints. Generally, the dupe negative contains only the picture and the music and effects tracks for later dialogue dubbing in the language of the country where the picture is to be released.

foreign production deal A motion picture production made by arrangement with a foreign producer or distributor who provides or guarantees any of the financing for the production or furnishes other consideration for the production.

foreign publication rights The rights granted by one publisher to another for the printing and distribution of copies of books in the same language as the original work.

foreign release A version of a film prepared for release in a language other than the original, either by dubbing voices in another language or sometimes by superimposing dialogue on the screen.

foreign version release print A release print made from a dupe negative containing foreign language dialogue and often foreign language titles.

forelengthening The exaggerated perspective obtained when an object is far from a lens. In a long shot with a telephoto lens the object appears to move toward the camera at an extremely slow rate. Cf. foreshortening.

foreman The person in charge of a composing room.

fore matter *See* front matter.

foreshadowing A script-writing technique used to develop expectancy in an audience by giving clues as to what is about to happen.

foreshortening The exaggerated perspective obtained when an object is close to a lens. At an extreme close-up with a wide-angle lens, the object is made to appear much wider than normal. Cf. forelengthening.

foreword A book preface; introductory remarks written by someone other than the author. Also called an *introduction.*

forfeiture □ The voluntary or involuntary surrender of an instrument of authorization from the FCC. □ *See* fines and forfeitures.

form □ A term generally synonymous with one page of material. □ Pages of type or other matter locked in a chase and ready for printing or duplicating.

formal application Any request for authorization where an FCC form for such request is prescribed. Cf. informal application.

formal ascertainment The specified procedures that were formerly required by the FCC for ascertainment. Now, the methods used for ascertainment may be decided by the licensee.

formalism A critical approach to film that stresses form over content; that meaning exists in the way that content is expressed rather than in the content itself.

format □ The general pattern of a television program or series. □ The type of programming carried by a radio station, for example, all-news, middle-of-the-road, and so on. □ A standardized intro and/or outro to a program. □ The aspect ratio of a television or film picture. □ The written form of a script. □ The varied types of magnetic tape recorders and reproducers, such as reel-to-reel, cassette, and cartridge. □ The varied types of television systems, for example, NTSC, PAL, and SECAM. □ Of a recorded videotape, the general arrangement of tracks or records on the tape. □ By extension, the totality of methods and standards used to produce a particular type of recorded tape. □ The shape, size, and general style of a book, magazine, brochure, or other publication. □ The design and layout of a page. □ To divide a computer disk into sectors so that information can be stored. □ The layout of a document to be printed. □ The arrangement of a data file into rows, columns, and so on. □ The physical form in which something appears. □ According to the Writers Guild of America, a written presentation consisting of the following: (a) as to a serial or episodic series, a framework intended to be repeated in each episode, the setting, theme, premise, or general story line of the proposed serial or episodic series and the central running characters being distinct and identifiable, including detailed characterizations and the interplay of such characters. The format may also include one or more suggested story lines for individual episodes. (b) As to a multipart series telling a complete story such format as described in (a) is called a ''bible'' if, in addition and at the request or upon the instructions of the company, it contains all of the following characteristics and requirements: 1. It is in much greater detail than a traditional format, and includes the context, framework, and central premises, themes, and progression of the multipart series or serial. 2. It sets forth a detailed overall story development for the multipart series or for the first broadcast season of the serial (or such lesser period as may be contracted for with the writer) and includes detailed story lines for (aa) all of the projected episodes of the multipart series or (bb) most of the projected episodes for the first broadcast season of the serial (or such lesser period as may be contracted for with the writer). 3. The characters must be not only distinct and identifiable but also must be set forth with detailed descriptions and characterizations. In a unit (anthology) series, the term means a written presentation consisting of the following: a detailed description of the concept of the proposed series, the context and continuing framework intended to be repeated in each episode, and the central premises, themes, setting (locale, time, and so on) flavor, mood, style, and attitude of the proposed series; and it may include suggested story lines for several of the projected episodes.

format code Computer code that is not printed but is used to control printing. Also called *formatting code. See also* flag.

format control Computer word processing printing commands used to format a page. Not used in manuscripts that will require generic codes for typesetting.

formatics The elements of a radio station format (proper music rotation, talk points, jingle points, and so on).

formatter A computer program that arranges a text file and adds the specified layout before the file is printed.

formatting □ The process of arranging a computer format. □ To arrange a page of type by coded computer instructions.

formatting code *See* format code.

form bit A bit that indicates whether a CD sector is form 1 or form 2.

forme The British spelling of form.

former buyer A person who has bought one or more times from a company but has made no purchase in the last 12 months.

form feed (FF) A special command or key that instructs a printer to move to the next page, or a display to move to the next screen. Cf. line feed.

form 1 The CD-I sector format with error detection code and error correction code. Equivalent to CD-ROM mode 1, but with the form identity included in a subheader to permit interleaving of form 1 and form 2 sectors to meet the requirements of real-time operation. Cf. form 2.

Form PA An application form for copyright registration for a work in the performing arts.

forms close date The final date for delivering advertising copy, cuts, and so on, to a printer.

forms down A notification that a newspaper form has been completed and locked.

form 2 The CD-I sector format with an auxiliary data field instead of error detection code and error correction code. Equivalent to CD-ROM mode 2, but with the form identity included in a subheader to permit interleaving of form 1 and form 2 sectors to meet the requirements of real-time operation. Cf. form 1.

formula □ A stock plot or dramatic action plan that is used again and again in motion pictures, books, television programs, and so on. Also called *formula writing*. □ The ingredients and their proportions required to make film processing solutions. □ The selection and balance of the materials used in a periodical. □ The various radio station programming formats; often used to indicate a top 40 station. □ Also used as The Formula: music, news, and sports.

formula writing *See* formula.

Fortnightly Decision A 1968 Supreme Court decision holding cable television systems immune from copyright infringement except for origination cablecasting.

fortyeightmo A book composed of 48 leaves.

45/45 A stereo disc recording and playback method using a V-shaped groove. Also called the *Westrex system*.

45 rpm A disc recorded for reproduction at 45 revolutions per minute. It is normally a seven-inch disc with a raised label area and a center hole 1.5 inches in diameter. Also called *extended play*. *See also* 33-1/3 rpm and 78 rpm.

45 rpm extended play *See* extended play.

forum A discussion program in which the participants deliver prepared speeches.

forwarding The work done in bookbinding after the stitching but prior to casing in.

FOT Fréquence Optimum de Travail. *See* optimum working frequency.

foto A variant spelling of *photo*.

fotog An abbreviation for *photographer*.

Fotosetter *See* Intertype.

foundation The base coat used in makeup.

foundation light *See* base-light.

Founders Medal An award given by the IEEE for "major contributions in leadership, planning and administration of affairs of great value to the engineering profession."

founders type A metal type used to print titles and credits.

foundry A place where type is cast, plates are made, and so on.

foundry proof A proof made before electrotype or stereotype plates are cast. *See also* proof.

foundry type Permanent type made for hand setting, as opposed to softer type intended for remelting after each use. Also called *hand type*.

fount The British spelling of font.

fountain The ink reservoir of a printing press.

four A's A reference to the American Association of Advertising Agencies.

four channel *See* quadraphonic.

four-color process A photomechanical process that reproduces color illustrations by printing in four colors from four separate plates: red, yellow, blue, and black.

Fourdrinier A machine for making paper in an endless web. Named after its early nineteenth century developers, Henry and Sealy Fourdrinier.

four stripe *See* four track.

Fourteenth Amendment The Amendment to the Constitution that makes the provisions of the First Amendment applicable to the states.

fourth class The postal service category of printed matter, books, magazines, and so on. Cf. first class, second class, and third class.

fourth cover The back cover of a book, magazine, or other printed matter.

fourth estate The press in general, newspapers specifically. Cf. fifth estate.

Fourth Estate Award A plaque given by the American Legion annually to the various media for ''outstanding service to community, state, or nation.''

fourth network The Public Broadcasting System (PBS), Fox, and the DuMont Television Network have been referred to at various times as the fourth network.

4to *See* quarto.

four track A film soundtrack that contains four channels of sound. Also called *four stripe. See also* fullcoat.

four track recording A system of recording a stereo signal on quarter-inch tape with tracks 1 and 3 used in one direction and tracks 2 and 4 used in the other direction. Also called *quarter-track recording.*

four walled set A completely enclosed set consisting of four walls instead of the usual three walls.

four walling The practice in which motion picture distributors rent a theatre for limited-run exhibitions instead of paying the owner of the theatre a percentage of the profits.

Fox Broadcasting Company (FBC) A late 1980s entry into the television scene as the fourth commercial television network.

foxing The brownish discoloration found on some paper.

fox message A common message used to test a typewriter, printer, keyboard, and so on, that prints all the letters of the alphabet: The quick brown fox jumps over the lazy dog.

FP □ Focal plane. □ Foreign program. An FCC file-number prefix. □ Front projection.

Fp Frontispiece.

FPA Foreign Press Association.

FPM Feet per minute. The speed of film through a camera.

FPS Feet per second. The speed of film or tape through a camera or recorder.

FPT Freight pass through.

FPT price The increase in price paid by the public for freight pass-through charges. Usually, 3 to 5 percent.

FR □ *Federal Register.* □ Facilities request. □ Folio recto.

fr An abbreviation for *frame.*

fractals A class of shapes that exist in fractal or noninteger dimensions, created by fractal geometry, which applies recursive subdivision to a basic form while introducing a random factor at each subdivision.

fractionalization The division of radio and television audiences by the presence of multiple sources of programming. Similar to fragmentation.

fractional page Periodical advertising space occupying less than a full page.

fractional showing A showing of outdoor advertising panels in a quantity of less than one-fourth that deemed adequate for coverage.

fragmentation □ A term applied to the increasing number of audience subdivisions that, together, constitute the total television receiver usage. Fragmentation can result from growth in the number of program alternatives, such as broadcast, pay cable, and basic cable; from an increase in the number of specific interests to which those alternatives appeal; or from other uses of the television receiver, such as VCR recording and playback, and videodisc playback. □ The use of a great variety of types of media for a single advertising campaign, with no single medium used predominantly or heavily.

fraktur A style of German type. Also spelled *fractur.*

frame □ In computing, the array of bits across the width of magnetic or paper tape. □ An individual picture on a film, filmstrip, or videotape. □ A single television tube picture scan combining interlaced information. □ In videotext, a page of data displayed on a terminal. □ In CD-DA, one complete pattern of digital audio information, comprising 6 PCM stereo samples, with CIRC and one subcode symbol, eight-to-fourteen modulated, with a synchronization pattern. □ A section of magnetic tape containing a group of bits. □ A unit of information. □ A display screen containing some form of data. □ A single illustration on a storyboard. □ A rack for holding type cases. □ One complete television picture consisting of two interlaced fields. □ To compose a picture. □ One of the series of pictures in a motion picture. □ The mask around a television receiver or monitor picture tube. □ A list, file, or some other way of identifying the sampling units that have a chance of being selected in a sample. For example, a list of telephone numbers or a map. It provides a means for selecting the sampling units.

frame accuracy The degree to which a videotape editing system is capable of editing precisely on a desired frame. If the system is precise, it is called *frame accurate*; if not, the accuracy is usually stated in terms such as plus or minus 1, 2, and so on. Also called *frame tolerance.*

frame accurate *See* frame accuracy.

frame address The precise frame on a videotape recording as identified by a time code number. Used in videotape editing.

frame bar *See* frame line.

frame-by-frame Filming in which each frame is exposed separately, as the object being photographed must be altered before each exposure in order to create the illusion of movement in the finished film; as opposed to the more usual method of filming in which the film runs through the camera at a steady, prescribed rate to record action taking place before it.

frame code *See* control track.

frame counter □ A digital counter attached to an animation camera which automatically records the number of frames that have been shot. □ A film counter that measures the number of frames that have been exposed.

frame frequency The number of times a complete television picture is scanned per second. In the United States, the standard is 30 frames per second; in Europe, 25 frames per second.

frame glass A British term for the sheet of glass used in an animation stand platen to hold the cels flat.

frame grabber □ In recording, an electronic technique for storing and regenerating a video frame from a helical videotape signal. This method avoids the need for the continuous head-to-tape contact that would otherwise be required in freeze-frame operation. □ An electronic device for extracting a complete frame from a video signal as it is being passed along a transmission channel and storing it in memory for further processing. *See also* framesnatch and frame store.

frame line □ The narrow bar that appears between film frames. Also called a *frame bar.* □ One of the four edges of a picture.

frame mask A cutout or marks used on some camera viewfinders to indicate the outer limits of a frame.

frame pulse □ One of a train of pulses derived from alternate vertical-interval signals of a composite video signal. □ A pulse superimposed on the control-track signal to identify the longitudinal position of a video track containing a vertical synchronizing pulse. Also called an *edit pulse.* □ By extension, the magnetic record of such a pulse.

framer The device on a film projector that may be adjusted to eliminate frame lines.

frame rate The speed at which film passes through a camera or projector. Also called *camera speed, frame speed,* and *projector speed.* Cf. foot.

frame roll A momentary roll of a television picture from top to bottom or viceversa.

framesnatch A control device allowing a home viewer to lock a single frame of a television picture on the screen.

frame speed *See* frame rate.

frames per foot *See* foot.

frames per second (fps) The number of frames of film exposed in a camera or run through a projector in one second. Normally, 24 frames per second.

frame store A memory unit capable of digitizing and storing a display screen containing text or graphics.

frame stretch The printing of extra identical frames to slow the action in a motion picture scene.

frame synchronizer *See* time base corrector.

frame tolerance *See* frame accuracy.

frame up A television director's command to adjust the picture composition.

framing □ The adjusting of a camera shot to improve picture composition. Also called *lining up*. □ To align a film in a projector gate so that the frame line does not show on the screen. Also called *racking*.

framing control *See* centering control.

framing shutter One of a series of internal flat metal plates used to limit the angle of coverage of a spotlight.

franchise □ An initial authorization, or renewal thereof, issued by a franchising authority, whether such authorization is designated as a franchise, license, resolution, contract, certificate, agreement, or otherwise, which authorizes the construction or operation of a cable system. □ An agreement granting an advertiser the right to retain the sponsorship of a radio or television program with no obligation to do so.

franchise area The geographic area subsumed by a cable television franchise.

franchise fee The money paid by a cable television system for a franchise to a municipal or county authority.

franchising authority Any governmental entity empowered by federal, state, or local law to grant a franchise for cable systems.

fraternal magazine A magazine designed for members of a fraternal order or society.

fraud A "scheme or artifice to defraud, or for obtaining money or property by means of false or fraudulent pretenses." The broadcasting of fraudulent messages is forbidden by Title 18 of the USC, section 1343 (The Criminal Code).

fraud order An order from the U.S. Postal Service to halt mail used for fraudulent or other unlawful purposes.

fraudulent advertising *See* false advertising.

fraudulent billing The issuing to any advertiser, advertising agency, station representative, manufacturer, distributor, jobber, or any other party, any bill, invoice, affidavit, or other document that contains false information concerning the amount actually charged by the licensee for the broadcast advertising for which such bill, invoice, affidavit, or other document is issued, or which misrepresents the quantity of advertising actually broadcast (number or length of advertising messages) or the time of day or date at which it was broadcast.

FRC Federal Radio Commission.

freak A slang term for an individual who is enamored of and knowledgeable in a specialized field, such as a computer freak or film freak.

FREC Federal Radio Education Committee. Now defunct.

free advertising □ The use of tradenames instead of generic names in news copy. □ Publicity releases aired or printed as news. Also called a *free puff*.

freebie A slang term for a complimentary ticket.

freeboard *See* E value.

free cinema A documentary film movement in Great Britain in the 1950s.

freedom of information (FOI) The access to government documents that do not compromise national security or violate privacy rights of individuals.

Freedom of Information Act (FOIA) A 1966 statute that requires all federal executive and administrative agencies to furnish information to the public when it is requested unless that information is in one of nine protected categories. The scope of the act was expanded in 1974.

freedom of the press □ The right granted under the First Amendment of the U.S. Constitution for access to newsworthy events. □ The right to publish books, pamphlets, and so on, without prior restraint. *See also* censorship.

free form □ A radio station format characterized by a lack of format. □ *See* free page.

free head A movable camera mount. *See* friction head.

freelance A person who contributes stories, news, artwork, skill, and so on, on a per assignment or contract basis. Not an employee of the company receiving the work or skill. Also called a *freelancer*.

free-lance player A player employed for a specific motion picture in a designated role on a weekly basis with a guarantee of less than $25,000. Cf. contract player, day player, deal player, multiple picture player, stunt player, and term player.

freelancer An individual who works freelance.

free linefall A typed page without hyphens at the right edge.

freely adapted A script based only generally on a novel; often, the plot and characters are changed.

free page A newspaper or magazine page that does not follow the conventional column format. Also called *free form.*

free perspective A technique of set design and execution used to provide an illusion of reality and depth. Cf. forced perspective.

free press/fair trial The dilemma that arises when the First and Sixth Amendments of the U.S. Constitution conflict: the right of the press to gather and publish information, and the right of a defendant to a fair trial.

free publication A magazine or other periodical sent free to a selected list of readers; a complimentary copy.

free puff *See* free advertising.

free reel *See* feed reel.

free-response question *See* open-end question.

free rider A retailer who takes advantage of mass media advertising without sharing in the costs of the advertising.

free space The area in line-of-sight transmission that does not contain natural objects or buildings that might reflect or absorb electromagnetic energy.

free space field intensity The field intensity that would exist at a point in the absence of waves reflected from the earth or other reflecting objects.

free space field strength The field strength that would exist at a point in the absence of waves reflected from the earth or other reflecting objects.

free space loss The attenuation of a signal due to distance and frequency only.

free speech *See* First Amendment.

freestanding insert A promotional piece loosely inserted or nested in a newspaper or magazine.

freestanding machine A video record and/or playback apparatus that includes all the equipment necessary for the recording or playback of a composite video signal.

free television A designation designed by broadcasters to distinguish commercial television from CATV or STV.

free-vee A slang term for free television as opposed to feevee.

freeze □ To approve a script, set design, camera shots, and so on, for final production. □ A director's command to stop all action or movement. □ In acting, to forget a line. □ The Freeze: the period from 1948 to 1952 when no new television construction permits were issued by the FCC. □ *See* freeze frame.

freeze frame □ The arrested picture motion created by holding one videotape or videodisc frame. Also called a *freeze. See also* stop action. □ The multiple printing of one film frame so that the picture is held on the screen during projection. Also called a *frozen frame, hold frame,* and *stop frame.*

F region A region of the earth's atmosphere 100 or more miles above the surface. *See also* ionosphere.

freight pass through (FPT) A method by which the cost of shipping books from a publisher to a bookseller is passed on to the consumer.

french curve A plastic template, used in artwork, containing a variety of curved edges.

french flag *See* flag.

French fold A sheet printed on one side and folded horizontally and vertically to form a four-page booklet.

French folio A lightweight paper.

French rule A type rule thicker in the middle than at the ends.

french scene A major or complete portion of an act, identified by a significant entrance or exit by a performer.

freon TF A rapidly evaporating fluid used to make frame pulses visible for videotape editing.

freq An abbreviation for *frequency.*

frequency (f) □ The number of complete excursions a periodic phenomenon makes in a unit of time, expressed in cycles per second or hertz. □ The average number of time periods, out of a set of specified time periods, in which households or individuals are in the audience of a given television or radio network, station, or program. Cf. reach. □ The average number of times households or persons viewed a given program, station, or advertisement during a specific time period such as one month. This number is derived by dividing the gross rating points (GRP) by the total nonduplicated audience (cume). Cf. cumulative audience and reach. □ The number of times an average individual or family has the opportunity to be exposed to an outdoor advertising message during a defined period of time. Frequency and reach in the outdoor medium usually refer to the calendar month as the basic reference, because this time period coincides with standard contract and exposure practices. *See also* repetition. □ The number of times a person orders goods by mail within a specific period of time. □ The average number of times the unduplicated viewers will be exposed to a schedule of commercials or spots.

frequency allocation *See* allocation.

frequency allotment *See* allotment.

frequency assignment *See* assignment.

frequency band *See* band.

frequency control The apparatus that automatically maintains the assigned frequency of a broadcasting station within the specified tolerance.

frequency curve A graphic representation of a frequency distribution. The most common is the bell-shaped curve.

frequency departure The amount of variation of a carrier frequency or center frequency from its assigned value.

frequency deviation The peak difference between the instantaneous frequency of the modulated wave and the carrier frequency.

frequency discount An advertising discount based upon the number and frequency of insertions or spots per year.

frequency distortion The distortion that occurs when all frequencies of an audio or video signal are not changed equally.

frequency distribution In general, a tabulation that shows the number, or the proportion, of times that given values or characteristics occur in a set of statistical observations.

frequency division multiplex (FDM) A process that allows two signals of differing frequencies to be transmitted over one communication channel.

frequency hopping system A spread spectrum system in which the carrier is modulated with the coded information in a conventional manner causing a conventional spreading of the RF energy about the carrier frequency. The frequency of the carrier, however, is not fixed but changes at fixed intervals under the direction of a pseudorandom coded sequence. The wide RF bandwidth needed by such a system is not required spreading of the RF energy about the carrier but rather to accommodate the range of frequencies to which the carrier frequency can hop.

frequency-hour One frequency used for one hour regardless of the number of transmitters over which it is simultaneously broadcast by a station during that hour.

frequency interleaving The process of joining the television luminance signal with the color subcarriers for transmission.

frequency modulation (FM) A system of modulation in which the instantaneous radio frequency varies in proportion to the instantaneous amplitude of the modulating signal, and the instantaneous radio frequency is independent of the frequency of the modulating signal. Cf. amplitude modulation.

frequency range The range of frequencies, from lowest to highest, that can be produced by a human voice, musical instrument, or electronic component or system. Cf. frequency response.

frequency record A disc containing various sine wave frequencies recorded at known amplitudes, for the purpose of measuring reproducing system frequency response characteristics. Also called a *test record.*

frequency response The relative output versus frequency of a recording or reproducing system, usually presented in the form of a curve plotted with frequency as the ordinate and dB as the abscissa. Cf. frequency range.

frequency reuse The use of a satellite transponder to transmit two signals at the same time; one vertically polarized, the other horizontally polarized.

frequency-shift telegraphy Telegraphy by frequency modulation in which the telegraph signal shifts the frequency of the carrier between predetermined values.

frequency spectrum *See* spectrum.

frequency swing The peak difference between the maximum and the minimum values of the instantaneous frequency of the carrier wave during modulation.

frequency tape A recording of various test frequencies at known amplitudes, usually for the purposes of testing and measuring reproducing equipment. Also called a *test tape.*

frequency tolerance The maximum permissible departure by the center frequency of the frequency band occupied by an emission from the assigned frequency, or by the characteristic frequency of an emission from the reference frequency. For example, AM stations must operate within 20 Hertz of the assigned center frequency.

frequency translation The conversion of one frequency to another, as by a television translator.

fresh air The white space on a newspaper or magazine page.

fresnel A luminaire embodying a lamp and a fresnel lens, with or without a reflector, which has a soft beam edge. The field and beam angles can be varied by changing the spacing between the lamp and the lens. Also called a *fresnel spotlight.*

fresnel effect The tendency of certain surfaces to absorb light rather than reflect it, which must be accounted for in modeling.

fresnel lens A lens that acts similar to a plano-convex lens but is thinner and lighter due to steps on the convex side. Often the flat side has a rough surface to smooth light beams by slightly diffusing the light.

friar A light colored smudge on a printed page. Cf. monk.

friction feed The method by which paper is moved in a standard typewriter or printer.

friction head A camera head with horizontal and vertical disks or springs used as pressure controls for smooth movement. Also called a *free head, pan head,* and *panning head.*

friction ring □ The surface of a reel hub. □ A cylindrical overlay of frictional material applied to a reel hub to facilitate threading. Also called a *friction sleeve* and *thread-up ring.*

friction sleeve *See* friction ring.

Friday hook The plot cliffhanger that a soap opera leaves in order to bring the audience back on Monday.

friend of a friend The result of one person sending in the name of someone considered to be interested in a specific advertiser's product or service. A third-party inquiry.

frilling The separation of a film emulsion from the edges of the base; usually caused by heat.

fringe □ *See* fringe time. □ A double outline produced by incorrect registration.

fringe area An area too far from a broadcasting station to receive a satisfactory signal at all times.

fringe candidate A legally qualified candidate for public office who has little, if any, hope of being elected, but who is nevertheless entitled to the rights granted all candidates under Section 315 of the Communications Act.

fringe light *See* back-light.

fringe time □ Generally, the two-hour period before (early fringe) and after (late fringe) prime time. □ Any period of time on radio and television with fewer viewers than during prime time.

fringing A halo effect caused by the superimposition of two or more images. *See also* halo.

frisket □ A protective stencil used in artwork. □ A paper cutout; a mask. □ A sheet stretched over an inked form so that only certain portions are printed.

from hunger A slang term for an inadequate script, program, book, article, and so on.

from the top To rehearse a scene or program from the beginning.

front □ The first page of a newspaper section. □ An abbreviation for *frontispiece.* □ The section of a theatre in front of the curtain.

front cover The outside cover on the front of a book, magazine, and so on. *See also* cover.

front curtain *See* curtain.

front end □ The activities necessary or the measurement of direct marketing activities leading to an order or a contribution. □ A computerized text processing system that eliminates the need for a composing room.

frontis An abbreviation for *frontispiece.*

frontispiece □ An illustration facing the title page of a book. □ The front of a stage or set.

front lighting Lighting from the general direction of the viewer.

frontload □ To schedule the use of the main part of an advertising budget for the first part of an advertising campaign to ensure that all of a budget is used for its originally designated use. Cf. backload. □ To schedule new radio or television programs or episodes at the beginning of a period of time in order to attract a new audience.

front matter The material in a book preceding the text: title page, frontispiece, table of contents, list of illustrations, acknowledgments, foreword, introduction, and so on. Also called *fore matter* and *preliminary matter.* Cf. back matter and body.

front office The office of the publisher, editor, business manager, station manager, theatre manager, or other executive where the major decisions are made.

front of the book The editorial matter of a magazine. Cf. back of the book matter.

front porch The portion of the composite picture signal that lies between the leading edge of the horizontal blanking pulse and the leading edge of the corresponding sync pulse. Cf. back porch.

front projection The projection of a background scene on an opaque screen from near the camera position. The projected image is not visible on performers or other scenery. Also called *front screen projection.* Cf. rear projection.

front screen projection *See* front projection.

front-to-back ratio A measure of the degree of a microphone's sensitivity to sounds received from various polar angles.

frost One of a series of color media that is translucent but colorless; used to diffuse light.

frosted A glass or plastic material coated to diffuse light.

frozen frame *See* freeze frame.

frying A hissing sound often caused by overheated equipment.

frying pan A type of diffuser.

FS □ Full shot. □ Follow shot. □ Filmstrip. □ Full stop.

F/S Frames per second. *See* frame frequency.

FSAPO Fade sound and picture out. A script notation.

fsc An abbreviation for *foolscap.*

F score A rating taken to determine an audience's familiarity with a performer.

FSK □ Frequency shift keying. □ The tones used at beginning and end of commercials for automatic cueing.

FSM Field strength meter.

f stop The setting that indicates the amount of light allowed through a lens; computed by dividing the focal length by the aperture diameter.

F. Supp. An abbreviation for *Federal Supplement,* an official publication of the U.S. district courts.

FSVDR File structure volume descriptor record.

FT FM broadcast translator. An FCC file-number prefix.

FTC Federal Trade Commission.

ft-c An abbreviation for *footcandle.*

FTM Flat tension mask.

fudge News that is inserted in a newspaper at the last minute, usually front page matter.

fudge box A space on a newspaper plate left for the insertion of last-minute news. Also called a *fudge column.*

fudge column *See* fudge box.

fugitive A slang term for printed or spoken matter of transitory or occasional use.

fulfillment house An organization that assists publishers with circulation and other problems.

full animation Animation that depicts movement and character as completely and smoothly as possible, giving the illusion of weight and motion in three dimensions. The object in motion is usually completely redrawn for each frame. Cf. limited animation.

full aperture (FA) The maximum aperture size of a camera or projector lens.

full apple An apple box 18 by 12 by 12 inches.

full binding A book binding made of leather.

full box A box with a border on each side.

full carrier single-sideband emission A single-banded emission without suppression of the carrier.

fullcoat A perforated film that is completely coated with magnetic oxide. Used for recording double system synchronized sound. *See also* magnetic film.

full duplex A transmission circuit in which communication between two points takes place in both directions simultaneously. Cf. half duplex and simplex.

fullface A boldfaced type.

full format A full-width 35 mm, 3:4 frame, as opposed to the academy aperture.

full frame The maximum image size that can be produced on a film frame.

full gilt A book with gilt on each edge.

full line A line of type that fills the available space completely without justification. Also called *full measure.*

full measure *See* full line.

full network All of the radio or television stations affiliated with a network.

full network station A commercial television broadcast station that generally carries in weekly prime time hours 85 percent of the hours of programming offered by one of the three major national television networks with which it has a primary affiliation (that is, right of first refusal or first call).

full point *See* full stop.

full position A preferred position for newspaper and magazine advertising, with reading matter on both sides or at the top of the page. More expensive than run-of-paper advertising.

full program sponsorship The sponsorship of a radio or television program by one sponsor.

full roll A roll of newsprint four pages wide.

full run □ The insertion of an advertisement in every edition of a daily newspaper during one day. □ *See* full showing.

full scale A photographic print that contains the full range of tonal values.

full screen A television station identification in which an advertiser or sponsor uses the entire screen. Cf. shared screen.

full service A client who purchases all the services of a given agency, ratings service, syndicator, and so on.

full service agency An advertising agency that offers its clients a full range of staff service capabilities, including marketing planning and management, creative, media, research, accounting, and often such services as merchandising and advertising-related legal counsel.

full shot A long shot that shows the entire body or object or group of persons or objects. *See also* camera shots.

full showing □ A transit advertising contract that requires a card to be placed on every bus, streetcar, and so on, in a given area. Also called *full run.* Cf. half showing and quarter showing. □ An outdoor posting of the number of boards conventionally regarded as adequate in a given geographical area.

full stop (FS) A period. Also called a *full point.*

full stripe A magnetic stripe running the full length of a piece of film's unperforated edge. Cf. fullcoat.

fulltimer A slang term for a radio station licensed for 24-hour-a-day operation.

full-time station A station authorized for unlimited time operation.

full track recorder A tape recorder that uses the entire width of a quarter-inch audiotape. Cf. half track recorder and quarter track recorder.

full up To operate a system or component or luminaire at its highest rating or power.

fully formed A typewriter or printer that produces letter quality output as opposed to characters formed by a dot matrix system.

fully scripted A script containing all the information concerning dialogue, shots, sound effects, and so on.

function That part of a computer program that specifies an operation to be performed.

functional FM *See* functional music.

functional lighting The ordinary, flat lighting of a scene or set that provides sufficient illumination for camera operation.

functional music The supplementary services offered by FM stations using an SCA from the FCC for multiplexing background music. Also called *functional FM. See also* musicasting, storecasting, and transitcasting.

functional set A practical set or setting used for a specific television function, such as a talk show, news, weather, and so on.

function key One of the 10 or 12 keys labeled F1 through F10 or F12 found on some computers.

fundamental frequency The basic frequency of a musical tone. Cf. harmonic.

fundraising list Any compilation or list of persons or companies based on a known contribution to one or more fundraising appeals.

funnel Metal tubes of various sizes that can be mounted on the front of spotlights to control stray light. On certain instruments, a funnel can be used to reduce beam size. Also called a *high hat, snoot,* and *top hat.*

furniture The pieces of wood or metal used to fill in spaces and separate material within a type form.

fuse (F) A protective device, usually a wire, used in electrical circuits to protect equipment from an overload. Cf. circuit breaker.

future A scheduled news event; often a political speech, dedication, meeting, and so on.

future book An assignment editor's calendar of future events to be covered. Also called a *datebook.*

future file □ A compilation of clippings, memoranda, notes, and so on, for insertion into a future book. □ A datebook of scheduled events. Also called an *advance file* and *futures book.*

futures book *See* future file.

fuzzy Music, sounds, or pictures that lack definition or clarity.

FV Family viewing (time).

FWH Fast weekly household audience report.

FX □ Extraneous effects. □ *See* Fax. □ Effects. □ Sound effects. □ Optical effects.

FYI For your information. Material received for information only; not for publication.

G

G □ General audiences; all ages admitted. A CARA classification for feature films. □ Ground.

GAAC Graphic Arts Advertising Council.

gadget Any piece of equipment not having a definitive name. Similar to *gizmo.*

gaffer An electrician. On a motion picture set, the chief electrician responsible for the lighting. Also called a *juicer.*

gaffer tape A pressure-sensitive sheet-metal duct tape used for various purposes in television and film. Cf. white tape.

gaffoon An engineer or sound effects person who accomplishes two or more effects at the same time.

gag □ A stunt performed by a stuntman or stuntwoman. □ Any laugh-producing joke, situation, or device. □ The forcible restraint of free speech. *See also* gag order. □ A hoax or falsified story reported as news. □ A humorous cartoon.

gag on gag order An order issued by a court restraining individuals from disseminating information about a gag order.

gag order An order by judicial authority to refrain from publishing information concerning a court proceeding. A form of prior restraint. Also called a *gag rule.* Courts prefer the terms *protective order* or *restrictive order.*

gag rule *See* gag order.

gagster *See* gag writer.

gag writer A radio or television writer who develops one liners or scripts containing humorous lines and situations. Also called a *gagster.*

gain □ The control of the volume of sound. □ The amplification of sound. □ The power increase derived from an antenna. Cf. loss. □ The ratio of voltage, current, or power with respect to a standard. □ The amplitude of a video signal.

gain boost A switch found on many EFP video cameras that allows the operator to increase the gain of the video amplifiers. Significantly increases the noise in the picture but allows shooting in low light levels.

gain control A potentiometer or fader used to vary the gain of an electronic system or component.

gain figure The ratio of the output to the input of an amplifier, vacuum tube, and so on. Also called *amplification factor.*

gallery □ The inexpensive seats in a theatre. □ The camera site and film developing area of a photoengraving or printing plant. □ A seating area for members of the press, as in the Senate and House of Representatives.

galley □ A shallow tray used to hold type after it has been set. □ An abbreviation for *galley proof.*

galley boy A person, regardless of age or sex, who does the menial tasks in a printshop. Also called a *printer's devil.*

galley press A press used to make galley proofs.

galley proof (GP) A proof made from the type set up in a galley, before it is set into pages. Also called a *galley* and *slip proof.* Cf. page proof.

galley slug A slug used to identify a section of a galley type.

gallows microphone A microphone hung from a support shaped like a gallows.

Gallup and Robinson A research firm that conducts print and broadcast media advertising effectiveness surveys.

Gallup Poll A public opinion poll. *See also* American Institute of Public Opinion.

galvanic process The metalwork that is accomplished for a conventional CD.

galvanic skin response (GSR) A physiological reaction to psychological stimuli, for example, fear or arousal. The intensity of response is measurable by the degree of skin conductivity created by various perspiration rates; used to determine a respondent's reactions to advertising.

galvanometer An electrical transducer used to convert sound waves into light waves for film soundtracks.

game show A radio or television program containing a host, participants selected in advance or from the audience, and a number of prizes won through skill or chance.

GAMIS Graphic Arts Marketing Information Service.

gamma □ A unit of magnetic intensity. □ A measure of the contrast of a film emulsion. It is represented by the slope of a straight line portion of the D log E curve of the emulsion. □ The degree of contrast in a television picture. For television cameras and receivers, the measurement is derived from the relationship of input or output voltage and the incident light or light output.

Gamma Alpha Chi An advertising people's society.

gamma-ferric oxide A magnetizable substance that is frequently used as the magnetizable medium of recording tapes.

gang □ To combine several film negatives into one flat for printing. □ A group of plates or type forms used to run several different printing jobs on one press at the same time. Also called *ganging up* or *gang run.* □ A group of reporters covering the same news event. □ To connect more than one lighting instrument to a stage circuit. □ Two or more switches, potentiometers, and so on, mechanically coupled together and controlled by a single knob.

gang duplication The simultaneous dubbing of an audio- or videotape from a single master.

ganging The coupling of two or more lengths of film in a gang synchronizer for editing.

ganging up *See* gang.

gang punching To enter identical information into a group of punched cards.

gang run *See* gang.

gangster film A film genre that usually depicts the inside story of the underworld and its members in relation to law and order. Often contains chase scenes, shootouts, and so on. Also called a *city western.*

gang synchronizer A film synchronizer with two, three, four, or more sprocket wheels.

gap □ In a magnetic head, the separation between the pole pieces, filled with a nonmagnetic spacing material. Also called a *head gap.* □ The space between two blocks of computer information in a magnetic storage device.

gap height *See* gap length.

gap leakage flux *See* magnetic flux.

gap length The physical distance between adjacent surfaces of the pole tips of a magnetic head measured in the direction of tape travel. Also called *gap height* and *gap width.*

gap loss While a magnetic record is being reproduced, the loss of high frequencies caused by the finite length of the gap in the reproduce head.

gap smear An undesirable physical condition of a video-head assembly characterized by a smearing of pole-tip material over the gap.

gap spacer Nonmagnetic material of known thickness placed in a gap during manufacture.

gap width *See* gap length.

garbage □ An accumulation of meaningless information in a computer storage device. Also called *gibberish* and *hash.* □ *See* garbled. □ *See* grass.

garbage collection A computer slang term meaning the elimination of unnecessary or unwanted data from memory.

garble A transmission breakdown that causes a partial or total loss of a message.

garbled An unintelligible message, often caused by transmission or reception equipment failure. Also called *garbage.*

gate □ The amount of money taken in by the box office or promoter of an event. *See also* box office. □ A general term for an electronic switch. □ The part of a film camera or projector that holds the film in place momentarily for exposure or projection. □ The symbol # that indicates the end of news copy or other matter. *See also* thirty.

gate float An undesirable intermittent movement of film in a camera or projector gate.

gatefold A magazine cover or insert that is larger than the size of the magazine and must be unfolded for viewing.

gatekeeper □ An individual who controls the flow of information. □ A reporter, editor, or other individual who decides whether to broadcast or print news stories.

gate mask A rectangular aperture in a camera or projector defining the film area to be exposed or projected.

gate pass A written authorization for an individual to enter a motion picture studio.

gate pressure The force exerted on film in a camera or projector gate to hold it in the proper position.

gateway A computer program that allows information from one system to be transferred to another dissimilar system; one videotex system to another.

gathering The process of assembling the signatures of a book or other publication in the proper order for binding. Cf. collate.

gathering machine A machine used to assemble the leaves of a book.

gathering table A surface on which book sections are laid out to be gathered.

gator clamp *See* gator grip.

gator grip A strong metal clamp with an alligator-type holder used to attach small luminaires, set pieces, cue cards, and so on, to pipes, flats, furniture, and so on. Also called a *gator clamp.*

GATT General Agreements on Tariffs and Trade. An intergovernmental organization.

gauffered *See* goffered.

gauge □ A device used for determining the length of a page. Also called a *page gauge.* □ *See* line gauge. □ The format of the film stock, i.e., super 8, 16 mm, or 35 mm.

gauge banding A type of banding characterized by a spurious chrominance variation within a headband and caused by a transverse variation in tape thickness. Cf. hue banding, noise banding, and saturation banding.

gauge pin A metal protrusion attached to a tympan to hold paper in place.

gauss The metric system electromagnetic unit of magnetic induction, equal to one line of flux per square centimeter.

gauze □ A material used for light diffusion. *See also* butterfly. □ In make-up, a material used for wig bases and moustache and beard foundations.

Gavel Award An award given by the American Bar Association to organizations that accurately inform the public of the vital role played by law enforcement agencies, the legal profession, and the courts.

gawkocracy A slang term for the television audience.

gaze motion The movement of a viewer's or reader's eyes. Cf. eye camera.

gazette A periodical publication; a newspaper.

Gc/S Gigacycles per second. *See* gigahertz.

GE Gilt edge.

geared head *See* gear head.

gear head A type of camera head using gears and cranks for pan and tilt movements. Also called *geared head.*

gear shift A slang term for the lever used to change the speed of a turntable.

gel □ An abbreviation for *gelatin.* A common color medium made by dyeing thin sheets of a glutinous material. Also spelled *jell* and called *jelly. See also* color media. □ Filled with artificial blood, gelatin capsules may be used in fight scenes. Also spelled *gelatine.*

gelatin □ A natural protein from animal hides and bones used as a binder in film emulsions. □ *See* gel.

gelatin printing *See* hectograph and photogelatin.

gem A small type size, approximately 4 points.

gemini A type of combined film and television camera using a common taking lens and a beam splitter to record an image on both tape and film at the same time.

gen *See* jenny.

gender changer A connector having two male or two female ends. Normally called an *adapter.*

general advertising *See* national advertising.

general American The speech sounds and patterns used by the majority of educated Americans. The typical sound of a radio or television network announcer or newscaster. Also called *network standard.*

general assignments reporter A reporter without a specific beat, but one who covers a mix of government, police, features, business, and so on.

general continuity link The theme or plot of a program. Cf. interior continuity link.

general damages *See* damages.

general direction The gross movements and action given by a director to a performer as opposed to interpretation and nuances.

general editor An editor who supervises other editors.

general editorial magazine A consumer magazine edited for a broad, general readership.

general extra An extra player in motion pictures performing any ordinary business, including normal action, gestures, and facial expressions.

general illumination Diffuse illumination of large areas with floodlights or striplights.

general interest magazine A magazine that contains information with a broad appeal for a wide range of readers. Also called a *general magazine*.

general magazine *See* general interest magazine.

general manager (GM) □ The chief executive officer of a broadcast station, either the licensee or the person responsible only to the licensee for the day-to-day operation of the station. Cf. station manager. □ The chief executive officer of a cable television system. Also called a *system manager*. □ The business manager of a publication.

general-purpose computer A computer designed to handle a wide range of applications.

general-purpose interface (GPI) A computer interface designed to control a number of external devices such as video switchers, audio recorders, and character generators.

general rate *See* national rate.

general release The simultaneous exhibition of numerous copies of a motion picture in theatres in widely dispersed locations. Cf. first run.

general sales manager (GSM) The individual in charge of the sales department of a radio or television station.

generation □ A term used to describe the history of tape or film to the original tape or film. It is always preceded by an ordinal number greater by one than the number of copying steps the tape or film represents. For example, an original recording is a first-generation tape; the first copy is a second-generation tape, and so on. There is, however, disagreement in usage. Many refer to the first duplicate made as a first-generation dupe or dub rather than second-generation. *See also* dub and dupe. □ Used with the correct ordinal number, the copy itself. □ A new development that derives from an earlier concept; as with a second-, third-, and so on, generation computer.

generator A device used to convert mechanical energy into electrical energy. Often used as a remote power supply.

generic Noting or pertaining to a product or service category as a whole.

generic advertising Print or broadcast advertisements that are specific about the product or service but do not mention local outlets where the product or service may be obtained.

generic code A set of unique symbols used in a word processor manuscript to label chapter titles, subheads, paragraphs, italics, and so on, for later conversion to typesetting codes.

generic lead A newspaper lead that begins with background or secondary information.

generic promo A radio or television promo that encourages the audience to stay tuned to the station, without specifically promoting a particular series, episode, personality, and so on.

generic tape An audio- or videotape that is prepared for use by a number of different stations in different markets. Each station may then insert its own ID, commercials, and so on.

geneva movement *See* maltese cross.

genlock □ An electronic device used to interlock sync generators. □ A capability planned for CDI-X in which the background plane will be synchronized to an external video source, allowing the CD-I application to interact with external video information.

genre A distinctive group or type of motion pictures, television programs, books, and so on, categorized by style, form, purpose, and so on. Examples include western, gangster, documentary, situation comedy, and gothic novel.

geodemographics A contraction of *geography* and *demographics*; the demographics of individuals or groups who reside in the same geographical area. Cf. psychographics.

geographic edition An edition of a publication designed for a particular geographic area.

geographics Any method of subdividing a mailing list based on geographic or political subdivisions (ZIP codes, sectional centers, cities, counties, states, or regions).

geographic split run A periodical advertising split run determined by geographical areas of distribution.

geographic weight *See* weight.

geometry error Any time base or velocity error caused between the recording and playback of a videotape by dimensional or positional changes.

George K. Polk Awards Awards given by Long Island University to recognize distinguished achievement in journalism.

geostationary orbit (GSO) The circular orbit followed by a geostationary satellite. Also called a *Clarke orbit.*

geostationary satellite (GSS) A geosynchronous satellite whose circular and direct orbit lies in the plane of the earth's equator and that thus remains fixed relative to the earth; by extension, a satellite that remains approximately fixed relative to the earth. Also called a *geosynchronous satellite. See also* synchronous satellite.

geostationary satellite orbit The orbit in which a satellite must be placed to be a geostationary satellite.

geosynchronous orbit (GSO) *See* geostationary orbit.

geosynchronous satellite *See* geostationary satellite.

German Expressionism A style of filmmaking common in the 1920s, characterized by dramatic lighting, distorted decor, and inner feelings instead of objective reality.

germanium A metallic element semiconductor used in transistors and diodes.

Gertrude A slang term for a large studio crane.

gestalt A psychological structure constituting a functional unit.

gesture The use of all or part of a performer's body to convey an idea, express an emotion, and so on.

getaway □ A passageway behind a set used by performers. □ Steps behind a set leading down to stage floor level.

ghetto blaster A slang term for a large, portable radio and cassette tape player. Also called a *box.*

ghost □ A foggy image produced by a lens defect. □ A soft photographic background. □ An image of the reverse side of a page caused by too much ink or thin paper. Also called *ghosting.* □ *See* ghost writer. □ The intentional double exposure of film to produce a second, paler image. □ A shadowy or weak image in the received television picture, offset to either the left or right of the primary image, the result of transmission conditions that create secondary signals that are received earlier or later than the main or primary signal. Also called a *double image* and *ghost image.* □ *See* phantom load.

ghost image *See* ghost.

ghosting □ The process of creating a double image, usually by double exposure or double printing. May also be accomplished on videotape. □ *See* ghost.

ghost load *See* phantom load.

ghost writer A person who writes so that someone else may take the credit for the work.

gHz Gigahertz.

GI Gross impression. *See* gross impressions.

gibberish *See* garbage.

gibbing *See* tongue.

gift buyer A person who buys a product or service for another.

gifts-in-kind Donations made to public broadcasting stations consisting of equipment, supplies, or other things of value.

gig A single paid engagement for a musician.

giga A prefix for one billion, as in a gigawatt, meaning one billion watts.

gigahertz (gHz) One billion hertz or cycles per second.

GIGO Garbage in/garbage out. The principle that the results of a program, experiment, and so on, will be only as good as the input.

gilt edge (GE) A book edge covered with gold leaf. *See also* full gilt.

gimbal A camera head support that allows a camera to remain parallel to the ground even though the camera mount is tipped.

gimcrack A typographic ornament.

gimme The pronunciation of the words "give me" in many situations; as in "gimme a level," "gimme a long shot," and so on.

gimmick □ Any device, idea, or trick used to attract attention. Also called a *hook*. □ Any characteristic of a radio or television program that sets it apart from other similar programs. □ An attention-getting device, sometimes three-dimensional, attached to a direct mail printed piece. □ A plot device used to resolve a situation.

gingerbread Artwork characterized by showy, overdone decoration.

GIs Gross impressions.

give A director's command to talent to put forth more effort.

giveaway □ A radio or television program that offers prizes to contestants. □ Anything distributed free for promotional purposes. *See also* premium.

give me *See* gimme.

gizmo A slang term applied to an object when the correct name is unknown. Similar to *gadget*.

gladiator A large, high-intensity, carbon arc spotlight.

glare To shine with brilliant reflected light.

glassine □ A thin, transparent paper. □ A method of making opaque letters with bronze powder on glassine paper to simulate a film positive. Also called a *bronze proof*.

glass master An optical master disc produced by exposing a photosensitive coating on a glass substrate to a laser beam, then developing the exposed coating and covering it with a silver coating. *See also* CD-disc master and mastering.

glass shot A camera shot taken through glass on which titles or a portion of a scene is painted. Also used as a background. Cf. front projection and rear projection.

G-line A wire with a dielectric coating used in microwave transmission.

glissando A musical tone that slides smoothly from one frequency to another. Often used as musical punctuation. *See also* sting.

glitch □ A form of low-frequency interference appearing as a narrow horizontal bar moving vertically through the television picture. □ Undesirable interference that causes errors in a computer system. □ Sometimes refers to any form of electronic distortion or disturbance.

global A full video screen. Cf. local.

global change A word, spelling, or other change accomplished by searching for and making the desired change in all occurrences of the word, spelling, or other element in a computer word processing document. Also called a *global search and replace*.

global search □ A computer routine that searches for every occurrence of a character sequence, word, or phrase in a text file. □ A search operation performed on a complete file or database. Cf. local search.

global village Marshall McLuhan's term for a world linked by electronic communication so that it becomes a worldwide village.

globe The glass enclosure of an incandescent lamp.

gloccamora A device used to produce the effect of flashing lights or fire.

gloomy beat *See* gloomy run.

gloomy run A reporter's beat that covers hospitals, police stations, and so on. Also called the *gloomy beat*.

glossary A collection or explanation of terms related to a specific subject; usually accompanying a book or other manuscript. In effect, a limited dictionary.

glossy □ A newspaper picture page printed on smooth paper. □ A photograph with a hard, shiny finish printed on smooth paper. Cf. matte.

gloves The white cotton gloves worn by film editors to protect the film from fingermarks and smudges.

glow-and-flow A concept that the act of watching television is the source of entertainment rather than the individual programs watched.

glycerine A syrupy alcohol used for artificial tears.

GM General manager.

Gm A symbol for the system rating of a microphone.

GMT Greenwich mean time.

gnd An abbreviation for *ground*.

GNH Gross night hour.

gobbledegook Slang for stories and scripts filled with incomprehensible jargon, redundancy, and indirect expression.

gobo □ A metal cutout pattern of suitable size to fit in the holder or aperture of an ellipsoidal reflector spotlight. □ A flag, usually opaque, that can be made with diffusing material. An opaque diffusing cookie. *See also* cucoloris. □ A cutout through which a camera may shoot. □ A sound reflector. □ Sound-absorbing material.

God slot A British term for a religious broadcast.

gofer An individual or grip who runs errands and performs other simple tasks, such as "gofer coffee." Also spelled *gopher.*

goffered Embossed or indented book edges.

go hunting A television director's command to a camera operator to find a good shot.

going off A script direction to a performer to speak the lines as he or she is moving off-stage or off-microphone.

going year A period of twelve consecutive months of advertising budgeting for a product or service. Cf. sustaining advertising.

gold A single record that has sold a million copies, or an album that has sold 500,000 copies. Cf. platinum.

Goldberg wedge A tinted gelatin wedge of varying thickness used in sensitometry.

gold book A list of records that have sold a million copies.

Golden Age of Radio Generally, the period from 1926 to 1948, from the advent of networks to the decline of network radio.

golden dimension *See* aspect ratio.

golden hours The hours for which a worker or performer receives pay greater than normal—often double or triple pay after working 12 to 16 hours. Also called *golden time.*

Golden Liberty Bell Award An award given by the Television and Radio Advertising Club of Philadelphia for distinguished service in broadcasting.

Golden Mike Award An award given by the American Legion Auxiliary for the best local radio and best local television programs presented "in the interest of youth."

golden oldies A slang term for the popular records of past years.

Golden Palm A motion picture award presented at the Cannes International Film Festival in France.

Golden Pen of Freedom An award given by the International Federation of Newspaper Publishers (FIEJ).

Golden Quill An award given by the International Society of Weekly Newspaper Editors.

golden rectangle A pleasing shape or layout; based on the Greek notion of beauty. Also called the *golden oblong* and *golden section.*

goldenrod A reddish yellow, opaque paper often used as a backing for negatives.

golden time *See* golden hours.

goldie A slang term for a gold record.

gold level The intermediate rate charge for satellite usage. Cf. bronze level and platinum level.

Gold Medal Award □ An award given by the International Radio and Television Society for "an outstanding contribution to, or achievement in" radio or television. □ An award given by the Broadcasters Promotion Association for creativity, originality, and effectiveness in audience promotion. □ An award given by the Audio Engineering Society for outstanding achievement in audio engineering.

gold record *See* gold.

Gold Screen Awards The awards given by the Television Bureau of Advertising for "outstanding performance in the art of total communication to promote an industry through advertising."

Goldwynism A term used to describe the malapropisms of Hollywood mogul Samuel Goldwyn. So named after Sheridan's Mrs. Malaprop, who was noted for her blundering use of words.

gone to bed A newspaper that has been printed. *See also* goodnight and put to bed.

good copy *See* clean copy. Cf. dirty copy.

good music A radio station music format characterized by instrumental standards or background music.

goodnight The closing of a newspaper news department after the last edition has been put to bed.

goodnight time Broadcast station sign off time.

good will The favor a business has accumulated or earned in a community. Examples include the assets of a radio or television station above the physical property, building, and equipment. Good will might include network affiliation contracts, station image, the license, and so on.

goof Any error or mistake, including beards, bloopers, blows, chokes, flubs, fluffs, and muffs.

gooseneck A flexible microphone support.

gopher *See* gofer.

gorilla A slang term for a highly successful novel, television program, motion picture, actor, and so on. From the motion picture *King Kong*.

gossip A person who writes a gossip column.

gossip column A newspaper column containing inconsequential material—juicy tidbits and idle remarks about people.

Gotham A film term derived from Washington Irving's *Salmagundi* to denote New York City.

Gothic A motion picture or novel characterized by a medieval, fearful atmosphere.

gothic *See* black letter.

go to black A television director's command to fade to black. Could be confused with *take black*.

Gouraud shading A smooth shading algorithm, developed by Henri Gouraud, that averages the light reflectance values of the polygons that make up a model, creating the illusion of a smoothly curving surface.

government channel A cable television channel assigned for use by a local government.

government document Any publication bearing a federal, state, or local government imprint, for example, annual reports, reports, rules and regulations, and so on.

Government in the Sunshine Act The 1976 statute that requires all agencies with two or more persons appointed by the president to hold all meetings open to the public, unless the information being discussed at the meeting is 1 of 10 protected categories. Also called the *Federal Open Meetings Law*.

government-owned stations Radio stations belonging to and operated by the United States and not subject to Sections 301 and 303 of the Communications Act.

governor An electronic or electromechanical device used to control a camera or projector motor so that it runs at a constant speed.

GP Galley proof.

GPI General Purpose Interface.

GPNITL Great Plains National Instructional Television Library.

GPO Government Printing Office. The largest single consumer of paper products in the world.

GPRA Government Public Relations Associations.

graceful degradation In CD-I, degradation of audio or video quality due to increasing error content.

gracing The continuation of a subscription without charge beyond the subscription's expiration date.

gradation The accuracy with which tonal values in a print or television picture are reproduced.

Grade A The coverage or service of a television station within the Grade A contour wherein satisfactory service is received at least 90 percent of the time by at least 70 percent of receivers.

Grade B The coverage or service of a television station within the Grade B contour wherein satisfactory service is received at least 90 percent of the time by at least 50 percent of receivers.

Grade 1 TASO television picture quality standard of excellent. The picture is of extremely high quality. It is as good as one could desire.

Grade 2 TASO television picture quality standard of good. The picture is of high quality and provides enjoyable viewing. Interference is perceptible.

Grade 3 TASO television picture quality standard of passable. The picture is of acceptable quality. Interference is not objectionable.

Grade 4 TASO television picture quality standard of marginal. The picture is poor in quality, and the viewer would prefer to improve it. Interference is somewhat objectionable.

Grade 5 TASO television picture quality standard of inferior. The picture is very poor, but one could watch it. Definitely objectionable interference is present.

Grade 6 TASO television picture quality standard of unusable. The picture is so bad that one cannot watch it.

grader An individual who determines the correct printing values for motion picture film. Also called a *timer.*

gradient The slope of the characteristic curve of a film emulsion and its contrast.

grading The subjective process of determining the proper printing exposure and color balance so that a film negative will produce a correctly exposed print.

grading print *See* answer print.

graduated filter A lens filter whose color or density varies from top to bottom or left to right so that various parts of a scene may be balanced.

graf An abbreviation for *paragraph.* Also abbreviated *graph.*

graftals A class of shapes created by graftal geometry, which recursively subdivides a basic form in a manner similar to fractal geometry, but without the randomness characteristic of fractals.

grain □ The minute silver granules that compose the tonal values of a film image. *See also* fine grain. □ The distribution of grain in a television picture when the source is a photograph or motion picture. □ The direction in which the fibers lie in a sheet of paper. □ The grouping of dots into squares to produce shading in a digital scanning device.

graininess A subjective measure of the appearance of a film emulsion due to the random clumps of silver grains that are visible under normal viewing conditions.

Grammy The awards given by the music recording industry to performers.

gramophone A British term for a record changer, record player, or turntable.

grand entrance A dramatic move onto a set by a performer.

grandfathering □ An exception made for existing enterprises to operate as they have in the past despite new laws or regulations to the contrary. □ The authority issued by the FCC exempting a cable television system (or broadcast station) from new rules and regulations; specifically, rules that would require deletion of television station signals carried by a cable television system before March 1972.

grandfather tape A tape that is two generations removed from the current tape.

grand jury A body of citizens charged with ascertaining whether sufficient evidence exists to bring the accused to trial. Cf. petit jury.

grand manner An elevated, formal, and stylized way of acting in the tradition of the great actors and actresses of the stage and early motion pictures.

grand master A lighting switch or dimmer that controls all switches or dimmers. Also called a *main gain control. See also* master. Cf. group master.

grangerize □ To mutilate books to obtain illustrations for other books. □ To illustrate a book extensively.

grant □ The authorization by the FCC for a construction permit or license for a radio or television station. □ Money given for various purposes, as in grants by the government or the CPB for construction of noncommercial educational television or radio facilities.

grant fee Payment made to the FCC by a licensee upon receipt of an initial license as authorized by Title 31 of the United States Code (USC), Section 483(a).

granulation A visual effect in which the pixels of an image are repeated, reducing its resolution.

grape □ An abbreviation for *grapevine.* □ Time copy. Also called *optional.*

grapevine □ Undated material used as a filler. □ An informal communications network.

graph An abbreviation for *paragraph.* Also spelled *graf.*

graphic □ A visual device of an informative, symbolic, or decorative nature. □ Clearly and vividly written or presented.

graphic arts The arts—such as printing, engraving, painting, and so on—that express ideas through line, color, characters, and other means.

graphic design The design of printed material.

graphic designer An individual who designs graphic materials.

graphic display terminal □ A computer terminal that enables the user to display works in graphic form. □ A computer terminal that enables the user to view a typeset page.

graphic equalizer An audio equalizer that displays a graphic representation of the frequency response curve selected.

graphics □ Illustrative material, as opposed to text. □ All artwork, pictures, charts, and so on, used in television and film production. *See also* character generator, crawl, credits, draw card, drum, flip card, flip stand, hod, graphics generator, pull, pull card, roller title, running title, still, title card, titles, and windmill.

graphics generator A device used to prepare graphics electronically. *See also* character generator.

graphics tablet A digitizing device using a stylus that allows charts, graphs, drawings, and so on, to be converted into digital information for input into a computer.

graphic work *See* pictorial work.

grass Electrical noise in a video picture. Also called *garbage* and *hash.*

grass roots A movement of a heterogeneous group of people having common ideals, opinions, or attitudes.

G rated *See* G.

graticule *See* reticle.

gratuitous Motion pictures that contain scenes of sex or violence that do not further the plot or characterization but are used to attract immature audiences. *See also* obligatory scene.

graver A tool such as an engraver's burin.

graveyard shift A late night shift, often from midnight to 6 a.m. *See also* lobster trick.

gravure □ An abbreviation for *rotogravure.* □ An abbreviation for *photogravure.* □ An intaglio print.

gray back *See* gray base.

gray base A film base made with a gray dye to reduce halation. Also called a *gray back.*

gray card A posterboard card with a gray tone used for taking light-meter readings of known reflectance.

gray out A newspaper page containing only text matter; hence a gray appearance.

gray scale An achromatic slide, test pattern, or other standard test card having 10 steps of gray ranging from white to black.

gray scale overlay strips Strips pasted over the corresponding sections of a resolution chart providing the correct logarithmic reflectance relationship for the scales on the chart.

gray screen *See* black screen.

grazing The quick scanning by viewers of television channels, usually accomplished by the use of remote control devices.

grease paint □ A make-up foundation. □ Make-up in general.

grease pencil A wax-like pencil used to mark tape edit points or crop marks on pictures.

Great Debates Law The Senate Joint Resolution in 1960 that provided for a suspension of the equal opportunities provision of Section 315 of the Communications Act for the two major presidential candidates.

Great Lakes Decision An oft-cited decision made by the FRC in 1928 calling for a "balanced program service."

Great Plains National Instructional Television Library (GPNITL) A producer and distributor of videotaped instructional television courses, film, and kinescopes.

great primer A type size; 18 points.

Greek An advertising artwork legend of meaningless shapes or garbled letters, intended to show the location and size of type to be added later or to test public response to the design alone of a package, advertisement, and so on.

green □ A newly developed photographic print or film that may be scratched easily. □ The motion picture studio department having the responsibility for landscaping, potted plants, flowers, and so on, on sets.

Green Book The listed standards for compact disc interactive (CD-I) systems. An informal name for the CD-I specification.

green copy *See* green proof.

greenery The live or artificial plants, trees, flowers, and so on, that decorate a set.

green eyeshade A green colored eyeshade formerly worn by editors and proofreaders.

green film *See* green.

green gun In a television camera, the electron gun whose beam strikes the phosphor dots emitting the green primary color.

greenman An individual who decorates sets with greenery.

green print *See* green.

green proof An uncorrected proof. Also called *green copy.*

green room A waiting room or lounge for performers.

green scale The same as gray scale, except that green is used.

Greenwich mean time (GMT) The mean solar time of the meridian at Greenwich, England, from which all times are measured. Synonymous with UTC, IAT, universal time, Z time, and zebra time. Now called *Coordinated Universal Time.*

green year A year in which an organization, station, newspaper, and so on, makes money.

grid □ A control element in a vacuum tube. □ *See* lighting grid. □ A television test pattern. □ A crosshatch pattern used for designing layouts.

grid card An advertising rate card in matrix form.

gridiron *See* lighting grid.

gridtronics A concept that would allow subscribers to select the programs they wish delivered to their television receivers.

grille cloth The material covering a baffle or loudspeaker housing.

grip A stagehand in the studio production crew. Also called an *arm swinger, cable puller, dolly pusher, facilities man, floor man, gopher,* and *key grip.*

grip chain A piece of metal chain used to secure movable pieces on a set.

gripper The leading edge on a sheet of paper as it passes through a printing press. Also called a *gripper edge* and *gripper margin.*

gripper edge *See* gripper.

gripper margin *See* gripper.

grippers The mechanical fingers that hold the edge of the paper in a printing press.

groove □ The elongated channel on the base of a piece of type. □ The elongated channel between the covers and the spine of a book binding.

groove angle The angle between the two side walls of a groove measured in a radial plane perpendicular to the disc surface.

groove run A skipped groove in a disc usually caused by a scratch.

groove speed The linear speed of a disc groove with respect to a fixed point such as a stylus tip. Also called *linear velocity.*

gross The amount charged for advertising time or space exclusive of discounts. Cf. net.

gross audience The total number of households or individuals in a television audience viewing for two or more time periods within a schedule of spots or programs without regard to duplication. Cf. cumulative audience.

gross billing □ The cost of print or broadcast advertising before discounts. □ The total amount of advertisers' funds handled annually by an advertising agency.

gross box office receipts The admission paid by the public at the box office.

gross circulation In outdoor advertising, the total number of persons passing an advertisement during a given period, without regard to the direction these persons may be facing. Cf. net circulation.

gross cost The cost for services by an advertising agency, including the agency commission.

gross distributor rental receipts *See* gross receipts.

gross impressions (GIs) □ The sum of the projected quarter-hour radio or television ratings for a given time period or spot schedule. *See also* gross rating points. □ The average number of persons who listen to a radio station multiplied by the number of times the commercial or spot is to run.

gross less An informal expression for the actual cost of an advertisement after a discount from the gross rate.

gross message weight The total gross weighting points received by an advertisement or advertising effort over a stated period of time.

gross night hour (GNH) The card rate for sponsorship of one hour of radio or television prime time; used as a basis for determining other commercial rates.

gross rate The published rate for advertising space or time charged by a communication medium without regard to advertising agency or seller's commissions. Also called *card rate.*

gross rating points (GRP) □ The sum of all rating points achieved for a particular period of time. Used for judging advertising delivery. When projected to actual audiences, these are referred to as gross impressions. Cf. net rating points. □ For outdoor advertising, the daily circulation, because there is duplicate circulation within the first day as contrasted to other media in which duplication usually begins on the second day of the advertising schedule.

gross receipts All money actually earned and received by a distributor of feature films. Also called *gross distributor rental receipts.*

grotesque *See* black letter.

ground □ An electrical connection to earth. □ A voltage reference point in an electric circuit. □ To tie together electrically.

ground absorption The transmission loss of a radio or television signal caused by power dissipation to ground.

ground bulletin A standard outdoor bulletin built on the ground as opposed to one on a building.

ground bus A bus used as an electrical ground.

ground cloth Canvas or other heavy material used to cover a stage or set floor to absorb sound.

ground conductivity The ability of the ground to conduct electromagnetic waves under various soil conditions.

ground cove A scenery piece, usually made of cloth or plywood, that visually merges the foreground into the background. Also called a *merging cove.*

grounded Connected to an electrical conductor.

ground glass A translucent viewing screen in a film camera or television camera viewfinder.

ground loop Feedback noise in an electronic component or system caused by a ground wire.

ground noise Noise in a system due to imperfections such as dust, scratches, and so on. Cf. system noise and unmodulated track.

ground rod A metal spike used to ground a system.

ground row □ Lighting strips aimed up from the base of a cyclorama or drop. □ A low partition placed in front of a cyclorama or flat on a set to give the illusion of depth and/or hide cables, wires, and so on, from the camera or audience.

ground station A transmitting and receiving station for satellites.

ground wave A low-frequency radio wave that travels along the earth's surface. Cf. direct wave, reflected wave, and sky wave.

ground wire A wire from an electrical component or system to a ground.

groundwood paper A paper, such as newsprint, made from groundwood pulp. Cf. chemical paper.

groundwood pulp Paper made by an inexpensive, mechanical method as opposed to a chemical process. Also called *mechanical pulp.* Cf. chemical pulp.

group □ A collection of sorted data records. □ A number of persons who are physically contiguous. Cf. mass.

Group A, B, C, D, E, F, G, H channels Channels used for cable television relay service as specified in Title 47 of the *Code of Federal Regulations* (CFR), paragraph 78.18.

group advertising Advertising by a group of independent retailers, often members of a voluntary chain.

group audience An audience that is assembled in one place. *See also* mass audience.

group delay The rate of change of phase with frequency.

group discount A discount offered to advertisers who buy time on group-owned radio or television stations.

group fader A fader that controls several others. Also called a *submaster fader.*

grouping The nonuniformity in spacing between the grooves of a disc caused by irregular motion on the recording lathe feed screw.

group interview An informal interview conducted for research purposes by a moderator.

group libel Libel of a small group of persons, usually less than 100. Large groups cannot normally successfully sue for libel.

group master A lighting switch or dimmer that controls only one set of switches or dimmers. *See also* master. Cf. grand master.

group ownership Two or more broadcasting stations or cable systems owned by the same individual or company. *See also* multiple ownership. Cf. cross-channel affiliation.

group quarters Residences of nine or more unrelated individuals. For example, persons living in college dormitories, homes for the aged, military barracks, rooming houses, hospitals, and institutions.

group shot A camera shot of several persons. Also, depending on the number in the group, a three-shot, four-shot, and so on.

Group W The name given to the radio and television stations owned by the Westinghouse Corporation.

GRP Gross rating points.

GSM General sales manager.

GSO Geostationary (or geosynchronous) orbit.

GSR Galvanic skin response.

GSS Geostationary (or geosynchronous) satellite.

GTS □ Geostationary technology satellite. □ Global telecommunications system.

guarantee □ A pledge of satisfaction made by the seller to the buyer and specifying the terms under which the seller will make good his or her pledge. □ The minimum amount of money required by union contract to be paid to an employee regardless of the actual time worked. □ A commitment from a medium assuring an advertiser of an agreed upon rate or audience level.

guard band □ The space between adjacent recorded tracks on a tape. □ A narrow band of frequencies between channels to prevent interference.

guarded A book section that is strengthened with cloth strips.

guide □ An overlay used in animation that indicates the positioning of the artwork, camera movement, or both. □ A manual or handbook that is used to explain filmed or taped educational materials. □ A mechanism that serves to hold a tape, film, and so on, in proper position. □ Any transport element whose function is to control the tape's location in the tape path, either transversely or perpendicularly. □ A publication that lists radio or television programs. □ An abbreviation for *vacuum guide.* □ To function as a guide.

guide height □ In quadruplex recording, the location of a guide relative to the reference plane. □ The displacement of a guide from its correct location, in a direction perpendicular to the reference plane. Often called *guide height error.*

guideline □ A drawing, pencil mark, or other indication of movement in animation, voiceovers, looping, and so on. □ An identifying name given to a story. Also called a *catchline* and *slug.*

guide number A figure used to calculate the proper f stop opening for a lens when flash is being used.

guide position □ In quadruplex recording, the location of a guide in the two directions perpendicular to tape motion. □ The location of the vacuum guide in the direction perpendicular to the tape neutral plane. □ The control that affects the guide position.

guide relief That portion of a guide surface that is recessed away from the tape.

guide rollers Wheels used in cameras, tape recorders, turntables, and so on, that serve to align film, tape, or moving parts.

guide servo In quadruplex recording, a servo mechanism that senses signal errors resulting from improper guide position and moves the guide to minimize these errors.

guide sheet A schedule outlining the details of a television production.

guide track *See* scratch track.

guild Generally, a union of performing artists, such as the Screen Actors Guild, American Federation of Radio and Television Artists, Directors Guild of America, and so on. May also be a nonunion association of persons interested in and associated with a particular profession.

guillemet A French quotation mark.

guillotine □ A paper or engraving cutter. □ A film splicer that uses clear or opaque pressure-sensitive tape. Cf. hot splicer.

gulp A slang term for a group of computer bytes.

gun *See* electron gun.

gun microphone *See* shotgun microphone.

Gunning formula A technique for assessing the ease with which a text may be read. It calls for measuring average sentence length, verb force, proportion of familiar and abstract words, and percentage of personal references and long words. Cf. Cloze procedure and Flesch formula.

Gutenberg Fifteenth century printer credited with the invention of movable type: Johann Gutenberg.

gutter □ The margin between facing pages. Also called a *back margin.* □ *See* river.

gutter bleed Printed matter that covers the gutter as opposed to edge bleed.

gutter position An advertising position beside the gutter on a page of a periodical.

guy wire A rope made up of a number of strands of high-strength steel wires used to reinforce an antenna tower or mast.

GW GigaWatt.

G-Y The green minus *Y,* or luminance, signal in a color television camera.

gyro An abbreviation for *gyroscope* and *gyroscopic.*

gyro head A camera head using a built-in gyroscopic flywheel to dampen any intermittent movement of the camera mount. Also called a *gyro stabilizer.*

gyro stabilizer *See* gyro head.

H

H □ FM. An FCC file-number prefix. □ Halt. □ Henry. □ Hexadecimal. □ Horizontal antenna polarization. □ Hyperfocal distance. □ Magnetic field strength.

Haas effect The result wherein a listener hears only the closest loudspeaker, if two loudspeakers are radiating equally.

HAAT Height above average terrain. *See* antenna height above average terrain.

hack A hired writer; usually willing to accept any assignment for money. Also called a *word jobber* and *word slinger.*

hacker A slang term for a person who is knowledgeable about sophisticated uses of computers.

hackle A make-up tool used for combing or carding skeins of hair.

hack writer *See* hack.

hair check A preliminary inspection of a camera lens and body for foreign matter such as lint and dust.

hairdresser An individual who styles and dresses performer's hair before and during filming or taping. Also called a *hair stylist.*

hair light *See* back-light.

hairline An extremely thin line or type rule.

hairline box A newspaper or magazine box set off by hairlines.

hairline register The exact superimposition of color plates for proper printing.

hair space A very thin space used to justify and space type.

hair stylist *See* hairdresser.

halation □ The halos or ghostlike images caused when a bright light is reflected from the film base to the emulsion. May be eliminated by the use of antihalation backing. □ The halos, streaks, and flares in a television picture caused by intense light entering the lens. Also called a *halo effect.*

half apple An apple box 18 by 12 by 6 inches.

half binding A book binding in which the material for the corners and back are different from the rest of the binding. Also called *half bound.*

half bound *See* half binding.

half broad A 1000-watt floodlight. *See also* luminaire.

half chase A chase used to make up a tabloid page.

half cloth A book binding having a cloth back and paper-covered boards.

half diamond *See* inverted pyramid.

half double A rule half as wide as a column.

half duplex A transmission circuit in which communication between two points takes place in one direction at a time. Cf. full duplex and simplex.

half inch A size of videotape used in home videotape recorders and, increasingly, in industrial and broadcast television.

half-lap The superimposition of a television picture that is held for a period of time.

half leather A book binding that has a leather back and cloth-covered boards.

half-page spread An arrangement for editorial matter or an advertisement consisting of the upper or lower half of each of two facing pages.

half run *See* half showing.

half scrim *See* scrim.

half showing A transit advertising contract that requires a card to be placed on every other bus, streetcar, and so on, in a given area. Also called a *half run.* Cf. full showing and quarter showing.

half-silvered mirror A mirror sometimes used in a multiplexer to perform the same function as a prism.

half stick Anything set in half-column width.

half title □ A book page containing the book title only; usually the first page of the book. Also called a *bastard title* and *fly title.* □ The first page of a book section. □ A book title placed on the first page of a chapter.

halftone □ A technique for reproducing pictures by photographing them through a screen wherein the image is formed by small dots of varying sizes. □ A printing plate used to make a halftone. □ A picture made by the halftone process.

halftone block A copper or zinc printing block used for halftones.

halftone blowup An enlargement made from a halftone negative; because the halftone dots are also enlarged, the effect is a rather coarse one.

halftone negative A photographic negative exposed through a halftone screen; used in preparing a halftone print or printing plate.

halftones The intermediate shades of gray between highlights and shadows.

halftone screen A grid of fine horizontal and vertical lines used in making halftones.

half track The combination of both optical and magnetic tracks on a sound film.

half track recorder An audio recorder with two heads for stereo recording or a head covering only the top 40 percent of the tape for mono recording. Also called a *dual track, twin track,* and *two track recorder.* Cf. full track recorder and quarter track recorder.

half track tape Quarter-inch audio tape that is physically identical to full track or quarter track tape, but only half of which is used to record sound; stereo in the same direction, mono in opposite directions.

Hall of Fame Award An award given by the Broadcast Pioneers to deceased persons who made an outstanding contribution to broadcasting.

halo A black aureole surrounding excessively bright regions and vice versa in a television picture; characteristic of the image orthicon. Also called *fringing.* Cf. halation.

halo effect □ A subjective reaction to an individual feature of an advertisement or product, conditioned by attitudes regarding the whole. □ *See* halation.

halogen Any of the elements of the chemical family of fluorine, chlorine, bromine, iodine, and astatine used in conjunction with silver in film emulsions.

halogen lamp A lamp made with halogen gas to reduce the blackening of the glass and retain the same color temperature throughout the life of the lamp.

halogen metal iodide (HMI) lamp An efficient halogen lamp that produces daylight color temperature light.

halo light *See* back-light.

halt (H) An instruction that stops the execution of a computer program.

ham □ A performer who overacts. □ An amateur radio operator.

hamfest A discussion held by performers after a radio or television program.

ham it To overact. Also called *bluster.*

hammer A short headline, usually in large type, placed above a regular headline.

Hamming code A method of checking for errors by comparing transmission and reception bits. Named after its inventor.

hammocking A television programming strategy wherein a new or weak program is placed between two strong programs in order to increase its ratings. Cf. tent polling.

hand art Illustrative material exclusive of photographs.

handback A British term for an outcue.

handbill A printed advertising sheet, usually distributed by hand. Also called a *flyer* and *throwaway.*

handbook A reference book for a particular subject.

handcam An abbreviation for a *hand-held camera.*

hand camera A relatively lightweight hand-held camera.

hand composition Type set by hand, as opposed to type set by machine. Also called *hand set* and *hand stuck.*

hand control A hand-operated device for manipulating a screen display. *See also* joystick and mouse.

hand cranked An old style of mechanical camera mechanism driven by a tightly wound spring.

hand cue A visual cue given to a performer by a director, floor manager, or other crew member.

H and D curve *See* characteristic curve.

handgrip A hand-held camera handle, often shaped to fit a human hand.

hand-held □ Any equipment, such as a camera, luminaire, or microphone, used without mechanical support. □ A camera shot taken without the benefit of a tripod or other mechanical support. Sometimes used to create the feeling of reality. □ An illustration or graphic held by a performer as it is shown on camera.

Handie Talkie A proprietary name for a hand-held two-way radio.

h and j Hyphenation and justification. The computer codes used in typesetting to automatically hyphenate and justify text.

handlaid *See* handmade paper.

handle A slang term for an amateur radio operator's name.

hand lettering Lettering done with a pen or brush as opposed to lettering done with metal or other type.

handmade paper Paper made from linen or other fibers a sheet at a time. Also called *handlaid paper.*

hand model An individual whose hands are the only visible part of the body that appear in a commercial.

handout A free film, tape, news or publicity release, and so on.

hand press A mechanically operated press as opposed to an electrically operated press.

hand prop A small item carried by an actor or used as set dressing. *See also* prop(s).

handset *See* headset.

hand set *See* hand composition.

handshaking The interaction between sending and receiving components of an electronic system such as a computer.

hands on Practical or actual experience as opposed to theoretical.

hand stuck *See* hand composition.

hand tooling The hand finishing of a printing plate to bring out highlights or otherwise improve reproduction quality.

hand type *See* foundry type.

handy-looky A slang term for a portable video camera.

hanger □ A stainless steel frame used to hold sheet film for development. □ *See* drophead.

hanger iron A piece of stage hardware with a ring at one end.

hanging indent *See* hanging indention.

hanging indentation *See* hanging indention.

hanging indention A stylistic device wherein the first line of a paragraph is printed full width and subsequent lines are indented from the left. Similar to *flush and hang.* Also called a *hanging indent* and *hanging indentation.*

hanging microphone Any microphone hung from a ceiling, lighting grid, and so on.

hanging punctuation Punctuation that overruns the right-hand margin.

hangover □ The blurring of a television picture in the direction opposite from the image movement. □ Blurred bass notes from a loudspeaker. Also called *tailing.*

hang up □ To terminate a telephone conversation. □ A situation in which a computer program stops and fails to continue its operation, or continues to perform the same command repeatedly.

happy news A radio or television news style characterized by informal banter between newscasters and by light news and features. *See also* infotainment.

happy talk The talking that takes place between or among anchors on a newscast. *See also* happy news.

hard Excess contrast in a television picture or film negative. Also called *hard image* and *hardness.*

hardback *See* hardbound.

hardbanding □ A tape fault characterized by variable thickness or variable elasticity across the width of the tape. Also called *hardcore.* □ The variation in recovered RF signal caused by such a fault.

hardbound A cloth-bound book as opposed to a paperbound book. Also called *hardback.*

hard copy A permanent, printed paper copy from a computer printer, as opposed to a video display copy. A computer printout. Cf. soft copy.

hardcore □ The type of film or videotape pornography that contains explicit and graphic sexual acts. Cf. softcore. □ *See* hardbanding.

hard cyc *See* cyclorama.

hard disk A rigid computer disk that is either sealed inside a mass storage device or loaded and unloaded into a hard disk system. A hard disk is capable of storing significantly more data than a floppy disk.

hard edge A photograph or illustration with distinct outlines. Cf. vignette.

harden A television director's command to a camera operator to sharpen focus.

hardener A chemical, such as formalin or sodium sulfate, used to make film or prints more resistant to scratching and abrasion.

hard focus A lens image that is defined as sharply as possible.

hard glass halogen lamp A tungsten-halogen lamp with a bulb of hard glass rather than of quartz or vycor. Due to hard glass fabrication techniques, these lamps generally cost less than a similar tungsten-halogen lamp and will have nearly equivalent performance. They are usually limited to low voltage, low wattage types.

hard hyphen A hyphen that is part of a word as opposed to an end-of-line hyphen. Cf. soft hyphen.

hard image *See* hard.

hard interconnect □ A linking of cable television systems by microwave, satellite, or hard wiring. Cf. soft interconnect. □ A system, series of components, and so on, that is hard wired.

hard lead A story lead that contains factual material as opposed to introductory or background material. Cf. soft lead.

hard light A light that produces hard or sharply defined shadows, such as light from an ellipsoidal spotlight. Cf. soft light.

hardness □ The degree to which talent overplays a role. □ *See* hard.

hard news Reports of immediate value as contrasted to feature stories and background material. Cf. soft news.

Hard Rock Somewhat derogatory reference to the ABC headquarters building in New York. *See also* Black Rock and Thirty Rock.

hard scrambling The use of sophisticated techniques to encode messages, programs, and so on. Cf. soft scrambling.

hard sell A radio or television commercial characteristically delivered in a rapid, forceful, and vigorous manner usually requesting listeners or viewers to buy *now*. Also called a *slug commercial*. Cf. soft sell.

hard shadow A single, definitive shadow; often produced by hard light.

hard sound The sound produced by a room with highly reflective walls.

hard ticket A ticket that has been paid for; a reserved seat ticket. Cf. comp.

hardware The physical equipment and components of a broadcast station, cable television system, printing plant, and so on, including antennas, cables, cameras, computers, presses, transmitters, and other pieces of equipment. Cf. software.

hardware net A distribution network.

hard wired □ Components that are permanently connected as opposed to components that are connected by plugs and jacks. □ A nonprogrammable computer that can perform only those tasks for which it is designed.

harlequin Any of various simple typographic ornaments.

harmful interference Interference that endangers the functioning of a radio navigation service or of other safety services or seriously degrades, obstructs, or repeatedly interrupts a radio communication service operating in accordance with International Radio Regulations.

harmonic A sinusoidal wave, the frequency of which is a multiple of the fundamental frequency.

harmonic distortion Nonlinear distortion characterized by the appearance, in the output, of harmonics of the fundamental input frequency. Cf. intermodulation distortion.

harmonic filter A network of capacitances and inductances tuned to suppress an undesired harmonic.

harmonics The branch of acoustics that deals with the physical characteristics of musical sounds.

harness A group of wires or cables tied together.

harsh A strident, unpleasant, or otherwise disagreeable voice or other sound.

Hartford experiment A broadcast pay television experiment begun in 1962 in Hartford, Connecticut.

hash □ *See* garbage. □ *See* grass.

hashing The interference caused by the mixing of two AM radio signals on the same or adjacent frequencies.

hash session A meeting held between the production personnel and the talent to discuss last-minute changes.

Hawthorne effect Bias introduced into research because of the subjects' knowledge that they are part of an experiment.

Hays office Motion picture industry self-regulatory organization formed in 1922 and named after former Postmaster General Will H. Hays, the first head of the MPAA.

haywire Any equipment that is not functioning properly.

hazard pay The additional remuneration earned by stuntpersons for taking a risk. Crew members may be entitled to hazard pay if their work requires a degree of risk.

haze filter A lens filter used to reduce blue and ultraviolet light and therefore the haze in the atmosphere.

hazel An abbreviation for *Hazeltine*, an electronic color film analyzer.

HB Highband.

h/b Hexadecimal to binary conversion.

hbk An abbreviation for *hardback*.

HBO Home Box Office.

h/d Hexadecimal to decimal conversion.

HDDR High density digital recording.

HDEP High definition electronic production.

HDTV High definition television. Also called *HQTV*.

head □ An abbreviation for *headline*. □ An electromagnetic transducer that reads, erases, or records information, as in a tape recorder. *See also* erase head, magnetic head, playback head, and recording head. □ The film projector mechanism that transports the film and produces illumination. □ The start or beginning of a tape or film. □ The top of a page. Cf. foot. □ The title of an article or other writing. □ An abbreviation for *heading*. □ *See* head margin. □ A title or heading of a chapter or division of a manuscript. □ *See* camera head. □ A transducer for converting electric currents into magnetic field patterns for storage on magnetic media, or for reconverting magnetic patterns so stored into electric signals, or for erasing such stored magnetic patterns. □ The body of a film camera.

head alignment The positioning of the record and the reproduce head on a tape recorder so that their gaps are mutually parallel and perpendicular to the path of travel of the tape.

head and tail The top and bottom of a book.

head assembly The heads and rotating drum that compose the read/write mechanism of a videotape recorder.

headband □ In quadruplex recording, a portion of the reproduced picture, 16 or 17 scan lines in height in a 525-line system, that is produced by a single head-pass along one video track. □ The visible picture fault characterized by a difference between that portion of the picture and adjacent portions. □ A printed or engraved border at the top of a page. □ A strip of material glued or sewn to the back of a book for appearance. Cf. tailband.

head channel The signal path assigned to a given magnetic head. In multiple head systems, such as quadruplex and certain helical systems, outputs of the several head channels are eventually combined to provide a continuous signal.

head clogging The accumulation of debris on an audio or video head, the usual result of which is a reduction of signal during playback or possible failure to record during the record mode.

head contouring *See* contouring.

head degausser *See* head demagnetizer.

head demagnetizer An electrical device for removing magnetism from a head. Also called a *head degausser*.

head drum The rotating mechanism that contains the video heads of a videotape recorder or player. *See also* drum.

head end □ The control center of a cable television system, where incoming signals are amplified, converted, and routed, and where cablecasting is originated. □ The electronic equipment located at the origination point of a transmitting system.

header □ A title or document identification printed at the top of a page. Cf. footer. □ Information, such as the writer's name, date, slug, and so on, placed at the top of a news story. □ In CD-ROM or CD-I, that part of a data sector containing the absolute sector address and mode byte. A header contains four bytes, indicating minutes, sector, sector number, and whether sector is mode 1, mode 2, or mode FF.

header record A computer list of the names given headers.

header sheet A computer listing of the available type fonts, sizes, lines per inch, column widths, and so on, for use in page make-up.

head gaffer The electrician in charge. *See also* gaffer.

head gap ☐ The space between the poles of a magnetic head. *See also* gap. ☐ The distance between the read/write head and a disk, drum, tape, and so on.

heading ☐ A title or other matter standing at the head of a chapter, subdivision, and so on. ☐ The largest display matter of an advertisement, setting the theme of the copy.

head leader *See* academy leader.

headletter The type used for headlines.

head librarian *See* librarian.

head life The span of time that a head or head assembly will operate in normal tape contact before the head or heads are worn down beyond the point of usability.

headline ☐ A caption, label, or other information set in large type above a story, article, editorial, and so on. ☐ A line at the top of a page containing the name of the chapter, author, page number, and so on. ☐ A short phrase or sentence used to introduce a broadcast news story. Cf. slug.

headline newscast A brief radio or television newscast of important events.

headliner ☐ A performer who is given top or star billing. ☐ *See* headwriter. ☐ A machine used to make large headlines.

Headliner Awards Awards given by the National Headliners Club for "consistently outstanding" news coverage, editorials, and community service.

headline schedule *See* head schedule.

headlinese Overused words or phrases in headlines.

head margin The margin at the top of a book page. Also called a *head.*

headnote ☐ A brief passage at the beginning of a chapter or other subdivision of a book that introduces the author or subject matter. ☐ A summary of a legal case or administrative agency decision printed at the top of the full text.

head of the desk The person in charge of a news desk.

head on An outdoor advertising structure built so that all traffic approaches perpendicular to the face of the structure.

head on shot A shot of a performer or performers moving directly toward the camera.

head optimization ☐ A procedure by which the signal current driving the record head is adjusted to the proper value. ☐ The condition obtained by such a procedure.

head out A film or tape with its head at the outside of the reel ready for projection or playback. Also called *head up.* Cf. tail out.

headpass The single excursion of a video head along a video track.

headphones A pair of electroacoustic transducers worn over the ears. Also called *cans.* Cf. headset.

headpiece A decoration placed at the beginning of a book chapter. Cf. tailpiece.

headroom ☐ The difference between the maximum recording level indicated on a VU meter and the point at which a tape actually becomes overloaded. ☐ The distance between the top of the framed subject or object and the top of the television or film picture.

head schedule A display of various headline types; used to select the proper size for a newspaper headline. Also called a *hed sked* and *headline schedule.*

headset A control room to studio intercommunication device worn on the head; consisting of headphones, mike, headband, and connecting cord. Also called a *handset.*

head sheet A photograph of a performer used for publicity purposes. Also called a *mug shot.* Cf. head shot.

head shot A photograph or television picture of a performer's head or head and shoulders. Also called *face shot* and *mug shot.* Cf. head sheet.

head slug The blank space that separates a headline from the text.

head stack A group of heads mounted together on a post, usually with their gaps on a common line perpendicular to tape motion.

head switching The transfer of the input terminal of the FM demodulator system from a given video playback head, just before it leaves the tape, to the subsequent video head, just after it has entered the tape.

head switching transient A momentary disturbance in the output video caused by head switching and occurring at a point corresponding to the time of the actual switch.

head to come (HTC) An indication that a story is to be set in type, but that the headline will be written later. Also spelled *hed to kum (HTK).*

head-to-tape speed The relative speed between tape and head during normal record or replay.

head trim A section of film edited from the front of a take. Cf. tail trim.

head unit The transmitting antenna of a microwave system.

head up *See* head out.

headwheel A rotatable wheel with magnetic heads mounted on its rim. This term is usually limited to small rotatable wheels, such as are used in quadruplex recorders. Larger wheels are usually referred to as *drums* or *head drums.*

headwheel servo A servo that controls the rotational velocity and phase of the headwheel in a videotape recorder. *See also* drum servo and rotary head servo.

headwriter A person who composes headlines. Also called a *headliner.*

hearing □ The process of perceiving sound. □ A presentation of testimony before the FCC as required by Sections 303(f) and 326 of the Communications Act in actions involving important actions or opposing interests. □ A legal proceeding in which evidence is heard.

Hearing Examiner *See* Administrative Law Judge (ALJ).

hearsay Second-hand information; information not based upon personal knowledge.

heartbreaker An audition, program, presentation, and so on, made purely on speculation.

heater The filament of a vacuum tube.

heat filter A filter that transmits visible light and either absorbs or reflects infrared in order to reduce the heat of the light beam.

heat sink A metallic base that dissipates the heat generated by a transistor or other semiconductor.

Heaviside layer *See* Kennelly-Heaviside layer.

heavy A casting term for a villain, outlaw, traitor; an antagonist.

heavy-up A brief or temporary increase in advertising activity. Cf. flight.

hectograph A spirit duplicator that produces purple copies. Often called a *ditto.*

hed A variant spelling of *head.* A headline.

hed sked *See* headline schedule.

hed to kum (HTK) *See* head to come.

height The vertical dimension of a television picture or film frame. Cf. width.

height control The vertical size control of a television receiver. *See also* vertical linearity control.

height to paper The standard height of type: 0.9186 inches.

held cel An animation cel that is held for several frames, often while other cels are changed. Also called a *hold* and *hold cel.*

helical Spiral shaped; from *helix,* meaning "spiral."

helical scan A method of video magnetic tape recording that uses one or more rotating video magnetic heads that engage a tape wrapped at least partially around a cylindrical column. The tape path describes a portion of a helix. The recorded video tracks lie at an angle substantially less than 45 degrees with respect to the length of the tape. Usually, one complete television field is recorded as one head passes across the width of the tape. Also called *slant track.* Cf. quadruplex.

helicopter mount A motion damping device for mounting cameras used in helicopters or other moving vehicles.

heliography A process for photoengraving using a polished metal plate, an asphaltic compound, and a high-intensity light source.

helix angle The angle formed between the path of the rotating pole tips and the tape reference edge-guiding elements in a helical scan television tape recorder.

hellbox A scrap box for type that is to be remelted.

hello The initial program used to boot some computer systems.

helmet camera A camera that is built into a helmet. Used in skydiving, skiing, and so on, to produce action shots.

help A special display on a computer that is designed to assist users in understanding the keystrokes necessary to accomplish the desired task.

help code A computer typesetting code used to alert the compositor when no code has been devised for the particular situation.

helps □ An abbreviation for *help wanted ads.* □ Advertising matter supplied to a dealer by a manufacturer.

Helvetica One of the most common typefaces.

HEMA Health Education Media Association.

hemisphere □ An integral part of a incident light meter designed to give ''average'' reading. □ An attachment for a reflected light meter, used to allow incident light readings. Also called a *photosphere.*

henry (H) The metric electromagnetic unit of inductance.

Henry Johnson Fisher Award An award given annually by the Magazine Publishers Association to individuals who contribute to the advancement of the magazine industry.

hero The principal character in a drama, story, poem, and so on. A protagonist having noble qualities.

heroic Anything or anyone larger than life; performer's roles, props, sets, and so on.

heroine A female hero.

herringbone Television picture interference characterized by parallel lines.

hertz (Hz) A unit of frequency equivalent to one cycle per second. Named in honor of Heinrich Hertz (1857–1894), a pioneer in electromagnetic wave research.

Hertzian waves *See* radio waves.

HeSCA Health Sciences Communications Association.

heterodyne To combine two different frequencies together to produce two other frequencies. A discovery by Reginald Fessenden that made possible a significant improvement in radio reception. Also called *beat. See also* superheterodyne. Cf. regenerative.

heterodyne color A system for time-stabilizing the chrominance components of a television signal without stabilizing the luminance components.

heterogeneity The degree to which an audience, population, sample, and so on, differs as to demographic characteristics, attitudes, opinions, and so on. Cf. homogeneity.

heuristic A general rule applicable to artificial language that serves to guide, discover, or reveal approaches to selecting among alternatives.

HEW Health, Education and Welfare, Department of.

hex An abbreviation for *hexadecimal.*

hexadecimal A computer numbering system that uses a base of 16, wherein each number from 0 to 15 can be expressed with one digit.

Heywood Broun Award An award for outstanding journalistic achievement in the spirit of Heywood Broun given by The Newspaper Guild.

HF □ High frequency. □ Hyperfocal.

HFR Hold for release.

HFWB High-frequency wire broadcasting.

HH Households.

HI Human interest.

hiatus □ Sometimes used as a euphemism for a television program that has been canceled. Also called an *out period.* □ The period of time a sponsor may discontinue radio or television advertising; often, the summer months. Also called an *interval.*

hickey □ A slang term for an electrical device. □ A defect on a printing plate.

hi con An abbreviation for *high contrast.*

hidden camera A production technique wherein the camera is not seen by the subject. Often used in making television commercials.

hidden line and hidden surface removal The process of removing those lines or faces of an object that are hidden by the parts of the object that face the viewer.

hidden microphone A production technique wherein a microphone is camouflaged behind props, greenery, furniture, and so on.

hide A camouflaged screen used to hide a camera operator while he or she is photographing wildlife.

HID lamps High-intensity discharge lamps; general lighting lamps of the mercury, metal halide, and high-pressure sodium types.

hierarchical database A graphics database that defines the parts of a scene in relationship to each other such that movements of one part are dependent on or independent of movements of another part.

hi-fi *See* high fidelity.

hi-fi color *See* hi-fi insert.

hi-fi insert A full-page, high-quality, four-color rotogravure advertisement that is preprinted on coated stock and furnished to a newspaper in roll form for insertion during a regular run. *See also* preprint.

hi fi quality In CD-I, the second of five audio quality levels. A bandwidth of 17 kHz is obtained using 8-bit ADPCM at a sampling frequency of 37.8 mHz. Comparable with LP record sound quality.

high-angle shot Any camera shot from an angle higher than eye-level. Also called a *high shot.* Cf. boom shot.

highband (HB) □ Pertaining to those frequencies specified in SMPTE Recommended Practice RP6, Practice HB. □ Pertaining to those recordings made in accordance with Practice HB of RP6, or equipment capable of making those recordings. □ The carrier frequencies that appear on a tape made in accordance with such practices. Cf. lowband. □ Television channels 7 through 13 (174 to 216 mHz).

high band recording A videotape recording made with a 20-mHz bandwidth. Standard on two-inch videotape recorders.

high-budget film A film with a negative cost that equals or exceeds a specific amount; for example, for a prime time television motion picture of 120 minutes or less, the sum of $900,000. In non-prime time, $450,000. Cf. low-budget film.

high comedy Comedy that derives from characterization and dialogue instead of situation.

high contrast □ A television or film picture in which intermediate tonal values are missing. □ A special film used for titles and matte work. □ A harsh lighting style. Cf. high-key lighting.

high definition *See* definition.

High Definition Electronic Production (HDEP) A proposed standard for an advanced television system with 1,125 scanning lines, 60 fields, an aspect ratio of 16:9, and a 90 mHz bandwidth. Often called HDTV.

high-definition television (HDTV) One of the terms sometimes used to include all advanced television (ATV) systems, or especially high-definition electronic production (HDEP).

high-density ethnic area A geographical area containing a relatively great number of black, Hispanic, or other minorities.

high end The treble frequencies of the audio spectrum. Cf. low end.

high-energy tape A tape whose coercivity is greater than that of a normal-coercivity tape, such as chromium dioxide tape.

high fidelity □ The accurate reproduction of sound within the full human hearing range; nominally 16 to 16,000 or 20,000 Hz. □ *See* hi-fi insert.

high frequency (HF) □ The band of frequencies from 3 to 30 mHz. □ Sound frequencies above 15,000 Hz. Also called *highs.*

high-frequency distortion Distortion effects that occur at high frequency. Generally considered as any frequency above the 15,750 line frequency in television.

high-frequency interference Interference effects that occur at high frequencies. Generally considered as any frequency above the 15,750-line frequency in television.

high-gain antenna An antenna that produces a high effective radiated power for a given input.

high-gain screen A projection screen that is capable of producing an extremely bright image.

high hat □ A low camera mount used where a tripod or other mount would be too high. Also called a *top hat. See also* camera mounts. □ *See* funnel.

high impedance A circuit or device in which the impedance is measured in thousands of ohms. Also called *high Z.* Cf. low impedance.

high-intensity arc A high-output carbon arc light.

high key Photographic tones rendered in light to medium grays or colors. *See also* highlight.

high-key lighting □ A type of lighting that, applied to a scene, is intended to produce a picture having gradations falling primarily between gray and white; dark grays and black are present but in limited areas. Intense, overall illumination. Also called *highlighting.* Cf. high contrast and low-key lighting. □ In motion pictures, high-level accent lighting with strong contrast (dark deep shadows with little or no middle gray).

high lead *See* high line.

high level A sound or light level that registers near the top of the scale.

high-level language A computer programming language, such as Basic, COBOL, Fortran, and Pascal, that allows the user to write instructions in almost-English or mathematical notation instead of in machine language. Cf. low-level language.

high-level modulation Modulation produced in the plate circuit of the last radio stage of a system.

highlight □ The brightest portion of a picture. □ To accentuate a portion of a scene by lighting or other effects. □ A high point in a story or drama; a climax.

highlight halftone *See* dropout.

high lighting *See* high-key lighting.

highlight tearing A picture fault characterized by random black streaks starting from the left edge of a highlight and extending toward the right. Usually caused by overmodulation or by excessively fast risetimes in the input signal.

high line A line of metal type that protrudes and prints incorrectly. Also called *high lead.*

high-pass filter An electronic filter that passes frequencies above a specified frequency only.

high pressure An intense, dynamic program, commercial, or performer. Cf. low pressure and soft sell.

high-res An abbreviation for *high resolution.*

high resolution □ The quality of a picture having closely spaced pixels. The closer the pixels, the higher the resolution. □ The degree of detailed visual definition (800 by 600 pixels) that gives readable 80 column text display. □ In CD-I, a display resolution mode of 768 horizontal pixels resolution by vertical 560 pixels—twice as many as normal resolution. Cf. double resolution and low resolution.

high shot *See* high angle shot.

High Sierra group An ad hoc standards group set up to recommend compatible standards for CD-ROM. The group includes representatives from hardware, software, and publishing industries and was named after the hotel in Lake Tahoe where it first met in 1965.

high-speed camera A film camera capable of speeds of from 150 to tens of thousands of frames per second.

high-speed duplication The dubbing of copies from a tape master at more than preferred or supplementary tape speeds.

high-speed duplicator Any apparatus for duplicating a tape at a rate greater than can be achieved by normal playback.

high-speed film □ Film with a high sensitivity to light; one with a high ASA number. □ A film with extra perforations for use in a high-speed camera.

high-speed photography *See* fast motion.

high-speed printer (HSP) □ A computer printer faster than a daisy wheel; a dot matrix, line printer, and so on. □ A continuous contact film printer that is capable of printing several hundred feet of film per minute.

high-speed reader A high-speed device for input into a computer; an optical reader, tape reader, softstrip reader, and so on.

high-speed scanning The viewing of a videotape at a speed faster than normal playback speed.

high spot bulletin A large outdoor advertising structure located at strategic places to permit opportunities for high audience levels of exposure. High spot bulletins are often larger than other bulletins sold in the market.

high technology A general term for complex devices such as computers and electronic equipment used in industry.

high tension Any electrical line or device that carries or uses thousands of volts of electricity.

high-ticket □ Merchandise with a high markup. □ Expensive merchandise.

highway A general term for a signal path.

high Z *See* high impedance.

hill and dale recording *See* vertical recording.

hinge A book joint that connects an insert or leaf to the spine.

hiss A high-frequency noise on a tape recording. *See also* Dolby system.

historical film A motion picture that portrays historical characters, actions, and situations.

hit □ A successful television program, motion picture, novel, and so on. Also called a *box office hit.* □ Any brief audible noise in an audio circuit caused by outside influences. □ *See* flash. □ A command or direction to turn on lights, sound, wind, and so on; as in "hit the lights."

hit black *See* bat blacks.

hitchhiker A commercial announcement, usually for a radio or television program sponsor, broadcast after the end of a program but before other commercials or a station break. Cf. cowcatcher.

hit it A radio or television director's command to start music, sound effects, and so on.

hit list A slang term for a list of possible donors or sponsors for nonprofit or educational programs.

hit radio *See* contemporary hit radio (CHR).

hit the mark A director's instruction to talent to stand at the marked position.

HLL High-level language.

HMI Halogen metal iodide.

hod *See* flip stand.

Hogarth's line A double curve in the shape of an *S* often used in composing camera shots. Also called an *S curve.*

hog calling contest An audition for radio or television announcers.

hold □ To freeze or stop the action. To achieve a hold in animation, the same cel or position of an object is photographed for several frames. □ To retain a television shot for later use. □ To maintain an audio level. □ *See* held cel. □ *See* hold for release.

hold cel *See* held cel.

hold control A potentiometer used to stabilize the horizontal or vertical scanning pulses.

holder A film container for a press camera.

hold for release (HFR) An order not to print or broadcast a news item or press release until a preset time or until authorized. Also called a *hold.*

hold frame *See* freeze frame.

holding A newspaper edition that is waiting for important news to be set in type. *See also* hold the press.

holding fee A residual payment to talent for previous work in a program or commercial that maintains the advertiser's or sponsor's right to use the property later for the same payment.

holding power The ability of a radio or television program to retain its audience.

hold it down A radio or television director's command for an audio console operator to reduce to or maintain the volume at a predetermined level.

holdover □ A motion picture that is exhibited in a given theatre for a period longer than that originally scheduled. □ News or other copy that is not used in one edition but saved for the next. *See also* overset.

holdover audience *See* inherited audience.

hold presses *See* hold the press.

hold the boards To hold the stage.

hold the paper *See* hold the press.

hold the press □ An order not to print a newspaper until important news can be set in type for inclusion in the paper. *See also* holding. □ An order not to admit the press to a meeting, motion picture or television set, and so on.

hold the stage To continue the performances of a production.

hole □ Any unused space in a newspaper or magazine page. □ *See* news hole. □ An intentional or inadvertent erasure of sound on a soundtrack.

Hollerith The standard punched card originated by Dr. Herman Hollerith.

hollow back A book back bound with a heavy paper between the spine and the cover.

Hollywood The motion picture headquarters located in and around the Los Angeles area.

Hollywood ten The 10 individuals who refused, in 1948, to testify before a House of Representatives Committee on Un-American Activities.

hologram *See* holograph.

holograph □ A handwritten document. □ A three-dimensional image produced by holography. Also called a *hologram*.

holography The production of three-dimensional images by splitting a laser beam so one part is directed to the object and then to a photographic film, the other directly to the photographic film. The result is an interference pattern that, when projected by laser light, produces a holograph.

holy factor A slang term for fill light.

holygate A slang term applied to the scandals concerning television evangelists in the 1980s.

home □ A computer command that moves the cursor to the upper left-hand corner of the display screen. □ The top left-hand corner of a computer display monitor. □ *See* household.

home ADI market An Arbitron designated market in which a station's home county is located. *See also* home county.

Home Box Office (HBO) A subscription cable service that provides motion pictures, sporting events, and specials. The first cable service to be delivered by satellite.

home county A county in which a broadcast station is licensed to operate, and, by extension, a newspaper is operated.

home interactive systems Systems that involve interactivity and that are used in the home. For example, a video game as opposed to passive devices such as television receivers.

home market The market in which a broadcast station is licensed to operate, although it may reach beyond its market by cable, satellite, or other means.

home number A unique four-digit number assigned to each household within a county being sampled.

home print Material that is printed in house as opposed to material that is sent out for printing.

homes *See* household.

home service book A magazine whose editorial content centers on various aspects of domestic living. Also called a *shelter magazine*.

homes passed The number of households that are connected or could be connected to a local cable system because the feeder lines are in the immediate area.

homes per dollar *See* households per dollar.

homes reached *See* households reached.

home station Any television station that is licensed to a city located within the Metro, Home County, and/or ADI of the market being reported in a survey. Cf. outside station.

homes-using-radio rating *See* households-using-radio rating.

homes-using-television rating *See* households-using-television rating.

home system Any system or unit intended for use in a domestic environment. For example, audio/video systems, heating units, and telephone systems.

home terminal A cable television subscriber drop.

Home Testing Institute, Inc. (HTI) The parent company of TVQ, an audience research firm.

Hometown Free Television Association A western broadcasters' political action group.

hometown story A general story written so that local persons may have their names inserted.

home track □ In quadruplex recording practice, the track in which the vertical interval is recorded. Also called *track 1*. □ The status of a quadruplex videotape recorder adjusted to play back track 1 with the head that would normally record on that track.

home video recorder (HVR) A videocassette recorder designed to be used in the home.

homogeneity The degree to which an audience, population, sample, and so on, is similar as to demographic characteristics, attitudes, opinions, and so on. Cf. heterogeneity.

honeywagon A transportable toilet used for location filming.

hood □ A headline boxed in on three sides with rules. □ A plastic or rubber shield that covers the rear end of a connector. *See also* cover. □ A shield placed over a television or film camera viewfinder to eliminate extraneous light.

hoofer A slang term for a dancer.

hook □ Any device used at the beginning of a story that is intended to capture and hold an audience or reader. *See also* gimmick. □ A surprise ending. □ A musical line that repeats itself. □ A brief musical excerpt. □ A premium offered to purchasers of a product or service. □ A form of television picture distortion wherein the top of the picture bends to the side. □ *See* spike.

hooker □ A local tie-in announcement. □ *See* teaser.

hooking A picture fault characterized by a left or right displacement of the scan lines at the top of the picture. Also called *broomsticking, flagging,* and *flag waving.*

hookup □ A connection between two or more circuits or broadcast stations. □ Two animation backgrounds that are matched, the end of one to the beginning of the next, so that there is no break in the picture.

hookup wire A single electrical conductor used to connect devices or components.

Hooper, C. E., Inc. A local radio audience survey company. The national rating portion of the company was sold to Nielsen in 1950.

Hooperating A radio program audience rating taken by C. E. Hooper, Inc.

hop The movement of a reflected radio wave from an antenna, to the ionosphere, and back to the earth.

hopper A device for holding punched cards.

horizontal back porch *See* back porch.

horizontal bars Relatively broad lines that extend over the entire television picture. The bars may be stationary or move up or down. Also called *hum bars* and sometimes *venetian blind effect. See also* strobing.

horizontal blanking *See* blanking.

horizontal buy *See* horizontal saturation.

horizontal competition The competition between broadcast stations of the same type, newspapers, magazines, and so on, in the same market.

horizontal contiguity The discount rate that some stations allow for advertising time purchased for horizontal saturation campaigns. *See also* continuous rate. Cf. vertical contiguity.

horizontal cume A cumulative audience rating for radio or television programs in the same time period on successive days. Cf. vertical cume.

horizontal discount A discount to an advertiser who buys radio or television time over an extended period, usually a year. Cf. vertical discount.

horizontal displacements A picture condition in which the scanning lines start at relatively different points during the horizontal scan.

horizontal documentary A documentary that is broadcast in several segments over a period of a few days or weeks. Cf. vertical documentary.

horizontal editor *See* flatbed.

horizontal front porch *See* front porch.

horizontal half-page The upper or lower half of a periodical page, especially as purchased for an advertisement. Cf. vertical half-page.

horizontal jitter □ Random timing errors in the placement of horizontal lines, occurring at a rate less than half the horizontal scanning frequency. □ The picture fault resulting from such errors.

horizontal linearity control *See* linearity control.

horizontal line update The modification of all or part of a single line in a video image.

horizontal lock The condition that exists when a videotape player is in synchronization with a television station's sync or a videotape recorder's sync.

horizontal look *See* horizontal make-up.

horizontal make-up The use of rules and other typesetting devices to make a page look wider than it actually is. Also called *horizontal look.*

horizontal polarization The placement of transmitting or receiving antennas in a horizontal plane. Horizontal polarization is used for television antennas. Cf. circular polarization and vertical polarization.

horizontal publication A trade publication for persons holding similar positions in different types of businesses. Cf. vertical publication.

horizontal repetition rate *See* scanning frequency.

horizontal resolution The number of elements or dots in a scanning line that can be discerned by the eye. *See also* resolution. Cf. vertical resolution.

horizontal retrace The return path of the electron scanning beam that is eliminated by blanking.

horizontal retrace period The time during which the horizontal line scan on a television screen returns to the beginning of the next line.

horizontal rotation The rotation of commercial messages on a broadcast station during the same time period on different days of the week or month. Cf. vertical rotation.

horizontal saturation A commercial advertising campaign using the same time slot on successive days on the same station or stations. Also called *horizontal buy. See also* reach. Cf. vertical saturation.

horizontal scanning frequency *See* scanning frequency.

horizontal spacing The fit of characters in a line by means of computer-generated calculations. Cf. vertical spacing.

horizontal sweep The movement of the scanning beam from left to right across the television screen.

horizontal timing stability That characteristic of a video signal that describes the regularity of occurrence of the horizontal scan lines.

horn □ A type of enclosure for a loudspeaker. □ The metal radiating portion of a high-frequency loudspeaker. Cf. driver. □ The flared portion of an antenna waveguide.

hornbook A sheet of parchment or paper containing the alphabet and mounted on a board. The sheet was protected by a transparent horn cover.

horns The ragged edges of a disc groove. Also called *shoulders.*

horror film A film genre characterized by dangerous monsters, dark houses, supernatural actions, and so on.

horse To read proof copy without the aid of a copyholder or copy. Also called *horsing.*

horse opera A slang term for a western. Also called an *oater.*

horseshoe □ A stage that thrusts out into the audience; a runway. □ An old term for a copy desk in the shape of a horseshoe.

horsing *See* horse.

host (hostess) The individual who performs the duties of a master of ceremonies on a radio or television program. *See also* communicator.

host-selling A device used on some radio or television programs wherein the host or other personality delivers the commercial messages. Prohibited by FCC rules on programs for children.

hot □ One of the most popular phonograph records in a given week as listed on the charts. □ Ungrounded. □ Any live circuit. □ Any luminaire that is turned on. □ Any lighting that is too bright. □ A film frame that is overexposed. □ A sound that is too loud.

hot background A set background that is so brightly illuminated that a lack of contrast results.

hot call letters Radio station call letters that have been changed.

hot camera A television camera that has been warmed up.

hot canary An accomplished photogenic or telegenic soprano.

hot clock A wheel divided into segments that shows the times that various items are to be broadcast on a radio station.

hot composition Typesetting accomplished through the use of molten metal. Cf. cold composition.

hot front An electrical panel or switchboard with exposed current-carrying parts. Cf. dead front.

hot kine A kinescope that is quickly processed for immediate transmission by a television station. Now obsolete.

hot light A concentrated light used to highlight or outline.

hot line An unofficial police or fire department telephone connection to various media outlets.

hot-line list The most recent names available on a specific list, but no older than three months. In any event, use of the term should be further modified by such adjectives as *weekly* or *monthly.*

hotliner The host on a call-in radio talk show.

hot melt A fast working, hot glue used in bookbinding and for many other purposes.

hot metal *See* hot type.

hot microphone A live microphone.

hot mirror A dichroic coated surface that transmits light but reflects infrared so that the transmitted beam contains less heat.

hot news Fast breaking, up-to-the-minute news stories. *See also* spot news.

hot press A machine designed to make graphics using pigmented foil, pressure, and heated type.

hot set A motion picture or television set that has been completed and is ready for use; not to be altered.

hot splicer A heated film splicer with stainless steel blocks, scrapers, and cutting knives. Cf. guillotine.

hot spot □ In animation, an area of a cel that is reflecting the lights back into the camera, causing that spot to be overexposed. □ An undesirable concentration of light on one portion of a set.

hot switch □ An energized switch. □ The rapid change of the program origination point during a broadcast.

hot type Type cast from molten metal. Also called *hot metal.* Cf. cold type.

hours of operation *See* minimum operation schedule.

house □ A motion picture theatre. □ An organization, company, manufacturer, publication, and so on. Also called *in house.*

house ad An advertisement promoting the publication in which it appears or another publication by the same publisher.

house agency An advertising agency owned by an advertiser.

house board A fixed switchboard serving the permanent equipment in a theatre.

housecleaning The firing of all or substantially all employees of a broadcast station or other medium, such as the editorial staff of a newspaper or magazine.

house curtain *See* curtain.

house drop The coaxial cable that connects a feeder line to a subscriber's home in a cable television system. Also called a *subscriber drop.*

house editor *See* acquisitions editor.

house electrician An electrician employed by a facility (theatre, arena, and so on) who is in control of audience lighting and performance electrical equipment.

household A group of individuals occupying a house, apartment, group of rooms, or single room that is considered a housing unit by the Bureau of the Census. *See also* housing unit. Cf. family.

household audience A tabulation of the number of households wherein at least one member was reached by some medium during a specified period of time.

household collector An attache case-sized microcomputer that collects meter data, checks transmission accuracy and stores tuning information in its memory. It is one piece of the meter service hardware, installed in the meter panel member's household.

household diary A diary that requires a record of behavior for all members of a household, rather than for only one individual. Cf. individual diary.

household meter An electronic device that identifies and records the station tuned to and the on/off status of each television receiver in a household.

household ranking The listing of television programs from highest to lowest based on the number of households reached during the average minute of the program.

households per dollar The ratio of the number of households estimated to be in a television or radio audience at the time an advertisement is broadcast to the cost of that advertisement in dollars. Cf. cost per thousand.

households reached The number of households that are estimated to be in the audience of a television or radio network, station, or program during a specified period of time, regardless of where located. Also called, inexactly, *homes reached.*

households-using-radio (HUR) The actual number of households in radio audiences at a given time. Cf. households-using-radio rating and sets-in-use rating.

households-using-radio rating A type of rating for radio in general, rather than for a specific network, station, or program; the percentage of households that are estimated to be in the audience for all stations in the area at any specified time. Cf. households-using-radio (HUR) and sets-in-use rating.

households using television (HUT) The percentage of all television households in the survey area with one or more receivers in use during a specific time period. The sum of the average ratings for a given time period will sometimes be higher than the HUT because of viewing in multiple receiver television households. When applied to persons the term is *persons viewing television (PVT).*

households-using-television rating A type of rating for television in general, rather than for a specified network, station, or program; the percentage of households that are estimated to be in the audience for all stations in the area at any specified time. Cf. households-using-television (HUT) and sets-in-use rating.

household tracking report (HTR) A report from Nielsen Television Index (NTI) that provides a 13- to 24-month "track record" of individual network program ratings.

House Interstate and Foreign Commerce Committee The House of Representatives Committee that acts as a watchdog over the FCC.

housekeeping □ Tasks performed within a computer program that are not directly related to the outcome of the program. □ The routine maintenance performed on electronic equipment.

house lights A general lighting system permanently installed in the audience area of either a theatre or studio that provides sufficient illumination for safe movement in the area. Cf. work lights.

house list Any list of names owned by a company as a result of compilation, inquiry or buyer action, or acquisition that is used to promote that company's products or services.

house-list duplicate Duplication of name and address records between the list user's own lists and any list being mailed by him or her on a one-time use arrangement.

house magazine An internal publication; a magazine edited and published within a company or organization, usually designed for internal use.

house manager The individual in charge of a motion picture or legitimate theatre.

house organ A periodical publication; a magazine, newspaper, newsletter, and so on, designed to keep employees informed about the company or organization, or to keep company customers outside the organization informed. Also called an *internal house organ.*

house representative A sales employee of a print medium who represents only one publisher. Cf. commissioned representative.

house seat A seat in a theatre saved until the last minute by the management for unexpected notables or guests.

house show A television program owned by a station or network.

house style The manner of copy presentation followed by a publisher from issue to issue.

house sync A sync generator that supplies the synchronization for a television studio or entire facility.

housewife time The hours usually used to reach homemakers with broadcast commercials, generally from 10 a.m. to 4 p.m.

housing □ The enclosure on a motion picture camera that protects the moving parts. □ A waterproof container used in underwater filming.

housing unit Defined by the U.S. Bureau of the Census as a group of rooms, or a single room, that is occupied (or is intended for occupancy) as separate living quarters. Housing units do not include institutions, barracks, dormitories, and other group quarters.

Howard Public Service Awards, Roy W. Awards given by the Scripps Howard Foundation for public service.

howl A wail produced in an audio circuit by feedback.

howl round A British term for feedback.

how to An instructional film or tape that explains and demonstrates a skill or process. Also called a *how to do it.*

how to do it *See* how to.

HPA High-power amplifier.

HQTV High-quality Television. *See* HDTV.

HR House of Representatives (of the United States Congress).

HRTS Hollywood Radio and Television Society.

HRTV High-resolution television.

HSD Home satellite dish.

HSN Home shopping network. A cable network.

HSP High-speed printer.

HT □ Half title. □ Halftone.

HTC Head to come.

HTI Home Testing Institute.

HTK Hed to kum.

HTR Household Tracking Report.

hub □ The central portion of a tape reel upon which the tape is wound. □ The protrusion over which the hole in a tape reel fits. □ A patch panel socket or receptacle. □ A raised band on the back of a book. □ A secondary cable headend used in large cities.

huckster A slang term for an advertising agency account executive.

hue Any pure color or wavelength without white. The red, orange, yellow, green, blue, violet, magenta aspect of color without regard to the other aspects such as saturation and brightness. Cf. chroma, intensity, luminance, and saturation.

hue banding Banding in which the visible difference is in color hue. Also called *hue shift banding. See also* color banding. Cf. gauge banding, noise banding, and saturation banding.

hue control The control on a television receiver that changes the color of the picture.

hue shift banding *See* hue banding.

hum A low-pitched noise in an audio circuit, often caused by 60-Hz alternating current.

human engineering *See* ergonomics.

human interest (HI) A news story or feature containing emotional as well as factual material. Also called a *human interest story.*

human interest angle The use of emotional material in a story, feature, screenplay, and so on, to arouse commonly recognized feelings and promote empathy.

human interest story *See* human interest.

hum bar A horizontal bar in a television picture caused by hum.

humidifier A device used to introduce moisture in the air to prevent film from drying out.

HUR Homes using radio.

Huston crane A type of large camera crane used for high-angle shots.

HUT Homes using television.

Hutchins Commission The 1940s commission headed by Robert Hutchins that delineated ideas on social responsibility coupled with freedom of the press.

HV □ High voltage. □ HomeVideo. A videocassette made for the home market.

HVR Home video recorder.

HW modulator *See* modulator.

hybrid □ An electronic circuit that contains both vacuum tubes and transistors. □ The use of two or more distinct technologies to perform a task. □ A communication satellite that combines both C band and Ku band payloads.

hybrid computer A computer that combines analog and digital capabilities.

hybrid spread spectrum systems Systems that use combinations of two or more types of direct sequence, frequency hopping, time hopping, and pulsed FM modulation to achieve their wide occupied bandwidths.

hydraulic pedestal A common form of camera mount that uses a counterbalancing fluid instead of springs and counterbalancing weights. *See also* pedestal.

Hydrotype process A photomechanical imbibition process for printing film by dye transfer.

hygroscope An instrument used to measure the amount of moisture in the air.

hype □ The stock-in-trade of a press agent; overly enthusiastic promotion. □ *See* hypoing.

hypercardioid A microphone pickup pattern that is more directional than a standard cardioid microphone.

hyperfocal distance (H) The distance between a lens set at infinity and the nearest object in acceptable focus.

hypergonar An anamorphic lens system developed in France in the 1920s.

hypersensitize To increase the emulsion speed of film using chemicals, vapors, or light.

hyphen A punctuation mark, often one-third the length of an em dash.

hyphenate A person who fulfills more than one production function, such as a writer-producer or producer-director.

hyphenated market A broadcast market that contains two or more communities. Examples are Minneapolis-St. Paul, Dallas-Fort Worth, and Albany-Schenectady-Troy.

hyphenation The breaking of words at the end of a line by the use of a hyphen.

hyphenless justification The justifying of lines of type by interletter and interword spacing.

hyping *See* hypoing.

hypo □ To add vitality to a program. □ An abbreviation for *hyposulfite of soda,* a photographic fixing agent. Actually, sodium thiosulfate.

hypodermic needle *See* magic bullet.

hypoing □ Any activity that is calculated to distort or inflate audience measurements using, for example, special contests, unusual advertising, and so on, during a survey period. □ An attempt by any medium to increase its listeners, viewers, or readers using any means to call attention to scheduled audience measurements. This includes the use of survey announcements by broadcast stations. Also called *hype* and *hyping.*

hypothesis A proposition offered as an explanation for the occurrence of phenomena. Often a working hypothesis to be studied and reported on, either descriptively or statistically.

hysteresis motor A synchronous motor in which the speed is governed by the frequency of the alternating current. Used in turntables, tape transport drive mechanisms, and so on, where a constant speed is required.

Hz Hertz.

I

I □ Current. □ Illuminance. □ Illuminated. □ Industrial. An FCC first letter file-number prefix. □ Informal. An FCC special temporary authorization for common carrier services. □ Input. □ Instructional programs. □ Interim. An FCC file number prefix. □ International. A wire service symbol for international news. □ Inverter. □ A single column inch.

IA An abbreviation for *IATSE.*

IAA International Advertising Association.

IAAB Inter-American Association of Broadcasting. A western hemisphere association of privately owned broadcast stations formed in 1948. Also abbreviated AIR.

IAB International Association of Broadcasting.

IABC International Association of Business Communicators.

IAEA International Advertising Executives' Association.

IAIP International Association of Independent Producers.

IAMS Instantaneous Audience Measurement Service. A CBS device for feeding a high-frequency audio signal to radio receivers equipped to return the signal to a central point.

IAPA Inter-American Press Association.

IAT International atomic time. *See* CUT and GMT.

IATSE International Alliance of Theatrical Stage Employees. A union representing various film and television workers; script supervisors, projectionists, make-up artists, screen cartoonists, and so on.

IAWRT International Association of Women in Radio and Television. An association, headquartered in West Germany, formed for the purpose of promotion and improvement of women's programs.

IB □ International Broadcast(ing). □ International television. An FCC file-number prefix.

IBA Independent Broadcasting Authority. British supervisory authority for commercial broadcasting. Formerly the Independent Television Authority (ITA).

IBC Inside back cover.

IBE Institute of Broadcast Engineers. Now SBE.

IBEW International Brotherhood of Electrical Workers. A union that represents some television technical personnel.

IBFM Institute of Broadcasting Financial Management, Inc. An association for financial executives in the broadcast industry founded in 1961. Publishes the *Broadcast Financial Journal* (BFJ).

IBI International Broadcast Institute. An international organization, based in London, to promote research and provide information and advice. Founded in 1968.

ibidem Latin for "in the same place." Usually abbreviated *ibid.*

IBPAT A union representing scenic artists.

IBS □ Intercollegiate Broadcasting System, Inc. An association of college and educational broadcasting stations. □ International Broadcasting Society. □ Iota Beta Sigma. A national collegiate honorary society for broadcasters.

IBTC A teamster's union representing theatrical teamsters, dispatchers, wranglers, trainers, mechanics, and others who work on motion pictures, television, and commercials.

IBTO International Broadcasting and Television Organization.

IBU International Broadcasting Union. Also abbreviated *UIB.* An international organization dissolved in 1946 when the EBU and the OIR (later OIRT) were established.

IC □ Aural broadcast intercity relay. An FCC file-number prefix. □ Input circuit. □ Integrated circuit.

ICA □ International Communication Association. □ Industrial Communications Association.

ICAO International Civil Aviation Organization. An intergovernmental organization. Also abbreviated *OACI.*

ICAS Interdepartment Council on Radio Propagation and Standards. A government advisory group.

ICB International Christian Broadcasters. A religious broadcasting organization, successor to WCMR and NRB.

ICC Interstate Commerce Commission.

ice cream cone A luminaire that contains a white reflector.

ICI International Commission of Illumination (or lighting). A lighting standards organization. Also abbreviated *CIE.*

ICIA International Communications Industries Association.

ICIE International Council of Industrial Editors.

ICI standards The standards of color description set forth by the ICI. Also called *CIE standards.*

icon □ A pictorial representation used instead of words to identify the proper place for the insertion of plugs and other connectors. □ A symbol that closely represents a symbolized object in a film. *See also* semiotics. Cf. motif. □ An ideogram used in some computer programs as a selection guide or menu for size of font, drawing lines, patterns, and so on.

iconograph An engraving or illustration made for a book.

iconography The art of representing symbolically through pictures or images.

iconoscope A camera tube in which a high-velocity electron beam scans a photoemissive mosaic that has electrical-storage capability. Developed by Vladimir K. Zworykin in 1923. *See also* pickup tube.

ICR Intercity relay.

ICRC International Committee of the Red Cross. Also abbreviated *CICR.*

ICSC Interim Communications Satellite Committee. The governing body of Intelsat.

ICSU International Council of Scientific Unions.

ICW Interrupted Continuous Wave.

ID Identification. *See* station identification. □ Item description.

IDA Identification data accessory. A feature of the ARCH system wherein the identity of a videocassette is automatically furnished to station personnel for comparison to the broadcast schedule.

ideal An item that is perfect in every aspect, for example, the perfect time for a program, the perfect piece of equipment, the perfect story, the perfect audience for an advertiser, and so on.

ideal copy A perfect copy of a first impression of a book; used for comparison purposes.

identification □ An element of defamation that occurs when an individual is identified by name, initials, or identifying characteristics. *See also* publication. □ The personal data used in a news story to describe an individual. □ The tendency of audiences to feel empathy for a character in a motion picture, story, play, and so on.

identification announcement *See* station identification (ID).

identification code The computer codes used by authors to indicate different parts of a manuscript, the kind of type, chapter titles, block quotations, and so on, for typesetting.

identification commercial A 10-second radio or television commercial. Also called an *identification spot.*

identification line A line of type that names the subject of a photograph or illustration.

identification signal The slate, tone, test card, or other marks at the start of a videotape that identify the program.

identification spot *See* identification commercial.

identifier A heading; often a newspaper or magazine classified ad heading.

ideogram A graphic symbol or picture used to represent or convey a particular idea or meaning.

idiot board *See* idiot card.

idiot card A derogatory term for a cue card. Also called an *idiot board* and *idiot sheet.*

idiot sheet *See* idiot card.

idiot tape Perforated tape to be used for computer typesetting containing only codes for type characters, not for justification and hyphenation. Also called *continuous tape, raw tape,* and *simple tape.*

idler □ The rubber-tired wheel that transmits the power from the drive spindle to the turntable. □ The rubber-tired wheel that presses the tape to the capstan of a tape transport. *See also* pressure roller.

idle rollers Guide rollers used in cameras, projectors, tape recorders, and so on.

idle time The time that an electronic system is not in use. Cf. down time.

IDT Improved definition television.

IDTV Improved definition television.

IEC International Electrotechnical Commission. An international standards organization. Also abbreviated *CEI.*

IEEE Institute of Electrical and Electronics Engineers, Inc. A professional organization formed by the merger of the IRE and AIEE.

IER Institute for Education by Radio. Now defunct.

IERT Institute for Education by Radio-Television.

IES Illuminating Engineering Society.

IF □ Instructional TV, fixed. An FCC file-number prefix. □ Intermediate frequency.

IFB Interrupted feedback.

IFC Inside front cover.

IFCJ International Federation of Catholic Journalists.

IFFA International Federation of Film Archives.

IFFJ International Federation of Free Journalists. An organization of Polish and Czech journalists based in London.

IFJ International Federation of Journalists.

IFMC International Folk Music Council.

IFNP International Federation of Newspaper Publishers.

IFPA □ Independent Film Producers of America. □ Information Film Producers of America.

IFPI International Federation of the Phonographic Industry. The international counterpart to the RIAA.

IFRB International Frequency Registration Board. A committee of the International Telecommunications Union (ITU) that maintains the records of international frequency assignments.

IFTC International Film and Television Council.

IHF Institute of High-Fidelity.

IHFM Institute of High-Fidelity Manufacturers.

IIA Information Industry Association.

IIC International Institute of Communications. An international forum for the study of the social, economic, political, and cultural legal issues in mass communication.

IJ Institute of Journalists.

ike An abbreviation for *iconoscope.*

IL An abbreviation for *illustrate, illustrated, illustration,* and *illustrator.*

ILAB International League of Antiquarian Booksellers.

ill An abbreviation for *illuminated.*

illuminaire *See* luminaire.

illuminated □ A book containing ornamental letters, designs, miniature pictures, and so on, usually in gold and brilliant colors. □ An outdoor advertising structure with electrical equipment installed for illumination of the message at night. Common coding used is Ill or I.

illuminated panel An illuminated outdoor poster or billboard.

illumination □ Generally, a synonym for lighting. □ The amount of light (flux) per unit area incident on a surface. The unit is either the footcandle or the lumen per square foot.

illumination meter *See* illuminometer.

illumination unit *See* footcandle and footlambert (fL).

illuminometer A light meter that measures in footcandles. Also called an *illumination meter.*

illus An abbreviation for *illuminated, illustrated,* or *illustration.*

illusion An effect created for listeners or viewers.

illusion of reality A scene that creates a believable atmosphere.

illustration A drawing, painting, photograph, and so on, designed to elucidate or decorate a book, magazine, brochure, and so on.

illustration board A heavy paper board that may be used for titles or other graphics.

illustrator An individual who uses nonphotographic techniques to create artwork for commercials.

ILO ☐ International Labor Office. An intergovernmental organization. Also abbreviated BIT. ☐ International Labor Organization. An intergovernmental organization. Also abbreviated *OIT.*

IM Intermodulation distortion.

image ☐ A photographically recorded object or person on a film that is made visible by processing. *See also* latent image. ☐ The picture on a television screen. ☐ The attitude of a person toward a product, brand, company, candidate, station, and so on. ☐ An exact copy stored in a different medium. ☐ The reputation that a station, newspaper, publisher, and so on, has within and outside of the industry. ☐ The area that is reproduced by printing.

image advertising Advertising designed to enhance the prestige of a company, product, service, or individual as opposed to advertising that explains the virtues of the company, product, service, or individual. *See also* institutional advertising.

image compression The amount of squeezing required by an anamorphic system so that the image will fit on the film. Cf. image expansion.

image dissector An early television camera pickup tube developed by Philo T. Farnsworth in 1927.

image duplication *See* freeze frame.

image enhancer An electronic circuit used in television to increase the resolution of the picture.

image expansion The amount of change in image size required by an anamorphic system so that the lens will expand the picture the required amount. Cf. image compression.

image orbiter An outdated device that automatically moved an image orthicon tube in order to reduce burn in.

image orthicon (IO) A type of television camera pickup tube developed by RCA that is extremely light sensitive.

image plane *See* focal plane.

image processing The manipulation and storage of computer text or graphics.

image resolution A measure of the number of dots per square inch produced on a dot matrix or other printer.

image retention A vidicon phenomenon that occurs with rapid motion of the actor or the camera and is especially noticeable at low light levels. Also called *lagging, sticking,* and *trailing.*

imagery transfer The hoped-for transfer of an audience's awareness of a program or personality to the commercial product being advertised.

image scanner An electronic device used to transform printed images into computer form.

image storage A device that is capable of storing a digitized frame of video information on a disk or tape.

image transform A computerized kinescope process.

imaginary line The line which, if crossed by a camera, reverses the audience's frame of reference. Also called *action axis* and *axis of action.*

Imax An extremely large wide-screen film process. The system utilizes a special film camera and projector that run the film horizontally. Cf. Omnimax.

IMBA International Media Buyers Association.

imbibition Any of the photomechanical reproduction processes used for printing color films by the selective absorption of dye by the three separation matrices. Also called *hydrotype.*

IMC International Music Council. Also abbreviated CIM.

immediacy The sometimes successful attempt by the electronic media to inform the public of events as they are happening.

immersion bath A method of processing motion picture film in which the film is automatically moved from the development stage through washing.

IMMI International Mass Media Institute. A nonprofit church-related organization.

impact The effect of the media on individuals, organizations, and ideas.

impact printer A printer such as a dot matrix or daisy wheel that prints characters on paper by striking dots or characters against an inked ribbon.

impact scheduling The presentation of two radio or television commercials for one product or service within a short period to expose the same audience to the same message twice.

impasto The thick application of paint to artwork.

impeachment A legal proceeding against a public official for misconduct in office.

impedance (Z) The sum of the resistance, inductance, and capacitance to the flow of alternating current in a circuit.

impedance matching A method of balancing two or more components to minimize attenuation or reflection.

impedance matching transformer A transformer used to match the impedance between two components.

impedance mismatch A condition that exists when two components are connected that have different impedances, such as a low-impedance microphone connected to a line input.

imperfection □ A book that is rejected because of damage or missing signatures, pages, and so on. □ A list of shortages at the end of a binding run noting the leftover signatures. Also called an *imperfection note.*

imperfection note *See* imperfection.

imperial octavo *See* octavo.

implication A writing technique that has the reader or audience create part of the action and characterization through drawing conclusions rather than having everything neatly laid out.

implode The opposite of explode; the inward shattering of a television picture tube or other vacuum tube.

import A book or other item brought into a country from another country.

imported signal A broadcast signal from outside the local area distributed to subscribers by a cable television system. *See also* distant signal.

imposing stone A flat table, usually metal or stone, on which page forms are locked in a chase for printing. Also called an *imposing surface* and *imposing table.*

imposing surface *See* imposing stone.

imposing table *See* imposing stone.

imposition The arranging of pages so that they will be in proper sequence when printed and folded.

impression □ The copies of a book or other publication that are printed at the same time. Cf. edition. □ A book that is reprinted without alteration. □ A measure of the number of copies printed per hour. □ The pressure of the type or plate against the paper.

impressionistic criticism A critic's or audience's judgment of a work on its own merits without regard to previous works by the same author or classical standards. Also called *new criticism.* Cf. authoritative criticism.

impressions The number of homes or individuals exposed to an advertisement or group of advertisements. *See also* gross rating points (GRP).

impression study A study made by Daniel Starch and Associates to determine the kinds of impression made on the public by advertisements in periodicals.

imprimatur The license to print or publish, usually issued under the official seal of church or state.

imprint □ The lines on the title page of a book containing the name, address, and so on, of the publisher. □ The name and address of a manufacturer or dealer on advertising material. □ The name of the printer on printed material. □ A strip on an outdoor advertising poster imprinted with the name, address, and phone number of the local dealer handling the product being advertised. It is common practice to place these imprint strips across the bottom 20 inches of the poster just above the blanking.

impromptu Speaking on the spur of the moment without specific preparation. *See also* ad lib.

improved-definition television (IDTV) A method for increasing the definition of television based on the 525-line NTSC system by using progressive scanning rather than interlace scanning. Also called *IDT.* Cf. high-definition television (HDTV).

improvisation The immediate creation of dialogue or action by a performer, often to cover forgotten lines.

impulse system A cable television interactive system that allows a subscriber to select pay-per-view programs by pushing buttons on a control panel instead of calling the cable television system.

imputation A process for assigning values for missing data.

in □ An abbreviation for *input.* □ A script notation meaning to start or begin.

in-ad coupon A coupon contained within a printed advertisement.

INAE International Newspaper Advertising Executives [Association].

in and under *See* up and under.

in banc *See* en banc.

in between breakdown The instructions given to an in betweener by an animator.

in betweener An artist who draws the sketches between the key or extremes drawn by the animator.

in betweening ☐ The creation of a smooth flow of animation by in between drawings. ☐ The computer interpolations in between key frames of an animation sequence.

in-betweens The drawings that fall between the extreme points of a movement. In studio animation, these drawings are done by an assistant animator or in-betweener. Cf. extremes.

in camera In judicial chambers; in private.

in camera editing The shooting of film or tape in the exact sequence it is to be used. Rarely used except for home movies.

in camera matte shot A film shot in which a portion of the action is masked, usually by a cutout in a matte box.

incandescence The emission of light caused by the heating of a filament or other body in a vacuum.

incandescent light The production of light by incandescence or by burning of two electrodes that cause an arc. Also called a *tungsten light*. Cf. fluorescent light.

incasting The process of sending signals from a subscriber to the head end of a CATV system.

incentive ☐ The payment in goods, services, or money that is given to survey participants to secure their cooperation. ☐ Any enticement made by a broadcast station, cable television station, newspaper, and so on, to secure an advertiser's business.

inch ☐ To move a tape, printing press, and so on, in small increments. ☐ Fourteen lines of vertical advertising space; a column inch. *See also* agate.

in character The ability of a performer to be immersed in a role and not revert during a performance.

inches per second (IPS) The measure of tape speed.

inching The movement of a film or tape forward or backward in small increments in a camera, projector, editor, and so on, to check for proper operation or location.

inching knob A handle or projection used to control inching in a camera, projector, editor, synchronizer, and so on.

incidence The percentage of an identifiable demographic group within a given geographic area.

incidental character A character in a novel, script, screenplay, and so on, who is not necessary to the main theme, but who serves to add color and reality to a plot.

incidental music *See* incidental sound.

incidental sound Effects or music that enhance the atmosphere during a scene. Also called *incidental music*. Cf. transition.

incident light The light that falls directly on a subject or object. Cf. reflected light.

incident light meter An exposure meter that measures the light falling on a subject.

incident ray A light ray that is at the point of entering a lens or other deflecting material. Cf. emergent ray.

incident reading A light-meter reading taken from the position of the subject in the direction of the light source. Cf. reflected reading.

in clear To begin speaking or using sound effects or music with no other sound.

inclination The angle determined by the plane containing the orbit of an earth satellite and the plane of the earth's equator.

inclinometer A device used to measure the angle a satellite is located above the earth's surface.

incoming An outdoor advertising structure that exposes the message to traffic approaching a central business district, city center, shopping center, and so on.

incue (IC) The first several words of a recorded news tape. Used to cue a tape to the proper place. Cf. outcue.

in cue A cue to start or begin a scene, line, or action.

incumbent A current sponsor, advertising agency, agent, and so on.

incunabulum A book printed in the fifteenth century. Also called a *cradle book* and *fifteener.*

indent To set copy in from the margin.

indentation *See* indention.

indention The beginning of a line or lines inside the margin; a recess in a border. Often referred to as *indentation.*

independent □ A television or film production company that is not owned or controlled by a major film studio. □ A film that is produced by an independent filmmaker. □ A cable television system that is not part of an MSO. □ Any circuit that is routed directly from the feed past the master or submaster so as to leave a circuit hot even when the master is thrown. □ *See* independent station. □ An animator who chooses not to be part of a studio, but works alone to produce his or her films.

independent animator An individual responsible for an animated motion picture. Cf. studio animator.

independent filmmaker An individual who produces, and often directs, motion pictures. Often, such individuals produce low-budget films.

independent network Generally, a broadcast network other than ABC, CBS, or NBC.

independent producer A motion picture or television producer who does not depend on a motion picture studio for financial backing or production facilities.

independent regulatory agency *See* administrative agency.

independent station □ A commercial television broadcast station that generally carries in prime time not more than 10 hours of programming per week offered by the three major national television networks. □ Any radio station not affiliated with a network. □ For the purposes of copyright, a commercial television broadcast station other than a network station.

independent television market The home market of an independent television station.

index □ A summary of the contents of a book, newspaper, magazine, and so on. □ In some computer programs, the first few lines of a story. □ A list, usually alphabetical, containing subjects and names, and the page numbers on which they can be found. Usually located in the back matter of a book. Cf. table of contents (TOC). □ A sign, such as a pointing finger, used to highlight a sentence, paragraph, and so on. Also called an *indicium.* □ An alphabetical list of items; a table of references.

index counter An audio- or videotape transport counter that indicates the approximate location of a specific point on a tape.

index letter A letter of the alphabet used to indicate subdivisions of type matter.

index of refraction □ The ratio of the velocity of light or other electromagnetic energy passing through one medium to the velocity of light passing through a second medium. □ The degree of change in the direction of a refracted beam. *See also* refraction.

India paper A very thin, durable paper used for printing bibles, dictionaries, and so on. Also called *bible paper.*

indicating instrument A meter that shows the value of the quantity being measured.

indicator A lamp, LCD, LED, or other device used as a visual display that a device is on or off, or in some state in between.

indicia □ The markings on envelopes used in place of stamps or postmarks to identify bulk mail. □ *See* index.

indictment A formal written statement charging a person with a crime.

indie A slang term for an independent radio or television station. Also spelled *indy.*

indigenous sound Any sound that matches exactly the action on film or tape. *See also* ambient sound.

indirect aggression Broadcast propaganda.

indirect interview An unstructured interview that uses open-ended questions to elicit responses.

indirect light Light from a source, such as a reflector, which is not itself luminous.

indirect media The media that communicate with large groups of individuals, and are not involved in one-on-one selling to individuals: radio, television, newspapers, and so on. Cf. direct media.

indirect method An FCC approved method for measuring antenna power; defined as the product of the plate voltage of the final radio stage, the total plate current of the final radio stage, and the efficiency factor. Cf. direct method.

indirect questioning An interview technique that asks a respondent about a related attitude or opinion instead of using a direct question.

indirect questionnaire A questionnaire containing questions disguised as to their specific use. Cf. direct questionnaire.

indirect quote An altered quotation, usually a change from first person to third person. Cf. direct quote, paraphrase, and partial quote.

indirect scanning *See* flying spot scanner.

indirect sound Sound produced by reflection.

indirect subscriber A person who orders magazines or other periodicals through an agency. Cf. direct subscriber.

indirect wave *See* sky wave.

individual diary A diary that includes a record of behavior; for example, television or radio activity for a particular individual, rather than for all members of a household. Also called a *personal diary.* Cf. household diary.

individual location An outdoor advertising location used for a single billboard.

individual reception The reception of emissions from a space station in the broadcasting-satellite service by simple domestic installations and in particular those possessing small antennae. Cf. community reception.

individuals reached The number of individuals that are estimated to be in the audience of a television or radio network, station, or program during a specified period of time, regardless of where located.

individuals-using-radio rating A type of rating for radio in general, rather than for a specific network, station, or program; the percentage of individuals who are estimated to be in the audience for all radio stations in the area at any specified time.

individuals-using-television rating A type of rating for television in general, rather than for a specific network, station, or program; the percentage of individuals who are estimated to be in the audience for all television stations in the area at any specified time.

individual voice tests *See* talent audition.

indoor film Film that has been color balanced for exposure under incandescent light. *See also* type A film and type B film. Cf. outdoor film.

inductance (L) A device that opposes any change in the current in a circuit. *See also* impedance.

induction □ The process of reasoning from the specific to the general. Cf. deduction. □ The process of establishing an electric field by using a magnet or magnetic field.

induction motor A form of motor that has its speed controlled primarily by the line frequency of the power source; often used in tape recorders, cameras, projectors, and so on.

induction period The time between the immersion of a film in a developer and the appearance of the developing image.

industrial advertising The advertising of industrial goods and services.

industrial film *See* industrial motion picture.

industrial motion picture A motion picture made to promote the image of an organization, to promote the use of its product or services, to offer training in the use of its products or services, or to provide education or instruction.

industrial union A union open to all members of an industry, whether skilled or unskilled. Cf. craft union.

indy A slang term for an independent radio or television station. Also spelled *indie.*

in edit □ In an insert edit, that point in the program where the inserted material begins and the original program disappears. Cf. out edit. □ The program material in the vicinity of such a point. □ The tape time at which such a point occurs.

inf An abbreviation for *information.*

inferior A subscript character or figure. Also called *inferior characters* and *inferior figures.*

inferior characters *See* inferior.

inferior court A court that is subordinate to another court. *See also* court of appeals and Supreme Court. Cf. superior court.

inferior figures *See* inferior.

infinite baffle A loudspeaker enclosure that has no openings except for the loudspeaker.

infinity □ Unlimited distance, quantity, or time. Practically, the distance from a camera that light rays appear parallel. □ The farthest distance marking indicated on a lens.

inflow The portion of the audience that changes channels at the beginning of a television program. Cf. outflow.

infomercial A long commercial, usually run on cable television, which emphasizes information about the product or service in addition to the sales pitch. Also spelled *informercial.*

informal application Any request to the FCC for authorization other than a formal application.

informal ascertainment Ascertainment accomplished by any means selected by an applicant for a broadcast license or renewal of license. *See also* ascertainment.

informal network A broadcast network created without a binding contract to share news, information, programs, and so on, on a semipermanent basis.

informatics The study of information processing; computer involvement in data processing.

information □ Generally, the communication of knowledge or intelligence. The reduction of uncertainty, randomness, or entropy. □ A general term encompassing any signals, sounds, signs, and so on, that are transmitted, received, or stored. □ The amount of material contained in a film frame, a page, and so on.

informational film *See* instructional film.

information capacity The ability of a computer system to transmit or store information.

information channel The hardware used in connecting two terminals or distant points.

Information Exchange Protocol (IXP) A protocol for labeling and describing data on a CD-I disc that is used in the mastering process. This data describes the media type and encoding techniques, among other characteristics. These data may also include other descriptions of the disc data that might be useful to the mastering facility.

Information Industry Association (IIA) An association of producers of information products.

information overload The condition that exists in an individual when he or she is presented more information than can be processed comfortably.

information pollution The profusion of unnecessary information produced by the mass media.

information processing A general term covering any operation performed by a computer.

information retrieval A computer system wherein stored data may be recalled instantly in one or more places or terminals.

information society A society in which more than half of the workforce is engaged in the accumulation, storage, and retrieval of information rather than producing goods.

information storage and retrieval (ISR) The process of obtaining stored documents, whether by hand or by machine.

information theory A theory that deals statistically with the processes of the transmission, distribution, and reception of knowledge or intelligence between individuals or between humans and machines.

information unit *See* bit.

informercial *See* infomercial.

infotainment Television news programs that are based on the concept of entertainment instead of enlightenment. Also called *trash TV. See also* happy news.

infra Below or following, the opposite of *supra.*

infrared □ Invisible light rays with wavelengths longer than visible light but shorter than radio waves. □ A type of film emulsion sensitive to infrared radiation. Cf. ultraviolet.

infrared film Film that is sensitive to the infrared portion of the spectrum; approximately 7000 to 13,000 angstrom units.

infrared filter A lens filter that is capable of reducing the effects of haze and fog.

infrared light *See* infrared.

infrared matte process A process wherein action is shot against a background illuminated by infrared lamps.

infrared photography The use of specially sensitized infrared film and filters to produce images in low light levels.

infrasonic Frequencies below the range of human hearing—below approximately 16 Hz. Sometimes called *subsonic,* a term that usually means below the speed of sound.

infringement The violation of any of the exclusive rights of a copyright owner or the importation of copies or phonorecords into the United States in violation of the Copyright Act.

ingenue An actress or female performer who appears to be in her late teens or early twenties. Cf. juvenile.

inherited audience The members of an audience who listened or watched the immediately preceding program on the same station. Also called a *carry-over audience* and *holdover audience.*

in-home Mass media that are consumed in the home as opposed to elsewhere, such as a car, theatre, bookstore, and so on.

in house □ The production facilities available within a company or organization. □ A production that is made within a company or organization for use by that company or organization. □ *See* house.

in house agency *See* house agency.

in house line A privately owned communications path.

initial A large capital letter set in display size at the beginning of a chapter, paragraph, magazine article, and so on. Also called an *initial letter* and *inset initial.*

initial compensation The amount received by a television or film writer for a script. Cf. additional compensation.

initial decision The first decision made by an FCC Administrative Law Judge in an adjudicatory case. Such decision may become final if no appeal is filed. Cf. final decision.

initialization □ The process of setting all switches, counters, and registers to the required values before beginning a computer program. □ The process of formatting a computer disk for use.

initial letter *See* initial.

initially designated households Households selected as part of a sample for survey purposes.

injection molding The process of forming a disc by injecting a liquefied plastic material into a die cavity.

injunction A temporary or permanent judicial order that requires a person to refrain from some act; a gag order.

ink To sign a contract for services with an agent, studio, network, and so on.

ink and paint □ The step in cel animation in which the animators' drawings are transferred to cels for photographing. □ In a studio, the department that performs this function. The drawings are first inked, by tracing them onto the front of the cels with a pen or fine brush, or transferred by a xerographic process. The backs of the cels are then painted, usually with special acrylic paints. Traditionally, this delicate work was one of the few jobs in the animation industry reserved for women; however, today both men and women perform these jobs.

ink bleed *See* bleed.

inker □ A roller or pad used to ink type. □ The person who traces the animators' drawings onto cels. *See also* ink and paint.

ink fountain An ink reservoir on a printing press. Also called a *fountain.*

inking The process of tracing the outlines from animated drawings to the animation cels.

ink jet printer A printer that creates characters by electrostatically aiming a spray of ink on specially coated paper.

ink jet printing A computer-controlled printing process in which characters are formed by spraying ink on paper. Also called *jet printing.*

ink smudge □ The overflow of ink outside the character outline. *See also* bleed. □ An extra amount of color added to the edges of artwork. □ To extend a color in multiple-color printing so that white does not show between colors.

inky A small fresnel spotlight with a 1.5- to 3-inch lens diameter. Also called a *midget.*

inky-dinky □ Any small incandescent lamp. Also called *inky,* from incandescent, and *dinky-inky.* □ A small 250-

watt spotlight often used as a camera light.

inlaid binding A decorative book binding made from different kinds or colors of leather. Also called a *mosaic binding* and *onlay.*

inlay The keyed insertion of one television picture for a portion of another. *See also* chromakey, key, and matte.

inline A display letter with a white line cut into it.

in-line heads *See* stacked heads.

inlooker An individual who has seen at least one major portion of the editorial section of a periodical. Cf. reader.

INN Independent Network News.

inner form The form that contains the inside pages. Also called an *inside form.* Cf. outer form.

innocent dissemination The unwitting broadcasting of defamatory remarks. *See also* defamation, libel, and slander.

INP International News Photo.

in phase Perfect coordination or synchronous operation between or among two or more components, waves, devices, currents, and so on. Cf. out of phase.

in point ☐ The film or television frame selected by an editor as the beginning of a shot. Cf. out point. ☐ The starting point of a scene.

in press In the process of being published.

in print A book or other publication that is available. Cf. out of print.

INPUT International Public Television. An international organization of public television access programmers.

input ☐ Information that flows from peripheral devices into a computer. ☐ The devices used to access data. ☐ A signal applied to an electronic device. ☐ The part of a circuit or component that receives power from an external source. ☐ The power, current, or voltage applied to a circuit or component. ☐ The terminals or jacks used to accept input signals. Cf. output.

input device Any of numerous devices that are used to feed a signal into another device, for example, tape players, disk drives, paper tape readers, and modems. Cf. output device.

input file A computer text file that contains the text matter before it is formatted with typesetting codes. Cf. output file.

input/output (I/O) The means by which information is sent between a computer CPU and its peripheral devices.

input port An interface used for transferring information into a computer. *See also* I/O port.

input power The product of the direct voltage applied to the last radio stage and the total direct current flowing to the last radio stage, measured without modulation.

input selector switch Any device that enables a cable television viewer to select between cable service and off-the-air television signals. Such a device may be more sophisticated than a mere two-sided switch, may use other cable interface equipment, and may be built into consumer television receivers.

input signal The signal that is introduced into an amplifier, tape recorder, and so on.

inquiry A request for literature or other information about a product or service. Unless otherwise stated, it is assumed no payment has been made for the literature or other information. A catalog request is generally considered a specific type of inquiry.

inquiry response mailing A bulk mailing that seeks an inquiry rather than one that solicits an order.

in re In the matter of; concerning.

INS International News Service. Merged with UP to form UPI.

ins An abbreviation for an *insert shot.*

inschool programming Instructional television programming designed for use by schools.

inscription A book dedication.

insert ☐ The post-production addition or substitution of a shot to a scene, often a close-up. Also called an *insert scene* and *insert shot.* ☐ A live portion of a radio or television program added to a recorded program, or vice-versa. ☐ *See* key. ☐ A type of edit in which new material is recorded between sections of existing program material. ☐ A word processing feature that allows the addition of characters at the cursor position, thus pushing any existing text in front of the new entries. Cf. overstrike. ☐ An addition to a news story or script. ☐ Additional matter added to a book during binding. □ A separate page bound into a publication. Also called an *inset*. Sometimes called an *insert section* in newspapers. □ A preprinted advertisement bound into a magazine. □ A mark (ˆ) used to indicate the place words are to be inserted in a story. □ A special segment for a photoplay done by extra players.

insert camera A television camera used for graphics.

insert card *See* bind-in card and blow-in cards.

insert earphone A small earphone that fits in the ear.

insert edit A type of video edit in which new audio and/or video is edited into existing footage. This type of editing uses the existing control track or time code. Cf. assemble edit.

insertion □ A single commercial on radio or television. □ An advertisement in a periodical.

insertion gain The increase in signal level caused by the addition of a component to a circuit.

insertion loss The decrease in signal level caused by the addition of a component to a circuit. Also called *attenuation loss.*

insertion order An authorization from an advertiser or advertising agency to print an advertisement of a specified size on a specified date. May specify the location on the page.

insert leader A printing rule used to separate columns of type matter.

insert mode The electronic recording of a picture segment between two previously recorded segments on a videotape recorder using a previously laid control track. Cf. assemble mode.

insert module A module that, when inserted into equipment or a system, enables it to perform additional functions.

insert rule A series of baseline dots used to separate columns of type matter.

insert scene *See* insert.

insert section *See* insert.

insert set A small portion of a set constructed for use in shooting brief scenes. Also called a *detail set. See also* wild set.

insert shot *See* insert.

insert space A type space that expands a line equally in both directions.

insert stage A miniature set used to shoot small objects. Also called a *table top.*

insert tape A program segment recorded on tape for later insertion into a live program.

inservice programming Instructional television programming designed for members of a profession or holders of jobs and used to upgrade specific skills.

inset □ A portion of a sheet that is cut and inserted in a signature. □ Artwork or a photograph that is made to appear as part of another piece of artwork or photograph. □ *See* insert.

inset initial *See* initial.

in sheets A book that is printed but unbound.

inside back cover (IBC) One of the preferred positions for advertising in a magazine. Also called a *third cover.*

inside form *See* inner form.

inside front cover (IFC) One of the preferred positions for advertising in a magazine. Also called a *second cover.*

inside panel All outdoor advertising panels erected as a group with several facing the same direction, except for the one closest to the traffic. The code is A for all the panels except for the one closest to the street, which is coded AE.

inside spread The two facing pages at the center of a newspaper or magazine.

inspection □ An on-site investigation by the FCC of a radio or television station's personnel and records, often held because of complaints against a licensee. □ A physical inspection of outdoor advertising structures to verify copy delivery, distribution, or other contracted values. □ The periodic checking on the quality of stored film or tape.

installation charge The charge made by a cable television system to a new subscriber.

installed sample Television households in which SIA equipment has been installed.

installer An individual who physically connects a subscriber to a cable television system, subscription television service, and so on.

installment buyer A person who orders goods or services and pays for them in two or more periodic payments after delivery of the products or services.

instantaneous audience rating The size of a television or radio audience as of a given instant, or point in time, expressed as a percentage of some specified base. Cf. total audience rating.

instantaneous disc *See* instantaneous recording.

instantaneous meter *See* meter.

instantaneous recording A disc that is intended for direct playback without further processing. Also called an *instantaneous disc.*

instant book A paperbound book describing a newsworthy event published shortly after the event.

instant lettering Letters, numbers, symbols, and so on, containing an adhesive backing for making signs, cards, graphics, and so on.

instant photography The use of cameras designed to furnish a picture within a few minutes, as with a polaroid camera.

instant publishing The use of type already set or completed computer typesetting tapes to reprint a book or other manuscript.

instant replay Action, often sports, recorded on special videotape or video disc recorders and immediately played back for the viewers.

Institute of Outdoor Advertising (IOA) The marketing, research, and promotion arm of the standardized outdoor advertising industry. Formed in 1974 and supported by outdoor companies and affiliates of the industry, it provides the advertising community with information needed for a more thorough understanding of the medium.

institutional advertising Advertising designed to promote good will for a company or sponsor rather than to promote a specific product or service. *See also* image advertising.

institutional loop An interconnection between a cable television system and an educational institution for sending and receiving programs.

institutional network An interconnection between institutions or businesses in the same field for the exchange of programs and information.

institutional program A radio or television program containing only institutional advertising.

instruction A single step in a computer program.

instructional film A film designed to assist in teaching skills, precepts, or other information. Also called an *informational film.*

instructional programs (I) Programs (other than those classified as A, N, PA, R, or S) involving the discussion of, or primarily designed to further an appreciation or understanding of, literature, music, fine arts, history, geography, and the natural and social sciences; and programs devoted to occupational and vocational instruction, instruction with respect to hobbies, and similar programs intended primarily to instruct. An FCC program type category.

instructional television (ITV) Television used for formalized instruction, either in-school or broadcast.

instructional television fixed service (ITFS) The frequencies set aside by the FCC for use by educational institutions in relaying ITV programs.

instructional television fixed station A fixed station operated by an educational organization and used primarily for the transmission of visual and aural instructional, cultural, and other types of educational material to one or more fixed receiving locations.

instrument A theatrical type luminaire.

instrumentation □ The process of orchestrating musical compositions. □ The use of meters or other devices to measure circuit values.

instrument of authorization A license, construction permit, or other written permission from the FCC to operate a broadcast station or cable television system.

insulation A nonconductive material used to coat wires to prevent grounding, shorts, or loss of current.

insurance □ A camera held on a wide shot to cover unexpected talent movement. Also called a *cover shot.* □ A duplicate film or tape made in case of damage to the master or original. □ Insurance may cover such items as cast insurance; negative film and videotape insurance; props, sets, and wardrobe insurance; animal mortality insurance; equipment insurance; bad weather insurance; extra expense insurance; property damage liability insurance; errors and omissions insurance (plagiarism, copyright infringements, and so on).

insurance print *See* insurance.

in sync The perfect matching of sound and picture. *See also* sync. Cf. out of sync.

int A script abbreviation for *interior.*

in-tab An abbreviation for *in tabulation. See also* in-tab sample.

in-tab goal The Arbitron usable in-tab diary sample objective for television households in the ADI. The size of the in-tab goal is relative to the number of television households in the ADI.

in-tab sample The number of usable returned diaries or meter households actually tabulated in producing a market report. In-tab consists of television households that returned one or more usable diaries, plus a selected percentage of Planned-No-Viewing households. This percentage will vary from county to county and from survey to survey. Often referred to as "in-tab."

in-tab sample size *See* sample size.

intaglio □ A printing method in which the design is engraved or incised into a metal plate. Cf. lithography, relief, and surface printing. □ A print made by this method.

integer A whole number; one that does not contain a fraction.

integral density The density of combined color images on tripak color film as measured through red, green, and blue filters. Cf. analytical density.

integral screen A motion picture screen designed for viewing images in three dimensions without glasses.

integral tripack The common form of color film; composed of three separate layers of emulsion, each sensitive to a different color of light, bonded to a common base.

integrate To insert a sequence of or from a film or videotape, such as a commercial, into a television program.

integrated amplifier An audio amplifier that contains both a preamplifier and a power amplifier.

integrated circuit (IC) A subminiature, solid state circuit that consists of interconnected semiconductors formed on a tiny chip of silicon; usually housed in a DIP.

integrated commercial □ A commercial delivered by the talent on a radio or television program. □ A commercial for a single sponsor that mentions two or more products. Cf. piggyback.

integrated format A radio or television program format that gives two or more sponsoring advertisers exposure according to the portion of the time purchased by each.

integrated home system A number of related home components used as part of a larger system.

Integrated Services Digital Network (ISDN) A proposal whereby a network can be created to carry everything from motion pictures to data to high-fidelity sound.

integrated software A group of application programs designed to be interactive.

integrated system □ An electronic system in which all components are designed to be compatible. □ A system in which several elements are connected and used for more than one function.

integration of ownership and management One of the criteria used by the FCC in comparative hearings. Credit is awarded if the applicant proposes to function in a managerial position with the proposed station on a day-to-day basis.

intelligence A meaningful signal conveyed by a carrier wave.

intelligent A computer device, interface, terminal, and so on, capable of processing information on its own.

intelligent player A CD player or LaserVision drive with additional computing facilities built in, enabling the player to interact with the user or to operate under program control. CD-I players are intelligent players.

intelligibility *See* articulation.

Intelsat International Telecommunications Satellite Organization. An organization, established in 1964, which operates a worldwide communications satellite system. COMSAT is the United States member of Intelsat.

intensification The process of increasing the density of an underdeveloped film by the use of chemicals. Cf. latensification.

intensity □ A measure of the "strength" of a light source in a particular direction. Intensity is independent of the distance from the source. The unit is the candela. *See also* candlepower. □ The strength or brightness of a display on a screen. □ *See* chroma. □ A measure of the "strength" of a magnetic field, sound, and so on. □ The advertising weight given to outdoor advertising posters. Common showing sizes are #50 and #100, but in a larger market, #25 and #75 are offered and other special showings may be negotiated.

intensity control The potentiometer used to control the strength of the electron beam in a cathode ray tube.

intensity distribution In lighting, a graph or diagram that describes how the intensity of a light source varies with direction.

intensity scale A series of film frame exposures in which the exposure remains the same but the intensity of the light differs. Used in sensitometry. Cf. step wedge.

interactive Having the capacity for communication flow in each direction.

interactive cable A cable television system that is capable of carrying signals both to and from the headend. Also called *two-way cable.*

interactive medium □ A medium that is designed for two-way communication. □ A medium that presents information in such a way that, by means of an application program, it is delivered in the course of a dialog with the user. The application may also be included in the medium. Examples include interactive LaserVision and CD-I.

interactive mode □ A cable television system operation that allows two-way communication between the subscriber and the cablecaster. □ The presentation of information in a sequence determined by a dialogue between the information medium and the recipient. Examples include CD-I and LaserVision. *See also* interactive medium. Cf. linear mode.

interactive system A system capable of using an interactive medium to supply information to a user.

interactive television A television system that is capable of two-way interaction when used with a computer and a modem. May include security systems, shopping services, banking facilities, games, and so on.

interactive video disc (IVD) The first attempt to merge the realism of motion video and audio with the interactivity of personal computers using an analog laser videodisc player with a digital computer interface.

inter alia In addition to other matters.

interchange □ The ability to play a tape on a television tape recorder other than the one used to record it. □ Picture faults resulting from such action. □ Pertaining to the degradations caused by interchanging.

interchangeability The characteristics that make it possible to change components of a system for other components from a different source and still obtain performance within the system specification. For example, CD-DA and CD-I discs and players are interchangeable. *See also* compatibility and standardization.

interchangeable lens A camera lens that is mounted so that it can be removed and replaced by a different lens.

intercity The main telephone lines that connect cities together. Also called *interexchange.*

intercity channel Telephone circuits between towns or exchange areas within a LATA that are used for radio remotes, network television, or to transmit a program from one station to another. Also called an *interexchange channel.*

intercity relay (ICR) *See* aural broadcast intercity relay station.

Intercollegiate Cooperative Broadcasting Network A network of cooperating radio stations that produces and syndicates interviews and documentaries.

intercom An intercommunicating system between a control room and a television studio.

interconnect □ The connection of customer-provided equipment to a telephone company's line. □ The connection between a cable television system and its program suppliers—such as satellite distribution, microwave, antennas, and so on—or between two or more cable television systems. □ Several cable television systems joined together in a specific area for purposes of selling advertising.

interconnectability The ability of two or more devices to be connected together.

interconnecting The ability to connect any load circuit to any line or control circuit by means of an interplugging or cross-connecting apparatus that permits the operation of groups of widely separated luminaires from adjacent, easily handled controls.

interconnection ☐ The use of microwave equipment, boosters, translators, repeaters, communication space satellites, or other apparatus or equipment for the transmission and distribution of television or radio programs to noncommercial educational television or radio broadcast stations. The preceding includes national, regional, state, and other interconnections. ☐ A tie line.

interconnection point The place where an interconnection takes place between a broadcast station or CATV system and the facilities of the telephone company or other distribution company.

Intercosmos An intergovernmental understanding between nine eastern European countries concerning the exploration and use of outer space.

intercut *See* cross cut.

intercutting The back and forth cutting between two or more independent scenes so that the separate actions appear to be taking place simultaneously. Also called *crosscut.*

Interdepartment Radio Advisory Committee (IRAC) A federal government advisory group begun by Secretary of Commerce Herbert Hoover in 1923. Membership includes the FCC, Air Force, Army, Federal Maritime Commission, Navy; and the Departments of Agriculture, Commerce, Interior, Justice, State, and Treasury.

interest *See* AIDA.

interested person Any person having a direct or indirect interest in the outcome of a restricted proceeding before the FCC.

interexchange *See* intercity.

interexchange channel *See* intercity channel.

interface ☐ A device, circuit, or protocol by which two or more units or systems interact. ☐ The point at which a connection is made between two compatible components or systems. ☐ The means of communication used at an interface. ☐ The exchange of information between two or more devices. ☐ The hardware and software that link a computer to a peripheral device. ☐ The physical connection between any two devices. ☐ A self-contained unit containing circuitry that allows two or more units to work together as a system or that allows a user to interact with a system. ☐ The point of interconnection between two distinct but adjacent communications systems having different functions. For example, the interface in the communication-satellite service is that point where communications terminal equipment of the terrestrial common carriers or other authorized entities interconnects with the terminal equipment of the communication-satellite earth station complex.

interference The effect of unwanted energy due to one or a combination of emissions, radiations, or inductions upon reception of a radiocommunication system, manifested by any performance degradation, misinterpretation, or loss of information that could be extracted in the absence of such unwanted energy. *See also* noise.

interference filter An optical filter that rejects unwanted radiation by reflecting those wavelengths.

Interim Communications Satellite Committee The governing body of Intelsat.

interim license A temporary broadcast license issued pending final action on the application by the FCC.

interim operation The operation of a broadcast station by one or more applicants for a license, pending final action on the applications.

interim statement A sworn, unaudited circulation statement by a periodical publisher, made quarterly or on special occasions.

interior (int) Scenes that are shot indoors or so as to appear to have been shot indoors. Abbreviated *int.* Cf. exterior (ext).

interior continuity link An individual continuity link used at one point in a program or scene. Cf. general continuity link.

interior monologue The use of an aside or the presentation of a stream-of-consciousness speech or narration spoken by a performer and heard by an audience.

interior sound The sound made by something inside a large object as heard from the outside of the object, such as an automobile.

interlace *See* interlaced scanning.

interlaced scanning A scanning process in which successively scanned lines are spaced an integral number of line widths, and in which the adjacent lines are scanned during successive cycles of the field frequency. Used to eliminate flicker. Also called *interlace* and *line interlace. See also* frame.

interleaving □ The insertion of blank or other sheets between printed sheets in a book. □ In CD-I, the process of physically separating data so it can be retrieved at the rate required for processing the data. It involves the interspacing of sectors at intervals that correspond to the nature of the data. For audio, a regular interspaced pattern is used that depends on the audio quality level required. The subheader indicates the interleaving pattern at file, channel, and data type levels. Blocks between consecutive audio blocks can be used for video or text data. □ The placing of the bands of the chrominance signal between the bands of the luminance signal in the transmission of a color composite television signal.

interlibrary loan A book or other manuscript transferred from one library to another on a temporary basis.

inter-list duplicate Duplication of name and address records between two or more lists, other than house lists, being mailed by a list user. Cf. intra-list duplicate.

interlock □ A system that electronically links a projector with a sound recorder; used during postproduction to view the edited film and sound track, to check timing, pacing, synchronization, and so on. *See also* interlock projector. □ A system for driving a sound head at the same speed as the claw in a projector. □ The integration of a set with a rear projection. □ A mechanism for temporarily interconnecting several lighting dimmer handles together. □ An electrical safety device that removes power from equipment when access covers are removed.

interlocked Lines of type that are so close the ascenders from one line overlap the descenders from the line above.

interlocking The mechanical joining of individual light control dimmers for simultaneous movement. Accomplished by twisting the dimmer handles so that a plunger is dropped into a slotted cam mounted rigidly on a shaft that is connected solidly to the master interlocking handles.

interlock motor *See* selsyn.

interlock projector A projector capable of running two reels of film at the same time; one containing the picture, the other the sound.

interlock system An electrical or mechanical system in which all the components work in synchronization.

Intermedia The religious programming branch of NCC/USA.

intermediate A positive or negative print derived from a tripack camera original. *See also* internegative and interpositive.

intermediate film A reversal color film.

intermediate frequency (IF) An electronic signal that has been changed partially during reception or transmission.

Intermedical TV Network A Washington, D.C., television network that ties major governmental medical institutions together.

intermessage A communication between two places or persons.

intermission A brief period between a double feature, acts of a play, and so on.

intermittent action *See* intermittent movement.

intermittent effect The difference between the density of an image shot a frame at a time and an image shot with the camera running at normal speed.

intermittent movement The periodic starting and stopping of the mechanism (claw, dog, or Maltese Cross) that moves the film in a camera or projector, thus allowing the exposure or projection of the film. Also called *intermittent action.* Cf. continuous motion.

intermittent pressure The pressure intermittently applied during intermittent movement in a camera or projector.

intermittent prism *See* rotating prism.

intermittent service area The area receiving service from the ground wave of an AM station but beyond the primary service area and subject to some interference and fading.

intermixture The allotment of both UHF and VHF channels to a market. Cf. deintermixture.

intermodulation The modulation of a complex wave by its components.

intermodulation distortion (IM) Nonlinear distortion characterized by the appearance of frequencies in the output, equal to the sums and differences of the component frequencies present in the input wave. Cf. harmonic distortion.

intern A student who works for experience in a media organization, usually without pay.

internal communication Communication within an organization, business, and so on.

internal house organ *See* house organ.

internal motivation Motivation that arises from the emotions of an actor rather than that necessitated by script requirements. Cf. external motivation.

internal publication *See* house organ.

internal reflector A focusing reflector (usually parabolic or elliptic) within a lamp. Cf. proximity reflector.

internal sync Synchronizing pulses that are generated within a piece of equipment, such as a video camera. Cf. external sync.

International Alliance of Theatrical Stage Employees (IATSE) A union that represents individuals in a number of different crafts, such as grips, projectionists, sound technicians, scenic artists, screen cartoonists, costume designers, and so on. Often abbreviated IA.

international broadcasting The transmission of programs from one country to the citizens of another country. International broadcasting may also include the exchange of programs between countries. Cf. comparative broadcasting systems.

International Broadcasting Awards Awards given by the Hollywood Radio and Television Society for commercials that "stimulate artistic, creative, and technical excellence" in broadcast advertising on an international basis.

International Broadcasting Society (IBS) A Scandinavian organization established in 1985 to promote cooperation and understanding in broadcasting between third world and developed countries.

international broadcasting station A broadcast station employing frequencies allocated to the broadcasting service between 5950 and 26,100 kHz, the transmissions of which are intended to be received directly by the general public in foreign countries.

International Brotherhood of Electrical Workers (IBEW) A union for stage, screen, and television electricians.

international character set A collection of letters, symbols, accents, and so on, available for computers that are needed to print materials using various languages.

International CIE system *See* ICI standards.

International Commission of Lighting *See* ICI.

international communication The transmission of news, information, opinions, beliefs, and so on, between or among different nations.

International Communication Association (ICA) An association composed primarily of teachers and researchers in the United States.

international copyright A copyright secured through agreement between cooperating nations. *See also* copyright.

international design *See* Swiss design.

International Electrotechnical Commission (IEC) A standards organization with headquarters in Geneva, Switzerland. Video recorders and many other electrical and electronic systems are internationally standardized by the IEC.

International News Service (INS) *See* United Press International (UPI).

International Organization for Standardization (ISO) A standards organization with headquarters in Geneva, Switzerland. Motion picture film systems are standardized by the ISO, together with many other mechanically based technologies.

international phonetic alphabet (IPA) A set of symbols that are used to describe the sounds made in human speech, regardless of the language being spoken.

International Radio and Television Organization (OIRT) A broadcasting association composed of broadcasting organizations from the Soviet Union and Eastern Europe, with associate members from other parts of the world. Cf. European Broadcasting Union (EBU).

International Radio and Television Society (IRTS) An organization, founded in 1952, of individuals in radio, television, and related industries. Provides industry faculty seminars, internship programs, publications, research, and so on.

International Radio Regulations The worldwide radio, television, satellite, and other types of regulations adopted by the International Telecommunications Union.

international reply coupon A coupon issued by various countries as postage for return mail.

international standard *See* picture line standard.

International Standard Book Number (ISBN) The number assigned to each published monograph identifying the title, author, publisher, and so on, and printed on the verso of the title page.

International Standard Recording Code (ISRC) Information about country of origin, owner, year of issue, and serial number of individual audio tracks that optionally appears in CD-DA subcode.

International Standard Serial Number (ISSN) A number similar to the ISBN but printed on the cover; it is assigned to each periodical publication.

International Standards Organization (ISO) An international standards coordinating body for, in addition to numerous other industries, standards for radio, television, and film.

International Telecommunications Union (ITU) (also UIT) An international organization of member nations designed to improve telecommunication services, to allocate frequencies, and to eliminate interference. Founded in 1865 as the International Telegraph Union.

International Television Center (ITC) An operational center for the transmission or reception of international television programs.

international track A film or tape soundtrack used to record dialogue in another language. *See also* foreign picture release negative.

International Typographical Union (ITU) A labor union for typesetters and others.

internegative (IN) □ A negative copy of a camera original color reversal film. Normally used to make release prints. □ A stage in the making of opticals.

interpersonal communication The communication that takes place in face-to-face situations.

interpolation □ A method of substituting estimated values for missing or erroneous data. In statistics, for example, the estimating of the intermediate steps between the data points described by the sample. □ In computer animation, the automatic generation of graphics or action to complete the sequence between specified frames.

interpositive (ip) A fine grain color positive print made from a color negative. Normally used to make color dupe negatives.

interpretative reporting The reporting of the facts of a news story with clarity but without editorial comment.

interrupt A computer program halt; a signal to a computer that a peripheral device needs attention.

interrupted continuous wave (ICW) A continuous wave interrupted by a sound frequency.

interrupted feedback (IFB) A wireless earphone used to communicate with a performer who is on camera.

interruption Any insertion of nonprogram material within the body of a radio or television program.

intersatellite communication *See* intersatellite link.

intersatellite link (ISL) The transmission and reception of signals between satellites in order to expand the footprint. Also called *intersatellite communication.*

intersatellite service A radio communication service providing links between artificial earth satellites.

interspacing *See* letterspacing.

intersplice To join together, electronically or mechanically, program material originally recorded separately.

Intersputnik An international satellite system, founded by members of Intercosmos in 1971, that is capable of delivering point-to-point communication as well as television broadcast signals.

interstate commerce Commerce between any state, the District of Columbia, the Commonwealth of Puerto Rico, or any possession of the United States and any place outside thereof that is within the United States; commerce between points in the same state, the District of Columbia, the Commonwealth of Puerto Rico, or any possession of the United States but through any place outside thereof, or commerce wholly within the District of Columbia or any possession of the United States.

interstate communication Communication or transmission □ from any state, territory, or possession of the United States (other than the Canal Zone), or the District of Columbia; to any other state, territory, or possession of the United States (other than the Canal Zone), or the District of Columbia, □ from or to the United States to or from the Canal Zone, insofar as such communication or transmission takes place within the United States; or □ between points within the United States but through a foreign country; but shall not, with respect to the provision of Title II of the Communications Act (other than Section 223 thereof), include wire or radio communication between points in the same State, Territory, or possession of the United States, of the District of Columbia, through any place outside thereof, if such communication is regulated by a State commission. Also called *interstate transmission.*

interstate transmission *See* interstate communication.

interstitial Material used to fill a gap in radio or television programming until the next program is scheduled.

Inter-sync An Ampex designed device for the synchronous mixing of the output of two tapes. Similar to the A and B roll in film postproduction mixing.

intertitles Motion picture titles that are used within the body of a film. Used mostly in the silent era but still used occasionally.

Intertype A tradename for a linecasting machine similar to a Linotype.

interurbia A metropolitan area containing two or more cities.

interval *See* hiatus.

intervalometer An automatic timing device for time-lapse photography.

intervening variable A nonobservable or nonidentifiable factor in the effect a message has on a receiver.

interview □ A process whereby one person seeks to obtain information from another person or group of persons. *See also* coincidental interview, personal interview, placement interview, recall interview, and telephone interview. □ According to SAG, an interview includes the reading or speaking of lines that the player has not been given to learn outside the studio, without photography or sound recording. Cf. audition and mass test. □ A story obtained by interview.

interviewee The person being interviewed.

interviewer The person who asks questions of respondents in a survey or on a radio or television program.

interviewer bias *See* interviewer effects.

interviewer effects Any differences or variations in responses to survey questions that can be attributed to differences between interviewers, rather than differences between respondents. Interviewer effects generally occur when interviewers fail to administer survey questionnaires in a highly standardized and consistent manner for all of the respondents interviewed. Also called *interviewer bias* and *interviewer variance.*

interviewer variance *See* interviewer effects.

interviewing bias A survey error that occurs when interviewers either fail to ask questions according to instructions or inadvertently influence the person being interviewed. *See also* nonsampling error.

Intervision A program exchange organization of East European countries operated by the International Radio and Television Organization (OIRT). Cf. Eurovision.

in the beam A performer within the angle of maximum microphone sound acceptance.

in the camera effects Effects—such as those achieved by filters, day-for-night, overcranking, and so on—in a camera as opposed to those achieved in a laboratory.

in the can □ A completed program on tape or film ready for use. Also called *on the shelf.* □ Film that is shot but not yet processed.

in the field A film or tape that is shot on location as opposed to one shot in a studio.

in-the-market traffic All traffic that originates within the market in which an outdoor advertising plant operates. Cf. out-of-market traffic.

in the mud □ Lifeless vocal quality. □ Sound picked up by the wrong microphone in a multiple microphone setup. □ Sound so low in volume it barely moves the indicator on a VU meter.

in the red Said of a VU meter that is driven past 100 percent modulation.

in tight A camera close-up.

into The period of time a radio or television production crew is ''into the program.''

intraexchange Located within one telephone exchange; normally one town.

intralata Located within a telephone LATA.

intra-list duplicate The duplication of names and address records within a given mailing list.

intrapersonal communication The communication that takes place within oneself.

intrastate commerce Commerce that is confined to within the borders of a single state. Cf. interstate commerce.

intro An abbreviation for *introduction.* The opening copy, lines, music, sound effects, picture, and so on, that set the scene for what is to follow. Cf. outro.

introduction □ Expository material written by someone other than the author of a book; usually included as part of the front matter. Also called a *foreword.* □ *See* intro. □ An opening tag for a taped or filmed commercial. Cf. ending. □ The initial stage of an advertising campaign. □ The first of the three major divisions of a speech. Cf. body and conclusion.

intrusion A violation of a person's right of privacy, such as by bugging, wiretapping, or using secret cameras or microphones.

INTV Independent Television Station Association.

invalid A computer command that has no function.

invasion of privacy A violation of the right of privacy; subjection of an unwilling person to unwarranted intrusions or undesired publicity. *See also* appropriation, false light, intrusion, and publication of private facts.

inventory □ The time periods on a broadcast station that remain unsold and are available to advertisers. A list of availabilities. □ The total number or amount of goods available; tapes, records, books, salable minutes, space, and so on.

inverse square law □ The physical law that states that electromagnetic radiation decreases in proportion to the square of the distance. □ An equation relating the intensity of a source to the illumination it produces at a given distance.

inversion □ The bending of a radio wave by differences in the atmospheric pressure, temperature, or moisture content between two layers of air. □ The quality of a lens that turns images upside down. □ A reversal of polarity in a black and white television picture.

inverted pyramid □ A headline in which each line is centered and shorter than the one above. □ The basic news story structure in which the major points are covered first, the minor points last. Also called a *half diamond.*

inverted telephoto lens A lens having a short focal length and a relatively long back focus. *See also* retrofocal lens.

inverter A device used to change direct current into alternating current. Cf. rectifier.

investigative reporter An individual who carries out investigative reporting. Also referred to as a *sleuth.*

investigative reporting A type of reporting that involves extended research and interviewing, often culminating in an exposure of wrongdoing in government or business or by public officials.

invisible The portion of artwork or design that is used as background to the primary focus of the work.

invisible cut A cut made from one camera to another during a performer's action. Cf. invisible edit.

invisible edit A cut made by matching the action from two successive camera shots. Cf. invisible cut.

invisible spectrum The portion of the spectrum containing the colors not visible to the eye: infrared and ultraviolet.

in vision *See* on camera (OC).

inward WATS The 800 number telephone system that allows calls from customers or other callers to be made to a company or organization without a toll charge. Also called *in WATS.* Cf. outward WATS.

in WATS *See* inward WATS.

IO Image Orthicon.

IOA Institute of Outdoor Advertising.

I/O error A message from a computer notifying the operator that a problem exists in the transfer of information to or from a peripheral device.

I/O functions In CD-I, the transfer functions Read and Play, which perform the physical transfer of data from the disc.

IOJ International Organization of Journalists.

ion An atom with a positive or negative electric charge.

ion burn A defect in the center of a CRT caused by ion bombardment. *See also* ion trap.

ionic loudspeaker *See* ionophone.

ionophone An electrostatic loudspeaker. Also called an *ionic loudspeaker.*

ionosphere The part of the earth's atmosphere from 25 to 250 miles above the surface containing layers that affect and reflect radio waves back to earth. *See also* Kennelly-Heaviside layer, D layer, E layer, and F layer.

ionospheric scatter The propagation of radio waves by scattering as a result of irregularities or discontinuities in the ionization of the atmosphere. Cf. tropospheric scatter.

ionospheric wave *See* sky wave.

ion trap A coating or magnetic field used in television picture tubes to prevent ions from hitting the screen.

I/O port An opening on a CD-I player in a microcomputer, enabling an external device to be connected for input/output operation.

IPA □ Independent Publishers Association. □ International Phonetic Alphabet.

IPI International Press Institute. An association, based in Switzerland, of newspaper and broadcast executives.

IPMPI International Photographers of the Motion Picture Industry. A trade association.

IPOSA International Photo Optical Show Association, Inc.

IP print A print made from an interpositive.

IPRA International Public Relations Association.

ips Inches per second.

IPTC International Press Telecommunications Council.

IQ International Quorum of Film and Video Producers.

IRAC Interdepartment Radio Advisory Committee.

IRB Intercollegiate Religious Broadcasters.

IRC International radio carrier. A common carrier that provides data links to overseas points.

IRE □ Institute of Radio Engineers. *See* IEEE. □ Investigative Reporters and Editors. An organization for the study of investigative reporting.

IRE standard scale A linear scale for measuring, in IRE units, the relative amplitudes of the components of a television signal from zero reference at blanking level, with picture information falling in the positive and synchronizing information in the negative.

Iris The NATPE awards given for local television programs and commercials.

iris □ In lighting instruments, an arrangement of thin plates that forms an opaque area with a circular opening in the center. The size of the circular opening is adjustable. As an example of its application, an iris diaphragm commonly is used in follow spots to vary the size of the beam. Also called an *iris diaphragm.* □ *See* iris wipe. □ The adjustable diaphragm used for vignettes. □ *See* aperture, diaphragm, and stop.

iris in A circular wipe that moves from the center of the screen to beyond the borders as a fade in from black or to reveal a new picture. Cf. iris out.

iris out A circular wipe that moves from beyond the borders of the screen to the center as a fade to black or to wipe in another picture. Cf. iris in.

iris wipe A circular wipe, either inward or outward. *See also* iris in and iris out.

iron oxide *See* ferric oxide.

irradiation The scattering of light rays as they fall on the silver halide crystals in a film's emulsion.

IRTF International Radio and Television Foundation, Inc. An organization that provides funds for the operation of IRTS.

IRTS International Radio and Television Society.

ISBD International Standard Bibliographic Description.

ISBDM International Standard Bibliographic Description for Monographs.

ISBDS International Standard Bibliographic Description for Serials.

ISBN International Standard Book Number.

ISDN Integrated Services Digital Network.

I Signal The signal used to convey the color difference or chrominance information in color television. *See also* color difference signal, luminance signal, M signal, and Q signal.

ISIT Intensified Silicon Intensifier Target.

ISL Intersatellite link.

island □ A mounted and positioned telecine film or film and slide chain. □ *See* island position.

island position □ Advertising in newspapers or magazines that is completely surrounded by print matter or margins. Also called an *island. See also* full position. □ A radio or television commercial announcement that is isolated from all other commercials by program material.

ISM Industrial, scientific, and medical.

ISO International Organization for Standardization.

iso Isolated. An isolated camera.

isolated A radio or television commercial with no other commercial immediately before or after it.

isolated camera □ A video camera reserved for close-ups of an action. Often used for instant replay in sports. Abbreviated *iso.* □ A video camera that is not connected to a system; a standalone camera and recorder.

isolation □ Electric or acoustic separation from one component or circuit. □ The complete electric or acoustic separation from one component, circuit, or device from others. Coupling between isolated circuits may be accomplished by isolation amplifiers, networks, or transformers.

isolation booth A small sound studio within a radio or television studio. *See also* announce booth.

ISO standards *See* International Standards Organization.

ISPC International Sound Program Center. An operational center for the transmission and reception of international broadcasts.

ISR Information Storage and Retrieval.

ISRC International Standard Recording Code.

ISRO Indian Space Research Organization.

ISSN International Standard Serial Number.

issue □ The total output of a newspaper in one day; may consist of more than one edition. □ All of the copies of a magazine or other periodical set from the same type.

issue life The period during which a given issue of a periodical is assumed to be read by the average reader, typically five weeks for a weekly and three months for a monthly.

IST Division of Information Science and Technology, National Science Foundation.

I symbol A signal that conveys the color difference information in television. Cf. M symbol and Q symbol.

ITA □ Independent Television Authority. Now IBA. □ International Tape Association. □ International Tape/Disc Association.

ital An abbreviation for *italic.*

italic A typeface that slants to the right while retaining the other characteristics of its roman counterpart.

itals An abbreviation for *italics.*

ITBC Instructional Television Funding Cooperative.

ITC □ International Television Center. An operational center for the transmission and reception of international and national television programs. □ International Television Committee. An organization for technical cooperation and standardization. Founded in 1947 and based in Paris.

ITCA Independent Television Companies Association. A British broadcasters' organization.

item A brief news story.

itemization A listing, in a news story, of the points to be covered in the story. Also called *itemizing*.

itemizer A person who furnishes a newspaper with news items.

itemizing *See* itemization.

iteration A method of solving a problem that uses repetitive calculations so that each time a better estimate is found. Used, for example, to select the best possible media mix.

ITFS Instructional Television Fixed Service.

ITFS response station A fixed station operated at an authorized location to provide communication by voice and/or data signals to an associated instructional television fixed station.

itn An abbreviation for *internegative.*

ITNA Independent Television News Association. A nonprofit news cooperative.

ITO Independent Television Organization.

ITSC International Telecommunications Satellite Consortium. *See* Intelsat.

ITSO International Telecommunications Satellite Organization (of the United Nations).

ITT International Telephone and Telegraph Company.

ITU □ International Telecommunication Union. □ International Typographical Union.

ITV □ Industrial Television. □ Instructional Television.

ITVA □ International Industrial Television Association. □ International Television Association.

IUAJ International Union of Agricultural Journalists.

IUE International Union of Electrical, Radio and Machine Workers.

IVD Interactive video disc.

IXP Information Exchange Protocol.

J

J □ Joule. □ Journal.

jack □ A female socket or receptacle. Cf. plug. □ A framed stage brace used to hold up scenery.

jacket □ The outside pages of a booklet or pamphlet. □ *See* dust jacket. □ A square plastic cover for a floppy disk. Cf. envelope. □ The outer insulating sheath of a wire or cable.

jacket copy The written material that is printed on a dust jacket concerning the book and/or its author.

jacketed lamp A lamp that has a double glass enclosure.

jack panel An assembly containing a number of female receptacles. Also called a *bay* and *patch panel.*

jaggies A slang term for one of the most common results of aliasing—jagged or stairstepped edges on diagonal lines in a television picture. *See also* aliasing.

jam □ A cluttered appearance caused by too little white space on a page. □ A film camera buckle. □ A stoppage in printer operation caused by paper wedged in the mechanism.

jammed A news story lead that contains too much information.

jamming The intentional transmission of interference on a frequency so as to obliterate the signals of a station. Carried on at various times by the Soviet Union, Communist China, Cuba, and others. Cf. transborder interference.

jam sync The synchronizing of the time code generator numbers with the time code on the edited master. Used in videotape assemble editing.

Janus Awards Awards given by the Mortgage Bankers Association for excellence in regularly scheduled financial news programming.

Japanese paper A strong, long-fibered paper made in Japan. Sometimes refers to domestic paper, Japanese vellum, which is made in a similar way.

Japanese style *See* Chinese style.

Japanese vellum *See* Japanese paper.

jargon The technical or characteristic terminology used by persons within a given industry; several thousand examples may be found in these pages.

jazz An unconventional, freeform page layout style.

jazz format A radio station format characterized by music with intricate rhythms and improvisation with a return to the original theme, and highly stylized instrumentalists and vocalists.

jazz journalism A 1920s style of tabloid newspaper designed to increase circulation by using startling pictures, flashy artwork, and shocking writing.

JCA Joint Communications Agency.

JCC Joint Communications Center.

JCEB Joint Council on Educational Broadcasting.

JCET Joint Council on Educational Telecommunications.

JCIC Joint Committee for Intersociety Coordination.

JEDEC Joint Electron Device Engineering Council.

jeep A closed-circuit television system.

jell *See* gel.

jelly *See* gel.

Jena glass An optical glass produced since the 1800s in Jena, Germany.

Jenkins system A mechanical scanning system for television introduced by Francis Jenkins in 1925.

jenny A slang term for a portable power generator. Also called a *gen.*

jeopardy A plot device or circumstance that threatens a character.

jet An orifice that injects air or nitrogen into film processing solutions to agitate the liquid.

JETEC Joint Electron Tube Engineering Council.

jet printing *See* ink jet printing.

jib The arm of a crane.

JIC A script notation for "just in case."

jig A guide or template used in hand lettering, layout, design, and so on.

jiggle A derogatory term for a television or film shot of irrelevant material.

jiggle show A television program that features an excess of female anatomy in motion. Also called a *T and A show.*

jim dash A short dash often used to separate headlines or paragraphs.

jingle A commercial musical signature or logo. Usually contains melodies and/or phrases that are easily recognized. Cf. theme song.

jingle house A production company that makes music tracks for commercials.

jingle package A series of radio station identification spots set to music; a musical logo.

jingle track The score of a melody written especially for a commercial.

JIP Join(ed) in progress.

jitter □ An unsteady television picture usually caused by improper synchronization or a time base error. □ *See* strobing. □ The fluctuation of a projected motion picture caused by an insufficient loop or gate malfunction.

job □ A unit of work done by a computer, printer, or other device. □ A commercial printing order.

jobber □ A book wholesaler. □ A job printer.

jobbing Commercial printing.

job case A shallow, compartmented tray used to hold type. *See also* California job case.

job font A small display type font.

job lot A miscellaneous collection of goods for sale; often leftovers, remainders, overruns, and so on.

job press A platen press used for short run, general printing work.

job printer A printer who undertakes miscellaneous printing jobs such as circulars, forms, cards, and so on. Cf. book printer.

job shop A printshop that handles miscellaneous jobs.

job ticket A form or envelope on which the directions for a printing job or commercial project are written.

job type Ornamental or display type.

job work The work done by a job printer in a job shop.

jock *See* disc jockey.

jog □ To move a magnetic tape forward or back. □ To move a magnetic tape quickly to a desired point in the program. □ To align the edges of sheets of paper. □ To cause the cylinders of a printing press to move. □ A narrow flat.

jogger A person or device used to jog sheets of paper.

jogging The process of moving a tape or film back and forth a frame at a time.

John Hancock Award An award for excellence given to writers who have contributed significantly to consumer understanding of business and finance.

join A British term for a film splice between two shots.

join(ed) in progress (JIP) A radio or television program that is broadcast from some point after it has begun.

joiner A British term for a person who splices film.

joint □ The edit point on a tape or film. □ A connection between two or more electrical conductors. □ One of the grooves where a book cover flexes or hinges.

joint author A person who works with another or others in writing a book.

Joint Committee Against Pay-TV An organization of broadcasting and motion picture interests opposed to pay television.

Joint Committee for Intersociety Coordination (JCIC) A coordinating organization composed of the SMPTE, EIA, NAB, IEEE, and others.

Joint Committee on Toll Television An organization of motion picture exhibitors opposed to pay television.

Joint Council on Educational Telecommunications (JCET) A consortium of organizations concerned with educational television. Formed in 1950 to persuade the FCC to reserve frequencies for noncommercial, educational broadcasting. Formerly Joint Council on Educational Television.

joint imprint The imprint of two or more publishers on one book as part of a cooperative marketing measure.

Joint Media Committee on News Coverage Problems An association of representatives from five professional news organizations concerned with the orderly coverage of news events.

joint newspaper operating arrangement Any contract, agreement, joint venture (whether incorporated or not), or other arrangement entered into by two or more newspaper owners for the publication of two or more newspaper publications, pursuant to which joint or common production facilities are established or operated and joint or unified action is taken or agreed to be taken with respect to any one or more of the following: printing, time, method, and field of publication, allocation of production facilities; distribution; advertising solicitation; circulation solicitation; business department; establishment of advertising rates; establishment of circulation rates and revenue distribution; provided that there is no merger, combination, or amalgamation of editorial or reportorial staffs, and that editorial policies be independently determined. *See also* Newspaper Preservation Act.

joint operating agreement *See* joint newspaper operating arrangement.

joint promotion A commercial in which more than one advertiser features or highlights more than one product or service.

Joint Technical Advisory Committee An organization representing various land-mobile interests.

joint use The use of a utility pole by two or more different utilities or services, such as power, telephone, cable television, and so on.

joint venture agreement A partnership or other arrangement created to produce motion pictures, television programs, publishing ventures, and so on, in order to minimize the risk.

joint work A work prepared by two or more authors with the intention that their contributions be merged into inseparable or interdependent parts of a unitary whole.

jokesmith A gag writer.

Jones plug A type of polarized connector having numerous contacts.

journal A general term for any periodical publication.

Journal Award, The An award given by the SMPTE for the outstanding paper published in the society's journal each year.

journalese The jargon of journalism.

journalism □ The business of publishing newspapers and magazines. □ The collecting, editing, and reporting of newsworthy persons, events, and developments.

journalism review A collection of articles concerned with the study of journalism and journalists.

journalist A somewhat formal name for a writer, reporter, editor, and so on.

journeyman A person who has completed an apprenticeship in a trade such as printing.

joystick □ A peripheral, hand-held user interface device with a rotary lever that enables a user to alter or respond to on-screen images. □ A hand-operated control used as a positioner, tape controller, motion effector, and so on, on a special effects generator, video switcher, computer, or other equipment.

joystick zoom control A two-way variable switch that allows remote operator control of a zoom lens.

JSA Japanese Standards Association. An association similar to the EIA.

J school An abbreviation for a school of journalism in a college or university.

JTA Jewish Telegraphic Agency, Inc. An American news agency.

JTAC Joint Technical Advisory Committee.

judder An annoying flicker effect seen around moving objects in a television picture.

judge-made law *See* common law.

judgment A decision of a court stating the outcome of a case. In a jury trial, the outcome is called a *verdict.*

judgment sample A nonprobability sample selected on the basis of someone's opinion about which elementary units will give a typical result. Cf. convenience sample.

judicial review The determination by a court about whether a statute, ordinance, rule, or executive action violates a federal or state constitution.

juice A slang term for electricity.

juicer A slang term for an electrician. Also called a *gaffer.*

jumbo roll Any roll of paper intended to be cut or rewound into smaller rolls.

jump □ To continue a story from one page to another. Also called a *breakover.* □ That portion of the story continued on another page. Also called a *breakover* and *jump page.* □ The distance from a remote to the studio or pickup point. □ To omit a planned shot, scene, or portion of a radio or television program. □ *See* jumping a cue.

jump cut An unnatural cut between two scenes without a bridging shot or transition, resulting in a loss of continuity. Cf. match cut.

jumped cue *See* jumping a cue.

jumper A short length of wire or cable used to bypass or complete a circuit.

jumper cable *See* jumper.

jump head The headline placed over the portion of a story continued on another page.

jumping a cue A performer beginning a line or action too soon.

jump line The line indicating the page on which a jumped story is continued, or the line indicating the page from which the story came.

jump out To eliminate frames from film or videotape.

jumpover □ A two-page spread, other than a double truck. □ Photographs, charts, illustrations, and so on, that interrupt the flow of printed text.

jump page *See* jump.

jump the gutter To make titles, illustrations, or other matter continue from one page to a facing page.

junction A connection between two or more conductors.

junction box A metal container for joining conductors. *See also* spider.

junction station A microwave relay station that distributes signals from the main trunk to other legs of the system.

junior A fresnel spotlight or floodlight that can accommodate lamps from 1000 to 2000 watts. Also called a *junior solarspot* and *junior spot. See also* deuce. Cf. senior.

junior page *See* junior unit.

junior panel □ A 6-sheet outdoor advertising poster, as opposed to the larger 24-sheet and 30-sheet posters. □ In transit advertising, any advertising display unit of smaller than standard poster size.

junior solarspot *See* junior.

junior spot *See* junior.

junior spread *See* pony spread.

junior unit A magazine advertisement produced in a single size, whose dimensions are a full page in some publications and a partial page in larger size publications with editorial matter on top or bottom and one side. Also called a *junior page.* Cf. digest sized page.

junket An expense-paid trip arranged for reporters and other media personnel by companies or organizations desiring favorable publicity. Acceptance of a junket is considered to be unethical by most media organizations and individuals.

junk mail A derogatory term for mail containing solicitations to buy goods or services.

jurisdiction The area or kinds of cases over which a court or administrative agency has control.

jury A number of persons selected to determine the facts of a case. Also called a *petit jury.* Cf. grand jury.

Justice Department The federal agency responsible for the enforcement of federal laws. In broadcasting, the enforcement of the antitrust laws and preservation of commerce; the Criminal Code concerning lotteries and obscene language; false advertising, and so on.

justification □ The process of spacing lines of type so that each line is the same length. Cf. ragged right. □ The spaces or pieces of type metal used in justification.

justified □ A camera movement, such as a dolly or truck, that is necessary because of the action. □ *See* justification.

justify □ To add interletter or interword spaces or both to lines of type. □ To arrange a page of type so that the left, right, or both margins are in line vertically.

Justowriter A trademark for a pair of typewriters that provide automatic justification.

juvenile □ A book for children. □ An actor or performer who appears to be in the late teens or early twenties. Cf. ingenue.

K

K ☐ Kelvin. ☐ Key. ☐ Kilo. ☐ Cathode. ☐ A wire service code for commentary. ☐ A thousand units of computer storage; actually, 1024 units. ☐ Kilobytes. Cf. M. ☐ *See* call letters.

Kahn system An AM broadcast stereo system.

kaleidoscope From the Greek meaning "to see a beautiful shape." A digital effects device used to manipulate two-dimensional objects in three-dimensional space.

Kalmus Gold Medal Award, Herbert T. An award given by the SMPTE for outstanding contributions in the development of color film and associated processes, techniques, or equipment.

Kalvar process A light-scattering instead of a light-absorption film process that uses a thermoplastic resin on a polyester base instead of the conventional silver halide crystals.

KB Kilobytes. *See* K.

KBN Kill bad name. *See* nixie.

KBPS Kilobytes per second.

KC Kilocycle.

KC/S Kilocycles per second. Now kHz.

keep down An instruction to a typesetter to use only lowercase letters. Cf. keep up.

keepsake An illustrated verse giftbook of the 19th century.

keep standing An instruction to a printer to hold type that has been used for possible future use. Cf. kill.

keeptake A camera shot that is considered good enough for possible inclusion in the completed motion picture. Cf. outtake.

keep up An instruction to a typesetter to use only capital letters. Cf. keep down.

keg light A cylindrically shaped spotlight that can hold a 500- or 750-watt lamp. *See also* luminaire.

kell factor A measure of human visual acuity, for example, the number of television scanning lines necessary for individuals to perceive a stated number of lines. The factor for television is 0.7 times the number of scanning lines. Also called a *scanning factor.*

Kelvin A temperature scale where each degree is the same size as a degree centigrade but has its zero at minus 273 degrees. This is the unit of temperature used to designate the color temperature of a light source.

kelvinometer A light temperature meter.

Kennelly-Heaviside Layer The region of the ionosphere that can reflect radio waves back to earth. Also called the *Heaviside layer. See also* sky wave.

Kenotron A hot cathode vacuum tube.

kern Any part of the face of a piece of type that extends past the edge and overhangs the next letter.

kernel The nucleus of CD-RTOS responsible for service request processing, memory management, system initialization after a reset, multiprogramming, input/output management, and exception and interrupt processing. The kernel must always be in main memory when any part of it or any other segment is loaded.

Kerner report A report by the National Advisory Committee on Civil Disorders that investigated the responsibility of the media for ghetto rioting.

kerning ☐ Reducing the space between certain pairs of characters to improve their appearance. ☐ The compression of a type line for justification purposes. Cf. letterspacing.

Kerr cell A device used to electrically modulate a beam of light. Used in film shutters that can expose a shot as fast as one millionth of a second.

key ☐ A switch used to open or close a pot, as on an audio control console. ☐

The intensity of light on a scene. *See also* high key and low key. □ Film that is used for rear projection. □ To insert or substitute one television picture for a part of another. *See also* chromakey and matte. □ A positioning guide used in letterpress printing, lithography, bookbinding, and so on. □ The range or tone of a picture. □ A device used to tighten or loosen quoins. □ To insert a coded word or symbol in an advertisement, such as a box number, in order to determine the source of a response. *See also* keyed advertisement. □ *See* key code. □ A black printing plate. Abbreviated *k.* □ *See* extremes. □ *See* keyline. □ To turn sound on or off.

key account A major client of an advertising agency.

key animator In studio animation, the artist who draws the key or extreme poses; a full-fledged animator.

keyboard □ The arrangement of keys on a typewriter, Linotype machine, computer, and so on. □ To set type using a keyboard.

keyboarding The use of a keyboard to type alphanumeric characters and symbols into a computer system.

key code A group of letters or numbers, colors, or other markings used to measure the specific effectiveness of media, lists, advertisements, and offers. Also called a *key.*

key drawing A drawing of one of the main poses in animation.

keyed advertisement A print or mail advertisement containing an identifying mark, number, code, and so on, so that the specific advertisement eliciting the response might be identified. Also called *keying an advertisement. See also* key.

keyed insertion *See* key.

keyed rainbow signal The color bars produced by a continuous sine wave used for checking or matching colors.

key frame In television digital animation, the beginning or ending extreme that defines the desired path of motion.

key grip The head grip; a grip in charge of other grips. Also called *first grip.*

key in □ The act of throwing a switch (key). □ A television director's command to key a picture.

keying an advertisement *See* keyed advertisement.

key insert *See* key.

key letters Footage letters marked along the edge of a film, usually after processing. *See also* edge numbers.

key-light The principal source of light that establishes the character of the actor together with the atmosphere and mood of the scene. Sometimes called the main light. *See also* high-key lighting and low-key lighting. Cf. back-light and fill light.

keyline □ A line, usually at the bottom of a page, that explains the symbols used on the page. □ Any one of a number of possible descriptions of past buying history coded into a mailing list. □ An outline used to indicate the exact size and placement of each element of artwork, type, photographs, and so on; usually camera ready material. Also called a *key* and *type mechanical.*

key line A line of dialogue that reveals a fact or idea necessary to the resolution of the plot.

key map A map used in newsrooms to locate the site of newsworthy events.

key number One of the edge numbers on motion picture film.

keypad □ A hand-held keyboard used for interactive responses to cable television inquiries, videotext, and so on. □ A computer keyboard containing a separate numerical set of keys. Also called a *numeric keypad* and *numeric pad.*

key plate In color printing, the first plate printed to which the other color plates must be registered. Also called a *keystone.*

key pose In animation, the characteristic or main pose in a movement. *See also* extremes.

key position An animation extreme.

keys A term synonymous with *extremes.*

key shot A master shot of a scene.

key sounds Sound effects used to evoke images in an audience of more than the single effect, such as multiple automobile horns to suggest a traffic jam.

key station A radio or television station that originates a network program.

keystone □ Picture distortion caused by a camera or projector not being at a right angle to the surface of the object being shot or occurring when the electron beam is not at a right angle to the face of the tube. □ A small piece of plywood used to reinforce joints on flats. □ *See* key plate.

keystroke A single strike of any key on a keyboard.

keyword A word used to classify a document for computer database reference.

K factor A rating system for television picture quality. *See also* Grades 1-6.

kHz Kilohertz.

kickback An unethical and sometimes illegal rebate on advertising rates or talent fee.

kicker □ A side- or back-light often near lens height; used to rim faces and model profile shots. Also called a *stinger.* □ A lighting instrument used to provide an additional highlight or accent on a subject. □ An eyelight. □ A brief, often humorous, news item used as the final story in a newscast. Also called a *brite, tag,* and *zipper.* □ A small headline, usually above and to the left of the main head. Also called a *stinger.* □ A device used to mark a predetermined number of newspapers after they are folded so that a count of papers can be made. Formerly used so flyboys could pick up a specified number of papers.

kiddult A slang term for a television program that appeals to both children and adults.

kidvid A slang term for a television program that appeals primarily to children.

kill □ To cut, cut off, delete, eliminate, or otherwise end, for example, a luminaire, line, scene, advertisement, news story, sound effect, picture, story, character, and so on. □ A request by a wire service not to use a story that has been sent. □ To designate news or other matter that is not to be printed. □ An instruction to a printer to distribute type or melt down plates after use. Cf. keep standing. □ To turn off stage or set lights.

kill copy A copy of a periodical marked to show material that is not to be run in the next issue.

kill fee A payment made to a freelance writer when a contracted story is not used.

kilo (K) A prefix for 1000, such as 1 kilohertz = 1000 hertz.

kilocycle An obsolete term now replaced by kilohertz.

kilohertz One thousand cycles per second.

kilroy Improper picture framing that cuts off a performer's chin.

kine □ An abbreviation of *kinescope.* □ A kinescope recording.

kinescope From the Greek term *kinema,* meaning "motion." □ The picture tube in a television receiver or monitor. □ *See* kinescope recording.

kinescope recording A recording made by a film camera from a television picture tube. Also called *electronic film transfer, kine, telerecording,* and *teletranscription. See also* videotape recorder.

kinestasis A method of imparting motion to static pictures or artwork, either by panning, zooming, and so on, or by moving the camera or object between frames. *See also* photokinestasis.

Kinetograph The camera patented by Thomas Edison in 1891.

Kinetoscope An early filmstrip device developed and devised by Thomas Edison and W. K. L. Dickson.

King Features Syndicate The major print media syndicator, furnishing cartoons, columns, games, and other features.

king size poster A 30- by 144-inch transit advertising poster used on the sides of buses and other vehicles. Cf. queen size poster.

kiss □ A light impression made by type on paper. □ A slang acronym meaning not to overwrite, overact, and so on, whose initials stand for Keep It Simple, Stupid. Also called *Keep It Short and Simple* and *Keep It Simple, Sir.*

kiss print Print through caused in tapes by the use of loopbin master duplicating.

Klieg light □ A high-intensity carbon arc spotlight, typically used in motion picture lighting. □ Any of the lighting instruments sold by Kliegl Brothers, but often used as a synonym for any stage or set luminaire.

klinker An obvious error, such as a wrong chord or note.

klystron A velocity-modulated electron tube often used as an oscillator or amplifier in ultrahigh-frequency transmitters.

knee shot A camera shot that covers a performer from the knees up.

knock A negative review or criticism.

knockdown □ To prepare a book for recovering. □ A location hut or dressing room that is capable of being taken apart and reassembled.

knock down □ To reduce the length of a news story. □ To take apart a set or piece of equipment.

knocker up A person who aligns sheets of paper. *See also* knock up.

knock off *See* knock out.

knockout A square or rectangular hole used to outline photographs or artwork.

knock out To write a news item quickly. Also called *knock off* and *knock up.*

knock up □ To make the edges of sheets of paper even for bookbinding. □ *See* knock out.

Kodalith A trademark film used in phototypesetting.

kookie *See* cucoloris.

kraft paper A strong, brown paper made from sulfate pulp, sometimes used as a backing paper in book bindings.

kraut A slang term for the fine ribbons of newsprint that result from the cutting of the newspaper in the folder.

krotoscope From the Greek term *krotos,* meaning ''handclapping.'' A device used to measure audience applause.

Ku band A set of frequencies from approximately 11 to 14 gHz. Used for satellite uplinks and downlinks. Cf. C band.

KV Kilovolt.

KW Kilowatt.

L

L □ Inductance. □ Land transportation. An FCC first letter file-number prefix. □ Left. □ License. An FCC file-number prefix. □ Limited time. □ Line (of print). □ Local program. □ Locking. A lamp base type. □ Lumen. Also abbreviated *lm.* □ A wire service code for lifestyle.

LA □ Live action. □ Low angle. □ Large aperture.

LAA League of Advertising Agencies.

lab An abbreviation for *laboratory.*

lab effects Special effects produced in a film lab using various optical or other techniques.

label □ A piece of paper affixed to a mass mailing containing the name and address of a mail order customer. □ *See* label head. □ A piece of paper containing the title, author, catalogue data, and so on, affixed to a library book. □ The identification printed in the center of a disc or on a tape reel, cartridge, cassette, and so on. □ A product name or other descriptor printed, keyed, or superimposed over an object. □ A symbol used to identify an item of data. □ A strip of paper or similar material affixed to a tape reel to identify the program recorded on the tape. □ To affix such a material.

label head An unimaginative or often repeated headline. Also called a *label.*

laboratory □ A place where motion picture film is processed or duplicated, or both. □ A postproduction facility for videotape editing, film-to-tape transfer, and so on.

laboratory color timer The technician who determines the printing light intensity and color for making motion picture prints.

laboratory effects Motion picture special effects that are accomplished in a laboratory as opposed to in-camera effects or library effects.

lace □ A base for tying hairpieces, beards, moustaches, and so on. Also called a *net.* □ A British term for thread (a projector).

lacing *See* threading.

lacquer □ A coating applied to film to protect it against abrasion. □ *See* lacquer disc. □ A slang term for a phonograph disc.

lacquer disc A recording disc consisting of plasticized cellulose nitrate lacquer coated on a rigid substrate such as aluminum or glass. Also called a *lacquer.*

lacquer master *See* lacquer original.

lacquer original An instantaneous recording on a lacquer disc made for the purpose of generating an original master by an electro-forming process. Also called a *lacquer master.*

ladder □ A ladderlike luminaire mounting assembly hung in the wings of a theatre, often with a cable-fed outlet box. □ An effect caused by the vertical rolling of a television picture.

Lady Macbeth *See* Macbeth.

lag □ The persistence of image in a television camera pickup tube that causes a momentary smearing of the picture when the camera is moved. Also called a *comet tail.* □ The time difference between the transmission and reception of a signal.

lagging ghost *See* following ghost.

lag time The time between the moment that a device is turned on or started and the time it is in operation, such as the lag time of a turntable, cart machine, delay device, and so on.

laid paper Paper with watermarked parallel lines; an imitation of wire-marked handmade paper.

lambda The Greek letter (λ) used as a symbol for wavelength.

lambert A unit of luminance equal to the luminance of a perfectly diffusing surface that reflects or radiates one lumen per square centimeter. *See also* footlambert.

laminate To bond a sheet of cellulose acetate, polyester, or other plastic to paper, books, and so on.

laminated stripe A magnetic tape stripe that is cemented to a length of film.

Lamme Medal An award given by the IEEE for ''meritorious achievement'' in the development of an electrical or electronic apparatus or system.

lamp A complete lighting unit, including filament or electrodes, bulb, base, and other components. Sometimes used synonymously for lighting instrument, especially a spotlight. Often incorrectly used to refer to a complete lighting instrument or luminaire.

lamp base *See* base (B).

lamp cord A pair of insulated wires used as a light-duty power cord. Also called *pot.* Cf. line cord.

lamp dip A colored transparent or translucent lacquer used on incandescent lamps in those instances when it is not possible to place color media in front of the equipment. This cannot be used on tungsten-halogen lamps due to the high bulb wall temperature.

lamphouse The lamp holder in a projector.

lamp lumens The maximum light available from a lamp.

lamppost interview A report of an interview in which the subject is unidentified.

LAN Local area network.

land The flat surface of a disc between adjacent grooves.

landline A telephone cable.

landmark case A legal opinion, often made by the Supreme Court, that establishes a new direction in the interpretation of a specific law and sets precedents for future cases.

land-mobile service A service that operates between fixed points and mobile units, such as police, fire, taxi companies, and so on.

land mobile-satellite service A mobile-satellite service in which mobile earth stations are located on land.

land mobile station A mobile station in the land mobile service capable of surface movement within the geographical limits of a country or continent.

Landrum-Griffin Act *See* National Labor Relations Board (NLRB).

land station A station, other than a mobile station, used for radio communication with mobile stations.

language □ A system of signs and sounds used to convey information or emotions. *See also* artificial language and machine language. □ The words and phrasing of a body of knowledge, such as the language of film.

language rights The rights granted by a copyholder to another to produce or publish a work in a different language.

Lanham Act The Federal Trade-Mark Act of 1946 that governs the application and protection of trademarks and other private marks.

lantern *See* luminaire.

lanyard microphone *See* lavaliere.

lap □ To begin anything before something else is finished. □ *See* dissolve. □ To deliberately abrade the pole tips of a headwheel or scanner in such a way as to shape them for more intimate tape contact in normal use.

lap dissolve *See* dissolve.

lapel microphone A small microphone clipped to a performer's clothing. Cf. lavaliere.

lapping tape A special tape having an abrasive surface that is used to lap the pole tips of a headwheel or scanner.

LAPS test *See* SLAPS test.

lap switch A dissolve that is so fast it appears to be a cut.

LARC An audio fader automatically changed by a computer-controlled motor.

large A size of paper; approximately 3 by 4-1/2 inches.

large format Any motion picture film greater than 35 mm in width, such as 55 mm, 65 mm, or 70 mm.

large post A size of paper; approximately 16-1/2 by 21 inches.

large scale integration The technology used whereby thousands of semiconductor devices are fabricated on a tiny silicon chip. *See also* integrated circuit.

large screen A motion picture projection screen capable of handling the aspect ratio of a large-format motion picture.

large screen television A projection television display that is larger than a system employing a direct view cathode ray tube.

laryngaphone A correct but somewhat pretentious name for a throat microphone.

LASCR Light-activated silicon controlled rectifier.

laser Light amplification by stimulated emission of radiation. A light source that emits highly concentrated and intense monochromatic light. May be used in the transmission of numerous messages at the same time; for photomicrography, surgery, and so on. Its potential uses may be limitless. Also called a *light maser* and *optical maser.*

laser disc Strictly, any disc recorded and read by a laser, but in general usage, a LaserVision disc. *See also* optical storage.

laser optical disk A storage medium on which a laser, instead of an electromagnetic head, stores and retrieves data.

laser printer A high-speed, high-quality printer that uses a laser beam to form characters and graphic images. Similar in operation to a photocopier. A relatively inexpensive alternative to phototypesetters for text and graphics printing.

LaserVision (LV) A trademark for an optical videodisc system developed by Phillips for reproducing color video pictures and two-channel sound. Uses the same optical readout principle as a compact disc, but the discs are larger and may be double-sided. The speed of rotation and the data rate are also higher. The program information is analog; the control information, digital.

lash line A rope used to tie flats together.

last issue The final copy of a periodical to be mailed on a subscription.

last radio stage The radio frequency power amplifier stage that supplies power to the antenna.

last telecast The last date on which a commercial or program is scheduled for broadcast.

LATA Local access and transport area.

late fringe The time period on television from 11 p.m. to 1 a.m. *See also* daypart.

late night The time period on television from 1 a.m. to sign off. *See also* daypart.

latensification The process of increasing the density of an undeveloped film by exposing it to a low-level light source. Cf. intensification.

latent edge number *See* edge numbers.

latent image □ The invisible image registered on a film emulsion by exposure to light that becomes visible after development. Cf. real image and virtual image. □ The momentarily stored image on a television camera mosaic screen.

lateral color A lens aberration that causes blurring around the edges of an image.

lateral compliance The ease with which a tone arm stylus can move from side to side.

lateral inversion *See* lateral reversal.

lateral orientation *See* lateral reversal.

lateral recording A disc containing groove modulation caused by radial recorder stylus motion in the plane of the disc surface. A monophonic recording.

lateral reversal The left to right or right to left change in an image because of the use of certain lenses, mirrors, viewfinders, electronic switches, and so on. Also called *lateral inversion, lateral orientation,* and *mirror image.*

lateral tracing angle error The angle, projected to the plane of the disc, between the vibration axis of the mechanical system of the pickup and a tangent to an unmodulated groove at the point of stylus contact.

late start A radio or television program that is broadcast after the program has started.

late watch *See* lobster trick.

latex A pure gum rubber in liquid form that is used in make-up for prosthetic devices.

latitude The range of a film emulsion's acceptance of different apertures and speeds to produce an acceptable picture. The faster the film, the greater the latitude. Also called *exposure latitude.*

laugh it up A radio or television director's command to talent to laugh at or among themselves.

laugh track A tape or record of people laughing added to a taped or filmed program to simulate or augment an audience. Laugh track machines are available and contain thousands of different laugh tracks—from one person giggling to thousands roaring.

lav An abbreviation for *lavaliere.*

lavaliere A small microphone worn on a cord hung around the neck. Also called a *lanyard mike, neck mike,* and *personal mike.* Cf. lapel microphone.

lavender *See* lavender print.

lavender print A fine grain positive print so called because of the color of the base. Also called a *lavender.*

law The aggregate of the rules, standards, practices, and customs that are recognized as binding; often enforced by the executive and legislative branches of governments. *See also* administrative law, common law, constitutional law, and statutory law.

law binding The plain, light-colored binding made of buckram, calfskin, or sheepskin used for law books. Also referred to as *law buckram, law calf, law lamb,* and *law sheep,* depending on the material.

law buckram *See* law binding.

law calf *See* law binding.

law lamb *See* law binding.

law sheep *See* law binding.

lay □ To place new type in a job case. □ The arrangement of the type in a job case. □ To place and arrange book pages on an imposing stone. □ The relation of the paper to the type or plate on a printing press. □ To record sound on film or tape.

lay an egg To produce a box office failure.

layback To add a sweetened or augmented audio track back to an edited videotape master.

lay down □ The arrangement of book sections in the proper sequence for assembly. □ To record sound; often to lay a single track of a multiple-track recording.

laydown *See* layover.

laydown speed The speed at which characters are exposed on the photographic material in phototypesetting.

lay edge The edge of paper that is closest to a printing press. *See also* gripper.

layer One thickness of a magnetic tape.

layercake The separation of a newspaper story from its headline because two headlines are stacked one above the other.

layer-to-layer adhesion *See* adhesion.

lay in To edit sound into the proper place on a film soundtrack or videotape.

laying down The process of recording sound or effects on a videotape for later transfer to the videotape master.

laying sound To edit a soundtrack to synchronize it with the picture. Also called *laying tracks.*

laying tracks *See* laying sound.

layout □ A diagram or sketch of a proposed printed page, showing the arrangement of text, headlines, illustrations, photographs, and so on. Also called a *spread. See also* comprehensive and rough. □ To plot the action, camera movement, lighting, and so on, within the confines of a set. □ *See* storyboard. □ In animation, a detailed drawing of a shot in which background elements, staging of the action, and camera moves are carefully worked out and plotted. □ The stage of production in which these are determined. *See also* scene planner. □ The design and arrangement of the various cels in an animated scene.

layout board *See* layout sheet.

layout editor A person who plans layouts.

layout paper An opaque paper containing nonreproducing lines used to draw layouts or arrange dummy copy. Also called *layout board* and *layout sheet.*

layout sheet *See* layout paper.

layover The process of transferring videotape soundtracks to audiotape for sweetening. Also called *laydown.*

lazy arm A simple microphone boom.

LBC Lowband color.

LBM Lowband monochrome. *See* lowband (LB).

LC Library of Congress.

lc Lowercase.

lca Lowercase alphabet.

LCD Liquid crystal display.

LCL Light center length.

LCS Loudness contour selector. *See* loudness control.

LCU Large close-up. *See* ECU.

LD □ Lighting director. □ Lighting designer. □ Long distance.

ld An abbreviation for *lead.*

LDE Lighting director engineer.

LDL Loudness discomfort level.

LDS Local distribution service.

Lea Act The congressional act that outlawed featherbedding and other coercive practices in broadcasting. It is contained in Section 506 of the Communications Act.

LEAA guidelines The regulations promulgated by the Law Enforcement Assistance Administration of the Department of Justice that restrict the dissemination of police records.

lead (pronounced *led*) □ A strip of metal used to space lines of type; usually one-half to three points in thickness. Sometimes spelled *ledd.* Cf. reglet. □ To space lines of type.

lead (pronounced *leed*) □ The most important news story or newscast of a day. Also called a *lead story.* □ *See* lead paragraph. □ The person who plays the lead. □ The first story in a newscast. □ A news tip. □ A fresh introduction to a news story. □ A wire from one part of a component to another part of the same component. □ The opposite of lag. □ The most important role in a play, screenplay, television drama, and so on. □ To maintain a space between a performer who is in profile and the edge of the frame.

lead all □ A lead that replaces an original lead. □ A lead that summarizes several stories. □ A lead that summarizes the parts of a single story.

leaded Type matter that has been expanded by inserting leads. Also called *leaded matter.* Cf. carding out.

leaded matter *See* leaded.

leader □ That section of tape that precedes a television program and provides setup signals and slate information. □ The information recorded on such a section of tape. □ The length of film that precedes the sound or picture. *See also* academy leader and head. □ Blank film or tape at the end of a reel. *See also* tail. □ Blank portions of tape or film inserted between segments of material. *See also* spacer. □ A series of baseline dots or dashes that direct the eye from one printed column to another, as in an index. Also called *leaders out.* □ An editorial article.

leaders out *See* leader.

leader tape Nonmagnetic tape made of plastic or paper.

lead-in □ An introduction to a commercial, news story, program, or scene. Also called a *down lead.* □ The wire from an antenna to a radio or television receiver or transmitter. □ *See* lead-in groove. □ A television program that precedes another program. *See also* hammocking and tent polling. Cf. lead out. □ An introductory segment that is used in more than one episode of a prime time dramatic and/or high-budget television series.

lead-in audience The audience from a previous radio or television program that continues to listen to or watch the following program.

leading To expand a column of type vertically by inserting leads. Also called *lead out.*

leading blacks The condition in a television picture where a white object appears to have a leading black border. Also called *edge effect.* Cf. following blacks.

leading ghost A ghost displaced to the left of the primary image in a television picture.

leading lady The female who plays the most important role in a production. Cf. leading man.

leading man The male who plays the most important role in a production. Cf. leading lady.

Leading National Advertisers-Publishers Information Bureau (LNA) A service that publishes monthly reports on advertising space and revenues of national and regional magazines, as well as the space usage and estimated spending of advertisers using these magazines.

leading question An interview question that may bias the response by the way the question is worded.

lead-in groove An unmodulated fast spiral groove from the edge of the disc to the start of the modulated groove area. Also called a *lead-in spiral.*

leading whites The condition in a television picture where a black object appears to have a leading white border.

Also called *edge effect.* Cf. following whites.

lead-in line The line on a script, audiotape, or videotape used to cue an announcer or newscaster.

lead-in spiral *See* lead-in groove.

lead off □ The first story in a radio or television newscast. □ The first radio or television program of a new series. □ The first radio or television program in a network feed during a day or daypart.

lead out *See* leading.

lead-out □ An outro to a commercial, news story, program, or scene. Cf. intro and lead-in. □ A musical outro. □ *See* lead-out groove. □ A television program that follows another program. *See also* hammocking and tent polling. Cf. lead in.

lead-out groove An unmodulated spiral groove at the end of a recording connecting the last groove at normal modulated groove pitch to a locked concentric or eccentric stopping groove.

lead-out track A track that follows the program material on a CD.

lead-over groove A fast spiral connecting two modulated sections or bands on a disc. Also called *crossover spiral* and *spread groove.*

lead paragraph The first paragraph of a news story; usually containing the who, what, when, where, and why material.

leads □ The leading man and leading lady of a production. □ *See* lead.

lead sheet □ A camera operator's shot sheet. □ Sheet music that contains the words and music, and sometimes the chord symbols, but not orchestration. □ An animation cue sheet containing complete sound and picture information. Also called a *bar sheet.*

lead story The news story given the most important position on page one of a newspaper or the first story in a newscast. Also called a *lead.*

lead-through A performance made by sideline musicians that is not intended for direct recording.

lead time The period between product, program, or commercial design and the completion or marketing of it.

leaf A book sheet with printing on both sides; two pages.

leaflet A printed sheet, usually consisting of two to six folded pages. Cf. pamphlet.

leaf shutter A camera shutter with a circular opening that is made from overlapping metal leaves.

League of Advertising Agencies (LAA) An association of advertising agencies.

leak □ An undesired sound heard on a tape or in a studio. □ *See* news leak.

leak light *See* spill light.

lean □ A thin or slender type character. □ Print that is difficult to set, and that therefore may be unprofitable. Also called *lean matter.*

lean matter *See* lean.

leapfrogging The FCC rule that required cable television systems to import signals from the closest of the stations carrying the same signal. The rule is no longer applicable.

leased access channel A specifically designated cable television channel available for lease on a first-come, nondiscriminatory basis.

leased channel □ A cable television channel available to users for a fee. □ *See* leased line.

leased line □ A communications channel reserved for a particular user. □ A rented telephone line. Also called a *leased wire.*

leased wire *See* leased line.

lease man An outdoor advertising plant employee who negotiates the right to build signs.

least objectionable program (LOP) The theory that audiences often select a television program, not on the basis of what they would enjoy viewing, but rather on the basis of which is the least objectionable of those available.

LED Light emitting diode.

L.Ed. U.S. *Supreme Court Reports, Lawyer's Edition.* A privately published record of decisions of the Supreme Court. *See also United States Reports.*

ledd *See* lead.

left (L) *See* camera left and stage left.

left (or right) signal The electrical output of a microphone or combination of microphones placed so as to convey the intensity, time, and location of sounds originating predominantly to the listener's left (or right) of the center of the performing area.

left (or right) stereophonic channel The left (or right) signal as electrically reproduced in reception of FM stereophonic broadcasts.

left-hand polarized wave An elliptically or circularly polarized wave, in fixed plane, normal to the direction of propagation, that rotates with time in a left-hand or counterclockwise direction as seen from the direction of propagation. Also called an *anticlockwise polarized wave.* Cf. right-hand polarized wave.

leftover matter Typeset copy not used in an issue of a periodical; usually set in case it is needed to fill empty space. Also called *overmatter* and *overset matter.*

leg ☐ An electrical circuit branch line. Cf. main. ☐ A branch of a network's interconnecting lines. ☐ *See* stack.

legal The legal notices printed in a newspaper.

legal advisor An attorney who is employed by or on retainer to a communication medium.

legal brief *See* brief.

legal considerations One of the basic eligibility criteria for a broadcast license. The others are financial, character, and technical.

legally qualified candidate Any person who has publicly announced that he or she is a candidate for nomination by a convention of a political party or for nomination or election in a primary, special, or general election—municipal, county, state, or national—and who meets the qualifications prescribed by the applicable laws to hold the office for which he or she is a candidate so that the person may be voted for by the electorate directly or by means of delegates or electors. (See Title 47 of the *Code of Federal Regulations* [CFR], paragraph 73.120, for a complete description.)

legal standing *See* standing.

leg-art *See* cheesecake.

legend ☐ A key to a map or illustration. ☐ A title accompanying an illustration. *See also* caption and cutline. ☐ Titles or credits keyed in or superimposed over a television picture.

legger *See* legman.

legibility A measure of the relative ease or difficulty of reading type matter. Cf. readability.

Legion of Decency An office of the Roman Catholic Church that—until it was disbanded in 1966—worked for the elimination of motion pictures it considered immoral.

legitimate theatre Plays performed on the stage. Originally used to distinguish theatre from vaudeville or burlesque.

legman A reporter who works a beat but usually does not write the story—or, on television, report on camera. Also called a *district man* and *legger.*

legs ☐ A slang term for a motion picture or television program that has or will achieve strong audience acceptance or interest. ☐ Vertical borders on a set.

leitmotif A musical selection or phrase that is associated with a character, idea, or situation. Usually used in a motion picture, television program, and so on, each time the character, idea, or situation appears.

Leko A trade name for an ellipsoidal spotlight.

lemon A television program, script, motion picture, book, and so on that leaves a sour taste with the viewer or reader.

lending library *See* circulating library.

length of approach The measured distance from which an outdoor advertising message is clearly visible.

lens An optical device consisting of a number of ground or molded elements of glass or plastic that focuses light by refraction. *See also* focal length, telephoto lens, wide-angle lens, and zoom lens.

lens adapter A device attached to a camera for easy lens changes.

lens angle The maximum angle of view as seen through a lens.

lens aperture *See* aperture.

lens axis The optical axis of a lens.

lens barrel The metal tube in which lens elements are mounted. Sometimes referred to as a *lens mount.*

lens cap A metal or plastic protective covering for a lens.

lens coating A magnesium fluoride covering used to neutralize reflected light within a lens.

lens element One of the pieces of optical glass contained in a lens barrel.

lens filter *See* filter.

lens flare *See* flare.

lens hood A tubular or rectangular attachment used in front of a lens to block stray light from entering. Also called a *lens shade*.

lens louse An individual who strives for publicity shots and gets in the way of a photographer so as to be in the picture.

lens markings The calibrating marks and numbers found on a lens that indicate the distance, diaphragm opening, depth of field scale, and so on.

lens mount □ The device by which a lens is attached to a camera or projector. □ The lens housing containing the elements of a lens.

lens projector A high-wattage scenic slide projector, usually of wide-angle coverage and sometimes with a motor drive to move a film strip.

lens shade *See* lens hood.

lens size For theatrical luminaires, the specification of diameter and focal length. A 6-by-9-inch PC would be a 6-inch diameter, 9-inch focal length plano-convex lens.

lens speed The maximum light-gathering power of a lens, equal to the focal length divided by the diameter of the lens. Lens speed is indicated by the maximum f or T number. *See also* aperture.

lens spotlight A luminaire embodying a lamp and a simple lens (plano-convex or bi-convex) with or without a reflector, which has variable field and beam angles obtained by changing the spacing between the lamp and the lens.

lens squeeze The amount of horizontal compression caused by an anamorphic lens.

lens stop *See* f stop.

lens support A reinforcing rod threaded into a long focal length lens to take the pressure off the lens mount.

lens tissue A soft, lintless paper used with a cleaning fluid to clean lenses.

lens turret A device for holding four or five lenses of differing focal lengths. Made largely obsolete by the introduction of zoom lenses. *See also* rack.

lenticular Having the shape of a double-convex lens, as in a lenticular screen used for projection.

lenticular screen A projection screen with a surface embossed with a pattern of light-scattering strips.

letter □ A size of paper; approximately 10 by 16 inches. □ One of the characters in the alphabet. Cf. symbol. □ A style of type. □ Type styles collectively. □ To title a book by impressing characters on the cover. □ To stamp the letters of the alphabet on thumb notches of a book. □ A written communication.

letterbox A motion picture version of a standard ratio film masked at the top and bottom so that it appears to be a wide-screen version.

letter gadget An object attached to or enclosed with an advertising mailing piece to arouse interest in an advertising message.

letterhead The printing on a letter that identifies the sender.

lettering safety *See* essential area.

letter of adherence A letter furnished by a union or guild by a producer, advertising agency, studio, and so on, certifying that the producer, advertising agency, studio, or other party will abide by and conform to the terms and conditions set forth in union or guild codes of fair practice, and other agreements and contracts.

letter of intent A letter stating an intention to enter a business relationship, such as to purchase media space or time.

letterpress A relief printing process in which the raised letters or cuts are inked and then printed on paper. Cf. gravure and photo offset lithography.

letterpress printing The movable type printing process invented by Johann Gutenberg in the fifteenth century.

letterpress supplement A newspaper supplement printed on newsprint or similar stock by letterpress rather than by the more common rotogravure process.

letter quality A document typed on a typewriter or set in type, as compared to dot matrix quality.

letterset *See* dry offset.

lettershop A business organization that handles the mechanical details of mailings such as addressing, imprinting, and collating. Most lettershops offer printing facilities, and many offer some degree of creative direct mail services.

letterspacing The insertion of spaces between the letters of a word in type composition for the purpose of justification. Also called *interspacing*. Cf. kerning.

level □ *See* sound pressure level (SPL). □ To take a VU meter reading for testing purposes. □ *See* blanking level. □ The amplitude of an audio or video signal. □ In animation, because individual elements or characters in a scene may move at different rates or be drawn by different animators, they may be put on separate cels for ease or economy of animation. The layers of cels are referred to as levels. In some cases, elements of a single character may be animated on different cel levels, for example, the flapping wings of a bird may be on the top level, the body on the second, and the opening and closing beak on the third. Usually the elements that move most frequently will be placed on the upper levels, making it easier for the camera operator to change them.

level indicator A device, such as a VU meter, that visually describes; an example is a record or playback level.

level of confidence *See* confidence level.

level of significance *See* statistical significance.

level sync The side-by-side alignment of a film picture frame with its corresponding sound. Used in double system editing. *See also* editorial sync. Cf. projection sync.

Lexis A legal database used for research. *See also* Westlaw.

LF Low frequency.

lf □ Line feed. □ Lightface.

libel A form of defamation usually consisting of written material; however, broadcast defamation, with or without a script, because of the media's widespread influence, is considered to be libel. *See also* defamation. Cf. slander.

libel per quod Libel that exists because of the circumstances surrounding the incident that may not be obvious through the words alone. Cf. libel per se.

libel per se Libel by or in itself; includes such expressions as calling someone a communist, calling an attorney a shyster, a physician a quack, or otherwise injuring someone in his or her business or profession.

libertarian theory One of the four theories of the press delineated by Wilbur Schramm. Based on the theory that humans are able to make intelligent decisions. Cf. authoritarian theory, social responsibility theory, and Soviet Communist theory.

librarian □ The head of a library. Also called a *head librarian* and *library director*. □ A professional member of a library staff. □ A person whose duties consist of the selecting and arranging of films, tapes, and so on, for the purposes of cataloging and filing, and for obtaining from the library stock shots of scenes, sound effects, and other material requested for the use of the editor or for sale.

library □ A film, music, sound effects, or stock shot storage facility. □ A company that sells stock shots. □ A collection of computer programs or routines. □ A collection of documents. □ A newspaper's collection of reference materials and its own stories. Also called a *morgue*. □ A collection of books. □ *See* circulating library. □ *See* Library of Congress.

library binding A binding made of a durable material.

library director *See* librarian.

library edition An identically bound set of books, usually by one author.

library effects Stock footage of special effects that may be rented or purchased for use in a production. Cf. camera opticals and laboratory effects.

library footage *See* stock footage.

library jobber *See* wholesaler.

library management system (LMS) An automated, digital, multicassette playback system.

library material *See* stock footage.

library music Recorded music licensed for use by broadcasting stations and available on disc or tape. Also called *stock music*. *See also* needle drop.

Library of Congress The library of the United States, established in 1800, which is the official repository for copyrighted materials.

Library of Congress system The classification system, commonly abbreviated *LC*, of the Library of Congress. *See also* Cataloging in Publication (CIP).

library service A business that rents music, stock footage, and so on, for use by broadcasting stations.

library shot *See* stock footage.

license For the purpose of the Administrative Procedure Act, the whole or a part of an agency permit, certificate, approval, registration, charter, membership, statutory exemption, or other form of permission.

license (L) A broadcast station instrument of authorization to operate; the term subsumes the words *permit* and *authorization. See also* station license. Cf. construction permit.

license deletion *See* deletion.

licensee The holder of a radio or television station license granted or continued in force under authority of the Communications Act of 1934. The term can also include the holder of a construction permit.

licensee qualifications *See* basic eligibility criteria.

license period *See* normal license period.

license renewal *See* renewal.

license revocation *See* revocation.

license transfer *See* transfer of control.

licensing □ For the purpose of the Administrative Procedure Act, agency process respecting the grant, renewal, denial, revocation, suspension, annulment, withdrawal, limitation, amendment, modification, or conditioning of a license. □ The granting of a permit to broadcast or operate a CATV system to an applicant by the FCC. Cf. allocation, allotment, and assignment.

Liebmann Award, Morris N. An award given by the IEEE for an "important contribution" to emerging technologies.

life □ The ability of an advertisement or promotion to elicit the intended action as indicated by the continuation of such reaction on repeated exposures of the advertisement. Cf. wearout. □ *See* rated life. □ *See* service life.

lifespan □ The number of years a radio or television program remains popular. □ The number of years a publication is issued, reprinted, and so on.

LIFO Last in, first out. A computer term for the order in which data may be processed. The term, however, applies to numerous situations, such as the latest subscribers to periodicals, first to drop out; and the latest subscribers to cable television, first to drop out.

lift □ To "borrow" a story or the facts from a story in another publication. □ To use an existing story or type that has been set. □ An unedited section of film or tape stored for later use. □ A short commercial made from a longer original. □ To increase the number of subscribers to a cable television system by offering additional channels, programs, or services. □ To use sound, pictures, or material from an earlier production or another source in a current production. □ The increase in basic cable television penetration brought about by the introduction of a new service or program; for example, pay television.

lift off During the fast forward or rewind tape modes, the removal of the tape from the heads by vacuum or mechanical means.

ligature A character formed by two or more letters joined together and cast on one type body. Cf. logotype.

light The radiant energy visible to the human eye with a wavelength between 400 to 700 millimicrons. *See also* ambient light, background light, back-light, base-light, counter-key, crosslighting, fill light, front lighting, high-key lighting, house lights, incident light, indirect light, key light, kicker, low-key lighting, modeling light, reflected light, rim light, set light, side light, specific light, stinger, three-point lighting, and top light. Cf. luminaire.

light amplifier *See* laser.

light balancing filter A lens filter used to make slight color temperature changes.

light bank *See* bank.

light board *See* lighting control console.

light box An enclosure with a translucent glass surface illuminated from below. Used in animation and as an inspection stand for transparencies and film. Also called a *light table.*

light bridge *See* bridge.

light center length (LCL) The distance between the center of an incandescent lamp filament and an arbitrary, but standard, point of the lamp base.

light change A point at which the exposure time is changed in the printing of motion picture film in order to correct for underexposure or overexposure.

light collector The photocell of a light meter.

light comedy Comedy characterized by wit and the lack of a serious message.

light distribution The uniformity or lack of uniformity of lighting or illumination on a set.

light emitting diode (LED) A display technology that allows a diode to emit light when biased in the forward direction; used for digital watches, calculators, meters, and so on.

light end The drying end of a film-developing machine. Cf. dark end.

light entertainment Motion pictures, television programs, novels, articles, and so on, that are produced or written to be enjoyed without much thought.

lightface (LF) The common text type used in printing as distinguished from boldface.

light flare *See* flare.

lighting ☐ The process of illuminating a scene or set. *See also* backlighting, cross-lighting, fill light, front light, highlighting, key light, kicker, light, luminaire, and top light. ☐ The amount of illumination on a scene or set.

lighting balance *See* lighting ratio.

lighting batten A pipe and wireway assembly suspended by wire cables with pigtails or receptacles that serves both to physically support the luminaires and to provide electrical power. Cf. lighting grid.

lighting cameraman A British term for a cinematographer.

lighting contrast *See* lighting ratio.

lighting control console The assembly —usually a desk-type housing—used to contain the controls required for adjusting the production lighting, such as dimmer, nondim, and other control functions. Also called a *light board.*

lighting designer (LD) ☐ An individual who plans lighting compositions; lays out hanging plans; directs the focusing of lighting units; and determines the various intensities, colors, and cues required in a production. ☐ A television lighting director.

lighting director A lighting designer who works in television.

lighting focus The spread of a light source, from a concentrated spot to a diffused illumination.

lighting grid A fixed structure of either aluminum or steel members, such as pipe, that is located above the studio floor for the purpose of supporting luminaires and to support the electrical outlets required. Also called a *gridiron.* Cf. lighting batten.

lighting instrument *See* instrument and luminaire.

lighting plan *See* light plan.

lighting ratio The ratio in intensity between the various light sources illuminating a scene or set. Often the mix among the key lights, back-lights, and fill lights. Also called *lighting balance, lighting contrast,* and *lighting ratio.*

lighting setup A detailed layout of a light plan.

light intensity *See* intensity.

light leak The streaking, flare, fogging, and so on, caused by an improperly closed camera, incorrectly seated lens, or other mechanical defect.

light level The intensity of light on a set, measured in footcandles.

light lift A pantograph or other adjustable height device used to support luminaires from a grid.

light lock *See* light trap.

light loss The loss of transmitted light in a lens caused by some of the light being reflected. Generally, the greater the number of elements in the lens, the greater the reflected light loss.

light meter A device for measuring the incident or reflected light. Also called an *exposure meter* and *photometer.*

light-on-dark An inking technique sometimes used to delineate very dark areas on a character, in which the ink lines are a slightly lighter color, adding definition and depth.

light pen A photoelectric device used to detect light on a display screen. The electrical response is then directed to write, edit, erase, or otherwise change the computer memory or display.

light plan *See* light plot.

light plot The complete layout of lighting equipment and its application in a production. Also called a *light plan* and *light script.*

light quality The extent to which the light on a scene is soft or hard.

light ratio *See* lighting ratio.

light reflection *See* light loss.

lights A request or command to turn on the house lights.

light script *See* light plot.

light source A computer graphics effect that increases the modeling effect with shadows and color enhancement.

light sourcing The definition of one or more sources of illumination for a scene.

light struck Film that has been fogged by unintentional exposure to light.

light table *See* light box.

light tight A camera, magazine, or darkroom that does not allow light to enter.

light trap □ A darkroom vestibule containing double doors so that light does not enter when only one door is opened at a time. Also called a *light lock.* □ A camera or magazine groove or baffle that does not allow light to penetrate to the film.

light valve A device used to print a motion picture soundtrack by passing a beam of light through an opening when it is triggered by electrical impulses.

light wave communication *See* fiber optics.

lily A color chart similar to color bars used in checking film processing.

limbo □ A black background having no detectable detail. □ A scene shot without a visible or distinguishable background.

limbo board A graphic that is mounted outside the set area.

limited animation A term used to describe animation in which full movement is not depicted but that relies on key poses and the movement of only those portions of the character that are essential to the motion. Because limited animation can be done more cheaply and quickly than full animation, it is widely used for television shows; however, some animators use it for aesthetic reasons. Cf. full animation.

limited edition A special edition of a book or set of books, restricted to a specific number of copies or sets.

limited engagement A brief appearance by a performer; a short run for a motion picture in a particular theatre, and so on.

limited response question A survey question to which there are only a few possible replies, such as yes/no, multiple choice, and so on.

limited run A television series that is not available for syndication because too few episodes were made.

limited time (L) Operation of a Class II (secondary) AM station on a clear channel with facilities authorized before November 30, 1959. Operation of the secondary station is permitted during daytime and until local sunset if located west of the dominant station on the channel, or until local sunset at the dominant station located east of that station. Operation is also permitted during nighttime hours not used by the dominant station or stations on the channel.

limiter □ An automatic protective device used to reduce volume when overmodulation occurs. □ A television circuit used to prevent the amplitude of a signal from exceeding a peak level.

limiting resolution The greatest resolution a film or television system can reproduce due to electronic or mechanical factors.

limp binding *See* flexible binding.

Lincoln Awards, Abe Awards given by the Southern Baptist Radio and Television Commission for outstanding contributions to the quality of life in America.

line □ The video and/or audio output from a radio or television control room. □ One of the 525 traces of the television scanning beam. *See also* dot, element, field, and frame. □ Any conductor of electrical energy, such as a wire. Cf. landline. □ The words spoken by a performer without interruption. □ A measure of printed space equal to one fourteenth of a column inch. *See also* agate. □ *See* banner. □ *See* line art. □ An abbreviation for *cutline.* □ A row of characters. □ A camera-positioning reference plane. *See also* imaginary line. □ According to the Screen Actors Guild, 1 line is 50 typewritten letters or spaces. A part of a line counts as 1 line unless it is only 1 word. Two such single words, either at the end of a speech or isolated are counted together as 1 line. Grunts, groans, screams, cries, sighs, laughter, or any other articulated sounds that form part of a speech are incorporated in the line count. All isolated articulated sighs of this kind will be counted as single words. □ According to the American Federation of Radio and Television Artists, a line consists of not more than 10 words, and part of a line will be considered a line. It is the intention of the 5-line-or-less category to include only those performers who have very minor parts to perform. A speech by a player consisting of not more than 10 words; part of a line is considered a line for payment purposes. □ *See* agate line.

lineage □ A measure of the amount of advertising space in a newspaper or magazine, based on the number of lines used. □ The total amount of advertising printed in an edition or issue or for a specified amount of time. □ A method of payment for written material based on the number of lines written.

line amplifier An amplifier used to supply a transmission line or distribution system with a signal of sufficient strength. Also called a *line extender* and *line stretcher.*

line animation Simple animation accomplished using plain line drawings only.

linear A circuit in which the output is directly proportional to the input.

linear editing Editing wherein the shots are selected in progressive sequence. Cf. nonlinear editing.

linearity The relationship between two quantities wherein a change in one is directly proportional to a change in the other.

linearity chart A test pattern used to help test geometric distortion of a television camera chain. Also called a *ball chart.*

linearity control A device for adjusting the rate of television picture scanning.

linear mode The presentation of information in a fixed sequence, uninfluenced by the recipient. Cf. interactive mode.

linear programming (LP) A BBDO mathematical model used in media planning that enables the media planner to specify reach, frequency, and seasonal and demographic goals for an advertising campaign.

linear reflectance chart A chart with the steps of gray scales in linear relationship used to align and measure the transfer characteristic of television camera systems. *See also* test pattern.

line art Artwork that appears as black or white rather than in continuous tones. Also called *line copy.* Cf. halftones.

linear velocity *See* groove speed.

linebeat Television camera pickup tube moire. Also called *beat* and *meshbeat.*

line blanking *See* blanking.

line-by-line correction In an automatic chrominance equalizer, the action of measuring and correcting the faults of each television line.

linecaster A hot metal typesetting machine capable of producing a complete, justified line of type on one slug. Also called a *linecasting machine* and *typecaster.* Cf. phototypesetter.

linecasting machine *See* linecaster.

line charge The cost of telephone company lines, cable, or microwave facilities.

line control table In CD-I, a two-dimensional array of instructions, each row of which is associated with the display line.

line conversion A method of converting continuous tone art to line art by the elimination of a halftone screen or by photographing.

line copy *See* line art.

line cord A two- or three-conductor power cord that is permanently attached to a receiver or other electrical device. Also called a *power cable* and *power cord.* Cf. lamp cord.

line cut A photoengraving, usually on zinc or copper, of a line drawing. Also called a *line engraving.*

line drawing A sketch, drawing, or illustration containing no gradations; line art. Also called a *line illustration.*

line editor □ A computer word processing procedure that allows the operator to edit lines of text after entry. □ A manuscript editor. Cf. acquisitions editor.

line engraving *See* line cut.

line equalizer An equalizer used to increase the intelligibility and quality of a telephone line.

line extender A cable television amplifier used to extend the effective length of a trunk cable.

line feed □ A feed from a remote location to a studio or transmitter. □ The distance between the scanning lines in a television picture. Also called *advance feed.*

line feed (LF) A control character that causes a printer to move the platen up one line. Cf. form feed.

line frequency □ The number of horizontal scans per second in a television picture: 15,750 (30 frames per second times 525 lines per frame). □ The power line frequency; in the United States, 60 Hz, in Europe, 50 Hz.

line gauge A printer's measuring ruler, marked in pica increments and inches. Also called a *measuring stick, pica rule, pica stick,* and *type gauge.*

line height The height of one line of type expressed as a fraction of the number of lines per inch.

line hit *See* spike.

line hold, line repeat The production of mosaic graphics in the vertical direction by holding and repeating lines.

line illustration *See* line drawing.

line input A high-level input. *See* line level.

line interlace *See* interlaced scanning.

line length The length of a printed line, measured in picas and points. Also called *line measure* and *measure.*

line level □ A signal of sufficient intensity so that it does not require preamplification. Cf. mike level. □ The intensity of a signal on a transmission line, as measured in decibels.

line-level microphone A combination microphone and amplifier that produces a line-level output.

line lighting The use of back and side lighting to silhouette a person or object.

linelock The electronic circuit that locks the sync pulses in a videotape recorder.

line loss The decrease in signal strength in a line due to the length of the line.

line measure *See* line length.

line microphone A British term for a shotgun mike.

line monitor *See* master monitor.

line multiplication A technique used in CD-I to make high-resolution line information compatible with a lower-resolution system.

linen A fabric used for book covers.

line negative A photographic negative of a line drawing, made without a halftone screen.

linen finish A paper made by impressing linen against the paper in a machine with rollers.

line noise Any noise in a transmission line.

linen paper A high-quality paper originally made from linen; now any paper with a linen finish.

line number A number assigned to each line of a draft manuscript or galley proof for ease of referencing and editing.

line-of-sight (LOS) □ The distance to the horizon from an antenna. □ The direct propagation path for FM and television. *See also* direct wave.

line of travel In outdoor advertising, the center of a lane of traffic moving in one direction.

line period The duration from the beginning of one television scanning line to the beginning of the next.

line printer A high-speed computer printer capable of printing a complete line at a time. Cf. character printer and page printer.

line pulling A picture fault characterized by the horizontal displacement of a single line.

liner □ The lighter shades of make-up used for highlights. □ The text printed on a record album. □ The banter of a disc jockey. □ *See* lining.

line radio *See* wire communication.

line rate □ The number of scanning lines in a television picture per second. □ The charge per line for newspaper space.

line rehearsal A run-through of lines by talent without cameras or other equipment. *See also* rehearsal.

lines □ Written material spoken by a performer. □ The ropes used to fly scenery.

line scanning *See* scanning.

line screen *See* screen.

line space The distance that paper moves between lines in a printer or typewriter; often one-sixth of an inch.

linespacing □ A measure of the vertical spacing between lines of type, measured in points and half points. On a typewriter, single spacing, double spacing, and so on. Cf. wordspacing. □ The addition of space between lines of type.

line speed The rate at which data can be transmitted over a communication path.

lines per minute (lpm)(l/m) A measure of printing speed.

line stretcher *See* line amplifier.

line terminator A device used to limit ghosting by using a coaxial stub or other impedance.

line test A British term for an animation pencil test.

line up To adjust the relationship between two or more components.

line-up □ The arrangement of signals through an audio control console. □ The products of an equipment manufacturer. □ The arrangement of stories in a newscast. Also called a *rundown.*

lineup □ The network television programs that will be broadcast during an upcoming season. □ The stations that will carry a particular network program.

line update In information presentation, the modification of a single line or part of a line of graphics stored in a file.

lineup sheet A rundown of the news stories that will be used on a radio or television newscast.

line-up time *See* warm-up.

line-up tone An audio signal used to align all VU meters in a system so they read at the same level.

lining The reinforcing paper that is glued to the spine of a book. Also called a *liner. See also* kraft paper and mull.

lining paper *See* end paper.

lining up □ The setting up of equipment, cameras, mikes, lights, and so on, for shooting. □ *See* framing.

link A receive-transmit booster that connects two locations, such as a microwave link. Also called an *extension.*

linkage editor *See* linking loader.

linked heads Newspaper headlines that refer to items on the same page having similar themes.

linker *See* linking loader.

linking loader In computer programming, an executive routine that assembles or compiles different program segments, renumbers them, and relocates them in main memory, so that the program can be run as one unit. Also called *linkage editor* and *linker.*

linkman A British term for a staff announcer.

link transmitter A signal booster usually used as a studio-transmitter link (STL) or from a remote to a radio or television studio.

Linnebach A lensless projector formed by a box painted black on the inside and containing a point source of light such as an incandescent lamp with a small filament. A cutout or a transparency (often painted on glass) is placed on the open side of the box. The Linnebach projector produces soft diffuse images.

lino An abbreviation for *Linotype.*

Linofilm A trademark phototypesetter that produces type on film as opposed to metal.

Linotype □ A trademark for a linecasting machine. Patented by Ottmar Mergenthaler in 1885. Now generally used as a term for all linecasting machines. □ A slug made by a Linotype.

lip flap A reporter's or performer's lip movements seen in a picture without sound, often found in single-system news film or improper videotape editing.

lip microphone A small microphone worn close to the mouth. Also called a *lip-ribbon microphone.*

lip-ribbon microphone *See* lip microphone.

lip-sync □ The synchronization of sound and picture. Also called *direct voice.* □ The mouthing of words or music by a performer to a recorded film or videotape. Also called *mouthing* and *post sync.*

liquid crystal display (LCD) A visual display made of two glass plates sandwiched together with a special fluid. When low power is applied, the light polarization in the liquid changes and, through a polarizing filter, an image becomes visible.

liquid duplicator *See* spirit duplicator.

liquid gate A printing machine attachment that coats the film with a refractive liquid to reduce the effects of scratches and abrasions. Also called a *wet gate.*

liquid gate printing The printing of copies of a film using a liquid gate at the time of exposure. Also called *wet gate printing.*

liquid head *See* fluid head.

LISP List Processor. One of two popular computer languages for artificial intelligence applications.

list □ A catalogue of a book publisher's current stock. □ The retail price of an item. □ *See* mailing list.

list ad A printed advertisement for more than one item of a kind, such as a list of books for sale.

list broker *See* mailing list broker.

list buyer *See* mailing list buyer.

list cleaning □ The removal of edits that are no longer necessary from an edit decision list. □ *See* mailing list cleaning.

list compiler *See* mailing list compiler.

listed sample Names, addresses, and telephone numbers of selected potential diary keepers derived from telephone directories and provided to Arbitron by Metromail, Inc.

listener An individual in the audience of a radio station.

listener diary A diary or log of radio or television programs heard or seen; the log is kept by a respondent to an audience rating survey.

listener sponsored A noncommercial radio station that is supported primarily by listener contributions.

listening □ Hearing a broadcast or other sound without participating. □ In survey work, a term that must be defined operationally in terms of the particular method of measurement used. The term should not be used if the survey question asks about tuning, hearing, hearing though not listening, paying attention, or any other term, regardless of whether someone considers that alternative term to be a synonym for listening. *See also* viewing. Cf. tuning.

listening area *See* coverage area.

listening level □ The volume of sound that is heard under normal conditions; this level may vary greatly, depending on the type of music, age of listener, and so on. □ A general term for the size of a radio station's audience. □ A general term for the length of time an individual listens to a radio station.

listening or viewing public Those members of the public who—using radio or television receivers—listen to or view programs broadcast by stations.

list exchange *See* mailing list exchange.

list maintenance *See* mailing list maintenance.

list management The changing, moving, shifting, and so on, of editing decisions entered into a computer-controlled edit decision list.

list manager *See* mailing list manager.

list owner *See* mailing list owner.

list price The published cost of a magazine, newspaper, book, and so on. Also called *list.*

list rental *See* mailing list rental.

list reproduction *See* mailing list rental.

list respondent An individual who is selected for a research study from a mailing list.

list royalty *See* mailing list royalty.

list salting *See* salting.

list sample *See* mailing list sample.

list segmentation *See* mailing list selection.

list selection *See* mailing list selection.

list sequence *See* mailing list sequence.

list sort *See* mailing list sort.

list test *See* mailing list test.

list usage *See* mailing list rental.

list user *See* mailing list user.

literal Any error in typesetting or printing found in proofreading, such as misspelled words and transpositions.

literary agent An individual who represents an author in dealing with a publisher.

Literary Market Place (LMP) The annual directory of the book publishing industry.

literary material Stories, adaptations, treatments, original treatments, scenarios, continuities, teleplays, screenplays, dialogue, scripts, sketches, plot outlines, narrative synopses, routines, and narrations for use in the production of television film formats.

literary property *See* copyright.

literary works Works—other than audiovisual works—expressed in words, numbers, or other verbal or numerical symbols or indicia, regardless of the nature of the material objects, such as books, periodicals, manuscripts, phonorecords, film, tapes, disks, or cards in which they are embodied.

literature □ Any printed matter, including advertising, promotions, and so on. □ The production of a literary work.

lith film A high-contrast film used in lithography.

litho An abbreviation for *lithography.*

lithography A printing method, invented by Alois Senefelder of Germany in the late 1790s, in which an image is applied to a stone or metal plate, then washed with an acid solution. Ink is then applied to the surface, adhering to the image portion only. *See also* photolithography, photo offset lithography, and planography. Cf. letterpress.

litho sheet A lithographed poster sheet.

little America method A technique for translating the media delivery of national advertising media plans into the media of one or more local areas, in a manner that attempts to match local deliveries to those that would be obtained nationally. Also called the *little U.S. method.* Cf. as-it-falls method, correct increment method, and media translation.

live □ A radio or television program broadcast as it is happening; not taped or filmed. □ A device or component that is turned on. □ Material that is not edited. □ News copy that is in use or ready to use. Also called *alive.* □ Plates, cuts, type matter, and so on, that is in use or set and ready for use. Also called *alive, live matter,* and *live type.* □ *See* live room.

live action □ Human action as opposed to animation. □ Not recorded.

live action camera A motion picture camera as opposed to a still camera.

live action log *See* log.

live action photography The recording on film of live actors and backgrounds, as opposed to animation photography.

live angle The angle of acceptance of sound by a microphone.

live animation Animation accomplished by moving an object or subject slightly between each frame.

live assist A local announcer who handles station breaks and other local insertions on an automated radio station.

live copy Written material read by an announcer, as opposed to recorded copy.

live end The end of the radio or television studio with the least amount of sound absorption. Cf. dead end.

live fade □ A fade created in a radio or television studio, as opposed to a fade created in a control room. □ *See* body fade.

live feed A network program that is carried by a radio or television station at the time it is received.

live matter *See* live.

live opener A newscaster's introduction to a filmed or taped story.

live recording The simultaneous recording of sound and picture.

live returns A shipment of books returned to a publisher unopened.

live room A studio or other space with a minimum of sound absorption and a long reverberation time. Also called *live studio.*

live side The face(s) of a microphone with the greatest sound sensitivity. Cf. dead side.

live sound Sound recorded at the scene of the filming or taping. Also called *location sound.*

livestock show A slang term for an audition for a large number of performers. Cf. hog calling contest.

live studio *See* live room.

live tag A local announcement following a recorded commercial that gives price, store address, and so on.

live television *See* live.

live time The period of time that network programs are fed to affiliates.

live titles Graphics shown on studio cameras rather than on a film chain.

live type *See* live.

ll An abbreviation for *leaves.*

LLL □ Low-level language. □ Low light level. *See* low key.

LLTV Low-light level television.

lm An abbreviation for *lumen.*

l/m Lines per minute. Also abbreviated *lpm.*

LMP □ *Literary Market Place.* □ Literary Market Plan.

LMS Library management system.

LNA Leading national advertisers. □ Low-noise amplifier.

LNB Low-noise block converter.

LNC Low-noise converter.

LO Local origination.

load □ The power consumed by an electrical device. Cf. overload. □ The device connected to the output of another device; for example, a loudspeaker connected to an amplifier. □ To add materials to paper to improve its surface qualities. □ To transfer data from a storage device into a computer. □ To insert a tape, cart, cassette, and so on, into a recorder or player. □ To position a tape so that the mechanism of a television tape recorder can use it as a medium for recording and reproduction.

loaded A script filled with difficult and complicated action, camera work, numerous cues, and so on.

loader □ A person who loads and unloads motion picture film magazines. □ In lighting, usually a plano-convex spotlight with lens removed so the spotlight can be used as a phantom load.

load factor In outdoor advertising, the average number of persons riding in each vehicle. This factor has been determined through national research as well as evaluation of government research and reports for highway capitalization. The Traffic Audit Bureau uses a load factor of 1.75 persons per car.

loading □ The addition of a filler—such as kaolin or talc—to pulp to produce the desired paper surface. □ The filler used in loading. □ The insertion of film into motion picture film magazines. Cf. threading. □ The insertion of videocassettes into a recorder or player.

load point *See* beginning of tape.

load time In video, the time taken to put a complete picture on the screen.

load up The process of offering a buyer the opportunity of buying an entire series at one time after the customer has purchased the first item in that series.

loanout An actor who is borrowed by a producer or company from another producer or company for a production.

loan-out company A corporation that is controlled by a performer and that furnishes a performer's services to others.

lobbying The performance of activities designed to influence the outcome of legislation. Cf. ex-parte presentation.

lobe An area of greater antenna radiation or microphone sound acceptance. *See also* polar pattern.

lobster shift *See* lobster trick.

lobster trick A newspaper shift that occurs after the paper has been put to bed —an afternoon shift for a morning paper or a night shift for an evening paper. Also called a *dog watch, graveyard shift, late watch, lobster shift, night side,* and *sunrise watch.*

local □ Radio or television station material that is produced internally. □ Nonnetwork. □ That which takes place in the area of publication or broadcast. □ *See* personal. □ A partially filled video screen. Cf. global.

local access and transport area (LATA) A geographic area designated by a telephone company to administer and provide communication services. May encompass one or more contiguous exchanges.

local advertising □ Advertising for a local merchant or business as opposed to regional or national advertising. □ Advertising placed at rates available to local merchants. □ *See* retail advertising.

local area network (LAN) A communications system usually confined to a building or small geographic area. Often includes a computer system containing various terminals, computers, and peripheral devices.

local cable system-originated program A program created by a cable system that usually is a live broadcast of news, local government, community activity, or high school sports; it may include cable-system-obtained commercially syndicated programs, such as movies.

local carriage The transmitting of local television stations by a cable television system.

local channel □ An AM channel on which several stations operate with a power no greater than 1 kilowatt nighttime and no greater than 250 watts daytime. (See Title 47 of the *Code of Federal Regulations* [CFR], paragraph 73.21(c) for exception.) Local stations are designated as Class IV. □ A local radio or television program channel furnished by a telephone company that is located within a single town or exchange area.

local color The use of mannerisms, regional dialects, incidents, and so on, that tend to add realism to a scene.

local cut-in *See* cut-in.

local distribution service station (LDS) A fixed CAR station used within a cable television system or systems for the transmission of television signals and related audio signals, signals of standard and FM broadcast stations, signals of instructional television fixed stations, and cablecasting from a local transmission point to one or more receiving points, from which the communications are distributed to the public by cable.

locale The environment or place where a scene is shot.

local government access channel A specifically designated cable television channel for local government uses.

local ID *See* station identification.

localism The FCC policy that tends to award broadcast licenses to individuals with residence in the city of license.

local item A news story about a local person or event.

localize □ To add local interest material to a wire service story. □ To emphasize the local angle of a news story.

locally edited supplement A Sunday newspaper supplement owned and edited by the newspaper itself; sometimes associated with other such supplements for the purpose of obtaining national advertising.

local media Communication media whose audiences are primarily drawn from the same locality as the media; these media customarily have a preferential rate for local advertisers.

local news News covered by the news staff of a local radio, television station, or newspaper.

local newsroom The working place of a newspaper's city staff.

local notice The FCC requirement that stations filing applications or designated for hearing publish information concerning the facts of the application or case.

local origination (LO) The programming produced by a broadcast station or cable television system. *See also* cablecasting.

local participating program A program available to more than one advertiser and not sponsored by any advertiser.

local program (L) Any program originated or produced by a broadcast station, or for the production of which the station is primarily responsible, that employs live talent more than 50 percent of the time. An FCC program source category.

Local Program Awards Awards given by the Corporation for Public Broadcasting for excellence in local public television programming.

local rate The advertising rate offered to local merchants by stations. Cf. national rate and regional rate.

local residence One of the many factors the FCC uses in selecting between or among mutually exclusive applicants for a broadcast license.

local sales The sale of radio or television station time to retail merchants and businesses. Cf. national sales.

local search A search operation confined to a part of a file or database. Cf. global search.

local service area □ For purposes of copyright (a) the local service area of a primary transmitter of a television broadcast station; comprises the area in which such station is entitled to insist on its signal being retransmitted by a cable system; and (b) the local service area of a primary transmitter of a radio broadcast station; comprises the primary service area of such station. □ The area in which telephone calls can be made without an additional charge. Cf. long distance.

local station □ A television station that places a Grade B or better signal over an area served by a cable television system. □ Any broadcast station that serves a city, town, or community.

local tag A radio or television tag that identifies a local dealer that is added to a recorded commercial announcement.

local talent The use of talent from the community that a station serves. Such use is looked on with favor by the FCC, according to the 1960 Programming Policy Statement.

location □ Any place other than a motion picture studio or lot used for filming. □ The site of a radio or television remote. □ The site of a news event. □ A place in computer memory where information can be stored.

location breakdown *See* breakdown.

location department A motion picture studio department in charge of finding appropriate sites for location filming.

location fee The payment made for the use of a remote site.

location filming *See* location shooting.

location list A list describing the location of all outdoor advertising panels sold and delivered. It is common industry practice that the posting's listing manager or other responsible person certifies delivery.

location manager *See* unit manager.

location production *See* location shooting.

location scout An individual who is selected by the location department of a motion picture studio or producer to find appropriate sites for location filming. Also called a *scout.*

location shooting The filming of motion pictures on location. Also called *location filming* and *location production.*

location sound Sound that is shot on location as opposed to sound added in editing. *See also* live sound.

location work Any work requiring transportation to a location away from the producer's regular broadcast studios. Cf. daily location work and overnight location work.

lock *See* locked.

lockbox A device that is attached to a cable television converter to allow parents to keep children from watching certain channels.

locked □ A film that has been edited and to which no further changes are to be made. □ Two or more components or circuits that are in complete synchronization. Also called *lock.* □ A television or film camera that is fixed in position by tightening the pan and tilt knobs. Also called *locked off.*

locked groove A circular continuous groove following a modulated groove section for the purpose of preventing further inward or outward travel of the pickup. Also called a *concentric groove.*

locked in A videotape recorder that is up to speed and ready to accept a feed. Also called *lock-up.*

locked off *See* locked.

lock out The closing credits of a program. *See also* standard close.

lock-up *See* locked in.

lockup The process of securing type in a chase. *See also* quoin.

Loeb Award, G. M. An award given for financial journalism.

Loewy panel A type of outdoor advertising poster panel designed by Raymond Loewy for the Outdoor Advertising Association of America (OAAA). Distinguished by light gray or white molding of metal or plastic.

lo-fi Low fidelity.

log □ One of the logs kept by a radio or television station as required by the FCC. □ To insert information in a log. □ An abbreviation for *logarithm.* □ A list of pages sent to a printer. □ *See* assignment book. □ To record a computer event. □ To sign on or off a computer system. *See also* log off and log on. □ A record of all film or television picture and sound takes. Also called *live action log* and *log sheet. See also* camera log. □ To record a series of events.

logarithmic reflectance chart A chart similar to the linear reflectance chart, except that the steps of reflectance difference follow a logarithmic, instead of linear, relationship. Used for the alignment and measurement of the transfer characteristic of television camera systems. *See also* test pattern.

log book A compilation of the logs for a particular filming or taping.

logging The process of entering information in a log, log sheet, maintenance report, and so on, either mechanically or automatically.

logic □ The science that deals with the formal principles of reasoning. □ The fundamental principles used in the design of electronic systems or devices.

logical operator A computer command string that allows embedded commands to be placed in material to be typeset.

logo An abbreviation for *logotype. See also* trademark.

log off To end the use of a terminal or computer. Cf. log on.

log on To begin the use of a terminal or computer for a period of time. Cf. log off.

logotype □ A single type body containing two or more spaced letters. Cf. ligature. □ An identifying name, device, or trademark used in advertising. □ *See* flag.

log sheet A record of the soundtracks made during filming or taping. Also called a *sound report. See also* log. Cf. camera log.

long approach A space position factor in outdoor advertising. Specifically, a term applied to a panel that is visible for more than 125 feet to pedestrian traffic, more than 350 feet to traffic traveling faster than 35 miles per hour, and more than 250 feet to traffic moving slower than 35 miles per hour. Cf. medium approach and short approach.

long distance (LD) A telephone call made to a number outside the local service area.

long distance microphone A shotgun microphone or a microphone with a parabolic reflector.

long focal length lens *See* telephoto.

long focus lens *See* long lens.

long form Television programs that are longer than the normal 30 or 60 minutes in length, such as motion pictures or specials.

long hair Classical music.

long handle posting A method of posting paper on an outdoor advertising panel from the ground or from a permanent platform by means of a long-handled brush.

longitudinal In tape recording, pertaining to directions or motions parallel to the tape-reference edge. Cf. transverse.

longitudinal recording □ The recording format used in audiotape recorders wherein the recording head is stationary and the writing speed equals the tape speed. Cf. helical scan and quadrature. □ To produce a magnetic representation of a video or audio signal having recorded track(s) lying parallel to the direction of tape travel.

longitudinal study A study that traces continuity and change over a period of years.

longitudinal time code (LTC) The time code recorded by audiotape recorders or on an audio track of a videotape recorder. Cf. vertical information time code (VITC).

long lens A lens with a focal length greater than the diagonal of the film negative. Frequently called a *telephoto*; however, a telephoto lens, because of its design, is shorter than a long lens of the same focal length. Also called a *long focus lens.*

long lines Telephone company long distance lines.

long pitch A filmstock containing perforations spaced for use in high-speed cameras.

long playing record (LP) A disc that has a playing time substantially greater than five minutes. Normally refers to a 10- or 12-inch 33-1/3 RPM disc recorded with approximately 150 to 300 grooves per inch. Cf. extended play.

long primer A size of type; 10 points.

long shot □ A television program that is produced with little expectation that it will be able to sustain itself. □ A camera shot taken at some distance from the set or object, often including the entire set. Also called a *distance shot. See also* camera shots and establishing shots. Cf. close-up (CU).

long take A camera shot held for an extended period of time.

longueur A dull passage or part in a book, play, program, motion picture, and so on.

long wave Electromagnetic radiation with a wavelength of more than 1000 meters or frequency below 300 kHz.

long wave band The band from 150 to 285 kHz used in Europe for broadcasting.

look ahead □ A news story that is written at least partially in advance of the event. □ The process of setting the next videotape edit by selecting the next edit from the edit decision list.

look angle The angle at which an earth station dish is pointed above the horizon toward a satellite.

looking room The space between a performer's face and the edge of the frame in the direction he or she is looking.

loop □ A folded antenna. Also called a *ring radiator* or *square loop,* depending on the shape. □ A telephone circuit between two points. □ The sections of slack film above and below the gate in a film projector or camera. Also called a *film loop.* □ A length of film or tape joined head to tail in a continuous band for continuous sound or picture. □ *See* feedback. □ A sequence of computer instructions that is repeatedly executed.

loopbin A tape holder that contains coiled audiotape for duplicating purposes.

loop elevator *See* loop tree.

looping A process used in dubbing dialogue, music, sound effects, and so on, to film or tape. A continuous picture loop is displayed to allow the performers to accurately lip sync to the picture. Also called *dubbing.* Cf. automatic dialogue replacement (ADR).

loop through A method of connecting two or more output devices to a machine or component to allow more than one output or display. Examples include a videotape recorder and a monitor connected to a cable television subscriber drop, and two or more monitors connected to a television receiver.

loop tree A series of rollers that allow a long loop to be used in looping.

loose ☐ A newspaper or magazine that is lacking in advertising or has excess white space. Also called *open.* Cf. tight. ☐ *See* loose shot.

loose framing *See* loose shot.

loose leaf binding A mechanical binding consisting of such items as rings, bars, cords, or pins that hold single sheets with or without punched holes.

looseleaf service A serial publication in one or more volumes that is revised on a regular basis using new and/or replacement pages to maintain current information. An example is Pike and Fischer, *Radio Regulation.*

loosen up A television director's command to dolly or zoom out.

loose shot Camera framing that leaves sufficient room for performer movement. Also called *loose* and *loose framing.* Cf. tight shot.

LOP ☐ Least objectionable program. ☐ Locally originated program. *See* local origination.

LOS ☐ Line-of-sight. ☐ Loss of signal.

lose super A television director's command to fade out a superimposed picture, leaving only the original shot.

lose the light ☐ A television director's command to move the camera to another shot after the tally light has gone out. ☐ To lose sunlight in outdoor shooting.

lose the loop The loss of the loop in a film projector that causes the picture to jump.

loss ☐ The decrease in the power of a signal with distance. Cf. gain. ☐ *See* attenuation.

loss leader An item of merchandise that is priced at or below cost in order to attract customers to a store.

lot The entire grounds of a motion picture studio, including soundstages, back lot, streets, and so on. *See also* back lot.

lottery The pooling of proceeds derived from the sale of tickets or chances and allotting those proceeds or parts thereof by chance to one or more chance takers or ticket purchasers. Prize, chance, and consideration must all be present before the drawing may be considered a lottery.

loudness The subjective sensitivity of the human ear to the intensity of sound. Cf. sound pressure level (SPL).

loudness control A control on a tuner designed to increase the bass and high-frequency response at low volume settings. *See also* Fletcher-Munson curve.

loudspeaker (LS) An electroacoustic transducer; used for converting an electrical signal into the mechanical vibrations that cause sound waves. Also called a *speaker.*

loudspeaker system A system containing two or more loudspeakers, a baffle, crossover networks, and so on.

louvers Thin parallel or cylindrical strips located in front of a reflector to reduce spill or direct light that falls outside of the main beam, usually of black finish. Also called a *spill shield.*

low-angle shot A shot normally taken from below eye level. Also called a *low shot.* Cf. high-angle shot.

lowband (LB) ☐ In quadruplex recording, pertaining to those frequencies specified in SMPTE Recommended Practice RP 6, Practice LBM or LBC. ☐ Pertaining to recordings made in accordance with Practice LBM or LBC of RP 6, or to equipment capable of making such recordings. ☐ The carrier frequencies appearing on a tape made in accordance with such practices. Cf. highband.

lowband standard The specifications for quadruplex recording practices specified in SMPTE Recommended Practice RP 6, Practice LBM or LBC.

low boy A short tripod.

lowbrow A variety of different forms of entertainment; primarily physical comedy such as slapstick.

low-budget film A film in which the negative cost does not exceed the figures listed for a high budget television feature film. *See also* negative costs. Cf. high budget film.

low-budget picture A feature-length motion picture, intended for theatrical exhibition, at a total production cost not exceeding $500,000.

low-budget production A motion picture or television production that is quickly shot, lacks well-known talent, contains few or no special effects, and so on.

low comedy Comedy that borders on farce.

low contrast A picture or lighting that lacks sharply defined shadows and highlights.

low cut filter A filter that eliminates the audio frequencies below a specified frequency. Also called a *low filter.*

low definition A television system that produces fewer than 200 scanning lines.

Lowell Medal, The Ralph An award given by the Corporation for Public Broadcasting to a programming oriented public broadcaster.

low end The bass frequencies of the audio spectrum. Cf. high end.

lowercase (lc) The small letters in a type font, as distinguished from capital letters. *See also* uppercase.

lowercase alphabet (lca) The length in points of all the lowercase letters of a given type font.

lower message key Character generator material placed in the lower third of a television picture's essential area. Formerly called a *lower message super* when superimpositions were used instead of keys.

lower message super *See* lower message key.

lower third The bottom one-third of a television screen; used for keying information, names, weather information, and so on.

lowest common denominator Television programming that is often designed to attract the largest possible audience; a program with a juvenile plot and characters.

lowest unit charge The highest rate for station time that may be paid by legally qualified candidates for public office who use a broadcast station. Computed at the highest frequency rate for the same class (rate) and amount of time for the same periods.

low filter *See* low cut filter.

low frequency (LF) The band of frequencies between 30 and 300 Hz.

low-frequency distortion Distortion effects that occur at low frequency. In television, generally considered as any frequency below the 15,750-Hz line frequency.

low-frequency interference Interference effects that occur at low frequency. In television, generally considered as any frequency below the 15,750-Hz line frequency.

low impedance A circuit or device with an impedance of less than 600 ohms. Also called *low Z.* Cf. high impedance.

low key □ A performer, program, motion picture, and so on, that is underplayed. □ *See* low-key lighting.

low-key lighting A type of lighting, which when applied to a scene, is intended to produce a picture having gradations from middle gray to black with comparatively limited areas of light grays and white. Cf. high-key lighting.

low-level language (LLL) A computer language that contains instructions in a code that is understandable to a computer. Cf. high-level language and machine language.

low noise amplifier (LNA) An earth station receiver amplifier that boosts the weak retransmitted signal from a satellite. *See also* low noise converter and low noise down converter.

low noise block converter (LNB) (LNC) An earth station receiver that contains both a low noise amplifier and a block downconverter. *See also* low noise amplifier and low noise converter.

low noise converter (LNC) An earth station receiver that downconverts satellite signals from C or Ku band to television frequencies.

low noise lamp An incandescent lamp having a special construction to minimize the generation of audio noise when operated on AC circuits and especially on dimmers that distort the sine wave. Used in recording studios and in filming where any noise would be objectionable.

low noise tape A magnetic tape with a higher signal-to-noise ratio and greater high-frequency sensitivity than standard tape.

low-pass filter An electronic filter that passes frequencies below a specified frequency only. Cf. high-pass filter.

low-power auxiliary station An auxiliary station authorized to transmit over distances of approximately 100 meters for uses such as wireless microphones, cue and control communications, and synchronization of TV camera signals.

low-power broadcast auxiliary station Devices—usually cue and control signal transmitters and wireless microphones—that are licensed to standard FM and TV broadcast stations and that have a maximum transmitter output not to exceed one watt.

low-power TV station (LPTV) A station authorized under the experimental, auxiliary, and special broadcast services that may retransmit the programs and signals of a TV broadcast station and that may originate programming in any amount greater than 30 seconds per hour and/or operate a subscription service.

low pressure A relaxed, easy-going program or performer. Cf. hard sell and high pressure.

low print tape Magnetic tape that is less susceptible to print-through.

low resolution A degree of detailed visual definition below the 400 by 300 pixels presented by normal color television receivers. Cf. double resolution, high resolution, and normal resolution.

low shot *See* low-angle shot.

low-speed film Film with a low sensitivity to light; one with a low ASA number. Cf. high-speed film.

low-speed photography The use of lower than normal camera speeds to increase the apparent speed of the action. *See also* fast motion. Cf. fast motion.

low to paper Type that is lower than standard height and unable to produce a uniform impression.

LP □ Linear programming. □ Long playing record. □ Long play. A four-hour-long recording mode on a VHS recorder. Cf. SP, and SLP or EP.

lp Line printer.

lpi Lines per inch.

LPM Literary Market Plan.

lpm Lines per minute. The number of lines a printer can print in one minute. Also abbreviated *l/m.*

LPNA Lithographers and Printers National Association.

lps Lines per second. The number of lines a printer can print in one second.

LPTV Low power television.

LPW Lumens per watt.

LQR Local qualitative radio. A Pulse rating service that breaks down the audience by occupation, income, education, and other demographic characteristics.

L + R Left plus right, the sum and difference in stereo signals. *See also* left (or right) stereophonic channel.

L – R Left minus Right. The sum and difference in stereo signals. *See also* left (or right) stereophonic channel.

LRC Long-range communications.

LS □ Local sunset. □ Long shot. □ Loudspeaker.

LSCC Line-sequential color composite.

LSI Large scale integration.

LT Last telecast.

LTC Longitudinal time code.

lubricant Any of several substances added to the magnetizable medium of a videotape during manufacture to diminish its coefficient of friction, thereby reducing headwear and lessening the incidence of tape stiction.

lubrication The application of a waxy substance to motion picture film to decrease noise and prevent damage during projection.

Ludlow A trademark for a Ludlow Typograph, a typecasting machine used primarily to cast display size type from matrices set by hand. Similar to an APL.

Lulu Awards Awards given by the Los Angeles Advertising Women, Inc., for "outstanding accomplishments" in broadcasting and related fields.

lumen (lm) A unit of (light) flux. Equal to the amount of light emitted by one candle.

lumen per square foot A unit of illumination; one lumen per square foot is equal to one footcandle.

lumens per watt (LPW) The number of lumens produced by a light source for each watt of electrical power supplied to the light source.

luminaire A complete lighting unit consisting of a lamp or lamps together with the parts designed to distribute the light, to position and protect the lamps, and to connect the lamps to the power supply. Also called a *fixture, instrument, lantern,* and *lighting instrument.* Also spelled *illuminaire. See also* arc light, ash can, baby, bank, base-light, basher, borderlight, broad, brute, camera light, catchlight, counter-key, crosslighting, dinky-inky, ellipsoidal spotlight, eyelight, five K, floodlight, footlights, fresnel, gladiator, half broad, inky-dinky, keg light, mini-brute, obie, pup, quadlite, scoop, senior, 750, single broad, sky light, sky pan, spotlight, standard junior, standard senior, striplight, sun arc, sun gun, Super-Beam 1000, Super-80, tenner, tiny mac, tru-broad, and variable beam light.

luminance □ A measure of the light (flux) per unit area leaving a surface in a particular direction. The unit is the footlambert. This quantity was formerly known as *brightness.* □ The measured radiance of a light source expressed by Y signals. Cf. chrominance.

luminance carrier *See* picture carrier.

luminance channel In a color television system, the channel that carries the monochrome signal.

luminance meter *See* exposure meter.

luminance signal The color television signal that varies with the light intensity of a scene. It is 11 percent blue, 59 percent green, and 30 percent red. *See also* M color difference signal and M signal. Cf. chrominance signal.

luminance unit *See* footlambert.

luminescence Fluorescent or phosphorescent light. Cf. incandescence.

luminous □ An adjective to indicate the production of light, such as *luminous source,* to distinguish from electrical source, and so on. The term is sometimes used before *intensity* or *flux.* □ A paint or powder used to reflect light on signs and billboards at night. Phosphorescent, fluorescent, and luminescent materials may be used.

luminous efficiency *See* efficacy.

luminous flux The rate of the flow of visible light; measured in lumens.

luminous intensity The amount of light emitted per second; measured in candela.

Lumitype *See* Photon.

lux The unit of illumination used predominantly in Europe; equal to one lumen per square meter, or 0.0929 footcandles.

LV LaserVision.

LW *United States Law Week.* An unofficial source of current court opinions, legislation, and federal agency rulings.

lx An abbreviation for *lux.*

M

M □ Magnification. □ Marine. An FCC first letter file-number prefix. □ Mega. □ Megabyte. □ Memory. □ Meter. □ Modification. An FCC file-number prefix. □ Monochrome. □ Thousand (the roman numeral for one thousand, as in CPM).

M A standard for television containing 525 lines and 30 frames per second. The NTSC standard.

m Milli.

MA Memory address.

mA Milliampere.

Ma Bell A slang term for the American Telephone and Telegraph Company (AT&T) or the Bell Operating Companies.

MAB Magazine Advertising Bureau, Inc.

Macbeth An overly dramatic performance by an actress. Also called a *Lady Macbeth.*

MacGuffin Alfred Hitchcock's term for a device that captures the attention of the motion picture audience, but has little to do with the plot.

machine A general term, like the word *device,* used to mean any mechanism or apparatus used to perform some kind of work.

machine coated An inexpensive paper coated by the paper-making machine rather than in a separate operation. Also called *process coated. See also* coated paper.

machine code *See* machine language.

machine composition *See* machine set.

machine finish (mf) An uncoated paper that has been calendered until it is relatively glossy and smooth.

machine gun microphone A directional microphone. *See also* shotgun microphone.

machine language A low-level language in binary form that a computer can understand without translation. Also called *machine code.*

machine leader A leader designed to take the additional strain of threading through the film processor first.

machine readable Information that is encoded in a form capable of being read by a machine, such as punched cards, paper tape, and magnetic storage materials.

machine readable cataloging (MARC) A Library of Congress system in which libraries can obtain magnetic tapes of catalog cards, acquisition printouts, and so on.

machine set Type composition performed by machine as opposed to hand composition. Also called *machine composition.* Cf. headset.

machine translation (MT) A translation from one language to another by computer.

mackle A blurred or double impression made in printing.

macro An abbreviation for *macro instruction.* A group of computer instructions that can be initiated with one or two keystrokes. Sometimes called *shorthand. See also* programmable key.

macrocinematography The motion picture filming of small objects with a macro lens. Cf. microcinematography.

macro focusing lens *See* macro lens.

macro instruction *See* macro.

macro lens A lens designed for macrophotography; one that will focus extremely close to an object. Also called a *macro focusing lens.* Sometimes referred to as a *micro lens.*

macro lever The device that enables or disables the operation of a macro lens.

macron A short stroke placed over vowels to indicate a long sound.

macrophotography The use of macro lenses to take extreme close-ups of small objects or portions of objects.

macro zoom lens A macro lens capable of zooming.

made □ A story of little value that is enhanced into a news story. □ Two sheets pasted together for bookbinding. □ A complete book made up from materials from other books.

made for pay A motion picture that is produced for pay cable television distribution.

made for television A generic term for any motion picture made for original showing on television; a telefilm.

Madison Avenue The highly publicized street in New York that has become a synonym for the home of the advertising agencies. Few of the major agencies are actually on Madison Avenue.

Madisonese The jargon of advertising. From Madison Avenue.

MADN Metropolitan area digital networks.

Madow Report A 1961 Congressional broadcast audience survey evaluation that helped lead to the formation of the Broadcast Rating Council (BRC).

Mae West A splicing block that cuts the edges of magnetic tape in a slightly curved manner.

mag □ An abbreviation for *magazine.* □ An abbreviation for *magnetic sound film.* □ An abbreviation for *magnetic,* as in *mag stripe.*

magazine □ A periodical publication containing stories, articles, advertising, and so on. A magazine may be specialized or designed for the general reader. □ The large metal container that holds the matrices in a linecasting machine. □ A hopper that holds punched cards. □ A mechanical assemblage designed to store a series of cassettes or cartridges and deliver them singly to a transport for playing or recording. □ A light-tight canister used to hold film before and after exposure in a camera or printer.

Magazine Advertising Bureau (MAB) An organization that is devoted to promoting magazines as an advertising medium. *See also* Magazine Publishers Association.

magazine concept The idea of a radio or television program having commercials by two or more advertisers rather than using program sponsorship. *See also* magazine format.

magazine format □ A radio or television arrangement wherein program time is sold to two or more advertisers. □ A format wherein a number of differing segments are broadcast within a program, similar to the format used in magazines.

magazine group An organization that publishes more than one magazine.

magazine plan A plan by which advertising aimed at a certain geographical zone can be placed only in magazines for distribution in that zone.

Magazine Publishers Association (MPA) An organization of magazine publishers, founded in 1919, for the purpose of promoting magazines as a means of improving the lives of their readers and as an advertising medium, as well as for the purpose of supplying its members with information and services; the Magazine Advertising Bureau is its sales arm.

magazine style The selection of type and layout common to magazines as compared to newspapers. *See also* up style.

magazine subscription agency *See* subscription agency.

magazine supplement A preprinted tabloid of magazine size supplement distributed in newspapers, usually in Saturday or Sunday editions.

magazinist An individual who writes for or edits a magazine.

mag card An abbreviation for *magnetic card.*

magenta A subtractive primary color; a reddish purple color. Used in process printing.

mag film *See* magnetic film.

mag head *See* magnetic head.

magic A bewitching scene, time, or place used as a plot device or shot.

magic bullet The theory that exposure to the mass media has an effect on audiences through a significant feature of the message. Also called *hypodermic needle.*

magic lantern The first projection device, invented in the 17th century by Athanasius Kircher, consisting of a metal box with a hole in one side covered by a lens; an image painted on a glass slide placed behind the lens is projected by means of a lamp inside the box.

magnafilm An early motion picture wide-screen process.

magna scale A larger-than-life model used on television to show detail.

magnascope An early motion picture wide-screen process.

magnesium plate A printing plate made of magnesium as opposed to the more common zinc or copper plate.

magnet A body having the property of attracting or repelling iron or iron compounds.

magnetic amplifier A series inductor type dimmer in which the control circuit changes the magnetic properties of the inductor core.

magnetic biasing □ The simultaneous conditioning of the magnetic recording medium during recording by superposing an additional magnetic field on the signal magnetic field. □ The AC magnetic biasing is magnetic biasing accomplished by the use of an alternating current usually well above the signal frequency range in the recording head.

magnetic card A flexible plastic card coated with magnetic material on which data can be stored.

magnetic cartridge *See* variable reluctance pickup.

magnetic-coated tape *See* magnetic tape.

magnetic coating The layer of magnetizable medium affixed to the base film of a magnetic tape.

magnetic deflection *See* deflection.

magnetic disk *See* floppy disk, hard disk, and magnetic medium.

magnetic drum A cylinder coated with magnetic material on which data can be stored.

magnetic field An area around a magnet or electromagnet containing magnetic forces.

magnetic film A perforated film base that has been completely coated with magnetic oxide for sound recording. Also called *full coat, mag film,* and *magnetic sound film.* Cf. mag stripe.

magnetic flux □ The total of the magnetic lines of force passing into a medium, perpendicular to a surface of that medium. □ In recording, the term often refers to the magnetic lines of force emanating from a head gap, or from magnetized areas on a recorded tape. These two quantities are more properly called *gap leakage flux* and *recorded flux,* respectively.

magnetic flux density The number of magnetic lines of force per unit area, perpendicular to that area. Also called *magnetic induction.*

magnetic head A structure whose essential elements are a coil of wire wound on a ring-shaped element made of magnetic material and having an insulated gap cut in it. The function of the head can be either the conversion of time-varying electrical signals introduced into the coil into time-varying magnetic fields in the gap, or the conversion of time-varying magnetic fields in the gap into time-varying electrical signals in the coil.

magnetic head core The high permeability structure that forms the head gap and supports the head winding.

magnetic induction *See* magnetic flux density.

magnetic ink An ink containing iron oxide used for character recognition in the sorting of coupons, bank checks, and so on.

magnetic ink character recognition (MICR) A magnetic ink used to allow the reading of graphic material by an automatic machine.

magnetic master The final edited magnetic film recording that is transferred to the motion picture film soundtrack.

magnetic medium A magnetically sensitive carrier for the storage and distribution of information: tapes, disks, drums, cores, and so on.

magnetic microphone *See* variable reluctance microphone.

magnetic original The original tape or magnetic film recording from which a magnetic master is made following editing.

magnetic oxide *See* oxide.

magnetic pickup A variable reluctance or moving coil used in a turntable pickup cartridge. Cf. crystal pickup.

magnetic printing The permanent transfer of a recorded signal from a section of a magnetic recording medium to another section of the same or a different medium when these sections are brought into proximity. *See also* print-through.

magnetic record (MR) Equipment incorporating an electromagnetic transducer and means for moving a ferromagnetic recording medium relative to the transducer for recording electric signals as magnetic variations in the medium.

magnetic recorder Any device that is capable of recording information on a magnetic medium, such as a tape recorder. Cf. optical recorder.

magnetic recording The use of any device capable of receiving magnetic information, such as a magnetic tape recorder, a magnetic disc recorder, or a magnetic stripe.

magnetic recording head A transducer used to convert magnetic signals on magnetic media into electric signals.

magnetic recording medium A magnetizable material used with a magnetic recorder for retaining the magnetic signals imparted during the recording process.

magnetic recording reproducer Equipment for converting magnetic signals on magnetic recording media into electric signals.

magnetic remanence The ability of a magnetic medium to retain the signal imposed on it after the removal of the magnetic field.

magnetic resolving *See* resolving.

magnetic sensitometry *See* sensitometry.

magnetic sound film *See* magnetic film.

magnetic sound stripe *See* magnetic stripe.

magnetic soundtrack A soundtrack in which the sounds are reproduced by electrically impressing the minute variations in the magnetic field on magnetic tape, magnetic film, or mag stripe. Cf. optical soundtrack.

magnetic stock New and unused magnetic film. Also called *mag stock.*

magnetic storage The storage of data on magnetic media.

magnetic stripe A thin strip of magnetic material attached to a motion picture film to carry a soundtrack. Usually called *mag stripe.* Cf. magnetic film.

magnetic tape A recording medium that consists of a thin tape with a coating of uniformly dispersed, ferromagnetic material on a nonmagnetic base that can be selectively magnetized. Used for recording analog or digital data in the form of changing magnetic levels in the tape coating.

magnetic tape leader The section of tape, usually recorded ahead of the program material, that contains engineering alignment signals and production information. *See also* leader.

magnetic track A magnetically recorded soundtrack or tape track.

magnetic transfer A magnetic soundtrack that is copied from one tape to another.

magnetism The physical phenomenon by which certain iron materials can exert a mechanical force on other magnetic materials.

magnetomotive force The force that has the power to produce a magnetic field. Analogous to an electromotive force, which can produce a current.

magneto-optical (MO) Erasable and reusable laser technological development in which the material is reheated while the external field changes bit polarity. *See also* erasable.

Magnetophone The original magnetic tape recorder. Developed in Germany by Telefunken.

magnetron A vacuum tube often used to generate high power in the UHF band.

magnification (M) The apparent enlargement of an object by a lens, as in a projector.

magnification ratio The ratio of the image size to the object size produced by a lens.

magnitude The size of one quantity compared with another of the same type.

magopt □ A motion picture film that carries both a magnetic and an optical track. Also called *magoptical track.* □ A film projector capable of reproducing both a magnetic and an optical track.

magoptical print A motion picture film print containing both magnetic and optical tracks.

magoptical track *See* magopt.

mag stock *See* magnetic stock.

mag stripe *See* magnetic stripe.

mag tape An abbreviation for *magnetic tape.*

mag track An abbreviation for *magnetic track.*

mail-ballot map A map prepared through returns from a mail survey questionnaire.

mail dates Dates on which a mailing list user has the obligation—by prior agreement with the list owner—to mail a specific list. No other date is acceptable without express approval of the list owner.

mail edition A newspaper edition distributed primarily by mail for out-of-town subscribers.

mailer □ A direct mail advertiser. □ A printed direct mail advertising piece. □ A folding carton, wrapper, or tube used to protect materials in the mail. □ Persons who physically handle mailings. □ A news story or feature that is sent by mail; usually a post-dated story or release.

mailers Promotional brochures and other mail sent by radio or television stations to advertisers, advertising agencies, station representatives, and so on.

mailgram A combination telegram-letter with the telegram transmitted to the postal facility close to the addressee and then delivered as first class mail.

mailing A large number of brochures, circulars, flyers, and so on, mailed at one time to potential buyers.

mailing list The names and addresses of individuals or companies having in common a specific interest, characteristic, or activity. Also called a *list.*

mailing list broker A specialist who makes all necessary arrangements for one company to make use of the lists of another company. A broker's services may include most or all of the following: research, selection, recommendation, and subsequent evaluation.

mailing list buyer Technically, this term should apply only to one who actually buys mailing lists. In practice, however, it is usually used to identify one who orders mailing lists for one-time use. A list user or mailer.

mailing list cleaning The process of correcting or removing a name or address from a mailing list because it is no longer correct. The term is also used in the identification and elimination of house list duplication.

mailing list compiler A person who develops lists of names and addresses from directories, newspapers, public records, sales slips, trade-show registrations, and other sources for identifying groups of people or companies with something in common.

mailing list exchange A barter arrangement between two companies for the use of mailing lists. The arrangement may be list for list, list for space, or list for comparable value other than money.

mailing list guarantee A guarantee furnished a mailing list buyer that a certain percentage of the names and addresses on the mailing list will be current and deliverable.

mailing list maintenance Any manual, mechanical, or electronic system for keeping name and address records (with or without other data) so that they are up-to-date at any (or specific) points in time.

mailing list manager A person who, as an employee of a list owner or as an outside agent, is responsible for the use, by others, of a specific mailing list. The list manager generally serves the list owner in several (or all) of the following: list maintenance (or advice thereon), list promotion and marketing, list clearance and record keeping, and collecting for use of the list by others.

mailing list owner A person who, by promotional activity or compilation, has developed a list of names having something in common. Also, one who has purchased (as opposed to rented, reproduced, or used on a one-time basis) such a list from the developer.

mailing list profile The demographic characteristics of a mailing list.

mailing list rental An arrangement in which a list owner furnishes names on his or her list to a mailer, together with the privilege of using the list on a one-time basis only, unless otherwise specified in advance. Also called *list reproduction* and *list usage.*

mailing list royalty A payment to list owners for the privilege of using their lists on a one-time basis.

mailing list salting *See* salting.

mailing list sample A group of names selected from a list for the purpose of evaluating the responsiveness of that list.

mailing list segmentation *See* mailing list selection.

mailing list selection The characteristics used to define smaller groups within a list.

mailing list sequence The order in which names and addresses appear in a list, such as ZIP code sequence, alphabetical, or chronological.

mailing list sort The process of putting a list in a specific sequence from another sequence or from no sequence.

mailing list test A part of a list selected for the purpose of trying to determine the effectiveness of the entire list. A list sample.

mailing list usage *See* mailing list rental.

mailing list user A person who uses names and addresses on someone else's list as prospects for the user's product or services. Similar to mailer.

mailing machine A machine that attaches labels to mailing pieces and otherwise prepares such pieces for deposit in the postal system.

mailing package A direct mail combination consisting of an envelope, letter, and return postcard or envelope.

mail merge A computer program that automatically combines database information with a word processor document. Used extensively in mass mailings.

mail order An order for goods or services that is received through the mail.

mail order action line (MOAL) A service of the Direct Mail/Marketing Association that assists consumers in resolving problems with mail order purchases.

mail order advertising A mail order solicitation accomplished through the mail. Cf. direct mail advertising.

mail order buyer A person who orders and pays for a product or service through the mail. Those who use the telephone or telegraph to order from direct response advertising may be included in this category although, technically, they are not mail order buyers.

mail order publication A book or other publication produced primarily for sale and distribution through the mail.

mail preference service (MPS) A service of the Direct Mail/Marketing Association wherein consumers can request to have their names removed from or added to mailing lists.

mail questionnaire A method of data collection that consists of sending a questionnaire to a respondent by mail, together with a request that the respondent answer the series of questions and return the completed questionnaire by mail.

mail response list A mailing list compiled from persons who have previously purchased goods or services through the mail.

mail survey map A map of radio or television station coverage prepared with the help of solicited or unsolicited mail to the station.

main The primary electrical service from a power company to a building where it is connected to the building's internal wiring system.

main channel □ The band of frequencies from 50 to 15,000 Hz that frequency-modulates the main carrier of an FM transmitter. □ The band of audio frequencies from 50 to 15,000 Hz that amplitude modulates the carrier of an AM transmitter. □ That portion of each authorized television channel used for the transmission of visual and aural information. □ In CD-ROM and CD-I, the only absolutely addressable information channel recorded on a disc. In CD-DA, the main channel carries the digital audio information. Cf. subcode channel.

main current *See* curtain.

main entry The primary entry for a catalogued book in a library card catalogue; author, title, or subject.

mainframe The central processing unit (CPU) of a computer with great processing power and memory capacity.

main gain control □ A British term for a grand master. □ *See* master control.

main head The principal display head of a body of printed matter such as an advertisement.

main light *See* key-light.

main memory *See* random access memory.

main plot The primary plot of a story, script, screenplay, and so on. Cf. subplot.

main stripe On a motion picture film that has more than one stripe, the magnetic stripe that is in the normal soundtrack position. Also called *first stripe* and *primary stripe.*

main studio A broadcast station studio from which the majority of local programs originate.

maintenance The inspection, servicing, and repair of equipment.

maintenance log One of the logs required by the FCC. Kept by a holder of a first-class radiotelephone license and reflecting results of maintenance procedures or observations performed. Cf. operating log and program log.

main title A title at or near the beginning of a motion picture or television program.

main trunk *See* trunk.

maizie A woolly pattern created with a cucoloris.

Major Award An award given by the Armstrong Memorial Research Foundation to encourage originality in FM programming.

major change A change in an FCC application involving significant changes in such items as power, antenna height, ownership, and so on.

major distributor One of the large motion picture studios.

major market *See* major television market.

major network One of the national radio or television networks and their affiliates.

major sponsor The sponsor using the majority of the commercial time on a program. Cf. minor sponsor.

major television market The specified zone of a commercial television station licensed to a community in the 100 largest markets, as listed in Title 47 of the *Code of Federal Regulations* (CFR), paragraph 76.51, or a combination of such specified zones where more than one community is listed. Also called a *major market.*

majuscule A capital or uppercase letter. Cf. minuscule.

make To close a relay or other contact.

make an out To omit a portion of the copy in setting type.

make good □ A commercial announcement presented after its scheduled time because of an error. □ A commercial announcement rerun because of technical difficulties the first time it was run. □ A newspaper or magazine advertisement reprinted because of an error.

make local To insert a station identification in a network program.

makeover The process of making a new page in order to add new or revised copy. Also called *replate.*

makeready The leveling of type matter in a letterpress form in order to produce a uniform impression on the paper.

make system To identify the radio or television network.

make-up □ The cosmetics, hairpieces, and so on, used by performers to enhance or change facial features. □ The retouching of commercial product packages for use on television. □ The physical transfer of several reels of film to one reel. □ The arrangement of type, illustrations, and other design elements on a page. Similar to layout.

make-up artist A individual who prepares, mixes, and applies cosmetics to the face or body of a performer.

make-up call The time a performer is scheduled to be available for make-up.

make-up department The department of a major film studio or production company in charge of applying cosmetics to performers.

make-up editor A newspaper or magazine editorial staff member who supervises the make-up of the pages.

make-up man The printer in charge of make-up.

make-up restriction A restriction on an advertising layout imposed by a periodical publisher to ensure that no unsalable advertising space is created by oddly proportioned advertisements.

make-up rule A thin, steel rule with a projecting top used to line up type.

male A part, such as a plug, adapted to fit into a female part, such as a jack.

malice In defamation, a statement made with knowledge that it is false, or with reckless disregard of the truth.

maltese cross An intermittent pull-down mechanism for film projectors and cameras. Also called a *geneva movement.*

management An ambiguous term covering the "art" of accomplishing objectives by working with subordinates.

Management Information System (MIS) A system for the day-to-day storage of operating and financial data.

management supervisor An advertising agency employee responsible for the successful management of designated accounts, and for liaison with client management. Cf. account supervisor.

manager □ An individual who supervises the business aspects of a career for a performer. Cf. agent. □ *See* general manager and station manager.

managing editor The newspaper or magazine editor who is responsible for personnel and the operation of the news department.

mandamus A writ from a superior to an inferior court commanding a specific act.

mandatory *See* mandatory copy.

mandatory carriage The broadcast station signals that the FCC requires a cable television system to distribute to subscribers. *See also* must carry.

mandatory copy Copy that is required by law to appear on the advertising of certain products, such as liquor and cigarettes. An example of such copy is ''Cigarette smoking is dangerous to your health.'' Also called *mandatory.*

mandatory kill An order from a wire service to delete a news story.

mandatory license *See* compulsory license.

mandatory message The legally required information broadcast as part of a commercial message or program, such as the products, prizes, and promotional fees paid by companies.

M and E Music and Effects. The film tracks used for dubbing music and effects. Dialogue is recorded separately.

M and E track Music and Effects track. A separate film track (or two) that contain only music and effects, not dialogue. Used extensively for foreign language release prints.

mangle A machine used in stereotyping.

man on the street An individual who is interviewed or performs in a commercial in a natural setting outside a studio.

manual A booklet containing detailed operating and technical instructions and diagrams.

manual control □ The processing of information without the aid of devices or machines. □ Hand operated control of electrical or electronic functions.

manual dimmer A dimmer that has only mechanical linkages between the control lever of the unit and the moving electrical contact that conducts the electrical power supplied to the luminaire load.

manual edit □ An electronic edit initiated by the judgment of the videotape operator. □ To perform or make such an edit, whose initiation is based on the judgment of an operator viewing the picture as the edit is made.

manual effects Sound effects operated by hand as opposed to recorded effects.

manual operation *See* manual control.

manual sequence A record album containing more than one disc on which even and odd numbered disc sides are on the same disc or discs. Cf. automatic sequence.

manufacturing The process of making a book; typesetting, printing, and binding.

manuscript (ms) □ Any handwritten or typewritten copy. □ Original or revised material written by an author, reporter, and so on. □ *See* script.

manuscript editor The individual who edits a final draft of a book manuscript for house style, physical layout, and so on; a copy editor.

manuscript reader Any individual who, in the process of preparing a book for publication, reads or checks a manuscript; a manuscript editor, copy editor, electronic manuscript specialist, and so on. Also called a *manuscript referee.*

manuscript referee *See* manuscript reader.

MAP Media Access Project. A public interest communications law firm representing groups and individuals.

map *See* dummy.

marbled calf A smooth calfskin etched with acid to resemble marbling. Also called *mottled calf.*

marbling The process of decorating the edges of books to look like veins of marble.

MARC Machine readable cataloging.

march on The title information used at the beginning of a radio or television program.

March season That portion of any year commencing 0100 GMT on the first Sunday in March and ending at 0100 GMT on the first Sunday in May. Cf. May season, November season, and September season.

margin The white space between the print or artwork and the edges of a page or layout. *See also* back margin, fore edge, gutter, and head margin.

marginal Writing, artwork, tape quality, personnel, and so on, that are barely adequate.

marginal head A heading placed in a margin.

marginalia Matter printed in margins: headings, footnotes, and so on.

marginal station A broadcast station that is on the borderline between economic success and failure.

mark □ An indicator or agreed on location to show where a performer is to stand, often marked by chalk or masking tape. □ To make notations on a script concerning cues, pronunciation, entrances, exits, and so on. □ *See* spike. □ Any device or expression that can be registered as a trademark, service mark, collective mark, or certification mark. □ *See* markup.

marker □ A grease pencil used to indicate edit points on magnetic tape. □ *See* markup. □ A physical or electronic mark placed at the beginning or end of a magnetic tape. May be used for sensing for automatic cueing or rewind.

market □ A population, group, industry, geographical area, and so on, regarded as a source of current or potential demand for a product or service. □ The extent of demand for a product or service. □ To offer a product or service for sale. □ Generally, any area reached by a radio or television signal. □ The television markets of the United States, and the stations in them, as identified in the latest publication of the Arbitron, together with any stations that have since become operational in the same community. □ An area established by an outdoor advertising plant operator. Larger markets often conform to counties or Metropolitan Statistical Areas.

market clustering The tying together of similar products such as books, records, and tapes in order to decrease the total cost of advertising and distribution.

marketer An individual or organization that offers a product or service for sale.

marketing Any business activities that affect the distribution and sales of goods and services from producer to consumer.

Marketing Communications Executives International (MCEI) An association of advertising and public relations people in all facets of the industry.

marketing concept *See* marketing plan.

marketing mix The functions considered in the selection of media for marketing a product or service: the product or service, the place it is sold, the price of the product or service, and the types of promotion to be used.

marketing plan □ A strategy devised for marketing a product or service. Also called a *marketing concept.* □ A comprehensive document containing background and supportive details regarding a marketer's objectives and strategies. Also called a *plan.*

marketing research The systematic gathering, recording, analyzing, and use of data used to promote the marketing of goods and services.

market penetration The degree or rate of usage of a product, service, or category among current users.

market position The reputation, or lack thereof, of a company as seen by members of the community. Similar to image.

market profile A summary of the characteristics of a market, including information on typical purchasers and competitors, and often general information on the economy and retailing patterns of the area.

market response The sales consequences of stimulation provided by marketing spending.

markets The name given to newspaper sections or pages containing financial, securities, and other market news.

market segmentation *See* segmentation.

market share □ The ratio of an individual company's sales to the total industry sales for a given product or service. □ *See* share.

market testing The selection of a geographical location to test the viability of a product or service before full-scale marketing is begun.

market totals The estimated number of persons in a market who listened to all radio stations that include qualifying stations, stations that did not meet the minimum reporting standards, noncommercial stations, and unidentified stations.

mark it A director's command calling for the use of clapsticks.

markup □ A proof or clipping of copy that is held and revised for a later edition of a paper. Also called a *mark* and *marker.* □ To place printing instructions on copy or layout. □ The difference in cost between the retail price of an item, such as a book, and the cost to the dealer.

marquee A canopy or neon sign in front of a theatre on which the title of the motion picture production and stars are displayed.

marriage □ A composite film of sound and picture. □ The combination of several different advertisements mailed together.

marriage split An arrangement between or among advertisers to purchase a certain space in different regular editions of a nationally distributed periodical jointly, with the advertisements appearing in copies delivered to their respective areas of the country.

married *See* married print.

married print A positive motion picture film print with synchronized picture and sound. Also called a *combined print, composite,* and *married.*

married sound The selection of sound and video by using the same television switcher. *See also* audio follow video.

marry *See* marriage.

martingale *See* twofer.

maser An acronym for microwave amplification by stimulated emission of radiation. A microwave amplifier signal booster.

mask □ To conceal a lighting instrument from an audience. □ To cut off part of a beam of light. □ The frame mounted in front of a television picture tube. □ A device used in enlargers to shield selected areas. □ A gobo. □ A device used to limit the field of view of a camera. □ Used to make a range of colors transparent. □ A sheet of opaque paper or black ink used in offset or engraving to prevent light from reaching the plate. □ A boundary set by a computer program to limit the space to be used for text or graphics. □ A template used to define the area of an integrated circuit.

masking □ The partial covering of a weak sound by a louder one. □ The hiding of a portion of a set by a flat or drape. Also called a *masking piece. See also* backing. □ The intentional covering of a portion of artwork so that it will not be printed.

masking piece *See* masking.

masking shot *See* matte shot.

mass □ A (usually) large number of heterogeneous, unorganized, physically separate individuals. Cf. group. □ A significant portion of a piece of artwork that has a unity of color or shading.

mass audience An audience that is physically separate from both the sender and the other receivers. Cf. group audience.

mass communication The process of expeditious distribution of mechanically or electrically produced duplicate copies of information to a heterogeneous and often large number of individuals. Cf. mass communications.

mass communications Individual messages delivered by various means: telephone, telegraph, radio, television, and so on. Cf. mass communication.

mass eraser *See* bulk eraser.

massification The tendency of television and cable television to ignore the diversity of audiences and program primarily for the mass audience.

mass magazine A magazine edited for the general public.

mass market A large number of prospective customers or consumers of products or services.

mass market paperback A low-priced, paperbound book, generally distributed to newsstands, chain stores, drugstores, supermarkets, and so on. Cf. quality paperback.

mass media The various vehicles used for sending information to a mass audience: radio, television, CATV, newspapers, magazines, books, discs, and so on.

Mass Media Bureau A division of the Federal Communications Commission, formed by the merger of the Broadcast Bureau and the Cable Television Bureau.

mass publication A periodical with a large, general circulation.

mass scene *See* crowd scene.

mass storage Memory that stores computer information outside the computer itself. Also referred to as *external memory.*

mass storage device Any computer peripheral that has a storage capacity greater than that of a floppy disk. Mass storage devices normally have a capacity of megabytes or gigabytes.

mass test An audition that includes a walk through. Cf. audition.

mass transportation Public conveyances such as buses, street cars, trains, subways, and rapid transit.

mast A pole used to mount an antenna.

master □ In disc recording, a metal part generated from a lacquer original. It may be used to generate metal molds by electroforming or to press discs. □ Any original audiotape, videotape, video disc, or film. Cf. dub and generation. □ Any control, such as a potentiometer or rheostat, that sets the level for a number of other controls. □ A switch or dimmer used to control other switches or dimmers for individual lighting circuits. *See also* grand master and group master.

master antenna television (MATV) A television distribution system that serves multiple unit dwellings, hotels, motels, and so on.

master clock A timing device used to control the operation of a system.

master control (MC) □ The room into which all of the video and/or audio outputs of the various studios within a station are fed. □ In lighting, a means for grouping a number of individual controls under a master switch or dimmer. *See also* lighting control console.

master control room A television or cable television control room that oversees the signals that are transmitted, as opposed to a studio control room that feeds into a master control room.

master copy □ A recording made in as few generations as possible and used as the highest quality finished product available. □ The edited copy of a manuscript; a printout from tape or disks. □ Artwork that is camera ready.

master disc An original disc from which copies can be made by a replication process.

master erase head A magnetic head capable of erasing the entire width of a magnetic tape.

master fader A video switcher fader that takes priority over any other faders on the console.

Master Frequency Record (MFR) The list kept by the FCC containing the frequencies and powers of stations in the radio communication service.

mastering □ The process of making a disk, tape, or other master. □ In optical disc technology, the production of a master disc.

master long shot A synonym for a cover shot.

master machine A television tape recorder used for generating a master recording or for playing such a recording to make copies of it.

master matching The cutting of shots from an original or master motion picture film to match the edited workprint. Also called *matching negative.*

master mix The combining of the various film or tape soundtracks into one.

master monitor The television control room high-quality monitor that shows the pictures being recorded or televised. Also called a *line monitor.*

master newspaper list A complete list of daily newspapers or of those newspapers used by an advertiser, for the running or ordering of advertising; usually includes rate and data circulation data. Cf. mock newspaper schedule.

master of ceremonies (MC) An individual who acts as a host on a radio or television program. Often spelled *emcee.*

master of properties *See* property master.

master original A recording made from any source and representing the highest quality recording available of that program.

master positive A positive film print from which duplicate negatives are made.

master pot The main gain control on the program output of an audio console.

master recording A recording dedicated to perform as the source in a dubbing session. It may be a master original or a copy of a master original.

master scene A major sequence in a script that uses one master shot.

master scene script A script that indicates the action and dialogue but does not specify camera shots or angles.

master script *See* shooting script.

master shot □ An uninterrupted long shot that is usually taken from a single camera position. Close-ups, cutaways, and so on, are usually added in editing. Cf. master scene. □ The widest possible shot in an animation scene.

master-slave A system, such as used in computing or videotape editing, where a master computer or controller determines the actions of the other computers or recorders.

master station A network origination control point.

master tape *See* master.

masthead The standing heading on the editorial page of a newspaper or magazine that contains the name, ownership, management, subscription rates, place of publication, and so on. Cf. flag and nameplate.

mat □ Any device attached to the front of a lighting instrument to shape the light beam. □ Soft light. □ A cardboard cutout used to mount artwork. □ *See* matrix and matte.

mat board Illustration board with a matte finish used for graphics.

match □ A direct mail term used to refer to the typing of addresses, salutations, or inserts onto letters with other copy imprinted by a printing process. □ *See* match cut.

match action cutting The editing of camera shots so that continuity is maintained between the shots.

match code A code determined either by the creator or the user of a direct mail file to be used for matching records contained in another file.

match cut Any cut from one shot to another showing the same object or talent. Cf. jump cut.

match dissolve (md) A dissolve from one shot to another where the second shot appears identical to the first but is revealed as different, often by zooming out or focusing. Also called a *match.*

matched frame edit *See* match frame edit.

matched groups Groups used for testing purposes who have similar demographic characteristics. Cf. control group.

matched pair Two devices that are mechanically or electronically identical to one another in operation, such as loudspeakers, resistors, tubes, and microphones.

match frame edit A videotape edit in which a portion of a scene already recorded is continued without interruption. Also called a *matched frame edit.*

matching □ The shading of television pictures to achieve balance. □ The assembling of a negative to match a workprint. *See also* master matching. □ *See* impedance matching. □ The visual assurance that performers and the set retain the identical appearance from one shot to the next. Especially important when portions of the same scene are shot on different days.

matching action The shooting and editing of videotape or film to ensure a smooth transition between shots and to ensure that no movement is switched, such as from camera right to camera left.

matching negative *See* master matching.

matching shot A match cut or match dissolve.

match stock Film stock that is from the same batch and can be used for filming the same scene.

material A writer or performer's jokes, songs, stories, and so on, used in a radio or television program.

materialist cinema An avant-garde type of film in which the materials of the art form become its primary subject matter.

material terms The factors that are significant in defining the operation of a contest; the omission of pertinent facts, misleading information, and so on.

matinee Any entertainment such as a motion picture shown or presented in the afternoon.

matrices The plural of matrix.

matrix □ The television circuit that transforms the I, Q, and Y signals into the three color signals. □ The mold from which discs are made. □ The piggyback system of carrying two extra sound channels on FM stereo for quadrasonic sound. Cf. discrete. □ The metal mold used to form the face of type. Sometimes called a mold. □ The brass Linotype plate containing the intaglio of the characters to be reproduced. □ The plaster, papier maché, or other material used as a mold in stereotyping and electrotyping. Also called a *mat.* □ A strip of film used for transferring dye in proportion to the density of the imposed relief images in some color film printing. □ An array of numbers arranged in rows and columns.

matrixing The processes of combining and decombining the luminance and chrominance components of a color television signal.

matrix printer *See* dot matrix printer.

mat roller A machine that makes matrices from page forms.

mat service A company that produces matrices for advertisements, borders, pictures, and so on.

matte □ A cutout or gobo used in front of a lens to cast a shadow, or give the effect of a foreground. □ A film with a cutout, printed with another film to prevent the cutout portion from being printed. □ An electronic matte inserted in a television picture. *See also* chromakey. □ A comparatively dull finish; not highly reflective. Also spelled *mat* or *matt.* Cf. glossy. □ An area on an image plane that cuts a hole, permitting the image behind it to show through like a window.

matte bleed The line around a matted image caused by imperfect alignment of the mattes.

matte box A camera lens attachment used to shield a lens from stray light and hold mattes or masks for simple special effects. Also called an *effects box.*

matte camera A television camera used for graphics.

matte finish *See* matte.

matteing amplifier A special effects generator.

matte line *See* matte bleed.

matte loop *See* matte roll.

matte out To eliminate a portion of a picture.

matter Any type set or in the process of being set. *See also* dead, fat matter, live, solid, and thin matter.

matte ringing *See* ringing.

matte roll The single or double roll of film used as light modulators in printing motion picture film. A single roll contains both clear and opaque areas; the double roll system uses one clear, the other opaque.

matte screen A low-gain projection screen with a plain white surface.

matte shot A camera shot made with a matte or mask in part of the frame to allow another shot to be printed in the opaque area. For example, a shot taken through a keyhole uses this technique. Also called a *masking shot.*

MATV Master antenna television system.

maxiline *See* maximil.

maximil The milline rate of a newspaper before any discounts. Also called *maxiline.* Cf. minimil.

maximum aperture The aperture of a camera, projector, printer, and so on, that allows the greatest amount of light to pass.

maximum depth requirement The maximum length of a periodical advertisement of less than a full column length allowed to pay less than a full column space rate.

maximum overall length (MOL) The maximum dimension of a lamp from base to base for double-ended lamps or base to extreme point of bulb for single-ended lamps.

maximum percentage of modulation The greatest percentage of modulation that may be obtained by a transmitter without producing in its output harmonics of the modulating frequency in excess of those permitted by the FCC.

maximum rated carrier power The maximum power at which a transmitter can be operated satisfactorily.

Maximum Service Telecasters (MST) An organization of local television broadcasters concerned with preserving over-the-air broadcasting and maintaining local stations as the basic element in the nationwide television broadcast system. Formerly the Association of Maximum Service Telecasters (AMST).

maximum usable frequency (MUF) The highest frequency that is returned by ionospheric radio propagation to the surface of the earth for a particular path and time of day for 50 percent of the days of the reference month.

maxipay A service for pay television, such as HBO, that has programs available at least eight hours per day. Also called *maxiservice.* Cf. minipay.

maxiservice *See* maxipay.

Mayflower Decision The 1941 FCC decision that held that broadcasters could not editorialize on the air. *See also* Fairness Doctrine and editorialization.

May season That portion of any year commencing at 0100 GMT on the first Sunday in May and ending at 0100 GMT on the first Sunday in September.

MB Megabyte.

MBN Mutual Black Network.

mbps Megabits per second.

MBS Mutual Broadcasting System.

MC □ Mass communication. □ Master control. □ Master of ceremonies.

Mc Megacycle. An obsolete term replaced by *megahertz.*

MCEI Marketing Communications Executives International.

McGuffin *See* MacGuffin.

McKittrick's Directory A quarterly guide to advertising agencies, their personnel, and their accounts.

MCQC Musicassette Quality Committee. A group instituted to improve the quality of audiocassettes.

MCR □ Master control room. □ Mobile control room.

Mc/s Megacycles per second. An obsolete term replaced by *megahertz.*

MCU Medium close-up.

MCW Modulated continuous wave.

MD □ Match dissolve. □ Music director. □ Magnetic disk. □ Magnetic drum. □ Message data.

MDR Magnetic disc recorder.

MDS □ Multipoint distribution service. □ Multipoint distribution system.

ME □ Managing editor. □ Marbled edges.

meal penalty The amount of money due a performer from a production company when he or she has worked more than a specified number of hours after the previous meal.

mean Normally, the arithmetic mean, the most common of the three means (arithmetic, geometric, or harmonic), computed by adding the values in a group together and dividing the resulting total by the number of values in that group. Cf. average, median, and mode.

mean line The line that marks the top of the primary lowercase letters that do not have ascenders, such as a, c, e, m, and n. Cf. baseline.

mean power of a radio transmitter The power supplied to the antenna during normal operation, averaged over a time sufficiently long compared to the period corresponding to the lowest frequency encountered in actual modulation. Cf. peak power of a radio transmitter.

mean time between failures (MTBF) The average amount of time from installation or repair until a device, component, and so on, may be expected to need replacement or repair.

measure The character space available in the width of a single column or line of type. *See also* line length.

measured service A telephone service wherein the customer is charged according to the time the service is used.

measurement techniques Methods used to measure radio and television audiences, such as meters, diaries, telephone coincidentals, and so on.

measuring stick *See* line gauge.

meat The essence of a news story or script.

mechanical A final layout of photographs, copy, proofs, and so on, ready for the engraver or printer; camera ready copy.

mechanical animation The animation of three-dimensional objects by physically moving the object's parts or limbs and using stop-motion photography.

mechanical binding A plastic spiral, metal ring, or other device used to bind pages of an inexpensive book, catalog, notebook, and so on. *See also* binding.

mechanical department The department of a newspaper or magazine that sets type, makes plates, and prints the edition or issue.

mechanical editing Editing accomplished by the physical cutting of a magnetic tape. Also called *physical editing.*

mechanical pulp *See* groundwood pulp.

mechanical requirements The layout and make-up specifications of a periodical to which prepared advertising printing material must conform.

mechanical reproduction A tape or disc of a radio or television program or announcement.

mechanical rights The rights to reproduce a copyrighted musical work on records or tapes. *See also* compulsory license.

mechanical rights organization An organization that grants licenses for the mechanical reproduction and synchronization of musical works. The Harry Fox Agency and SESAC, Inc., grant such licenses.

mechanical scanning The original, but now obsolete, type of television scanning that used rotating drums, discs, vibrating mirrors, and so on. Based on Paul Nipkow's 1884 invention and used into the 1930s.

mechanical spacing The spacing of the letters in a word without regard to appearance. Cf. optical spacing.

mechanical splice An editing of tape performed by physically cutting a tape and then rejoining (splicing) sections of the tape with an adhesive foil.

mechanical television *See* mechanical scanning.

med A script notation for a medium shot. Also MS.

Medal of Honor An award given by the IEEE to persons making "a particular contribution which forms a clearly exceptional addition to the science and technology" of concern to the IEEE.

media □ The plural of medium; the vehicles used to convey information to an audience. Includes radio, television, newspapers, magazines, car cards, motion pictures, direct mail, cable television, books, records, tapes, and so on. □ The materials on which data and instructions are recorded.

media association An organization of individuals or companies formed to promote a particular mass medium, such as the National Association of Broadcasters and the American Newspaper Publishers Association.

Media Award An award for the advancement of economic understanding given by the Champion International Corporation through the School of Business at Dartmouth.

media buy The purchase of time or space in an advertising medium.

media buyer An advertising agency employee who recommends time, availabilities, or space in media schedules for clients and, if approved, places the orders for the ad or campaign.

media conversion The use of some form of interface to convert such items as the information on a computer disk to information usable by a typesetter.

media coverage The reach of an advertising schedule expressed as a percentage of the target audience.

media department An advertising agency department that schedules advertising campaigns and buys magazine and newspaper space and/or station and network time.

media director The advertising agency employee responsible for the selection and purchasing of media time or space for a client's advertising efforts.

media event □ A press conference or other event that is designed to draw media attendance. □ An event deliberately staged by the media. □ An event given excessive coverage by the media. □ A special event covered by the media.

media generation The people who have grown up with the media; those who cannot remember the time before television.

mediagenic An individual who is photogenic, telegenic, or otherwise appealing when seen or heard on the mass media.

media imperialism The transplanting of media models from developed nations into geographic areas they control or influence. Cf. cultural imperialism.

media junkies Individuals who spend their free time absorbing almost anything the media have to offer, such as one known as a television couch potato.

media kit An advertising sales folder; usually contains a rate card, survey results, information about the station or periodical, and other sales literature.

media market The geographic area covered by the medium being used or measured. *See also* market.

media mix □ A record of the media time or space bought during a campaign or specific period of time. Also called a *media schedule.* □ The use of two or more of the mass media to advertise or promote a product or service.

mediamorphosis The distortion of facts or ideas by the media.

median A measure of central tendency; that value above which and below which half of the values in the set fall. Cf. average, mean, and mode.

media objectives The statement of the specific goals of an advertising campaign.

media palette In CD-I, the range of technology functions that permit specific design applications.

media plan A sales plan designed to select the proper demographics for an advertising campaign through the proper selection of the media. *See also* marketing plan.

Media Records, Inc. An organization that records information about newspaper advertising, given by paper in agate lines, and total dollar expenditures.

media representative A salesperson who works for a radio or television station or network. Also called a *media salesman* and *station representative.*

media salesman *See* media representative.

media schedule *See* media mix.

media shy An individual who is nervous about being interviewed by the media.

Mediastat An abbreviation for *Media Statistics, Inc.* An audience research organization.

media strategy A plan of action by advertisers and/or their agencies for bringing advertising messages to the attention of consumers.

media survey A survey taken to determine the particular medium's penetration of a market. *See also* survey.

media synergism The use of the electronic media to add impact to the messages of the print media, or vice versa.

media translation An adaptation of a media spending plan from a national to a local level, or vice versa, as for testing purposes. Cf. as-it-falls method, correct increment method, and little America method.

media vehicle *See* vehicle.

media voices The different mass media outlets that are available to the residents of a given community.

Mediawatch An electronic monitoring system devised by the Arbitron Company that measures network, spot, and syndicated programming, and cable television commercial spots 24 hours a day in the top 75 markets.

media weight The number and size or length of advertisements, or the total audience delivery level, produced by an advertising effort.

medium The singular of media. □ A means of transmitting information. □ A substance capable of transmitting electromagnetic radiation or sound—air, water, and so on. □ *See* mass media. □ The substance on which information is recorded or stored. □ A gel used to change the color of the light source. □ A size of paper; 18 by 23 inches.

medium and half A size of paper; 24 by 30 inches.

medium approach An outdoor advertising space position value factor. Specifically, it is applied to a panel that is fully visible for 75 to 125 feet to pedestrian traffic, 200 to 350 feet to traffic traveling faster than 35 miles per hour, and 150 to 250 feet to traffic moving slower than 35 miles per hour. Cf. long approach and short approach.

medium close shot *See* medium close-up.

medium close-up (MCU) A camera shot between a close-up and a medium shot. Also called a *medium close shot. See also* camera shots.

medium frequency (MF) The frequencies between 300 and 3000 kHz.

medium long shot (MLS) A camera shot between a medium shot and a long shot. *See also* camera shots.

medium octavo A size of paper; one-eighth the size of medium.

medium quarto A size of paper; one-quarter the size of medium.

medium shot (MS) A camera shot approximately halfway between a close-up and a long shot. Also called a *mid shot. See also* camera shots.

medium wave band The band of frequencies from 535 to 1605 kHz. Used for AM radio.

Med.L.Rptr. *Media Law Reporter.*

meg An abbreviation for *megacycle, megawatt, megohm,* and so on. *See also* mega.

mega (M) A prefix denoting one million, such as megahertz (mHz), megawatt (mW), and so on.

megabyte (M) Actually 1,048,576 bytes, but commonly referred to as 1 million bytes.

megahertz (mHz) One million hertz.

megamedia event A news event that transcends the ordinary, such as the Iran-Contra affair or Watergate.

megaphone A cone-shaped voice amplifying device, still used sometimes by film directors.

megaverdict A jury verdict that awards an extremely large sum of money to a plaintiff in a defamation case. Also called a *monster verdict.*

melodrama A script or play that depends primarily on plot action. Loosely, melodrama is to tragedy what farce is to comedy.

mem An abbreviation for *memory.*

membrane keyboard A keyboard with a flexible plastic overlay.

memo An abbreviation for *memorandum.*

memorandum opinion and order (MO&O) A document containing a decision by an administrative agency.

memory □ A device for storage of intensity information for combinations of luminaires (cues or presets) for use during the course of a production. □ Any recording device into which information can be stored and later retrieved. Also called *storage.* □ The integrated circuits in a computer that store instructions in ROM or information in RAM. *See also* disc storage, random access memory (RAM), and read-only memory (ROM).

memory capacity The number of units of data that can be stored in a computer's RAM; usually expressed in bytes.

memory control logic The circuitry used to control the movement of information to, from, or within a memory.

memory counter A magnetic tape transport device that returns a tape automatically to a preset location. Also called *memory rewind.*

memory management The optimum allocation of disc space during the design process. Also called *disc mapping.*

memory rewind *See* memory counter.

memory system An automatic device using controls such as punched cards or magnetic tape to control successive settings of lighting dimmers or cross connect systems.

meniscus lens An inexpensive, concave-convex lens sometimes used as a close-up attachment to a camera.

mention A brief, on-air reference to a product or person.

mentions The number of different diaries in which a radio or television station is mentioned once with at least five minutes of listening in a quarter hour; does not indicate all the entries to a station in one diary.

menu A list of options or programs displayed by a computer or editor from which the operator selects the next procedure to be performed.

MEOV Maximum expected operating values.

MEP Mogul end prong. A lamp base type.

merc An abbreviation for a *mercury vapor lamp.*

mercer clips Small flexible clips used to mark film for editing.

merchandising □ Any activity directed toward stimulating interest in a product or advertising campaign. □ The activity of a station or network and advertiser that promotes a product or service in addition to the on-air commercials. The term merchandising is often used interchangeably with marketing.

merchandising rights The right to manufacture and to sell or otherwise dispose of any object or thing first described in literary material written by a writer, provided such object or thing is fully described therein and by such description appears to be unique and original.

merchandising service Any of various services offered, usually free of direct charge, by a communication medium to help in promoting an advertiser's products or to gather marketing information of interest to the advertiser.

mercuric chloride A white, corrosive substance used in film intensification.

mercuric iodide A red substance used in film intensification.

mercury vapor lamp A lamp that produces a cold blue light by the use of vaporized mercury.

merge To combine the information from two or more computer databases, a database and a word processor file, and so on.

merge-purge To join different mailing lists and automatically remove identical names, addresses, and so on.

merger The absorption of one company by another. Numerous mutually exclusive applications have been resolved by mergers.

merging The combining of two or more computer files into one.

merging cove *See* ground cove.

meridian A type size; approximately 44 points.

MERPS Multiple event record and playback systems. MERPS cannot only play spots and programs, according to a preset log, they can even locate, insert, remove, and replace tapes automatically.

meshbeat Television camera pickup tube moire. Also called *beat* and *linebeat.*

message ☐ What passes between a communicator and a receiver. ☐ A modulated wave. ☐ A combination of characters designed to communicate information.

message channel A cable television channel on which time is sold to individuals for want ads, personal messages, and so on.

message research Any analysis of print or broadcast mass media content, either micro or macro.

message sector A sector containing caution encoded as CD-DA audio data to warn users of a CD-DA player to lower the volume.

message switching A communication system wherein a message is received and stored, then transmitted when a channel is available. Also called *packet switching.*

messenger A steel cable used between telephone poles to support a coaxial cable.

META Metropolitan Educational TV Association.

metal ☐ Type metal; an alloy of lead, antimony, and tin. ☐ Type that has been set.

metalanguage A complex language, such as that used to create and ''read'' television texts, which is based on and interrelated with cultural codes from semiotics.

metal father A recording mold formed by nickel plating on a master disc. Can be used directly for replication or as the basis for the production by two further stages of plating of stampers for large-quantity production.

metal head A magnetic head whose pole piece is made of metal, such as Sendust, rather than a ferrite.

metal master A metal negative produced from an original disc.

metal oxide semiconductor (MOS) A device that permits bidirectional flow of current. Used for field effect resistors, capacitors, and transistors.

metal particle tape A magnetic tape that has high coercivity and corresponding sensitivity.

metal positive *See* mold.

metamorphosis An animation technique wherein one shape is changed into a different form or object.

meter (M) ☐ Any automated recording device that, when connected to a radio or television receiver, will record whether the receiver is turned on or off and, usually, the channel or station to which the receiver is tuned. If the information thus obtained is electronically relayed back to a central office location, it may be called an instantaneous meter. ☐ The beat of a speech, line, or music. ☐ An electrical or electronic measuring device, such as a multimeter, voltmeter, ammeter, VU meter, light meter, and so on. ☐ A metric system unit of length equal to 39.37 inches.

metered market service (MM) Nielsen's meter-based local market television audience measurement service that operates in New York, Los Angeles, Chicago, San Francisco, Philadelphia, Detroit, and other markets.

meter reading The measure of the intensity of light, the current, voltage, resistance in a circuit, and so on.

method Usually referred to as ''The Method.'' A style of acting based on Stanislavsky's ideas of characterization. Also called *method acting.*

method acting *See* method.

methodology ☐ The study and principles underlying development of research design and analysis. ☐ Techniques and procedures used to attain an end. An example is the total telephone frame (TTF) methodology employed by NSI in all U.S. counties and markets to incorporate unlisted telephone households into NSI samples.

metro An abbreviation for *metropolitan;* a densely populated area.

metro area An abbreviation for *metropolitan area.* A standard metropolitan statistical area as defined by the Bureau of the Budget, although it is sometimes used to refer to an area that is geographically broader or narrower than the corresponding SMSA. Used in estimating household ratings and audience shares.

metropolitan area *See* metropolitan statistical area and metro area.

metropolitan daily A daily newspaper published in a large city.

Metropolitan Statistical Area (MSA) An urban area designated by the Bureau of the Budget for statistical reporting purposes; a metro area in audience measurement studies. An MSA has a population of at least 50,000; larger areas are designated as CMSAs and PMSAs. MSA is generally synonymous with the former term standard metropolitan statistical area (SMSA).

metro rating A rating computed for the households or the individuals in a well-defined metropolitan area; normally, the metropolitan statistical area.

Metro Rating Area A separate reporting area where Arbitron reports television household ratings, shares, and HUTs. The Metro Rating Area generally includes the entire "corresponding" MSA (Primary Metropolitan Statistical Area, as defined by the U.S. Office of Management and Budget) except in those instances in which an MSA county (or portion of a geographically split MSA county) is not in the ADI of the market.

metro share Television households in the metro area tuned to a specific station as a percent of metro area television households with a receiver turned on.

metro survey area (MSA) (metro) An area generally corresponding to a metropolitan statistical area, CMSA, or PMSA, and subject to exceptions dictated by historical industry usage and other marketing considerations.

metteur en scene The director or person responsible for the final quality of a motion picture.

mezzotint □ A process for engraving a copper or steel plate by roughening and burnishing in different areas. □ An engraving produced by this process.

MF Medium frequency.

mf Machine finish.

MFR Master frequency record.

MH Magnetic head.

MHz Megahertz.

MI Move in.

mic An abbreviation for *microphone.* Often abbreviated *mike.*

Mickey Mouse □ A slang term for anything that is not constructed or accomplished in a professional manner. □ A type of music used to describe action.

MICR Magnetic ink character recognition.

micro □ From the Greek, meaning "small" or "minute." □ One-millionth part of a unit. □ Anything very small.

microcam A small electronic news gathering (ENG) type television camera.

microcassette A miniature audiocassette approximately one-fourth the size of a standard cassette.

microcinematography A photographic process for taking pictures of objects too small for a macro lens using a combination of a film camera and a microscope. Cf. macrocinematography.

microcircuitry The use of integrated circuits in electronic devices.

microcomputer A somewhat general term indicating a computer with limited capabilities; a personal or desktop computer. Cf. minicomputer.

microcopy A photograph that is reduced in size to fit on microfilm.

microelectronics Essentially, miniaturized electronics.

microfiche A microfilm format from 3 by 5 inches to 6 by 9 inches in size.

microfilm A photographic medium on which data is stored in a greatly reduced size.

microfloppy A 3-1/2-inch floppy disk.

microform A general term for the photographic technique of reducing the size and bulk of records, card catalogs, books, and so on, and storing the information on film. Includes microfilm, microfiche, and micro-opaque processes.

microgroove A disc groove that has a nominal top width of 3 mils suitable for reproducing with a 1/2- to 1-mil stylus. Also called a *fine groove.*

microgroove record *See* long playing record (LP).

micro lens *See* macro lens.

micron A unit of measurement equal to one-millionth of a meter.

microphone A transducer used to change acoustical energy into electrical energy. Abbreviated mic or mike. *See also* capacitor (C), carbon (C), condenser, dynamic, eight ball, electrostatic, lapel, lavaliere, lip, moving coil, pressure, ribbon, rifle, ring, shotgun, variable reluctance, velocity, vibration, and wireless microphones. *See also* mike pattern.

microphone boom *See* mike boom.

microphone cable *See* mike cable.

microphone howl *See* feedback.

microphone input A low-level input. *See also* mike level.

microphone mixer *See* mike mixer.

microphone pattern *See* mike pattern.

microphone pickup pattern *See* mike pattern.

microphone presence *See* presence.

microphone stand *See* mike stand.

microphone transformer An impedance-matching transformer used between a microphone and an amplifier or mixer.

microphonic bars Wide horizontal lines on a television picture caused by interference.

microphonics □ The audio noise caused by mechanical vibration or shock. □ In video transmission, the mechanical vibration of the elements of an electron tube resulting in a spurious modulation of the normal signal. This usually results in erratically spaced horizontal bars in the picture.

microprocessor The primary or central processing unit of a computer; the computer's "brain."

micropublishing The publication of information using microform techniques.

microsecond One-millionth of a second.

microvolts/meter/mile A method of stating the field strength of a radiated wave.

microwave The line-of-sight and point-to-point transmission of signals. *See also* microwaves.

microwave antenna A truncated parabolic reflector. *See also* dish.

microwave link One of the relay stations in a microwave relay system that receives, amplifies, and retransmits a signal. Also called a *relay* and a *relay station.*

microwave relay A method of transmitting and receiving television (and other) signals by means of geographically spaced microwave links.

microwaves The radio frequencies above approximately 1000 mHz. *See also* microwave.

midband The channels on a cable television system that are between channels 6 and 7 on broadcast television.

middle break A station identification made at or near the midpoint of a radio or television program.

midband converter A device that transforms information on a midband to a channel that may be watched by a cable subscriber.

middle break A commercial break in a radio or television program that interrupts the flow of the story.

middle-of-the-road (MOR) A radio station format characterized by popular music other than country and western, folk, jazz, rock, and so on.

middle range The audio frequencies from approximately 400 Hz to 3000 or 4000 Hz. Also called *midrange.*

middle tones The shades of gray in a photograph or halftone engraving.

mid fi quality In CD-I, the third of five audio quality levels. A bandwidth of 12 kHz is obtained by using 4-bit ADPCM at a sampling rate of 37.7 kHz. Comparable with FM broadcast sound quality.

midget A small spotlight used for fill light. *See also* inky.

MIDI Musical Instrument Digital Interface. An event-oriented protocol devised as a means of allowing electronic musical instruments to communicate control information within a system.

MIDI clock A device used to start and stop MIDI source and destination sequencers.

MIDI recorder A musical multitrack polyphonic recorder with editing features.

MIDI sequence A continuous stream of MIDI messages.

mid point The halfway moment of a superimposition, dissolve, fade, and so on.

midrange *See* middle range.

midrange loudspeaker The loudspeaker in a three-way system that carries the middle range sounds. Also called a *squawker.* Cf. woofer and tweeter.

midseason replacement A television series that is substituted for one canceled after several months, often in January.

mid shot *See* medium shot.

midtone A picture level that is neither light nor dark, bright nor dim.

Midwest Case The 1972 Supreme Court decision that upheld the FCC's right to require local program origination by CATV systems.

M-II A second generation M format videotape system.

mike An abbreviation for *microphone.* Also abbreviated *mic.*

mike amplifier *See* mike preamplifier.

Mike Berger Memorial Award An award presented to New York reporters given in honor of the Pulitzer Prize-winning reporter.

mike boom A boom with a long telescoping arm capable of being raised or lowered and swung in an arc.

mike button A switch or button that is used to activate and deactivate a microphone.

mike cable A shielded cable used to attach a microphone to a preamplifier.

mike channel The key, fader, preamplifier, and associated circuits in an audio control console used for a microphone.

mike fade *See* body fade.

mike fright A common fear and reaction to being placed in front of a microphone. Similar to stage fright and other situations that are new and different.

mike hog A performer who constantly edges other talent away from a microphone. The audio equivalent of upstage.

mike level A signal of such low intensity that it requires preamplification. Cf. line level.

mikeman A microphone boom operator or other television or film crew member who places microphones on a set.

mike mixer A small audio console.

mike mugger A performer who always works too close to a microphone.

mike pattern The polar pattern of a microphone. *See also* bi-directional, cardioid microphone, directional microphone, nondirectional mike, omnidirectional microphone, polydirectional microphone, semidirectional microphone, and unidirectional microphone.

mike preamplifier An audio frequency amplifier used to increase the minute signal level produced by a microphone. Also called a *mike amplifier.*

mike stand A floor or desk device for holding a microphone.

mike stew A slang term for extraneous unwanted sounds picked up by a microphone.

mike technique An awareness of the characteristics of microphones and an ability to use the knowledge to achieve the most effective results.

mike wise A performer who is knowledgeable in microphone technique.

miking The arranging of microphones for a broadcast or recording.

mil A unit of measurement equal to one-thousandth of an inch.

milk □ To rearrange and repeat a news story after it has lost its freshness. □ To work an audience to extract a maximum of applause or reaction.

milk glass A translucent glass used to diffuse light. Also called *opal glass.*

mill A slang expression for a typewriter on which stories are ground out.

milli (m) In the metric system, a prefix denoting one-thousandth.

millimeter One-thousandth of a meter. One inch equals 25.4 millimeters.

millimeter wave The electromagnetic radiation from 30 to 500 gHz. The satellite Ku band is in this portion of the spectrum from 20 through 30 gHz.

millimicro *See* nano.

milline An agate line of advertising space in one million copies of a publication.

milline rate The cost of a milline.

millivolts per meter (mv/m) A measure of television or radio signal strength.

MIM Morality in Media. A citizens' group.

Mimeograph A trademark name for a stencil duplicating machine. The term is often used generically.

mimeographed newspaper A newspaper printed from stencils.

Mimeoscope A trademark name for an illuminated easel.

mimic A computerized display of a stage lighting plot.

min An abbreviation for *minute* and *minimum*.

miniature Any small scale model of an object or scene; a diorama. Generally made for motion picture production when the cost of a full-size set would be prohibitive.

miniature camera Generally, a 35-mm camera used for taking slides and prints; a popular personal as well as professional still camera.

miniaturization The use of transistors, integrated circuits, and so on, to make electronic equipment smaller and thus more mobile.

mini-brute A high-intensity fill light. Cf. brute.

minicable A cable system in which an earth station serves an apartment complex. Minicable companies do not need a municipal franchise because they do not cross public rights-of-way.

minicam A contraction of *miniature camera*; a small, lightweight television camera used primarily for news or remotes.

minicassette □ A smaller videocassette designed to fit in portable videocassette recorders. □ A smaller audio cassette that is driven by the take-up reel instead of by a capstan.

minicomputer A somewhat general term for a computer with more power, storage capacity, and sophistication than a microcomputer but less than a mainframe.

minidisk A 5.25-inch computer floppy disk. Also called a *diskette*.

minidoc An abbreviation for a *minidocumentary*.

minidocumentary □ A documentary program shown on television on successive days. □ A brief radio or television documentary; sometimes a short news item.

minikin A British term for the smallest size of type made in England; 3-1/2 points.

minimal cinema A type of film production that attempts to reduce the importance of the medium and use it only to record the dialogue and action. Also called *minimal film*.

minimal film *See* minimal cinema.

minimil The milline rate of a newspaper after all possible discounts for space and frequency purchases have been calculated. Also called *minimilline*. Cf. maximil.

mini-mount A small camera mount used in helicopters.

minimum The pay negotiated in a union contract. *See also* scale.

minimum channel capacity The FCC requirement that cable television systems have the equivalent of 20 broadcast channels available for immediate or potential use.

minimum depth requirement A newspaper requirement that advertisements have a certain proportion of depth to width, usually one inch per column.

minimum focusing distance The minimum distance between an object and a camera wherein the object is in focus.

minimum frequency A level of exposure to or scheduling of advertising that is believed to represent the lowest level at which the advertising will be effective in attaining its ends, while permitting the greatest degree of advertising continuity.

minimum mileage separation The distance a broadcast station must be separated from co-channel and adjacent-channel stations or assignments.

minimum operation schedule The minimum amount of time a broadcast station may operate, as delineated in Title 47 of the *Code of Federal Regulations* (CFR), paragraphs 73.71, 73.262, 73.561, and 73.651.

minimum reporting standards (MRS) The standard minimum requirements (minimum amounts of listening during a survey) that a radio or television station must meet in a given market, in order to be listed in the report of that market.

minimum scale The minimum amount to be paid to performers, players, actors, and so on, as set forth in union or guild agreements.

minimum service The minimum number of television signals a cable television system may carry.

minion A common type size; 7 points.

minionette A size of type; 6-1/2 points.

minipage A computer screen display that shows how a completed page will look when printed. The page and type are less than normal size. Also called a *page preview.*

minipay □ A cable television programming service that charges cable television systems according to the number of subscribers. □ A service for pay television that has programs available less than eight hours a day. Cf. maxipay.

miniplug A small connector, 3-1/2 mm or 1/8 inch, used for earphones, microphones, and so on.

miniseries A short television series, often run on succeeding nights and usually consisting of only three or four episodes. Often based on a novel. Also called a *closed-end series.*

miniwave A microwave camera-to-control link; normally used on remotes.

minor change An insignificant change made to an application to the FCC. Cf. major change.

minor character A performer's role, more than a walk on, but less than a supporting role. Also called a *minor part.*

minor part *See* minor character.

minor sponsor The sponsor who presents only one of the commercials on a radio or television program. Cf. major sponsor.

Minporen The national association of commercial broadcasters in Japan.

mint A collector's item, such as a book or other publication, in like-new condition.

minuscule A lowercase letter. Cf. majuscule.

minute A 60-second commercial.

minute-by-minute profile An estimate of the varying numbers of listeners to a radio or television program at closely spaced periods during the program; used to determine the most advantageous times for scheduling commercials.

minute of program (MOP) A specified program minute based on the program's start time.

MIP Marche International des Programmes de Télévision International. A marketplace for buyers and sellers of television programs.

MIPS Millions of instructions per second. A measure of a computer's performance.

MIRED Micro reciprocal degrees. A unit of measurement of color temperature obtained by dividing the color temperature into one million.

mirror ball An approximately spherical ball whose surface is covered with small plane mirrors. When a spotlight is shone on the ball and it is rotated, multiple moving spots of light sweep across surrounding surfaces.

mirror image *See* lateral reversal.

mirror shot A camera shot taken by reflection.

mirror shutter A reflex camera shutter that allows continuous viewing of the scene being photographed.

MIS Management information system.

miscast To select a performer for a role for which he or she is not suited.

miscellany □ A book containing miscellaneous writings. □ Matter used as a filler in a newspaper page.

misdemeanor An offense less serious than a felony and punishable by a fine or imprisonment.

mise en scene □ The scenery, props, camera angles, lighting, and so on, of a stage setting. □ The preparations that are made for a stage setting.

misleading advertising *See* false advertising.

mismatch The condition existing when two components with different impedances are connected.

misprint A typographical error made by a typesetter. Cf. printer's error (pe).

misregistration An error in the alignment of components or parts of a device or system, as in color television camera tubes that are not aligned properly.

misrepresentation Any false statement. Misrepresentation to the FCC may be grounds for denial of an application or revocation of license under Section 312 of the Communications Act.

miss □ A failure to cover a news story. □ A failure by a performer to reach or stop on a mark.

mistracking □ An undesirable condition characterized by a failure of the playback video head to scan directly over the recorded track. □ The picture fault resulting from such improper scanning. □ The inability of a tonearm to properly follow the grooves on a phonograph disc.

mist shot A camera shot taken through gauze or one that is slightly out of focus.

Mitchell One of the most popular brands of motion picture cameras.

miter □ To join the corners of a book without overlapping. □ To join lines or rules at a 45-degree angle.

mix □ To combine electrically any two sound or video sources. □ An optical dissolve. □ A film rerecording. □ The selection of different media for an advertising campaign. □ The combination of two or more images into a single image.

mixdown A collapsing technique used to reduce multitrack recordings to one track.

mixed field A television camera pickup tube that uses both electromagnetic and electrostatic deflection.

mixed highs The method of transmitting the color information as part of the luminance signal, thus not increasing the bandwidth necessary for transmission.

mixed market A television market that contains both VHF and UHF stations. *See also* deintermixture.

mixed media The use of two or more media in a program, such as slides and tapes or sound effects, rear screen projection, and live performers. *See also* multimedia.

mixer □ A device having two or more inputs, usually adjustable, and a common output, which operates to combine linearly the separate input signals to produce an output signal. *See also* console. □ The individual who supervises a motion picture rerecording crew. An individual who operates a mixer. □ The technician responsible for sound recording on a motion picture. □ The technician responsible for mixing various soundtracks.

mixing □ The use of two or more typefaces within a line, column, or page. □ The process of combining two or more audio signals or tracks. *See also* rerecording.

mixing board A console used in a mixing studio.

mixing console *See* mixing board.

mixing panel *See* control panel.

mixing room *See* mixing studio.

mixing sheet *See* cue sheet.

mixing studio A studio with facilities for combining sound sources. Also called a *mixing room.*

mix minus A method of eliminating feedback in a performer's earphone. The program mix minus the performer's audio is fed to the earphone. May be automatically accomplished through a circuit in an audio console.

mix session A time period wherein a soundtrack is prepared for use.

mix sheet A log of all the transitions, levels, and so on, of a recording session made in preparation for mixing the various soundtracks. *See also* cue sheet.

ML □ Machine language. □ Modified license. An FCC file-number prefix.

M-load *See* M-wrap.

MLS Medium long shot.

MM Metered market service.

mm Millimeter.

MMDS Multiple multipoint distribution service.

MNA Multinetwork area.

mnemonic An acronym, symbol, or other mental device used to assist human memory. Also called a *mnemonic code.*

mnemonic code □ A system of substituting letters and symbols for translation into typesetting commands. Cf. generic code. □ *See* mnemonic.

MO □ Magneto-optical. □ Move out.

MOAA Mail Order Association of America.

MOAL Mail Order Action Line.

MO&O Memorandum opinion and order.

mobile camera A portable, hand-held television camera.

mobile control room (MCR) A control room, often in a truck or trailer, used at a remote site.

mobile earth station □ An earth station intended to be used while it is in motion or during halts at unspecified points. □ An earth station in the mobile-satellite service intended to be used while in motion or during halts at unspecified points.

mobile link A microwave system that connects a remote crew to a television station or other receiving point.

mobile mike *See* wireless microphone.

mobile production unit (MPU) A van or truck used for on-site television recording and production.

mobile recording unit *See* mobile unit.

mobile reporter A news reporter who broadcasts live from the scene of a newsworthy event.

mobile-satellite service A radio communication service between mobile earth stations and one or more space stations; or between space stations used by this service; or between mobile earth stations by means of one or more space stations. This service may also include feeder links necessary for its operation.

mobile service A radio communication service between mobile and land stations or between mobile stations.

mobile station A station in the mobile service intended to be used while it is in motion or during halts at unspecified points.

mobile unit A car, truck, or trailer equipped with the facilities to originate a remote broadcast. Cf. remote unit.

mobility The ease with which broadcast equipment may move from place to place.

Mobilux A proprietary name for a television animation device.

mob scene *See* crowd scene.

mock newspaper schedule A selective list of daily newspapers of the United States, chosen for their high milline rate and coverage and arranged in the population order of their communities; used to facilitate mass purchasing of advertising space. Cf. master newspaper list.

mock-up A full-scale interior or exterior reproduction of an object, building, commercial product, and so on; often used in the making of motion pictures. Cf. miniature and model.

mockup A rough sketch or design for artwork. *See also* rough. Cf. dummy.

MOD Magneto-optical disc.

mod An abbreviation for *model, modular,* and *module.*

mode □ The operation of a recorder or other device to accomplish a specific function, as playback mode, record mode, insert mode, assemble mode, and so on. □ The point(s) in a statistical measurement at which most of the values lie. A measure of central tendency. Cf. average, mean, and median. □ The arrangement of lines of type; justified, ragged right, or ragged left. □ The condition in which a computer system operates.

mode 1 One of the two physical sector formats defined for CD-ROM. Incorporates EDC/ECC error detection and correction.

mode 2 One of the two physical sector formats defined for CD-ROM. Incorporates an auxiliary data field instead of EDC/ECC error detection and correction.

mode byte In CD-ROM, the byte in the header field of a sector that defines whether a sector is mode 1 or mode 2.

mode FF *See* IXP.

model □ A set constructed in small scale and used for planning camera shots and talent movement. Cf. miniature. □ A person hired to pose, usually for a commercial product.

model drawing *See* color model.

modeling The use of light or shading to impart a three-dimensional quality to a two-dimensional surface.

modeling light An illumination that reveals the depth, shape, and texture of a subject. Key light, crosslighting, counter-key light, side light, back-light, and eye-light are types of modeling lights. *See also* light.

model release The formal, legal permission granted by the subject of a photograph to use the picture for commercial purposes.

model sheet A series of drawings of a character showing how it is constructed, its size relative to other characters and objects in the film, and how it appears from various angles and with various expressions. Used as a reference by animators to make sure the characters have consistent appearances throughout the film.

model shot Any camera shot in which a miniature is used.

modem An acronym for *modulator/demodulator.* A device that converts a digital signal to an analog signal and vice versa in order to use a telephone line for communication between computers. *See also* acoustic coupler.

moderator A person who serves as an MC and directs a discussion program.

modern A typeface characterized by symmetrical letters and thin, straight serifs. Bodoni exemplifies this class of typefaces. Cf. old style and transitional.

modification (M) □ A change in the design of a system component. □ A change filed for or granted by the FCC in a construction permit or license. □ A change in a computer program.

modified probability sample A misleading term sometimes used to describe a sample selected by using probability sampling methods at one stage of a sample design and nonprobability sampling methods at other stages. The result is a nonprobability sample.

modular □ Constructed of standard units or dimensions, often plug-in or easily changed. □ A page make-up system consisting of rectangular areas for text and graphics. Also called *modular make-up*.

modular agency *See* a la carte agency.

modular make-up *See* modular.

modulate To vary the frequency, amplitude, or phase of a wave by impressing another wave on it.

modulated carrier A carrier wave that has been changed in amplitude, frequency, or phase by the signal carried.

modulated groove *See* groove.

modulated stage The radio frequency to which the modulator is coupled and in which the continuous wave (carrier wave) is modulated in accordance with the system of modulation and the characteristics of the modulating wave.

modulation □ The process of superimposing a sound wave on a carrier wave so that it may be transmitted. *See also* amplitude modulation (AM) and frequency modulation (FM). □ The process of impressing a sound picture on tape, film, or disc. □ The act of changing a musical key within a song.

modulation envelope *See* envelope.

modulation frequency The frequency in the FM domain associated with or corresponding to a particular video level. For example, for SMPTE Practice HB (highband), the modulation frequency corresponding to the tip of sync is 7.2 mHz.

modulation monitor A monitor required by the FCC to measure the percentage modulation.

modulation noise The component of noise that exists only in the presence of a recorded signal.

modulator □ In a television tape recorder, the circuit that converts the input video signal to a frequency-modulated signal for recording. Sometimes further identified as FM modulator or video modulator. □ The circuit that converts the error signals from a servomechanism to motor-control voltages or currents. Sometimes further identified as servo modulator, HW modulator, drum modulator, scanner modulator, reel-servo modulator, tension-control modulator, or capstan modulator. □ Any device used to modulate.

modulator stage The last amplifier stage of the modulating wave that modulates a radio frequency stage.

module □ A defined portion of a printed page, usually a rectangle. □ An integrated component of a system. □ A single unit of an educational whole. □ A part of a computer program. □ A subassembly of a larger electronic system. Sometimes called a *component*.

mogul □ One of the former heads of the major Hollywood motion picture studios during their heyday. □ A type of base for lamps used in television and motion pictures.

moire □ A pattern of wavy lines in a halftone, often caused by making a halftone from a halftone print. □ A picture fault characterized by the presence of wavy lines over all or portions of a picture, so named because of its resemblance to the light and dark patterns seen in watered silk fabric. Called linebeat or meshbeat in image-orthicon cameras.

MOL □ Maximum overall length. □ Machine oriented language.

Molarc A trademark name for a large arc spotlight used for key lighting. Also called a *brute*.

mold □ A metal part derived from a master by electroforming. It has grooves similar to those on a disc and thus may be played as a disc. Also called a *metal positive* and *mother*. □ An impression made from a letterpress engraving, usually on a vinyl sheet under heat and pressure. □ *See* matrix.

molding A trim strip of metal, wood, or plastic surrounding an outdoor advertising panel.

mold made paper Paper made by machine to imitate handmade paper.

Molefay A trademark name for a lighting instrument containing a cluster of fay lamps that produce light at a color temperature of 5000 degrees Kelvin.

Molepar A trademark name for a lighting instrument containing a single or cluster of par lamps that produce light at a color temperature of 3200 degrees Kelvin.

mom and pop operation A small, family operated business, such as a retail store or a small-town radio station.

mon An abbreviation for *monitor.*

monaural Literally, one-eared; therefore the less used but correct term is *monophonic,* except in the case of a hearing aid.

monaural recorder A single-channel tape recorder. Also called *single track.*

monetary value Total expenditures by a direct mail customer during a specified period of time, generally 12 months.

monitor □ A high-quality television receiver used in a control room or studio. □ A loudspeaker used in a radio or television production facility. □ To listen to or view a program or tape. □ To watch equipment operated by remote control. □ A device used to indicate the output of equipment. □ A television display device that receives its picture and/or sound from a non-RF signal, such as baseband composite video, RGB video, or Y and C components. Cf. receiver. □ To maintain continuous control over the operation of a studio, program, editing session, and so on.

monitor head A special tape recorder head that allows monitoring of material as it is being recorded.

monitoring □ The controlling of picture and sound quality during a broadcast or taping. □ The act of censoring a program. □ To listen to foreign broadcasts for the purpose of obtaining information, especially during wartime.

monitor pot A potentiometer on an audio control console that controls the volume of a monitor speaker.

monitor printer A computer printer that produces a hard copy of the display screen.

monitor speaker A high-quality loudspeaker used to check the acoustics and overall mix of the sound in a studio.

monitor viewfinder A film camera viewfinder that is external to the camera and, therefore, must be equipped with parallax correction.

monk An ink blot or smudge on a printed page. Cf. friar.

monkey chatter A garbled signal caused by adjacent channel interference.

mono An abbreviation for *monaural* and *monophonic.*

monochromatic Pertaining to a single color. *See also* hue.

monochrome (M) Having one color. In television, black and white.

monochrome receiver A television receiver capable of displaying only a black and white picture.

monochrome television Black and white television.

monochrome transmission The transmission of television signals that can be reproduced in gradations of a single color only.

monofilm A typesetting machine, similar to a monotype, except that the output is film instead of metal.

monograph A treatise on a particular subject; a paper, an article in a journal, a pamphlet, or a book.

monologue □ A long speech given by a single character in a drama. □ A literary soliloquy.

monomorphic station A radio station format characterized by the continuous programming of one type of material, such as all-news.

monopack A general term for a film with two or more emulsion layers.

monophonic Sound heard from a single channel. Cf. binaural and stereophonic. *See also* monaural.

monophoto A typesetting machine, similar to a monotype, except that the output is film instead of metal.

monopod A single, extendible pole used to support the weight of a camera; a one-legged tripod.

monopoly The exclusive possession of a commodity by one party. In broadcasting, a concentration of media control to a point that might restrain competition and trade within the media. *See also* diversification of control and restraint of trade.

monoscope A television camera pickup tube or slide designed for test purposes.

monotone *See* black and white.

Monotype A tradename for a typesetting machine, similar to a Linotype, except that each type character is formed individually rather than in a solid line of type.

monster □ A slang term for a current musical superstar. □ A slang term for a large crane.

monster verdict *See* megaverdict.

montage □ A sequence of rapid shots designed to evoke an image or illustrate events. □ A rapid sequence of varying sounds. □ A picture containing a number of different scenes or shots. □ Also called a *photomontage.* □ The process or result of editing shots together.

monthly A periodical that is issued monthly.

mood commercial A commercial message that is designed to establish an atmosphere or lure an audience.

mood lighting Lighting used to establish an audience attitude or intensify atmosphere.

mood music Music used to establish an audience attitude or intensify atmosphere. Also called *background music* and *program music.*

mood programming *See* block programming.

moonlight Printed material used as a filler.

moot □ A question having no further significance. □ A point of law unsettled by judicial decision.

mooz A slang term for a fast zoom out.

MOP Minute of program.

MOR Middle-of-the-road.

mordant □ A chemical compound used in color film processing. □ A corrosive substance used in etching plates.

more □ An add to a previous news story from a wire service. □ The word placed at the bottom of a page of news copy to indicate that a story continues on the another page.

more wax A direction to sing or speak more softly.

morgue The room or place where newspaper and magazine files are kept. Usually contains clippings, photographs, and other pertinent information. Also called a *library.*

morning drive The time period on radio from 6 a.m. or sign on to 10 a.m. Also called *drivetime. See also* daypart.

morning man The announcer on a radio station who works the morning drive shift.

morning zoo A radio station format characterized by a humorous cast of characters.

morocco A fine, durable goatskin leather used for expensive book covers.

mortality □ The rate of failure to complete interviews in a survey. □ The loss of respondents to a continuing survey over a period of time.

mortise □ A cutout made in a halftone plate so that type matter or another picture may be inserted. Cf. notch. □ To make a cutout in a halftone plate.

MOS □ Man on the street. A program type. □ Mit out sound. A slang term for silent. □ Metal oxide semiconductor.

mosaic □ The small color elements through which a film is exposed in some processes. □ The light-sensitive surface of a television camera pickup tube that is scanned by the electron beam. *See also* target.

mosaic binding A leather bookbinding with inlaid designs in color. Also called an *inlaid binding.*

mosaic graphics In CD-I, low resolution graphics achieved by repeating pixels or lines by a specified factor.

Moss-Magnuson Act *See* Federal Trade Commission Improvements Act of 1975.

mother □ In disc replication, a negative mold intermediate between a metal father and stamper. Formed by nickel plating on the metal father. □ *See* mold.

motherboard A large piece of insulating material on which components, integrated circuits, banks of memory, and so on, are mounted.

motif □ A recurring technique or theme used in a motion picture, television drama, and so on. Cf. icon. □ The theme or dominant feature of a work of art.

motion An application made to the FCC (or a court) to enlarge, change, or delete issues in a hearing.

motion blur The deformation of an object along the longitudinal axis of movement, designed to give motion.

motion picture □ A series of pictures photographed with a camera on a thin, flexible plastic and projected in a rapid sequence so as to give the illusion of motion. *See also* film. □ A film made for theatrical showings. □ For union purposes, a film, whether made on or by film, tape, or otherwise, and whether produced by means of motion picture cameras or devices, tape devices, or any combination of the foregoing or any other means, methods, or devices now used or which may hereafter be adopted.

Motion Picture Association of America (MPAA) A film industry group founded in 1922. Organizations and individuals who promote American motion pictures and rate them as to audience suitability. *See also* Hays office.

motion picture camera *See* camera.

Motion Picture Patents Company The so-called motion picture trust that was formed in the late 1800s and found guilty of conspiring to monopolize the production, distribution, and exhibition of motion pictures in 1914.

motion picture photography An alternate term for *cinematography.*

motion picture producer □ According to the FCC, a person or organization engaged in the production or filming of motion pictures. □ *See* producer.

motion picture projector *See* projector.

Motion Picture Radio Service (MPRS) A communication service that may be used by broadcasters while they are engaged in the production or filming of motion pictures.

motion picture trust *See* Motion Picture Patents Company.

motion to quash A request to a court to invalidate a subpoena or other order.

motivation The inducement or incentive for a character's actions in a play or script.

motivational research (MR) The application of research techniques in advertising and marketing to determine the bases of brand choices and product preferences.

motor A device used to convert electrical energy into mechanical energy.

motor board *See* tape transport.

motorboating Audio frequency interference caused by oscillation in an amplifier.

motor cue The first film cue that alerts a projectionist to start the other projector. *See also* changeover.

motor governor *See* governor.

motormouth A slang term for an announcer who speaks too rapidly or too much, or both.

motor route manager A newspaper employee who supervises motor route drivers for newspaper delivery.

mottled A film with a spotted or cloudy surface.

mottled calf *See* marbled calf.

moulage A reversible impression material used in make-up casts.

moulding The frame of wood or metal that surrounds the face of an outdoor advertising structure.

mount □ A flange or socket used to hold a lens. □ A device used to hold a camera, luminaire, microphone, and so on. □ A structure that is designed to support a microwave or satellite dish. □ *See* base (B). □ To place a compact disc in operation.

MOUSE Minimum Orbital Unmanned Satellite, Earth.

mouse A hand-held x-y pointer device used to manipulate a screen display and invoke utility functions. The mouse is rolled over a flat surface and movement is measured and fed into the computer. Control functions are invoked by moving the mouse to designated tablet areas or pressing a control button on it. It may be employed to input graphics or to manipulate text on displayed documents.

mouth The large end of a horn.

mouthing *See* lip sync.

movable type Type that contains one body and face for each character, and that can be reused without melting. Invented by Johann Gutenberg about 1450.

move The transmission of news copy of pictures by a wire service.

move in (MI) A director's command to a camera operator to move the camera closer to the subject.

movement □ The change in position of talent, as set in the blocking. □ The intermittent mechanism in a camera or projector that pulls the film into position.

move out (MO) A director's command to a camera operator to move the camera farther from the subject.

movie A commonly accepted slang term for a motion picture.

movie for television *See* made for television.

movie library A motion picture that is available for television station broadcast.

movie license A television station that has paid the necessary fee to broadcast a motion picture.

movielight A small, high-intensity luminaire used primarily as a camera light.

movie palace A large, often ornate motion picture theatre, such as Radio City Music Hall or Grauman's Chinese.

moving coil loudspeaker *See* dynamic loudspeaker.

moving coil microphone *See* dynamic microphone.

moving coil pickup *See* dynamic pickup.

moving off To fade off.

moving on To fade on.

moving shot A camera shot taken from a moving object. *See also* following shot.

Moviola A tradename for a film-editing machine; however, the term has become generic and is applied to many devices that are capable of synchronizing pictures and sound.

MOW Movie of the week. A made-for-television movie.

MP □ Modified construction permit. An FCC file-number prefix. □ Motion picture.

MPA □ Multiple product announcement. □ Music Publishers Association of the U.S. A trade association of music publishers. □ Motion Picture Alliance. □ Magazine Publishers Association.

MPAA □ Motion Picture Association of America. □ Musical Performing Arts Association.

MPAA Code The former self-regulatory code designed and enforced by the Motion Picture Association of America. The code was superseded by a suitability rating system. *See also* CARA.

MPATI Midwest Program for Airborne Television Instruction. A program of the 1960s that used aircraft to transmit instructional programming to schools over a six-state region.

MPEA Motion Picture Export Association. A trade association.

MPEAUS Master Printers and Engravers Association of the United States.

MPG Magazine Promotion Group.

MP/L Modified construction permit and license. An FCC file-number prefix.

MP/ML Modified construction permit and modified license. An FCC file-number prefix.

MPMO Motion Picture Machine Operators. A union; part of IATSE.

MPPA Music Publishers Protective Association.

MPRF Motion Picture Relief Fund.

MPRS Motion Picture Radio Service.

MPS Mail preference service.

MPU □ Mobile production unit. □ Microprocessor unit.

MPX Multiplex. *See* multiplexing.

MR □ Magnetic recorder. □ Media Report, The. A periodical. □ Motivational research.

mr An abbreviation for *master.*

MRA Metro rating area. *See* metro area and metro rating.

Mr. and Mrs. show A talk show hosted by a man and a woman.

MRDA Media Research Directors Association.

MRIA Magnetic Recording Industries Association. A standards organization; merged with the EIA in 1965.

MRS Minimum reporting standards.

MS □ Medium shot. □ Miniature screw. A lamp base type. □ Master scene. □ Master shot.

ms An abbreviation for *magnetic storage, manuscript,* and *millisecond.*

MSA □ Metropolitan Statistical Area. □ Metro survey area.

msec An abbreviation for *millisecond.*

M signal The television luminance signal that provides the monochrome picture and the brightness information for color pictures. Also called the *Y signal. See also* color difference signal, I signal, and Q signal.

MSO Multiple systems operator.

MSP Medium side prong. A lamp base type.

mss Manuscripts.

MSSA Modification of special service authorization. An FCC file-number prefix.

MST Maximum Service Telecasters. An organization of major market television broadcast stations. Formerly AMST.

M system The 525-line, 30-frames-per-second, 6-mHz bandwidth, FM sound television system used in the United States, other western hemisphere countries, and Japan. Cf. A system, B system, D system, and E system.

MT □ Magnetic tape. □ Miniature tube. □ Machine translation.

MTBF Mean time between failures.

MTF Modulation transfer function.

MTR Magnetic tape recorder.

MTS □ Message telecommunications service. An intrastate WATS line. □ Multichannel television sound.

MTV Music Television. A concept or performance video of single recordings made by contemporary artists.

M-II A component analog video (CAV) format that uses metal-particle tape. Cf. Betacam, Betacam SP, S-VHS, and U-Matic SP.

mu The English equivalent of the Greek letter μ. The abbreviation for the prefix *micro* or the word *micron*.

muckraking A sensationalized newspaper or magazine crusade that seeks to expose or charge public figures with corruption. Based on a character in Bunyan's *Pilgrim's Progress* and on a group of journalists in the early 1900s.

muddy □ Dull, lifeless sound. *See also* in the mud. □ A dark, lifeless picture.

MUF Maximum usable frequency.

muff To fluff a line. *See also* goof.

mugger □ A performer who uses broad facial antics. □ A mike or camera hog.

mugging The use of broad facial movements to attract attention on camera.

mug shot A close-up of talent. *See also* head sheet and head shot.

mull A soft, sheer fabric of cotton, silk, or rayon sometimes used as a lining paper. *See also* kraft paper and lining.

mult An abbreviation for *multiple*.

multbox An audio patching system used to feed the output of several microphones to a number of recorders. Used in pool coverage.

multiaffiliate A radio or television station that is affiliated with two or more networks.

multiband antenna An antenna designed to receive more than one frequency band.

multibuyer *See* multiple buyer.

multicamera operation The use of two or more cameras at the same time in the photographing of a scene. Used primarily as protection shots that could not be repeated, such as of a building explosion, dangerous stunt, and so on.

multicasting The former practice of broadcasting stereo programs using two radio stations; often an AM and FM combination with each station transmitting one of the two channels.

multicel The use of two or more layers of animation cels at the same time.

multichannel multipoint distribution service (MMDS) A microwave system that combines multipoint distribution service (MDS) and instructional television fixed service (ITFS) channels to offer service to subscribers. An over-the-air substitute for cable television.

multichannel sound Film, radio, television, or another source furnishing two or more channels of sound.

multichannel television sound (MTS) Any system of aural transmission that uses aural baseband information between 15 kHz and 120 kHz to convey information or that encodes digital information in the video portion of the television signal that is intended to be decoded as audio information.

multidirectional microphone A microphone that has the capability of being switched between two or more polar patterns.

multifax *See* Fax.

multifiber cable A cable containing two or more optical fibers.

multifilm system A film system in which two or more projectors are used simultaneously to project a scene, such as for Cinerama.

multifrequency monitor A video monitor that is compatible with two or more different systems.

multifunctional workstation A computer-based terminal, usually with a display screen and sometimes with a printing device, that enables a user to perform different tasks.

Multigraph A tradename for a duplicating machine that produces copy resembling typing.

multihead printer A film printing machine that is capable of printing two or more copies of a motion picture negative.

multi-image A motion picture containing two or more separate pictures on one film or television screen. Cf. multiscreen.

multilateral A radio or television program that originates from two or more locations.

multilayer film A motion picture film containing more than one emulsion layer, usually a three-color separation negative to be used in the imbibition process.

Multilith A tradename for an offset duplicator.

multilock An Ampex development for synchronizing separately recorded sound to a videotape picture.

multimedia A play, program, event, and so on, designed to use several different media. Also called *mixed media.*

multimedia study A study that combines research in two or more of the mass media.

multimedia survey A survey that secures information from a respondent about activity of a household or an individual with respect to two or more media.

multimedia system In computers, a system architecture based on the use of different media to carry the data and application programs. A CD-ROM system, for example, carries the data on a CD-ROM disc, whereas the application program is stored on a magnetic medium.

multimeter A meter capable of measuring several different electrical quantities, such as current, resistance, and voltage.

multinational A company that conducts business in more than one country, such as a worldwide motion picture distributor. Cf. transnational.

multinetwork area (MNA) A compilation of television markets used by Nielsen's Television Index (NTI) to provide estimates of television audiences on a geographic base where all three national networks have approximately comparable facilities.

multipass To expose the same piece of film two or more times during filming, usually to produce semitransparent effects, such as clouds or shadows.

multipath effect The phase difference effect caused by the reception of two different signals from the same broadcast station due to reflection. May cause echoes, fading, or ghosts.

multipath signals *See* multipath effect.

multipay A cable television subscriber who receives two or more pay cable channels.

multiplane □ The use of animation cels placed at different levels in order to obtain a feeling of depth. □ A video image in which various planes are overlaid.

multiplane camera A special animation stand developed at the Disney studio and first used in The Old Mill in 1937. The background artwork is divided into foreground, middle, and distant elements and painted on sheets of glass placed several inches apart. During trucking or panning moves, the background elements move in relation to each other, creating an illusion of realistic depth and perspective.

multiple □ A parallel electric circuit used in lighting. □ A unity gain amplifier with numerous mike level outputs used in pool remotes to eliminate the need for an excessive number of microphones. Also called a *presidential patch.* □ *See* floating multiple.

multiple approach The use of advertising in two or more media channels to persuade an audience to buy goods or services.

multiple buyer A person who has bought products two or more times by direct mail; not one who has bought two or more items. Also called a *multibuyer* and *repeat buyer.*

multiple camera technique The use of a television camera and recorder mounted with a motion picture camera in order to produce dailies or to check the setup of shots.

multiple chain Two or more film chains.

multiple color press A printing press capable of printing more than one color at a time.

multiple contract A contract between an author and a publisher for more than one book.

multiple destination A radio or television program received by more than one country; usually by satellite.

multiple dwelling A structure, such as an apartment, that contains more than one family unit.

multiple echo A succession of separately distinguishable echoes from a single source.

multiple exposure A special effect achieved in film by exposing the film two or more times or by combining several images in printing. A television superimposition. Cf. double exposure and multiple image.

multiple franchise A geographic area that is served by more than one cable television system. Also called a *nonexclusive franchise.*

multiple image □ An optical effect in film wherein the same image is repeated 2, 4, 8, 16, and so on, times in the same frame. □ A television split screen. Sometimes called multiscreen. *See also* montage. Cf. multiple exposure.

multiple insertion The use of two or more enclosures in a direct mailing.

multiple lead A news story lead that contains two or more newsworthy items.

multiple microphone interference The problems that occur when two or more microphones that are receiving the same signal are fed into a single channel. *See also* phasing.

multiple multipoint distribution service (MMDS) A closed circuit, multichannel MDS system.

multiple network A network that owns or operates two or more networks. Formerly forbidden by FCC rules; however, waivers have been authorized.

multiple operation In international broadcasting, the broadcasting by a station on one frequency over two or more transmitters simultaneously. If a station uses the same frequency simultaneously on each of two (or more) transmitters for an hour, it uses one frequency-hour and two (or more) transmitter-hours.

multiple ownership The ownership or control of radio and television broadcast stations. The maximum number of stations any individual or corporation may control is 36; 12 AM, 12 FM, and 12 TV. Exceptions to the rule may be made for minority ownership. *See also* duopoly rule.

multiple picture player A player who is employed for two or more pictures per year, whose contract with respect to services in the production of motion pictures is nonexclusive, and whose compensation may be more or less than $2500 a week or who is guaranteed more or less than $25,000 per picture depending under which category the player is compensated. Cf. contract player, day player, deal player, free-lance player, stunt player, and term player.

multiple printing *See* multihead printer.

multiple processing The Nielsen procedure used to remove duplicate viewing within the same household for program or HUT computation.

multiple product announcement (MPA) An announcement in which two or more products or services are presented as a unit. *See also* integrated commercial and piggyback.

multiple recording The recording of more than one audio-or videotape simultaneously; often done for protection with unrepeatable events.

multiple regression A statistical technique used to measure the relationship between responses to a mailing with census demographics and list characteristics of one or more selected mailing lists. Used to determine the best types of recipients and geographic areas. Can also be used to analyze customers, subscribers, and so on.

multiple-set television households An Arbitron estimate of the number of television households with more than one television receiver, based on information obtained during diary placement.

multiple soundtrack A group of soundtracks recorded side-by-side; used for stereophonic, quadraphonic, or multiple audio track recording.

multiple sponsorship The dividing of the cost of a radio or television program between or among different and noncompetitive advertisers. *See also* sponsor.

multiple submission The submission of a manuscript to more than one publisher at a time, in the hope that at least one publisher will accept it.

multiple system operator (MSO) A cable organization that owns more than one cable television system.

multiple tracking □ The rerecording over the original soundtrack or adding an additional track—electronically or mechanically—containing the same material as recorded on the original track. Also called *overdubbing.* □ The singing of the same part two or more times where separate soundtracks are recorded and a composite is made of separate renditions.

multiple transmission A subchannel added to the regular aural carrier of a television broadcast station by means of frequency-modulated subcarriers.

multiplex To send two or more signals by means of one carrier or optical fiber.

multiplexer □ A mechanical device consisting of movable mirrors or prisms used in a film chain to direct several projection sources into one television camera. □ Any device used to mix two or more signals.

multiplex FM *See* FM multiplex.

multiplexing □ A technique used to carry a significant number of messages on a single communication channel. □ The electronic encoding of the color television signals for transmission on a common channel. □ The mixing of audio and video signals for transmission on a common channel.

multiplexor (mux) A computer communication control device that allows a central processor to handle data from several different devices or terminals at the same time.

multiplex transmission The simultaneous transmission of two or more signals within a single channel. Multiplex transmission as applied to FM broadcast stations means the transmission of facsimile or other signals in addition to the regular broadcast signals. *See also* FM multiplex.

multipoint distribution service (MDS) A common carrier authorized to transmit specialized private television programming within a metropolitan area on 2150 to 2160 mHz.

multipoint distribution system (MDS) □ A closed circuit television transmission system that uses UHF frequencies to deliver premium programming. □ A wireless cable system for distributing premium channels.

multisatellite link A radio link between a transmitting earth station and a receiving earth station through two or more satellites, without any intermediate earth station. A multisatellite link is composed of one up-link, one or more satellite-to-satellite links, and one down-link.

multiscreen □ The use of a number of film projectors or television screens to show images from different cameras. Cf. multi-image. □ *See* multiple image.

multiset household A household that has two or more television (or radio) receivers.

multiset TVHH A television household that has two or more television receivers.

multispot plan A package rate for commercials on radio or television.

multistage sample A sample in which sampling elements are selected in stages. At each stage, a sample of elements is selected from the sample of elements chosen at the previous stage. *See also* probability sample.

multistandard A television receiver or monitor capable of presenting signals from two or more different types of signals, such as NTSC, PAL, and SECAM.

multistation lineup A group of radio or television stations in a single market area that carry the announcements of an advertiser.

multistripe magnetic film A mag film containing two or more sound stripes. Cf. fullcoat.

multitrack An audiotape recorder capable of recording a number of audio tracks side-by-side on a tape; often two, four, eight, or more tracks.

multitrack magnetic recording system A recording system that provides, on a medium such as magnetic tape, two or more recording paths that are parallel to each other and that may carry either related or unrelated program material in common time relationship.

multitrack sound A motion picture release print that contains two or more soundtracks.

multiuser machine A computer, such as a mainframe, that can be used by more than one person at a time.

Multi-Vision *See* Tri-Vision.

mumetal A high-permeability magnetic alloy widely used for screening recording heads, pickups, television picture tubes, and so on, from stray magnetic fields.

Munsell scale A color definition scale based on the hue, value, and chroma.

mural A large photograph used for a set background.

Murrow Award, Edward R. An award, established in 1977, made for outstanding contributions to public radio.

mus A script abbreviation for *music.*

MUSE Multiple sub-Niquist sampling encoding. One of a number of sampling and encoding systems for the transmission of high definition television.

mushy A sound lacking in clarity; often caused by incorrect microphone placement.

musical □ A program consisting primarily of music and dancing. □ A musical comedy.

musical clock A type of radio station program consisting of music, news, weather reports, and frequent references to time. Usually broadcast in the morning.

musical comedy A program or presentation in which music and dance predominate and plot is secondary. Also called a *musical.*

musical contractor An individual who obtains musicians for a specified motion picture or television production.

musical curtain The music used to end a radio or television program or program segment.

musical cushion *See* cushion.

musical director The individual in charge of the music for a motion picture or television program. The individual may be the composer, the music editor, or someone selected by a musical contractor or a music department.

musical echo A flutter echo in the audible range.

musical format The radio station format under the general heading of music. Subheadings vary, and few agree as to standardized definitions; however, they may include middle-of-the-road, top-40, rock, good music, classical, contemporary, underground, country and western, religious, popular, jazz, rhythm and blues, progressive, and so on.

musical format service company An organization that supplies taped musical programs to radio stations on a subscription basis.

musical ID *See* musical logo.

musical logo A musical signature associated with a product, advertiser, program, or station. Also called a *musical ID* and *musical signature. See also* logo.

musical score Any music written or selected to enhance a motion picture, television program, and so on.

musical signature *See* musical logo.

musical variety A program format used on radio and television characterized by comedy skits, music, and dance.

music and effects track *See* M and E track.

music and news The format of a radio station that programs music and news.

musicasting An FM service furnishing background music to businesses and waiting rooms. *See also* functional music, storecasting, and transitcasting.

music bed A musical background used for commercials, transitions, station breaks, and so on.

music bridge A musical transition. *See also* bridge.

music clear *See* music cold.

music clearance The securing of the rights to use a copyrighted musical selection. *See also* clearance.

music cold Music used without other sound. Also called *music clear.*

music consultant An individual hired by a radio station to evaluate its music programming. Also called a *music doctor.*

music department The motion picture studio department responsible for hiring and/or assigning musicians for work on a film.

music director A radio station employee who selects and programs the station's music.

music doctor *See* music consultant.

music down A radio or television director's command to lower the volume of the sound.

music editor The individual who scores the music used in a motion picture. *See also* musical director.

music fade A radio or television director's command to lower the volume of sound until it is out. Also called *music fadeout.*

music fadeout *See* music fade.

music in A radio or television director's command to start the music.

music in and under A radio or television director's command to start the music at normal volume to establish, then fade and hold under dialogue or other sound. Also called *music up and under.*

music library A motion picture, television, or radio repository for stock music and sound effects.

music licensing fee The payment made to the music licensing companies by broadcast stations for the performing rights to musical compositions. *See also* ASCAP, BMI, and SESAC.

music line A telephone company line capable of carrying the full range of the sound spectrum. *See also* class AAA line.

music negative A motion picture film negative on which sound has been recorded.

music out A radio or television director's command to cut the music.

music package A complete musical logo used by a radio station.

music power A rating of the reproduction capabilities of an amplifier. The standards are set by the Institute of High Fidelity (IHF).

music sheet A form used to check clearances, talent, and so on, of the music used in a program.

music sweep The uninterrupted, back-to-back playing of two or more musical selections by a radio station.

music track The optical or magnetic track on which music is recorded. Dialogue and effects are also recorded on separate tracks.

music up A radio or television director's command to raise the volume of the sound.

music up and out A radio or television director's command to increase the volume of the sound, then fade out.

music up and under *See* music in and under.

music video A song, usually contemporary, that is accompanied by pictures of the performer and, usually, other shots that help enhance the entertainment value of the production.

must □ A book, motion picture, and so on, that is popular, important, or critically acclaimed, that people "must" see. □ An item in a newscast or newspaper that "must" be broadcast or printed, as opposed to other items that might be cut or omitted if time or space runs short. Also called a *must story.* □ *See* business office must (BOM).

must-buy A network policy that required advertisers to purchase time on certain stations when ordering the network. This policy was voluntarily dropped in the 1960s.

must carry An FCC rule that required cable television systems to carry all qualified local television stations. Declared unconstitutional in 1987.

must story *See* must.

mut *See* quad.

mute □ A motion picture negative or positive on which the soundtrack has not yet been married. □ A silent film. □ To eliminate or deaden a sound.

mute negative A motion picture negative that does not contain a soundtrack.

mute print A motion picture print that does not contain a soundtrack.

muting relay A relay used to disconnect a loudspeaker when a microphone is activated in the same studio so as to prevent feedback.

Mutoscope A viewing machine, manufactured in 1895 by the American Mutoscope Company, which used the "flip book" principle to create the illusion of movement. It contained a series of continuous photographs arranged on a horizontal axis. A coin was dropped into the machine to operate the hand crank that moved the pictures rapidly and created the illusion of motion.

mutted Type that is indented one em. Cf. nutted.

mutton *See* em.

mutton quad *See* em quad.

Mutual Black Network (MBN) A radio network begun in 1973 by the Mutual Broadcasting System to serve black audiences.

Mutual Broadcasting System (MBS) The national radio network serving the greatest number of stations. Founded in 1934.

mutually exclusive An application by two or more prospective licensees for the same allotment or frequency in which the granting of one would preclude the granting of the other or others.

MUX An abbreviation for *multiplexor.*

Mv Megavolt.

mV Millivolt.

MVC Manual volume control.

mv/m Millivolts per meter.

MW □ Medium wave. □ Megawatt. □ Microwave.

mw Milliwatt.

M wrap The description of the shape of a tape path for particular television tape recorders that results in a configuration resembling the uppercase letter M. Also called *M-load.* Cf. alpha wrap and omega wrap.

mx An abbreviation for *matrix* and *multiplex.*

mylar The duPont tradename for a highly durable polyester plastic film used to manufacture magnetic tape. Cf. acetate.

mystery A genre in which the cause or circumstances of the uneasy feeling the audience has is not explained or revealed. Cf. suspense.

N

N □ Nano. □ Network. An FCC program source designation. □ News programs. □ Nighttime. □ Number. The number of respondents in a sample. □ A wire service designation for regional.

NA □ Not applicable. □ Not assigned. □ Not available. □ No answer.

NAAN National Advertising Agency Network.

NAAP National Association of Advertising Publishers.

NAB □ National Audience Board. A citizens' group. □ National Association of Broadcasters. A Japanese broadcasting association. □ National Association of Broadcasters. □ Newspaper Advertising Bureau, Inc.

NAB-A, NAB-B, NAB-C The three standard sizes of magnetic tape cartridges. Type A is 4 inches wide by 5-1/2 inches long; Type B is 6 inches wide by 7 inches long; Type C is 7-5/8 inches wide by 8-1/4 inches long. Each type has a maximum height of .9375 inches.

NABB National Association for Better Broadcasting. A citizens' group; formerly NAFBRAT.

NAB curve The standard playback equalization curve for tape recording set by the National Association of Broadcasters (NAB). Cf. RIAA curve.

NABET National Association of Broadcast Engineers and Technicians.

NABOB National Association of Black Owned Broadcasters.

NABTFP National Association of Black Television and Film Producers.

NABTS North American Broadcast Teletext Standard. A high resolution teletext standard similar to NAPLPS.

NABUG National Association of Broadcast Unions and Guilds. A consultative union organization.

NAC □ Net advertising circulation. □ National audience composition.

NACP National Academy of Cable Programming.

NACS National Association of College Stores.

NAD □ National Advertising Division (of the Council of Better Business Bureaus). □ National Audience Demographics report.

NAEA Newspaper Advertising Executives' Association.

NAEB National Association of Educational Broadcasters.

NAEIR National Association for the Exchange of Industrial Resources.

NAET National Association for Educational Television.

NAFB National Association of Farm Broadcasters.

NAFBRAT National Association for Better Radio and Television. Now NABB.

NAFD National Association of Farm Directors.

NAFMB National Association of FM Broadcasters.

NAG National Association of Gagwriters.

Nagra The Polish word for tape recorder. A high-quality tape recorder designed by Stefan Kudelski and manufactured in Switzerland.

NAIRD National Association of Independent Record Dealers and Manufacturers.

NAITPD National Association of Independent Television Producers and Distributors.

NAJD National Association of Journalism Directors.

NAK An abbreviation for *negative acknowledgment.* The opposite of ACK.

NAM National Association of Manufacturers.

name □ A single entry on a mailing list. □ A personality of star caliber used to attract an audience.

name acquisition The technique of soliciting response to obtain names and addresses for a mailing list.

name credit Talent whose name appears in the credits of a motion picture or television program.

nameplate *See* flag.

name-removal service That portion of the mail preference service offered by Direct Mail/Marketing Association wherein a consumer is sent a form that, when filled in and returned, constitutes a request to have the person's name removed from all mailing lists used by participating members of the association and other direct mail users.

NAMM National Association of Music Merchants.

NAMP National Association of Magazine Publishers.

NAMSCO National Association of MDS Service Companies.

NAMSRC National AM Stereophonic Radio Committee. Also NASC.

NAMW National Association of Media Women.

NANA □ National Advertising Newspaper Association. □ North American Newspaper Alliance, Inc.

NANBA North American National Broadcasters Association. A group organized in 1978 to study problems in international broadcasting.

nano (n) A prefix for one-billionth; as in nanosecond, nanovolt, and so on. Formerly called *millimicro.*

NAP National Association of Publishers.

NAPA National Association of Performing Artists.

NAPIM National Association of Printing Ink Manufacturers.

NAPL National Association of Printers and Lithographers.

NAPLPS North American Presentation Level Protocol Syntax. A videotex standard for North America developed by AT&T.

NAPTS National Association of Public Television Stations.

NARA North American Radio Archives.

NARAS National Academy of Recording Arts and Sciences.

NARB □ National Advertising Review Board. □ National Association of Radio Broadcasters.

NARBA North American Regional Broadcasting Agreement.

narcotizing dysfunction The effect that arises from overexposure to the mass media; results in a lack of concern, such as that overexposure to violence on television leads to apathy toward violence.

NARCU National Association of Railroad and Utility Commissioners.

NARDA National Appliance and Radio-TV Dealers Association.

NARM National Association of Recording Merchandisers.

narr An abbreviation for *narration.*

narratage The story of a program, film, play, and so on, as told by one of the characters.

narration □ The comments or descriptions spoken by a narrator. □ Material used, typically off camera, to explain or relate sequences or action.

narration script A script prepared especially for use by a narrator.

narrative □ A story characterized by description rather than dramatic action. □ The chronological dialogue and action that structure and move a screenplay.

narrative action The events that structure a screenplay.

narrative lead A newspaper, magazine, or television news story that begins chronologically instead of with a traditional lead.

narrative synopsis An outline of a story owned by a writer; prepared for the purpose of determining the suitability of the story for teleplay purposes. The outline indicates characters and plot line but need not be sufficiently developed to meet the definition of a story.

narrator The talent or commentator who tells the story. The term usually implies an offstage or offcamera voiceover.

narrator over *See* voiceover.

narrow angle lens *See* telephoto.

narrow band A band of frequencies sufficient for voice-grade radio transmissions but insufficient for television. Cf. wide band.

narrow band frequency modulation (NBFM) Frequency modulation transmission using only a portion of the normal 200 kHz bandwidth. Used primarily for police, taxi, and other such two-way communication.

narrowcast □ A distribution of information by a mass medium to a select or limited audience. □ A nonbroadcast, closed-circuit electronic communication. Cf. broadcast.

narrowcasting □ The process of programming to a selected, highly defined demographic group. □ The transmission of programs by cable television.

narrow gauge A motion picture film smaller than 35 mm in width. Also called *substandard*.

NARTB National Association of Radio and Television Broadcasters. Now NAB.

NARUC National Association of Regulatory Utilities Commissioners. An association concerned with cable television regulation.

NAS National Academy of Sciences.

NASA □ National Aeronautics and Space Administration. A federal government satellite organization. □ Newspaper Advertising Sales Association.

NASC National AM Stereo Committee. A temporary committee organized to study FM stereo; composed of the EIA, IEEE, NAB, and NRBA.

NATAS National Academy of Television Arts and Sciences.

NATESA National Alliance of Television and Electronic Service Associations.

national Of or pertaining to media, products, or services distributed throughout the country.

National Academy of Cable Programming (NACP) An organization of individuals and companies that presents the ACE awards for cable.

National Academy of Television Arts and Sciences (NATAS) A national professional organization responsible for conferring annual awards of excellence in television production and performance called the Emmy awards. The organization also holds educational seminars relating to various aspects of television.

national advertising Advertising placed by an advertising agency. Also called *agency advertising* and *general advertising*.

National Advertising Division (NAD) A division of the Council of Better Business Bureaus that evaluates the truthfulness of advertising claims.

national advertising rate A periodical or broadcast advertising rate charged by local media for advertising placed by national advertisers; customarily higher than the rate for local advertising.

National Advertising Review Board (NARB) An advertising industry organization that provides self-regulatory review and approval of advertising proposed for use in any medium.

National Advertising Sales Association (NASA) An organization, founded in 1907, for the promotion and development of newspaper advertising.

national Arbitron A national television rating made by the Arbitron Company.

National Association of Broadcast Engineers and Technicians (NABET) A union that represents technical and other employees of broadcast stations.

National Association of Broadcasters (NAB) The major voluntary commercial broadcasting association in the United States. Founded in 1923, the NAB promulgates self-regulatory codes, serves as an industry representative before the FCC and Congress, and offers a number of legal, engineering, research, and so on, services to its members. Other more specialized associations are also available to broadcasters: AMST, CCBS, DBA, NAEB, NAFMB, NATPE, RAB, RTNDA, state broadcasting associations, and so on.

National Association of Educational Broadcasters (NAEB) A professional organization of individual public broadcasters, teachers, and others involved in the educational aspects of broadcasting. Established in the 1920s.

National Association of Television Program Executives (NATPE) An organization consisting of television programming executives representing television networks, independent and network-affiliated stations, cable interests, and program suppliers.

National Association of Transportation Advertising *See* Transit Advertising Association.

national audience composition (NAC) Nielsen Television Index persons sample providing estimates of audiences to television and to network programs.

national audience demographics report (NAD) Report from Nielsen Television Index (NTI) that provides estimates of

U.S. television usage and sponsored network program audiences in terms of both households and persons by household market divisions.

National Black Network (NBN) A radio network founded in 1973 to serve the black communities with news and sports.

National Book Awards Awards established in 1950 to recognize distinguished fiction, nonfiction, and poetry books.

National Broadcasting Company (NBC) The first of the three major radio and television networks in the United States, first organized in 1926. For years a subsidiary of the Radio Corporation of America (RCA); now a subsidiary of General Electric. *See also* blue network and red network. Cf. ABC and CBS.

national broadcasting systems The various methods of controlling and operating the internal broadcasting of the countries of the world; government ownership and operation, private ownership and operation, government ownership and public operation, and public ownership and operation.

National Bureau of Standards (NBS) The federal government agency charged with setting standards for weights, measures, and so on.

National Business Publications *See* American Business Press.

National Cable Television Association (NCTA) The major association of CATV operators in the United States. Founded in 1952, the association works for limiting the regulatory power of government over cable operation and serves the CATV industry much as the NAB serves broadcasters.

national circuit A radio or television circuit that originates and terminates within a country.

National Citizens Committee on Educational Television A committee founded in 1952 by the Fund for Adult Education to study the problems of educational television.

National Committee for the Full Development of Instructional Television Fixed Service A committee formed in 1965 to plan the use of ITFS frequencies. Committee members included FCC staff members and educational representatives.

National Defense Emergency Authorization (NDEA) The authorization by the FCC for a station to operate during an emergency action condition in a manner consistent with the needs of national security and defense. *See also* Emergency Broadcast System.

National Editorial Association (NEA) The former name of the National Newspaper Association.

National Electrical Code (NEC) A code established by the American National Board of Fire Underwriters detailing the construction and installation of electrical wiring and equipment for safety purposes.

National Industrial Advertisers' Association (NIAA) An association of advertisers, agencies, and communication media formed for the purpose of promoting industrial advertising and marketing.

National Instructional Television Library A library established in 1961 by the Eastern Educational Television Network (EEN) with funds furnished by the United States Office of Education.

National Labor Relations Act (NLRA) *See* National Labor Relations Board.

National Labor Relations Board (NLRB) The government agency that was created by the National Labor Relations Act of 1935. The board has two functions: preventing and correcting unfair labor practices, and holding secret ballot elections for employees.

National League of Cities (NLC) An organization of major cities that advocates city interests and concerns to government. Active in cable television interests.

National Library Week A promotional program that encourages the use of libraries; sponsored by the American Library Association.

National Magazine Awards Annual awards given for editorial excellence and innovation in magazines.

National Museum of Communications An outgrowth of the National Broadcast Museum.

National News Council (NNC) An organization founded in 1973 to review complaints of unfairness, inaccuracy, or bias by wire services, networks, news syndicates, and news magazines.

National Newspaper Association (NNA) An organization of small town newspaper editors, founded in 1885; formerly the National Editorial Association.

National Outdoor Advertising Bureau, Inc. (NOAB) A national organization cooperatively owned and used by advertising agencies for buying and servicing outdoor advertising campaigns. It maintains a staff of field service representatives throughout the country for on-the-spot evaluation and inspection of advertising structures and other out-of-home media.

national plan A strategy for a nationwide marketing effort.

National Program Production and Acquisition Grant (NPPAG) A Corporation for Public Broadcasting grant of funds to radio stations for the production and distribution of programs.

National Project for the Improvement of Televised Instruction A program established by a grant from the Ford Foundation in 1964 to provide consultant services and conduct seminars under the auspices of the NAEB.

National Public Radio (NPR) A national educational network of public radio stations, funded by the Corporation for Public Broadcasting (CPB), which produces and distributes programming.

National Radio Broadcasters Association (NRBA) A former association of radio broadcasters, now a part of the National Association of Broadcasters.

National Radio Conferences (NRC) A series of conferences convened in the early 1920s by Secretary of Commerce Herbert Hoover in an attempt to develop a workable set of broadcast regulations.

national radio network broadcast A broadcast carried simultaneously by one or more stations in excess of the stations composing a regional radio network.

National Radio Systems Committee (NRSC) A committee formed to study and recommend ways to improve AM radio. Composed of members from the broadcast and receiver manufacturer industry.

national rate The advertising rate charged by a communication medium to national advertisers. Also called *general rate.* Cf. local rate and regional rate.

national rating Any rating calculated for a television or radio network or program over the United States.

national representative *See* station representative.

national sales The purchase of time on a local radio or television station by national advertisers through advertising agencies or station representatives. Cf. local sales.

national spot □ Advertising time purchased by a national advertiser. □ A broadcast station availability that is sold through national sales.

National Telecommunications and Information Administration (NTIA) A federal agency formed in 1978 by combining the Office of Telecommunications Policy and the Office of Telecommunications. NTIA's goals include formulating policies to support the development, growth, and regulation of telecommunication and information services.

National Television Systems Committee (NTSC) An industry-wide committee organized in 1940 that formulated the standards for monochrome and color television.

NATO National Association of Theatre Owners.

NATOA National Association of Telecommunications Officers. A national cable television organization.

NATPE National Association of Television Program Executives.

NATRA National Association of Television and Radio Announcers.

nat sound □ An abbreviation for *natural sound.* □ *See* ambient sound.

NATTKE National Association of Theatrical, Television, and Kine Employees. A British trade union.

natural break A break designed to interrupt a radio or television program with a minimum of obtrusiveness.

natural image *See* natural picture.

natural interference Any electromagnetic interference caused by atmospheric disturbances or solar flares.

naturalism A literary theory that forces the portrayal of a character's actions as being controlled by sociological and psychological forces.

natural language A language spoken by humans as opposed to a computer language.

natural lighting A term generally synonymous with sunlight, although it may be used to indicate any lighting that does not appear augmented. Also called *existing light.*

natural picture In video, a picture of a real-life subject. Also called a *natural image.*

natural sound □ The actual sounds that are heard at a given location. □ The sounds that are heard in synchronization with a picture.

nature film A short or full-length feature, usually produced in documentary style, that concentrates on the environment, plants, animals, marine life, and so on.

NATVAS National Academy of Television Arts and Sciences. Now NATAS.

NAVA National Audio-Visual Association, Inc.

NBC □ National Broadcasters' Club. □ National Broadcasting Company.

NBCC National Book Critics Circle.

NBEA National Broadcast Editorial Association.

NBFM Narrow Band Frequency Modulation.

NBI Nielsen Broadcast Index.

NBL National Book League.

NBMC National Black Media Coalition. A citizens' group that is attempting to increase black representation and ownership of the mass media.

NBN National Black Network. A radio network.

NBP National Business Publications.

NBS National Bureau of Standards. The U.S. government standards organization. *See also* time signal.

NBW National Book Week.

NC □ Network channel. A telephone company circuit. □ Noiseless Camera.

NCAE National Center for Audio Experimentation.

NCATA National Cable Antenna Television Association of Canada.

NCCAS National Center of Communication Arts and Sciences.

NCCB National Citizens Committee for Broadcasting. A citizens' group.

NCCBN National Council of Churches Broadcasting Network.

NCC/USA National Council of Churches of Christ in the USA.

NCE Noncommercial Educational. An FCC designation.

NCES National Center for Educational Statistics.

NCFDITFS National Committee for the Full Development of Instructional Television Fixed Services.

NCORT National Catholic Office for Radio and Television.

NCPAC National Conservative Political Action Committee.

NCS □ National communication system. □ National Cartoonists Society.

NCSA Noncommercial spot announcement. A PSA.

NCSCT National Center for School and College Television.

NCTA National Cable Television Association.

NCUR National Committee for Utilities Radio.

NCWC National Catholic Welfare Conference News Service. An American news agency.

ND □ News director. □ Nondirectional. *See also* nondirectional mike. □ Neutral density.

nd No date.

NDEA National Defense Emergency Authorization.

NE □ New edition. □ News editor.

NEA □ National Editorial Association. □ National Endowment for the Arts. □ Newspaper Enterprise Association, Inc.

near letter quality *See* NLQ.

Nebraska Press Association v. Stuart The 1976 case in which the Supreme Court held that a judge could not gag the press concerning information prior to a trial. *See also* gag order.

NEC □ National Electrical Code. □ The National Entertainment Conference (of the recording industry).

necessary bandwidth For a given class of emission, the minimum value of the occupied bandwidth sufficient to ensure the transmission of information at the rate and with the quality required for the system employed, under specified conditions.

neck □ That portion of a piece of type between the face and the body. *See also* beard. □ The narrow, cylindrical part of a television picture or pickup tube.

neck microphone *See* lavaliere.

NEDA National Electronic Distributors Association.

needle □ The pointer or indicator on a meter or dial. □ A popular term for a *stylus.*

needle chatter The unwanted sounds made by a stylus. Also called *needle talk.*

needle drag *See* stylus drag.

needle drop The recording of one band from a stock music library. Payment is usually made on the basis of a variable fee for each use.

needle force *See* stylus force.

needle scratch *See* surface noise.

needle talk *See* needle chatter.

neg An abbreviation for *negative.*

negative □ A value less than zero. □ An electrode that has an excess of electrons. □ The opposite of positive. □ Raw film stock designed to be used for negative images. □ Developed film that has tonal values that are opposite from those of the original subject. □ Any negative film image.

negative appeal An advertising message that does not promote the good qualities of the product or service, but intimidates the reader or viewer with the consequences of not using the particular product or service.

negative assembly *See* negative cutting.

negative costs □ Generally, the expenses incurred in the production of a motion picture, television program, book, and so on. *See also* above-the-line and below-the-line. □ The total expenditures made to complete a motion picture, exclusive of publicity, distribution, and exhibition expenses. □ The gross film rentals less the expenses of distribution. □ All actual costs and expenses of production, including overhead, excluding deferments.

negative cutting The editing of a film negative to match a workprint. Also called *negative assembly, negative matching,* and *negative pulling. See also* master matching.

negative film *See* negative.

negative ghost A ghost in which the colors are reversed.

negative image *See* negative.

negative lens A lens that is thicker at the edges than at the center, thus producing light ray divergence. Cf. positive lens.

negative numbers *See* edge numbers (EN).

negative option A buying plan in which a customer or club member agrees to accept and pay for records, tapes, books, or other products that are announced in advance at regular intervals unless the person notifies the company not to ship within a reasonable time after each announcement.

negative perforation A type of perforation with two parallel flat edges; used in 35-mm negative film stock and for animation registration. Cf. positive perforation.

negative pickup An agreement between a motion picture distributor and a producer wherein the producer delivers the finished motion picture negative for an advance payment.

negative pitch A camera film stock with a short pitch from one perforation to the next. Cf. positive pitch.

negative pulling *See* negative cutting.

negative space The white space around artwork or in photographs.

negative splice A cemented film splice with a narrow overlap between the two pieces of film. Cf. positive splice.

negative transmission The transmission of a television picture in which a decrease in initial light intensity causes an increase in the transmitted power.

negligence In defamation, a failure to act as a responsible or prudent individual. Cf. actual malice.

NEH National Endowment for the Humanities.

neighborhood showing A closely spaced group of outdoor posters advertising a product or service available in the same neighborhood.

NEM New electronic media. Also called *neovideo.*

NEMA National Electrical Manufacturers Association.

nemo An acronym for *not emanating main office* or *not emanating main origination.* A remote broadcast.

ne/nd New edition in preparation; no date.

neologism An existing word used in a new sense, such as lavaliere for a type of microphone.

neon An inert gas used in tubes for display purposes in outdoor advertising.

neonized An outdoor advertising display using neon tubes.

neon lamp A lamp containing an inert gas that glows when excited by electricity. Used in glow lamps, timing circuits, and extensively in display signs.

neorealism A type of film that relied heavily on nonprofessional actors and extensive location filming. Evolved in Italy shortly after World War II.

neovideo *See* NEM.

nep New edition pending.

NER National Educational Radio. *See* NPR.

NERC National Electronic Reliability Council.

NERN National Educational Radio Network. A former educational radio network of the Educational Radio Division (ERD) of the NAEB.

NERTF National Educational Radio Task Force. A former instructional radio committee.

NES News Election Service.

NESC National Electrical Safety Code. *See* National Electrical Code.

NESDA National Electronics Service Dealers Association.

nesting □ Placing one enclosure within another before the contents are inserted into a direct mail envelope. □ Placing one computer subroutine or sequence within another, such as in multilevel loops.

NET □ National Educational Television. Formerly the primary television network for educational programming. Now a program production arm of PBS. Formerly NETRC. □ *See* network program. □ An abbreviation for *network.* Any program furnished to a broadcast station by a national, regional, or special network. An FCC program source category.

net □ An abbreviation for *network.* □ Interconnecting lines between radio or television stations or organizations. □ A light diffuser. □ The amount paid to a radio or television station by an advertising agency after the commission has been deducted. □ *See* lace. □ The price to be paid for a book or other item, with no further discount. Also called *net price.* Cf. gross. □ *See* net cost.

net advertising circulation (NAC) *See* net circulation.

net audience Unduplicated audience. *See* cumulative audience.

net circulation The total number of persons passing an outdoor advertisement within a given period who face the advertisement easily. Also called *net advertising circulation.* Cf. gross circulation.

net controlled circulation The number of purchased and unpurchased copies of a controlled-circulation publication that are actually distributed to the intended readership.

net cost □ The cost of a service provided by an advertising agency aside from the agency commission. Also called *net.* □ An advertising rate applied after deduction of applicable discounts, the agency commission included. Also called *net* and *net plus.*

netCUE An alert system developed by National Public Radio (NPR) for program advisory announcements, technical matters, and Emergency Broadcast System transmission notification.

net name arrangement An agreement between a list owner and a list user at the time of ordering or before in which the list owner agrees to accept adjusted payment for less than the total names shipped.

net paid The number of copies of a newspaper or magazine, less the number unsold, held back, defective, and so on, actually paid for.

net paid circulation The net circulation of a periodical for which not less than 50 percent of the newsstand or subscription has been paid; the minimum is that of the Audit Bureau of Circulations.

net plus *See* net cost.

net price *See* net.

net profit The profit made on a single sale of a book or other item.

net rating points (NRP) A relative measure of cumulative audience expressed as a percentage of either a specified group of television households, or individuals residing in a specified area estimated to be in the audience at least once during two or more time periods. Cf. gross rating points.

NETRC National Educational Television and Radio Center. *See* NET.

net reach The number of different people reached by a given schedule. Available through Arbitron Information on

Demand (AID), net reach is reported for single station and multiple station schedules. *See also* cumulative audience and reach.

net run The total number of salable copies of a publication.

net unduplicated audience The actual number of persons who may be exposed to advertising, regardless of how many exposures each person may have. *See also* cumulative audience. Cf. gross audience.

net weekly circulation The number of noncable television households that viewed the station for five minutes or more during the entire week, expressed as a percentage of the total noncable television households in the survey area. *See also* significantly viewed.

network □ A national, regional, or state organization distributing programs for a substantial part of each broadcast day to broadcasting stations, generally by interconnection facilities. □ A combination of interconnected electrical circuits or components. □ A group of independent and noncompeting advertising agencies that exchange ideas and services. Also called *agency group* and *agency network*. □ A system of interconnected electronic devices, such as computers.

network affiliate *See* affiliate.

network affiliation contract An agreement between a network and a station for the station to carry the programs of a network. Such contracts may not require the station to carry all the network programs or prohibit or hinder a station from carrying the programs of another network.

network architecture *See* architecture.

network case The 1943 Supreme Court decision that resulted in the FCC's authority to regulate affiliation agreements and in the divestiture of the Blue Network by NBC.

network clipping The illegal practice of a broadcast station deleting the end of a network program or commercial.

network compensation The money paid to affiliates by radio and television networks for carrying programs and commercials. Cf. reverse compensation.

network cooperative program *See* cooperative program.

network cue A visual or audible cue from a network to its affiliates that a program is ending or being interrupted for local announcements.

network delay machine A television tape recorder dedicated to recording and storing a network program for replay at some later time, usually within the same or subsequent broadcast day.

network exclusivity The right of a network affiliate to telecast programs on an exclusive basis within the affiliate's service area.

network exhibition The telecasting of a motion picture over the network facilities of the United States of NBC, CBS, or ABC, or any other network, for the exhibition of an entertainment product by any means, including cable television or satellite distribution.

network feed The transmission of a network program to affiliated stations by microwave or wire. The feed may be aired live or taped for later broadcast. Cf. bicycle network.

network identification (NI) An announcement and cue to affiliates, such as, "This is NBC, the National Broadcasting Company."

networking □ The business of procuring stations or scheduling programs for a network. □ The interconnection of two or more computer systems.

network news News delivered to listeners or viewers by a national or regional network.

network option time *See* option time.

network owned and operated *See* O&O.

network primary affiliate *See* primary affiliate.

network program □ Any program delivered simultaneously to more than one broadcast station, regional or national, commercial or noncommercial. □ A program broadcast over two or more television stations in the United States, its territories, and possessions. It may include regularly affiliated stations, if any, of each network in Canada, Mexico City, Tijuana, and/or Bermuda.

Network Program Analysis (NPA) An Arbitron term for an analysis of the network television programs broadcast during the major sweep periods.

network programs by DMA report (NPD) A report by Nielsen Station Index that provides a market-by-market compilation of audience estimates to network programs.

network programming The programming supplied by a national or regional network, whether commercial or noncommercial.

network rating Any rating calculated for a television or radio network.

network standard *See* general American.

network station *See* affiliate.

network switching The connection of various possible paths for the transmission of items such as telephone messages.

network syndication An FCC rule that prohibits television networks from syndicating their own programs in the United States.

Network Transmission Committee (NTC) A subcommittee of the Video Transmission Engineering Advisory Committee concerned with promoting uniform technical practices in television transmission systems.

neutral □ Music used under voiceover announcements. □ Neither positive nor negative. □ A gray scale or card used to assist in the proper exposure of a scene.

neutral angle A camera shot in which the subject moves in line with the axis of the lens.

neutral balance A film print that correctly displays the proper ratio between the three primary colors.

neutral density (ND) filter A filter that reduces the power at all wavelengths equally, thus dimming the light without affecting the color quality.

neutral reportage In defamation, the accurate reporting of newsworthy statements, even if the reporter doubts the accuracy of the statements.

neutral wire The grounded wire in a three-wire electrical system.

new American cinema The American cinema from the mid-1940s.

new build A cable television system that has laid cable in a new housing development before the construction of the dwellings.

new business man An advertising agency employee or principal responsible for developing new agency clients.

new connect A new subscriber to a cable television system.

new criticism *See* impressionistic criticism.

new edition (ne) A book edition containing substantial changes from the original or previous edition. Also called a *revised edition.* Cf. impression and reprint.

new head (NH) *See* new lead.

new journalism A style of journalistic writing begun in the 1960s that is characterized by colorful, subjective stories.

new lead (NL) A fresh beginning for a news story, usually containing new material. May be a rewrite for an unacceptable lead. Also called a *new head* and *new top.*

new media Media that are now becoming available, or envisaged as becoming available for mass information presentation.

news □ An abbreviation for *newspaper* and *newsprint.* □ An event or material suitable for a news story. □ The timely accounts of recent or significant events involving people, governments, or phenomena.

news agency An organization, such as AP or UPI, that collects news for distribution to subscribers.

news agent □ A news dealer. □ A person who collects and supplies news to media.

news analyst A person who attempts to interpret the news rather than just report it.

news assistant An entry-level position in a radio or television news department. Also called a *desk assistant.*

news beat *See* beat.

news block An uninterrupted or segmented extended period of news reporting on radio or television.

newsboy A person who distributes or sells newspapers.

news case A type case set up for news composition.

newscast A radio or television broadcast containing news.

newscaster A person who presents the news on radio or television. Cf. reporter and standupper.

news clip A short film or videotape of a news highlight.

news conference *See* press conference.

news consultant An individual or company hired to improve the news department of a radio or television station to enhance the ratings. Also called a *news doctor.*

news cruiser A radio station news mobile unit.

news cycle □ The length of time on an all-news station before the news is repeated. *See also* news wheel. □ The length of time before the major news of the day is rewritten by a wire service.

news dealer A person or store that sells newspapers and magazines.

news digest *See* budget.

news director (ND) The news department executive charged with overall responsibility for news production, personnel, and often scheduling and budgeting.

news doctor A slang term for a news consultant.

news editor *See* editor.

News Election Service (NES) A pool used to gather election returns.

news feature *See* feature.

news film Any film used in presenting a news broadcast. Now replaced by videotape.

news flash □ A news item important enough to interrupt a broadcast program in progress. □ *See* flash.

news gap □ The time difference between a newsworthy event and its reporting. □ The difference between the amount of newsworthy material and the time available for its presentation.

news handout A press release, often concerning future events, to be used at a later date or time.

newshawk A slang term for a reporter.

newshen A somewhat outmoded term for a female reporter.

news hole The amount of space available in a newspaper for news after the space necessary for advertising has been determined. Also called a *hole.*

news hook *See* hook.

newshound A slang term for a reporter.

news leak A story containing confidential information secured by a reporter and often released on purpose by a government official. Cf. off the record.

newsletter A periodical publication, usually letter size and without advertising.

news magazine A broadcast program that contains features, reports, human interest stories, investigative reports, and so on.

newsman An employee of a newspaper; a man or woman who reports, writes, or edits the news.

news management Any of a number of techniques used by governments and officials to control the flow or reporting of news by the media.

newspaper □ A publication that contains news, opinions, features, advertising, and so on, usually distributed on a daily or weekly basis. Also called a *paper. See also* newspaper publication. □ An organization that publishes a newspaper. □ The newsprint that a newspaper is printed on.

Newspaper Advertising Bureau, Inc. (NAB) An association of daily newspapers, founded in 1913 to promote the use of newspapers and supplements as an advertising medium.

Newspaper Advertising Executives Association (NAEA) The former name of the International Newspaper Advertising Executives.

newspaper chain *See* newspaper group.

Newspaper Enterprise Association (NEA) A feature syndicate.

newspaper group An organization that owns two or more newspapers in different markets. Also called a *newspaper chain* and sometimes a *newspaper syndicate.*

Newspaper Guild, The A union that represents editors and other journalists.

newspaper owner Any person who owns or controls directly, or indirectly through separate or subsidiary corporations, one or more newspaper publications.

Newspaper Preservation Act The 1970 statute that created antitrust exemptions for newspapers in economic distress so that they could operate jointly. Also called the *Failing Newspaper Bill. See also* joint newspaper operating arrangements.

newspaper publication A publication produced on newsprint that is published in one or more issues weekly (including as one publication any daily newspaper and any Sunday newspaper published by the same owner in the same city, community, or metropolitan area), and in which a substantial portion of the content is devoted to the dissemination of news and editorial opinion.

newspaper syndicate □ *See* newspaper group. □ *See* syndicate.

newspaper wire The wire services news feed that is written for newspapers.

news peg *See* angle.

news pool □ An organization or group of individuals who exchange news on a regular basis. □ *See* pool.

newsprint An inexpensive, machine-finished paper usually made from wood pulp and used for printing newspapers. *See also* groundwood pulp.

news programs (N) Programs dealing with current local, national, and international events, including weather and stock market reports; also include commentary, analysis, and sports news if an integral part of the news programs. An FCC program type category.

newsreader A person who reads broadcast news but who may or may not participate in its writing; an anchor.

newsreel □ A short—usually not more than 10 minutes—news film made for theatrical showing. □ Any film or tape report of current events.

news release An item of information distributed to the media, often promoting some cause or person.

newsroom □ The room or office in a newspaper where news is written and edited. □ A room set aside for reporters in courthouses, executive buildings, and other government locations. □ A radio or television station newsroom. □ A library reading room containing newspapers and magazines. □ A place where periodicals are sold.

news satellite A mobile transmitter used for news.

news sense The indefinable quality of a reporter or editor to uncover, select, or write news of interest to readers or viewers. Also called a *nose for news.*

newssheet A slang term for a newspaper.

news sleuth A sometimes inaccurate slang term for a reporter.

news source The person, files, documents, tips, and so on, that furnish news to reporters.

news staging An unethical and deliberate attempt by the media to cause a newsworthy scene or action in order to have something to report. Cf. nonevent.

newsstand Formerly, an open air structure on the street that sold newspapers and magazines. Now a vendor of newspapers and magazines in office buildings, malls, airports, and so on.

newsstand circulation The sales of a periodical through retail outlets, rather than by subscription; usually considered with respect to the total number of issues sold in this manner, or the percentage of the total relative to total circulation.

news summary □ A brief overview or recap of the news that is to be presented on a newscast. □ A column, usually on the first page of a newspaper, that lists the major news stories and the pages on which they can be found.

news value A subjective measure of the importance of a news story. *See also* newsworthy.

news wheel A news program that is repeated, either on videotape or live, with updated material.

news wire A teletype news service from one of the press associations. *See also* wire service.

newswire service *See* wire service.

newsworthiness A traditional defense in an invasion of privacy lawsuit claiming that the information published was newsworthy and, therefore, not an invasion of privacy.

newsworthy An item that has news value.

news writer A reporter, rewrite person, or editor.

Newton rings The concentric, colored rings that are caused by optical interference between two surfaces of film that are not in contact.

new top *See* new lead (NL).

Newvicon A trademark for an improved vidicon television pickup tube.

new wave □ A series of motion pictures made on location by French directors in the 1950s and 1960s. Also called *nouvelle vague.* □ Generally, any new group of filmmakers.

New World Information Order (NWIO) A United Nations-approved resolution about the Third World concerning the flow of information. Under this concept, the media are supposed to support the goals set by governments.

New York Times v. Sullivan The precedent-setting 1964 Supreme Court decision that held damages could not be awarded to public officials for defamation unless the statement was made with "actual malice."

NEXIS A trademark for a computer database that contains the complete text of newspaper stories and wire service matter.

next to reading matter (nr) The position of advertising matter placed next to text instead of other advertising. *See also* preferred position.

nexus The point in an electronic network at which the interconnections meet.

NF □ Noise figure. □ Normal frequency. □ Nonfiction.

NFAA National Federation of Advertising Agencies.

NFB National Film Board (of Canada).

NFCB National Federation of Community Broadcasters.

NFLCP National Federation of Local Cable Programmers. An organization that provides assistance in the production of local cable television programs.

NFPB National Friends of Public Broadcasting. A citizens' group.

NFPW National Federation of Press Women.

NG No good. A bad take, shot, sound, and so on. Cf. OK.

NH New head.

NHI Nielsen HomeVideo Index.

NHK Nippon Hoso Kyokai. The Japanese national broadcasting system.

NI Network identification.

NIAA National Industrial Advertisers Association.

NIAC National Industry Advisory Committee. An advisory group to the government that recommended, among other things, the two-tone EBS system.

NIAC order A service order previously filed with AT&T providing for program origination reconfiguration of the major radio and television networks voluntarily participating in the national-level EBS.

nibble Four bits; a half a byte. Sometimes spelled *nybble.*

NiCad Nickel cadmium; used in rechargeable batteries.

nick A groove in a piece of type that allows for visual alignment.

nickel cadmium (NiCad) An alloy of nickel and cadmium used extensively in rechargeable batteries.

nickelodeon □ An old-time motion picture theatre that charged five cents for admission. □ A juke box.

nickel type A copper type body plated with nickel for increased durability.

Nielsen (ACN) The A. C. Nielsen Company, an audience research service that operates in 23 countries, begun in 1950 when the Nielsen Company purchased the national services of the C. E. Hooper Company. Nielsen is best known for its television ratings.

Nielsen Broadcast Index (NBI) The Canadian counterpart of the Nielsen Station Index in the United States.

Nielsen HomeVideo Index (NHI) A division of Nielsen's Media Research Group responsible for syndicated and nonsyndicated measurement of cable, pay cable, VCRs, video discs, and other new television technologies.

Nielsen Market Section Audiences (MSA) Report by Nielsen Television Index (NTI) that provides estimates of U.S. television household usage and program average audiences for the total country and by a variety of market sections.

Nielsen Post-Buy Service (NPBS) A special analysis facility of the Nielsen Station Index that enables agency/advertiser clients to analyze the audiences achieved by their network or spot schedules.

Nielsen rating In the public mind, usually refers to percent of U.S. television households tuned to a particular network program during the average minute of a particular telecast, as reported by Nielsen Television Index (NTI).

Nielsen Station Index (NSI) A service of Nielsen's Media Research Group that provides syndicated local market television audience measurement.

Nielsen Television Index (NTI) A service of Nielsen's Media Research Group.

NTI is Nielsen's syndicated national network television service that provides audience estimates for all sponsored U.S. network television programs.

night The time period on radio from 7 p.m. to sign off. Also called *nighttime* and *teen. See also* daypart.

night effects The techniques used in photography to film scenes in daylight so that they appear to be shot at night.

night filter A camera lens filter that is used to produce night effects.

night for day The shooting of film at night but compensating so that the film appears to have been shot during the day. Cf. day for night and night for night.

night for night Night scenes that are photographed at night instead of during the day. Cf. day for night and night for day.

night shift *See* night side.

night side A newspaper or wire service staff that works at night. Also called a night shift. Cf. day side.

nighttime (N) □ The period of time between local sunset and local sunrise. □ *See* night.

night work For the purpose of television and motion picture production, work between 8:00 p.m. and 6:00 a.m., except that a first call for the day at 5:00 a.m. or thereafter does not constitute night work.

nihil obstat Latin for "nothing hinders." An official approval of material for publication.

nine point five mm film An obsolete film gauge, now largely replaced by super 8 mm film.

1960 Programming Policy Statement A comprehensive programming statement issued by the FCC as a guide to licensee programming decisions. The actual title is "Report and Statement of Policy re: Commission en banc Programming Inquiry." Cf. Blue Book.

ninety A radio or television commercial 90 seconds in length.

Nipkow disk A round disc with openings; once used for mechanical scanning in television.

NIR color television system A Russian variation of the SECAM color television system.

NIS News and Information Service. An NBC station program service.

NIT National Instructional Television. Now AIT.

nit The metric unit of luminance; equal to one candela per square meter.

NITA National Instructional Television Association.

NITC National Instructional Television Center.

nitrate base A highly flammable film base made of cellulose nitrate. Used until the 1950s when it was replaced by safety film bases made primarily of cellulose triacetate.

nitrogen burst agitation The use of bubbles of nitrogen gas to keep film developing solutions in motion.

nixie □ A glow tube that changes electrical signals into visual information. □ A mailing piece returned to a mailer (under proper authorization) by the U.S. Postal Service because of an incorrect or undeliverable name and address.

NL □ New lead. □ New line.

NLC National League of Cities.

NLMC National Latino Media Coalition. A citizens' group.

NLQ □ Near letter quality. An advertising slogan used to describe the type quality of high-resolution dot matrix printers. □ Nonlinear quantization.

NLRA National Labor Relations Act. *See* National Labor Relations Board.

NLRB National Labor Relations Board.

NMA National Micrographics Association.

NMPA National Music Publishers Association. A trade association of music publishers.

NMRS National Mobile Radio System.

NNA National Newspaper Association.

NNC National News Council.

NO Not our (publication). Same as NOP.

NOAA National Oceanic and Atmospheric Administration.

NOAB National Outdoor Advertising Bureau, Inc.

no claims bonus A percentage of a completion guarantor's fee that is paid to producers upon timely completion and delivery of a film.

no commitment A book club that does not require a specified number of purchases.

noctovision A television system that used infrared light for scanning.

nodal head A camera mount that retains its relationship to the scene by pivoting around the nodal point of the camera lens.

nodal point Either of the two points on the axis of a lens through which the incident ray and the emergent ray are parallel.

no date (nd) A book or other undated publication.

noddies A British term for cutaways of interviewers.

node A point where electrical or physical lines converge; a terminal.

nodules Small clusters of magnetic oxide on the surface of a magnetic tape.

no fax A television rehearsal accomplished without the use of technical facilities.

NOI Notice of inquiry.

noise □ Any undesired stimuli in a communication channel. □ Any undesired disturbance in an electrical or electromagnetic circuit or wave generated by random electrical variations. *See also* distortion, hiss, and snow.

noise banding Banding of a video picture in which the visible difference is in noise level. Cf. gauge banding, hue banding, and saturation banding.

noise factor *See* noise figure.

noise figure (NF) The ratio of the noise of a component or system at the output as compared to the input. Also called *noise factor.*

noise gate A variable threshold circuit that can be set to eliminate various low-frequency noises.

noiseless camera A self-blimped motion picture camera.

noise level The existing sound at any given location.

noise limiter An electronic circuit that clips the noise above the highest received signal or lowers the gain of an amplifier in the absence of a signal.

NOL Naval Ordnance Laboratory.

nom de plume An author's pen name.

nominal bandwidth The maximum usable bandwidth of a channel not including the guard bands.

nominal damages *See* damages.

nominal power The power of a standard broadcast station as specified in the FCC's system of classification. The following values are included: 50 kW, 25 kW, 10 kW, 5 kW, 2.5 kW, 1 kW, 0.5 kW, and 0.25 kW.

nomograph A chart on which equations may be solved graphically.

non-ADI market A non-ADI market may be established when the city of license of a commercial station that does not have a rebroadcast arrangement with any other station located in a county that is in the ADI but not in the Metro of a Metro market. A non-ADI market includes only the home county of such a station.

non-ADI station A broadcast station that is not located in the major market of an ADI.

non-air commercial A commercial not intended for broadcast use, such as nonbroadcast audience reaction commercials, copy testing, or client demonstrations.

nonbroadcast A system for the distribution of electronic signals by a means other than broadcasting, such as ITFS, SCA, teletext, and cable.

noncommercial broadcasting Radio and television broadcasting that receives no advertising revenue and that is designed to serve the educational, cultural, and other needs of a community.

noncommercial educational broadcast station A radio or television broadcast station that is eligible to be licensed by the Federal Communications Commission as a noncommercial educational radio or television broadcast station and that is owned (controlled) and operated by a state, political or special purpose subdivision of a state, public agency or nonprofit private foundation, corporation, institution, or association, or owned (controlled) and operated by a municipality and transmits only noncommercial programs.

noncommercial FM translator An FM broadcast translator station that rebroadcasts the signals of a noncommercial FM radio broadcast station.

noncommercial program *See* sustaining program.

noncommercial radio *See* noncommercial broadcasting.

noncommercial telecommunications entity Any enterprise that is owned (controlled) and operated by a state, a political or special purpose subdivision of a state, a public agency, or a nonprofit private foundation, corporation, institution, or association; and that has been organized primarily for the purpose of disseminating audio or video noncommercial educational and cultural programs to the public by means other than a primary television or radio broadcast station, including, but not limited to, coaxial cable, optical fiber, broadcast translators, cassettes, discs, satellite, microwave, or laser transmission.

noncommercial television *See* noncommercial broadcasting.

noncompatible Two or more pieces of equipment that are incapable of working together or are mismatched. Cf. compatible.

noncomposite A video signal that contains the video and blanking signals only. Cf. composite.

nonconductor An insulating material.

noncooperation *See* nonresponse.

noncustom commercial Any commercial other than a custom commercial.

nondecision-making Commission personnel All FCC personnel other than decision-making Commission personnel.

nondim A circuit supplying electrical power to a luminaire by means of a switch or a relay in order to permit an on/off function rather than a dimming function.

nondirected move A movement by a performer not called for by the script, director, or motivation.

nondirectional mike An omnidirectional microphone. *See also* mike pattern.

nondirective probe A technique used in interviews to solicit further information to the initial response to an open-end question. *See also* probe.

non-DMA station A broadcast station that is not located in the major market of a DMA.

nondrop frame A method of numbering videotape frames for editing, such as 30 frames for every second instead of 29.97 frames per second. *See also* drop frame.

nonduplicated income For public broadcasting stations, the income received from outside the public broadcasting system.

nonduplication □ The FCC rule imposed on cable television systems that forbids the importation of distant signals if such signals are carried by a local station. □ The FCC rule that prohibits two commonly owned stations in the same market from programming the identical material.

nonduplication protection editing The editing of household diaries to give credit to local stations for cable household viewing that has been improperly credited to a distant signal by the diary keeper.

non-EQ'd sound *See* dry sound.

nonevent An event caused by the mere presence of television cameras, microphones, and so on, which would not take place if it were not for the mass media. Cf. news staging.

no news lead A news story lead that is devoid of facts.

nonexclusive A news story, film clip, tape recording, and so on, received by more than one reporter, broadcast station, newspaper, or other recipient. Cf. exclusivity.

nonexclusive contract A contract between a writer, performer, director, and so on, and a company that does not prohibit him or her from accepting other employment.

nonexclusive franchise A cable television franchise awarded to more than one individual or company. *See also* multiple franchise.

nonfiction (NF) The narration or presentation of real events, actions, and ideas concerning real persons.

nonfiction film A motion picture that uses real-life characters, plot, and setting.

nonflammable film *See* safety film.

nonilluminated An outdoor poster panel that is not artificially lighted.

noninterlaced A television scanning method that produces picture lines sequentially.

nonlens spotlight A luminaire embodying only a lamp and a reflector that has variable field and beam angles obtained by changing the spacing between the lamp and the reflector.

nonlinear amplifier An amplifier in which the output is not directly proportional to the input.

nonlinear distortion Distortion caused by a deviation from a linear relationship between the input and output of a system or component.

nonlinear editing The computer-controlled flexible manipulation of original material. Cf. linear editing.

nonlinear quantization Quantization using steps of different sizes to distribute the steps more efficiently over the dynamic range. Takes advantage of the fact that quantization errors are less perceptible when signal changes are large.

nonmagnetic A material that is incapable of being magnetized or attracted by a magnet.

nonoxide side *See* backside.

nonpareil □ A size of type; 6 points. □ A 6-point slug.

nonparticipating station A broadcast station that is not voluntarily participating in the national-level Emergency Broadcasting System and does not hold an EBS authorization.

nonphased color (NPC) □ A color television signal that lacks the normal precise lock between the horizontal scanning frequency and the color subcarrier frequency. □ Pertaining to a television tape recorder video playback mode adapted for the replay of such a recorded signal.

nonprint Material that is recorded on tape, film, disc, and so on, rather than material produced in books, magazines, newspapers, and so on.

nonprinting comments A message inserted in a manuscript, enclosed within delimiters, that a computer will ignore when the document is printed.

nonprobability sample A nonscientific sample from which legitimate conclusions may not be drawn. *See also* convenience sample and judgment sample.

nonprofit A foundation, corporation, institution or association, to which no part of the net earnings inures, or may lawfully inure, to the benefit of any private shareholder or individual.

nonprogram material Broadcast items including billboards, commercials, all credits in excess of 30 seconds, and promotional announcements. Usually, nonprogram material does not include public service announcements and promotional announcements for the same program.

nonprotected speech Speech that is outside the protection of the First Amendment, such as fighting words, obscenities, and some forms of defamation.

nonrenewal A denial of license renewal by the FCC or federal court.

nonresponse (NR) The failure of a household or person selected as part of a sample to provide usable information. Also called *noncooperation.*

nonresponse error A survey error that occurs if respondents differ in some characteristics from nonrespondents. Increases in sample size will not lessen any bias that is due to nonresponse. *See also* bias of nonresponse and nonsampling error.

nonresponse rate The percentage of respondents to a survey who fail to respond, either totally to a questionnaire in a predetermined sample, or to an individual question in a survey.

nonsampling error The result of imperfect survey procedures. This may be caused by several factors: nonresponse error, conditioning bias, interviewing bias, prestige bias, and response error. Cf. sampling error.

nonsegmented A videotape recorder format in which a full frame of video information is recorded during one revolution of the video record head. Cf. segmented.

nonstandard film □ Film with the emulsion wound facing out. □ *See* narrow gauge.

nonstructured interview An interview in which the respondent talks freely, with little or no guidance about subject matter.

nonsync An abbreviation for *nonsynchronous.*

nonsynchronous Unrelated in frequency or phase to other components. Cf. synchronous.

nonsynchronous color A color recording, typically for home or industrial applications, in which the phase of the chrominance may vary from the original signal's chrominance phase.

nonsynchronous sound Film or videotape in which the sound and picture are not recorded simultaneously.

nonsynchronous soundtrack *See* wild track.

nonsynchronous switch (NSS) □ A transition made between two video signals that are being generated by independent sync generators. □ Such a transition recorded on tape. □ The visible results of such a transition.

nontelevised A program that is blacked out.

nontheatrical distribution The rental of motion pictures by schools, colleges, and other nonprofit organizations. Such motion pictures may be nontheatrical films or regular motion pictures.

nontheatrical film A motion picture, such as a training film, not intended for screening in a motion picture theatre.

nonverbal communication Communication accomplished without the use of written or spoken words.

nonvolatile memory *See* nonvolatile RAM.

nonvolatile RAM (NVRAM) A memory that retains data when its power supply is removed. Also called *nonvolatile memory.*

nonwrinkle posting A method of dampening outdoor advertising poster sheets prior to posting. When posted, the wet sheets stretch and eliminate wrinkles when the poster dries.

noodle A musical improvisation. Often referred to as *noodling.*

NOP Not our publication. Same as *NO.*

NOPA National Office Products Association.

no pay A person who has not paid for goods or services ordered. Also called a *deadbeat, delinquent,* and *uncollectible.*

NORAD North American Air Defense.

NORDICOM Nordic Documentation Center for Mass Communications Research. A research organization based in Finland.

norm Any mean, median, or mode; an average.

normal □ The orientation of a surface; that is, the direction the surface faces. □ *See* normalled.

normal angle A medium shot taken with a normal lens from in front of the subject.

normal curve *See* normal distribution.

normal development Film that is developed using a standard strength developer and a normal development time; not pushed.

normal distribution The most common of the frequency distribution curves in statistical measurement. A normal distribution produces a plot that is unimodal and symmetrical with the mean, median, and mode at the midpoint. Also called a *bell curve* and *normal curve.*

normal focus lens *See* normal lens.

normalled A contact in a patch panel that is always connected unless a plug is inserted to divert the input or output elsewhere.

normal lens A lens that approximates the view of the human eye, such as for 35-mm film, a 50-mm lens; for 16-mm film, a 25-mm lens.

normal license period For AM and FM stations, seven years; for television broadcast stations, five years; for experimental television broadcast stations, experimental facsimile broadcast stations, and developmental broadcast stations, one year; for cable television relay stations, five years.

normal resolution In CD-I, a display resolution of 384 horizontal pixels by 280 vertical pixels. The lowest-resolution picture defined by the CD-I system. Cf. double resolution, high resolution, and low resolution.

north The direction of an animation stand farthest from the operator. Cf. south.

North American Newspaper Alliance, Inc. (NANA) A news syndicate.

North American Regional Broadcast Agreement (NARBA) An agreement first made in Havana, Cuba, in 1937 and subsequently revised; it allocates frequencies among the nations of North America.

no seam paper A wide paper used for backdrops.

nose for news *See* news sense.

nose room The distance, as seen in profile, between an individual's nose and the edge of the picture frame.

nostalgia radio A radio format characterized by musical standards.

nostril shot An extreme close-up that distorts a performer's features.

not available (NA) A term used to identify the reason for missing data in a table.

notch □ A recess cut into the edge of negative film that is read by some printers to change the light intensity. □ A physical mark made on film for identification in a darkroom. □ *See* notch code. □ A cutout made on one or two sides of an illustration for the insertion of type matter. Cf. mortise.

notch code A recess cut into sheet film so that it may be identified in a darkroom.

notch filter A device or arrangement of electronic components that is designed to attenuate a specific frequency band, usually with a sharp rolloff at each end.

note A musical tone.

noted A term used by the research firm of Daniel Starch & Associates to designate persons who have seen a certain advertisement in a certain periodical. Cf. read/most and seen/associated.

note session A production crew meeting held after a rehearsal.

noted score A term used by the research firm of Daniel Starch & Associates to designate the percentage of ad-noters for a certain issue of a certain periodical. Cf. ad-noter.

not for attribution A news source that may not be identified.

not for profit *See* nonprofit.

notice of inquiry (NOI) An administrative agency's method of soliciting comments by publishing information about a question at issue, proposed rules and policies, and so on.

notice of proposed rulemaking (NPRM) An administrative agency's method of soliciting comments by announcing a possible rule modification or new rule.

notification *See* local notice.

notification date A radio or television deadline for notification by an advertiser of the option of exercising the right to new or continued sponsorship.

nouvelle vague *See* new wave.

novelization The writing of a novel based on a play, screenplay, or other literary form.

novelty *See* ornamental.

novelty format An attention-getting direct mail format.

novelty printing Advertising slogans or names printed on pens, pencils, badges, matchbooks, and so on.

November season That portion of any year commencing at 0100 GMT on the first Sunday in November and ending at 0100 GMT on the first Sunday in March.

Novosti The news agency of the Soviet Union.

NOW National Organization for Women. A citizens' group. Cf. WWWW.

NP □ No place (of publication). □ No publisher (listed). □ No printer (listed).

NPACT National Public Affairs Center for Television. An organization that produces news and public affairs programming for public television stations.

NPC □ Nonphased color. □ National Press Club.

NPITI National Project for the Improvement of Televised Instruction.

NPPA National Press Photographers Association.

NPPAG National Program Production and Acquisition Grant.

NPR National Public Radio.

npr Night press rate. Formerly, the less expensive rate charged by telegraph companies for sending news. Cf. dpr.

NPRC National Opinion Research Center.

NPRM Notice of Proposed Rulemaking.

NPWC National Press Women's Club.

NQRC National Quadraphonic Radio Committee. A standards committee organized by the EIA to study the feasibility of quadraphonic radio. Similar in operation to the former NSRC committee.

NR □ Nonresponse. □ Next to reading matter. Same as NRM. □ Not required.

nr An abbreviation for *number.*

NRB National Religious Broadcasters, Inc. An international association of Christian broadcasters. Now ICB.

NRBA National Radio Broadcasters Association.

NRC □ National Radio Conference. □ National Research Council.

NRI National Research Institute. An audience research organization.

NRM Next to reading matter. Same as NR.

NRP Net rating points.

NRSC National Radio Systems Committee.

NS □ No sound. A script notation. □ Nanosecond. □ New series. □ Noise suppressor (radio).

NSA □ Nashville Songwriters Association, The. An organization for the advancement of the songwriting profession. □ National Standards Association.

NSD No significant difference.

nsec An abbreviation for *nanosecond.*

NSF National Science Foundation.

NSI Nielsen Station Index rating. A local market rating service offered by the A. C. Nielsen Company.

NSI area A group of counties including the Metro or central area of a given market, plus additional counties to encompass approximately 95 percent of the average quarter-hour audience to the stations in that market. This is not a reported area but constitutes that area that must be sampled each time a given market is measured and reported. It is not a basis for calculating station total audiences.

NSI Plus A computerized special analysis service for clients of Nielsen Station Index. Provides such studies as audience flow, reach and frequency, audience duplication, and exclusive viewing using standard or specially tailored geography.

NSPA National Scholastic Press Association.

NSRC National Stereophonic Radio Committee. A temporary committee organized by the EIA to study the feasibility of FM stereo. Cf. NQRC.

NSS Nonsynchronous switch.

NSSC National Society for the Study of Communication.

NSTP National Society of TV Producers.

NTA □ National Telefilm Associates, Inc. □ National Translator Association. □ Nielsen Television Areas. U.S. market areas established by the A. C. Nielsen Company.

NTC Network Transmission Committee.

NTC-7 The standards set by the Network Transmission Committee of the VITEAC for video transmission.

NTFC National Television Film Council.

Nth name selection A fractional unit that is repeated in sampling a mailing list. For example, in an "every 10th" sample, you would select the 1st, 11th, 21st, and so on, records after you selected the starting point at random.

NTI Nielsen Television Index. A network rating made by the A. C. Nielsen Company.

NTIA National Telecommunications and Information Administration.

NTI rating In general, the percent of U.S. television households tuned to the average minute of a network program during a given telecast, as reported by Nielsen Television Index.

NTIS National Technical Information Service. A service of the National Bureau of Standards, Department of Commerce.

NTSC National Television Systems Committee.

NTSC-M The U.S. standard of television transmission; 525 lines and 30 frames per second.

NTSC signal The National Television System Committee signal of 3.58 mHz that is varied with the hue and saturation of the color.

NTSC triangle A diagram showing the phosphor colors used in television.

nudie *See* skin flick.

null □ Relating to zero. □ The absence of information. □ The state of a receiver when no reception is taking place. □ Having no legal force. □ A place on the radio dial where no signal is received.

null instruction A computer instruction to do nothing.

null modem A cable that joins two computers as if they were connected through a modem.

num An abbreviation for *number* and *numeric.*

number □ A relatively brief act or sketch, often involving music. □ A musical selection.

number board A display containing the film title, scene number, take number, and so on, photographed at the beginning of a take. Also called a *take board. See also* clapstick.

numbering machine A device used to print edge numbers on film stock at regular intervals.

numbers Usually referred to as "The Numbers," the all-important radio and television ratings.

numeric display A digital indicator that displays relevant numbers on a tape recorder, memory system, computer screen, and so on.

numeric keypad *See* keypad.

nut □ *See* en. □ The total cost of a radio or television program, production, or sponsorship.

NUTN National University Teleconference Network.

nut quad *See* en quad.

nuts and bolts film A slang term for an educational how-to-do-it film or tape.

nutted Type indented one en. Cf. mutted.

nV Nanovolt.

NVC Nonverbal communication.

NVRAM Nonvolatile RAM.

NWG National wire gauge.

NWIO New World Information Order.

NWS National Weather Service.

NY No year (listed).

nybble *See* nibble.

NYP Not yet published.

O

O □ Octal. □ Octavo. □ Ohm. □ Output. □ Other programs.

OAAA Outdoor Advertising Association of America, Inc.

OACI Organization de l'Aviation Civile Internationale. Also abbreviated *ICAO.* An intergovernmental organization.

OANA Organization of Asian News Agencies.

O&O Owned and operated. The major market radio and television stations that are owned and operated by the networks.

OASD/PA Office of the Assistant Secretary of Defense/Public Affairs.

OAT On air test.

oater A slang term for a western. Also called a *horse opera.*

OB □ Outside broadcast. □ Output buffer.

OBC Outside back cover (of a book).

obie A small eye-light.

obit An abbreviation for *obituary.*

obiter dictum A judicial remark or opinion that is not essential to the decision in the case. The plural is *obiter dicta.*

obituary □ A death notice printed in a newspaper. □ Biographical information about a well-known person kept in a news file.

object An inanimate body that is used in a scene or shot. Cf. subject.

object animation An animation technique, similar to puppet animation, in which objects are made to appear to move by manipulating them slightly before each exposure. In this technique, the object animated retains its identity and is recognizable as itself.

objective News stories written in an impersonal style and point of view. Cf. subjective.

objective camera The use of a camera to show action as it would be seen by the eyes of a viewer. Cf. subjective camera.

objective lens Any light-collecting lens.

objective reporting *See* objective.

objective research *See* quantitative research.

objective time The passage of time as presented by objective camera shots and scenes. Cf. expanded time, experienced time, and screen time.

objectivity That lack of distortion, prejudice, or bias a news reporter or critic strives for but never quite achieves.

obligatory That scene in a play or script demanded by the writer's promise of a confrontation.

obligatory scene □ A scene demanded by an audience because of implied or suggested action or dialogue earlier in the production. □ The scenes that are included in motion pictures because of audiences' desires, not scenes demanded by the script. Such scenes include nudity, violence, or gratuitous sex.

oblique □ A camera shot taken from a tilted position. □ A sans serif typeface that slants to the right. Cf. italic.

oblong An elongated book, sheet of paper, or picture.

obscene language A yet to be satisfactorily defined term. Title 18 of the United States Code, Section 1464 reads: "Whoever utters any obscene, indecent or profane language by means of radio communication shall be fined not more than $10,000 or imprisoned not more than two years, or both."

obscenity Material unprotected by the First Amendment that appeals to prurient interest, or patently offensive works of sexual conduct, and material that lacks serious literary, artistic, political, or scientific value. *See also* SLAPS test.

obstacle effect The absorption or reflection of sound by objects that have dimensions larger than the wavelengths of the sound striking them.

obstruction light An aviation red tower light used to mark antenna structures.

obtained score The actual percentage of respondents who prove recall of a printed advertisement; the term is that of Gallup and Robinson.

OC □ On camera. □ An abbreviation for the Latin term *opere citato,* meaning "in the place cited." □ Order canceled. □ Outcue.

OCB Operations Coordinating Board. A U.S. government board for coordinating national security matters.

occasion A radio or television time interval intended or used for a commercial announcement.

Occupational Safety and Health Act The federal statute that created the Occupational Safety and Health Administration (OSHA).

Occupational Safety and Health Administration (OSHA) The administrative agency charged with establishing standards and regulations to protect workers from unsafe working conditions.

occupied bandwidth The width of a frequency band such that, below the lower and above the upper frequency limits, the mean powers emitted are each equal to a specified percentage Beta/2 of the total mean power of a given emission. The value of Beta/2 is normally 0.5 percent.

OCDM Office of Civil Defense Mobilization. Now OEP.

OCR □ Optical character recognition. □ Optical character reader.

OCST Office of Cable Signal Theft.

oct An abbreviation for *octal* and *octavo.*

octal Referring to the numbers 0 through 7 in the base 8 system.

octave The interval between two sounds or frequencies having a ratio of two to one. For example, the note A above middle C is 440 Hz; the next higher A is 880 Hz.

octavo The size of a sheet of paper folded into eight leaves. Abbreviated *8vo.*

octopus A box containing a number of electrical connectors or wires.

OD Optical density.

odd-line interlace *See* interlaced scanning.

oddment □ The extra pages (not divisible by 16 or 32) in a book that are not included in sections. □ Separate parts of a book, other than text.

odd parity *See* parity.

ODM Office of Defense Mobilization. Now OEP.

OEC Office of Emergency Communications of the FCC.

OEM Original equipment manufacturer.

OEP Office of Emergency Planning. A U.S. government agency.

oersted The CGS unit of magnetizing force (symbol H), equal to a magnetomotive force of 1 gilbert acting over a length of 1 cm. Named after Hans C. Oersted, a Danish physicist.

OFC Outside front cover (of a book).

OFF Organization for Femininity. A citizens' group. Cf. NOW and WWWW.

off *See* offstage.

off air □ A television program that a viewer receives by an antenna as opposed to one received by cable or other means. □ A broadcast that is taped for later playback.

off beam A performer working a microphone outside the optimum angle of acceptance of sound.

offcamera □ Action that occurs out-of-sight. Also called *off scene.* □ *See* voiceover.

offcamera announcer An announcer whose voice is heard but who does not appear on camera. Cf. off screen announcer.

off card A special rate not shown on a radio or television rate card.

off center zoom A zoom in that is combined with a pan or tilt.

offcut The part of printed pages or sheets that is trimmed off to reduce them to the proper size.

offer □ An invitation to carry a specific radio or television program made by a network to an unaffiliated station. *See also* acceptance. □ The terms under which a specific mail order product or service is promoted. □ Any premium or prize an audience may compete for or receive by submitting labels, facsimiles, and so on.

office correction A change made in copy after it has been set, usually because of a mistake.

Office of Administrative Law Judges The FCC office concerned with conducting adjudicatory cases.

Office of Cable Signal Theft (OCST) A division of the National Cable Television Association. It works for the passage of laws to prevent the sale and use of illegal pirating equipment.

Office of Chief Engineer The FCC office concerned with planning and advising the Commission in technical matters.

Office of Executive Director The FCC office concerned with the coordination of staff activities.

Office of General Counsel The FCC office concerned with advising and representing the Commission in matters of litigation, legislation, and other legal functions.

Office of Management and Budget (OMB) The federal government office that oversees and controls the administration of the federal budget. Formerly, the Bureau of the Budget.

Office of Opinions and Review The FCC office concerned with assisting with and making recommendations to the Commission and individual Commissioners in matters relating to adjudicatory cases.

Office of Plans and Policy The FCC office concerned with advising and recommending communication policies to the Commission.

Office of Telecommunications Policy An office of the federal executive branch to which is delegated the responsibility of advising the president on communication policies, spectrum management, FCC matters, and so on.

off its feet Type that does not rest evenly on its base and thus makes a poor impression on the paper.

off line □ Devices that are not under the control of the CPU of a computer. Cf. on line. □ *See* off line editing.

off line editing □ Videotape editing that is accomplished in order to produce an edit decision list. This type of editing is not meant to produce a final finished master. □ A technique of dubbing quad tapes to helical scan recorders for logging frame pulses by specific frame numbers. The editing is then accomplished on the quad tapes. Cf. on line editing.

off mike □ A performer working the dead side of a microphone. □ A performer within the optimum angle of sound acceptance, but at a distance from the microphone. Cf. on mike.

off-network program A television program that is no longer on a network and thus available to independent stations and cable television systems.

off-network series A series whose episodes have had a national network television exhibition in the United States or a regional network exhibition in the relevant market.

off-network syndication The use by an independent television station or cable television system of a program series that was originally on network television.

offprint A copy of an article or chapter in a journal, magazine, or book. May be run at the same time as the original work or reprinted later. Cf. reprint.

off register □ The off center changing of an animation compound to produce special effects such as vibrations. □ A printing plate that is not aligned properly and that smears or prints slightly off center. □ The movement, often relatively violent, of a camera to show the effects of an earthquake, explosion, and so on.

off scene *See* off camera.

off screen (OS) *See* off stage.

off screen announcer An announcer in a television program who is heard but not seen. Cf. off camera announcer.

off screen narration *See* voiceover.

off screen sound *See* lip-sync.

offset □ The transfer of ink from one sheet of paper to another; caused by placing sheets together before they are dry. Also called *setoff*. □ *See* photo offset lithography.

offset angle In lateral disc reproduction, the smaller of the two angles between the projections into the plane of the disc of the vibration axis of the pickup stylus and the line connecting the vertical pivot (assuming a horizontal disc) of the pickup arm with the stylus point.

offset lithography *See* photo offset lithography.

offset paper Paper designed for use in offset lithography.

offset printing *See* photo offset lithography.

offset scrapbook A book of camera ready copy in a scrapbook format, reproduced for promotional purposes.

offset sheet *See* slip sheet.

offside An off-color line. *See also* blue.

off stage (OS) A performer or object not within camera range. Also called *off screen.* Cf. on stage.

off the air □ Pertaining to material not broadcast. □ Facilities not used in the process of broadcasting. □ *See* off air. Cf. on the air.

off the cuff A slang term for a performance or speech made without specific preparation. *See also* impromptu.

off the record □ A release of information by a government official with the understanding that the information will not be attributed to the source. Also called a *backgrounder. See also* authoritative source. □ Any statement that is not to be quoted or reported. Cf. news leak and on the record.

OFS Operations fixed service.

O Henry The final speech or tag line of a radio or television program, usually one with a surprise ending. *See also* twist.

ohm (Ω) The basic unit of electrical resistance and reactance.

ohmmeter A device for reading the resistance of a circuit. *See also* multimeter.

Ohm's law A basic law of electricity: The voltage (E) of a circuit is equal to the product of the current (I) and resistance (R).

OIR Organization Internationale de Radio. Now OIRT.

Oirovision The original name of Intervision.

OIRT Organization Internationale de Radio et Télévision (International Radio and Television Organization). Also abbreviated *IBTO.* An Eastern European broadcasting organization, similar in function to the European Broadcasting Union (EBU). The OIRT member nations are affiliated with Intervision, a program exchange service. OIRT was formerly OIR and until 1946 was part of the International Broadcasting Union (IBU).

OIT □ Organization Ibéroamericaine de Télévision. □ Organization International du Travail. Also ILO. An intergovernmental organization.

OK A film shot, take, or sound that is considered acceptable for use. Cf. NG.

OK with corrections Used in signed approvals of art, keyline, or proof material where corrections (usually minor) have been noted as needed.

OL On line.

OLC On line computer.

old cow hand An experienced radio or television station employee.

Old English (OE) A style of black letter type.

old face *See* old style (OS).

oldie A recording that has retained its popularity; often accompanied by nostalgic feelings.

old man The old man. A designation for the person in charge of a newspaper, magazine, broadcast station, and so on.

old style (OS) A class of type, derived from early printers such as Caslon and Garamond, characterized by oblique emphasis and bracketed serifs. Also called *old face.* Cf. modern and transitional.

OLE Office of Library Education (of the American Library Association).

oleo □ A backdrop. □ A show curtain.

olivette An early type of floodlight with a box shaped enclosure and a diffuse painted reflecting surface.

OM Operations manager.

OMB Office of Management and Budget.

ombudsman From the Swedish term for "grievance man." A radio or television station employee who attempts to solve viewers' problems with local government or business firms. Often featured as part of a news program. *See also* action line.

omega wrap A type of videotape format in which the tape covers the drum in a shape similar to the Greek letter omega. Cf. alpha wrap and M wrap.

omni An abbreviation for *omnidirectional.*

omnibus book A book containing articles by a number of authors.

omnibus clause A statute or rule containing general provisions for items not specifically covered.

omnidirectional An electronic device that does not emit or receive signals from any particular direction. Also called *nondirectional.*

omnidirectional microphone A microphone with a 360-degree polar pattern acceptance of sound. Also called a *nondirectional microphone. See also* mike pattern.

omnies Atmospheric words or sounds uttered by anyone in a scene.

Omnimax A trademark name for a system of filming and projection using an even larger screen than Imax.

omni player A player capable of playing CD-DA, LaserVision, and CD-I discs.

OMS Organization Mondiale de la Sante. Also WHO. An intergovernmental organization.

on A performer who is on stage, on the air, on the board, and so on.

ONA Overseas News Agency. An American news agency.

on a daily A performer who is working as a daily player.

on-air *See* over-the-air.

on-air light □ A warning light located outside a radio or television control room or studio indicating that a program is being broadcast or taped. □ *See* tally light.

on air test (OAT) A test of a commercial or program that uses a real broadcast of the test material on radio or television as the stimulus for a measurable audience response, such as recall, attitude or purchase interest change, interest, or audience size.

on approval *See* approval plan.

on approval copy A textbook sent by a publisher to a college instructor for possible adoption. The copy must be returned or paid for if the textbook is not adopted.

on approval plan *See* approval plan.

on a roll A slang term for a performer, director, writer, and so on, who has had several successes in a row.

on board Additional or supporting functions incorporated into a printed circuit board or within the housing of equipment.

on call A television or film performer or crew member who has been hired and is awaiting orders to report for work.

on camera (OC) The talent or object being shot by an on-the-air camera. Also called *in vision.*

on camera narration A narration that takes place with the narrator seen on camera; usually in lip-sync. Cf. voiceover.

on consignment Books, magazines, and so on, shipped to a dealer with the understanding that they need not be paid for until sold.

on demand A publication printed to order. Also called *on request.*

one act A play that has only one act, as opposed to the usual three-act play.

one and one An instruction to a musical group to play one verse and one chorus.

one and two An instruction to a musical group to play one verse and two choruses.

one hundred eighty degree rule *See* imaginary line.

one K *See* ace.

one light printing The printing of ungraded film dailies using a single light setting.

one liner A joke, retort, or witty remark made in few words. Also called a *zinger.*

one nighter *See* one shot.

one on one A news interview between a reporter and an interviewee.

one percent TALO rule An Arbitron radio procedure that establishes a cut-off point for resolving conflicts over listening credit through ascription. In order to be included in the ascription process, a station must have received at least one percent of the total number of in-tab diary mentions in a given county during the previous available year. TALO is the total number of in-tab diary mentions, for all stations combined, in each county during that preceding year.

one reeler A short motion picture, usually not more than approximately ten minutes.

one-sheet *See* sheet.

one sheet □ A motion picture theatre poster of current or coming attractions. □ A single page resume.

one sheet poster An outdoor poster consisting of a single sheet 28 inches by 42 inches or 30 inches by 46 inches used especially on subway and railroad station platforms.

one shot □ A radio or television program scheduled for one broadcast. Also called *OTO.* □ A radio or television program that is not part of a series. Also called a *one nighter* and *one spot.* □ A noncontinuing guest appearance on a radio or television program. □ A film developer that is used one time and then discarded. □ *See* single. □ A magazine that is issued only once.

one-shot color camera A special camera in which three-color separation negatives may be made with a single exposure.

one spot *See* one shot.

one step recording An inexpensive method of disc recording. Cf. two step recording.

ones, twos, threes The number of motion picture frames to be exposed for each animation drawing.

one take A program or scene that is done correctly the first time.

one-time buyer A mail order purchaser who has not ordered a second time from a given company.

one-time rate The basic cost for a single advertisement; one that does not earn a frequency discount. Also called a *basic rate, open rate,* and *transient rate.*

one-time use An intrinsic part of the normal mail order list usage, list reproduction, or list exchange agreement in which it is understood that the mailer will not use the names on the list more than one time without specific prior approval of the list owner.

one-to-a-market rule Another name for the *duopoly rule.*

one to one □ A photographic copy that is neither enlarged or reduced. □ A sound recording that is reproduced without change.

one way screen A halftone screen with lines running in one direction only, instead of the customary two.

on film animation Animation accomplished by drawing or painting directly on film stock.

on hold □ A television or film production that has been temporarily discontinued. □ A performer who has worked on a production but is awaiting further reporting orders.

onionskin A thin paper used for carbon copies.

onlay *See* inlaid binding.

on line Any data processing system in which the operator is in control of the application running on a computer system. Cf. off line.

on line editing □ Manuscript editing that takes place at a computer terminal. □ Videotape editing that is accomplished to produce a master tape. Cf. off line editing.

on location A motion picture or television cast and crew that film or tape a production away from the studio.

on mike A performer who is within the beam of maximum sound acceptance of a microphone. Cf. off mike.

on-off switch *See* power switch.

on ones, twos, or threes In animation, refers to the number of frames each drawing is held during filming. The smoothest animation is done on ones and twos, which means 24 or 12 drawings are used per second of screen time. Animating on threes will work for some movements; if the drawings are held for more than three frames, the movements will appear jerky or stiff.

on order A network affiliate that has been ordered by an advertiser but that has not yet cleared the time.

on request *See* on demand.

on screen sound Sound that appears to come from a projected image as opposed to voiceover sound.

on spec □ A television pilot made without a network or premium cable channel commitment to air the program. □ A motion picture made without a commitment for distribution. Also called *on speculation* and *shoot on spec.* □ Photography, artwork, advertising campaigns, and so on, that are made without a contract but with some expectation that an agreement to use the material will be reached.

on speculation *See* on spec.

on stage A performer or object within camera range. Cf. off stage.

on the air □ The period of a radio or television program transmission. □ A performer who is on camera or on mike. □ Pertaining to material that is broadcast. □ Facilities that are used in the process of broadcasting. *See also* over the air. Cf. off the air.

on the beach A slang term for an unemployed performer. *See also* at liberty.

on the board The radio or television station employee on duty at a control console.

on the button *See* on the nose.

on the cuff To perform without pay.

on the fly The setting of edit points or timing while a videotape is moving.

on the head □ A radio or television program that begins or ends exactly on time.

□ A radio or television program that is running exactly on time. Also called *on the money* or *on the nose.*

on the line The picture that is being telecast or taped.

on the log An entry made in the program, operating, or maintenance log.

on the money *See* on the head.

on the nose □ A visual signal for correct. Also called *on the button.* □ *See* on the head.

on the record A statement that may be quoted or reported. Cf. off the record.

on the run A late insertion into a press run that has already begun.

on the shelf A completed production. Also called *in the can.*

ONU Organization des Nations Unis. Also UN.

OOP □ Out of pocket. □ Out of print. Also OP.

OOT Out of town.

OOV Out of vision. A British term for a voiceover.

ooze leather A soft calfskin or sheepskin used in bookbinding.

OP Out of print. Also OOP.

opacity The property of paper that determines whether print from one side will show through to the other. The opposite of transparency.

opal glass *See* milk glass.

opaque □ To touch up a negative to remove spots, defects, and so on. Also called *opaquing.* □ A material that does not transmit light. Cf. translucent.

opaque leader Film leader that is opaque.

opaque projector A device that will project an image of opaque material such as a printed page. Cf. overhead projector.

opaquer The artist who applies the opaque colors to animation cels. *See also* painter.

opaquing □ Another term for cel painting, used primarily in the eastern United States; a painter is referred to as an opaquer. □ *See* opaque.

Op.Att'y Gen. Opinions of the Attorney General. The official government reporter published by the Government Printing Office.

OPC Overseas Press Club of America.

op cit Latin for "in the work cited."

op ed Opposite editorial. The page facing the editorial page in a newspaper. Sometimes called *page opposite.*

open □ The beginning of a broadcast program. □ A computer command requesting that a file be displayed on the screen. □ Artwork or page make-up that has a large amount of white space. □ A book with separate leaves. □ *See* outline. □ To begin a theatrical run; a premiere. □ A style of punctuation characterized by as few punctuation marks as possible. □ A standard open. □ *See* open circuit. □ *See* loose.

open account A mail order customer record that, at a specific point in time, reflects an unpaid balance for goods and services ordered, without delinquency.

open architecture A device that is designed to accept components in addition to those originally furnished, such as extra slots in a computer. Cf. closed architecture.

open back A book binding that is not firmly attached to the back. Also called *looseback.* Cf. tight back.

open call The notification of a nonrestricted talent tryout or audition.

open circuit □ An incomplete path for current flow. □ Programming that is broadcast, as opposed to closed circuit.

open cold To begin without rehearsal. *See also* cold.

open end □ A recorded commercial that has time left at the end for a tag. □ A radio or television program that has no specified time to end. □ A program furnished to a station with time left for the local insertion of commercials. □ A story or screenplay without a definitive conclusion. □ A series of books published in which the number of volumes is not designated. Cf. closed end.

open-end diary A diary that does not list specific time segments. Cf. closed-end diary.

open-end edit A videotape edit that contains an in point but no designated out point.

open-end question A question for which the possible answers are not prelisted on a questionnaire or schedule, and that therefore does not restrict the respondent to any fixed set of answers. Also called a *free-response question.* Cf. fixed-alternative question.

opener A news story lead.

open face A category of display type that has open letters defined with strokes of uneven thickness that give a three-dimensional effect. Cf. in-line and outline.

open form A technique of camera framing that purposefully cuts off part of the action.

open house A hospitality event wherein guests are invited to observe the operation of a newspaper, broadcast station, equipment manufacturer, and so on.

opening □ The first sounds or pictures of a broadcast program. □ The first performance of a motion picture or theatrical production. Also called a *premiere.* □ Any two facing pages in a book.

opening billboard *See* opening credits.

opening credits The credits that appear at the beginning of a motion picture or television program. Also called an *opening billboard.* Cf. closing credits.

opening night The first performance of a production.

opening shot The first camera shot used in a production. Cf. closing shot.

open left A director's command to a camera operator to place the subject or object at the extreme left of the picture.

open meeting laws The federal and state laws that require meetings of government agencies to be held open to the public. *See also* Government in the Sunshine Act.

open mike □ A microphone that is left on during a taping or broadcast. □ A radio or television director's command to turn on a microphone.

open negotiation A negotiation between a broadcast station or station representative and a buyer in which they ultimately agree on a price for an advertising campaign at a specified rating. Cf. closed negotiation.

open rate *See* one-time rate.

open records law A law that guarantees access to public records not specifically exempted by law.

open reel *See* reel to reel machine.

open reel machine An audio- or videotape machine whose transport design accepts tape on reels only, in contrast to a cassette or cartridge machine.

open right A director's command to a cameraman to place the subject or object at the extreme right of the picture.

open shelf Library shelves that allow unrestricted access to users. Cf. closed shelf.

open shop A business in which eligibility for employment is not governed by membership or nonmembership in a union. Cf. closed shop.

open space Outdoor advertising availabilities; poster or bulletin space not under contract and for sale.

open spacing Type that is set loosely; not crowded.

open track A track on a multitrack audio recorder that does not contain any sound.

open university A system wherein students may receive college or university credit for classes conducted on television.

open up To increase the aperture opening of a lens.

operating instructions The step-by-step procedures outlined in a device's manual that describe how to make the device function.

operating level In general, an audio signal amplitude suitable for recording or playback, especially a signal amplitude previously standardized or agreed on.

operating log One of the logs required of stations by the FCC. The operating log records the time a station begins to supply power to the antenna, notations of EBS tests, plate voltage and current, antenna current, and so on. *See also* maintenance log and program log.

operating permit The authorization received to construct and operate a cable television system.

operating power Depending on the context within which it is employed, the term may be synonymous with *nominal power* or *antenna power.*

operating sheet *See* program log.

operating side The side of a web press where the controls are located. Cf. drive side.

operating system (OS) Routines that run the functions of a computer and its peripheral devices. MS-DOS, ProDos, CP/M, UNIX, and OS/2 are typical mini- and microcomputer operating systems. *See also* disk operating system (DOS).

operation A defined action that a computer carries out by a programmed instruction.

operational (local) area A geographical area that encompasses a number of contiguous communities, as determined by the State Industry Advisory Committee (SIAC) and as shown in the State EBS Operational Plan.

operational communications Communications related to the technical operation of a broadcast station and its auxiliaries, other than the transmission of program material and cues and orders directly concerned therewith.

operational cost Those approved costs incurred in the operation of an entity or station, such as overhead, labor, material, contracted services, and including capital outlay and debt service.

operational station A station authorized and operating as of June 10 (with respect to programs beginning October 1) or as of December 10 (with respect to programs beginning April 1), or a station authorized and that gives notice to the FCC by such June 10 or December 10 date that it will be on the air by such October 1 or April 1 date, and commits itself to remain on the air for six months after such October 1 or April 1 date.

operation prime time (OPT) A group of television stations that carries a number of prime time miniseries.

operations □ A station or network department concerned with scheduling and sometimes personnel. □ The function of scheduling programs and personnel.

operations fixed service (OFS) A microwave service used by private businesses.

operations manager (OM) □ An individual who schedules and coordinates production facilities for a radio or television station. □ A newspaper employee who supervises customer accounts, circulation accounting, office record keeping, and so on. □ An individual who is responsible for all production aspects of a printing company.

operations research (OR) The application of such mathematical methods as models to a system of variables, to project probable changes in the system resulting from changes in one or more variables.

operator □ A person assigned to perform a specific task or function, such as a camera operator or board operator. □ The owner of a cable television system.

operator error A mistake usually caused by an operator's failure to follow defined procedures.

opinion □ The overt expression of an attitude. □ The statement of a court giving the reasons for a decision. *See also* concurring opinion and dissent.

opinion leader Any person who is exposed to the media and directly or indirectly influences the attitudes or opinions of others.

opinion meter *See* program analyzer.

opinion research Research that concentrates on the opinions of respondents rather than on facts.

OPP □ Office of Plans and Policy (of the FCC). □ Out of print at present.

opportunity of exposure The amount of reasonable expectation that an advertisement will be seen or heard.

opposing viewpoint *See* Fairness Doctrine.

opposition The competition; usually said of newspapers.

OPS Out of print, searching.

OPT Operation Prime Time.

opt An abbreviation for *optical.*

optical *See* optical soundtrack.

optical alignment *See* optical spacing.

optical answer print A print of a film in which all color corrections and optical effects have been incorporated; used to obtain final approvals of a production.

optical axis The line through the center of an optical system such as a camera or projection lens.

optical center The center of a page as it appears to the eye; approximately five-eighths above the bottom of the page.

optical centering *See* optical framing.

optical character reader (OCR) A device that uses optical character recognition to feed information into a computer. Also called an *optical reader* and *reader.*

optical character recognition (OCR) A process in which photosensitive devices are used to analyze the light patterns of printed characters.

optical code reader *See* reader.

optical communication *See* fiber optics.

optical digital disc An optical disc on which information is stored digitally.

optical disc A disc on which information is impressed as a series of pits in a flat surface and is read out by optical means such as a laser.

optical effects □ A general term for film image modifications, such as fades and dissolves, accomplished in the laboratory, usually by means of an optical printer. Also called *opticals*. □ Television visual effects, such as fades, wipes, and superimpositions, accomplished either on line or off line. *See also* special effects.

optical fiber conductor *See* fiber optics.

optical filter The glass in front of a television picture tube used to prevent reflections.

optical framing A method of centering motion picture film in a projector gate mask without changing the position of the picture on the screen. Also called *optical centering*.

optical glass A fine quality flint or crown glass made for lenses.

optical house A laboratory that specializes in producing special effects for film.

optical input In optical media, the light signal before it is converted into an electrical signal.

optical lens *See* lens.

optical maser *See* laser.

optical master A motion picture film used to make release prints.

optical medium A medium employing optics for the storage and distribution of information.

optical mix The combining of videotape A and B rolls into a finished product.

optical negative *See* negative.

optical outrider A device for prompting talent. *See also* telecuer.

optical pattern A light pattern that can be observed when the surface of a recorded disc is illuminated radially by a collimated parallel beam of light. The outline of the envelope or pattern is the function of the maximum modulation slope or recorded stylus velocity inscribed in the groove wall. Also called a *light pattern*.

optical print *See* answer print.

optical printer A device that combines the functions of a film camera and a projector. Used to make optical and special effects, make reduction prints, and so on. Cf. contact printer.

optical printing The process of transferring the image contained on one piece of film to another by projection. Also called *enlargement printing* and *projection printing*. Cf. contact printing.

optical reader *See* optical character reader.

optical recorder Any device that is capable of recording information on a film's optical soundtrack. Also called *optical sound recorder*. Cf. magnetic recorder.

optical recording □ The process of recording sound on film in which the sound is converted into modulated light. *See also* variable area and variable density. Also called *optical sound* and *optical sound recording*. Cf. magnetic recording. □ The recording of information in such a way that it can be read by a beam of light.

optical reduction The process of reducing the size of film prints using an optical printer.

optical scanner A visual scanning device used to generate a digital representation of written data such as a typeset page.

optical scanning The process of using various optical techniques to interpret printed information for input to a computer system.

optical sound *See* optical recording.

optical sound head A device used to convert optical sound on film to electronic signals.

optical sound recorder *See* optical recorder.

optical sound recording *See* optical recording.

optical soundtrack A soundtrack in which the changes in the pitch and volume of the sound are recorded as optical variations along the edge of a motion picture film. Also called *optical* and *optical track*. Cf. magnetic soundtrack.

optical spacing The spacing of type characters to present a more pleasing appearance on a page. Also called *optical alignment*. Cf. mechanical spacing.

optical storage The storage of information in such a way that it can be read using optics. Characterized by very high storage density, such as that used in audio compact discs and optical videodiscs.

optical system The lens systems used in cameras or projectors.

optical technology Technology based on the use of optical effects for the transmission and storage of information.

optical track *See* optical soundtrack.

optical transfer The dubbing of a tape or magnetic stripe to optical sound.

optical type font A type font that can be read by an optical scanner as well as by the human eye.

optical viewfinder *See* viewfinder.

optical waveguide A medium constructed of glass fibers.

optical wedge *See* step wedge.

optical weight The visual impact that a page makes on a reader or viewer.

optical window A portion of a television picture containing a second or alternate message; often used in a commercial.

optics The branch of science concerned with electromagnetic radiation of light.

optimization The design or modification of a system to allow it to perform with maximum efficiency.

optimum format The format of a book, magazine, newspaper, and so on, that is most legible and pleasing to the reader.

optimum line length The length of a printed line that is the easiest for a reader to comprehend.

optimum working frequency (FOT) The highest frequency that is returned by ionospheric radio propagation to the surface of the earth for a particular path and time of day for 90 percent of the days of the reference month.

option □ A contract in which one party is given the rights, for a specified time period, to a literary property, motion picture proposal, television series, and so on, for the payment of a fee. □ The opportunity for first refusal granted by an author to a publisher. □ The rights granted to a publisher by another publisher for reprint or foreign rights.

optional *See* grape.

optional cut A predetermined portion of a script that may be eliminated if the radio or television program is running over its allotted time. *See also* provisional cut.

option time □ Any contract, arrangement, or understanding—express or implied—between a radio or television station and a network organization that prevents or hinders the station from scheduling programs before the network agrees to use the time during which such programs are scheduled, or that requires the station to clear time already scheduled when the network organization seeks to use the time. □ That portion of the day during which, by contract between a network and affiliated station, one or the other may exercise control over programming.

optoelectronics The science of coupling electronic circuits by the use of light waves.

opus The singular of *opera.* A single script or musical composition.

Oracle Optical Reception of Announcements by Coded Line Electronics. The teletext system of the British Independent Television Authority.

oral argument A presentation before a court in which each litigant argues the merits of his or her case.

ORBIS Orbiting Radio Beacon Ionosphere Satellite.

orbit □ A method of scheduling commercials in a variety of programs or time periods to reach the greatest number of different members of the audience. □ The circular or elliptical path followed by a satellite. Also called an *orbit path* and *satellite orbit.*

orbital position The fixed point above the earth in which a geostationary satellite is located. Also called an *orbital slot.*

orbital slot *See* orbital position.

orbiter A device used on old image orthicon cameras to automatically move the mechanism so that the picture would not burn in on the face of the tubes.

orbit path *See* orbit.

orchestration A director's arrangement of script elements—blocking, pauses, tempo, emphasis, and so on—to give the program life.

order □ The whole or a part of a final disposition, whether affirmative, negative, injunctive, or declaratory in form, of an agency in a matter other than rule making but including licensing. □ To arrange elements, data, numerals, and so on, in a sequence.

order blank envelope An order form printed on one side of a sheet with a mailing address on the reverse. The recipient simply fills in the order, folds the form, and seals it like an envelope.

order card A reply card used to initiate an order by mail.

order edit The checking of a customer's orders to determine whether they are being properly handled.

order form A printed form on which a customer can provide information to initiate an order by mail. Designed to be mailed in an envelope.

order letter A preliminary letter of agreement, sent by a buyer, between an advertising buyer and a communication medium specifying the terms of purchase of advertising space or time.

order wire A telephone company line used for remote communication.

ordinance A law or regulation enacted by a local government. Cf. law and regulation.

organ ☐ A slang term for a lighting control console. ☐ An in-house publication.

organization The logical progression of a script brought about by unity, simplicity, clarity, transition, coherence, emphasis, and so on.

organizational chart A line drawing, usually with boxes, showing how people or departments within a company relate to each other.

Oriental Missionary Society, The A religious broadcasting organization.

orientation shot An establishing shot.

orig An abbreviation for *original*.

original ☐ A camera negative. ☐ An unedited audio- or videotape recording. *See also* first generation. ☐ The first recording of a film, tape, soundtrack, and so on, as opposed to a dub or duplicate. ☐ A script written for motion pictures, radio, or television, as opposed to one that has been adapted from another medium. ☐ A camera negative. ☐ Not copied or reproduced. ☐ Camera ready copy. ☐ The covering used on books as first released.

original binding The covering used on books as first released; original boards, cloth, wrappers, and so on.

original color negative The color negative film that is exposed in a camera.

original color positive A color positive reversal film that is exposed in a camera.

original equipment manufacturer (OEM) ☐ A company that supplies nonlabeled products to other companies for marketing under their own names. ☐ The primary manufacturer of devices or components as compared to a manufacturer who makes copies or replacement parts.

original film *See* camera original.

original jurisdiction The first court to hear a case initially, as compared to an appellate court. Although the Supreme Court is an appellate court, it has both original and appellate jurisdiction. Cf. appellate jurisdiction.

original lacquer An original disc recording used to produce a master.

original license A license granted by the FCC on completion of the terms, conditions, and obligations of a construction permit.

original master *See* master.

original picture negative A black and white negative film that is exposed in a camera.

original purchase unit An actual purchase or subscription to a periodical. Used in readership surveys.

original sample The estimated number of households originally drawn for a survey.

original screenplay *See* original.

original sound negative The initial sound recording that is exposed in a film recorder.

original syndication A showing of syndicated television programs that have not been on network television first.

original treatment An original story written for motion picture purposes in a form suitable for use as the basis of a screenplay. *See also* treatment.

originate ☐ To develop a script or program idea. ☐ To feed a radio or television program to another station or stations.

originating organization A person or legal entity that decides what programs a satellite will carry.

origination The point from which a program is fed, either by a network or a station. Also called an *origination point*.

origination cablecasting Programming, exclusive of broadcast signals, carried on a cable television system over one or more channels and subject to the exclusive control of the cable operator.

origination point *See* origination.

ornament A decorative design or character used in printing.

ornamental A decorative type face. Also called a *novelty.*

orphan An isolated line of type left at the bottom of a page; often the first line of a paragraph that is continued on the next page. Cf. widow.

ORTF Office de Radiodiffusion-Télévision Française. A French national broadcasting organization.

orthicon A storage camera tube developed in 1939 in which a low-velocity electron beam is used to scan a photosensitive mosaic. Also called *orth* and *orthiconoscope. See also* pickup tube.

orthiconoscope *See* orthicon.

orthochromatic A film stock that is sensitive to the blue and green regions of the visible spectrum. Cf. panchromatic.

orthopanchromatic A film stock that is sensitive to all the colors of the visible spectrum, but with little variation in the red region.

OS □ Off screen. □ Off stage. □ Old style (type). □ Over-the-shoulder. □ Out of stock. □ Operating system.

OSC Out of stock, canceled (book orders).

Oscar The statuette awarded by the Academy of Motion Pictures Arts and Sciences yearly to the best actor, best actress, best director, and so on, in motion pictures.

Oscars in Agriculture An award given by DeKalb Agresearch, Inc. for "superior contributions furthering the advancement of American Agriculture."

oscillation A regular vibration at an audio or radio frequency.

oscillator A device used to produce an alternating signal at a particular frequency.

oscillograph A device used to graphically portray the instantaneous values of varying electrical quantities.

oscilloscope A device using a cathode ray tube for the visual display of electrical quantities. *See also* waveform monitor.

OSF Out of stock, to follow (books).

OSHA Occupational Safety and Health Administration.

OSI Out of stock, indefinitely (books).

OS-9 The real-time operating system that forms the basis for the CD-I operating system, CD-RTOS.

OST Out of stock, temporarily (books).

OT Office of Telecommunications of the Department of Commerce.

other programming service Information that a cable operator makes available to all subscribers generally. *See also* cable service.

other programs Radio and television programs not falling in the FCC program type categories A, E, N, PA, R, I, or S.

OTO One time only. *See* one shot.

OTP Office of Telecommunications Policy.

OTS Orbital test satellite.

out □ A script mark used to indicate the end of an action, sound, picture, and so on. □ A sound or picture that is no longer heard or seen. □ A book that is not available from a library; a book in circulation. □ A book or other publication that is available; newly published. □ Type matter inadvertently omitted in printing. □ An abbreviation for *output.*

outact To surpass another performer in the same production.

outcue □ A script or verbal cue that a film or tape is about to end. □ The last few words of a soundbite. Used to cue an announcer, director, and so on. Cf. incue.

outdated Material, such as news, that can no longer be used because of incorrect time references.

outdoor advertising Posters, painted displays, spectaculars, billboards, and other display advertising placed along highways, on walls, roofs, and so on. Cf. transit advertising.

Outdoor Advertising Association of America, Inc. (OAAA) The trade association of the outdoor business, founded in 1891, that monitors the activities of the Congress and federal agencies and reports to members so that policies can be developed by the members of the association.

outdoor advertising company A firm that specializes in building and maintaining outdoor advertising space on a national and local basis.

outdoor film Color film that is balanced for exposure by daylight, approximately 5600 degrees Kelvin. Cf. indoor film.

outdoor plant *See* plant.

outdoor service The maintenance and repair of outdoor advertising structures.

outdoor space buyer An advertising agency employee who is responsible for buying outdoor advertising space.

out edit □ In an insert edit, that point in the program where the inserted material ends and the original program reappears. Cf. in edit. □ The program material in the vicinity of such a point. □ The tape time at which such a point occurs.

outer form The printing form that contains the first and last pages. Also called an *outside form.*

Outer Space Treaty, The The 1967 treaty, signed in Washington, London, and Moscow that called for international cooperation in the peaceful exploration and use of outer space for the benefit of all people.

outflow The portion of the audience that changes channels at the conclusion of a television program. Cf. inflow.

outgoing Outdoor advertising poster panels or bulletins that expose the advertiser's message to traffic leaving the central business district of a town or market. The term has lost considerable meaning due to urbanization of many cities into complexes of adjacent urban areas.

outgrade To eliminate a performer from a scene or program by editing. Cf. downgrade and upgrade.

out in the alley A performer who is out of range of the microphone or camera.

outlet □ An electrical receptacle. □ A terminal that connects a television receiver to a 75 or 300 ohm tap. □ A network affiliate. □ The market for a commodity.

outline □ A written synopsis for a proposed book, script, story, program, and so on. □ Type that is in the form of an outline; not solid. Also called *open.* □ A sketch without shading. □ *See* silhouette. □ Any display type that has open letters defined with strokes of even thickness. Cf. inline and openface. □ *See* development.

outline cut *See* silhouette.

outlined cut *See* silhouette.

outline halftone *See* silhouette.

outline processor A computer program designed to allow the generation of a logical outline for word processing tasks.

out-of-band emission Emission on a frequency or frequencies immediately outside the necessary bandwidth that results from the modulation process but excludes spurious emissions.

out of character A performer who fails to sustain the role by using actions or speech that are inconsistent with the character.

out of date A piece of equipment, mailing list, program, and so on, that is obsolete or dated.

out of focus A picture that is not sharp; fuzzy.

out of focus dissolve *See* defocus transition.

out of frame □ A performer or object not in view of the camera. □ A film projector showing parts of two frames at the same time.

out of his time A person who has just completed an apprenticeship; a new journeyman.

out-of-home Mass media that are consumed away from home as opposed to in-home consumption, such as in a car, theatre, bookstore, and so on.

out-of-market traffic Traffic originating beyond the area in which an outdoor plant operates.

out of phase Imperfect coordination or nonsynchronous operation between or among two or more components, waves, devices, currents, and so on. Cf. in phase.

out of print (OP) A book that is sold out; no copies remain. Cf. in print.

out of round A roll of newsprint that has become oblong in shape.

out-of-service An outdoor advertising structure temporarily or permanently unavailable for advertising purposes.

out of sorts A set of type in a job case that is missing some characters. *See also* sort.

out of stock (OS) A book that is not available immediately; a temporary condition.

out of sync □ A lack of synchronization between a transmitted and received television picture, usually resulting in a vertical roll. □ A lack of synchronization between sound and picture. Cf. in sync.

out of vision a British term meaning off camera.

out period *See* hiatus.

out point The videotape or film frame selected as the ending point of a scene. Cf. in point.

output □ The voltage, current, or power from a circuit or component. Cf. input. □ The terminals of a piece of equipment or component. □ The program or programming transmitted or taped. □ A visible record of the information contained in a computer file; a printout or screen display. □ Data already processed by a computer. Cf. input.

output converter *See* upconverter.

output device Any device that stores or presents information, such as a printer, loudspeaker, display screen, or disk drive. Cf. input device.

output display processor A DVI processor that produces resolution modes and pixel formats. The resolution capability ranges from 256 to 1024 pixels horizontally and up to 512 pixels vertically. It can also select any one of 16 million colors available in each pixel to produce television-quality pictures on a computer screen.

output file A computer text file containing typesetting and formatting codes as well as the text matter. Cf. input file.

output port An interface used for transferring information out of a computer.

outro A slang term meaning the end of a program. The opposite of intro.

outs *See* outtake.

outside broadcast (OB) A British term for a remote.

outside form *See* outer form.

outside mortise *See* notch.

outside source A program or portion thereof fed from a remote location to a radio or television studio.

outside station Any station that is not classified as "home" to a market but is receivable in a market other than its home market. Superstations (outside of their home market) and cable services are treated as "outside" stations.

outtake A scene or shot that is edited out and not used in the production. Also called *outs*. Cf. keeptake.

out time The time a program is scheduled to end.

outward WATS A telephone company service that allows customers to make unlimited calls within a specified service area for a fixed monthly rate. Cf. inward WATS.

over A program or program segment that runs longer than scheduled. Also called *overboard* and *overrun*. Cf. under.

overact To play a role with too much exaggeration or overstatement. Cf. underplay.

overage The leftover copies of a printing run.

overboard □ Overacting, overproducing, overdirecting, overspending, or overanything. □ *See* over.

overbreadth doctrine The policy that requires laws to be declared unconstitutional if they are too broad in scope.

overbuild A geographic area that contains competing cable television systems.

overcasting *See* oversewing.

overcommercialization An excessive number of, amount of time devoted to, or interruptions by commercial matter in a radio or television program. An excessive number of commercials is also called *clutter*.

overcrank To operate a film camera at greater than normal speed in order to produce slow motion. Cf. undercrank.

overcutting In disc recording, the effect of excessive level characterized by one groove cutting into an adjacent one.

overdevelop To develop film for more than the required time, resulting in too much contrast. Cf. underdevelop.

overdeviation □ The excessive deviation of the FM carrier, especially that exceeding the limits specified by SMPTE recommended practices. □ Picture distortions resulting from excessive deviation. *See also* bearding.

overdrive The application of an excessive signal to a system.

overdubbing □ The adding of audio tracks to the original sound source of a scene or picture. *See also* sweetening. □ *See* multiple tracking.

overexposure The film or print condition caused by too much light on a negative. Cf. underexposure.

overflow The condition that exists when a component or system is unable to handle any additional input.

over frame *See* voiceover.

overhang □ The amount that a book cover exceeds the dimensions of the pages. Also called *extended cover* and *squares*. □ The amount a tonearm stylus reaches past the center post of a turntable. □ The length of time that a sound continues after the sound is no longer being emitted. □ The amount of signal that remains at the output of a component after the input signal has ended.

overhaul To revise a story, script, equipment, and so on.

overhead □ An outdated term for a story sent by telegraph instead of leased wires. □ The general expenses of a business that cannot be charged directly to a production, book, or product, such as rent, lighting, office expenses, depreciation, taxes, and so on.

overhead projector A device that projects an image of a horizontal transparency on a vertical screen. The transparency may be a copy of printed material, illustrations, and so on, or it may be writing done with a special pen directly on the transparent material on the projection device. Cf. opaque projector.

overhead shot A camera shot taken from a position directly above the action or object.

overhead strip A striplight positioned above the action or object for diffuse illumination.

overlap □ The condition caused by talent picking up cues too quickly. □ To shoot scenes longer than necessary to facilitate editing. □ The portion of a dissolve in which the images are superimposed. □ The sound heard with the wrong film picture. □ The time during which two separate video playback machines or projectors are running to allow synchronization before changeover. □ *See* extended cover. □ To begin a film or videotape sequence with the same lines the previous sequence ended with. Used to assist in editing. Also called *overlapping*. □ *See* overlap splice. □ A book binding that overhangs the leaves. *See also* overhang. Cf. flush.

overlap action The continuation of action from one camera shot to the next. Cf. cutaway.

overlapping *See* overlap.

overlapping circulation The advertising of a product or service in two or more media having the same coverage area.

overlap sound A sound that is not changed at the same instant a picture is changed and that thus overlaps or precedes the next picture.

overlap splice A film splice in which a portion of the two sections of film are doubled in thickness. Cf. butt splice.

overlay □ A thin piece of paper used in a letterpress to make a more uniform impression on the paper being printed. Cf. underlay. □ A plastic sheet used to protect artwork. □ A paper or plastic sheet used to record instructions for a platemaker. □ A paper strip or price designation, such as a dealer imprint, that is pasted on the face of an outdoor advertising poster. □ A chromakey shot that places a performer in front of a selected background. □ A technique in cel animation in which foreground elements of the setting are painted on a cel and placed over the characters to give an illusion of depth to the scene.

overlay control In CD-I, the mechanism that controls transparency between planes.

overline □ A caption placed above a cut. □ *See* kicker.

overload A load greater than the design capacity of the component or system.

overmatter Matter that was left out of a publication because of a lack of space. *See also* leftover matter and overset.

overmodulation The exceeding of the maximum permissible amplitude of a signal for recording or transmission. The result is usually distortion.

over music To speak or act with a musical background.

overnight □ A reporting assignment made the previous evening to be covered the next day. Also called an *overnighter*. □ Radio or television programming from sometime after midnight until approximately dawn.

overnight location work Work on an assignment at a location requiring a performer to stay from home overnight. Cf. daily location work and location work.

overnighter *See* overnight.

overnights A slang term for the television ratings received through metered households and delivered the morning of the day following the telecast.

overplay To overact.

overpower To dominate another actor by an intense performance in a role.

overprint □ To print on top of other print. Also called *surprint.* □ *See* overrun. □ *See* overwrite.

overrecord To record more material than is necessary in a videotape edit. The extra material is then edited out by the next edit.

override A manual control that is operated to negate a predetermined setting or circuit.

overrun □ The leftover copies from a printing order. Also called *overage* and *overprint.* □ To move words from one line to the next because of an insertion or deletion. □ A percentage of paper prepared and delivered in excess of the amount ordered. □ *See* over.

overrunning To be behind time at any point in a script or program.

overs *See* cutout and overset.

over-scale contract The engagement of a performer or player with terms or conditions greater than the minimum scale for the type of work assigned.

overscanning The deflection of the scanning beam beyond the mask on a television picture tube.

over scene *See* voiceover.

over schedule A production, publication, commercial, and so on, that is not completed within the planned timetable. Cf. under schedule.

Overseas Press Club Awards A series of annual awards for news reporting from abroad.

overset Type matter set but not used, usually because of a lack of space. Also called *overs* and *runovers. See also* holdover and overmatter.

oversewing □ The sewing of a book binding by machine in imitation of hand sewing. □ The reinforcing of a book by additional sewing through the back.

overshoot □ To overmodulate. □ To transmit a greater distance than normal because of atmospheric conditions. □ To take a wider camera shot than intended. Also called an *over shot.* □ An excessive response to an unidirectional signal change. Sharp overshoots are sometimes referred to as spikes. □ To use so much film or tape that it is wasted. Cf. undershoot.

overshot *See* overshoot.

overstock To order more books, tapes, or other material than can be handled or sold.

overstrike □ A word processing mode that allows the replacement of characters by typing over existing text. Also called *strikeover.* Cf. insert. □ *See* boldface.

over the air Broadcasting as opposed to cable transmission. Also called *on-air.*

over the horizon propagation *See* scatter propagation.

over-the-shoulder (OS) A shot where the camera is positioned behind and slightly to the side of one performer and takes a full face shot of the other performer.

over the transom Unsolicited manuscripts, articles, and so on, sent to publishers. Also called *slush.*

overtones A harmonic with a higher pitch than the fundamental frequency in a complex tone.

overwire hanger *See* banner.

overwrite □ To record over existing material. □ To print on top of other printing. Cf. overstrike. □ To retype over existing text in order to darken the print. Also called *overprint.* □ To write in a literary or labored style unsuited to the needs of the publication. Sometimes caused by too many revisions.

OWI Office of War Information. A World War II federal government organization.

owned and operated *See* O&O.

owner The holder or holders of a copyright.

ownership report The report required by the FCC of licensees on initial application and at renewal describing full information concerning station ownership.

Oxford corner A book cover having two horizontal and two vertical rules that form a square at each corner.

Oxford rule A border consisting of two parallel rules, one thick and one thin. Also called a *double dash* and *Scotch rule.*

oxidation A chemical reaction wherein a chemical solution, such as a developer, loses its potency.

oxide □ The magnetizable medium employed in magnetic recording tapes, specifically such oxides as gamma-ferric oxide and chromium dioxide, both of which are employed as magnetizable media. □ Pertaining to that portion of a recording tape where the magnetizable medium is applied, as the oxide side.

oxide buildup The accumulation of particles of oxide, abraded from a tape, on the various surfaces of a tape transport that normally contact and support the oxide side.

oxide shedding The loss of oxide particles from the binder system during normal tape usage, ultimately resulting in degradation of output signal level uniformity and increased dropout activity.

oxide side The surface of an audio-or videotape that bears the magnetizable medium.

Ozalid A trademark process for producing copies on sensitized paper. *See also* whiteprint.

ozone A form of oxygen found near electrical discharges and in the atmosphere.

ozotype *See* carbro process.

ozzie A pattern of concentric rings created with a cucoloris.

P

P □ Construction permit. An FCC file-number prefix. Normally, CP is used to designate a construction permit. □ Paragraph. □ Power. □ Public safety. An FCC first letter file-number prefix. □ Page. □ A wire service symbol for national politics. □ Pico.

PA □ Public address. □ Public affairs (radio or television programs). □ Personal appearance. □ Press association. □ Production assistant.

PABX Private automatic branch exchange. An automated private telephone switching system interconnected with the telephone company. Cf. PBX.

PAC Political action committee.

PACCT Political Action Committee for Cable Television. A citizens' group.

pace The timing, tempo, and rhythm of a performance, motion picture, program, and so on.

pacing *See* orchestration and timing.

pack A collection of punched cards. Also called a *deck.*

package □ A number of radio or television programs sold as a unit. □ *See* package program. □ A number of radio or television commercials sold as a unit. □ A proposal presented to prospective backers for a motion picture, consisting of the rights to the script, a budget, the major actors and actresses, director, and so on. □ A computer program. □ A complete television news story. □ All of the assembled enclosures (parts or elements) of a mailing effort. Includes an envelope, letter, and reply device.

package dimmer Modular units containing several dimming circuits; units can be arranged in various numbers and combinations.

package insert Any promotional piece included in a product shipment. It may be for different products (or refills and replacements) from the same company or for products and services of other companies.

package plan □ The purchase of multiple time periods by an advertiser at a discount from one-time rates. Also called a *package rate.* □ The purchase by a television station of a series, multiple programs, or group of films.

package program A complete program, except for commercials, furnished to a sponsor, network, or station. Also called a *package* and *package show.*

packager □ An individual or organization that combines all the elements that make up a radio or television program. □ An individual or organization that packages products, such as books, for a fee or sale.

package rate *See* package plan.

package show *See* package program.

package test A test of elements, in part or in their entirety, of one mailing piece against another.

packet A data unit that is a proper size for transmission.

packet switching A method of transmitting data wherein each message is broken down into small blocks of data, called *packets.* The message is then reassembled at the receiving station.

packing density □ A measure of the video or audio information recorded per unit tape area. □ The number of digital bits that a given area of computer storage can hold.

PACT Protective Action for Children's TV. A citizens' group.

pact A contract or agreement to produce or perform in a production.

pad □ To add material to a radio or television program that is running short. □ A resistance in a circuit to match impedances or introduce a transmission loss. □ A base on which an antenna or dish is erected. □ To increase the length of a news item, story, and so on. □ A story that contains superfluous details. □ To increase the number of copies of a publication. □ *See* fill. □ *See* padding.

pad copy News copy that is available for use should the radio or television newscast run short.

padding □ The words added to the end of a line by a performer for transitional purposes. □ *See* fill. □ The binding of loose paper into pads.

paddle plug *See* stage plug.

page □ A television (and formerly radio) employee who guides tours and serves as an audience usher. □ A unit of information consisting of a single display or printout. □ A segment of computer memory. □ Information on a video display screen. □ A single still picture. □ One side of a leaf of a book, manuscript, magazine, and so on. □ The matter that is printed on a page. □ The 20 lines of type on a video display screen. □ The type that is set and ready to print. □ To page up. □ In interactive videotex, a unit of information containing one or more pages.

page break □ That point in a book, manuscript, periodical, and so on, at which type matter is carried over to the next page. □ A calculated indication in a computer program of where page breaks will occur when the material is printed.

page brightener *See* brite.

page cord The twine used to tie up pages of type.

page dummy *See* dummy.

page gauge *See* gauge.

page make-up *See* make-up.

page map A location indicator in a computer page make-up program showing the relative positions of text and graphics.

page opposite *See* op ed.

page plan A draft made of a page layout for discussion purposes.

page preview *See* minipage.

page printer A computer-controlled printer that composes an entire page at once. Cf. line printer.

page proof The first proof of type matter that has been made up in page form. *See also* proof. Cf. galley proof.

page pull A video effect in which one picture appears to pull another onto the television screen. Cf. page push.

page push A video effect in which one picture appears to push another onto the television screen. Cf. page pull.

pager A small electronic device used to contact an individual.

page reader An optical character reader that is capable of reading a full page at a time.

page size The size of a full-page, nonbleed advertisement.

page turn A video effect in which the picture appears to fold over like a page in a book, thus revealing the next page.

page up To make up type into pages.

pagination □ The process of numbering the pages of a book or other publication in consecutive order. □ The numbers that indicate the sequence of the pages. □ The total number of pages. □ The arranging of type forms so that they will print in the proper order. □ The process of laying out a page using a computer program.

paid cancel Refers to a person who completes a basic buying commitment or more before canceling a commitment. *See also* completed cancel.

paid circulation Distribution of a publication to persons or organizations that have paid for a subscription.

paid during service A method of paying for magazine subscriptions in installments, usually weekly or monthly; generally collected in person by the original salesperson or a representative of the company.

paid spot A radio or television commercial.

paint box *See* paint system.

paint bulletin *See* painted bulletin.

paint department The motion picture studio department responsible for set painting.

painted bulletin A large outdoor advertising structure; commonly 14 feet by 48 feet. Copy is reproduced by two methods: painting directly on the surface or posting paper with the advertising preprinted. If painting is the method of reproduction, the bulletin is called a *paint* or *painted bulletin*; if posting is the method of reproduction, the bulletin is called a *posted* or *printed bulletin*. Also called a *bulletin*. Cf. poster panel.

painted display An advertisement on a painted bulletin.

painted display plant An outdoor advertising company that owns and maintains bulletins.

painter The person responsible for coloring in the inked drawings on a cel with paint. Also called an *opaquer*. *See also* ink and paint.

painter's guide A line rendering with color overlays that indicates the forms and colors for a painted bulletin.

painting The adjustment of the color controls on a camera or camera control unit to achieve balance or the desired effect.

paint out To obliterate copy on an outdoor advertising painted bulletin in preparation for a change in design. Also called *blank-out* and *coat-out*.

paint pots The video controls that are used to adjust the color balance in a camera.

paint room The shop or area where a scene painter works.

paint system A digital electronic system designed for the direct display of artist or operator generated high-quality video images. Also called a *paint box*.

pair Two electrical conductors, usually wires, used to form a circuit or connect components.

pairing A partial or complete failure of interlace in which the scanning lines of alternate fields do not fall exactly between one another but tend to fall in pairs one on top of the other.

PAL □ Permanent artificial lighting. □ Phase alternation line. *See* PAL color system.

palaeotypography Ancient typography.

PAL color system The color television system developed in Germany, similar to the NTSU system, but in which one of the color signals is reversed in polarity between alternate lines. *See also* SECAM.

paleography □ Ancient writings. □ The study of ancient writing.

palette □ The range of colors available to a computer graphics artist. □ In CD-I, a palette is used by the user communications manager to support the color lookup table. The maximum size of the palette at any instant in time is 256 colors, with the red, green, and blue components each defined to 8-bit accuracy. □ *See* media palette.

palimpsest An ancient parchment or tablet that has been erased and used a second or third time.

pallet □ A tool used to gild books. □ A wooden form used to ship and hold paper, machinery, and so on.

pamphlet A booklet with pages of printed matter—usually eight or more—and a paper cover. Cf. leaflet.

pan □ An abbreviation for *panchromatic, panorama,* and *panoramic.* □ The horizontal movement of a camera from a stationary position. *See also* camera movement. □ To criticize a book, television program, motion picture, and so on, negatively.

pan and tilt head A camera head that allows both pans and tilts.

Panavision The most widely used 35-mm anamorphic process for motion pictures. *See also* Super-Panavision and Ultra-Panavision.

pan background A wide background used in animation to permit long east or west movements.

pan blur *See* whip.

pancake □ A type of make-up foundation. □ A low, movable platform used to raise the height of performers or objects. *See also* riser. □ A slang term for a disc.

Pancake turner A slang term for a disc jockey.

pan cel An animation cel that is several times as wide as a standard cel; used as a pan background.

pan chart In animation, the charted camera calibrations affixed to the top of the artwork for a pan.

panchromatic A film that is sensitive to all colors of the visible spectrum. Cf. orthochromatic.

pandering The commercial exploitation of erotic matter considered to be obscene.

pandering act The 1970 statute that allows recipients of unwanted sexually oriented mail to have their names removed from the sender's mailing list.

P and H Postage and handling.

panel □ A group of respondents that are surveyed continuously over time, or perhaps periodically over time, rather than only once. □ An audio control console. □ *See* patch panel. □ A small group of judges sitting to hear a case. Cf. en banc. □ A group of persons summoned as jurors. □ A group of players or participants on a radio or television program. □ A block of type or an illustration that is indented from the margins, sometimes with rules at top and bottom. □ An area or label on a book cover that is enclosed by a border. □ A wide photograph, often panoramic. □ An outdoor advertising display board, whether regular or illuminated; usually of billboard size.

panelize To appear on a television panel program.

panel number A number given to outdoor advertising panels to aid employees in the painting or posting of advertising structures.

pan film *See* panchromatic.

pan focus A depth of field that is great enough to allow the action to remain in focus throughout a camera pan.

pan handle A metal rod attached to a camera head that assists the operator in panning and tilting the camera. Also called a *panning handle.*

pan head *See* friction head.

panic button The often imaginary, but sometimes real, button needed when a deadline is imminent or when an equipment operator is unable to cope with a situation.

panic period *See* panic time.

panic time The period immediately preceding and during a radio station break or other difficult or complicated periods. Also called *panic period.*

pan left A director's command to a camera operator to pan to the left.

panning handle *See* pan handle.

panning head *See* friction head.

panning peg bars In animation, specialized movable pegs on the compound, calibrated and controlled by dials, which allow the artwork to be moved to accommodate moving shots such as pans. Also called *traveling peg bars.*

panorama □ An extremely wide-angle camera shot. □ A print made from a series of slightly overlapping wide-angle shots.

panorama cloth *See* cyclorama.

panoram dolly A large camera dolly with a tongue and a pan and tilt head.

panoramic projection The projection of motion pictures that cover a 360-degree horizontal arc.

pan pot A potentiometer used to vary the amount of an audio signal when it is split between two or more outputs, as from one loudspeaker to another or from one program channel to another.

pan right A director's command to a camera operator to pan to the right.

pans A bank of fluorescent lights.

pan shot □ A fast or slow horizontal camera movement. If the movement is fast, it is called a *whip.* □ A shot that encompasses a wider area than can be viewed by the camera at one time and that will be scanned by the camera by means of panning.

pan stick A pancake foundation makeup in stick form.

pan to A director's command to a camera operator to pan to an object or follow talent movement.

pantograph □ A device having a scissor-type mechanism that permits the variable height hanging of luminaires. □ In animation, a pointer attached to the compound that moves over a field guide to indicate the exact position of the compound during an off-center pan or truck. Also called a *pantograph unit.*

pantograph chart A drawing used in conjunction with an animation pantograph to indicate the proper positioning of each movement.

pantograph unit *See* pantograph.

pantomime A wordless performance using gestures and movement.

paparazzi The crowds of photographers who follow stars and other celebrities in order to obtain candid shots.

paper □ The sheets made from wood, rags, straw, or other fibrous material manufactured by hand or with a Fourdrinier machine. The better grades of paper are made from linen rags; the lesser grades from groundwood pulp. Also called *paper stock.* □ A printed or written document. □ A periodical such as a newspaper. □ A slang term for a free pass to a theatrical event. □ To affix end papers to books. □ A general term for photographic printing and enlarging stock.

paper advance The mechanism that drives the perforated paper through a tractor feed printer.

paperback A colloquial term for a book bound in paper. More properly called *paperbound.*

paper bail *See* bail.

paper boards Book boards that are covered with paper instead of leather or cloth.

paperbound A paper-covered book. Also called a *paperback* and *softcover*. *See also* mass market paperback and quality paperback.

Paperbound Books in Print A periodical index of paperbound books printed and available.

paperbounder A publisher of paperbound books.

paper cover A paper wrapper used on a book. Sometimes a synonym for a *paperback*.

paper hanger *See* billposter.

papering The use of paper strips to mark the beginning and ending of a film, videotape, or audiotape shot or segment to be edited.

paper machine A machine used to change pulp into paper. *See also* Fourdrinier.

paper out sensor A small switch located near a computer printer platen used to detect and signal the absence of paper.

paper punch tape *See* paper tape.

paper stock *See* paper.

paper tape A former computer storage medium on which punched holes were used to save data.

paper throw The movement of paper through a printer at a rate faster than printing speed.

paper weight *See* basis weight.

papier-mache A mixture of paper, water, and glue used to make irregularly shaped three-dimensional objects, stereotype mats, and so on.

papyrus □ A paper made in ancient Egypt from the pith of the papyrus plant. □ An ancient document printed on papyrus.

PAR Parabolic aluminized reflector. *See* PAR light.

par An abbreviation for *paragraph, parallax, parallel,* and *parameter*.

para An abbreviation for *paragraph*.

parabola □ A curve generated by a point moving an equidistance from a line and a fixed point. □ A directional microphone reflector in the shape of a parabola. Also called a *dishpan* and *parabolic reflector*. □ Graphics that are curved so as to remain perpendicular to camera panning movements.

parabolic antenna An antenna that concentrates the radiated power in a tight beam. Also called a *dish*.

parabolic microphone A microphone that is mounted at the focus of a parabolic dish. Similar in effect to a shotgun mike.

parabolic reflector A concave reflector in the form of a truncated paraboloid used in floodlights, spotlights, striplights, and some antennas.

parabolic spotlight *See* beam projector.

parabroadcasting The transmission of information by nonbroadcast means using broadcast type equipment. Examples of uses include closed-circuit, medical, and industrial.

paragon A size of type; 20 points.

paragraph □ An arbitrary but logical division of a body of written or printed material, usually indented, containing a developed thought. □ A symbol (¶) used to indicate a paragraph.

parallax The apparent difference in direction to an object seen from two different points, as in a film camera's viewfinder and the lens of the camera.

parallax check A measurement taken before shooting to assure the camera operator that the viewfinder and the lens will see the identical scene.

parallax compensation Any method used to control the errors in framing due to parallax.

parallax error The difference in the field of view between a viewfinder and a camera lens. The error increases as the distance between the subject and camera is decreased.

parallel □ A collapsible platform used on a set as a riser or to hold cameras, lighting stands, and so on. □ Two or more components or circuits connected so that the current is divided between them. Cf. series. □ The sending or receiving of computer information in blocks of bits that are transferred over parallel wires. Cf. serial. □ An outdoor advertising panel built at an angle of less than 6 degrees to the line of travel. These panels generally are visible to traffic in both directions, but because of their construction, the advertising message may be distorted to the audience. □ *See* bed.

parallel action Action that is taking place simultaneously, usually shown through the use of cutbacks. Also called *parallel development.*

parallel circuit. *See* parallel.

parallel cutting The editing of two or more different scenes so as to show parallel action.

parallel development *See* parallel action.

parallel editing *See* cross cut.

parallel interface *See* interface.

parallel location The location of an outdoor advertisement parallel to a street or road.

parallel plot A subplot that is developed at the same time as the main plot through the use of parallel action.

parallel recording The recording of the same source simultaneously on two or more recorders.

parallel rule A rule of two or more parallel thin lines. Cf. double rule and Oxford rule.

parallel single (PS) An outdoor advertising panel considered to be a single panel if it is the only panel visible to approaching traffic or if no other panel is visible within 25 feet along the line of travel and no painted display is visible within 50 feet.

parallel sound *See* synchronous sound.

parallel sync *See* level sync.

parallel tracking A method of mounting a pickup arm on a turntable so that the arm is always at a tangent to the groove.

parallel transmission A method of data transmission wherein each bit of a byte is sent at the same time. Cf. serial transmission.

parameter □ In a computer system, a constant defined by the user. □ The defining of the make-up of a page. □ A quantity or fact that describes a statistical population.

parametric equalizer A continuously variable audio device that can increase or decrease the sound in the selected frequency bands.

parametric surface patches Objects, used to define a three-dimensional object, that are created with a limited number of control points to define the surface's shape and curve, with remaining points determined computationally. Also called *bicubic patches.*

paraphrase A restatement of a quotation in another form; usually in the third person. Cf. direct quote, indirect quote, and partial quote.

paraxial The parallel rays of light near the optical axis of a lens. Cf. abaxial.

parchment □ An early writing material made from sheepskin or goatskin. □ *See* vellum.

parens An abbreviation for *parentheses.*

parenthesis One of the two curved marks, (and), used in writing. Cf. bracket.

parent station A broadcast television station that supplies programming and commercials to another station to expand the coverage of the parent.

parity □ A computer feature that checks accuracy by counting the number of odd or even bits. □ The quality of being equal or equivalent; an example is two newspapers in the same community that have approximately equal shares of the market.

parity bits The bits used during data transmission to detect, and possibly correct, errors.

park To hold a tape at a stop in preparation for running.

Park Row A street in lower New York City; formerly a well-known publishing center.

par lamp *See* par light.

par light A spotlight-like luminaire using a par lamp. The beam characteristics depend upon the par lamp used.

parody A humorous imitation of a literary or other work; a caricature of an author's style or manner.

parroting □ The imitation by a novice broadcaster of the speech patterns and vocal inflections of a well-known announcer. □ The imitation of the writing style of another by a novice writer. □ An introductory sentence in a news script that is identical to, or almost identical to, the first sentence of a sound bite or standupper.

parse To analyze the structure of a sentence using its component parts of speech.

part □ A character in a drama, screenplay, and so on. Cf. role. □ To play a role in a production.

partial One frequency of a complex tone.

partial grant The grant by the FCC of any privilege, term, or condition other than those requested in an application.

partial network station A commercial television broadcast station that generally carries in prime time more than 10 hours of programming per week offered by the three major national television networks, but less than the number of hours carried by a full network station.

partial quote A portion of a direct quotation. Cf. direct quote, indirect quote, and paraphrase.

partial remaindering Books that are offered to booksellers by publishers at discounted prices for resale to the public at less than the published price.

partial sponsorship A radio or television program that is sponsored by two or more advertisers. Also called *segment sponsorship*. Cf. magazine concept.

partial update In information presentation, the modification of part of the text, graphics, or natural image displayed on screen.

participating advertiser An advertiser who buys time for commercials within a radio or television program.

participating agency An advertising agency that has a commercial announcement on a radio or television program but is not the agency of record.

participating announcement A commercial message used in a participation program.

participating sponsors Two or more sponsors of the same radio or television program.

participating writer A writer who accomplished some of the writing of a story or screenplay and who received screen credit for the writing of a motion picture.

participation The acceptance of a percentage of the profits from a motion picture or television program in lieu of or in addition to a salary.

participation program □ A radio or television program designed to carry the commercial messages of a number of advertisers. The announcements are usually delivered by the program talent; if not, it is called an *announcement program*. □ *See* audience participation program.

participation shot A camera shot in which the audience sees what a performer sees. *See also* point of view.

participation spot The time reserved by a station for a commercial.

part-time station A station authorized by the FCC to broadcast on a restricted schedule. *See also* daytime operation and sharing time.

party □ For the purposes of the Administrative Procedure Act, a person or agency named or admitted as a party, or properly seeking and entitled as of right to be admitted as a party, in an agency proceeding, and a person or agency admitted by an agency as a party for limited purposes. □ A participant in a legal action.

party in interest *See* interested person.

party line A shared communication channel.

pass □ A single passage of a tape through a tape recorder. □ A single passage of a head over a tape. □ A single passage of a tape over a head. □ A single run of film through a camera or projector.

pass-along audience. *See* pass-along reader.

pass-along circulation. *See* pass-along reader.

pass-along reader The number of persons who receive a periodical from the original subscriber or purchaser; does not include others in the homes of such persons. Also called *pass-along audience, pass-along circulation,* and *secondary readership.*

pass band A band of frequencies that may be filtered without attenuation.

passing shot A camera shot in which the camera is panned to follow the action, extensively used in car chase scenes. Cf. following shot and follow shot.

passive device An electronic device that is controlled only by an input signal and does not amplify or in any other way change the signal, such as splitters, passive mixers, and resistors.

passive media The mass media wherein the consumer is required to do nothing except watch or listen, as in television, cable television, and direct broadcast satellites.

passive satellite An earth satellite intended to reflect radio communication signals without amplification. Also called a *reflecting satellite, reflector satellite,* and *relay satellite.* Cf. active satellite.

passive switcher An inexpensive switcher that is mechanically activated by the operator. Cf. active switcher.

passive viewing *See* passive media.

password A secret, identifying word used by an operator to gain access to a computer system.

past broadcast record The broadcast history of a licensee or prospective licensee wherein there is or was ownership of a station involved. One of the comparative criteria often used in mutually exclusive hearings. Cf. previous broadcasting experience.

paste To assemble news stories furnished by wire services.

pasteboard □ A stiff material made by pasting several sheets of paper together. □ A slang expression for a theatre ticket.

pastedown *See* end paper.

pasteup A camera ready layout with the text proof and engraver's proofs or photostats pasted in the proper position. Also called a *paste up dummy. See also* mechanical.

pasteup dummy *See* pasteup.

pasting □ A method of affixing inserts into magazines. □ A paper used to make a high grade pasteboard.

pasting in *See* tipping.

past tense story A news item written about a future event as though it had already occurred.

PA system *See* public address system.

patch □ A temporary equipment connection. □ To connect circuits or equipment together temporarily, often by a patch cord. □ A short length of transparent plastic used to join or repair motion picture film. □ A section of a printing plate or keyline corrected or revised by new material stripped in or pasted over the original material. □ To repair a pasteup by inserting new material. □ To make connections on a lighting patch panel.

patch bay *See* patch panel.

patch board *See* patch panel.

patch cord □ A short cord with plugs at each end used to temporarily connect two pieces of equipment or signal paths together. □ A short cord with a plug at one end and a pair of clips at the other.

patch in To connect one circuit to another electrically.

patching The act of interconnecting components or signal paths by means of patch cords and patch panels.

patch jack *See* jack.

patch panel □ A plug and jack assembly that permits studio outlets to be temporarily connected to various dimmer and nondim circuits output. Also called a *switchboard.* □ An assembly of jacks into which various circuits are permanently tied and into which patch cords may be inserted. Also called a *patch board.*

patch plug *See* plug.

patchwork A quick fix for a news item that is poorly written.

patent □ A grant issued by the United States government giving an inventor or discoverer of a new and useful process, machine, manufacture, composition of matter, or any new and useful improvement of these items the right to exclude all others from making, using, or selling the invention. Cf. copyright. □ *See* patent insides.

patent base A device used to raise the type form in a letterpress.

patent infringement The illegal use of an invention or process registered to another person or corporation.

patent insides Newspaper sheets purchased preprinted on one side with features, articles, and other miscellaneous matter, sold to small weekly newspapers who print local news on the other side. Rarely used now. Also called *patent, patent outsides,* and *readyprint.*

patent outsides *See* patent insides.

patent pending A term used by a manufacturer or seller of an article to inform the public that an application for patent has been filed in the United States Patent and Trademark Office.

paternalism The media condition wherein a government controls the flow of information to fulfill what it believes is in the public's best interest.

path □ The channel along which information may flow. □ One of the sound-carrying circuits in a stereophonic system. □ A complete circuit between two points within a component or system.

path attenuation The power loss that occurs between a transmitter—a broadcasting station, a satellite transponder, and so on—and a receiver. Also called *path loss* and, for satellites, *space loss*.

path descriptor A data structure used to represent an open file; each open file is associated with a path descriptor.

path loss *See* path attenuation.

path name A computer file name consisting of, at a minimum, a slash, a volume name, another slash, and the file name.

path of action In animation, the movement of a character through a scene; used in layout.

pathos The emotions of pity and sympathy that are awakened in an audience by some works of art.

path table A branching structure that provides simplified format access to files and directories on a disk.

patron An individual or corporation that donates money to causes such as public television stations for the underwriting of programs.

patter The words, sentences, phrases, and so on, used by a disc jockey.

pattern *See* polar pattern.

pattern plate □ A reinforced electrotype plate made from original engravings or other electrotype plates. □ A molding plate used as a master for the reproduction of other printing plates.

pattern projector A spotlight used to project shapes and forms on a backdrop. *See also* cucoloris.

pattern spotlight An ellipsoidal reflector spotlight, especially one with a pattern or gobo slot at the focal point of the unit to permit insertion of pattern templates for projection.

pause An interruption in a computer program's execution.

pause control A feature of some audio- and videotape recorders that allows the tape to stop until the pause control is pressed again.

pay cable Pay television programs distributed on a cable television system and paid for on an individual basis in addition to the monthly cable charge. *See also* pay television.

pay cable channel A cable television system channel that carries a pay cable network, channel, or pay-per-view channel.

pay cable household A household that subscribes to one or more cable television premium services.

pay cable network A cable television service, usually delivered to the cable television system by satellite.

pay off □ A tag line. □ A musical curtain. □ The climax of a program or play. □ The use of a previously planted character, idea, or object, such as a gun, in the climax of a motion picture, novel, play, and so on. Cf. plant.

payola Money, service, or anything of value directly or indirectly paid or promised to a radio or television station employee for the broadcast of any matter that is not disclosed. Payola has often been received for the promotion of records on radio stations. Cf. plugola.

pay-per-view A pay cable or subscription television service that charges viewers for each program watched.

pay radio A cable radio satellite music channel that does not contain commercials. As with pay television, the cost of the service is in addition to the monthly cable fee.

pay saturation The pay television subscriber population, expressed as a percentage of passings (first) and basic subscribers (second). In a system of 100 passings and 59 basic subscribers, 20 pay subscribers represent pay saturation of 20 percent of passings and 33.9 percent of basics.

pay television A system of distributing motion pictures, television programs, and so on, over the air or by cable where a separate channel is provided for which the subscriber pays on an individual per-program basis. Pay television systems use some form of scrambling of either sound or picture. Also called *fee-vee, pay-TV, payvision, STV, toll television,* and *toll video. See also* pay cable and subscription television.

pay TV Another name for pay television.

payvision Another name for pay television.

pay window The length of time a program or motion picture is available to pay cable television. *See also* window.

PB □ Pull back. □ Pocket book.

PBL Public Broadcasting Laboratory.

PbO Lead oxide.

PBS □ Public Broadcasting System. Also called, derogatorily, *Primarily British Shows* and *Primarily British Syndication.* □ Paginated by sections.

PBX Private branch exchange. An internal telephone system connected to telephone company lines and used in organizations and businesses. Cf. PABX.

PC □ Personal computer. □ Provisional cut. □ Press club. □ Press council. □ Printed circuit.

PC board *See* printed circuit.

P channel One of the eight compact disc subcode channels (P–W). The P channel carries the music flag, indicating the presence or absence of a music track.

PCIRC Preparatory Committee for International Radio Conference.

PCM Pulse code modulation.

PD □ Program director. □ Production director. □ Public domain. □ Professional digital. *See* PD recording.

PDR Primary demographic report.

PD recording Professional digital recording. One of the two professional digital audio formats. Cf. DASH.

PDT Published data tapes.

PE □ Printer's error. □ Professional engineer.

Peabody Awards George Foster Peabody Awards are given by the University of Georgia School of Journalism for distinguished achievement in the public interest.

PEACESAT Pan-Pacific Education and Communications Experiments by Satellite. An experiment in direct broadcast satellite transmission.

peak □ A momentary period of high volume or amplitude. □ To raise the level of an audio or video signal. □ A high point in a performance. □ To adjust electronic components to perform at optimum levels. Also called *tweak.*

peak envelope power The average power supplied to the antenna transmission line by a transmitter during one radio frequency cycle at the crest of the modulation envelope taken under normal operating conditions.

peak indicator A light on some recording devices that flashes when the input signal exceeds a specified level.

peak limiter An electronic device that maintains the maximum instantaneous volume level of an amplifier below a specified value. Cf. volume limiter.

peak load The increase in power, transmissions, and so on, up to the maximum capabilities of the system to handle the burden.

peak power The power, over a radio frequency cycle, corresponding in amplitude to synchronizing peaks.

peak power of a radio transmitter The mean power supplied to the antenna during one radio frequency cycle at the highest crest of the modulation envelope, taken under conditions of normal operation. Cf. mean power of a radio transmitter.

peak program meter (PPM) *See* VU meter.

peak time A British term for prime time.

peak-to-peak The algebraic difference between the maximum positive and negative amplitude excursions (peaks).

pearl A size of type; 5 points.

pebbling The process of embossing paper to give it the appearance of pebbles, ripples, imitation leather, and so on. Also called *roller embossing.*

pedal pusher A slang term for a studio organist.

pedestal □ A camera dolly with a counterbalanced vertical column. □ A luminaire support unit. □ The black level of a television signal that elevates the base level for another wave. Now considered an obsolete term. *Blanking level* is preferred. □ To move a camera up or down.

pedestal down A director's command to a camera operator to lower a camera mounted on a pedestal.

pedestal housing A protected, underground box used to house cable television distribution equipment. Also called *underground housing.*

pedestal level *See* blanking level.

pedestal up A director's command to a camera operator to raise a camera mounted on a pedestal.

peel □ Paint pulling away from the face of an outdoor advertising structure. □ A variation of a special effects curl, wherein the edge is creased.

peel-off label A self-adhesive label attached to a backing sheet that is attached to a mailing piece. The label is intended for removal from the mailing piece and for attachment to an order blank or card.

peepie-creepie *See* walkie-lookie.

PEG □ Professional Emphasis Group; a division of the NAB. □ Public, educational, government. Access channels on cable television.

peg □ The angle or main point on which a story hangs. □ To increase sound volume so that the indicator on a VU meter hits the metal stop; to overmodulate. □ *See* stage screw.

pegbar A strip of metal containing pins that hold animation cels in place. Also called a *registration pegbar.*

pegs In animation, small metal or plastic projections that are affixed to all surfaces that will support the artwork during production. They correspond to holes punched in drawing paper, cels, and background artwork; they are used to maintain registration through all stages of production. First used by Raoul Barre in 1913 and further developed (and patented in 1915) by Earl Hurd and John Randolph Bray.

pel An abbreviation for *pixel.*

pellicle An extremely thin transparent plastic material used as a reflecting surface.

pels An abbreviation for *picture elements* and *pixels.*

PEN Poets, Playwrights, Essayists, Editors, and Novelists. An international association of writers.

pen To write a book, screenplay, script, and so on.

pencil □ A narrow beam of light that converges or diverges from a point. □ A thin, theatrical make-up cosmetic. □ A slang term for a rough drawing or layout.

pencil test A film of the animators' pencil drawings, used during production to check the timing and smoothness of the animation. In recent years, videotape has generally replaced film for this use because of its immediacy. Also called a *line test.*

pending The time from the filing of an application with the FCC until it is no longer subject to rehearing by the Commission or to review by any court.

penetration □ The percentage of households in a given area that have a radio or television receiver. Also called *saturation* or, incorrectly, *set saturation.* □ The percentage of households in a given area that have subscribed to a CATV service. □ The relationship of the number of individuals or families on a particular mailing list—such as in total, by state, ZIP code, or SIC—compared to the total number possible.

penny press The low-priced newspapers that began in the 1830s that sold for one penny.

Pentagon papers The massive government volumes that covered the causes of the Vietnam War. A legal decision in equity forced the government to release the papers in 1971.

penumbra A double shadow produced by a floodlight. Cf. umbra.

people journalism Journalism devoted primarily to pictures and captions of famous or interesting people or groups.

people meter A home television audience measurement device that requires interaction by the members of the family to record audience composition. *See also* AGB, Arbitron, and Nielsen (ACN).

perambulator A microphone stand dolly.

perceived color The color as seen by the interaction of hue, brightness, and saturation.

percentage An agreement in which an actor, director, and so on, receives a percentage of a film's profits instead of or in addition to a fixed amount.

percentage modulation The ratio of the actual frequency deviation to the frequency deviation as 100 percent modulation, expressed in a percentage. For FM broadcast stations, a frequency deviation of plus or minus 75 kHz is defined as 100 percent modulation; for TV broadcast stations, the deviation is an aural frequency deviation of plus or minus 25 kHz.

percent distribution The proportion of TSA television households within specified survey areas viewing a home market station (or all home market stations in the case of total percent distribution).

percentile A statistical point on a scale of values; the 90th percentile is that point on the scale below which 90 percent of the values fall.

per-channel deviation In a frequency-modulated radio transmitter, the amount of frequency deviation produced by a standard test tone in a single telephone channel at the characteristic baseband frequency.

per curiam opinion Latin for "by the court." An opinion issued in the name of a court without identification of the writer or writers of the opinion.

per diem Latin for a sum of money, computed on a daily basis, paid to cast and crew members when they are on location.

perf An abbreviation for *perforation.*

perfect To print both sides of a sheet or web of paper in one pass through a press.

perfect binding A book binding accomplished by gluing the pages and cover together without stitching. Also called an *adhesive binding.*

perfecting machine *See* perfecting press.

perfecting press A printing press capable of printing on both sides of a sheet or web of paper in one pass. Also called a *perfecting machine* and *perfector press.*

perfector press *See* perfecting press.

perfect ream A ream that contains 516 sheets of paper.

perforated paper. *See* pinfeed paper.

perforated tape A paper tape on which data are recorded by means of punched holes.

perforating The punching, scoring, or laser cutting of paper so that it may be separated easily. Used extensively for continuous-feed computer paper.

perforation One of the series of holes punched along either or both edges of film stock and mag film (single perf or double perf) and computer paper. Also called a *sprocket hole.*

perforation pitch *See* pitch.

perforator ☐ A machine used to perforate paper. ☐ A keyboard computer device used to automate the punching of holes in perforated tape. ☐ A person who operates a perforator. ☐ An extremely accurate device that uses precise steel punches to perforate film.

perform To recite, render, play, dance, or act a copyrighted work, either directly or by means of any device or process or, in the case of a motion picture or other audiovisual work, to show its images in any sequence or to make the sounds accompanying it audible.

performance ☐ The effectiveness of a component or system. ☐ A public presentation or appearance by talent. ☐ *See* promise versus performance.

performance art A combining of live presentations with motion pictures, photography, or other forms of media.

performance bond A sum of money that is pledged to ensure that a contract will be completed. Used extensively in the motion picture industry.

performance for profit The performance of a musical composition for which money or other consideration is received.

performer An individual who acts a part or presents a routine.

performing arts Those disciplines that have a major component of performance: dance, music, theatre, and so on. Cf. visual arts.

performing rights The rights granted through the payment of fees to ASCAP, BMI, or SESAC for playing the recordings of composers and lyricists associated with that company.

performing rights society An association or corporation that licenses the public performances of nondramatic musical works on behalf of the copyright owner, such as ASCAP, BMI, and SESAC.

periaktos A tall, slender, triangular piece of scenery mounted on casters so that it can be turned quickly for set changes.

perigee The point in a satellite's orbit at which it is closest to the earth. Cf. apogee.

per inquiry (PI) A type of advertising wherein the media and the promoter or manufacturer split the profit. This type of advertising is not highly regarded.

period ☐ The time that elapses between two consecutive passages of a satellite through a characteristic point on its orbit. ☐ The time required for one complete cycle.

periodical A publication that is issued at regular intervals of more than one day containing a variety of articles by different authors; a magazine or a journal. The term does not include newspapers.

Periodical Publishers' Association (PPA) An organization founded in 1900 for the purpose of aiding good relations within the periodical publishing industry and for checking the credit standing of advertising agencies.

period of operation A single uninterrupted transmission or a series of intermittent transmissions from a single location or continuous or intermittent transmission from a television pickup station covering a single event from various locations, within a single day.

period piece A noncontemporary program or play.

peripheral An input or output device on a computer.

peripheral card. *See* card.

peripheral device Any device that is connected to a computer or other system. Such equipment includes tape recorders, modems, disk drives, printers, and magnetic drums. Also called *peripheral equipment.*

peripheral equipment *See* peripheral device.

peripheral slot *See* slot.

periscope A device containing two mirrors that can be used to take camera shots over the heads of crowds or shots from the ground.

perk An abbreviation for *perquisite.*

permanent memory Computer memory that is retained when power is turned off. Cf. volatile memory.

permanent set A frequently used film or television set that is not removed or struck after each use.

permanent sign on The sign on time (other than local sunrise) authorized by the FCC for some daytime stations.

permissible interference Observed or predicted interference that complies with quantitative interference and sharing criteria contained in International Radio Regulations, in CCIR Recommendations, or in special agreements. This term is used in the coordination of frequency assignments between administrations in various countries. Cf. accepted interference.

permission The granting by a copyright owner of the right to quote from a book, article, or other copyrighted source.

permit for construction *See* construction permit (CP).

permittee The holder of a radio or television broadcast station construction permit.

per program license A music performing right issued to a broadcast station for a single program. Cf. blanket license.

perquisite An item or privilege granted by an employer in addition to wages or salary; examples include stock options, automobiles, residences, free tickets, and vacations.

per quod *See* libel per quod.

per se *See* libel per se.

persistence The length of time a phosphor dot on a television screen remains visible.

persistence of vision The ability of the eye to perceive a series of rapid still images as a single moving image by retaining each impression on the retina for a fraction of a second, thus overlapping the images. This phenomena makes it possible to see the sequential projected images of a motion picture as life-like continuous motion. Cf. phi phenomenon.

person □ As used by the FCC, a term for an individual, corporation, company, association, firm, partnership, society, joint stock company, or any other organization or institution. □ For the purposes of the Administrative Procedure Act, an individual, partnership, corporation, association, or public or private organization other than an agency.

persona One of the characters in a play, novel, and so on. The Latin plural is *personae,* as in Shakespeare's *dramatis personae.*

personal A brief news story about one or more persons, usually local in nature. Also called a *local.*

personal appearance (PA) A visit by a performer, director, novelist, or other well-known person to a motion picture theatre, bookstore, television program, and so on, in order to promote a movie, book, or other work.

personal attack An attack upon the honesty, character, integrity, and so on, of an identified person or group. A personal attack on the air requires the offer of a reasonable opportunity to respond over the licensee's facilities.

personal computer (PC) A mini or microcomputer designed for use in a home, office, or school. Cf. mainframe.

personal diary *See* individual diary.

personal endorsement *See* testimonial.

personal interview A type of interview in which the interviewer is in the physical presence of the respondent. Cf. telephone interview.

personality □ An individual who is well-known for his or her distinctive character or magnetism. □ An individual selected for use in an advertisement.

personality plug A radio or television station promo that informs the listeners or viewers about a disc jockey, newscaster, talk show host, and so on.

personality test A filmed screen test of an individual who is being considered for a part in a production.

personalized book □ A self-published book about the affairs of an individual or family. □ An autographed book.

personalized letter *See* personalizing.

personalizing The individualizing of direct mail pieces by adding the name or other personal information about the recipient. Cf. personal letter.

personal letter A direct mail letter containing an individual's name in the salutation. Cf. personalizing.

personal manager An individual who informs and counsels a performer in his or her career.

personal microphone A lavaliere or other small microphone used by an individual in order to leave his or her hands free.

personnel director The employee of an organization in charge of recruiting and hiring.

persons-per-diary value (PPDV) The numerical value assigned to each in-tab diary for the process of projecting audience estimates to the entire 12 + population in a market. The PPDV reflects the number of persons in the geographic age/sex group represented by each in-tab diary after sample balancing has been performed.

persons ranking The ranking of television programs (highest to lowest) based on the number of persons reached by selected age groups.

persons reached *See* individuals reached and reach.

persons-using-radio rating *See* individuals-using-radio rating.

persons using television (PUT) The percentage of all persons or of total persons within a given demographic category in the survey area who are viewing television during a specific time period. *See also* persons viewing television.

persons-using-television rating *See* individuals-using-television rating.

persons viewing television (PVT) The number of persons in Canadian television homes by network area or DMA using their receivers for more than five minutes in each quarter hour, expressed as a percentage of the network area or DMA persons in television households. Also called *persons using television (PUT).*

perspective □ The converging of lines at a point that creates a three-dimensional illusion of distance. □ The feeling of depth created in a drawing, stage set, and so on, by the spatial relationships of the objects. □ The subjective relationship between the sound level and distance or direction.

persuasive documentary A documentary that attempts to persuade the audience to a particular point of view. Cf. analytic documentary.

PES Private earth station.

petition An application filed with the FCC requesting intervention in a proceeding by a party in interest or for reconsideration of a Commission action, final decision, or application for review, and so on.

petitioner *See* plaintiff.

petition to deny A legal action filed with the FCC asking that agency to deny a license renewal application, usually on the grounds that the licensee has failed to operate in the public interest.

petit jury A trial jury, usually composed of 12 persons. Cf. grand jury.

Petzval lens A projection lens using widely separated elements.

PF Power factor.

pF Picofarad.

PFVEA Professional Film and Video Equipment Association.

PG Parental guidance suggested; some material may not be suitable for children. A CARA classification for feature films.

PG-13 Parental guidance; some material may be inappropriate for children under thirteen. A CARA classification for feature films.

PGA Producers Guild of America. A union.

pgm An abbreviation for *program.*

pH A chemical scale that measures the degree of acidity or alkalinity of a liquid. Used extensively in photography and some forms of printing. A neutral solution has a pH of 7.

phantom channel A combination of the left and right stereo signals fed into a third loudspeaker.

phantom load An off-stage load applied to resistance type dimmers when the functioning load is less than the minimum rating of the dimmer. This is necessary because resistance dimmers do not dim effectively unless the total connected load meets the dimmer rating.

phantom power The DC voltage that is fed by the microphone cable to power a condenser microphone.

phantom stage A studio where rain, wind or hail renders sound recordings unusable. The Screen Actors Guild allows weather-permitting calls for work on such stages.

phase □ The point reached in a cycle of recurring waves. □ The angular relationship between two or more electrical quantities in a circuit. □ *See* in phase and out of phase. □ Additive acoustical energy; mikes and loudspeakers are said to be in phase when their input or output is additive. □ The synchronous operation of a camera or projector shutter with the intermittent movement of the film. □ Broadly, the synchronous operation of sound and picture.

phase alternation line *See* PAL.

phased array antenna *See* flat plate antenna.

phase distortion The unwanted shift in phase from the input to the output of a circuit or component. *See also* phase shift.

phase modulation (PM) The modification of a signal by a change in its phase by the information to be carried. *See also* multiplexing. Cf. amplitude modulation (AM) and frequency modulation.

phase response The phase shift of a circuit versus its frequency.

phase shift □ The difference in phase angle between input and output signals. □ The lead or lag displacement of a waveform in time. Phase shift may cause cancellation of signals in microphones and loudspeakers and hue shift in a television picture.

phasing □ The controlling of two circuits or systems so that they operate in phase. □ The installing of wires to stereophonic loudspeakers so that they both have the same polarity. □ *See* flanging.

phat *See* fat matter.

Phenakistiscope An early animation device that uses a disc with sequential drawings around its border in front of a mirror to create the illusion of motion.

phi phenomenon The apparent motion of a rapid succession of different pictures shown in slightly different positions. One of the two characteristics of apparent movement. Cf. persistence of vision.

phon A unit of loudness. One phon is equal to 1 dB at 1000 Hz.

phonation The act of producing sound by the movement of the vocal chords.

phone □ An abbreviation for *telephone.* □ *See* headphones.

phone beat A reporter's beat that he or she is assigned to cover by telephone. Also called a *beat check.*

phone coupler A device used to record both sides of a telephone conversation.

phone jack A female connector designed to be used with a phone plug. Also called a *telephone jack.*

phone list A mailing list compiled from names listed in telephone directories.

phoneme The smallest unit of speech that is distinguishable from another unit.

phone plug A common audio connector used with headphones, microphones, and so on, that fits into a phone jack. Also called a *telephone plug.*

phone screener *See* screener.

phonetics The study and systematic classification of speech sounds.

Phonevision A device developed by the Zenith Radio Corporation in 1947 to test pay television.

Phong shading A smooth shading algorithm, developed by Phong Bui-Tuong, that incorporates diffuse reflection and specular reflection to create a smoothly curving surface with light-reflecting highlights.

phonogram □ A character or symbol used to represent a sound or word. □ A message sent by telephone but delivered by a letter appearing to be a telegram. □ An obsolete term for a phonograph record.

phonograph A device used for playing discs. It includes a turntable, tone arm, pickup cartridge, motor, and stylus. Called a *gramophone* in Britain.

phono jack A female connector designed to be used with a phono plug.

phono plug A small plug often used to connect preamplifiers, amplifiers, turntables, and so on.

phonorecords Material objects in which sounds, other than those accompanying a motion picture or other audio-visual work, are fixed by any method now known or later developed, and from which the sounds can be perceived, reproduced, or otherwise communicated, either directly or with the aid of a machine or device. The term "phonorecords" included the material object in which the sounds are first fixed.

Phonovision □ A device developed by John Baird of Great Britain to store a television image on a disc. □ A general term for a personal telephone television system.

phosphor The layer of luminescent material on the inner face of a television picture tube or cathode ray tube.

phosphor dots The red, green, and blue dots on a television screen that glow when excited. In a three-gun color tube, the dots are often placed in a triangular relationship.

phosphorescence The emission of light by a material after excitation. *See also* electroluminescence.

phosphorescent printing A method of making signs that give off light after exposure to a light source.

phosphors Substances that emit light when exposed to the excitation of electrical energy.

phosphor strip One of the strips of color that is used instead of phosphor dots on the inner surface of some television receivers and monitors.

phot A unit of luminescence equal to one lumen per square centimeter.

photo □ A prefix derived from the Greek word *phot,* meaning "light." □ An abbreviation for *photograph, photographer, photographic, photography,* and so on.

photo agency A commercial organization that sells photographs from an extensive picture library.

photoboard A set of still photographs made from a television commercial, accompanied by a script, and printed on a single sheet of paper; used primarily for recordkeeping or merchandising purposes.

photo call A film, television, stage show, or other call for the purpose of taking publicity stills.

photocathode An electrode that, when exposed to light, emits electrons. Used in television camera tubes and other devices.

photocell A device that transduces light into electrical impulses. Also called a *photoelectric cell.*

Photocolor A special television newsphoto service of the Associated Press.

photocomposer A photomechanical device used in photo offset lithography to make multiple copies of the same image.

photocomposition A method of setting type by exposing negatives of the characters on film or photographic paper. Also called *photographic typesetting* when only type is being composed. Also called *phototypesetting* and *phototypography. See also* photo offset lithography.

photocopy A reproduction of a page, advertisement, picture, and so on, made by whiteprint processes, xerography, or other such process.

photo double *See* double.

photodrama A tragic or melodramatic photoplay.

photo editor An individual who is in charge of the photography department of a newspaper or magazine and who selects, or assists others in selecting, photographs for inclusion in stories, articles, and so on. Also called a *picture editor.*

photoelectric The property certain substances have of creating an electrical potential when they are excited by light.

photoelectric cell *See* photocell.

photoelectrotype An electrotype produced through photographic means.

photoemissive Emitting or capable of emitting electrons upon exposure to radiation in and near the visible region of the spectrum.

photoengraver A person who makes photoengravings.

photoengraving The photochemical process of making relief printing plates from artwork, proofs, photographs, and so on.

photo essay □ A story told with photographs or slides. □ An article or book detailing one subject or person in photographs.

photofabrication The manufacture of metal parts using photographic and etching processes.

Photofax A wire picture service of the Associated Press.

photofinishing The process of producing prints from negatives.

photoflash The firing of oxygen-filled glass bulbs for photographic purposes. Now largely obsolete in professional use because of the development of electronic flashguns.

photoflood An incandescent lamp used to produce a high-intensity light.

photogelatin A screenless, continuous-tone printing process that uses gelatin-coated plates. Also called *collotype.*

photogelatin plate A plate used in the photogelatin printing process.

photogenic A person or object that photographs well. *See also* telegenic.

photogram □ A landscape or other pictorial photograph. □ A picture made by placing an object on photographic paper and exposing it to light.

photograph □ A picture or image made by photography. □ A still or series of stills, in the form of prints, slides, motion pictures, and so on.

photographer An amateur or professional skilled in the art of making motion pictures or taking stills. *See also* cinematographer. Cf. videographer.

photographic emulsion *See* emulsion.

photographic filter *See* filter.

photographic image □ An image formed on an emulsion by photography. □ Any image formed on a light-sensitive surface such as a cathode ray tube.

photographic speed A measure of the sensitivity of a film emulsion. *See also* film speed.

photographic type *See* cold type.

photographic typesetting *See* photocomposition.

photography Literally, from the Greek meaning "writing with light." □ The formation of a image on a photosensitive surface by the action of light or other radiant energy. □ The art or process of making pictures.

photogravure □ A photomechanical intaglio process. □ A print made by this process.

photojournalism The art of reporting news or supporting news stories through photographs—still, tape, or film. Sometimes called *pictorial journalism.*

photokinesis *See* photokinestasis.

photokinestasis An animation technique in which an illusion of movement is achieved by moving static artwork—usually photographs, collages, or reproductions of paintings—under the camera. Also called *kinestatis* and *photokinesis.*

photolettering The production of photographic images of display type by various means on film or photographic paper. *See also* photocomposition and phototypesetting.

photolithography *See* photo offset lithography.

photomacrography The process of photographing visible small objects so that they appear larger than life size. Cf. photomicrography.

photomatic A television commercial produced from filming a sequence of still photographs; usually used only for testing purposes. Cf. animatic.

photomechanical Any process that combines photographic and mechanical means to produce a printing plate. *See also* intaglio, lithography, and photoengraving.

photomechanical transfer (PMT) *See* velox.

photometer A precision instrument used to measure the intensity of light. *See also* light meter.

photometry The branch of science that deals with the measurement of the intensity of light.

photomicrography The process of photographing small objects through a microscope. Cf. photomacrography.

photomontage A picture composed of two or more other, smaller pictures or portions of pictures. *See also* montage.

Photon A trademark for a phototypesetting machine.

photon The smallest unit of electromagnetic energy, in light equal to one candle per square meter.

photonovel A paperback that contains a novel and stills from the motion picture that was made from the novel.

photo offset *See* photo offset lithography.

photo offset lithography A planographic printing process in which a photographic image is transferred from a printing plate or cylinder to a rubber blanket and "offset" to paper. Also called *offset, offset printing, photolithography,* and *photo offset. See also* dry offset and lithography. Cf. letterpress.

photo opportunity A time set aside for the media to take pictures of celebrities or political figures.

photoplastic recording A reusable, electrostatic recording process using a photoconductive polymeric layer that is deformed by a light beam. Cf. thermoplastic recording.

photoplay □ A motion picture produced and/or exhibited with sound and voice recording, reproducing and/or transmitting devices, radio devices, and all other improvements and devices—including television—that are now or may hereafter be used in connection with the production and/or exhibition and/or transmission of any present or future kind of motion picture production. □ A stage play that has been made into a motion picture.

photopolymer A classification of plastic material capable of receiving an image from film when the plastic is exposed to light. Used for both direct printing and for molding duplicate reproduction products, such as newspaper mats.

photoprint A print made of a page by any photographic copying process.

photo release *See* release.

photoscript A photographic record of a motion picture, commercial, television program, and so on, made from original footage.

photosensitive A substance or surface capable of emitting electrons when it is excited by light rays.

photosensor Any device that converts light into an electrical signal.

photosetting A method of setting type by photocomposition. *See also* photocomposition.

photosphere *See* hemisphere.

Photostat □ A trademark for a photocopying machine. □ A photographic reproduction sometimes used as an inexpensive title card.

phototelegraphy The transmission of still photographs by wire or radio.

phototype A printing plate or block made from a photograph.

phototypesetter A computerized machine for photographically setting type. Cf. linecaster.

phototypesetting The method of setting type using the output of a computer. *See also* photocomposition.

phototypography *See* photocomposition.

phrasing The inflection, tempo, and pauses given a line by a performer or singer.

physical A scene in a motion picture, television program, story, and so on, that contains strong physical action, such as fight scenes.

physical editing *See* mechanical editing.

PI □ Per inquiry. □ Public information. □ Programmed information. □ Programmed instruction. □ Parallel input. □ Program interrupt.

pi Metal type that is mixed or disarranged. Also spelled *pie.* Also called *pied.*

piano board Originally, a portable resistance dimmer switchboard in an upright castered wooden box and used as a road board. Now, the term is sometimes used for other types of portable dimmer switchboards. Also called a *piano box.* Cf. road board.

PIB Publishers Information Bureau, Inc.

pic An abbreviation for *picture,* either still or moving. The plural is abbreviated *pix.*

PICA Press Independence and Critical Ability. An index of a country's freedom of the press issues.

pica □ A size of type; 12 points. □ A standard measure for the width of a line of type; 6 picas equal 1 inch. □ The most common size of typewriter characters; 10 characters to the inch. Cf. elite.

picaresque A novel, motion picture, and so on, that centers on the adventures of a rogue.

pica rule *See* line gauge.

pica stick *See* line gauge.

pi character A little used special character or symbol.

picket fencing The "fffff" noise that occurs on a car radio when the car moves through rapidly varying FM signal strength areas.

picking The lifting, during printing, of paper fibers by the inked type or plates.

pick it up □ A director's command to talent to pick up cues faster. □ A director's command to increase the tempo of the lines, music, and so on. □ To begin a scene rehearsal from a specific point in a script, usually at a place where something went wrong.

pick up (PU) To retake part of a previously shot film sequence.

pickup □ An electromechanical transducer that is actuated by modulations present in the groove of the recording medium and that transforms this mechanical input into an electric output. □ Any device used to transform a sound picture into corresponding electric impulses. □ The sound received by a microphone. □ The picture received by a television or film camera. □ A feed received from a multiple. □ *See* pickup point. □ The origination point of a remote broadcast. □ Material that is added to a story already in type; often a new lead or updated information. □ Type matter that has been used previously and held for future use. □ To use information in a news story that was obtained second hand. □ *See* pickup material. □ Supplemental music recorded by musicians after a motion picture has been completed.

pickup arm A pivoted arm arranged to hold a pickup. Also called a *tone arm*.

pickup cartridge The removable portion of a pickup containing the electromechanical translating elements and the reproducing stylus.

pickup line A line at the top of wire service copy that indicates the continuation of previous information about a story by the use of the word *add*.

pickup material Advertising material created for one advertisement and used in some form in a different advertisement. Also called a *pickup*.

pickup pattern *See* polar pattern.

pickup point The place of origin of a broadcast. Usually refers to a remote.

pickup tube An electronic device that converts optical images into an electrical current or a charge-density image by scanning in order to provide an electric signal. *See also* calnicon, cathode ray tube (CRT), iconoscope, image dissector, image orthicon, orthicon, plumbicon, and vidicon.

pico (p) A prefix for one-trillionth. Formerly referred to as *micro-micro*.

pics An abbreviation for *pictures*; more commonly spelled *pix*.

pictograph A chart or graph that uses pictures for comparison purposes.

pictorial, graphic, and sculptural works Two-dimensional and three-dimensional works of fine, graphic, and applied art, photographs, prints and art reproductions, maps, globes, charts, technical drawings, diagrams, and models. Such works include works of artistic craftsmanship insofar as their form but not their mechanical or utilitarian aspects are concerned; the design of a useful article is considered a pictorial, graphic, or sculptural work only if, and only to the extent that, such design incorporates pictorial, graphic, or sculptural features that can be identified separately from, and are capable of existing independently of, the utilitarian aspects of the article.

pictorial journalism *See* photojournalism.

pictorial work *See* pictorial, graphic, and sculptural works.

picture □ The motion picture industry. □ The art or business of making motion pictures. □ A motion picture. □ The video portion of a television signal. □ A still picture. □ One frame of a motion picture.

picture area That portion of a film or videotape that carries the image.

picture brightness *See* brightness.

picture car A vehicle that is used in a motion picture, television program, and so on.

picture carrier The luminance signal of a television picture. Also called *luminance carrier.*

picture channel The circuits that carry a television picture signal from the pickup tubes through the associated equipment to the transmitter.

picture chaser A slang term for a news photographer.

picture definition *See* definition.

picturedom The world of the motion picture.

picture dupe negative A film negative printed from a master positive or from a picture negative. Also called a *dupe.*

picture editor *See* photo editor.

picture element *See* pixel.

picture elements *See* element.

picture field *See* field.

picture frame *See* frame.

picture frequency The complete number of times a television picture is scanned per second. *See also* frame frequency.

picture gate *See* gate.

picture house An outdated term for a *motion picture theatre.*

picture image A visual likeness of an object recorded on film or videotape.

picture line standard The total number of horizontal lines in a complete television picture. In the United States, Japan, and other countries, 525. Some systems used 405; others use 819 lines. The international standard is 625 lines. Some advanced television systems, such as HDTV, use 1125 lines.

picture master positive A film print used to produce a picture dupe negative.

picture matching *See* camera balance.

picture monitor *See* monitor.

picture negative Any film that produces a negative image, whether camera original or print.

picture palace A slang term for a motion picture theatre.

Picturephone □ An AT&T development in the 1920s and 1930s that included a video picture as well as voice. □ A telephone capable of video transmission as well as voice.

picture play An outdated term for a screenplay. *See also* photoplay.

picture print A positive print made from a picture negative.

picture quality standards *See* Grade 1, Grade 2, Grade 3, Grade 4, Grade 5, and Grade 6.

picture release negative An edited film negative used to print the picture portion of release prints.

picture safety The border around the essential area of a picture.

picture scanning *See* scanning.

picture service The major press associations' service providing visual material to television stations.

picture signal The composite video signal that lies above the blanking level.

picture size □ The area of a received picture. □ The diagonal measurement of the screen of a television receiver or monitor.

picture tube A television receiver or monitor cathode ray tube in which electrical signals are converted into picture information by a scanning beam traversing a photosensitive surface. Also called a *kinescope.*

picture work print A positive work print that is used to edit the various scenes of a motion picture.

picturize To make into a motion picture.

PI deal *See* per inquiry.

Pi Delta Epsilon A journalism society.

pie A variant spelling of *pi.*

piece □ A leather insert on a book back. □ A play, drama, picture, painting, and so on. □ *See* story.

piece accent A typographical accent cast on a type body.

piece fraction A type body consisting of two pieces; one piece the numerator, the other the denominator.

piece to camera A British term for a standupper.

pied *See* pi.

pie formula A slang term for a television series format wherein the crust, or cast, stays the same each week but the filling, or story line, changes.

piezoelectric crystal A quartz crystal or other crystalline substance that generates a voltage when the crystal is subjected to mechanical stress.

pig A large piece of type metal.

pigeon □ A film or tape courier for a network, station, or wire service. □ A movable platform used to increase the height of talent or cameras. *See also* apple box, pancake, and riser.

pigeonhole A white space in several lines of type caused by too much spacing between words.

pigeons Noise observed on television picture tubes as pulses or bursts of short duration at a slow rate of occurrence.

piggyback □ A direct mail offer that hitches a free ride with another offer. □ Two commercial messages promoting different products by the same manufacturer played back-to-back. *See also* integrated commercial and multiple product announcement. □ A cable television channel that is used for two or more services.

pig iron Dull or overly serious news reports.

pigment The coloring substance in ink, paint, and so on.

pigskin A leather used in bookbinding.

pigtail □ A wire or optical fiber used for terminating a circuit. □ An electrical connector consisting of a plug and two jacks.

pile-on To override a lighting preset with another higher preset.

pi line A throwaway line set by a compositor when a mistake has been made in the line.

pillar A tall, tube-shaped column used as a set piece.

pilot □ A videotape or film of a proposed television series prepared for presentation to prospective sponsors, networks, and advertising agencies. Also called a *pilot film* and *pilot program.* Cf. de facto pilot. □ A signal sent through a system to control or monitor its function.

pilot film *See* pilot.

pilot light A small incandescent lamp usually covered with a colored cap used to indicate that a circuit is on or functional.

pilot pin One of the camera or projector registration pins that engage the perforations on motion picture film. Also called a *pin* and *register pin.*

pilot pins *See* registration pin.

pilot print *See* answer print.

pilot program *See* pilot.

pilot script A story and/or teleplay intended to be used for the production of a pilot film for a proposed serial or episodic series and setting forth the framework intended to be repeated in subsequent episodes, including the setting, theme, and premise of the proposed serial or series and its central running characters.

pilot study A testing version of a proposed large-scale investigation in such contexts as marketing, direct mail, and audience preferences.

pilot subcarrier □ A subcarrier serving as a control signal for use in the reception of FM stereophonic broadcasts. □ A subcarrier used in the reception of TV stereophonic aural or other subchannel broadcasts.

pilot test A screening of a television pilot in which members of the audience, who are often pulled in off the streets, evaluate the potential of the program.

pilot tone □ A standardized waveform recorded on a tape for audio synchronization purposes. □ An audio tone recorded at the beginning of a tape to indicate the level of sound for playback. □ An audio tone recorded on tape with the motion picture audio to serve as a reference for later synchronization of sound and picture.

pin □ A terminal on a plug or vacuum tube. □ To sharpen the beam of a luminaire. □ To drive the needle on a VU meter, or other indicator, past the maximum limit. Also called *peg.* □ To establish a point or thought in an audience. □ One of the series of sharp pins that hold the newspaper in the folder. □ A small nail used in mounting printing plates on wood. □ *See* pilot pin.

pinboard animation *See* pinscreen.

pinch effect A pinching of the reproducing stylus tip twice each cycle in the reproduction of lateral recordings, due to a decrease in angle measure in a plane perpendicular to the modulation slope at any given instant.

pinch roller A cylinder of rubber or similar material that holds the tape in contact with the capstan. *See also* pressure roller.

pincushion distortion A type of distortion characterized by an inward curving of straight lines.

pin feed A mechanism used on some printers that use attached, perforated, or fanfold paper. Also called *tractor feed.*

pinfeed paper Paper that is attached and perforated. Designed to fit tractor feed printers. Also called *perforated paper.*

ping ponging □ The back-and-forth switching between anchors in the presentation of television newscasts. □ The mixdown of two or more audio tracks into one on a multiple-track tape recorder. □ To change the time code and audio on a videotape to different tracks. Accomplished by rerecording the information one track at a time.

pinhole □ A transparent spot on a film negative; usually caused by dust on the film during exposure. □ An old fashioned, simple box camera that used a pinhole opening instead of a lens. □ One of the small perforations made by the folding machine in the bottom of newspaper pages.

pink noise Any audio noise that is inversely proportional to the frequency of the signal; contains the same energy level in all frequencies.

pin plug An electrical connector using round cross section pins. Also called a *connector.*

pin rack The wire hooks above an editing bin used for holding motion picture film.

pin rail The device containing wooden pegs that are used to tie off scenery or lighting instruments flown from the flies.

pins The teeth in a camera or projector that fit into the perforations of the film.

pinscreen An animation technique invented by Alexander Alexeieff and Claire Parker that uses the shadows of hundreds of thousands of tiny steel pins to form black and white pictures; the configuration of the pins is altered before each exposure. Also called *pinboard animation.*

pin spot A low-wattage spotlight.

PIO □ Public Information Office of the FCC. □ Public information officer.

pipe □ To distribute a program or signal, usually by wire or cable. *See also* feed. □ A slang term for telephone. □ The galvanized iron pipe that is used to construct lighting grids.

pipe clamp A device that connects the yoke or pipe arm of a lighting instrument to a pipe batten or boomerang.

pipe grid *See* lighting grid.

pipeline The communication link between a source of information and the ultimate user.

piping The act of feeding a radio or television program by wire or cable.

PIQ Program Idea Quotient. A Home Testing Institute measure of audience reaction to new program ideas.

piracy □ The misappropriation of an individual's efforts; often used in the sense of copyright infringement. □ The theft of satellite programming services in violation of Title 47 of the United States Code (USC), Section 705. □ The theft of cable television or pay cable services without payment. □ *See* pirating.

pirate A person or company guilty of piracy or pirating.

pirated copy A reproduction of a copyrighted work.

pirate station A radio or television station that operates without authority; often in international waters.

pirating The illegal (unlicensed) reproduction and subsequent sale of records or tapes made to look like the original product. Also called *counterfeiting.* Cf. bootlegging.

PISA Public Interest Satellite Association. A citizens' group.

pistol grip A handle in the shape of a handgun used to steady small cameras while someone shoots the image.

pit The ''groove'' in a CD.

pitch □ The number of grooves per inch in a disc recording. □ The property of a musical tone that is determined by the highness or lowness of its frequency. □ The distance between typeset letters. *See also* character pitch. □ An appeal or plea to an audience or sales prospect. □ The distance between successive film perforations.

pitch control A turntable or tape recorder potentiometer or signal processor that controls, within narrow limits, the speed of the device. Also called a *pitch shifter* and *pitch transposer.*

pitchman A high-pressure salesperson employing a hard sell.

pitch program A high-pressure radio or television program that runs longer than one minute and that attempts to sell a product through the use of high-pressure techniques.

pitch shifter *See* pitch control.

pitch transposer *See* pitch control.

pivoting A camera pan in which one of the edges of the picture remains relatively stationary while the rest of the picture changes. Accomplished by moving the camera.

pivot printing The printing of type characters vertically instead of horizontally.

pix An abbreviation for *pictures.* The singular is abbreviated *pic.*

pixel An abbreviation for *picture element.* The smallest element of a display space that can be addressed, manipulated, or effectively reproduced; the smallest unit of raster graphics.

pixel depth The number of bits used by a computer to describe each pixel; a measure of intensity resolution.

pixel multiplication In CD-I, a technique used in decoding pictorial information to make high-resolution pixel information compatible with a lower-resolution system.

pixel paring The joining together of two pixels to make one byte; the pair are then regarded for most purposes as a single unit. Occurs in three-bit run-encoded images, and four-bit CLUT encoded pictures.

pixel processor A DVI video display processor that is designed to process 12.5 million instructions per second.

pixel repeat A visual effect function that repeats pixel values from an image memory to produce horizontal magnification. Used in RGB 555 and CLUT image decoding.

pixillation An animation technique using stop-motion photography to photograph live actors and sets in order to create unusual motion effects.

pixlock A videotape recorder feature that synchronizes the output with other input sources to a switcher so that fades and dissolves may be accomplished without tearing. *See* amtec and linelock.

PL □ Combined construction permit and license. An FCC file-number prefix. □ Private line. □ Public law. □ Public library. □ Programming language.

PLA Public Library Association.

placement call *See* placement interview.

placement interview The initial contact with a member of a household in order to secure permission to install a people meter or diary in the household. The primary aim is to secure an agreement of the individual to participate in a survey.

plagiarism The unauthorized use of ideas, writing, photographs, and so on, by an individual without acknowledgment or permission of the originator or copyright holder.

plain ASCII A computer ASCII format file that does not contain any codes from a specific word processing program. A plain ASCII file may contain generic codes for typesetting. Also called *pure ASCII.*

plain lighting Indoor lighting that approximates the position of sunlight.

plaintiff The person who brings a civil lawsuit. Sometimes known as the *petitioner.* In a criminal action, the government is the plaintiff. Cf. defendant and respondent.

plan □ *See* floor plan. □ *See* package.

plane In video, one layer of a bit-mapped display. *See also* image plane.

plane of critical focus The area of a picture that is in critical focus.

planer A wooden block used to make the type level in a form before it is locked up.

planned-no-viewing households Television households that indicated at the time of diary placement that no television viewing would occur during the survey week and that did not return a usable diary.

plano-convex lens A simple lens with one flat and one convex side.

plano-convex spotlight An old form of spotlight similar to a fresnel spotlight but using a plano-convex lens that produces a less uniform beam and a sharper beam edge. Also called a *P.C. spot. See also* ellipsoidal spotlight.

planography Any process that prints from a plane surface, including lithography and photogelatin. Cf. halftone, intaglio, and relief.

plan rate The cost to an advertiser who purchases time in quantity; based on the number of spots.

plant □ The physical buildings, equipment, and so on of a broadcast station or CATV system. □ A factory or workshop designed to produce equipment or products; a printing plant, a photographic plant, and so on. □ A performer who pretends to be a member of an audience. □ To send publicity materials to the media. □ An object, idea, or character that is established in one scene of a motion picture, novel, play, and so on, and used as a payoff later. □ All of the outdoor advertising structures in a given city, town, or area operated by an outdoor company or plant operator. Also called an *outdoor plant.*

plant capacity In outdoor advertising, the number of "100" showings available in a plant. This is determined by dividing the total number of panels in a plant by the number of panels that make up the 100 GRPs or 100 showings.

plant operator An individual or company that operates and maintains outdoor advertising structures.

plant owner An individual or company that owns outdoor advertising structures.

plasma display A flat panel containing highly ionized gases; used as an alternative to cathode ray tubes.

plastic A resin or polymer suitable for molding discs by the application of heat and pressure in a mold (die) cavity.

plastic binding *See* mechanical binding.

plasticizer An additive to the tape base material, usually to ensure flexibility.

plastic plate A plate made from plastic, as opposed to mats, electrotypes, or stereotypes.

plate □ A film that is used for front or rear projection as a background. Also called a *process plate.* □ A sheet of glass coated with an emulsion. □ The anode of a vacuum tube. □ Any printing surface from which ink is transferred to paper, except for surfaces made from individual pieces of type or slugs. A letterpress plate usually indicates a duplicate electrotype, stereotype, plastic plate, and so on. *See also* cut, engraving, gravure, and photogelatin plate. □ To finish paper with a high gloss by pressing between metal plates. □ A book illustration, especially a large and relatively important one. □ A single resistance dimmer unit. Also applied to other types.

plateau A level that is reached and maintained, such as in newspaper subscriptions, audience ratings, cable penetration, or advertising agency billings.

plated disks Computer disks that are coated with a hard metal alloy instead of iron oxide.

plated stock High gloss, smooth paper that has been pressed between polished metal sheets.

plate input power The product of the direct plate voltage applied to the tubes in the last radio stage and the total direct current flowing to the plates of these tubes, measured without modulation.

plateless engraving *See* thermography.

platemaker A person who produces printing plates.

platen □ The part of a turntable assembly on which the disc lies. Also called a *platter plate.* □ The flat metal plate that presses the paper against the type in a platen press. □ The roller of a typewriter or printer that printing mechanisms hit in order to form characters on paper. □ In animation, a sheet of heavy glass used to hold cels flat and still during shooting. The use of the platen also prevents shadows from the painted areas from falling on the background.

platen press A relief printing press with a movable vertical platen and upright type form.

plate proof A proof made from an electrotype, stereotype, plastic plate, and so on.

platform The stated editorial policy of a publication. Also called a *policy.*

platinum A record album that has sold a million copies. Cf. gold.

platinum level Time purchased on a satellite transponder that is not preemptible. Cf. bronze level and gold level.

platter □ The thin, round plate used for a hard disk. □ A flat disc used for holding a quantity of tape, usually in the form of a large roll. □ A slang term for a phonograph disc or electrical transcription. *See also* pressing.

platter plate *See* platen.

platter spinner A slang term for a disc jockey.

play □ A representation of an action or story. □ To create a role in a drama or program. □ To reproduce the audio and/or video records of a tape recording. □ The length of time a news story is emphasized. □ To emphasize or deemphasize a story. □ To operate a device, such as a tape recorder, projector, turntable, and so on, so that it reproduces recorded material. □ A showing of a licensed program or motion picture.

play back To play a tape. Cf. playback.

playback □ An expression used to denote the reproduction of a recording. □ The recounting of the content of a commercial by a respondent in an interview. □ Recorded music that is used instead of musicians during a rehearsal. □ A soundtrack used to cue performers during the filming of the action. □ The process of playing a tape. Cf. play back. □ A survey respondent's recall of specific elements in an advertisement, story, program, and so on.

playback equalization *See* postemphasis.

playback head □ The magnetic head used to pick up the sound or picture information from a tape. Also called a *play head* and *replay head.* □ A read head on a computer disk drive.

playback loss *See* translation loss.

playbill A printed theatre, concert, or other program that contains a list of the cast, director, crew, title, and so on.

play-by-play A sporting event broadcast that includes all major actions in sequence, as opposed to a summary. May be live, delayed, or re-created.

play-by-play announcer A radio or television sportscaster who reports the action of a sporting event.

play control block A data structure indicating what information is to be accessed on the disc for the current or next real-time record play function of the compact disc file manager.

play control list A structure list that controls the destination of the data.

playdate The date on which a motion picture, television program, and so on, will be shown.

play down To deemphasize the importance of a story by, for example, placing in on an inside page of a publication or late in a newscast. Cf. play up.

player The talent—actor, actress, performer, and so on—used in a motion picture, program, show, or commercial. *See also* contract player, day player, deal player, free-lance player, multiple picture player, stunt player, and term player.

playgoer A general term for an individual who attends productions in the legitimate theatre, motion pictures, and so on.

play head *See* playback head.

playing area The area encompassed by a set, or the area outlined in which talent is to perform.

playing time □ The maximum amount of tape or film on a reel or in a cassette or cartridge, usually measured in feet or minutes. □ The running time of a tape, motion picture, laser disk, and so on. □ The total time of a program or play exclusive of interruptions or intermissions. Cf. cumulative time.

playlist The records that have been or will be broadcast by a radio station.

playoff The final showing of a motion picture or other program under the rights granted to broadcast the motion picture or program a specific number of times.

play off The curtain or exit music used to end a scene or performance.

play on The music used to begin a scene or performance.

play-only machine A television tape machine used only for the reproduction of tapes.

play theory A theory that the user of mass media does so primarily to derive pleasure rather than receive information.

play up To emphasize the importance of a story by, for example, placing it on the front page of a publication or early in a newscast. Cf. play down.

playwright An individual who has written at least one play; a dramatist.

pleading □ Any written notice, motion, petition, request, opposition, reply, brief, proposed findings, exceptions, memorandum of law, or other paper filed with an administrative agency in a hearing proceeding. □ A statement of the parties to a lawsuit that contains their allegations and defenses.

plop A slang term for a plosive sound.

plopping focus A quick refocusing from one object or performer to another in a shot. Also called *throwing focus*.

plosive An explosive sound made by overemphasizing a letter such as B and P. Also called a *plop* and *pop*.

plot □ The story line of a play, drama, novel, program, or commercial. □ A lighting plot. □ In animation, to plan and calibrate the movements of the artwork and/or camera for pans, trucks, and rotations.

plot gimmick *See* gimmick.

plot line *See* story line.

plot music Any music that is an integral part of the plot, such as a song sung by one of the characters, as opposed to background music.

plot plan *See* floor plan.

plot plant *See* plant.

plotter □ A device used for producing hard copies of graphic materials. □ A device that mechanically draws computer-driven graphs, charts, drawings, and so on.

PLP Presentation Level Protocol.

plug □ To promote an advertiser, product, program, station, and so on. □ The casual mention of a product or advertiser on the air for which no payment is received. □ Fill copy. □ A connector, usually male, that fits into a fixed jack. *See also* phone plug and phono plug. □ To fill out a form by inserting spacing material. □ A book that has not sold well. *See also* remainder.

plugging box A portable receptacle with one electrical feed, and outlets for two or more branch circuits; often contains branch fuses.

plug in A device or component having the connectors necessary for use already attached.

plug-in module *See* insert module.

plugola The promoting of products on the air for which the radio or television station does not receive payment; record plugola, song plugging, or "accidental" mentions of products by performers for which payment is received. *See also* payola.

plumbicon A photoconductive type of television camera pickup tube similar to the vidicon but with improved capabilities because of the use of a lead (hence the use of the word *plumb*; Pb for lead) monoxide target. *See also* pickup tube.

plumbing A colloquial term for rf lines.

plus lens A lens with a positive diopter factor; a close-up lens.

PM □ Permanent magnet. □ Phase modulation. □ Post meridiem. □ Preventive maintenance. □ People meter.

p.m. An afternoon newspaper. Cf. a.m.

PMA □ Phonograph Manufacturers Association. □ Photo Marketing Association.

PMB Print Measurement Bureau.

PMPEA Professional Motion Picture Equipment Association.

pmt Photomechanical transfer.

PNS Publishers Newspaper Syndicate.

pocket □ Individual or groups of outlets for stage circuits, often located under a protective trapdoor; examples include floor pockets, wall pockets, and fly pockets. □ An envelope-like receptacle on one of the inside covers of a book.

pocketpiece (PP) A biweekly rating report designed to fit in a coat pocket, issued by Nielsen Television Index.

pocket shot A medium close-up usually taken from the lapel pocket of a man's coat up.

Poe Awards, Edgar Allen Awards given by the Mystery Writers of America, Inc. for outstanding crime and mystery writing in television and other fields.

poid The curve traced by the center of a sphere when it rolls or slides over a surface having a sinusoidal profile.

point □ A place in time where disc jockeys and announcers place material, such as a talk point, jingle point, or time point. □ To emphasize or punch a line. □ To indicate a cue physically. □ A rating point. □ A unit of type measurement, approximately 1/12 of a pica or 1/72 of an inch. *See also* point system. □ A punctuation mark; usually refers to a period but may be a comma, semicolon, or other mark.

pointer □ A needle or indicator used in a meter. □ A master of ceremonies.

pointillage The building up of a flat surface by painting.

point of attack The beginning of a story or play.

point of departure In story telling, beginning the story at the beginning of a script. Each character has a history, and each story has events that happened before the point of departure.

Point-of-Purchase Advertising Institute, Inc. (POPAI) A nonprofit organization, founded in 1938, by makers of point-of-purchase advertising displays; also members are the advertisers and retailers who use the displays.

point of view (POV) □ A camera shot that shows the scene from the position of one of the performers. Also called a *first person shot.* Cf. objective camera and subjective camera. □ The perspective or specific character through which or from which a story line is written or narrated. □ An auteur's attitude as it is seen in the finished product.

point set A piece of type whose width is a multiple or fraction of a point. Cf. unit set.

point system A system adopted in 1886 by the United States Type Founders Association for the vertical measurement of type; based on a then-standard pica type body. One point is .013837 inches. *See also* point.

point to point The transmission of signals between two points by microwave or cable.

POL An abbreviation for *polarized* and *political programs.*

polar characteristics *See* polar pattern.

polar curve A graph showing the characteristics of a light source.

polar diagram *See* polar pattern.

polarity □ The direction of current flow. □ The north and south poles of a magnet. □ The black portion of a television signal with respect to the white portion.

polarity control A switch on a camera control unit that allows the reversing of negative or positive images.

polarity reversal The electronic change of the black portions of a television picture to white and the white portions to black.

polarization The direction of transmission of electromagnetic signals from an antenna that have been vertically, horizontally, or circularly radiated.

polarized glasses Glasses used for stereoscopic viewing; one lens is horizontally polarized; the other, vertically polarized.

polarized light Light that is transmitted in one plane only by blocking the other light planes.

polarized plug An electrical plug that may be inserted in one direction only.

polarized projection The projection of superimposed images to form a stereoscopic picture.

polarizing filter A lens filter mounted on a lens that restricts light waves from entering from more than one angle. Used to reduce glare and reflections. Cf. pola screen.

polar mount A satellite dish that is mounted so that it can track a geosynchronous satellite by movement on only one axis.

polaroid fade A camera fade accomplished by rotating one of two polarizing lens filters.

polaroid filter *See* pola screen.

Polaroid Land A trademark for a process that is used to produce a print from a camera shortly after film exposure. Sometimes called an *instant camera.*

polar pattern □ The angle of acceptance of sound by a microphone as seen from directly above. □ The radiation pattern of a loudspeaker or antenna. Also called *polar characteristic, polar diagram,* and *field pattern.*

pola screen A large polarizing filter mounted in front of a camera lens to decrease glare and reflections. Also called a *polaroid filter.* Cf. polarizing filter.

Polavision A trademark for a motion picture camera that develops the film in the cartridge automatically.

pole One of the ends of a magnet, battery, switch, lamp, and so on.

pole attachment Any connection by a cable television system to a pole, duct, conduit, or right-of-way owned or controlled by a utility.

Polecat A trademark for a telescoping metal tube used to hang luminaires.

pole climber An individual who attaches and repairs telephone lines and/or cable television coaxial cables to utility poles.

pole face The surface of a pole tip that is parallel to and in contact with the gap spacer.

pole piece The magnetic core structure of a video-head assembly, part of which is wound with the head windings that carry record and reproduce current to and from the head, and part of which is formed into the pole tip.

pole rights The rights obtained by a cable television system to attach cables to poles owned by utility companies.

pole tip That part of the video head that protrudes radially beyond the surface of the headwheel or drum and forms the magnetic path to and from the tape.

police blotter A police record of arrests, bookings, and so on.

police power The inherent authority of a government to exercise power to protect the general welfare of its citizens.

policy □ A statement issued by an administrative agency concerning a regulatory matter. □ *See* platform.

Policy Statement on Comparative Broadcast Hearings A 1965 policy statement issued by the FCC to delineate the comparative criteria and their application to mutually exclusive applicants for a broadcast license.

policy story A printed story designed to promote a publication's platform.

polish To write changes in dialogue, narration, or action of a teleplay or screenplay. Cf. rewrite.

Polish notation *See* reverse polish notation (RPN).

political action committee (PAC) An organization formed to raise and distribute campaign funds to candidates for political office.

political broadcasting Programs and/or commercials that are presented on radio, television, or cable by legally qualified candidates for public office or their supporters.

political candidates *See* legally qualified candidates.

political editorial An editorial broadcast by a station endorsing or opposing a legally qualified candidate for public office. Such editorials require that the station offer reasonable opportunity to respond to the editorial.

political programs (POL) Programs that present candidates for public office or that give expression (other than station editorials) to views on such candidates or on issues subject to public ballot. An FCC program type category.

Polk Memorial Awards, George Awards given by The Long Island University Journalism Department for distinguished achievements in journalism.

poll □ A method by which communication devices such as a computer or data transmission system are asked in sequence whether they need processing or transmitting time. Also called *polling.* □ *See* convenience sample.

polling □ *See* poll. □ An interactive computer method of interrogating a respondent or terminal from a central point.

pollster □ A slang term for an organization that conducts public opinion polls and/or surveys. □ An individual who works for a polling organization.

poly bag A transparent polyethylene bag used instead of an envelope for mailing.

polydirectional microphone A microphone with an adjustable polar pattern. *See also* mike pattern.

polyester Polyethylene glycol terepthalate. A high-quality synthetic resin used as a magnetic tape backing. Cf. acetate and mylar.

polyglot A book that contains the same text in two or more languages; usually in parallel columns.

polygon A three-dimensional shape used extensively in designing complex images by computer graphics.

polygonal rendering A basic modeling technique that defines polygonal surfaces defined by vertex points and filled in with color or gray scale shading.

polystyrene A thermoplastic material used as a dialectric.

polyvinyl chloride (PVC) A thermoplastic material used as a substitute for rubber to insulate wires and cables.

POM Professionals, owners, and managers. A demographic category reported by NTI.

pony *See* pony service.

pony report *See* pony service.

pony service A report, often by telephone, from a press association to a newspaper giving a summary of the day's news. Also called *pony* and *pony report.*

pony spread A periodical page arrangement in which an advertisement occupies a portion of each of two facing pages. Also called a *junior spread.*

pony unit A reduced size version of a standard advertisement. Also called a *junior unit.*

pool □ The sharing of information, facilities, microphones, cameras, tapes, and so on, by two or more competing media. Often used to cover news events. □ *See* commercial pool.

pool lighting The illumination of one area of a set or stage. *See also* limbo.

pool out To develop one or more commercials for use in a commercial pool.

pool partner A commercial that is used in a commercial pool; usually in reference to a two-commercial pool or a newly developed commercial.

pool reporter A reporter who is selected from among a number of reporters to represent them when the allowable number of reporters is limited.

poop sheet *See* dope sheet.

pop □ A slang term for popular music. □ A heavy crash on a line caused by thunder or other disturbance. □ *See* plosive. □ A musical fanfare or flourish.

POPAI Point of Purchase Advertising Institute.

pop filter An interior or exterior device that decreases the plosive sounds that reach a microphone. Most commonly refers to a foam windscreen.

pop in The instantaneous appearance of a performer, product, title card, and so on, in a television picture. Also called a *bump in* and *pop on.*

pop music *See* popular music.

pop off *See* pop out.

pop on *See* pop in.

pop out The instantaneous deletion of a performer, product, title card, and so on, from a television picture. Also called a *bump off* and *pop off.*

popping The breaking up of a signal from a microphone by excessive air pressure, often caused by plosive sounds.

POPSI Precipitation and Off Path Scatter Investigation.

popular A euphemism for overpriced; often used in connection with theatre ticket prices.

popular culture A general term for contemporary music and drama that pervades the electronic mass media, and to a lesser extent, the print media. Usually lacking in depth or value.

popular music The music that is currently most popular as shown by record sales, juke box plays, radio station programming, and so on; the term may include showtunes, standards, middle-of-the-road, jazz, swing, and so on. Also called *pop music.*

popular press The print media publications, especially newspapers, that contain more entertainment than information and are geared toward the less educated segment of the population.

population *See* statistical population and universe.

pop-up A printed piece containing a paper construction pasted inside a fold and that, when the fold is opened, "pops up" to form a three-dimensional illustration.

pop-up coupon A tear off perforated coupon stitched into the binding of a periodical as a separate, small space unit. Also called a *preclipped coupon. See also* bind in card and blow in cards.

pop zoom An extremely fast zoom.

porch The interval between a line-scanning period and the start of the sync pulse and between the end of the sync pulse and the succeeding line-scanning period. *See also* back porch and front porch.

pork □ Material that is reprinted in a later edition of a newspaper. □ *See* time copy.

porn An abbreviation for *pornographic.*

porno An abbreviation for *pornographic.*

pornographic film An exploitation film, usually lacking any real plot or characterization, produced to appeal to prurient interests through showing explicit sex. Also called a *porn film, porn flick,* and *sexploitation film.*

pornography Literally, from the Greek meaning "the writing of harlots." The depiction of erotic behavior so as to appeal to prurient interests. *See also* obscenity.

port □ A hole in a bass reflex loudspeaker enclosure that allows air to escape. □ A series or parallel interface connection between a computer and peripheral devices.

portable A system or piece of equipment designed to be used for radio or television remotes.

portable dressing room A mobile home or house trailer that is used on motion picture locations.

portable recorder An audio- or videotape recorder that is powered by a battery.

portable transmitter A transmitter so constructed that it may be moved about conveniently from place to place but not ordinarily used while in motion.

portapak A miniaturized, lightweight portable videotape recorder and camera.

porta-panel A mobile outdoor advertising poster panel that may be wheeled to a given location. Frequently used for merchandising purposes at retail outlets.

portrait lens A camera lens with a fairly long focal length used for close-up work.

pos An abbreviation for *positive.*

pose-to-pose animation A method of animation in which the animator plans the movements in advance, enabling him to draw the extremes, and the assistant animator to draw the in-betweens; as opposed to straight-ahead animation. Pose-to-pose is the method commonly used in studio animation.

posing The arrangement of people to make a pleasing picture composition.

position □ The place a commercial is inserted in a radio or television program. □ The location of an object or performer on a set. □ The location of a camera, microphone, luminaire, and so on. □ The location of a specific scene, line, picture, and so on, on a tape. □ The statement of an advertiser or advertising agency with regard to a proposed advertising campaign. □ The page and location on a page of printed material.

positioner A joystick or other control on a television switcher that allows the movement of an insert to the desired position in the television frame.

positioning □ An advertiser's, broadcast station's, newspaper's, or other party's attempt to persuade the general public that a certain product or service is somehow different from and superior to the competition. □ An advertiser's or programmer's attempt to select the proper places or times for ads or programs to reach the maximum or target audiences.

position paper A detailed statement on a question at issue made by an individual or organization.

position request A request by an advertiser for a certain location in a periodical or time on a radio or television program, if available.

positive □ A value greater than zero. □ An electrode or point to which electrons are attracted. □ The opposite of positive. □ Raw film stock designed to produce positive images. Cf. negative. □ Developed film that has tonal values that are the same as those of the original subject. Also called a *positive image.* □ Any positive film image. Cf. negative.

positive film *See* positive.

positive image *See* positive.

positive lens A lens that is thicker at the center than at the edges, thus producing light ray convergence. Also called a *converging lens.* Cf. negative lens.

positive option A method of distribution of products and services incorporating the same advance notice technique as negative option but requiring a specific order on the part of the member or subscriber each time. Generally, it is more costly and less predictable than negative option.

positive perforation A common form of film perforation that is shaped in the form of a rounded rectangle. Used primarily for projection prints. Cf. negative perforation.

positive pitch A print film stock with a long pitch from one perforation to the next. Cf. negative pitch.

positive print *See* positive.

positive splice A cemented film splice with a wide overlap between the two pieces of film. Cf. negative splice.

post □ A stationary structure that contacts the tape in the tape path and serves to alter its direction; a stationary guide. A post may also support one or more stationary heads. □ To update a data file.

postal service prohibitive order A communication from the U.S. Postal Service to a company indicating that a specific person or family considers the company's advertising mail to be pandering. The order requires the company to remove all names listed on the order from its own mailing list and from any other lists used to promote that company's products or services. Violation of such order is subject to fine and imprisonment. The names listed on the order are to be distinguished from names removed, voluntarily, by the list owner at an individual's request.

post-buy analysis An evaluation based on the audience viewing levels at the time a commercial ran. A post-buy analysis is used to determine the effectiveness of an advertising buy.

postcard A single-sheet self-mailer on card stock.

postcard mailer A booklet containing business reply cards that are individually perforated for selective return to order products or obtain information.

postcard renewal *See* simplified renewal application.

post dubbing The process of adding dialogue to the picture portion of a motion picture. *See also* dubbing.

postecho □ The effect caused by the deformation of the groove walls of a disc in which the sound of the previous groove is faintly heard. □ The effect caused by print-through on a magnetic tape in which the sound of the previous layer of tape is heard faintly. Cf. preecho.

posted bulletin A large outdoor advertising structure. The most common size is 14 feet by 48 feet. Copy is reproduced by two methods: posting paper with the advertising preprinted or painted directly onto the surface. If paper is put on the bulletin, it is called a *posted bulletin.*

postemphasis An operation whereby certain frequencies of a signal are changed in relative amplitude during playback. *See also* deemphasis and postequalization.

postequalization The technique of increasing the quality of sound after it has been recorded. Also called *deemphasis* and *postemphasis.* Cf. preequalization.

poster An advertising message that is posted on an outdoor advertising structure. Also called a *bill. See also* outdoor advertising.

poster frame A framed panel used for holding a poster on or in a bus, terminal, station, store, and so on.

posterization □ A photographic technique that converts a halftone into three shades: black, white, and one intermediate gray. □ The changing of chrominance or luminance information of a television signal to produce a shimmering video effect. □ A tone separation process that produces sharply defined tones for poster-like effects in film prints.

posterize A design that is developed in a manner or style that is characteristic of outdoor advertising pictorial posters. All elements are eliminated except for the ones that identify the product.

poster panel The smaller of the two standardized outdoor advertising structures on which 30-sheet posters or 24-sheet posters are displayed. Its overall dimensions are 12 feet high and 25 feet wide. Cf. bulletin.

poster plant An outdoor advertising plant that specializes in posters and poster panels.

poster showing An outdoor advertisement showing that consists of a number of posters.

poster type A type that is larger and more striking than display type.

postflashing An additional exposure to a subdued light source given to exposed motion picture film to reduce the contrast. Also called *post fogging.* Cf. preflashing.

postfogging *See* postflashing.

posthouse *See* postproduction service.

posting The physical placement of an outdoor advertisement.

posting date The date on which the outdoor advertising posters of a showing are scheduled for display.

posting instructions The detailed information sent to an outdoor advertising plant operator covering the display of a particular poster design.

posting leeway A grace period of five working days after an outdoor advertising scheduled posting date allowed to a plant operator to complete the posting of a showing without penalty.

posting listing The process of selecting the individual panels that will compose an outdoor advertising poster showing under contract.

posting period The length of time during which one outdoor advertising poster design is displayed; usually one month. Figured as 30 days for the purpose of costing and credits.

postmark advertising An advertising slogan or design printed by a postage meter.

postproduction □ The final stage of feature film production, including editing, the director's and producer's cuts, synchronization of dialogue, sound track, special effects, music, and so on. □ Any work done on a film or tape production after it is recorded. Cf. preproduction.

postproduction house *See* postproduction service.

postproduction service A company that specializes in finishing a motion picture, television program, audio program, or other work. Usually accomplishes special effects, post dubbing, titles, and so on. Also called a *posthouse* and *postproduction house.*

postrecording A general term for the recording of sound or effects after the filming or taping has been completed, from narration to lip sync. *See also* postsynchronization. Cf. prerecording.

postscoring The addition of a soundtrack to a film or videotape after production. Cf. prescoring.

postscript □ A note appended to a book, manuscript, letter, and so on, containing additional information. □ A newspaper page amended between editions.

postsync *See* postsynchronization.

postsynchronization The recording of dialogue or other sound to match the existing lip movements on the picture track of a film or tape. Also called *postsync* and *postsynchronized sound.* Cf. presynchronization.

postsynchronized sound *See* postsynchronization.

Post-Telephone-Telegraph Administration (PTT) The government or government-controlled agency in many countries of the world that regulates broadcasting and other telecommunication systems.

posttest The testing of the acceptance or quality of a commercial or program after it has been aired. Cf. pretest.

posture The relative aggressiveness of an advertising campaign or personality.

pot An abbreviation for *potentiometer.*

potboiler A book, article, and so on, hastily written for the sole purpose of making money.

pot cut A brief cut or fade to eliminate an unwanted sound. *See also* cough button.

potential audience □ The audience, measured in households or persons, viewing television at a given time and therefore theoretically available to a particular network, station, or cable television system. □ The total number of readers of a publication who might read a specific advertisement.

potential viewer (PV) A projection of the maximum number of persons who have the opportunity to see an outdoor advertising poster.

potentiometer An electromechanical device containing a resistance used to control the output of a circuit or component. Also called an *attenuator, fader, mixer, rotary fader, rotary pot,* and *variable pad.* Cf. slider.

potting The changing of audio sound levels through the use of a potentiometer.

pounce pattern The method most frequently used for enlarging art copy to full painted outdoor advertising bulletin size. The design is projected onto large sheets of paper and traced in outline form. The outline is then perforated with an electric needle. The perforated sheets, known as *pounce patterns,* are held against the painting surface and dusted with charcoal to reproduce the outline of the design on the surface to be painted.

POV Point of view.

poverty row The minor motion picture companies of the 1920s to the 1940s, such as Republic, that specialized in creating B pictures.

POV shot *See* point of view.

powderless etching A process for making etchings without using powdered resin.

powderman An individual who designs and executes special effects involving explosions, gunpowder blasts, and so on.

power (P) The rate at which work is done. In an electric circuit, power is expressed in watts and is the product of the voltage and the current ($P = EI$). The power of a broadcast station is regulated by the FCC. An AM station may have a maximum of 50,000 watts; an FM station, 100,000 watts; and a television station, from 316,000 to 5 million watts.

power amplifier An amplifier designed for driving loudspeakers.

power belt A belt used as a power source for cameras, recorders, lights, and so on, containing batteries in compartments.

power cable *See* line cord.

power consumption The power used by an electronic or electrical device.

power cord *See* line cord.

power down To cut the electrical power to a device. Often the term implies a slow decrease in power.

powerhouse A slang term for a Class I AM station operating on a clear channel.

powerpack A rechargeable, battery-operated power supply used to power portable tape recorders and other devices.

power splitter *See* splitter.

power strip An electrical device usually containing four or six outlets.

power supply An electrical device used to furnish power to another device or component.

power switch A switch used to turn power on and off. Also called an *on-off switch.*

power zoom A zoom lens in which the mechanism for changing the focal length is driven by a battery or other power supply.

PP □ An abbreviation for *pages.* □ Privately printed. □ Postpaid. □ Pocketpiece.

PPA □ Periodical Publishers Association. □ Publishers Publicity Association. □ Professional Photographers of America.

PPDSE Plate Printers, Die Stampers, and Engravers Union. An international union.

PPM □ Peak program meter. □ Pictures per minute.

PPS Pictures per second.

PPV Pay per view.

PR □ Public relations. □ Publicity release.

pr An abbreviation for *print, printed,* and *printing.*

practical A set prop, light, window, door, and so on, that is designed to be operated or used by a performer.

practical set □ An actual location used as a set for filming or taping. □ A completely realistic set constructed on a stage or studio property.

Praxinoscope A 19th century form of animation, created by Emile Reynaud, that used mirrors and painted pictures.

PRB □ Press-Radio Bureau. □ Private Radio Bureau (of the FCC).

prealerted survey A survey in which respondents are notified of their selection for the survey in advance of the actual data collection. This prenotification to the sampled person or household is usually made by telephone or mail contact. It has been shown to increase both response and data quality relative to similar surveys having no prenotification of respondents.

preamp An abbreviation for *preamplifier.*

preamplifier An amplifier positioned between a source such as a microphone or turntable cartridge and a potentiometer or another amplifier, and designed to amplify the low level source. A preamplifier is often associated with an equalizer.

prebinding The reinforcing or double binding given a book.

prebuy A payment made for the rights to show a motion picture on television even before the film is produced. Cf. presold.

precede News copy that comes after a headline but before the lead; often new material for an old story. Sometimes used to indicate a new lead.

precedent The legal principle that courts should make decisions based on previous decisions in the same types of cases. *See also* stare decisis.

precision □ A measure of the accuracy of a calculation, usually expressed by the number of digits to which the calculation is carried. □ *See* reliability.

preclipped coupon *See* pop-up coupon.

precoding The use of codes on an interview questionnaire so that later coding is unnecessary.

predate A publication printed before its release date, such as a morning newspaper printed the previous night.

predesignated sample The elementary units initially selected for a survey, including any units that ultimately turn out to be nonrespondents.

prediction filter A filter used in ADPCM encoding to achieve effective response to audio frequency distribution fluctuations.

pre-echo □ The effect caused by the deformation of the groove walls of a disc in which the sound of the next groove is heard faintly. □ The effect caused by print-through on a magnetic tape in which the sound of the next layer of tape is heard faintly. Cf. post-echo.

pre-edit To edit data before it is sorted or evaluated.

preemphasis The preequalization of a recording system where the system response is the reciprocal of a standard reproduce characteristic. Also called *preequalization* and, in disc recording, *record equalization.*

preempt To replace a regularly scheduled radio or television program or commercial with another program or commercial. Sometimes due to a special or political broadcast. *See also* preemption.

preemptible □ *See* preemptible rate. □ Satellite service that is not guaranteed and may be canceled. Cf. protected.

preemptible rate The amount charged on a radio or television station for commercial time that is not guaranteed. The time may be sold to another advertiser who is willing to pay the full rate for the time. The preemptible rate is usually sold at a discount. Cf. fixed rate.

preemptible spot A radio or television commercial time period that is subject to cancellation.

preemption □ A right taken by the federal government under the Supremacy Clause of the Constitution to make laws that do not allow for state interpretation or action. □ The cancellation of a network program by an affiliate. □ The cancellation by a network of a regularly scheduled program in order to substitute a special program. □ *See* preemptible spot.

preequalization A change made in a signal to reduce distortion or to improve the signal to noise ratio. Also called *preemphasis.* Cf. postequalization.

preface A short introduction or explanation of a book written by its author. Cf. foreword.

prefade To roll back-timed music at a predetermined time so that it will end on time. The music is then faded in when needed.

preferred position □ A First Amendment theory that holds that freedom of expression is to be considered before other important rights granted under the Constitution. □ The position in a newspaper or magazine desired by an advertiser. Often charged at a higher rate. Cf. run of paper (ROP).

preferred speed The preferred speed of magnetic tape is 7-1/2 inches per second; the preferred speed of turntables is either 33-1/3 or 45 revolutions per minute. *See also* supplementary tape speed.

prefiling announcements The first and sixteenth day of the month announcements required by the FCC of licensees applying for renewal of license.

preflashing An exposure of motion picture film to a subdued light source before use to reduce the contrast. Also called *prefogging.* Cf. postflashing.

prefocus □ A lamp base type. □ To set the focus on each lens in a turret so that it will be in focus when it is racked into position.

prefogging *See* preflashing.

prefreeze station One of the 108 television broadcast stations operating or authorized prior to the Freeze of 1948.

prehearing A meeting between the parties to an adjudicatory proceeding before the FCC or other administrative agency held to reduce the complexity of a hearing and lead to a more expeditious disposition of the proceeding.

preinterview An interview between a reporter and an interviewee that takes place before the recorded interview. Used, for example, to define the limits of the interview or to place the interviewee at ease.

prejudicial publicity The presentation of information by the mass media that may tend to lessen a defendant's right to a fair trial. Also called *pretrial publicity.*

preliminaries *See* preliminary pages.

preliminary matter *See* front matter.

preliminary pages The front matter of a book, usually identified by roman numerals. Also called *preliminaries.*

prelims An abbreviation for *preliminaries* or *preliminary pages.*

premastering □ In recording, the process in which basic program material is processed to produce a master tape. In CD-I and interactive LaserVision, the stage between authoring and mastering. □ The sweetening of the sound accomplished before analog recordings are reissued.

premiere The first showing of a motion picture or television program or series. Also called *first night.* Cf. first run, preview, and rerun.

premiere week The sometimes staggered weeks that present the new fall lineups of the major television networks.

premise A basis, thesis, or theme, often generated by a question, that furnishes the basic idea for a script, story, novel, and so on.

premium □ An item offered to a buyer, usually free or at a nominal price, as an inducement to purchase or obtain for trial a product or service offered. Also called a *giveaway.* □ A token cash payment mailed with survey diaries to serve as an inducement for a diarykeeper to participate in the survey and return the diary. A premium is sent for each person 12 years of age and older in a consenting household. The amount of the premium may vary.

premium buyer A person who buys a product or service to get another product or service, usually free or at a special price, or who responds to an offer of a special product (premium) on the package or label, or sometimes in the advertising, of another product.

premium channel A cable television channel, such as HBO or Showtime, for which an additional fee is charged above that charged for basic service.

premium network A pay radio or television service, such as pay cable, SMATV, STV, pay radio, DBS, and MMDS.

premium rate An above-normal amount paid to a broadcast station to secure a special time period on the air.

premium television Any television distribution system wherein there is a charge made to the viewer for service. *See also* cable television and pay television.

premix To combine a number of sound sources or tracks to be later mixed with other sources to make a final soundtrack. *See also* prerecorded.

preoperational expenses All nonconstruction costs incurred by new public telecommunications entities before the date on which they begin providing service to the public, and all nonconstruction costs associated with the expansion of existing public telecommunications facilities before the date on which such expanded capacity is activated, exclusive of any portion of the salaries of any personnel employed in an operating public telecommunications entity.

prepasting A technique for applying paste to the surface of outdoor advertising posters in the plant rather than in the field. The method uses a modern conveyor belt system for paste application. Posters are then sealed in plastic bags and stored until the posting date.

preplanner/checker A film animator; formerly called a *senior checker.*

prepress production The mechanical and electronic steps necessary to prepare text and graphics for output on a printing press.

preprint □ A roll of paper that has been printed with advertisements, then rewound and shipped to a newspaper for later additions. □ A newspaper section that is printed and folded for later insertion in an edition. □ A book or periodical section bound and distributed before the publication date. □ An advertising insert printed in advance and supplied to a newspaper or magazine for insertion.

preproduction Any work done on a production before filming or taping begins; the director hired, principal cast committed, budgets developed, shooting schedules set, and locations planned. Preproduction is the second step in feature film production. *See also* development. Cf. postproduction.

prepub An abbreviation for *prepublication* or *prior to publication.*

prepublication agreement A nondisclosure agreement that is required of some government officials and employees that restricts their ability to speak as private citizens.

prepublication price A special price for a book prior to its publication date offered by the publisher to booksellers.

prequel A book or screenplay that is written about characters or events that predate an already-written book or screenplay. Cf. sequel.

prerecorded □ A commonly used misnomer for a recorded tape. The term is redundant when it refers to a tape that has been previously recorded. □ A recording made of several sounds or pictures that are later to be mixed with other sounds or pictures.

prerecorded tracks Tracks on magnetic tape containing timing information, such as a time code.

prerecording A general term for the recording of sound or effects before the filming or taping has been completed. *See also* prerecorded. Cf. postrecording.

preroll □ The time required for a given tape mechanism to achieve operating speed from a nonoperating mode. □ The amount of time a videotape machine takes to produce a stable picture or achieve synchronization with other machines. Depending on the equipment, the time may vary from a fraction of a second to several seconds.

preroll time The interval, often approximately five seconds, between the time a tape is started and the time it is switched to an on air signal. Cf. runup time.

prerun Any showing of a motion picture —in theatres or pay cable—before it is seen on network television.

prescoring □ The recording of a soundtrack for use during the filming of a motion picture scene. Cf. postscoring. □ The recording of a soundtrack on videotape before recording the video. Cf. postscoring.

preselection The selection of records, tapes, and so on, for systematic presentation by an automated radio station.

presence The quality of sound that makes it seem real, natural, close, warm, and so on. Often accomplished by working close to a microphone or by boosting the signal in the 2-to 8-kHz range. Cf. balance and room tone.

presence control A potentiometer used to control the midrange loudspeaker in a three-way system.

presentation □ Any communication going to the merits or outcoming of any aspect of a restricted proceeding before the FCC. □ A display, dummy, demonstration, and/or explanation of a motion picture, television program, advertisement, and so on, made by an advertising agency or individual to a client or prospective buyer.

presentational A form of delivery wherein the announcer or speaker talks to the camera as if it were the audience. Cf. representational.

presentation copy An autographed copy of a book presented to an individual.

Presentation Level Protocol (PLP) AT&T's videotext system.

presenter A British term for a television anchor.

preservative □ A chemical added to a film developer to retard oxidation. □ A substance, such as wax, applied to a film to help protect it from scratches.

preset □ To fix the value or level of a circuit, control, or potentiometer before use. □ A set of predetermined lighting levels that can be mechanically or electronically set up on a system in advance of need and to which the console operator may fade when desired. □ The provision for such sets of levels.

preset camera A camera fixed and locked into position for a shot.

preset control A control, usually a potentiometer, located on a lighting control console, used to program or preset the output of a dimmer, and in turn, the light output of the luminaire connected to the dimmer.

preset fade A fade of a previously selected group of different lighting instruments at the same time by an automated light board.

preset switcher A video switcher used to change from one source to another and back again.

presidential patch *See* multiple.

Presidential Task Force A committee formed in 1967 to study communications policy. It recommended the establishment of a new federal agency for radio spectrum allocation and management.

presoak To immerse film in water immediately prior to development.

presold An idea for a motion picture or television program for which a payment is made before the motion picture or program is produced. Cf. prebuy.

presort Mail that is sorted by ZIP code; eligible for a lower rate.

press □ Originally, a reference to newspapers and magazines; the print media. Now includes the electronic media. □ A synonym for journalism generally. □ A printing press. □ Employees of a mass medium. □ The process or act of gathering and disseminating of news. □ The members of the news profession. □ The process of printing.

press agent A person hired to promote and publicize performers or organizations. Also called an *axe grinder, drumbeater,* and *flack.*

press agentry The promotion of an individual, product, or service through the use of free publicity obtained from the mass media.

press association (PA) An organization that gathers news for dissemination to subscribers. *See also* wire service.

press book *See* press kit.

press box □ The location from which a sportscaster or sports reporter views and reports a sporting event. □ The section of a sports arena, meeting room, courtroom, or other location reserved for members of the press.

press camera The traditional bellows camera used by news photographers for years. Now replaced by miniature and reflex cameras.

press card An official or unofficial document used to identify a reporter or other news-gathering personnel.

press clipping *See* clipping.

press conference A meeting between members of the press and a newsworthy figure at which statements are made and/or questions asked. Also called a *news conference.*

press corrector An obsolete term for a proofreader.

press council (PC) A private or public organization that serves a watchdog on print media publications.

press counter A device used to count the number of completed newspapers in a press run.

press coverage The amount of media attention received by an organization, business, individual, and so on.

press gallery A press box in a legislative chamber.

pressing A disc produced in a molding press from a master or stamper. Also called a *platter* and *record.*

press kit A portfolio of news releases, pictures, background information, and so on, distributed to the press for publicity purposes. Also called a *press book.*

pressman A person who operates a printing press.

press manager An employee in charge of a pressroom.

press mark □ A number in a library book designating its location on the shelves. □ A mark on paper designating the press on which it was run. □ *See* colophon.

press operator An employee who operates a commercial press.

press pass □ A card or other document issued by a mass media organization to identify reporters and other employees. □ A card or other document issued by an organization that allows a reporter access to the site of an event without payment.

press plate *See* plate.

press proof One of the first copies of a press run; used for checking.

Press-Radio Bureau (PRB) A news service formed in 1936 by the AP, UP, and INS to furnish news to radio stations after the material had been given to newspapers. The PRB was disbanded in 1940.

press release A story or information distributed by an organization; a handout for media reporters. *See also* press kit.

press revise A final proof made before a press run.

pressroom The room in which the printing presses are operated.

press run The total number of copies of a book, newspaper, magazine, and so on, made at one time.

press secretary An individual employed by another individual or organization to present information to the press by holding news briefings, issuing press releases, and so on. An example is the press secretary to the U.S. president.

press time The time at which newspaper presses begin a run; the time when it becomes too late for additional news to be incorporated in the newspaper.

press to talk switch A switch that must be held in order to operate a microphone or other device. Also called a *push to talk switch.*

pressure The force per unit area. Often measured in pounds per square inch (psi).

pressure group An interest group formed to influence governmental policy.

pressure microphone *See* dynamic microphone.

pressure pad □ The material on spring-loaded arms that press the tape against the heads in inexpensive tape recorders. □ *See* pressure plate.

pressure plate The flat metal plate in a camera, projector, or optical printer that presses on the back of the film to keep the emulsion surface in the lens focal plane.

pressure plate pad The sheet of glass and cloth or paper that holds an animation cel flat.

pressure roller □ A rubber-tired wheel that holds the tape tightly against the capstan. Also called a *capstan idler, pinch roller,* and *puck.* □ A rubber-tired wheel used to drive a turntable.

pressure sensitive labels Gummed mailing labels that do not need moistening to adhere to paper.

presswork The part of the printing process that involves putting the ink on the paper.

Prestel The viewdata system used in Great Britain.

prestige advertising The use of advertising to raise or maintain a corporate image as opposed to advertising goods and services. *See also* institutional advertising.

prestige bias A survey error that results if the respondent unconsciously or consciously tries to upgrade his or her social image or cultural level by reporting what he or she believes are more desirable activities. *See also* bias and nonsampling error.

prestriped film Film that has a mag stripe added before processing.

presunrise service authority (PSA) Authority issued by the FCC to certain class II and III stations to operate before local sunrise.

presync *See* presynchronization.

presynchronization The recording of a synchronized film soundtrack before the picture information is added. Also called *presync* and *presynchronized sound.* Cf. postsynchronization.

presynchronized sound *See* presynchronization.

pretest □ An evaluation made by a test audience of a radio or television commercial or program before it is aired. □ A preliminary tryout of a survey questionnaire to evaluate its workability and suitability. Also called a *field test.* Cf. posttest.

pretransmission The period of time immediately preceding a broadcast.

pretrial publicity *See* prejudicial publicity.

preventive maintenance (PM) The periodic maintenance performed on equipment in order to identify and repair potential problems before they can affect the operation of the system or device. Also called *routine maintenance* and *scheduled maintenance.*

preview □ To view a program or commercial before it is aired. □ A pilot. □ To rehearse a videotape edit before it is recorded. □ A performance of a scheduled broadcast that is performed before a studio audience prior to broadcast. Cf. after-shows.

preview bus The bus on a television switcher that selects the picture seen on the preview monitor.

preview key A switch on a videotape controller that selects the preview mode. Cf. record key.

preview monitor The television monitor that shows the director the next camera shot to be used. Often used to set up special effects, inserts, chromakeys, and so on, before they are used on the air.

preview reports Optional advance reports that provide basic audience data on the early weeks of regular report periods, available in selected major markets from Nielsen Station Index.

previous broadcasting experience The time a licensee or prospective licensee has had in working in a broadcast station for which there was no ownership responsibility. One of the comparative criteria often used in mutually exclusive hearings. Cf. past broadcast record.

previous restraint *See* prior restraint.

primacy recency theory The theory that it is advantageous to a speaker to have his or her argument presented first or last.

prima facie Latin for "on the face of it." Evidence that is legally sufficient; self-evident. May be later disproved.

PRIMA Public Radio in Mid-America.

primary affiliate A television network affiliate that carries a majority of a single network's programs and commercials.

primary audience □ The potential audience for a single advertising message. □ The persons or places to which a periodical is sold or delivered for use. □ The persons to whom the editorial content of a periodical is directed. Also called *primary readership.* □ The total number of primary readers of a periodical.

primary circulation The recorded circulation of a periodical, based on subscription and newsstand sales figures.

primary color A color that may not be produced by the mixture of other colors, but that, when mixed with other primary colors, can produce all visible colors. In pigments or subtractive primary colors, the primaries are red, yellow, and blue (actually magenta, yellow, and blue-green); in light or additive primary colors, they are red, green, and blue (actually red-orange, green, and blue-violet).

primary coverage *See* primary service area.

primary data Material and information collected from original sources. In a survey, the information collected from respondents.

primary demographic report (PDR) A simplified July report formerly issued by Nielsen Station Index (NSI) for markets beyond the top 70. Discontinued when NSI started to issue complete Viewers in Profile reports in all DMA markets.

primary household A household that includes a subscriber or purchaser of a periodical.

primary journal A journal designed primarily for research and library use.

primary marketing area The principal area of editorial and advertising coverage of a newspaper.

primary medium The advertising vehicle used for the major portion of an advertising campaign. Cf. secondary medium.

Primary Metropolitan Statistical Area (PMSA) A geographic area containing a population of more than 1 million. Cf. Consolidated Metropolitan Statistical Area (CMSA) and Metropolitan Statistical Area (MSA).

primary movement Any movement by talent in front of a camera. Cf. secondary movement and tertiary movement.

primary news The major news stories of the day.

primary reader A person who resides in a primary household who has looked at the content of a periodical.

primary readership *See* primary audience.

primary relay station An FM or TV station responsible for relay service of EBS national-level common emergency programming that also functions as part of a state relay network.

primary research Research that collects original data as opposed to using data that are from other studies.

primary service area The area in which the ground wave is not subject to objectionable interference or objectionable fading.

primary standard of frequency The standard of frequency maintained by the National Bureau of Standards of the Department of Commerce in Boulder, Colorado. The operating frequency of all radio stations is determined by comparison with signals of stations WWV, WWVH, or WWVB of the National Bureau of Standards.

primary station □ The FM radio broadcast station radiating the signals retransmitted by an FM broadcast translator station or an FM broadcast booster station. □ The television broadcast station that provides the programs and signals being transmitted by a television broadcast translator station. □ A station that broadcasts a common emergency program for the duration of the activation of the national-level EBS. *See also* alternate station.

primary storage The internal memory of a computer.

primary stripe *See* main stripe.

primary transmission In copyright, a transmission made to the public by the transmitting facility whose signals are being received and further transmitted by the secondary transmission service, regardless of where or when the performance or display was first transmitted. Cf. secondary transmission.

prime lens A fixed focal length lens.

prime meridian The meridian that separates east from west and from which the location of satellites is measured in degrees of longitude.

primer One of a series of explanatory documents issued by the FCC from time to time, such as the Fairness Primer or Primer on Ascertainment of Community Problems.

prime time □ Generally, those broadcast periods viewed or listened to by the greatest number of persons and for which a station charges the most for air time. □ The time period on television from 8 p.m. to 11 p.m. (or Sundays from 7 p.m. to 11 p.m.). *See also* daypart and drivetime.

prime time access rule (PTAR) A 1970 FCC rule that denied networks the right to feed programs to affiliates in the top 50 markets for more than three hours per night. Also called an *access rule.* Later modified.

principal □ An individual cast in the major role in a production. □ An owner or partner of an advertising agency or broadcast station.

principal action axis *See* imaginary line.

principal axis The straight line that passes through the center of all the elements of a lens.

principal community contour The signal contour that a television station is required to place over its entire principal community.

principal headend The location of the cable system equipment used to process the signals of television broadcast stations for redistribution to subscribers. Where more than one location meets this definition, the cable operator designates a single location as the principal headend.

principal performer Anyone who is seen and who speaks a line or lines of dialogue, whether directly employed for such work or after being hired as an extra performer. This includes anyone whose face appears silent, alone in a stationary camera shot; anyone who is the subject of a close-up and who is identifiable; clowns in proprietary make-up that is identifiable; stunt performers if they perform an identifiable stunt; specialty dancers or specialty acts; anyone whose voice is used off camera except omnies; persons appearing in stop action or squeeze action or still photographs; performers operating hand, stick, or string manipulated puppets or marionettes; pilots under certain circumstances; a featured foreground performance by specialty acts, dancers, or stunt performers; or anyone who speaks lines or performs a stunt for a commercial.

principal photography The actual filming or shooting of a screenplay. Principal photography shooting is the third step in feature film production.

print □ A positive copy made from a film negative. □ The output of a teletype service. □ A printed publication such as a newspaper or magazine. □ An abbreviation for *newsprint.* □ An intaglio impression. □ To make a photographic print, intaglio, and so on. □ Positive raw film stock that has been exposed but not processed. Also called *print stock.* □ *See* print media.

print and tumble *See* work and tumble.

print and turn *See* work and turn.

printed bulletin A printed copy, either lithographed or silk screened, posted on an outdoor advertising bulletin structure. A paint embellishment may be combined with the printed element in some designs.

printed circuit (PC) An electronic circuit in which conductive strips are affixed to an insulated board in place of wires.

printed word media All media for advertising prepared by printing; examples include periodicals, posters, shopping bags, and matchbooks. Also called *print media.*

printer □ Any device that produces a hard copy of information. □ A device used to type messages automatically from a news wire service. Also called a *teleprinter* and *teletypewriter.* □ A device used to print a processed film onto a piece of raw film stock. □ An individual who operates a printer. □ A person who operates a motion picture printer, printing press, and so on; sometimes refers to a typesetter.

printer diaphragm The device on some optical film printers used to change the light intensity falling on the film being exposed.

printer driver A computer program that formats the output of a computer so that it produces the desired results on paper.

printer light *See* printing light.

printer light scale A series of exposure increments used to measure and control the light output on an optical printer.

printer's devil A printer's apprentice or helper. Cf. galley boy.

printer's error (pe) An error made by a typesetter that is caught in proofreading. *See also* author's alterations (aa) and editor's alteration (ea). Cf. misprint.

printer's flower *See* flower.

Printers' Ink Statute A model statute developed in 1911 by the magazine Printers' Ink designed to control false or deceptive advertising.

printer's mark A visible mark used to identify the work of a particular printer. Cf. colophon.

printer sync *See* projection sync.

print format *See* format.

printing □ The process of impressing type or other matter on paper or other materials. □ In photography, usually refers to the production of positives from negatives. □ A reprinting of a book; a new impression. □ The process of using a processed film as a light modulator to expose raw stock, either negative or positive.

printing broker A person who locates printing facilities needed by a client.

printing couple A combination of an impression cylinder and a plate cylinder.

printing density The density of the image on the film printed in an optical printer.

printing depth The minimum depth that a plate or cylinder must be etched or engraved in order to print properly.

printing element Any typeface, thimble, daisy wheel, plate, cut, and so on, capable of impressing an image on paper or other material.

printing frame A wood or metal frame used in enlarging to hold the negative and outline the area to be printed.

printing light The light source in any type of film printer. Also called a *printer light.*

printing master A first-generation dupe used to print release prints.

printing plate *See* plate.

printing press Any of a number of machines capable of making an inked impression on paper or other material. *See also* flatbed press, platen press, and rotary press.

printing roll A roll of film used in optical printing.

printing surface The area of the paper that is printed.

printing sync *See* projection sync.

print journalism The gathering, writing, and editing of news for newspapers and magazines, as opposed to radio and television news. Cf. broadcast journalism.

print media The mass media that includes newspapers, magazines, periodicals, and direct mail. Also called *print.*

printout The copy produced by a computer printer.

print press The reporters, editors, and so on, of newspapers and magazines.

printshop A company whose primary business is printing.

print spooler A temporary storage area for material to be printed that is used when a computer printer is outputting another block of data.

print stock *See* print.

print-through □ The usually undesirable transfer of recorded magnetic patterns from one layer of a magnetic tape wound on a reel to an adjacent layer. Also called *feed through.* □ The resulting spurious magnetic pattern. □ The audible result from such a spurious magnetic pattern.

print up □ To make a positive print of a motion picture in a format larger than the original. □ To make a soundtrack louder by changing the optical track of a motion picture.

print wheel A typewriter or printer print element, such as a daisy wheel.

priority The precedence according to importance assigned to messages to be transmitted.

Priority Four EBS national programming and news.

Priority One An EBS presidential message.

Priority Three EBS operating (local) area programming.

Priority Two EBS state programming.

prior restraint The essential element of censorship; a restriction on expression before broadcast or publication. Cf. subsequent punishment.

prism A triangular shaped piece of glass or plastic capable of splitting, through diffraction, a ray of white light into its component colors. Often used in multiplexers, and in television cameras to split the light beam so that each color is sent to a different pickup tube.

prismatic lens A camera lens with a number of facets that is capable of producing multiple images. Also called a *prism lens.*

prism block *See* prism.

prism lens *See* prismatic lens.

prism shot A photographic image taken through an image-multiplying prism so as to reproduce the image many times.

prism shutter A camera prism that deflects light to both the film and the viewfinder.

privacy *See* right of privacy.

Privacy Act The 1974 statute that forbids government disclosure of information about individuals and gives individuals the right to see, make copies of, and correct inaccuracies in their files.

Privacy Protection Act The 1980 statute that made it unlawful for federal, state, or local governments to search for or seize any material intended for dissemination to the public.

private automatic branch exchange- *See* PABX.

private branch exchange *See* PBX.

private facts An invasion of privacy in which the disclosure of intimate and personal information about an individual would be highly offensive to a reasonable person and not of legitimate concern to the public.

private land mobile service A mobile service that provides a regularly interacting group of base, mobile, portable, and associated control and relay stations for private one-way or two-way land mobile radio communications by eligible users over designated areas of operation.

private law The law governing relationships between individuals; property law, domestic relations law, torts, and so on. Cf. public law.

private line (PL) An intercom between television studio and control room personnel.

Private Line News Exchange A closed-circuit wire interconnecting CBS radio station affiliates.

privately printed A book or other manuscript printed by a private press or distributed privately; generally not for sale to the general public.

private mail Mail handled by special arrangement outside the U.S. Postal Service.

private places Intrusion into a nonpublic place by trespassing, hidden cameras or microphones, bugging, eavesdropping, wiretapping, and so on.

private press A noncommercial press that prints special editions or limited quantities of books.

private screening A motion picture or television program that is shown to a select audience.

private viewing The viewing for private use in an individual's dwelling unit by means of equipment, owned or operated by such individual, capable of receiving satellite cable programming directly from a satellite.

privatization The removal of a duty or responsibility from the government and giving it to the private sector.

privileged □ A communication that a court may not require to be disclosed, such as communications between a husband and wife, lawyers and clients, and so on. □ In defamation law, the immunity granted to individuals under certain circumstances. *See also* absolute privilege and qualified privilege.

prize One of the three elements that constitute a lottery. Money or anything of value. *See also* chance and consideration.

prize broker An individual who arranges barter merchandise given as prizes on radio or television shows in return for mentions of brand names of the merchandise donated.

PRO Public relations officer.

probability □ More than a possibility, less than a certainty. □ A mathematical basis for predicting the outcome of some event.

probability sample A sample in which the elements are selected from a sampling frame with a known nonzero probability of selection. *See also* area probability sample, cluster sample, multistage sample, replicated sample, simple random sample, stratified sampling, and systematic selection sample. Cf. convenience sample and judgment sample.

probable cause The requirement for a search warrant that a search of a specific place will probably uncover evidence for a specific case.

probable error An indicator of the margin of sampling error in survey results that has been superseded in statistical work by the standard error.

probe □ An electrical testing device used to make contact with a point in a circuit. □ A type of light meter often used in printing and enlarging. □ A survey question asked by an interviewer as a follow-up to a previous question in order to elicit additional information or response.

proc An abbreviation for *procedure, processor,* and *programming computer.*

proc amp An abbreviation for *processing amplifier.*

procedural bias *See* nonsampling error.

procedural law The law that deals with the rules governing the application of substantive law. Also called *adjective law.*

procedural modeling Modeling based on a series of instructions that defines the elements of a scene and the rules for combining them.

proceeding An official record of a legal process, as in a case before the FCC or a court.

process □ A general term for a series of actions or operations. □ To develop or print film. □ *See* process shot.

process camera □ A camera that contains a single-frame motor drive used for optical printing and animation. □ A camera used for making halftones and plates.

process cinematography Cinematography that uses process photography.

process coated *See* machine coated.

process color *See* color separation.

processing The chemical and other operations necessary to convert an exposed film into a visible picture: developing, fixing, washing, and drying.

processing amplifier An amplifier designed to restore the synchronizing signal portion of a composite video signal by inserting new sync, blanking, and color burst. Commonly referred to as a *proc amp.*

process letter A letter whose body is printed so as to imitate typing.

processor □ A device in a television camera that inserts gamma correction in the video signal or processes the RGB signals. □ An automatic device for processing film. □ Any device used to perform operations on data.

process photography The use of back or front projections in photographing live action. *See also* process shot.

process plate One of the plates used to print a color, usually black, blue, red, and yellow, in a color separation print. *See also* plate.

process printing A method of producing a halftone with a full range of colors by using a color separation process.

process projection The projection of an image on a screen using front or back projection.

process screen The front or back projection screen used in process photography.

process shot A shot in which foreground action is filmed against a front or back projection containing a previously filmed scene.

proclamation An executive order or official public pronouncement.

produce □ To create the physical material—film, printing plates, magnetic tapes, and so on—to be used by a medium as an advertisement or production. □ To manage the development of a planned public event, especially entertainment.

producer □ An individual who is ultimately responsible for a production, commercial, television series, and so on.

Sometimes, the financial backer of a production. Cf. director. □ A third person to whom a commercial has been sold, assigned, transferred, leased, or otherwise disposed of. □ An individual or company that packages books for distribution by a publisher. Also called a *book packager* and *packager.* □ An advertising agency employee responsible for the production of commercials; includes such functions as selection of a production supplier, cost control, and quality control. Also called a *production director.* □ In studio animation, the administrative head of the film, usually responsible for budget, staff, legal contracts, distribution, scheduling, and so on.

producer-director An individual who handles the combined functions of a producer and a director.

producer's gross The worldwide total gross receipts derived by the distributor of a motion picture from licensing the right to exhibit on free television.

product awareness A measure of audience familiarity with or knowledge of a commercial product.

product copy □ All copy, sets, and so on, used for a specific program. □ The portions of the prose in an advertisement devoted to product descriptions and claims.

product identification The ability of individuals to identify a radio or television program with a program sponsor or a commercial with a well-known line or logo.

product image The relative quality of a commercial product as perceived by an audience.

production □ A single radio or television program or commercial. □ The organizing, casting, set design, rehearsing, taping, and so on, of a program or commercial. □ The four stages in the making of a motion picture: planning, breakdown, scheduling, and budgeting. A production includes the development, preproduction, principal photography, and postproduction. □ The process of preparing, typesetting, and printing a work. □ The transformation of an idea into a finished product, such as a book, advertising campaign, commercial, and so on.

production aids The stock music, sound effects, props, equipment, and so on, available for a production.

production assistant (PA) An assistant to a radio, television, or film producer or director. *See also* gopher.

production audio The sound that is recorded at the same time as the video is shot.

production auditor The person responsible for setting up an auditing office, opening production bank accounts, reviewing the budget, furnishing cost reports, and paying the bills incurred by the production.

production board □ A bulletin board containing the information concerning the performers to be used, scenes to be shot, extras needed, and so on, for a production. □ An audio control console used in a production studio.

production company *See* production house.

production control The general and specific limits placed on a director by a producer or the front office regarding the expenditures for a motion picture. Expenditures are usually examined on a daily basis.

production coordinator *See* production office coordinator.

production credits *See* credits.

production crew *See* production team.

production department □ A motion picture studio department that carries out preplanning for proposed productions. □ The composing room and pressroom of a newspaper or magazine. □ A station, network, or advertising agency department that designs and executes programs or commercials.

production designer The individual in charge of the aesthetic appearance of a set and who may coordinate other designers, such as lighting, costumes, special effects, and so on.

production director □ A person in charge of a production, as for a publishing house, advertising agency, television station, and so on. Cf. producer and production manager. □ A radio or television director.

production facilities (fax) The physical sets, props, art work, costumes, and so on, necessary to a television or radio production. Cf. facilities (fax).

production fade *See* board fade.

production hours □ The total time necessary to build, rehearse, and tape or broadcast a television production. □ The total number of hours of programs produced by public broadcasting stations during a fiscal year.

production house An organization that specializes in making television commercials, although it may produce programs. Also called a *production company.*

production insurance Insurance purchased for a production to cover such risks as weather, death of principal actor, or production delays.

production manager □ An individual in charge of the day-to-day operation of a production. Responsible to the producer, director, or sometimes, the assistant director. □ An individual who coordinates and supervises the work of the various department heads for a production: sets, props, make-up, costumes, talent, and so on. □ The individual responsible for the development of advertising materials for an advertising agency. □ The individual responsible for the final reproduction in print of a periodical, book, or collateral printed piece. Cf. producer and production director.

production notes *See* production report.

production number A motion picture musical extravaganza.

production office coordinator A liaison between the producer, production manager, assistant directors, script supervisor, and so on. Responsibilities include the efficient operation of the production office. Also called a *production coordinator.*

production personnel *See* production team.

production report A daily summary made of all the notes made by various personnel on a film or videotape crew concerning the camera shots, sound, problems, and so on. Also called *production notes.*

production run The final output of publications, equipment, supplies, and so on, for sale to consumers. Cf. test run.

production schedule The day-by-day timetable for the shooting of a motion picture.

production secretary An individual who provides clerical support to a production unit or producer.

production still A still picture taken at the same time a motion picture scene is being shot, one taken from a single motion picture frame, or one that is staged.

production supervisor □ A motion picture studio employee who assists a producer in routine administrative duties. □ In studio animation, an assistant to the producer, in charge of routine administrative duties.

production team All individuals who are members of the crew of a motion picture or television production. Also called *production crew* and *production personnel.*

production time The real time used in the broadcast of a production. Cf. dramatic time.

production unit A complete production team, consisting of a director, camera crew, sound crew, and so on.

production values The sometimes insignificant items or ideas that add depth, richness, or appeal to a motion picture or other production.

product manager The individual in charge of a company's merchandising.

product programming Product information presented in greater detail than normal advertising time span allows.

product protection The amount of time a station, network, newspaper, periodical, and so on, guarantees between the broadcasting of competing commercials or the physical proximity of advertisements for competitive products. Also called *protection.*

product use study A survey conducted to determine if there is a difference in total use or frequency of use of a product between viewers and nonviewers of a commercial message or campaign.

profane language Terms that debase or defile that which is holy. Forbidden by Title 18 of the United States Code (USC), Section 1464. *See also* obscene language.

pro-fax An abbreviation for *production facilities.*

professional An individual who is paid for his or her knowledge or skill; as a professional actor. The term often implies a code of ethics, specific training, and so on; an example is a professional journalist.

professional book A book written primarily for a specific field, such as computer science, engineering, architecture, or law.

professional journal A journal written primarily for a specific group of individuals, such as lawyers, physicians, or journalists.

professional magazine A magazine designed for members of a specific profession or related professions. Cf. consumer magazine and trade magazine.

Professional Motion Picture Equipment Association (PFVEA) A group of manufacturers, dealers, and distributors of professional film equipment.

professional singer A person who is employed primarily to sing a set piece of music on a given pitch either as a solo or in a group requiring unison, melody, and harmony.

Professional Systems Network, Inc. (PSNI) An association of professional video dealers.

professional trade title A specific industry-oriented book carried by a retail bookstore but that has limited appeal to the general public.

professional writer Any person who has (a) received employment for a total of 13 weeks as a television, motion picture, or radio writer, (b) has received credit on the screen as a writer for a television or theatrical motion picture, (c) has received credit for three original stories or one teleplay for a program one-half hour or more in length in the field of live television, (d) has received credit for at least three radio scripts for radio programs one-half hour or more in length, or (e) has received credit for at least one professionally produced play on the legitimate stage or one published novel. Cf. writer.

profile □ A feature or story about an individual or organization that reveals something about the inner character of the person or organization. □ A delineation of audience, reader, or buyer demographic or psychographic characteristics. □ In computers, a specific set of preferred parameter values for use in a given application. □ *See* audience profile.

profile chart A graph made from the results of a program analyzer. Also called a *program profile.*

profile piece A three-dimensional background used on a set.

profile spotlight *See* ellipsoidal spotlight.

profit The money gained in excess of expenditures.

profit and loss statement A balance sheet showing the revenues, costs, and expenses of a company.

pro forma As a matter of form; a formality.

pro forma invoice A publisher's statement made up to show what the cost of certain books would be; not an invoice showing books that have been shipped.

prog An abbreviation for program and programming.

program □ A complete, self-contained broadcast presentation, either commercially sponsored or sustaining. Also called a *show.* □ One program of a series. □ To write instructions for a computer or other device. □ The instructions given to a computer to perform specific tasks. □ A plan for a public relations campaign. □ A printed list of acts, cast, crew, and so on, given to an audience in a theatre. □ To input information into a memory light board.

program analyzer Any of a number of devices used to measure test audiences' instantaneous reactions to programs or commercials, usually accomplished by having the audience push buttons indicating "like" or "dislike." *See also* big annie, black box, opinion meter, and Stanton-Lazarsfeld analyzer.

program audio track The area reserved on the tape for the program audio record, usually associated with the accompanying video recording. Also known as *audio #1 record.*

program audition A performance of a program that is used to determine whether the program shall be broadcast at a future date or time. Such auditions are not shown to the public generally but may be performed before a studio audience.

program availability One of a number of nonnetwork television programs that has not yet been purchased for use in a market.

program balance The arrangement of the various program elements to provide the desired audience reaction.

program billboard *See* billboard.

program bus The television switcher bus that is used for takes and that usually overrides all other buses.

program campaign An advertising campaign using programs, as opposed to spots.

program channel The high-level audio output that feeds a program line. Cf. audition channel and cue channel.

program circuit An equalized telephone company line capable of carrying a wide range of frequencies.

program clip A brief clip taken from a television program.

program closing *See* commercial billboard.

program compatibility The appropriateness of advertising to a radio or television program and vice versa.

program continuity *See* continuity.

program contribution The credit that may be received by an advertiser from a station for talent costs.

program coverage factor The percentage of television households in a market with fewer than three stations able to receive a network program.

program cycle The length of time, measured in years, that elapses between the peaks of popularity for a given television genre.

program deletion The elimination of one or more programs by a cable television system; occurs where a local broadcast station is protected against program duplication from an outside source or where the system elects to preempt one program in order to carry another.

program delivery rating The percentage of households within a given area estimated to be tuned in to a radio or television program at a given moment.

program department The radio or television station or network department concerned with the development of individual programs and series to serve the overall programming philosophy of the station or network.

program director (PD) The manager of a radio or television station program department. Also called a *program manager.*

program disk A computer disk that contains an operating system and usually a self-starting program.

program duplication (AM-FM) The simultaneous broadcasting of a particular program over both the AM and FM station or the broadcast of a particular FM program within 24 hours before or after the identical program is broadcast over the AM station.

program effectiveness □ A measure of audience acceptance as determined by ratings. □ A measure of sponsor acceptance as determined by sales results.

program exclusivity *See* exclusivity.

program fair A showing of television programs to television station programmers; often syndicated shows or public television programs.

program fee A sum of money paid to performers for each television program in which they appear.

program following The radio or television program that follows another. *See* lead-out.

program interruption Any occurrence of nonprogram material within a program.

program length commercial A pitch program of unspecified length consisting of a continuous demonstration or sales presentation.

program level The VU meter reading at the output of an audio control console.

program library A collection of computer programs or routines.

program line The feed from a studio to a transmitter or recorder.

program lineup A listing of stations carrying a program either on a live or delayed basis. Stations are as supplied by the network or as received directly from their affiliates.

program log A radio or television station log listing the time of programs, classification, source, commercial matter, station identification, and so on. Also called an *operating sheet.* Cf. maintenance log and operating log.

programmable key A computer keyboard letter or symbol that may be used as a substitute for typing a complete character string. *See also* macro.

programmable sound generator An audio signal generator with an integrated microprocessor to control the output signal according to a program set up by the user.

program manager *See* program director.

programmer □ A person who writes computer programs. □ A slang term for a program director.

programming □ The process of producing instructions for a computer. □ The planning, arranging, and scheduling of programs for broadcast, cable television, MMDS, DBS, and so on.

programming language A language, other than machine language, used to write a computer program. *See also* high-level language.

program music *See* mood music.

program opening *See* commercial billboard.

program opposite A radio or television program that is on the air at the same time on another station.

program origination Any transmissions other than the simultaneous retransmission of the programs and signals of a TV broadcast station. Origination shall include locally generated television program signals and program signals obtained via video recordings, microwave, common carrier circuits, or other sources.

program packager An independent program producer.

program picture An inexpensively made motion picture; formerly shown as the B movie in a double bill.

program practices *See* continuity acceptance.

program preceding The radio or television program that is broadcast immediately before. *See also* lead-in.

program profile *See* profile chart.

program rating Any rating calculated for a radio or television program.

program rating service Any of a number of audience research organizations such as the A. C. Nielsen Company, The Arbitron Company, Pulse, Trendex, or AGB.

program rating summary report (PRS) *See* household tracking report (HTR).

program related data Data in the form of executable object code to be read and processed by the CD-I MPU.

program related data signal A signal, consisting of a series of pulses representing data, that is transmitted simultaneously with and directly related to the accompanying television program.

program report form The form required by the FCC for requests for changes in facilities, transfers of control, and so on.

program research Research that is primarily concerned with broadcast and cable programs, the scheduling of programs, and other programming matters.

program responsibility The nondelegable duty of a licensee to retain control over all material broadcast over a station's facilities.

program selector The individual who has the greatest control over the others in a household who wish to watch television at the same time.

program signal The video and/or audio signal that is sent from a studio or remote to a transmitter.

program source □ The origination point of a broadcast. □ The device from which a program is received, such as a tape recorder, turntable, cart, or film projector. □ A local program (L), a network program (NET), or recorded program (REC).

program station basis The percentage of radio or television receivers in a coverage area tuned in to a given program at a given moment, taken as a basis for a rating of the program's success against all individual competition.

program substitution The substitution by a cable system of one program for another on a given channel. *See also* cherry picking.

program syndication *See* syndication.

program test authority The authority from the FCC for a station to broadcast programs after the completion of the equipment test but before the license is issued.

program types The various kinds of radio and television programs defined by the FCC; categories are A, E, ED, EDIT, I, N, O, PA, POL, R, and S.

program use A commercial used on two or more interconnected stations. *See also* Class A, Class B, and Class C. Cf. dealer use and wild spot.

progression □ The development of conflict between characters in a play or script. □ The heightening of tension in a novel or screenplay.

progressive proof One of a series of proofs made from each of the color plates; shown separately and in combination in the order they are to be printed.

progressive scanning The sequential line scanning of a television picture rather than by interlace scanning.

Progress Medal An award given by the SMPTE for research, inventions, or developments making a "significant advance" in film or television.

proj An abbreviation for *projection* and *projector.*

project To increase voice production so as to be heard at a distance.

projectall A device used to project opaque slides.

projected audience Expressing a rating in terms of households reached by applying universe estimates.

projected audience size The number of persons or households predicted for the audience of a commercial, radio broadcast, or television program.

projection □ The process of reproducing a film or videotape image on a screen. □ The extrapolation of raw data to represent estimates of household or population information for the respective geographic area surveyed. Estimates of households tuning and persons viewing in a specific sex/age group are projected and rounded to the nearest thousand.

projection booth The room at the rear of a theatre that houses the projectors.

projection cue *See* changeover cue.

projection gate *See* gate.

projectionist The individual in a studio or motion picture theatre who operates projectors.

projection lamp A high-intensity light source used in film projectors.

projection leader *See* leader.

projection lens That lens in a projection system that images the slide, film, and so on, onto the screen; the lens closest to the screen.

projection printing *See* optical printing.

projection receiver A television receiver that uses a combination of mirrors and lenses to form an enlarged picture.

projection room A screening room specially designed and designated for projecting motion pictures.

projection screen Any one of a number of types of surfaces used for projecting film or videotape. May be paper, vinyl coated, aluminum coated, beaded, and so on.

projection shuttle *See* shuttle.

projection speed The rate at which the film moves through the projector; twenty-four frames per second is the standard for sound films.

projection sync The synchronization of picture and sound in a projector by displacing the soundtrack in relation to the picture. The amount of displacement varies with the size of film and the type of soundtrack. For example, the sound is 20 frames ahead of the corresponding picture for 35-mm film and 26 frames ahead for 16-mm film. Also called *printer sync, printing sync, printing synchronization, sound displacement,* and *sound separation.* Cf. editorial sync.

projection synchronism *See* projection sync.

projection television A method of casting a television image on a large screen by using mirrors and lenses. May be either front or rear projection.

Project Officer A military officer assigned to work with a production company if the project is found to qualify under general Department of Defense guidelines.

projector Any optical or electronic device used to project film, slides, video signals, and so on. *See also* balop, projectall, and telop projector.

prologue An introduction to a dramatic work, either written or performed. The lines are sometimes delivered by an individual who is not a character in the work.

promise versus performance The comparison between a station licensee's proposed programming made for an original license or at renewal, and the actual programming broadcast.

promo An abbreviation for *promotional announcement.* □ Generally, any announcement that plugs a network, station, sponsor, product, and so on. □ Specifically, an announcement that identifies the sponsor of a future program beyond the mention of the sponsor's name.

promoter An individual who brings others together to form an organization, business, business enterprise, and so on.

promotion The methods and techniques designed to attract and retain listeners, viewers, readers, and so on, to one of the mass media, through attempts to demonstrate that the station or publication is different from and somehow superior to the competition.

promotional announcement *See* promo.

Promotion Award Plaque, The An award given by the Corporation for Public Broadcasting for the outstanding radio or television promotion of the preceding year.

promotion department A network, station, publishing firm, or other body's department concerned with audience and sales promotion.

promotion manager The individual in charge of a small station's promotion or in charge of a large station's promotion department.

prompt □ A symbol used by a computer to indicate that it is waiting for the operator to supply further input. □ To furnish a forgotten line to talent by a prompter.

prompter □ A person who holds cue cards for or whispers a forgotten line to talent. □ A mechanical device mounted on or near a camera and used to display the continuity or lines for a performer. Also called a *prompting device. See also* telecuer.

prompter card *See* cue card.

prompting device *See* prompter.

prompt key A switch that allows the sound of a program to be cut momentarily so that a performer may be prompted. Cf. cough button.

pronouncer A phonetic spelling of a word in the copy for a newscast. The pronouncer is usually enclosed in parentheses immediately following the word in question.

proof □ A trial print made from a negative. □ An inked impression made from type, plates, cylinders, and so on, to determine whether there are any printer's errors. Also called a *proof leaf* and *proof sheet.*

proofing *See* proofreading.

proofing press *See* proof press.

proof leaf *See* proof.

proof of performance □ An FCC technical requirement that certain measurements be made at specified intervals: field strength measurements, audio frequency response, FM signal-to-noise ratio rate, and so on. □ The certification that an outdoor advertising service has been delivered.

proof paper Photographic paper used for exposure timing in printing or enlarging.

proof press A simple printing press used to take proofs. Also called a *proofing press.*

proofreader An individual who reads proofs and marks them for correction.

proofreader's marks *See* proofreading marks.

proofreading The procedures used to find and eliminate errors in typography, punctuation, spelling, and grammar in printed material. May include the use of spelling and punctuation checkers in computer written copy. Also called *proofing.*

proofreading marks The marks and symbols used by proofreaders in correcting copy. Corrections are normally indicated in the margins rather than on the copy itself, as in copyediting. Also called *proofreader's marks* and *proofreading symbols.*

proofreading symbols *See* proofreading marks.

proof sheet *See* proof.

prop(s) □ An abbreviation for *property (properties).* Anything used to dress a set that is not structurally a part of the set: decorations, pictures, books, flowers, and so on. *See also* hand prop. □ An object that is part of a news story.

propaganda The use of ideas, information, opinion, and so on, for the purpose of furthering or hindering a cause, promoting or denigrating an idea, and so on.

propaganda film A motion picture designed to further the ideological purposes of an individual or group.

propagation The transmission of electromagnetic or sound waves through the air or other medium.

propagation loss The loss of power sustained by a signal as it passes between the transmission and receiving points.

propagation path The route taken by a radio or television signal between the transmitter and receiver, or between a satellite and an earth station, and so on.

prop box A cart or cabinet that is used to hold props on a set.

properties *See* prop.

property □ *See* prop. □ Any vehicle used in the media, such as a book manuscript, screenplay, novel, musical composition, and so on.

property department The motion picture studio department responsible for procuring, storing, maintaining, and checking out props.

property manager *See* property master.

property master The individual in charge of the props for a motion picture, television program, and so on. Also called a *master of properties, prop man,* and *property manager.*

property plot *See* property sheet.

property sheet A list of the props that are necessary for a production. Also called a *property sheet*; sometimes called a *poop sheet.*

property truck A wheeled vehicle that contains the props necessary for a production.

prop list *See* prop plot.

prop man *See* property master.

proportion The relationship in a design, layout, printed page, and so on, that is pleasing to the eye.

proportional printing Printing in which the space allotted for each character varies with the width of the character.

proportional scale A wheel-shaped device used in figuring enlargements and reductions.

proportional spacing Type that is printed taking into consideration the varying widths of printed characters.

proposal A written proposition submitted to prospective backers or producers concerning a possible motion picture or television program venture. Also called a *prospectus.*

proposed programming The programming schedule, based partially on ascertainment, that a prospective licensee submits to the FCC. One of the criteria used in deciding between or among mutually exclusive applicants for a license.

prop plot A list of all properties necessary to a production; detailing when, where, and by whom they are to be used. Also called a *prop list.*

proprietary Information—such as trade secrets, survey results, computer programs, or methods—that is protected from disclosure by those holding the proprietary information.

prop set A representational set that uses a minimum number of items to indicate a locale or specific place or room.

prop truck A small, wheeled cabinet used to store and move hand props and other small items used in set decoration.

prosateur A formal term for a prose writer.

proscenium The wall that divides a stage or set from an audience. Also called a *proscenium arch.*

prospect □ A name of a person on a mailing list who is regarded as a potential buyer for a given product or service but who has not previously made such a purchase. □ A potential buyer of advertising, air time, magazines, and so on.

prospecting A mailing to obtain leads for further sales contacts rather than to make direct sales.

prospectus □ A printed statement issued by a publisher or other business firm designed to arouse interest in a forthcoming book or other product. □ *See* proposal.

prosthetics Artificial features constructed of latex or other materials used in make-up to change natural features.

protagonist The hero or main character of a story; the character the audience is most interested in. Cf. antagonist.

protected *See* protection.

protection □ The safeguard from objectional interference afforded stations by the minimum mileage separation between cochannel or adjacent channel stations. □ A duplicate made in case the original is lost or damaged. *See also* protection master. □ A film or videotape of a news event taken upon arrival at the scene so that something is recorded. □ Satellite service that is guaranteed and may not be canceled. Cf. preemptible. □ A policy allowing a bookseller to return unsold books to a publisher. □ The amount of time before and after the assigned mailing date during which the list owner will not allow the same names to be mailed by anyone other than the mailer cleared for that specific date.

protection copy *See* protection master.

protection master □ A master positive used to make a new dupe negative if the original is damaged. Also called a *protection print* and *protective master.* □ A high-quality duplicate made of an audio- or videotape. Also called a *protection copy.*

protection print *See* protection master.

protection shot *See* cover shot.

protective filter A clear optical glass or ultraviolet filter used to protect the front surface of a lens.

protective flat A flat positioned at the edge of a set so that a camera shot does not accidentally show the backstage area.

protective leader Clear or raw stock used at the head and tail of a reel of motion picture film. It is replaced as small sections are broken off during use.

protective master *See* protection master.

protective order *See* gag order.

protocol A set of conventions used in the exchange of communication between two devices or within a system. The conventions contain the code structure and recognition signals as well as the speed at which the information is to be sent.

prove To take a trial proof of a printed page. Also called *prove up.*

prove up *See* prove.

provisional cut (PC) A story, scene, lines, and so on, designed to be cut from a television program if necessary. Also called a *tentative cut. See also* optional cut.

proximity effect The change in the frequency response of a microphone caused by a minimal distance between the speaker and the microphone. Cf. presence.

proximity pickup A device designed to sense a piece of aluminum foil on film and automatically mark videotape for later editing.

proximity reflector A small, nonfocusing reflector with a lamp mounted immediately behind a planar filament. Cf. internal reflector.

proxy A character written into a story to provide a platform for a writer's views.

PRS Program rating summary report. *See* household tracking report.

PRSA Public Relations Society of America.

prt An abbreviation for *printer.*

prurient interest A portion of the definition of obscene material; that which appeals to lascivious, shameful, or morbid interest in sex.

PR wire A wire service received by both the print and electronic media.

PS □ Postscript. □ Power supply. □ Programming system. □ Proof shot. □ Parallel single. □ Public service. *See* PSA.

PSA □ Photographic Society of America. □ Presunrise Service Authority. □ Public service announcement.

pseudoevent According to Daniel J. Boorstin, manufactured news that is used to gain publicity for the person or cause of the event.

pseudonym An author's or writer's pen name.

pseudonymous work In copyright, a work on the copies or phonorecords of which the author is identified under a fictitious name.

pseudostereo The use of electronic devices to produce a semblance of stereo from a monaural signal.

PSP model Pre-Season Predictor Model. A BBDO computerized system for predicting the rating success or failure of new and returning television programs.

PSSC Public Service Satellite Consortium.

psychoacoustics The branch of science that deals with the subjective factors involved in audio acoustics.

psychographics □ The study of the characteristics of a mass audience. □ The characteristics or qualities used to denote the lifestyle or attitude of customers and prospective customers.

PT A telephone company designation for a radio loop.

PTAR Prime Time Access Rule.

PTFP Public Telecommunications Facilities Program.

PTFP director An employee of the National Telecommunications and Information Administration who recommends final action on public telecommunications facilities applications and grants.

PTL Public Television Library.

PTLA *Publishers' Trade List Annual.*

PTT Post-Telephone-Telegraph Administration.

PTV Public television.

pu An abbreviation for *pick up.*

PUAA Public Utilities Advertising Association.

pub An abbreviation for *publication, publicity, publish, published, publisher,* and *publishing.*

pub date An abbreviation for *publication date.*

public A particular body, regardless of size, of people who have common bonds or interests; an example is an author's public.

public access channel A specially designated, noncommercial cable television channel available to the public on a first-come, nondiscriminatory basis.

public address (PA) system A system for amplifying and controlling the sounds in a large room or before a large audience. Also called a *PA system.*

public affairs programs (PA) Radio or television programs that include talks, commentaries, discussions, speeches, editorials, political programs, documentaries, forums, panels, roundtables, and similar programs that primarily concern local, national, and international public affairs. An FCC program type category.

publication □ The sale, placing on sale, or public distribution of copies of a work. □ The communication of defamatory remarks to one or more persons. Cf. fault and identification. □ In copyright law, the distribution of copies or phonorecords of a work to the public by sale or other transfer of ownership, or by rental, lease, or lending. The offering to distribute copies or phonorecords to a group of persons for purposes of further distribution, public performance, or public display, constitutes publication. A public performance or display of a work does not of itself constitute publication.

publication date The date on which a book or other publication becomes available for sale to the public.

publication of private facts In privacy law, the publication of information about an individual that is not a matter of public concern and not a matter of public record.

publication rights The right to publication of a work in book form or in magazine or periodical form, including serial publications.

publication-set Type or other printed materials for an advertisement set or prepared by the periodical in which it is run rather than supplied in some form by the advertiser or agency. Also called *pub-set.* Cf. composition-set type.

public broadcasting Broadcasting by noncommercial radio and television stations.

Public Broadcasting Act The 1967 Congressional Act that established the Corporation for Public Broadcasting (CPB).

Public Broadcasting Service (PBS) A private organization that manages the public television network and selects, schedules, and distributes programming. Established by the CPB in 1969.

Public Broadcast Laboratory (PBL) An experiment, funded by the Ford Foundation in 1967, in which NET offered live programming to public television stations.

public broadcast station *See* noncommercial educational broadcast station.

public comments The comments solicited through a licensee's prefiling announcements.

public correspondence Any telecommunication that the offices and stations, by reason of their being at the disposal of the public, must accept for transmission.

public display *See* public performance.

public domain (PD) A musical or literary work for which no copyright was issued or for which the copyright has expired. Therefore, such a work is not subject to copyright protection and is available for use without payment of royalties.

public, educational, or governmental access facilities A channel capacity designated for public, educational, or governmental use; facilities and equipment for the use of such channel capacity.

public figure A prominent or well-known person or an individual who has voluntarily thrust himself or herself into the limelight.

public file The information—including letters, applications, exhibits, and other documents—that broadcasters must maintain for perusal by the general public.

publici juris Latin for the history of the day. News itself is not copyrightable, although a news article is.

public interest *See* public interest, convenience, and necessity.

public interest, convenience, and necessity A phrase borrowed from the Transportation Act of 1920 and various state public utility legislation. It now serves as a broad mandate to the FCC to operate in the best interest of the public. The phrase simply defies precise definition, because no definition would be able to cover all possible contingencies. Often abbreviated *public interest.*

publicist *See* press agent.

publicity Information regarding a person, product, idea, institution, and so on, that is executed and distributed through one or more of the mass media. Publicity is often disguised as news.

publicity crime A criminal act performed to gain media attention.

publicity director An advertising agency or advertiser employee responsible for obtaining publicity for clients or the employer. Also called a *public relations director.*

publicity release A news story distributed by a press agent concerning a client. Sometimes called a *blurb* or *puff. See also* news release and publicity.

publicity still A photograph taken of a performer, often a head shot, used for publicity. *See also* photo call.

public law □ The law governing the relationship between the government and individuals, and the organization and conduct of the government itself; includes constitutional law, international law, administrative law, and so on. □ A statute passed by the U.S. Congress; for example, Public Law 416, 73rd Congress, June 19, 1934, is the Communications Act of 1934. Cf. private law.

public library (PL) A privately or publicly owned library open to the public without charge.

publicly *See* public performance.

public official An individual who is elected to public office. An individual who would have to prove actual malice in a defamation case.

public opinion The expression of an attitude by members of a group who are in some way informed about a subject.

public opinion survey A scientific sampling of the expressed attitudes of the public. *See also* survey.

public performance To perform or display a work at a place open to the public or at any place where a substantial number of persons outside of a normal circle of a family and its social acquaintances is gathered; or to transmit or otherwise communicate a performance or display of the work to a place specified or to the public, by means of any device or process, whether the members of the public capable of receiving the performance or display receive it in the same place or in separate places and at the same time or at different times.

public radio A noncommercial radio station that is affiliated with National Public Radio.

public record □ Any document that law requires a government body to make available to individuals. *See also* Freedom of Information Act. □ Source material for which the right of inspection is available.

public relations (PR) The art and science of influencing the attitudes and opinions of a group of persons in the interest of promoting a person, product, idea, institution, and so on.

public relations director *See* publicity director.

Public Relations Officer (PRO) An individual employed by an organization to promote the organization's point of view to the public. Often refers to a member of the armed forces.

Public Relations Society of America (PRSA) A professional organization, formed in 1948, to provide professional development and placement services for members.

public service advertising Advertisements placed in a medium with or without charge in the interest of promoting the general welfare and good will of its audience.

public service announcement (PSA) An announcement for which no charge is made and that promotes programs, activities, or services of federal, state, or local governments; the programs, activities, or services of nonprofit organizations and other announcements regarded as serving community interests, excluding time signals, routine weather announcements, and promotional announcements.

public service copy Copy of a civic or philanthropic nature posted on an outdoor advertising structure in the interest of community welfare.

public service programs *See* public affairs programs.

Public Service Responsibility of Broadcast Licensees *See* Blue Book.

Public Service Satellite Consortium (PSSC) An organization of users of communications satellites for health, education, and other social services.

public station A radio or television station that receives programming or funds from the Corporation for Public Broadcasting (CPB).

public telecommunications entity Any enterprise that is a public broadcast station or noncommercial telecommunications entity and that disseminates public telecommunications services to the public.

public telecommunications facilities Apparatus necessary for production, interconnection, captioning, broadcast, or other distribution of programming; the apparatus includes, but is not limited to, studio equipment, cameras, microphones, audio and video storage, towers, antennas, and transmitters, except that the term does not include the buildings to house such apparatus, other than small equipment shelters that are part of satellite earth stations, translators, microwave interconnection facilities, and similar facilities.

Public Telecommunications Facilities Program (PTFP) A program designed to ensure the fair, equitable, and uniform treatment of applications for planning and construction grants for public telecommunications facilities.

public telecommunications services Noncommercial instructional, community service, public service, public affairs, educational, and cultural radio and television programs that may be transmitted by means of electronic communications by a public telecommunications entity.

Public Television (PTV) A term suggested by the Carnegie Commission on Educational Television to replace the term *educational television (ETV).*

Public Television Library (PTL) A PBS-operated library that distributes public television programs.

public utilities commission (PUC) A state agency delegated the responsibility for regulating public utilities such as power, water, and light.

public utility A regulated business that supplies the public with necessary services, such as the telephone company.

publish To print and disseminate printed matter, such as newspapers, magazines, and books.

published data tapes (PDT) Report book data in magnetic tape form for computer processing by subscribers or by service bureaus retained for that purpose.

publisher □ A person who issues, or causes to be issued, printed matter such as books, magazines, and music. □ The owner or designated chief executive officer of a newspaper or other periodical.

Publishers' Information Bureau (PIB) A firm that publishes syndicated reports on advertising schedule expenditures, by product or service, of advertisers in consumer magazines.

publisher's interim statement A circulation statement issued by a periodical publisher belonging to the Audit Bureau of Circulations at optional intervals between the regular publishing statements.

publisher's letter A second letter enclosed in a mailing package to stress a specific selling point.

publisher's representative An individual who solicits the purchase of advertising from advertisers on behalf of a periodical publisher. Cf. representative.

publisher's statement A sworn statement made by a publisher as to the circulation of a publication. *See also* Audit Bureau of Circulations (ABC).

Publishers' Trade List Annual (PTLA) An alphabetical reference to the catalogs and publications of publishers.

pub-set *See* publication-set.

puck *See* pressure roller.

puff □ A flattering review of a program, story, or performance. □ A publicity release containing more than the usual number of superlatives. Also called a *puff piece.*

puffery The extravagant praise lavished on a product by an advertiser that stops just short of deception.

puff piece *See* puff.

puff sheet A newspaper, usually small, that prints only favorable news about advertisers.

Pulitzer Prizes The best-known journalism prizes. Endowed by Joseph Pulitzer, the founder of the *St. Louis Post-Dispatch,* and administered by Columbia University. First awarded in 1918.

pull □ A graphic card with a movable insert used to simulate a simple form of animation. Also called a *pull tab.* □ A slang term for the number of amperes a lighting or other circuit draws. □ *See* pulling power. □ *See* pull a proof.

pull a proof To make an impression on paper from type. Also called *pulling a proof.*

pull back □ *See* dolly out. □ *See* zoom out.

pull card A studio title card that is removed by hand to reveal another card. Also called a *pull-off card.*

pull down The process of moving film a frame at a time in a camera or projector.

pull down mechanism A device, usually a claw or maltese cross mechanism, that produces the intermittent movement necessary for motion picture projection.

puller A tape transport.

pull focus *See* focus pull.

pulling a proof *See* pull a proof.

pulling focus *See* focus pull.

pulling power The effectiveness of an advertisement, radio or television program, motion picture, and so on, in persuading the public to buy a product, watch a program, attend a motion picture, or take some other positive action. Also called *pull.*

pull-off card *See* pull card.

pullout A self-contained section of a newspaper designed to be removed.

pull out □ *See* dolly out (DO). □ *See* zoom out.

pull tab *See* pull.

pullup A film projector or camera loop.

pulp □ The mixture of wood fibers and/or rags and water from which paper is made. *See also* chemical pulp and groundwood pulp. □ A magazine printed on comparatively rough paper, often newsprint. Cf. slick.

pulp magazine *See* pulp.

Pulse The Pulse, Inc. A broadcast audience survey organization founded in 1941.

pulse An instantaneous change in voltage used to activate or generate a signal for blanking, synchronization, and so on.

pulse code editor *See* control track editor.

pulse code modulation (PCM) A technique for converting analog information into digital form. The analog signal is sampled at a rate equal to at least twice the maximum signal frequency component, and the sampled value is represented by a fixed-length binary number. This number is then transmitted as a corresponding set of pulses.

pulse count A method of tracking videotape frames by counting the individual control track pulses in control track editing.

pulsed track *See* pulse track.

pulse lamp A high-intensity light source used in cinematography, motion picture projectors, and telecine machines.

pulse modulation The modulation of a carrier wave by a series of pulses to carry binary codes or other information.

pulse sync The synchronizing pulse used on a pulse track.

pulse track A series of brief sounds recorded on tape to lock a film camera to a tape recorder so that they are in synchronization. Also called *pulsed track. See also* resolving.

pulsing The use of heavy advertising in cyclical or intermittent periods of time.

pump A slang term meaning to feed or generate a signal.

punch □ To deliver a line with emphasis. Also called *point* and *punch up.* □ An end mark on a film. □ To take; to punch up or cut from one picture to another. □ To write copy in a vigorous, forceful manner. □ A relief design on metal used to impress wax or plastic for intaglio printing. □ To make a hole in a punched card or paper tape. □ In animation, the device that cuts the registration holes in cels and drawing paper, so they can be placed over corresponding pegs.

punch card *See* punched card.

punched card A standard Hollerith stiff paper card used for storing information by the calculated placement of punched holes.

punched paper tape A strip of paper used for storing information by the calculated placement of punched holes.

punched tape A tape used to initiate light changes in an optical printer.

puncher A person who operates a machine to punch tapes or cards.

punching The editing of audiotape by pressing the record button at the edit point.

punch line *See* tag line.

punch tape A former method of storing videotape edit decision lists using paper tape with holes punched in it.

punch the mike To turn a microphone on.

punch up *See* punch.

punitive damages *See* damages.

punk *See* filler.

pup A small spotlight similar to a baby.

puppet animation An animation technique in which three-dimensional articulated figures are manipulated on miniature sets and photographed frame-by-frame.

puppetoon An animated feature using carved figurines.

purchase proposition *See* position.

pure ASCII *See* plain ASCII.

pure research *See* basic research.

pure tone *See* simple tone.

purge The process of eliminating duplicates or unwanted names and addresses from one or more mailing lists.

purity The property of a color unmixed with white or other colors.

purity control A potentiometer in a color television receiver that controls the magnetic coils directing the electron beams to the proper phosphor dots.

purposive sample *See* judgment sample.

push The forced development of film beyond its emulsion rating. Also called *force*.

pusher A grip who moves a camera dolly.

push in *See* dolly in (DI).

pushing *See* forcing.

push off A wipe in which the image seems to be propelled off the screen by another picture. Also called a *pushover*. Cf. push on.

push on A wipe in which the image seems to be pulled off the screen by an invisible force. Cf. push off.

pushover *See* push off.

push processing *See* forced development.

push-pull An electronic circuit containing two identical components that operate 180 degrees out of phase.

push to talk switch *See* press to talk switch.

PUT Persons using television.

put to bed To complete a newspaper edition, with the forms locked up and ready to print; all in hand.

PV Potential viewer.

PVC Polyvinyl chloride.

PVT Persons viewing television.

pylon □ A tall, triangular-shaped column used as a set piece. □ A support for an outdoor advertising display. □ A tall outdoor sign.

pyramid □ The arrangement of printed advertisements to resemble a pyramid. □ *See* inverted pyramid.

pyramid ad *See* pyramid.

pyramid head A headline of three or more lines in inverted pyramid style.

pyramiding A method of testing mailing lists in which one starts with a small quantity and, based on positive indications, follows with larger and larger quantities of the balance of the list until the entire list is mailed.

pyro Pyrogallic acid, a film-developing agent.

pyrotechnics □ The art of making and using fireworks for display purposes. □ A fireworks-like display of acting.

pyroxylin A cellulose nitrate material used in the manufacture of celluloid film bases.

Q

Q □ A script notation meaning cue. □ A symbol for likability or degree of public acceptance. □ Low-power TV. An FCC file-number prefix. □ A symbol for a quantity of electrical charge. □ A wire service symbol for the result or period score of a sporting event. □ An abbreviation for *quarterly.* □ An abbreviation for *quarto.* □ Quality factor.

Q and A Question and answer.

QC □ Quad center. □ Quick connect. □ Quartz crystal. □ Quality control.

Q channel □ The band of frequencies used to transmit the red and green color television information. □ One of the eight compact disc subcode channels (P–W). The Q channel carries the main control and display information. It identifies tracks, indexes, and running times, and the absolute playing time of the disc. It also indicates whether the recorded information is audio or data, whether preemphasis is applied, and whether digital copying is permitted. It also includes its own cyclic redundancy check.

Q8 Quadraphonic eight. An eight-track tape cartridge format.

Q factor □ The ratio of the reactance of the series resistance of an inductor or capacitor in an electronic circuit. □ *See* Callier coefficient.

QHY Quantized high Y.

QI Quartz iodide (or iodine).

QK Quick kinescope.

QL Quad left.

QM Quadrature modulation.

QR Quad right.

Q rating A rating of the percentage of radio or television listeners or viewers who are aware of a given program and who regard it positively.

Q signal A signal used to convey the color difference of chrominance information in color television. *See also* color difference signal, I signal, luminance signal, and M signal.

Q-sort A research procedure in which a respondent sorts printed statements into piles that represent the degree of truth or agreement the respondent finds in the statements.

quad □ Pertaining to the number four. □ An abbreviation for *quadraphonic, quadrature,* and *quadruplex.* □ A cable consisting of four separately insulated conductors twisted together. □ An abbreviation for *quadrat.* □ A piece of metal, shorter than type high, used for spacing material in hand typesetting. An em quad is the square of the type size; it occupies the same space as the letter *m.* Also called a *quadrat.*

quadcast A four-channel FM radio broadcast.

quad center (QC) A centered line of type. Cf. quad left (QL) and quad right (QR).

quad crown A size of paper; 30 by 40 inches.

quadding □ The mechanical process of filling spaces with quads. Also called *quadding out.* □ The computer process for controlling the positioning of less than a full line of type matter.

quadding out *See* quadding.

quad eight Thirty-five-mm film that is slit after printing and processing into four super 8-mm films.

quad left (QL) Less than a full line of type matter that is positioned flush left.

quad line A blank type slug.

quadlite A luminaire containing four floodlights.

quad out To expand a line with blank quads.

quadradisc *See* CD-4.

quadraphonic □ A system for broadcasting four signals on FM radio. Also called *quadraphonic broadcasting.* □ A four-channel recording or transmission. *See also* stereophonic sound. Cf. biphonic and triphonic. □ A recording and playback system using four separate loudspeakers into which four separate signals are fed. Also called *quadrasonic.* Also spelled *quadriphonic. See also* discrete and matrix. Cf. stereophonic.

quadraphonic broadcasting *See* quadraphonic.

quadraphonic microphone A single microphone containing two pairs of directional microphone elements.

quadraphonic sound Sound produced by the use of four separate audio channels and four loudspeakers. Also called *quad sound.*

quadrasonic *See* quadraphonic.

quadrat *See* quad.

quadrature In quadruplex recording, the geometric relationship among the four magnetic pole tips mounted on the headwheel. Ideally, the pole tips are precisely 90 degrees apart.

quadrature error In quadruplex recording, the time base error in the reproduced video signal that results when the four video magnetic pole tips are not 90 degrees apart.

quadrature modulation The modulation of two AM or FMX carrier components 90 degrees apart in phase by separate modulation.

quad right (QR) Less than a full line of type matter that is positioned flush right. Cf. quad left.

quadriphonic *See* quadraphonic.

quadruplex Literally, four-headed. Pertaining to a standardized method of videotape recording that uses four magnetic pole tips mounted around the rim of a headwheel. The headwheel rotates in a plane perpendicular to the direction of the tape motion. Cf. helical scan.

quadruplex recorder A videotape recorder using four heads for video record and playback. Cf. helical scan.

quadruplex transverse scanning *See* transverse scanning.

quad sound *See* quadraphonic sound.

quad split A video switcher effect that permits up to four different pictures on the screen at one time.

qualified circulation The readership eligible to receive a controlled circulation periodical.

qualified issue reader An individual who qualifies for examination on his or her reactions to a periodical advertisement by giving evidence of having read the issue in which the advertisement appeared. Also called a *qualified reader.*

qualified privilege A legal privilege that is less than absolute but is nevertheless entitled to protection under the law. An example is the fair and accurate reporting of defamatory statements made of official proceedings. Also called *conditional privilege.*

qualified professional actor According to the Screen Actors Guild, a person who has had prior employment as a motion picture actor at least once during the period of three years prior to the date of the proposed employment.

qualified reader *See* qualified issue reader.

qualified respondent An individual who has met the standards established for respondents in a consumer or audience research project.

qualified station Any television broadcast station, except where such station would be considered a distant signal for copyright purposes, that, with respect to a particular cable system: is licensed to a community whose reference point is within 50 miles of the principal headend of the cable system; and, if a commercial station, receives an average share of total viewing hours of at least 2 percent and a net weekly circulation of at least 5 percent in noncable households in the county served by the cable system or has been operational for less than one year. Noncommercial educational television station translator stations with a higher power are also qualified stations.

qualified viewer An individual who qualifies for examination on his or her reaction to a television commercial by giving some evidence of having watched the program on which the commercial was presented.

qualitative research The systematic study of individuals, groups, phenomena, and so on, in an attempt to determine the nature of that which is being studied. Often used to develop insights and develop hypotheses. Also called *subjective research.* Cf. quantitative research.

quality □ The faithfulness to or fidelity of sound or picture reproduction. □ A term sometimes used as a theatrical synonym for *color.*

quality circulation Readership demographics that are highly desirable to the newspaper or magazine.

quality control (QC) An organizational process for maintaining product or service quality at a designated standard.

quality demographics The middle- to upper-income households containing individuals in the upper-20s-to-50 age bracket.

quality paperback A paperbound book, often a reprint of a hardbound book, that is sold in bookstores. Also called a *trade paperback*. Cf. mass market paperback.

quality print *See* reference print.

quantitative audience measurement *See* quantitative research.

quantitative research The systematic study of individuals, groups, phenomena, and so on, in an attempt to determine the composition and proportions of that which is being studied. Also called objective research. In broadcasting also called quantitative audience measurement. Cf. qualitative research.

quantitizing *See* quantize.

quantity discount A rate reduction offered to time or space buyers who agree to spend a specified amount of money during a given period. *See also* frequency discount.

quantity prints □ Multiple film or videotape prints of a commercial prepared in order to permit its simultaneous airing on a number of broadcast stations at the same time. □ Multiple glossy prints of a still photograph, made from an original negative and used for mailings, sales kits, and so on.

quantization *See* quantize.

quantization error The distorted sound caused in digital recording due to aliasing problems.

quantize To assign one of a fixed set of values to an analog signal as part of an analog-to-digital conversion process. For example, in pulse code modulation, an analog signal is sampled and quantized, and a corresponding set of binary pulses is produced. Also called *quantization* and *quantitizing*.

quantized high Y (QHY) A coding technique used to reduce the quantity of data required to encode a high-resolution-type picture. A normal resolution DYUV image is recorded, together with the data that needs to be added to it to turn the luminance (Y) of the picture to the equivalent of high resolution. The latter data further compressed is termed *QHY*.

quantizer A device or circuit that assigns fixed binary values to sample analog signals in analog-to-digital conversion.

quarter apple An apple box 18 by 12 by 3 inches.

quarter binding A style of book binding in which the back is of a different material from the sides. Also called *quarter bound*.

quarter bound *See* quarter binding.

quarter-hour audience An estimate of the average audience having viewed a station for a minimum of five minutes within a specific quarter-hour. These quarter-hour total audiences, when accumulated over larger time periods, become average quarter-hour audiences.

quarter inch tape The standard width of magnetic audiotape.

quarterly A publication that is issued every three months.

quarterly issues/programs list The list required by the FCC of commercial radio stations that delineates the programs and announcements that treated ascertained community problems.

quarterly measurement A broadcast audience survey taken for a period of 12 consecutive weeks. Cf. sweeps.

quarter roll A roll of newsprint one page wide. Also called a *cheese roll* and *dinky roll*.

quarter run *See* quarter showing.

quarter service *See* quarter showing.

quarter showing A transit advertising contract that requires car cards to be placed on one of every four buses, streetcars, and so on, in a given area. Also called a *quarter run* and *quarter service*. Cf. full showing and half showing.

quarter track *See* four track.

quarter track recorder A tape recorder that uses one-quarter (less the width of the guard band) of a tape to record each signal. Cf. full track recorder and half track recorder.

quarter wave (QW) One quarter of a wave cycle. Often, the length of an antenna cut to a quarter of the wavelength of the signal to be transmitted or received.

quartile The three percentile points that divide a frequency distribution into four equal parts.

quarto A book the size of a fourth of a sheet of paper. A size obtained when a sheet is folded twice, making four leaves or eight pages.

quartz The hexagonal-shaped mineral silicon dioxide, used extensively to make crystals.

quartz crystal A piezoelectric crystal used to control the frequency of an oscillator. Also called a *crystal.*

quartz halogen lamp *See* quartz lamp.

quartz iodine A bright lamp using iodine as the gaseous element and enclosed in quartz instead of glass.

quartz iodine lamp *See* quartz lamp.

quartz lamp A tungsten filament enclosed in quartz instead of glass and containing a trace of iodine or xenon.

quartz light The light emitted by a quartz lamp.

quartz lights A generic term for small luminaires of various types (usually open reflector) that use tungsten-halogen lamps.

quash To set aside, vacate, or overthrow by judicial action.

quasi Latin for "seeming" or "resembling."

quasi-equal opportunities Another name for the Zapple Doctrine.

quasi-judicial An administrative agency (independent regulatory commission), such as the FCC, FTC, or FDA, that also handles adjudicatory matters within its area of expertise.

quasi-laser A microwave link designed to replace trunk coaxial cables in a CATV system. Cf. amplitude modulated link (AML).

quasi-optical The line-of-sight transmission of electromagnetic energy.

Qube A trademark for an interactive cable television system.

queen size poster A 30-by-88-inch transit advertising poster used on the sides of busses and other vehicles. Cf. king size poster.

query □ A question mark placed in the margin of manuscript or other copy by a proofreader or copy editor to indicate a possible error. □ A brief summary or outline of a story sent by a correspondent, writer, or stringer to determine whether the publisher or station wants to use the story. Also called a *query letter.* □ A question from a subscriber or customer as to the status of his or her account or about a product or service.

query letter *See* query.

question and answer (Q and A) □ A format for copy for advertisements, in which consumers pose questions answered by advertisers or spokespersons. □ An interview format. □ A format for meetings, in which an individual presents material only in response to questions.

questionnaire A form that lists a series of closed-ended or open-ended questions to be answered and filled out by the respondent. Cf. schedule.

question shot A television interviewer's question or questions taped after an interview so that the questions fit the edited answers by the individual interviewed.

queue □ A line of persons waiting to buy tickets to a theatre or other performance. □ A line or list of jobs waiting for computer processing. Queues may be FIFO or LIFO.

quick and dirty A slang phrase for any motion picture, radio or television program, spot, publication, production, and so on, that is done as quickly and cheaply as possible.

quick change A performer who is able to make fast costume changes; a quick change artist.

quick cue □ Any fast cue. □ An intentional interruption of the end of one performer's line by another performer.

quick cutting A series of rapid television or film takes.

quick disc An optical disc produced on a very short delivery (normally one working day) to a special requirement or for program validation prior to disc replication.

quick disconnect A type of electrical connector that is designed to break away easily in case of emergency.

quickie A somewhat derogatory term for a low-budget motion picture or television program made in a relatively brief period of time.

quick kinescope (QK) Originally, a film kinescope processed rapidly for rebroadcast. Now seldom used, the term may mean any immediate replay of a recorded program.

quick motion *See* fast motion.

quick-study A performer who has the ability to memorize lines rapidly.

quiescence The condition of an electrical circuit when no signal is applied to the circuit.

quiet A radio or television director's command for silence on a set.

quiet tuning A radio receiver that automatically eliminates the sound between stations.

Quincy decision The court of appeals for the District of Columbia decision that overturned the FCC's must carry rules as an infringement on First Amendment rights.

quinol A common film-developing agent; hydroquinone.

quintaphonic A five-channel motion picture theatre sound system, such as THX.

quintile analysis The dividing of an audience into five equal groups for the purpose of analysis and comparison.

quintile ranges A set of summary statistical measures—referred to as the first, second, third, fourth, and fifth quintile ranges—that divide a complete set of values, arrayed in order of magnitude, into five groups of equal frequency.

quipster A performer who uses sarcastic or witty remarks.

quire □ A quantity of paper, either 24 or 25 sheets of the same size and quality. □ A small book or booklet.

quiz program A radio or television game or audience participation program wherein contestants must answer questions to win a prize.

quiz scandals The television quiz program problems that arose in the late 1950s when it was discovered that some of the quiz programs were rigged by giving the answers to some of the questions to certain contestants.

quoin A keyed metal device used to lock up type in a form.

quoin key A key used to lock type forms or galleys.

quonking Any noise or movement by individuals not connected with the scene being shot but nevertheless picked up by a microphone or seen on camera.

quota □ A sales goal set for an individual, usually expressed either in receipts or as a percentage. □ A media plan goal set in terms of, for example, individuals or households to be reached. □ A number or proportion to be reflected by one element in a population sample; intended to produce a suitably balanced sample. *See also* quota sample.

quota sample A survey sample in which desired sample sizes or quotas are established for various universe subclasses (controls). The purpose is to ensure that the characteristics of the sample being examined are distributed in proportion to the characteristics of the total population. Cf. probability sample.

quotation *See* quote.

quote □ An abbreviation for *quotation.* □ The words inside quotation marks. Cf. direct quote, indirect quote, paraphrase, and partial quote. □ To record the exact words of a speaker or writer. □ A price estimate given for supplies, printing, equipment, and so on.

quotes An abbreviation for *quotation marks.*

QW Quarter Wave.

qwart A luminaire that can produce both a spotlight or soft light.

qwerty The traditional typewriter keyboard layout that contains the six letters *qwerty* in order on the top row of letters. Cf. Dvorak keyboard.

QZ An abbreviation for *quartz.*

R

R □ Registered; a symbol used to identify a registered trademark: a circle containing an *R*. □ Read. □ Reader. □ Recto. □ Religious programs. □ Reluctance. □ Renewed license. An FCC file-number prefix. □ Resistance. □ Resistor. □ Reverse. □ Right. □ A wire service symbol for regular priority. □ Restricted; A CARA classification for feature films. Under 17 years requires accompanying parent or guardian. Cf. G, PG, PG-13, and X.

RA Reduced aperture.

RAB Radio Advertising Bureau, Inc.

rabbit ears An inexpensive, V-shaped indoor television receiver antenna.

RAC Radio Advisory Committee of the CPB.

race The major classification of typefaces: roman, text, italic, square serif, sans serif, and ornamental. *See also* type classification.

raceway A channel, often located under a floor, used to protect and run wires, cables, and so on.

raceway flooring *See* computer flooring.

rack □ A vertical cabinet used to mount equipment; usually 19 inches wide. □ A turret for holding camera lenses. □ To rotate a camera lens turret from one lens to another. Also called *flip* and *rack over*. □ *See* pin rack. □ The process of threading film in a camera. □ To adjust a film in a projector gate. □ To change the distance between the lens and the pickup tube in a television camera by moving the focusing control. □ A support that holds the camera and subject in process photography. □ A frame that holds type cases. □ A film-drying or -editing frame.

racked up Equipment and components permanently mounted in a rack.

rack focusing The focusing on a performer or object so as to keep the background or foreground out of focus in order to concentrate a viewer's attention. Also called *selective focusing*.

racking □ To change lenses on a turret. Also called *rack*. □ To move the focusing control knob on a camera. □ *See* framing.

rack mount *See* turret.

rackover □ A method of checking the precise center of a camera's field, in which the body of the camera is temporarily shifted to one side to allow the camera operator to look through a special viewfinder with cross hairs; the camera is shifted back into position for shooting to continue. Rackovers are often used to check the accuracy of off-center shots. □ To move a rackover viewfinder into place. □ *See* rack.

rack sale The sale of newspapers from unattended open racks or boxes, payment dependent on the honesty of the takers. Seldom used now.

rack through focus To move the focusing control on a camera from one extreme to the other.

rack up The movement of the lines in a video display wherein they move up one at a time as the cursor moves down.

RADAR □ Radio's All-Dimension Audience Research. A project of the four national radio networks in audience research. Cf. ARMS and CRAM. □ Radio detection and ranging.

RADI Radio area of dominant influence.

radiant energy Energy in the form of electromagnetic radiation.

radiate To emit electromagnetic energy from an antenna.

radiating element The portion of an antenna that radiates electromagnetic energy. Also called a *radiator*.

radiating system The transmitting antenna, supporting structures, transmission lines, and so on, of a broadcast station.

radiation The outward flow of energy from any source in the form of radio waves.

radiation pattern A cross-sectional graph of the vertical and horizontal radiation planes of an antenna. Also called *directional pattern.*

radiator *See* radiating element.

radio From the Latin radius, a ray. □ The wireless transmission of signals by electromagnetic energy. Heinrich Hertz of Germany in 1886 demonstrated experimentally the propagation of electromagnetic waves based on the 1867 theories of James Clerk Maxwell of Scotland. Radio may be used as a noun, verb, or adjective. □ A radio receiver. □ To send a wireless message. The term, when used in the Communications Act or by the FCC, often subsumes the word *television.* □ A general term applied to the use of radio waves.

Radio Act of 1912 The second radio law passed in the United States. The act required a license from the secretary of Commerce and Labor to operate a radio station but failed to provide for efficient broadcast regulation. *See also* Wireless Ship Act of 1910.

Radio Act of 1927 The Act that created the Federal Radio Commission (FRC) with broad powers to regulate broadcasting. Replaced by the Communications Act of 1934.

Radio Advertising Bureau (RAB) The radio industry's sales promotion organization. Similar in function to TvB.

radio area of dominant influence (RADI) A term used by The Pulse, Inc., to describe counties where most of the radio reception is of programs from home stations.

Radio Beijing An international broadcasting organization beaming programs worldwide from the People's Republic of China.

radio broadcast *See* broadcast.

radio broadcast station A station equipped to engage in radio communication or transmission of energy by radio. Also called a *station* in the Communications Act.

radio channel A band of frequencies wide enough for the transmission of radio signals. In AM radio, a channel is 10 kHz wide; in FM radio, 200 kHz.

Radio Club of America, Inc. (RCA) An association of persons interested in wireless founded in 1909 as the Junior Wireless Club, Ltd.

Radio Code The self-regulatory code first adopted in 1929 by the National Association of Broadcasters that set forth program and advertising standards for member radio stations. The code was eliminated.

Radio Code Board An 11-member panel empowered to "enact, amend, and promulgate Radio Standards of Practice or Codes" of the Radio Code of the National Association of Broadcasters. Now defunct.

radio communication □ The transmission by radio of writing, signs, signals, pictures, and sounds of all kinds, including all instrumentalities, facilities, apparatus, and services (among other things, the receipt, forwarding, and delivery of communications) incidental to such transmission. Also called *communication by radio* in the Communications Act. □ Telecommunication by means of radio waves.

radio communication service A service involving the transmission, emission, and/or reception of radio waves for specific telecommunication purposes.

radio conferences *See* National Radio Conferences (NRC).

radio equipment list A list of equipment approved for use in broadcast stations by the FCC.

radio family *See* radio household.

radio feed *See* feed.

radio format *See* format.

Radio Free Europe (RFE) A private United States broadcasting organization that broadcasts to the countries of Eastern Europe from overseas transmitters. Cf. Radio Liberty.

radio frequency (RF) Any frequency at which the radiation of electromagnetic energy is possible.

radio frequency interference *See* RF interference.

Radio Group An early broadcast operational group consisting of General Electric, Westinghouse, and RCA. Cf. Telephone Group.

radio home *See* radio household.

radio household A household that owns any type or model of radio, even when the radio is temporarily out-of-order, being repaired, or not being used for any other reason. Also called a *radio family* and *radio home.*

Radio Information Center (RIC) An organization that tracks radio formats on a monthly basis.

Radio Liberty A U.S. broadcasting organization that transmits programs from Germany to the Soviet Union. Cf. Radio Free Europe.

radio link A narrow radio beam used for point-to-point communication.

radio loop A line from a customer's premises to a telephone company central office. Used for rate determination.

Radio Marti The Voice of America radio station that broadcasts to Cuba. Named for Cuban patriot and writer Jose Marti.

radio microphone A portable microphone with a low power transmitter capable of sending a signal a short distance.

Radio Moscow An international broadcasting organization beaming programs worldwide from the Soviet Union.

radio music box David Sarnoff's 1916 name for a radio receiver.

radio order circuit A communication circuit used by stations for information concerning program service.

radiophonic sound Electronic sound effects used in conjunction with other sounds.

radio president A name given to Franklin D. Roosevelt because of his extensive use of radio.

radio programming *See* programming.

radio rating point A unit of radio audience size equal to one percent of the radio-owning households in the area under study.

Radio Regulation (RR) The oft-cited and much-used looseleaf publication by Pike and Fischer containing indexed decisions, reports, cases, and so on, of the FCC, courts, and other agencies.

radio relay A transmission booster or translator.

radio rights The right to broadcast by radio for aural reception only and unaccompanied by any recordation, transmission, or broadcast intended for visual reception.

radio service An administrative subdivision of the field of radio communication. In an engineering sense, the subdivision may be made according to the method of operation, such as mobile service and fixed service. In a regulatory sense, the subdivisions may be descriptive of particular groups of licensees, such as the groups of persons licensed under experimental radio services.

radio spectrum The total spectrum range that is capable of being radiated and used for radio communication, from approximately 10,000 Hz to more than 300 gHz.

radio station *See* radio broadcast station.

radio station license *See* station license.

radio superstation A radio station whose signal is distributed to cable television systems by satellite.

Radio Technical Planning Board (RTPB) A committee organized in 1943 to advise government, industry, and the public of plans for frequency allocation and standardization.

radiotelegram A telegram, originating in or intended for a mobile station or a mobile earth station transmitted on all or part of its route over the radio communication channels of the mobile service or of the mobile-satellite service.

radiotelephone call A telephone call, originating in or intended for a mobile station or a mobile earth station, transmitted on all or part of its route over the radio communication channels of the mobile service or the mobile-satellite service.

radiotelephony Two-way radio communication.

radiotelegraphy Radio communication by means of coded signals.

radiotelex call A telex call, originating in or intended for a mobile station or a mobile earth station, transmitted on all or part of its route over the radio communication channels of the mobile service or the mobile-satellite service.

radiotorial A radio editorial.

radio transmission A means of distributing information by modulating a high-frequency carrier wave with a signal, amplifying it, and radiating the resultant signal to be picked up by a receiver.

radio transmission of energy *See* transmission of energy by radio.

radio transmitter *See* transmitter.

radio-TV camera A portable television camera containing a radio link to a mobile van, studio, transmitter, and so on.

radio-TV wire The wire service copy that is written in broadcast style.

radio waves Electromagnetic waves of frequencies arbitrarily lower than 3000 gHz, propagated in space without artificial guides. Also called *Hertzian waves.*

radio wire A news wire carrying news written in broadcast style. Cf. A-wire and B-wire.

radix The base of a number system.

radome A fiberglass or plastic cover used to protect microwave antennas from dirt and weather.

rag A slang term for a newspaper.

rag content The percentage of linen or cotton contained in some paper. Usually stated as 25, 50, 75, or 100 percent.

ragged edge Type set ragged left or ragged right, although it usually refers to ragged right.

ragged left A typed page or column that has an even right margin but an uneven left margin. Cf. justification and ragged right.

ragged right A typed page or column that has an even left margin but an uneven right margin; the usual appearance of a page produced by a typewriter. Cf. justification and ragged left.

rag paper Paper made from linen or cotton scraps instead of wood fibers. Generally, a superior quality paper.

rail □ A wooden cross piece in a flat. □ A pipe batten.

rail light *See* balcony spotlight.

railroad □ To use copy without editing or type without proofreading. □ To use a type form that has not been completely proofed.

railroad showing A bulletin or poster used alongside a railroad track or in a station. Also called a *station poster* and *transportation display poster.*

rain □ A television interference pattern consisting of small vertical marks. □ The vertical scratches on film caused by frequent use. *See also* cinch marks.

rain-lap Outdoor advertising posters trimmed so that the upper sheets overlap the lower sheets, similar to the way in which shingles are laid on a roof. This lessens the possibility of flags, due to rain seepage between the poster and the panel face.

raised eyebrow One of the methods used by administrative agencies to regulate an industry. Usually consists of questions, letters, or statements made in speeches by Commissioners about specific practices by licensees or others.

raised printing *See* thermography.

rake □ The angle of a flat or set in relation to a camera. □ The slope of a set floor. □ To change the angle or slope of a flat.

raking angle The amount of rake in a camera shot or set.

RALPH Royal Association for the Longevity and Preservation of the Honeymooners. An organization of fans of the Jackie Gleason television series.

RAM □ Radio audience measurement. □ Random access memory.

ramp A platform with a rake, used for moving a camera mount in relation to the action.

ranch A location for shooting western films.

R and B Rhythm and blues.

R and F Reach and frequency. *See* cumulative audience.

random A frame with a sloping top used to hold type galleys.

random access □ A method of obtaining or storing data to or from computer storage on a nonsequential basis. Cf. sequential access. □ The retrieval of picture or sound information stored on a tape without respect to its location.

random access memory (RAM) □ A memory chip used with microprocessors. Information can be read from and written into the memory, but the contents are lost when the power supply is removed. Also called *main memory.* Cf. nonvolatile RAM and ROM. □ Any form of storage in which the access time for any item of data is independent of the location of the data most recently obtained.

random area update In video, an area of any shape, updated as a succession of horizontal whole or partial line updates.

random digit dialing (RDD) A procedure for sampling all telephone households in an area through the use of a random digit sample. Under this method unlisted numbers are also included in the sample. *See also* random digit sample.

random digit sample (RDS) A random sample of possible telephone numbers made without the use of a telephone book in order to obtain a representative sample containing unlisted as well as listed numbers.

random error A spontaneous bit error in computing; usually not reproducible and independent of the data.

random noise Any noise generated in a circuit that has no specific period or is irregular and unpredictable.

random number A number produced from a set of numbers free from statistical bias.

random numbers A set of the digits 0, 1, 2, . . . 9 in scrambled order that has passed certain statistical tests to provide a means for selecting a probability sample mechanically.

random sample *See* probability sample.

range □ The maximum distance at which a radio or television signal can be received. □ An index of variability, often stated as the number or distance between maximum and minimum or lowest and highest. □ The maximum effective pickup distance of a microphone or camera. □ The difference between the lowest and highest notes an instrument or singer can reach.

rangefinder An instrument used to measure the distance between a camera and the subject or object.

rank □ To arrange in order of importance, desirability, use, or value. □ A program, book, motion picture, and so on, of questionable quality.

RARC Regional Administrative Radio Conference. An ITU regional conference.

rarefaction The portion of a soundwave in which the vibrating molecules are farthest apart. Cf. compression.

RASO Radio Allocations Study Organization. An organization that was similar in function to TASO.

raster The illuminated area of a television picture tube produced by the scanning lines.

raster graphics Graphics based on a raster display, in which the electron beam of the CRT scans each line in turn, illuminating only those points (pixels) where information is found. Cf. vector graphics.

raster scan The standard television display technique wherein an image is created by lines of elements of varying intensities.

rate □ The charge for time made by broadcast stations and networks. □ The charge for space made by newspapers and magazines. □ To estimate media audience size based on a research sample. □ The price charged to a customer for a telecommunication service. Usually based on a tariff.

rate base □ A minimum guaranteed circulation used as a basis for determining advertising space rates. □ A minimum audience size guaranteed by a medium in return for a stated advertising rate.

rate book A publication listing rates and other data concerning the advertising media, such as Standard Rate and Data Service.

rate card A list issued at various times by a periodical, broadcast station, and so on, detailing the medium's charges for time, space, rate inclusions, commission allowed, rate protection, spot length, and similar considerations.

rate class The amount charged for broadcast time during a specific period of the broadcast day. *See also* class rate.

rate cutting The practice of selling time or space for less than the price set on the rate card or the offering of bonus space or time.

rated An outdoor advertising structure that has been evaluated for visibility, competition, direction of traffic (incoming or outgoing), type of area, and circulation.

Rated Exposure Unit (REU) A BBDO measure of an advertising medium's value.

rate differential The difference in rates charged by local media for local and national advertisers.

rated life The average lamp life as determined on a group of lamps under controlled laboratory conditions of constant applied voltage and other controls. Cf. service life.

rated speed The speed at which a computer printer or typesetting device can produce its output; generally stated in characters per second or lines per minute.

rate holder A broadcast spot or printed advertisement that is run to maintain a long-term advertising contract with a radio or television station or publication.

rate inclusions The facilities and personnel available without extra charge to advertisers at rate card prices.

rate of decay The rate at which the sound pressure level decreases.

rate of response The ratio of the number of elementary units in a survey that report information that is usable for tabulations to the number of elementary units, predesignated for the survey, that properly belong to the statistical population of study. Also called *cooperation rate, rate of return,* and *success rate. See also* bias of nonresponse, call-back, and nonresponse.

rate of return *See* rate of response.

rate protection A contractual agreement between an advertiser and a radio or television station that rates will not be raised during the contract period.

rate sheet A price list furnished by a laboratory, equipment rental company, print shops, and so on.

rating □ *See* Classification and Rating Administration (CARA). □ The size of an audience expressed in relative or percentage terms. The estimated percent of total television households, or persons within those households, tuned to a particular station or program service for a given period of time, daypart, or program for the ADI, Metro, or Home County. *See also* quarter-hour audience. □ *See also* audience, average audience rating, households-using-radio rating, households-using-television rating, individuals-using-radio rating, individuals-using-television rating, instantaneous-audience rating, national rating, network rating, program rating, sets-in-use (SIU), share, station rating, and total audience rating.

rating distortion An activity by a broadcast station that may affect the way survey respondents or diary keepers record or report their listening or viewing without changing their actual listening or viewing.

rating point One point of the theoretically possible 100 points on a rating scale.

rating scale □ The scale from 0 to 100 that indicates a station or network rating. □ A scale on which survey respondents may indicate their intensity of feeling, information, preferences, and so on. Usually a bipolar scale.

rating service A research organization that accomplishes quantitative and/or qualitative audience measurements. *See also* AGB, Arbitron, Hooper, Nielsen (ACN), Pulse, Trendex, and Videodex.

ratio □ The numerical relationship obtained by dividing one number by another. □ *See* aspect ratio.

ratio decidendi The rationale for a judicial decision.

rats nest A tangle of undressed wires and cables.

rave A slang term for a review or critique that is extremely positive.

raw data Data not yet edited or processed.

raw stock Unexposed and unprocessed film. Also called *stock.*

raw tape □ Unused audio-or videotape. Also called *blank tape, uncut tape,* and *virgin tape.* □ *See* idiot tape.

raw wrap *See* dutch break.

ray A narrow beam of radiant energy.

ray tracing A method for tracing the path of light rays from their source to the viewer's eye as they reflect from and/or pass through the objects that make up a scene.

RC □ Remote control. □ Remote control authority. An FCC file-number prefix.

RCA □ Radio Club of America, Inc. □ Radio Corporation of America. The former parent company of the National Broadcasting Company. Formed in 1919. □ Research Corporation of America.

RCEEA Radio Communications and Electronic Engineers Association.

R channel One of the eight compact disc subcode channels (P–W). At present allocated to CD graphics.

RCMA Research Council of Makeup Artists.

RC paper Resin-coated paper.

R-DAT Rotating digital audiotape.

RDD Random digit dialing.

RDG Radio Directors Guild. A former union.

RDS Random digit sample.

RE □ Revised edition. □ Remote pickup. An FCC file-number prefix. *See also* remote pickup broadcast station.

reach □ The number of households, or individuals, that are estimated to be in the audience of a given television or radio program, group of programs, or announcement, at least once over some specified period of time. May also be expressed as *cume* or *net circulation*. Also called *net reach*. Cf. circulation and frequency. □ The percentage of the population or households covered by an advertising campaign in outdoor advertising.

reach and frequency (R and F) Two criteria used to determine the cumulative audience for a program, motion picture, billboard, and so on. *See also* frequency and reach.

reactance (X) The opposition of a capacitor or inductance to the flow of alternating current. The unit of reactance is the ohm.

reaction pan A reaction shot obtained by panning rather than cutting.

reaction shot A cut to a shot showing the effect of action or dialogue on a character.

reaction time The length of time between a television director's command and the response from the individual switching shots. The term also applies to such timings as how long a performer takes to react to another performer's cue or line.

read □ To obtain data from a peripheral storage device. □ *See* reader.

readability □ The intelligibility of received signals. □ A measure of the relative ease or difficulty of comprehending written material. Cf. legibility.

reader □ An individual who reads manuscripts, screenplays, and so on, as an occupation. □ A proofreader. □ An uncomplimentary term for a performer or anchor who sounds as though he or she is reading lines instead of acting or speaking. □ A computer device for converting information from one form to another for storage. □ A person who reads manuscripts submitted to a publisher to see whether the submission might interest the publisher. □ *See* sound reader. □ *See* copyreader. □ An abbreviation for *proofreader*. □ *See* optical code reader. □ A radio or television news story that is read on camera without the use of additional visuals or soundbites. Also called a *read*. □ Any device capable of sensing data stored on magnetic media.

reader ad An advertisement in a printed publication that appears to be news or editorial matter. Nearly always marked as advertising. Also called a *reading notice*.

reader confidence The loyalty of a regular readership to a periodical.

reader exposure *See* exposure (X).

reader impression study A study conducted by the research firm of Daniel Starch and Associates to determine the significance of a periodical advertisement to ad-noters.

reader interest A newspaper or magazine feature that evokes a response from the reader.

reader profile A demographic description of the readers of various print media.

reader response Actions taken by readers of a publication, especially letters or orders prompted by a print advertisement.

read error An error in accessing data from a storage medium.

reader service card A return postal card bound into a magazine containing numbers corresponding to various suppliers from whom information may be requested by circling the proper numbers and returning the card.

readership The total number of people actually reached by a publication; the primary and pass-along audiences together. Cf. circulation.

readership survey A survey of a publication's readers as to their attitudes toward the publication and its content.

readers per copy A ratio of a publication's readership to its circulation; usually stated as an average number of readers per copy.

reader traffic The pattern of attention shift from one part of a periodical to another on the part of its readers.

read for story A quick reading of a script.

read head An electromagnetic head used to access information from magnetic media.

read in A cutline or head that leads (reads in) to the head or text that follows. Cf. read out.

reading A tryout or audition for a part in a production.

reading circle A group of book lovers who meet to exchange and discuss books. Also called a *reading group.*

reading days of issue exposure The total readership of a periodical multiplied by the average number of days the average individual reader is exposed to its contents.

reading diagonal The path a reader's eye follows on a page; from upper left to lower right.

reading group *See* reading circle.

reading matter In a newspaper, editorial and news matter, as opposed to advertising matter.

reading notice *See* reader ad.

reading room ☐ A library room or space provided with newspapers and magazines. ☐ A room or space set aside for proofreading.

reading time The average time spent by the average reader of a periodical on any given issue.

readmost A category used by the research firm of Daniel Starch and Associates to designate persons who read more than half of an advertisement in a periodical.

read only memory (ROM) A storage device whose contents can only be changed by a particular user, by particular operating conditions, or by a particular external process. ROM implies a storage device that is designed not to be modified by conventional write procedures and that is used to store permanent information in computers and microcomputers. Cf. erasable, RAM, and write once.

read out ☐ To transfer data from the internal memory of a computer to an output device, such as a printer or disk. ☐ A subordinate head that leads (reads out) to the text that follows.

readout ☐ The printing or visual display of computer information. ☐ A television camera picture displayed on a viewfinder or monitor. ☐ A visual indication of the state of a device or component.

read through The first reading of a script by a cast. *See also* rehearsal. Cf. dry run, run through, and walk through.

read/write head The electromagnetic head used to read from or write to a magnetic storage medium.

read/write medium A medium that can be both written (recorded) and read (played back). Magnetic media can generally be written, read, erased, and rewritten repeatedly. Optical carriers are at present read only, or write once, read many times (WORM). Erasable optical discs are the subject of extensive research.

ready A television director's preparatory command to a switcher, camera operator, board operator, or other crew member to prepare to take, dissolve, fade, and so on. Usually followed by a word or phrase indicating the specific instruction to be followed, such as, "Ready camera 1," "Ready to dissolve to 1," or "Ready on the set." Cf. stand by.

read-y The quality of acting by someone who is a reader. Pronounced *reedy.*

readyprint *See* patent insides.

real focus The point at which converging rays of light meet. Cf. virtual focus.

real image ☐ An image that is intended to be recorded on film. Cf. latent image and virtual image. ☐ One of the two images formed in a hologram; the other is the virtual image.

realism A fidelity to real life, in literature, motion pictures, television, and so on, in the way the work is presented. Cf. naturalism.

real motion video DVI technology that produces real-time motion by compressing megabytes of information into 150K of data. Compression is accomplished by digitizing the video and running it through a compression algorithm on a computer.

real time ☐ The actual length of a radio or television broadcast, as opposed to dramatic time. ☐ The actual time in which an event or process takes place. ☐ The processing or recording of events that are occurring simultaneously. Also called *clock time.* ☐ Any film or video production that is recorded at the speed at which it will be reproduced. ☐ In CD-I, the smallest amount of real-time data that can be randomly accessed. Contains audio, video, and/or computer data that must be retrieved from a disc at a precise rate.

real-time animation The use of computer techniques to photograph computer graphics in real-time, as opposed to stop motion photography.

real-time capture and compression *See* edit-level video (EVL).

real-time control area A disc sector preceding some real-time records that contains all control data and specific instructions for playback.

real-time data In CD-I, data taken directly from a disc, whose flow cannot be interrupted or stopped within the bounds of a real-time record.

real-time edit A videotape edit that takes place in actual clock time on several videotape recorders.

real-time file A file containing at least one real-time record.

real-time interactive system An interactive system that responds to events directly as they occur, that is, in real time. CD-I is a real-time interactive system.

real-time operating system (RTOS) An operating system that functions within the constraints of real time, such as CD-RTOS, the OS-9 based operating system of CD-I. Such an operating system is essential for full interactivity.

real-time record interpreter A trap-handler module that an application can use to assist in the playback of real-time records.

real-time sector In CD-I, a sector with the real-time bit set. The data in this sector must be processed without interrupting the real-time behavior of the CD-I system.

ream Formerly, 480 sheets of paper, or 20 quires; now, 500 sheets of paper.

Reardon Report The recommendations adopted in 1968 by the American Bar Association concerning guidelines for reporting information about judicial proceedings.

rear projection (RP) The projection of slides or film on a translucent screen to provide a background for a studio set. Also called *back projection* and *rear screen projection.* Cf. front projection.

rear screen A translucent screen used for rear projection.

rear screen projection *See* rear projection.

reasonable access Section 312(a)(7) of the Communications Act states that broadcast licenses may be revoked for willful or repeated failure to allow reasonable access for candidates for federal elective office. What is ''reasonable'' is left to the good-faith judgment of the licensee.

reasonably comparable facilities Station transmitting facilities powerful enough such that the station's Grade B coverage area is at least two-thirds as large as the smallest of the market affiliated station's Grade B coverage areas. Applies to the carriage of network programs by stations other than the affiliate in a market.

reback To replace a book backing.

rebate A refund given to an advertiser who uses more than the contracted number of spots, thus earning a lower rate.

rebroadcast The reception by a broadcast station of a program or part thereof, and the simultaneous or subsequent retransmission of such a program by a broadcast station.

rebuild A complete reconstruction of a cable television system. Cf. retrofit.

rebuild rule An FCC rule requiring that cable television systems having more than 3500 subscribers conform to the minimum specifications for number of channels, equipment, and so on.

REC □ Recorded program. □ Radio Executives Club.

rec An abbreviation for *record, recorder,* and *recording.*

recall □ A bona fide offer to a day player of work for the next day as an actor. □ To use a previous edit from an edit decision list again, usually with some modification.

recall interview A type of interview in which an interviewer asks a respondent to remember behavior for some period of time in the past. Recall interviews may be either aided or unaided. Cf. coincidental interview.

recap □ A recapitulation, especially of news. □ A news summary at the end of a newscast. □ A brief newscast. □ To summarize the news.

recapture *See* preemption.

recase To rebind a book.

recast To replace one or more cast members of a motion picture, television program, or other cast.

receive only A device designed to receive information but not to transmit.

receiver □ An electronic device capable of converting electromagnetic waves into visual and/or sound information. A radio or television receiver. Often erroneously called a *radio set, set,* or *television set.* □ A television display device that receives its picture and/or sound from an RF or broadcast television signal. Cf. monitor. □ In information theory, the decoder of a message.

recency The latest purchase or other activity recorded for an individual or company on a specific customer mailing list. *See also* frequency and monetary value.

recency-frequency-monetary-value ratio (RFMVR) A formula used to evaluate the sales potential of names on a mailing list.

recent reading technique A technique employed by Target Group Index for analyzing magazine readerships by asking respondents whether they have read any issue of a certain magazine in the last week or month.

receptacle An electrical outlet.

reception The listening to or viewing of a broadcast.

reciprocal dealings The advertising and promoting of a radio or television licensee's nonbroadcast interests.

reciprocity failure The inability to rely on the reciprocity law when the exposure times are extremely short or long.

reciprocity law The inverse relationship between the length of exposure and the intensity of the light source. Theoretically, doubling one should halve the other.

reckless disregard A high degree of awareness of the probable falsity contained in a publication. Used to determine whether actual malice is present in a defamation case.

recognition □ The ability of individuals in a research study to recall a commercial message. □ The agreement by a communication medium to regard an advertising agency as bona fide, competent, and ethical, and thus entitled to discounts. Also called *agency recognition. See also* recognized agency.

recognition method An aided-recall method for determining whether a respondent in a survey has been exposed to an advertisement.

recognition news News stories that laud the accomplishments of individuals or groups.

recognized agency An advertising agency that is allowed agency commissions from the media because it meets certain industry standards. *See also* recognition.

recognized private operating agency A nongovernmental national communications organization that provides international telecommunications facilities.

recommendation The approval of an advertising agency by a communication medium for recognition by its members.

recommended agency An advertising agency that is a member of a standards-setting media association.

reconditioning □ The laboratory treatment of motion picture film to remove oil, scratches, and so on, from the film. □ The rebuilding of cassettes and cartridges using new tape, new pressure pads, and so on.

reconfiguration A change made in the relative arrangements of parts of a system or device.

reconstruction A documentary account produced at the scene of an event.

record □ The magnetic pattern on the tape corresponding to a signal. A record is recorded on a track. □ A disc or electrical transcription. □ The process of recording. □ The transcript of testimony and exhibits, together with all papers and requests filed in a proceeding. □ According to the Freedom of Information Act, items that can be copied or reproduced, such as paper documents, photographs, or tape recordings. □ A collection of data. □ A set of related data fields in a database. □ The logical component(s) of a CD-I file.

record amplifier Electronic circuitry that processes the input video or audio signal prior to actual recording.

record changer A device used for playing discs in succession automatically. Also called a *changer.* Cf. record player.

record compensator *See* equalizer.

recorded flux *See* magnetic flux.

recorded level The level measured by a standard reproducing system with respect to the NAB standard reference level, expressed in decibels.

recorded program (REC) Programs primarily featuring discs, transcriptions, or tapes. An FCC program source category.

recorded tape Any magnetic tape on which sound and/or picture is recorded. Often referred to as a *prerecorded tape.*

record equalizer *See* equalizer.

record equalization *See* preemphasis.

recorder Any electronic device used to make a permanent record of audio or video information, such as a tape recorder, videotape recorder, or wire recorder.

record film A picture taken for the sole purpose of making an archival copy or proving a fact.

record head *See* recording head.

Recordimeter (RM) A trademark for a Nielsen clock measuring the amount of television receiver usage in the National Television Index (NTI) sample of households used in conjunction with viewing diaries called *Audilogs. See also* National Audience Composition (NAC).

Record Industry Association of America (RIAA) A standards organization of the recording industry.

recording □ The process by which audio or video information is stored for later playback. □ A disc or tape. Also called a *mechanical reproduction* by the FCC. □ The process of producing a record on a tape. □ Pertaining to the process of producing a record on a tape.

recording artist An individual or group that has signed a contract to record songs or other material for a recording company.

recording chain The entire system of equipment used for recording audio and/or video. Cf. reproducing chain.

recording channel One of a number of independent recorders in a recording system or independent recording tracks on a recording medium.

recording characteristic The electrical parameters relating the video or audio input signals to the corresponding records on tape, especially with regard to the amplitude-frequency response of the recording current.

recording company An organization that records, produces, and distributes phonograph records and tapes.

recording contract A legal agreement signed between a record company and a recording artist.

recording current The flow of electrons corresponding to the changes in amplitude of the input signals, which are routed to the audio, video, and control heads.

recording disc A blank disc used for recording. Also called a *blank disc.*

recording engineer The engineer in charge of microphone placement, balance, and proper recording techniques.

recording error An error in a research study caused by the failure of an interviewer or respondent to record necessary information or to enter information in a questionnaire improperly. Also called a *response error.*

recording head The electromagnetic transducer used in an audio- or videotape recorder to impress the sound or video information on magnetic tape. *See also* head.

recording lamp A light source used to record sound on film.

recording level The level at which a signal is recorded.

recording level indicator *See* VU meter.

recording loss The loss in recorded level whereby the amplitude of the wave in the recorded medium differs from the amplitude of the recording current in a tape recording or the amplitude executed by the stylus in disc recording.

recording medium Any medium capable of storing information for later playback, such as a tape, disc, or film.

recording room *See* recording studio.

recording session The time spent making a recording.

recording stage A motion picture studio soundstage that is used for recording music or sound effects.

recording studio A soundproof studio used for the production of audiotapes. Also called a *recording room.*

recording stylus The tool that inscribes the grooves into the disc medium. Tips may be designed for either cutting or embossing the groove. Cf. reproducing stylus.

recording supervisor The individual in charge of servicing clients or other employees in a recording company, post production facility, and so on.

recording surface The magnetic particles coating the base material on magnetic media.

recording sync *See* editorial sync.

recording system The equipment necessary for recording audio or video; cameras, microphones, tape recorder, cables, and so on.

recording tone The note—often 440 Hz —recorded on tapes and used to set levels for playback.

recordist ☐ A motion picture sound technician who supervises or operates the sound equipment. ☐ An amateur recording engineer.

record key A key on a videotape recorder that causes material to be recorded. Cf. preview key.

record level *See* recording level.

record-mostly machine A television tape recorder used for recording, as opposed to playback, the majority of the time. Cf. record-only machine.

record-only machine A television tape recorder used for recording, as opposed to playback, all of the time. Cf. record-mostly machine.

record-playback head *See* record-reproduce head.

record player A nonautomatic device for playing discs one at a time. Cf. record changer.

record-reproduce head A dual-purpose head used in some inexpensive tape recorders. Also called a *record-playback head.*

record rotation The length of time that elapses between the playing of the same record on a radio station.

records The books, documents, papers, and so on, used for audits, research, or other purposes.

records column The newspaper columns that report vital statistics: births, deaths, marriages, divorces, and so on.

recovery time The interval between a sudden decrease in sound pressure level and the return to a normal state in an audio system. Also called *response time.*

rectifier A device used to change alternating current into direct current. Cf. inverter.

recto ☐ The right-hand page of a book. Cf. verso. ☐ The front of a sheet. Cf. verso. ☐ Sometimes, the front of a book.

recycle ☐ To reuse print, program, or other material two or more times. ☐ To listen to or view broadcast or cable programs two or more times.

red book ☐ An informal name for the CD-DA specification. ☐ An informal name for the Standard Directory of Advertising Agencies and for the Standard Directory of Advertisers.

red button ☐ The emergency button or switch used to stop a printing press or other device. ☐ A button or switch on a tape recorder that must be pressed or thrown in order to record.

Red Channels A 1950 publication that named blacklisted directors, performers, writers, and so on.

red dog *See* filler.

redeeming social value One of the tests used to determine whether a work is obscene.

red flag words Words that could lead to defamation lawsuits, such as *communist, quack,* or *ambulance chaser. See also* libel per se.

red gun In a television camera, the electron gun whose beam strikes the phosphor dots emitting the red primary color.

rediffusion A system used to relay radio or television programs to subscribers or individuals from a common source or receiver by means of lines or cables. *See also* wire broadcasting. Cf. CATV.

red light The warning device placed outside a soundstage, television studio, radio control room, and so on, to indicate that something is being recorded or the station is on the air.

Red Lion decision The landmark 1969 Supreme Court decision that upheld the constitutionality of the Fairness Doctrine.

Red Network The NBC radio network formed from the Telephone Group in 1927. Cf. Blue Network.

reduce To decrease the size of a picture, artwork, and so on, during reproduction.

reduced aperture (RA) *See* academy aperture.

reduced power The operation of a broadcast station using less than the authorized power because of technical difficulties.

reducer *See* reducing agent.

reducing agent The active ingredient in a film-developing solution. Also called *developing agent.*

reducing glass A double concave lens mounted in a frame and used to reduce the apparent size of artwork, and so on, to judge its effect at reduced scale.

reduction □ Any film print that is smaller than its negative. □ The process of changing the intensity or contrast of a negative in developing film.

reduction negative A film negative made from a larger negative.

reduction print A film print made from a larger negative.

reduction printer A machine used to accomplish reduction printing.

reduction printing The process of optically producing a smaller film negative or print from a larger one.

reduction ratio The ratio between the size of the original material and the size of the reduced image.

redundancy □ The use of two identical components to improve the reliability of a system. □ The portion of a message that can be eliminated or is eliminated by noise or distortion without the loss of essential information. □ The use of more than one of the same device to provide a backup in case of equipment failure. □ The transmission of unnecessary or repetitious information. □ The carriage by a cable television system of two television stations affiliated with the same network.

reel □ A metal or plastic spool on which tape or film is wound. *See also* feed reel and take-up reel. □ A quantity of videotape mounted on a hub and usually supported by two flanges. □ The hub and associated flanges. □ The period of time it takes to project one reel of film; approximately 10 minutes. □ Any length of edited motion picture film. Cf. roll.

reel motion controller A rotary potentiometer on a videotape-editing controller that governs the speed and direction of a videotape recorder or player.

reel number A number assigned to a film reel, audio- or videotape reel, and so on, for identification purposes.

reel servo A closed-loop servo system that regulates the torques applied to the supply and take-up reels to stabilize tape tension.

reel-servo modulator *See* modulator.

reel-to-reel machine An audio- or videotape recorder that uses open supply and take-up reels rather than a cassette. Cf. cartridge and cassette.

reentry The ability of a video switcher to produce a second special effect as part of one already displayed.

reestablishing shot A return to the camera shot that established the scene originally. *See also* establishing shot.

reetch To etch a halftone plate further in certain areas to sharpen contrasts or highlights, in order to achieve a closer match to the copy.

refer A line of type that indicates related material is printed elsewhere in the newspaper or magazine.

referee An expert in a field who reviews manuscripts for content.

reference beam The second beam of coherent light used in holography.

reference black level The level corresponding to the specified maximum excursion of the luminance signal in the black direction.

reference book A book written to be consulted for information about a particular subject.

reference dimension A standard usually without tolerance, used for informational purposes. It may result from other values. Cf. basic dimension and derived dimension.

reference edge In video recording, the designated edge of a recorded tape that is used as a measurement reference for the dimensions stipulated by the tape format specification.

reference level An arbitrary point selected for use in comparing loudness, power, voltage, and so on.

reference list A book bibliography.

reference mark Formerly, any symbol used to indicate an accompanying note; now refers also to superior numbers indicating footnotes.

reference matter *See* back matter.

reference media The publications that contain statistical and other useful information issued periodically for commercial use.

reference month That month of a season that is used for determining predicted propagation characteristics for the season; either January, April, July, or October.

reference print A motion picture release print that is retained as a comparison for subsequent prints. Also called a *quality print.*

reference recording A disc or tape recording made for test purposes. *See also* frequency record and frequency tape.

reference signal An electronic waveform used to balance different components of a system, such as the green gun television signal, or the luminance signal.

reference strip A piece of film used as a comparison to the density of a processed film.

reference tone A tone, often 440 Hertz, placed on an audio track at 0 dB, as an indication of the program or soundtrack level.

reference white level The amplitude of the video signal that represents maximum luminance.

reflectance A measure of how effectively a surface will reflect light, such as the ratio of the reflected lumens to the incident lumens on the surface. Also called *reflection factor* and *reflectivity.*

reflectance mapping An algorithm for causing the surface of an object to display a realistically distorted reflection of a background scene.

reflectar lens A 16-inch lens with a 40-inch effective focal length.

reflected light Light that is reflected on contact with an object. Cf. incident light.

reflected light meter A light meter that measures the amount of light reflected by an object or subject.

reflected reading A light meter reading taken toward the subject. Cf. incident reading.

reflected signal *See* reflected wave.

reflected wave A wave that is redirected on contact with a different medium. Also called a *reflected signal.* Cf. diffracted wave, direct wave, ground wave, refracted wave, and sky wave.

reflecting satellite A communication satellite that does not contain a transponder and is designed only to bounce signals back to the earth. Also called a *relay satellite. See also* passive satellite. Cf. active satellite.

reflection The characteristic of light and radio waves that redirects the wave in another direction. *See also* angle of incidence, angle of reflection, and echo.

reflection button A small glass or plastic reflector, used in combination with others to create letters or designs in nonilluminated outdoor advertisements.

reflection factor *See* reflectance.

reflective optics The system of lenses and mirrors used in projection television.

reflectivity *See* reflectance.

reflector □ An antenna element used to reflect or block energy. Cf. director. □ The part of a luminaire that reflects light. □ A large piece of metal or other reflective material used to direct sunlight for location shooting. □ A round button, visible at night by reflected light, used to form letters on outdoor advertising signs.

reflector lamp A lamp with a built-in reflector.

reflector satellite *See* passive satellite.

reflector spotlight A spotlight that contains a parabolic mirror but no lens.

reflex A camera that allows through-the-lens viewing.

reflex baffle *See* bass reflex.

reflex camera A film camera with a mirrored shutter that allows the operator to observe the scene on a ground glass viewing screen. *See also* single lens reflex (SLR) and twin lens reflex.

reflex finder A viewfinder that eliminates parallax by allowing the operator to view the scene through the taking lens of the camera. Also called a *reflex viewfinder.*

reflex mirror *See* reflex shutter.

reflex screen A highly reflective, glass-beaded material used as a front projection surface. Also called a *reflex surface.*

reflex shutter A combination mirror and shutter that is fixed at a 45 degree angle to the lens of a reflex camera.

reflex surface *See* reflex screen.

reflex viewfinder *See* reflex finder.

refocus To sharpen focus on a soft picture.

refracted wave A transmitted wave that moves from one medium into another. Also called a *transmitted wave.* Cf. diffracted wave and reflected wave.

refraction The change in direction of a wave caused by its passing obliquely through media of differing densities.

refresh The process of reinforcing visual material on a cathode ray tube by rescanning the screen 30 times a second.

refresh rate The frequency with which new visual information is replaced on a video display.

reg An abbreviation for *register.*

regenerative A major development in radio circuitry patented by Edwin H. Armstrong in 1913, and Lee DeForest in 1914. Four claimants to the patent filed suit, which was finally settled by the Supreme Court in 1934 in favor of DeForest.

regenerator A horizontal drive compensator in a television camera that advances the sync pulse delayed by cable length.

region ☐ A geographical area of a country, usually including several states, designated for analytic or administrative purposes. Cf. unit and zone. ☐ An area in Great Britain served by an IBA station or a regional studio of the BBC.

regional channel An AM channel occupied by a number of stations with a power not to exceed 5 kilowatts. Regional stations are designated as class III stations.

regional edition An edition of a national periodical distributed within one geographical area; its advertising space may be purchased separately.

regional feed ☐ A feed from a network to one region of the country. ☐ A feed of a special announcement to a group of network affiliated stations in a region. Also called a *sectional feed.*

regionalism Speech that is characteristic of a particular geographic region. *See also* general American.

regional network An educational (such as the Eastern Educational Network) or commercial (such as the Texas State Network) chain of radio or television stations covering a relatively large geographical area.

regional publication A magazine or book designed to appeal to regional tastes and lifestyles.

regional radio network A network maintained by a company for regional coverage as distinguished from national or transcontinental coverage.

regional rate The rate offered by some radio or television stations to regional advertisers at less than the national rate but more than the local rate.

regional split A period of time on the news wires devoted to the transmission of regional news.

regional wire The major press associations' news wire serving a region or state.

region generation In video, an overlay technique defining the overlay area separate from the image contents.

register ☐ The exact alignment of color plates in the color separation process, or of any other printing images. ☐ An area of computer memory designed for a specific function. ☐ The exact adjustment of printing pages so that printing on facing pages will correspond properly. ☐ The inner part of a type mold. ☐ A list of book signatures. ☐ A bookmark. ☐ A table of contents. ☐ In acting, to show emotion. ☐ The range of the human voice or other instrument. ☐ To hold a drawing or graphic card in place. ☐ To stabilize a film in a camera or projector gate. ☐ *See* registration.

register mark An indicator, usually in the shape of a plus, printed in the margins of pages to assist in proper registration.

Register of Copyrights The director of the Copyright Office of the Library of Congress.

register pin *See* pilot pin.

register pins *See* registration pin.

registration ☐ The accurate alignment of two or more images on separate animation cels. ☐ The accurate relationship between the placement of a camera and the animation cel being photographed. ☐ The accurate alignment of the three electron guns in a television camera or receiver. Also called *register.* ☐ The act of submitting materials, works, and so on, for the purpose of obtaining a patent, copyright, or trademark.

registration hole One of the punched holes in an animation cel.

registration peg One of the projecting metal pins that fit in the punched holes of an animation cel.

registration pegbar A strip of metal containing pegs and pins used to hold animation cels.

registration pin One of the pins in a camera mechanism that engage the film perforations. Sometimes called *pilot pins* and *register pins.*

reglet A thin wooden or metal strip used for spacing type matter. Cf. lead.

regular □ An individual who consistently attends a motion picture theatre, watches a particular television program, reads a specified magazine, and so on. □ A member of the continuing cast of a radio or television program. □ A guest on a continuing radio or television program or series who is seen often. □ A term used by some to designate outdoor advertising structures that do not have illumination. The Transit Advertising Bureau recommends two designations to increase standardization of the terms: illuminated advertising structures and unilluminated advertising structures. Terms such as *regular* or *dark* are sometimes used for identifying a structure that is unilluminated. Also called *nonilluminated.*

regular audit An audit of a periodical's circulation conducted at established regular intervals.

regular 8 Eight millimeter film. *See also* Super 8.

regulation □ The rule-making process of administrative agencies. □ A term used synonymously with *rule. See also* rules and regulations.

regulatory agencies *See* administrative agency and independent regulatory agencies.

regulatory underbrush The policies and rules of the FCC that were eliminated as a part of deregulation, such as the use of sirens and sound effects, repetitious broadcasts, and the broadcast of astrology information. Most of the regulatory underbrush is covered under other laws or regulations.

rehash A book, screenplay, script, and so on, written by an author that contains little new material, but uses the plot from a previous work.

rehearing The reopening of a case before the FCC involving an order, decision, report, or action that has been taken. A petition for rehearing must be filed within 30 days from the date of public notice of the order, decision, report, or action.

rehearsal The individual and/or collective preparation accomplished before a production is broadcast or taped. *See also* camera rehearsal, cue rehearsal, dress rehearsal, dry run, line rehearsal, no fax, read through, run through, and walk through.

rehearsal hall A large room, often rented, used to rehearse a performance.

rehearse To practice a role, lines, characterization, and so on.

reinforcement □ The boost given a sound by adding indirect sound before it reaches a microphone. □ A theory that televised violence reinforces an individual's existing patterns of behavior.

reissue □ A reprint of a book or other publication from the original type, tape, plates, and so on. Cf. revised edition. □ The rerecording, reprinting, and so on, and releasing of old tapes, records, magazines, and so on.

rejection slip A card or letter sent by a publisher, editor, literary agent, and so on, notifying the person submitting a book manuscript, article, screenplay, and so on, that the submission will not be published or used.

rekeyboarding The retyping of an edited manuscript by typesetting personnel.

related Two or more advertisements by two or more advertisers that are published in such a way as to support one another's message.

relational editing The placement of camera shots to suggest contrasts and comparisons or an association of ideas. Also called *associative editing.*

relative aperture The relationship between the focal length of a lens and its aperture that determines the effective aperture for other lenses.

relative pitch The relationship of one tone to another without an absolute reference point.

relative speed The effective speed of tape movement in a videotape recorder or player. Determined by the sum of the speeds of the longitudinal tape movement and the rotational speed of the head(s).

relative standard error thresholds The thresholds indicate the approximate relative degree of variations due to sampling error in the audience estimates reported. Thresholds are shown for two levels of relative error: 25 percent and 50 percent. One standard error is used in the calculation of thresholds.

relative unit (ru) One of a number of vertical slices that a typeface em is divided into for calculating the number of characters per line.

relax To ease the tension on a tape by shuttling it by fast forwarding and rewinding.

relay □ An electromechanical device used to open or close a circuit. *See also* muting relay. □ *See* microwave link. □ To amplify and retransmit a signal without changing its characteristics.

relay lens A lens used in an optical printer.

relay point The place to and from which a signal is relayed. Also called a *repeater point.*

relay satellite *See* reflecting satellite.

relay station □ A retransmitting station used as a link between a remote and a broadcast station. *See also* microwave link. □ One of the stations used in a relay system.

relay system A series of highly directional microwave relay stations separated by approximately 30 miles and used to feed television signals to distant points.

relay transmitter *See* repeater.

release □ To free a camera for movement after a completed shot. □ A completed radio or television program made available for use. □ A legal statement received from talent or an individual authorizing a station or advertiser to use his picture or words. □ *See* news release. □ A motion picture that has been made available for distribution and exhibition. □ *See* release form. □ Copy received in advance of its release time. Also called *release copy.* □ *See* release date. □ To release news or promotional material to the mass media. *See also* news release.

release copy *See* release.

release date □ The earliest date on which advertising, publicity, or advance copy sent to media may be used. □ The date that motion pictures, videotapes, books, records, and so on, are placed on sale or available for viewing. Also called *release.*

release form □ An signed instrument that permits media to use a person's likeness, words, and so on. Also called a *model release form.* □ A form submitted with a script absolving the reader from later suit for the supposed theft of an idea. Also called a *release.*

release negative A motion picture composite negative that is used to print release prints.

release print A motion picture composite print that is made for distribution and exhibition. Also called a *show print. See also* composite print.

release studio A radio or television director's final command indicating the end of a rehearsal, taping, or broadcast.

release time The length of time it takes for an audio signal limiter or compressor to return to its normal state after the input signal has been removed.

reliability □ A measure of the performance of a device based on a predetermined standard. □ The extent to which a sample result reproduces the same result that would be obtained by attempting a complete census with the same care and the same survey methodology as was used with the sample. Reliability is often referred to as stability or precision. The degree of reliability of estimates based on probability samples is usually expressed in terms of standard error, or the error around the estimate. The smaller the standard error the more reliable the estimate. Cf. accuracy.

relief □ A raised printing surface. □ A sequence designed to relieve audience tension in dramatic action. □ A three-dimensional prop, set, drawing, and so on. □ For the purposes of the Administrative Procedure Act, the whole or a part of an agency grant of money, assistance, license, authority, exemption, exception, privilege, or remedy; recognition of a claim, right, immunity, privilege, exemption, or exception; or taking of other action on the application or petition of, and beneficial to, a person.

relief printing A general term for printing, such as letterpress, that is accomplished from raised surfaces.

religious programs (R) Programs including sermons or devotionals; religious news; and music, drama, and other types of programs designed primarily for religious purposes. An FCC program type category.

reluctance (R) The resistance to the flow of magnetic lines of force.

rem An abbreviation for *remote*.

remainder A unit of a product, especially a book, that remains unsold at the regular price after the demand for the product at that price level has expired; usually sold at a discount. Cf. overstock.

remainder dealer A book dealer who buys publishers' overstocked books for resale. Also called a *remainder house*.

remainder house *See* remainder dealer.

remake □ A motion picture made years after the original film that uses the same title, but a different cast. □ To rearrange a page, publication, or book.

remand The action of an appellate court in returning a case to the original lower court or administrative agency for appropriate action.

remanence The extent to which a magnetized material retains its flux density after the removal of the magnetizing field. Also called *magnetic remanence*.

remarketing A campaign designed to reach individuals or organizations that did not respond to an initial effort to sell a product or service, such as periodical subscriptions, book clubs, or cable television services.

remarque A small design etched on a plate to indicate the stage of completion. The remarque is removed before the final printing.

Rembrandt lighting Performer lighting that is characterized by soft light and dark shadows.

remelt To make pigs from used type.

remembrance advertising *See* reminder advertising.

reminder advertising □ Advertising in the form of brief allusions to a product or service that is assumed to be familiar to the reader or listener. Also called *remembrance advertising*. □ Advertising intended to remind prospects of the benefits of a product or service, or the immediacy of their need for such benefits.

remix To mix a greater number of tracks into a lesser number. *See also* mixdown.

remnant space Magazine advertising space sold at a discount to ensure that it will be occupied; most common in regional editions.

remote A broadcast that originates from outside a station. Also called a *field pickup, field production, nemo, outside broadcast, pickup,* and *remote pickup*.

remote control □ The operation of any system or component from a distance, such as a television receiver or videotape recorder. □ The device used in such an operation. □ The operation of a station by a qualified operator at a control position from which the transmitter is not visible. The control position is equipped with suitable control and telemetering circuits so that the essential functions that could be performed at the transmitter can also be performed from the control point.

remote controlled camera A camera focused and moved by a servomechanism.

remote controlled dimmer A dimmer that requires an electrical circuit or circuits as part or all of the transmission system between the central lever and the dimmer unit.

remote line The program line between a remote location and the studio or transmitter.

remote metering The checking on the condition of a circuit or device from a distance. Often used to check broadcast transmitter operation from a control room.

remote pickup *See* remote.

remote pickup broadcast base station A base station licensed for communicating with remote pickup broadcast mobile stations.

remote pickup broadcast mobile station A land-mobile station licensed for the transmission of program material and related communications from the scene of events that occur outside a studio, to broadcasting stations and for communicating with other remote pickup broadcast base and mobile stations.

remote pickup broadcast stations A term used to include remote pickup broadcast base stations and remote pickup broadcast mobile stations.

remote station *See* remote terminal.

remote survey An on-the-scene scouting of a television remote to determine if there is a line-of-sight problem.

remote terminal A terminal that is physically distant from a computer. Also called a *remote station.*

remote unit The equipment necessary to produce a live or recorded broadcast signal from a remote. Often contained in a car, van, or truck. *See also* mobile unit.

rendering □ The process of completing a computer animated sequence after the lighting, color, model, and so on, information has been designated. □ An advertising layout.

renewal □ The regranting by the FCC of a license to broadcast for another fixed period. □ The extending of a contract on or before its expiration date. □ A subscription to a periodical that has been renewed prior to or at expiration or within six months thereafter.

renewal right The right of an incumbent to renew sponsorship of a radio or television program before it is offered to others. Cf. right of first refusal.

renewals Extra outdoor advertising posters sent to plant operators to replace those that may be damaged during the display period. The number of posters printed for renewal purposes varies from 10 to 20 percent of the total order.

RENG Radio Electronic News Gathering.

rent a citizen A cable television and broadcast station practice of offering selected local citizens a financial interest in a new station or cable television franchise in return for their influence and/or names on an application.

rental *See* mailing list rental.

rental library *See* circulating library.

rep An abbreviation for *representative.*

repeat □ The use of the same animation drawings to show the same action two or more times. *See also* cycle. □ A periodic broadcast of a specific, single program over a number of years. Also called a *rebroadcast* and *rerun.*

repeat buyer *See* multiple buyer.

repeat cycle *See* cycle.

repeater □ One of a number of television booster stations operating during the 1950s without authorization from the FCC. □ An amplifier used in a telephone company line. □ A relay station transmitter. □ An amplifier used at various points in a microwave, wire transmission channel, or fiber optics system, and so on, to boost the signal.

repeater point *See* relay point.

repeater satellite A satellite that can both receive and retransmit a signal. *See also* active satellite.

repeat function A tape recorder designed to allow the automatic replay of a sequence or selection.

repeating groove A defect that causes a stylus to return to a previously played groove.

repeat key A computer key that repeats a keystroke by being held down.

reperf An abbreviation for *reperforator.*

reperforator A machine that perforates tapes for automatic typesetting. Also called a *reperf.*

repetition □ The reiteration of an advertisement, slogan, or theme to strengthen its impression. □ The average number of times each person is exposed to an outdoor advertising showing during the display period. The more common media term is frequency.

replacement □ A host or performer who substitutes for the regular host or performer. □ A television program that temporarily or permanently substitutes for another. Often a summer replacement.

replacement animation Animation in which parts of objects or puppets are changed between frames.

replacement medium A local communication medium used in place of a national medium, as for advertisement testing or market expansion in the area.

replacement string A computer program string that replaces words or characters on a one by one or global basis. Cf. search string.

replate *See* makeover.

replay To watch a videotape recording.

replayed A television program that is broadcast more than 60 days after an original telecast in any area where the original telecast was shown.

replay head *See* playback head.

replenisher A chemical added to a film developer to extend its useful life.

replicated sample A probability sample selected in parts or subsamples to facilitate administration of a survey, processing of data, and interpretation of results. Each subsample may be thought of as a replication of a basic survey design.

Sometimes referred to as *replicated subsamples.*

replicated subsamples *See* replicated sample.

replication The production of copies from a master, usually for commercial distribution.

reply card A sender-addressed card included in a direct mailing on which the recipient may indicate his or her response to the offer.

Reply-O-Letter One of a number of patented direct mail formats for facilitating replies from prospects. It features a die-cut opening on the face of the letter and a pocket on the reverse. An addressed reply card is inserted in the pocket, and the name and address that appear thereon show through the die-cut opening of the letter.

report □ To work as a reporter. □ An account of a judicial decision printed by a reporter. □ A written or verbal account of a news event made by a reporter.

reportage The production of a documentary program.

Report and Order The public notification and publication of the results of deliberations by the FCC on a specific matter, such as the formulation of rules, policies, investigations, and so on.

reporter □ A published source for legal documents, such as the *United States Reports, Federal Reporter,* or *Federal Supplement.* □ An employee of a newspaper, magazine, broadcast station, news service, and so on, who gathers and writes news. Cf. newscaster.

reporter certification The accreditation afforded to news personnel by various federal, state, and local governments and used to identify them. *See also* press card.

Reporters Committee for Freedom of the Press A watchdog association concerned with the actions of the judicial branches of Federal, state, and local governments.

reporter-source privilege *See* shield laws.

reporting The act of obtaining and writing or broadcasting the results of newsworthy events or developments.

reporting error *See* response error.

reporting forms The forms required by an administrative agency of licensees or others, such as employment reports, ownership reports, and so on.

Report on Syndicated Programs (ROSP) A supplementary report by Nielsen Station Index that contains a comprehensive profile of the audiences, competition, and lead-in programs to over 300 syndicated shows. Published three times a year.

reportorial Noting or pertaining to a style or format for advertisements imitating the factual, objective editorial.

report sheet *See* camera log.

repositioning The changing of broadcast television channel numbers to different numbers on a cable television system. Often a source of aggravation and confusion for users.

reposting charge An additional cost incurred for posting a change of design to an outdoor advertising poster before the expiration of a display period.

representational A form of delivery wherein the announcer or speaker talks to others as if there were no camera present. Cf. presentational.

representative □ A talent agent, literary agent, or other individual who represents a performer, writer, and so on. □ An individual who solicits the purchase of advertising space or time on behalf of a medium. □ *See* station representative.

representative sample A misleading term. *See also* accuracy and reliability.

reprint □ Copy that is used in one edition of a newspaper and available for use in the next edition. □ A new impression of a book or other publication. *See also* offprint, reissue, and revised edition. □ To print a page again. Sometimes called a tear sheet.

reprint publisher A publisher that specialized in reprint editions of books originally produced by another publisher.

reprint rights The rights granted by a copyright holder to a publisher to reprint a book or other manuscript.

reprise To repeat a portion of a song or jingle.

repro □ An abbreviation for *reproduce* and *reproduction.* □ *See* reproduction proof.

reproducer □ Any device capable of copying a disc, tape, and so on. □ *See* transducer.

reproducing chain All of the equipment used to play back a radio or television program previously recorded. Cf. recording chain.

reproducing head An electromagnetic transducer used to convert magnetic patterns into electrical variations in a magnetic tape recorder. *See also* head.

reproducing stylus A mechanical transmission element consisting of a suitable tip to follow the modulation of a recorded groove and a means for transferring the resultant vibration to the transducer element of the pickup. Cf. recording stylus.

reproduction □ The process of playing back a radio or television program tape to recreate the program. □ The process of duplicating sounds or pictures. □ The conversion of electronic signals into sound or picture. □ The process of duplicating on film the original tonal values of a scene. □ A copy of artwork, a page, an etching proof, and so on.

reproduction proof A camera ready, carefully made proof of copy used to make a printing plate. Also called an *etching proof, repro,* and *repro proof.*

reproduction right An authorization by a mailing list owner for a specific mailer to use that list on a one-time basis.

repro proof *See* reproduction proof.

request for proposal (RFP) A notification by a municipality or community that it is accepting applications for a cable television franchise.

re-rating A motion picture previously rated by CARA that is resubmitted for the purpose of having its rating changed.

rerecording □ The process of making a new recording from an existing one. □ The process of reproducing a recorded sound source and recording this reproduction. *See also* dub.

reregulation *See* deregulation.

rerelease A motion picture that is released again for exhibition.

rerouting The selecting of a different channel of communication when the primary transmission path is unavailable or inoperative.

rerun A program, program series, or motion picture that is repeated on a television station or network. Cf. first run, premiere, preview, rebroadcast, and syndication.

res adjudicata From the Latin, a matter that has been settled by a court and may not be the subject of litigation again between the same parties.

resale common carrier A communication company that leases telephone, microwave, and satellite services for further resale to users.

resale number A tax number obtained from a state that allows a wholesaler or manufacturer to buy goods without paying sales tax.

rescale *See* resize.

reschedule To select a new time period to broadcast a radio or television program that was preempted.

rescind To revoke or cancel a law, rule, court order, contract, and so on.

research □ The use of source material to improve a program. □ Any studious examination or inquiry. □ *See* audience measurement.

research and development The conception, design, and first creation of experimental or prototype operational devices. May apply to such devices as a communications satellite system, as distinguished from the term *production,* which relates to the construction of such devices to fixed specifications compatible with repetitive duplication for operational applications.

research department □ An advertising agency department that collects and analyzes data on products, advertisers, and the media. □ A motion picture studio department that investigates the speech, period pieces, and other visual sets or props used in a motion picture. □ A network or station department that is involved in deciphering and preparing reports on ratings and the competition.

research director An advertising agency or advertiser employee responsible for procurement, analysis, and dissemination of information on factors influencing the market for goods. Also called a *consumer research director, director of research,* and *marketing research director.*

researcher A media employee who accomplishes the research necessary to a story; usually concerned with background material.

reserve *See* filler.

reserved seat A theatre ticket that identifies the holder as having the right to a certain seat reserved for that ticket holder.

reserve price The minimum amount that is acceptable to a seller for goods or services. Usually goods and services that are subject to bids, such as television programs or auction items.

reset □ To set a counter or device to zero or a predetermined state. Also called *restore.* □ To set type over again in order to change type style, add new material, and so on.

reset button A push switch found on some devices that acts as a circuit breaker.

residual A talent fee paid for reruns of programs, commercials, announcements, narration, and so on, according to a set or negotiated scale that is usually established by union agreements. Cf. reuse fee.

residual magnetism The magnetism that remains in an electromagnetic material after the current has been removed.

residual rights The rights granted under an agreement for the use of previously performed material.

resin coated (RC) paper A printing paper coated with a resinous substance and used for photographic prints and typeset output.

resist A protective coating applied to a printing plate to keep the acid from the printing area. Also called an *acid resist.*

resistance (R) The property of a material that impedes the flow of current. The unit of resistance is the ohm and is determined by dividing the voltage in a circuit by the current. *See also* Ohm's law.

resistance dimmer A variable resistance placed in series with a lighting load. Also called a *rheostat.*

resistor (R) A device that impedes the flow of electric current. *See also* resistance.

resize To alter the dimensions of an advertisement for use in a periodical space other than that for which it was originally designed. Also called *rescale.*

reslate To place an audio beeper, tone, visual identification, and so on, on the beginning of a tape for another take.

resolution □ The degree of clarity and definition in a picture. Usually stated as the maximum number of lines easily discernible on a picture tube at a specified distance. *See also* horizontal resolution and vertical resolution. □ The ability of a lens to produce detail. Also called *resolving power.* □ *See* display resolution. □ The portion of a play or script after the climax that resolves the conflict.

resolution chart A diagram used to help measure the resolution of a television system or a part of it, such as a television camera chain. The resolution chart has horizontal and vertical resolution wedges that cover the range from 200 to 800 lines. *See also* test pattern.

resolve chord The last musical notes of a program or scene.

resolver A device used to transfer sound from an audiotape to motion picture film. *See also* resolving.

resolving The process of transferring a synchronized soundtrack from a quarter inch audiotape to sprocketed magnetic film. A control signal is used to maintain synchronization during the transfer. *See also* pulse track.

resolving power *See* resolution.

resonance □ The reinforcement of a sound by its harmonics. □ The reinforcement of a voice by the resonating cavities.

resonant frequency □ The frequency at which an object or system naturally resonates. □ The frequency of a crystal.

resonating cavities The portions of the human body that reinforce sound; the mouth, pharynx, chest, and nose.

respondent □ A cable television system operator or a utility against whom a complaint is filed. □ The defendant in a civil action; at the appellate level, the individual who is against the appeal. Cf. defendant. □ A person selected for a sample. May also be used to label only those sampled persons who provide information in response to survey questions.

response □ The sensitivity of a microphone or other device. *See also* polar pattern. □ The relationship of the output of a device or system to the input. □ *See* frequency response. □ A reply to an interviewer's question. □ An action prompted by an advertisement. Cf. return.

response curve The plot of the sensitivity of a microphone, amplifier, or other device at various frequencies.

response device In direct mail, any card or envelope used to respond to an advertisement, such as a business reply card.

response error A survey error that occurs if a respondent or interviewer fails to record information according to the instructions. Also called *recording error* and *reporting error.* *See also* nonsampling error.

response list A compilation of names of individuals who have purchased an item as a result of direct mail advertising.

response rate The proportion of originally designated sample persons who provide usable data to a survey. In practice, the calculation of final response rates generally involves certain adjustments to account for (a) unusable sample and (b) incomplete or otherwise unusable diaries or questionnaires. In radio surveys, response rates are most appropriately determined by dividing the total number of in-tab diaries or interviews obtained by the total usable starting sample. The resulting fraction may then be converted to a percentage. Also called *cooperation rate.*

response time □ The time from the initiation of an action to the completion of the action. □ *See* recovery time. □ The time required for an indicator on an instrument to come to rest after excitation.

restore *See* reset.

restorer As used by the telephone company, a network designed to remove the effects of predistortion or preemphasis, thereby resulting in an overall normal characteristic.

rest period □ The length of time that a motion picture, television program, commercial, and so on, is not shown in order to avoid audience wearout and apathy. □ A 12-hour consecutive period of time from the time a performer is dismissed from his or her first call.

restrainer A substance, such as potassium bromide, used to retard film fogging and the action of a photographic developer.

restraining order A judicial order, similar to a temporary injunction, which restricts an action until a hearing is held on a request for an injunction.

restraint of trade An act or agreement by manufacturers, stations, licensees, broadcasters, and so on, that tends to lessen or prohibit the free flow of goods or services. *See also* monopoly.

restricted *See* R.

restricted music Music that is not available for broadcast.

restricted proceeding An adjudicative matter before the FCC from the time it is designated for hearing until it is removed from hearing status or has been decided by the Commission and is no longer subject to reconsideration by the Commission or to review by any court.

restrictions □ The conditions imposed on writers and performers in regard to offensive material, controversial issues, and so on, by stations, networks, or self-regulatory codes. Also called *taboos.* □ The conditions placed on a station by its license or any rule of the FCC.

restrictive order *See* gag order.

resume An outline of personal information, educational background, work experience, and so on, prepared for use in applying for a job. Usually written, but may include, depending on the job sought, a portfolio of artwork, writing samples, audio- or videotape samples, and so on.

resume tape An audio- or videotape that demonstrates an individual's work. May be used as part of a resume. *See also* aircheck.

retail advertising □ Advertising designed to promote local merchants and their goods and services. □ Advertising placed by local merchants. Also called *local advertising.*

retail rate *See* local rate.

retail trading zone The area beyond the city zone whose residents regularly trade in the city zone.

retained image *See* burn-in.

retainer A fee paid to a consultant, freelance writer, communication attorney, and so on, by a newspaper, broadcast station, and so on, to obtain advice, right of first refusal, information, and so on.

retake □ The photographing or recording of a scene again, often because of some defect in the previously taken picture or sound. □ The subsequent recording.

retentivity The ability of a material to retain magnetization after the removal of the magnetizing force.

reticle A system of lines or cross-hairs in a camera viewfinder. Sometimes spelled *reticule*. Also called *graticule*.

reticulation □ The clumping of granules on a film. □ The wrinkling of a film emulsion due to excessive heat in processing.

reticule *See* reticle.

retina The sensory membrane of the eye or an optical scanning device.

RETMA Radio Electronic Television Manufacturers Association. The former name of the EIA.

retouching The process of removing blemishes or improving the appearance of photographic negatives, prints, artwork, and so on, by hand.

retrace The return of the scanning line to its starting point. Also called *flyback*, *return line*, and *return trace*.

retrace blanking The blanking of a television signal during the retrace interval.

retrace line The blanked out return line from the end of one scanning line to the start of the next scanning line. Also called a *return line*.

retraction A printed or broadcast admission and correction of an error or false statement made in earlier reporting or writing. A retraction is usually given as prominent a space or air time as the error or false statement received. *See also* defamation.

retransmission *See* rebroadcast and repeat.

retransmission consent □ The right granted by a broadcast station to other stations for rebroadcasting. □ The right granted to a resale common carrier to retransmit copyrighted material to cable television systems.

retransmit To transmit a signal that has been received from another transmitter.

retree Paper that is imperfect or slightly damaged during manufacturing.

retrieval □ The extraction of data from a computer file for display on the screen. □ The process of searching for and locating court records.

retrieve □ To recall information from a memory lighting board. □ To recover information stored in a computer or on a tape.

retro A revival or rerelease of an old motion picture, play, song, and so on.

retrofit To update an existing system in order to take advantage of new developments or inventions or to upgrade services, such as a cable television system. Cf. rebuild.

retrofocal lens A lens with a greater than normal distance between the rear element of the lens and its focal plane. Used in television cameras and reflex shutter film cameras. Also called an *inverted telephoto lens*.

retrospect *See* flashback.

return □ A narrow flat normally attached to the end of a set. Also called a *corner post*, *return flat*, and *return post*. □ A key on a keyboard that moves the cursor or carriage to the start of the next line. *See also* carriage return (CR). □ A direct response by a member of the public to an advertiser in consequence of a sales offer, contest, or coupon promotion. Cf. response.

return envelope An addressed reply envelope, either stamped or unstamped, as distinguished from a business reply envelope that carries a postage payment guarantee; included with a mailing.

return flat *See* return.

return line *See* retrace.

return postage guaranteed A legend that should be imprinted on the address face of envelopes or other mailing pieces if the mailer wishes the U.S. Postal Service to return undeliverable third class bulk mail. *See also* mailing list cleaning.

return requested An indication that a mailer will compensate the U.S. Postal Service for return of an undeliverable mailing piece.

returns □ The mail received by a broadcast station or advertiser as the result of a commercial or campaign. □ Election returns. □ Responses to a direct mail program.

returns per thousand circulation A figure used in gauging the effectiveness of an advertising campaign in a given communication medium by the percentage of direct responses to an advertisement.

return trace *See* retrace.

REU Rated Exposure Unit.

Reuben Award An award, a statuette created by Rube Goldberg, given by the National Cartoonists Society for the outstanding cartoonist of the year.

reuse fee The payment made to talent for the use of commercials on the air. *See also* dealer use, program use, and wild spot. Cf. residual.

Reuters A British news agency, one of the five major agencies in the world. The other four are Agence France Presses, AP, TASS, and UPI.

rev An abbreviation for *reversal film, reverse, reverse shot, revised,* and *revision.*

revamp To give a new look or form to old copy without rewriting the material. *See also* rewrite.

reveal A dolly or zoom out that shows other performers or objects.

revelation pan A camera pan that reveals an unexpected person, device, or action.

revenue split The division of money between a motion picture distributor and a theatre owner, a cable television system and a pay cable network, and so on.

reverb An abbreviation for *reverberation.*

reverberation The persistence of sound due to repeated reflections. Reverberation may be caused accoustically or electronically. Often abbreviated *reverb. See also* echo and echo chamber.

reverberation period *See* reverberation time.

reverberation receive A potentiometer that is used to adjust the signal from the reverberation unit. Cf. reverberation send.

reverberation send A potentiometer that is used to adjust the signal sent to the reverberation unit. Cf. reverberation receive.

reverberation time (RT) The time necessary for a sound to decrease to one millionth of its original intensity. Equal to 60 dB. Also called *reverberation period.*

reverberation unit Any device that is capable mechanically or electronically of delaying a sound signal. *See also* tape delay.

reverb unit *See* reverberation unit.

reversal □ Film producing a positive image. *See also* reversal film. □ To change the origination point of a program feed, such as from Los Angeles to New York or vice versa.

reversal film A motion picture film that will produce a positive image after exposure and development.

reversal master print A 16-mm reversal print used to make other prints.

reversal original A positive image produced by reversing the emulsion of the camera original in order to obtain a picture that is transposed from left to right.

reversal print A print made on reversal film and processed to produce a positive image.

reversal process The process of forming a positive image from a reversal film by developing, bleaching, redeveloping, fixing, and washing.

reverse □ Type or plates that are printed the opposite from normal, such as white letters on a dark background. Also called *reverse plate* and *reverse type.* □ *See* flop. □ To set aside a decision by a lower court by an appellate court. □ *See* reverse angle.

reverse action *See* reverse motion.

reverse angle A camera shot taken from the opposite side of the original shot. Also called a *reverse* and *reverse shot.*

reverse compensation A situation in which an affiliated television station pays the network for programs. Cf. network compensation.

reverse kicker *See* barker.

reverse lead *See* back lead.

reverse motion The recording or projection of movement that is the opposite of normal movement; usually done for comic effect. Also called *reverse action.*

reverse plate *See* reverse.

reverse polish notation (RPN) A form of mathematical notation wherein the numbers follow the signs.

reverse programming The rescheduling of a radio or television program to a time different from a competing program.

reverse scene The printing of a film with the right and left sides exchanged.

reverse shot (RS) *See* reverse angle.

reverse type *See* reverse.

reverse video A picture containing dark characters or graphics on a light background.

reversible error A mistake by an inferior court that causes a superior court to invalidate the inferior court's decision.

reversion In copyright, the act of returning exclusive rights in a work to the original owner or his or her heirs or assigns on the effective date of termination of the agreement.

review □ A critical evaluation of a motion picture, radio or television program, or performance. □ To write a critical evaluation. □ A judicial or administrative reexamination of a case. *See also* application for review. □ A summary of events of a news story. □ A summary of a motion picture or television program. □ A periodical containing critical articles. □ A judicial reexamination of the records or decisions of a lower court by an appellate court.

Review Board A permanent body composed of three or more FCC employees designated by the Commission to review initial decisions and other hearing matters.

review copy A copy of a new book sent to reviewers, teachers, and so on, for the purpose of review, adoption, or purchase.

reviewer A person who comments on or sometimes evaluates a program or performance. Cf. critic.

review slip A card enclosed with a review copy that solicits comments about the book.

revise □ A proof taken to determine if corrections on a previous proof were properly made. Also called a *revised proof.* □ To remake a book, copy, layout, proof, and so on.

revised edition A book published with changes made from the previous edition. Also called a *new edition.*

revised proof *See* revise.

revision A revised form or version of a book.

revival A new presentation or publication of a book, play, motion picture, and so on.

revocation The nullification of a broadcast license by the FCC for false statements, willful or repeated failure to operate as set forth in the license, for violation of Title 18 of the United States Code relating to broadcasting, and so on, or by a federal court for violation of monopoly or restraint of trade laws.

revolving stage A stage that is mounted on wheels so that it will turn to reveal a different set, performers, locale, and so on.

revue A production that contains songs, skits, dances, and so on.

rew An abbreviation for *rewind.*

rewind □ To return a tape or film from the take-up reel to the feed reel. □ The motion opposite to fast forward on a tape transport. □ To wind unused newsprint butts onto one roll. □ A hand or motor driven geared device used in editing and projection to move film from one reel to another. Used in pairs. Also called a *rewind arm* and *rewinder.*

rewind arm *See* rewind.

rewind control The knob, button, or lever used to place a tape recorder in the rewind mode.

rewinder *See* rewind.

rewinds The hand-operated editing devices used to hold film take-up and feed reels. *See also* rewind.

rewind tension The amount of tension exerted on the tape during rewind.

rewind time The time required to rewind a reel of tape.

rewrite □ To write a story again to improve it. Cf. revamp. □ To write a story based on material that appeared elsewhere, as in another newspaper. □ To write a story from information supplied by a newspaper reporter. □ The writing of significant changes in plot, story line, or interrelationship of characters in a teleplay or screenplay. Cf. polish. □ A complete revision of an act of Congress, as opposed to amending an act.

rewrite editor *See* rewrite man.

rewrite man A person who writes news stories from material supplied by others, often by telephone. Also called a *rewrite editor.*

RF □ Radio frequence. □ Reported frequency.

RF dub □ To dub by rerecording the RF signal recovered, without demodulation from the tape being copied. □ A copy made by this process. Cf. video dub.

RFE Radio Free Europe.

RFI Radio frequency interference. *See* RF interference.

RF interference □ Any electrical interference that degrades or distorts any portion of the electromagnetic spectrum. □ The high frequency interference that appears on a television picture as a herringbone pattern.

RF line A waveguide or coaxial cable used to carry radio frequency energy.

RF modulator A device used to convert television audio and video signals to radio frequency signals for use by a television receiver.

RFMVR Recency-frequency-monetary-value ratio.

RFP Request for proposal.

RF pattern A term sometimes applied to describe a fine herringbone pattern in a picture. May also cause a slight horizontal displacement of scanning lines resulting in a rough or ragged vertical edge of the picture. Caused by high-frequency interference.

RGB Red, green, blue.

RGB channels The red, green, and blue channels of color television.

RGB encoding *See* RGB (555).

RGB (555) One of the video encoding techniques used for images in CD-I. For each pixel the colors red, green, and blue are each quantized and represented by 5 bits of information, giving 32 levels of intensity from one extreme value to the other.

RGB monitor A type of television monitor requiring separate inputs for each color in order to produce high resolution color images.

RH □ Report heading. □ Right hand.

rheostat A variable resistor with one fixed terminal and a movable wiper. Often used in lighting circuits. Also called a *resistance dimmer.*

RHSA Radio Historical Society of America.

rhythm The beat, cadence, accent, tempo, and so on, of a musical composition or a performer's speaking.

rhythm and blues A radio station format characterized by ballads with a strong rhythm.

rhythm track(s) An audio track(s) on a multitrack recorder that contains the recorded rhythm instruments.

RIAA Record Industry Association of America, Inc.

RIAA curve The recording and equalization standards set by the RIAA. Cf. NAB curve.

rialto The theatre district on Broadway in New York City.

RIAS Radio in the American Sector (of Berlin). A United States international broadcasting organization.

ribbon □ A headline that runs the full width of a newspaper page, usually beneath a banner. □ A cloth strip fastened to the top of a book as a bookmark. □ A narrow strip of aluminum foil suspended between two magnets in a ribbon microphone.

ribbon cable A flat cable that consists of a number of insulated wires joined side-to-side.

ribbon microphone A bidirectional, sensitive, velocity microphone.

Richardson effect *See* Edison effect.

ride □ To control the gain or level of the input or output of a device or component such as an audio control console. Also called *ride gain, ride the needle,* and *ride the pot.* □ An ad-libbed musical selection.

ride gain *See* ride.

ride the boards *See* riding the showing.

ride the needle *See* ride.

ride the pot *See* ride.

riding the showing A physical inspection of the outdoor advertising panels that comprise an advertising buy. Also called *ride the boards.*

rifle □ An elongated, highly directional microphone. Also called a *rifle mike. See also* shotgun approach. □ A luminaire with a light-diffusing corrugated reflector. Also called a *rifle spot.*

rifle approach A newswriting style characterized by pointed, concise language. Cf. shotgun approach.

rifle mike *See* rifle.

rifle spot *See* rifle.

rig □ To set up lights, sets, and so on. □ A remote or mobile unit. □ To illegally fix a contest or broadcast program so that the prize need not be awarded, the winner is selected dishonestly, or clues are given to certain participants that are not given to others, and so on.

rigger An individual who works at rigging a set.

rigging ☐ The process of positioning luminaires on a set. ☐ The scaffolding, flys, catwalks, and so on, that are used to suspend luminaires, flats, microphones, and so on.

right A privilege conferred by law, regulation, or custom; as the right of free speech.

right (R) *See* camera right and stage right.

right-hand polarized wave An elliptically or circularly polarized wave, in which the electric field vector, observed in any fixed plane, normal to the direction of propagation, rotates with time in a right-hand or clockwise direction from the direction of propagation. Also called a *clockwise polarized wave.*

right justify *See* flush right.

right of access The right of news agencies and reporters to attend public meetings and have access to records. *See also* access and Canon 3(a)(7).

right of first refusal ☐ A clause written into a contract that gives the publisher the authority to determine whether or not to publish the author's next book before other publishers are offered the manuscript. Also called *first call.* ☐ An offer of a prior claim to sponsorship made by a medium to an advertiser.

right of privacy The right of a nonnewsworthy individual to demand that his private affairs not be publicized.

right of publicity The concept that well-known persons should have control over the use of their names for commercial or advertising purposes.

right of reply The right granted to individuals under Section 315 or the Fairness Doctrine to respond to opponents or ideas presented on broadcast stations. Also called *right to reply.*

right side The felt side of paper.

right (or left) signal The electrical output of a microphone or combination of microphones placed so as to convey the intensity, time, and location of sounds originating predominately to the listener's right (or left) of the center of the performing area.

right (or left) stereophonic channel The right (or left) signal as electrically reproduced in reception of FM stereophonic broadcasts.

rights The privileges granted to use copyrighted material. *See also* copyright, royalty, and subsidiary rights.

right to know The right of the people, news agencies, and reporters to investigate and report on governmental affairs.

right to refuse The right of the media to refuse advertising or any other material.

right to reply *See* right of reply.

rim The outside of a horseshoe shaped newspaper copy desk where copyreaders sit. *See also* slot.

rim drive A method of driving turntables by using a small rubber pressure roller at the inside edge of the turntable.

rim light A light directed from behind a subject or object for highlighting. Cf. modeling light.

rim man A copyreader.

ring ☐ Any undamped resonance. ☐ The audible signal made by a telephone. ☐ To draw a circle around a word or symbol in copy editing to indicate that it should be spelled out or vice versa.

ringback line *See* ringdown line.

ring bank A composing room stand where corrections to type are made.

ringdown A method of signaling on a telephone line.

ringdown line A telephone company line used for control purposes between a remote and a radio or television studio. Also called *ringback line.*

ring head A magnetic head in which the magnetic core material forms an enclosure with one or more gaps. The magnetic recording medium bridges one of these gaps and is contacted by the pole pieces on one side only.

ringing ☐ A sound made by an alternating or pulsating current. ☐ Television picture interference characterized by a ghost or edge effect. Often seen on all sides of a sharply defined object. Also called *matte ringing.*

ring microphone A microphone used over a boxing ring or, by extension, one used in other sporting events that use a stationary microphone.

ring radiator *See* loop.

RIO Radio Information Office (of the NAB).

rip and read To take news copy directly from news wire and air it without rewriting and, often, without preparation.

rip open To remake a newspaper page for late-breaking news.

ripple □ A ripple like rolling of the lines in a computer display caused by a change in the information. □ A wave-like variation caused by inadequate filtering that results in spikes in the output of a power supply.

rippled edge A tape edge that exhibits curvature perpendicular to the plane of the tape.

ripple dissolve A special effects dissolve in which the pictures seem to wave or ripple.

riser □ A low platform used to elevate cameras, performers, or set pieces. *See also* apple box, pancake, pigeon, and stacker. □ *See* ascender.

risers The ridged surfaces on a stepped lens or a fresnel lens between sections of active lens surfaces. These are sometimes blackened to reduce stray light.

rising initial A large initial letter that aligns with the base of the first line of body type. Cf. drop initial.

RIT Red Interamericana de Telecomunicaciones (Inter-American Telecommunications Network). An international organization.

RITAL Red Internacional de Telecomunicaciones de America Latina (International Telecommunication Network for Latin America). An international organization.

RITC Radio Interference Technical Committee.

river An irregular streak of white space that runs down incorrectly printed pages. Also called a *gutter.*

river novel A long novel that often traces a family through a number of generations. From the French *roman fleuve.*

RL Radio Liberty.

RLC Real-time lens error correction. An automatic PROM correction of registration errors caused by manipulating a lens.

RLE Run-length encoding.

RM Recordimeter.

RMA Radio Manufacturers Association. Now the EIA.

RMS Root-mean-square. The "average" value of a periodic quantity equal to the square root of the squares of the values.

RNA Religious Newswriters Association.

RNS Religious News Service.

RO □ Read out. □ Receive only. □ Runover.

roadblock The purchase of commercial time on a number of radio or television stations simultaneously in order to obtain maximum reach within a certain time period.

road board A portable lighting switchboard brought into a theatre for a show. Cf. piano board.

road manager An individual in charge of making traveling and living accommodations for a performer or company on tour.

road show A series of performances or motion pictures performed or presented in various theatres.

roan An imitation morocco book binding made of sheepskin.

Robinson-Patman Act An act of Congress, passed in 1936, that forbids unfair trade practices such as price and payment discrimination in interstate commerce.

rock □ To prepare the surface of a mezzotint plate with a rocker. □ A type of music or music format characterized by repetition, driving rhythms, and a lack of subtlety. Also called *rock and roll.*

rock and roll □ The back and forth movement of picture and film in synchronization during editing. □ *See* rock.

rocker □ A slang term for a radio station with a rock format. □ A hand tool used in preparing mezzotint plates. Also called a *cradle.* □ *See* camera rock.

rocket head A headline that sets several of the words of a news story in display type.

rocking The movement of an audio-or videotape back and forth by hand to locate an edit point.

rocumentary A documentary motion picture that consists primarily of a rock performer's appearances.

rod One of the monochromatic sensory organs of the retina. Cf. cone.

ROFA Radio of Free Asia. A United States international broadcasting organization.

role □ The character an actor portrays in a drama, screenplay, and so on. Cf. part. □ For a freelance player, a role as written at the time the freelance contract is entered into, or as it may from time to time thereafter be rewritten, lengthened, or shortened by the producer.

role playing technique An interview technique in which a respondent is encouraged to imagine the part he would play in an imaginary situation as a way of determining his or her attitudes.

roll □ The unwanted vertical movement of a television picture. Also called a *rollover.* □ An uncut, complete length of motion picture film or magnetic tape. Cf. reel. □ A command to start a machine such as a film camera or recorder. Also called *roll 'em.* □ *See* scroll. □ A movement similar to a curl except the image is rolled tightly. □ To cause a tape machine's transport to be set in motion.

roll cue A cue mark on a tape or film.

roll down *See* scroll.

roll 'em *See* roll.

roller □ One of a number of pulleys over which motion picture film passes during processing. □ A tape-path element that turns on a bearing in response to the tape passing over it.

roller caption *See* roller title.

roller embossing *See* pebbling.

roller title A device used to move titles up, down, or across in front of a television or film camera. Also called a *roller caption* and *roll title. See also* crawl.

roll film Any film designed to take a series of pictures, as opposed to sheet film.

roll in An insertion and integration of a commercial into a radio or television broadcast.

rolling over Replacing cable network programs and/or advertisements with local events.

rolling sample An audience measurement technique that averages samples that are taken over a period of time.

rolling split A cumulative purchase of space in syndicated newspaper supplements on a market-by-market basis in such a way that full national advertising coverage is obtained.

roll it A radio or television director's command to roll a film or tape.

rolloff □ A gradual attenuation of frequencies at either end of the sound spectrum. Called *bass rolloff* or *treble rolloff.* □ The attenuation of treble frequencies to compensate for preemphasis in recording or transmission. Also called *slope.*

roll out To mail the remaining portion of a mailing list after successfully testing a portion of that list.

roll-out The advertising of a product in a limited geographical area before a national campaign is executed.

rollover □ A conversion of a computer software program, book, or other existing material to CD-I. □ *See* roll.

roll-thru A blank portion of film or tape that continues to run but is not seen by the audience. Often used in newscasts when a number of stories have film or tape clips.

roll title *See* roller title.

roll up □ A special effect in which one picture changes to another by a wipe from the bottom of the picture up. □ *See* scroll. □ A two second interval of filmed images preceding the start of the audio tracks at the beginning of a film.

ROM Read only memory.

rom An abbreviation for *roman.*

roman A style of type, either old-style or modern, characterized by upright thick and thin strokes with serifs. Also called *antiqua. See also* race.

roman fleuve *See* river novel.

roman type *See* roman.

ROM cassette A plug-in memory unit containing data and machine code.

rondel A round, convex, heat resistant glass, color filter primarily used on some border lights or footlights, also available as clear cover glass. Also spelled *roundel.*

roof bulletin An outdoor advertising bulletin built on the roof of a building.

room noise The unwanted vibrations and ambient sounds that can cause a lack of presence in a studio or other enclosed space.

room presence *See* room tone.

room sound *See* room tone.

room tone □ The ambient sound present in any given enclosed space. Also called *room sound.* □ The quality of sound in a studio or other enclosed space; often determined by the size and shape of the area. Also called *room presence.* Cf. presence.

ROP □ Run of paper. □ Run of press. □ Run of publication.

ROP color The use of color, other than spot color, run on a press in a newspaper.

Roper and Associates, Elmo A research organization that conducts media studies.

ROS □ Run of schedule. □ Reporter on scene. □ Read only storage.

rosin A substance used in soldering to promote the fusion of the metals.

ROSP Report on Syndicated Programs.

ROSR Real-time on-scene report. A radio news report from the scene of a newsworthy event.

roster recall *See* aided recall.

roster study *See* aided recall.

rostrum □ A horizontal board used to hold titles, artwork, pictures, and so on, with a camera and lights mounted on a vertical column above the board. □ *See* animation stand.

rostrum camera A still or motion picture camera mounted on the column of a rostrum.

rotary cart *See* carousel.

rotary fader *See* potentiometer.

rotary head A head that moves in a circular path while recording or reproducing a tape program.

rotary head servo The closed-loop servo system that ensures accurate speed and phase (synchronization) of head rotation. *See also* headwheel servo.

rotary plan *See* rotate.

rotary pot *See* potentiometer.

rotary press A fast, efficient printing press that has two or more curved plates fastened to a cylinder. The paper is fed in a continuous web for impression, either offset or direct. Cf. flatbed press.

rotary shutter An adjustable rotating shutter used in some film cameras.

rotary transformer An inductive device for transferring signals from the video headwheel to the main playback circuitry, and from the recording circuitry to the video headwheel. One winding of this transformer is stationary while the other rotates with the headwheel or scanner.

rotate To move an advertisement from one outdoor board location to another in order to give it wide exposure. Used if a showing is scheduled for more than 30 days. Also called a *rotary plan.*

rotating bulletin The process of moving an advertiser's message from an outdoor advertising location to another at stated intervals in order to achieve a more balanced coverage of a market. Cf. set showing.

Rotating digital audiotape (R-DAT) A digital tape system that uses high-coercivity metal particle or barium ferrite tape about one-seventh of an inch wide.

rotating prism A prism used to replace the shutter in some cameras, projectors, and viewers. Also called an *intermittent prism.*

rotating wipe A wipe that moves in a line as does the hand on a clock.

rotation □ The horizontal or vertical rotation of commercial messages on a broadcast station or network. □ The scheduling of motion pictures on cable networks at different times of the day and different days of the week during a given period so as to reach the greatest possible audience. □ A camera movement in which the camera is moved in a complete circle to give a spinning effect in the film. A partial rotation is called a *Tilt.*

rotational latency In computer disc drive systems, the average delay time, caused by the disc rotation needed to gain access, between a request for read or write action and the commencement of that action.

rotator A motor-driven device used to turn an antenna.

Roth v. United States The 1957 Supreme Court case in which the standards of obscenity were defined as material that is sexually lewd and appeals to prurient interests. *See also* SLAPS test.

roto An abbreviation for *rotogravure.*

rotogravure □ A long-run printing process accomplished by means of a gravure on a web-fed press. □ A newspaper supplement with a magazinelike format printed by this process.

Rotoscope □ A trademark name for a device patented by Max Fleischer in 1917, that projects live-action film, one frame at a time, onto a small screen from the rear. Drawing paper is placed over the screen allowing the animators to trace the live-action images as a guide in capturing complicated movements. □ An image traced on an animation cel using a Rotoscope.

rough □ A dummy or layout in sketchy form with a minimum of detail. Also called a *rough dummy* and *rough layout*. *See also* layout. Cf. comprehensive. □ A draft of a commercial message. □ An animation sketch.

rough cut A preliminary arrangement of film or tape shots in the early stages of editing. Also called a *slop cut*. *See also* assemble. Cf. final cut.

rough dummy *See* rough.

rough layout *See* rough.

rough mix A preliminary joining of music, effects, and dialogue on one track. Also called a *scratch mix* and *slop mix*.

rough print *See* slop print.

roughs The animators' original drawings, which are usually broad and sketchy, rather than finished drawings, and which are refined by the cleanup artist.

round A British term for a reporter's beat.

rounding The process of curving the back of a book before backing.

round robin An interconnecting circuit between or among radio or television stations that allows instantaneous switching between origination points.

roundup □ A news story prepared using information from different sources, as in a weather roundup or sports roundup. □ *See* wrapup.

rout To remove unwanted areas of a metal printing plate or casting.

route □ To lay wires or cables. □ A communication path.

router A high-speed tool or machine used to cut metal from printing plates.

routine □ A performer's act. □ A self-contained dramatic unit constituting fifty percent or less of the entertainment portion of a comedy-variety program, provided that such is an adaptation of material previously used in television or any other medium, or original and written to fit the special talents and personality of the particular actor or actors in the film involved. Cf. sketch. □ A sequence of instructions or a part of a computer program.

routine maintenance *See* preventive maintenance.

routing □ The assignment of communication facilities and lines for the transmission of information. □ The selecting of a path for a signal.

routing switcher A switcher in which the multiple inputs can be assigned to any of the outputs.

row □ A horizontal line of letters, figures, symbols, and so on. Cf. column. □ A low profile scenery piece. *See* ground row.

royal A size of paper; 19 by 24 or 20 by 25.

royalty The payment made to a copyright holder that secures duplication, performance, or other rights. Cf. public domain (PD).

royalty statement An accounting received by a writer or copyright holder of the money earned within a given period.

royola Payola in the recording industry.

RP □ Rear projection. □ Remote pickup. Also RPU, remote pick up.

rp An abbreviation for *reprint* and *reprinting*.

RPAC Radio Propagation Advisory Committee.

RPM Revolutions per minute.

RPN Reverse Polish notation.

rpnd An abbreviation for *reprinting, no date* (books).

R print An inexpensive color print suitable for use in comprehensive layouts, although not suitable for use for print reproduction. Also called a *type R print*. Cf. C print and dye transfer.

RPU Remote pickup. *See* RP.

RR Radio regulation.

RRC Radio Research Council. Now defunct.

RS □ Radio station. □ Reverse shot.

RS-232 A standard defined for asynchronous communication between two devices. A standard developed by the EIA, the Bell System, and computer manufacturers. Also *RS-232C*.

RS-232 interface An electronics industry standard connector used to connect computers to peripheral devices. Also *RS-232C* and *RS-422*.

RSC Recessed single contact. A lamp base type.

RT □ Real time. □ Radio telephony. □ Remote terminal. □ Reverberation time.

RTC Radio Technical Committee for Aeronautics.

RTCA □ Radio and Television Correspondents Association. □ Real-time control area.

RTCM Radio Technical Commission for Marine Services.

RTDG Radio and Television Directors Guild. A union.

RTES Radio and Television Executives Society.

RTMA Radio Television Manufacturers Association. Now the EIA.

RTNDA Radio-Television News Directors Association. An industry trade association that also sets self-regulatory standards.

RTNDA Code A self-regulatory code of the Radio and Television News Directors Association.

RTOS Real-time operating system.

RTPB Radio Technical Planning Board. A former standards organization.

RTR Real-time record.

RTRC Radio and Television Research Council.

RTRI Real-time record interpreter.

RTS □ Rapid transmission and storage. A video invention by Peter C. Goldmark. □ Royal Television Society (of Great Britain). An association of broadcasters.

RU Relative unit.

rubbed A worn or abraded book binding.

rubber cement A nonwrinkling paper adhesive used in layout, artwork, and so on.

rubber plate A printing plate made of rubber, as opposed to metal.

rub off *See* rub on.

rub on Letters, numerals, and symbols that can be affixed to paper or other materials by rubbing. Also called *rub off* and *transfer letters.* Used for layout and graphics.

rubout A news wire mistake that is later "rubbed out."

rubric A title page, initial letter, and so on, of a book printed in red.

ruby A size of type; 5-1/2 points.

rule □ For the purposes of the Administrative Procedure Act, the whole or a part of an agency statement of general or particular applicability and future effect designed to implement, interpret, or prescribe law or policy or describing the organization, procedure, or practice requirements of an agency, which includes the approval or prescription for the future of rates, wages, corporate or financial structures or reorganizations thereof, prices, facilities, appliances, services or allowances therefor or of valuations, costs, or accounting, or practices bearing on any of the foregoing. *See also* rules and regulations. □ An order of a court. □ A judicial or quasi-judicial decision. □ A strip of type high metal, used horizontally or vertically, to separate lines of type, underline, create boxes, and so on. A column rule, hairline rule, border, and so on.

ruled insert A story that is divided into parts by a rule.

rule for insert *See* turn rule.

rule for pickup *See* turn rule.

rulemaking The government administrative agencies' procedure for formulating, amending, or repealing rules and regulations.

rule of thirds A concept in picture composition wherein subjects or objects are placed one-third of the way from the top to the bottom or the left to the right of the picture.

rules and regulations The guides, standards, and orders, and so on, made by an administrative agency in order to carry out the mandates of Congress. For example, the Rules and Regulations of the Federal Communication Commission are published as Title 47 of the Code of Federal Regulations (CFR).

ruling line A line made by a rule or by a program in computer-set copy.

rumble A low-frequency vibration mechanically transmitted to the recording or reproducing turntable and superimposed on the reproduction. Also called *turntable rumble.*

rumble filter A filter used to eliminate low-frequency vibrations.

run □ A reporter's beat. □ *See* press run. □ To execute a computer program. □ A complete showing of all the episodes of a television series. □ The number of days or weeks a play is performed or motion picture is shown in the same location. □ To operate a piece of equipment, such as a printing press or audio control console.

run-around A block of type, where a portion is set to less than full measure to leave space for an illustration, large initial, and so on. Also spelled runaround. Also called *set around.*

runaway A remote location out of union jurisdiction.

runaway production A motion picture production in which production costs have far exceeded the budget.

rundown sheet A timing sheet that lists the order of performances or scenes in a production. Also called a *fact sheet* and *timing sheet.*

run flat To set matter in type without change.

run in An instruction by a copy editor or proofreader to print copy without a paragraph or other break. Also called *run on.*

run length In a data stream, the number of bits between transitions.

run length encoding (RLE) In digital video, an encoding technique that compresses the data required to store a given image by recording the values of distances between transitions or changes from one color or intensity to the next, as well as the values of the colors or intensities between transitions.

runners *See* pipe.

running charge The price charged by a mailing list owner for names run or passed but not used by a specific mailer. When such a charge is made, it is usually made to cover extra processing costs. However, some mailing list owners set the price without regard to actual cost.

running dummy A dummy page that is in a state of revision.

running foot *See* running head.

running gag A joke or humorous action that is repeated during a motion picture or television program or from program to program.

running head The title, date, folio, and so on, of a publication that may appear on the top of each page. If the information appears at the bottom of the page, it is called a running foot.

running log A radio or television station program log containing a complete listing by hour and minute of the day's programming.

running part A continuing role in a series.

running shot *See* following shot.

running speed The rate at which film passes through a camera or projector.

running story □ A story or plot told in serial form, as in a soap opera. □ A continuing news story that is updated and run a number of times as the news changes. Also called a *sectional story.* □ A story that is sent to the composing room as the material is written.

running text The main text on a printed page, as opposed to its display lines.

running time □ The actual duration of a motion picture, television program, film or tape segment, and so on. Cf. cumulative time. □ *See* absolute playing time.

running title *See* crawl.

run of book The placement of advertising at the discretion of the publisher instead of the advertiser.

run of paper (ROP) The placement of advertising at the discretion of the newspaper instead of the advertiser.

run of paper color (ROP color) □ Color advertising run anywhere in a newspaper that is convenient. □ Color advertising run in the main section of a newspaper rather than in a supplement.

run-of-schedule (ROS) The purchase of spots by an advertiser for which the broadcast station selects the time. ROS spots are always preemptible, but cost less. Also called *floating time* and *run-of-station.*

run-of-station *See* run-of-schedule.

run on □ A book chapter that begins on the same page as the end of the previous chapter. □ Any additional copies made on a press run after the required number has been printed. □ *See* run in.

run out □ An instruction by a copy editor or proofreader to make a hanging indention at the place indicated. □ To fill the end of a line of type with blank quads. □ The extra motion picture film spliced to the end of a reel of film. *See also* protective leader.

runover (RO) □ A part of a news story that breaks to another page. *See also* jump. □ *See* overset.

run over ☐ To review a script or program. ☐ A radio or television program that exceeds its allotted time.

run through ☐ Usually considered to be the first complete rehearsal of a scene or program with cameras, sound effects, and so on Cf. walk through. ☐ *See* run through shot.

run through shot A camera shot in which a performer or object enters one side of the picture and exits the other side.

run up ☐ Tape or film pictures that are shown before the VTR or projector is up to speed. A video wow. ☐ To start a second projector in preparation for changeover.

run up time The time from the application of power to a camera or projector mechanism until it is up to speed. Cf. pre roll time.

runway *See* horseshoe.

rush Copy that is to be handled expeditiously. Also called *rush copy.*

rush copy *See* rush.

rushes Motion picture film that is processed quickly, often overnight, to determine if a retake is necessary. Also called *dailies.*

rush print *See* rushes.

RUT Rooms using television. A Nielsen acronym for motel and hotel rooms using television.

R/W Read/Write.

rwd An abbreviation for *rewind.*

RWG Radio Writers Guild. Now defunct.

rx An abbreviation for *receiver.*

S

S □ Official number of station. An FCC file-number prefix. □ Second. □ Senate (of the United States Congress). □ Sharing time. □ Sized. □ Sports programs. □ A wire service symbol for sports. □ A wire service priority symbol for an advance for weekend use.

SA Studio address.

SAA Specialty Advertising Association.

Sabattier effect *See* solarization.

saccadic movement A quick eye movement from one point to another.

SACD Société des Auteurs et Compositeurs Dramatiques (Society of Dramatic Authors and Composers), an international organization.

sacred cow An idea, profession, product, and so on, that is not to be denigrated on the air or in print.

SACT (President's) Special Advisory Committee on Telecommunications.

saddleback A softback binding.

saddle stitch A type of stitching in which two wire staples are driven through the center fold of a magazine or pamphlet. Also called *saddle wiring.* Cf. side stitch.

saddle wiring *See* saddle stitch.

safe action area *See* essential area.

safe area *See* essential area.

safe harbor The time period from midnight to 6 a.m. when the FCC has indicated that it will not prosecute stations for broadcasting indecent material. The subject is, in 1990, the subject of both litigation and legislation.

safelight A light used in a darkroom that will not affect a film's emulsion.

safe track The audio track farthest from the edge of a videotape, and thus least likely to be damaged.

safety □ A second original or dub of an audio- or videotape made in case of damage to the original. Also called a *safety copy.* □ The distance between a magazine's page edge and printed copy. □ *See* essential area.

safety area *See* essential area.

safety base A slow-burning acetate or polyester base used for manufacturing film.

safety copy *See* safety.

safety curtain A fireproof curtain used in theatres to separate the stage and backstage areas from the audience in case of fire.

safety film A film made with a noncombustible film base.

safety footage *See* bumper.

safety shell A thin copper replica of an original printing plate from which duplicates may be obtained in case of injury to, or loss of, the original. Also called a *protection shell* and *safety mold.*

SAG Screen Actors Guild.

SAG fee *See* residual.

salad A slang term for the buckling of film in a camera or projector. *See also* jam.

sales department The radio or television station department concerned with the sale of time to advertisers and advertising agencies.

salesman *See* time salesman.

sales manager (SM) The person in charge of a broadcast station sales department.

sales network A linking together of a number of media outlets for the purpose of selling joint time or space at a discounted rate.

sales presentation *See* presentation.

sales promotion *See* promotion.

sales quota The minimum dollar amount required of an individual selling media time or space.

sales representative *See* station representative.

salting The deliberate placing of decoy or dummy names in a mailing list to trace list usage and delivery. *See also* decoy and dummy name. Also called *seeding.*

SAM Station acquisition marketing plan.

same size (SS) An instruction to a photographer, printer, and so on, to reproduce the material without changing the size of the picture submitted.

SAMP Stuntmen's Association of Motion Pictures.

SAMPAC Society of Advertisers, Musicians, Producers, Arrangers, and Composers. A trade association of professionals involved in the creation of advertising music.

sample Elementary units that have been selected from a statistical population according to some specified procedure intended to serve as a basis for generalizing to a statistical population. *See also* area probability sample, cluster sample, convenience sample, judgment sample, modified probability sample, multistage sample, nonprobability sample, probability sample, quota sample, replicated sample, representative sample, simple random sample, stratified sample, and systematic selection sample.

sample and hold A circuit that is used to convert an analog signal into digital information. Used, for example, in digital television. *See also* sampling.

sample area The geographical area in which a survey respondent sample is obtained.

sample buyer A person who sends for a sample product, usually at a special price or for a small handling charge, but sometimes free.

sample copy A free copy of a publication distributed to a prospective subscriber or advertiser.

sample error *See* sampling error.

sample frame The number of elementary units from which a survey sample is drawn. *See also* frame.

sample in-tab *See* in-tab sample.

sample package An example of the mailing piece to be mailed by a list user to a particular list. Such a mailing piece is submitted to the list owner for approval prior to commitment for one-time use of that list.

sample page A page of a book or other publication made up by a printer for approval.

sample print □ A motion picture final trial composite print. □ A rough print used to demonstrate the overall effect of a scene.

sampler A phonograph album, primarily designed for radio stations, that contains selections from a number of new albums from that company.

sample reel *See* demo.

sample size The number of elementary units in a survey that supply information that is used in tabulations. In this sense, also called in-tab sample size. In contrast, the number of units initially selected in a survey should be referred to as the ''size of the predesigned sample.'' For most sampling plans, the appropriate statistical formula shows that the size of the standard error is, approximately, inversely proportional to the square root of the sample size. *See also* accuracy.

sampling □ A method of recording a short segment of a sound and storing it in computer memory. Cf. sequencing. □ The process of examining a variable signal at periodic intervals. □ The primary method for turning an analog signal into a digital signal. □ A technique for creating sounds electronically by manipulating a digital recording. □ The technique of using a mathematically selected portion of a statistical population to describe or evaluate the entire statistical population. □ The rapid selection of different radio or television programs by a member of the audience in order to select one that is satisfactory for the moment.

sampling error The difference between the survey result obtained with a sample, and the result that would be obtained by an attempted census of the sampling units in a frame, conducted in the same manner and with the same care as the sample survey. Cf. nonsampling error.

sampling frequency The rate at which analog signals are sampled for conversion to digital signals.

sampling rate □ The ratio of the sample size to the size of the statistical population. □ The rate that an analog signal is looked at and then given a number (quantized). The more often a signal is sampled, the higher the frequency of the sampling rate. Higher sampling rates generally mean a higher quality. The standard rates are 32 kHz, 44.1 kHz, 44.056 kHz, and 48 kHz.

sampling unit A geographic area, normally consisting of a county or independent city. Some counties, however, may be divided into two or more sampling units due to topography or ethnicity.

SAN Standard address number.

sanction □ For the purposes of the Administrative Procedure Act, the whole or a part of an agency prohibition, requirement, limitation, or other condition affecting the freedom of a person; withholding of relief; imposition of penalty or fine; destruction, taking, seizure, or withholding of property; assessment of damages, reimbursement, restitution, compensation, costs, charges, or fees; requirement, revocation, or suspension of a license; or taking other compulsory or restrictive action. □ A disqualification imposed by the FCC on a party to an adjudicatory proceeding for unauthorized ex parte presentations or the failure to report same.

sandbag A canvas bag filled with sand for use as a weight; often for holding flats of other set pieces in place.

Sanders Brothers case The 1940 Supreme Court decision that was interpreted by the FCC to mean that it need not consider economic injury in licensing. Cf. the Carroll case.

S and SC Sized and supercalendered (paper).

sandwich □ A radio or television spot that contains live advertising or promotional copy between a music intro and outro. Also called a *donut* and *wraparound.* □ A radio or television network program that is scheduled between two local programs; often news, or vice versa. □ A number of different cylinder dressings for letterpress machines. Also called *sandwich dressing.*

sandwich dressing *See* sandwich.

sanner dolly A large, versatile, crane arm camera dolly. *See also* camera mounts.

sans serif A class of typeface with strokes of equal thickness and without serifs. Also called *block letter.* Cf. serif.

SAP □ Second audio program. □ Soon as possible.

sapphire A gem used for bearings in precision instruments. Also used as a substitute for a diamond stylus.

Sarnoff Gold Medal, David An award given by the SMPTE for meritorious achievement in television engineering.

Sarnoff Medal, David An award given by the IEEE for an outstanding contribution to the field of electronics.

SASI Shugart Associates System Interface. An industry standard that preceded SCSI.

sat An abbreviation for *satellite.*

satcom □ An abbreviation for *satellite communication.* □ A domestic satellite network.

satellite □ A broadcasting station licensed by the FCC to retransmit the programs of another station. *See also* booster and television broadcast translator station. □ Any device in extraterrestrial space capable of transmitting signals. □ An active or passive orbiting earth satellite used to relay signals from one point on the earth to another or others. □ A body that revolves around another body of preponderant mass and that has a motion primarily and permanently determined by the force of attraction of that other body.

satellite antenna A parabolic reflector used to capture signals from a space satellite. *See also* dish.

Satellite Broadcasting and Communications Association of America (SBCA) An organization formed by the merger of DBSA and STIA in 1986.

satellite broker An individual or company that purchases time on communication satellites for resale.

satellite cable programming Video programming that is transmitted via satellite and that is primarily intended for direct receipt by cable operators for retransmission to cable subscribers.

satellite carrier A common carrier that uses satellites to provide communication facilities.

satellite communication The transmission of information in which transmission to or from a satellite is at least one link in the signal path.

satellite link A radio link between a transmitting earth station and a receiving earth station through one satellite. A satellite link comprises one uplink and one downlink.

Satellite Master Antenna Television (SMATV) A television distribution system that uses large earth stations to receive signals that are then distributed to users without crossing city streets. Cf. cable television and MATV.

satellite network A satellite system or a part of a satellite system, consisting of only one satellite and the cooperating earth stations.

satellite news vehicle (SNV) A mobile van or truck with uplink capabilities used to feed transmissions from a remote site to a satellite for relay to a television station or network. Also called a *star truck.*

satellite orbit *See* orbit.

satellite piggybacking *See* piggybacking.

satellite position *See* slot.

satellite receiver The earth station equipment that downconverts and processes downlink signals.

satellite relay □ A microwave repeater that receives and transmits television signals from one repeater to another on the earth. □ A satellite transponder.

satellite station A station that has entered into a rebroadcast arrangement with a primary broadcaster in order to service an area not normally reached by the parent station. It is the passive recipient of broadcast, transmitted or fed programming of the active parent station. The satellite station is assigned separate call letters and channel numbers by the FCC.

satellite subscription television The transmission of premium channels directly from satellites to homes.

satellite system A space system using one or more artificial earth satellites.

Satellite Television Corporation (STC) A subsidiary of Comsat.

satellite terminal station A complex of communication equipment located on the earth's surface, operationally connected with one or more terrestrial communication systems, and capable of transmitting telecommunications to or receiving telecommunications from a communications satellite system.

Saticon A television pickup tube containing selenium arsenic tellurium.

satire A literary composition, motion picture, play, and so on, that exposes human or individual vices, follies, or shortcomings to ridicule.

sat link An abbreviation for a *satellite link.*

saturation □ A property of color that determines the difference from white at constant hue, such as the sequence strong red, light red, pink, and white. □ An advertising campaign that uses a heavy schedule well above the normal levels of frequency and coverage. Also called a *saturation campaign* and *saturation schedule.* □ Banding in which the visible difference is in saturation. □ A condition wherein an increase in input power does not increase the output power in a circuit. □ The point at which further magnetization of a tape is impossible. □ *See* penetration.

saturation banding Banding in which the visible difference is in reproduced video color saturation. Cf. gauge banding, hue banding, and noise banding.

saturation campaign *See* saturation.

saturation control The control that regulates the amplitude of the chrominance signal in a color television receiver.

saturation point The level at which a tape, microphone, loudspeaker, and so on, will not accept greater signal strength.

saturation schedule *See* saturation.

saturation showing An outdoor advertising showing well above the 100 intensity.

saturation speech A political program that is carried by all networks at the same time.

Saturday morning television A term that has its roots in the child-oriented, limited animation cartoon shows that began to dominate this time slot in the 1950s, but has come to stand for this genre of mass-produced animation.

save □ To store information on a magnetic recording medium. □ To stop or preserve a process or action, in photography, motion pictures, or television.

save the food A direction to performers to run through the lines and action of a scene and save the food for the performance.

save the lights A command to turn off the set lights to conserve lamps and energy. Also called *save 'em.*

SAWA Screen Advertising World Association.

sawtooth □ A studio wall constructed in the shape of the teeth of a saw to reduce reflected waves. □ An electronically generated waveform used for scanning pulses.

SB Single bayonet (lamp base).

SBCA Satellite Broadcasting and Communications Association of America.

SBE Society of Broadcast Engineers.

SBME Society of Business Magazine Editors.

SBN *See* International Standard Book Number (ISBN).

SBPA Southern Baptist Press Association.

SC □ Small caps. □ Supercalendered. □ Single column. Used in ordering advertising space. □ Single contact. A lamp base type.

SCA □ Subsidiary communications authorization. □ Speech Communication Association. □ Screen Composers' Association.

scale □ The division of the audio spectrum by musical frequency ratios. □ A defined set of values. □ The markings on a meter or other instrument. □ The minimum pay received by members of a union. Also called *scale rate.* □ The degree of contrast in a picture. □ To increase or decrease the relative size of a photograph, artwork, drawing, and so on, keeping the proportions the same. □ The ratio between the size of the subject and the size of a produced image.

scale rate □ A standard cost for printing, engraving, and so on. □ *See* scale.

scaling The process of determining and producing the proper size for artwork, photographs, and so on, for printed advertisements. Also called *sizing.* Cf. casting off.

scalloping A form of horizontal picture distortion in which the sides of a television picture repeatedly curve during videotape playback. *See also* skewing.

scalp To buy and sell tickets in short supply for a quick profit.

scan □ One sweep of the television scanning line. □ To sweep the scanning lines successively. □ To examine items in a list or data file.

Scan-a-graver A trademark for an engraving machine that makes halftones on a plastic printing plate.

ScanAmerica The Arbitron Company's syndicated research service that uses people meter technology to measure television viewing and a scanner wand to measure household product purchases within the same household.

scan converter □ A device used in presenting a noninterlaced picture on a normal television screen containing the same number of lines as the original interlaced picture. *See also* double-frequency scanning. □ A device used to convert a video frequency to an audio frequency for transmission over telephone lines or narrow bandwidth radio lines.

scandal sheet A tabloid or newspaper that emphasizes sensationalism.

scan line *See* scanning line.

scanned print A 4:3 aspect ratio motion picture print or videotape made from an anamorphic or wide-screen print by means of a pan and scan optical printer or film chain.

scanner □ *See* optical character reader (OCR). □ An electronic device that is able to read colors from a photograph automatically for use in color separation. □ A mechanical assembly containing a drum, rotating pole tips, and tape guiding elements used to record and reproduce videotape recordings.

scanner modulator *See* modulator.

scanning □ The process of analyzing successively, according to a predetermined method, the light values of picture elements constituting the total television picture area. □ The process of drawing an animation image on a monitor.

scanning area The total area scanned by the television camera as seen on a studio monitor. Cf. cutoff and essential area.

scanning beam An electron beam used for scanning.

scanning device An electronic device, such as those used in airports to check luggage, that may fog film and ruin magnetic media.

scanning disk □ The color wheel developed by CBS in the 1940s for use in color television. □ A disk used in early mechanical television systems. *See also* Nipkow disk.

scanning factor *See* kell factor.

scanning frequency The number of scanning lines per second in a television picture. In the NTSC system, 15,750 (30 frames times 525 lines). Also called *horizontal repetition rate, horizontal scanning frequency,* and *stroke speed.*

scanning line A single, continuous, narrow horizontal strip of a television picture area containing highlights, shadows, and halftones, determined by the process of scanning.

scanning rate *See* scanning frequency.

scanning spot The point on the face of a television pickup or picture tube at the instant it is being scanned.

scarcity doctrine The idea that licensing of broadcast stations is allowable under the First Amendment because the available spectrum is limited.

scatter □ The random change in direction of a transmitted wave caused by reflection or refraction. □ The unsold commercial time on a radio or television station or network.

scatter buying *See* scatter plan.

scattering loss The decrease in intensity of a transmitted wave due to scattering.

scatter market The unsold time on a network after the preseason up-front buying is completed.

scatter plan The use of a number of different advertising vehicles at different times and frequencies so as to reach the greatest possible audience. Also called *scatter buying. See also* participation program.

scatter propagation The transmission and reception of high-power radio waves beyond line-of-sight distances by tropospheric or ionospheric scatter. Also called *over-the-horizon propagation* and *scatter transmission.*

scatter transmission *See* scatter propagation.

SCC Specialized common carrier.

scenario □ A basic script or screenplay containing a plot and dialogue, from which a final script is derived. Less complete than a shooting script. *See also* treatment.

scenarist A playwright or scriptwriter.

scene □ A part of a motion picture, television program, and so on, consisting of one or more interrelated shots. □ A part of a sequence. □ A division of a play, program, act, and so on. □ The setting of an action or script. □ A series of unified camera shots. □ A numbered series of camera shots.

scene dock *See* bay.

scene master A device for controlling a group of dimmers that are assigned to a specific set or scene.

scene planner In studio animation, the person who works with the director and storyboard artist to do detailed drawings of the scene, indicating the path of action, background elements, camera moves, etc. Also called a *layout artist. See also* layout.

scener A radio report from the scene of a newsworthy event.

scenery The flats and other set pieces that form an acting area.

scenery dock *See* bay.

scenescope A device designed to show talent in front of a projected background. *See also* rear projection (RP).

scene sheet *See* shot sheet.

scene shift The changing of scenery between acts or portions of a program.

scene shop An area used for scenery construction.

scenic artist A person who supervises painters, sign writers, and others in the production of sets.

scenic designer An individual who supervises the design elements of a set.

scenic elements *See* construction units.

scenic lead A lead, used primarily in features, that sets a scene or mood.

scenic projection The projection of large photographic images. *See also* front projection and rear projection (RP).

scenic projector *See* effects projector.

scented ink A printing ink to which a fragrance has been added.

SCF Sectional center facility.

SCG Screen Cartoonists Guild.

S channel One of the eight compact disc subcode channels (P-W). At present allocated to CD graphics only.

schedule □ In surveys, a question-and-answer form that is filled out by an interviewer. The terms ''schedule'' and ''questionnaire'' are often used interchangeably. Cf. questionnaire. □ The program log of a broadcast station. □ A list of assignments given to a reporter. □ An editor's list of completed stories. Also called a *budget* and *directory*. □ *See* head schedule. □ A wire service list of stories to be sent. □ The times and dates that the individual spots of an advertising campaign are to be broadcast or printed. □ A maintenance schedule. □ A shooting schedule. □ A tabular list of lighting units to be used on a production, usually including type of unit, hanging position, lamp type and size, color media, accessories, cabling instructions, and use.

scheduled maintenance A preventive maintenance plan for servicing equipment on a regular basis. *See also* preventive maintenance.

schedule reach A statistical estimate of the number of different individuals (unduplicated audience) who are exposed to an advertising message.

scheduling The organization of the priorities in performing maintenance, operations, or transmissions.

Scheiner scale A system, used primarily in central Europe, of rating film emulsion speed. Replaced by DIN.

schematic A drawing that shows the components and proper connections in a circuit. Also called a *circuit diagram*.

Schenck v. United States *See* clear and present danger.

schlock A slang term for heavy, tasteless copy or advertising matter.

schmaltz Any music, action, or writing that is overly sentimental.

Schufftan process An optical method, using a large silvered mirror, of combining a miniature set with live action. Originated by Eugen Schufftan.

Schwerin Research Corporation An organization that tests the advertising effectiveness of commercials.

science fiction A literary and film genre that combines scientific hypotheses with life in future times, sometimes on other worlds, perhaps with bug-eyed monsters, and often, with realistic human characterization.

sciopticon An optical effects projector for moving effects. In principle, it is similar to a slide projector with a continuously moving slide.

scoop □ A deep floodlight with a diffuse, generally elliptical contoured reflector; the field angle commonly is less than 100 degrees. Also called a *basher* and *floodlight*. □ The dead air caused by the failure to roll the music or open a microphone. □ An exclusive news story or one that is printed or broadcast ahead of the competition. Also called a *beat*.

SCOP Single copy order plan.

scope An abbreviation for *CinemaScope*. Also refers to other wide-screen processes. □ An abbreviation for *oscilloscope*.

scope print A CinemaScope or other wide-screen process print.

scophony television A mechanical projection television system developed in Great Britain.

scorcher A hot news story.

score □ The musical elements of a radio or television program. *See also* musical score. □ To write music for use on a television program or motion picture.

scoring □ A musical recording session for television or motion pictures. Also called a *scoring session*. □ The process of composing, orchestrating, and arranging music. □ The compressing of heavy paper stock so that it will not tear upon folding. Cf. creasing.

scoring session *See* scoring.

Scotchlite process A trademark material used for front projection screen.

scotch rule *See* Oxford rule.

scout A person who searches for talent or locations; often an employee of a motion picture studio. *See also* book scout, location scout, and talent scout.

scouting report A written summary concerning the location(s) available for a motion picture or concerning talent. *See also* scout.

SCPC Single channel per carrier. A satellite transmission system that uses a separate carrier for each channel.

SCR Silicon controlled rectifier.

scramble To encode an audio or video signal. Used, for example, in pay cable, cable television, SMATV, and so on, to prevent unauthorized reception of a program or service. *See also* encode.

scrambler A device used to encode or alter an audio or video signal.

scrap Visual material derived from clippings, labels, and so on, used to roughly illustrate an intended visual or scenic treatment.

scrape To remove old or "expired" outdoor advertising posters from a poster panel face in order to ensure a smooth posting surface. Usually performed with a long handled, sharp edged tool shaped like a chisel or putty knife.

scraper The knife-like portion of a film splicer used to remove the emulsion before cementing.

scratch □ Tape damage that results in the removal of the magnetic surface, typically in a long line. □ The resulting picture impairment caused by this damage. □ An undesirable physical mark on a disc, disk, or film.

Scratch-and-Sniff A trademark for a microencapsulation process, used to convey a specific scent to readers of the print media; such scents are released by scratching a properly treated area, or paper, or scratching a tape affixed to the printed piece, which breaks the microscopic sized plastic "scent bubbles," thus releasing the aroma.

scratchboard A clay-coated and inked drawing board used to achieve woodcut and other effects.

scratched print *See* scratch print.

scratch filter A filter used to lessen the effects of stylus scratch on a disc.

scratch mix *See* scratch track.

scratch off □ An animation technique wherein parts of an inked and opaqued cel are removed between frames. If it is shot in reverse, it is called a scratch on. □ A device used in direct mail that is removed by using a coin to reveal the message underneath. Usually for a prize or a chance for a prize.

scratch on *See* scratch off.

scratch print □ A stock shot print from a library that is deliberately defaced so that it cannot be used. If the shot is acceptable, a fine grain positive is ordered. Also called a *scratched print.* □ A low quality motion picture print that is used for sound track scoring or preparation. Also called a *slash print.*

scratch track A temporary, low quality soundtrack used for motion picture or television editing and synchronization. Also called a *guide track* and *scratch mix.*

SCR dimmer A type of control used to vary the intensity of lamps by rectifying the alternating current.

screamer □ A large, bold headline; a banner. □ A printer's slang expression for an exclamation point. □ A rapid-paced, loud disk jockey. □ A radio station with a loud, unsophisticated sound. □ A jingle with an ID.

screen □ The face of the television picture tube or monitor. □ An absorbing or reflecting panel used to change the acoustic properties of a studio. □ An opaque or translucent material onto which pictures may be projected. □ *See* windscreen. □ To view motion pictures or videotapes, often as part of an evaluation process. □ To view a screening. □ The cross-ruled plate or film that converts continuous tone images into halftones. Also called a *line screen.* □ To photograph an illustration through a screen. □ The number of lines in a screen; the greater the number of lines, the greater the resolution.

Screen Actors Guild (SAG) One of the major acting unions, representing some 70,000 professional actors and performing artists. It was formed in 1933, and is chartered as part of the Associated Actors and Artistes of America (AAAA).

Screen Advertising World Association (SAWA) An organization that promotes motion pictures as an advertising medium.

screen brightness The luminance of a motion picture screen as measured without film in the projector.

screen continuity *See* continuity.

screen credits *See* credits.

screen direction The axis along which action moves along a motion picture or television screen, as seen from the position of the audience or camera. The opposite of stage direction.

screen dump A computer routine that allows the immediate printing of a display screen.

screened A British term for shielded.

screener An individual, usually a producer, who screens telephone calls for a radio or television call-in talk show. Also called a *call screener* and *phone screener.*

Screen Extras Guild (SEG) A union comprising individuals who work as extras in motion pictures.

screen gain The ratio of the luminance of a screen to the luminance of a reference screen that reflects all of the incident light and reflects it uniformly in all directions, that is, has a uniform luminance in all directions. The gain of an actual screen will vary with the viewing direction. Screen gain may be greater than unity over a limited range of directions.

screening □ A preview of a motion picture shown to a limited audience. □ The showing of a motion picture to exhibitors prior to executing licensing agreements.

screening question An item in a questionnaire that is designed to determine if the next or following questions are to be asked of the respondent.

screening room A small motion picture projection room used primarily for screenings.

screen lumens The quantity of light flux reaching a screen from a projector.

screenplay □ A final script with individual scenes, full dialogue, and camera setups. Cf. first draft. □ A final script (as represented on the screen) with individual scenes and full dialogue, together with such prior treatment, basic adaptation, continuity, scenario, dialogue, and added dialogue as shall be used in and represent substantial contributions to the final script. Cf. scenario, teleplay, and treatment.

screen print *See* velox.

screen ratio *See* aspect ratio.

screen saturation The point at which a cathode ray tube begins to burn in.

screen size The diagonal measurement of a cathode ray tube.

screen test A test of an actor or actress made to determine if he or she is to be cast in a part or offered a studio contract. Now rarely used.

screen time The time span covered by the screenplay, as opposed to running time.

screenwriter An individual who writes stories, treatments, and scripts for motion pictures and made for television movies. Sometimes called a *scriptwriter.*

screwball comedy A type of comedy typical of the 1930s and characterized by verbal exchanges, sexual innuendo, and incongruous situations. Cf. slapstick.

screw base A lamp socket with screw threads.

screw mount A lens mount containing threads. Cf. bayonet mount.

scribe □ A pointed tool used to scratch the emulsion of a film to conform it for splicing. Also called a *scriber.* □ A term sometimes applied to journalists and other writers.

scriber *See* scribe.

scrim □ A flag made of translucent material, such as gauze or glass fabric, and used to diffuse or soften light. □ A gauze-like theatrical curtain. When properly lighted from the front, this curtain can appear opaque. If light is brought up behind the scrim, it becomes transparent.

script □ An abbreviation for *manuscript.* The complete written representation of the words, music, sound effects, and so on, of a program, motion picture, and so on. A nontheatrical scenario. *See also* continuity. □ Radio or television news copy. □ A typeface in which the letters are connected to resemble handwriting. *See also* cursive.

script breakdown *See* breakdown.

script clerk *See* script supervisor.

script doctor An individual called in to rewrite or revise a script or screenplay in need of help.

scripted show *See* script show.

scripter An individual who writes scripts, screenplays, teleplays, and so on.

script girl *See* script supervisor.

script rack A small stand used to hold a performer's script.

script scene A portion of a script that may be filmed or taped in one continuous camera shot.

script show A fully scripted radio or television program, as opposed to an ad lib program. Also called a *scripted show.*

script supervisor A script supervisor is a liaison between the producer, director, and editor and is required (by union rules) for the production of any motion picture that involves timing, matching, cast, continuity, maintaining lined scripts, or preparing notes for the film editor. Usually makes breakdowns of wardrobe and props, rough timing, keeping script continuity, numbering picture and sound takes, and so on. Also called a *script clerk* and formerly a *script girl.*

scriptwriter □ An individual who writes scripts. □ *See* screenwriter.

scroll □ A roll of paper or parchment. □ To move a cursor vertically through a computer file. □ The continuous horizontal or vertical movement of video information displayed, such that as old data disappears at one edge, new data appears at the opposite edge. □ To move a picture, lines of type, and so on, toward the top of a television screen or monitor. Also called a *roll.*

scroll down To move the information on a display screen toward the top of display. Also called *roll down.* Cf. scroll up.

scrolling *See* scroll.

scroll up To move the information on a display screen toward the bottom of the display. Also called *roll up.* Cf. scroll down.

scrub To delete or remove a rehearsal, set, scheduled performance, and so on.

SCSI Small Computer System Interface. An IEEE standard for interfacing a computer to multiple, disparate high speed peripherals.

S.Ct. Supreme Court Reporter. A privately published reporter covering the decisions of the Supreme Court. Cf. *United States Reports* (U.S.).

SCTE Society of Cable Television Engineers.

scum A slang term for the atmospheric pollution that causes photographic prints to become dull.

scumble The process of aging a set by painting.

S curve *See* Hogarth's line.

SD Standard Deviation.

SDG Screen Directors Guild.

SDIG Screen Directors International Guild.

S distortion A waving distortion of vertical lines in a television picture.

SDX Sigma Delta Chi.

SE □ Sound effects. □ Standard error.

seal □ A bookbinding leather made from the skin of a seal. □ *See* wafer.

sealed beam lamp A tungsten lamp with an internal, silvered reflector surface.

sealed beam spotlight A light source with integral filament, reflector, and lens.

sealer A rapid drying liquid plastic used as a coating in make-up.

Seal of Approval □ A symbol granted by a publication, especially a magazine, for use in advertising, stating that the magazine has tested the product advertised and found it satisfactory. □ The former Television Code symbol of the NAB that signified station membership.

search □ To seek a specific point in an audio- or videotape. □ To scan material in a document, card file, and so on. □ To shuttle tape in order to select an edit point. □ A device on an audiotape recorder that remembers a selected point and returns to it automatically.

search and replace A word processing function that can find a specified word or phrase and automatically replace it.

search program A computer program that searches a data file or database to find a key phrase supplied by an operator or another program. *See also* retrieval.

search string A computer program string that seeks specified words or characters for replacement. Cf. replacement string.

search warrant A court order authorizing a search of private property by an officer to obtain evidence.

season The period of time that begins with the introduction of new television programs in the Fall and ends in the Spring. Also called the *Fall season.* Cf. second season.

seasonal commercial A commercial that is especially related, by audio or video reference, to a particular season, such as a Christmas commercial, June bride commercial, Valentine's Day commercial, and so on.

seasonal schedule An assignment by the FCC of a frequency or frequencies to an international broadcasting station for transmission to particular zones or areas of reception during specified hours.

season average Household and persons estimates for each program reported as an average of all telecasts included in the NTI pocketpiece from the fall "premiere" through the current report interval.

sec An abbreviation for *second.*

SECA Southern Educational Communication Association.

SECAM Séquentiel Couleur à Mémoire (sequential color and memory). A color television system developed in France that utilizes a single-frequency modulated subcarrier for transmission of the chrominance channel.

secondary affiliate A radio or television station that carries programs from other than its primary network. Cf. primary affiliate.

secondary AM station Any AM station, except a Class I station, operating on a Class I frequency.

secondary audience □ The readers of a publication other than those for whom its editorial content is intended. Also called *secondary readership.* □ *See* pass-along.

secondary audio program *See* second audio program.

secondary boycott A labor union boycott of a station, newspaper, magazine, and so on, wherein the union urges the public not to patronize advertisers on a station, newspaper, magazine, and so on. Secondary boycotts are forbidden by the Landrum-Griffith Act.

secondary color The color produced by the combination of two of the three primary colors, cyan, magenta, or yellow. *See also* complementary color.

secondary coverage *See* secondary service area.

secondary cue tone *See* cue tone.

secondary data Information collected in a survey that is not used at the time in reporting results.

secondary emission The release of electrons when they are struck by other electrons.

secondary entry *See* added entry.

secondary meaning A common word that has become identified with a specific product and is thus eligible for registration as a trademark.

secondary medium An advertising medium that is selected to supplement the advertising carried for the same product or service on another medium. Cf. primary medium.

secondary movement Any intended motion of a camera. Cf. primary movement and tertiary movement.

secondary news News of minor importance.

secondary readership *See* secondary audience.

secondary relay An intermediate microwave relay used when a single relay is impossible because of distance or the line-of-sight is physically blocked.

secondary service area The area served by the skywave of an AM station and not subject to objectionable interference, but subject to intermittent variations in intensity.

secondary station Any station in the AM band except a Class I station operating on a clear channel.

secondary transmission In copyright law, the further transmission of a primary transmission simultaneously with the primary transmission. Nonsimultaneous transmission may be considered secondary transmission in Hawaii if the transmission is permitted under the rules and regulations of the FCC.

second assistant director The individual assigned to assist the first assistant director in conducting the business of the set or the location site.

second audio program (SAP) A BTSC encoded monophonic television channel that may be used for a different language, a video service for the blind, weather information, and so on. Also called a *secondary audio program.*

second class A U.S. Postal Service mail classification for newspapers and magazines.

second color A color other than black used in color separation processes.

second coming The largest display type used for newspaper headlines; reserved for news of the highest importance.

second cover The inside front cover of a periodical.

second cycle story *See* follow.

second day lead A newspaper lead for a story carried on any day but the first day.

second day story *See* follow.

second feature The second of two theatrical motion pictures shown on the same bill. Now rare except for less successful motion pictures.

second front The front page of a newspaper's second section. Also called a *second page one* and *split page.* Cf. section page.

second generation □ A technological advance in equipment, hardware, software, and so on, over the original design in speed, ease of operation, power, and so on. Styling changes are not included in this concept. □ A copy of an original or master tape, disc, or film. *See also* generation.

second generation computer The first computers that used transistors instead of vacuum tubes.

second impression The second side of a newspaper page printed on a web press.

Second Mayflower decision A name sometimes given to the Fairness Doctrine.

second page one *See* second front.

second person narration A personal type of narration wherein the viewer is addressed as "you."

second season The television programming season that begins in January with programs to replace those that have not received audience support in the preceding months. Also called the *Spring season.* Cf. season.

second serial rights The rights granted to a magazine or periodical to publish portions of a book after the publication of the book. Cf. first serial rights.

second string The writers, talent, photographers, and so on, who are called in to substitute for individuals on vacation or who are ill.

second unit □ A director and crew assigned to film location scenes. □ A motion picture unit that photographs scenes to be used in a motion picture and requires the services of persons whose actions before the camera need direction.

second unit director The individual in charge of directing a motion picture second unit.

secrecy agreement A compact entered into between the government and individuals or private companies and individuals to protect classified information or trade secrets.

Secretary □ The secretary of an administrative agency such as the FCC. □ A presidential cabinet-level post.

section □ The use of several items to suggest a setting or locale. □ A division of a legislative statute. □ One leg of a relay system. □ Any of three levels of rates for spot television announcements. □ *See* signature.

sectional announcement A network announcement heard or seen in specific geographical areas of the country only. Also called a *cut-in.*

sectional center facility (SCF) A U.S. Postal Service distribution unit comprising different post offices whose ZIP codes start with the same three digits.

sectional feed *See* regional feed.

sectional magazine A magazine intended to appeal to people in one geographical area.

sectional story *See* running story.

section flag A flag on a newspaper section. Also called a *section logo.* Cf. flag.

section logo *See* section flag.

section page The first page of a newspaper section or pullout. Cf. second front.

Section 315 The section of the Communications Act of 1934 that deals with legally qualified candidates for public office. *See also* equal opportunities.

sector □ A section of a track on a magnetic disk where data is stored. □ The smallest unit of absolutely addressable information in a CD-ROM or CD-I disc. A sector contains 2352 sequential bytes with a synchronization pattern, header field, and digital data. It may also contain a subheader and EDC/ECC error protection. *See also* sector structure.

sector address In CD-ROM and CD-I, the physical address of a sector expressed in minutes, seconds, and sector number. Contained in the address part of the sector header.

sectoral horn A loudspeaker horn that is divided into sections.

sector structure In CD-ROM and CD-I, the 2352 sequential bytes of a sector may be divided in one of four ways, depending on the system and the degree of data integrity required. *See also* form 1, form 2, mode 1, and mode 2.

secular priesthood The image some viewers assign to television personalities.

security □ The safety code requirements that specify the number of exits in a place for public performances. □ A motion picture studio or other media police department or guards.

sedition The incitement to resist government authority.

seditious libel Political criticism of the government or its officials.

see copy An instruction to a printer to compare the marked proof to the original.

seeding *See* salting.

seefee A colloquial term for pay television.

seek The action of changing the location of a pointer to another specified location in a CD-ROM disc.

seek latency The delay between a request for search action and arrival at the location sought.

seen/associated Noting or pertaining to ad-noters who claim to have seen a given advertisement and to have recognized the advertiser; used by the research firm of Daniel Starch and Associates.

SEG □ Screen Extras Guild. A union. □ Special effects generator.

seg An abbreviation for *segment.*

segment □ A part of a radio or television program. □ A portion of a computer program or file.

segmentation □ The division of a market into demographic and geographic parts for the purpose of identifying target audiences for advertising campaigns and public relations efforts. Also called *market segmentation.* □ *See* mailing list selection.

segmented □ A computer file that is too large to be contained on one disk and is therefore automatically saved on two or more disks. □ A radio or television program that is sold to advertisers in segments. □ A videotape recorder format that records a half frame of video information in one revolution of a video head. Cf. nonsegmented.

segmented recording In video recording, a technique of using multiple heads on the headwheel and time division multiplexing of each television field into groups of scanning lines (segments) that are recorded in turn by each head. Examples include the quadruplex and Type-B formats.

segmented video A videotape format that records a field of information in two or more passes of the video heads. Cf. nonsegmented.

segment sponsorship *See* participating sponsorship.

segue To dissolve from one musical selection or sound effect to another. Pronounced "seg-way."

segway *See* segue.

SelectaVision A tradename for a home video recording machine formerly produced by RCA. *See also* EVR.

selected take An approved film or video scene or shot.

selection A book, television program, radio station, and so on, chosen from a number of choices.

selection criteria The definition of characteristics that identify segments or subgroups within a mailing list.

selective A periodical of interest to a certain type of reader rather than to the public generally.

selective attention The conscious choice made by a reader or viewer on where to focus attention, such as on a particular portion of a page or television picture. Cf. selective exposure, selective perception, selective reinforcement, and selective retention.

selective clubbing An offer to prospective subscribers of a certain number of magazines from a list at a reduced rate.

selective exposure The choice made by a reader, listener, viewer, and so on, as to whether or not to read, listen to, or view a particular program, speaker, writer, and so on.

selective filter *See* separation filter.

selective focusing *See* rack focusing.

selective magazine A magazine published for persons with special interests. Also called a *special interest magazine* and *specialized magazine.*

selective multiple address radio and television service (SMARTS) Satellite service from RCA that provides earth stations free to broadcasters and then leases satellite transponder time to program suppliers.

selective perception The predisposition of a reader, viewer, or listener to discern that information with which he or she agrees.

selective recall The degree of memory of things experienced that is influenced by preexisting attitudes, subsequent experiences, and so on.

selective reinforcement The conscious choice made by a reader or viewer as to what to read or view that supports attitudes or opinions already held. Cf. selective attention, selective exposure, selective perception, and selective retention.

selective retention The predisposition of a reader, viewer, or listener to retain that information with which he or she agrees. Cf. selective attention, selective exposure, selective perception, and selective reinforcement.

selectivity □ A measure of the degree to which a receiver differentiates between signals from two or more broadcast stations. □ The action that viewers, listeners, or readers take in choosing their content from the mass media.

selector switch system A system that contains one or more multiposition switches to permit one or more conductors to be connected to any of the other conductors. Cf. cross connect circuit and patch panel.

self-administered diary *See* diary.

self-administered questionnaire A questionnaire filled out by a respondent rather than by an interviewer.

self-blimped A motion picture camera containing padded components so that it is comparatively noiseless in operation. *See also* blimp.

self-contained A newspaper or magazine picture without a caption.

self-cover A pamphlet with its cover made of the same kind of paper as the inside pages. May be used as a self-mailer. Also called a *self-wrapper.*

self-mailer A direct mail piece that can be mailed without an envelope. *See also* self-cover.

self-matteing *See* chromakey, matte, and traveling matte.

self-publishing □ *See* desktop publishing. □ *See* vanity publisher.

self-regulation The standards and regulations set by an industry, profession, individual station, network, and so on, itself, as opposed to government or external regulation. Self-regulation is manifested by, for example, the RTNDA code or continuity acceptance departments.

self-represented station A broadcast station that does not use a station representative for national time sales.

self-synchronizing A system that is locked together in synchrony by a Selsyn.

self-test A test of a computer printer wherein all characters stored in ROM are automatically printed.

self-threading □ A tape reel that automatically winds the start of a tape around the hub. □ A projector or camera that automatically winds the film around the takeup reel.

self-wrapper *See* self-cover.

selenium An element having photosensitive properties. Widely used in electronics.

sell □ To present a news story, article, advertising campaign, and so on, to an editor, advertiser, and so on. □ A portion of an advertisement devoted to encouraging a sale of the product or service advertised.

sellathon An auction held by a public television station to raise money for programs and operation.

selling idea An advertising execution element that compellingly summarizes or expresses a creative strategy.

sell-off □ The sale of a broadcasting station when the licensee would exceed the maximum 12–12–12 limit. □ The resale to another advertiser of advertising space or time for which one has contracted.

sellout rate The percentage of radio or television availabilities that are sold.

Selsyn An abbreviation for *self-synchronous*; a tradename for a motor that is used to synchronize sound and picture. Also called an *interlock motor.*

semantic differential A bipolar adjectival scale often used to measure the strength of a respondent's attitudes.

semantic noise Any interference in communication due to misunderstanding.

semantics The study of the meaning of words, forms, symbols, and so on.

semiclassical A type of music or music format characterized by the use of well-known classical compositions.

semiconductor One of a class of materials such as germanium or silicon that conducts electricity at high temperatures and acts as an insulator at low temperatures.

semidirectional microphone A microphone in which the frequency response varies only partially with the angle of incidence of the sound source. *See also* mike pattern.

semimonthly A periodical issued twice a month. Cf. bimonthly.

semiotics The theory of signs, including the study of semantics, syntactics, and pragmatics.

semipilot An unfinished pilot for a television program; complete except for design elements.

semiportable A remote video system that is too complex to be easily carried; usually contained in a van or other vehicle.

semiscripted A radio or television program that is only partially scripted. Cf. ad lib and fully scripted.

semispectacular A painted outdoor advertising bulletin to which special lighting, animation, or three-dimensional features have been added but that does not have the elaboration of a true spectacular. Also called an *embellished painted bulletin.*

semiweekly A periodical issued twice a week. Cf. biweekly.

Senate Interstate Commerce Committee The Senate watchdog committee that oversees FCC activities. *See also* House Interstate and Foreign Commerce Committee.

send down To send newspaper copy to the composing room. Also called *send out.*

sender The originator of a message.

send out *See* send down.

senior A large, 5000-watt spotlight. Also called a *five* and *senior solarspot.* Cf. junior.

senior checker *See* preplanner/checker.

senior solarspot *See* senior.

sensationalism The overemphasis by the mass media of items of a morbid, sexual, or violent nature.

sense □ To perceive a meaning. □ To detect electronic signals. □ To detect the state of a switch setting.

sensing A tape recorder device used to stop a tape or cue another tape in an automatic operation.

sensing foil A metallic material used on a tape for sensing.

sensitivity □ The degree to which a receiver is able to reproduce weak signals. □ A measure of a film emulsion's susceptibility to light. □ The degree to which a television camera is able to produce an acceptable picture under adverse light conditions.

sensitivity control □ The potentiometer on a radio receiver that changes the amplitude of the RF amplifier stages. □ The control in a television camera that changes the size of the iris opening.

sensitized material A general term for any materials that have been made light sensitive, such as film, photographic paper, or plates.

sensitizer A chemical dye that increases a photographic film's sensitivity to light.

sensitometry □ The science of the measurement of light sensitive materials. □ A device used to measure a film emulsion's sensitivity.

sensor □ A detector of some parameter, such as light, heat, or ambient humidity, that may affect or control machine operation. □ *See* paper out sensor.

Sensurround A trademark for a motion picture sound system that produces low frequency vibrations that are felt by an audience.

sentence completion A method for determining preexisting attitudes or information by having a respondent in a survey complete partial sentences.

sep An abbreviation for *separation.*

separate A separately issued copy of an article, essay, and so on.

separation □ The ratio of the signal in the recorded channel to the signal in the unrecorded channel of a stereophonic disc groove. □ The degree of complete isolation of the three colors in television or film. □ The degree to which stereophonic or quadraphonic recording channels are isolated. □ The degree of microphone isolation from other microphones. □ The period of time between two competing commercials. □ The isolation of the three primary colors from full color copy by means of camera filters in preparing four color (including black key) film negatives; used in producing process printing plates.

separation filter One of the three (red, green, or blue) filters used to separate the three primary colors from one another. Used for making separation negatives. Also called a *selective filter* and *tricolor filter.*

separation lighting Lighting used to separate the subject from the background; a back light.

separation negative One of the three black and white negatives made from the three colors of the original color film.

separation of powers The state of government in which the duties and responsibilities of the branches of government do not overlap, but are divided: executive, legislative, and judicial.

separation positive One of the three black and white positives made to retain as a protection master.

separator A short jingle.

sepia □ A type of monotone film or photographic printing paper yielding brown tones instead of gray to black. □ Noting or pertaining to the brown tones characteristic of such photographs.

sepmag An abbreviation for *separate magnetic*; the use of two different film stocks for sound and picture. Also called *double band.*

sepmag projector A projector containing two separate sets of mechanisms, reels, and so on; one for the soundtrack, the other for the picture.

sepopt An abbreviation for *separate optical;* the use of two different film stocks; one for the soundtrack, the other for the picture.

September season That portion of any year commencing at 0100 GMT on the first Sunday in September and ending at 0100 GMT on the first Sunday in November.

seq An abbreviation for *sequence.*

sequel A new theatrical motion picture, novel, and so on, in which the principal characters of the first theatrical motion picture or novel participate in an entirely new and different story. Cf. prequel.

sequel rights The right to use the leading character or characters of a work participating in a substantially different story in an episodic series or serial type filmed television program or radio program.

sequence □ To place or arrange objects in order. □ A series of sounds, pictures, words, programs, and so on. □ An arrangement of selected shots or scenes in a filmed or taped television program or motion picture. □ A series of film or video shots that cover a single event or time period. □ A series of photographs taken at short intervals. □ A series of pages arranged in logical order. □ An arrangement of items according to a specified set of rules or instructions. In direct mailing, it refers generally to a ZIP code or customer number sequence. □ An arrangement of related data. □ A succession of two or more interrelated scenes; the equivalent of a chapter in a novel. □ A group of related scenes in a film that combine to tell a particular portion of the story, and that are usually set in the same location or time span.

sequence outline A written presentation for a proposed motion picture or television program containing a rundown of the plot and action. Sometimes called a *treatment outline.*

sequencer A digital electronic device used in automation to initiate and continue a broadcast sequence.

sequence shot A long, sometimes involved camera shot containing an entire sequence.

sequencing □ A method of recording music by storing a sequence of note parameters in computer memory. □ The order in which programs are placed in a broadcast schedule.

sequential access A method of storing information in which data can be retrieved only in the order it was stored. *See also* serial access. Cf. random access.

sequential color television A color television system wherein the three primary colors are transmitted sequentially. *See also* SECAM.

sequential interlace The method of television interlace in which the lines of one field are positioned between the lines of the other field.

sequential scanning The scanning of a television picture from top to bottom without interlace.

sequester To isolate a jury under court supervision so that they are not influenced by publicity.

ser An abbreviation for *serial.*

serial □ A publication issued in successive parts on a regular and continuing basis, such as newspapers, magazines, and annuals. *See also* periodical. □ A series of films in which generally the same characters carry on a continuing narrative. □ A radio or television program in which a continuing story is presented in installments. *See also* series. □ The sending or receiving of computer information sequentially rather than in parallel.

serial access The transfer of data wherein each bit of information follows the previous bit as compared to parallel transfer.

serial data Data sent by serial transmission.

serial interface *See* interface.

serial operation *See* serial transmission.

serial rights The reprint rights for a book. *See also* first serial rights and second serial rights.

serial service *See* looseleaf service.

serial time code *See* longitudinal time code.

serial transmission A method of data transmission wherein each bit of information is sent sequentially. Cf. parallel transmission.

series □ A group of two or more works that are centered around, and dominated by, the same individual, or that have the same, or substantially the same, cast or principal characters or a continuous theme or plot. □ A circuit in which the same amount of current flows throughout. Cf. parallel. □ The range of fonts in one type family. □ A number of volumes by the same author or publisher, often having the same title and similar subjects. □ A continuing story printed for a number of days in a newspaper.

serif A typeface with fine cross strokes on the letters. Cf. sans serif.

serigraphy *See* silk screen.

serrated The roughly finished edges of a newspaper.

serration A television picture distortion characterized by ragged vertical or almost vertical lines.

service area *See* intermittent service area, primary service area, and secondary service area.

service fee □ The annual license fee for broadcast stations and the annual cable television authorization fee prescribed by the FCC. *See also* filing fee and grant fee. □ An amount paid by an advertiser to an advertising agency, either as a retainer for general services or compensation for unusual services.

service life □ The estimated useful life of a device. □ Lamp life in service as affected by voltage variations, vibrations, shock, excessive heat conditions, and so on. Cf. rated life.

service literature Information sent by direct mail detailing operating and maintenance procedures for products.

service magazine *See* women's publications.

service mark A word or name used in industry and protected under the Federal Trademark Act, such as program titles, character names, or distinctive features. *See also* trademark.

service news Radio station reports on weather, school lunch programs, traffic updates, and so on.

service tier A category of cable service or other services provided by a cable operator and for which a separate rate is charged by the cable operator.

servicing The steps taken to assure advertiser satisfaction after the sale of time or space in a mass medium.

servo An abbreviation for *servomechanism.* An electrical device used to control the speed or motion of different types of interrelated equipment.

servo capstan The servomechanism that controls the motion of the capstan in a videotape recorder.

servo lens A zoom lens in which the focus and zoom controls are driven by a servo.

servomechanism *See* servo.

servo modulator *See* modulator.

servo system The servomechanism that controls the speed of tape movement in an audio- or videotape recorder or player.

SESAC One of the music licensing organizations. Formerly, SESAC stood for the Society of European Stage Authors and Composers. *See also* ASCAP and BMI.

session A meeting of performing talent, such as actors, singers, announcers, and so on, with production personnel for the purpose of creating some form of record of a performance, whether on film, tape, or phonographic record.

session fee A payment made to a musician, performer, singer, dancer, and so on, for recording commercials, music, and so on. A session is normally two or three hours in length, depending on union contracts. Cf. residual and reuse fee.

set □ A complete arrangement of flats, props, backgrounds, furniture, and so on, in which a scene or program takes place. □ To assemble the scenic elements for a program or scene. □ A popular misnomer for a radio or television receiver. □ A predisposition to expect something. Also called *expectancy set.* □ A selection of songs played consecutively by an orchestra, singer, or group. □ The environment in which filmed or taped action takes place. □ To enter the time code on a videotape editing system keyboard. □ To compose or arrange type by hand or machine. Also called *set up.* □ The amount of lateral spacing between letters. □ The prepared stage on which the action for three dimensional animation takes place. A set may be as simple as a plain table top or as elaborate as props and decorations can make it.

set and hold An instruction to set type and hold it for later use.

set around Also called *runaround.*

set aside To overrule or annul a decision.

setback The distance measured from the line of travel to the center of an outdoor advertising structure.

set close To set type with minimum spacing between letters or words. Also called *set tight.*

set color To adjust the ink fountains on a printing press for the proper flow of ink. The term color is used even if the ink is black.

set decorator *See* set dresser.

set designer An individual who designs and supervises the construction of theatrical, motion picture, or television sets.

set dresser An individual responsible for set decoration and prop placement. Also called a *set decorator.*

set dressing The placement and arrangement of the elements, such as props, that lend atmosphere to a set.

set flat *See* flat.

set flush An instruction to a printer to set type even with the left margin without indention.

set light Separate illumination of the background or set other than that provided for principal subjects or areas.

set list An enumeration of the number of sets to be used in a production.

set noise The undesirable noise on a set caused by cameras, switches, wind machines, and so on.

setoff *See* offset.

set open To set lines of type or other matter with leads for extra white space.

set piece A piece of scenery that is self-supporting, such as a ground row, pillar, pylon, periaktos, step unit, or sweep.

set saturation *See* penetration.

set showing An outdoor advertising poster arranged between the plant operator and the advertiser in which the same locations are used for the duration of the contract. Cf. rotating bulletin.

sets-in-use (SIU) An obsolete term for the actual number of radio or television receivers that are being used during some period of time. Cf. sets-in-use rating.

sets-in-use rating An obsolete term for the percentage of some specified group of radio or television receivers that are being used during some period of time. Cf. sets-in-use (SIU).

set size *See* set width.

set solid To set lines of type without leads between the lines.

set tight *See* set close.

setting The physical surroundings and music or sound effects used to create an atmosphere for a production.

setting up □ The positioning of the camera, cels, compound, and so on, in preparation for an animation shot. □ To furnish information to an audience about a future action in a play, motion picture, and so on.

set up □ The ratio between the reference black level and reference white level as measured from the blanking level in a television system. □ To prepare a disc or tape for playing. □ To position cameras, microphones, and so on. □ To mount, aim, and focus luminaires. □ *See* set.

setup day The day or days scheduled for the construction of a set in a studio.

set width The width of typeface characters; based on em measurement. Also called *set size. See also* relative units.

seven dirty words The seven words from a 1978 George Carlin album that led to at least one definition of indecent.

7-1/2 ips The preferred speed for audiotape recording. Cf. supplementary tape speeds.

750 A small spotlight.

seven seven seven rule *See* multiple ownership.

78 rpm The former standard disc speed; actually 78.26 rpm. The preferred speeds are now 33-1/3 and 45 rpm.

seventy-mm film Currently, the largest size of motion picture film; used for wide-screen processes.

sewing A means of holding book pages together. Cf. stitching.

sexploitation film An abbreviation of *sex* and *exploitation.* A motion picture designed to appeal to prurient interests. *See also* pornographic film.

SF Soft focus.

SFX Sound effects. Also SE.

SH Specified hours.

shade □ In pigments, a color less than medium gray in brilliance, and one often low in saturation. □ To eliminate false signals and exaggerated contrast from a television image. □ To change the hue of a color by adding black.

shaded Noting or pertaining to display type having certain strokes repeated so that a three-dimensional effect is produced.

shader A broadcast technician, sometimes the technical director, who balances and peaks the cameras during a performance. Also called a *shaker* or *video engineer.*

shading □ The spurious variations in the brightness gradient of a television picture generated by the camera pickup tube. □ To control the spurious signals. □ In make-up, the grayed or shadow colors. Cf. countershading.

shading sheet A piece of transparent plastic with any one of numerous patterned surfaces for adding gray tones to a line cut.

shading tints *See* Benday.

shadow area The geographical area in which radio or television signals are subject to reflections or degradations in strength.

shadow box □ A device mounted around a screen to shield it from light. □ A device used to show two or more title cards or pictures at one time by the use of mirrors.

shadow cable An unused cable television system cable that is reserved for future use, such as interactive communication.

shadowing The use of luminaires to create a desired shadow.

shadow mask *See* aperture mask.

shake A blur in printing caused by vibration.

shaker *See* shader.

shallow A narrow depth of field.

shallow focus The use of a narrow depth of field to place one performer or object in sharp focus, the other performers or objects out of focus. Cf. deep focus.

shank □ The portion of a stylus that is attached to the cartridge. □ The rectangular main body of metal type.

shape To change the quality of a sound with a filter.

share The size of a station's audience expressed as a percent of the total viewing audience. The calculation includes those households tuned to a specific station or programming service divided by the total number of homes using television for a daypart or program. Also called *share of audience.* Cf. rating.

shared ID A station ID containing commercial copy.

shared screen A television station identification that contains the ID on a portion of the screen; the other portion is used by an advertiser or sponsor. Cf. full screen.

shared system A multiuser computer system.

share of audience *See* share.

share of viewing hours The total hours that noncable television households viewed the subject station during the week, expressed as a percentage of the total hours these households viewed all stations during the period. *See also* significantly viewed.

share point A share, as of market or audience, equal to one percent of the total.

sharing time (S) A division of time between or among one or more other radio stations using the same AM channel.

sharp A camera shot or print that is crisply outlined and in complete focus. Cf. soft.

sharpening The process of electronically peaking a television picture. Also called *crispening.*

sharpness control The television receiver control that adjusts picture definition.

shave A slang term for a percentage of the house receipts paid to performers.

SHB Super highband.

sheave A grooved pulley wheel used for scenery lines.

shedding □ The loss of magnetic coating from a tape, especially in small flakes. □ The resulting picture impairment caused by this damage. *See also* dropout.

sheet □ An individual piece of paper made for writing or printing. □ A slang term for a newspaper. □ An obsolete size of outdoor display advertising. A 24-sheet display covers a standard billboard. □ An outdoor advertising poster size. A one-sheet is actually one sheet measuring the full dimensions of an advertising poster. The original one-sheet was 28 inches by 41 inches in size. One-sheets were combined to make larger posters to fit different size frames. A two-sheet is produced on one sheet; a three-sheet is produced on two sheets. Other posters have lost their original relationship of name to sheets. The 24-sheet poster was originally designated because the complete poster was made up of 24 separate sheets. Today, the number of sheets used are determined by the press size and the artwork. The 24-sheet posters are usually cut in sheet layouts known as 10-sheet or 12-sheet layouts. A 30-sheet poster is often cut in 11-sheet layouts. In general practice, the number of separate sheets range from 8 to 14.

sheetage The ratio of the surface area of a sheet to its weight.

sheet fed A printing press that accepts single sheets of paper. Cf. web fed.

sheet film Film that is cut into individual pieces for use. Also called *cut film* and *flat film*. Cf. roll film.

sheet imposition *See* sheetwise.

sheets The unbound pages of a book.

sheetwise The process of printing the two sides of a sheet from different forms. Also called *sheet imposition*. Cf. work and turn.

sheetwork The work done in binding a book, from the printing to the sewing.

shelfback *See* backbone.

shelf life □ The period of time that batteries, photographic materials, and so on, remain usable. □ The period of time that news, advertising, and other timely material are usable.

shell □ The outer covering of a plug or jack. □ The metal case that contains a phonograph cartridge.

shellac □ The material that was used in the manufacture of 78 rpm discs. □ A colloquial term for a 78 rpm disc.

shelter A book or magazine that features home furnishings, decoration, and the like.

shelter magazine *See* home service book.

Sherman Antitrust Act *See* antitrust laws.

SHF Super high frequency.

shield A metal plate or other material placed around a component to reduce the effects of electric or magnetic fields.

shielded cable A cable surrounded by a metallic sheath in order to decrease the effects of stray electrical or magnetic fields.

shielded pair A two-wire conductor surrounded by a metallic sheath.

shielding A metal covering used on a cable, wire, or component to protect it from undesirable radiation, hum, stray magnetic fields, and so on.

shield laws The various laws that protect a reporter's source of information. The right of a reporter to refuse a court order to disclose his or her source of information is not absolute and the laws vary from state to state.

shift □ The period of time an individual is assigned to work during a day. □ *See* board shift. □ A displacement in time, phase, color, and so on. □ To move type to the left or right.

shim A piece of non-metallic material placed in the head gaps of magnetic tape recorders.

shimmer dissolve A wavy dissolve sometimes used to signify a flashback.

shipping instructions An itemized list of shipping information for the use of lithographers in shipping posters to outdoor advertising plants.

shirttail □ A short item added to a news story. □ *See* follow.

SHL Studio to headend link.

shock The use of an unexpected sound, music, or picture to attract immediate viewer attention. Also called a *shocker*.

shocker *See* shock.

shock jock A shock radio disc jockey.

shock mount A resilient support for microphones that helps isolate them from mechanical movement.

shock radio A late 1980s name for radio stations that broadcast raunchy, usually sexually indecent, material.

shoehorn A slang term for adding a visual to an already crowded advertisement.

shoot To film or tape.

shoot around To continue to film or tape a production without the services of one of the necessary characters. Often done if an actor or actress is ill.

shooter A slang term for a camera operator.

shooting breakdown *See* shot sheet.

shooting call *See* call.

shooting date The day scheduled to tape or film a program, scene, and so on.

shooting log *See* shooting schedule.

shooting off To show an area beyond the horizontal limits of a television set.

shooting over To show an area above the vertical limits of a television set.

shooting ratio The ratio between the amount of film or tape shot and the amount used in the edited motion picture or program.

shooting schedule The order and timing of the scenes in a motion picture or television program, without regard to their sequence in the finished product. Also called a *shooting log.* Cf. shot sheet.

shooting script The script from which a motion picture, television program, commercial, and so on, is made. Contains extensive details as to the action, shots, and so on. Also called a *director's script* and *master script.*

shooting sequence The order in which scenes in a production are to be filmed or taped. *See also* shooting schedule.

shooting speed The number of frames per second a motion picture camera is set to record.

shooting the blue A chromakey shot.

shooting wild *See* wild sound.

shootoff *See* border.

shoot on spec *See* on spec.

shopper *See* shopping newspaper and throwaway.

shopping The submission of literary material to a third party or parties.

shopping channel A cable television channel devoted to shop-at-home services. Merchandise is displayed on the screen and viewers are given an 800 number to call for ordering.

shopping newspaper A newspaper primarily edited for local shoppers, containing advertisements, information about local events, and so on. Also called a *controlled circulation newspaper, shopper,* and *throwaway.*

short □ An accidental or undesired low resistance connection made in a circuit that causes component damage, a blown fuse, or tripped circuit breaker. Also called a *short circuit.* □ A motion picture that usually runs between 5 and 30 minutes. Formerly used as a prelude to the main feature in a motion picture theatre. Also called a *featurette* and *short subject.* Cf. feature. □ According to the Director's Guild of America, any picture that when released is 2700 lineal feet or less in length on 35-mm film, or 1080 lineal feet or less in length on 16-mm film. Cf. short subject. □ A brief film or tape used as a filler. □ A brief news story or filler. □ The copies of the different sheets necessary to complete a signature or book. □ A brief radio or television program. □ The term often refers to the cartoons made in the Hollywood studios during the 1930s, 1940s, and 1950s, which ran between 6 and 7 minutes long. Today, shorts range from 1-1/2 to over 20 minutes in length and cover a variety of styles and subjects.

short and A slang term for an ampersand.

short approach An outdoor advertising space position value factor specifically applied to a poster panel that is fully visible for 40 to 75 feet to pedestrian traffic; 100 to 200 feet to traffic moving faster than 35 miles per hour, and 75 to 150 feet to traffic moving slower than 35 miles per hour. Cf. long approach and medium approach.

short circuit *See* short.

short discount The small discount allowed for items not usually sold at wholesale.

short end A leftover piece of film in a magazine. Also called a *tail.*

short focal length lens A wide-angle lens; one that has a focal length less than the diagonal size of the film or camera tube. Also called a *short focus lens* and *short lens.* Cf. long focal length lens.

short focus lens *See* short focal length lens.

short form A television program generally less than 30 minutes in length. Cf. long form.

short lens *See* short focal length lens.

shorthand □ Any system of abbreviated notation. □ A term sometimes used for *macro.*

short handle posting A method of outdoor advertising posting in which the poster hanger works from a scaffold hung against the face of the panel and posts the paper with a short handled brush.

short pitch film Motion picture negative film that has its perforations spaced slightly closer than normal.

short rate An additional charge incurred by an advertiser when insufficient space is purchased to meet the contractual obligation.

shorts *See* short and short subject.

short short An article that fills up less than the equivalent of one page in a magazine.

short-spaced assignments Broadcast assignments or allotments that are spaced closer together than originally planned by the original Table of Assignments.

shortstop *See* stop bath.

short subject According to the Writer's Guild of America, a motion pictures that when released is 3600 lineal feet or less in length. Cf. short.

short take A brief piece of copy set into type.

short-term license A broadcast license issued by the FCC for less than the normal license period. A form of sanction. Also called a *short term renewal. See also* conditional renewal.

short-term renewal *See* short term license.

short-term subscription A periodical subscription of less than one year.

short-title catalog (STC) An abbreviation for a two-volume list of books published in England, Scotland, Ireland, Wales, British America, and other English books printed from 1475 to 1700.

short voice An individual with a restricted speaking or singing range.

short wave (SW) The high-frequency broadcast bands (6 to 21 megahertz) used for international long distance AM broadcasting. *See also* seasonal schedule.

shot □ A slang term that refers to an outdoor advertising structure, either a poster or bulletin. □ The noise responsible for audio hiss or video grass or snow. □ A worn-out component. □ A continuous piece of film or tape containing a single series of pictures, uncut and uninterrupted. Generally synonymous with the term *scene. See also* camera shots.

shot box □ The preset controls for a zoom lens. □ *See* Bretz box.

shot breakdown *See* shot sheet.

shot card *See* shot sheet.

shotgun approach A generalized method of newswriting that does not present specific information. Cf. rifle approach.

shotgun interview An interview made by a reporter without an appointment; often of an unwilling or reluctant subject.

shotgun microphone An ultracardioid microphone with a highly directional pickup pattern used to gather sound from a distance. Also called a *gun microphone* and a *rifle.*

shot list *See* shot sheet.

shot sheet □ A cinematographer's or camera operator's printed list of shots for a production. Also called a *breakdown sheet, camera script, crib card, crib sheet, scene sheet, shooting breakdown, shot breakdown, shot card,* and *shot list.* □ Any list of shots, sequences, lines, and so on.

shoulder The upper surface of a type body on which the character rests.

shoulder brace *See* shoulder pod.

shoulder mount *See* shoulder pod.

shoulder note A note printed at the top outer edge of a page.

shoulder pod A camera support designed to brace a camera on an operator's shoulder. Also called a *shoulder brace* and *shoulder mount.* Cf. body pod.

shoulders *See* horns.

shoulder shot A camera shot taken from the shoulders of the subject to just above the head. Cf. over-the-shoulder shot.

shout A slang term for an exclamation point.

shout shop A slang term for an advertising agency.

show A radio or television program.

show bill A large advertising poster containing information about a play, motion picture, and so on.

show biz □ A slang term for the entertainment industry. Also called *show business.* □ A somewhat derogatory term for a radio or television newscast that overemphasizes entertainment.

show board A small outdoor advertising billboard.

showboating The increase in attention or in extreme cases, the change in behavior of judges, legislators, witnesses, and other people caused by the mere presence of television cameras in a courtroom, legislative chamber, and so on.

show business *See* show biz.

show card □ A hand-lettered poster. □ A small advertising placard.

showcase To exhibit one of a number of motion pictures.

show cause order An order from the FCC to a licensee to give reasons for actions taken by the licensee. A show cause order must be issued before a cease and desist order is issued or revocation proceedings are instituted.

show copy *See* show print.

show curtain *See* curtain.

showing □ A single presentation of a motion picture, tape, film, and so on. □ A number of outdoor advertisements offered as a unit. Cf. intensity. □ A number of transit advertisements, especially car cards, offered as a unit. Also called a *run.* □ The total number of panels in an outdoor advertising buy. The common advertising weight is #100, #75, #50, and #25 showings or better defined as gross rating points, which relate directly to the population of a market. For example, a #50 showing will deliver 500,000 daily exposures in a market with one million people in it. A showing size does not indicate the number of poster panels utilized.

showmanship The quality or ability to produce, direct, act, and so on, with aural and visual effectiveness.

show print □ A British term for a motion picture release print. Also called a *show copy.* □ *See* release print.

show reel A portfolio of a filmmaker, animator, actor, and so on, demonstrating the quality of his or her work.

show stopper A performance that exceeds expectations; usually followed by prolonged applause.

show through □ Colors from a previous outdoor advertising poster that show through the current poster. In most cases, this is caused by printing posters on stock that is not up to standard specifications. □ Printed matter that is seen from the back of a page because of a lack of paper opacity.

shrinkage □ The loss in length and width of motion picture film due to processing and time. □ The reduction in size during molding and drying of a matrix from which printing plates are cast; requires overdimensioning of the original if final agate line size is to be retained.

shutter □ Movable metal gates used within a lighting device or projector to block light, such as the elements used to shape the beam of an ellipsoidal spotlight. □ The mechanical or optical device in a film camera or projector that eliminates the light while the film is moving.

shutter angle The angle of the wedge-shaped sector or sectors of a shutter.

shutter bar A horizontal line that moves up or down in a television picture. Also called a *shuttle bar.*

shutter control A mechanism used to control the shutter angle.

shutter efficiency The ratio of the amount of light a shutter transmits to the amount of light it would transmit if it were continuously open.

shutter mirror A camera mirror used to deflect light to a viewfinder during the pulldown period.

shutter release A mechanical device used to open and close a camera shutter from a short distance.

shutter speed The length of time that a shutter remains open for the transmission of light. Also called *shutter time.*

shutter time *See* shutter speed.

shuttle □ To fast forward and rewind tape in order to relax it before recording. □ To move a tape rapidly backward and forward, usually while reproducing the audio record, for cueing purposes. □ The camera mechanism that holds the film in place during exposure.

shuttle bar *See* shutter bar.

shuttle pin The protrusion in a camera shuttle that engages the film perforations during pulldown.

shuttle time The length of time it takes to move a tape to a desired point on the tape.

SI □ Sponsor identification. □ Station identification.

SIA Storage Instantaneous Audimeter.

SIAC State Industry Advisory Committee. A part of the EBS system.

SIA dailies Daily reports based on Nielsen Television Index Audimeters, providing household audience estimates for network television programs, generally 36 hours after telecast.

sibilance The production of accented *S* sounds in speech.

SIC Standard Industrial Classification.

sic From the Latin for "correct."

SID Society for Information Display.

side □ A single speech in a script. □ A portion of a script containing one performer's lines and cues. □ One side of a phonograph recording. *See also* flip side. □ The front or back cover of a book. □ One surface of a folded sheet. □ To apply covers to a book.

side back light Illumination of the subject from behind to produce a highlight along its pictured edge; light is from a direction substantially not parallel to a vertical plane through the optical axis of the camera or view. *See also* light.

sideband The frequency band on each side of the carrier frequency caused by the modulation of the carrier wave.

sidebar □ A secondary story that elaborates on another, more prominent news story. Also called a *side story* and *with story.* □ A steel bar used to lock the side of a type form. □ A news wire story written as a follow up but that may be used without reference to the original story.

side bind *See* side stitch.

side-by-side shot *See* half-lap.

side drift A defect in a zoom lens that causes an object to become off center during a zoom.

side head □ A heading set flush to the left margin. □ A heading that is run in to text matter. Also called a *sidesaddle.*

sidelight A sidebar that deals with information about the person or organization covered in the main story.

side light Lighting from the side to enhance subject modeling and place the subject in depth; apparently separated from the background. *See also* kicker.

sideline musician An individual who is engaged to mime the playing of a musical instrument.

side note A marginal note. *See also* marginalia.

side panels □ The area of a wide-screen television or motion picture image that is cut off when shown on standard television. □ The areas in some advanced television systems (ATV) that are transmitted separately to form the complete picture at the receiver.

side position □ In transit advertising, a car card placement above the side windows of a vehicle; the common position. □ The position of advertising posters on either side of the exterior of a public transit vehicle.

side saddle *See* side head.

side stitch □ A type of binding used in some books in which wire staples are inserted through the side of the book. Also called *side wiring.* Cf. saddle stitch. □ To bind a magazine, pamphlet, or booklet by stapling or sewing the folded sheets next to the edge of the fold, on the outside. Also called *side bind.* Cf. saddle stitch.

side story *See* sidebar.

side thrust The radial component of force on a pickup arm caused by stylus drag.

sidetone The reception of one's own voice in a headset.

side wiring *See* side stitch.

Sidney Hillman Awards An annual series of prizes to honor works in civil liberties, race relations, social welfare, world understanding, and so on.

sig An abbreviation for *signal* and *signature.*

sigalert A traffic advisory from the highway patrol or other police unit.

sight cue A cue given by the action of a performer.

sight gag A nonverbal piece of stage business, such as a pratfall. Also called a *visual gag.*

sight lines The maximum angles from which an audience may view a motion picture, television screen, play, and so on.

Sigma Delta Chi (SDX) The Society of Professional Journalists. A professional journalism fraternity of publishers, editors, and reporters.

Sigma Delta Chi Awards Annual awards given by the Society of Professional Journalists/Sigma Delta Chi, for distinguished service in print and broadcast journalism.

sign □ An ideographic mark, abbreviation, design, picture, and so on, used to identify a person or organization. □ A gesture, as in pantomime. □ To communicate by signing, as in a visual language. □ A generic term for billboards, transit cards, posters, and so on.

signage A series of signs of varying content but sharing a common design system.

signal □ The audible or visible intelligence or message to be transmitted. □ A modulating current. □ A modulated, transmitted electromagnetic wave. □ A cue. □ The medium of communication.

signal area The geographical area in which a broadcast station's signal can be received with regularity.

signal carriage Stations that are carried by a cable television system, including local stations that request carriage by system, plus stations that are significantly viewed off-air within the community, plus distant signals imported by the system.

signal contour *See* contour.

signal converter An electronic device or circuit that changes one form of signal to another, as analog to digital, downconverter, and so on.

signal distortion *See* distortion.

signal fading The attenuation of a signal due to atmospheric conditions.

signal generator An electronic device used to produce a standard voltage for test purposes.

signal grade Any of several degrees of signal strength in various parts of a radio or television station coverage area.

signal importation Carriage of station signals originating outside the specified zone in which the cable community is located.

signaling A process of informing a receiver that a message is to be transmitted.

signaling rate The rate at which signals are transmitted.

signal level The amplitude of a signal, often expressed in decibels.

signal processor An electronic device or circuit that changes the amplitude, frequency, phase, and so on, of a signal.

signal range The distance from an antenna that a broadcast signal can be received. The range depends on the power of the station, the antenna height, antenna gain, atmospheric conditions, the frequency of the carrier wave, ground conductivity, and so on.

signals The bells used by the wire services to indicate a bulletin.

signal service zone The primary service area of a radio or television station.

signal strength The intensity of a signal at a given distance from an antenna, usually expressed in millivolts per meter.

signal-to-interference ratio The signal strength of a radio or television station necessary to blank out cochannel or adjacent channel signals.

signal-to-noise ratio (S/N)(SNR) The ratio, usually expressed in decibels, between the signal and the noise levels in a component, amplifier, transmitter, receiver, and so on.

signatory An advertising agency, network, station, motion picture studio, and so on, that has signed a union contract.

signature □ A folded sheet containing 4, 8, 12, 16, and so on, pages that are folded to form a part of a book or pamphlet. Also called a *section.* □ A letter or figure placed at the bottom of the first page of a signature to assist in gathering. Also called a *signature mark.* □ A logo used in an advertisement.

signature (sig) □ A musical theme or sound effect used on a program or commercial. Abbreviated *sig.* Cf. theme song. □ A logo. □ A musical theme at the beginning or end, or both, of a television program.

signature mark *See* signature.

significance level *See* statistical significance.

significant interest A cognizable interest for attributing interests in broadcast, cable, and newspaper properties pursuant to *FCC Rules and Regulations.*

significantly viewed Television signals that are viewed in other than cable television households as follows: for a full or partial network station, a share of viewing hours of at least 3 percent (total week hours), and a net weekly circulation of at least 25 percent; and for an independent station, a share of viewing hours of at least 2 percent (total week hours), and a net weekly circulation of at least 5 percent.

sign language The gestures used to indicate commands or questions between radio or television control room personnel and studio personnel or between a floor manager and talent.

sign off □ The time a broadcast day ends. □ The announcement made at the end of a broadcast day. □ The announcement made at the end of a program. □ To terminate a communication from a terminal to a computer system. Also called *log off.*

sign on □ The time a broadcast day begins. □ The announcement made at the beginning of a broadcast day. □ The announcement made at the beginning of a program. □ To begin a communication from a terminal to a computer system. Also called *log on.*

SII Sponsor identification index.

sil A script abbreviation for *silent.*

silence The absence of sound or noise.

silence alarm A non-audible alarm used in automation radio.

silent A film or videotape without a soundtrack. Abbreviated *sil. See also* MOS.

silent bit An extra player performing pantomime of such significance that it portrays a point essential to the staging of the scene involved.

silent film *See* silent.

silent night The one night a week when local radio stations signed off the air so that listeners might receive distant signals. The practice was discontinued in the 1920s.

silent speed The exposure and projection rate of 16 frames per second. Most silent film is shot at the standard sound speed of 24 frames per second. Cf. sound speed.

silent zone The geographical area between the maximum range of a ground wave and the minimum range of a sky wave. Also called *skip zone* and *zone of silence.*

silhouette □ A halftone in which the background has been cut away or otherwise eliminated. Also called an *outline, outlined cut, outline halftone,* and *silhouette halftone.* Cf. vignette. □ The lighting of a subject or object from behind so that little or no detail may be discerned. Cf. limbo.

silhouette animation A type of cutout animation in which only the shapes of the figures are shown against a background; brought to its highest development by Lotte Reiniger.

silhouette halftone *See* silhouette.

silica gel A desiccator used to reduce the moisture absorbed by equipment.

silicon A metallic element used as a semiconductor.

silicon controlled rectifier (SCR) A solid state semiconductor device that operates as a high-speed switch for most modern lighting dimmers.

silk A material formerly used as a light diffuser.

silk screen A printing process that may be used for graphics and posters. In the process, ink is passed through unblocked areas on a silk screen onto an area to be printed. Also called *serigraphy.*

silly season The time of year, often late summer, when newspapers resort to reporting inconsequential matters because of a lack of important news.

silver An element used in the production of the halogen salts for photographic emulsions, such as silver bromide, chloride, and iodide.

Silver Anvil Award An award given by the Public Relations Society of America, Inc., for outstanding public relations programs.

silver halide A general term for any of the halogens used in a compound with silver. *See also* silver.

silvering In disc recording, the process wherein the lacquer original is metallized by precipitating onto this surface the metallic silver in ammoniated silver nitrate.

Silver Medal Award, The An award given by the Audio Engineering Society to recognize an outstanding development in the field of audio engineering.

silver nitrate A chemical compound used in intensifiers and sensitizers.

silver print □ A final proof of a negative for an offset plate. Also called a *blue* and *Vandyke*. □ A photographic print on paper covered with silver salts and used for making pen and ink drawings for engravings.

silver screen A name originally applied to glamorize the motion picture industry.

silver spraying In disc recording, metallizing the lacquer original using a dual spray nozzle wherein the ammoniated silver nitrate and reducer are combined in an atomized spray to precipitate the metallic silver.

Simmons Market Research Bureau, Inc. (SMRB) A service that reports multimedia viewership by users of products and product categories.

simple random sample A survey sample in which each element and all possible equal-sized combinations of elements have an equal chance of selection. *See also* probability sample.

simple tape *See* idiot tape.

simple tone A tone without harmonics. Also called a *pure tone*.

simplex A communication channel capable of transmission in only one direction at a time. Cf. duplex and half duplex.

simplex operation The operating method in which transmission is made possible alternately in each direction of a telecommunication channel, such as by means of manual control.

simplified renewal application The one page form (303-S) filed with the FCC for license renewal. Also called *postcard renewal*.

SIMPP Society of Independent Motion Picture Producers.

simulation □ A computerized representation of a real-time action. □ A mockup of how a CD-I application will play, using whatever hardware and software may be necessary.

simulcast The broadcast of a single performance of a program by radio or television, whether or not the radio and television broadcasts are made at the same time, provided that the original broadcasts by radio and television take place within twenty-one days of each other.

simulcasting □ The broadcasting of a program over AM and FM stations simultaneously to provide for the two channels necessary for stereophonic reproduction. Now obsolete since the advent of stereo radio. □ The broadcasting of a program over a radio and a television station simultaneously.

simulkine A kinescope recording made at the same time as a videotape recording.

simultaneous contrast The perception resulting from the placing of two colors side-by-side, as when a medium shade appears lighter against a dark background, complementary colors appear brighter than noncomplementary colors, and so on.

simultaneous program substitution A form of protection favoring Canadian broadcasters who are carrying U.S. programs. Should a Canadian and U.S. station telecast the same episode of a program, the Canadian station has the right to ask cable companies to replace the American identification and commercials with Canadian.

simultaneous publication The publication of hardbound and softbound covers at the same time.

simultaneous submission The presentation of a manuscript, script, and so on, to two or more publishers, producers, and so on, at the same time.

simultaneous transmission The transmission of data between two points in both directions at the same time. *See also* full duplex.

Sindlinger and Company An audience research company that utilizes telephone interviews on a national basis.

sine qua non Latin for without which not; an absolutely indispensable part.

sine wave A wave that can be graphically expressed as the trigonometric sine of a linear function of time or space, or both.

sing A spurious high-frequency audio noise.

singing commercial A commercial set to music. Also called a *jingle.*

single □ A camera shot of one individual or object. Also called a *one shot.* □ A phonograph disc containing one song on each side. Cf. album. □ A performer who works alone.

single broad A rectangular floodlight.

single camera production A production in which one camera is used. Angles and shots are varied by camera movement during and between shots.

single card A screen credit that contains only one name in the frame.

single chain A program or news story that uses only one film chain. Cf. double chain.

single channel antenna An antenna with elements cut to respond at maximum efficiency to one frequency. Cf. multiband antenna.

single column *See* SC.

single copy order plan (SCOP) *See* single title order plan (STOP).

single copy sales Newsstand sales of periodicals.

single 8 An obsolete size of narrow gauge film; now replaced by super 8.

single field *See* single frame exposure.

single frame *See* single frame exposure.

single frame animation *See* single frame exposure.

single frame exposure The exposure of a single frame of film at a time, as opposed to running the film through the camera continuously. Used extensively in animation. Also called *single framing.* In television, the effect may be accomplished by single frame or single field.

single frame photography The exposure of one frame of film at a time, as opposed to live-action photography. Also called *stop motion photography.*

single frame release A motion picture camera control that allows single frame exposures.

single framing *See* single frame exposure.

single gun A color television picture tube that uses only one electron gun to illuminate the three color phosphors sequentially.

single instance rule The judicial opinion that defamation does not normally occur in a single statement that someone has made a mistake or error.

single lens reflex (SLR) A film camera in which the viewfinder moves out of the light path just before the picture is taken.

single medium system In computers, a system architecture based on the use of a single medium that carries all the software needed for a given application. In CD-I for example, all the program data (video, sound, text, and computer), application, and driver software is held on the CD-I disc itself. Only the basic operating system kernel is stored in ROM in the base case CD-I player external to the disc. Cf. multimedia system.

single perf An abbreviation for *single perf.*

single perforation A film with perforations along one edge and a soundtrack on the other edge. Often abbreviated *single perf.* Cf. double perforation.

single phase An alternating current circuit in which two wires (plus a ground wire) are 180 degrees out of phase.

single publication rule The judicial opinion that holds that defamation occurs only once regardless of the number of copies that are circulated.

single rate card A radio or television rate card that does not differentiate between national and local rates.

single roll editing The editing of A and B rolls into one single roll.

single-sideband emission An amplitude modulated emission with one sideband only.

single sideband transmission (SSB) The transmission of one sideband and the suppression of the other sideband.

single system The process of recording both sound and picture on the same film or videotape. Also called *single system recording* and *single system sound.* Cf. double system.

single system sound camera A film camera in which the picture and sound are recorded on the same length of film.

single title order plan (STOP) A system designed by the American Bookseller's Association to minimize handling on special orders for single titles through the use of a special form available from the ABA. Formerly called Single Copy Order Plan (SCOP).

single track *See* monaural recorder.

single unit A filmed television program intended for broadcast as a single show or program, and not as a part of a unit series or episodic series.

single width A press the width of two plates.

sink *See* sinkage.

sinkage The distance from the top of a page to the heading or first line of type. Also called *sink.*

SINPO code A rating that indicates the reception quality of a signal, its strength, interference, noise, propagation, and overall merit on a scale of one to five in each category.

sinusoidal A wave, such as ordinary alternating current, that varies with the sine of an angle.

SIP □ Station independence program. □ Society of Independent Producers.

siphoning The purchase of special events, sports, movies, and so on, that are seen on commercial television by cable television and pay television operations.

SIRSA Special Industrial Radio Service Association, Inc.

sister media The other types of the mass media in addition to the one being referred to: radio, television, print, motion pictures, and so on.

sister station A broadcast station under common ownership with another.

SIT Silicon intensifier target. A low-bloom television camera pickup tube.

sit □ A substitute copy editor. Also called a *sit in.* □ An abbreviation for a *situation wanted advertisement.*

sitcom An abbreviation for *situation comedy.*

SITE Satellite instructional television experiment.

sit in *See* sit.

sitting microphone A microphone mounted on a table or desk.

situation □ The combination of circumstances surrounding the characters in a plot. □ A plot conflict that is to be resolved.

situation comedy A dramatic program with continuing characters that derives its comedy from the interaction of its characters and from their reactions to normal, unusual, or ridiculous predicaments. Each episode is usually complete in itself. Usually abbreviated *sitcom.*

situationer A news story that contains sufficient information to explain complex situations.

situation show A radio or television program, often ad lib, based on the circumstances of the moment.

SIU Sets-in-use.

625 lines The international standard for the number of lines in a television frame.

six sheet poster panel An outdoor advertising poster panel 5 feet 4 inches high by 11 feet 7 inches wide.

16-mm A standard gauge of film; used by amateurs and professionals alike. Formerly used for television news until the advent of ENG cameras and recorders. Cf. standard film and super-8.

16-mm release A motion picture release print made on 16-mm film.

sixteenmo A book made up of sheets with sixteen leaves.

Sixth Amendment The Sixth Amendment of the Constitution of the United States that provides for a fair trial for the accused. *See also* First Amendment and Fourteenth Amendment.

Sixth Report and Order The FCC report that ended the television licensing Freeze in 1952, and, among other items, allocated the frequencies to be used for UHF television.

sixty *See* sixty seconds.

sixty-cycle current The standard alternating current frequency in the United States.

65-mm film A gauge of film used for wide-screen photography. Usually used to make 70-mm positive release prints.

sixtyfourmo A book made up of sheets with sixty four leaves.

sixty seconds One of the standard spot lengths on radio or television. Others are 10, 15, 20, and 30 seconds.

size control The control that varies the horizontal or vertical dimension of a television picture.

sized (S) Paper that has been chemically treated to make it smooth. *See also* calendered.

sized and supercalendered (S and SC) A finely finished book paper. *See also* supercalendered.

sizing □ A glue used on paper to make it impermeable to water. □ A glue that is used to prepare flats for painting.

skating The unwanted, fast movement of a turntable tonearm across a record. Often caused by insufficient stylus pressure.

sked An abbreviation for *schedule*.

skeletonize News copy that was sent by wire with unnecessary words eliminated.

sketch A self-contained dramatic unit having a plot and constituting fifty percent or less of the entertainment portion of a "comedy-variety" program, provided that such is either an adaptation of material previously used in television or any other medium; or original and written to fit the special talents and personality of the particular actor or actors in the film involved. Cf. routine.

sketch dummy A page dummy.

skew □ The angle between the center line of a tape head gap and a line perpendicular to the tape center line. □ To italicize characters with a word processing program.

skewed distribution An asymmetrical frequency distribution in which the mode and the mean do not correspond.

skewing The zig-zag distortion caused by improper horizontal alignment in a television receiver.

skid □ A small triangular, wheeled platform used to mount camera tripods. □ A wooden platform used to move large quantities of paper.

skimming Advertising or programming that is directed to high income households.

skin flick A motion picture that displays generous portions of the human anatomy. Often a pornographic motion picture. Also called a *nudie*.

skip distance The distance from a transmitter where the reflected sky wave can be received. Cf. silent zone.

skip fading The fading of a sky wave caused by variations in the density of the ionosphere.

skip field The recording of every second field in a helical scan recorder with two heads. Playback is accomplished by playing back each field twice.

skip frame The process of printing every other frame or selected frames in a film in order to double the effective action or shorten a film. Also called a *skip print*. *See also* step frame.

skip-interval A number, k, that represents the ratio of the number of sampling units in the frame to the number of sampling units to be selected for the sample. *See also* systematic selection sample.

skipping *See* strobing.

skip print *See* skip frame.

skip zone *See* silent zone.

skiver An inexpensive sheepskin used in bookbinding.

skull shot A slang term for a closeup containing a performer's head movements or reactions.

sky cloth A British term for a cyclorama.

sky cyc A tightly-stretched cyclorama.

sky filter A graduated filter used to darken the sky on black and white film.

sky hook A luminaire or microphone mount hung from the ceiling of a studio.

skylight Reflected sunlight.

sky light *See* sky pan.

skylight filter An ultraviolet filter used to eliminate the blue cast in film caused by reflected sunlight.

skyline A newspaper headline placed above the nameplate on page one.

sky pan A very shallow scoop or floodlight of extremely wide beam spread, generally near 180 degrees. Often used for shadowless lighting on sky cycs. Also called a *sky light*.

sky shade A camera lens shade used to shield the lens from direct sunlight.

sky wave A radio wave that is reflected by the ionosphere back to the earth. Also called an *indirect wave* and *ionospheric wave*. Cf. direct wave, ground wave, and reflected wave.

SLA Special Libraries Association.

slab serif *See* square serif.

slander The oral defamation of a person's reputation. Cf. libel.

slant □ A news story written with editorial, policy, or political bias. □ To write a story from a particular point of view. Also called a *slant.* □ *See* virgule.

slant track The preferred term is *helical scan.*

SLAPS test Obscenity, as defined in Miller v. California in 1973, included the acronym SLAPS (serious literary, artistic, political, or scientific value). *See also* obscenity.

slapstick A type of comedy that depends on broad physical action and unsophisticated humor. Cf. screwball comedy.

slash *See* virgule.

slash head A two part headline separated by a virgule.

slash print *See* scratch print.

slate □ An identifying sequence preceding or following a scene or program. □ *See* clapstick. □ The frames containing the clapper board information.

slate board *See* slate.

slating The process of identifying the beginning and end of a film sequence, but using a slate or clapper board or both.

slave □ Any mechanical or electronic unit or device that is controlled by another unit, such as a computer peripheral or an audio or video recorder used for editing. In computing, it may be called a slave station or slave terminal. □ *See* slave machine.

slave machine A video record and/or playback apparatus that is under the control of some other device or apparatus. Also called a *slave.*

slave station *See* slave.

slave terminal *See* slave.

slaving The process of interconnecting a master station with remote stations to work in synchronization.

SLCB Single line color bar.

sled A mount used to hang overhead luminaires.

sleeper □ A book, motion picture, television series, phonograph record, and so on, for which there is little demand or acceptance, but that later becomes a success. Also called *slow* and *slow builder.* □ A question used in a survey interview to determine if an earlier response was valid.

sleeper effect A delayed change in an individual's attitude or behavior from a previously applied or perceived stimulus.

sleeve A device that aligns two plugs.

sleuth A slang term for an investigative reporter.

slewing The process of synchronizing videotape recorders and players during editing.

slice of life From the French *tranche de vie.* A motion picture, book, television program, or commercial, and so on, that purports to display a segment of real life.

slick □ A popular magazine printed on glossy paper. Cf. pulp. □ A proof pulled on glossy paper, clean in appearance, and suitable for reproduction. Also called an *enamel proof.*

slide □ A film transparency, usually 2 by 2 in., but may be larger. □ An opaque slide. Also called a *balop* and *telop.* □ A shelf in a galley storage rack used for type forms.

slide chain *See* film chain.

slide film □ The film used to take 2 by 2 transparencies. □ *See* filmstrip (FS).

slide in A television director's command to take a slide.

slide projector An optical projector designed to project transparencies.

slider A potentiometer controlled by straight line motion rather than rotary motion. Also called a *sliding pot.* Cf. fader.

sliding cel An animation cel that is wider than normal; often used for panoramic views.

sliding pot *See* slider.

sliding rate A media rate for advertising that diminishes per unit of space or time as the number of units purchased increases. Also called *sliding scale.*

sliding scale □ A variable payment made for the exhibition of feature motion pictures instead of a flat rental fee or percentage. □ *See* sliding rate.

sliding track An overhead luminaire or cyclorama support that allows the movement of the instruments or cyclorama along the length of the track.

slime hole A defect in paper caused by slime growth.

slip □ A change made in a newspaper for circulation to different areas. □ The end of the tape or cord that is attached to the boards. □ A proof taken from a column of type in a galley. □ The name of an unemployed printer posted on a slipboard.

slipboard A newspaper composing room bulletin board.

slipcase A protective cover, usually cardboard, for books.

slip clutch A device that allows a camera or projector mechanism to adjust to slight differences in feed and take-up reel speed.

slip cover A book dust jacket.

slip cueing *See* slip start.

slip frame The use of four or more frames of each animation cel to produce a desired fast or jerky motion.

slip law A separately printed bill enacted by Congress. *See also* United States Code (USC).

slipping The television picture distortion caused by mechanical drive failure in the recorder or loss of horizontal or vertical sync.

slip proof *See* galley proof.

slip sheet A sheet of paper placed between printed sheets to prevent offset. Also called an *offset sheet.*

slip start A method of starting a disc exactly on cue. The record is held in position while the turntable rotates, then released on cue. Also called *slip cueing.*

slit The fixed or variable-width narrow opening used to record or playback optical film sound.

slit card A poster that is slit to fit around a book for display purposes.

slit scan cinematography A motion control technique for producing special effects, in which backlit artwork is photographed through a narrow slit in an opaque mask.

slitter The steel knife that cuts a newspaper web in the press.

slitting The process of cutting a wide roll of film, tape, or printing paper into the required sizes.

SLM Signal level meter.

slogan □ A word or phrase used to identify an advertiser's product or service. *See also* logo. □ A phrase used in packaging a candidate or politician.

slogan identifier (ID) Another means, aside from call letters, for a radio station to identify itself. Each station is allowed to maintain slogan ID's of up to 25 characters on Arbitron's local listings.

slo mo An abbreviation for *slow motion.*

slope *See* rolloff.

slop mix *See* rough mix.

slop print An uncorrected film print that is used primarily to check shot composition and timing. Also called a *rough print.*

slot □ The position of a commercial or program. □ The position of a story in a newscast. □ The job function assigned to an individual. □ The inside space of a horseshoe-shaped desk in which a newspaper copy editor sits. *See also* rim. □ The location of a satellite in its geosynchronous orbit. □ A means of expanding the capabilities of a microcomputer by adding additional memory, faster processing, interfaces for printers and disk drives, and so on. □ One of several narrow, elongated sockets inside a computer where peripheral cards are inserted.

slotman A newspaper copy editor.

slow □ A lens with a small maximum aperture. □ A film with a low emulsion speed. Also called *slow stock. See also* fine grain. Cf. fast. □ *See* sleeper.

slow builder *See* sleeper.

slow film *See* slow.

slow in/slow out Refers to the fact that panning and trucking moves usually begin slowly, gradually attain their full speed, then slow to a stop, to avoid a sense of jerkiness in the movement.

slow lens *See* slow.

slow motion The movement that appears when film is projected at a speed slower than that at which it was shot. Cf. fast motion.

slow scan television (SSTV) A low-quality, inexpensive television system used to transmit still pictures by slow horizontal scanning.

slow stock *See* slow.

SLP Standard long play. The six-hour playing time mode on a VHS recorder. Cf. SP, EP, and LP.

SLR Single lens reflex.

slug □ A one or two word label or phrase used to identify a news story. Also called a *catchline, guide, guideline,* and *slugline.* Cf. headline. □ To give a catchline to a news story. □ A line of metal type cast in one piece. □ A piece of metal, usually six points, used for spacing copy. □ A piece of leader used in a film workprint to replace damaged or missing footage. □ A piece of leader used to fill a gap between sound bites. *See also* spacing. □ A portion of blank leader used between news stories on film.

slug casting machine A machine that casts a line of metal type in one solid piece, such as a Linotype or Ludlow.

slug commercial *See* hard sell.

slug in To insert blank leader in a film workprint.

slugline *See* slug.

slung microphone A suspended microphone.

slush □ An unsolicited manuscript or article sent to a publisher. *See also* over the transom. □ Inconsequential, gushy, and emotional copy. □ A mixture of water and paper pulp.

slushpile The collection of unsolicited manuscripts received by magazines.

SM □ Sales manager. □ Spectrum management. □ Stage manager. □ Station manager.

SMA □ Society of Make-up Artists. □ Special market area.

small atlas A size of paper; 25 by 31 inches.

small capitals (sc) Letters in capital form but approximately two thirds the size of the capital letters for that font.

small caps An abbreviation for *small capitals.*

small double cap A size of paper; 16 by 26 inches.

small double post A size of paper; 19 by 29 inches.

smaller television market The specified zone of a licensed television station that is not included in the FCC list of first fifty or second fifty major television markets. Cf. major television market.

small format A reference to film or tape sizes of less than standard width, such as 8-mm film. *See also* substandard.

small letter *See* minuscule.

small market A geographical area that does not contain a city; usually less than 100,000 population. *See also* smaller television market.

small pica A size of type; 11 points.

small post A size of paper; 13-1/2 by 16-1/2.

small sweeps Television ratings that are taken in the summer.

small time A term derived from vaudeville, meaning repetitive theatrical performances for little pay. Cf. big time.

small town weekly A weekly newspaper published in a town physically separate from a larger city; not a suburban paper.

SMART Stop Advertising Alcohol on Radio and Television. A citizens' group.

smart device A computer peripheral or terminal that contains its own microprocessor. Also called a *smart terminal.*

SMARTS Selective multiple address radio and television service.

smart terminal *See* smart device.

smash A sensational news story, motion picture, television program, and so on.

smasher □ The operator of a smashing machine. □ *See* smashing machine.

smashing The compression of book signatures in preparation for binding.

smashing machine A mechanical device used to smash book signatures. Also called a *smasher.*

SMATV Satellite master antenna television.

smear A television picture distortion in which objects have a blurred horizontal trailing edge, caused by lag in a camera tube.

Smellovision A short-lived attempt in which motion picture theatres included fragrances and odors to add another sense to films.

smile *See* brite.

SMN Satellite Music Network.

smoke machine A device used to furnish smoke for special effects.

smooth shading A computer effect that allows the addition of modeling to shapes, edges, and surfaces so that their appearance is more realistically three-dimensional. *See also* Gouraud shading and Phong shading.

SMPAD Society of Motion Picture Art Directors.

SMPE Society of Motion Picture Engineers (since 1949 SMPTE).

SMPTE Society of Motion Picture and Television Engineers.

SMPTE time code A standardized form of time code used for videotape editing.

SMPTE universal leader A film projection leader that counts down the seconds to the beginning of a film. Also called a *society leader.* Cf. academy leader.

SMRB Simmons Market Research Bureau, Inc.

SMSA Standard Metropolitan Statistical Area.

SMTF Spectrum Management Task Force.

smudge ☐ To damage a piece of artwork, photographic film or print, or a freshly printed sheet in a manner that results in a blurred spot, as a fingerprint. ☐ To blur a well-focused advertising idea by excessive manipulation.

SMW Society of Magazine Writers.

Smyth sewing A form of sewing in which adjacent book signatures are sewn together.

S/N ☐ Signal-to-noise ratio. Also SNR. ☐ Serial number.

snake A multiple channel cable capable of carrying several signals simultaneously.

SNAP Society of National Association Publications.

snap ☐ A sharply-defined television picture. ☐ An audible cue to change slides. ☐ A slang term for a snapshot. ☐ A British term for an important news bulletin.

snap on mount A camera lens mount in which the lens is held by spring clips. Cf. bayonet mount and screw mount.

snapper ☐ A performer's exit line. ☐ A sales clincher.

snappy A photograph with high contrast and yet with a full range of tones.

snapshot A still photograph.

snap switch ☐ A cut from one television camera to another. ☐ An ordinary household light switch.

snatch To hide a newsworthy person or item from other reporters in order to maintain an exclusive.

sneak ☐ To slowly fade in or fade out a sound or picture. ☐ *See* sneak preview.

sneak in To fade in music slowly.

sneak out To fade out music slowly.

sneak preview The showing of a new motion picture, often unannounced, in order to gauge audience reaction before the film is released.

SNG A trademark acronym for Satellite News Gathering.

sniffing A slang term for searching for newsworthy information.

snipe Originally a small advertisement illegally pasted on an outdoor advertising surface. Legitimate dealer imprints across the bottom of a poster are now often referred to as snipes. Sometimes called an *overlay.*

snoot *See* funnel.

snorkel A periscope attachment for a camera.

snow A television picture random noise characterized by white flecks. Often caused by a weak signal. Also called *video noise.* Cf. confetti.

SNPA Southern Newspaper Publishers Association.

SNR ☐ Signal-to-noise ratio. Also S/N. ☐ Subject to nonrenewal.

snuff film A pornographic motion picture in which someone is actually murdered.

SNV Satellite news vehicle. Also called a *star truck.*

soap *See* soap opera.

soaper A slang term for a soap opera.

soaperatic Of or pertaining to soap operas.

soap opera A dramatic program, usually presented daily, with continuing characters and multiple plots. The action, which deals with contemporary problems and their solutions, continues from episode to episode. Called soap operas because many of the original sponsors were soap manufacturers. Also called a *daytime drama, soap,* and *soaper.*

soap sudder A slang term for a writer of soap operas.

sob sister A reporter who writes sob stories.

sob story A news story or feature with a sentimental, emotional appeal. Also called *sob stuff.*

sob stuff *See* sob story.

soc An abbreviation for *society.* Newspaper pages devoted to society news, women's fashions, and so on. Also abbreviated *sox.*

socialist realism The type of motion picture, book, article, and so on, that stresses realism to serve the doctrines of the State. Also called *Soviet social realism.*

Social Responsibility Theory One of the four theories of the press delineated by Wilbur Schramm, based on the theory that it is not enough to report facts, but the truth about the facts must be reported. Cf. Authoritarian theory, Libertarian theory, and Soviet Communist theory.

society leader *See* SMPTE universal leader.

Society of Advertisers, Music Producers, Arrangers, and Composers (SAMPAC) A trade association of individuals involved in the creation of advertising music.

Society of Broadcast Engineers (SBE) An association of Broadcast Engineers formed in 1963 as the IBE.

Society of Cable Television Engineers (SCTE) A technical organization for engineers involved in the cable television industry.

Society of Motion Picture and Television Engineers (SMPTE) A major organization that was founded in 1916 as the Society for Motion Picture Engineers, which has its headquarters in White Plains, New York. SMPTE writes standards for video recording and other systems used in North America.

Society of Professional Journalists *See* Sigma Delta Chi (SDX).

Society of Professional Stunt Women An association of female stunt players.

socket A holder for a lamp base, chip, or other device; normally female.

sock it To punch a line, commercial, and so on.

soda pulp A caustic soda wood pulp used in papermaking.

sodium A chemical used in numerous ways in photography: as an ingredient in developers, fixing baths, stop baths, and so on.

sodium lamp A gas-discharge lamp that contains sodium vapor. The emitted light is yellow in color. Also called a *sodium vapor lamp.*

sodium process A process developed to produce traveling mattes using sodium lamps to illuminate a yellow background.

sodium vapor lamp *See* sodium lamp.

SOF Sound on film.

soft A camera shot or print that is not well-defined and lacking in detail. *See also* soft focus. Cf. sharp.

soft contrast A photographic print that contains well-reproduced mid-tones, but is lacking in sharp contrast.

soft copy A message seen on a display screen, as opposed to one displayed on paper. Cf. hard copy.

softcore A motion picture that depicts simulated sexual situations. Also called *soft pornography.* Cf. hardcore.

softcover *See* paperbound.

soft cut A transitional device somewhere between an instantaneous cut and a fast dissolve.

soft edge A controlled transitional wipe, quad split, border between pictures, and so on, containing edges that are intentionally blurred.

soft error A momentary error that is not repeated in reading a computer disk.

soft focus □ A slightly out-of-focus picture or shot created by filters or lenses in order to create an atmosphere or provide a hazy effect. □ A picture that is sharp in one plane only.

soft focus lens A camera lens containing spherical aberrations that soften its focus.

soft hyphen A hyphen used to break a word at the end of a line, as opposed to a hyphen that is part of a word. Cf. hard hyphen.

soft interconnect A linking of cable television systems through the exchange of programs. Cf. hard interconnect.

soft lead A news lead that contains a quotation, background information, and so on, as opposed to the traditional five W's. Also called a *feature lead.* Cf. hard lead.

soft light A well-diffused light source that produces soft or poorly defined shadows when an object is placed between the luminaire and the light background. Cf. hard light.

soft news Features, kickers, and so on, that may be used with little regard to the age of the story. *See also* feature. Cf. hard news.

soft pornography *See* softcore.

soft scrambling The encryption of satellite signals using analog techniques instead of digital. Cf. hard scrambling.

soft sell The use of low-pressure techniques in commercials and advertisements. Cf. hard sell.

software □ Radio and television station programming, computer programs, and so on, as opposed to equipment. Cf. hardware. □ The programs and instructions that are used to tell the computer how to carry out its tasks. Cf. hardware.

solar cell A semiconductor that converts light into electricity. Used extensively in satellites, calculators, and so on.

solarization The reversal of image tones caused by subjecting a photographic image to extreme overexposure. Also called the *Sabattier effect.*

solder A mixture of tin and lead used to join metal surfaces and wires. *See also* rosin.

soldier *See* bang.

solenoid An electromagnet used to activate or deactivate a device.

sole sponsor An advertiser who purchases all the availabilities in a radio or television program.

solid Lines of type set without additional interlinear spacing. Also called *solid matter* and *solid set.*

solid matter *See* solid.

solid set *See* solid.

solid state A circuit or component that uses semiconductors, as opposed to vacuum tubes.

solo mailing A mailing that promotes a single product or a limited group of related products. It usually consists of a letter, brochure, and reply device enclosed in an envelope.

sone A unit of loudness. One sone is equal to a 1000-Hz tone, 40 dB above the threshold of hearing.

song plugger A music publishing firm representative who promotes the company's recordings.

songshark An individual or company that charges a fee to publish a musical composition. Similar to a subsidy book publisher.

sonic Relating to sound.

Sonovox An electronic device used to convert sound effects into intelligible speech.

SOP Standard operating procedures.

sort □ A printer's term for an individual piece of type. □ To arrange items of information in a particular order such as alphabetical or numerical, either by computer or by hand.

SOS Sound on sound.

SOT □ Start of tape. □ Sound on (video) tape.

sotto voce The use of half-whispered, half-vocalized sounds by a performer.

soubrette An actress who plays a coquettish young woman.

sound □ The auditory sensations derived from the stimulation of the auditory nerves in the brain through vibrations received by the ear. □ A series of compressions and rarefactions of air particles caused by the vibration of an object. Also called a *sound wave.* □ Film or videotape containing soundtracks, as opposed to silent. □ The music, disc jockeys, format, and so on, that make one radio station seemingly different from another.

sound absorption The absorption of sound by a nonreflective surface such as a screen.

sound-actuated *See* voice-actuated.

sound advance A measure of the number of frames the sound precedes the corresponding picture on film or tape. Also called *sync advance. See also* projection sync.

sound balancer A British term for an audio console operator.

sound band *See* soundtrack.

sound bars The horizontal bars in a television picture caused by an audio frequency sound.

sound bed A musical background, usually instrumental, over which commercials, promos, and so on, are recorded.

sound bite □ The voice portion of a videotape shot; usually applies to news shot on location. A television actuality. □ An audio sound effect used to enhance a video shot. □ Sometimes used to mean any sound on tape. *See also* bite.

sound boom *See* boom.

sound booth *See* announce booth (AB).

sound bridge *See* bridge.

sound camera A motion picture camera designed for noiseless operation, so that sound may be recorded in synchronization.

sound carrier The frequency modulated carrier that transmits the audio portion of a television signal.

sound channel An audio frequency channel.

sound chart A British term for a bar sheet.

sound chip An integrated circuit used in audio recording and playback. Also called an *audio chip.*

sound crew The personnel who work sound in a television or film production.

sound cue A cue given by a sound effect to a performer.

sound cutter An individual who specializes in editing soundtracks.

sound daily print A photographic print made for evaluation purposes from an original sound negative.

sound department A motion picture studio department charged with maintaining and operating sound equipment.

sound displacement *See* projection sync.

sound dissolve An alternative term for a *segue.*

sound distortion The resultant amplitude, attenuation, harmonic, intermodulation, or phase distortion that occurs in a sound system due to imperfect equipment.

sound drum The cylindrical flywheel around which the film moves in a projector.

sound editing The process of synchronizing sound and picture.

sound editor □ The equipment used in editing sound film. □ The editor who is in charge of splicing soundtracks.

sound effects (SFX)(SE) The electrical, mechanical, recorded, or other sounds, exclusive of music and dialogue, which imitate or reproduce actual sounds, such as breaking glass, dogs barking, and trains whistling.

sound effects filter An electronic filter used to alter normal sound by reducing the low and/or high frequencies.

sound effects library A catalogued collection of sound effects recorded on film, tape, records, and so on.

sound effects negative A motion picture negative film on which sound effects have been recorded.

sounder A brief musical passage used on radio to identify a network, station, news brief, station identification, and so on.

sound film A single perforation film with an optical soundtrack or magnetic stripe.

sound gate The mechanical opening in a projector in which the film soundtrack is exposed to the exciter lamp.

sound group In CD-I, part of the user data field in an ADPCM audio sector. Each ADPCM audio sector has 18 sound groups.

sound head □ The film projector device which converts the optical or magnetic sound information into electrical signals. □ The sound reproducing head on an audio- or videotape recorder.

sound image A photographically produced variable area or variable density soundtrack.

sounding □ The process of transferring audio information from one form to another, as in film or videotape editing. □ A memory area that preloads audio data from a disc in CD-ROM.

sound jeep *See* sound truck.

sound level *See* level.

sound lock A small passageway between a studio and an outside corridor with a soundproof door at each end. Also called a *sound trap.*

sound log *See* log.

sound loop A length of film with its head spliced to its tail. Used in editing to obtain longer or continuous sounds.

sound macro A predefined sound or sound sequence stored in computer form.

soundman An individual who operates sound effects, an audio control console, or makes audio setups.

soundmap A RAM location containing ADPCM audio data in CD-ROM. Cf. drawmap.

sound master positive A sound print made from a negative to produce sound dupe negatives for making release prints.

sound mixer □ An individual who mixes the various soundtracks for television or film. □ A simplified audio console used for uncomplicated sound mixing.

sound, music, effects, and dubbing editor An individual who creates or selects music and soundtracks for the purpose of rerecording; times and cues the picture for scoring, prepares tracks, and so on.

sound negative A negative soundtrack produced either by direct recording or exposure to a positive sound image.

sound on film (SOF) A film that contains a recorded soundtrack, often single system sound.

sound on sound (SOS) The addition of new sounds to an existing soundtrack. Usually accomplished by dubbing the new material and the recorded soundtrack on a second track. In some systems this may be accomplished with varying results, by recording sounds on the original track without erasing it completely.

sound on tape (SOT) A videotape that contains a recorded soundtrack.

sound perspective The impression that distance makes in the perception of sound.

sound picture A wide range of individual sounds used to represent a scene. An audio montage.

sound presence *See* presence.

sound pressure level (SPL) An objective measure of the ratio of a sound pressure to a reference pressure.

sound print A positive film printed from a sound negative.

soundproof A room, studio, announce booth, and so on, which is insulated against the passage of sound. Cf. anechoic chamber.

sound reader An editing device which is capable of playing back optical or magnetic soundtracks.

sound recordings For the purposes of copyright, works that result from the fixation of a series of musical, spoken, or other sounds, but not including the sounds accompanying a motion picture or other audiovisual work, regardless of the nature of the material objects, such as disks, tapes, or other phonorecords, in which they are embodied.

sound recording system A combination of transducing devices and associated equipment suitable for storing sound in a form capable of subsequent retrieval and reproduction.

sound reinforcement (SR) The use of loudspeakers to raise the level of sound for an audience.

sound release negative A release negative used to print the soundtrack of a release print.

sound report *See* log sheet.

sound reproducing system A combination of transducing devices and associated equipment for reproducing recorded sound.

sound separation *See* projection sync.

sound spectrum The audible frequencies within the range of human hearing; from approximately 16 to 16,000 or 20,000 hertz.

sound speed The standard frame rate of film through a camera or projector of 24 frames per second. Also called *synchronous speed.* Cf. silent speed.

soundstage A large, soundproof studio used for taping or filming as well as sound recording.

sound stripe A thin band of magnetic material attached to the edge of film stock.

sound system The electronic components necessary for a complete sound path from one or more microphones, or other transducers, through preamplifiers and amplifiers, to one or more loudspeakers, or other transducers.

sound table *See* sound truck.

sound tape *See* tape.

soundtrack □ The thin band occupying the full length of motion picture film used to supply audio information. The band may contain single or multiple magnetic tracks, or variable density or variable area optical tracks. Sometimes called a *sound band.* □ A separate audio recording made to accompany a film or series of slides. □ The portion of a videotape that carries the audio information. Often spelled *sound track.*

soundtrack advance *See* sound advance.

sound trap *See* sound lock.

sound truck A large, movable box mounted with turntables and other devices for playing or making sound effects. Also called a *cocktail bar, sound jeep,* and *sound table.*

sound under *See* under.

sound wave *See* sound.

sound workprint An intercut soundtrack synchronized with the picture, and usually containing dialogue, music, and effects.

soup A slang term for film developing solutions.

soupy Any sound that is mushy or unintelligible.

sour ☐ A wrong note. ☐ A poor radio or television program.

source The originator or origination point of a message, news item, program, signal, lighting, and so on.

source book A reporter's address book, listing important names and telephone numbers for obtaining information.

source code A unique alphabetical or numerical identification for distinguishing one mailing list or media source from another. *See also* key code.

source count The number of names and addresses in any given list for the media or mailing list sources from which the names and addresses were derived.

source image The absolute RGB picture that is to be recorded on a CD-ROM disc using DYUV compression techniques.

source material All material on which a screenplay is based, including other material on which the story is based.

source music Music used in a film or television program in which the originator or originators are seen by the camera, as opposed to mood or other music on a soundtrack.

source recorder A videotape recorder or player that is used to playback a tape for editing.

source volume A computer disk that is being loaded into a computer's RAM. Cf. destination volume.

south The direction of an animation stand closest to the operator. Cf. north.

Soviet Communist Theory One of the four theories of the press delineated by Wilbur Schramm; based on the theory that the press exists only to further the interests of the state. Cf. Authoritarian Theory, Libertarian Theory, and Social Responsibility Theory.

Soviet social realism *See* socialist realism.

sox An abbreviation for *society.* Also spelled *soc.*

SP ☐ Standard play. The two hour playing time mode on a VHS recorder. Cf. EP and SLP. ☐ Special performance. ☐ Special publication. ☐ Stop press.

SPA Syndicated program analysis.

SPACE Society of Private and Commercial Earth Stations; now STIA. An association of satellite dish owners.

space ☐ An interval in which nothing is being transmitted on a radio or television station. ☐ Time available for broadcast advertising. ☐ An area of a printed page; often refers to space purchased by advertisers. ☐ *See* white space. ☐ A small piece of type used to separate words or letters in a line of type. ☐ *See* space out. ☐ The portion of an outdoor or transit display area that may be purchased for advertising.

space advertising Display advertising, as opposed to classified advertising.

spaceband A pair of tapered steel wedges used to space lines automatically on linecasting machines.

space bar The lever that activates the dropping of spacebands.

space book A record of news stories or features filed by a space writer.

space buyer A person who buys advertising space in a newspaper, magazine, and so on.

space charge The charge made by publishers, billboard owners, transit advertising companies, and so on, for advertising space. Also called *space rate.*

spaced Microphones that are separated for stereo or multiple sound sources.

space discount The discount offered to advertisers for the purchase of space above specified minimum amounts.

space grabber A slang term for a publicity agent.

space mailman A communication satellite.

space opera A slang term for a science fiction novel, motion picture, story, and so on.

space operation service A radio communication service concerned exclusively with the operation of spacecraft, in particular space tracking, space telemetry, and space telecommand. These functions will normally be provided within the service in which the space station is operating.

space out To increase the spaces between words to fill out a line of type, or to use leads or furniture to extend the length of a column.

space position value (SPV) One of the factors used to determine the showing value in outdoor advertising. It is an index of visibility of a poster panel, based on four factors: length of approach, speed of travel, angle of the panel to its circulation, and its relationship to adjacent panels.

spacer A length of paper or plastic tape used between recorded segments on audiotape. Cf. leader.

space radio communication Any radio communication that involves the use of one or more space stations or the use of one or more reflecting satellites or other objects in space. Cf. terrestrial radio communication.

space rate *See* space charge.

space schedule A schedule, often made out by an advertising agency, showing the media to be used, the times, costs, positions, and so on, in an advertising campaign.

space segment The telecommunications satellites, and the tracking, telemetry, command, control, monitoring, and related facilities and equipment required to support the operation of these satellites.

space spot Any of a number of low-cost newspaper advertising spaces sold in specified quantities, to appear at unspecified intervals over a specified period.

space staging A well-worked-out plan for a set that allows for easy movement of talent and cameras.

space station A station located on an object which is beyond, is intended to go beyond, or has been beyond, the major portion of the earth's atmosphere. Cf. earth station.

space system Any group of cooperating earth stations and/or space stations employing space radio communication for specific purposes.

space telecommand The use of radio communication for the transmission of signals to a space station to initiate, modify or terminate function of the equipment on a space object, including the space station.

space telemetering The use of telemetering for the transmission from a space station of results of measurements made in a spacecraft, including those relating to the functioning of the spacecraft.

space tracking The determination of the orbit, velocity, or instantaneous position of an object in space by means of radiodetermination, excluding primary radar, for the purpose of following the movement of the object.

space writer A freelance writer who is paid by the number of words in a story, article, and so on, or the amount of space the material uses.

spacing □ The distance between stereo loudspeakers or microphones. □ The distance between fixed relay points. □ The distance between line amplifiers in a cable television system. □ *See* leading. □ *See* letterspacing. □ Lengths of film used to fill sections of the soundtrack where there is no sound. Also called *fill* and *slug.*

spacing guide An indicator used to indicate the number of frames and the amount of movement that should be made between animation extremes.

spacing loss The undesirable reduction in magnetic flux transferred to or from magnetic tape due to head-to-tape separation.

spaghetti □ A tubular insulation material used to insulate electrical conductors. □ Thin strips of waste newsprint.

spaghetti western A somewhat derogatory term for a western motion picture shot in Italy.

spark A brief, brilliant electrical discharge between two bodies, at least one of which must be electrically charged.

sparkle dust A set decoration of tinsel, glass, or other iridescent material.

sparkles The little flecks seen in a television picture due to insufficient signal strength.

sparks A slang term for a studio electrician. *See also* gaffer.

SPARS Society of Professional Audio Recording Studios.

SPARS code A three-letter code that appears on a CD indicating the type of recording, either analog or digital. The first letter indicates the original recording, A or D; the second how the music was mixed or edited, A or D; and the third the type of mastering used to produce the CD.

spatial cutting The cutting from one picture to another utilizing two or more projection screens.

spatial distortion The distortion that occurs in the reproduction of a stereophonic signal due to improper microphone or loudspeaker relationships.

SPC Station Program Cooperative.

SPD Spectral power distribution.

speak back *See* talkback.

speaker □ An individual delivering a speech, talking into a microphone, and so on. □ An abbreviation for *loudspeaker.*

speakerine A television program hostess.

speaker system *See* loudspeaker system (LS).

speaking part A member of a cast who speaks lines, as opposed to an extra.

spec An abbreviation for *specification* and *speculation. See also* specs.

special □ A single network television program that is not carried on a regular basis. Formerly called a *spectacular.* Cf. series. □ A news story filed by an out-of-town correspondent.

special ability extra An extra who has special skills such as riding horses, handling livestock, skating, skiing, and so on.

special character A character that is not normally available on a computer or typewriter keyboard or a character that requires an addition mark: umlaut, cedilla, and so on.

special damages *See* damages.

special effects (se)(sfx) Illusions that are generated by a wide range of processes or equipment using trick photography, optical effects, multiple images, models, miniatures, inserts, animation combined with live action, and so on.

special effects department A motion picture studio department that handles natural special effects such as fires and explosions.

special effects generator (SEG) The electronic device used to create special effects. An SEG is often built into a television switcher.

special events Radio or television programs of news interest that are usually scheduled on an irregular basis, such as Senate investigations and parades. Cf. special.

special extra □ An extra who is addressed individually by a principal performer, is alone in the scene, or speaks individually as part of a group or crowd. □ An extra who performs work requiring special ability, such as horseback riding, swimming, and skating.

special interest magazine *See* selective magazine.

specialization The use of specific formats, music, language, and so on, to attract a target audience for a broadcast or to a radio or television station.

specialized common carrier (SCC) A common carrier, other than a telephone company, authorized to provide communication services.

specialized copy desk A newspaper copy desk that handles a specific type of story. Also called a *specialized desk.* Cf. universal desk.

specialized desk *See* specialized copy desk.

specialized magazine *See* selective magazine.

specialized network A television network, usually pay cable, that provides programming to defined audiences, including sports, movies, and so on.

specialized publisher A publishing firm that specializes in certain types of books, such as technical, romance, and foreign language.

specialized telecommunications services Telecommunications services that can be made available by means of satellites except for those services that are made available to the public.

special library A specialized library organized and maintained by an individual, group, association, and so on, for specific subject matter or specialized services.

special market area (SMA) A special area measured and reported by Nielsen Station Index usually for a small market that does not qualify for its own designated market area (DMA).

special opening A prepared intro that identifies sponsors of a radio or television program.

special order An order placed with a retailer by an individual or group for an item such as a single book.

special relief (SR) Authority granted by the FCC for a waiver of the rules relating to cable television systems, for additional or different requirements, or for a ruling on a complaint or disputed question, on petition by a cable television system, a franchising authority, an applicant, permittee, or licensee of a television broadcast, translator, or microwave relay station, or by another interested person.

special risk insurance Insurance purchased to cover performers and property during potentially dangerous filming situations.

special sale A publisher's clearance for unwanted or overstocked books, usually carried out through nontraditional channels.

special sort A character that is not usually included in a typical font. *See also* sort.

special temporary authorizations (STA) The authority granted to a permittee or licensee to permit the operation of a broadcast facility for a limited period at a specified variance from the terms of the station authorization or requirements of the FCC Rules applicable to the particular class of station.

specialty act Any performer or group of performers who render and perform a self-contained theatrical performance with material and theatrical routines of their own (as distinguished from material and routines furnished or provided by the producer), which performance has been previously rehearsed and/or used by such specialty act prior to its engagement by the producer. A specialty act is a standard act, a variety act, and a vaudeville act.

specialty advertising Advertising accomplished by printing messages and logos on items to be given away, including pens, matches, calendars, and so on.

Specialty Advertising Association (SAA) An association of individuals and companies involved in specialty advertising.

specialty singer A professional singer employed for a solo or employed as a part of a "name" group.

specialty station A radio or television station carrying religious or foreign language programming during one-third of the hours of the average broadcast week and one-third of the weekly hours during prime time.

specification A description specifying the physical format of a CD-I disc and how various types, audio data and program related data are coded.

specific illumination Illumination of localized areas by means of controlled illumination.

specific light The mixture of light sources to create a feeling of depth or dimension.

specified hours (SH) The exact operating hours specified in the license for some AM stations.

specified zone The area extending 35 air miles from the reference point in a community to which a television broadcast station is licensed or authorized by the FCC.

speckling Television picture spots caused by an imperfection in a plumbicon pickup tube.

specs An abbreviation for *specifications.* □ The detailed instructions given for the construction of a set, the purchase of equipment, and so on. □ Specifications as to size, font, and so on, of type to be used. □ Manuscripts, stories, news, and so on, written without a contract but in hopes of selling the writing.

spec sheet □ A list of information about a product or advertiser. □ An equipment manufacturer's detailed description of a product.

spectacle A motion picture that is impressive in scope, range, cast size, remarkable special effects, or other notable dramatic scenes or devices. Similar to a *spectacular.*

SpectaColor A trademark for preprinted advertising with defined margins; often rotogravure.

spectacular □ An outdoor advertising display built with structural steel and designed for a particular advertiser on a long-term contract. The advertising copy is presented in a spectacular fashion through the use of incandescent lamps, luminous tubing flashers, chaser borders, motographs, or any combination of these electrical devices. Cf. semispectacular. □ A television program or motion picture that is lavishly produced and usually employs well-known stars. Similar to a *spectacle. See also* special.

spectral Of or pertaining to the spectrum.

spectral power distribution (SPD) A plot showing the relative amounts of power at the various wavelengths for a particular light.

spectral purity The color saturation of a small portion of the light wave band.

spectral recording (SR) A Dolby high quality noise reduction process.

spectral sensitivity The color response of a photosensitive device or film.

spectrogram A graph that displays the color sensitivity of film as measured by using a neutral density wedge.

spectrometry The process of measuring the wave lengths of rays of light.

spectroscope A device used to measure the wave lengths of rays of light.

spectrum □ The continuous range of electromagnetic energy radiations encompassing the entire electromagnetic spectrum from the longest radio waves, through the light waves, to the shortest cosmic rays. □ A definable portion of the electromagnetic spectrum, such as the AM band and light waves. □ *See* sound spectrum.

spectrum management (SM) The regulation of the use of the electromagnetic spectrum so as to make available interference-free service for as many services and audiences as possible.

specular Description of a mirror-like surface. When used to describe a light, it implies a hard light.

speculation Scriptwriting, filming, taping, and so on, on a contingency basis in hopes of selling the book, script, product, and so on, at a later date. Also called *on spec* and *spec.*

speech □ The communication of sounds or signs between individuals. □ A talk delivered by an individual to a group or mass audience.

speech channel *See* voice grade.

speech coil A British term for a voice coil.

speech frequency *See* audio frequency (AF).

speech quality In CD-I, the fourth of five audio quality levels. A bandwidth of 8.5 kHz is obtained using 4-bit ADPCM at a sampling frequency of 18.9 kHz. Comparable with AM broadcast sound quality.

speed □ A measure of the sensitivity of a film. □ A cue given by a film or videotape operator when the device is rolling and ready for use. *See also* film speed, sound speed, and tape speed. □ A measure of the light-gathering power of a lens.

speed of action The relative speed between the movement in a scene and the location of the camera.

speed of light The speed at which light and electromagnetic waves travel; approximately 186,300 miles per second, or 300 million meters per second, or approximately 7-1/2 times around the world in 1 second.

speed of sound The speed at which sound travels through air; approximately 750 miles per hour, or 1080 feet per second.

spell □ To enunciate a line clearly. □ To accent a movement precisely.

spell checker *See* spelling checker.

spelling checker A computer program that proofreads text by comparing each word to a dictionary, then indicates misspelled or questionable words. Also called a *spell checker.*

SPERDVAC The Society to Preserve and Encourage Radio Drama, Variety, and Comedy. A volunteer support group.

spherical aberration The blurring of an image due to a lens defect that does not allow all light rays to focus at the focal point.

spherical dish An antenna or microphone that uses a truncated sphere as a reflector.

SPI Society of Photographic Illustrators.

spider □ A multiple outlet extension cord. *See also* junction box. □ The flexible ring in a loudspeaker used to center the voice coil. □ *See* crowfoot. □ A folding device used to hold the legs of a tripod stationary on slippery surfaces. Also called a *crab, crowfoot,* and *spreader.*

spider box *See* junction box.

SPIE Society of Photo-Optical Instrumentation Engineers.

spiel A slang term for the continuity used in commercial copy.

spieler An old term for a person who tells a story; formerly used to describe a person who furnished dialogue live to accompany silent movies. Sometimes used to describe a radio or television announcer.

spike □ A mark on a studio floor indicating the proper position for scenery or props. Also called a *mark.* □ An electrical transient. *See also* overshoot. □ To remove a story from a newscast. □ A pointed spindle used to hold unused or unwanted news copy. Also called a *hook.*

spill □ Light directed at one area of a set that accidentally strikes another area. Also called *leak light.* □ To unspool a quantity of tape from a reel by accident. Often caused by tape recorder malfunction or by using two different sized reels. □ The portion of a split newspaper story continued on another page.

spill-in The percentage or number of households in a home market viewing stations originating in an outside market. Cf. spill-out.

spill-in circulation Circulation within a given urban area of a newspaper published outside the area.

spill-in coverage The coverage of a market by a communication medium located outside the market.

spill light □ Stray light outside of the main beam of a luminaire. □ Light that is misplaced or undesired within a scene.

spill-out The percent or number of households in an outside market viewing stations originating in a home market. Cf. spill-in.

spillover □ A VU meter reading in excess of 100 on the scale. □ The flow of electronic signals beyond the border of the originating country.

spill ring A band of concentric rings attached to a luminaire to eliminate light spill.

spill shield *See* louvers.

spin □ To rotate a graphic or picture around its center. □ A promotional emphasis or idea that is attributed to a product or individual by an advertiser or press agent.

spindle □ The center post of a turntable. □ The rotating shafts of a tape transport or turntable mechanism.

spine □ The back edge of a book or magazine. *See also* backbone. □ The basic plot of a play, screenplay, novel, and so on.

spinner A disc jockey; a platter spinner.

spinoff □ A book, usually a novel, based on a character or situation in a previously published book. □ A new radio or television program derived from or based on a character in an exiting program.

spin start □ *See* slip start. □ A method of fast-starting a nonrim drive turntable wherein the turntable is spun by hand on cue.

spiral binding A book binding consisting of a coiled wire inserted through holes in the pages.

spiral wipe A basic television wipe; wherein one picture displaces another as if a hand of a clock were accomplishing the effect.

spirit duplicator A common office duplicating machine. Also called a *fluid duplicator. See also* hectograph.

SPJ Society of Professional Journalists. *See* Sigma Delta Chi (SDX).

SPL Sound pressure level.

splash The main front page story in a newspaper.

splash light Any light, other than from a projector, that strikes a projection screen.

splatter Adjacent channel interference caused by overmodulation.

splay To angle sets, flats, lights, and so on, at an angle to the cameras. *See also* rake.

splice □ A mechanical joining between two pieces of tape, usually held together by a strip of self-adhesive foil. □ A butt splice between two pieces of film. □ To join two pieces of tape or film together. Also called a *splice patch.*

splice patch *See* splice.

splicer Any device used to cut and join pieces of film or magnetic tape. *See also* Mae West and splicing block.

splicing The process of joining film or tape together.

splicing block A rectangular metal casting with a groove for holding magnetic tape in place for cutting and splicing. Also called an *editing block.*

splicing tape The self-adhesive foil used to secure a tape splice.

split The division of money between, for example, a media outlet and an advertising agency, a theatre owner and a motion picture distributor, and so on.

split channel A network that feeds two or more legs with different programs.

split commercial *See* piggyback.

split edit A videotape edit in which the sound and video edits begin at different times.

split entry A broadcast ratings company procedure for dividing the credit for listening or viewing when the reported time periods overlap for two or more stations.

split fader A device that allows the control of two electronic signals or lighting instruments at the same time, usually increasing the level of one while decreasing the level of the other.

split feed A circuit that separates a single signal into two or more.

split field lens A closeup lens that has been cut to cover only part of the main camera lens so that close and distant objects may be in focus.

split focus *See* differential focus.

split fountain An ink fountain that is divided into spaces for two or more colors.

split frame *See* split screen.

split image *See* split screen.

split image rangefinder A camera focusing device that produces two halves of an image; when the two are joined, the image is in focus.

split logging A commercial or program that is placed in two or more FCC categories.

split network A network that offers two or more programming services.

split page □ A script that contains television audio and video in two columns on one page. □ *See* second front.

split play The reporting of one side of a news item in a publication, and the other side in a later issue or edition.

split reel □ A film reel with removable flanges. Also called a *split spool.* □ Two or more different short motion pictures spliced together on one reel. Seldom used today.

split roller The separately inked rollers that are used in split fountain printing.

split run □ The regional division of a national publication containing advertising directed toward a specific geographical area. □ The division of a publication into two or more slightly different versions in order to verify the effectiveness of different advertisements.

split run test *See* split test.

split screen □ An electronically divided television picture using two or more picture sources. Also called *split image.* □ A process used to duplicate an actor's image. Also called *split frame.* □ A film technique in which two parts of the frame are exposed separately, usually from different sources. □ The use of a split screen to display two news stories side-by-side on a video display terminal.

split setup The arrangement of talent to correspond to a microphone's angle of acceptance.

split sponsor *See* cosponsored.

split spool *See* split reel.

splitter A device used to divide an antenna's output so that two or more receivers may use the same antenna.

split test A technique in which two or more samples from the same list, each considered to be representative of the entire list, are used for package tests or to test the homogeneity of the list. Also called a *split run test.*

split thirties A 30-second television advertising spot that contains two or more related products.

split track recording The recording of separate sounds side-by-side on a multitrack tape recorder.

spoilage Printed matter that is spoiled in printing or binding; considered and allowed for in advance when ordering.

spokesman An individual who presents a radio or television commercial; often someone familiar to the audience. *See also* testimonial.

sponsor □ Generally, any advertiser who pays for broadcast time. □ Specifically, an advertiser who purchases an entire program. *See also* alternate sponsor, cosponsored, major sponsor, minor sponsor, and participating sponsor. □ An advertiser who purchases all of the available commercial minutes in a radio or television program.

sponsored Paid for.

sponsored book A specialized book published without financial risk by the publisher. Often, a specified number of copies are ordered by the sponsoring organization or group before publication. Cf. vanity publisher.

sponsored program A radio or television program paid for by an advertiser or advertisers, as opposed to a sustaining program.

sponsor identification (SI) □ The disclosure required by the Communications Act of 1934 and the FCC Rules and Regulations. □ *See* sponsor identification index.

sponsor identification index (SII) The percentage of viewers who are able to identify the sponsor of a radio or television program. Also called *sponsor identification.*

sponsoring editor A term sometimes used for an acquisitions editor.

sponsor relief The withdrawal from sponsorship of a radio or television program during an off-season period.

spook A slang term for a ghost writer.

spool □ To wind a tape onto a reel or hub. □ *See* reel. □ A British term for a reel.

sports blackouts *See* black out.

sportscaster A play-by-play or color announcer.

sports programs (S) Programs including play-by-play and pre- or post-game related activities and separate programs of sports instruction, news, or information. An FCC program type category.

SPOT A computer-controlled system for the control of commercials, promos, and so on, aired during radio or television station breaks.

spot □ A brief commercial or PSA, presented on a local radio or television station. Also called a *spot announcement* and *spot commercial.* □ The time purchased from an individual station for a spot. Also called *spot sales.* □ The selling of print space in national magazines on a market-by-market basis. □ An abbreviation for a *spotlight.* □ Any point on the face of a cathode ray tube. □ A brief radio news story fed from a remote. □ To retouch film negatives to remove imperfections. □ To adjust a luminaire, usually by moving the lamp away from the lens, reducing the diameter of the beam of light emitted. □ The narrowest beam possible from a focusable light.

spot advertising campaign A non-network advertising campaign utilizing local, regional, or national programs or announcements. Also called a *spot campaign.*

spot announcement *See* spot.

spot beam A signal being transmitted from a satellite to earth for a specific geographic area.

spot brightness meter An exposure meter that is used to measure small areas of the scene to be shot from the vantage point of the camera. Also called a *spot exposure meter* and *spot meter. See also* incident reading and reflected reading.

spot buy A purchase of commercial time on a local radio or television station.

spot campaign *See* spot advertising campaign.

spot carrier A participation program that contains a number of availabilities.

spot checking The comparison of portions of an updated electronic manuscript printout with a previous version for proofreading purposes. Used to determine if a complete proofreading is advisable.

spot color □ Color printing other than process printing. □ A color applied for emphasis to areas of a basically black and white print advertisement.

spot commercial *See* spot.

spot drawing A small drawing in an advertisement or periodical page that is otherwise basically text. Also called a *vignette.*

spot exposure meter *See* spot brightness meter.

spotlight □ Any of several different types of luminaires with relatively narrow beam angle designed to illuminate a specifically defined area. *See also* ellipsoidal spotlight and fresnel. Cf. floodlight. □ In motion pictures, generic for *fresnel lens luminaires.* □ To feature a performer on a radio or television program.

spot load The number of commercials broadcast by a radio station per hour.

spot meter *See* spot brightness meter.

spot microphone *See* accent microphone.

spot news Live news, often unexpected, obtained at the scene and at the time of the event. Also called *stop news. See also* hot news.

spot programming The purchase of radio or television program time on a market-by-market basis from individual stations.

spot radio Commercial time purchased on local stations by national or regional advertisers.

Spot Radio Rates and Data A monthly publication by Standard Rate and Data Service (SRDS) that lists the rate cards and other information about all commercial radio stations in the United States.

spot reading A light reading taken with a spot brightness meter.

spot sales *See* spot, spot radio, and spot television.

spot schedule The schedule of local purchases of radio or television spot time.

spot sheet □ A list of commercial times purchased in an advertising campaign. □ *See* dope sheet.

spot speed The rate of travel of a television scanning beam.

spotted map A map of a market with dots (spotted) to show the placement of outdoor advertising panels or bulletins for a specific buy. Also called a *spotting map.*

spot television Commercial time purchased on local stations by national or regional advertisers.

Spot Television Rates and Data A monthly publication by Standard Rate and Data Service (SRDS) that lists the rate cards and other information about all commercial television stations in the United States.

spotter An individual who works with a play-by-play sportscaster to help identify players.

spotting □ The process of determining the precise location of individual words or sounds on a film soundtrack, usually accomplished by utilizing a moviola or other sound reader. □ The process of listing the sound cues, special effects, narration timing, and so on, on a tape or film. □ The use of spotlights, as opposed to floodlights. □ *See* spot programming.

spotting map *See* spotted map.

spotting session A meeting held to determine the proper places to insert music and sound in a motion picture film.

spot up To place patches of thin paper on low spots on a sheet to make it print more evenly.

spot wobble The fluctuation of a scanning beam used to eliminate the horizontal lines in a television picture.

spray processing The use of jets to spray processing chemicals on film, instead of immersing the film in conventional baths.

spread □ To widen the beam of light from a luminaire. □ To stretch a radio or television program so as to fill the allotted time. □ The length of time used in a program by nonplanned material, such as laughter, applause, and ad libs. □ A news story important or large enough to require a headline at the top of a column. □ A news story or related stories, usually with illustrations, that requires more than one column. □ Another term for a *layout.* □ *See* double spread. □ *See* spread head.

spreader *See* spider.

spread groove *See* lead-over groove.

spread head A newspaper headline covering a spread; often three or more columns wide. Sometimes called a *spread.*

spread posting date The separated posting dates for a single outdoor advertising showing, in which individual boards are posted at different times.

spread spectrum systems An information-bearing communications system in which information is conveyed by modulation of a carrier by some conventional means, and the bandwidth is deliberately widened by means of a spreading function over that which would be needed to transmit the information alone.

spring drive A film camera that contains a hand wound motor.

sprites Small images on a screen, movable under program control, and normally ranging from characters or cursor shapes to specific patterns as in computer games.

sprocket The toothed gear in a camera or projector that engages the perforations on a film.

sprocket holes *See* perforation.

sprocket modulation A distortion in projected sound caused by the movement of the film perforations close to the soundtrack.

SPSE Society of Photographic Scientists and Engineers.

SPU Special power unit.

spur A projection on the lower right side of some capital G's.

spurious emission Emission on a frequency or frequencies that are outside the necessary bandwidth and the level of which may be reduced without affecting the corresponding transmission of information. Spurious emissions include harmonic emissions, parasitic emissions, intermodulation products, and frequency conversion products, but exclude out-of-band emissions. Also called *spurious radiation.*

spurious radiation *See* spurious emissions.

sputtering A process sometimes used in the production of a metal master wherein the original is coated with an electric conducting layer by means of an electric discharge in a vacuum. Now obsolete. Also called *cathode sputtering.*

SPV Space position value.

spyder A small dolly. *See* camera mounts.

spy film A film genre that covers a broad range of plots centering around international espionage.

squabble Type matter that has been set and then disarranged.

square The portion of a book cover that projects beyond the trimmed pages.

square brackets One of the characters "[" or "]"; sometimes used as delimiters in electronic manuscripts. Cf. angle brackets and braces.

square finish halftone *See* square halftone.

square halftone A halftone with square or rectangular sides, as opposed to, for example, a silhouette. Also called a *square finish halftone.*

square indention A form of indention wherein all lines are indented from the left even with the paragraph intention. Cf. flush left and hanging indention.

square loop *See* loop.

squares *See* overhang.

square serif A typeface that has monotonal strokes and serifs of the same or greater weight than the body of the type. Also called *block serif, Egyptian,* and *slab serif.*

squash In animation, the intentional distortion of the shape of a character or object; often flattened to show the character or object impacted against an unyielding surface. *See also* stretch.

squash and stretch An element of character animation which involves the exaggeration of the normal tendency of an object in motion to undergo a degree of distortion, lengthening as it travels, and compressing as it stops.

squawk box □ The talkback loudspeaker in a radio or television studio. □ A slang term for a sound reader.

squawker A midrange loudspeaker in a three-way system. Cf. tweeter and woofer.

squeal The noise caused by friction between a tape and the pressure roller in a tape transport.

squeegee A rubber or plastic wiper or roller used to remove liquid solutions from film being processed.

squeeze A technique that uses multiple still pictures to create the effect of motion.

squeeze frame A television picture that is decreased in size until it occupies only a portion of the frame.

squeeze lens A slang term for an anamorphic lens.

squeeze ratio The horizontal compression of an image on film by an anamorphic lens in wide-screen systems.

squeeze track □ A soundtrack whose variations in pitch are determined by variations in its playing time. □ A 16-mm sound film with an optical soundtrack, prepared by direct, integrated reduction from separate 35-mm optical sound and visual film elements.

squelch To eliminate unwanted sounds by reducing the gain of a receiver.

squib □ A brief newspaper or magazine story, often used as a filler. □ Writing, often political, characterized by wit or sarcasm. □ A small container used to hold a powder charge for gunshots and other noises.

SR □ Sound reinforcement. □ Spectral recording. □ Special relief. An FCC cable file-number prefix prior to March 31, 1972.

SRA Station Representatives Association.

SRDS Standard Rate and Data Services, Inc.

SRO Standing room only.

SRTCA Senate Radio-Television Correspondents Association.

SS □ Same size. A photographic abbreviation for no change in picture size during printing or enlarging. □ Stock shot. □ Sans serif. □ Solid state.

SSA □ Solid state amplifier. □ Special service authorization. An FCC file-number prefix for nonbroadcast services.

SSB Single sideband.

SSP Society for Scholarly Publishing.

SSTV Slow scan television.

ST □ Aural STL. An FCC file-number prefix. □ Screw terminal. A lamp base type.

STA □ Special temporary authority. □ Subscription Television Association.

stab □ *See* sting. □ To puncture sheets, signatures, and so on, to make book sewing easier.

stabilization □ The process of rendering a processed film or print permanent in a short time by the use of a stabilizing agent. □ The methods used to minimize the vibration effects caused by using long focal length lenses.

stabilization process A process for making fast, temporary proofs for phototypesetting.

stable The authors, writers, actors, or other people who are under contract to a particular agency, publisher, and so on.

stack □ A group of bookshelves or cases with narrow aisles; usually refers to library book storage. Often used in the plural. □ A column of type in a newspaper. Also called a *leg.* □ A slang term for an antenna.

stacked A commercial print advertisement containing information about two or more products or services.

stacked antenna *See* stacked array.

stacked array An antenna with two or more elements mounted one above the other. Also called a *stacked antenna.*

stacked heads Two tape recorder heads, one mounted directly above the other, and used for multitrack recording. Also called *head stack* and *in-line heads.*

stacked type Type set without interlinear spacing.

stacker A platform used to elevate cameras for high-angle shots. *See also* riser.

stacking □ The orderly arrangement of radio or television newscasts. □ *See* block programming.

stacking tracks The recording of different performances on parallel tracks of an audiotape so that different segments may be selected for the master tape.

staff All of the regularly employed personnel of a station, network, advertising agency, publishing firm, and so on.

staff opinion letter A nonbinding letter from the FTC to an advertiser concerning whether or not a proposed action or advertisement might violate a law or regulation.

staff writer A radio or television station, network, or advertising agency writer who is employed to write continuity, scripts, newscasts, commercials, and so on. Cf. commissioned writer and freelance.

stage □ The floor of a radio or television studio. □ The general area on which a set is erected. □ The area behind the proscenium in a theatre. □ To present a production to an audience. □ One step of an amplifier. □ To display publicly.

stage brace An adjustable device used to hold a flat in place.

stage business The small moves and actions of a performer that help add believability to a role.

stage cloth A canvas used to cover the acting area of a stage.

stage direction The movement of characters opposite to that of screen direction.

stage directions The blocking and stage business given to talent by a director.

staged news News that is created by the media, press agents, candidates for public office, and so on.

stage door An entrance to a theatre, soundstage, studio, and so on, used by performers and crew members.

stage fright The nervousness felt by performers in front of an audience, camera, microphone, and so on.

stagehand An individual who works behind the scenes on a production. *See also* grip.

stage hog A performer who attempts to direct an audience's attention to himself or herself.

stage left The direction from a performer's point of view. The opposite of camera left. Cf. stage right.

stage manager (SM) □ An individual who serves as a liaison between the director or producer-director, associate director, and all persons and facilities in the studio, on location or on the stage during rehearsals, prerecording, and performances. □ The person in charge of a theatrical show during performances. Cf. staging coordinator. □ *See* floor manager.

stage monitor A loudspeaker or television monitor that allows a performer to hear or see his or her performance.

stage mother *See* studio mother.

stage name A professional name used by a performer, actor, and so on.

stage picture The aesthetic view of a scene composed by a director as seen from the perspective of the audience.

stage play A play that is produced in the legitimate theatre.

stage plug A flat two- or three-conductor lighting connector. Also called a *paddle plug.*

stage right The direction from a performer's point of view. The opposite of camera right. Cf. stage left.

stage screw A large tapered screw used to secure stage braces to the stage floor. Also called a *peg.*

stage setting The scenery, props, lighting, and costumes that help set the mood, locale, scene, and so on, for a production.

stage spacing The distance between set pieces and talent in relation to the cameras.

stage struck A person who is fascinated by the entertainment industry and who wishes to become a part of it.

stage wait □ A planned hesitation or pause in stage speech or action. □ An unplanned hesitation in stage speech; usually due to forgotten lines.

stage whisper A loud whisper directed by an actor to an audience but supposedly not heard by other actors.

stageworthy A play, script, and so on, deserving dramatic presentation.

staggered heads A seldom used method of mounting stereo recording heads. Cf. stacked heads.

staggered schedule An advertising plan wherein advertisements are published in two or more different publications on alternate dates.

stagger head *See* drop head.

stagger through A slang term for the first complete runthrough of a production.

staging The creation of the entire atmosphere in a production through the use of sets, costumes, lighting, blocking, and so on.

staging coordinator A production facilities supervisor for television; comparable to a stage manager. Also called a *staging director.*

staging director *See* staging coordinator.

staging plan *See* blocking.

staircase A test signal that contains a number of steps of increasing luminance levels. Used to measure luminance linearity.

stake out *See* provisional cut (PC).

STAM Sequential Thermal Anhysteric Magnetization. A system for duplicating helical scan videotapes at high speed.

stamper A metal negative made by electro-forming from which finished record pressings or optical discs are molded.

stamping The process of impressing a design on a book cover or other item, usually with gold leaf, foil, or ink. Also called *blocking.*

stamping die The engraved plate used in stamping.

stamping press A mechanical device for stamping book covers.

stand □ A heavy iron base to which are attached vertical telescoping pipes. A spotlight or floodlight attached to the top can be located 5 or 10 feet above the floor. Also used to hold scrims, microphones, and so on. □ A geographical location where a traveling troupe entertains; as in a one night stand. □ In animation, the entire photographing unit, including the compound, camera, and crane.

stand alone □ A microprocessor-based machine used by an individual for producing relatively short, uncomplicated documents. Cf. mainframe, microcomputer, minicomputer, and multiuser. □ A news picture without accompanying text. □ Programming that is received on film or videotape by a cable television system. □ A device that can operate by itself without any other equipment. Cf. component. □ A radio or television station that is not part of a group or combination.

stand alone service Nonsatellite cable service programmed by videotapes secured directly from program suppliers.

standard □ A gauge or criterion established by law, custom, or agreement against which quantities, values, weights, procedures, and so on, may be measured. □ An adjustable luminaire or set support. □ A popular song that has withstood the test of time. Also called an *evergreen.* □ A bannerlike sign bearing the identification of an advertiser. □ A vertical member used to support an advertising sign. Also called an *upright.* □ A normal typeface as distinguished from boldface, italic, condensed, and so on. Usually refers to width of type.

standard address number (SAN) The identification code for each organization that is a member or is served by the book industry.

Standard Advertising Unit A set of uniform advertising procedures adopted by many newspapers.

standard art *See* stock art.

Standard Book Number *See* International Standard Book Number (ISBN).

standard broadcast band The band of frequencies extending from 535 to 1605 kHz in the United States (to be increased to 1705 kHz).

standard broadcast channel The band of frequencies 10 kHz wide occupied by the carrier and two sidebands of a broadcast signal.

standard broadcast station A broadcasting station licensed for the transmission of radiotelephone emissions primarily intended to be received by the general public and operated on a channel in the band 535 to 1605 kHz.

standard cel *See* standard field.

standard close A uniform close used each time a radio or television program is broadcast. Also called a *lock out* and *stock close. See also* outro. Cf. standard open.

standard colors Ink or paint colors adopted by a medium as acceptable for use by advertisers at no extra charge.

standard consolidiated area *See* Standard Metropolitan Statistical Area.

standard consolidated statistical area (SCSA) A combination of contiguous standard metropolitan statistical areas.

standard deviation A statistical measure of the variability among a set of values. *See also* standard error (SE).

Standard Directory of Advertisers A periodical published by the National Register Publishing Company listing leading advertisers, their advertised products and services, and the positions of key marketing and advertising employees. Cf. *Standard Directory of Advertising Agencies.*

Standard Directory of Advertising Agencies A periodical published by the National Register Publishing Company listing advertising agencies, their accounts, and key employees' positions. Also called the *Red Book.* Cf. *Standard Directory of Advertisers.*

standard eight The original form of 8-mm film, as opposed to Super-8.

standard English *See* general American.

standard error (SE) A measure of the sampling variability that may occur because audience estimates are derived from less than perfect probability samples. A universally accepted measure of the expected range of error in audience estimates created from the results of a sampling survey. The one standard error value is interpreted to mean that there are 68.26 chances out of 100 that a complete census would yield a rating estimate in the range defined by adding and subtracting the one standard error value to the estimate. For example, if rating estimate equals 10 and one standard error equals 1.5, then one can be 68 percent confident that a complete census would yield a corresponding rating in the range 8.5 to 11.5. Standard error does not reflect nonsampling errors. *See also* standard deviation.

standard field A transparent plastic cel used in animation of varying sizes. Also called a *standard cel. See also* field.

standard film The nominal film gauge of 35 mm. Narrower films are referred to as substandard. Also called *standard gauge.*

standard frequency and time signal-satellite service A radio communication service using space stations on earth satellites for the same purposes as those of the standard frequency and time signal service.

standard frequency and time signal service A radio communication service for scientific, technical, and other purposes, providing the transmission of specified frequencies, time signals, or both, of stated high precision, intended for general reception.

standard frequency and time signal station A station in the standard frequency and time signal service.

standard gauge *See* standard film.

standard highway bulletin A painted bulletin 41 feet 8 inches long by 13 feet high.

Standard Industrial Classification (SIC) The classification of businesses as defined by the U.S. Department of Commerce.

standardization □ The establishing of agreed practices and specifications within an industry to allow for coordination and interchangeability of parts. □ A specific standard set for a particular function, such as tape dimensions, speeds, and so on, that allows a tape recorded on one manufacturer's device to be played on one manufactured by another. Also called *interchangeability.* □ The selection of equipment so that redundancy is possible.

standard junior A luminaire that may be used as either a floodlight or spotlight.

Standard Metropolitan Statistical Area (SMSA) The former area designated by the U.S. Office of Management and Budget. Now called Metropolitan Statistical Area (MSA).

standard newspaper A newspaper of the standard size, normally 21-1/2 inches in depth, 14-1/2 inches wide, with 8 columns totaling 2400 agate lines, or 6 columns totaling 1800 agate lines. Cf. tabloid.

standard open A uniform opening used each time a radio or television program is broadcast. Also called a *stock open. See also* intro. Cf. standard close.

Standard operating procedures (SOPs) □ Detailed operational instructions that are used for activating, terminating, and testing the National-Level EBS. □ Substantially uniform and regularly and widely used procedures for operating equipment, producing reports, and so on, within an organization or industry.

standard order blank An order form for media space and time purchases.

standard pitch The tone A, 440 hertz, from which other tones are measured.

Standard Rate and Data Service (SRDS) A commercial firm that publishes a number of reference volumes that quote advertising rates and other data for periodical, radio, television, and transit advertising.

standard reference level The 400-Hz level that is equal to the recorded level on the NAB primary reference tape.

Standards and Practices A network department responsible for evaluation of programs and commercials that are to be aired. Also called *program practices. See also* continuity acceptance.

standards converter Any device used to change signals from one standard to another, such as from 525 television scanning lines to 625.

standard senior A large 5000-watt luminaire.

standard streamliner bulletin A painted outdoor advertising bulletin 14 to 15 feet high by 46 to 48 feet wide.

standard structure An outdoor advertising structure built in accordance with the specifications of the Outdoor Advertising Association of America, Inc.

standard tape *See* alignment tape.

standard television signal A signal that conforms to the television transmission standards.

standard type *See* standard.

standard value A statistical result that could conceivably be obtained by carrying out a survey rigorously, according to what one considers to be an ideal set of definitions, rules, and procedures. Often loosely referred to as a *true value. See also* accuracy.

stand by □ A command given by a television director or floor manager that a program is about to start. □ A director's command given during a program to talent or crew to prepare for a cue. Stand by is often used as a preparatory command for sound effects, tape and film operations, and so on; reserving "ready" for camera and switching cues.

standby A performer, program, component, and so on, to be used as a replacement in case of trouble.

standby mode An operational mode of a tape recorder in which all functions of the machine are in operation except for tape motion.

standby signal *See* stand by.

standby space Unscheduled periodical advertising space, offered to an advertiser at a discount with the understanding that the advertisement will appear only when the space happens to be available.

standby switch A switch that is used to preserve the batteries and circuits of a video camera when it is not being used temporarily.

stand-in A performer, of the same general physical characteristics, who is engaged to substitute for a member of a cast during rehearsals.

standing □ Matter that is retained in type because it is used frequently, such as advertisements, box heads, or tables. Also called *constant, standing matter,* and *standing elements.* □ The right to intervene in a court or adjudicatory proceeding of an administrative agency.

standing ad *See* standing.

standing box *See* standing.

standing committee A committee of one of the independent regulatory agencies that is assigned specific functions.

standing elements *See* standing.

standing head *See* standing.

standing matter *See* standing.

standing order (SO) An order given by a subscriber or buyer for future publications to be shipped without further authorization. Also called a *continuation order.*

standing press A mechanical press used to flatten folded sheets or books.

standing room only (SRO) A theatrical production or studio audience program that is sold out.

standing set *See* permanent set.

standing type *See* standing.

stand of paper The sheets of paper needed to compose a complete outdoor poster advertisement.

standup *See* standupper.

standup copy A script designed to be used without visuals.

standupper A news story delivered by a television reporter from the scene of the incident. Also called a *standup.*

Stanislavski method *See* method.

Stanton-Lazarsfeld analyzer A program analyzer named after its designers.

stanza A recurring unit of lines, music, program, and so on.

stapling The common method of attaching the pages of pamphlets or magazines together with wire staples. Cf. stitching.

star □ An extremely well-known actor or actress. □ The individual who receives top billing in a production. Also called a *lead.* □ A method of identifying different editions of a multiedition newspaper—one star for the first edition, two stars for the second, and so on.

star billing A performer's name listed above the title of a production. Cf. top billing.

starburst lens A lens that produces the same effect as a star filter.

Starch, Daniel, and Associates A research firm that specializes in syndicated sales of measures of consumer response to and recognition of periodical advertising.

star commercial A radio or television commercial presented in a program by the star of the radio or television program. *See also* host selling. Cf. cast commercial.

stare decisis To stand by decided matters; to follow judicial precedence unless overriding reasons compel a different decision.

star filter A camera filter that produces star-shaped images on film.

stargazer An individual who watches well-known motion picture stars and other celebrities.

starlet An aspiring, young actress.

star performer A performer whose average gross compensation as measured by his or her last four comparable appearances (excluding exchanges), is more than $1500.

star system The system popularized in the 1920s, '30s, and '40s by the motion picture studios, that made their stars and contract players household words.

start marks *See* sync marks.

star truck A slang term for a satellite news vehicle.

start up *See* boot.

start up disk The first disk used when powering up a computer; contains the operating system.

stat □ An abbreviation for *photostat.* □ A prefix for the cgs system electrostatic units, such as *statampere.*

state □ As used in the Communications Act of 1934, the 50 states, the District of Columbia, the Commonwealth of Puerto Rico, the Virgin Islands, Guam, American Samoa, and the Trust Territory of the Pacific Islands. □ For the purposes of cable television regulation, any state, territory, or possession of the United States, the District of Columbia, or any political subdivision, agency, or instrumentality thereof. □ The condition of a book with respect to wear or damage.

state association Any of a number of different mass media groups that bring together individuals for the purpose of discussing common interests, such as the Texas Association of Broadcasters.

state count The number of names and addresses in a given mailing list for each state.

state educational radio agency A board, commission, state officer, or agency established by law or appointed by the Governor for the purpose of promoting educational radio.

state educational television agency A board, commission, state officer, or agency established by law or appointed by the Governor for the purpose of promoting educational television.

state farm paper A periodical for farm families in a certain state of the union.

state film commission A state government organization that attempts to persuade motion picture producers to film in that state. Provides assistance in securing necessary permits, accommodations, and so on.

statement of ownership The yearly statement required by the Postal Service of all publishers of periodicals.

statement stuffer A small printed piece designed to be inserted in an envelope carrying a customer's statement of account.

state network primary control station An FM station that acts as the originating station for the state relay network, and is programmed directly by the Governor or his designated representatives.

state of the art Usually refers to equipment that is the most up-to-date available; not outmoded.

state operated lotteries A lottery operated by or conducted under state law.

state relay network A relay network composed primarily of FM stations, and augmented, if necessary, by TV stations and leased common carrier communications facilities, for disseminating statewide emergency programming originated by the Governor or his designated representative.

static Any noise of electrical origin. *See also* atmospherics.

static background An animation background without movement or a background lacking motion.

static cutting Editing that is lacking in imagination or smooth flow of images. Cf. dynamic cutting.

static marks Random lines caused in film by the discharge of static electricity. Usually caused by improper raw film handling.

static position A performer who remains in one position throughout a scene or performance.

station □ One or more transmitters or receivers or a combination of transmitters and receivers, including the accessory equipment, necessary at one location for carrying on a radio communication service. □ A radio or television broadcast station. *See also* radio broadcast station and television broadcast station. □ A computer terminal.

station acquisition marketing plan (SAM) A PBS marketing plan for programs wherein each station purchases programs based on the size of the station's market. Cf. station program cooperative.

station authorization Any construction permit, license, or special temporary authorization issued by the Federal Communications Commission. *See also* authorization.

station break An interruption in a radio or television program or the time between programs utilized for station identification.

station break announcement A commercial or PSA broadcast during a station break.

station classification *See* Class I-IV station and Class A-D station.

station compensation *See* network compensation and reverse compensation.

station format *See* format.

station identification (ID)(SI) The announcements required by the FCC at the beginning and ending of each time of operation and hourly, as close to the hour as feasible. Each station identification must include the call letters of the station and the name of the community or communities specified in its license as the station's location. Television stations may make these announcements visually or orally.

station image *See* image.

station independence program (SIP) A public television project designed to increase the number of subscribers to public television stations.

station information form A computer-generated form that lists essential station information including power, frequency, sign-on/sign-off times, simulcasting (if any), slogan ID, network affiliates, and national representative (if applicable). The form is part of the station information packet that is forwarded to qualifying stations for verification prior to a survey period. Also called a *facility form.*

station information packet A set of forms mailed by The Arbitron Company to qualifying radio stations approximately 50 days prior to each survey; allows the station to change its slogan ID, sign-on/sign-off times, and programming changes.

station license The instrument of authorization required by the Communications Act of 1934 and the Rules and Regulations of the FCC pursuant to the Communications Act, for the use or operation of apparatus for transmission of energy, or communications, or signals by radio by whatever name the instrument may be designated by the Commission. Also called a *license* and *radio station license.*

station lineup The number of radio or television stations that carry a particular radio or television program.

station log *See* log.

station logo *See* logo.

station manager The chief executive officer of a single radio or television station. Cf. general manager.

station operator An individual classified and authorized by the FCC to sign logs and perform specified duties.

station option time *See* option time.

station panel A standard outdoor advertising poster panel erected on the property of a gasoline station.

station policy book A book or pamphlet outlining the long and short range radio or television station goals, continuity acceptance rules, job descriptions, office procedures, and so on.

station poster *See* railroad showing.

station program cooperative (SPC) A system wherein public television stations select the PBS programs they desire and defray the cost for the programs on a cooperative basis. Cf. station acquisition marketing plan (SAM).

station rating Any rating calculated for a radio or television station.

station reach listing A county-by-county listing of radio or television stations that can be received in a county. This listing is based on previous diary history and is updated with recent diary information as well as changes in power/antenna height.

station rep An abbreviation for *station representative.*

station representative An individual or agency that represents a radio or television station on a fee or percentage basis in the sale of time to regional and national advertisers or agencies. Often abbreviated *station rep* or *rep.*

Station Representatives Association (SRA) A trade association promoting the use of spot advertising.

station time The time on a radio or television station that is not available for network programs.

station total area Station total audiences based on viewing data obtained from counties both within and outside a station's NSI area.

statistic A sample fact in a collection made from sampling units. Cf. parameter.

statistical error *See* standard error (SE).

statistical population The complete set of elementary units that are deemed pertinent for a given problem. Also called a *population* and *universe.*

statistical significance A measure of observed differences in statistical tests; that an observed difference between a sample result and some hypothesized population value is unlikely to have occurred simply due to sampling error.

statistics The branch of mathematics dealing with the design, collection, analysis, and interpretation of data.

status The condition of a device, machine, component, and so on.

status conferral The ability of the mass media to bestow importance or legitimacy on individuals or ideas by merely presenting information.

status line The display line in a word processing program that indicates the page, the position of the cursor, the file name, and the amount of memory remaining.

statute A single enactment by a legislative body; such as the Communications Act of 1934, enacted by the U.S. Congress.

statute of limitations A law that requires that legal action be initiated within a specified period of time.

statutory construction The judicial position taken in the interpretation of statutes.

statutory law The body of laws enacted by legislative bodies.

stay A temporary or permanent order by a court enjoining an action.

staying power The ability of a performer, television series, magazine, and so on, to retain its popularity over time.

STC □ Satellite Television Corporation. A subsidiary of COMSAT. □ Short-title catalog.

std An abbreviation for *standard.*

STD average Season-to-date average.

Steadicam A tradename for a self-balancing and movement damping body brace worn by a camera operator. *See also* body pod.

steamy A slang term for a pornographic motion picture.

steel engraving *See* engraving.

Steenbeck A horizontally mounted film editing device made in Germany. *See also* flatbed. Cf. Moviola.

stem The main vertical strokes of a letter. Cf. apex, arm, bar, cross stroke, ear, spur, tail, and vertex.

stencil □ A mask used to expose or hide a portion of an image being animated. □ A paper coated with paraffin from which lettering or designs are reproduced. *See also* Mimeograph and silk screen.

step A single instruction in a computer routine.

step deal An arrangement wherein payment for services is made after the completion of various phases of a project, such as the production of a television pilot or motion picture. Also called *step funding* and *step process.*

step frame The elimination of television or film frames in a preselected pattern in order to produce a strobed effect. *See also* skip frame.

step funding *See* step deal.

step head *See* drop head.

step it up □ To increase the tempo of a scene or program. Cf. pick it up. □ To increase the volume level.

step lens A lens that acts similar to a plano-convex lens but is thinner and lighter due to steps; the term is often used when a lens is stepped on the plano side and is without diffusion to distinguish it from a fresnel lens.

step lines Printed lines that are successively indented. Also called *drop lines.*

step on To begin a line before another performer has finished his or her line.

step optical printer *See* step printer.

step outline The development of a story in the form of a condensed scene-by-scene progression indicating action and the substance of essential story dialogue, but without dialogue. Also called a *step sheet.*

stepped head *See* drop head.

stepped lens *See* fresnel lens.

stepper motor A motor that is controlled by pulses to produce discrete rotation movements rather than continuous movement.

stepping out The American Federation of Television and Radio Artists requires that if a soloist or duo steps out of a group and sings eight or more cumulative bars or speaks ten words or more, he will be classified and paid as a principal performer.

step printer An optical or contact printer that holds the positive and negative motionless during the printing of each frame. Also called a *step optical printer.* Cf. continuous printer.

step process *See* step deal.

steps *See* color bars.

step sheet *See* step outline.

step up The use of special premiums to get mail order buyers to increase their quantity of purchase.

step wedge A series of exposures, from light to dark, made on film that increases the exposures in predetermined steps. Also called an *optical wedge.* Cf. intensity scale.

stereo An abbreviation for *stereophonic* and *stereotype.*

stereocasting *See* stereophonic broadcasting.

stereo mat A mold, usually of papier maché, for a stereotype.

stereo matrixing *See* matrix.

stereophonic The recording and reproducing of sound using two or more channels for the music or other information. Also called *stereophonic sound* and, sometimes, *stereosonic.* Abbreviated *stereo.* Cf. binaural, monophonic, and quadraphonic.

stereophonic amplifier An amplifier that has two separate channels for sound.

stereophonic broadcasting The broadcasting of two signals for the reception of stereophonic sound, either by one AM, FM, or TV station. Formerly accomplished by a combination of AM, FM, or TV stations. Also called *stereocasting.*

stereophonic cartridge A high-compliance cartridge with one stylus and two elements for the reproduction of stereophonic discs. Also called a *stereophonic pickup.*

stereophonic channel The band of audio frequencies from 200 to 15,000 Hz containing the stereophonic information that modulates the radio frequency carrier.

stereophonic crosstalk An undesired signal occurring in the main channel from modulation of the stereophonic channel or that occurring in the stereophonic channel from modulation of the main channel.

stereophonic microphone Two microphones encased in one housing.

stereophonic miking The use of two microphones, one for each channel, for recording or transmitting.

stereophonic pickup *See* stereophonic cartridge.

stereophonic pilot tone An audio tone of fixed or variable frequency modulating the carrier during the transmission of stereophonic programs.

stereophonic recording □ On discs, a system wherein two channels are recorded in a single groove. □ On tape, a system wherein two channels are recorded on separate tracks on the same tape.

stereophonic separation The ratio of the electrical signal caused in the right (or left) stereophonic channel to the electrical signal caused in the left (or right) stereophonic channel by the transmission of only a right (or left) signal.

stereophonic sound The audio information carried by plurality of channels arranged to afford the listener a sense of the spatial distribution of sound sources. Stereophonic sound broadcasting includes, but is not limited to, biphonic (two-channel), triphonic (three-channel), and quadraphonic (four-channel) services.

stereophonic sound subcarrier A subcarrier within the FM broadcast baseband used for transmitting signals for stereophonic sound reception of the main broadcast program service.

stereophonic sound subchannel The band of frequencies from 23 kHz to 99 kHz containing sound subcarriers and their associated sidebands.

stereophonic television *See* stereophonic broadcasting.

stereo plate *See* stereotype.

stereoscopic A television system that is capable of producing images that appear three-dimensional.

stereoscopic camera A film camera containing two closely spaced lenses and film paths for recording an image.

stereoscopic cinematography The production of motion pictures that present the illusion of depth when two paired images are projected on a flat screen. Normally, a viewer must wear glasses that separate the two projected pictures.

stereosonic *See* stereophonic.

stereotype □ A simplified interpretation of ideas or people. □ Casting performers in roles by physical characteristics only. □ A performer who appears the same from role to role. □ A printing plate cast in metal from a papier maché mold. Often called a *stereo* and *stereo plate.* Cf. electrotype. □ To cast a printing plate. □ *See* bromide.

stet □ From the Latin for "let it stand." A proofreading term meaning to let the copy remain as it originally was; to ignore marked changes. Stet may be indicated by the word or by a series of dots. □ A standard open and close used in a radio or television program.

STIA Satellite Television Industry Association; formerly SPACE. *See also* SBCA.

stick □ A metal receptacle for handset type; a composing stick. □ *See* stickful. □ A slang term for a vertical antenna.

stickful □ A full composing stick; approximately two column inches of type matter. Also called a *stick.* □ A request to a reporter to write a few lines.

sticking *See* burn.

sticks □ A clap stick. □ The command to use a clap stick.

stick up initial A cut in or rising initial.

stiction The tendency for a tape to adhere to itself in adjacent winding layers, or to adhere to surfaces that it contacts in a recorder transport system.

stilb A unit of luminance equal to one candela per square centimeter.

stile One of the two vertical members of a flat.

still □ A single photograph taken by a camera. □ A single frame of a videotape or motion picture. □ A publicity photograph of a performer.

still background An animation background that is not moved.

still frame A single shot held for a number of television or motion picture frames.

still man A photographer who takes stills for publicity purposes.

still store A computer storage device that is capable of storing pictures digitally for later editing and use on electronic, optical, or magnetic storage devices.

sting An emphatic, sudden musical chord or phrase used to accentuate or emphasize a dramatic moment, serve as a bridge, and so on. Also called a *stab* and *stinger. See also* glissando.

stinger □ *See* sting. □ *See* kicker.

stipple To draw or engrave using fine dots in a random pattern, often on a drawing board containing the stippled surface.

stipulation An agreement entered into before a hearing between or among parties as to fact.

stitcher A machine for laying underground cable.

stitching The use of wire staples in book, magazine, and pamphlet binding. *See also* saddle stitch and side stitch. Cf. sewing.

STL Studio-transmitter link.

STM □ Short-term memory. □ Scientific, technical, and medical. A publishing house that specializes in STM.

stn An abbreviation for *station.*

stock □ Unexposed film. Also called *filmstock* and *raw film.* □ Unexposed print film. □ *See* stock footage. □ *See* raw tape. □ The paper used for printing.

stock art Artwork created and sold for use for a number of purposes or by a number of advertisers. Also called *standard art.*

stock character *See* stock part.

stock close *See* standard close.

stock company A repertory group that presents plays without the services of a star.

stock cut Printing engravings kept by the printer or publisher for occasional use, in contrast to exclusive use.

stock footage Film clips from already exposed and processed film or from a commercial film library. Also called *library footage, library material, library shot, stock material,* and *stock shot.*.

stock format A direct mail format with illustrations or headings preprinted and to which an advertiser adds his own copy.

stock material *See* stock footage.

stock music A library of musical intros, bridges, backgrounds, and so on, usually purchased; often a charge is made for each use. Also called *library music. See also* needle drop.

stock open *See* standard open.

stock part A stereotyped role played in a production. Also called a *stock character* and *stock role.*

stock photo A generic photographic still used when no up-to-date pictures are available.

stockpiling The buying of syndicated programs, motion pictures, and so on, by a television station before they are needed in order to prevent other stations from obtaining them.

stock poster A standard outdoor advertising design that covers a specific category of business. It may be purchased and used by advertisers in that category merely by adding their trade names to the stock poster.

stock reel *See* feed reel.

stock role *See* stock part.

stock set A set constructed from existing flats and set pieces. Also called a *unit set.*

stock shot □ An unimaginative camera shot with the appearance of stock footage. Also called a *clipping.* □ *See* stock footage.

stock size One of the various sizes of film or tape, such as 35 mm, 16 mm, 1 inch, 2 inch.

stock solution A photographic chemical that must be diluted before use.

STOC-TV Satellite Technical and Operational Committee-Television.

stone A smooth, flat table, once made of stone but now of steel, on which printing forms are assembled. Also called an *imposing stone.*

stone man A printing shop employee who assembles printing forms.

stone proof A proof made of a printing form without using a press. *See also* proof.

STOP Single title order plan.

stop □ One of the marks on a potentiometer dial. □ A metal stud in a potentiometer with which the wiper makes contact. □ A radio or television program brought to a complete halt by spontaneous laughter or applause by the audience. □ The size of a lens diaphragm opening. *See also* f stop. □ A punctuation mark; especially a period.

stop action □ The freezing of one videotape frame on the screen. □ *See* stop motion.

stop bath An acid solution used after the film developer to eliminate further development.

stop down To reduce the diameter of a lens diaphragm so as to decrease the amount of light in the camera. Also called *stopping down.*

stop frame *See* freeze-frame.

stop leader The blank leader between two film or tape segments.

stop motion photography A technique by which objects can be animated by adjusting their positions or changing drawings between shooting the next frame in a sequence. Also called *stop action. See also* animation and single frame photography.

stop motion printing The repeated printing of a single frame of film. *See also* freeze-frame.

stop news *See* spot news.

stop out □ To sear a portion of an electrotype to prevent the deposit of metal. □ To cover a portion of a negative with an opaque material or resist to prevent etching.

stopper A striking headline or illustration intended to attract immediate attention.

stopping down *See* stop down.

stopping groove *See* concentric groove.

stopping up *See* stop up.

stop pull The changing of the aperture of a lens during the course of a shot.

stop set A group of commercials, announcements, or both aired between sets of music.

stop up To increase the diameter of a lens diaphragm in order to increase the amount of light in the camera. Also called *stopping up.*

storage □ The erasable memory in a computer. □ A device, such as a disk drive, used to hold data for later retrieval. □ The act of storing data on a recording medium.

Storage Instantaneous Audimeter (SIA) A Nielsen-developed microcomputer used by both NTI and NSI metered measurement of television tuning.

storage switcher An electronic device that stores information about shots or radio or television programs and automatically switches the proper source on line at the selected time.

store To place information in a storage device for later retrieval.

store and forward A technique in which a number of messages are stored in memory and transmitted in a batch on demand. Used, for example, in electronic mail and pay-per-view services.

store audit A measurement of consumer sales made at the point of sale.

storecasting An FM service that furnishes background music to retail stores. *See also* functional music, musicasting, and transitcasting.

story □ A narrative of something that has occurred. □ A synonym for *plot.* Also called a *story line.* □ A literary or dramatic story indicating the characterization of the principal characters and containing sequences and action suitable for use in, or representing a substantial contribution to, a final script. □ All writing representing a contribution distinct from screenplay and consisting of basic narrative, idea, theme, or outline indicating character development and action. Cf. narrative synopsis. □ A report of an event; an article written for publication except for advertising and editorials. Also called a *piece.* □ A prose narrative, usually less extensive than a novel.

story analyst An individual hired by a motion picture studio or production company to synopsize and analyze potential scripts.

storyboard □ A series of small consecutive drawings with accompanying caption-like descriptions of the action and sound, which are arranged comic-strip fashion and used to plan a film. The drawings are frequently tacked to corkboards so that individual drawings can be added or changed in the course of development. Invented at the Disney studio, the technique is now widely used for live-action films and commercials, as well as animation. Also called a *layout.* □ An illustration of the design elements of an application.

story conference A meeting held between a producer, writer, and others to discuss a story, play, treatment, screenplay, and so on.

story count The number of stories that appear on a single page in a publication, or the total number of stories in a publication.

story editor An individual who reads, rewrites, and edits scripts and other manuscripts.

story line An outline of the plot of a story, novel, program, screenplay, and so on. Also called a *plot line.*

story treatment *See* treatment.

stow □ To place a story on a newspaper page that will be completed early in the make-up of the paper. □ A slug placed on copy that will not be changed.

straddle show A radio or television network program that begins during and runs beyond network option time.

straight □ An unequalized line or recording. □ *See* straight news.

straight commercial A radio or television commercial delivered during a station break or program interruption.

straight copy *See* straight matter.

straight cut A redundant term for a *cut.*

straight make-up Make-up that makes a character appear normal to the eye, as opposed to younger, older, character, and so on.

straight man A performer who sets lines or situations for a comic or comedian.

straight matter Copy set without embellishment—italics, boldface, rules, tables, and so on. Also called *straight copy.* Sometimes referred to as *body type. See also* text.

straight news News that is written in a clear, unembellished, straightforward manner; without interpretation. Also called *straight.*

straight part A role that calls for acting in a normal manner. Also called a *straight role.* Cf. heavy.

straight reading Lines or material delivered by a performer without undue emotion or emphasis.

straight role *See* straight part.

straight run A method of printing a newspaper to double the capacity of a press using different plates top and bottom. Cf. collect run.

straight shot A camera shot taken from directly in front of the subject or object.

straight up Refers to the beginning of a radio or television program; when the second hand points at 12.

strain relief A wire or clamp that is connected between a connector and a cable to provide protection against accidental wire breakage.

strand A steel cable that supports coaxial cable strung between utility poles.

stranded conductor *See* stranded wire.

stranded wire A flexible wire composed of a number of individual wires wound together. Also called a *stranded conductor.*

strap A subordinate headline, usually placed over the main head.

strategy A statement of the communications goal and basic message (not specific content) to be used in an advertisement or series of advertisements; usually consists of a stated intent (such as to persuade), target prospect description, the benefit or benefits to be promised, and the facts to be used to support the believability of the benefits promised. Also called *creative strategy.*

stratified sampling A survey sample that divides the original sampling frame into mutually exclusive sub-frames (strata) wherein separate and independent samples are selected from each strata. *See also* probability sample. Cf. quota sample.

Stratovision A plan proposed by Westinghouse in 1945 to use airplanes equipped with television transmitters to relay programs from coast to coast.

stray light Any unwanted reflected, diffused, extraneous light on a set or in a theatre.

streaking A television picture distortion that stretches objects horizontally.

streaky noise A low-frequency random noise in the chrominance signal. *See also* chroma noise.

streamer ☐ A long scratch on a looped film used as a cue. ☐ *See* banner.

streamer head *See* banner.

stream of consciousness A type of first-person narration in which the narrator reveals his or her inner thoughts.

street correspondent A newspaper, radio, or television reporter who works a beat, such as the White House, police beat, and so on. Also called a *street job.*

street job *See* street correspondent.

stress marks Streaks on film caused by tight winding.

stretch ☐ A direction to talent to slow down so as to fill time. ☐ An elongation of an object in an animation drawing. *See also* squash. ☐ A limousine used to transport highly paid personnel.

striations The series of density lines that produce the modulations on variable density soundtracks.

strike ☐ To dismantle and store a set after a production. ☐ To remove an object from a set. ☐ A work stoppage by employees. ☐ To make a duplicate. ☐ To make a copy of a film. ☐ To make an impression on a book cover with a hot tool. ☐ To form an arc between two electrodes as in a film projector or luminaire.

strike application An application made to the FCC for a broadcast license for the purpose of delaying or impeding a legitimate application by another party.

strike on A method of producing an image through the direct contact of type on paper as in typewriting. Also called *direct impression.*

strikeover *See* overstrike.

strikethrough The forceful impression of type that shows through the opposite side of a printed page.

string ☐ A series of newspaper clippings attached end to end or affixed in a scrapbook. ☐ The "output" of a stringer. ☐ The amount of type set by a Linotype operator on one shift. ☐ A connected set of characters.

stringer A freelance camera operator, news reporter, and so on, usually paid on a per-story, per-film, per-inch, and so on, basis.

string man *See* stringer.

strip ☐ To remove insulation from a wire. ☐ *See* striplight. ☐ A series of comic cartoons, usually in a series of horizontal rectangles. ☐ To remove computer codes from tapes. ☐ To affix strips of cloth to the lining or insert of a book. ☐ To separate an electroplating from its mold. ☐ *See* stripping.

stripe *See* magnetic stripe.

stripe filter A filter used to separate the three colors in a single-tube video camera.

strip in *See* stripping.

striping The process of attaching a stripe of magnetic tape to the edge of a film.

striplight A luminaire with a number of lamps arranged in a line. Often each lamp is in an individual compartment. There may be a reflector behind the lamp and/or a color medium in front of the lamp. Striplights are normally wired in three or four circuits.

stripping □ The combining of negatives on a flat for photoengraving or photolithography. Also called *strip* and *strip in.* □ To make a roll of paper ready for use in a press. □ The practice of broadcasting a syndicated television series at the same time each day during the week. Also called *strip in, strip programming, strip run,* and *strip show.*

strip programming *See* stripping.

strip run *See* stripping.

strip show *See* stripping.

strip slot The time period that is used for stripping a television program.

strip title *See* subtitle.

strobe □ An electronic flash used for still cameras. □ An abbreviation for *stroboscope.*

strobing □ The visual effect caused by rapid panning. □ The flicker in a television picture caused by horizontal lines. Also called *venetian blind effect. See also* horizontal bars. □ A visual effect caused by the difference in frame rate and the movement of an object. Also called *jitter, skipping,* and *stroboscopic movement.*

stroboscope A light that pulsates at a known frequency.

stroboscopic disc A disc, usually made of paper, printed with alternate dark and light areas and used with a stroboscope to measure the speed of a turntable or tape transport.

stroboscopic movement *See* strobing.

strobotron A gas filled vacuum tube with a cold cathode used especially as a source for stroboscopic light.

stroke speed *See* scanning frequency.

structural film *See* structuralism.

structuralism The study of society and psychological phenomena in art forms. The structural film exemplifies this arrangement of photographic images. Also called *cine structuralism.*

structured interview An interview that requires the interviewer to ask the questions exactly as written. Cf. unstructured interview.

structured question *See* fixed-alternative question.

structuring The combining of story elements into a plot.

stub A short length of transmission line.

stud One of the metal contacts in a potentiometer.

studhorse A large, dark display typeface.

studio □ A motion picture studio. □ Any room or series of rooms equipped for the production of motion pictures, broadcast programs, sound mixing, and so on. *See also* soundstage.

studio address (SA) *See* talkback.

studio animation Animation characterized by the fact that the various aspects of production are done by different people and, in the case of larger studios, different departments; the finished product is the result of a coordinated group effort.

studio animator An individual responsible for drawing the characters used in animation. Cf. independent animator.

studio audience A group of persons present in a broadcast studio for the presentation of a program, either live or taped.

studio camera A camera designed primarily for work in a television studio. Cf. field camera.

studio card A graphic shot with a television studio camera, as opposed to one on film or tape.

studio coordinator An individual responsible for the operation of a radio or television studio. Also called a *studio manager.*

studio manager The individual in charge of a motion picture studio. *See also* studio coordinator.

studio mother The parent of a child performer who sometimes becomes particularly demanding of special treatment for her offspring. Also called a *stage mother.*

studio program A radio or television program that originates in a studio, as opposed to a remote.

studio set-up The production facilities: sets, cameras, microphones, and so on, in position and ready for use.

studio teacher A teacher who presents a telelesson.

studio-to-headend link (SHL) A local relay used to join a studio to a transmitter site.

studio workweek Any workweek other than an overnight location workweek.

studio zone A location within a specified area for which no travel time is paid by a motion picture studio.

stuff □ A slang term for the raw material of a news story. □ *See* filler. □ To enclose advertising material in envelopes. □ Paper stock ground.

stuffer An advertising piece enclosed in an envelope, newspaper, magazine, and so on.

stump The end of a roll of newsprint.

stunt □ A difficult or dangerous piece of business accomplished by a stunt player. □ An event created by a newspaper, publicity agent, broadcast station, and so on, in order to attract attention or gain recognition or applause.

stunt coordinator The individual in charge of stunts on a motion picture.

stunting The scheduling of special programs on television so as to confound or confuse the competition. Stunting may also include the shifting of regular program days and times.

stunt man A male stunt player.

Stuntmen's Association of Motion Pictures, Inc. An association of stunt players.

stunt player A person who is employed to perform the risky or hazardous action(s) designated in a script. Cf. contract player, day player, deal player, freelance player, multiple picture player, and term player.

stunt woman A female stunt player.

STV □ Subscription television. □ Subscription television authority. An FCC file-number prefix. □ Subscription TV, Inc.

STVRC Satellite Television Viewing Rights Coalition; formerly part of SPACE.

STWP Society of Technical Writers and Publishers.

style □ A distinguishing characteristic or manner in speaking, writing, or acting. □ Audience applause encouraged by a cue from a member of a production team. □ A consistent approach to the presentation of ideas, designs, performances, writings, and so on. □ The typographical plan for a written work as to punctuation, spelling, display, capitalization, and so on.

stylebook A manual that sets forth the rules for style of a particular publisher, publication, wire service, and so on. Also called a *style sheet.*

style sheet *See* stylebook.

stylized Lighting, sets, artwork, and so on, that are designed to evoke an abstract feeling or effect.

stylus □ A small needle-shaped object used to cut or reproduce a disc groove; usually diamond, sometimes sapphire. The term may refer to a subassembly comprising the entire moving system of the pickup cartridge. Also called a *needle. See also* embossing stylus, recording stylus, and reproducing stylus. □ A penlike device that is used with a graphics tablet or to control the movements in a computer graphic system.

stylus drag The force resulting from friction between the surface of the recording medium and the reproducing stylus. Also called *needle drag.*

stylus force The vertical force exerted by a stylus on a groove. Also called *needle force, stylus pressure,* and *tracking force.*

stylus pressure *See* stylus force.

sua sponte Voluntarily; as when a court or administrative agency acts on its own initiative.

sub □ An abbreviation for *substitute.* A news story substituted for one already in type or written. □ An abbreviation for *substance.*

subaudible tones and pulses Tones and pulses used by SCA holders to activate and deactivate subscribers' multiplex receivers. *See also* pulses and superaudible tones.

subbing The process of coating film with a layer between the base and the emulsion. *See also* subbing layer.

subbing layer The layer of gelatins and solvents used to increase adhesion between a film base and emulsion. Also called a *substratum.*

subcarrier A modulated carrier that is used to modulate another carrier.

subcode A channel that can contain other information besides music and that is not heard when the disc is played; a CD digital audio data stream.

subcode channel In CD, one of eight subchannels, referred to as P to W, that exist in parallel to the main channel. They are used for control and display information.

subcontrol station A station that originates an international television broadcast.

subdistrict A cable television system area that receives specific channels that are different from other areas serviced by the same system.

subharmonic A submultiple of a fundamental frequency.

subhead □ A subordinate heading or title within the body of a story; often used to separate long blocks of type. □ A display line within the body of a text, serving as a subtitle for the portion of the text that follows.

subheader In CD-I, a field indicating the nature of the data in a sector, thus allowing real-time interactive operation. The subheader can be thought of as a series of realtime switchers that reduce load on the microprocessor and coprocessors and save decoding time.

subject □ A speech topic. □ An animate being that is used in a scene or shot. Cf. object.

subject heading A topical index used in card catalogs, indexes, and so on. Also called a *subject index*.

subject index *See* subject heading.

subjective That which is perceived by the mind, as opposed to objective.

subjective camera Action that is photographed from an actor's position in order to intensify a scene. Also called *subjective viewpoint*. *See also* point-of-view. Cf. objective camera.

subjective loudness A redundant term for loudness.

subjective research *See* qualitative research.

subjective shot A camera shot that contains the often strange or bizarre actions or thoughts of a character in a story.

subjective time The length of time experienced by a character in a scene, regardless of real time. Cf. expanded time, experienced time, objective time, and screen time.

subjective tracking A camera shot in which the lens becomes the eyes of an actor in a scene. *See also* subjective camera.

subjective viewpoint *See* subjective camera.

subjective writing A feature or story colored by the writer's opinions, prejudices, and point of view.

subject to nonrenewal (SNR) A radio or television announcement that is available only if a sponsor or advertiser does not exercise renewal rights.

sub judice A matter not yet decided by a court.

subliminal advertising The advertising of a visual message that is too brief to be consciously recognized.

subliminal perception The subconscious recognition of a message below the threshold of normal awareness.

submaster □ An audio control console potentiometer that controls the output of two or more other potentiometers. □ *See* group master. □ An audio- or videotape made from a master, and used for duplicating other tapes.

submaster fader *See* group fader.

submission A script, novel, story, and so on, that is offered for sale by the author.

subplot A separate story within the main story that is designed to enhance and expand on the main plot of a novel, motion picture, and so on. Often used to provide relief from the main plot. Cf. main plot.

subpoena A court order requiring an individual to appear in court or produce documents (subpoena duces tecum).

subprint The superimposition of type on artwork so that the type remains solid in appearance.

subrefraction Atmospheric refraction of radio waves that is less than normal.

sub rights An abbreviation for *subsidiary rights*.

subroutine A computer program routine that is used repeatedly by the main program or used in different programs.

subsample A selected portion of a sample, such as men between 39 and 54 or households with income above $30,000.

subscreen The horizontal position of a single CD frame that can use different decoding and resolutions from other subscreens in the same plane.

subscriber □ An individual who purchases services from a pay television system, telephone company, and so on. □ An individual, group, or organization that has paid to receive a subscription to a periodical or book. □ A member of the general public who receives broadcast programming distributed by a cable television system and does not further distribute it.

subscriber drop □ The line from a telephone company pole to a subscriber's building. □ A cable from a utility pole to a cable television subscriber's terminal.

subscriber line □ The telephone line between a central exchange and a subscriber's telephone. □ *See* subscriber drop.

subscriber study A demographic or psychographic study of the subscribers to a periodical.

subscriber tap *See* subscriber terminal.

subscriber terminal The cable television system terminal to which a subscriber's equipment is connected. Separate terminals may be provided for delivery of signals of various classes. Also called a *subscriber tap.*

subscript A letter or other character written below the base line. Also called a *figure* and *inferior letter.* Cf. superscript.

subscription An order for a periodical, book, or other publication; usually a magazine or newspaper.

subscription agency An organization that orders subscriptions to periodicals in bulk and distributes them to various libraries and other users.

subscription book □ A book set or series purchased as the various volumes are published. □ A special set of books, often bound alike, sold only to subscribers. Also called a *subscription edition.*

subscription cablecasting Origination or access cablecasting operations for which a per-program or per-channel charge is made.

subscription edition *See* subscription book.

subscription list A list of subscribers or subscriptions or both.

subscription music channel *See* subsidiary communications authorization (SCA).

subscription television (STV) A system whereby subscription television broadcast programs are transmitted and received. *See also* pay television.

subscription television broadcast program A television broadcast program intended to be received in intelligible form by members of the public only on payment of a fee or charge.

subscription television market The area included by the signals of all commercial broadcast stations that place a Grade A contour over the entire community to which the subscription station is licensed.

subscription television program A television program intended to be received in intelligible form only for a fee or charge.

subscription television station (STV) A broadcasting television station that can be received only in homes that have subscribed to the television service offered by the station. The station sends out a scrambled signal, then unscrambles the signal in the subscribing household. Generally, STVs share time on the facilities of a commercial television station.

subsequent punishment Sanctions that are imposed after publication. The effect can be similar to prior restraint.

subsidiary channel Any portion of an authorized channel not used for main channel transmissions.

subsidiary communications authorization (SCA) The authority granted by the FCC to an FM broadcast station to multiplex a number of services. *See also* functional FM.

subsidiary contrast A subordinate portion of a picture. Cf. dominant contrast.

subsidiary rights The rights to a book, such as reprint, translation, paperbound, and so on, granted by a copyright holder to another or others.

subsidy publishing □ *See* sponsored book. □ *See* vanity press.

subs previous A news wire story that supersedes everything previously received concerning a particular item.

substance *See* basis weight.

substandard Any film less than 35 mm. *See also* narrow gauge.

substantially duplicates A cable television system that regularly duplicates the network programming of one or more stations in a week during the hours of 6 to 11 p.m., local time, for a total of 14 or more hours.

substantially true A recognition of the general validity of a news story.

substantiation The requirement that advertisers have a reasonable basis for making claims about products or services.

substantive law The law concerned with the rights and duties of individuals. Cf. procedural law.

substantive process The incorporation of color-forming materials in the emulsion layers of film instead of in the processing solution.

substratum *See* subbing layer.

subtext The secondary meanings and implications of a novel, story, motion picture, and so on, that must be discovered by the reader or viewer.

subtitle □ A secondary or subordinate book title. Also called a *strip title.* □ A half title. □ The explanatory words used to set or advance a scene or translate foreign dialogue.

subtractive color film Film that is designed to be used in the subtractive process.

subtractive color mix The removal of energy of various wavelengths from a light, such as by filtering or reflection. When colorants (paints, dyes, and so on) are mixed or when filters are superimposed, each tends to remove energy at the wavelengths it would have if acting independently. Cf. additive color mix.

subtractive filter A filter that is sensitive to all colors but its own color.

subtractive primary colors The pigment colors of red, yellow, and blue that, when mixed in the proper proportions, form the other colors. Cf. additive primary colors. *See also* primary color.

subtractive process The major method of reproducing the colors of a film through the use of three transparent dyes that each remove unwanted portions of the spectrum. Cf. additive process.

Suburban case A landmark case wherein the Court of Appeals for the District of Columbia upheld the FCC's right to require ascertainment of community needs and problems from a prospective licensee.

suburban copy Newspaper copy primarily concerned with news and features about outlying areas of a metropolitan area.

success rate *See* rate of response.

sudser A slang term for a soap opera.

suds scenario A slang term for a soap opera script.

sulfate paper Paper made by boiling wood chips in an alkaline solution under pressure.

sulfite paper Wood pulp paper whitened by bleaching. *See also* chemical pulp.

sum channel The monophonic signal derived by combining the left and right stereophonic channels.

summary □ A brief statement of the facts of a news story. □ A brief newscast.

summary contempt The judicial power to hold an individual in contempt of court without the necessity of a trial.

summary head A headline that encapsulates the news.

summary index An index of brief summary heads; often found on the front page of a newspaper.

summary judgment A judicial decision based on the law instead of issues of fact.

summary lead A lead that contains the 5 Ws, or most of the main points of a news story.

summer program Any program that is broadcast between June 1 and September 15 of any year. A period during which summer rates may be paid.

sun arc A large, intense arc light.

Sunday ghetto A time period in which the networks and local stations air public service programs.

Sunday supplement Any of various nonnews sections included with a Sunday newspaper, as comics, or television schedules, and especially general interest magazines.

sun gun A small, portable luminaire.

sunlight The light that reaches a set directly from the sun, as opposed to reflected light. Cf. daylight.

sunrise and sunset For each particular location and during any particular month, the time of local sunrise and sunset as specified in the instrument of authorization by the FCC.

sunrise watch *See* lobster trick.

sun screen A gauze screen used to diffuse sunlight.

sunscreen A diffusing light screen mounted in front of a television receiver picture tube to reduce glare.

sunset The time frame for phasing out an existing law or regulation.

sunset law A law that sets the date for the termination of agencies or programs.

sunshade A lens shade, often a rectangular box on film cameras, designed to decrease the amount of stray light reaching the lens. Also called a *lens hood.*

Sunshine Act *See* Government in the Sunshine Act.

sunshine legislation Any legislation that requires any level of government to hold open meetings. Especially applies to the 1976 federal law that requires approximately 60 federal agencies subject to the Freedom of Information Act to hold open meetings in most circumstances.

sunspot number The 12-month running average of the number of sunspots for any month as indicated in the U.S. Department of Commerce Telecommunications Research and Engineering Report.

sunspots The dark spots on the surface of the sun that may cause interference with electromagnetic waves.

super □ An abbreviation for *superimpose* and *superimposition.* □ To superimpose. □ A director's command to superimpose one shot over another.

super □ A thin, open mesh fabric used for reinforcing book bindings. Cf. crash. □ An abbreviation for *supercalendered.*

superaudible tones and pulses Tones and pulses used by SCA holders to activate and deactivate subscribers' multiplex receivers. *See also* pulses and subaudible tones.

superband The cable television channels (J–W) that are located between the VHF and UHF frequencies, and, therefore, require a cable converter or cable compatible receiver or VCR.

Super-Beam 1000 A circular, 1000-watt quartz luminaire.

super blanking *See* supersync.

supercalendered (sc) An uncoated paper that has been given an extremely glossy finish.

supercardioid A unidirectional microphone with a narrower angle of acceptance than a standard cardioid microphone.

supered titles *See* superimposed titles.

super-8 A film format 50 percent larger than the obsolete 8-mm format.

super-80 A large luminaire used in floodlighting.

superheterodyne An improved version of the heterodyne receiver developed by Edwin H. Armstrong in 1919.

super highband □ Pertaining to those frequencies specified in SMPTE Recommended Practice RP 6, Practice SHB. □ Pertaining to recordings made in accordance with Practice SHB or RP 6, or equipment capable of making such recordings.

super high frequency (SHF) The frequencies between 3 and 30 gigahertz.

superimpose □ The technique of using two separate television picture sources simultaneously, each at approximately half strength. □ To combine two picture sources. Also called a *super, super-imp, super-impose,* and *superimposition.* Cf. chromakey and key.

superimposed titles The use of lettering over a static or moving background. Also called *supered titles.*

superimposure A double exposure on film. Also called a *burn-in.*

super in sync To superimpose titles or other words at the same time an announcer reads the material.

superior character *See* superscript.

superior court A court of law higher in standing than a lower court. Cf. inferior court.

superior figure *See* superscript.

superior letter *See* superscript.

Super Panavision A Panavision process using a 65-mm negative.

Super Panavision 70 A 70-mm Panavision print from a 65-mm Panavision negative.

super power A radio station authorized a power greater than that normally granted for a given class of service. For example, radio station WLW was authorized 500,000 watts temporarily in the 1930s.

superregenerative receiver An improved version of the regenerative receiver designed by Edwin H. Armstrong in 1922.

super royal octavo An English book size; 10 inches in height by 6-3/4 in width.

SuperScope A wide-screen process that utilized standard 35-mm film that was anamorphically printed.

superscript A letter or other character written above the waist line. Also called a *superior character, figure,* or *letter.* Cf. subscript.

super-16 A 16-mm film that eliminates the soundtrack to allow for wide-screen filming.

super slide A slide used in a television superimposition.

supersonic Faster than the speed of sound.

supersonic bias The use of high frequency impulses to reduce distortion in magnetic recording systems.

superstation An independent television broadcast station whose programs are distributed nationally by satellite to cable television systems, and then retransmitted by cable to subscribers.

supersync A horizontal and vertical signal pulse generated at the end of each scanning line. Also called *super blanking.*

super table of contents (super TOC) In CD-I, synonymous with disc label; the information that is required to start up the CD-I player. Stored in the first track on the disc, it concerns the disc type and format, the status of the disc as a single entity or part of an album, the data size, and the position of the file directory and bootstrap. Cf. table of contents.

Super Technirama A Technirama process producing 70-mm prints from 65-mm negatives.

super TOC *See* super table of contents.

super trunk The cable television transmission lines from the antenna or head end to the distribution points.

supertrunk A cable used to link a cable television headend with a hub or antenna site.

super VHS *See* S-VHS.

supervising editor An individual who functions as an editor and who is also responsible for the work of any other editor or editors working on a given production or series.

superzoom lens An easily adjustable zoom lens.

supplement □ A separately printed section of a newspaper. □ Material, often extensive, added to a book; either new material or material intended to continue the body of the book. Cf. appendix. □ A separate book intended to update material contained in a previously published book, as an encyclopedia yearbook.

supplemental Television that is used as an adjunct to classroom work in schools.

supplemental market The sale, rental, or exhibition of theatrical motion pictures on cassettes for exhibition on a home-type screen in the home, in other closed circuit use such as in hotel rooms, or on pay-type cable television or pay television, or on any common carrier such as commercial airlines, trains, ships, and buses.

Supplemental Register A register for certain marks not eligible for entry in the Principal Register under the Trade Mark Act of 1946.

supplementary lens A lens, usually positive, that is attached to the front of a camera lens to enable it to focus on objects close to the lens.

supplementary story *See* follow.

supplementary tape speeds Fifteen, 3-3/4, and 1-7/8 inches per second are supplementary tape speeds. *See also* preferred speed.

supplier An individual or company that furnishes equipment, programs, records, advertising material, and so on.

supply reel The reel from which the tape is unwound during the normal play or record modes of the tape recorder. Also called a *feed reel.* Cf. take-up reel.

support *See* advertising weight.

supporting cast The cast of a motion picture or television program or series that reinforces the plot or characters.

supporting role A motion picture or television role that is more than a walk on or minor character, but less than a leading role.

suppress To prohibit publication or withhold from circulation. *See also* censorship.

suppressed carrier A sideband that is not transmitted. Also called a *suppressed sideband.*

suppressed sideband *See* suppressed carrier.

suppression □ The elimination of a portion of a transmitted wave. □ The elimination of sounds, signals, interference, and so on, by filtering, grounding, or shielding.

supra Above; the opposite of *infra.*

Supreme Court The highest court in the United States judicial system. Cf. court of appeals.

surface induction The flux density normal to the surface of the magnetic tape.

surface noise The noise component in the electric output of a pickup due to irregularities in the surfaces of the groove walls at or close to the points of stylus contact. Also called *needle scratch.*

surface paper Paper that is sized and calendered.

surface printing Printing by any method, such as lithography, that uses a flat printing surface. Cf. intaglio.

surface wave A ground wave that travels along the surface of the earth.

surge A sudden change in current or voltage.

surge protector A device that is designed to eliminate alternating current line surges.

surprint To superimpose lettering on a photograph or illustration. Also called *doubleprint* and *overprint.*

surprise The writing technique of using the least likely character in a story as the guilty person.

surrealism An art movement from the 1920s often characterized by distorted and incongruous sequences and pictures.

surround sound An alternative term for quadraphonic or multiple channel sound.

survey □ A method of estimating audience size, habits, viewing patterns, and so on, by using a sample selected from a statistical population. Cf. census and poll. □ A reconnaissance made of a proposed location for a motion picture or television program or series.

survey announcements *See* hypoing.

survey area The geographic area from which a sample is developed for a study. Cf. coverage area.

suspended interest A news story that withholds the main point until near the end of the story.

suspense The generation of concern in an audience for a protagonist through a writer's or director's use of curiosity and tension. Cf. mystery.

suspenser A television suspense program.

sustain To hold a camera shot, musical note, sound, and so on.

sustainer *See* sustaining program.

sustaining advertising Advertising for the purpose of maintaining the demand for a product rather than creating or increasing it.

sustaining program A program broadcast by a network or station that receives no advertising revenue. Also called a *noncommercial program* and a *sustainer.*

S-VHS A VHS format that is basically an improved consumer product with greater resolution (430 lines horizontal resolution), improved audio, and some compatibility with standard VHS. Cf. Betacam, Betacam SP, M II, and U-Matic SP.

SW □ Short wave. □ Switch.

swan cube *See* beam splitter.

swarf *See* chip.

swash Letters in some typefaces, usually italic, that contain elongated, sweeping lines.

swatching The attaching of samples of material to a printed piece.

sweating To anchor a printing plate to its base by soldering. Also called *anchoring.*

sweep □ A tall, concave or convex set piece. □ The movement of the electron beam in a cathode ray tube. *See also* scanning. □ A period, usually of four weeks duration, during which all local television markets are simultaneously measured and reported by a rating service. Traditional sweep months are November, February, and May. In addition, NSI measures and issues complete Viewers in Profile reports on all Designated Market Areas (DMAs) in July.

sweephand The large second hand on a stopwatch or clock used extensively in timing. Now somewhat replaced by digital readouts.

sweep reversal The horizontal or vertical electronic reversal of a television picture that results in a mirror image.

sweeps □ *See* sweep. □ Radio ratings taken at various times.

sweetening □ Music, sound effects, applause, bass boost, and so on, added to a soundtrack or live performance to improve the quality of the sound. □ The singing of different parts or notes recorded at different times where separate soundtracks are made and a composite is made of separate renditions. □ The addition of a new or variant soundtrack over an original track.

sweetening session A recording session that adds voice, strings, or other sounds to an already recorded rhythm track.

swell A smooth, fast increase in the volume of sound.

swell dash *See* diamond dash.

swelled rule A rule that is thicker in the center than at the ends.

swing A line or paragraph used as bridging material in a story.

swinger A slang term for a phonograph disc with an off-center center hole.

swinging arm The most common type of turntable tone arm.

swing man A newspaper employee who temporarily fills in for another.

swipe A compilation or file of artwork, designs, photographs, and so on, used for inspiration or as a substitute for inspiration.

swish pan *See* whip.

Swiss design A layout system that uses grids and is characterized by clean, flowing lines and spaces. Sometimes called *international design*.

switch □ A change from one camera to another. *See also* take. □ To accomplish a take. □ To act as a switcher. □ To change a camera angle. □ A mechanical device used to open or close an electrical circuit.

switchboard □ A lighting switch panel, control board, or console of any type. □ A portable control board of the piano box type. □ A telephone termination board used to interconnect various telephones. □ *See* patch panel.

switched line A communication path that may vary with each usage.

switcher □ An electronic device that permits instant cuts between television cameras. Also called a *video mixer*. *See also* special effects generator. □ The individual who performs the function of switching. □ A device in a videotape recorder that activates the recording, playback, and erase heads.

switching □ The process of electrically transferring from one signal to another. □ The process of selecting between or among video or audio sources.

switching overlay In video, a technique in which every pixel in the displayed image is selected from one or another of the corresponding source images.

switching transient Electrical noise that may be caused by switching from one signal to another.

switchover To change from one device to another. *See also* changeover.

switch pitch An attempt on the part of a radio or television station to persuade an advertiser to place a spot announcement or schedule using funds currently employed for advertising on a competitive station.

swivel To move a microphone or camera boom in a horizontal plane.

SWR Standing wave ratio.

SWS Slow wave structure. A delay tube for a satellite.

SWT Short wave transmitter.

syllable A unit of language consisting of one or more vowel sounds and sometimes a consonant or consonants.

symbol □ A letter or simplified design used to represent words or components in schematics and formulas. □ A sign used to represent an operation, quantity, process, element, relation, quality, or data item. □ An arbitrary or conventional sign, letter, number, and so on, used in place of a word or words. □ Anything that represents an object or person. □ In CD, the basic unit of digitized data, parity, and subcode data. Initially 8 bits long, it is expanded to 17 (14 + 3) bits by 8-to-14 modulation.

symbolic speech Nonverbal communication, usually in the form of a negative reaction to public policy.

symmetrical lens A lens consisting of two identical or similar sets of elements. Cf. asymmetrical lens.

symmetry □ The potentiometer on many video switchers that controls the shape of an insert. □ The balance obtained in a camera shot.

sympathy A writing technique used to create concern for a character in a drama.

symposium A collection of writings on a particular subject published in a periodical.

sync An abbreviation for *synchronization, synchronous,* and so on.

sync advance The number of film frames the sound precedes the picture. *See also* projection sync.

sync beep An audible synchronizing pulse used to mark sound on tape or magnetic film.

sync cable A connection carrying a sync pulse between a film camera and a magnetic tape recorder. Also called a *sync lead.*

sync generator An electronic device used to supply the sync pulses in a television system.

synch An alternative spelling of *sync.*

sync head The head on a double system sound recorder used to record the sync pulses. Also called a *sync pulse head.*

synchronism The relationship between the sound and picture of a motion picture film.

synchronization □ The maintenance of one operation in step with another, such as between sound and picture, between a scanning beam and the blanking pulse, and so on. □ The process of maintaining common timing and coordination between two or more operations, events, or processes, under the control of CD-RTOS.

synchronization field In CD-ROM and CD-I, the first 12 bytes of a sector containing synchronization information.

synchronization pattern A distinctive pattern in a transmitted waveform, used to establish synchronization.

synchronization pulse *See* sync pulse.

synchronization rights The rights granted by a mechanical rights agency to use copyrighted music in conjunction with motion pictures, television programs, or other visuals.

synchronization signals In CD-I, real-time software interrupts, often generated by a device driver during hardware interrupt processing when a predefined condition has been met.

synchronize □ To make sound correspond to a picture on film. □ To lock one element of a system to the others.

synchronizer A mechanism that maintains synchronization between two or more lengths of film. It consists of two or more sprockets mounted on a common revolving shaft.

synchronizing mark *See* sync marks.

synchronizing pulse *See* sync pulse.

synchronous The ability of transmitting and receiving devices to run continuously at the same frequency.

synchronous logic The electronic circuit in a television system that generates the composite sync signals.

synchronous mark *See* sync marks.

synchronous motor An induction motor that runs at a speed controlled by the frequency of the power source.

synchronous pulse *See* sync pulse.

synchronous satellite A satellite that rotates at the same speed as the earth. *See also* geostationary satellite.

synchronous sound Sound that is in synchronization with a picture; usually refers to lip synchronous sound. Also called *parallel sound.* Cf. nonsynchronous sound.

synchronous speed *See* sound speed.

synchronous transmission *See* synchronous.

sync lead *See* sync cable.

sync leader A length of film leader that contains numbers indicating the seconds until the beginning of a picture. Usually refers to academy leader.

sync level The amplitude of the sync pulses.

sync marks The marks used on both a soundtrack and picture to indicate the synchronous starting point for editing. Also called *start marks.*

syncom An acronym for synchronous communication. A satellite system designed to provide worldwide coverage through the use of three synchronous satellites.

sync plop *See* sync pop.

sync point Any sound or mark that indicates synchronized points on a film or tape.

sync pop A sound placed at the beginning of a soundtrack for later synchronization. Also called a *sync plop.*

sync pulse An electronic pulse produced by a sync generator.

sync pulse head *See* sync head.

sync punch A hole in a film soundtrack used as an audible cue.

sync roll The vertical rolling of a television picture caused by switching between sources that are not in synchronization or by a poor videotape edit.

sync separation *See* video filter.

sync signal The television signal used for synchronizing scanning.

sync sound Sound that matches the picture on film or videotape frame for frame.

sync tone A recorded high-frequency signal used to drive a slave recorder or playback unit.

sync tone oscillator A crystal controlled oscillator that produces an electrical signal that is fed to a magnetic tape recorder for synchronous sound and picture.

syndex Syndicated exclusivity.

syndicate □ An organization that buys and then sells stories, comic strips, features, and so on, to newspapers and magazines. □ To sell and distribute a newspaper column, Sunday supplement, comic strip, and so on, to a number of periodicals for simultaneous publication.

syndicated art *See* standard art.

syndicated exclusivity The FCC rule that prohibited the importation by cable television systems of programs for which local broadcasters had exclusive local rights. The rule was reinstated effective January 1990. Often referred to as syndex.

syndicated feature A short audio or video program containing news, personalities, critiques, and so on, that is sold to individual broadcast stations.

syndicated mailing A mailing prepared for distribution by firms other than the manufacturer or syndicator.

syndicated program Any program sold, licensed, distributed, or offered to television station licensees in more than one market within the United States other than as network programming. Also called *syndication.*

Syndicated Program Analysis (SPA) An Arbitron term for a special rating and share analysis of syndicated programs to aid in programming decisions.

syndicated program exclusivity *See* syndicated exclusivity.

syndicated service □ Music programming on tape sold to individual radio stations. □ A radio and television ratings service sold to individual stations and networks.

syndicated supplement A newspaper supplement sold on a syndicated basis.

syndicated writer A writer who is carried by a number of different newspapers.

syndication The distribution of programs to individual broadcast stations, as opposed to network distribution. *See* bicycling and syndicated program.

syndication window The length of time that a motion picture is available to television stations.

syndicator □ A person who makes available prepared direct mail promotions for specific products or services for mailing by a mailing list owner for his or her own list. Most syndicators also offer product fulfillment services. □ The production company or distributor of a radio or television program or series available to stations or cable television systems for syndication. □ *See* packager.

synopsis □ A condensed version of a proposed or completed script, program, novel, and so on. □ A brief narrative of a plot.

syntax A set of rules governing the structure of a language, human or machine.

synthesis parameters The parameters used to regenerate audio information from data stored in a compressed or encoded format on media such as CD.

synthesized speech quality In CD-I, the fifth and lowest audio quality level. Artificially generated speech using phonetic coding.

synthesizer An electronic device that is capable of producing original audio signals either by internally generating them or by accepting external signals.

synthetic distortion Television picture distortion introduced electrically or mechanically.

synthetic sound Sound that is created by drawing, computer input, and so on, as opposed to live sound.

system □ Any method of classification, codification, regulation, and so on. □ A combination of components joined in an orderly fashion to form a complete operating unit, such as a loudspeaker system or telephone system.

systematic sample *See* systematic selection sample.

systematic selection sample A survey sample that consists of taking every *k*th element after a random start, where *k* is the sampling interval, as in the number of elements in the frame divided by the desired sample size. This is the equivalent of selecting a single cluster consisting of *k* elements. *See also* probability sample.

system community unit A cable television system, or portion of a cable television system, that operates or will operate within a separate and distinct community or municipal entity (including unincorporated communities within unincorporated areas and including single, discrete unincorporated areas). Also called a *community unit.*

system cue A time, voice or visual cue from a network to affiliates that a station break is due.

system interconnect An informal network between two or more cable television systems.

system manager A cable television system general manager. Also called a *general manager.*

system microphone A microphone design wherein different microphone elements may be interchanged using a common base and power supply to produce varied pickup patterns.

system noise □ That combination of undesired and fluctuating disturbances within a cable television channel that degrades the transmission of the desired signal and that is due to modulation processes or thermal or other noise-producing effects but does not include hum and other undesired signals of discrete frequency. □ *See* ground noise.

system of public telecommunications entities Any combination of public telecommunications entities acting cooperatively to produce, acquire, or distribute programs, or to undertake related activities.

system operator The owner or manager of a cable television system.

system software Programs that form part of a computer operating system or its support utilities. Cf. applications software.

system text In CD-ROM and CD-I, a message processed by the operating system without the need to load and process any special text processing application program.

T

T □ Television. An FCC file-number prefix. □ Time. □ Transformer. □ Telephone. □ Telegraph. □ Terminal. □ Time. □ Transmission. □ Transmission stop. □ True. □ A wire service code for travel news.

TA Total audience.

TAA □ Textbook Authors Association. □ Transit Advertising Association.

TAB □ Television Bureau of Advertising. *See* TvB. □ Traffic Audit Bureau, Inc.

tab □ An abbreviation for *tabloid.* □ A recessed or protruding book index marker. □ A set drop suspended by a single line.

tab curtain A curtain that opens from the center. Also called a *tableau curtain.*

table □ An arrangement of data in columns and rows. *See also* matrix. □ Material printed in tabular form, usually with three or more columns.

tableau A camera shot of persons who remain motionless and silent.

tableau curtain *See* tab curtain.

Table of Allotments The list of FM or TV channel assignments for the various communities of the country published by the FCC. Formerly called a *Table of Assignments.*

Table of Assignments *See* Table of Allotments.

table of contents (TOC) □ A list of the parts of a book or other extensive printed matter such as chapter headings, major divisions, and so on; part of the front matter. Sometimes called a *register.* □ Subcode information defining the sequential number, start, length, and end times of tracks on a compact disc, together with their type, including digital audio or data. The table of contents is contained in the Q channel of the lead-in area of all compact discs. Cf. super table of contents.

tabletop *See* compound.

tabletop photography The photography of miniatures and models on a small table or animation compound. Also called an *insert stage.*

table work □ To set type in a tabular format. □ Type matter set in tabular form.

tabloid □ A newspaper format approximately one-half the size of a standard newspaper, and usually containing five or six columns. □ A small format newspaper characterized by extensive pictorial matter and sensational stories. □ A preprinted advertising insert of four or more pages, usually about half the size of a regular newspaper page, designed for insertion into a newspaper.

taboo A prohibition placed on ideas, words, actions, and so on, in a script, advertisement, or production by a sponsor, broadcast station, newspaper, and so on, because of social pressure, or self-regulatory procedures.

tabulate To arrange data in a table.

TAC Television Advisory Committee of Great Britain.

TACET Television Advisory Committee for Educational Television.

tachistocope A device used to expose an object to respondents in a survey for a precisely measured and extremely small time interval, such as a tenth of a second; used in advertisement and package recognition tests. Also called a *T-scope.*

tachometer A device used to measure or indicate the rotational speed of a shaft or associated moving part.

tack A measure of the ''stickiness'' of ink used for printing.

TACOMA Television Advisory Committee of Mexican Americans. A citizens' group.

TAD Telephone answering device.

tag □ A voice or musical ending added to a commercial. □ The closing words to a news story on film or tape delivered by an announcer on camera. □ *See* kicker. □ A punch line. Also called a *tag line.*

tag business A visual tag.

tagging The delineation of a script character accomplished by revealing his or her dominant traits.

tag line The last line of a scene, program, joke, and so on. Also called a *punch line.*

tagline A line added to the address on a mailing list that directs the piece to a specific person in an organization.

tag scene *See* tag line.

tail □ The downward projection on certain letters; a descender. Cf. apex, arm, bar, cross stroke, ear, spur, stem, and vertex. □ The bottom margin of a printed page. Cf. head. □ The end of a book chapter. □ A part of a stereotype casting that is cut away. □ The end of a piece of film or tape. Also called *foot. See also* short end. □ The last few seconds of a radio or television program, commercial, or recording. □ A ghost image or pulse in a television picture or signal. Also called an *afterimage.*

tailband A strip of cloth sewn into the bottom of a book back. Cf. headband.

tailing *See* hangover.

tail leader A leader attached to the end of a piece of film or tape.

tailor To slant news to conform to the policy of the publisher.

tailor-made A group of radio or television stations that form a network for a single program.

tail out A tape or film that has not been rewound. *See also* tail. Also called *tail up.* Cf. head out.

tailpiece A decoration placed at the end of a book chapter or story. Cf. headpiece.

tail sync *See* end sync.

tail trim The frames that are edited from the end of a shot.

tail up *See* tail out.

take □ A length of film or videotape, often one of several similar shots. □ A cut from one camera to another. □ A television director's command to cut; as "take one." Also called a *direct take.* □ A page of newspaper copy ready to be set in type. □ A portion of the copy of a large printing job. One of a number of takes. □ In videotape program production, a segment of the total program recorded in time isolation from other segments for later assembly into the complete program. □ A reaction by a character. Tex Avery was famous for his use of wildly extreme takes in his films; eyes would bulge to the size of watermelons, jaws would drop and knock holes through tables, tongues would unroll to several feet, and so on.

take a balance To audition various audio sources for proper balance.

take a level To set an audio level by having talent speak into a microphone.

take board *See* number board.

take cue An audio or video cue marked on tape or film as a starting point.

take five A director's command to take a brief break. Also take ten or other indication of time.

take it away A cue to begin that is given to a remote, announcer, following program, and so on.

take it from the top A director's rehearsal instruction to a cast or crew or both to begin again from the start.

take list A detailed list of the videotape or film takes. Also called a *take sheet.*

take number The sequential number assigned to a camera take.

take-one A transit car card that is used inside a vehicle and that bears a pouch or printed leaflets, reply cards, and so on, intended for passengers to take.

takeout A comprehensive news story.

takes A number of individual shots.

take sheet *See* take list.

take timings To measure the exact time of each take.

take up The mechanism used to wind the film or tape on a take-up reel.

take-up reel The reel onto which the tape is wound after it has passed through the tape transport, in the normal play or record modes of the machine. Cf. supply reel.

taking lens The lens through which a scene is photographed, as opposed to a viewfinder lens.

Talbotype *See* calotype.

talent A generic term for all persons who perform, including actors, comedians, masters of ceremonies, quiz masters, disc jockeys, singers, dancers, announcers, sportscasters, specialty acts, stunt persons, walk-ons, extras, puppeteers, reporters, and analysts.

talent agency An organization that represents and promotes performers and others in contract negotiations.

talent agent An individual who acts as a performer's booking representative.

talent audition A tryout period wherein a performer or group of performers is tested for ability, talent, physical attributes, and/or suitability for inclusion in a broadcast or motion picture. Also called an *individual video test* and *individual voice test.*

talent cost The above the line cost for the performers in a radio or television program.

talent payment *See* residuals.

talent raid The hiring of two or more individuals by a network, agency, newspaper, and so on, from the competition.

talent release *See* release.

talent scout An individual employed by a network, production company, and so on, who searches for new talent for a program or series. Also called a *scout.*

talent union A union or guild that represents performers, such as AFTRA, SAG, SEG, AEA, AGVA, or AGMA.

talk □ A radio station format. □ A broadcast speech.

talkback □ A system of loudspeakers between a television studio and a control room. Also called a *speak back* or *studio address.* Cf. intercom. □ A system for intercommunication between a control room and a remote. Also called a *ring down line.*

talkback switch A switch that activates a talkback system.

talk down To speak with condescension to an audience. Cf. talk up.

talkie A slang term for a motion picture with sound. The term was used primarily in the late 1920s.

talking book A recorded reading of a book, usually on records or tapes, made especially for the visually handicapped.

talking clock *See* edit sync guide.

talking head □ A style of shooting in which only the person on camera is shown. Often a dull, monotonous shot or program lacking in visual impact. □ An individual close-up on television.

talk jockey (TJ) A radio talk show host.

talk program A program that consists of interviews, roundtable discussions, speeches, and so on. Cf. talk show.

talk radio A radio format in which a host interviews well-known personalities and accepts calls from the audience.

talk sets The talk between records by disc jockeys.

talk show A program that has a well-known host interviewing celebrities. Cf. talk program.

talk up To speak with obfuscatory or pleonastic sesquipedalian words to an audience. Cf. talk down.

tall copy A book containing larger than normal top and bottom margins.

tally light The red light mounted on a television camera that indicates to performers and cameramen when the camera is on. Also called a *camera cue light* or *cue light.* Cf. check light.

TALO Total audience listening output.

TAMI Television Accessory Manufacturers Institute.

tampon A variant spelling of *tympan.*

T and A show A television program that highlights the anatomical details of female performers. Also called a *jiggle show.*

T and E Travel and entertainment.

tandem □ The use of two anchors in a television newscast. □ A system in which signals pass between two devices or components. □ A telephone interconnection between two exchanges.

T&M Test & Measurement.

tank □ A container in which film is processed. □ A pool in which underwater scenes are photographed.

tank shot An underwater shot.

tanning The process of hardening the gelatin in a film emulsion.

TAP Total audience plan.

tap □ A contact on a rheostat, potentiometer, or other device from which a portion of a voltage, signal, and so on, is derived. □ A device on the feeder line of a cable television system that diverts the television signal to the subscriber's line drop.

tape □ A flexible ribbon consisting of an acetate, polyester, or mylar base on which is coated a magnetic material, used as a recording and playback medium for audio or video signals. Standard tape widths are 1/4 inch, 1/2 inch, 3/4 inch, 1 inch, and 2 inches. □ To record a program, picture, or sound. □ A narrow ribbon of perforated paper used in setting type. □ Formerly, copy received on ribbons of tape from wire services. □ A band of material used to strengthen book bindings. □ A flexible band used to guide sheets into or from a printing press, folder, and so on.

tape cartridge A plastic case that contains audio magnetic tape. Usually called a *cart.* Also called a *tape magazine. See also* cartridge.

tape cassette A plastic case that contains magnetic audio- or videotape and associated supply and take-up reels. *See also* cassette.

tape chatter The vibration caused by the audio- or videotape sticking to the tape guides.

tape counter *See* counter.

tape cross section The configuration of the tape through its various layers, typically including the backside coating, the base, the binder, and the oxide.

tape curvature The deviation of an untensioned length of videotape from straightness. Most video recorder format specifications indicate maximum values for tape curvature and define measurement methods.

taped announcement An announcement made by broadcasting stations that the program or material being presented is taped, filmed, or recorded. Required only when the element of time is of special significance.

tape deck The tape transport, heads, and often the preamplifier of a tape recorder or reproducer.

tape delay A system used by radio stations on call-in shows to briefly delay the material before it airs, so that possible objectionable remarks can be deleted. Also called *time delay. See also* delay line.

tape density A measure of the number of bits per inch that can be recorded on tape, such as 800 or 1600 bits per inch.

tape drive The mechanism used to move the audio- or videotape.

tape guide A roller or post used to position the tape correctly along its path on the tape transport.

tape-input guide In quadruplex recording, the last guiding element encountered by the tape as it approaches the vacuum guide. The tape-input guide combines with the tape-output guide to define the tape neutral plane. Cf. tape-output guide.

tape leader The neutral section of audio- or videotape, usually recorded ahead of the program material, that contains technical alignment signals and production information.

tape lifter The mechanism that removes the tape from contact with the heads in the fast forward and rewind modes.

tape log A list of all the cuts or shots on an audio- or videotape.

tape loop A tape with the ends spliced together. *See also* loop.

tape magazine *See* tape cartridge.

tape network An informal radio network wherein tapes are bicycled between stations.

tape neutral plane In quadruplex recording, a plane located between and defined by the tape-input guide and the tape-output guide in which the tape would lie if it were undeflected by the vacuum guide.

tape noise Noise that is inherent in an audio- or videotape.

tape operator A television station employee who loads and unloads videotape reels and cartridges from videotape recorders and players.

tape-output guide The first guiding element encountered by the tape after it leaves the vacuum guide. The tape-output guide combines with the tape-input guide to define the tape neutral plane. Cf. tape-input guide.

tape oxide The material affixed to a flexible base for recording and reproducing magnetic signals.

tape pack The degree of tightness with which magnetic tape is wound on a reel.

tape path The path described by the tape as it passes through the tape transport during normal operation of the machine.

tape player A tape reproducer.

tape puncher An individual who produces punched paper tapes by keyboarding information.

tape reader A device capable of reading information stored on a punched paper tape.

tape recorder An electromechanical device capable of impressing audio or video information on a magnetic tape in the form of magnetic patterns.

tape reproducer A device used to play recorded tapes, but that does not have the capability of recording.

tape speed The linear rate of travel of the undeformed recording medium past any stationary portion of a tape transport. The most common tape speeds are 1-7/8 ips, 3-3/4 ips, 7-1/2 ips, and 15 ips. *See also* preferred speed.

tape splice A film splice made with an overlay of transparent adhesive plastic.

tape splicer *See* splicer.

tape tension The tension applied longitudinally to the tape by the tape transport.

tape threader A device used to wind tape on a reel.

tape timer A readout device that indicates the running or elapsed time of a tape in motion. *See also* counter.

tape-to-film transfer The transfer of a program from a videotape master recording to a motion picture film. Cf. film-to-tape transfer.

tape transport The basic mechanism of a tape recorder or reproducer, not including electronic parts. Also called a *motor board* or a *puller.*

tape transport geometry The configuration of the tape path through a video recorder.

tapologist A slang term for a sound recording specialist.

target □ A designation for an obstruction blocking the view approach to an outdoor advertising structure. □ The plate in a television camera pickup tube that stores the electrons emitted from the photosensitive surface and that is scanned by the electron beam. □ A round flag.

target audience □ The group of individuals, identified by age, sex, or other demographic or psychographic characteristics, that an advertiser wishes to reach in an advertising or public relations campaign. Also called a *target group* and *target market.* □ The specific demographic audience for which a program, motion picture, novel, and so on, is designed.

targetcasting Broadcast station, and especially cable television, programming that is designed to appeal to a select audience. *See also* narrowcasting.

target demographics Audience groupings containing multiple discrete demographics, such as men and/or women 18+, 18 to 34, 18 to 49, 25 to 49, as opposed to discrete demographics, such as men and/or women aged 18 to 24, 25 to 34, 35 to 44.

target group *See* target audience.

Target Group Index (TGI) A syndicated study of national media audiences and their product purchase behavior.

targeting Designing or aiming programs, articles, periodicals, motion pictures, and so on, toward a specific audience.

target market *See* target audience.

tariff The charge made to users of a communication service for equipment and/or services. Common carrier services are subject to Federal or state tariff regulations.

TARPAC Television and Radio Political Action Committee. The political action fund of the NAB.

TASO Television Allocations Study Organization. An industrywide committee that studied UHF allocation problems, set standards for picture quality, and so on.

TASS Telegrafnoie Agenstvo Sovietskavo Soyuza. The major Soviet news agency.

TAT Thematic Apperception Test.

tax certificate A document issued by the FCC to broadcast station licensees who sell to minority owners. The certificate allows the seller certain tax breaks.

TBA □ Television Bureau of Advertising. *See* TvB. □ To be announced.

TBC Time base corrector.

TBD To be determined.

TBDF Transborder data flow.

T-bone A metal bracket used to hold luminaires.

TC □ Telecine. □ Title card. □ Time code. □ Transcontinental. □ Transfer of control. An FCC file-number prefix.

TCAF Temporary Commission on Alternative Financing for Public Telecommunications.

TCC □ Telecommunications Coordinating Committee. A government committee formed in 1946 to develop plans and policies in frequency allocation and spectrum management. □ Television control center.

T channel One of the eight compact disc subcode channels (P-W). At present allocated to CD graphics only.

TCU Tight close-up.

TD Technical director.

TDMA Time division multiple access.

TE □ Telecommunication engineering. □ Test equipment.

TEA Technical Engineers Association.

TEAM Top European advertising media.

tearing A condition of a television picture wherein diagonal or horizontal lines appear to move apart. Also called *bearding.*

tearjerker Any sad motion picture, novel, television program, and so on; often used to refer to a soap opera.

tear sheet □ A page torn from a publication and sent to an advertiser as proof of insertion. Cf. checking copy. □ *See* reprint.

tease A brief news item, often at the top of a radio or television newscast, that is designed to hold listeners or viewers for a story to be reported on later in the newscast.

teaser □ A short program segment broadcast before the titles. □ An announcement or promo designed to arouse curiosity in the audience. Also called a *come-on spot* and *hooker.* □ A horizontal border above a set used to prevent cameras from shooting into the lights or to hide the grid from an audience. □ An advertisement or promotion planned to excite curiosity about a later advertisement or promotion. □ A curiosity arousing device or slogan placed on a direct mail piece. □ *See* kicker. □ A headline used to arouse curiosity in a reader. Also called a *teaser head.*

teaser campaign A series of commercial announcements designed to arouse curiosity and create interest in an audience. Teaser commercials violate section 317 of the Communications Act unless the advertiser's name is included in the announcement.

teaser head *See* teaser.

tea wagon A slang term for a small, wheeled audio console.

technical An acting interpretation that appears underplayed or wooden to an audience.

technical advisor An expert in a subject hired to assist with background, technical, or other information on a subject. Extensively used in motion picture production.

technical considerations One of the basic eligibility criteria for a broadcast license. *See also* character considerations, financial considerations, and legal considerations.

technical coordinator An individual who assists the director on a multicamera television motion picture film production that is photographed before a live audience, or as though a live audience were present, in planning the placement and movement of cameras.

technical difficulties (TD) □ Time periods of five or more minutes during a survey in which a station had technical problems such as transmitter failure, power failure, loss of audio or video, and so on. □ A generic term used when anything goes wrong with a camera, printing press, and so on, and sometimes, operator error.

technical director (TD) A technician who is responsible for the performance of technicians for a particular television program. Often serves as the switcher, or may operate the video controls during a production.

technical editor A videotape editor who works under the creative decisions made by another.

technical log *See* operating log.

Technical Merit Award An award presented by the American Radio Relay League to amateur radio operators or groups of amateurs for technical contributions to amateur radio.

technical run through A run through designed to test the capabilities and readiness of the equipment used in a production.

technician An individual skilled in the operation and maintenance of equipment. The term is often used to mean an engineer.

Technicolor A trademark for the most widely used motion picture color film processing.

Technirama A system in which 35-mm film moves horizontally through the camera to produce a wide-screen motion picture.

Techniscope A system in which a half-height frame of 35-mm film is used to produce a wide-screen motion picture.

technological determinism The theory that new technologies are discovered by research and development rather than brought about by societal changes, and then lead to social change.

teen □ A medium or product that appeals primarily to adolescents. □ *See* night.

tel An abbreviation for *telegraphic, telegraphy, telephonic, telephony, teletype, teletypewriter,* and *television.*

telco A contraction of telephone company.

tele An abbreviation for *telephoto* and *television.* From the Greek for "far off."

telecamera A television camera.

telecast A television broadcast.

telecasting Television broadcasting.

telecensus A census of television receiver owners.

telechrome A paint made especially for television scenery.

telecine (TC) □ The equipment used in television to show film and slides. *See also* film chain and multiplexer. □ The room that houses the telecine and equipment. Also called a *film chain room* and *telecine studio.*

telecine camera A camera permanently mounted on a film chain pedestal.

telecine studio *See* telecine (TC).

telecine transfer A film-to-tape transfer process using a film chain and videotape recorder.

telecom An abbreviation for *telecommunication.*

telecommunication □ Literally, the process of communicating at a distance by means of wire, radio waves, light waves, and so on. □ Any transmission, emission, or reception of signs, signals, writing, images, and sounds or intelligence of any nature by wire, radio, optical, or other electromagnetic systems. Cf. broadcasting.

telecommunications The individual messages that are sent by telecommunication.

telecommuting The use of telecommunication facilities that allows employees to accomplish their work at home.

telecon An abbreviation for *telephone conversation.*

teleconference A conference between or among persons who are physically separate but linked together by telecommunication devices.

telecourse Instructional material presented on television.

telecruiser A mobile television van.

telecuer A device used to prompt a television performer. It may be mounted on or near a camera, in front of a lens or nearby, and consist of words on a transparent or opaque scroll, tape, paper, and so on. Also called a *prompter. See also* autocue, teleprompter, and tele-q.

telefac An abbreviation for *television facsimile.*

telefacsimile A system for the transmission and reproduction of graphic materials. Also called *telefax.*

telefax *See* telefacsimile.

telefeature A made-for-television movie.

Telefex A trademark for a rear projection system.

telefilm Television film. A film made specifically for use on television. Also called a *made-for-television movie.* Cf. kinescope.

telegenic A person or object with a pleasing appearance on television. Similar to *photogenic.*

telegogue A television demagogue.

telegram Written matter intended to be transmitted by telegraphy for delivery to the addressee. This term usually includes *radiotelegrams. See also* telegraphy.

telegraph □ To give an obvious hint to an audience of what is to come in a play or script. □ A device that uses coded signals to send messages by wire.

telegraph editor The newspaper editor in charge of editing wire service news. Also called a *wire editor.*

telegraphic news An older term for news received from a wire service.

telegraphy A form of telecommunication that is concerned in any process providing transmission and reproduction at a distance of documentary matter, such as written or printed matter or fixed images, or the reproduction at a distance of any kind of information in such a form. For the purposes of the International Radio Regulations, the term also means a form of telecommunication for the transmission of written matter by the use of a signal code.

teleinformatics A general term for information sent and received by a telecommunication system.

telejector A slide projector joined with a television camera. *See also* telecine.

telelecture A television lecture. Usually used in conjunction with a telecourse.

telelesson A school lesson, usually grammar school or high school, presented on television.

telemarketing The use of telephone services for the promotion, sale, and solicitation of goods and services.

telematics The combination of telecommunication and computer technology; from the French *télématique.*

telemessage A message sent by a telecommunication system.

telemetry The remote sensing and measuring of systems, such as a broadcast transmitter.

teleordering The use of computers connected by telephone lines for the ordering of merchandise by retail stores such as booksellers.

telephile A person who is enamored of television; often a couch potato.

telephone An instrument that converts sound waves into electrical impulses for transmission by wire, and vice versa.

telephone adapter *See* telephone pickup.

telephone coincidental A type of audience survey made by telephone. *See also* coincidental interview.

telephone coupler *See* modem.

telephone exchange service Service within a telephone exchange, or within a connected system of telephone exchanges within the same exchange area operated to furnish to subscribers intercommunicating service of the character ordinarily furnished by a single exchange, and that is covered by the exchange service charge. Cf. telephone toll service.

telephone filter A filter used to pass voice-range audio frequencies.

Telephone Group The radio stations owned by AT&T and Western Electric in the 1920s. These stations became NBC's Red Network in 1926. Cf. Radio Group.

telephone interview A question and answer session conducted by telephone. *See also* coincidental interview. Cf. personal interview.

telephone jack *See* phone jack.

telephone pair Two wires in a circuit designed to carry telephone lines.

telephone pickup A device used to monitor telephone conversations without connection to the telephone line. Also called a *telephone adapter.*

telephone plug *See* phone plug.

telephone quality *See* voice grade.

telephone recall *See* recall and telephone interview.

telephone talk program A radio talk program that invites telephone calls from the audience.

telephone toll service Telephone service between stations in different exchange areas for which there is made a separate charge not included in contracts with subscribers for exchange service. Cf. telephone exchange service.

telephony A form of telecommunication set up for the transmission of speech or, in some cases, other sounds.

telephoto □ A long focal length lens with a narrow angle of vision that magnifies the size of objects from a distance. Also called a *narrow angle lens.* Cf. long lens. □ A photograph transmitted by telegraph lines or radio. Now usually called a *wirephoto.*

telephoto effect The change in perspective caused by a telephoto lens when the camera to subject distance is great.

telephoto lens *See* telephoto.

telepix Made-for-television movies.

teleplay A dramatic script written especially for television.

teleplay A final script with individual scenes, full dialogue or monologue (including narration in connection therewith), and camera setups if required; provided that if the company desires any script to consist in part of suggested or indicated dialogue (so that an actor portraying a role may extemporize therefrom) such suggested or indicated dialogue shall be deemed to satisfy the requirement of "full dialogue or monologue."

teleport An uplink and downlink facility for satellite communication.

teleprinter A printing device containing a keyboard used in telecommunication systems. *See also* printer and teletype.

teleprocessing The remote processing of data through the use of telecommunication facilities.

teleprompted Assisted by a teleprompter or other telecuer.

Teleprompter A proprietary name for a *telecuer.*

telepublishing Publishing accomplished by electronic means; without paper.

Tele-Q An automatic telecuer.

telerecording A British term for kinescope recording. *See also* kinescope and videotape recording.

telescreenwriter An individual who writes dramatic material for television.

telescript A final script with individual scenes, full dialogue or monologue, and camera setups if required. Cf. first draft telesplay.

telescription A television transcription. *See also* kinescope recording.

telesee A slang term for television.

teleshopping The purchase of goods or services from the home using telephone, interactive videotex, cable television shopping channels, and so on.

telespeak A canned interview.

telestrator A visual television device used by sportscasters to draw and demonstrate plays during sporting events.

telestudent A student taught by means of a telecourse.

telestudio A television studio.

teleteaching Teaching by television.

Teletel The French videotext system.

teletex A system of data transmission between computer terminals by telephone lines. Cf. teletext, videotex, videotext, and viewdata.

teletext The one-way transmission of digitally coded text and graphics to television receivers using the vertical blanking interval of the television broadcast signal. Also called *data radio.* Cf. teletex, videotex, videotext, and viewdata.

telethon A television marathon. A long program, usually broadcast for the purpose of raising money.

teletranscription A kinescope recording.

teletrial A televised legal proceeding.

teletron A television picture tube formerly made by DuMont.

Teletype □ A device, developed by the Teletype Corporation, used for sending and receiving messages worldwide by telegraph. *See also* Telex and TWX. □ An automatic printer used to print news from a wire service. Also called a *teleprinter* and *ticker.*

teletypesetter (TTS) □ A general term for equipment that converts Linotype machines to automatic operation; specifically, an attachment to a Linotype machine that is capable of setting type from the instructions contained on perforated tape. □ A wire service machine that transmits and sets type automatically, often at a number of different locations.

teletypewriter A teleprinter used for telegraphic communication. *See also* printer.

televangelist A television evangelist.

televaudeville Television vaudeville. Television programs that present varied performers and acts.

televenglish The jargon of television performers.

televerbiage The words used by television performers.

teleview To watch by means of television.

televiewer A television viewer; a member of the audience.

televise To transmit pictures and sound by television.

television Literally, to see at a distance. A system of telecommunication used for the transmission of transient images of fixed or moving objects.

television auxiliary broadcast stations A general term encompassing television pickup stations, television STL stations, television intercity relay stations, and television translator relay stations.

television auxiliary services *See* television auxiliary broadcast stations.

television band *See* television broadcast band.

television booster *See* booster.

television broadcast *See* broadcast.

television broadcast band The band extending from 54 to 806 mHz that may be assigned for television broadcast stations; 54 to 72 mHz (channels 2–4), 76 to 88 mHz (channels 5–6), 174 to 216 mHz (channels 7–13), and 470 to 806 mHz (channels 14–69). Channels 70 through 83 were previously allocated to television; they were reallocated to land-mobile services in 1970.

television broadcast booster station A station in the broadcast service operated by the licensee or permittee of a full service broadcast television station for the purpose of retransmitting the programs and signals of such primary station without significantly altering any characteristic of the original signal other than its amplitude. A television broadcast booster station may only be located such that its entire service area is located within the protected contour of the primary station it retransmits.

television broadcast channel *See* television channel.

television broadcast station A station in the television broadcast band transmitting simultaneous visual and aural signals intended to be received by the general public.

television broadcast translator station A station in the broadcast service operated for the purpose of retransmitting the programs and signals of a television broadcast station, without significantly altering any characteristic of the original signal other than its frequency and amplitude, for the purpose of providing television reception to the general public. The term *translator* is now used to include a booster.

Television Broadcasters Association An association of television broadcasters formed by Allen B. DuMont in 1944.

television broadcasting *See* broadcasting.

Television Bureau of Advertising (TvB) An advertising trade development organization of the television industry. It assists member networks and stations in promoting television broadcasting as an advertising medium and thus increasing television's share of advertising dollars.

television camera A device used to convert an optical image formed by a lens into electrical signals by a scanning process.

television channel A band of frequencies 6 mHz wide in the television broadcast band and designated either by number or by the extreme lower and upper frequencies.

Television Code The self-regulatory code, first adopted in 1952 and frequently revised by the National Association of Broadcasters, which set forth program and advertising standards for member television stations. The Television Code and Code Review Board were abolished by the NAB after a court decision found the advertising standards to be anticompetitive.

Television Code Review Board *See* Television Code.

television cropping The amount by which the size of a television picture is reduced during transmission and reception. Also called *television cut off.*

television cut off *See* television cropping.

television director An advertising agency employee responsible for the production management of television programs or commercials produced by the agency.

television film *See* television motion picture.

television household A household having one or more television receivers, even though the receiver(s) may be out of order or not used.

television households (TVHH) An Arbitron estimate of the number of households (including those on military installations) having one or more television receivers.

Television Information Office (TIO) An office within the National Association of Broadcasters until 1989, when it was dissolved and moved to the Museum of Broadcasting in New York City.

television intercity relay station A fixed station used for intercity transmission of television program material and related communications for use by television broadcast stations.

television market A single or multiple city or geographical area served by one or more television stations.

television modulator A low-power television transmitter used in closed-circuit television.

television motion picture The entertainment portion of motion pictures, whether made on or by film, tape, or otherwise, and whether produced by means of motion picture cameras, electronic cameras or devices, or any combination of the foregoing, or any other means, methods, or devices, now used or that may hereafter be adopted for the recordation of motion pictures produced primarily for exhibition by free television. Also called a *television film*. Cf. theatrical motion picture.

television operating center (TOC) A telephone company control location for monitoring and switching television network signals.

television optical *See* telop.

television penetration The percentage of households in a given area that have television receivers.

television pickup station A land-mobile station used for the transmission of television program material and related communications from the scenes of events occurring at points removed from television broadcast station studios to television broadcast stations.

television program A program made for free television, pay television, video discs/video cassettes, and basic cable, including television programs that consist substantially of excerpts from theatrical motion pictures.

television program producer A person or organization engaged in the production of television programs.

television programming *See* programming.

television receive only (TVRO) A satellite dish that is designed to accept a signal but not to transmit a signal.

television receiver *See* receiver.

television recording A videotape made of a television program.

television rights *See* rights.

television satellite *See* satellite.

television screen The fluorescent screen of a television receiver or monitor picture tube.

television set □ A commonly used term for a television receiver. □ *See* set. □ *See* receiver.

television signal The simultaneously transmitted audio and video signals of a television program.

television station *See* television broadcast station.

television STL station A fixed station used for the transmission of television program material and related communications from the studio to the transmitter of a television broadcast station. *See also* STL.

television survey season The twelve-month period beginning April 1 of one year and ending March 31 of the following year.

television tape recorder A machine used to record and play back a magnetic video recording tape. Also called a *videotape recorder.*

television translator *See* television broadcast translator station.

television translator relay station A fixed station used for relaying the signals of television broadcast stations to television broadcast translator stations.

television transmission standards The standards that determine the characteristics of a television signal as radiated by a television broadcast station.

television transmitter The transmitter or transmitters used for the transmission of both visual and aural television signals.

Televisor The first commercially produced television receiver. Developed by Baird in England using a mechanical scanning device.

Telex An acronym for teletype exchange. The worldwide telegraphic communication service provided by Western Union. *See also* Teletype and TWX.

Telidon A Canadian teletext system.

tell story A television news item read without accompanying visuals.

telly A British nickname for television.

telop An acronym for television optical. An opaque photograph or graphic projected on a telop projector. Cf. balop.

telop projector An opaque projector used for television.

Telpak Telephone package. A wideband point-to-point telecommunication service by the telephone company.

telsat An acronym for a *television satellite.*

Telstar The first of the experimental low-altitude active satellites, launched July 10, 1962.

template □ An opaque mask with patterned cutouts used in the gate of an ellipsoidal reflector spotlight. □ A picture or window shaped design used as an aid in computer graphics.

tempo The rate or pace of a performance or program.

Temporary Commission on Alternative Financing for Public Telecommunications (TCAF) The 1981 authorization that allowed noncommercial television stations to test the feasibility of airing commercial messages.

temporary fixed ITFS station An ITFS station used for the transmission of material from temporary unspecified points to an ITFS station.

temporary restraining order (TRO) *See* restraining order.

temporary storage *See* random access memory.

ten A 10-second commercial.

ten add One method of sending a part of a news story to the composing room before the lead is written. The first take is labeled ten add, the second eleven add, and so on. *See also* A matter.

ten-K *See* tenner.

tenner A 10-kW fresnel spotlight. Also called a *ten-K*.

tension The act or degree of stretching; as in tape tension.

tension arm A movable lever over which tape passes. The lever is spring loaded to provide a specific force parallel to the direction of tape travel.

tension control A switch found on professional audio recorders that changes the tension for different sized reels.

tension control modulator *See* modulator.

ten state rule To be considered a national presidential or vice presidential candidate, a person must make a substantial showing that he or she is qualified for a place on the ballot in at least 10 states, or 9 states and the District of Columbia.

tentative cut *See* provisional cut.

tent card A display card printed and folded so as to be legible from two directions.

tent polling A television programming strategy wherein a strong program is placed between two new or weaker programs in order to strengthen their audiences. Cf. hammocking.

teracycle One million megahertz per second.

term □ The period of time for a contract, agreement; engagement, subscription, and so on. □ An entry in a dictionary.

terminal □ A point at which two or more connectors join. □ A fitting or device attached to the end of a conductor. □ The point of connection between a house drop and a CATV subscriber's television receiver. □ A communication device that is capable of sending or receiving information. □ A point at which data may be sent or received in a communication network. □ A device with a keyboard and a display screen used for sending and receiving information to a mainframe or communication system. □ A final syllable, word, page, subscription, area of a page, and so on. □ The mechanism that collects newspapers at the end of the conveyor line.

terminal board *See* terminal strip.

terminal isolation The attenuation, at any subscriber terminal, between that terminal and any other subscriber terminal in the cable television system.

terminal station The final station of a microwave system.

terminal strip A multiterminal, nonconducting board used to connect wires. Also called a *terminal board.*

terminated □ A program or contract that is not renewed. □ A circuit, transducer, and so on, that has been closed on one end.

terminator *See* line terminator and stub.

terminator record The last record in the disc label, signifying the end of the disc label of a compact disc.

term player A player who is guaranteed a minimum of 20 out of 26 weeks (or 10 out of 13 weeks) who works in a television episode or episodes but who does not have a continuing role in a series. Cf. contract player, day player, deal player, free-lance player, multiple picture player, and stunt player.

terms The conditions under which a television program, motion picture, and so on, are licensed for broadcast or distribution.

terrestrial radio communication Any radio communication other than space radio communication or radio astronomy.

terrestrial relay A radio communication service that transmits or receives messages on the earth.

terrestrial station A station effecting terrestrial radio communication.

territorial exclusivity The right of a broadcast station to the exclusive use of a network program within its coverage area.

tertiary color A color produced by the mixing of two secondary colors.

tertiary cue tone *See* cue tone.

tertiary movement The motion caused in a scene by the use of two or more cameras. Cf. primary movement and secondary movement.

test □ A short piece of film used to determine whether the exposure or other variable is correct. *See also* test strip. □ A short on-camera interview or reading to determine the suitability of an actor for a part. □ To interview a random sample of individuals to determine their attitudes or opinions concerning products, services, programs, publications, and so on.

testboard A telephone company switchboard that is equipped to make tests of temporary interconnections.

test commercial *See* test market commercial.

test exposure A short length of film, often from the end of a scene, developed to determine the correct processing procedures.

test film A short film designed to determine whether a projector is in proper working order.

test group A selection of individuals for the purpose of measuring reactions to products or services.

testimonial An advertising technique in which a prominent person endorses a commercial product or service.

testimony An oral statement made under oath by a witness in a courtroom proceeding.

testing The pretesting of a survey questionnaire for completeness, competency, understandability, and so on.

test mailing *See* mailing list test.

test market A single, well-defined geographical area used to test an advertisement or advertising campaign.

test market commercial A commercial that is to be used to test a product in a market. Also called a *test commercial* and *test spot.*

test market profile (TMP) A compilation of marketing data by Designated Market Area (DMA) published annually by the A. C. Nielsen Company.

test panel A term used to identify each of the parts or samples in a split test.

test pattern Any of a number of charts used for television camera or VTR alignment. *See also* color registration chart, linear reflectance chart, linearity chart, logarithmic reflectance chart, and resolution chart.

test record *See* frequency record.

test run A trial made to examine equipment, supplies, or format before beginning a production run.

test spot *See* test market commercial.

test strip A short piece of film or photographic paper used to determine the proper development procedure.

test tape □ A selection of representative records within a mailing list designed to enable a list user or service bureau to prepare for reformatting or converting the list to a form more efficient for the user. □ *See* frequency tape.

test tone An audio tone used for adjusting a circuit or tracing trouble.

text □ The portions of a signal that carry information, as opposed to control information in a computer or data processing circuit. □ The actual words of an author's work. □ The main body of matter on a printed page. □ An abbreviation for *textbook.* □ The body of a book or other manuscript, as opposed to front and back matter. □ Solid reading matter, as opposed to display matter, headlines, and so on. Also called *body copy* and *straight matter.* □ Any one of two or more different versions of an author's work. □ The content of a speech or official document. □ A race of type. *See also* black letter. □ The information in a message. □ The main body of printed matter on a page. □ The principal part of a book.

textbook A manual of instruction covering a portion of a specific subject.

text edition A textbook edition of a book intended primarily for classroom use. Cf. trade book.

text letter □ Black letter type. □ The type used for the body of a book.

text paper A semismooth paper used for numerous purposes.

text processing The use of computers to prepare electronic manuscripts.

text size The size of type generally used for the body of printed material. Nine to 12 points are common for reading matter. Also called *body type* and *text type.* Cf. display size.

text stream The flow of characters in an electronic manuscript in the order necessary for computer typesetting.

text type *See* text size.

texture An irregularly painted or covered surface used to give a set "character."

texture mapping A computer imaging algorithm for "wrapping" a two-dimensional pattern or texture around the surface of a three-dimensional object so that the pattern curves and distorts realistically.

textures *See* video textures.

text writer □ A textbook writer. □ Before the invention of printing, a manuscript copier.

TF □ Till forbid. □ To fill.

Tf Trufocus. A lamp base type.

TFE Television film exhibit.

TFN Till further notice. *See* till forbid (TF).

TFT Thin film technology.

TGI Target group index.

Thaumatrope An early animation device that consisted of a disc with one image painted on each side; when the disc was spun on a loop of string, the images seemed to appear together.

THD Total harmonic distortion.

The Academy In the motion picture industry, the Academy of Motion Picture Arts and Sciences.

theatre □ A building for dramatic presentations; originally referred to as the *legitimate theatre.* Now any location where performances are given. □ A collection of dramatic works. Also spelled *theater.*

theatre advertising Commercial messages that are shown before feature motion pictures in a motion picture theatre.

theatre television A projection television system used in auditoriums or theatres. Demonstrated as early as 1930. *See also* Eidophor.

theatrical distribution The distribution of motion pictures to exhibitors.

theatrical film A motion picture designed for theatre exhibition rather than on television.

theatrical motion picture A motion picture or photoplay, whether made on or by film, tape, or otherwise, and whether produced by means of motion picture cameras, electronic cameras or devices, or any combination of the foregoing or any other means, methods, or devices now used or that may be hereafter adopted for the recordation of motion pictures produced primarily for exhibition in a theatre or similar location in which a fee or admission charge is paid by the viewing audience. Cf. television motion picture.

theft of service The unauthorized use of a cable television system or pay television service.

thematic apperception test (TAT) A projective psychological test in which a respondent, shown a series of ambiguous pictures, is asked to compose a story to fit them, the theory being that his or her own concerns, attitudes, and experiences will emerge.

thematic montage A type of editing characterized by a lack of time and space continuity. Cf. classical cutting.

theme □ The basic subject matter or topic of a play or script. Sometimes called a *thesis* or *premise.* □ The recurring melody of a song. □ *See* motif.

theme music A melody or song, often instrumental, that is designed to accompany a motion picture or television drama. Cf. theme song.

theme scheduling The scheduling, over a short period, usually a week, of motion pictures of a particular genre or performer on independent television stations.

theme song A song or melody identified with a particular radio or television performer, program, or series. Cf. jingle and theme music.

theory A set of general propositions used for study into a series of phenomena. Theory deals with principles and methods as distinguished from actual practice.

thermal duplication Copying a tape by means of heat and contact using a special kind of master tape having a relatively low Curie point.

thermal printer An inexpensive printer that uses heated pins or plates to transfer waxy ink characters to heat-sensitive paper. Also called a *thermal transfer printer.*

thermal protector A circuit breaker that turns off equipment that is overheating.

thermal transfer printer *See* thermal printer.

thermistor A resistor whose resistance varies sharply with temperature.

thermoelectricity Electricity produced by the action of heating two dissimilar metals.

Thermofax A trademark copy machine. *See also* thermography.

thermography A printing process using a powder sprinkled on freshly inked paper to simulate embossing. Sometimes called *plateless printing.*

thermoplastic A material capable of being formed when heated. Used for the manufacture of discs. *See also* vinyl resin.

thermoplastic recording A recording process in which a special electron gun deforms a heated plastic with a low melting point. The resulting film can be projected or viewed by using a flying spot scanner.

thesis *See* theme.

Theta Sigma Phi Now Women in Communications, Inc.

thickness piece A wooden board or other material used to add a third dimension to a flat or other construction on a set.

thin □ An advertising campaign that uses too few spots to be effective. □ Sound that is lacking in richness and resonance. □ An underexposed negative. Cf. dense.

thin film technology (TFT) A method of plating extremely thin components to serve as semiconductors, integrated circuits, capacitors, and so on.

think piece An interpretative article or feature. Sometimes called a *dope piece.*

thin lens A lens in which the surfaces of the elements are close together.

thin print A photographic print lacking in density.

thin space A metal space used to space out a line of matrices.

third A size of paper used for cards; approximately 1-1/2 by 3 inches.

third class An inexpensive mailing category used for bulk mailings.

third coast The Dallas-Fort Worth metroplex; a major market in television and film production.

third cover The inside back cover of a book or periodical.

third generation computer A computer with smaller circuits and more complete miniaturization than a second generation computer.

third hand News that is of questionable reliability or value.

third party A participant in a legal action who is neither the plaintiff nor the defendant.

third person narration Narration in which an outside voice provides the viewer with the emotions and ideas of a character.

thirds rule A principle of photographic and artistic composition that the subject matter should be divided horizontally, vertically, or both one-third of the way from the selected edge of the composition. Also called *rule of thirds.*

third stick A column of type one-third of a column wide.

third world The technologically undeveloped countries of the world, particularly those in Asia and Africa.

third world cinema The motion picture productions of the developing countries of the world.

thirty □ A thirty-second commercial. □ A word or symbol used to indicate the end of a news story, article, program, and so on. Also called an *end dash, end sign, gate, thirty dash,* and *thirty mark. See also* end mark.

thirty bar A rule used as a thirty.

thirty dash *See* thirty.

35 mm The standard gauge of film for motion picture production. Now, several other sizes have become standard for wide-screen projection, such as 70 mm.

35-mm blow up A 35-mm negative made from a 16-mm or 8-mm positive or negative.

thirty mark *See* thirty.

Thirty Rock A somewhat derogatory reference to the NBC headquarters building. *See also* Black Rock and Hard Rock.

thirty sheet poster An outdoor advertising space providing a copy area measuring 21 feet 7 inches by 9 feet 7 inches, usually covered with a single poster printed in sections on twelve paper sheets.

33-1/3 rpm The standard speed of long-playing microgroove discs.

thirtytwomo □ A book having thirty two leaves to a sheet. □ A book measuring approximately 3-1/2 by 5-1/2 inches.

Thompson Memorial Prize, Browder J. An award given by the IEEE for each author under 30 years of age for the most outstanding paper published in an IEEE publication.

thread To place tape or film in the proper operating position in a tape transport, camera, or projector.

threading The guiding of film or tape through the proper path in the transport mechanism of a film camera, projector, tape recorder, editor, and so on. Also called *lacing*. Cf. loading.

threading slot The elongated opening adjacent to the heads of a tape transport.

thread-up ring *See* friction ring.

three color printing *See* color separation.

three color system A design used in television and film in which the colors of the visible spectrum are divided into three parts: usually red, blue, and green.

three cornered publication A newspaper that publishes morning, evening, and weekend editions.

three D A three-dimensional picture.

three decker □ A three-volume novel. □ Any unusually long novel.

three-dimensional effects The use of edging, borders, and so on, to produce titles with the appearance of depth.

three-gun A color television picture tube that utilizes one gun for each of the three primary colors. Cf. single gun.

three head A standard configuration for professional audiotape recorders; erase, record, and playback heads.

360 *See* 360 pan.

360 pan A camera pan that moves in a complete circle to return to its starting point. Also called a *360*.

three motor A standard configuration for professional tape recorders; separate motors for the tape drive, feed reel, and take-up reel.

three-point lighting A basic lighting setup that uses key, fill, and back lights after the base-light has been set.

three quarter binding A book binding in which the back material covers approximately one-third of the sides and is different from the rest of the binding.

three-quarter inch The width of a standard videotape format.

threes In animation, the exposure of three frames for each drawing.

three sheet poster □ An outdoor advertising poster 6 feet high by 12 feet wide. □ A transit advertising poster, used in train stations, 7 feet high by 3 feet 6 inches wide.

three shot A camera shot, often a medium shot, of three performers. Cf. two shot.

three strip camera A film camera in which the three colors are recorded on three separate strips of film.

three stripe *See* three track.

three track The use of three magnetic tracks on sound motion picture film.

three tube A standard configuration for video cameras; three pickup tubes: red, green, and blue.

three two scanning *See* two three scanning.

three unities The classical conception of unity: time, place, and action.

three wall The typical motion picture or television set, composed of three walls. The audience and the camera are the fourth wall.

three-way system A loudspeaker system using a separate loudspeaker for different portions of the sound spectrum. The loudspeakers are fed through a crossover network. *See also* squawker, tweeter, and woofer.

three-year rule An FCC rule that, except in certain circumstances, a hearing must be held on applications for transfer of control of a broadcast station if the licensee has not owned the station for at least three years. The rule was designed to reduce trafficking. Now eliminated, but may be reinstituted.

threshold □ The minimum amount of exposure that may be given to produce an image on film. □ The minimum amount of light necessary to produce an acceptable television image.

threshold of audibility *See* threshold of hearing.

threshold of hearing The minimum sound pressure level capable of being detected by the human ear, expressed in decibels. Also called the *threshold of audibility.*

throat The narrow portion of a loudspeaker horn.

throat microphone A contact microphone worn around and touching the throat.

throughput The length of time it takes a computerized typesetting system to complete a task.

through-the-book method A survey research technique used to determine whether a survey respondent actually read an issue of a magazine, by leading the respondent through the issue asking questions section by section.

through the lens (TTL) □ A system for measuring light directly through a lens. □ A single lens reflex camera.

throw □ To direct the light of a luminaire in a particular direction. □ The effective distance between a luminaire and the area being lighted. □ The effective distance between a projector and the screen.

throw a cue To cue a performer by pointing.

throwaway □ A line that is delivered by a performer casually. Also called a *throw line.* □ An advertisement or promotional piece intended for widespread free distribution. It is generally printed on inexpensive paper and most often distributed by hand, either to passersby or house-to-house. Also called a *shopper.*

throwaway lead A printed or spoken lead to a story that is unnecessary or lacks specific information.

throw focus *See* plopping focus.

throwing focus *See* plopping focus.

throw it away □ A direction to deliver a line casually. □ To deliver a line casually. □ A television director's command to fade out sound and/or picture.

throw line □ *See* throwaway. □ *See* writeup.

throw-out groove *See* lead-out groove.

thumb index An alphabetical index consisting of rounded notches incised into book pages, as in a dictionary. Cf. edge index and tab.

thumbnail □ A rough layout containing little detail; often used in advertising layouts. □ A half-column illustration or photograph. □ A short literary sketch.

thump A low-frequency, transient, muffled noise in an audio circuit.

THX A trademark for the theatrical multichannel sound from Lucasfilm, usually accompanied by Dolby encoding.

thyristor *See* silicon controlled rectifier.

TI TV Intercity. An FCC file-number prefix.

TICCIT Time Shared, Interactive Computer Controlled Information Television.

ticker A slang term for a teletypewriter: a news service printer. *See also* teletype.

ticket □ An admittance authorization to, for example, a motion picture theatre. □ A slang term for an authorization, such as a radiotelephone operator's permit.

ticket agency An organization that sells tickets to public events.

ticket night A performance for which the proceeds from ticket sales are given to charity.

tickler A collection or file of anecdotes, fillers, items, and so on, assembled for future use.

tie back *See* tie in.

tied letters *See* ligature.

tied off □ A set rigging line fixed in position. □ A camera locked in position for a shot.

tiedown Any device used to anchor a prop on a set.

tie in □ A reference in a news story to previously printed information in order to refresh a reader's memory. Also called a *tie back.* □ A retail dealer's advertising placed with or near a manufacturer's advertising. □ Two products advertised in one advertisement or commercial. □ A cooperative mailing effort involving two or more advertisers. □ A story that is related to a newsworthy event. □ A simultaneous release of information or media properties. □ An advertising strategy in which one medium is promoted in another.

tie-in advertisement □ A periodical advertisement that makes reference to an advertisement in the same issue run by the same advertiser. □ A single advertisement that advertises more than one product or service, and, at times, involving more than one advertiser.

tie-in announcement A commercial announcement for a local retailer who carries the product or products advertised on the network program immediately preceding. Also called a *trailer.*

tie-in promotion A single promotion event intended to encourage the sale of more than one product or brand.

tie line An interconnecting private communications channel between two points.

tier □ A radio antenna that has each element stacked one above the other. □ A cable television service available in levels; from the basic service to two or more separate tiers. Also called *tiered service.* □ Two or more cable networks or channels sold as a package.

tiered service *See* tier.

tiering The act of charging the customer separately for an additional cable service or services. A tier can be one service or a grouping of services, and may or may not include a traditional pay television offering.

tie tac microphone A small microphone that is attached to clothing with a small clip.

tie up The use of the name of a well-known person for advertising purposes, especially a testimonial.

tight □ Anything that allows little leeway. □ A newspaper or other publication with so much advertising there is little or no space left. Also called a *tight paper.* Cf. loose. □ A line of copy without adequate spacing. □ *See* tight shot. □ *See* tight board.

tight back A book binding that is glued firmly to the cover. Cf. open back.

tight board The operation of a radio station audio control console with a minimum of dead air. Also called *tight.*

tight close-up (TCU) A camera shot usually between a close-up and an extreme close-up. *See also* camera shots.

tighten up A director's command to a camera operator to zoom in or dolly in slightly.

tight framing *See* tight shot.

tight paper *See* tight.

tight shot A camera shot that allows for little movement by performers. Also called *tight framing.* Cf. loose shot.

tight show A radio or television program that has no leeway in timing and may run over if problems develop.

tightwinder A device used to wind film on a core.

tight writing Writing without excess verbiage.

till forbid (TF) An advertising campaign or spot schedule that runs until canceled by the advertiser. Also called *till further notice (TFN).*

tilt □ The vertical arc inscribed by camera movement from a fixed position. □ To move a camera in a vertical arc. Cf. pan. □ The changes in amplitude on a cable system caused by unequal frequency attenuation. □ *See* rotation.

tilt down A film or television director's command to point the camera farther down.

tilting The vertical movement of a camera, as opposed to panning.

tilt up A film or television director's command to point the camera farther up.

tilt wedge A device used to increase the degree of camera tilt.

TIM Transient intermodulation distortion.

timbre The quality or color of a tone imparted by a voice or musical instrument.

time (T) □ A measure of duration in seconds, minutes, and so on. □ A broadcast time period available for a program or announcement. □ The number of repetitions, occasions, or insertions specified in an advertising schedule or rate card.

time address code *See* time code.

time bank A barter by a radio or television station in which an advertiser supplies a program in return for advertising time in the program.

time base A reference scale used in film and television.

time base corrector (TBC) A device that electronically compensates for fluctuations in the time relationships of a signal.

time base error Any variation in the relationship between the various sync pulses and the other information on a videotape.

time brokerage The purchase of blocks of station time for resale by an intermediate party. The practice is not allowed.

timebuyer A person employed by an advertising agency media department, or by a media buying service, to negotiate with stations or their representatives for the efficient placement of spot advertising in accordance with a previously formulated media plan.

time charge The amount a station charges for air time. *See also* rate card.

time check ☐ The synchronization of clocks before a broadcast. ☐ *See* time signal.

time classification ☐ The breakdown of a radio or television rate card into categories for the various time periods, such as AAAA to A, or A to D, from the most expensive time to the least expensive. ☐ The hours of operation for an AM station are designated by the FCC. The various classes are unlimited time, limited time, daytime, sharing time, and specified hours.

time clearance The process of making time available on a station for a program or commercial.

time code An encoded digital signal that indexes a tape recording by providing a time indication in each field of the program. Also called *time address code. See also* longitudinal time code (LTC), SMPTE time code, and vertical interval time code (VITC).

time code generator An electronic device used to produce an 80 bit code for use in videotape editing.

time code character generator An electronic device used to convert time code into a video display on a monitor.

time code key One of the keys used to input time code information.

time code reader A nixie or LED used to display the time code for precise location in videotape editing.

time compression ☐ The use of edited material to fit the time available for presentation. ☐ The automatic increase in the speed of a tape being played back so as to shorten the time fractionally. Cf. time expansion.

time contract An agreement between an advertising agency and a radio or television station or network, covering all time purchased by the advertiser through all agencies in order to earn the greatest possible discount. Cf. AAAA spot contract.

time copy News copy that is written or composed in advance and held for use; often filler material. Also called *pork.*

time-date generator A device used to produce the time and date visually on a videotape.

timed cut A videotape edit that is selected for length rather than content.

time delay ☐ The time between a cue or command and its execution. ☐ The time between the transmission and reception of a sound or signal. Also called *time lag.* ☐ *See* tape delay.

time delay system *See* tape delay.

timed fader An automatic lighting fader that fades the lighting instruments according to a preset length of time.

time discount ☐ A rate reduction for advertisers who make quantity purchases of time. ☐ A discount offered by periodicals if a certain number of insertions are run within a given period of time. Also called *frequency discount* and *quantity discount.*

time division multiple access (TDMA) The conversion of various messages into digital signals for transmission in packets by satellites. The return signals are then converted into their original forms.

time domain reflectometer A device used to test and locate defects in coaxial cable.

timed print A motion picture print that has been timed for the correct exposure for density and color when duplicated.

time expansion The automatic decrease in speed of a tape so as to fill the available time. Cf. time compression.

time exposure A film exposed for more than one second.

time hand A British term for a person, such as a printer, who works by the hour, as opposed to piecework.

time hopping systems A spread spectrum system in which the period and duty cycle of a pulsed RF carrier are varied in a pseudorandom manner under the control of a coded sequence. Time hopping is often used effectively with frequency hopping to form a hybrid time-division, multiple-access (TDMA) spread spectrum system.

time lag *See* time delay.

time lapse □ A passage of time indicated by a shot of a calendar, clock, and so on. □ A break in script continuity. □ *See* time lapse photography.

time lapse motor *See* intervalometer.

time lapse photography The exposure of film frames at timed intervals. Often, hours are compressed into minutes.

time period An interval of time, usually defined by day and hour without regard to the television programming aired. Thus, audience researchers may speak of four-week time period averages, as differentiated from pure program averages in evaluating a television station or in looking at audience trends.

time period rating A rating calculated for a specific time interval such as 15 or 30 minutes, as opposed to a specific program. *See also* rating.

time, place, and manner regulations Laws, ordinances, or rules that place limitations on the time, place, or manner of speaking or publishing that do not limit freedom of speech or of the press. Cf. content regulation.

timer □ A circuit that provides pulses, blanking, and so on. □ A frame or tape length counter. □ A clock used to time programs, commercials, and so on, that can be reset. □ *See* grader.

time sales The process of selling station time to advertisers or sponsors.

time salesman An individual who sells radio or television station or network time.

time sharing □ A computer system in which the central processor is shared by two or more terminals or operators. □ *See* sharing time (S).

time sheet □ A tabulation of the running time of a script, rehearsal, or program. *See also* timing. □ A record of broadcast media purchases. Also called a *buy sheet.*

time shifting The use of videotape recorders to record a television program and retain it for playback at a later time.

time signal □ A broadcast announcement of the correct time. Also called a *time check.* □ The precisely timed signals broadcast by the National Bureau of Standards over WWV, WWVB, and WWVH.

time slot The time a program or commercial is broadcast.

time spent listening (TSL) An estimate of the number of quarter-hours the average person spends listening to radio during a specified period of time.

time spent viewing (TSV) An estimate of the amount of time the average person spends watching television during a specified period of time.

time spent viewing/turnover factor Indicators of relative reach and frequency. Reach aims for broad coverage with minimum duplication (low time spent viewing/high turnover), whereas the goal of frequency is the maximum amount of repetition or duplication (high time spent viewing/low turnover).

Times rule The rule that grew out of the New York Times v. Sullivan case; the definition of "actual malice."

time standards The limits that were set by the NAB Radio and Television Codes for the maximum allowable time to be used for nonprogram material. For radio, the maximum was 18 minutes per hour; for television, the maximum was 16 minutes per hour, with varying maximums in special situations. The NAB Radio and Television Codes are no longer in operation.

time transition An audio or video device used to indicate a passage of time between scenes.

timing □ The noting of time intervals on a script during a rehearsal so that the elapsed time during production may be compared to them. □ A performer's sense of pace. □ *See* grading. □ A laboratory process that involves balancing the color of a film to achieve consistency from scene to scene. Also includes adjusting exposure settings in duplication.

timing card A list of printer light values used in printing motion picture film.

timing sheet *See* rundown sheet.

timing tape Audio leader tape that is cut to a specific length according to the time desired between audio cuts.

tin ear An individual who has trouble carrying a tune or who cannot direct others in musical endeavors.

tinny A sound or recording that lacks low frequencies.

tin pan alley The area in New York City that contained the leading music publishing firms before the turn of the century.

tinseltown A somewhat derogatory term for Hollywood.

tint A shade created by mixing white with a color.

tint block □ A solid area of color used under photographs or text matter. □ The printing plate used to produce the color background. Also called a *tint plate.*

tint plate *See* tint block.

tintype A photograph made on a wet collodion emulsion on metal. Used in the late 19th and early 20th centuries. Also called a *ferrotype.*

tiny mac A small spotlight.

TIO Television Information Office.

tip □ Information received concerning a possible newsworthy event. Also called a *tip off.* □ The contact end of a jack. □ *See* tipping in. □ One of the small heads found on videotape recorders and players.

tip engagement The preferred term is *tip penetration.*

tip height A synonym for *tip projection.*

tip in *See* tipping in.

tip off *See* tip.

tip on *See* tipping in.

tip penetration The momentary radical deflection of the tape in the vacuum guide caused by the passage of a video head pole tip.

tipping in A page or section of a book, magazine, or printed piece inserted by gluing. Often used for adding illustrations. Also called *pasting in, tip, tip in,* and *tip on.*

tip projection In a videotape recorder, the measured radial difference between a pole tip and the headwheel rim. Also called *tip engagement, tip height,* and *tip protrusion.*

tip protrusion *See* tip projection.

tip sheet A racing form or other odds-giving publication. The advertising of tip sheets was forbidden by the NAB Radio and Television Codes.

tipster An individual who furnishes news information to a radio or television station. Cf. stringer.

tissue A gauze-like paper used in books to prevent damage to engravings.

title □ The heading of a story or article. □ A newspaper headline. □ The section of a book containing the title page. □ A motion picture subtitle. □ To stamp a book cover with a title. □ The name given to a novel, story, article, motion picture, and so on. □ A caption or other written material used on the screen in motion pictures.

title card (TC) A graphic card shown on camera, as opposed to one on film or slides. Also called a *caption.*

title catalog An alphabetical listing of books and other publications.

title crawl *See* crawl.

title drum A cylindrical device used to mount a long title card.

title letter *See* title type.

title line *See* byline and nameplate.

title music Theme music that is used with the titles of a motion picture, television program, and so on. *See also* signature and theme song.

title page A book page containing the title of the work, and, usually, the author's and publisher's names, date, and place of publication. *See also* front matter. Cf. imprint.

titler □ A device used to hold title cards and a camera for photographing the title cards. □ An inexpensive character generator.

title roll *See* crawl.

titles □ Any graphics used on television. □ The specific credit information listing the name of a program, cast, sponsor, and so on.

title slide A title card that has been photographed for use in a telecine.

title song A vocal that is used with the titles of a motion picture, television program, and so on.

title type The full-size capital letters found on some title pages. Now rare.

TJ Talk jockey.

TK To come. *See also* HTK.

TM Trademark.

TMA Total market coverage.

TMDA Training Media Distributors Association.

TMP □ Test market profile. □ Test market plan.

TNO Track number.

TNT Target Network Television. A cable television network.

T number A lens calibration number that takes optical efficiency of the lens into account. Also called a *transmission number.*

TO Turnover.

TOA Theatre Owners of America.

TOC □ Table of contents. □ Television operating center.

today story A news story brought up-to-date by new material.

Todd AO One of the wide-screen motion picture systems that utilizes a 65-mm camera negative and a 70-mm print for projection.

toenail A slang term for a parenthesis.

to fill (TF) An instruction to a typesetter: set to fill space indicated.

toggle To change back and forth between two stable electric or mechanical states.

toggle switch A switch that has two positions; a flip-flop switch.

token In direct mail advertising, an involvement device usually consisting of a perforated portion of an order card that is designed for removal from its original position and then placed in another designated area on the order card to signify desire to purchase the product or service offered.

tolerance The allowable deviation of a quantity or component from a specified value.

toll A charge made for a service, such as a long distance telephone call.

toll broadcasting The first form of radio sponsorship, wherein an advertiser leased the facilities of WEAF in New York in 1928 to advertise an apartment complex.

toll television *See* pay television.

toll video *See* pay television.

tombstone □ The effect produced by the side-by-side placement of two or more headlines of the same type size. *See also* bumped heads. Also called *tombstoning.* □ A small print advertisement for a professional person or organization, designed to meet the legal and customary restraints observed in such advertising. □ A print advertisement that contains text matter only.

tombstoning *See* tombstone.

tonal key The relative appearance of a set due to lighting. *See also* high-key lighting and low-key lighting.

tonal lighting *See* lighting.

tone □ A sound that has a definite pitch. □ The style or manner of speaking or writing. □ To blend or harmonize color, sound, and so on. □ A color tint. □ The mood or atmosphere of a story, novel, motion picture, and so on.

tone arm The turntable or record player device that holds the pickup cartridge. Also called a *pickup arm.*

tone control A potentiometer used to vary the bass and treble frequency response of an amplifier.

tone deaf A derogatory term for an individual who cannot carry a tune or an actor who cannot take vocal direction.

tone generator An audio oscillator used to generate a tone to set audio levels.

tone wheel A geometrically symmetrical disk of ferromagnetic material that moves in front of a coil, thus inducing a continuous waveform.

tongue □ A boom mount for a camera. *See also* camera mounts. □ To move a boom mounted camera in a horizontal plane. Also called *gibbing* and *tonguing. See also* camera movement.

tonguing *See* tongue.

toning The process of changing or converting a photographic image to another color by the addition of a chemical dye.

toning sheet *See* shading sheet.

tonnage The total mass audience delivered by a television program regardless of the demographics of the audience.

Tony The legitimate theatre award similar to television's Emmy and motion picture's Oscar. Named after Antoinette Perry.

tooling □ Impressions made on book covers, usually by stamping. □ A hand operation to cut fine lines in a halftone or engraving.

TOP Temporarily out of print (books).

top □ The high frequency notes of the audio spectrum. □ To surpass a previous performer or performance. □ The beginning of a script or scene. □ A lead for a news story. □ The price of the most expensive seats for a performance.

top billing The name listed above all other performer's names in the program billing. Also called a *headliner.*

top deck *See* top line.

top forty A radio station format characterized by the most popular music as indicated by current sales charts.

top hat *See* funnel.

top head A headline at the top of a newspaper column.

topical A promotional announcement that contains specific information concerning a radio or television program.

topless radio Sex-oriented radio programming; usually a radio station call-in program in which callers discussed intimate sexual matters with the talk show host.

top light Any light that comes from above a set.

top line A line of type that forms the upper part of a headline. Also called a *top deck.*

top 100 The 100 largest television markets. *See also* major television market.

top peg One of the upper set of pegs on an animation compound table.

tormentor A vertical flat or curtain at the edge of a set.

tormentor light A spotlight mounted on a boomerang just off stage from either tormentor.

tort A private wrong other than a breach of contract that violates the rights of another, such as libel or invasion of privacy.

torus A geographic area either wholly or partially surrounding another geographic area.

TOS Temporarily out of stock (books).

toss To introduce another radio or television news story by a different reporter or anchor.

TOT An abbreviation for *total.*

total (TOT) The summation of estimated average quarter-hour viewing in the total survey area to the home stations by households and demographic categories. This ''total'' excludes viewing to outside stations, non-ADI stations and home stations whose audiences were below minimum standards.

total audience (TA) A rating that represents the percentage of a given universe that viewed a station for a given interval of time, or a specific program, for six minutes or longer. The total audience typically is greater than the average audience.

total audience impressions The total number of exposures to a specific number of issues of a given periodical or to the issues of a given group of periodicals appearing at one time; used for survey purposes.

total audience listening output (TALO) The number of diaries in which a radio or television station is mentioned in a market, a county or other designated geographic area; a county-by-county printout of the number of mentions in in-tab diaries for each station; can be used to rank stations and to calculate weekly cumes and raw bases.

total audience plan (TAP) A package of radio spots designed to reach the maximum or target audiences by varying the times of the day from day to day.

total audience rating A cumulation of instantaneous audiences excluding those that are in the audience for less than a specified time (such as the length of a television or radio program). Cf. average audience rating.

total circulation The full number of copies of a publication distributed, including copies sold both to subscribers and single-copy buyers, as well as complementary copies.

total harmonic distortion (THD) The difference between the signal recorded on a tape or disc and the quality of the sound that is heard.

total marketable audience The portion of the audience most sought after by radio or television stations, as opposed to the total audience. Generally the 18 to 49 age group.

total market coverage (TMA) An advertising concept whereby a newspaper attempts to reach all households in a market through the use of subsequently mailed or distributed pamphlets, newspapers, circulars, and so on.

total net paid The total circulation of a publication that is listed as being paid for by the end user.

total running time (TRT) The actual time of a taped segment from beginning to end.

total story time (TST) The estimated time that a radio or television news story will take over the air, including intro, outro, soundbites, voiceovers, and so on.

total survey area (TSA) A geographic area composed of those counties that, by Arbitron estimates, account for approximately 98 percent of the net weekly circulation of all commercial home market stations, exclusive of counties located outside the MSA or ADI reached solely by communications satellite transmission. The TSA includes all of a market's Metro and ADI counties, plus all other additional counties necessary to account for 98 percent of the viewing to that market's home commercial stations.

total teaching All instruction of a particular course presented by broadcast or closed-circuit television.

total telephone frame (TTF) A sampling frame of telephone households, both listed and unlisted, used for NSI samples.

touch control A control activated by the capacitance of an operator's hand.

touch screen A cathode ray screen that is activated by a pen or other device contacting the conductive coating.

Touch-tone A trademark for a telephone system that uses dual tones to represent numbers; replaces the rotary dial pulse system.

tower ☐ A fixed or movable high stand or platform on which to mount lighting fixtures, generally with a built-in ladder. ☐ A tall, metal structure used to mount an antenna. Cf. mast.

tower light *See* obstruction light.

town crier A singer who belts a song.

town marker A symbol used to identify the end of a geographical unit of a mailing list. It was originated for towns but is now used for ZIP codes, sectional centers, and so on.

TP ☐ TV pickup. An FCC file-number prefix. *See also* television pickup station. ☐ Test procedure. ☐ Two pin. A lamp base type.

tp An abbreviation for (magnetic) *tape.*

TPC Telecommunications Planning Committee. A government advisory committee.

TPEA Television Program Export Association.

TPI Tracks per inch.

TPIB Technical Panel for International Broadcast. A government advisory committee.

TPO Transmitter power output.

TR Turn rule.

tr An abbreviation for *translation, translator,* and *transpose.*

Trace An audience research organization using an automobile coincidental survey method.

trace ☐ To record on a library catalog card the other headings under which added entries are recorded. ☐ A display line on a cathode ray tube. ☐ An electrical path on a printed circuit board.

traceable expenditure An expenditure for media space or time attributed to a specific communication medium and advertiser that is reported by published sources; given usually on a nondiscounted basis. Also called *reported spending.*

tracer An individual who copies animated drawings onto cels.

tracing distortion The nonlinear distortion introduced in the reproduction of discs, because the curve traced by the motion of the spherical tip stylus is limited to a function of the tip radius and its instantaneous acceleration in the groove.

track ☐ In recording and computing, a path along which data is recorded on a continuous or rotational medium, such as magnetic tape or a magnetic disk. ☐ An area in a tape format that is to contain a record. ☐ To adjust a videotape playback apparatus so that correct control-track phasing is obtained. ☐ An area on the tape containing a record. ☐ A film soundtrack. ☐ A band on a disc. ☐ To follow a performer's movements with a camera. ☐ An audio, video, or control track on a videotape. ☐ In a compact disc, a sequence of contiguous data, the beginning, length, mode, and end of which are defined in the table of contents. The two types of tracks currently defined are the CD-DA track according to the CD-DA specification and the data track according to the CD-ROM specification, which is also used in CD-I. In CD-DA the length of a track is related to playing times between 4 seconds and 72 minutes. □ An audio section of a radio or television remote news story. May consist of a number of separate tracks. □ The rails used to guide a camera mount during a moving shot. □ One of a series of concentric circles on a computer disk.

track angle The angle of the video record with respect to the reference edge of the tape in a helical-scan videotape recording.

track bouncing The submixing of several audio tracks down to one or two tracks in order to make room for adding new material, such as on an 8-track ATR.

track configuration For tape, the relative position of the active recording area referenced to the entire cross-sectioned surface of the magnetic recording medium.

track curvature The deviation from straightness of a single video track record.

tracking □ The accuracy with which a stylus follows a disc groove. □ The process of adjusting the three guns of a television pickup tube or picture tube. □ The process of positioning a recorded tape so that its tracks are correctly scanned on playback. Usually accomplished by a servo mechanism. □ A British term for trucking. □ An animation zoom. □ A letterspacing option on some computer typesetting equipment. Also called *character compensation.* □ To monitor a syndicated program over a period of time to determine its long-term ratings. Also called *trending.* □ A research study that follows a group or idea over a period of time. □ The following of a track by a readout or pickup device, such as a laser.

tracking control A control on a videotape playback apparatus that permits the operator to adjust the equipment to obtain correct tracking.

tracking control signal The preferred term is *control track signal.*

tracking error The degree of deviation from a specified point or angle in a disc, disk, record, tape, and so on.

tracking force *See* stylus force.

tracking shot A forward, backward, or sideways movement of a camera made in order to remain at the same distance from the performers. Also called a *traveling shot.* Cf. following shot and trucking shot.

track layer An individual who specializes in track laying.

track laying The process of synchronizing and editing the various soundtracks that are to accompany a motion picture or videotape.

track 1 □ In quadruplex recording, the video track that includes the location for recording the vertical interval. □ The record contained in track 1.

tracks per inch (TPI) The number of tracks on a computer disk.

track width The dimension of a track measured perpendicular to its longer dimension. These dimensions vary from cassettes to cartridge to reel-to-reel and from monaural to stereophonic to quad.

tract A pamphlet, usually religious or political, issued for propaganda purposes.

tractor feed *See* pin feed.

trade advertising Advertisements for consumer products that are intended to appeal to wholesalers and retailers rather than consumers.

trade allowance *See* trade discount.

trade association An organization established to promote the interests of a particular trade or industry; manufacturers, professionals, dealers, and so on.

trade binding The standard or publisher's book binding.

trade book A book intended for sale to the general public through normal distribution channels. Cf. book club, subscription book, and text edition.

trade catalogue A publication distributed by a manufacturer, dealer, distributor, and so on, describing specific lines of products.

trade deal *See* trade out.

trade discount A discount from the list price of merchandise given by publishers, distributors, and so on, to a retailer. Also called a *trade allowance.*

trade edition A book intended for use by libraries and for sale to the general public; generally synonymous with *trade book.* Cf. text edition.

trade guild An association of members of a single craft or profession.

trade journal *See* trade press.

trade libel The disparagement of products, as opposed to persons.

trade list A publisher's catalogue of available book titles.

trade magazine *See* trade press.

trademark A word, name, symbol, or device, or any combination of these, adopted and used by a manufacturer or merchant to identify his goods and distinguish them from those manufactured or sold by others. The trademark is registered with the U.S. Patent Office. Broadcast station call letters may be considered trademarks. Sometimes called a *brand name* or *logo.*

trade name A business name used by manufacturers, merchants, or others to identify themselves or their products or services.

trade out The bartering of station time for goods or services. Also called a *trade deal.*

trade paper *See* trade press.

trade paperback *See* quality paperback.

trade-practice conference A conference between members of the Federal Trade Commission and representatives of an industry to establish fair trading practices.

trade press A newspaper or magazine that serves the interests of a particular trade, such as broadcasting, publishing, and cable television. Also called a *trade journal, trade magazine, trade paper, trade publication,* and *trades.*

trade publication *See* trade press.

trade publisher A publisher that specializes in trade books.

Trade Regulation Rules (TRR's) Federal Trade Commission rules that formally interpret the Commission's regulations. TRR's may be nationwide in effect or limited to particular areas, industries, products, or geographic markets. Also called *trade rules.*

trade review A review published in the trade press.

trade rules *See* Trade Regulation Rules.

trades □ The publications of a trade. □ *See* trade press.

trade sale A book auction.

trade secret A formula, process, pattern, device, and so on, that is not divulged so as to give the business an advantage over competitors.

trade show A special temporary exhibit of goods or services to trade buyers, often conducted in concert with other exhibitors at a single location.

trade spots *See* trade out.

trade title A general term for a fiction or nonfiction book carried in a typical bookstore.

trade union An industry union or guild, such as NABET, AFTRA, and SAG.

trade up To sell a radio or television station or cable system in order to purchase a larger station or system.

trading area The geographical area encompassing the homes of individuals who would normally use the metropolitan area as their primary buying location.

TRAFCO TV, Radio and Film Commission of the Methodist Church.

traffic □ The amount or composition of the use of a communication service. □ Messages that are transmitted by a system. □ The programs and announcements that are broadcast on a radio or television station. □ The two-way flow of copy and other information between an advertising agency and a radio or television station.

traffic audit An authentication of circulation out-of-doors as applied to outdoor advertising structures.

Traffic Audit Bureau, Inc. (TAB) A tripartite organization with equal representation from advertisers, advertising agencies, and outdoor companies. It validates outdoor companies' claims of capacity (number of boards), quality (space position value), and quantity (authenticated circulation or number of potential viewers passing each board daily).

traffic builder A direct mail piece intended primarily to attract recipients to the mailer's place of business.

traffic count A recording of the vehicles and pedestrians passing a given outdoor advertising point in order to establish daily effective circulation.

traffic department □ The department of a network or station responsible for day-to-day scheduling of programs and announcements. □ The section of an advertising agency responsible for coordinating the work of the various departments.

traffic flow A graphic presentation of the traffic volume for outdoor advertising on any system of streets, arteries, or highways, shown by widths of lines that vary with the amount of traffic carried.

traffic flow map A graphic representation of traffic densities used in planning outdoor advertising showings.

trafficking The acquisition of broadcast properties by persons having a history of short-term buying and selling such properties, or seeking waiver of the three-year rule when the seller will realize a profit.

traffic manager An individual who handles the flow of work in an advertising agency.

tragedy A literary genre in which a noble character fails through a flaw in his or her character.

trailer □ A commercial announcement following the apparent end of a radio or television program. *See also* hitchhiker. □ An uncoated segment of tape or blank film at the end of a reel. □ A short preview of a future radio or television program. Also called a *teaser*. □ *See* tie-in announcement. □ A short commercial pitch for a new motion picture. Sometimes shown after the main feature in a motion picture theatre.

trailers Dark or light streaks in a television picture.

trailer tag A motion picture trailer containing the MPAA CARA rating.

trailing blacks *See* following blacks.

trailing edge *See* video track trailing edge.

trailing whites *See* following whites.

training film A motion picture that is designed to teach the use of equipment, procedures, company policy, and so on.

tramp printer A printer who moves from job to job and often from city to city.

trannie A British slang term for a transistor radio.

transaction A process wherein information is transmitted and received in both directions, such as an interactive videotex service.

transactional television A general term for interactive cable or interactive television.

transborder communication The flow of information across national borders.

transborder interference Interference that occurs when radio or television stations close to a border transmit on channels that are the same as or adjacent to those across the border. Cf. jamming.

transceiver An abbreviation for *transmitter-receiver*; any device that is capable of transmitting and receiving a signal.

transcoder A device used to change one television system standard to another without changing the number of lines or field rate.

transcoding The changing of a television signal from one system to another, as from SECAM to PAL.

transcribe To copy information from one system to another.

transcribed program A program broadcast by means of a previously recorded transcription.

transcript The official record of proceedings of a court or adjudicatory hearing.

transcription □ A recording on a disc, tape, or film. □ A somewhat obsolete term for a disc containing a complete radio program. *See also* electrical transcription (ET). □ A script of a transmitted program.

transducer A device used to convert energy from one form to another. For example, a loudspeaker is an electroacoustic transducer. Also called a *reproducer*.

transfer □ To send and receive information. □ To rerecord a program from one tape to another, or from one medium to another. *See also* copy and dub. □ To change from one format to another, as in film to videotape. □ The movement of an individual performing a stunt from a vehicle to another moving object. □ To copy data from one computer memory to another.

transfer letter *See* rub on.

transfer of control (TC) The sale of a broadcast station from one licensee to another or to a prospective licensee. *See also* control and trafficking.

transfer of ownership The conveyance of any or all of the exclusive rights granted to a copyright holder.

transfer printing *See* decalcomania.

transfer rate The rate of data transfer in a computer system measured in bits or characters per second.

transformer (T) An electromagnetic device used to change the voltage or current in a circuit, or to match the impedances of two dissimilar components or lines.

transient □ A momentary surge in power or sound. □ Something that passes in and out of existence in a short time.

transient rate The cost of a single newspaper insertion or radio or television spot.

transient response The ability of a system or component to handle a momentary surge.

transistor A semiconductor device, usually made of silicon or germanium, which can control and amplify. Widely used as a replacement for vacuum tubes. Developed by Bell Telephone Laboratories in 1948.

transistorized A device or component utilizing transistors, as opposed to vacuum tubes.

transit advertising Advertising associated with public transportation, placed inside and outside vehicles and in train stations. Also called *transportation advertising.*

Transit Advertising Association (TAA) An organization of sellers of transit advertising, formed in 1942 to provide educational support for members. Formerly National Association of Transportation Advertising.

transit case A shipping container for tape or film reels.

transitcasting An FM service furnishing background music to public transportation vehicles. Also called *transit radio. See also* functional music, musicasting, and storecasting.

transition The continuity, action, sound, or device that leads from one scene to another. Transitions may include music, sound effects, dissolves, fades, silence, and so on. Also called a *bridge.*

transitional A typeface that contains characteristics of both old style and modern faces.

transition focus A transition accomplished by throwing a camera out-of-focus and then focusing in with the same or another camera.

transition point The place at which a change in scene begins.

transit radio *See* transitcasting.

transit spectacular An advertising display that occupies all of one or both sides on the inside or outside of a public transportation vehicle.

translate To change a computer language into another form. *See also* low-level language and machine language.

translation □ The use of a national advertising campaign in a test market that duplicates the proposed national campaign. □ In computer graphics, the movement of an object in a straight line. □ The conversion of one computer language to another. □ The conversion of one set of symbols to another.

translation loss The loss in the reproduction of a mechanical recording whereby the amplitude of motion of the reproducing stylus differs from the recorded amplitude in the medium. Also called *playback loss.*

translation rights The granting by a publisher of the legal right to publish a translation of a book.

translator *See* television broadcast translator station.

transliteration The representation of a word in one language by the use of characters in a different language that does not contain exact equivalents.

translucent A material that transmits light but breaks up the rays so that an image cannot be seen through the material. Cf. opaque and transparent.

translucent screen A rear projection screen.

Translux A trademark for a rear projection system designed for television.

transmission The process of sending information from one point to another or others.

transmission band *See* channel.

transmission factor *See* transmittance.

transmission line A conductor used to carry electrical energy from one point to another.

transmission link Any path by which information flows from a sender to a receiver.

transmission loss Any reduction in signal due to the characteristics of the transmission system. *See also* attenuation.

transmission medium Any environment in which information is transmitted, including wire, cable, fiber optic cable, air, space, and so on.

transmission number *See* T number.

transmission of energy by radio Transmission and all instrumentalities, facilities, and services incidental to such transmission. Also called *radio transmission of energy.*

transmission program For the purposes of copyright, a body of material that, as an aggregate, has been produced for the sole purpose of transmission to the public in sequence and as a unit.

transmission rate The speed at which information is sent on a communication network; usually expressed in bits per second, number of characters, or words per second or per minute.

transmission speed The rate at which data are sent over a communication circuit, expressed in bits per second, characters per second, words per minute, and so on.

transmission stop *See* T stop.

transmit □ To send information, power, light, from one point to one or more others. □ For the purposes of copyright, a performance or display communicated by any device or process whereby images or sounds are received beyond the place from which they are sent.

transmittance A measure of how effectively a material will transmit light, that is, the ratio of the transmitted lumens to the incident lumens on the material. Also called *transmission factor.*

transmitted wave *See* refracted wave.

transmitter □ A fiber optics device that converts an electrical signal into an optical signal. □ In information theory, the encoder of a message.

transmitter (TX) □ A device used to generate, modulate, and amplify a carrier wave so that it may be radiated by an antenna. □ A telephone mouthpiece microphone.

transmitter-hour One frequency used on one transmitter for one hour.

transmitter microphone *See* wireless microphone.

transmitter site The location of a radio or television station antenna and transmitter.

transmitting station □ A transmitter designed to propagate radio communication signals. □ A terminal in a computer network.

transmutation The changing of the timbre of a sound.

transnational A corporation that controls companies in the same field in other countries. Cf. multinational.

transparency □ A still or graphic on glass, film, or other transparent material for viewing by transmitted light. □ An editing system's ability to allow creativity without interference. □ The function of a computer or communication system without the obvious intervention of other equipment. □ The ability to see through from one plane to another.

transparency bit In CD-I, a dedicated bit controlling overlay transparency in the cursor plane and the RGB (555) plane.

transparency control The three mechanisms used to control the display of superimposed planes.

transparent □ A material that transmits light without breaking up the rays. Cf. opaque and translucent. □ An automatic operation or activity performed by a computer that is unnoticed by the operator. □ A transmission wherein the medium does not change or alter the essential information in any way.

transponder A transmitter-receiver facility the function of which is to transmit signals automatically when the proper interrogation is received.

transport □ The mechanism of a tape recorder that moves the tape. *See also* tape transport. □ The mechanical parts of a film mechanism. *See also* film transport.

transportation advertising *See* transit advertising.

transportation department A motion picture studio department responsible for the vehicles used at the studio and on location.

transportation display poster A train or bus station or depot display poster that comes in various sizes: one, two, or six sheets; viewed mainly by commuters.

transpose (tr) □ To change the position of letters, words, lines, and so on, that are in the incorrect order. □ Copy marked for transpositional changes.

transposer A device used to change the distance between the sound and picture on magnetic stripe film.

transverse Pertaining to dimensions or motions perpendicular to the tape reference edge. Cf. longitudinal.

transverse curl *See* cupping.

transverse recording □ In general, a method of recording in which the recording head moves perpendicular to the direction of tape motion. Quadruplex recording is a specific standardized example of this method. □ Quadruplex recording.

transverse scanning The quadruplex system of scanning magnetic tape wherein the heads read and write vertically.

trap □ A filter or circuit designed to attenuate undesired frequencies or signals. □ The clean superimposition of the yellow, red, blue, and black inks used in four color wet printing, to attain the specific hues and color density desired in the final printed image.

trapeze A device used to suspend luminaires from ropes or wires.

trapezoidal distortion The distortion of an image in which the image is trapezoidal in shape rather than rectangular. Common in television pictures and projected images.

trapping routine In computer programming, a routing used to identify and trap a specified event.

trash TV □ The theory that television in the 1980s is involved in the coarsening of our public life in the United States. □ *See* infotainment.

TRAV Television, Radio and Audio-Visuals of the Presbyterian Church in the United States.

traveler □ A publisher's representative who visits prospective buyers (bookstores, professors, and libraries,) to promote books, solicit orders, and so on. □ A mechanism used to make performers appear to fly. □ A slotted track used to hang stage or set curtains. □ A traveler curtain. Also spelled *traveller*.

traveling display A form of transit advertising in which the display is placed on the outside of buses, taxicabs, and so on. Cf. car card.

traveling pegbars *See* traveling pegs.

traveling peg bars *See* panning peg bars.

traveling pegs One of the two sets of movable pegs mounted on an animation table. Also called *traveling pegbars*.

traveling tympan A shifting tympan used in offset printing to avoid soiling the paper.

traveling matte □ A matte shot in which the foreground and background scenes are shot separately and in which the matte changes from frame to frame. Also called *self matteing*. □ An insert that changes position in a television picture.

traveling shot *See* tracking shot.

travelogue A radio or television program that describes people or places.

travel shot *See* truck.

travel time For location shooting, the time spent traveling between the place of reporting and the location and, if applicable, the time between the location and the place of housing.

TRE Telecommunications Research Establishment.

treatment □ An adaptation of a story, book, play, or other literary, dramatic or dramatic-musical material for motion picture purposes in form suitable for use as the basis of a screenplay. According to the Copyright Office, a treatment is often an intermediate stage between the script idea and the shooting script. Also called a *story treatment* and *treatment outline*. Cf. original treatment. □ A detailed version of a proposed story or script. *See also* scenario. □ The interpretation imposed on a script by a director. □ An overview of a proposed CD-I title, including information on the logistics involved in the title's creation. □ The general approach to or tone of an advertising campaign or advertisement.

treatment outline Generally synonymous with *treatment*, but sometimes equivalent to a *sequence outline*.

treble The higher part of the vocal or instrumental range; normally, above middle C.

treble boost An intentional accentuation of the higher audio frequencies. Cf. bass boost.

treble response The ability of a loudspeaker, microphone, or amplifier to reproduce high frequencies.

treble rolloff *See* rolloff.

tree A high stand or tower with horizontal arms on which to mount lighting fixtures.

tree calf A chemically treated calfskin book binding with a grain similar to that of the bark of a tree.

tree network A comparison of a cable television system to a tree, from the headend through the trunk and feeders to subscribers.

trend analysis A research study that attempts to locate trends through tracking or by comparing other studies.

Trendex, Inc. An audience research firm organized in 1950, which takes audience measurements for networks and advertising agencies.

trending *See* tracking.

trespass The tort of unlawful entry on the real property of another.

triacetate base Cellulose triacetate, a safety film base.

triad A cluster of the three different color phosphors on a television picture tube. Also called a *trio*.

trial balloon A project designed to test public opinion as to the advisability of a contemplated action.

trial buyer A person who buys a short-term supply of a product or who buys the product with the understanding that it may be examined, used, or tested for a specified time before a decision is made whether to pay for it or return it.

trial court A court of original jurisdiction, either civil or criminal, as opposed to an appellate court.

trial lead *See* bunk lead.

trial print A first trial composite print. *See also* answer print.

trial subscriber A person who orders a publication or service on a conditional basis. The condition may relate to delaying payment, the right to cancel, a shorter than normal term, or a special introductory price.

triangle *See* spider.

triaxial A loudspeaker with three independent, coaxially mounted drivers.

trichromatic camera A television camera employing three color tubes.

trick □ A skillful, but expedient method of writing a story, shooting a scene, and so on. □ An optical illusion.

trick angle A camera shot taken from an unusual angle. Also called a *dutch angle*.

trickle charger A battery charger that recharges at a slow rate and then maintains the charge. Used extensively for portable radio and television equipment.

trickle down A technological effect, wherein innovative and costly electronic systems, components, features, and so on, become the commonplace features of tomorrow.

trick shot Any shot that creates an unnatural or unusual illusion. Trick shots may be accomplished by opticals, supers, mirrors, and so on.

tricolor A television camera that separates light into the three primary colors.

tricolor filter *See* separation filter.

trigger An electronic device used to initiate an action.

triggyback A commercial with three segments. Cf. piggyback.

trim □ To adjust the capacitance, inductance, or resistance of a circuit. □ The materials used to finish a set. □ To dress a set. □ To tighten or condense copy to remove excess verbiage. □ To cut a publication's or document's pages to their final size. *See also* trim size. □ A border or molding strip used to frame an outdoor advertisement. □ The addition or subtraction of a frame or two in videotape editing in order to make the transition between shots more precise. □ To eliminate unwanted shots during editing. □ To edit.

trim bin A large rectangular, cloth lined container used during editing to hold pieces of film hung from pins.

trim flush To trim a book cover even with the pages.

trim mark The lines used to indicate the points at which pages or sheets are to be trimmed.

trimmed edge A book edge that has had the projecting edge removed. Also called *trimmed flush.* Cf. uncut edge (UE).

trimmed flush *See* trimmed edge.

trimmed size *See* trim size.

trimming The cutting of book edges.

trim pot A variable resistor.

trims Unused pieces of film or tape that are left over after editing. Also called a *clip* and *cut. See also* outtake.

trim size The dimensions of book signatures, pages, sheets, or other printed matter after trimming. Also called *trimmed size.*

trim tab A small marker used to identify pieces or rolls of film.

trio □ A group of three. Often refers to musicians. □ *See* triad.

triode A three-element vacuum tube. *See also* audion.

tripack Originally, three emulsions on three separate lengths of film; now, on three layers of the same length of film.

triphonic A three-channel stereophonic recording or transmission. *See also* stereophonic sound. Cf. biphonic and quadraphonic.

triple associates method A research technique in which a respondent, being given an advertising campaign theme and product type, is asked to name the brand of product or manufacturer associated with it.

triple spotting The broadcasting of three consecutive commercials.

triplet A lens with three elements.

tripod A collapsible, three-legged camera support. *See also* camera mounts.

triptych A picture in three parts. Sometimes refers to early attempts to produce a wide-screen picture with three projectors.

Tri-Vision A painted outdoor advertising display embellishment that, through use of a triangular louver construction, permits the display of three different copy messages in a predetermined sequence. Also called *Multi-Vision.*

trolley *See* dolly.

trombone A tubular device used to suspend luminaires from lighting grids.

troposphere The portion of the earth's atmosphere extending from sea level to a varying altitude of approximately 6 to 12 miles. Cf. ionosphere.

tropospheric scatter The propagation of radio waves by scattering as a result of irregularities or discontinuities in the physical properties of the troposphere. Cf. ionospheric scatter.

trouble number The telephone number of a survey supervisor given to each interviewer in case of problems.

troubleshoot To seek the cause of defective equipment.

TRR's Trade regulation rules.

TRT Total running time.

tru-broad A floodlight capable of being focused.

truck □ A camera movement parallel to a set or to talent, normally perpendicular to a dolly or zoom. Also called a *crab, crabbing,* and *travel shot.* □ *See* turtle. □ In animation, a camera move in which the camera seems to move toward (Truck In) or away from (Truck Out) the subject. The same effect is called a zoom in live-action filmmaking.

trucking shot A camera shot taken from the side of a set or talent. Cf. tracking shot.

truck left A television or film director's command to move a camera to the left.

truck right A television or film director's command to move a camera to the right.

true rating *See* standard value.

true value *See* standard value.

tru-line rate The milline rate of a newspaper based on the circulation in the trading area only.

truncate □ To drop digits from a number. □ To use only a section of a geometrical shape, such as a portion of a parabola for use as a reflector (a truncated paraboloid).

trunk □ A message circuit or line between two offices. □ A telephone company cable, microwave, fiber optics cable, and so on, main interconnecting system that moves calls to and from a central office or between branch exchanges. □ The main line of a cable television system that extends from the headend to the feeder cables. □ The primary wire of a wire service.

trunk amplifier One of a series of amplifiers used in a cable television system trunk.

TRUST □ *See* Motion Picture Patents Company. □ Television relay using small terminals.

truth The best defense against a charge of defamation; that the alleged defamation was a true representation of the facts. Sometimes called *justification.*

tryout An audition.

TS □ TV STL. An FCC file-number prefix. □ Typescript. □ Type specification.

TSA Total survey area.

T-scope *See* tachistoscope.

TSL Time spent listening.

TSP □ Telecommunication science panel. □ Theta Sigma Phi.

TST Total story time.

T stop The calibration of the actual light gathering power of a lens, unlike an f stop. Also called a *transmission stop.*

TSV Time spent viewing.

TT □ Teletype. □ Teletypewriter. □ Total time. □ UHF translator. An FCC file-number prefix.

TTB UHF signal booster. An FCC file-number prefix.

TTF Total telephone frame.

TTL Through the lens.

TTR TV translator relay. An FCC file-number prefix.

TTS Teletypesetter.

tts code A computer code used to operate a teletypesetter.

TTV VHF translator. An FCC file-number prefix.

TTY Teletypewriter.

tubby *See* boomy.

tube □ A slang term for a video display terminal, television receiver, and so on. □ *See* vacuum tube.

tube carriage The cradle that holds a television camera pickup tube in place.

tube socket The receptacle that holds a vacuum tube in place and provides for electrical connections.

tub thumper A slang term for a press agent. Also called a *tubman.*

tune □ To adjust a receiver to a particular frequency. □ To adjust the pitch of a musical instrument. □ The melody of a song.

tuned A circuit or component adjusted to operate or resonate at a given frequency.

tune in To select a radio station for listening. Cf. tune out.

tune out To turn a radio station or receiver off. Cf. tune in.

tuner A radio receiver, not including the amplifier and speakers.

tungsten A metal used in the manufacture of filaments for vacuum tubes and lamps.

tungsten film A film stock balanced for use under tungsten lighting.

tungsten-halogen Incandescent light sources utilizing the halogen regenerative cycle to prevent blackening of the lamp envelope during life. Usually more compact and with a longer life than comparable standard incandescent sources. Also called *halogen types, quartz, quartz halogen,* and *quartz iodine.*

tungsten-halogen lamp A tungsten filament, quartz lamp that is filled with halogen gas. Designed for a color temperature of 3200 degrees Kelvin.

tungsten light *See* incandescent light.

tuning The process of a radio or television receiver being adjusted to receive a broadcast. Usually, a radio or television receiver is considered to be tuned as long as it is turned on. Cf. listening and viewing.

tuning control The radio receiver control knob that is used to select the desired radio station. Cf. channel selector.

tuning indicator A meter or electric eye that is used to tune a receiver accurately.

tuning inertia The tendency of some radio and television listeners or viewers to stay tuned to the same channel unless a disliked program is next.

turkey A slang term for a book, television program, motion picture, and so on, that is a flop.

turn □ A news story that continues from one column to the next. Cf. turn story. □ A variety show act. □ A performer in a variety show.

turnaround □ A union term for a rest period between the time of dismissal and the recall to work on a production. □ A screenplay that is not produced by a studio and made available to other producers or studios. □ A radio or television station that has been made financially successful after losing money.

turnaround time □ The time required to complete a task or repair equipment. □ The time from the completion of an electronic or typeset manuscript to the completion of a proof or finished printing.

turn column *See* turn story.

turned letter A type character used as a substitute for a turn rule. Also called a *turned sort.*

turned sort *See* turned letter.

turnkey The installation of a station, printing plant, electronic system, and so on, in complete and operational form. Often vendor installed.

turn over To relinquish control or operation of a radio or television studio to another operator or for another program.

turnover □ Printed material that extends beyond the allotted space. Also called *runover.* □ *See* turn story. □ The ratio of new subscribers to those discontinuing service for, for example, cable television, MMDS, newspapers, and periodicals. □ The departure of members of an audience (households or persons) during the course of a single program or a broadcast schedule, and the arrival of other members not tuned in or viewing earlier. Audience turnover is sometimes regarded as the opposite of audience loyalty or station holding power.

turnover cartridge A turntable pickup having a stylus for both microgroove and 78 rpm discs. Also called a *dual pickup* and *turnover pickup.*

turnover factor In survey estimates, the ratio of the number of cume persons to the AQH persons. *See also* audience turnover.

turnover pickup *See* turnover cartridge.

turn rule A rule inserted with its base up to indicate that a story is not complete and that additional material is to be inserted at that point. Also called a *rule for insert* and *rule for pickup.*

turn story A news story that runs from the right hand column of one page to the left hand column of the next page, thus eliminating the need for a jump head. Also called a *turn column* and *turnover.* Cf. turn.

turntable The complete mechanism used to play a disc. Cf. platen, record changer, record player, and tone arm.

turntable hit A record played often by a radio station, but one that sells few copies.

turntable platen *See* platen.

turntable rumble *See* rumble.

turntable speed The standard speeds for turntables are 33-1/3 rpm and 45 rpm. The standard speed was formerly 78.26 rpm, but discs designed to rotate at that speed are no longer manufactured.

turret □ A rotatable lens mount positioned in front of a camera that permits rapid switching of lenses. Also called a *rack* and *rack mount.* □ A television receiver channel selector in the shape of a rotary drum or disc in which the coils are pretuned to the various channels.

turret tuner *See* turret.

turtle A wheeled composing room table on which forms are made up. Also called a *truck.*

tusche □ A lithographic ink. □ A substance used as a resistant in the etching process.

TV Television.

TVA Television Authority. A former television talent union that combined with AFRA to form AFTRA.

TvB Television Bureau of Advertising.

TVBS Television Broadcast Satellite.

TV cutoff *See* essential area

TV mask A cardboard cutout or lines drawn on a television camera viewfinder to show the limits of the safe action area.

TV print A composite color print balanced for xenon projection.

TVHH Television households.

TVI Television interference.

TV microwave booster station A fixed station in the TV broadcast auxiliary service that receives and amplifies signals of a TV pickup, TV STL, TV relay, or TV translator relay station and retransmits them on the same frequency.

TVN Television News, Inc. Now INTA.

TVola A videotape editing machine similar in function to the picture portion of a moviola.

TV pickup station A land mobile station used for the transmission of TV program material and related communications from the scenes of events occurring at points removed from TV broadcast station studios to TV broadcast or low power TV stations or other purposes as authorized.

TvQ An audience research company stressing qualitative measurements. A division of Marketing Evaluation, Inc.

TvQ score The percentage of television viewers familiar with a particular program who consider the program as one of their favorites.

TVR Television recording. A kinescope recording.

TV relay station A fixed station used for transmission of TV program material and related communications for use by TV broadcast and low power TV stations or other purposes as authorized.

TVRO Television receive only.

TV STL station A fixed station used for the transmission of TV program material and related communications from the studio to the transmitter of a TV broadcast or low-power TV station or other purposes as authorized.

TV translator relay station A fixed station used for relaying programs and signals of TV broadcast stations to LPTV, TV translator, and to other communications facilities that the Federal Communications Commission may authorize or for other purposes as permitted.

tweak *See* peak.

tweeter A high-frequency loudspeaker, usually used in conjunction with a woofer. *See also* squawker.

twelve-twelve-twelve rule *See* multiple ownership.

twenty A twenty-second commercial.

twentyfourmo □ A book having twenty four leaves to a sheet. □ A book measuring approximately 3-3/4 by 6 inches.

twenty-four sheet panel *See* twenty four sheet poster panel.

twenty four sheet poster An outdoor advertising space providing a copy area measuring 8 feet 8 inches by 19 feet 6 inches, usually covered with a single poster printed in sections on 10 paper sheets. Also called a *twenty-four sheet.*

twenty four sheet poster panel An outdoor advertising structure 25 feet long and 12 feet high to which outdoor posters are pasted. Also called a *twenty-four sheet panel.*

twentymo A sheet folded so as to have 20 leaves.

TWG Television Writer's Guild. A union.

twin filament lamp A lamp containing two filaments; one or both may be activated.

twinkling A television picture distortion that looks like stars twinkling. Also called *edge beat.*

twin lead A two-conductor line with parallel wires commonly used to connect an antenna to a television receiver. Normally, 75- or 300-ohm impedance. Also called a *video pair.*

twin lens reflex A two lens still camera, one lens for viewing on a ground glass screen, the other for taking the picture.

twin track recorder *See* half track recorder.

twist A surprise ending to a script or program. *See also* O Henry.

twisted pair Two insulated wires that are wrapped around each other.

TWNS Trans World News Service.

two brand rate The station time rate discount offered to advertisers who purchase two time periods.

two color A print made with black and one other color. Cf. color separation.

two color process An obsolete film process using two colors (orange-red and blue-green) instead of the current three colors.

twofer A load connector wired in parallel to two-line connectors so that two luminaires can be connected to a single electrical circuit. Also called an *asbestos tapoff, martingale,* and *Y-cord.*

two-fold Two flats hinged together. Also called a *book, book flat, two-fold flat, wing,* and *wing flat.*

two-fold flat *See* two-fold.

two inch A professional size of videotape used on quadruplex recorders.

two-K *See* deuce.

two-line figure A letter or numeral having a type height of two lines. May also be a three-line figure, four-line figure, and so on. Also called a *two-line initial.*

two-line initial *See* two-line figure.

two page spread A layout that covers two opposing pages.

two phase (double) samples A survey sample in which a sample of elements is selected and some information is collected from the elements in the first phase sample. Using the information, a second phase sample is selected and additional information is collected. Sampling may be extended to more than two phases. *See also* probability sample.

twos In animation, the exposure of two frames for each drawing.

two sheet poster A transportation station poster. Not standardized but usually 60 inches high by 42 inches wide.

two shot A close-up of two persons or objects. Cf. three shot.

two step flow of communication A process by which information is disseminated; the listener, viewer, or reader passes on the information received from a mass medium to others.

two step recording The usual method of disc recording. *See also* master, mold, and mother. Cf. one step recording.

two three scanning The method of scanning a motion picture for conversion to television. A frame is scanned twice, the next three times, the next two times, and so on, to make 60 fields or 30 frames per second.

two track *See* half track recorder.

two way A communication circuit that allows messages to pass in both directions, such as telephone, interactive cable television, and walkie-talkie. *See also* two way communication.

two way cable The potential capacity of cable television to provide services in which information can flow from the subscriber as well as to the subscriber. *See also* interactive cable.

two way communication Radiocommunication between two fixed or mobile points, each of which is capable of transmission and reception. Also called *two way radio.*

two way radio *See* two way communication.

two-way system A single loudspeaker containing two electrically independent radiating elements, one for low frequencies, the other for high frequencies.

TWR Trans World Radio. A religious broadcasting organization.

TWX □ Teletypewriter Exchange. A teleprinter data communication service by Western Union. □ A teletype message sent by TWX. *See also* Telex.

tx An abbreviation for *telex* and *transmitter.*

tying in A radio or television station that joins a network program in progress.

Tyler mount A gyroscopically controlled television camera mount used in helicopters.

tympan A sheet of paper or other material used to cover the platen or impression cylinder on a printing press. The term sometimes includes the backing material. Also spelled tampon.

typage *See* typecasting.

type □ An individually cast metal printing element containing a raised character or symbol on one end. □ Metal type collectively. □ The typographic image produced by type, phototypesetting, strike on, laser printing, and so on. □ To typewrite or keyboard. □ A performer especially suited to one kind of role in a production.

Type A1 A telephone company transmission line that carries frequencies from approximately 200 to 3500 Hz.

Type A2 A telephone company transmission line that carries frequencies from approximately 100 to 5000 Hz.

Type A3 A telephone company transmission line that carries frequencies from approximately 50 to 8800 Hz.

Type A4 A telephone company transmission line that carries frequencies from approximately 50 to 15,000 Hz.

type acceptance The recognition by the FCC that specific electronic equipment is acceptable for broadcast use, including transmitters, antennas, and so on.

Type A dealer commercial A commercial made and paid for by the manufacturer or distributor of a product or service that the commercial advertises. Cf. Type B dealer commercial.

Type B dealer commercial A commercial made and paid for by a national manufacturer or distributor of a product or consumer service that is delivered to a chain of local retail stores owned and operated by the national manufacturer or distributor. The commercial is telecast as a wild spot, which advertises only a product sold or service marketed exclusively under the brand or trade name of the national manufacturer or distributor. The commercial is used only by its own retail stores or service outlets and is "tagged" to identify the local retail stores or service outlets in the local markets in which it is telecast. Cf. Type A dealer commercial.

Type A film A color film balanced for shooting in tungsten light with a color temperature of 3400 degrees Kelvin.

type area *See* type page.

type A reel A metal or plastic audiotape reel with a three-inch center hole that has a diameter of 10-1/2 inches. Cf. type B reel.

type B A less used one-inch videotape format. Cf. type C.

typeball A golfball size printer element containing raised characters.

type bar A slug containing a line of type. Also called a *type slug.*

Type B film A color film balanced for shooting in tungsten light with a color temperature of 3200 degrees K.

type book A printed book showing the typefaces, rules, ornaments, and so on, available from a particular printer, computer program, and so on. Also called a *type library* and, if a single sheet, a *type sheet.*

type B reel A plastic 5/16-inch center hole audiotape reel that has a diameter of 3, 5, 7, or 10-1/2 inches. Cf. type A reel.

type C The major one-inch videotape format; manufactured by Ampex, Sony, and others. Cf. type B.

typecaster *See* linecaster.

typecasting The selection of actors and actresses on the basis of their physical appearance rather than for their acting ability. Also called *typage.*

type classification A somewhat nonstandardized categorization of typeface designs. Often, type is divided into roman, sans serif, serif, script or cursive, and novelty, decorative, or display. However, some systems of classification use black letter, roman, and italic only.

Type D film A color film balanced for shooting in daylight with a color temperature of 5600 degrees K.

typeface The varied styles of printed letters, numbers, characters, identified by family names, such as Baskerville, Bodoni, Caslon, and so on.

type family A group of related typefaces; generally known by their tradenames, such as Helvetica, Caslon, Garamond, and so on. Cf. font and type series.

type gauge *See* line gauge.

type G film An amateur film suitable for shooting under various light temperature sources.

type height *See* type high.

type high The standard printing height of a line of type in this country: 0.9186 of an inch. Also more properly, but less often, called *height to paper.*

type library *See* type book.

type louse The imaginary bug responsible for typographical errors and other mistakes in a printshop, composing room, and so on.

type M The half-inch VHS videotape format.

type measurement *See* point.

type mechanical *See* keyline.

type metal The alloy, consisting of lead, antimony, tin, and sometimes copper, used for making type, plates, and so on.

type page The portion of a page that type or other printed matter will utilize. Also called *copy area* and *type area.* Cf. gutter and margin.

typescript Typewritten matter. *See also* copy.

type series All of the fonts of one typeface.

typeset Printed matter made from movable type.

typesetter □ A keyboard machine capable of setting type; a Linotype, intertype, or monotype. Also direct impression or cold type machines. □ A person who sets type; a compositor.

typesetting The arranging of type into lines from a manuscript.

typesetting codes The symbols understood by a computer-driven typesetting machine that are derived from the writer's generic codes.

typesetting computer A computer capable of translating text and codes from disks or tapes.

typesetting machine *See* typesetter.

typesetting pass One complete cycle in the keyboarding of a manuscript.

type sheet *See* type book.

type size Before 1886 when the point system of type measurement was adopted by the Unites States Type Founders' Association, each size of type was designated by a name. The names used and the nearest equivalent point sizes were: excelsior, 3; brilliant, 3-1/2 or 4; diamond, 4-1/2; pearl, 5; agate, 5-1/2; nonpareil, 6; emerald, 6-1/2; minion, 7; brevier, 8; bourgeois, 9; long primer, 10; small pica, 11; pica, 12; English, 14; Columbian, 16; great primer, 18; paragon, 20; double small pica, 22; double pica, 24; double English, 26; double great primer, 36; double paragon, 40; meridian, 44; canon, 48. Above this, the sizes were called five line pica, six line pica, and so on.

type slug *See* type bar.

type style *See* typeface.

type wash A solvent used for cleaning type.

typewriter An electronic, electric, or manual device consisting of keyboard connected types that strike a carbon or ink coated ribbon to make impressions on the paper.

typewriter composition Copy prepared by a typewriter or other direct impression machine.

typo □ An abbreviation for *typographical error.* □ A printer or compositor.

typographer A person who is skilled in typographic design.

typographical error A mistake made by a typist or typesetter.

typographical style The rules concerning punctuation, capitalization, abbreviations, and so on, set by a publisher.

typography □ The art and process of composing a printed page, including the selection of paper, typeface, and so on. □ The use of type to impress images on paper or other materials. □ The effect obtained from the style of a printed page.

U

U □ Unlimited time. □ Urgent; a wire service priority code for important news, but less important than a bulletin.

UA Urban area.

U and lc Upper- and lowercase.

UAPRE University Association for Professional Radio Education. *See* BEA.

UAR Universal asynchronous receiver. *See* UART.

UART Universal asynchronous receiver-transmitter.

UC □ Uppercase. □ Uncut edges (of paper or books).

UCC □ Universal Copyright Convention. An intergovernmental organization. □ Uniform Commercial Code.

U channel One of the eight compact disc subcode channels (P-W). At present only allocated to CD graphics.

UCM User communications manager.

UDC Universal Decimal Classification.

U desk Another term for a horseshoe shaped copy desk.

UE United Electrical, Radio and Machine Workers of America. A union. An abbreviation for the UERMWA.

UER Union Européenne de Radiodiffusion. *See* EBU.

UERMWA United Electrical, Radio and Machine Workers of America. A union. Also UEW.

UEW United Electrical, Radio, and Machine Workers of America. A union. Also UERMWA.

UF Underground feeder (cable).

UHF Ultra high frequency.

UHF connector A barrel-shaped connector used for video.

UHF converter A device formerly used to convert UHF signals to VHF so that the signals could be displayed on VHF only television receivers.

UHF to VHF converter A device used to convert UHF signals to lower frequencies for use on cable systems.

UHF translator A television broadcast translator station operating on a UHF television broadcast channel.

UHF translator signal booster A station in the broadcasting service operated for the sole purpose of retransmitting the signals of a UHF translator station by amplifying and reradiating such signals that have been received directly through space, without significantly altering any characteristic of the incoming signal other than its amplitude.

UHF translator station A television broadcast translator station operating on a UHF television broadcast channel.

UIB United Independent Broadcasters.

UIE Union Internationale des Editeurs (International Union of Publishers). An international organization.

UIR Union Internationale de Radiodiffusion. *See* IBU.

UIT Union Internationale des Telecommunications. An intergovernmental organization. *See also* ITU.

UL Underwriter's Laboratories.

ultimate consumer The final user: the reader, the broadcast audience, and so on. Also called *final consumer.*

ultracardioid A microphone with an extremely narrow angle of acceptance. A shotgun microphone.

Ultrafax A tradename for a high-speed television communication system.

ultrafiche A form of microfiche that may contain thousands of pages of text.

ultra high frequency (UHF) The band of frequencies from 300 to 3000 mHz. It is within this band that UHF television channels 14–69 are located.

ultra large scale integration (USLI) A microprocessor that contains tens of thousands of components.

Ultra Panavision A wide-screen process that produces 70-mm prints with a 2.7:1

aspect ratio. *See also* Panavision and Super Panavision.

Ultra Semi-Scope A nonanamorphic Japanese wide-screen process that produces an aspect ratio of 2.35:1. Similar in format to Techniscope.

ultrasonic Above audible frequencies.

ultrasonic cleaning The cleaning of motion picture prints through the use of a solvent agitated by ultrasonic energy.

ultraviolet (UV) Radiation that is of the same basic nature as light—that is, electromagnetic energy—but of wavelengths too short to be seen by the eye. Wavelengths close to the visible spectrum (320–380 nanometers) are called black light and are used to excite fluorescent materials, paint, dyes, and so on, in theatrical applications. Cf. infrared.

ultraviolet filter A lens filter used to reduce haze, produce fluorescent photographs, and so on. Also called a *colorless filter.*

ultraviolet light The invisible light immediately above violet on the visible spectrum. Also called *black light.*

ultraviolet matte A self-matteing system using ultraviolet filters and differently lit foregrounds and backgrounds.

ultra vires Literally, beyond power. Exceeding permissible power or authority.

U Matic A Sony tradename for a videotape cassette format.

U-Matic SP A videotape cassette format compatible with U-Matic, but with improved video using a special oxide tape. Cf. Betacam, Betacam SP, M-II, and S-VHS.

umbilical A cable between a film camera and a sound recorder. *See also* cable synchronization.

umbra The darkest portion of a shadow. Cf. penumbra.

umbrella An umbrella-shaped light reflector.

umbrella promotion A promotional method that employs a theme to cover a number of different products sold or manufactured by the same company.

UN United Nations Organization. Also ONU.

unaffiliated network A network not having an affiliated station in a particular market, even though it may have other types of agreements or per-program arrangements.

unaffiliated station A television station not having an affiliation arrangement with a national television network, even though it may have other types of agreements or per-program arrangements with it. Cf. affiliated station.

unaided recall A recall interview in which the interviewer does not give the respondent any assistance in remembering past behavior. Used extensively in advertising content surveys. Cf. aided recall.

unattended operation The operation of a station by automatic means whereby the transmitter is turned on and off and performs its functions without attention by a qualified operator.

unauthorized A book printed without authorization from the copyright holder. *See also* piracy.

unauthorized communications Communications that are not allowed, unless specifically authorized, under the Communications Act of 1934, such as radio, television, and wire communications not intended for reception by the general public; police and fire public safety messages; FAA radio transmissions; and rebroadcasts.

unavailable, on order (UOO) A radio or television time slot that is not available to air a network program, but will air at a later time or date.

unbalanced A circuit that has one side grounded.

unbalanced line A transmission line that has unequal voltages on the conductors.

unblanking The turning on of a scanning beam. *See also* blanking.

unbuilt station A standard, FM, or television broadcast station for which a construction permit is outstanding, and for which program test authority has not been issued.

unbundling The dissolution of cable television services that were formerly available as a package. Cf. bundling.

UNCA United Nations Correspondents Association.

uncial An ancient form of capital letter. *See also* majuscule and minuscule.

uncollectable A person who hasn't paid for goods and services at the end of a normal series of collection efforts.

uncombined listening estimates *See* discrete demographics.

unconstitutional A law not in conformance or consistent with a federal or state constitution.

uncontested renewal A radio or television station license renewal application that is not subjected to petitions to deny, competing applications, and so on.

uncontrolled documentary *See* direct cinema.

uncorrected proof A rush copy of a book galley released for review purposes.

UNCTAD United Nations Conference on Trade and Development.

uncut edge (UE) Books or periodicals that have not had their edges trimmed, although the signatures or pages have been slit. Cf. trimmed edge.

uncut tape *See* raw tape.

UNDA Catholic International Association for Radio and Television. A religious broadcasting organization. From the Latin meaning ''wave.''

undated A news story that has no dateline.

undated story A news story without a dateline, often from a wire service, that summarizes news from several geographical areas or related events.

under □ A radio or television program that runs shorter than its allotted time. Also called *underrun.* Cf. over. □ To subordinate one sound to another. Also called *sound under.*

underbrush proceeding *See* regulatory underbrush.

undercrank To run a film camera at less than 24 frames per second so that the action speed is increased when the film is projected. Cf. overcrank.

undercut An overetched halftone printing plate in which acid has eaten into the sides of the dots, leaving a mushroom surface dot; though usable for printing, the plate cannot be used for molding duplicate printing plates.

under dash matter Previously prepared news stories that are held for use when needed. New material is written, then following a dash, the previously prepared material is used. Also called *under dash material.*

underdevelop To develop film for less than the required time, resulting in a thin negative. Cf. overdevelop.

underexposure To expose a film for an insufficient amount of time, resulting in a picture lacking in detail. Underexposure is due to insufficient light, incorrect lens aperture, or incorrect shutter speed. Cf. overexposure.

underground cable A cable designed to be installed beneath the surface of the earth.

underground cable system A cable television system that locates its trunk, feeder, or subscriber drop cables below ground level, as opposed to utilizing utility poles.

underground cinema *See* underground film.

underground film A low budget, often nontraditional motion picture, made without studio backing and distribution. Also called *underground cinema* and *underground movie.*

underground housing *See* pedestal housing.

underground movie *See* underground film.

underground press Publications that are designed as an alternative to established newspapers. Generally, publications, especially those of the 1960s, that questioned current social and political ideology.

underground radio A radio station format characterized by a lack of traditional content with a heavy emphasis on progressive rock. Also called *alternative radio.*

underground television A type of television format, or lack of format, seen on CATV public access channels.

underlap *See* underscanned.

underlay A piece of paper placed under type to raise it to proper printing level. Cf. overlay.

underlighting □ The condition that exists when insufficient illumination is used for proper lighting. □ Light that is directed from beneath the subject or object. *See also* bottom lighting.

underline □ An explanatory cutline beneath an illustration. □ A horizontal line beneath type matter; often used to indicate italics.

undermodulation A broadcast signal that has insufficient modulation, thus decreasing the signal-to-noise ratio. Cf. overmodulation.

underpart A subordinate acting role.

underplay To act in a subdued manner. Cf. overact.

underprint To print with insufficient pressure to produce an acceptable impression.

underrun □ A shortage in the number of copies of printed matter ordered. Often caused by damage in printing, binding, or both. □ *See* under.

underscanned A television picture in which the borders are visible on the screen. Also called *underlap*.

under schedule A production, publication, commercial, and so on, that is completed ahead of schedule. Cf. over schedule.

underscore To add weight to a line of type by underlining.

underscoring The use of music to reinforce dialogue.

undersell To sell a product, service, space, air time, and so on, for less than the competition.

underset An insufficient number of lines of type and illustrative matter set to fill the available space. *See also* loose and tight.

undershoot □ To shoot an insufficient amount of film or tape. Cf. overshoot. □ A form of television signal distortion.

undersized Paper that has not been sufficiently sized.

understudy A performer who is prepared to play a major role in a production if necessary. An understudy usually has a minor role in the same production.

underwater housing A waterproof camera case used in shooting underwater scenes.

underwriter An organization that subsidizes a public broadcasting program or series.

Underwriter's Laboratories (UL) An independent laboratory that tests equipment to see if it meets certain safety standards.

underwriting The subsidizing or financing of a production, publication, announcement, and so on. Often, a grant by a corporation to fund a program or series on PBS.

undeveloped Film that has been exposed but not processed.

undirected scene A public event open to the general public; the crowd in attendance must number at least 1000 persons, and the event must be publicized or advertised and not staged for motion picture purposes, and the event must not be directed by or be under the control of a producer.

undirectional microphone A microphone with a maximum angle of acceptance pattern in one direction. Often refers to a cardioid microphone. *See also* mike pattern.

undisplay advertising Classified advertising without display type or artwork.

UNDP United Nations Development Program. An intergovernmental organization.

undupe To remove duplicate names or addresses from a mailing list. *See also* purge.

unduplicated A radio or television program that is available on only one station in a market.

unduplicated audience *See* cumulative audience.

UNESCO United Nations Educational, Scientific and Cultural Organization. An intergovernmental organization.

uneven right margin *See* ragged right.

unexposed Raw film stock.

unfair advertising Advertising prohibited by the FTC under the Magnuson-Moss Warranty-Federal Trade Commission Improvement Act. For example, the FTC suggested a ban on all advertising to children on television as inherently unfair.

unfair competition The misappropriation of that which belongs to a competitor. Unfair competition has been extended to include the pirating of news from newspapers by broadcast stations.

unfair labor practice A practice that interferes with the rights of employees to organize and bargain collectively. Included in the National Labor Relations Act, as amended by the Taft-Hartley Act.

unfair producer A producer who engages a bargaining unit performer and who breaches any material term or condition of a union or guild code or agreement.

UNFB United Nations Film Board.

unformatted A computer disk that has not had tracks or sector information recorded on it. Also called *uninitialized.*

UNGA United Nations General Assembly.

ungrounded A component or system that is not directly grounded.

UNIATEC International Union of Technical Motion Picture Associations.

unidirectional One direction.

unidirectional antenna An antenna that has a single direction of maximum gain.

unidirectional microphone A microphone that has an angle of response in one direction only. Also called a *directional microphone.*

unidirectional printing Printing in which the print head moves from left to right across the page. Cf. bidirectional.

Unifax II A UPI wirephoto service.

Uniform Commercial Code (UCC) A codification of the commercial laws of the various states designed to provide some degree of uniformity.

Uniform Deceptive Trade Practice Act Legislation enacted by a number of states that provides for injunctions to prevent the disparagement of another manufacturer's product.

uniformity A measure of the lack of variation in a magnetic tape; the greater the uniformity, the higher the quality of the tape.

uniform system A lens marking method in which the numbers are in proportion to the f stop values. Also called the *U.S. System.*

unilateral A term sometimes substituted for unidirectional.

unilluminated panel A standard outdoor advertising poster panel not equipped with illumination. *See also* regular.

unilux A computer-operated strobe lighting system.

uninitialized *See* unformatted.

uninterruptable power supply (UPS) A power supply for a computer that is backed by batteries in case of power failure.

union A confederation of individuals who work in an industry. Formed to improve working conditions and wages. See also AFTRA, AGVA, IATSE, NABET, SAG, and WGA.

union card An identification card issued to members by unions, indicating their active affiliation.

union catalog □ A catalog that combines a number of catalogs into one. □ A catalog that lists the holdings of a number of libraries.

union list A blacklist of companies and organizations a union deems to be engaged in unfair practices against a union.

union shop A company that retains workers who agree to join the union within a specified period; usually 30 days. *See also* closed shop.

unique selling proposition (USP) The original and different benefit claimed for an advertised product or service.

unisette An oversized cassette designed for broadcast purposes.

unit □ A name applied to theatrical type luminaires; basically jargon for a lighting unit. □ A measure of the width of a letter or space; usually, one eighteenth of the width of the widest character of a font. *See also* em. □ A base or practical unit of measurement, such as volt, ampere, or footcandle. □ A section of a printing press; one that prints both sides of a web. □ A standard volume unit by which a single product item sale is measured. □ A single copy of an advertisement or medium. □ The members of the crew engaged in making a motion picture. □ One-eighteenth the width of the widest character in a font. □ A single part of a number of items, such as one audio track in a four-track system.

unit count The number of em space equivalents available in a line of type of specified length. Cf. character count.

United Independent Broadcasters (UIB) A radio network formed January 27, 1927. Later became the Columbia Broadcasting System (CBS).

United Press International (UPI) A major American news agency, formed by the merger of UP and INS.

United Scenic Artists (USA) A union.

United States (U.S.) The several states, the District of Columbia, the Commonwealth of Puerto Rico, and the possessions of the United States, but not including the Canal Zone.

United States Bureau of the Census The federal government agency that creates and publishes census data. A part of the Department of Commerce.

United States Code (USC) The laws of the United States, including amendments.

United States court of appeals *See* court of appeals.

United States district court A federal court that conducts trials to determine the facts in particular cases. Inferior to a court of appeals.

United States Postal Service (USPS) A semiautonomous organization established in 1972 to collect, distribute, and deliver mail.

***United States Reports* (U.S.)** The official reports of Supreme Court decisions.

United States Statutes at Large The series of volumes that contain all enactments by the Congress.

United States Supreme Court *See* Supreme Court.

unit manager □ The individual in charge of a motion picture location unit; primarily concerned with budget control. Sometimes called a location manager. Cf. unit production manager. □ An individual in charge of network program coordination. □ An individual in charge of a remote. □ The individual in charge of the facilities for a production.

unit of sale A description of the average dollar amount spent by customers on a mailing list.

unit production manager (UPM) The individual who coordinates, facilitates, and supervises a motion picture's budget, breakdown, and scheduling. Cf. unit manager.

unit series A series of films each of which contains a separate complete story, without a character or characters common to each of the films in the series but held together by the same title, tradename or mark or identifying device or personality common to all the films in the series. Cf. episodic series.

unit series format *See* format.

unit set □ Type that is cast on a monotype in multiples of one eighteenth of an inch. Cf. point set. □ *See* stock set.

unit split A division of a single radio or television commercial unit into two even parts, each with its own announcement. Cf. piggyback.

unit weighting The assigning of weights based on the size of a television market. Used in pricing wild spot unit rates except for New York, Chicago, and Los Angeles.

unity □ A design principle that all elements of a page, set, layout, and so on, create a single cohesive impression. □ One of Aristotle's three principles of dramatic structure; unity of time, place, and action.

unity gain A condition in which the output of a circuit is equal to the input.

universal asynchronous receiver-transmitter (UART) A device that converts parallel data to serial. Also called a *universal asynchronous receiver (UAR).*

universal copy desk *See* universal desk.

universal desk A newspaper copy desk that handles all copy except for highly specialized departments. Also called a *universal copy desk.* Cf. specialized copy desk.

universal finder A viewfinder used to show the field of view obtainable from a variety of lenses. Cf. Bretz box.

universal focus A picture that has all portions of a scene in sharp focus.

universal output transformer An audio output transformer that has a variety of output impedances to match the impedances of various loudspeakers. Common impedances are 4, 8, and 16 ohms.

universal product code (UPC) A series of vertical parallel bars that are used to identify a product. Increasingly used in supermarkets, bookstores, magazines, and so on.

universal receiver A radio receiver capable of operating on either alternating or direct current. Also called an *ac/dc receiver.*

universal time *See* Coordinated Universal Time (UTC) (CUT).

universe □ The total number of cable television subscribers within a system or in all systems. □ The population chosen for study. *See also* statistical population.

University of Mid-America The first attempt in the United States to deliver higher education on a mass basis. Headquartered in the University of Nebraska.

university press A nonprofit publisher of scholarly books and journals; usually owned by a university.

Univision An international Hispanic broadcasting network.

unjustified Not justified; having uneven left and right margins.

unlimited time (U) Authorized radio or television station operation without a maximum limit as to time. *See also* time classification.

unlisted sample Telephone numbers that are not in the data bank of numbers listed in telephone directories. *See also* expanded sample frame (ESF).

unload To sell merchandise quickly through various promotional expedients.

unmerging To extract a single channel of MIDI data from tracks that have been merged previously.

unmodulated A carrier wave that is not modulated at any given instant.

unmodulated groove A groove in a disc that has been recorded with no signal applied to the cutter. Also called a *blank groove* or *dry groove.*

unmodulated track A tape or film soundtrack on which no sound has been recorded.

unopened Book or periodical leaves or pages that have not been separated by trimming or slitting. *See also* uncut edge.

unp An abbreviation for *unpaged.*

unpaid copy A copy of a periodical distributed free or at a price lower than the minimum prescribed by the Audit Bureau of Circulations.

unpublished material A work that has not been published but may be registered under the 1976 Copyright Act.

unquote The end of a quotation, whether written or read aloud.

unregulation *See* deregulation.

unrestricted random sample An unmodified random sample. *See also* simple random sample.

unscaled Not to scale. A diagram or plot plan that is used to show rough approximations of the location of components, set pieces, and so on.

unscramble To decode an encrypted message or scrambled signal.

unsolicited A manuscript, script, program idea, and so on, that has not been contracted. *See also* over the transom.

unsqueeze To project an anamorphic print through an anamorphic lens.

unsqueezed print A normal motion picture print made from an anamorphic negative.

unstructured A radio station that lacks a defined format or formula.

unstructured interview An interview in which the interviewer is free to ask questions about the survey subject in a form and manner that seem appropriate. Cf. structured interview.

until forbid *See* till forbid (TF).

unusable diaries Returned diaries determined to be unusable according to established Arbitron Ratings diary edit procedures.

unusable sample Any household included in the original designated sample determined to be ineligible for survey participation for a variety of reasons, including disconnected telephone with no new listing within the survey area; those that volunteer that they are institutional housing with nine or more occupants; nonresidential listing; and those that state that a member of the household is media affiliated.

unwanted emissions An undesired emission consisting of spurious emissions and/or out-of-band emissions.

unweighted average A simple average. Also called an *unweighted mean.* Cf. weighted average.

unweighted noise The noise measured within the audio frequency pass band using a measuring instrument that is uniform in response with respect to frequency over some specified pass band. Cf. weighted noise.

unwired A group of radio stations that is not physically linked, but sold as a network on a national or regional basis.

UOO Unavailable, on order.

UP □ A direction to set type in upper case. □ United Press. Now UPI.

up □ To increase the volume of sound. □ A radio or television program that is on the air. □ The direction away from an audience. *See also* upstage. □ A performer who is at least momentarily at his or her peak.

up and over To bring music or sound effects up to the point where it covers the dialogue or other sound. Used as a transitional device.

up and under A radio or television director's command to bring the music up to establish it, then lower it and hold under the dialogue or other sound.

UPC Universal Product Code.

up conversion A conversion of standards from, for example, 525 to 625 lines in television. Cf. down conversion.

upconverter An electronic device that increases the frequency of a signal. Used to change channels in cable television systems. Also called an *output converter.*

upcut □ The intentional overlapping of one sound with another, often caused when switching from one source to another. □ To take a new sound source before the current source is cut, thus causing a clash of disparate sounds. □ A loss of words at the beginning of a sentence, either live or on tape. □ The elimination of part of a network or syndicated program by a radio or television station in order to make room for a local commercial. *See also* clipping.

update □ To bring a news story up-to-date by adding new information or rewriting to emphasize a different angle. □ Adding recent transactions and current information to the master mailing list to reflect the current status of each record on the list.

up fade An increase in lighting intensity on a set.

up front □ The securing of payment for a product offered by mail order before the product is sent. □ The purchase of air time from a television network before the start of a new season. □ *See* up front money.

up front money Remuneration received before any work is begun.

upgradability A facility allowing easy extension of the performance of a basic unity by adding extra hardware or software, often in the form of add-on modules.

upgrade □ To improve a cable television system. □ The selection of a premium channel service by a cable television subscriber. □ To increase the importance of a performer's role from the original plan or script. Cf. downgrade and outgrade.

UPI United Press International.

UPIA United Press International Audio.

UPI Audio A radio service of United Press International (UPI).

UPIN United Press International Newsfeatures.

UPI Radio Network (UPIRN) A radio news network furnished by UPI.

UPIRN United Press International Radio Network.

UPITN United Press International Television News. A former UPI news service purchased by TVN.

UPI Unifax A news service that furnishes still photographs to television stations.

uplink An earth station that is capable of sending signals to a satellite for distribution to other points on the earth.

upload To transfer information from a computer bulletin board or another computer. Sometimes used to mean the transfer of disc or tape files to RAM.

UPM Unit production manager.

up on one (two, three, and so on) A television director's command to fade in a picture.

upper and lowercase (U and lc) □ The upper and lower cases of the two cases holding handset type. Also referred to as C and lc (caps and lowercase). □ The use of capital letters on each word of a headline, sentence, and so on.

uppercase (UC) □ The capital letters of a font. □ The top case of a pair of type cases. □ An instruction to a printer to use uppercase letters.

upper drum That part of the drum in a helical scan videotape recording system that does not contact the reference edge of the tape. *See also* drum.

uprating To shoot film as though it had a higher emulsion rating than that indicated. *See also* push.

upright □ A book that is taller than it is wide. □ *See* standard. □ A vertical film editing machine. Cf. flatbed.

UPS □ Uninterruptible power supply.

upscale A market or audience that has a higher than average socioeconomic, educational, and so on, base. Cf. downscale.

upscale audience *See* upscale.

up shot A shot taken from a low angle. Cf. down shot.

upside The upper portion of a rotating digital video effect (DVE). Cf. downside.

upstage □ The direction away from the cameras or audience. Cf. downstage. □ A position assumed by a performer that forces another performer to act with his or her back to the audience. □ To move deliberately so as to become the center of attention.

upstream □ Pertaining to locations on a tape longitudinally displaced from a given reference point in a direction opposite to tape travel. Cf. downstream. □ The flow of communication or signal in the direction opposite to the normal flow, such as from a subscriber to the headend of a cable television system or from a receiver to a sender. Also called an *upstream signal. See also* utility services.

upstream capacity The number or amount of signals that may be carried from a receiver to a sender.

upstream signal *See* upstream.

up style A style of writing or printing that emphasizes the use of capital letters. Cf. downstyle.

up time The time a computer, device, or other system is available for use. Cf. downtime.

up to speed A motion picture camera that is running at the desired speed.

uptrend To increase radio or television ratings over a period of time. Cf. downtrend.

urban A contemporary radio station music format primarily aimed at black audiences.

urban contemporary station A radio station designed to appeal to black audiences.

urgent News wire material that is ranked below bulletin and flash.

URI Université Radiophonique Internationale (International University of the Air). An international organization that provides a pool of educational and cultural films and recordings.

URSI Union Radio Scientifique Internationale (International Scientific Radio Union). An international organization.

URTI Université Radiophonique et Télévisuelle Internationale (International Radio and Television University).

US □ Upstream. □ Microsecond.

U.S. *United States Reports.*

USA □ United Scenic Artists. A union. □ A cable television network.

usable activated channels Channels engineered at the headend of the cable television system for the provision of services generally available to residential subscribers of the cable system, regardless of whether such services are actually provided, including any channel designated for public, educational, or governmental use but excluding channels whose use for the distribution of broadcast signals would conflict with technical and safety regulations.

usable area *See* essential area.

usable space The space on a utility pole above the minimum grade level that can be used for the attachment of wires, cables, and associated equipment.

usage pull The ability of advertising to persuade people to purchase the advertised product or service.

U.S. App. D.C. The legal citation for the Court of Appeals, District of Columbia (CADC).

USASCII United States of America Standard Code for International Interchange. *See* ASCII.

USASI United States of America Standards Institute. Formerly ASA; also abbreviated *ASI.* Now ANSI.

USC □ United States Code. □ United States Congress.

USCA United States Code Annotated. An unofficial publication of the United States Code with notations as to changes in the original laws.

USCS United States Code Service. An unofficial publication of the United States Code with notations as to changes in the original laws. Formerly FCA.

use An identifiable appearance on radio or television by a legally qualified candidate for public office. Appearance on a bona fide newscast, news documentary, news interview, or on-the-spot coverage of news is not considered a ''use'' under Section 315 of the Communications Act of 1934.

use fee The residual paid to performers. Also called a *use payment.*

useful article In copyright, an article having an intrinsic utilitarian function that is not merely to portray the appearance of the article or to convey information. An article that is normally a part of a useful article is considered a ''useful article.''

useful spectrum The total number of frequencies that may be used for radio communication.

use payment *See* use fee.

user □ A general term for an individual or group that is authorized for use of computer facilities. □ An individual who sends or receives messages on a communication system. □ An individual who benefits from communication services but is not a member of a specific organization.

user application A program or related set of programs designed for the user of a system, rather than for programmers or service technicians. *See also* application software.

user bits A portion of the data included in the SMPTE time and control code that can be utilized for user-selected information.

user communications manager (UCM) A CD-RTOS module used by an application to manipulate the audio and video output devices and user input devices of CD-I players.

user data In CD-ROM and CD-I, data supplied by an information provider for an application.

user data field In CD-ROM and CD-I, a 2048-byte-long portion of the data field in an addressable sector, dedicated to user data.

user definable Keys on a computer keyboard whose functions can be defined by the user.

user defined A code or special character selected by an author to use as a typesetting code in electronic manuscripts. The code or special character is set off from the text by delimiters selected by the compositor.

user friendly Equipment, hardware, and software that is easy to learn and operate. Primarily used to indicate computer hardware and software.

user interface The interface through which the user and a system communicate. Includes input and output devices such as a joystick, mouse, printer, and display. Also the software-controlled means by which the user is prompted to supply data needed by the application, notified of errors, and told how to correct them.

user number A code or password by means of which an authorized user can gain access to a computer or to stored information.

user shell In computers, a program between the operating system and application on the one hand, and the user on the other, to enhance the manner of information presentation and command.

uses and gratifications model An approach to the mass media that contends that the members of an audience seeks gratification rather than being used by the media.

USIA United States Information Agency. The State Department agency that operates the Voice of America.

USIBA United States International Book Association.

USICA United States International Communication Agency. Formerly the USIA.

USIS United States Information Service. The overseas branches of the USIA.

USITA United States Independent Telephone Association.

USITT United States Institute for Theatre Technology.

USLI Ultra Large Scale Integration.

USOE United States Office of Education.

USP Unique selling proposition.

USPS United States Postal Service.

USRN United Stations Radio Networks, Inc.

U.S. System *See* uniform system.

USTA United States Trademark Association.

UT □ Universal time. □ Uptime.

UTC Universal Coordinated Time. *See* Coordinated Universal Time (UTC) (CUT).

utility Any company whose rates or charges are regulated by the federal government or a state and that owns or controls poles, ducts, conduits, or rights-of-way used in whole or in part for wire communications. Such term does not include any railroad, any company that is cooperatively organized, or any company owned by the federal government or any state.

utility pole A telephone company or power company pole that may be used to carry cable television cables.

utility program □ A program that enhances computer operation by adding functions to another program. □ A computer program used for "housekeeping" functions. Also called a *utility routine.*

utility routine *See* utility program.

utility services Cable television operations that may be used for fire and police alarms, meter reading, two-way communication, and so on. *See also* upstream.

UUUU Unidentified; in surveys, listening that could not be interpreted as belonging to a specific station.

UV Ultraviolet.

UV filter *See* ultraviolet filter.

V

V □ Verbal. □ Verso. □ Versus. □ Vertical. *See* vertical polarization. □ Voice. □ Volt. □ Voltmeter. □ A wire service code word for advisories. □ Volume.

VA Voltampere.

VAC □ Verified Audit Circulation Corporation. □ Value added carrier.

vacate To void a legal order or judgment.

VACC Value added common carrier.

vac-pack posting Outdoor advertising posters collated, properly treated with adhesives, and placed in a sealed plastic container. This ensures uniform, wrinkle free brilliant appearance of posters, eliminating pop-outs, tears, and cracks, as well as past accumulation on rims and panel moldings.

vacuum capstan A capstan in which an internal vacuum is used to hold the videotape against the capstan.

vacuum forming A method of making duplicates from heated plastic.

vacuum guide The part of a quadruplex video-head assembly used to maintain the tape in the correct position relative to the headwheel by means of a vacuum system. Also called a *female guide.*

vacuum tube An electronic device used for detection, amplification, control, and so on, from which air and gases have been evacuated. Most vacuum tube applications are now accomplished by transistors and integrated circuits. Also called a *tube* or *valve.*

vagueness A doctrine a court might use to overturn a statute that is imprecise or overbroad.

VAI Video assisted instruction.

val An abbreviation for *value.*

validation □ A procedure used in surveys to verify the accuracy of an interviewer's methods and to verify that the interviews actually were accomplished. Also called *cross-validation* and *verifying.* □ The power of the mass media to set social norms, behavior patterns, judge, and otherwise perform instant miracles of gratification.

validity *See* accuracy.

valuable consideration The receipt by a radio or television station of anything of value other than money or services. "Valuable consideration" is used in connection with the requirement for radio and television sponsor identification.

value □ The luminance of a color; the lightness or darkness displayed or measured. □ The tone or detail of a picture or artwork in relation to its lightness or darkness. □ The utility of a product or service to a user or prospect, as measured by the rate of sale of such products or services at varying prices.

value added carrier (VAC) A common carrier that offers services in addition to transmitting messages; usually computer services by means of leased lines. Also called a *value added common carrier (VACC)* and *value added network (VAN).*

value added network (VAN) *See* value added carrier.

value added theory A supposition that advertising raises the expectations of consumers for products and services.

value theory A combining of aesthetics and ethics as a basis for judging programs, performances, novels, and so on.

valve A British term for a vacuum tube.

vamp A silent screen sex goddess.

vampire video A television commercial action or scene deliberately unrelated to, or not synchronized with, the contents of the accompanying soundtrack.

VAN Value added network.

van A truck containing television cameras, VTR's, lighting equipment, and so on.

Van Allen belts The two areas of high energy radiation that surround the earth.

vandyke □ A blueprint that is brown instead of blue. *See* blueprint and brownprint. □ A proofing print made of an offset on sensitized paper.

vanishing cream A make-up foundation.

vanishing point An imaginary point at which receding lines appear to meet.

vanity press *See* vanity publisher.

vanity publisher A book publishing firm that prints books paid for by authors, generally without regard to literary value, need, salability, and so on. Also called *self publishing, subsidy publisher,* and *vanity press.* Cf. sponsored book.

variability The extent to which individuals, objects, and so on, differ from one another.

variable A symbol that can substitute for any object, number, and so on.

variable area recording A method of producing film soundtracks by utilizing a photographic process. *See also* variable area soundtrack.

variable area soundtrack An optical film soundtrack on which the sound modulations are divided into opaque and transparent areas. Cf. variable density soundtrack.

variable beam light A luminaire that is capable of being adjusted from a floodlight to a spotlight.

variable capacitor A capacitor that can be changed in value, as in a radio tuner.

variable contrast An enlarging paper that is capable of producing prints of different contrast grades.

variable density recording A method of producing film soundtracks by utilizing a photographic process. *See also* variable density soundtrack.

variable density soundtrack An optical film soundtrack on which the sound modulations are shown in the form of gradations from dark to light. Cf. variable area soundtrack.

variable diffuser A light diffuser containing two rotatable diffusers.

variable equalizer A sound filter that allows selected frequencies to be eliminated.

variable focal length (VFL) lens A lens capable of producing an infinite number of image sizes between given limits. Also called a *variable focus lens. See also* zoom lens.

variable focus lens *See* variable focal length (VFL) lens.

variable groove A disc recording groove that varies in width as changes in volume occur. On quiet passages, for example, the width of the groove is decreased.

variable indention The indenting of lines of type that vary in length from line to line; generally found in some forms of poetry.

variable input phototypesetter One of the second generation of phototypesetters.

variable length record A computer program capable of allowing database records of varying lengths. Also called a *variable record format.*

variable pad *See* potentiometer.

variable record format *See* variable length record.

variable reluctance microphone A microphone that uses the variations in reluctance of a magnetic circuit for its output. Also called a *magnetic microphone.*

variable reluctance pickup A common form of turntable pickup cartridge that uses the variations in reluctance of a magnetic circuit for its output. Also called a *magnetic pickup.*

variable shutter A camera shutter in which the angle of the opening can be changed in order to alter the exposure time.

variable space The spaces that are expanded or contracted in order to justify a line of type. Cf. fixed space.

variable speed A telecine that offers the capability of running videotape through a still store for slow motion effects.

variable speed control A device on a record turntable or tape recorder that alters the speed of the machine.

variable speed motor A motor that is capable of running at a number of different speeds. Also called a *wild motor.*

variable word length A computer word length that does not have a prescribed number of characters or bits. Cf. fixed word length.

Variac A tradename for an autotransformer.

variance A statistical measure equal to the square of a standard deviation.

variant A modification or change as in spelling, typefaces, books, and so on.

variety program A radio or television program characterized by music, comedy, dramatic sketches, dancing, and so on. *See also* comedy-variety program.

varifocal lens A variable focal length lens.

variorum A book edition, usually of a classical author, containing notes by different persons.

varistor A two electrode semiconductor that changes resistance with the current flowing through it.

VariTyper A trademark name of a composing machine that works like a typewriter but justifies lines and has changeable type.

varnish A coating of varnish or lacquer often given to book covers or other printed matter.

vast wasteland A name applied to television in 1961 by the then chairman of the FCC, Newton Minow.

vaudeo A slang term for a television vaudeville program.

vaudeville A variety show. Originally applied to the stage, vaudeville is sometimes used to mean any variety program or act. Cf. legitimate theatre.

vault □ A temperature and humidity controlled room used to store film and tape. □ An underground enclosure for cable television connections.

VBI Vertical blanking interval.

VCA Voltage controlled amplifier.

V channel One of the eight compact disc subcode channels (PW). At present only allocated to CD graphics.

VCR □ Video cartridge recorder. □ Videocassette recorder.

VCS Videocassette.

VCU Very close-up or very extreme close-up. Usually referred to as an XCU.

v.d. Various dates.

VDA Video distribution amplifier.

VDP Video display processor.

VDP chip set *See* video display processor (VDP).

VDR Video disc recorder.

VDSQ Video data sequence.

VDT Video display terminal.

VDU Video display unit.

vector graphics An image composed of lines and dots that are described by television screen coordinates. Cf. raster graphics.

vectorscope An oscilloscope with a stable time base. Used to check time delay between two signals. *See also* waveform monitor (WFM).

veejay A video disc jockey.

vehicle □ An advertising or communication medium. □ A specific newspaper, magazine, and so on, used for advertising. □ A program used to carry commercial matter. □ The commercial matter itself. □ A script or act used by a performer to demonstrate his or her talent. □ A solution used to make ink, paint, and so on.

VEL Verified encoded logging. A logging system used in automation.

vellum Originally, a finely grained lambskin or calfskin used for bookbinding or writing material. The term now also refers to a fine grade of writing paper. Cf. parchment.

vel non From the Latin for "or not."

velocilator A movable camera mount; smaller than a crane, but larger than a dolly.

velocity compensator A VTR accessory that eliminates horizontal banding. Also called a *velocity error compensator.*

velocity error A television picture defect that appears as horizontal hue banding.

velocity error compensator *See* velocity compensator.

velocity microphone A bidirectional microphone that utilizes a thin metal ribbon mounted between the poles of a magnet. Also called a *ribbon microphone.*

velocity of light *See* speed of light.

velocity of sound *See* speed of sound.

velour A material with a pile or napped surface used for draperies.

Velox A screened and highlighted photographic print frequently used in newspaper advertising as an inexpensive substitute for halftones. Also called a *screen print. See also* benday.

vendor A seller of newspapers, periodicals, or other products.

venetian blind effect In segmented recordings, where groups of scanning lines are recorded by different pole tips, an effect caused by misadjustments that resembles venetian blinds. *See also* horizontal bars and strobing.

venie A venetian blind effect pattern created with a cucoloris.

venire A group of persons from which a jury is selected.

venue The city, county, or district in which a court is located.

verbal storyboard A series of written instructions concerning the action to take place in a scene.

verbatim A word-for-word report of an interview.

verification □ The process of determining the truth or accuracy of a news story. □ The process of determining the validity of a mail order by sending a questionnaire to the customer.

verification card A card issued by the FCC to the holder of a radiotelephone operator's permit attesting to the original permit.

Verified Audit Circulation Corporation (VAC) A corporation that audits periodical circulations.

verifying *See* validation.

verisimilitude The state or quality of being real or true; often said of an exceptional novel, motion picture, and so on.

verism The theory that in art, the ugly and vulgar have their place if they are true and present aesthetic value.

vernacular The common speech of a region, trade, profession, and so on. *See also* jargon.

vernier A small, auxiliary device or knob used to make fine adjustments. Used for tuning, focusing, precision movements, and so on.

verse style The style of composition wherein copy is set as poetry.

version One reporter's story as compared to another's account of the same incident.

verso (V)(VO) □ The left-hand page of a book. Cf. recto. □ The back of a sheet. Cf. recto.

vertex The bottom of a character where the stems join, as at the bottom of a *V.* Cf. apex, arm, bar, cross stroke, ear, spur, stem, and tail.

vertical blanking The signals that occur at the end of each field of a television picture.

vertical blanking interval (VBI) The period of time between the end of one television field and the beginning of the next field during which the scanning beam is inactive.

vertical blanking pulse The pulse used to begin the vertical blanking interval.

vertical buy An advertising schedule wherein time is purchased on radio or television programs that appeal to the same types of viewers or listeners. Cf. vertical saturation.

vertical centering control A control used to move a television picture or pickup tube up or down.

vertical compliance The ease with which a stylus is able to move in a vertical direction.

vertical contiguity The discount rate that some stations allow for advertising time purchased for vertical saturation campaigns. *See also* contiguous rate. Cf. horizontal contiguity.

vertical cume A cumulative rating for two or more radio or television programs broadcast on the same day. Cf. horizontal cume.

vertical cumulative audience *See* vertical cume.

vertical discount A reduction given for purchase of radio or television time at a given frequency during a limited time period, such as a week. Cf. horizontal discount.

vertical documentary A radio or television documentary broadcast in segments on the same day. Cf. horizontal documentary.

vertical file A file in which pamphlets, clippings, tear sheets, illustrations, and so on, are kept.

vertical half-page Half the entire width of the full height of a periodical page purchased for an advertisement. Cf. horizontal half-page.

vertical hold control *See* hold control.

vertical information time code (VITC) The time code recorded vertically on professional videotape recorders. Cf. longitudinal time code (LTC).

vertical integration The common ownership of more than one level in the traditional multilevel supply and distribution chain, as in the control of the production, distribution, and exhibition of motion pictures. Also called *vertical ownership.*

vertical interval switching The common method of switching between television picture sources using the time between the end of one frame and the beginning of another.

vertical interval test signal (VITS) A signal inserted during the vertical blanking interval to test a remotely controlled television transmitter.

vertical interval time code (VITC) The time code information that is recorded during the vertical blanking interval of a television signal.

vertical-lateral recording A technique for recording stereo discs wherein one channel is recorded laterally, the other vertically.

vertical linearity control The television picture control that adjusts the upper portion of the picture. Cf. vertical size control.

vertical ownership *See* vertical integration.

vertical pan A sometimes used pair of words that are contradictory. A pan is a horizontal camera movement, and a vertical camera movement is a tilt.

vertical polarization The placement of transmitting or receiving antennas in a vertical plane. *See also* circular polarization and horizontal polarization.

vertical publication A publication intended for persons in a specific trade, profession, interest group, life style, and so on. Cf. horizontal publication.

vertical recording A mechanical recording in which the groove modulation is in a direction essentially perpendicular to the surface of the recording medium. The method is now obsolete. Also called *hill and dale recording.*

vertical resolution The maximum number of horizontal wedge lines that can be clearly distinguished on a test pattern.

vertical retrace The return of the scanning beam from the bottom of a television picture to the top during the vertical blanking interval.

vertical retrace period The time during which the vertical field scan on a television screen returns to the beginning of the next field.

vertical riser A cable television subscriber drop that either enters or leaves the ground.

vertical rotation The rotation of commercial messages on a broadcast station at different times during a day.

vertical saturation A heavy advertising schedule used during one or two days on a station in order to reach all members of the station's audience. Cf. horizontal saturation and vertical buy.

vertical size control The television picture control that adjusts the lower portion of the picture. Cf. vertical linearity control.

vertical spacing The distance between lines in printed matter. Cf. horizontal spacing.

vertical sweep The vertical movement of the scanning beam through the 525 lines of a television picture.

vertical sync The series of pulses that control the vertical scanning of a television picture.

vertical sync pulse One of the pulses transmitted at the end of each television picture field.

vertical tracking angle error The angle between the mechanical axis of the pickup, projected on a plane perpendicular to the disc surface and containing the tangent to the groove at the point of contact, and the effective axis of the vertical modulation of the groove.

vertigrate To vertically integrate the advertising and promotion efforts of a retail dealer, franchiser, or licensee into the broader advertising and promotion plans of a manufacturer or licensor, to permit greater impact and efficiency.

very high density (VHD) *See* video high density (VHD).

very high frequency (VHF) The band of frequencies between 30 and 300 mHz. The VHF band includes television channels 2 through 13 and the entire FM band.

very large scale integration (VLSI) The process of making integrated circuits that contain in excess of 10,000 semiconductor devices.

very low frequency (VLF) The band of frequencies below 30 kHz.

vestigial sideband transmission A system of transmission wherein one of the generated sidebands is partially attenuated at the transmitter and radiated only in part.

VF □ Video frequency. □ Voice frequency.

VFL Variable focal length.

VHD Video high density.

VHF Very high frequency.

VHF translator A television broadcast translator station operating on a VHF television broadcast channel.

VHS Video home system. The most widely used half inch videotape recording and playback system.

VI Volume indicator.

VIA Videotex Industry Association.

vibration A mechanical oscillation.

vibration microphone A microphone that is excited by mechanical vibrations, as opposed to sound.

vibrato A rapid variation in pitch used to enrich a sound.

vid An abbreviation for *video.*

video From the Latin *videre,* meaning "to see." □ A synonym for *television.* □ A prefix used for numerous television components and circuits. □ The picture portion of the television signal. □ The left column of a television script. Cf. audio. □ A brief film or videotape made for television; usually a rock video.

video amplifier An amplifier capable of passing the wide range of frequencies necessary for television picture information.

video animation stand A special unit designed to photograph animation on videotape. The recorder moves the tape in one twenty-fourth of a second increments that correspond to frames of film. Its instant replay capacity makes it useful for pencil tests.

video art Art that uses videotape and television cameras as the medium to produce aesthetic works.

video assist A motion picture camera with a video camera and recorder attached. Used to view and edit scenes quickly before the film is developed.

video band The frequency band used to transmit a composite video signal.

video black The synchronizing and pedestal levels of a television picture.

video carrier The television signal containing the picture, sync, and blanking information.

video cartridge A plastic container designed to hold videotape for automatic threading.

videocassette A plastic container designed to hold videotape for automatic threading. *See also* Beta, U-Matic, and VHS.

videocassette recorder (VCR) A recorder that is capable of recording and playing back a videotape in either half, three-quarter, or one inch videotape.

videocast A television program.

video chip A dedicated integrated circuit designed to fulfill specific video functions. Also called *digitized video.*

video club A nightclub that shows videos, usually rock videos.

video compression A technique for reducing the bandwidth necessary to carry a television signal by reducing the amount of redundant information carried. *See also* compressed video.

videoconferencing A long-distance teleconference using video as well as audio. *See also* teleconference.

video control The monitoring and adjusting of video equipment in order to control the quality of the picture.

video data In CD-I, data related to one or more units of video information as encoded in DYUV, RGB (555), CLUT, or run-length encoding techniques.

Videodex, Inc. An audience research organization.

Video Disc A home video recording machine produced by Teldec. *See also* EVR.

video disc A magnetically coated aluminum laser or capacitance disc capable of storing video information. Also spelled *videodisc. See also* capacitance disc and laser disc.

video disc player A device used to play video discs, but that is incapable of recording video discs.

video disc recorder (VDR) A recording device using an aluminum disc with a magnetic coating. Used for instant replay and stop action.

video display A device to display visual information, text, or graphics. Usually a CRT but may also be LED's or plasma panels.

video display processor (VDP) A two-chip microprocessor consisting of a pixel processor and an output display processor that provides extremely powerful programming capability for processing and displaying video images interactively on a computer screen or a television receiver.

video display terminal (VDT) A computer device by which keyboarding produces an image on a cathode ray tube for writing or editing. Also called a *video display unit.*

video display tube A cathode ray tube used in a video display terminal.

video display unit (VDU) *See* video display terminal.

video distribution amplifier (VDA) A device used to feed a video signal to a number of different monitors or receivers.

video dub □ To dub by recording the video signal from a tape being replayed. □ A copy made by this method. Cf. rf dub.

video editing terminal A term generally synonymous with *video display terminal* but a terminal used primarily for editing.

video engineer The engineer or technician who monitors and adjusts the camera pictures for balance and quality. Also called a *shader. See also* technical director (TD).

video error concealment In digital video, a technique to reduce the visual effect of disturbances arising from erroneous video data.

videofilm A process for transferring videotape to film.

video filter The circuit used to clip the sync pulses from the composite video signal.

video frequency (vf) The frequencies from approximately 30 Hz to 4 mHz that contain the television picture information.

video gain The brightness control in a television circuit.

video game An inexpensive device that allows electronic computer games to be attached to a television receiver.

videograph □ An obsolete term used to describe the process of taking pictures with a television camera. □ An alphanumeric character generator. □ A high-speed printer using a cathode ray.

videographer An individual who uses a video camera and recorder. Cf. photographer.

video head The electromechanical device in a videotape recorder that reads and writes the video portion of the signal to the tape.

video high density (VHD) A capacitance videodisc system using a laser recorded glass master disc. Also termed *very high density.*

video insert *See* insert edit.

video inversion A method of scrambling downlinked satellite signals by inverting the video signal.

video jockey (VJ) A disc jockey on a rock music program. Also called a *video jock.*

videola A kinescope editing device.

video layout system *See* video layout terminal.

video layout terminal (VLT) A video display terminal with the capability of displaying text and graphics in the order the material is to be printed.

video mixer A device used to combine the pictures from several television sources. *See also* switcher.

video monitor *See* monitor.

video noise *See* snow.

video pair *See* twin lead.

videophone A telephone with video capabilities.

video player *See* videotape player.

video pointer An electronic device that is designed to highlight information on a television screen.

video-pool pickup *See* pool.

Videoprobe Index, Inc. A cable television audience measurement organization.

video programming Cable television programming provided by, or generally considered comparable to programming provided by, a television broadcast station. *See also* cable service.

videoprompter *See* teleprompter.

video quality level The reproduction quality of a video signal. In CD-I, for example, provides for four video quality levels: natural picture, RGB (555) graphics, CLUT graphics, and run-length coded animation.

video record The magnetic facsimile of the picture that is placed within a track area on a videotape.

video recorder *See* videotape recorder.

video recording A method of preserving a television picture and associated soundtrack on a magnetic tape.

VideoScene A process that links two cameras with servo mechanisms so that live action may be perfectly synchronized with backgrounds, miniatures, film, and so on.

video scene process An early form of electronic matteing.

Videoscope A trademark for a wide-screen mat that masks the top and bottom of a projected picture.

video signal The television picture information, and the sync and blanking pulses.

video switcher A device that allows several video sources to be selected or mixed. *See also* switcher.

video synthesizer A computer-controlled device that is used to manipulate the colors and shapes of a video image.

videot A contraction of video and idiot.

videotape □ Magnetic recording tape intended for recording and playback of video signals. Standard tape widths are one-half inch, three-quarter inch, 1 inch, and 2 inches. Also spelled *video tape. See also* magnetic tape and tape. □ For the purposes of copyright, the reproduction of the images and sounds of a program or programs broadcast by a television broadcast station licensed by the Federal Communications Commission, regardless of the nature of the material objects, such as tapes or films, in which the reproduction is embodied.

videotape leader *See* leader.

videotape operator A technician who operates videotape recorders.

videotape player (VTP) An electromechanical device used to play back magnetic video recording tape, but lacks the circuitry necessary to record videotapes. *See also* play-only machine. Cf. videotape recorder.

videotape recorder (VTR) An electromechanical device used to record and play back images on magnetic-coated tape. Videotape recorders are not standardized; users must select from a number of tape widths, numerous speeds, different reel sizes, and a number of different formats: quadruplex recorder, helical scan, cassette, and so on. *See also* television tape recorder. Cf. videotape player.

videotape recording Any form of recording made by a videotape recorder.

videotape replication The duplication of videotapes through the use of high-speed devices.

videotape winder A power driven machine used to wind and rewind videotape to save wear and tear on videotape heads.

videotex A generic term for an interactive, computer-based, electronic data transmission system. Sometimes used for interactive television. Cf. cabletext, teletext, videotext, and viewdata.

Videotex Industry Association (VIA) An association of suppliers, industry representatives, and others interested in furthering the use of videotex.

videotext An interactive home video information service that delivers text and graphics by telephone lines or cables. Cf. cabletext, teletex, teletext, videotex, and viewdata.

video textures Synthetic video created by a computer model of a desired scene or object, and then wrapping the surfaces of the computer model with video images.

video to film transfer *See* kinescope.

video track A track containing the video record.

video-track curvature The departure from a straight line of the video record.

video-track pitch The distance, measured along the direction of tape travel, between two adjacent video tracks. Also called *video-track spacing.*

video-track spacing *See* video-track pitch.

video track trailing edge The upstream edge of the video track.

Video Transmission Engineering Advisory Committee A committee composed of telephone company and network representatives for the purpose of coordinating engineering standards.

Videovoice A device developed by RCA for the transmission of television pictures over telephone lines using slow-scan television.

videowall A computer-based system that projects images from a videotape to a number of direct view monitors or rear projectors.

vidicon An abbreviation for *video iconoscope.* A relatively inexpensive television camera pickup tube often used for industrial and educational applications in place of the more expensive plumbicon or IO tubes.

vidifont A name or other title produced by a character generator.

Vidimag A tradename for one of the rapidly evaporating fluids (Freon TF) used to make the frame pulses on videotape visible for mechanical editing. No longer used.

Vidnews The alphanumeric format used by UPI and AP in broadcasting news for cable television systems.

vidoc A video documentary made for television.

Vidtronics A system for transferring videotape to film using three film negatives.

view camera A still camera in which the taking lens forms an image on a ground glass screen.

viewdata A system for producing computerized information on television receivers. An interactive videotex system. *See also* cabletext, teletex, teletext, and videotext.

viewer □ An individual who watches a television program. *See also* viewing. □ A simple, mechanical-optical device used in film editing to enlarge the film frames for viewing. □ A film processing technician who judges the quality of a print.

viewer impression A study accomplished to determine the effectiveness of television commercials.

viewer loyalty The ability of a television program to build and maintain an audience.

viewership A generic term for television viewers in general; a term similar in scope to readership.

Viewers in Profile (VIP) The regularly scheduled television market reports for over 220 markets published by NSI.

viewers per household (VPH) The average number of persons viewing a television program in both viewing and nonviewing households.

viewers per set (VPS) The number of persons watching a single television receiver in a household at the same time.

viewers per viewing household (V/VH) (VPVH) The estimated number of viewers, usually classified by age and sex, recorded as comprising the audience within those households tuned to a given station or program or using television during a particular time period.

viewer's script A script containing a motion picture's dialogue.

view finder A registration device mounted near the top of the animation stand that allows the camera operator to check whether or not the camera is trained on the center of the field. *See also* rackover.

viewfinder An electronic or optical device attached to a television or film camera that allows the camera operator to see the picture being shot. Also called a *finder.*

viewfinder hood *See* hood.

viewing □ The act of seeing. Cf. listening. □ In survey work, a term that must be defined operationally in terms of the particular method of measurement used.

viewing angle The angle through which the audience may see a television or motion picture without excessive loss of screen brightness.

viewing area *See* coverage area.

viewing distance The distance from a viewer to the motion picture or television screen.

viewing glasses Glasses used to check the contrast in a scene and thus indicate any needed lighting or filter changes.

viewing lens A camera lens through which the scene is observed by a camera operator.

viewing mirror A mirror used in a projection television system to change the angle of viewing.

viewing screen □ The ground glass screen in a view camera. □ The face of the television picture tube, monitor, or viewfinder.

viewpoint □ The relationship of the camera angle and distance to the scene to be shot. □ The relationships in a scene as seem by one of the characters.

vignette □ A brief, often poignant news item or feature. □ A photograph, halftone, and so on, in which the background is faded away gradually. Cf. silhouette. □ A picture that has soft edges; often accomplished through the use of cutouts or masks. □ A brief word picture.

vignetting The softening of the edges of a scene or picture.

villain The "heavy" in a book, script, program, and so on.

VIMCAS Vertical Interval Multi-Channel Audio System. A system for adding high-quality audio to new or existing video.

vinylite A plastic used in electrotype moldings, phonograph records, and so on.

vinyl resin A thermoplastic material used for making discs.

violation A failure to follow the law or the rules and regulations of the FCC or other administrative agency. Violations often involve failure to make required entries in logs, failure to control modulation, failure to have a licensed operator on duty, and so on.

violence profile An annual record made by George Gerbner and Associates of the number of violent incidents on network television.

VIP □ Variable input phototypesetting. □ Viewers in profile.

VIR Vertical interval reference.

virgin Raw tape or film that has not been used. Also called *virgin stock* and *virgin tape*.

virgin medium Any medium that has not been used.

virgin stock *See* virgin.

virgin tape *See* virgin.

virgule The "/" symbol. Also called a *slant* and *slash*.

virtual focus The point from which divergent rays of light appear to diverge. Cf. real focus.

virtual image An image on the opposite side from a light source; the optical image formed behind a lens. Cf. latent image and real image.

virtual storage (VS) The combining of two or more computer memory devices in order to increase the available storage capacity.

viscous damped tone arm A tone arm that contains a thick fluid that protects the stylus in case the tone arm is dropped on a disc.

viscous processing The processing of film through the use of heavy solutions instead of baths of chemicals.

visible Capable of being seen.

visible spectrum The narrow band of electromagnetic waves, from approximately 400 to 750 millimicrons, to which the human eye is sensitive.

visible surface algorithm A modeling method that describes solid objects with filled-in surfaces; characteristic of raster based systems.

Visimag A tradename for a rapidly evaporative fluid (Freon TF) that is mixed with iron particles and used to identify frame pulses on videotape for mechanical editing. No longer used.

vision control operator A British term for a technical director.

vision mixer A British term for an individual who works a television switcher, and also a television switcher itself.

vision switcher A British term for an individual who works a television switcher.

Vistascope A device used to create a background behind a performer.

VistaVision A 35-mm wide-screen process that runs film through the camera sideways, using the width of two standard frames for one picture.

visual □ Of or relating to sight. □ Any graphic material, such as illustrations, slides, videotape, pictures, and so on. □ An advertising sketch showing product arrangement. □ Any picture or image, as opposed to any sound that might accompany the picture or image.

visual arts Those disciplines that have sight as a major component of art: architecture, painting, sculpture, and so on. Cf. performing arts.

visual captioning The broadcast of messages by television stations visually as well as aurally as a service to the hearing impaired.

visual carrier The portion of a television carrier that contains the picture information. Cf. aural carrier.

visual carrier frequency The frequency of a television carrier modulated by the picture information.

visualcast A transparency projector.

visual device Any device, such as a telop, miniature, and so on, designed to achieve a visual effect on television.

visual effects A term generally synonymous with *special effects* but limited to visual images.

visual effects function In CD-I, one of the set of functions, such as signal mixing and color palette control, used to achieve visual effects.

visual gag *See* sight gag.

visualization □ The process of producing a sketch, layout, and so on, from a mental image. □ The script treatment that describes the setting and action of a drama or program to an audience.

visual primary A scene in which the sound is subordinate to the picture in importance.

visual scanner *See* optical scanner.

visual show A radio or television program taped or broadcast before a live audience.

visual squeeze An animation technique in which images are shot in rapid succession to produce more information in a given time.

visual station identification (VSI) A television station ID containing only the station's call letters without audio reinforcement.

visual transmissions Communications or messages transmitted on a subcarrier intended for reception and visual presentation on a viewing screen, teleprinter, facsimile printer, or other form of graphic display or record.

visual transmitter The equipment used for the transmission of the visual television signal only.

visual transmitter power The peak power output that transmits a standard television signal.

Vitaphone The sound-on-disc film system used for the first full length sound feature, *The Jazz Singer*, in 1927.

Vitascope A motion picture projector invented by Thomas Armat in 1895.

VITC Vertical interval time code.

VITEAC Video Transmission Engineering Advisory Committee.

VITS Vertical interval test signal.

viz An abbreviation for *vizmo*.

vizmo A device used for rear screen projection. Abbreviated *viz*.

VJ Video jockey.

VLF Very low frequency.

VLSI Very large scale integration.

VLT Video layout terminal.

VM Voltmeter.

VO □ Verso. □ Voiceover. □ Video operator. *See* video engineer.

VOA Voice of America.

vocabulary The special languages, codes, and instructions used for writing computer programs.

vocal stop A short break occurring before certain consonants in vocalized speech.

voice □ A sound produced by the vocal cords and resonated by the cavities in the head and throat. □ To express an opinion.

voice activated A microphone or other device that is started by the sound pressure of the human voice. Also called *sound actuated* and *voice actuated*.

voice actor A performer who specializes in offcamera narration.

voice actuality A report from the scene of a news event that contains an actuality. *See also* wraparound.

voice artist An actor who performs the voices for the animated characters during a recording session.

voice channel *See* voice grade.

voice coil The coil attached to a loudspeaker diaphragm that is moved by the electrical signal. Called a speech coil in Great Britain.

voice cue A cue, usually a line delivered by another performer.

voice filter A filter used to eliminate low frequencies or to imitate the sound of someone speaking on a telephone.

voice frequency (vf) *See* audio frequency (AF).

voice grade A telephone channel capable of carrying only the frequencies of the human voice or low speed data transmission. Also called *telephone quality*.

voice grade audio information Audio information of a quality sufficient for reproducing the human voice, normally having a bandwidth of 408 kHz. *See also* speech quality.

voice grade channel A channel capable of transmitting only the frequency range of the human voice.

voice input Human voice input to a given device, such as a computer, where it is normally used for control or information entry purposes. *See also* voice recognition.

voice level *See* level.

Voice of America (VOA) The broadcasting service of the USIA. Authorized by Congress in 1948.

voice off (VO) An off stage voice.

voiceover (VO) The use of an announcer, newscaster, narrator, and so on, speaking over film, slides, or other visual material. Also called *over frame*. *See also* off camera and off stage.

voiceover commercial A typical method of producing a television commercial; the announcer's voice describes or enhances the visual presentation of the product.

voiceover credits The use of a voiceover instead of visual words at the beginning or end of a television program or motion picture.

voice processor An electronic device that combines a microphone preamplifier, compressor, limiter, expander, equalizer, and notch filter.

voice quality *See* voice grade.

voicer □ An audio news report narrated by an individual other than an anchor, newscaster, or disc jockey. □ A radio news report from a remote.

voice recognition The ability of a computer to translate words spoken by a human into computer accepted commands. Also called *voice input*.

voice switching The opening or closing of an electronic circuit by the use of sound.

voice test An audition for a part in a radio or television program.

voice track A film or videotape soundtrack used for voices.

voice tracker A device that enables recorded audio tracks to be run at a faster speed without increasing the pitch of the audio.

void □ The blank areas of a layout, type matter, photographs, and so on. □ Without legal force or effect.

voir dire A preliminary competence examination of a witness or prospective juror by a court.

vol An abbreviation for *volume*.

volatile memory A storage medium, such as computer RAM, that loses its information with an interruption in the power source, or when the device is turned off. Cf. permanent memory.

volt (V) The unit of electromotive force, equal to the potential difference across a resistance of one ohm when a current of one ampere is flowing through it. Named after Alessandro Volta of Italy.

voltage (E) The electromotive force required to move an electrical current through a circuit. *See also* Ohm's law.

voltage controlled amplifier (VCA) An amplifier that digitally controls analog functions, as in faders.

voltage regulator An electronic circuit or device that maintains the output voltage at a predetermined value in the circuit.

voltage standing-wave ratio (VSWR) The ratio of the maximum to the minimum voltage in a transmission line that is terminated in an impedance different from the characteristic impedance of the line.

voltmeter An instrument used to measure the voltage in a circuit.

volume □ The collected or combined issues of a newspaper published within a one-year period. □ A collection of leaves, signatures, and so on, fastened together; a book. □ A floppy disk or a portion of a hard disk. □ The magnitude of a sound expressed in decibels or volume units (VU) relative to a standard reference. *See also* level. Cf. loudness.

volume compression □ The limiting of the volume level of a recording in order to increase the signal-to-noise ratio. □ The limiting of the volume level at a transmitter in order to increase the modulation without causing overmodulation.

volume control A potentiometer used to control the output volume of a receiver or amplifier.

volume descriptor In CD-I, that part of the disc label identifying a given disc.

volume discount A discount offered for the purchase of a certain amount of advertising in a medium.

volume flag In CD-I, the field in the file structure volume descriptor containing the logical name of the CD-I disc.

volume indicator (VI) A meter that indicates the volume of sound. *See also* VU meter.

volume limiter An electronic circuit that controls the average volume level in an amplifier. Cf. peak limiter.

volume name A file name of a computer volume directory.

volume unit (VU) A unit of audio frequency power, referenced to 1 milliwatt in a circuit with 600 ohms impedance.

volume unit meter *See* VU meter.

voluntary An individual who orders a noncommercial classified ad in a newspaper.

volunteer An individual who offers his or her services for a media study.

VOM Volt-ohm-milliammeter.

vortex public figure *See* public figure.

VO/SOT Voiceover/sound on tape. The use of a voiceover with a sound on tape bite. Often used in television newscasts.

vowel A speech sound in which the breath is not blocked: A, E, I, O, U, and sometimes Y. Cf. consonant.

voxel A discrete unit of volume.

vox pop An abbreviation for *vox populi,* the voice of the people. Sometimes used to indicate brief man on street interviews.

V.P. Various publishers.

VPA Videotape Production Association.

VPH Viewers per household.

VPR Video production recorder. A VTR with built-in editing facilities.

VPS Viewers per set.

VPVH Viewers per viewing household.

VS □ Versus. □ Variable speed. □ Virtual storage.

VSB Vestigial sideband system.

VSI Visual station identification.

VSWR Voltage-standing-wave ratio.

VT □ Vacuum tube. □ Videotape. □ Video terminal.

VTR □ Videotape recorder. □ Videotape recording.

VTR control track *See* control track.

VTR operator The individual responsible for recording a program on a VTR.

VTRS Videotape recording system.

VTVM Vacuum tube voltmeter. An electronic voltmeter.

VU Volume unit.

VU meter A volume unit meter. An audio level meter calibrated in decibels and percentage of modulation. Also called a *peak program meter.*

VV □ Verses. □ Volumes.

V/VH Viewers per viewing household.

V.Y. Various years (of publication).

W □ A wire service code for news from Washington. □ *See* call letters. □ Watt. □ Write.

WABE Western Association of Broadcast Engineers.

WACB World Association for Christian Broadcasting. A religious broadcasting organization.

WACC World Association for Christian Communication.

wafer A sticker used to attach advertising cards in windows, seal envelopes, and so on. Also called a *wafer seal.*

wafer seal *See* wafer.

Wagner Act *See* National Labor Relations Act (NLRA).

wagon A low, wheeled platform used to mount a portion of a set for quick scene changes.

waist shot A camera shot taken from a performer's waist to just above his or her head. *See also* camera shots.

wait □ An unintentional pause in a radio or television program caused by technical failure or a performer's dropped line or missed cue. □ An intentional pause, often for audience laughter or applause.

wait order An instruction to set advertising copy in type and hold for later insertion in a publication.

waiver □ An exception made by a union or guild with respect to working conditions in order to meet program or other requirements. □ A signed statement by a prospective licensee relinquishing any claim to the use of any particular frequency because of previous use of a frequency, whether by license or otherwise. Required by Section 304 of the Communications Act of 1934.

Walker report A study by the National Commission on the Causes and Prevention of Violence, which found that the police were primarily responsible for the crime and rioting that took place at the 1968 Democratic National Convention in Chicago.

walkie-lookie A small, portable, battery operated television camera used for remote broadcasts. Also called a *peepie-creepie.*

walkie-talkie A small, portable, battery operated radio receiver and transmitter.

walking The sideways movement of a web while the press is running.

walking shot □ A shot taken by a moving camera. □ A shot taken of a performer moving.

walking standupper A standupper in which the reporter walks toward the camera as he or she is speaking.

walk-on A person who performs in a television program or motion picture but who does not speak any lines whatsoever as individuals but who may be heard, singly or in concert, as part of a group or crowd. An extra.

walk-through A rehearsal without cameras to acquaint performers with the blocking; a dry run.

walkway *See* catwalk.

wall The side of a disc groove.

walla walla The sounds made to imitate a mumbling crowd. *See also* omnies.

wall banner □ An outdoor advertising sign; often placed on a wall but may be hung on a wire across a street. □ A hanging advertisement in a retail store.

wall bracket *See* wall plate.

wallpaper video A generic visual used on television, such as a library stock shot.

wall plate A bracket from which to hang luminaires. Also called a *wall bracket.*

wall sled A bracket attached to the top of a flat from which to hang luminaires.

Wall Street Journal Radio Network A satellite-delivered hourly news and features radio network.

wall television An electroluminescent panel used as a television picture tube.

wall-to-wall □ A motion picture, radio, or television production without space or time for additional material. □ A radio station music format that runs a number of songs back-to-back without interruption. □ A channel that has 24 hours of programming.

wall treatment The use of paint, wallpaper, pictures, and so on, to produce a lifelike set.

want list A library list of desired books.

WAPOR World Association for Public Opinion Research. A research organization based in Canada.

warbler A slang term for a singer or vocalist.

WARC World Administrative Radio Conference (of the ITU).

WARC-BS World Administrative Radio Conference for Broadcast Satellite service (of the ITU).

WARC-ST World Administrative Radio Conference for Space Telecommunications (of the ITU).

wardrobe □ Any clothes used by performers before the camera. □ The costume department.

wardrobe call An appointment for an actor or actress to be fitted for a costume.

wardrobe department A motion picture studio department responsible for designing, constructing, and maintaining costumes.

wardrobe master *See* wardrobe mistress.

wardrobe mistress An individual responsible for supervising the wardrobe for a motion picture, play, and so on. Also wardrobe master.

wardrobe truck A wheeled box used to move clothes from storage to a set.

warehousing □ The purchasing of the rights to motion pictures, syndicated programs, and so on, with the intention of holding them for later sale at a higher price. □ The gathering of cable television franchises by an individual or company that has no intention of building, but holds them for later sale.

war film An often violent motion picture that depicts war and its ramifications and consequences.

warm □ The colors toward the red end of the spectrum. Cf. cool. □ Between hot and cold.

warm boot The process of initiating action in a computer system that has already been turned on. Also called a *warm start.* Cf. boot.

warm color Generally a color in the range of yellow-orange-red. Warm light sources are of low color temperature. Cf. cool color.

warming filter A filter designed to reduce the blue portion of the spectrum. *See also* warm.

warm start To begin a different operation on a computer while the power is still on. The opposite of cold start. *See also* boot and warm boot.

warm-up □ A planned entertainment for a studio audience immediately preceding a broadcast or dress rehearsal. □ The individual who attempts to place an audience in a receptive mood for a broadcast. □ The time necessary to wait before beginning to use an electronic device after the power is turned on. Also called *line up time.*

warning bell The bell that is rung on a motion picture soundstage to signal the start or end of a take.

warning light The light outside a studio or soundstage, sometimes blinking or rotating, that indicates filming or taping is taking place. *See also* on-air light and tally light.

warrant A court order authorizing a law enforcement official to make an arrest, search premises, and so on.

warranty A stated or implied guarantee of the fitness and quality of goods or services.

wash □ Even, overall light on performance space or background. □ *See* wash drawing.

wash drawing A black and white watercolor, often intended for halftone reproduction. Also called a *wash.*

washed out A negative or print lacking in contrast.

washing The process of using water to remove developer or fixer from film.

washtub weeper Another term for *soap opera.*

washup The cleaning of a printing press when the ink color is changed or at the end of a shift or day's use.

waste circulation □ A figure reflecting the readers of a periodical who are unlikely to purchase a certain product or service advertised in it. □ The advertising of a product or service in an area where the product or service is not available.

watchdog A group that is unusually attentive to the mass media; often suggests or demands improvements, changes, eliminations of actions, and so on.

water haul Fruitless or futile research or work done for a news story.

watermark A faint impression integrated into paper that can be seen when held up to the light; often used as a papermaker's trademark, an organizational logo, and so on.

waterproof paper Paper that is impervious to water.

water spots Spots on film caused by drops of water that were not removed before drying.

watertight camera *See* underwater housing.

WATS Wide Area Telecommunications Service.

watt (W) The unit of electrical power, equal to the rate of work done by one ampere under a pressure of one volt (PEI). Named after the Scottish engineer, James Watt.

wattmeter An electrical instrument designed to measure the power in a circuit.

wave □ A regular or irregular periodical variation in frequency propagated through space or through a medium. *See also* electromagnetic wave and sound wave. □ A cyclic use of air time or space by advertisers. *See also* flight.

wave analyzer An instrument used to measure the voltage or frequency of a wave.

wave band (WB) A band of frequencies.

waveform A graphic representation of a wave plotted against time.

waveform monitor (WFM) An oscilloscope used to show a graphic representation of a wave. Used extensively to analyze and adjust television pictures. Also called an *A scope.*

waveguide A hollow tube transmission line used for microwaves.

wavelength The measure of the distance between successive cycles of a periodic wave. Wavelength is inversely proportional to the frequency of a wave.

wave plan An advertising strategy that programs commercials in intermittent periods, such as two weeks of saturation, two weeks without commercials, and two weeks of saturation.

wave posting A concentration of outdoor advertising poster showings in a succession of areas within a market. Usually coincides with special promotions in each of these areas.

wave propagation *See* propagation.

wave rule A rule that prints a rippling line.

wave trap A circuit that is tuned to eliminate undesirable frequencies.

wax □ In mechanical recording, an obsolete term meaning a blend of waxes with metallic soaps. □ In make-up, a material such as nose putty, plastic wax, dental inlay wax, and so on, used for making minor changes to teeth and features. □ A resinous preparation used as an adhesive, such as sealing wax, etching wax, paste up wax, and so on.

waxing The application of wax to the edges of motion picture film to decrease the piling up of emulsion.

wax master *See* wax original.

wax mold electrotype *See* wax process.

wax original An obsolete term meaning an original recording on a wax surface for the purpose of making a master. Also called a *wax master.*

wax pencil A China marker pencil used to mark edit points on magnetic tape.

wax process An electrotype process in which the design is impressed or photographed on a metal plate coated with wax. Also called a *wax mold electrotype.*

waybill A freight company invoice used in shipping film, tape, equipment, and so on.

wayzgoose An annual holiday, such as a company picnic, for printers.

WB □ White balance. □ Wave band.

WBPA Western Book Publishers Association.

WBS World Broadcasting System. An organization that furnished programs to stations on electrical transcriptions.

WBVTR Wide band videotape recorder.

WCA Wireless Cable Association.

W channel One of the eight compact disc subcode channels (P–W). At present only allocated to CD graphics.

WCMR World Conference on Missionary Radio. Now ICB.

WEAC West European Advisory Committee of RFE.

wearout The point at which an advertisement or advertising campaign loses its sales effectiveness due to excessive exposure and consequent disregard. Cf. life.

weathercaster An individual who presents the weather information on radio or television.

weather day A day in which a production is delayed because of inclement weather and for which additional costs are incurred.

weave The undesired side-to-side movement of motion picture film in a camera or projector due to faulty threading or misalignment.

weaver A nervous performer who sways back-and-forth or from side-to-side in front of a camera or microphone.

weaving The side-to-side movement of magnetic tape as it passes through a recorder or player.

web □ A continuous roll of paper, such as newsprint, threaded through a rotary press; used especially for newspapers, magazines, and long-run collateral pieces. □ A slang term for a radio or television network.

web break The tearing of a web during a run.

weber The MKS unit of magnetic flux, which is the magnetic field strength that generates an electromotive force of one volt in a single moving turn of a conductor.

web fed A rotary printing press into which a web is fed. Cf. sheet fed.

web fed press *See* web press.

web offset An offset printing press fed by a web instead of single sheets.

web perfecting press A rotary printing press that prints on both sides of the web simultaneously. Also called a *web perfecting rotary press.*

web perfecting rotary press *See* web perfecting press.

web press A rotary printing press using curved plates to print on a continuous roll of paper at high speeds. Also called a *web fed press. See also* rotary press.

wedge □ A wedge-shaped formation of alternating black and white lines used in a test pattern to determine camera resolution. □ *See* step wedge.

wedge spectrogram A graphic representation of the color sensitivity of film. Made by exposing a strip of film to light through a neutral density wedge.

weeding The process of culling out-of-date, unnecessary, or duplicate records, books, tapes, and so on, from a library.

weekly □ A publication issued each week. □ *See* weekly player.

weekly "500" net test transmissions Test transmissions of the National-Level EBS interconnection facilities conducted on a random basis once a week.

weekly player A player who is employed on a weekly basis. Also called a *weekly.*

weekly unit of television films The number of television films of a particular series of variety (including comedy-variety), quiz, or audience participation programs prepared by the same writer or writers for initial broadcast within one week.

week-to-week employment The employment of a writer on a week-to-week basis that may be terminated by the company or writer at any time.

weight □ The basis on which the thickness of paper is determined and sold. For example, a ream of bond paper 17 by 22 inches weighs 20 pounds, and is referred to as 20 pound bond. □ The relative heaviness of a typeface, from lightface to extra bold. □ The amount of advertising in support of an effort; expressed in terms of gross rating points, reach and frequency, impressions, spending levels, and so on. □ The number of advertising exposures received by an individual. □ An adjustment made in a survey sample to correct for demographic or geographic imbalance.

weighted average A statistical quantity calculated by multiplying each value in a group by an assigned weight, summing those products, and dividing the total by the sum of the weights. Also called a *weighted mean. See also* weighting. Cf. unweighted average.

weighted in-tab An audience measurement survey that is adjusted for over- or under-representation of the statistical population.

weighted mean *See* weighted average.

weighted noise The noise measured within the audio frequency pass band using a measuring instrument that has a frequency selective characteristic. The sensitivity is usually greatest in the frequency range where the ear is most sensitive. Cf. unweighted noise.

weighting □ The numerical score assigned a market and used to determine the reuse fees paid to talent. □ In general, the application of ratio estimation to adjust in-tab sample data from samples so that the weighted sample is in balance with the universe for various household or persons' characteristics.

weighting characteristic Response-frequency characteristic of a measuring device used to measure weighted noise.

well *See* well make-up.

Welles Award, Orson An award given by the Radio Advertising Bureau (RAB) for excellence in local radio commercial production.

well format *See* well make-up.

well make-up An advertising arrangement with a deep, narrow opening for news or editorial matter between two or more columns of advertisements, often in the shape of a "U." Also called a *well* and *well format.*

WEMA Western Electronic Manufacturers Association.

west The direction of an animation stand to the left of the operator. Cf. east.

Westar One of a number of domestic satellites owned by Western Electric.

West Coast feed A radio or television program broadcast at a convenient hour on the West Coast that originates in New York or some other easterly point.

western An idealized form of drama, usually depicting a glorified form of cowboy hero who vanquishes the forces of evil. Also called a *classic western.* Cf. adult western.

Western Union sports wire A wire service for broadcast stations that emphasize sports.

Westinghouse rule A modification of the Prime Time Access Rule made in 1972 on an appeal by the Westinghouse Corporation, which included network film reruns among the network material restricted.

Westlaw A legal database used for research. *See also* Lexis.

west of Denver Any technical problem that is difficult to solve.

Weston speed An obsolete numerical system for rating emulsion speeds.

Westrex system *See* 45/45.

wet gate *See* liquid gate.

wet printing □ A film-processing procedure in which a negative is coated with a liquid to cover physical defects in the film. □ Printing in which another color is printed before the previous color has had time to dry.

wet sound Any sound that contains reverberation or equalization of any kind. Also called *EQ'd sound.* Cf. dry sound.

wetting agent A chemical used in film processing to prevent water spotting by lowering the surface tension of the water.

wf A proofreader's mark for wrong font.

WFM Waveform monitor.

WGA Writers' Guild of America (West).

WGAE Writers' Guild of America (East).

WHCA White House Correspondents Association.

wheel □ A pictorial representation in the shape of a clock of the format of a radio station showing the segments to be broadcast during an hour. Contains segments for records, promos, commercials, station identifications, traffic reports, and so on. Also called a *clock.* □ *See* wheel printer.

Wheeler-Lea Act. The amendments to the Sherman and Clayton Acts that allowed the FTC to regulate unfair or deceptive acts or practices in commerce.

wheel printer A printer that prints characters that are spaced around a disk.

when room Filler material that may be used in a publication at any time.

whiff Publicity material with little news value; a puff.

whip □ An extremely fast camera pan in which the image blurs. Also called a *blue pan, flash pan, pan blur, swish pan, whip pan, whip shot, whiz pan,* and *zip pan. See also* camera shots. □ A videotape editing defect that causes horizontal distortion in the picture.

whip antenna A slim, flexible, vertically mounted antenna.

whip pan *See* whip.

whip shot *See* whip.

white □ An achromatic light, that is, one without hue; an achromatic surface of high reflectance. □ In television color, a mixture of the red, green, and blue phosphor dots in the proper proportion. □ *See* white space.

white area □ The area or population that does not receive interference-free primary service from an authorized AM station or does not receive a signal strength of at least one mV/m from an authorized FM station. □ An area that is outside the normal range of a particular class of broadcast service; a rural area. □ A rural area that is the principal market for satellite-delivered programming to home dish owners.

white balance (WB) A control used to vary the white level of each of the three color television channels.

white coat rule A Federal Trade Commission restriction that prohibits advertisers from using individuals who purport or appear to be medical professionals (physicians, dentists, and so on) in commercials and other advertisements.

white compression The reduction of the amplitude of the signal corresponding to the light areas of a television picture to reduce contrast. Also called *white saturation.*

white crush The ability of television cameras to mask seams and overlaps on white surfaces. Cf. black crush.

white level The television signal level corresponding to the maximum picture luminance.

white light A mixture of all the wavelengths of the visible spectrum; sunlight.

white line □ In printing, a blank line. □ *See* woodcut.

white mail Mail order requests for information or goods that do not indicate the advertisement that prompted the requests.

white noise Random audio or video background noise that is constant over the frequency range of the circuit.

white paper □ An extensive letter or document prepared as a report on a specific topic or issue. □ A blank piece of printing paper regardless of color.

white peak The maximum excursion of a television signal in the white direction.

whiteprint An improved blueprint process. *See also* diazo. Cf. blueprint.

white saturation *See* white compression.

white space The unprinted areas between blocks of type, illustrations, headlines, and so on. Used to improve the appearance of the printed page. Also called *air* and *white.*

white tape An adhesive tape used to seal film cans. Cf. gaffer tape.

whiz pan *See* whip.

WHO World Health Organization. Also OMS. An intergovernmental organization.

whodunit A slang term for a mystery film, story, program, novel, and so on.

whoduniteer A person who writes whodunits.

whole bound A book bound in one type of material.

wholesale bookseller *See* wholesaler.

wholesaler An individual or company that buys books from publishers for resale to libraries and bookstores. Also called a *book jobber* and *wholesale bookseller.*

whole step *See* whole tone.

whole tone A musical interval of two half steps, as C to D. Also called a *whole step.*

WIC Women in Cable. A cable television industry professional organization.

WICI Women in Communications, Inc.

wicket A kicker or other material placed at the side of a headline.

wide-angle distortion The perceived changes in perspective when a wide-angle lens is used close to a subject.

wide-angle lens A short focal length lens that subsumes a wide field of view. Cf. telephoto lens.

wide-angle shot A camera shot taken with a wide-angle lens or a shot taken from a distance.

Wide Area Telecommunications Service (WATS) A telephone service that allows long distance calls to be made for a monthly fee, as opposed to a fee for each call. Extensively used for 800 number service.

wideband Any communication system or component capable of passing a wide range of frequencies. *See also* broadband.

wideband channel A communication channel with a bandwidth greater than a voice grade channel.

wideband communications network A communications system capable of providing a number of channels. *See also* broadband.

widen To dolly or zoom out.

wide open □ Said of a newspaper that has more than enough room for news copy because of insufficient advertising. Cf. tight. □ Said of a lens that is at maximum aperture.

wide-screen Any of a number of processes used to produce motion pictures with an aspect ratio greater than 1.33:1. *See also* CinemaScope, Cinerama, Panavision, Super Panavision, Technirama, Techniscope, Todd-AO, Ultra Panavision, and VistaVision.

wide-screen aperture A nonstandard frame mask used for various wide-screen processes, usually with a ratio greater than 2:1. Cf. academy aperture.

wide-screen print A print with an aspect ratio greater than 1.33:1.

wide-screen process One of three types of systems for producing other than standard motion pictures: A. anamorphic processes, B. multiprojector systems, and C. projector aperture masking to change the normal aspect ratio.

wide shot In general, a long shot.

wide type *See* enlarged type.

widow A one- or two-word line at the end of a paragraph. A widow is not acceptable when it is the first line of a new column or page or when it is contained in a caption. Cf. orphan.

width □ The horizontal dimension of a television screen. *See also* aspect ratio. □ The horizontal dimension of a typeface.

width control The control used to vary the width of the television picture.

wild □ The separate nonsynchronous recording of sound and picture. □ A scene or program shot without a script. □ News or feature material that may be inserted wherever there is space available.

wild camera A camera that is not in sync with the sound.

wild card □ In a word processing program, a character or symbol that matches any character in a search and replace operation. □ Television signals imported by a cable television system in addition to the mandatory signals carried.

wild cel An animation cel that is not controlled by registration pegs.

wild commentary Commentary that is recorded separately from a picture for later editing and synchronizing.

wild line A spoken line that is added to the soundtrack of a film or tape after the scene is shot.

wild motor A variable speed motor.

wild picture □ A picture used in a publication without an accompanying caption or story. □ The recording of a picture without sound. *See also* MOS.

wild recording *See* wild and wild sound.

wild set A small set, or portion of a larger set that is detached to permit the free movement of cameras. *See also* insert set.

wild shot A film or tape sequence shot without sound.

wild sound Sound that is recorded separately from a picture for later editing and synchronizing.

wild sound bite A wild sound effect used in a newscast.

wild spot A commercial broadcast by noninterconnected single stations that is used independently from any program or used on a local participating program. Cf. dealer use and program use.

wild track A soundtrack recorded separately from a picture and therefore not in synchronization.

wild wall A freestanding flat.

Winchester A type of hard disk drive in which the disk is permanently sealed in the mechanism.

wind The way that tape or film is wound on a reel. *See also* A-wind and B-wind.

wind filter *See* windscreen.

winding The process of transferring film or tape from one reel to another.

wind it up A radio or television director's command to conclude an interview, go to the finish, increase the tempo, and so on. Also called *wrap it up.*

wind machine A large fan used to create special effects such as driving rain and hurricanes.

windmill A rotating device used to hold title cards. Cf. crawl and drum. *See also* graphics.

window □ A clear space on a film negative. □ *See* window envelope. □ An FCC filing window; a period of time during which the FCC will accept certain types of applications. □ An insert in a display screen that is used to display information, such as help screens and menus. □ A word processor or other computer application program feature that allows portions of two or more files to be viewed at the same time. □ A period of time during which a film distributor, network, pay cable operator, and so on, has the rights to show a feature film or other program. □ The period of time during which a communications satellite may be launched. □ The period of time during which there is an unobstructed path between a satellite and an earth station.

window banner *See* window streamer.

window card An advertising card used for display purposes in store windows.

window dub A copy of a videotape that has an insert containing the time code information. Also called a *window dupe.*

window dupe *See* window dub.

window envelope An envelope with a die-cut portion on the front to permit the viewing of the name and address printed on an enclosure. The die-cut window may or may not be covered with a transparent material. Also called a *window.*

windowing The preferred term is *cinching.*

window streamer An advertising strip posted in a store window. Also called a *window banner.*

windscreen A thick foam covering placed over a microphone to decrease the effects of the wind when the microphone is used outdoors. Also called a *screen* and called a *windshield* in Great Britain.

windshield *See* windscreen.

windshield wiper effect Television picture distortion caused by cross modulation between two channels in a cable television system.

wing □ To ad lib or improvise. □ *See* two-fold.

wing flat *See* two-fold.

winging *See* wing it.

wing it To direct or perform without rehearsal. Also called *winging.*

wing mailer A label-affixing device that uses strips of paper on which addresses have been printed.

wings The left and right off stage areas.

wipe □ A transitional television and film technique, either optically or electronically produced, in which one scene is gradually replaced by another. Hundreds of geometrical wipe patterns are available from large special effects generators: horizontal, vertical, diagonal, circular, square, and so on. Also called a *wipe over.* □ To erase a magnetic tape.

wipe over *See* wipe.

wiper The moving arm of a potentiometer.

wire □ An abbreviation for *wire service.* □ An insulated or uninsulated solid or stranded metallic conductor.

wire broadcasting The use of wires for the distribution of programming, as opposed to over the air broadcasting. The term is self-contradictory. Used in some countries to deliver a radio signal from a central location to the audience. Also called *line radio* and *wire radio. See also* wire communication.

wire communication The transmission of writing, signs, signals, pictures, and sounds of all kinds by aid of wire, cable, or other like connection between points of origin and reception of such transmission, including all instrumentalities, facilities, apparatus, and services (among other things, the receipt, forwarding and delivery of communications) incidental to such transmission. Also called *communication by wire.*

wire copy News stories furnished by a wire service.

wired city A concept that would be similar to present cable television systems, but that would increase the number of channels and broaden the use to provide a wide range of services.

wired microphone Any microphone that is connected by a cable to the input of an electronic device. Cf. wireless microphone.

wired wireless A method of low-power broadcasting often used on college and university campuses in which line transmitters are used to distribute the signal over wires. Also called *line radio. See also* wire broadcasting.

wire editor *See* telegraph editor.

wire frame An animation graphic that displays only the edges of a polygon.

wire frame modeling A method of model construction that produces objects defined by a network of straight lines; characteristic of vector based systems.

wireless □ A British term for radio. The invention of the wireless has been attributed to many, but Guglielmo Marconi of Italy demonstrated its practicality in 1895. □ A device that is not connected by cable to another device, such as a wireless microphone.

wireless cable A system of making multiple programming services available to subscribers by using a mix of ITFS and MDS channels. *See also* MMDS.

Wireless Cable Association (WCA) An association of MMDS operators.

wireless intercom An intercommunicating device containing two or more stations connected by low-power transmitter-receivers.

wireless microphone A microphone that transmits a low-power signal capable of being picked up at a distance. Also called a *transmitter microphone.* Cf. wired microphone.

Wireless Ship Act of 1910 The first American radio law. The act, which was concerned with marine communication, was superseded by the Radio Act of 1912.

wireless telegraphy The early use of radio to send messages by Morse code.

wire lines *See* wire marks.

wire marks The lines made on paper by a paper machine.

wire overhead The use of the telephone or telegraph to send news.

wirephoto A trademark for a process of transmitting still pictures by wire.

wire printer A high-speed printer. *See also* dot matrix printer.

wire radio *See* wire broadcasting.

wire recorder A magnetic recorder used primarily in the 1940s that used a thin stainless steel wire as the recording medium instead of magnetic tape.

wire re-creation The broadcasting of a sporting event by an announcer who is not at the scene of the action. Re-created by using sound effects and wire service reports of the game.

wire service A news wire of one of the press associations that serve the broadcast and print media with news for a fee. Also called a *press association.* The major U.S. services are AP and UPI. *See also* A-wire, B-wire, and radio wire.

wire service codes □ The letters used to indicate the importance of news (priority code): a, b, d, f, r, s, and u. □ The codes that indicate the type of story: a, b, c, e, f, i, k, l, n, p, q, s, t, v, w, and y.

wire side The slightly rougher side of a sheet of paper; the side that was next to the wire during manufacturing. Cf. felt side.

wire stitch A saddle or side wire stitch used in bookbinding.

wire strip The elimination of the computer codes contained in the news stories received from a wire service.

wire tape Typesetting tape transmitted from a wire service.

wiretapping The act of connecting a listening device to a telephone line or other wire communication service or system.

wiring diagram A drawing that shows the components of a device and the interconnections between them.

withholding A Canadian term for the preemption of radio or television time for the presentation of programs of special interest, but not of any emergency or nationally important nature.

within house *See* in house.

without □ A news item that needs a picture to tell a story. □ A picture that does not have a related story; a standalone.

with story *See* sidebar.

with the grain The direction in line with the fibers in a sheet of paper *See also* grain. Cf. against the grain.

WL Wavelength.

W/M Watermark.

WMPI Women in the Motion Picture Industry.

WNBA Women's National Book Association.

WNPC Women's National Press Club.

WNRC Women's National Radio Committee. A former citizens' group founded in 1934.

WNU Western Newspaper Union.

Women in Cable (WIC) An organization devoted to the interests of women in the cable industry.

Women in Communications, Inc. (WICI) An organization of women in journalism, broadcasting, public relations, and so on.

women's publications Magazines and other publications designed primarily to serve a feminine audience or cater to feminine tastes. Also called a *service magazine* and *women's service magazine.*

women's service magazine *See* women's publications.

womp A momentary surge of power in a television receiver that results in a corresponding increase in picture brightness.

woodcut ☐ An illustration or design cut into or photomechanically transferred to a wood block for relief printing. Also called *white line.* ☐ A print made by this process. Also called *wood engraving.* ☐ A scenery piece made of canvas and wood; often to resemble a tree.

wood engraving *See* woodcut.

wooden head A dull, uninspired headline.

wood pulp The pulp used to make paper. *See also* chemical pulp and groundwood pulp.

woodshed To rehearse a script or copy in private.

Wood's lamp An ultraviolet lamp named after its developer.

woof ☐ A television engineer's slang for okay. ☐ A word used to replace "now" in a non-broadcast time check.

woofer A relatively large loudspeaker used to reproduce the lower audio frequencies in a two or three way system. Cf. squawker and tweeter.

woolly Sound that is lacking in clarity.

word ☐ A unit of data or memory. In computing, a group of bits, bytes, or characters, considered as an entity, and capable of storage in one memory location. ☐ A unit of information. ☐ As in a "word from your local station"; usually a commercial break.

word association test A test used for evaluating attitudes, in which a respondent is asked to reply to a word spoken to him or her with the first word that comes to mind.

wordbook A collection of words; a dictionary.

word count A computer word processing program that can count the number of words in a document.

word cruncher An individual who is employed in the media to write or edit.

word jobber *See* hack.

word length The number of characters or bits in a word.

word of mouth advertising The advocacy of action regarding a product or service that is passed from one person to another without a sponsor's paid support; hence, not truly advertising. Cf. two step flow of communications.

word picture A graphic, vivid, or expressive piece of writing.

word processing (WP) Letters, reports, documents, manuscripts, and so on, made by using a computer program. The program allows the user to write, edit, manipulate, format, and print text.

word processing code A generic code, identification code, command, special character code, and so on, embedded in an electronic manuscript to format portions of the text matter.

word seller An somewhat obsolete term for a writer.

word slinger *See* hack.

word space ☐ The white space between words in a line of type. ☐ *See* wordspacing.

wordspacing The increase or decrease of units between words in a line of type. Cf. letterspacing.

word wrap A word processing feature that automatically moves a word down to the start of the next line when the word would overlap the right hand margin. Also called *wraparound.*

work ☐ To use a microphone properly. ☐ The amount of power expended in a given period of time. ☐ *See* work made for hire.

work a fight To stage a fight scene.

work and tumble A method of printing both sides of a sheet similar to work and turn except that the sheets are turned from front to back instead of left to right. Also called *print* and *tumble*. Cf. sheetwise and work and turn.

work and turn A method of printing both sides of a sheet of paper from the same form. The work is printed on one side, then turned and printed on the other side, which results in two complete printed copies when the sheets are cut in half. Also called *print and turn*. Cf. sheetwise and work and tumble.

worked up A news story that goes beyond the ordinary and results in imaginative, intelligent coverage.

worker An electrotype used for printing, as opposed to one used for a pattern.

work for hire *See* work made for hire.

working aperture *See* effective aperture.

working distance The distance from a camera to a subject.

working dummy The artwork from which an advertisement, electrotype, and so on, is made; a working drawing.

working press The individuals who report, write, and edit the news.

working solution A photographic processing chemical diluted to the proper strength.

working title A tentative title given to a motion picture, novel, script, and so on, until a decision is reached.

working women (WW) An estimate of females aged 18+ who work outside the home 30 or more hours per week.

work lights A general lighting system permanently installed in a studio or stage production area that provides sufficient illumination for moving scenery and general work when the production lighting system is not in use. Cf. house lights.

work made for hire For the purposes of copyright, a work prepared by an employee within the scope of his or her employment; or a work specially ordered or commissioned for use as a contribution to a collective work, as a part of a motion picture or other audio-visual work, as a translation, as a supplementary work, as a compilation, as an instructional text, as a test, as answer material for a test, or as an atlas, if the parties expressly agree in a written instrument signed by them that the work shall be considered a work made for hire.

work of the United States government For the purposes of copyright, a work prepared by an officer or employee of the United States government as part of that person's official duties.

work order *See* job ticket.

work picture *See* workprint.

workprint (WP) A duplicate positive picture or soundtrack print used for editing purposes to determine the final composition of the motion picture, and to guide the cutting of the original. Also called a *cut picture* and *work picture*.

workstation *See* multifunctional workstation.

work up An ink smudge caused on printed matter by slugs, spaces, and so on, moving up to the level of the typefaces and becoming inked.

world disc A CD-I disc on which the video data is encoded in such a way that it can be played and displayed on any CD-I player, irrespective of 525- or 625-line television standard.

worldize To record background sounds on location.

Worldnet A worldwide television service of the USIA.

World System Teletext (WST) A North American teletext system based on the British Ceefax and Oracle systems. Cf. NABTS.

WORM Write once read many (times) medium. The typical configuration of optical laser discs; which, once written, cannot be erased to permit rewriting.

worm's eye view A camera shot taken from a low angle.

wove paper A rough-textured paper that contains the impression of a fine wire screen. Cf. laid paper.

wow □ A slow variation of tape speed in recording or playback, resulting in pitch error. Use of this term is usually confined to audio recording. □ A cyclic deviation occurring at a relatively low rate, as for example, a once-per-revolution speed variation of a phonograph turntable. Cf. drift and flutter.

WP □ Word processing. □ Workprint.

WPA Women's Press Association.

WPM Words per minute.

WPS Words per second.

WR An abbreviation for *write.*

wrangler The individual in charge of livestock used in a television program or motion picture.

wrap □ To finish or conclude a rehearsal, taping, or filming session. □ To complete a television program or motion picture. □ A single layer of magnetic tape on a reel. □ A length of magnetic tape in contact with an audio or video recording or playback head. □ The geometric path of the tape in the vicinity of the head scanner in a videotape recorder. Three common types of wraps, denoted by their similarity to certain letters, are the alpha, omega, and M wraps. □ To continue a story from one column to the next. *See also* jump. □ *See* word wrap. □ An insert in a book, pamphlet, magazine, and so on, that has been stitched to the binding. Also called a *wraparound.* □ An algorithm that runs on a DVI chip set to place textures on a wireframe computer model. Relatively complex images containing hundreds of surfaces can be texture-mapped in a fraction of a second.

wrap angle The angle measured at the center of rotation of a scanner or the center of a tape guide that is subtended by the tangent points of the tape to the scanner or guide.

wraparound □ The curve of a magnetic tape across or around a recorder's heads. □ The intro and outro copy for a film or tape news story. Also called a *wrapper. See also* donut. □ A relief printing press that utilizes a curved plate wrapped around a cylinder. □ An advertising banner used around a display case. □ *See* wrap. □ *See* word wrap.

wrap in To tie one news item to another with information common to both.

wrap it up A director's command to stop a rehearsal or production and return everything to its proper place.

wrapped up *See* wrapup.

wrapper □ A paperbound book or pamphlet cover. □ A hardbound book promotional cover. □ A paper cover bound to the front and back of a newspaper or magazine. □ A paper enclosure for a product, used as a package or label. □ An abbreviation for *wraparound.*

wrapup □ A complete news story, often containing all the elements of previous takes of the story. Also called a *roundup.* □ A summary of the most important stories presented on a newscast. Also called a *roundup.* □ A wire service story containing the material from previous leads of the same story. □ The kraft paper formerly used to wrap newspapers.

Wratten filter One of a series of optical filters used to control light.

wrinkle A crease or crinkling of paper caused by incorrect feeding to a printer or by using damaged paper.

writ A court order requiring the performance or nonperformance of a specific act, as in a writ of certiorari.

write (W) To transcribe data from RAM into a storage device.

write enable A procedure that allows a user to save information on a disk. On a floppy disk a notch is cut into the disk jacket to allow writing to the disk. Cf. write protect.

write head A magnetic head that transfers digital information from a computer to a magnetic storage device.

write in □ An addition made to a completed script prior to or during production. □ Fan mail received by performers, stations, agencies, and so on.

write once A disc that is not erasable or may be read only.

write protect A procedure that does not allow information to be saved on a disk. On a floppy disk no notch is cut into the disk jacket or an existing notch is covered. Cf. write enable.

writer □ A creative and professional individual who is employed by a company to write literary material or make revisions, modifications, or changes. The term writer shall not be deemed to include any corporate or impersonal purveyor of literary material or rights therein. Cf. professional writer. □ A script, continuity, or news writer who works as a staff writer, commissioned writer, or freelance writer for a broadcast station, network, advertising agency, and so on.

write/read medium *See* read/write medium.

Writers' Guild of America (WGA) (WGAE) A writer's union that sets minimum fees for scripts, commercials, and so on.

writer's script A properly formatted screenplay.

writeup A sentence that immediately precedes a news bite. Also called an *intro, lead in,* and *throw line.*

write up To write an account of a news event, review, discrepancy report, and so on.

writing rate *See* writing speed.

writing speed □ The speed at which a magnetic tape passes the heads of a tape recorder. □ The speed at which a scanning beam traverses the face of a cathode ray tube. Also called *writing rate.*

writ of certiorari *See* certiorari.

writ of mandamus A process of a court ordering a public official to perform an act required by law.

wrong face *See* wrong font.

wrong field edit A videotape edit that is made out of sequence, that is, at the end of the first field of a frame instead of the second, or at the beginning of the second field of a frame instead of the first.

wrong font (WF) A notation indicating a printer's error in using one or more type characters in a different size or type font.

wrong reading A photograph printed with the emulsion facing the wrong way.

WRTH *World Radio and Television Handbook.* A publication offering a complete listing of international broadcasting stations, their frequencies, times of operation, and so on.

WSAAA Western States Advertising Association.

WST World system teletext.

W/T □ Walkie-talkie. □ Wireless telegraphy. □ Wireless telephony.

WW Working women.

WWA Western Writers of America.

WWV The call letters of the National Bureau of Standards radio station located in Fort Collins, Colorado. WWV broadcast services include: standard audio frequencies, standard time intervals, time signals, universal time corrections, and official announcements.

WWVB The call letters of the National Bureau of Standards radio station located on the same site as WWV. WWVB transmits a standard radio frequency of 60 kHz, standard time signals, time intervals, and universal time corrections.

WWVH The call letters of the National Bureau of Standards radio station located in Kikaha, Kauai, Hawaii. WWVH performs the same services as WWV.

WWWW Women Who Want to be Women (Association of the W's). An organization of women opposed to the Equal Rights Amendment. Cf. NOW.

WX An abbreviation for *weather report.*

WYSIWYG What you see is what you get. A word processing program feature that displays exactly what will be printed.

X □ Exposure. □ Frame of film. □ Reactance. □ An abbreviation for *trans*, as in Xcription or Xmitter. □ A script notation for a stage direction for an actor's cross. □ A script notation for dissolve. □ A mark a performer is to hit. □ Experimental. An FCC first letter file-number prefix. *See also* experimental station. □ An abbreviation for *italic*. □ Seventeen and under not admitted. A CARA classification for feature films generally considered to be pornographic.

X axis *See* XYZ axes.

Xcription An abbreviation for an *electrical transcription*.

XCU A script notation for an Extreme close-up. Also called a *VCU*.

X-dissolve A cross-dissolve. *See also* dissolve (D).

Xenon A rare gas used in long-life, high-efficiency quartz lamps.

xenon lamp A high efficiency discharge lamp used in xenon projectors to produce a bright light with good color balance. Now used instead of carbon arc lamps. Also called a *xenon tube*.

xenon projector A common theatrical projector.

xenon tube *See* xenon lamp.

xerography □ A patented electrostatic process for reproducing printed matter wherein a negatively charged powder is fused to the paper by heat. The name is now loosely applied to all copy machines. □ A special form of photocopying on cels; developed by the Disney studio in conjunction with the Xerox Corporation. Used instead of inking to transfer the animation drawings onto cels.

Xfer An abbreviation for *transfer*.

x height □ The height of lowercase letters of a given font; the height of a lowercase x. □ The distance between the base line and the mean line of a line of type. □ A type character without ascenders or descenders. Also spelled *ex height*.

Xister An abbreviation for *transistor*.

XL An abbreviation for *existing light*.

X lighting Cross lighting, wherein the backlighting for one performer is accomplished by the key lighting for the other.

XLR connector A standard professional microphone connector containing three shielded conductors.

Xmit An abbreviation for *transmit*. Also *XMT*.

Xmitter An abbreviation for *transmitter*.

XMT An abbreviation for *transmit*. Also *Xmit*.

XO An abbreviation for *crystal oscillator*.

X off An abbreviation for *transmitter off*.

X on An abbreviation for *transmitter on*.

xpndr An abbreviation for *transponder*.

XR A notation for no returns permitted.

X-rated An X-rated film. *See also* X.

X-ray *See* borderlight.

X/S A script notation for an over the shoulder shot. Also abbreviated *OS*.

X-sheet An abbreviation for *exposure sheet*.

Xtal An abbreviation for *crystal*.

X-talk An abbreviation for *crosstalk*.

xylograph □ An engraving on wood. □ A print made by xylography.

XY miking A form of coincident or crossed pair stereo miking that uses matched cardioid microphones usually placed at 90 degrees to each other.

X-Y pointer device An input device for entering X and Y coordinates, mainly used for accurate cursor positioning.

XYZ axes The mathematical coordinates that define three dimensional space. X is the horizontal axis; Y, the vertical axis; and Z, the depth axis. Used in describing computer generated three-dimensional images and graphics.

XY zoom A zoom that moves off-center to enlarge or decrease the size of a portion of a film or television frame.

Y

Y □ Monochrome. *See also* M signal. □ A wire service code indicating the message is for internal routing among wire bureaus or for reruns.

yagi An antenna that consists of a dipole, directors, and reflectors usually mounted in the same plane.

yak A slang term for often unnecessary talk or narration.

yapp A book binding with a limp cover. Also called a *divinity circuit binding.*

Y axis *See* XYZ axes.

Y cable An electrical cable with a Y at one end to allow more than one luminaire or other electrical equipment to be plugged in. *See also* Y connector.

Y connector A cord or cable in the shape of a Y. Used to feed two different inputs from one output. *See also* Y cable.

Y-cord *See* twofer.

Y/C output An S-video output compatible with S-VHS and ED-Beta.

yellow □ One of the three subtractive primary colors. The other two are cyan and magenta. Cf. additive primary colors. *See also* primary color. □ *See* yellow journalism.

yellow back An obsolete term for a cheap novel, usually bound in a yellow cover.

yellow book An informal name for the CD-ROM specification.

yellow journalism Sensationalized, often inaccurate, indecent, or vulgar stories; often combined with crude headlines and pictures. Writers and publishers were referred to as yellow journalists, newspapers as yellow journals or yellow press.

yes response A technique used to gain audience agreement for a major point by first mentioning minor points with which they will agree.

yield The ratio of the number of usable questionnaires in a survey to the number obtained by interview.

YIG Yttrium iron garnet. A crystal that resonates at microwave frequencies. Used for tuning.

yoke □ The horizontal and vertical coils placed around the neck of a cathode ray tube to deflect the scanning beam. □ A luminaire support that surrounds or forms a Y around the instrument.

young adult A book designed for adults and mature teenagers.

Y signal *See* M signal.

yupcom A slang term for a television situation comedy aimed at yuppies.

yuppie An term coined for young, urban professional. An upwardly mobile group of people who are the target of extensive advertising.

YUV In video, a symbol denoting the luminance signal (Y) and the two chrominance signals (U and V). *See also* YUV encoding.

YUV encoding A video encoding scheme taking advantage of the human eye's reduced sensitivity to color variations, as opposed to intensity variations. In each picture line, the luminance (Y) information is encoded at full bandwidth, whereas on alternate lines the chrominance (U and V) signals are encoded at half bandwidth. *See also* delta YUV.

Z

Z □ Impedance. □ Authority to determine operating power by direct measurement. An FCC file-number prefix. *See also* direct method.

zap □ A slang term for an electrical shock. □ A component that is burned out. □ To erase something unintentionally. □ *See* zapping.

zapping The use of an electronic device or remote control unit to stop a videotape recorder while commercials or other undesired material is being broadcast. Cf. zipping.

Zapple Doctrine A political corollary to Section 315 that requires that supporters of legally qualified candidates be allowed to buy comparable time on radio or television to respond to authorized supporters of other candidates for the same office.

Z axis *See* XYZ axes.

Z channel A pay television channel.

zebra color tube A single-gun color picture tube that has alternate red, green, and blue phosphors in narrow vertical stripes.

zebra time *See* Coordinated Universal Time.

zener diode A two-layered semiconductor that is used for voltage regulation, circuit protection, and so on.

zero To set a mechanical or electronic counter to zero.

zero access storage Computer storage for which there is no real wait time.

zero cut A method of cutting A and B rolls so that at least two frames overlap, thus making invisible splices when rolls are printed.

zero duration dissolve In editing videotape, an instantaneous dissolve between two television frames on two separate tapes. The equivalent of a cut. Also called a *zero frame dissolve.*

zero frame dissolve *See* zero duration dissolve.

zero hour The last minute before a radio or television program goes on the air, a newspaper is put to bed, and so on.

zeroing The act of setting a frame, footage, or other counter to zero.

zero level *See* reference level.

ZI Zoom in.

zigzag reflection A series of multiple reflections of radio waves from the ionosphere.

zilch A slang term for a stranger in the studio.

zinc □ A photoengraving made of zinc; usually a linecut, but may refer to a halftone. Also called a *zinc etching* and *zinc halftone.* Now obsolete. □ A zinc etching or cut.

zinc engraving *See* linecut and zincograph.

zinc etching *See* zinc.

zinc halftone *See* zinc.

zinco An abbreviation for *zincograph.*

zincograph □ A relief etching process used to produce a zinc lithographic plate. Also called *zinc engraving.* □ A print made by zincography.

zine A science fiction newsletter or magazine.

zinger *See* one liner.

ZIP Zoning improvement plan.

zip *See* zipping.

Zip-A-Tone A trademark for a brand of shading sheet with a pattern of dots or lines.

ZIP code A group of five digits used by the U.S. Postal Service to designate specific post offices, stations, branches, buildings, or large companies or organizations.

Zip code count The number of names and addresses on a mailing list, arranged by ZIP code.

ZIP code selection A process carried out by computer that selects individuals to receive promotional mail by ZIP code.

ZIP code sequence The arrangement of names and addresses in a list according to the numeric progression of the ZIP code in each record. This form of list formatting is mandatory for mailing at bulk third class mail rates based on the sorting requirements of the U.S. Postal Service regulations.

zip pan *See* whip.

zipper *See* kicker.

zipping The practice of fast forwarding through commercials or other undesired material while watching television programs that were videotaped. Cf. zapping.

zirconium lamp A film projection lamp containing an oxide of the element zirconium.

ZO Zoom out.

Zoetrope An early animation device that uses strips of sequential drawings that are spun and viewed through slits in a rotating drum to create an illusion of motion.

zombie composition The breaking of words from one line to the next without the use of hyphenation.

zone □ A geographical area that is covered by different editions or sections of newspapers. □ A geographical subarea, used to define sales territories, mailing areas, and so on. Cf. region and unit. □ One of the three major regions of the United States specified by the FCC in setting minimum cochannel mileage separations for television stations.

zone coverage The reporting of news and features appropriate to different newspaper zones.

zoned edition A newspaper edition that contains material appropriate to a specific geographical area of a newspaper's readership.

zone focusing The focusing of a camera so that a relatively great depth of field is set to allow for the movement of talent.

zone of privacy The physical area surrounding a person that may not lawfully be intruded on. *See also* right of privacy.

zone of reception Any geographic zone indicated in 47 CFR 73.703 in which the reception of particular programs is specifically intended and in which broadcast coverage is contemplated.

zone of silence *See* silent zone.

zone plan An advertising and marketing plan wherein a product or service is experimentally introduced into a limited geographical area.

zones Areas delineated by the FCC for the purpose of allocation and allotment of FM and television channels.

Zoning Improvement Plan (ZIP) A system of mail sorting and delivery instituted by the U.S. Postal Service. *See also* ZIP code.

zoom □ To alter the size of an image on a cathode ray tube or other video display tube. □ The facility to enlarge or diminish the area of interest in an image. □ To alter the focal length of a variable focal length lens. The effect of a zoom is approximately the same as that of a dolly, except that the perspective does not change. □ *See* truck.

Zoomar A tradename for a zoom lens.

zoom chart A list of the distances an animation camera is to be moved between frames in a zoom.

zoom happy Said of a novice camera operator who overuses a zoom lens.

zoom in (ZI) □ To change the focal length of a zoom lens so as to make the subject or object appear to move toward the camera. Cf. dolly in. □ A television director's command to a camera operator to zoom in.

zoom keyer A device that has varied shapes on slides and that is used to electronically key various pictures of various sizes.

zoom lens A variable focal length lens that allows an infinite number of shots from close-ups to long shots without moving the camera.

zoom out (ZO) □ To change the focal length of a zoom lens so as to make the subject or object appear to move away from the camera. Cf. dolly out. □ A television director's command to a camera operator to zoom out.

zoom range The difference between the shortest and longest focal lengths of a zoom lens. The ratio is often 12:1 or 15:1.

zoom ratio *See* zoom range.

zoom ring An electrical or manual attachment to a zoom lens that allows the focal length of the lens to be changed.

zoom shot A camera shot during which the focal length of a zoom lens is changed.

Zoopraxiscope A device designed in 1880 that projected photographs in quick succession. The forerunner of modern motion pictures.

Z page The first page of a newspaper section.

Z time *See* Coordinated Universal Time.

Zworykin Prize Award, Vladimir K. An award given by the IEEE for ''outstanding technical contributions in electronic television.''

TITLES OF INTEREST IN PRINT AND BROADCAST MEDIA

Essentials of Media Planning, by Arnold M. Barban, Steven M. Cristol, and Frank J. Kopec
Strategic Media Planning, by Kent M. Lancaster and Helen E. Katz
Media Math, by Robert W. Hall
Introduction to Advertising Media, by Jim Surmanek
Media Planning, by Jim Surmanek
Advertising Media Planning, by Jack Sissors and Lincoln Bumba
Advertising Media Sourcebook, by Arnold M. Barban, Donald W. Jugenheimer, and Peter B. Turk
The Future of Television, by Marc Doyle
How to Produce Effective TV Commercials, by Hooper White
How to Create Effective TV Commercials, by Huntley Baldwin
The Radio and Television Commercial, by Albert C. Book, Norman D. Cary, and Stanley Tannenbaum
Dictionary of Broadcast Communications, by Lincoln Diamant
Children's Television, by Cy Schneider
Fundamentals of Copy & Layout, by Albert C. Book and C. Dennis Schick
Creating and Delivering Winning Advertising and Marketing Presentations, by Sandra Moriarty and Tom Duncan
How to Write a Successful Advertising Plan, by James W. Taylor
Advertising Copywriting, by Philip Ward Burton
Strategic Advertising Campaigns, by Don E. Schultz
Writing for the Media, by Sandra Pesmen
The Advertising Portfolio, by Ann Marie Barry
Public Relations in the Marketing Mix, by Jordan Goldman
Handbook for Business Writing, by L. Sue Baugh, Maridell Fryar, and David A. Thomas
Handbook for Public Relations Writing, by Thomas Bivins
Handbook for Memo Writing, by L. Sue Baugh
Handbook for Proofreading, by Laura Anderson
Handbook for Technical Writing, by James Shelton
UPI Stylebook, by United Press International
Fundamentals of Successful Newsletters, by Thomas Bivins
Business Magazine Publishing, by Sal Marino
The Publicity Handbook, by David R. Yale
NTC's Mass Media Dictionary, by R. Terry Ellmore
NTC's Dictionary of Advertising, by Jack Wiechmann
Dictionary of Broadcast Communications, by Lincoln Diamant
How to Produce Creative Advertising, by Ann Keding and Thomas Bivins
How to Produce Creative Publications, by Thomas Bivins and William E. Ryan

For further information or a current catalog, write:
NTC Business Books
a division of *NTC Publishing Group*
4255 West Touhy Avenue
Lincolnwood, Illinois 60646–1975